International Business

The New Realities

International Edition

Second Edition

S. Tamer Cavusgil
Georgia State University

Gary Knight
Florida State University

John R. Riesenberger
Thunderbird School of Global Management,
Clinical Professor of Executive Development,
Corporate Learning Group

PEARSON

Boston   Columbus   Indianapolis   New York   San Francisco   Upper Saddle River   Amsterdam
Cape Town   Dubai   London   Madrid   Milan   Munich   Paris   Montréal   Toronto   Delhi
Mexico City   São Paulo   Sydney   Hong Kong   Seoul   Singapore   Taipei   Tokyo

Editorial Director: Sally Yagan
Editor in Chief: Eric Svendsen
Director of Editorial Services: Ashley Santora
Director of Development: Steve Deitmer
Editorial Project Manager: Meg O'Rourke
Editorial Assistant: Carter Anderson
Director of Marketing: Patrice Lumumba Jones
Marketing Manager: Nikki Ayana Jones
Marketing Assistant: Ian Gold
Senior Managing Editor: Judy Leale
Sr. Production Project Manager/Supervisor:
  Lynn Savino Wendel
Senior Operations Supervisor: Arnold Vila
Creative Director: Christy Mahon

Sr. Art Director/Design Supervisor: Janet Slowik
Art Director: Steven Frim
Interior Designers: Rob Aleman / Steven Frim
Cover Designer: Jodi Notowitz
Manager, Rights and Permissions: Hessa Albader
Editorial Media Project Manager: Denise Vaughn
MyLab Product Manager: Joan Waxman
Media Project Manager: Lisa Rinaldi
Full-Service Project Management: Christian Holdener,
  S4Carlisle Publishing Services
Composition: S4Carlisle Publishing Services
Printer/Binder: Courier Kendallville, Inc.
Cover Printer: Lehigh-Phoenix Color/Hagerstown
Text Font: 10/12 Palatino

Credits and acknowledgments borrowed from other sources and reproduced, with permission, in this textbook appear on appropriate page within text (or on page 628).

10 9 8 7 6 5 4 3 2 1

ISBN 10: 0-13-245327-4
ISBN 13: 978-0-13-245327-1

Dedicated to. . .

This book is dedicated to my parents, Mehmet and Naciye Cavusgil, who never received much formal education but passed on a deep sense of appreciation for knowledge to their children; my wife, Judy, and my children, Erin and Emre Cavusgil, who graciously provided much-needed understanding, support, and encouragement; and my students whom I had the opportunity to mentor over the years.

S. Tamer Cavusgil
Atlanta, Georgia

This book is dedicated to my wife, Mari, for her patience, intellect, and adventurous spirit; to Bill and Audrey, for being great parents and role models; and to the numerous students I have had the good fortune to influence over the years.

Gary Knight
Tallahassee, Florida

This book is dedicated to my parents, Richard and Marie Riesenberger, for their example, many sacrifices, and love. To my wife and best friend, Pat, for her enthusiasm and loving support. To my daughters, Chris and Jen, and their husbands, Byron and Martijn, of whom I am so very proud and thankful. To my amazing grandchildren, Ryan, Paige, and Ethan—the future of the New Realities.

John R. Riesenberger
Basking Ridge, New Jersey

> About the Authors

S. Tamer Cavusgil

Georgia State University, Fuller E. Callaway Professorial Chair
Executive Director, Center for International Business Education
and Research, J. Mack Robinson College of Business

Professor Cavusgil has been mentoring students, executives, and educators in international business for the past three decades. A native of Turkey, Professor Cavusgil's professional work has taken him to numerous other emerging markets.

Professor Cavusgil has authored more than 190 refereed journal articles and three dozen books, including *Doing Business in the Emerging Markets* (Sage). His work is among the most cited contributions in international business. He is the founding editor of the *Journal of International Marketing* and *Advances in International Marketing*. He serves on the editorial review boards of professional journals.

Professor Cavusgil is an elected Fellow of the *Academy of International Business*, a distinction earned by a select group of intellectual leaders in international business. He also served as Vice President of the AIB, and on the Board of Directors of the *American Marketing Association*. Michigan State University bestowed him with its highest recognition for contributions to the international mission: the Ralph H. Smuckler Award for Advancing International Studies. He was named International Trade Educator of the Year in 1996 by the National Association of Small Business International Trade Educators (NASBITE). At Michigan State University, he also earned the distinction of University Distinguished Faculty, the highest award given to a faculty member. In 2007, he was named an Honorary Fellow of the Sidney Sussex College at the University of Cambridge.

Professor Cavusgil holds MBA and PhD degrees in business from the University of Wisconsin. Previously, he held positions at the Middle East Technical University in Turkey, University of Wisconsin-Whitewater, Bradley University, and Michigan State University. He also served as Senior Fulbright Scholar to Australia and taught at Monash University and other Australian institutions. He serves as a visiting Professor at Manchester Business School and was Gianni and Joan Montezemolo Visiting Chair at the University of Cambridge, the United Kingdom.

Gary Knight

Florida State University, Associate Professor
and Director of Program in International Business

Professor Knight has extensive experience in international business in the private sector. In his position as Export Manager for a medium-sized enterprise, he directed the firm's operations in Canada, Europe, Japan, and Mexico, supervising the business activities of some fifty distributors in these regions. Previously, he worked for several years in Tokyo, Japan.

At Florida State University, Professor Knight developed the study abroad programs in business in Britain, France, Japan, and Spain, as well as FSU's online courses in international business. He has been an invited speaker at numerous institutions worldwide. He has won several awards for research and teaching, including best teacher in the MBA program and the Hans Thorelli Best Paper Award for his article "Entrepreneurship and Strategy: The SME Under Globalization." His research emphasizes international business strategy, international services, emerging markets, and internationalization of small and medium-sized firms.

Professor Knight is a member of the Academy of International Business. He has authored six books and more than 100 refereed articles in academic journals and conference proceedings, including *Journal of International Business Studies, Journal of World Business, International Executive,* and *Management International Review.* Recently, he was ranked one of the top fifteen most prolific scholars in the United States, and one of the top thirty worldwide, in the six leading international business journals. He is on the editorial review boards of several international journals. The U.S. House of Representatives' Committee on Small Business invited Professor Knight to provide expert testimony on international business topics.

Professor Knight earned his MBA at the University of Washington and PhD at Michigan State University, both in international business. Earlier degrees were in Finance and Modern Languages. He also attended the University of Paris in France and Sophia University in Japan and is fluent in French, Japanese, and Spanish.

John R. Riesenberger
Thunderbird School of Global Management, Clinical Professor of Executive Development, Corporate Learning Group

Mr. Riesenberger's international business career spans over three decades in the global pharmaceutical industry. He has conducted business transactions in twenty-one countries. His passion is to help students develop the managerial skills frequently required of new graduates entering careers in international business.

Currently, Mr. Riesenberger is the President of Consilium Partners, Inc., a pharmaceutical consulting firm with clients in pharmaceutical, biotechnology, and pharmaceutical agency firms.

He worked for 30 years with Pharmacia & Upjohn and The Upjohn Company as a senior executive. His experience covered a diverse range of divisional, geographic, and functional accountabilities. His most recent position was Vice President, Global Business Management. Mr. Riesenberger also served as Corporate Vice President and Chief Commercialization Officer for a biotechnology firm and as the Executive Vice President of a pharmaceutical science agency.

Mr. Riesenberger served as a member of the Global Advisory Board of the American Marketing Association. He serves as an Executive in Residence at the Michigan State University Center for International Business Education and Research. He served on the Editorial Review Board of *The Journal of International Marketing.* He served as Chairman, Industry Advisory Board, "Value of Marketing Program," SEI Center for the Advanced Studies in Management, The Wharton School of the University of Pennsylvania. He is the former Chairman of the Pharmaceutical Manufacturing Association Marketing Practices Committee. John is the coauthor, with Robert T. Moran, of *The Global Challenge: Building the New Worldwide Enterprise* (McGraw-Hill, London).

John holds a Bachelor of Science degree in Economics-Business and an MBA in Management from Hofstra University. He attended the Harvard Business School's International Senior Management Program.

> Brief Contents

> Contents

3   Organizational Participants That Make International Business Happen   94

Part 3 Strategy and Opportunity Assessment   342

12   Strategy and Organization in the International Firm   342

> Preface

What's New in This Edition

The authors have received an overwhelmingly positive response and many comments regarding the first edition of *International Business*. Since the last edition, the international business environment has experienced radical change with the impact of the global financial crisis and the rapidly changing dynamics among firms conducting business in advanced economies, emerging markets, and developing economies. Many business practices have experienced significant change in focus and direction. This new edition has undergone significant revision to capture these changes and priorities.

Ethics

We have added a new chapter devoted entirely to ethical conduct in international business. This chapter focuses on the most current and relevant topics associated with five critical topics: (1) ethics, (2) corruption, (3) corporate social responsibility, (4) sustainability, and (5) corporate governance. We have developed an ethical decision-making framework for analyzing questionable occurrences and practices in international business and created new Apply Your Understanding exercises for each chapter.

Case Studies

The second edition features six new case studies that address contemporary dynamics and the latest trends in international business. The new cases feature Siemens, Tata, AIG, Wolverine, and H&M. We have also substantially revised existing cases featuring Hyundai and DHL, FedEx, and UPS. All other existing cases have been updated as well.

Opening Vignettes

We have developed a number of new opening vignettes that emphasize such themes as corruption, the EU, the euro, and cultural differences between Western and Japanese consumers. All remaining opening vignettes have been updated to reflect the current environment.

Exhibits

The new edition contains more than 150 new and updated exhibits. A major graphical redesign has been incorporated in a large number of the exhibits in this edition to enhance reading and retention.

Balanced Geographical Coverage

Geographical coverage of companies and issues affecting African and Latin American countries has been significantly expanded.

Videos

Fifteen new customized videos have been developed to support the specific major themes of *International Business: The New Realities*. Topics include: Globalization and the Growth of International Business, Internationalization of Born Globals and Other Small and Medium Enterprises, Impact of Culture on International Business, Ethics and Corporate Social Responsibility in the Global Marketplace, Comparative and Competitive Advantages in Global Competition, Growing Role of Emerging Markets in International Business, New Global Challengers from Emerging Markets, Contrasting Government Intervention in China and Germany, Regional Economic Integration—Will the Euro Survive?, Can Acer Surpass HP, Entering the Chinese Market, Walmart in China and Mexico—Sourcing and Selling, International Marketing at P&G and Unilever, The G20 and the Global Monetary and Financial Systems, and Airbus versus Boeing.

Major Content Revisions

Each chapter has received extensive updating based on changing environmental conditions and the focus of new emerging topics in international business. Some of these updates include, but are not limited to, the global financial crisis, global corporate citizenship, ethics, corporate social responsibility, governance, sustainability, corruption, contagion, globalization of the service sector, sovereign wealth funds, Africa, Latin America, political and legal systems, government takeover of corporate assets, updated content on comparative advantage and competitive advantage, women in international business, and several new "Recent Grad in IB" profiles.

Why We Created This Book and Teaching System

The book you are holding, *International Business: The New Realities*, is a component of an innovative educational system we have developed over the past decade. The system represents an innovative and exciting approach to teaching international business. The insights we gained from comprehensive research and discussions with hundreds of practitioners, students, and faculty have been instrumental in refining our pedagogical philosophy and resources. The book attempts to impart the core body of knowledge in international business in an interesting and lively manner. Our teaching system works from the ground up, where cases and exercises are seamlessly integrated and matched to the topics covered in each chapter.

The New Realities

The new realities in international business are critical for today's students to embrace. We are witnessing remarkable changes in the cross-border flow of products, services, capital, ideas, and people. Today's volume of international trade, ease of communication and travel, and technological advances compel, and help, large and small firms to internationalize. We designed the content, organization, and features of the book and other resources to motivate and prepare future managers to grasp these new realities. These include: global sourcing, the impact of technological advances on globalization, globalization of finance, and the success of the smaller firm in international markets. Three other new realities are worth elaborating here: emerging markets, the diversity of international business participants, and corporate social responsibility.

Emerging Markets Students need an improved understanding of the changing nature of the international business landscape, not just the Triad regions (Europe, North America, and Japan). Over the past two decades, some thirty high-growth, high-potential countries have sprung into the forefront of cross-border business with rapid industrialization, privatization, and modernization.

We introduce emerging markets in Chapter 1, "Introduction: What Is International Business?" and discuss how companies achieve efficiencies by sourcing to low labor-cost countries. In Chapter 10, "Emerging Markets, Developing Economies, and Advanced Economies," we explain what makes emerging markets attractive for international business and the risks and challenges of doing business in these markets. In Chapter 10 we also discuss Mexico's Cemex, Egypt's Orascom Telecom, and China's Shanghai Automotive.

The Diversity of International Business Participants Multinational enterprises (MNEs) have historically been the most important type of focal firm. However, students need to be familiar with a variety of firms active in international business. We therefore provide balanced coverage of MNEs, small and medium-sized enterprises (SMEs), and born globals. We introduce these three types of firms in Chapter 1 and revisit them throughout the book. Here are a few examples of the firms we discuss:

- Diesel, a fashion design company that grew from an SME into an MNE (Chapter 1, "Introduction: What Is International Business?")
- Electrolux, a Swedish MNE in the kitchen appliance industry (Chapter 2, "Globalization of Markets and the Internationalization of the Firm")
- Geo Search, a Japanese born global in the electronics industry (Chapter 3, "Organizational Participants That Make International Business Happen")
- L'Oreal, a French MNE in the cosmetic industry (Chapter 4, "The Cultural Environment of International Business")
- The challenges MNEs and SMEs encounter in Russia (Chapter 7, "Political and Legal Systems in National Environments")
- Trade barriers affecting SMEs (Chapter 8, "Government Intervention in International Business")
- IKEA, a Swedish MNE in the furniture industry (Chapter 12, "Strategy and Organization in the International Firm")
- Widespread emergence of SME exporting firms (Chapter 14, "Exporting and Countertrade")

Ethics and Corporate Social Responsibility Firms are increasingly aware of their role as good corporate citizens. We address ethics and corporate social responsibility (CSR) in Chapter 5, "Ethics and International Business," and provide examples from firms such as Motorola, Petrobras, and Siemens. In the chapter we also address such issues as adopting and adhering to ethical practices and values, fostering economic development through profitable projects, and creating more equitable working environments for foreign employees. We address ethics and CSR as appropriate in various other chapters as well.

globalEDGE™ Knowledge Portal

globalEDGE™ was developed at Michigan State University's Center for International Business Education and Research (CIBER) under the direction of S. Tamer Cavusgil. globalEDGE™ has become the leading knowledge portal for professionals in international business, providing a gateway to specialized knowledge on countries, cross-border transactions, culture, and firm practice. In each chapter, the authors provide several globalEDGE™ exercises as the basis for student assignments and projects. For more information, visit http://globaledge.msu.edu/.

Textbook Features of Special Note

Maps

In today's globalized business environment, it is more important than ever for students to understand world geography. Our maps are large, easy to read, and colorful. Below is an example of a map from Chapter 9. Note the clear labeling of countries, the use of color coding, and the cut-out of Europe to make countries easy to identify:

Recent Grad in IB

Selected chapters include a special feature entitled *Recent Grad in IB*, which highlights IB graduates now working in exciting international careers. We hope this feature will motivate today's students to travel, learn another language, and be open to working internationally. We have added several new Recent Grad features for the second edition.

The most active economic blocs

- EU
- EFTA
- NAFTA
- MERCOSUR
- CARICOM
- CAN
- ASEAN
- APEC
- CER

Closing Case

Each chapter closes with an extensive case study that is new, developed specifically to address the learning objectives in the chapter, and written or co-written by the authors. The cases help students build their managerial skills by applying what they have learned in the chapter to a situation faced by a real-world manager. Questions accompany the case for assignment as homework. Class discussion helps students sharpen their analytical and decision-making skills. Here are a few examples of the closing cases:

- Chapter 1: Whirlpool's Dramatic Turnaround Through Internationalization
- Chapter 2: Debating the Merits of Globalization
- Chapter 4: Hollywood's Influence on Global Culture
- Chapter 5: Corruption at Siemens
- Chapter 7: Political, Legal, and Ethical Dilemmas in the Global Pharmaceutical Industry
- Chapter 10: Tata Group: India's New Global Challenger
- Chapter 11: AIG and Global Financial Contagion
- Chapter 13: Advanced Biomedical Devices: Assessing Readiness to Export
- Chapter 15: AUTOLATINA: A Failed International Partnership
- Chapter 18: H&M: International Marketing Success Story
- Chapter 19: Evolving Human Resource Challenges at Sony
- Chapter 20: International Financial Operations at Tektronix

This Book Supports Association to Advance Collegiate Schools of Business (AACSB) International Accreditation

Each chapter ends with a collection of exercises: Closing Case, Test Your Comprehension, Apply Your Understanding, and globalEDGE™ Internet Exercises. In every chapter, next to each exercise, we provide a specific AACSB tagging logo to help instructors identify those exercises that support AACSB learning goals. We also provide AACSB tagging for all the questions in the Test Item File that accompanies the textbook.

What Is the AACSB? AACSB is a not-for-profit corporation of educational institutions, corporations, and other organizations devoted to the promotion and improvement of higher education in business administration and accounting. A collegiate institution offering degrees in business administration or accounting may volunteer for AACSB accreditation review. The AACSB makes initial accreditation decisions and conducts periodic reviews to promote continuous quality improvement in management education. Pearson Education is a proud member of the AACSB and is pleased to provide advice to help you apply AACSB Learning Standards.

What Are AACSB Learning Standards? One of the criteria for AACSB accreditation is the quality of the curricula. Although no specific courses are required, the AACSB expects a curriculum to include learning experiences in such areas as:

- Communication abilities
- Ethical understanding and reasoning abilities
- Analytic skills
- Use of information technology
- Dynamics of the global economy

- Multicultural and diversity understanding
- Reflective thinking skills

These seven categories are AACSB Learning Standards. Questions that test skills relevant to these standards are tagged with the appropriate standard. For example, a question testing the moral questions associated with externalities would receive the ethical understanding and reasoning abilities tag.

How Can I Use These Tags? Tagged exercises help you measure whether students are grasping the course content that aligns with AACSB guidelines noted previously. In addition, the tagged exercises may help to identify potential applications of these skills. This, in turn, may suggest enrichment activities or other educational experiences to help students achieve these goals.

Resources in Support of the Text

Instructor's Resource Center

At **www.pearsonhighered.com/irc**, instructors can access a variety of print, media and presentation resources available with this text in downloadable, digital format. Registration is simple and gives you immediate access to new titles and new editions. As a registered faculty member, you can download resource files and receive immediate access and instructions for installing course management content on your campus server.

If you ever need assistance, our dedicated technical support team is ready to help with the media supplements that accompany this text. Visit **http://247pearsoned.custhelp.com** for answers to frequently asked questions and user support.

Instructor's Manual Authored by Marta Szabo White, professor at Georgia State University and winner of numerous teaching awards, the Instructor's Manual offers much more than just the traditional, limited chapter outline and answers to the end-of-chapter materials. In addition to these basic items, each chapter includes a variety of resources such as exercises, critical-thinking assignments, debate topics, and research assignments. This manual is available for download by visiting www.pearsonhighered .com/irc.

Test Item File The Test Item File (available for download from www.pearsonhighered .com/irc) contains approximately seventy-five questions per chapter, including multiple-choice, true/false, short answer, and essay questions. Cara Cantarella, the author of this supplement, is an assessment expert with extensive experience in test authoring. Each question has been carefully reviewed and edited to ensure accuracy and appropriateness.

Test questions are annotated with the following information:

- Page number from the main text where the question's topic is covered
- Learning Objective from the main text
- Difficulty level: Easy for straight recall, Moderate for some analysis, or Analytical for complex analysis
- Skill: concept, application, critical thinking or synthesis

For each question that tests a standard from the Association to Advance Collegiate Schools of Business (AACSB), we use one of the following annotations:

- Communication abilities
- Ethical understanding and reasoning abilities
- Analytic skills

- Use of information technology
- Dynamics of the global economy
- Multicultural and diversity understanding
- Reflective thinking skills

TestGen Test Generating Software This easy-to-use software allows instructors to custom design, save, and generate classroom tests. Instructors can edit, add, or delete questions from the test bank, analyze test results, and organize a database of tests and student results. It provides many flexible options for organizing and displaying tests, along with a search-and-sort feature. TestGen can be downloaded from www.pearsonhighered.com/educator.

PowerPoint Slides Fully updated PowerPoints offer helpful instructional support by highlighting and clarifying key concepts. The PowerPoints are available for download from http://www.pearsonhighered.com/irc.

Image Library All of the exhibits from the textbook are available electronically for instructors to download, print, display in class, or produce customized materials. The Image Library is available for download from www.pearsonhighered.com/irc.

Videos on DVD

Video segments illustrate the most pertinent topics in international business today and highlight relevant issues that demonstrate how people lead, manage, and work effectively. Contact your Pearson representative for the DVD. Additional videos are available to myiblab users at www.myiblab.com.

myIBlab

myIBlab (**http://www.myiblab.com**) is an easy-to-use online tool that personalizes course content and provides robust assessment and reporting to measure individual and class performance. All of the resources you need for course success are in one place—flexible and easily adapted for your course experience. Some of the resources include quizzes, video clips, assessments, and PowerPoint presentations that engage students while helping them study independently. Students can purchase access to myIBlab by visiting http://www.myiblab.com. They can also purchase an access card packaged with the text from http://www.pearsonhighered.com at a reduced price using ISBN 0132622734.

> Acknowledgments

Our Reviewers

Through three drafts of the manuscript, we received guidance and insights at several critical junctures from many trusted reviewers who provided specific recommendations on how to improve and refine the content, presentation, and organization. Their contributions were invaluable in crystallizing our thinking. We extend our gratitude to:

Anil Agarwal, University of Arizona

Raj Aggarwal, University of Akron

Richard Ajayi, University of Central Florida

Hamid Ali, Chicago State University

Allen Amason, University of Georgia

Gary Anders, Arizona State University

Mathias Arrfelt, Arizona State University

Bulent Aybar, Southern New Hampshire University

Nizamettin Aydin, Suffolk University

Peter Banfe, Ohio Northern University

Eric Baumgardner, Xavier University

Mack Bean, Franklin Pierce University

Lawrence Beer, Arizona State University

Enoch Beraho, South Carolina State University

David Berg, University of Wisconsin-Milwaukee

Jean Boddewyn, Baruch College, City University of New York

Henry Bohleke, Owens Community College

Santanu Borah, University of Northern Alabama

Darrell Brown, Indiana University, Purdue University, Indianapolis

Linda Brown, Scottsdale Community College

Diana Bullen, Mesa Community College

Kirt Butler, Michigan State University

Michael Campo, Regis University

Tom Cary, City University, Seattle

Kalyan Chakravarty, California State University, Northridge

Aruna Chandra, Indiana State University

Kent Cofoid, Seminole State College

Tim Curran, University of South Florida

Madeline Calabrese Damkar, California State University-East Bay

Donna Davisson, Cleveland State University

Seyda Deligonul, St. John Fisher College

Peter Dowling, Victoria University of Wellington, New Zealand

Juan España, National University

Bradley Farnsworth, University of Michigan

Aysun Ficici, Southern New Hampshire University

John Finley, Columbus State University

Ian Gladding, Lewis University

Jorge Gonzalez, University of Texas–Pan American

David Griffith, Michigan State University

Tom Head, Roosevelt University

Bruce Heiman, San Francisco State University

David Hrovat, Northern Kentucky University

Douglas Johansen, Jacksonville University

Paul Jones, Regis University

Ali Kara, Pennsylvania State University-University Park

Daekwan Kim, Florida State University

Konghee Kim, St. Cloud State University

Ahmet Kirca, Michigan State University

Leonard Kloft, Wright State University

Anthony Koh, University of Toledo

Stephanie Kontrim-Baumann, Missouri Baptist University

Tatiana Kostova, University of South Carolina

Chuck Kwok, University of South Carolina

Ann Langlois, Palm Beach Atlantic University

Romas Laskauskas, Stevenson University

Yikuan Lee, San Francisco State University

Bijou Lester, Drexel University

Phil Lewis, Eastern Michigan University

Minghua Li, Franklin Pierce University

Bob McNeal, Alabama State University, Montgomery

Janis Miller, Clemson University

Barbara Moebius, Waukesha County Technical College

Bruce Money, Brigham Young University

Bill Murray, University of San Francisco

Matthew B. Myers, University of Tennessee

Max Grunbaum Nagiel, Daytona State College

Kuei-Hsien Niu, Sacramento State University

Bernard O'Rourke, Caldwell College

Braimoh Oseghale, Fairleigh Dickinson University

Jeffrey W. Overby, Belmont University

Susan Peterson, Scottsdale Community College

Iordanis Petsas, University of Scranton

Zahir Quraeshi, Western Michigan University

Roberto Ragozzino, University of Central Florida

Brandon Randolph-Seng, Texas Tech University

Michelle Reina, Wisconsin Lutheran College

Michael Rubach, University of Central Arkansas

Carol Sanchez, Grand Valley State University

Hakan Saraoglu, Bryant University

Jeff Sarbaum, University of North Carolina at Greensboro

Deepak Sethi, Old Dominion University

Karen Sneary, Northwestern Oklahoma State University

Kurt Stanberry, University of Houston-Downtown

John Stanbury, George Mason University

William Streeter, Olin Business School, Washington University in Saint Louis

Philip Sussan, University of Central Florida

Charles Ray Taylor, Villanova University

Deanna Teel, Houston Community College

Gladys Torres-Baumgarten, Ramapo College of New Jersey

Kimberly Townsend, Syracuse University

Thuhang Tran, Middle Tennessee State University

Joseph Trendowski, Old Dominion University

Sameer Vaidya, Texas Wesleyan University

Cheryl Van Deusen, University of North Florida

Linn Van Dyne, Michigan State University

Davina Vora, State University of New York at New Paltz

William Walker, University of Houston

Paula Weber, St. Cloud State University

Mindy West, Arizona State University

Sidney Wheeler, Embry-Riddle Aeronautical University

Marta Szabo White, Georgia State University

Richard Wilson, Hofstra University

Jennifer Woolley, Santa Clara University

Alan Wright, Troy University

Attila Yaprak, Wayne State University

Betty Yobaccio, Bryant University

Pierre Yourougou, Whitman School of Management, Syracuse University

Bashar Zakaria, California State University, Sacramento

Anatoly Zhuplev, Loyola Marymount University

Focus Group Participants

We were also fortunate that so many colleagues generously gave their time and offered perspectives on our teaching resources. We met with these colleagues in person, teleconferenced with them, or otherwise received their input. The insights and recommendations of these educators were instrumental in the design and format of our teaching system. We extend our gratitude and thanks to the following reviewers and colleagues:

David Ahlstrom, The Chinese University of Hong Kong

Yusaf Akbar, Southern New Hampshire University

Victor Alicea, Normandale Community College

Gail Arch, Curry College

Anke Arnaud, University of Central Florida

Choton Basu, University of Wisconsin-Whitewater

Eric Baumgardner, Xavier University

Mark Bean, Franklin Pierce College

Enoch Beraho, South Carolina State University

Paula Bobrowski, Auburn University

Teresa Brosnan, City University, Bellevue

Darrell Brown, Indiana University, Purdue University-Indianapolis

Nichole Castater, Clark Atlanta University

Aruna Chandra, Indiana State University

Mike C. H. (Chen-Ho) Chao, Baruch College, City University of New York

David Chaplin, Waldorf College

Dong Chen, Loyola Marymount University

Chen Oi Chin, Lawrence Technological University

Patrick Chinon, Syracuse University

Farok J. Contractor, Rutgers University

Angelica Cortes, University of Texas–Pan American

Michael Deis, Clayton State University

Les Dlabay, Lake Forest College

Gary Donnelly, Casper College

Gideon Falk, Purdue University-Calumet

Marc Fetscherin, Rollins College

Charles Fishel, San Jose State University

Frank Flauto, Austin Community College

Georgine K. Fogel, Salem International University

Frank Franzak, Virginia Commonwealth University

Debbie Gilliard, Metropolitan State College

Robert Goddard, Appalachian State University

Kenneth Gray, Florida A&M University
Andy Grein, Baruch College, City University of New York
Andrew C. Gross, Cleveland State University
David Grossman, Florida Southern College
Seid Hassan, Murray State University
Wei He, Indiana State University
Xiaohong He, Quinnipiac University
Christina Heiss, University of Missouri-Kansas City
Pol Herrmann, Iowa State University
Guy Holburn, University of Western Ontario
Anisul Islam, University of Houston-Downtown
Basil Janavaras, Minnesota State University
Raj Javalgi, Cleveland State University
Ruihua Jiang, Oakland University
Yikuan Jiang, California State University-East Bay
James Kennelly, Skidmore College
Ken Kim, University of Toledo
Leonard Kloft, Wright State University
Anthony C. Koh, The University of Toledo
Ann Langlois, Palm Beach Atlantic University
Michael La Rocco, University of Saint Francis
Romas A. Laskauskas, Villa Julie College
Shaomin Li, Old Dominion University
Ted London, University of Michigan
Peter Magnusson, Saint Louis University
Charles Mambula, Suffolk University
David McArthur, Utah Valley State College
Ofer Meilich, Bradley University
Lauryn Migenes, University of Central Florida
Mortada Mohamed, Austin Community College
Robert T. Moran, Thunderbird
Carolyn Mueller, Stetson University
Kelly J. Murphrey, Texas A&M University

Lilach Nachum, Baruch College, CUNY
William Newburry, Florida International University
Stanley Nollen, Georgetown University
Augustine Nwabuzor, Florida A&M University
Bernard O'Rourke, Caldwell College
David Paul, California State University-East Bay
Christine Cope Pence, University of California Riverside
Heather Pendarvis-McCord, Bradley University
Kathleen Rehbein, Marquette University
Liesl Riddle, George Washington University
John Rushing, Barry University
Mary Saladino, Montclair State University
Carol Sanchez, Grand Valley State University
Camille Schuster, California State University-San Marcos
Eugene Seeley, Utah Valley State College
Deepak Sethi, Old Dominion University
Mandep Singh, Western Illinois University
Rajendra Sinhaa, Des Moines Area Community College
John E. Spillan, Pennsylvania State University-DuBois
Uday S. Tate, Marshall University
Janell Townsend, Oakland University
Sameer Vaidya, Texas Wesleyan University
Robert Ware, Savannah State University
Marta Szabo White, Georgia State University
Steve Williamson, University of North Florida
Lynn Wilson, Saint Leo University
Attila Yaprak, Wayne State University
Rama Yelkur, University of Wisconsin-Eau Claire
Minyuan Zhao, University of Michigan
Christopher Ziemnowicz, Concord University

Our Colleagues, Doctoral Students, and Practitioners

Numerous individuals have contributed to our thinking over the years. Through conversations, conferences, seminars, and writings, we have greatly benefited from the views and experience of international business educators and professionals from around the world. The senior author also had many rich conversations with the doctoral students whom he mentored over the years. Their names appear below if they have not been previously mentioned. Directly or indirectly, their thoughtful ideas and suggestions have had a significant impact on the development of this book. Our appreciation goes to many individuals, including:

John Abbott, The Upjohn Company
Billur Akdeniz, University of New Hampshire
Catherine N. Axinn, Ohio University
Nizam Aydin, Suffolk University

Ted Bany, The Upjohn Company
Christopher Bartlett, Harvard Business School
Simon Bell, University of Melbourne
Daniel C. Bello, Georgia State University

Muzaffer Bodur, Bogazici University
Jacobus Boers, Georgia State University
Nakiye Boyacigiller, Sabanci University
John Brawley, The Upjohn Company
David Bruce, Georgia State University
Pedro Carrillo, Georgia State University
Erin Cavusgil, University of Michigan-Flint
Brian Chabowski, University of Tulsa
Emin Civi, University of New Brunswick, St. John, Canada
Tevfik Dalgic, University of Texas at Dallas
Guillermo D'Andrea, Universidad Austral-Argentina
Angela da Rocha, Universidad Federal do Rio de Janeiro, Brazil
Fernando Doria, Georgia State University
Rick Della Guardia, The Upjohn Company
Deniz Erden, Bogazici University
Felicitas Evangelista, University of Western Sydney, Australia
Cuneyt Evirgen, Sabanci University
Carol Finnegan, University of Colorado at Colorado Springs
Harold Fishkin, The Upjohn Company
Michael Fishkin, Stony Brook University
Richard Fletcher, University of Western Sydney, Australia
Esra Gencturk, Ozyegin University
Pervez Ghauri, Kings College London
Tracy Gonzalez-Padron, University of Colorado at Colorado Springs
Bill Hahn, Science Branding Communications
Tomas Hult, Michigan State University
Destan Kandemir, Bilkent University
George Kaufman, The Upjohn Company
Ihsen Ketata, Georgia State University
Irem Kiyak, Michigan State University
Tunga Kiyak, Michigan State University
Yener Kndogan, University of Michigan-Flint
Phillip Kotler, Northwestern University
Tiger Li, Florida International University
Karen Loch, Georgia State University
Mushtaq Luqmani, Western Michigan University
Robert McCarthy, The Upjohn Company
Myron Miller, Michigan State University (ret.)

Vincent Mongello, The Upjohn Company
Robert T. Moran, Thunderbird
G. M. Naidu, University of Wisconsin-Whitewater
John R. Nevin, University of Wisconsin
Gregory Osland, Butler University
Aysegul Ozsomer, Koc University
Ed Perper, Science Branding Communications
Morys Perry, University of Michigan-Flint
Alex Rialp, Universidad Autonoma de Barcelona, Spain
Tony Roath, University of Oklahoma
Carol Sanchez, Grand Valley State University
Michael Savitt, The Upjohn Company
Peter Seaver, The Upjohn Company
Linda Hui Shi, University of Victoria
Rudolf R. Sinkovics, The University of Manchester
Carl Arthur Solberg, Norwegian School of Management, Norway
Elif Sonmez-Persinger, Eastern Michigan University
Douglas Squires, The Upjohn Company of Canada
Barbara Stoettinger, Wirtschaftuniversitaet Wein, Austria
Detmar Straub, Georgia State University
Berk Talay, University of New Hampshire
Cherian Thachenkary, Georgia State University
David Tse, University of Hong Kong
Mithat Uner, Gazi University
Nukhet Vardar, Yeditepe University
Marta Szabo White, Georgia State University
Fang Wu, University of Texas-Dallas
Shichun (Alex) Xu, University of Tennessee
Goksel Yalcinkaya, University of New Hampshire
Attila Yaprak, Wayne State University
Ugur Yavas, East Tennessee State University
Sengun Yeniyurt, Rutgers University
Poh-Lin Yeoh, Bentley College
Eden Yin, University of Cambridge
Chun Zhang, University of Vermont
Shaoming Zou, University of Missouri

Our Prentice Hall Team

This book would not have been possible without the tireless efforts of many dedicated professionals at our publisher, Prentice Hall. We are especially grateful to Eric Svendsen, Editor-in-Chief; Meg O'Rourke, Editorial Project Manager; Carter Anderson, Editorial Assistant; Nikki Jones, Marketing Manager; Ian Gold, Marketing Assistant; and Lynn Savino Wendel, Production Project Manager. Kathleen McLellan helped organize numerous focus groups with insightful educators and assisted with marketing efforts. Our appreciation goes to many other individuals at Prentice Hall, including: Linda Albelli, Steve Deitmer, Jerome Grant, Patrice Jones, Brian Kibby, Judy Leale, Patrick Leow, Ben Paris, and Ashley Santora.

International Business

PART 1

CHAPTER 1

LEARNING OBJECTIVES In this chapter, you will learn about:

1. What is international business?
2. What are the key concepts in international trade and investment?
3. How does international business differ from domestic business?
4. Who participates in international business?
5. Why do firms internationalize?
6. Why study international business?

Introduction: What Is International Business?

A Typical Day in the Global Economy

Julie Valentine is a college junior majoring in business. On a recent Saturday, she went shopping at a local mall. First, she ordered a big breakfast, unaware that most of her meal was imported from abroad: bacon from Spain, juice from Brazil, and French-branded yogurt. Julie then headed to the department store to buy a gift for her father. She perused neckties with Italian and French brand names, and others made in China and Romania. She also considered electric shavers made by Braun (a German brand) and Philips (a Dutch brand). She eventually bought a Panasonic (a Japanese brand). Next, she headed to the perfume counter, where she tried various brands, including Chanel (France), French Connection (United Kingdom), and Shiseido (Japan).

Julie was dreaming of buying a laptop computer. At the electronics store, she explored several models made in China, Ireland, and Malaysia. As she passed a travel agency, she remembered her spring vacation was just around the corner and decided to consult her best friend, Melissa. Whipping out her Nokia cell phone (a Finnish brand, but made in Hungary and South Korea), Julie reached Melissa, who answered on her Motorola phone (from a U.S. firm, but made in Malaysia). The two chatted about their dream trip to the beaches of southern Spain, considered Mexico, but decided they will probably end up in Florida. Julie looked at a blouse made in Vietnam, but hesitated to buy it because she had read that some products from Southeast Asia are made with child labor.

Julie left the mall and drove away in her Hyundai (a Korean brand, made from Chinese, Korean, and U.S. parts). She liked Melissa's car, a BMW (German, but made in the United States from Asian and European components). Over the following weeks, Julie and her exchange-student friend, Anders (her favorite Norwegian import), met several times at restaurants featuring food from various countries, including France, India, and Lebanon. On Friday night, they watched *The Dark Knight* (made in Britain, Hong Kong, and the United States, and featuring Australian and British actors) on a friend's big-screen TV (a Dutch brand, but made in Indonesia). Over dinner, Julie and Anders enjoyed pasta from Italy and shrimp from El Salvador and chatted about their future. Julie was dreaming of an international career.

What Is International Business?

International business Performance of trade and investment activities by firms across national borders.

As you can see from the opening vignette, international business touches our daily experiences. **International business** refers to the performance of trade and investment activities by firms across national borders. Because it emphasizes crossing national boundaries, we also refer to international business as *cross-border business*. Firms organize, source, manufacture, market, and conduct other value-adding activities on an international scale. They seek foreign customers and engage in collaborative relationships with foreign business partners. While international business is performed mainly by individual firms, governments and international agencies also undertake international business activities.[1] Firms and nations exchange many physical and intellectual assets, including products, services, capital, technology, know-how, and labor. In this book, we are mainly concerned with the international business activities of the individual firm.

While international business has been around for centuries, it has gained much momentum and complexity over the past three decades. Firms seek international market opportunities more today than ever before, touching the lives of billions of people worldwide. Daily chores such as shopping and leisure activities such as listening to music, watching a movie, or surfing the Internet involve transactions that connect you to the global economy. International business gives you access to products and services from around the world and profoundly affects your quality of life and economic well-being.

Globalization of markets Ongoing economic integration and growing interdependency of countries worldwide.

The growth of international business activity coincides with the broader phenomenon of globalization of markets. The **globalization of markets** refers to the ongoing economic integration and growing interdependency of countries worldwide. While internationalization of the firm refers to the tendency of companies to systematically increase the international dimension of their business activities, globalization refers to a macro trend of intense economic interconnectedness between countries. Globalization is associated with the internationalization of countless firms and dramatic growth in the volume and variety of cross-border transactions in goods, services, and capital flows. It has led to widespread diffusion of products, technology, and knowledge worldwide.

The globalization of markets is evident in several related trends. First is the unprecedented growth of international trade. In 1960, cross-border trade was modest—about $100 billion per year. Today, it accounts for a substantial proportion of the world economy, amounting to some $13 trillion annually—that is, $13,000,000,000,000! Second, trade between nations is accompanied by substantial flows of capital, technology, and knowledge. Third is the development of highly sophisticated global financial systems and mechanisms that facilitate the cross-border flow of products, money, technology, and knowledge. Fourth, globalization has brought about a greater degree of collaboration among nations through multilateral regulatory agencies such as the World Trade Organization (WTO; www.wto.org) and the International Monetary Fund (IMF; www.imf.org).

Globalization both compels and facilitates companies to expand abroad. Simultaneously, company internationalization has become easier than ever before. A few decades ago, international business was largely the domain of large, multinational companies. Recent developments have created a more level playing field that allows all types of firms to benefit from active participation in international business. In this book, you will read about the international activities of smaller firms, along with those of large, multinational enterprises. While international business once was conducted mainly by firms that manufacture products, this is no longer the case. Companies in the services sector are also internationalizing, in such industries as banking, engineering, insurance, and retailing.

A recent manifestation of globalization is the global financial crisis, which began in 2008. The global economy is more integrated than ever, and, like a virus, economic problems spread quickly across porous national borders. The crisis began in the United

States and moved to other countries, triggering a severe global *recession*, a condition in which national economies undergo a sustained period of negative growth.[2] Canada's recession resulted largely from its intense trading relationship with the United States. Mexico's exports to the United States declined substantially, worsening Mexico's already high unemployment rate. Job losses also ensued in Japan and other Asian countries as exports to the United States fell sharply. The economies of both China and India, the world's most populous countries, slowed significantly due to the crisis. In short, integration and interdependency of national economies quickly spread the crisis throughout the world ... t has affected most firms and individuals in an increasingly in- ... ddress globalization and the global financial crisis in more de-

... Key Concepts
... l Trade and Investment?

... ternational business transactions are international trade and ... trade refers to an exchange of products and services across ... nvolves both products (merchandise) and services (intangi- ... ough **exporting**, an entry strategy involving the sale of prod- ... rs located abroad, from a base in the home country or a third ... o take the form of **importing** or **global sourcing**—the pro- ... rvices from suppliers located abroad for consumption in the ... country. While exporting represents the outbound flow of products and services, importing is an inbound activity. Both finished products and intermediate goods, such as raw materials and components, are subject to importing and exporting.

International investment refers to the transfer of assets to another country or the acquisition of assets in that country. These assets include capital, technology, managerial talent, and manufacturing infrastructure. Economists refer to such assets as *factors of production*. Trade implies that products and services cross national borders. By contrast, investment implies the firm itself crosses borders to secure ownership of assets located abroad.

The two essential types of cross-border investment are international portfolio investment and foreign direct investment. **International portfolio investment** refers to the passive ownership of foreign securities such as stocks and bonds for the purpose of generating financial returns. It does not entail active management or control over these assets. The foreign investor has a relatively short-term interest in the ownership of these assets. **Foreign direct investment (FDI)** is an internationalization strategy in which the firm establishes a physical presence abroad through acquisition of productive assets such as capital, technology, labor, land, plant, and equipment. It is a foreign-market entry strategy that gives investors partial or full ownership of a productive enterprise typically dedicated to manufacturing, marketing, or management activities. Investing such resources abroad is generally for the long term and involves extensive planning.

The Nature of International Trade

Exhibit 1.1 contrasts the growth of total world exports to the growth of total world *gross domestic product (GDP)* since 1970. GDP is the total value of products and services produced in a country over the course of a year. Following a 27-year boom, world trade declined in 2009 due to the global recession. The hardest hit imports were consumer goods, cars, and car parts.[3] Overall, however, export growth has outpaced the growth of domestic production during the last few decades, illustrating the fast pace of globalization. In

International trade Exchange of products and services across national borders, typically through exporting and importing.

Exporting The strategy of producing products or services in one country (often the producer's home country), and selling and distributing them to customers located in other countries.

Importing or global sourcing Procurement of products or services from suppliers located abroad for consumption in the home country or a third country.

International investment The transfer of assets to another country or the acquisition of assets in that country.

International portfolio investment Passive ownership of foreign securities such as stocks and bonds for the purpose of generating financial returns.

Foreign direct investment (FDI) An internationalization strategy in which the firm establishes a physical presence abroad through acquisition of productive assets such as capital, technology, labor, land, plant, and equipment.

Exhibit 1.1 Comparing the Growth Rates of World GDP and World Exports

SOURCE: World Investment Report 2009 (New York: United Nations, 2008), retrieved from http://www.unctad.org, June 4, 2010; World Trade Organization, World Trade Report 2009 (Geneva, Switzerland: WTO Publications, 2009), retrieved from http://www.wto.org, June 4, 2010; and International Monetary Fund, World Economic Outloo, (Washington, DC: IMF database 2010), retrieved from http://www.imf.org, June 4, 2010.

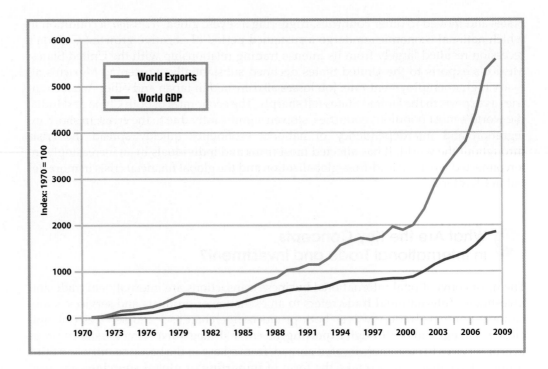

fact, during this period, world exports grew more than thirty-fold, while world GDP grew only tenfold. To illustrate this point, consider the journey of a shirt sold in France. Initially, the cotton to produce the shirt is exported from the United States to China. After the shirt is manufactured in China, it is exported to France. Eventually, after the French owner discards her used shirt, it is exported once again and sold on the used clothing market in Africa. In total, the value generated in exporting the shirt greatly exceeds the cost to produce it.

Much of the difference in the growth of exports versus GDP is due to advanced (or developed) economies such as Britain and the United States now sourcing many of the products they consume from low-cost manufacturing locations such as China and Mexico. For example, although the United States once produced most of the products it consumed, today it depends much more on imports. Rapid integration of world economies is fueled by such factors as advances in information and transportation technologies, decline of trade barriers, liberalization of markets, and the remarkable growth of emerging market economies.

Exhibit 1.2 identifies the nations that lead in the exporting and importing of products (but not services)—that is, international merchandise trade. Panel (a) shows the total value of products traded in billions of U.S. dollars. Panel (b) shows the annual value of products traded as a percentage of each nation's GDP. While the United States is the leading country in terms of the absolute value of total merchandise trade, trade accounts for only 23 percent of its GDP. In contrast, merchandise trade is a much larger component of economic activity in countries such as Belgium (171 percent), the Netherlands (138 percent), and Germany (72 percent). These percentages show that some economies are very dependent on international trade relative to the value of all goods and services they produce domestically. Indeed, in Singapore, Hong Kong, South Korea, and Malaysia, trade accounts for more than 100 percent of GDP. These countries are known as *entrepôt* economies. *Entrepôt* is from the French for 'intermediate depot'. Such countries import a large volume of products, some of which they process into higher value-added products and some they simply re-export to other destinations. For example, Singapore is a major *entrepôt* for petroleum products received from the Middle East, which it then exports to China and other destinations in Asia.

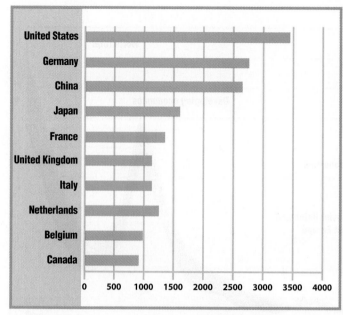

(a) Total annual value of products trade (exports + imports) in billions of U.S. dollars

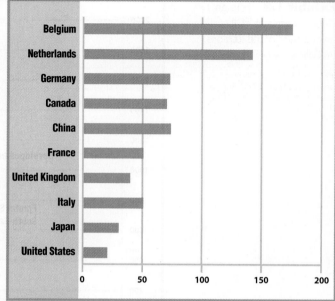

(b) Total annual value of products trade (exports + imports) as a percentage of nation's GDP

Exhibit 1.2 Leading Countries in International Merchandise Trade

SOURCE: World Trade Organization http://(www.wto.org); data for 2007. © 2009 World Trade Organization. Reprinted with permission.

The Nature of International Investment

Of the two types of investment flows between nations—portfolio investment and foreign direct investment—we are concerned primarily with FDI, because it is the ultimate stage of internationalization and encompasses the widest range of international business involvement. FDI is the foreign entry strategy practiced by the most internationally active firms. Companies usually engage in FDI for the long term and retain partial or complete ownership of the assets they acquire.

Firms undertake FDI for a variety of strategic reasons, including to (1) set up manufacturing or assembly operations or other physical facilities, (2) open a sales or representative office or other facility to conduct marketing or distribution activities, or (3) establish a regional headquarters all in foreign countries. In the process, the firm establishes a new legal business entity, subject to the regulations of the host government in the country where the entity is established.

FDI is especially common among large, resourceful companies with substantial international operations. For example, many European and U.S. firms have invested in China, India, and Russia to establish plants to manufacture or assemble products, taking advantage of low-cost labor and other resources in these countries. At the same time, companies from these rapidly developing economies have begun to invest in Western markets. For example, in 2008, the Turkish company Yildiz acquired the premium chocolate maker Godiva from U.S.-based Campbell Soup Company in a deal valued at $850 million. More recently, Ford invested some $3 billion to build a new car factory in Mexico to manufacture Fiesta automobiles.

Exhibit 1.3 illustrates the dramatic growth of FDI into various world regions since the 1980s. The exhibit reveals that the dollar volume of FDI has grown immensely since the 1980s, especially in advanced economies such as Japan, Europe, and North America. FDI inflows were interrupted in 2001 as investors panicked following the September 11 terrorist attacks in the United States, but the trend has remained strong and growing over time. Particularly significant is the growth of FDI into *developing economies*, which are nations with lower incomes, less-developed industrial bases, and less investment capital than the advanced economies. Most of the developing economies are located in parts of Africa, Asia, and Latin America. Despite lower income levels, developing

Exhibit 1.3 Foreign Direct Investment (FDI) Inflows into World Regions (in Billions of U.S. Dollars per Year)

SOURCE: UNCTAD, World Investment Report 2008, © United Nations. The United Nations is the author of the original material. Reproduced with permission.

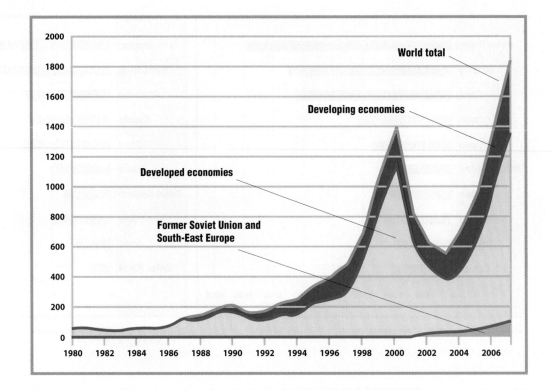

economies collectively comprise a substantial and growing proportion of international trade and investment.

Services as Well as Products

Historically, international trade and investment were mainly the domain of companies that make and sell products—tangible merchandise such as clothing, computers, and cars. Today, firms that produce *services* (intangibles) are key international business players as well. Services are deeds, performances, or efforts performed directly by people working in banks, consulting firms, hotels, construction companies, retailers, and countless other firms in the services sector. For example, if you own a house, your mortgage may be underwritten by the Dutch bank ABN Amro. Perhaps you eat lunch in a cafeteria owned by the French firm Sodexho, which manages the food and beverage operations on numerous university campuses. In the United States and several European countries, travel and tourism are now the number-one source of revenue from foreigners.

International trade in services accounts for about one-quarter of all international trade and is growing rapidly. In recent years, services trade has been growing faster than products trade. Exhibit 1.4 identifies the leading countries in total international services trade, including both exports and imports. Panel (a) shows the total annual value of services trade in billions of U.S. dollars. Panel (b) shows the total annual value of services trade as a percentage of each nation's GDP. As with products, larger advanced economies account for the greatest proportion of world services trade. This is expected, because services typically comprise more than two-thirds of the GDPs of these countries. Compare the value of merchandise trade in Exhibit 1.2 with the value of services trade in Exhibit 1.4 for each country. Although services trade is growing rapidly, the value of merchandise trade is still much larger. One reason is that services face greater challenges and barriers in cross-border trade than merchandise goods.

Not all services can be exported. For example, you cannot export the construction work to build a house, repair work done on your car, or the experience of eating a meal in a restaurant. Although some services can be digitized and moved across borders, most service providers can operate internationally only by establishing a physical presence

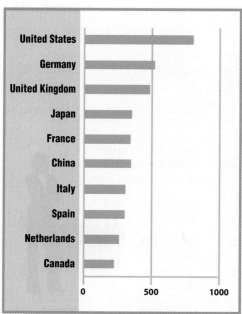
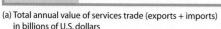
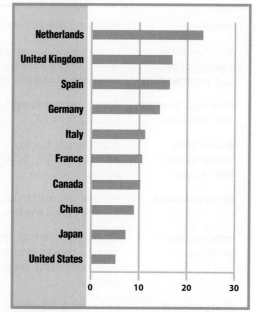

Exhibit 1.4 Leading Countries in International Services Trade

SOURCE: Copyright © 2008 World Trade Organization. Reprinted with permission.

(a) Total annual value of services trade (exports + imports) in billions of U.S. dollars

(b) Total annual value of services trade (exports + imports) as a percentage of nation's GDP

abroad through direct investment. Firms employ FDI to set up restaurants, retail stores, and other physical facilities through which they sell trillions of dollars worth of services abroad every year.

There are numerous industries in the services sector with strong potential for internationalization. The giant Internet retailer eBay earned nearly $9 billion in 2009, of which more than 50 percent came from international sales. The company expects most future revenue growth will come from abroad. When developing its business in India, eBay acquired the Mumbai-based e-retailer Baazee. This acquisition followed eBay's expansion into China, Korea, and Europe.[4] Exhibit 1.5 illustrates the diversity of service sectors that are internationalizing, extending their reach beyond the countries where they are based. If you are considering a career in international business, keep these industries in mind.

The International Financial Services Sector

International banking and financial services are among the most internationally active service industries. Explosive growth of investment and financial flows has led to the emergence of capital markets worldwide. It resulted from two main factors: the internationalization of banks and the massive flow of money across national borders into pension funds and portfolio investments. In the developing economies, banks and other financial institutions have been fostering economic activity by increasing the availability of local investment capital, which stimulates the development of financial markets and encourages locals to save money.

International banking is flourishing in such regions as the Middle East, where the return on equity in Saudi Arabia, for instance, often exceeds 20 percent (compared to 15 percent in the United States and much less in France and Germany). Citibank, Deutsche Bank, BNP Paribas, and other international banks are thriving because of higher oil prices, a boom in consumer banking, and low taxes. National Commercial Bank, the biggest bank in the region, calculates that non-interest-bearing deposits comprise nearly 50 percent of total deposits in Saudi Arabia. Banks lend this free money to companies and consumers at high margins. By structuring loans as partnerships, they comply with Islamic rules that forbid banks to pay interest.[5]

Exhibit 1.5 Service Industry Sectors that Are Rapidly Internationalizing

SOURCE: International Trade Administration, Washington, DC: U.S. Department of Commerce.

Industry	Representative Activities	Representative Companies
Architectural, construction, and engineering	Construction, power utilities, design, engineering services, for airports, hospitals, dams	ABB, Bechtel Group, Halliburton, Kajima, Philip Holzman, Skanska AB
Banking, finance, and insurance	Banks, insurance, risk evaluation, management	Bank of America, CIGNA, Barclays, HSBC, Ernst & Young
Education, training, and publishing	Management training, technical training, language training	Berlitz, Kumon Math & Reading Centers, NOVA, Pearson, Elsevier
Entertainment	Movies, recorded music, Internet-based entertainment	Time Warner, Sony, Virgin, MGM
Information services	E-commerce, e-mail, funds transfer, data interchange, data processing, computer services	Infosys, EDI, Hitachi, Qualcomm, Cisco
Professional business services	Accounting, advertising, legal, management consulting	Leo Burnett, EYLaw, McKinsey, A.T. Kearney, Booz Allen Hamilton
Transportation	Aviation, ocean shipping, railroads, trucking, airports	Maersk, Santa Fe, Port Authority of New Jersey, SNCF (French railroads)
Travel and tourism	Transportation, lodging, food and beverage, aircraft travel, ocean carriers, railways	Carlson Wagonlit, Marriott, British Airways

How Does International Business Differ from Domestic Business?

Firms that engage in international business operate in environments characterized by unique economic conditions, national culture, and legal and political systems. For example, the economic environment of Colombia differs sharply from that of Germany. The legal environment of Saudi Arabia does not resemble that of Japan. The cultural environment of China is very distinct from that of Kenya. Not only does the firm find itself in unfamiliar surroundings, it encounters many *uncontrollable variables*—factors over which management has little control. These factors introduce new or elevated business risks.

The Four Risks in Internationalization

Internationalizing firms are routinely exposed to four major types of risk, as illustrated in Exhibit 1.6: cross-cultural risk, country risk, currency risk, and commercial risk. The firm must manage these risks to avoid financial loss or product failures.

Cross-cultural risk occurs when a cultural misunderstanding puts some human value at stake. Cross-cultural risk arises from differences in language, lifestyles, mindsets, customs, and religion. Values unique to a culture tend to be long-lasting and transmitted from one generation to the next. These values influence the mind-set and work style of employees and the shopping patterns of buyers. Foreign customer characteristics differ significantly from those of buyers in the home market. Language is a critical

Cross-cultural risk

A situation or event where a cultural misunderstanding puts some human value at stake.

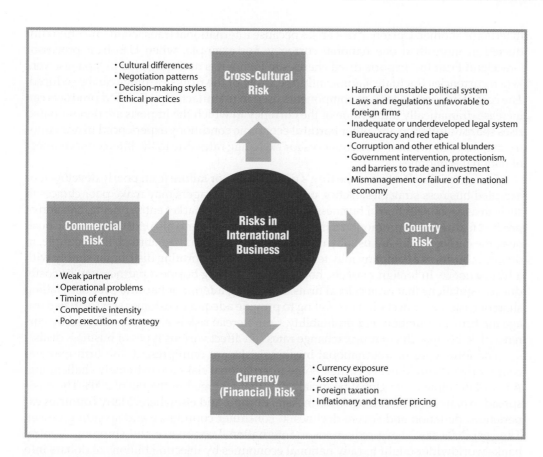

Exhibit 1.6 The Four Risks of International Business

dimension of culture. In addition to facilitating communication, language is a window on people's value systems and living conditions. For example, Inuit (Eskimo) languages have various words for snow, while the South American Aztecs used the same basic word stem for snow, ice, and cold. When translating from one language to another, it is often difficult to find words that convey the same meanings. For example, a one-word equivalent to *aftertaste* does not exist in many languages. Such challenges impede effective communication and cause misunderstandings. Miscommunication due to cultural differences gives rise to inappropriate business strategies and ineffective relations with customers. Cross-cultural risk most often occurs in encounters in foreign countries. However, the risk also can occur domestically, as when management meets with customers or business associates who visit company headquarters from abroad.

Country risk (also known as *political risk*) refers to the potentially adverse effects on company operations and profitability caused by developments in the political, legal, and economic environment in a foreign country. Country risk includes the possibility of foreign government intervention in firms' business activities. For example, governments may restrict access to markets, impose bureaucratic procedures on business transactions, and limit the amount of income that firms can bring home from foreign operations. The degree of government intervention in commercial activities varies from country to country. For example, Singapore and Ireland are characterized by substantial economic freedom—that is, a fairly liberal economic environment. By contrast, the Chinese and Russian governments regularly intervene in business affairs.[6] Country risk also includes laws and regulations that potentially hinder company operations and performance. Critical legal dimensions include property rights, intellectual property protection, product liability, and taxation policies. Nations also experience potentially harmful economic conditions, often due to high inflation, national debt, and unbalanced international trade. Indeed, the global financial crisis plunged many nations into a deep recession in 2009.

Currency risk (also known as *financial risk*) refers to the risk of adverse fluctuations in exchange rates. Fluctuation is common for *exchange rates*—the value of one currency

Country risk Exposure to potential loss or adverse effects on company operations and profitability caused by developments in a country's political and/or legal environments.

Currency risk Potential harm that arises from changes in the price of one currency relative to another.

in terms of another. Currency risk arises because international transactions are often conducted in more than one national currency. For example, when U.S. fruit processor Graceland Fruit Inc. exports dried cherries to Japan, it is normally paid in Japanese yen. When currencies fluctuate significantly, the value of the firm's earnings can be reduced. The cost of importing parts or components used in manufacturing finished products can increase dramatically if the value of the currency in which the imports are denominated rises sharply. Inflation and other harmful economic conditions experienced in one country may have immediate consequences for exchange rates due to the interconnectedness of national economies.

Commercial risk

Firm's potential loss or failure from poorly developed or executed business strategies, tactics, or procedures.

Commercial risk refers to the firm's potential loss or failure from poorly developed or executed business strategies, tactics, or procedures. Managers may make poor choices in such areas as the selection of business partners, timing of market entry, pricing, creation of product features, and promotional themes. While such failures also exist in domestic business, the consequences are usually more costly when committed abroad. For example, in domestic business a company may terminate a poorly performing distributor simply with advance notice. In foreign markets, however, terminating business partners can be costly due to regulations that protect local firms. Marketing inferior or harmful products, falling short of customer expectations, or failing to provide adequate customer service may damage the firm's reputation and profitability. Commercial risk is also often affected by currency risk, because fluctuating exchange rates can affect various types of business deals.

The four types of international business risks are omnipresent; the firm may encounter them around every corner. Some international risks are extremely challenging. A recent example is the global financial crisis that emerged in the fall of 2008. The crisis spread to banks and insurance firms in Asia, Europe, and elsewhere. Many countries experienced deflation and severe declines in consumer confidence and spending power. The year 2009 saw sharp reductions in international commerce and shipping. Central banks worldwide sought to rally national economies by injecting billions of dollars into their financial systems.[7]

Although risk cannot be avoided, it can be anticipated and managed. Experienced international firms constantly assess their environments and conduct research to anticipate potential risks, understand their implications, and take proactive action to reduce their effects. This book is dedicated to providing you, the future manager, with a solid understanding of these risks as well as managerial skills and strategies to effectively counter them.

Who Participates in International Business?

What types of organizations are active in international business? Among the most important are *focal firms*, the companies that directly initiate and implement international business activity. Two critical focal firms in international business are the multinational enterprise and the small and medium-sized enterprise.

Multinational Enterprise (MNE)

Multinational enterprise (MNE)

A large company with substantial resources that performs various business activities through a network of subsidiaries and affiliates located in multiple countries.

Multinational enterprises (also known as *multinational corporations*) historically have been the most important type of focal firm. A **multinational enterprise (MNE)** is a large company with substantial resources that performs various business activities through a network of subsidiaries and affiliates located in multiple countries. MNEs carry out research and development (R&D), procurement, manufacturing, and marketing activities wherever in the world the firm can reap the most advantages. For example, Alcon is a Swiss pharmaceutical firm that established major R&D facilities in the United States to take advantage of the country's superior know-how in the chemicals sector. Verizon Wireless has located much of its technical support operations in India, to take advantage of high-quality, low-cost customer support personnel located there. Royal Dutch Shell owns several oil refineries and nearly 2,000 gasoline stations in Canada. In addition to a home office or headquarters, the typical MNE owns a worldwide network of subsidiaries. It collaborates with numerous suppliers and independent business partners abroad (sometimes termed *affiliates*).

Typical MNEs include Barclays, Caterpillar, Disney, DHL, Four Seasons Hotels, Samsung, Unilever, Vodafone, and Nippon Life Insurance. In recent years, the largest MNEs have been firms in the oil industry (such as Exxon-Mobil and Royal Dutch Shell) and the automotive industry (General Motors and Honda), as well as retailing (Walmart). Exhibit 1.7 shows the geographic distribution of the world's largest MNEs, drawn from *Fortune*'s Global 500 list. As shown, these firms are concentrated in the advanced economies. The United States is home to 140 of the top 500 MNEs, a number that has declined over time as other countries' firms increase in size. Japan has the second-most MNEs (68 firms), followed by France (40 firms), Germany (39 firms), and Britain (26 firms). Collectively, the European Union countries have more top 500 firms than the United States.

In recent years, large MNEs have begun to appear in emerging market countries, such as China, Mexico, and Russia. China currently hosts 37 of the top 500 MNEs, a fairly recent development. The "new global challenger" firms from emerging markets are fast becoming key contenders in world markets. For example, the Mexican firm Cemex is one of the world's largest cement producers. In Russia, Lukoil has big ambitions in the global energy sector. China Mobile dominates the cell phone industry in Asia. The new global challengers make best use of home-country natural resources and low-cost labor to succeed in world markets. Thousands of firms from emerging markets have big global dreams and pose competitive challenges to companies from the advanced economies.

Although MNEs are among its leading participants, international business is not the domain of large, resourceful firms alone. Many **small and medium-sized enterprises (SMEs)** participate as well. An SME is a company with less than 500 employees, as defined in Canada and the United States. In the European Union, SMEs are defined as firms with less than 250 employees. In addition to accounting for smaller market shares of their respective industries, SMEs tend to have limited managerial and other resources and primarily use exporting to expand internationally. However, in most nations, SMEs constitute the great majority of all firms.

Small and medium-sized enterprise (SME) A company with 500 or fewer employees (as defined in Canada and the United States).

With the globalization of markets, advances in various technologies, and other facilitating factors, many more SMEs are pursuing international opportunities. SMEs account for about one-third of exports from Asia and about a quarter of exports from the affluent countries in Europe and North America. In some countries—for example, Italy, South Korea, and China—SMEs contribute roughly 50 percent of total national exports.[8]

One type of contemporary international SME is the **born global firm**, a young entrepreneurial company that initiates international business activity very early in its evolution, moving rapidly into foreign markets. Born globals are found in advanced economies, such as Australia and Japan, and in emerging markets, such as China and India.

Born global firm A young entrepreneurial company that initiates international business activity very early in its evolution, moving rapidly into foreign markets.

International business requires specialized knowledge, commitment of resources, and considerable time to develop foreign business partnerships. How do SMEs succeed in international business despite resource limitations? First, compared to large MNEs, smaller firms are often more innovative and adaptable and have quicker response times when it comes to implementing new ideas and technologies and meeting customer needs. Second, SMEs are better able to serve niche markets around the world that hold little interest for MNEs. Third, smaller firms are usually avid users of information and communication technologies, including the Internet. Fourth, as they usually lack substantial resources, smaller firms minimize overhead or fixed investments. They rely on external facilitators such as FedEx and DHL, as well as independent distributors in foreign markets. Fifth, smaller firms tend to thrive on private knowledge that they possess

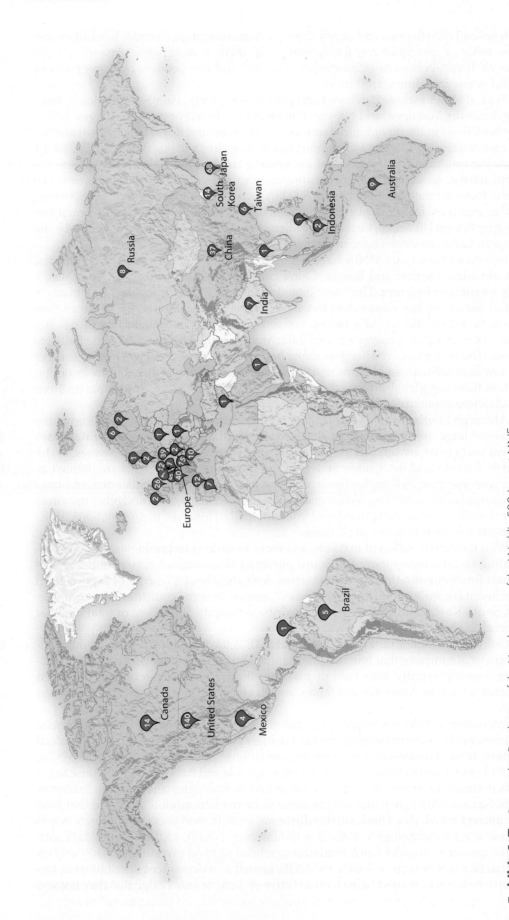

Exhibit 1.7 Geographic Distribution of the Headquarters of the World's 500 Largest MNEs

GL🌐BAL TREND

DIESEL: A Smaller Firm's Smashing International Success

The global youth culture loves Diesel jeans, Europe's hottest brand. Founded in Italy, Diesel began as an SME and grew to achieve annual sales of more than $1 billion (U.S.), 85 percent of which comes from abroad. Diesel produces unusual but popular men's and women's casual wear, like $150 jeans in exotic shades and styles, that competes with Donna Karan and Tommy Hilfiger brands. Its style is futuristic. Company management sees the world as a single, borderless macro-culture, and Diesel staff includes an assortment of personalities from all parts of the globe who create an unpredictable, dynamic vitality and energy. The firm focuses on design and marketing, leaving production to subcontractors.

Diesel has expanded distribution to department stores and specialty retailers in over 80 countries, as well as to 400 company-owned stores from Paris to Miami to Tokyo, and recently entered a marketing partnership with Adidas. Controversial advertising has propelled it to enormous international success. Ads have featured sumo wrestlers kissing, a row of chimpanzees giving the fascist salute, and inflatable naked dolls in a board meeting with a hugely overweight CEO. Some people see the prankish campaigns, which poke fun at death, obesity, murder, and do-gooders, as politically incorrect. Under pressure from activists, Diesel withdrew ads that applauded smoking and gun ownership with slogans such as "145 cigarettes a day will give you that sexy voice and win new friends." Another ad featured nuns in blue jeans below the copy, "Pure, virginal 100 percent cotton. Soft and yet miraculously strong."

Diesel was one of the first firms to have a major Internet presence (www.diesel.com), selling jeans via an online virtual store. Its web advertising is also hip, with a powerful, market-friendly message that drives its popularity among youth worldwide. The firm introduces some 1,500 new designs every 6 months and employs a multicultural team of young designers who travel the globe for inspiration and weave their impressions into the next collection. Diesel is a classic success story in international business by a smaller firm.

SOURCES: Web site, http://www.diesel.com; Gail Edmondson, "Diesel Is Smoking But Can Its Provocative Ads Keep Sales Growth Hot?" *Business Week*, February 10, 2003, p. 64; Diesel corporate profile at http://www.hoovers.com; Kevin Helliker, "Teen Retailing: The Underground Taste Makers—Is Diesel Apparel a Bit Too Trendy for Its Own Good?" *Wall Street Journal*, December 9, 1998, p. B1; Y. Moroz, "Adidas Refuels with Diesel Collaboration," *Retailing Today*, March 17, 2008, p. 4.

or produce. They access and mobilize resources through their cross-border knowledge networks or their international social capital.[9]

In each chapter of this text, you will find a feature entitled *Global Trend,* profiling an important new development in international business. The first *Global Trend* features Diesel, an SME that eventually grew into a large firm.

Non-governmental Organizations (NGOs)

In addition to profit-seeking focal firms in international business, numerous *non-profit organizations* conduct cross-border activities. These include charitable groups and *non-governmental organizations (NGOs).* They pursue special causes and serve as advocates for the arts, education, politics, religion, and research, operating internationally either to conduct their activities or to raise funds. Examples of non-profit organizations

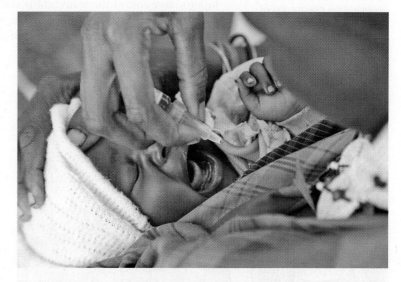

The British Wellcome Trust funds non-governmental organizations (NGOs) and research initiatives to work in collaboration with private businesses to develop remedies for diseases in Africa and other less developed areas around the world.

include the Bill and Melinda Gates Foundation and the British Wellcome Trust, both of which support health and educational initiatives. CARE is an international non-profit organization dedicated to reducing poverty. Many MNEs operate charitable foundations that support various initiatives. GlaxoSmithKline (GSK), the giant pharmaceutical firm, operates a number of small country-based foundations in Canada, France, Italy, Romania, Spain, and the United States.

Why Do Firms Internationalize?

There are multiple motives for international expansion. Some motives are strategic in nature, while others are reactive. An example of a strategic, or proactive, motive is to tap foreign market opportunities or acquire new knowledge. An example of a reactive motive is the need to serve a key customer that has expanded abroad. Nine specific motivations include:

1. *Seek opportunities for growth through market diversification.* Substantial market potential exists abroad. Many firms—for example, Gillette, Siemens, Sony, Biogen—derive more than half of their sales from international markets. In addition to offering sales opportunities that often cannot be matched at home, foreign markets can extend the marketable life of products or services that have reached maturity in the home market. One example is the internationalization of automatic teller machines (ATMs). The first ATM was installed outside a London branch of Barclays Bank in 1967. The machines were next adopted in the United States and Japan. As growth of ATMs began to slow in these countries, they were marketed throughout the rest of the world. Today there are more than 1.5 million ATMs worldwide; a new one is installed somewhere every few minutes.

2. *Earn higher margins and profits.* For many types of products and services, market growth in mature economies is sluggish or flat. Competition is often intense, forcing firms to get by on slim profit margins. By contrast, most foreign markets may be underserved (typical of high-growth emerging markets) or not served at all (typical of developing economies). Less intense competition, combined with strong market demand, implies that companies can command higher margins for their offerings. For example, compared to their home markets, bathroom fixture manufacturers American Standard and Toto (of Japan) have found more favorable competitive environments in rapidly industrializing countries such as Indonesia, Mexico, and Vietnam. Just imagine the demand for bathroom fixtures in the thousands of office buildings and residential complexes going up from Shanghai to Singapore!

A young workforce in emerging markets is accelerating integration of these economies with the rest of the world. Here affluent young people shop in downtown Shenzhen, China.

3. *Gain new ideas about products, services, and business methods.* International markets are characterized by tough competitors and demanding customers with various needs. Unique foreign environments expose firms to new ideas for products, processes, and business methods. The experience of doing business abroad helps firms acquire new knowledge for improving organizational effectiveness and efficiency. For example, just-in-time inventory techniques were refined by Toyota in Japan and then adopted by other manufacturers around the world. Numerous foreign suppliers learned about just-in-time from Toyota and then applied the method to manufacturing in their own countries.

4. *Better serve key customers that have relocated abroad.* In a global economy, many firms internationalize to better serve clients that have moved into foreign markets. For example, when Nissan opened its first factory in the United Kingdom, many Japanese auto parts suppliers followed, establishing their own operations there.

5. *Be closer to supply sources, benefit from global sourcing advantages, or gain flexibility in product sourcing.* Companies in extractive industries such as petroleum, mining, and forestry establish international operations where these raw materials are located. One example is the aluminum producer Alcoa, which established operations in Brazil, Guinea, Jamaica, and elsewhere to extract aluminum's base mineral bauxite from local mines. Some firms internationalize to gain flexibility from a greater variety of supply bases. Dell Computer has assembly facilities in Asia, Europe, and the Americas that allow management to quickly shift production from one region to another. This flexibility provides Dell with *competitive advantages* over less agile rivals—a distinctive capability that allows Dell to outperform competitors and skillfully manage fluctuations in currency exchange rates.

6. *Gain access to lower-cost or better-value factors of production.* Internationalization enables the firm to access capital, technology, managerial talent, and labor at lower costs, higher quality, or better value. For example, some Taiwanese computer manufacturers established subsidiaries in the United States to access low-cost capital. The United States is home to numerous capital sources in the high-tech sector, such as stock exchanges and venture capitalists, which have attracted countless firms from abroad seeking funds. More commonly, firms venture abroad in search of skilled or low-cost labor. For example, the Japanese firm Canon relocated much of its production to China to profit from that country's inexpensive and productive workforce.

7. *Develop economies of scale in sourcing, production, marketing, and R&D.* Economies of scale reduce the per-unit cost of manufacturing due to operating at high volume. For example, the per-unit cost of manufacturing 100,000 cameras is much cheaper than the per-unit cost of making just 100 cameras. By expanding internationally, the firm greatly increases the size of its customer base, thereby increasing the volume of products it manufactures. On a per-unit-of-output basis, the greater the volume of production, the lower the total cost. Economies of scale are also present in R&D, sourcing, marketing, distribution, and after-sales service.

8. *Confront international competitors more effectively or thwart the growth of competition in the home market.* International competition is substantial and increasing, with multinational competitors invading markets worldwide. The firm can enhance its competitive positioning by confronting competitors in international markets or preemptively entering a competitor's home markets to destabilize and curb its growth. One example is Caterpillar's entry into Japan just as its main rival in the earthmoving equipment industry, Komatsu, was getting started in the early 1970s. Caterpillar's preemptive move hindered Komatsu's international expansion for at least a decade. Had it not acted proactively to stifle Komatsu's growth in Japan, Komatsu's home market, Caterpillar would certainly have had to face a more potent rival sooner.

9. *Invest in a potentially rewarding relationship with a foreign partner.* Firms often have long-term strategic reasons for venturing abroad. Joint ventures or project-based alliances with key foreign players can lead to the development of new products, early positioning in future key markets, or other long-term, profit-making opportunities. For example, Black and Decker entered a joint venture with Bajaj, an Indian retailer, to position itself for expected long-term sales in the huge Indian market. The French computer firm Groupe Bull partnered with Toshiba in Japan to gain insights for developing the next generation of information technology.

At the broadest level, companies internationalize to enhance competitive advantage and to seek growth and profit opportunities. Throughout this book, we explore the environment within which firms seek these opportunities, and we discuss the strategies and managerial skills necessary for achieving international business success.

International trade is encouraging faster diffusion of consumer products and brands around the world.

Why Study International Business?

There are many reasons to study international business. We can examine them from the perspectives of the global economy, the national economy, the firm, and you as a future manager.

Facilitator of the Global Economy and Interconnectedness

International business is transforming the world as never before. In the last 50 years, international trade and investment have experienced unprecedented growth. Since the 1980s, *emerging markets* have provided new impetus to worldwide economic interconnectedness. These fast-growth developing economies—some thirty countries, including Brazil, Russia, India, and China, the so-called BRICs—are experiencing substantial market liberalization, privatization, and industrialization, which are fueling global economic transformation. Located on every continent, they are gradually breaking away from the stagnation typical of developing economies. The emerging markets are home to the largest proportion of world population and participate increasingly in foreign trade. In the opening vignette, Julie sampled products from several emerging markets, including China, Hungary, and Mexico.

Along with market globalization, *advances in technology* are another megatrend helping to transform the global economy. The rise of information and communication technologies, as well as production and process technologies, has dramatically reduced the cost of conducting business with customers around the world. E-commerce makes international business increasingly imperative for firms of all sizes and resource levels. Technological advances are allowing globalization to progress more rapidly. Globalization, in turn, is accelerating the development of the latest technologies.

Contributor to National Economic Well-Being

International business contributes to economic prosperity, helps countries use their resources more efficiently, and provides interconnectedness to the world economy and access to a range of products and services. Consequently, governments have become more willing to open their borders to foreign trade and investment.

International trade is a critical engine for job creation. It is estimated that every $1 billion increase in exports creates more than 20,000 new jobs. In the United States, cross-border trade directly supports at least twelve million jobs. One of every seven dollars of U.S. sales is made abroad. One of every three U.S. farm acres and one of every six U.S. jobs is producing for export markets. On average, exporting firms create jobs faster and provide better pay than nonexporting firms.[10]

There is a strong relationship between national prosperity and participation in international trade and investment. Nations once suffering from economic stagnation are now increasingly prosperous. For example, China, India, and Eastern European nations are active international traders. The proportion of affluent citizens in these countries is growing rapidly. In terms of material gain, households in many developing economies have recently experienced huge increases in the ownership of televisions, refrigerators, and other mass-produced products. While these gains are attributable to various causes, the benefits of free exchange of products, services, capital, and technology among nations are paramount.

Rising prosperity associated with international trade and investment helps improve literacy rates, nutrition, and health care in nations around the world. Trade and investment promote freedom and democracy and may reduce the likelihood of cross-border conflict. In an era of economic turmoil and strained global relations, international business is helping to decrease such tensions, by reducing world poverty and increasing interactions that help soothe relations among nations.[11]

Cross-border business also helps integrate world economies. Development of the European Union (EU) is transforming Europe into a new powerhouse in global trade. The North American Free Trade Agreement (NAFTA), launched in 1994, has integrated the economies of Canada, Mexico, and the United States into a giant market of roughly 450 million consumers. Following NAFTA's launch, the volume of trade among the three countries jumped dramatically. In Mexico, NAFTA led to substantially higher wages and higher employment rates.[12] Recently, a new accord was launched between the United States and Costa Rica, El Salvador, Guatemala, Honduras, Nicaragua, and the Dominican Republic. Known as the Dominican Republic Central American Free Trade Agreement (DR-CAFTA), it is invigorating the economies of the member countries.

International business contributes to national economic well-being. Nations once suffering from economic stagnation are now increasingly prosperous. This trendy shopping mall is in Kuala Lumpur, Malaysia.

A Competitive Advantage for the Firm

To sustain a competitive advantage in the global economy, firms must readily participate in cross-border business and acquire the necessary skills, knowledge, and competence. Procter & Gamble sells shampoo, disposable diapers, and other consumer products in more than 150 countries. MTV broadcasts its programming in some 140 countries. Nestlé sells its food and beverage products worldwide, obtaining nearly all its revenue from foreign operations. As these examples imply, going international offers countless opportunities for firms to grow and earn additional profits.

In addition, international business allows firms to maximize the efficiency of their operations. Companies secure cost-effective factor inputs by establishing manufacturing in emerging markets like Malaysia, Mexico, and Poland, or sourcing from foreign suppliers. For example, Microsoft cuts the costs of its operations by having much of its software written in India. Renault achieves efficiency by assembling cars at low-cost factories in Romania.

International business also allows firms to access critical resources that may be unavailable at home. It helps firms reduce the costs of new product development, after-sales service, and other critical business activities. Companies access foreign sources of information and knowledge that provide the basis for future R&D, improved production and administrative processes, and other innovations. Finally, internationalization broadens the firm's options for dealing with competitors. It offers opportunities to make globally strategic moves and countermoves that help the firm compete more effectively with rivals.[13]

A Competitive Advantage for You

Julie, the student in the opening vignette, is touched every day by a variety of international business transactions. She is considering a career in international business because she grasps its growing importance. She is beginning a path full of intrigue and excitement. While most international careers are based in one's home country, managers travel the world and meet people from various cultures and backgrounds. Traveling abroad leads to exciting challenges and learning experiences. Managers rising to the top of most of the world's leading corporations honed their managerial skills in international business. In this text you will learn about the merits of gaining international business proficiency, through the experiences of people like you, in a special feature called *Recent Grad in IB*. Read about Ashley Lumb, a recent graduate who is enjoying her early experiences in international business.

Recent Grad in IB

Ashley's majors: Finance and International Business

Objectives: Adventure, international perspective, self-understanding, career growth, and the opportunity to learn foreign languages

Internships during college: Merrill Lynch

Ashley Lumb

Jobs held since graduating:

- Junior Analyst at KPMG, London, England
- Marketing Representative, Vins Sans Frontieres, Nice, France
- Account Representative, The Ultimate Living Group, Monte Carlo, Monaco
- Marketing Associate, Made in Museum, Rome, Italy
- Advertising/Marketing Coordinator, *Italian Vogue*, New York, United States

In Ashley Lumb's senior year in college, a six-week study abroad program to Europe sparked a desire for an international career. Following graduation, Ashley interned as a Junior Analyst at KPMG in London, where she gained technical training and analytical skills. She wanted to work in the luxury goods industry in Europe and eventually took a six-month contract job at Vins Sans Frontieres. VSF enrolled Ashley in its wine courses at the company headquarters in the south of France. VSF imports wine from around the world and sells it exclusively to private yachts along the French Riviera. Ashley gained experience in various marketing methods. For example, VSF attends yacht trade fairs and hosts wine tastings. VSF's marketing reps like Ashley scour the ports from San Remo, Italy, to St. Tropez, France, daily, speaking with yacht chefs, stewards, or captains about wine and distributing wine catalogs.

Ashley next worked as an account representative for The Ultimate Living Group in Monte Carlo, Monaco. The company caters to the corporate jet set that travels to Cannes for meetings and conferences. The key event of the year is the Cannes Film Festival.

Ashley then took up a position as a marketing associate at Made in Museum (MIM) in Rome, Italy. MIM specializes in the design, production, and delivery of authorized museum reproductions. It markets jewelry, sculptures, mosaics, and Etruscan pottery. Ashley organized the products into groups and restructured the inventory and Web site.

While in Italy, Ashley developed a passion for the fashion industry, so she decided to move to New York. Before leaving Italy, Ashley took a course at the prestigious Polimoda International Institute of Design and Marketing in Florence entitled "Business and Marketing in the Fashion Industry." In New York, Ashley worked at the headquarters of fashion houses Hermès and J. Crew. Subsequently, she leveraged the services of a bilingual recruiting agency, Euromonde Inc., to land a job at *Italian Vogue* magazine in Times Square to work as the U.S. advertising/marketing coordinator.

Ashley's Advice for an International Career

"Working abroad helped me sort through my career goals, as Europe offered a view into other industries that the U.S. lacked. I was able to experience different cultures and work environments and, although they might seem far apart, I saw a shared passion for exceptional products and dynamism. Back in the U.S., my international experience was an impressive asset to prospective employers; it is valued as proof of one's ability to handle challenging assignments and work with people from diverse cultures and backgrounds."

Success Factors

"The two most important factors in working abroad were *hard work* and *networking*. I cast a wide net and met many people, sent a lot of résumés, asked many questions, and researched the market. To keep myself afloat between assignments, I took some unglamorous jobs. Some days I wanted to give up and go home, but instead I just kept going. . . . Hard work and persistence are crucial."

Challenges

"The decision to work abroad carries some risks. After all, you're leaving much of what you know behind and stepping outside a clearly defined career path. The language barrier is always present. The work was usually in English, though I did pick up Italian and a bit of French through classes and immersing myself in the culture."

What's Ahead?

"I'd like to continue my path in the fashion magazine industry and work in a merchandising, special events, or promotions capacity. I'm also studying French and eventually I would like to attend the graduate school ESSEC, Paris, to pursue an MBA program that specializes in international luxury goods management."

An Opportunity for Global Corporate Citizenship

As the world's population grows, so do pressures to meet consumer demand. Increasingly, companies operate in environments characterized by limited resources, vulnerable human conditions, and stakeholder consciousness on issues that affect all society. In response to this trend, companies are increasing their awareness about the social and environmental implications of their actions.

Rather than being caught off guard, firms increasingly develop socially responsible policies and practices. For example, Starbucks began selling coffee only from growers certified by the Rain Forest Alliance (www.rainforest-alliance.org), a non-profit organization that promotes the interests of coffee growers and the environment. Such multinational enterprises as Philips, Unilever, and Walmart follow business practices that promote sustainable development. McDonald's buys beef from farmers who meet special standards on animal welfare and environmental practices. Its outlets in Britain, Germany, Sweden, and Austria sell only organic milk.[14] Internationally active firms must embed corporate citizenship into their strategic decisions as well as their ongoing processes and practices. Ethics and responsible behavior in firms' international activities are of such importance that we devote Chapter 5 to this topic.

 Closing Case

Whirlpool's Dramatic Turnaround Through Internationalization

Home appliance maker Whirlpool Corporation, headquartered in Benton Harbor, Michigan, generated over $19 billion in annual sales in 2006, an increase of 26 percent from the previous year. Key factors influencing this performance include the acquisition of the Maytag Corporation in 2006 and an increased global demand for its brands and innovative products. During the next several years, the company expects growth in Asia and Latin America to be significantly higher than in North America and Europe.

Whirlpool employs more than 80,000 employees in over 60 manufacturing and technology centers worldwide. The firm manufactures washers, dryers, refrigerators, dishwashers, freezers, ranges, compactors, and microwave ovens in 13 countries and sells them in 170 others under brand names such as Whirlpool, Maytag, Magic Chef, Jenn-Air, Amana, KitchenAid, Kenmore, Brastemp, and Bauknecht. Whirlpool generates almost 60 percent of its sales from North America, 25 percent from Europe, 15 percent from Latin America, and just 2 percent from Asia.

International Expansion

As the U.S. appliance market matured in the 1990s, Whirlpool faced intense domestic competition and more demanding buyers, resulting in lower profit margins. Meanwhile, international market trade barriers fell, consumer affluence grew, and capitalism flourished. Management realized that it could best deal with these threats and opportunities by undertaking a systematic program of internationalization. As a result, Whirlpool engaged in a series of moves over the next decade.

Whirlpool acquired the appliance business of Philips in Europe, 65 percent of Italian cooling compressor manufacturer Aspera, and purchased Poland's second largest appliance maker. In Eastern Europe, Whirlpool created subsidiaries to sell and service appliances in Bulgaria, Hungary, Romania, Russia, Slovakia, and the Czech Republic.

In China, Whirlpool formed a joint venture to produce air conditioners and established a corporate headquarters and product development/technology center in Shanghai. The company also opened regional offices in

Hong Kong, New Delhi, and Singapore. In Mexico, Whirlpool acquired Vitromatic, a former joint venture partner in Mexico. It also developed low-cost versions of popular models to target customers in low-income markets in Latin America, China, and India.

Three factors have driven this global expansion. First, Whirlpool sought to reduce its costs of R&D, manufacturing, and service by locating plants and other operations in lower-cost locations such as China, Mexico, and Poland. Second, flat to declining sales growth in the United States pressured management to target sales in new markets abroad. Third, Whirlpool realized the firm's manufacturing and assembly operations would benefit from a more global approach. Management redesigned products with more standardized parts and ramped up marketing to make Whirlpool a globally recognized brand. The company integrated the activities of regional subsidiaries so that Whirlpool's most advanced expertise in appliance technology, production, and distribution could be shared with the firm's divisions worldwide.

Innovation

Whirlpool conducted an internal critical assessment in the late 1990s. It became apparent that a consumer walking into any appliance store anywhere in the world would witness a "sea of white" appliances with little differentiation, even between manufacturers. The industry became known as the "white goods business." Consumers perceived the products as commodities, which offered little differential advantage and commanded ever lower prices due to increasing competition.

In 1999, Whirlpool management launched a major campaign to differentiate the firm's offerings by emphasizing innovative, value-added products. In early 2000, Whirlpool enlisted 75 employees from almost every job classification and assigned them in groups to Benton Harbor, Italy, and Brazil. Training lasted nearly a year and was conducted by an outside consulting group.

The next step was to get the rest of the global workforce involved. Whirlpool established an intranet site and created a do-it-yourself course in innovation. Throughout 2001 and 2002 Whirlpool's "knowledge management" intranet site recorded up to 300,000 hits per month. The company established a rating system to identify high potential, innovative ideas. Since 2003, revenue has quadrupled annually. Whirlpool estimates that the new appliances in development from this system, once marketed, could produce $3 billion in annual sales, up from projections of $1.3 billion in 2003. Whirlpool developed microwave ovens that can grill steaks, bake pizzas, or come in the form of a drawer that slides out for easy access to large dishes. The firm invented a washer with a built-in sensor that detects the size of the load and automatically picks the water level, spin speed, and type of wash cycle, essentially making all decisions for the user.

Local Preferences

Cross-regional R&D teams also collaborate on innovations to adapt offerings to meet local demands in diverse international environments. For example, due to very different climates, Italians often line-dried their clothing, while the Danes need to spin-dry their clothes. Capacity requirements vary greatly for refrigerators. The Spanish care about capacity for meats, the British want well-constructed units, and the French are more concerned about the capacity for keeping fruits and vegetables fresh. Germans are particularly concerned about environmental features, while child safety features are very important to the Italians. In India, Whirlpool developed a washing machine that delivers a higher level of cleanliness for consumers who believe whiteness of clothing expresses purity. The washer's gentle hand-scrub movement and unique "hot wash technology" maximize the effectiveness of laundry detergent.

Whirlpool has benefited immensely from international business. The firm is a leading example of how internationalization can revive declining sales and optimize cost structures. It has developed international distribution that reduces expenses, leading to higher profits, and has positioned itself to challenge competitors on a global scale. The firm has thrived through sensitivity and commitment to consumers in diverse cultural and economic settings around the world.

Growing Competitive Threat from Abroad

Yet not all is bright and sparkling on Whirlpool's horizon. Haier, China's largest appliance maker, established a production base and a distribution center in South Carolina in the United States. The firm also bought a six-story landmark structure in New York, dubbed the Haier Building, to house its U.S. headquarters. The world's fifth-largest kitchen appliance maker, Haier has captured nearly 20 percent and 50 percent of the markets for window air conditioners and small refrigerators, respectively. Now it is expanding into full-size refrigerators. Haier's moves are especially troubling given that Whirlpool generates very little of its sales from Asia, the world's most populous region, where Haier already has a strong presence.

Ironically, Haier's South Carolina factory is creating new jobs in a state that witnessed a mass exodus of textile jobs to factories in China. South Carolina receives foreign direct investment from various countries and is home to four Japanese and 18 European facilities. These trends show that globalization both benefits and poses new threats to Whirlpool's international ambitions.

As it struggles to remain a world-class player in a key industry, Whirlpool faces new challenges. Management wants to expand sales in emerging markets while defending the home market from global rivals from China and elsewhere. The firm seeks to continue to leverage and enjoy all the benefits of international business.

AACSB: Reflective Thinking Skills, Analytic Skills

Case Questions

1. What is the nature of Whirlpool's domestic and international business environments? What types of risk does the firm face?

2. How can Whirlpool benefit from going international? What types of advantages can the firm obtain? What advantages acquired abroad can help management improve Whirlpool's performance in its home market?

3. What actions has Whirlpool management taken to ensure that the firm succeeds in local markets throughout the world? To what extent is the appliance business local/regional rather than global?

4. How can Whirlpool effectively compete with new rivals originating from low-cost countries, such as Haier from China? Should Whirlpool's response differ in its home and foreign markets? If so, how?

5. The "Careers" section at Whirlpool's website (www.whirlpool.com/) advertises "opportunities you never knew existed . . . everywhere across the globe." Visit the site and report on the types of jobs available at Whirlpool and the locations of these positions worldwide. What positions interest you most? Would you like to work in Whirlpool's international operations? Why or why not?

SOURCES: Association of Home Appliance Manufacturers Web site, www.aham.org/News; Cavusgil, Tamer. (2001). "Globalization Headaches at Whirlpool" *Global Marketing 3rd Edition*. Boston: McGraw-Hill. Hoover's online Web site for Whirlpool Corporation www.hoovers.com; Spors, Kelly. (2004). "Against the Grain: A Chinese Appliance Maker has Placed Its Bet on a Counterintuitive Strategy: It's Bringing Jobs to the U.S." *Wall Street Journal*, September 27, p. R6; Stepanek, Marcia. (2000). "As I Was Saying to My Refrigerator. . .," *Business Week*, September 18, p. 40; Stevens, James. (2002). "In Hot pursuit of Mexico: Whirlpool," *Appliance Manufacturer*, October 50(10), pp. 12–13; *Whirlpool Corporation Annual Report 2005*. Whirlpool's corporate Web site; press release, February 7, 2007, www.whirlpoolcorp.com; May 8, 2006. "Creativity Overflowing" www.businessweek.com; May 8, 2006. "Whirlpool's Future Won't Fade" www.businessweek.com

CHAPTER ESSENTIALS

Key Terms

born global firm, p. 49
commercial risk, p. 48
country risk, p. 47
cross-cultural risk, p. 46
currency risk, p. 47
exporting, p. 41

foreign direct investment (FDI), p. 41
globalization of markets, p. 40
importing or global sourcing, p. 41
international business, p. 40
international investment, p. 41
international portfolio investment, p. 41

international trade, p. 41
multinational enterprise (MNE), p. 48
small and medium-sized enterprise (SMEs), p. 49

Summary

In this chapter, you learned about:

1. What is international business?

International business refers to the performance of trade and investment activities by firms across national borders. **Globalization of markets** is the ongoing economic integration and growing interdependency of countries worldwide. International business is characterized by international trade and investment.

2. What are the key concepts in international trade and investment?

International trade refers to exchange of products and services across national borders, typically through exporting and importing. **Exporting** is the sale of products or services to customers located abroad, from a base in the home country or a third country. **Importing** or **global sourcing** refers to procurement of products or services from foreign suppliers for consumption in the home country or a third country. **International investment** refers to international transfer or acquisition of ownership in assets. **International portfolio investment** is passive ownership of foreign securities such as stocks and bonds for the purpose of generating financial returns. **Foreign direct investment** is an internationalization strategy in which the firm establishes a physical presence abroad through acquisition of productive assets such as capital, technology, labor, land, plant, and equipment.

3. How does international business differ from domestic business?

International firms are constantly exposed to four major categories of risk that must be managed. **Cross-cultural risk** refers to a situation or event where some human value has been put at stake due to a cultural misunderstanding. **Country risk** refers to the potentially adverse effects on company operations and profitability caused by developments in the political, legal, and economic environment in a foreign country. **Currency risk** refers to the risk of adverse fluctuations in exchange rates. **Commercial risk** arises from the possibility of a firm's loss or failure from poorly developed or executed business strategies, tactics, or procedures. The risks are ever-present in international business and firms take proactive steps to reduce their effects.

4. Who participates in international business?

A key participant in international business is the **multinational enterprise (MNE)**, a large company with many resources whose business activities are performed by a network of subsidiaries located in multiple countries. Also active in international business are **small and medium-sized enterprises (SMEs)**, companies with 500 or fewer employees. **Born global firms** are entrepreneurial firms that initiate international business from or near their founding. Non-governmental organizations (NGOs) are nonprofit organizations that pursue special causes and serve as an advocate for the arts, education, politics, religion, and research.

5. Why do firms internationalize?

Companies internationalize for various reasons. These include the ability to increase sales and profits, better serve customers, access lower-cost or superior production factors, optimize sourcing activities, develop economies of scale, confront competitors more effectively, develop rewarding relationships with foreign partners, and gain access to new ideas for creating or improving products and services.

6. Why study international business?

There are many reasons to study international business. It enhances a firm's competitive positioning in the global market, facilitates development of the global economy and of the interconnectedness among nations, and contributes to national economic well-being. From a career standpoint, learning about international business will provide you with a competitive edge and enhance your ability to thrive in the job market. Firms have various opportunities for ethical corporate citizenship abroad.

Test Your Comprehension AACSB: Reflective Thinking Skills

1. Distinguish between international business and globalization of markets.

2. What is the difference between exporting and foreign direct investment?

3. What makes international business different from domestic business?

4. What are the various types of risks that firms face when they conduct international business?

5. Who are the major participants in international business?

6. What is the difference between a multinational enterprise (MNE) and a small and medium-sized enterprise (SME)?

7. What are some of the key motivations for firms to engage in international business?

8. Why should you care about international business?

Apply Your Understanding AACSB: Communication Abilities, Reflective Thinking Skills, Ethical Understanding and Reasoning Abilities

1. Richard Bendix is the marketing manager at a firm that makes and sells high-quality prefabricated houses. He believes that there is little difference between his home-country market and foreign markets and that he can use the same methods for selling in Asia or Latin America as he does in his home country. Write a memo in which you explain to Richard the differences between domestic and international business. Explain the risks and other differences that Richard's firm will likely encounter if it expands abroad.

2. Suppose that after graduation you get a job with Cottonwood Corporation, a small firm that does business only in its domestic market. You have just completed coursework in international business, are aware of various business opportunities abroad, and believe that Cottonwood should internationalize. Write a memo to your boss in which you explain why your company should pursue international business. What are the benefits to Cottonwood of venturing abroad? Explain why firms internationalize.

3. You have become the president of the International Business Club at your school. You are trying to recruit new members and find that many students do not recognize the importance of international business or the career opportunities available to them. You decide to give a presentation on this theme. Prepare an outline of a presentation in which you explain what types of companies participate in international business, why students should study international business, and what career opportunities they might find.

globalEDGE Internet Exercises
(http://globalEDGE.msu.edu)

AACSB: Communication Abilities, Use of Information Technology, Analytic Skills

1. You can gain valuable insights into international business by examining how countries compare to each other. Various research groups and international agencies systematically examine economic, political, and other features of nations and provide annual rankings. Visit globalEDGE™ Resource Desk and click on "Research: Rankings." You will find more than two dozen country rankings based on: degree of globalization, attractiveness with respect to FDI or global sourcing, retail development, extent of e-readiness, degree of economic freedom, quality of living, global competitiveness, and many other factors. Choose the ranking study that is of most interest to you. Learn about the methodology and the specific indicators used to rate countries. Then, examine how the following three countries rank in this study: Germany, Singapore, and South Africa. Based on your examination of their relative standing, provide an explanation of why they rank where they do. Indicate whether their relative positions make sense to you.

2. In this chapter, we reviewed the four major risks that firms face in international business: cross-cultural risk, country risk, currency risk, and commercial risk. Identify one or more countries that interest you, then visit globalEDGE™ and research the countries to uncover examples of each of the four types of risks. For example, China is characterized by various cultural differences and a national government that tends to intervene in business. Research by entering the country name into the search engine. Then, under Quick Links, visit links such as the Country Commercial Guide and Economist Country Briefing. Illustrate each risk with examples.

3. You have recently been hired by a smaller firm that is beginning to expand internationally. When first starting out, most firms choose exporting as their main foreign market entry strategy. However, no one in your firm knows how to conduct exporting. Therefore, your boss has given you an assignment: Prepare a presentation for your coworkers on how to engage in exporting. Using globalEDGE™, find and review a "Guide to Exporting" that you can use to create your presentation.

CHAPTER 2

LEARNING OBJECTIVES In this chapter, you will learn about:

1. Why globalization is not new
2. Market globalization: An organizing framework
3. Dimensions of market globalization
4. Drivers of market globalization
5. Technological advances
6. Societal consequences of market globalization
7. Firm-level consequences of market globalization: Internationalization of the firm's value chain

Globalization of Markets and the Internationalization of the Firm

Bangalore: IT's Global Destination

Weekday evenings in Bangalore, thousands of young men and women commute by bus to call centers throughout the city, the fifth largest in India. As the business day begins in Eastern Canada and the United States, these young Indians put on their telephone headsets to begin the overnight shift. They assist North American customers with service problems regarding credit cards, product purchases, and Internet transactions. To put callers at ease, they often use Western-sounding names (e.g., Bill, Mary) and may receive language training that includes specific accents and cultural tips on callers' geographical locations.

In all, more than 100,000 Indians work in Bangalore writing software, designing chips, running computer systems, reading X-rays, processing mortgages, preparing tax forms, and tracing lost luggage for firms in Australia, China, Europe, Japan, and North America. The same trend is found in Delhi, Chennai, Hyderabad, and other emerging high-tech centers across India. Accenture, AOL, British Airways, Cisco, Philips, and Ernst & Young all have located operations in the country.

The number of people working in outsourced information technology (IT) services in India surpassed one million in 2008. What is the attraction? First, Indians are paid roughly one-quarter of what Westerners receive for similar work, and in many cases they do a better job. Second, India is home to several million highly educated knowledge workers. Third, English is widely spoken. Fi-

nally, being located in a different time zone from Europe and the United States allows Indians to take advantage of time-sharing: When North Americans are ending their workday, Indians are arriving at the office to start theirs. Thanks to instant data transmission technologies, Europeans and North Americans can e-mail the projects they are working on to their Indian counterparts, who then submit the completed work by the next morning. For firms in the knowledge economy, welcome to the 24-hour workday.

Infosys (www.infosys.com) is India's leading software company. CEO Nandan Nilekani has a video conference room with wall-size flat screen TVs through which he regularly holds virtual meetings with suppliers around the world. The firm's U.S. designers can be on the screen speaking with their Indian software writers and their Asian manufacturers simultaneously. "That's what globalization is all about today," says Nilekani. Above the screen are eight clocks that sum up the Infosys workday: 24/7/365. The clocks are labeled U.S. West, U.S. East, London, India, Singapore, Hong Kong, Japan, and Australia.[1]

Nilekani explains that computers are becoming cheaper and commonplace around the world, and there has been an explosion of e-mail software and search engines like Google. Proprietary software can chop up any piece of work and send one part to Boston, one part to Bangalore, and one part to Beijing, making it easy for anyone to do remote development. "When all these things came together, they created a platform for intellectual work that could be delivered from anywhere. It could be disaggregated, delivered, distributed, produced, and put back together again. What you see in Bangalore today is really the culmination of all these things coming together." Emerging markets like India, Brazil, and China can compete equally for global knowledge work as never before.[2]

Ravi Patel is typical of the knowledge workers that Bangalore IT firms employ. He drives a Suzuki car, uses a Sony Ericsson mobile phone, and banks with Citibank. He hangs out with friends drinking Starbucks coffee or Bacardi and Sprite. He watches U.S. movies on a Samsung TV, brushes his teeth with Colgate, and owns a pair of Reeboks. At work Ravi drinks Coca-Cola, and uses an Acer computer with Microsoft software, a Lucent telephone, and a Mita copy machine.

Ravi's life illustrates the phenomenon of globalization. Globalization has several implications:

- It is increasingly difficult to distinguish where you are in the world based on the products and services you consume.
- Important technologies can be developed in most locations worldwide.
- Jobs in the knowledge sector are being performed wherever the firm can ex-

tract maximal advantages, anywhere in the world.

- In the long run, by emphasizing free trade and global sourcing, globalization allows consumers worldwide to receive maximum quality at minimum price. Buyers in both producer and consumer nations can increase their income and quality of life.[3]

Meanwhile, Bangalore is also experiencing the downside of globalization. Before leading software companies made it their headquarters, it was considered one of India's most livable cities, with cheap housing and a rich cultural environment. But Bangalore may be choking on its own success: The arrival of hundreds of thousands of IT workers has brought congestion, pollution, high rents, a raucous nightlife, and Western values. In 2008, Bangalore opened a new, $500 million airport to support the city's rapid growth, even though fewer than 5 percent of Bangalore residents have ever been inside an airplane. And while a shortage of affordable housing has forced long-time residents out of the city or into slums, government construction projects focus on high-rise apartments for the wealthy.

SOURCES: Mehul Srivastava, "A Backlash Grows in Bangalore Over Tech Revolution," *Business Week*, November 6, 2008; John Heilemann, "In Through the Outsourcing Door." *Business 2.0*, November 2004; "Where Is Your Job Going?" *Fortune*, November 2003; Thomas Friedman, "It's a Flat World, After All," *The New York Times Magazine*, April 2005; Jeremy Siegel, *The Future for Investors* (New York: Crown Business, 2005).

Globalization of markets Ongoing economic integration and growing interdependency of countries worldwide.

The chapter-opening vignette highlights two megatrends that, more than any others, have altered the international business environment: technological advances and the **globalization of markets**. As we discussed in Chapter 1, globalization of markets refers to the gradual integration and growing interdependence of national economies. Globalization allows firms to view the world as an integrated marketplace that includes buyers, producers, suppliers, and governments in different countries. Market globalization is manifested by the production and marketing of branded products and services worldwide. Declining trade barriers and the ease with which international business transactions take place due to the Internet and other technologies are contributing to a gradual integration of most national economies into a unified global marketplace.

Ongoing technological advances characterize the other megatrend that has transformed contemporary business. Developments in information, manufacturing, and transportation technologies, as well as the emergence of the Internet, have facilitated rapid and early internationalization of countless firms, such as Neogen (www.neogen .com). The firm's founders developed diagnostic kits to test for food safety. Compared to test kits available from other firms, Neogen's products were more accurate, more efficient, and easier to use. As word spread about the superiority of its products, Neogen was able to internationalize quickly and acquired a worldwide clientele. Farmers use Neogen test kits to test for pesticide residue; veterinarians use them for pharmaceuticals, vaccines, and topicals; government agencies use them to test for *E. coli*. Today, Neogen is a highly successful international firm.

Modern technology is promoting a higher level of international business activity than ever before. For example, many companies in software, gaming, and entertainment maintain a presence only on the Web. Advances in transportation and communication technologies have greatly aided express delivery service providers such as DHL, UPS, and FedEx to serve clients around the world.

The twin trends of market globalization and technological advances now permit firms to more readily engage in both marketing and *procurement* activities on a global scale. Companies increasingly sell their offerings throughout the world. Firms source raw materials, parts, components, and service inputs from suppliers located around the globe. Such trends are transforming national economies. Growing world trade and foreign direct investment (FDI), coupled with the spread of technology, provide consumers and industrial buyers with a much wider choice of products and services. The competitive and innovative activities of internationally active firms are helping to reduce the prices people pay for products and services. Job creation by internationally active firms is contributing to higher living standards around the world. At the same time, preferences for some consumer products appear to be converging across markets, exemplified by the universal popularity of certain music, entertainment, consumer electronics, and food. Globalization is helping disseminate values from liberalized economies about free trade and respect for intellectual property rights to an ever-widening international audience.[4]

 ## Why Globalization Is Not New

Globalization is not new; it has simply accelerated and acquired a more complex character in recent decades. In early history, civilizations in the Mediterranean, Middle East, Asia, Africa, and Europe all contributed to the growth of cross-border trade. Globalization evolved out of a common desire of civilizations, no matter where they developed, to reach out and touch one another.[5] It is a culmination of people's recognition, thousands of years ago, of the wonders of difference and discovery. Exchange with others gave societies the opportunity to expand and grow. Trade through the ages fostered civilization; without it, we would be a world of warring tribes bent on getting what we need through combat.[6] Cross-border trading opened the world to innovations and progress.

Phases of Globalization

We can identify four distinct phases in the evolution of market globalization since the 1800s. Each phase, as illustrated in Exhibit 2.1, was accompanied by revolutionary technological developments and international trends.

The first phase of globalization began about 1830 and peaked around 1880.[7] International business became widespread due to the growth of railroads, efficient ocean

Phase of Globalization	Approximate Period	Triggers	Key Characteristics
First phase	1830 to late 1800s, peaking in 1880	Introduction of railroads and ocean transport	Rise of manufacturing: cross-border trade of commodities, largely by trading companies
Second phase	1900 to 1930	Rise of electricity and steel production	Emergence and dominance of early MNEs (mainly from Europe and North America) in manufacturing, extractive, and agricultural industries
Third phase	1948 to 1970s	Formation of General Agreement on Tariff and Trade (GATT); conclusion of World War II; Marshall Plan to reconstruct Europe	Focus by industrializing Western countries to reduce trade barriers; rise of MNEs from Japan; development of global capital markets; rise of global trade names
Fourth phase	1980s to present	Privatization of state enterprises in transition economies; revolution in information, communication, and transportation technologies; remarkable growth of emerging markets	Rapid growth in cross-border trade of products, services, and capital; rise of internationally-active SMEs and services firms; rising prosperity of emerging markets

Exhibit 2.1   Phases of Globalization Since the Early 1800s

transport, and the rise of large manufacturing and trading firms. Invention of the telegraph and telephone in the late 1800s facilitated information flows between and within nations and greatly aided early efforts to manage companies' supply chains.

The second phase of globalization began around 1900 and was associated with the rise of electricity and steel production. This phase reached its height just before the Great Depression, a worldwide economic downturn that began in 1929. In 1900, Western Europe was the most industrialized world region. Europe's colonization of countries in Asia, Africa, and the Middle East led to establishment of some of the earliest subsidiaries of multinational enterprises (MNEs). European companies such as BASF, Nestlé, Shell, Siemens, and British Petroleum had established foreign manufacturing plants by 1900.[8] In the years before World War I (pre-1914), many firms were already operating globally. The Italian manufacturer Fiat supplied vehicles to nations on both sides of the war.

The third phase of globalization began after World War II. At war's end in 1945, substantial pent-up demand existed for consumer products, as well as for input goods to rebuild Europe and Japan. The United States was least harmed by the war and became the world's dominant economy. Substantial government aid helped stimulate economic activity in Europe. The pre-war years had been characterized by high tariffs and strict controls on currency and capital movements. After the war, leading industrialized countries, including Australia, Britain, and the United States, sought to reduce international trade barriers.

The Bretton Woods Conference of twenty-three nations in 1947 led to the *General Agreement on Tariffs and Trade (GATT)* and a series of negotiations that, over time, reduced barriers to international trade and investment. Participating governments recognized that liberalized trade would stimulate industrialization, modernization, and better living standards. The GATT eventually transformed into the **World Trade Orga-nization (WTO**; www.wto.org), a multilateral governing body that grew to include 149 member nations. The WTO aims to regulate and ensure fairness and efficiency in global trade and investment. Global cooperation in the post-war era gave birth to other international organizations such as the International Monetary Fund and the World Bank.

Early multinationals from this third phase of globalization originated in the United States, Western Europe, and Japan. European firms like Unilever, Philips, Royal Dutch-Shell, and Bayer organized their businesses by establishing independent subsidiaries around the world, often in former colony countries. Many companies developed inter-nationally recognized trade names, including Nestlé, Kraft, Kellogg, Lockheed, Cater-pillar, Coca-Cola, Chrysler, and Levi's. Foreign subsidiaries of such companies operated as miniature, autonomous versions of the parent firm, selling much the same products in markets worldwide. Gradually, MNEs began to seek cost advantages by locating fac-tories in developing countries with low labor costs. In the 1960s, trade liberalization and growing MNE activity led to substantial growth in international trade and investment. Recovered from World War II, MNEs in Europe and Japan began to challenge the global dominance of U.S. multinationals. With the easing of trade barriers and currency con-trols, capital began to flow freely across national borders, leading to integration of global financial markets.[9]

The fourth phase of globalization began in the early 1980s, which saw enormous growth in cross-border trade and investment. The phase was triggered by the development of personal computers, the Internet, and Web browsers; the collapse of the Soviet Union and ensuing market liberalization in Central and Eastern Europe; and industrialization and modernization in East Asian economies, including China.

Growing international prosperity began to reach emerging markets such as Brazil, In-dia, and Mexico. The 1980s witnessed huge increases in FDI, especially in capital- and technology-intensive sectors. Technological advances in information, communications, and transportation made it feasible for the rise of internationally active small and medium-sized enterprises (SMEs) and for managers to organize far-flung operations around the world, geographically distant yet electronically interconnected. These tech-nologies also facilitated the globalization of the service sector in such areas as banking, en-tertainment, tourism, insurance, and retailing. The merger of major firms once viewed as strongholds of national corporate power exemplified the growing integration of the world economy.

Today, countless firms configure and coordinate trade and investment activities in a giant global marketplace. In their own way, globalization and technological advances have triggered the "death of distance"[10]—shrinkage of the geographic and cultural dis-tances that long separated nations. Exhibit 2.2 reveals the progression of this trend. Glob-alization is gradually shrinking the world into a manageable marketplace.

World Trade Organization (WTO)
A multilateral governing body empowered to regulate international trade and investment.

In This Time Period . . .	Fastest Transportation Was Via . . .	At a Speed of . . .
1500 to 1840s	■ Human-powered ships and horse-drawn carriages	10 miles per hour
1850 to 1900	■ Steamships	36 miles per hour
	■ Steam locomotive trains	65 miles per hour
Early 1900s to today	■ Motor vehicles	75 miles per hour
	■ Propeller airplanes	300– 400 miles per hour
	■ Jet aircraft	500– 700 miles per hour

Exhibit 2.2 The Death of Distance

SOURCE: Adapted from P. Dicken (1992), *Global Shift*. New York: Guilford, p. 104.

Market Globalization: An Organizing Framework

Exhibit 2.3 presents an organizing framework for examining market globalization. The exhibit makes a distinction between: (1) drivers or causes of globalization; (2) dimensions or manifestations of globalization; (3a) societal consequences of globalization; and (3b) firm-level consequences of globalization. In the exhibit, the double arrows illustrate the interactive nature of the relationship between market globalization and its consequences. As market globalization intensifies, individual firms respond to the challenges and new advantages that it brings. However, keep in mind that firms do not expand abroad solely as a reaction to market globalization. As discussed in Chapter 1, they also internationalize proactively, in order to pursue new markets, find lower-cost inputs, or obtain other advantages. Often, adverse conditions in the home market, such as regulation or declining industry sales, push firms to boldly venture abroad. Firms that do so tend to be more successful in global competition than those that engage in international business as a reactive move.

Vodafone (www.vodafone.com), one of the leading wireless phone service providers, is a good example of firms pursuing internationalization as a strategic growth alternative. Its main offerings include telecommunications and data services, multimedia portals, cellular operations, satellite services, and retail shops. Vodafone

Exhibit 2.3 The Drivers and Consequences of Market Globalization

① DRIVERS OF MARKET GLOBALIZATION

- Worldwide reduction of barriers to trade and investment
- Market liberalization and adoption of free markets
- Industrialization, economic development, and modernization
- Integration of world financial markets
- Advances in technology

② DIMENSIONS OF MARKET GLOBALIZATION

- Integration and interdependence of national economies
- Rise of regional economic integration blocs
- Growth of global investment and financial flows
- Convergence of buyer lifestyles and preferences
- Globalization of production activities
- Globalization of services

③a SOCIETAL CONSEQUENCES OF MARKET GLOBALIZATION

- Contagion: Rapid spread of financial or monetary crises from one country to another
- Loss of national sovereignty
- Offshoring and the flight of jobs
- Effect on the poor
- Effect on the natural environment
- Effect on national culture

③b FIRM-LEVEL CONSEQUENCES OF MARKET GLOBALIZATION: INTERNATIONALIZATION OF THE FIRM'S VALUE CHAIN

- Countless new business opportunities for internationalizing firms
- New risks and intense rivalry from foreign competitors
- More demanding buyers who source from suppliers worldwide
- Greater emphasis on proactive internationalization
- Internationalization of firm's value chain

has annual sales of $70 billion and more than 200 million customers worldwide. Founded in 1983 as a joint venture between a British and a U.S. firm, the company had set up mobile phone networks in Australia and Hong Kong and throughout Scandinavia by 1993. It then launched or bought stakes in operations throughout Africa, Asia, Europe, and the Americas. Vodafone has internationalized mainly via foreign direct investment. Today it has equity interests in some 25 countries and owns a 45 percent stake in the U.S. provider Verizon Wireless.

Vodafone took advantage of such globalization trends as harmonization of communications technologies, convergence of buyer characteristics, and reduced trade and investment barriers. As emerging markets develop economically, they leapfrog older telecom technologies (typically landline systems) and embrace cell phone technology instead—a boon to Vodafone. In Turkey in 2008, the firm acquired Telsim, the country's second-biggest mobile phone operator. It also bought stakes in cell phone firms in India and South Africa, moves that leveraged these countries' rapid economic growth and need to upgrade their phone systems.

Vodafone's proactive global strategy emphasizes selling standardized products and services and pursuing standardized marketing programs across the globe. To minimize costs, many of its cell phones are essentially identical worldwide, with adaptations to accommodate local languages, regulations, and telephone standards. Vodafone's advertising aims at developing and maintaining a global brand that people recognize everywhere. Convergence of buyer lifestyles and incomes worldwide help facilitate the global approach. Management coordinates operations on a global scale and applies common business processes in procurement and quality control. The strategies of product standardization, global branding, and selling to customers worldwide owe much of their success to the globalization of markets. Vodafone's strategic internationalization allows the firm to benefit from economies of scale, which make its products more price-competitive.[11]

 ## Dimensions of Market Globalization

Globalization has been studied within various disciplines, including economics, anthropology, political science, sociology, and technology. In terms of international business, market globalization can be viewed simultaneously as a: (1) consequence of economic, technological, and government policy trends; (2) driver of economic, political, and social phenomena; and (3) driver and consequence of firm-level internationalization. Globalization of markets is a multifaceted phenomenon, with six major dimensions:

1. *Integration and interdependence of national economies.* Internationally active firms devise multicountry operations through trade, investment, geographic dispersal of company resources, and integration and coordination of value-chain activities. A **value chain** is the sequence of value-adding activities performed by the firm in the course of developing, producing, marketing, and servicing a product. The *aggregate* activities of such firms give rise to *economic integration*. Governments have facilitated this integration by lowering barriers to international trade and investment, harmonizing their monetary and fiscal policies within *regional economic integration* blocs (also known as *trade blocs*), and developing *supranational* institutions—the World Bank, International Monetary Fund, World Trade Organization, and others—that seek further reductions in trade and investment barriers.

Value chain The sequence of value-adding activities performed by the firm in the course of developing, producing, marketing, and servicing a product.

2. *Rise of regional economic integration blocs.* Closely related to the first trend is the emergence since the 1950s of regional economic integration blocs. Examples include the North American Free Trade Agreement area (NAFTA), the Asia Pacific Economic Cooperation zone (APEC), and Mercosur in Latin America. These blocs consist of groups of countries within which trade and investment flows are facilitated through reduced trade and investment barriers. In more advanced arrangements, such as the "common market," barriers to the cross-border flow of factors of production (mostly labor and capital) are removed. For example, the European Union (www.europa.eu), in addition to adopting

The French supermarket Carrefour is one of many multinational enterprises that contribute to convergence of consumer lifestyles and preferences.

free trade among its member countries, is harmonizing fiscal and monetary policies and adopting common business regulations.

3. *Growth of global investment and financial flows.* In the process of conducting international transactions, firms and governments buy and sell large volumes of national currencies (such as dollars, euros, and yen). The free movement of capital around the world—the globalization of capital—extends economic activities across the globe and is fostering interconnectedness among world economies. Commercial and investment banking is a global industry. The bond market has gained worldwide scope, with foreign bonds representing a major source of debt financing for governments and firms. Information and communications networks facilitate heavy volumes of financial transactions every day, integrating national markets. Nevertheless, widespread integration can have negative effects. For example, when the United States experienced a banking crisis in 2008, the crisis quickly spread to Europe, Japan, and emerging markets, triggering a global recession.

4. *Convergence of consumer lifestyles and preferences.* Around the world, consumers spend their money and time in increasingly similar ways. Lifestyles and preferences are converging. Shoppers in Tokyo, New York, and Paris demand similar household goods, clothing, automobiles, and electronics. Teenagers everywhere are attracted to iPods, Levi's jeans, and BlackBerry cell phones. Major brands have gained a global following, encouraged by greater international travel, movies, global media, and the Internet, which expose people to products, services, and living patterns from around the world. Movies such as *The Lord of the Rings* and *Slumdog Millionaire* receive much attention from a global audience. Convergence of preferences is also occurring in industrial markets, where professional buyers source raw materials, parts, and components that are increasingly *standardized*—that is, very similar in design and structure. Yet, even as converging tastes facilitate the marketing of highly standardized products and services to buyers worldwide, they also promote the loss of traditional lifestyles and values in individual countries.

5. *Globalization of production.* Intense global competition is forcing firms to reduce their costs of production and marketing. Companies strive to drive down prices through economies of scale, by standardizing what they sell, and by shifting manufacturing and procurement to foreign locations with inexpensive labor. For example, companies in the auto and textile industries have relocated their manufacturing to low labor-cost locations such as China, Mexico, and Eastern Europe.

6. *Globalization of services.* The services sector is undergoing widespread internationalization. First, banking, hospitality, retailing, and other service industries are rapidly expanding abroad. The real estate firm REMAX has established more than 5,000 offices in over fifty countries. Second, as noted in the opening vignette, firms increasingly outsource business processes and other services in the value chain to vendors located abroad. Finally, in a relatively new trend, many people go abroad to take advantage of low-cost services. For example, many U.S. consumers regularly travel to India, Latin America, and other international destinations to undergo medical procedures like cataract and knee surgeries. Several U.S. health insurance companies view international "medical tourism" as a means to reduce costs.[12]

Drivers of Market Globalization

Various trends have converged in recent years as causes of market globalization. Five are particularly notable:

1. *Worldwide reduction of barriers to trade and investment.* The tendency of national governments to reduce trade and investment barriers has accelerated global economic integration. For example, tariffs on the import of automobiles, industrial machinery, and countless other products have declined nearly to zero in many countries, encouraging freer international exchange of goods and services. Falling trade barriers are facilitated by the WTO. After joining the WTO in 2001, China made its market more accessible to foreign firms. Reduction of trade barriers is also associated with the emergence of regional economic integration blocs, a key dimension of market globalization.

2. *Market liberalization and adoption of free markets.* Built in 1961, the Berlin Wall separated the communist East Berlin from the democratic West Berlin. The collapse of the Soviet Union's economy in 1989, demolition of the Berlin Wall that same year, and China's free-market reforms all signaled the end of the 50-year Cold War and smoothed the integration of former command economies into the global economy. Numerous East Asian economies, stretching from South Korea to Malaysia and Indonesia, had already embarked on ambitious market-based reforms. India joined the trend in 1991. These events opened roughly one-third of the world to freer international trade and investment. China, India, and Eastern Europe have become some of the most cost-effective locations for producing goods and services worldwide. Privatization of previously state-owned industries in these countries has encouraged economic efficiency and attracted massive foreign capital into their national economies.

3. *Industrialization, economic development, and modernization.* Industrialization implies that emerging markets—rapidly developing economies in Asia, Latin America, and Eastern Europe—are moving from being low value-adding commodity producers, dependent on low-cost labor, to sophisticated competitive producers and exporters of premium products such as electronics, computers, and aircraft.[13] For example, Brazil is now a leading producer of private aircraft, and the Czech Republic excels in the manufacture of automobiles. As highlighted in the opening vignette, India has become a leading supplier of computer software. Economic development is enhancing standards of living and discretionary income in emerging markets. Perhaps the most important measure of economic development is *Gross National Income (GNI)* per head.[14] Exhibit 2.4 maps the levels of GNI worldwide. The exhibit reveals that Africa is home to the lowest-income countries, along with India and a few other countries in Asia and Nicaragua. These areas are also characterized by low levels of market globalization. The adoption of modern technologies, improvement of living standards, and adoption of modern legal and banking practices are increasing the attractiveness of emerging markets as investment targets and facilitating the spread of ideas, products, and services across the globe.

4. *Integration of world financial markets.* Integration of world financial markets makes it possible for internationally active firms to raise capital, borrow funds, and engage in foreign currency transactions. Financial services firms follow their customers to foreign markets. Cross-border transactions are made easier partly as a result of the ease with which funds can be transferred between buyers and sellers, through a network of international commercial banks. For example, as an individual you can transfer funds to a friend in another country using the SWIFT network. Connecting more than 7,800 financial institutions in some 200 countries, the network facilitates global financial transactions. The globalization of finance contributes to firms' abilities to develop and operate world-scale production and marketing operations. It enables companies to pay suppliers and collect payments from customers worldwide.

5. *Advances in technology.* Technological advances are a remarkable facilitator of cross-border trade and investment. Let's elaborate on this important driver of globalization and company internationalization in detail.

Exhibit 2.4 Gross National Income in U.S. Dollars

SOURCE: World Bank (2008); World Bank Development Indicator database. Reprinted with permission. http://data.worldbank.org.

ARCTIC OCEAN

NORWAY
SWEDEN
FINLAND

ESTONIA
NETHERLANDS
UNITED
KINGDOM
IRELAND
DENMARK
LATVIA
LITHUANIA
RUSSIA
BELARUS
GERMANY
POLAND
LUXEMBOURG
CZECH
REP.
SLOVAKIA
UKRAINE
FRANCE
AUSTRIA
LIECH.
SWITZ.
SLOVENIA
HUNGARY
MOLDOVA
CROATIA
ROMANIA
BOSNIA
SERBIA AND
HERZEGOVINA
MONTENEGRO
BULGARIA
MONACO
ANDORRA
ITALY
MACEDONIA
ALBANIA
SPAIN
GREECE
TURKEY
PORTUGAL
GEORGIA
AZERBAIJAN
ARMENIA
TUNISIA
CYPRUS
SYRIA
LEBANON
IRAQ
ISRAEL
JORDAN
KUWAIT

RUSSIA

KAZAKHSTAN

MONGOLIA

NORTH
KOREA
SOUTH
KOREA
JAPAN

UZBEKISTAN
KYRGYZSTAN
TURKMENISTAN
TAJIKISTAN
AFGHANISTAN
IRAN
PAKISTAN

CHINA

PACIFIC
OCEAN

MOROCCO
ALGERIA
LIBYA
EGYPT
WESTERN
SAHARA
MAURITANIA
MALI
NIGER
CHAD
SAUDI
ARABIA
QATAR
UNITED ARAB
EMIRATES
OMAN
YEMEN
NEPAL
BHUTAN
BANGLADESH
INDIA
MYANMAR
(BURMA)
LAOS
TAIWAN

SENEGAL
GAMBIA
GUINEA-BISSAU
GUINEA
SIERRA LEONE
LIBERIA
BURKINA
FASO
IVORY
COAST
GHANA
TOGO
BENIN
NIGERIA
CENTRAL AFRICAN
REPUBLIC
CAMEROON
SUDAN
ERITREA
DJIBOUTI
ETHIOPIA
SOMALIA
THAILAND
CAMBODIA
VIETNAM
PHILIPPINES
SRI
LANKA
BRUNEI
MALAYSIA
SINGAPORE

EQUATORIAL
GUINEA
GABON
CONGO
REPUBLIC
CONGO
DEMOCRATIC
REPUBLIC
(ZAIRE)
UGANDA
RWANDA
BURUNDI
KENYA
TANZANIA
INDIAN
OCEAN
INDONESIA
PAPUA
NEW
GUINEA
SOLOMON
ISLANDS

SOUTH
ATLANTIC
OCEAN

ANGOLA
ZAMBIA
MALAWI
MOZAMBIQUE
NAMIBIA
ZIMBABWE
BOTSWANA
MADAGASCAR
MAURITIUS
RÉUNION
VANUATU
FIJI
NEW
CALEDONIA

SWAZILAND
SOUTH
AFRICA
LESOTHO

AUSTRALIA

NEW
ZEALAND

GNI in U.S. Dollars Per Capita, 2007

- 7,490 or more
- 2,350 - 7,490
- 1,110 - 2,350
- 430 - 1,110
- less than 430
- No data

Technological Advances

Perhaps the most important driver of market globalization since the 1980s has been technological advances in information, communications, manufacturing, and transportation. While globalization makes internationalization imperative, technological advances provide the *means* for it to happen. Initially, technology greatly eased the management of international operations. Now firms interact more efficiently with foreign partners and value-chain members than ever before. They transmit all kinds of data, information, and vital communications that help ensure the smooth running of their operations worldwide. They use information technology to improve the productivity of their operations, which provides substantial competitive advantages. For example, information technology allows firms to more efficiently adapt products for international markets or produce goods in smaller lots to target international niche markets.

In addition, technological advances have made international operations affordable for all types of firms, explaining why so many SMEs have internationalized during the past two decades. Panel (a) of Exhibit 2.5 shows how the cost of international communications has plummeted over time. Panel (b) shows how the number of Internet users has grown dramatically in recent years.

Managers use the latest technologies to manage international operations: iPads that combine laptop functionality with smartphone convenience; BlackBerry phones with cross-national Wi-Fi capability that can take phone calls from anywhere on Earth; iPods for listening to audio books or mini Sony Playstations for that ride home on the train after work.

Technological advances have spurred the development of new products and services that appeal to a global audience. Leading examples include the Wii and iPhone. Emerging markets and developing economies also benefit from technological advances, partly due to technological leapfrogging. For example, Hungary and Poland went directly from old-style analog telecommunications (with rotary dial telephones) to cell phone technology, bypassing much of the early digital technology (push-button telephones) that characterized advanced economy telephone systems.

Exhibit 2.5

Declining Cost of Global Communication and Growing Number of Internet Users

SOURCE: IMF (2007), World Economic Outlook. International Monetary Fund and United Nations International Telecommunications Union. Washington DC: International Monetary Fund. Copyright © 2008. Used with permission.

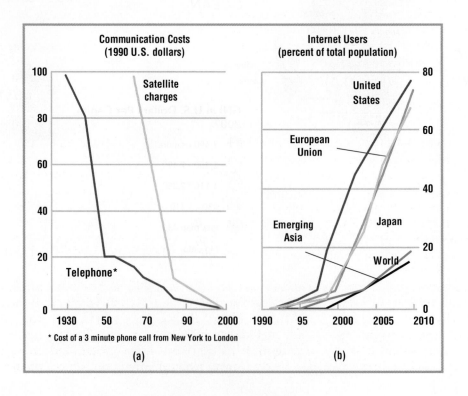

China and India are the new beachheads for technological advances. The chapter's opening vignette revealed how India has become a focus of global Internet- and knowledge-based industries. Top management at Intel and Motorola, two leading technology companies, agree that China is the place to be when it comes to technological progress. Both firms generate substantial sales there. Management predicts double-digit increases in demand for technology products in China far into the future. Intel's CEO commented, "I come back from visiting China and feel as if I've visited the fountain of youth of computing."[15]

In broader terms, technological advances have had the greatest impact in several key areas—information technology, communications, manufacturing, and transportation—which we review next.

Information Technology

Information technology (IT) is the science and process of creating and using information resources. Its effect on business has been nothing short of revolutionary. The cost of computer processing fell by 30 percent per year during the past two decades and continues to fall. The remarkable performance of the U.S. economy in the 1990s was substantially due to aggressive integration of IT into firms' value-chain activities, which accounted for 45 percent of total business investments at the time. IT alters the structure of industries and, in so doing, changes the rules of competition. By giving companies new ways to outperform rivals, IT creates competitive advantage.[16] For example, geographically distant subsidiaries of a multinational firm can be interconnected via intranets, facilitating the instant sharing of data, information, and experience across company operations worldwide.[17] MNEs also use collaboration software that connects global product development teams scattered around the world, enabling them to work together. IT benefits smaller firms as well, allowing them to design and produce customized products they can target to narrow, cross-national market niches.

IT has spawned new products, such as cell phones, and new processes, such as automated factory controls. Google, Yahoo, and other online search engines provide easy access to unlimited data for researching markets, customers, competitors, and countries' economic conditions. At a higher level, IT supports managerial decision making, such as the selection of qualified foreign business partners, by allowing firms to quickly access key information and intelligence.

Communications

It took five months for Spain's Queen Isabella to learn about Columbus's voyage in 1492, two weeks for Europe to learn of President Lincoln's assassination in 1865, and only seconds for the world to witness the collapse of New York's World Trade Center towers in 2001. At one time, the only way to communicate with foreign suppliers was through slow postal service, expensive phone calls, and clunky telex machines. In 1930, a 3-minute phone call between New York and London cost $3,000. By 1980, the cost had fallen to $6. Today, the call is virtually free. Scanners and fax machines send documents worldwide for almost nothing. Bank transactions are relatively costly when performed via ATM machines or telephones but are virtually free when handled via the Internet.

The Internet, and Internet-dependent systems such as intranets, extranets, and e-mail, connect millions of people across the globe. Today, the widest range of products and services—from auto parts to bank loans—is marketed online. Transmitting voices, data, and images is essentially costless, making Seoul, Stockholm, and San Jose next-door neighbors, instantly. South Korea has nearly 100 percent Internet access and among the fastest broadband networks worldwide. Korean schoolchildren use their cell phones to

Increasing availability of cell phones in Africa has helped spur economic growth there. Some farmers use cell phones to monitor crop prices in various local markets where they can sell their harvests.

get homework from teachers and play games online with gamers worldwide. Adults use their phones to pay bills, do banking, buy lottery tickets, and check traffic conditions.

Widespread availability of the Internet and e-mail makes company internationalization cost effective. For instance, Amdahl, a manufacturer of computers, uses the Internet to order circuit boards from factories in Asia and to arrange international shipments of parts and components via firms like FedEx. The Internet opens up the global marketplace to SMEs and other firms that normally lack the resources to do international business. By establishing a presence on the Web, even tiny enterprises can take the first step in becoming multinational firms. Thanks to the Internet, services as diverse as designing an engine, monitoring a security camera, selling insurance, and doing secretarial work have become easier to export than car parts or refrigerators. The *Global Trend* feature highlights the emergence of e-commerce and its effect on company internationalization.

In order to support economic development, countries need modern infrastructure in communications, such as reliable telephone systems. Recently, the cell phone has become the most transformative technology for developing economies. Compared to landline-based telephony, mobile phone infrastructure is inexpensive and relatively easy to install. Africa is benefiting from a rapid increase in mobile telephone ownership. The continent has the fastest growth rate of cellular subscribers in the world. For example, in six years, Nigeria increased its telecom infrastructure from just 500,000 phone lines to more than 30 million cellular subscribers. One consequence has been a dramatic rise in productivity and commerce, which helps improve living standards. Among other advantages, the mobile telephone saves wasted trips, provides access to banking services, supplies information about crop prices, and facilitates communication between suppliers and customers. The rapid penetration of cell phones into Africa helps account for much of the continent's economic growth in recent years.[18]

Manufacturing

Computer-aided design (CAD) of products, robotics, and production lines managed and monitored by microprocessor-based controls are transforming manufacturing, mainly by reducing the costs of production. Revolutionary developments now permit low-scale and low-cost manufacturing. Firms can make products cost effectively even in short production runs. These developments benefit international business by allowing firms to more efficiently adapt products to individual foreign markets, profitably target small national markets, and compete more effectively with foreign competitors that already have cost advantages.

Transportation

Managers consider the costs of transporting raw materials, components, and finished products when deciding to either export or manufacture abroad. For example, if transportation costs to an important market are high, management may decide to manufacture its merchandise in the market by building a factory there. Beginning in the 1960s, technological advances led to the development of fuel-efficient jumbo jets, giant ocean-going freighters, and containerized shipping, often through the use of high-tech composites and smaller components that are less bulky and lightweight. In the 20-year period through 2008, the number of container-carrying ships quadrupled to over 4,000 vessels.

GL🌐BAL TREND
Globalization and E-Business in the Online World

Information technology and the Internet are transforming international business by allowing firms to conduct e-commerce online and to integrate e-business capabilities for activities such as sourcing and managing customer relations. E-business drives the firm's globalization efforts by helping it beat geography and time zones, and do business around the world all day, every day. E-business levels the playing field for all types of firms, large and small. Even new companies can be active abroad. Born global firms are among the most intensive users of the Web for global selling, procurement, and customer service.

E-business provides at least three types of benefits. First, it *increases productivity* and reduces costs in worldwide value-chain activities through online integration and coordination of production, distribu-

tion, and after-sale services. Second, it *creates value for existing customers and uncovers new sales opportunities* by increasing customer focus, enhancing marketing capabilities, and launching entrepreneurial initiatives. Using online technologies, firms routinely organize marketing strategy on a global scale. Virtual interconnectedness facilitates the sharing of new ideas and best practices for serving new and existing international markets. Third, e-business *improves the flow of information and knowledge throughout the firm's worldwide operations*. In this way, the Internet enhances the ability to interact with customers, suppliers, and partners worldwide. Managers can make instantaneous changes to strategies and tactics in value-chain activities. The firm can accommodate real-time changes in market conditions almost as quickly as they occur.

Cisco uses e-business solutions to minimize costs and maximize operational effectiveness in its international supply chain. The firm uses the Internet to remain constantly linked to suppliers and distributors. This helps Cisco manage inventory, product specifications, purchase orders, and product life cycles. E-procurement systems help Cisco save money on transaction processing, reduce cycle times, and leverage supplier relations.

Customer relationship management is especially critical in foreign markets where buyers often favor local vendors. Internet-based systems provide real-time information, help forecast shifting short- and long-term market needs, and increase after-sales service effectiveness. E-commerce greatly enhances competitive advantages and performance objectives in the global marketplace.

Containers are the big boxes, usually 40 feet long (about 12 meters), loaded on top of ships, trucks, and rail cars that carry the world's cargo. Today, the typical ocean-going container ship holds more than 2,300 containers, double the average of the 1980s. As a result, the cost of transportation, as a proportion of the value of products shipped internationally, has declined dramatically. Lower freight costs have spurred rapid growth in cross-border trade. Technological advances have also reduced the costs of international travel. Until 1960, it was common to travel by ship. With the development of air travel, managers quickly travel the world.

 ## Societal Consequences of Market Globalization

Our discussion so far has highlighted the far-reaching, positive outcomes of market globalization. Major advances in living standards have been achieved in virtually all countries that have opened their borders to increased trade and investment. Nevertheless, the

Advances in transportation and low freight costs have helped spur market globalization. This cargo ship is approaching the Port of Miami, Florida.

transition to an increasingly single, global marketplace poses challenges to individuals, organizations, and governments. Low-income countries have not been able to integrate with the global economy as rapidly as others. Poverty remains a major problem in Africa and populous nations like Brazil, China, and India. Let's turn to some of the unintended consequences of globalization.

Contagion: Rapid Spread of Monetary or Financial Crises

Beginning in late 2008, the world economy experienced a severe financial crisis and global recession, the worst in decades.[19] The crisis was precipitated by pricing bubbles (excessively high prices) in housing and commodities markets around the world. For example, by mid-2008, oil prices climbed to an all-time high of nearly $150 a barrel, and gasoline prices reached record levels in many countries. High commodity prices resulted partly from rising demand, especially in emerging markets such as China and India. As bubbles in real estate markets burst, home values crashed, leaving owners with mortgage debts greater than the value of their homes. Many homeowners found themselves unable to repay their debts, a situation that worsened as people lost jobs or experienced pay cuts. Meanwhile, thousands of mortgages had been securitized—that is, sold as investment vehicles on stock markets worldwide. As the value of these securities plunged or became uncertain, the stock markets crashed.[20]

A recession occurs when a national economy undergoes a prolonged period of negative growth. Exhibit 2.6 shows how GDP growth in advanced, developing, and emerging economies varies over time. It declined substantially in recent years, due to the global recession and the financial crisis. However, one lesson of the exhibit is that, even following deep recessions, the global economy has always returned to net GDP growth.

Contagion The tendency of a financial or monetary crisis in one country to spread rapidly to other countries, due to the ongoing integration of national economies.

The crisis began in the United States and, like a contagious disease, spread around the world. In international economics, **contagion** refers to the tendency for a financial or monetary crisis in one country to spread rapidly to other countries, due to the ongoing integration of national economies. The origins of the global financial crisis include the "easy money" policy followed by the U.S. Federal Reserve Bank throughout most of the 2000s.[21] By charging very low interest rates to banks, the Federal Reserve enabled them to make loans that injected billions of dollars into the U.S. economy. Experts also point to China's rapid economic growth and high savings rate, which have endowed the country with an enormous pool of funds. The Chinese used the funds to buy U.S. Treasury bonds (nearly $800 billion in 2009), in effect, making huge loans to the United States. The savings glut in China, other emerging markets, and the oil-producing countries further contributed to low interest rates in the United States and elsewhere, which

Exhibit 2.6   Percent Change in Annual GDP Growth

SOURCE: IMF, World Economic Outlook Update (Washington, DC: International Monetary Fund, January 28, 2009). Accessed at: http://www.imf.org/external/pubs/ft/weo/2009/update/01/index.htm, 3/24/09. Used with permission.

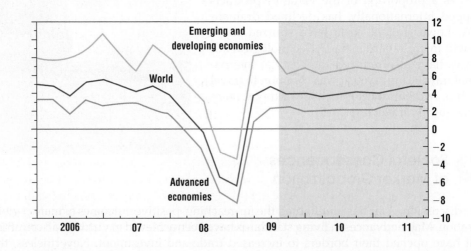

facilitated additional borrowing. These trends set the stage for widespread borrowing by consumers to purchase homes and durable goods, which led to an unsustainable overheating of the U.S. economy. Another cause of the financial crisis was inadequate regulation of mortgage markets and the banking sector in the United States. As we will see later in this text, having a strong legal and regulatory framework is critical to national economic well-being.

The financial crisis raised questions about the merits of globalization. Modern technology facilitated the integration of national economies and banking systems. As a result, although the crisis began in the United States, it quickly spread to other countries.[22]

Consumer confidence also dwindled, triggering substantial declines in spending on cars, consumer electronics, home appliances, luxury goods, gasoline, bank loans, and new homes. Decreased spending, in turn, has been a drag on global commerce.[23] Trade has especially slowed or flattened in consumer durables, energy, financial services, new construction, and related industries. In 2009–2010, global growth declined sharply to levels not seen since World War II.

Canada and Mexico slipped into recession partly due to their heavy reliance on trade and investment with the United States. Hong Kong, Japan, Iceland, New Zealand, Singapore, Turkey, the United States, and most countries in the European Union all experienced significant recessions. Of the largest world economies, only China's continued to grow at a fast rate, over 6 percent per year. While advanced economies were particularly affected, emerging markets and developing economies have been more resilient than in previous global downturns, although growth in these countries has slowed considerably. Living standards have been severely affected, and millions of people worldwide have fallen into severe poverty. This occurred largely because developing economies depend on exports to, and direct investments from, the advanced economies that have all been hurt by the crisis.[24]

Meanwhile, central bankers and finance ministers have struggled to keep up with rapidly evolving events. To stimulate economic activity, governments worldwide pumped hundreds of billions of dollars into their national economies. A key implication of recent events is that, when financial markets are unchecked or unregulated, crises spread quickly and take on global scale. Governments are increasingly intervening in national economies, with some taking ownership stakes in private-sector firms. We will consider the role of government intervention later in this text.

Loss of National Sovereignty

Sovereignty, the ability of a nation to govern its own affairs, is a fundamental principle that underlies global relations. One country's laws cannot be applied or enforced in another country. Globalization can threaten national sovereignty in various ways. MNE activities can interfere with the sovereign ability of governments to control their own economies, social structures, and political systems. Some corporations are bigger than the economies of many nations. Indeed, Walmart's internal economy—its total revenues—is larger than the GDP of most of the world's nations, including Israel, Greece, and Poland. Large multinationals can exert considerable influence on governments through lobbying or campaign contributions. They often lobby their government for, say, devaluation of the home currency, which gives them greater price competitiveness in export markets. MNEs influence the legislative process and extract special favors from government agencies.

At the same time, even the largest firms are constrained by *market forces*. In countries with many competing firms, one company cannot force customers to buy its products or force suppliers to supply it with raw materials and inputs. The resources that customers and suppliers control are the result of free choices made in the marketplace. Company performance depends on the firm's skill at winning customers, working with suppliers, and dealing with competitors. Corporate dominance of individual markets is rare. In reality, market forces generally dominate companies. Gradual integration of the global economy and increased global competition, combined with privatization of industries in various nations, are making some companies less powerful within their national markets.[25] For example, Ford, Chrysler, and General Motors once dominated the U.S. auto market. Today many more firms compete in the United States, including Toyota, Honda, Hyundai, Nissan, and BMW. In annual sales, Toyota now leads the U.S. market, and home-country market shares of domestic U.S. automakers have tumbled.

Today, globalization and the spread of financial crises compel governments to pursue sound economic policies and managers to manage their firms more effectively. To minimize globalization's harm and reap its benefits, governments should strive for open and liberalized economic regimes. Specifically, governments should ensure the freedom to enter and compete in markets, protect private and intellectual property, enforce the rule of law, and support voluntary exchange through markets rather than through political processes. Banks and financial institutions should be regulated appropriately. Transparency in the affairs of business and regulatory agencies is critical. One example is the Sarbanes-Oxley Act, which the U.S. Congress passed in 2002. It addresses the flaws in financial reporting practices that became apparent following corporate and accounting scandals in such firms as Enron, Tyco International, and WorldCom. It introduced new and enhanced standards for all U.S. public company boards, management, and public accounting firms.

Offshoring and the Flight of Jobs

Globalization has created countless new jobs and opportunities around the world, but it has also cost many people their jobs. Ford, General Motors, and Volkswagen have all transferred thousands of jobs from their factories in Germany to countries in Eastern Europe. This occurred partially because mandated shorter working hours (often just 35 hours per week) and generous benefits made Germany less competitive, while Eastern Europe offers abundant low-wage workers. Recognizing this, the German government loosened Germany's labor laws to conform to global realities. These changes have disrupted the lives of tens of thousands of German citizens.[26] General Motors and Ford have also laid off thousands of workers in the United States, partly the result of competitive pressures posed by carmakers from Europe, Japan, and South Korea.

Offshoring is the relocation of manufacturing and other value-chain activities to cost-effective locations abroad. For example, the global accounting firm Ernst & Young relocated much of its accounting support work to the Philippines. Massachusetts General Hospital has its CT scans and X-rays interpreted by radiologists in India. Many IT support services for customers in Germany are based in the Czech Republic and Romania.[27]

Offshoring has resulted in job losses in numerous mature economies. The first wave of offshoring began in the 1960s and 1970s with the shift of U.S. and European manufacturing of cars, shoes, electronics, textiles, and toys to cheap-labor locations such as Mexico and Southeast Asia. The next wave began in the 1990s with the exodus of service-sector jobs in credit card processing, software code writing, accounting, health care, and banking services.

High-profile plant closures and relocation of manufacturing have received much media attention in recent years. Critics have labeled many MNEs as "runaway" or "footloose" corporations—quick to relocate production to countries that offer more favorable access to inputs. For example, Electrolux, the Swedish manufacturer of home appliances, recently moved its Greenville, Michigan, refrigerator plant to Mexico. Closure of the plant, which once provided 2,700 jobs, devastated the small Michigan community. Management shifted production to Mexico despite repeated appeals by the local community, the labor union, and the state of Michigan.

Effect on the Poor

MNEs are often criticized for paying low wages, exploiting workers, and employing child labor. Child labor is particularly troubling because it denies children educational opportunities. The International Labor Organization (www.ilo.org) reported in 2010 that there are approximately 153 million children aged 5–14 at work around the world.

Nike was criticized for paying low wages to shoe factory workers in Asia, some of whom work in sweatshop conditions. Critics complained that while founder Phil Knight is a billionaire and Nike shoes sell for $100 or more, Nike's suppliers pay their workers only a few dollars per day.

Labor exploitation and sweatshop conditions are major concerns in many developing economies.[28] Nevertheless, consideration must be given to the other choices available to people in those countries. A low-paying job is usually better than no job at all. Studies suggest that banning products made using child labor may produce unintended negative consequences such as reduced living standards.[29] Legislation passed to reduce child labor in the formal economic sector (the sector regulated and monitored by public authorities) may have little effect on jobs in the informal economic sector, sometimes called the *underground economy*. In the face of persistent poverty, abolishing formal sector jobs does not ensure that children leave the workforce and go to school.

In many developing countries, work conditions tend to improve over time. The growth of the footwear industry in Vietnam translated into a five-fold increase in wages. While still low by advanced economy standards, increasingly higher wages are improving the lives of millions of workers and their families. For most countries, globalization tends to support a growing economy. Exhibit 2.7 shows the GDP growth rate worldwide from 2000 to 2009. Note that most nations generally experienced positive growth. However, the recent global financial crisis has dealt a setback, as numerous countries slipped into recession. As shown in the map, the world's fastest-growing large economies are China and India. Chile, Ireland, and Vietnam have also been on the fast-growth track. Former Soviet Union countries in Eastern Europe faltered in the 1990s as they transitioned to market-based economic systems. Most African countries continue to suffer low or negative GDP growth and alarming poverty, which worsened during the recent global recession.

Critics insist that workers in developing economies should receive a decent wage. However, as wages rise, countries that attract investment due to low-cost labor can lose their attractiveness. Legislation to increase minimum wage levels also can reduce the number of available jobs. By contrast, over time the evidence suggests that globalization helps to stimulate higher wages. As Exhibit 2.8 illustrates, countries that liberalize international trade and investment enjoy faster per-capita economic growth. The exhibit shows how, during the 1990s, developing economies that sought integration with the rest of the world had faster per-capita GDP growth than already integrated advanced economies, which, in turn, grew faster than nonintegrating developing economies.

Governments are responsible for ensuring the fruits of economic progress are shared fairly. Developing countries can undertake proactive measures to reduce poverty. They can improve conditions for investment and saving, liberalize markets and promote trade and investment, build strong institutions that ensure good governance, and invest in education and training to promote productivity and encourage upward mobility for workers. Advanced economies can

Media attention and consumer concern are helping wages and sweatshop conditions to slowly improve in developing economies, such as those in Central America.

Exhibit 2.7 The Growth of World GDP, Average Annual Percent Change, 2000–2009, Average annual GDP growth rate, 2000–2009 (percent)

SOURCE: International Monetary Fund, World Economic Outlook Database

ARCTIC OCEAN

NORWAY
SWEDEN
FINLAND
ESTONIA
UNITED KINGDOM
IRELAND
DENMARK
LATVIA
LITHUANIA
RUSSIA
BELARUS
NETHERLANDS
POLAND
BELGIUM
GERMANY
LUXEMBOURG
CZECH REP.
SLOVAKIA
UKRAINE
FRANCE
LIECH
AUSTRIA
SLOVENIA
HUNGARY
MOLDOVA
SWITZ.
ROMANIA
MONACO
CROATIA
BOSNIA SERBIA AND
HERZEGOVINA MONTENEGRO
BULGARIA
ANDORRA
ITALY
MACEDONIA
SPAIN
ALBANIA
PORTUGAL
GREECE
TURKEY
TUNISIA
CYPRUS
SYRIA
LEBANON
ISRAEL
JORDAN
IRAQ
MOROCCO
ALGERIA
LIBYA
EGYPT
GEORGIA
ARMENIA
AZERBAIJAN
UZBEKISTAN
KYRGYZSTAN
TURKMENISTAN
TAJIKISTAN
AFGHANISTAN
IRAN
PAKISTAN

RUSSIA

KAZAKHSTAN

MONGOLIA

NORTH KOREA
SOUTH KOREA
JAPAN

CHINA

PACIFIC OCEAN

WESTERN SAHARA
MAURITANIA
MALI
NIGER
CHAD
SUDAN
ERITREA
YEMEN
SENEGAL
GAMBIA
INEA-BISSAU
GUINEA
BURKINA FASO
NIGERIA
BENIN
SIERRA LEONE
IVORY COAST
GHANA
TOGO
LIBERIA
CENTRAL AFRICAN REPUBLIC
ETHIOPIA
CAMEROON
EQUATORIAL GUINEA
CONGO REPUBLIC
GABON
CONGO DEMOCRATIC REPUBLIC (ZAIRE)
UGANDA
RWANDA
BURUNDI
KENYA
TANZANIA
QATAR
SAUDI ARABIA
UNITED ARAB EMIRATES
OMAN
DJIBOUTI
SOMALIA
NEPAL
BHUTAN
BANGLADESH
INDIA
MYANMAR (BURMA)
LAOS
THAILAND
VIETNAM
CAMBODIA
PHILIPPINES
SRI LANKA
TAIWAN
BRUNEI
MALAYSIA
SINGAPORE
INDONESIA
PAPUA NEW GUINEA
SOLOMON ISLANDS

SOUTH ATLANTIC OCEAN

ANGOLA
ZAMBIA
NAMIBIA
BOTSWANA
ZIMBABWE
MALAWI
MOZAMBIQUE
SWAZILAND
SOUTH AFRICA
LESOTHO
MADAGASCAR
MAURITIUS
RÉUNION

INDIAN OCEAN

AUSTRALIA

VANUATU
FIJI
NEW CALEDONIA

NEW ZEALAND

Average annual GDP growth rate, 2000-2009 (%)

negative
○ less than -2.5
○ -2.5 to 0
○ no data available

positive
○ 0 to 1
○ 1 to 2
○ 2 to 3
○ 3 to 4
○ 4 to 5
○ over 5

Exhibit 2.8 Relationship between Globalization and Growth in Per-Capita Gross Domestic Product (adjusted for purchasing power parity)

SOURCE: Dollar, D. (2004). "Globalization, Poverty and Inequality since 1980," World Bank Policy Research Working Paper 3333, June 2004, Washington, DC: World Bank. © 2004 World Bank. Reprinted with permission. http://data.worldbank.org.

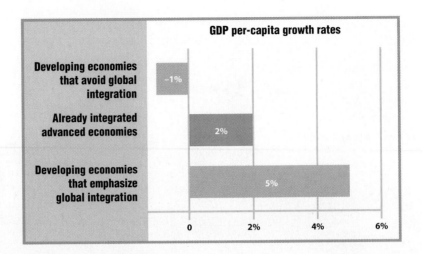

help reduce global poverty by making their markets more accessible to low-income countries; providing debt relief to heavily indebted nations; and facilitating the flow of technology, private capital, and direct investment into poor countries.

Effect on the Natural Environment

Globalization can harm the environment by promoting increased manufacturing and economic activity that results in pollution, habitat destruction, and deterioration of the ozone layer. For example, economic development in China is attracting much inward FDI and stimulating the growth of numerous industries. However, the construction of factories, infrastructure, and modern housing can spoil previously pristine environments. In Eastern China, growing industrial demand for electricity led to construction of the Three Gorges Dam, which flooded agricultural lands and permanently altered the natural landscape. See the *Apply Your Understanding* exercise at the end of this chapter that presents an Ethical Dilemma on the environmental damage done by a large oil company in Nigeria.

While it is generally true that globalization-induced industrialization produces considerable environmental harm, this effect tends to decline over time. The evidence suggests that environmental destruction diminishes as economies develop, at least in the long run. As globalization stimulates rising living standards, people focus increasingly on improving their environment. Over time, governments pass legislation that promotes improved environmental conditions. For example, Japan endured polluted rivers and smoggy cities in the early decades of its economic development following World War II. But as their economy grew, the Japanese passed tough environmental standards to restore natural environments.

Evolving company values and concern for corporate reputations also lead most firms to reduce or eliminate practices that harm the environment.[30] For example, in Mexico, big U.S. automakers like Ford and GM have gradually improved their environmental standards. Benetton in Italy (clothing), Alcan in Canada (aluminum), and Kirin in Japan (beverages) are examples of firms that embrace practices that protect the environment, often at the expense of profits.[31] The Conservation Coffee Alliance, a consortium of companies, has committed approximately $2 million to environmentally friendly coffee cultivation in Central America, Peru, and Colombia.

Effect on National Culture

Globalization exerts strong pressures on national culture. Market liberalization leaves the door open to foreign companies, global brands, unfamiliar products, and new values. Consumers increasingly wear similar clothing, drive similar cars, watch the same movies, and listen to the same recording stars. Advertising leads to the emergence of societal values modeled on Western countries, especially the United States. Hollywood dominates the global entertainment industry. In this way, globalization can alter people's norms, values, and behaviors, which may tend to homogenize over time.

Critics call these trends the "McDonaldization" or the "Coca-Colonization" of the world. To combat such trends, governments try to block cultural imperialism and prevent the erosion of local traditions. In Canada, France, and Germany, the public sector attempts to prevent U.S. ideals from diluting local traditions. Hollywood, McDonald's, and Disneyland are seen as Trojan horses that permanently alter food preferences, lifestyles, and other aspects of traditional life. For better or worse, however, such trends are probably inevitable in a globalizing world.

Information and communications technologies speed the homogenization of world cultures. People worldwide are exposed to movies, television, the Internet, and other information sources that promote lifestyles of people in the United States and other advanced economies. Appetites grow for Western products and services, which are seen to signal higher living standards. For example, despite low per-capita income, many Chinese buy consumer electronics such as cell phones and TV sets. Global media have a pervasive effect on local culture, gradually shifting it toward a universal norm.

Western companies such as McDonald's can influence people's food preferences, but cultural values tend to remain stable over time.

At the same time, the flow of cultural influence often goes both ways. Advanced Fresh Concepts is a Japanese food company that is transforming fast food by selling sushi and other Japanese favorites in supermarkets throughout the United States. It sells some $250 million worth of sushi to U.S. buyers every year.[32] As the influence of the Chinese economy grows over time, Western countries will likely adopt cultural norms from China as well. Chinese restaurants and some Chinese traditions are already a way of life in much of the world outside China. Similar influences can be seen from Latin America and other areas in the developing world.

Although some tangibles are becoming more universal, people's behaviors and mind-sets remain stable over time. Religious differences are as strong as ever. Language differences are steadfast across national borders. While a degree of cultural imperialism may be at work, it is offset by the countertrend of nationalism. As globalization standardizes superficial aspects of life across national cultures, people resist these forces by insisting on their national identity and taking steps to protect it. This is evident, for example, in Belgium, Canada, and France, where laws were passed to protect national language and culture.

Globalization and Africa

Exhibit 2.8 highlighted how countries that liberalize international trade and investment enjoy faster per-capita GDP growth. Among all regions, Africa is home to the poorest countries. The majority of its nearly one billion people live on less than two dollars a day. It is the area least integrated into the world economy and accounts for less than 3 percent of world trade. Although it has abundant natural resources, Africa remains underdeveloped due to such factors as inadequate commercial infrastructure, lack of access to foreign capital, high illiteracy, government corruption, wars, and the spread of AIDS.

Experience of the past half-century suggests that traditional methods of trying to help Africa—mainly foreign aid provided by advanced economies—have achieved little success.[33] Despite billions of dollars of aid to Africa since the 1960s, per-capita income has not increased significantly.[34]

In recent years, experts have suggested that the most effective way to alleviate African poverty is to employ business-based models.[35] After decades of stagnation, several sub-Saharan African countries have experienced rapid economic growth thanks to increasing international trade in commodities. For example, Africa is a major supplier of petroleum to Europe and the United States. The top supplier of oil to China is the African country of Angola. There is a ripple effect to economic development and, as certain sectors in Africa have boomed in recent years, foreign banks, retailers, and MNEs have set up operations in the continent. In formerly war-torn Rwanda, countless business opportunities have emerged in sectors as diverse as mining, tourism, telecommunications, and real estate. China and India are beating out U.S. firms and quickly increasing their business dealings in Africa. Chinese companies are investing billions of dollars in the continent. International trade and investment are helping to address many of Africa's most pressing development needs.[36]

 ## Firm-Level Consequences of Market Globalization: Internationalization of the Firm's Value Chain

The globalization of markets has opened up countless new business opportunities for internationalizing firms. At the same time, globalization means that firms must accommodate new risks and intense rivalry from foreign competitors. Globalization results in more demanding buyers who shop for the best deals worldwide. A purely domestic focus is no longer viable for firms in most industries. Managers should replace parochial attitudes with a more cosmopolitan orientation. Internationalization may take the form of global sourcing, exporting, or investment in key markets abroad. Proactive firms seek a simultaneous presence in major trading regions, especially Asia, Europe, and North America.

The most direct implication of market globalization is on the firm's value chain. Market globalization compels firms to organize their sourcing, manufacturing, marketing, and other value-adding activities on a global scale. In a typical value chain, the firm conducts research and product development (R&D), purchases production inputs, and assembles or manufactures a product or service. Next, the firm performs marketing activities such as pricing, promotion, and selling, followed by distribution of the product in targeted markets and after-sales service. The value-chain concept is useful in international business because it helps clarify what activities are performed *where* in the world. For instance, exporting firms perform most "upstream" value-chain activities (R&D and production) in the home market and most "downstream" activities (marketing and after-sales service) abroad.

Each value-adding activity in the firm's value chain is subject to internationalization; that is, it can be performed abroad instead of at home. Exhibit 2.9 portrays a value chain in a typical international firm. As examples in the exhibit suggest, companies have considerable latitude regarding where in the world they locate or configure key value-adding activities. The most typical reasons for locating value-chain activities in particular countries are to reduce the costs of R&D and production or to gain closer access to customers. Through offshoring, the firm relocates a major value-chain activity by establishing a factory or other subsidiary abroad. A related trend is global outsourcing, in which the firm delegates performance of a value-adding activity to an external supplier or contractor located abroad. We discuss these trends in greater detail in Chapter 16.

In the same month that German carmaker BMW launched a new factory in South Carolina, Jackson Mills, an aging textile plant a few miles away, closed its doors and shed thousands of workers. Globalization created a new reality for both these firms. By establishing operations in the United States, BMW found it could manufacture cars cost-effectively while more readily accessing the huge U.S. market. In the process, BMW created thousands of high-paying, better-quality jobs for U.S. workers. Simultaneously, Jackson Mills had discovered it could source textiles of comparable quality more cost-effectively from suppliers in Asia. Globalization drove these firms to relocate key value-adding activities to the most advantageous locations around the world.

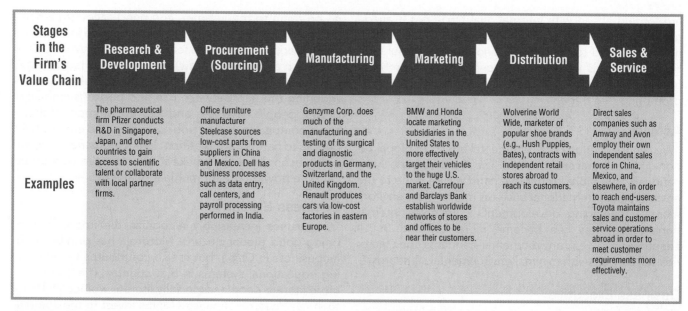

Stages in the Firm's Value Chain	Research & Development	Procurement (Sourcing)	Manufacturing	Marketing	Distribution	Sales & Service
Examples	The pharmaceutical firm Pfizer conducts R&D in Singapore, Japan, and other countries to gain access to scientific talent or collaborate with local partner firms.	Office furniture manufacturer Steelcase sources low-cost parts from suppliers in China and Mexico. Dell has business processes such as data entry, call centers, and payroll processing performed in India.	Genzyme Corp. does much of the manufacturing and testing of its surgical and diagnostic products in Germany, Switzerland, and the United Kingdom. Renault produces cars via low-cost factories in eastern Europe.	BMW and Honda locate marketing subsidiaries in the United States to more effectively target their vehicles to the huge U.S. market. Carrefour and Barclays Bank establish worldwide networks of stores and offices to be near their customers.	Wolverine World Wide, marketer of popular shoe brands (e.g., Hush Puppies, Bates), contracts with independent retail stores abroad to reach its customers.	Direct sales companies such as Amway and Avon employ their own independent sales force in China, Mexico, and elsewhere, in order to reach end-users. Toyota maintains sales and customer service operations abroad in order to meet customer requirements more effectively.

Exhibit 2.9   Examples of How Firms' Value-Chain Activities Can Be Internationalized

Closing Case

Debating the Merits of Globalization

Recently, a university sponsored a roundtable on the broader implications of international business. The participants were an anti-international business activist, a business executive with extensive international dealings, and a government trade official. Excerpts from the exchange present the diverse perspectives of market globalization held by different interest groups.

Activist

"One problem with international business is that it often ignores human rights and basic labor standards. Low-wage factories abroad create substandard working conditions. The activities of multinational companies not only result in job losses here at home, but also in low wages and exploited workers around the world. Just think of the sweatshops in Asia that make imported clothing. Think of the auto workers in Mexico who live in horrible conditions and make only a few dollars a day. Also consider the poverty caused worldwide by the recent global financial and economic crisis."

Business Executive

"Our country needs to participate in the global economy. Companies that export provide better-paying jobs, have more profits, pay higher taxes, and stimulate purchases from local suppliers. Foreign companies that invest here create new jobs, enhance local living standards, and pressure our firms to stay competitive in a challenging global marketplace. Exporters pay higher wages and provide better benefits than nonexporting firms. Many companies need access to foreign markets because of the huge, upfront research and development costs they accumulate. One more pill is cheap; it's the cost of research to find a cure for AIDS that is prohibitive. I think it's a pretty strong argument for the human basis of doing international business. Companies need big markets to amortize the costs of big projects. Africa is getting decimated by AIDS. But pharmaceutical firms can't do the necessary R&D unless they can amortize those costs over a huge, global marketplace. In the long run, uninterrupted international commerce is good."

Trade Official

"The current administration believes in the value of free trade. The government strongly supported NAFTA, and this has already had a positive effect on the economy through increasing exports to Mexico, creating jobs, and leading to improved investment opportunities. Countries are forging ahead with international trade ties. Canada has completed a free trade agreement with Chile. Economic ties lead to cultural ties and more peaceful relations. Also, it is hard for our government to promote freedom and democracy around the world if we are not promoting free trade."

Activist

"We cannot overlook the detrimental effects of globalization on the natural environment. The more we trade internationally, the more irreparable harm will be done to the environment. International business means more environmentally damaging development. Companies internationalize so they can become more efficient. But if countries have weak environmental standards, then factories will be built with minimal environmental standards."

Business Executive

"If we trade internationally, then living standards will increase everywhere. As living standards rise, awareness of and care for the environment will also increase. International business is good for the world because it creates wealth. The more affluent the people, the more they will care about their environment and pass laws to protect it. We are also becoming more responsive to concerns over social responsibility and environmental degradation. We have shown that a good economy and a clean environment are not mutually exclusive. We can have it both ways: a clean planet and a better economic quality of life."

Trade Official

"I think part of the solution is to negotiate trade agreements that take environmental factors into account. International trade that runs roughshod over legitimate environmental concerns is counterproductive and defeats the political agendas of most governments around the world. It is clear that international trade must take environmental concerns into account."

Activist

"International trade interferes with the sovereignty of national governments. When General Motors is the nation's biggest company, like it is in Canada, it is harder for governments to manage policies regarding taxes, monetary policy, social issues, and exchange rates. And who are we, trying to impose our own cultural standards on the world? When I travel in Asia or Latin America, I see McDonald's all over the place. They see Western powers exploiting globalization, harming the economic, cultural, and environmental interests of the rest of the world.

"Global corporations claim they spread modern technologies around the world. But technology is good only if you have access to it. In most of Africa, you have no on-ramp to the Internet. You need access to a computer, which is awfully difficult or impossible in countries where people make only a few dollars a day. When you're paid such a low wage, how can you afford technology? How can you afford to see a doctor? Globalization is widening the gap between rich and poor. As inequality grows, people have less and less in common. Multinational companies exploit poor countries and expose their people to harmful competition. Infant industries in developing economies can't make it when they're confronted with the power of giant multinational firms."

Business Executive

"Companies increasingly recognize the importance of being good global citizens. Motorola has profited from its business in China, but it also contributes to developing educational systems in that country. There are a lot more literate people, especially literate women, in China than ever before. Japanese MNEs invest in the communities where they do business. Companies are not all evil; they do a lot of good for the world, too. Bill Gates is going to do more than any government to get people computers and get them hooked up on the Internet. He has created the world's biggest fund to combat diseases of the poor. He and Warren Buffett are tackling many of these diseases. GlaxoSmithKline is working with the World Health Organization to find a cure for Elephantiasis, a terrible disease that ravages people in Africa."

Trade Official

"Globalization is complex and it's hard to tease out what is bad and what is good. Globalization has made rapid progress; global poverty has declined. Social indicators for many poor countries show improvement over several decades. It's true that income disparities have increased dramatically over the last 50 years while international trade has integrated the world economy. The world has experienced a generally rising tide in terms of people's standard of living. People everywhere are better off than they were 50 years ago. There are some exceptions to this, especially during recessions, but it's better to live in a world where 20 percent of the people are affluent and 80 percent are poor, than a world in which nearly 100 percent of the people are poor, as was the case throughout most of history. There is a strong role for government in all this. Countries benefit from trade, but governments are responsible for protecting citizens from the negative or unintended consequences that trade may bring."

Activist

"Governments have not done enough to regulate the excesses of capitalism. We saw this clearly in the global financial and economic crises, from which the world is still recovering."

AACSB: Reflective Thinking Skills, Ethical Understanding and Reasoning Abilities

Case Questions

1. Do you think globalization and MNE activity are creating problems for the world? What kinds of problems can you identify? What are the unintended consequences of international business?

2. Summarize the arguments in favor of globalization made by the business executive. What is the role of technology in supporting company performance in a globalizing business environment?

3. What are the roles of state and federal governments in dealing with globalization? What is government's role in protecting citizens from the potential negative effects of foreign MNEs conducting business in your country? What kinds of government actions would you recommend?

4. What is the role of education in: (i) addressing the problems raised in the roundtable; (ii) creating societies in which people can deal effectively with public policy issues; and (iii) creating citizens who can compete effectively in the global marketplace?

SOURCES: C. Higgins and P. Debroux, "Globalization and CSR in Asia," *Asian Business & Management* 8, no. 2 (2009): 125–27; F. Mishkin, "Globalization and Financial Development," *Journal of Development Economics* 89, no. 2 (2009): 164–73; J. Pellet, "Next-Generation Globalization," *Chief Executive*, January/February 2009, pp. 50–55; S. Sethi, "Globalization and the Good Corporation," *Journal of Business Ethics* 87 (April 2009): 1–2; "Does Globalization Cause Poverty?" Retrieved from Emory University Globalization Web site http://www.sociology.emory.edu/globalization/issues03.html; Frank Lechner, "Does Globalization Diminish Cultural Diversity?" Retrieved from Emory University Globalization Web site http://www.sociology.emory.edu/globalization/issues05.html; Frank Lechner, Deborah McFarland, Thomas Remington, and Jeff Rosensweig, "Is a Globalization Backlash Occurring?" Retrieved from Emory University Globalization Web site http://www.emory.edu/ACAD_EXCHANGE/1999/mayjune99/global.html.

CHAPTER ESSENTIALS

Key Terms

contagion, p. 80

globalization of markets, p. 66

value chain, p. 71

World Trade Organization (WTO), p. 69

Summary

In this chapter, you learned about:

1. Why globalization is not new

Globalization of markets refers to the gradual integration and growing interdependence of national economies. Early civilizations in the Mediterranean, Middle East, Asia, Africa, and Europe all contributed to the growth of cross-border trade. International trade was triggered by world events and technological discoveries. Globalization has progressed in phases, particularly since the early 1800s. The current phase was stimulated particularly by the rise of IT, the Internet, and other advanced technologies. The **World Trade Organization** is a multilateral governing body empowered to regulate international trade and investment.

2. Market globalization: An organizing framework

Market globalization can be modeled in terms of its drivers, dimensions, societal consequences, and firm-level consequences. As market globalization intensifies, firms are compelled to respond to challenges and exploit new advantages. Many firms proactively pursue internationalization as a strategic move. They become more aggressive at identifying foreign market opportunities, seeking partnerships with foreign firms, and building organizational capabilities to enhance their competitive advantage.

3. Dimensions of market globalization

Market globalization refers to the growing integration of the world economy from the international business activities of countless firms. It represents a growing global interconnectedness of buyers, producers, suppliers, and governments. Globalization has fostered a new dynamism in the world economy, the emergence of regional economic integration blocs, growth of global investment and financial flows, the convergence of buyer lifestyles and needs, and the globalization of both production and services. At the business enterprise level, market globalization amounts to reconfiguration of company

value chains—the sequence of value-adding activities including sourcing, manufacturing, marketing, and distribution—on a global scale.

4. **Drivers of market globalization**

   Market globalization is driven by several factors, including falling trade and investment barriers; market liberalization and adoption of free market economics in formerly closed economies; industrialization and economic development, especially among emerging markets; integration of world financial markets; and technological advances.

5. **Technological advances**

   Advances in technology are particularly important in driving market globalization. The most important advances in technology have occurred in information technology, communications, the Internet, manufacturing, and transportation. These systems help create an interconnected network of customers, suppliers, and intermediaries worldwide. They have made the cost of international business affordable for all types of firms.

6. **Societal consequences of market globalization**

   There is much debate about globalization's benefits and harm. Globalization was a major factor in the recent global recession and financial crisis. Critics complain that globalization interferes with national sovereignty, the ability of a state to govern itself without external intervention. Globalization is associated with *offshoring*, the relocation of value-chain activities to foreign locations where they can be performed at less cost by subsidiaries or independent suppliers. Globalization tends to decrease poverty, but it may also widen the gap between the rich and the poor. Unrestricted industrialization may harm the natural environment. Globalization is also associated with the loss of cultural values unique to each nation. Trade and investment can help address many of Africa's development needs.

7. **Firm-level consequences of market globalization: Internationalization of the firm's value chain**

   Market globalization compels firms to organize their sourcing, manufacturing, marketing, and other value-adding activities on a global scale. Each value-adding activity can be performed in the home country or abroad. Firms choose where in the world they locate or configure key value-adding activities. Firms internationalize value-chain activities to reduce the costs of R&D and production, or to gain closer access to customers.

Test Your Comprehension

1. Define market globalization. What are the underlying dimensions of this megatrend?

2. Is globalization a recent phenomenon? Describe the phases of globalization.

3. Summarize the six dimensions of globalization. Which of these do you think is the most visible manifestation of globalization?

4. Describe the five drivers of globalization.

5. What is the role of the World Trade Organization?

6. In what areas have technological advances had their greatest effect on facilitating world trade and investment?

7. What are the pros and cons of globalization?

8. What effect does globalization have on national sovereignty, employment, the poor, the natural environment, and national culture?

9. What are the implications of globalization for company internationalization?

Apply Your Understanding AACSB: Communication Abilities, Reflective Thinking Skills, Ethical Understanding and Reasoning Abilities, Use of Information Technology, Analytic Skills

1. Imagine you are studying for your international business class at a local coffee shop. The manager spies your textbook and remarks, "I don't get all that foreign business stuff. I don't pay much attention to it. I'm a local guy running a small business. Thank goodness I don't have to worry about any of that." The manager's comments make you realize there is much more to business than just local concerns. What is the likely value chain of a coffee shop? For example, how did the varieties of coffee beans get there?

What is the likely effect of market globalization on coffee shops? Do technological advances play any role in the shop's value chain? Does globalization imply any negative consequences for the worldwide coffee industry? Justify your answer.

2. Globalization provides numerous advantages to businesses and consumers around the world. At the same time, some critics believe globalization is harming various aspects of life and commerce. In what ways is globalization good for firms and consumers? In what ways is globalization harmful to firms and consumers?

3. *Ethical Dilemma:* Northern Energy, Inc. (Northern) is a large oil company with production and mar-

keting operations worldwide. You are a recently hired manager at Northern's subsidiary in Nigeria, which provides jobs to hundreds of Nigerians and supports many local merchants and suppliers. Suppose Northern's drilling and refining practices have severely damaged the natural environment in Nigeria, polluting the air, land, and water. As a result, Northern has faced violent protests and much negative publicity in Nigeria. Develop suggestions on how Northern should address these issues. Keep in mind that top management is reluctant to invest significant new resources in Nigeria, given the firm's weakening business performance there.

globalEDGE Internet Exercises

(http://globalEDGE.msu.edu)

AACSB: Reflective Thinking Skills, Ethical Understanding and Reasoning Abilities, Use of Information Technology, Analytic Skills

Refer to Chapter 1, page 62, for instructions on how to access and use globalEDGE™.

1. The KOF Swiss Economic Institute prepares the annual *KOF Index of Globalization*, which ranks the most globalized countries (enter "KOF Index of Globalization" at globalEDGE™ or other search engine). The index uses three different dimensions to measure globalization: *economic globalization*, *political globalization*, and *social globalization*. Visit the index and explain what each dimension represents, and why each is important for a nation to achieve a substantial presence in the global economy.

2. Service sector jobs are increasingly outsourced to lower-cost locations abroad. The globalEDGE™ Web site has various resources that detail the nature and location of jobs that have been transferred abroad. Some experts believe the resulting foreign investment and increased demand in lower-cost countries will cause wages to rise in those countries, eliminating cost advantages from offshoring and narrowing the income gap between developed economies and low-cost countries. In other words, offshoring will help to reduce global poverty. Others believe that

manufacturing jobs will be consistently moved to low-cost countries, making China and India the world's center of innovation and production. What do you think? Find three articles on outsourcing at globalEDGE™ by doing a search using the keywords "global outsourcing" or "offshoring," and write a report on the most likely consequences of these trends for your country, its workers, and consumers.

3. A key characteristic of globalization is the increasingly integrated world economy. MNEs and many nations have a vested interest in maintaining the globalization trend. If the trend were somehow reversed, participants in international business, such as exporters, would likely suffer big economic losses. In many ways, globalization's role in the world economy is critical. But just how big is the global economy? What is the extent of international trade relative to the size of the global economy? What is the proportion of international trade in the GDPs of each of the following countries: Australia, Canada, Sweden, United Kingdom, and the United States? Consult globalEDGE™ to address these questions.

CHAPTER 3

LEARNING OBJECTIVES In this chapter, you will learn about:

1. Four types of participants in international business
2. Participants arranged by value-chain activity
3. Focal firms in international business
4. International entry strategies of focal firms
5. Distribution channel intermediaries in international business
6. Facilitators in international business
7. Governments in international business

Organizational Participants That Make International Business Happen

The Emergence of Born Global Firms

Geo Search Ltd. is a Japanese company that develops high-technology equipment to help engineers survey ground surfaces for cavities and build safe roads, airports, and underground utility lines. At the request of the United Nations, Geo Search (www.geosearch.co.jp) designed the world's first land-mine detector, called Mine Eye. The firm had an immediate international market because there are millions of mines buried in countries like Afghanistan, Cambodia, and Kuwait. The firm works with non-governmental organizations (NGOs) to search for mines worldwide. Removing land mines is risky, particularly plastic mines that cannot be found with metal detectors. Geo Search's electromagnetic radar can distinguish between mines and other objects buried underground. Images appear in three dimensions on a liquid crystal display, and there is no need to touch the ground surface.

Geo Search is one of an increasing number of small- and medium-sized enterprises (SMEs) active in international business. SMEs make up the majority of all firms in a typical country and often account for more than 50 percent of national economic activity. Compared to large multinational enterprises (MNEs), historically the most common types of international firms, the typical SME has far fewer financial and human resources. In the past, international business was often beyond their reach. But globalization and technological advances have made venturing abroad much less expensive, cre-

ating a commercial environment in which many more small firms do international business than ever before. Since the 1980s, companies that internationalize at or near their founding, *born global firms*, have been springing up all over the world.

Management in born global firms targets products and services to a dozen or more countries within a few years after launching the firm. By internationalizing as early and rapidly as they do, these firms develop a borderless corporate culture. Despite the limited resources that characterize young firms, their agility and flexibility help them serve both foreign and domestic customers well.

Born globals internationalize early for various reasons. Some specialize in a product category for which demand in the home market is too small. Management may perceive big demand for the firm's products abroad or have a strong international orientation. Neogen Corporation (www.neogen.com) is a U.S. born global that manufactures chemicals to kill harmful bacteria and toxins in food crops. The fact that certain toxins are more common in foreign locations led Neogen to internationalize shortly after its founding.

The widespread emergence of born globals shows that any firm, regardless of its size, age, or resource base, can participate actively in international business. Today, born globals and other SME exporters make up a sizable proportion of internationally active firms. The trend is especially relevant to college students who specialize in international business, because SMEs provide numerous job prospects as they aggressively pursue opportunities abroad.

SOURCES: S. Tamer Cavusgil and Gary Knight, *Born Global Firms: The New International Enterprise.* (New York: Business Expert Press, 2009); Oystein Moen, Roger Sorheim, and Truls Erikson, "Born Global Firms and Informal Investors: Examining Investor Characteristics," *Journal of Small Business Management* 46, no. 4 (2008): 536–49; Terence Fan and Phillip Phan, "International New Ventures: Revisiting the Influences Behind The 'Born-Global' Firm," *Journal of International Business Studies* 38, no. 7 (2007): 1113–32; G. Knight and S. T. Cavusgil, "Innovation, Organizational Capabilities, and the Born-Global Firm," *Journal of International Business Studies* 35, no. 2 (2004): 124–41; C. Mambula, "Relating External Support, Business Growth and Creating Strategies for Survival," *Small Business Economics* 22, no. 2 (2004): 83–109; B. Oviatt and P. McDougall, "Toward a Theory of International New Ventures," *Journal of International Business Studies* 25, no. 1 (1994): 45–64.

I n Chapter 2, we learned that market globalization is the growing integration of the world economy through the activities of firms. Factors that drive globalization include falling trade and investment barriers and technological advances. In this chapter, we discuss the people and organizations that make globalization happen and their role in the value chain.

Four Types of Participants in International Business

International business requires numerous organizations, with varying motives, to work together as a coordinated team, contributing different types of expertise and inputs. There are four major categories of participants:

Focal firm The initiator of an international business transaction, which conceives, designs, and produces offerings intended for consumption by customers worldwide. Focal firms are primarily MNEs and SMEs.

1. A focal firm is the initiator of an international business transaction. It conceives, designs, and produces offerings intended for consumption by customers worldwide. Focal firms take center stage in international business. They are primarily large multinational enterprises (MNEs; also known as multinational corporations or MNCs) and small and medium-sized enterprises (SMEs). Some are privately owned companies, others are public, stock-held firms, and still others are state enterprises owned by governments. Some focal firms are manufacturing businesses, while others are in the service sector.

Distribution channel intermediary A specialist firm that provides various logistics and marketing services for focal firms as part of the international supply chain, both in the home country and abroad.

2. A distribution channel intermediary is a specialist firm that provides various logistics and marketing services for focal firms as part of the international supply chain, both in the focal firm's home country and abroad. Typical intermediaries include independent distributors and sales representatives, usually located in foreign markets where they provide distribution and marketing services to focal firms on a contractual basis.

Facilitator A firm or an individual with special expertise in banking, legal advice, customs clearance, or related support services that assists focal firms in the performance of international business transactions.

3. A facilitator is a firm or an individual with special expertise in banking, legal advice, customs clearance, or related support services that helps focal firms perform international business transactions. Facilitators include logistics service providers, freight forwarders, banks, and other support firms that assist focal firms in performing specific functions. A **freight forwarder** is a specialized logistics service provider that arranges international shipping on behalf of exporting firms, much like a travel agent for cargo. Facilitators are found in both the home country and abroad.

Freight forwarder A specialized logistics service provider that arranges international shipping on behalf of exporting firms.

4. Governments or the public sector are also active in international business as suppliers, buyers, and regulators. State-owned enterprises account for a substantial portion of economic value added in many countries, even rapidly liberalizing emerging markets such as Russia, China, and Brazil. Governments in advanced economies like France, Australia, and Sweden have significant ownership of companies in telecom, banking, and natural resources. The global financial crisis that began in 2008 led governments to step up their involvement in business, especially as regulators. Governments in many countries introduced new regulations in the financial sector aimed at resolving flaws and abuses that came to light following the crisis.

The activities of firms, intermediaries, and facilitators in international business overlap to some degree. The focal firm performs certain activities internally and delegates other functions to intermediaries and facilitators when their special expertise is needed. In other words, the focal firm becomes a client of intermediaries and facilitators who provide services on a contractual basis.

While focal firms, intermediaries, and facilitators represent the supply side of international business transactions, customers or buyers make up the demand side. For the most part, customers are individual *consumers and households, retailers* (businesses that purchase finished goods for the purpose of resale), and *organizational buyers* (businesses, institutions, and governments that purchase goods and services as inputs to a production process, or as supplies needed to run a business or organization). Governments and non-profit organizations such as CARE (www.care.org) and UNICEF (www.unicef.org) also often constitute important customers around the world.

 ## Participants Arranged by Value-Chain Activity

It is useful to think of the four categories of participants in terms of the firm's value chain. Focal firms, intermediaries, and facilitators in particular all are engaged in one or more critical value-adding activities such as procurement, manufacturing, marketing, transportation, distribution, and support—configured across several countries. The value chain is thus the complete business system of the focal firm, comprising all the activities the focal firm performs. In international business, the focal firm may retain core activities such as production and marketing within its own organization and delegate distribution and customer service responsibilities to independent contractors, such as foreign-market-based distributors. In this way, the resulting business system is subject to internationalization; that is, individual value-adding activities can be configured in multiple countries. Exhibit 3.1 shows the stages in the value chain where channel intermediaries and facilitators usually operate. It also identifies typical intermediaries and facilitators critical to the functioning of international business transactions.

In exporting firms, much of the value chain is concentrated within one nation—the home country. In highly international firms, management may perform a variety of

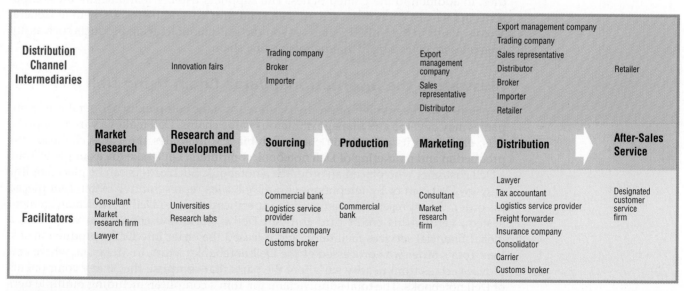

Exhibit 3.1 Typical Positions of Intermediaries and Facilitators in the International Value Chain

Exhibit 3.2 Sample Suppliers of Components for the Chevrolet Malibu

SOURCE: Automotive News.

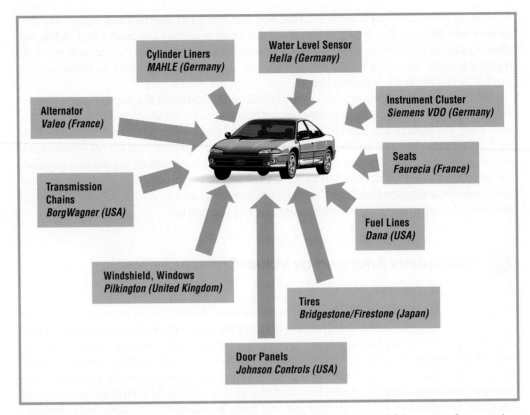

Cylinder Liners
MAHLE (Germany)

Water Level Sensor
Hella (Germany)

Alternator
Valeo (France)

Instrument Cluster
Siemens VDO (Germany)

Seats
Faurecia (France)

Transmission
Chains
BorgWagner (USA)

Fuel Lines
Dana (USA)

Windshield, Windows
Pilkington (United Kingdom)

Tires
Bridgestone/Firestone (Japan)

Door Panels
Johnson Controls (USA)

value-chain activities—production, marketing, distribution—within several countries. In highly internationalized focal firms, the value chain is configured in numerous countries and often from multiple suppliers. MNEs strive to *rationalize* each of their value chains by locating each activity in a country with the most favorable combination of cost, quality, logistical considerations, and other criteria.

As an example, Exhibit 3.2 shows the national and geographic diversity of suppliers that provide content for the Chevrolet Malibu. General Motors sources components for the Malibu from several dozen primary (also called *tier one*) suppliers, such as alternators from Valeo, transmission chains from BorgWagner, and tires from Bridgestone/Firestone. These suppliers are headquartered in Britain, France, Japan, and numerous other countries, in addition to the United States. The suppliers usually manufacture the components in low-cost countries, such as China and Mexico, and then ship them to General Motors plants in the United States. As you can see, manufacturing products such as automobiles involves a truly international value chain.

Illustrating the International Value Chain Using Dell Inc.

Depending on the number of products offered and the complexity of operations, companies may develop and manage numerous value chains. Dell makes a variety of products, each with its own value chain. Exhibit 3.3 illustrates the value chain for the production and marketing of Dell notebook computers. Let's take the example of Tom, a Dell customer who placed an order for a notebook. Such orders can be placed online at www.Dell.com or by telephone with a Dell sales representative. After Tom placed his order, the representative entered the specifications into Dell's order management system; verified his credit card through Dell's work-flow connection with Visa, a global financial services facilitator; and released the order into Dell's production system. Tom's order was processed at the Dell notebook factory in Malaysia, where employees access from nearby suppliers the parts that comprise the 30 key components of Dell notebooks. The total supply chain for Tom's computer, including multiple tiers

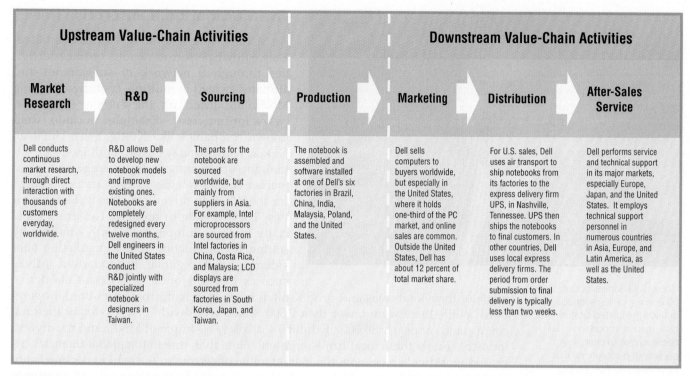

Upstream Value-Chain Activities				Downstream Value-Chain Activities		
Market Research	**R&D**	**Sourcing**	**Production**	**Marketing**	**Distribution**	**After-Sales Service**
Dell conducts continuous market research, through direct interaction with thousands of customers everyday, worldwide.	R&D allows Dell to develop new notebook models and improve existing ones. Notebooks are completely redesigned every twelve months. Dell engineers in the United States conduct R&D jointly with specialized notebook designers in Taiwan.	The parts for the notebook are sourced worldwide, but mainly from suppliers in Asia. For example, Intel microprocessors are sourced from Intel factories in China, Costa Rica, and Malaysia; LCD displays are sourced from factories in South Korea, Japan, and Taiwan.	The notebook is assembled and software installed at one of Dell's six factories in Brazil, China, India, Malaysia, Poland, and the United States.	Dell sells computers to buyers worldwide, but especially in the United States, where it holds one-third of the PC market, and online sales are common. Outside the United States, Dell has about 12 percent of total market share.	For U.S. sales, Dell uses air transport to ship notebooks from its factories to the express delivery firm UPS, in Nashville, Tennessee. UPS then ships the notebooks to final customers. In other countries, Dell uses local express delivery firms. The period from order submission to final delivery is typically less than two weeks.	Dell performs service and technical support in its major markets, especially Europe, Japan, and the United States. It employs technical support personnel in numerous countries in Asia, Europe, and Latin America, as well as the United States.

Exhibit 3.3   Dell's International Value Chain

SOURCES: Adapted from Ben Charny, "Dell Widens U.S. Computer-Share Lead," *Wall Street Journal*, January 17, 2008, p. B4; Thomas Friedman, *The World Is Flat* (New York: Farrar, Straus, & Giroux, 2005); Gartner, Inc., http://www.gartner.com; A. Lashinsky, "Where Dell Is Going Next," *Fortune*, October 18, 2004, pp. 115–20.

of suppliers, encompasses about 400 companies, primarily in Asia, but also in Europe and the Americas.

On a typical day, Dell processes orders for 140,000 computers, which are sold and distributed to customers worldwide. Although Dell is based in Texas, non-U.S. orders account for roughly half its total sales (about $61 billion in 2009). As growth in U.S. sales flattens over time, the proportion of non-U.S. sales will grow. Shipping is handled via air transport. For example, from the Dell Malaysia factory to the United States, Dell charters a China Airlines 747 that flies to Nashville, Tennessee, six days a week. Each jet carries 25,000 Dell notebooks that together weigh more than 100,000 kilograms, or 220,000 pounds. A hallmark of Dell's value chain is collaboration. CEO Michael Dell and senior managers constantly work with their suppliers to make process improvements in Dell's value chain.

 ## Focal Firms in International Business

Imagine a typical theatrical production. There are script writers, stage managers, lighting technicians, musicians, set directors, business managers, and publicity staff, in addition to performing actors. Each participant contributes in different ways, and much coordination among them is required. Advance planning, preparation, timeliness, and synchronization are critical to ultimate success. In the same way, international business transactions require the participation of many specialist organizations, exact timing, and precision.

Focal firms are the most prominent international players. They include well-known multinational enterprises and small and medium-sized exporting firms, as well as contemporary organizations such as the born globals featured in the opening vignette. Let's learn more about each of these key actors in international business.

Coca-Cola derives about 80 percent of its revenues outside the United States. U.S. market importance has declined due to changing consumer preferences that favor healthier options like water and juices. Pictured is company CEO Muhtar Kent.

Multinational enterprise (MNE)

A large company with substantial resources that performs various business activities through a network of subsidiaries and affiliates located in multiple countries.

The Multinational Enterprise (MNE)

An MNE is a large company with substantial resources that performs various business activities through a network of subsidiaries and affiliates located in multiple countries. Leading MNEs are listed on the *Fortune Global 500* (www.fortune.com). Examples include well-known companies like Nestlé, Sony, Unilever, Nokia, Ford, Barclays, ABB, and Shell Oil. Although such firms employ a range of foreign market entry strategies, MNEs are best known for their foreign direct investment (FDI) activities. They operate in multiple countries, especially in Asia, Europe, and North America, by setting up production plants, marketing subsidiaries, and regional headquarters. MNEs such as Exxon, Honda, and Coca-Cola derive much of their total sales and profits, often more than half, from cross-border operations. While there were fewer than 7,500 MNEs worldwide in 1970, today the total count stands at nearly 80,000.[1] Exhibit 3.4 displays a sample of MNEs and the diverse industry sectors these focal firms represent. Note that, due to the global financial crisis and worldwide recession, the market value of sectors in the exhibit declined substantially in recent years. The largest drops occurred in the financial and consumer discretionary sectors, each of which declined in value by almost 50 percent between 2005 and 2009.

Some focal firms operate in the services sector, including airlines, retailers, and construction companies. Examples include HSBC in banking, CIGNA in insurance, Bouygues in construction, Accor in hospitality, Disney in entertainment, Nextel in telecommunications, and Best Buy in retailing. Although retailers are usually classified as intermediaries, some large ones such as IKEA, Walmart, and Gap are considered focal firms themselves. In addition, nontraditional Internet-mediated businesses that deliver knowledge-based offerings such as music, movies, and software online have joined the ranks of global focal firms. Amazon and Netflix are examples.

Not all focal firms are private businesses. In developing countries and centrally planned economies, some focal firms are partly or wholly owned by the government. Lenovo Group is China's leading computer maker. It owns the former PC business of IBM and is about 25 percent government-owned. CNOOC is a huge oil company that tried to buy Unocal in the United States in 2005. It is 70 percent owned by the Chinese government. Numerous other leading Chinese MNEs—China Mobile and China Netcom in telephony, Dongfeng Motor Corporation and Shanghai Automotive in cars, and China Life in insurance—are wholly or partly owned by the Chinese government.

MNEs have played a major role in the current phase of globalization. In the years following World War II, most multinationals, typically from the United States and the United Kingdom, went abroad seeking raw materials, production efficiencies, and foreign-based customers. Today, these firms undertake sourcing, manufacturing, servicing, and marketing activities that span all areas of the world.

A typical MNE, and one whose products you may have sampled, is Sodexo (www.sodexo.com), the world's second-largest contract foodservice provider. Sodexo is the second-largest employer in France, number six in Europe, and twenty-second globally. Its 355,000 employees provide cafeteria-style food to universities, hospitals, corporations, and public institutions at 33,900 sites in more than 80 countries. Sodexo serves more than 40 million consumers per day and earns revenues topping $20 billion annually. Typical customers include the British-Dutch firm Unilever, Germany's Ministry of Foreign Affairs, and the U.S. Marine Corps. Sodexo is the food source for numerous

Sector	2008 Market Value (US $ billions)	Percentage of World Total	Representative Firms
Financials	$2,949	18.2%	Capital One, Danske Bank, Mitsui Sumitomo Bank
Energy	1,929	11.9	Mobil, Total, China Oilfield Services
Health Care	1,850	11.4	GlaxoSmithKline, Novartis, Baxter International
Consumer Staples	1,812	11.2	Procter & Gamble, Unilever, China Mengniu Dairy, Honda
Industrials	1,699	10.5	Landstar Systems, Shenzhen Expressway, Haldex
Information Technology	1,684	10.4	Microsoft, Oracle, Hoya, Taiwan Semiconductor Manufacturing
Consumer Discretionary	1,344	8.3	Coach, Adidas, Salomon, Matsushita Electric
Materials	1,013	6.3	Dow Chemical, Alcan, Vitro SA
Telecom Services	1,007	6.2	AT&T, China Mobile, Royal KPN
Utilities	924	5.7	Duke Energy, Empresa Nacional de Electricidad SA, Hong Kong and China Gas, Ltd.
TOTAL	**16,211**	**100.0**	

Exhibit 3.4
Typical Multinational Enterprises as Focal Firms (Ranked by Industry Sector Size)
SOURCE: S&P Global 1200, 2008, accessed at http://www.standardandpoors.com. Reprinted with permission.

college cafeterias in Australia, Canada, and the United States. Chances are, if you eat in a university cafeteria, it's a Sodexo operation.

Small and Medium-Sized Enterprises

Another type of focal firm that initiates cross-border business transactions is the SME. As defined in Canada and the United States, **small and medium-sized enterprises (SMEs)** are manufacturers or service providers with fewer than 500 employees (in the European Union and numerous other countries, they are defined as having fewer than 250 employees). SMEs now make up the majority of companies active in international business. Nearly all firms, including large MNEs, started out small. Compared to the large multinationals, SMEs can be more flexible and quicker to respond to global business opportunities. They are usually less bureaucratic, more adaptable, and more entrepreneurial and are often the basis for entrepreneurship and innovation in national economies.

Being smaller organizations, SMEs are constrained by limited financial and human resources. This explains why they usually choose exporting as their main strategy for entering foreign markets: Their limited resources prevent them from undertaking FDI, an

Small and medium-sized enterprise (SME) A company with 500 or fewer employees (as defined in Canada and the United States).

expensive entry mode. To compensate, SMEs leverage the services of intermediaries and facilitators to succeed abroad. As their operations grow, some gradually establish company-owned sales offices or subsidiaries in key target markets.

Because of their size and relative inexperience, SMEs often target specialized products to market niches too small to interest large MNEs. SMEs owe much of their international success to support provided by distributors in foreign markets and globe-spanning logistics specialists such as FedEx and DHL. Smaller firms also rely on information and communications technologies that allow them to identify global market niches and efficiently serve specialized buyer needs. As a result, SMEs are gaining equal footing with large multinationals in marketing sophisticated products around the world.

In Eastern Europe, the development of emerging market countries is driven increasingly by the rise of fast-growing SMEs. Examples include the Latvian coffee shop chain Double Coffee and the Hungarian employment recruiter CVO Group. Many of Eastern Europe's small firms operate not in manufacturing but in intellectual, knowledge-intensive industries such as software and consulting. The rise of Eastern European SMEs has resulted mainly from two trends: the access these firms have gained in recent years to the massive European Union and direct investment by foreign investors in emerging markets.[2]

Born Global Firms

Born global firm

A young entrepreneurial company that initiates international business activity early in its evolution, moving rapidly into foreign markets.

Born global firms, such as Geo Search Ltd., featured in the opening vignette, represent a relatively new breed of international SME—those that undertake early and substantial internationalization. Despite the scarce resources typical of most small businesses, born globals usually internationalize within three years of their founding and may export to twenty or more countries, generating more than 25 percent of their sales from abroad. One example is History and Heraldry (www.historyandheraldry.com), a born global in Britain specializing in gifts for history buffs and those with English ancestry. In its first five years, the firm expanded its sales to sixty countries, exporting about 70 percent of its total production. The firm's biggest markets are France, Germany, Italy, Spain, and the Americas. It recently opened a North American subsidiary in Florida.[3]

Some successful born globals grow large enough to become large multinational firms. For example, QualComm (www.qualcomm.com) was founded in California in 1985 and eventually grew to become a major MNE on the strength of huge international sales. QualComm developed the e-mail software Eudora and OmniTRACS, a two-way satellite messaging and position reporting system used in the global transportation industry. Just four years after its founding, QualComm began exporting to Europe and soon followed with market entry in Brazil, China, India, Indonesia, and Japan. QualComm's founders were entrepreneurs who, from the beginning, made little distinction between domestic and foreign markets. Technological prowess and managerial vision were strong factors in making the firm an early international success.

The born global phenomenon represents a new reality in international business. In countries like Australia, Denmark, Ireland, and the United States, born globals account for a substantial proportion of national exports. In many cases, born globals offer leading-edge products with strong potential to generate international sales. They leverage the Internet and communications technologies to facilitate early and efficient international operations.

The emergence of born globals is associated with *international entrepreneurship,* in which

Born global firms are international from their founding. Vix ERG is an Australian born global that produces fare management systems for the public transit industry worldwide.

innovative, smaller firms pursue business opportunities everywhere, regardless of national borders. Communications and transportation technologies, falling trade barriers, and the emergence of niche markets worldwide have increased the ability of contemporary firms to view the whole world as their marketplace. Entrepreneurial managers are creative, proactive, and comfortable dealing with risk. They are usually quick to adapt company strategies as circumstances evolve. The widespread emergence of born globals implies that any firm, regardless of size or experience, can succeed in international business.[4]

 ## International Entry Strategies of Focal Firms

One way to analyze focal firms in international business is in terms of the entry strategies they use to expand abroad. Earlier, we noted that the larger MNEs tend to expand abroad through FDI. By contrast, smaller firms tend to be exporters. Both MNEs and SMEs often rely on contractual relationships such as franchising and licensing.

A Framework for Classifying International Entry Strategies

Exhibit 3.5 shows the array of foreign market entry modes that focal firms use and the foreign partners they seek. The first column lists three categories of international business transactions: (i) transactions that involve the trade of products; (ii) transactions that involve contractual exchange of services or intangibles; and (iii) transactions based on investing equity ownership in foreign-based enterprises.

The second column in Exhibit 3.5 identifies the types of focal firms engaged in international business. Some focal firms are manufacturing businesses such as Sharp, John Deere, and Land Rover. They use manufacturing processes to produce tangible products

Nature of International Transaction	Types of Focal Firm	Foreign Market Entry Strategy	Location of Major Activities	Typical Foreign Partners
Trade of products	Small manufacturer	Exporting	Home country	Distributor, agent, or other independent representative
	Large manufacturer	Exporting	Mainly abroad	Company-owned office or subsidiary
	Manufacturer	Importing (e.g., sourcing)	Home	Independent supplier
	Importer	Importing	Home	Trader or manufacturer
	Trading company	Exporting and Importing	Home	Trader or manufacturer
Contractual exchange of services or intangibles	Service provider	Exporting	Usually abroad	Agent, branch, or subsidiary
	Supplier of expertise or technical assistance	Consulting services	Abroad (temporarily)	Client
	Licensor with patent	Licensing	Home	Licensee
	Licensor with know-how	Licensing (technology transfer)	Home	Licensee
	Franchisor	Franchising	Home	Franchisee
	Service contractor	Management/Marketing service contracting	Abroad	Business owner or sponsor
	Construction/Engineering/ Design/ Architectural Firm	Turnkey contracting or build-own-transfer	Abroad (temporarily)	Project owner
	Manufacturer	Non-equity, project-based, partnerships	Home or abroad	Manufacturer
Equity ownership in foreign-based enterprises	MNE	FDI via greenfield investment	Abroad	None
	MNE	FDI via acquisition	Abroad	Acquired company
	MNE	Equity joint venture	Abroad	Local business partner(s)

Exhibit 3.5 International Business Transactions, Types of Focal Firms, and Foreign Market Entry Strategies

that they sell in foreign markets. Trading companies are brokers of goods and services. Service providers are firms in the services sector, such as insurance companies and hotel chains. Some services firms supply expertise—purely intangible offerings such as advice and training, often one on one—to clients. Examples include lawyers and consulting firms.

The second column also identifies licensors of various types of intellectual property, including patents and know-how. A **licensor** is a firm that enters a contractual agreement with a foreign partner to allow the partner the right to use certain intellectual property for a specified period of time in exchange for royalties or other compensation. A **franchisor** is a firm that grants another the right to use an entire business system in exchange for fees, royalties, or other forms of compensation. Franchisors are essentially sophisticated licensors and include companies like McDonald's and Hertz Car Rental. Other firms, particularly in the construction, engineering, design, or architectural industries, provide their offerings via turnkey contracting. **Turnkey contractors** are focal firms or a consortium of firms that plan, finance, organize, manage, and implement all phases of a project and then hand it over to a foreign customer after training local personnel.

The third column in Exhibit 3.5 identifies the foreign market entry strategy, or the mode of internationalization that the abovementioned companies employ. A foreign market entry strategy refers to the manner in which the focal firm internationalizes, whether through exporting, importing, licensing, or FDI. The type of entry mode depends on the nature of the business as well as the nature of the focal firm, its products, and its goals. When the nature of business is dealing in intangibles, such as professional services, the focal firm may enter into agency relationships with a foreign partner. This is common among banks, advertising agencies, and market research firms. Licensing and franchising are common in the international transfer of intangibles. A franchisor makes a contract with a foreign franchisee; a supplier of expertise makes a contract with a foreign client, and so forth.

In undertaking international business, the focal firm has the option of serving customers either through foreign investment or by relying on the support of independent intermediaries located abroad. In the former case, the firm will set up *company-owned* manufacturing and distribution facilities abroad. The fourth column in Exhibit 3.5 identifies the location of major activities. For example, most exporters carry out major activities—manufacturing, marketing, and sales—in their home country; they produce goods at home and ship them to customers abroad. MNEs and other large firms, however, tend to carry out major activities in multiple countries; they produce goods and sell them to customers primarily located abroad.

The last column in Exhibit 3.5 identifies the nature of the foreign partner. In almost all cases, the focal firm relies on intermediaries as well as support firms located in foreign markets. Significant activities are typically delegated to these foreign partners, including marketing, distribution, sales, and customer service. MNEs have seen a strong trend in recent years away from fully integrated operations toward the delegation of certain noncore functions to outside vendors, a practice known as *outsourcing*. Outsourcing involves the firm in a variety of foreign partnerships. For example, Nike maintains its design and marketing operations within the firm, but outsources production to independent suppliers located abroad.

Other Types of International Entry Strategies

Let's develop a fuller understanding of focal firms other than the MNEs and SMEs that are highlighted in Exhibit 3.5. Some focal firms expand into foreign markets by entering into contractual relationships with foreign partners. Licensing and franchising are examples of contractual relationships. Occasionally, the licensor sells essential components or services to the licensee as part of their ongoing relationship. Licensing allows companies to internationalize rapidly while remaining in their home market. For instance, Anheuser-Busch signed a licensing agreement with the Japanese beer brewer Kirin, under which Kirin

Licensor A firm that enters a contractual agreement with a foreign partner to allow the partner the right to use certain intellectual property for a specified period of time in exchange for royalties or other compensation.

Franchisor A firm that grants another the right to use an entire business system in exchange for fees, royalties, or other forms of compensation.

Turnkey contractors Focal firms or a consortium of firms that plan, finance, organize, manage, and implement all phases of a project and then hand it over to a foreign customer after training local personnel.

produces and distributes Budweiser beer in Japan. The agreement has substantial potential, given Japan's $30 billion-a-year beer market.[5] In another example, Canadian toymaker Mega Bloks signed an agreement with Disney that gives the SME the right to produce toys that feature Disney characters such as Winnie the Pooh and the Power Rangers.[6]

Like licensors, the franchisor remains in its home market and permits its foreign partners to carry out activities in *their* markets. The franchisor assists the franchisee in setting up its operation and then maintains ongoing control over aspects of the franchisee's business, such as operations, procurement, quality control, and marketing. The franchisee benefits by gaining access to a proven business plan and substantial expertise. Major international franchisors include Subway, Curves, Pizza Hut, KFC, RE/MAX, and McDonald's.

Turnkey contractors specialize in international construction, engineering, design, and architectural projects, typically for airports, hospitals, factories, power plants, oil refineries, campuses, and upgrades to public transportation such as bridges, roadways, and rail systems. In a typical turnkey contract, the contractor plans, finances, organizes, manages, and implements all phases of a construction project, providing hardware and know-how to produce what the project sponsor requires. Hardware includes buildings, equipment, and inventory that comprise the tangible aspects of the system. Know-how is the knowledge about technologies, operational expertise, and managerial skills that the contractor transfers to the customer during and after completing the project.[7]

Turnkey projects are typically awarded on the basis of open bidding, in which many potential contractors participate. Some are highly publicized megaprojects, such as the European Channel Tunnel, the Hong Kong Airport, and the Three Gorges Dam in China. Typical examples of turnkey projects include upgrades to public transportation networks such as bridges, roadways, and rail systems. Most metro projects are financed largely by public funding. They are typically in Asia and Western Europe, where demand is driven by intensifying urbanization and worsening congestion. One of the world's largest publicly funded heavy-rail projects is underway in Delhi, India. Delhi Metro Rail Ltd. (www.delhimetrorail.com) commissioned the estimated $2.3 billion turnkey project to build roads and tunnels that run through the city's central business district. The turnkey consortium includes numerous local firms as well as Sweden's Skanska AB, one of the world's largest construction companies.[8]

An increasingly popular type of turnkey contract in the developing economies is the *build-own-transfer* venture. In this arrangement, the contractors acquire an ownership stake in the facility for a period of time until it is turned over to the client. The contractors also provide ongoing advice, training, and assistance in navigating regulatory requirements and obtaining needed approvals from government authorities. At some point after a successful period of operation, the contractors divest their interest in the project.

Exhibit 3.6 identifies the top construction contractors in the world based on revenues from projects outside their home countries. The list reveals the highly global nature of the large-scale construction industry. Top firms come from Europe and the United States and derive much of their total revenues from international projects. Many have established reputations in specialized project areas such as airports, steel plants, refineries, high-speed rail, and environmental projects.[9]

An *international collaborative venture* is a cross-border business alliance in which partnering firms pool their resources to create a new venture, sharing the associated costs and risks. Collaborative ventures represent a middle ground between exporting and FDI. Collaborative arrangements help the focal firm increase

ABB and Alstom are among the international construction contractors that have built the Three Gorges Dam on the Yangtze River in China's Hubei province. The project, which aims to control the country's mighty Yangtze River and tame the floods, is thought to have cost more than any other single project in China's history, with unofficial estimates as high as $75 billion.

Rank, based on 2008 International Revenues	Contractor (Home Country)	Approximate 2008 (U.S.$ millions)		Example of Recently Completed Mega Project
		International	Total	
1	Vinci (France)	$33,061	$45,936	Channel tunnel, Britain-France
2	Hochtief AG (Germany)	23,189	25,789	New airport, Berlin
3	FCC, SA (Spain)	17,976	18,922	N6 highway, Ireland
4	Bechtel (United States)	17,873	30,753	Hong Kong Airport, China
5	Skanska AB (Sweden)	17,005	21,802	Oresund Bridge, Denmark
6	Bouygues (France)	13,247	44,158	Groene Hart Tunnel, Netherlands
7	Fluor (United States)	12,502	22,326	Shell Rayong Refinery, Thailand
8	Strabag SE (Austria)	11,863	14,829	Xiaolangdi Dam, China

Exhibit 3.6 Top International Construction Contractors (Based on Revenues from Projects Outside the Home Country)

SOURCES: *Engineering News-Record* (2008). "The Top 225 International Contractors," August 18, p. 32; *Fortune* "GLobal 500" at http://money.cnn.com/magazines/fortune/global500, accessed June 26, 2009; Company profiles at Hoovers.com; and Web sites of the indicated corporations.

international business, compete more effectively with rivals, take advantage of complementary technologies and expertise, overcome trade barriers, connect with customers abroad, configure value chains more effectively, and generate economies of scale in production and marketing.

Joint ventures (JV) and project-based, nonequity ventures are both examples of international collaborative ventures. A **joint venture partner** is a focal firm that creates and jointly owns a new legal entity through equity investment or pooling of assets. Partners form JVs to share costs and risks, gain access to needed resources, gain economies of scale, and pursue long-term strategic goals. For example, Hitachi formed a joint venture with MasterCard to promote a smart card system for banking and other applications. The Japanese electronics giant invested $2.4 million to take an 18 percent stake in the JV, established in San Francisco.[10]

Partners in a **project-based, nonequity venture** are focal firms that collaborate to undertake a given project with a relatively narrow scope and well-defined timetable, but without creating a new legal entity. In contrast to JVs, which involve equity investment by the parent companies, project-based partnerships are less formal, short-term, nonequity ventures. The partners pool their resources and expertise for a limited time to perform some mutually beneficial task, such as joint R&D or marketing, but do not form a new enterprise.[11]

One example is Cisco Systems (www.cisco.com), the worldwide leader in Internet networking technology, which expanded its operations by partnering with key foreign players. Cisco formed an alliance with Japan's Fujitsu to jointly develop routers and switches that enable clients to build Internet protocol networks for advanced telecommunications. In Italy, Cisco teamed with Italtel to jointly develop network solutions for the convergence of voice, data, and video to meet growing global demands. Cisco also formed an alliance with the Chinese telecom ZTE to tap Asian markets. The two companies are collaborating to provide equipment and services to telecommunications operators in the Asia-Pacific region.[12]

Joint venture partner A focal firm that creates and jointly owns a new legal entity through equity investment or pooling of assets.

Project-based, nonequity venture partners A collaboration in which the partners create a project with a relatively narrow scope and a well-defined timetable, without creating a new legal entity.

 ## Distribution Channel Intermediaries in International Business

A second category of international business participant is the distribution channel intermediary. Intermediaries are physical distribution and marketing service providers in the value chain for focal firms. They move products and services in the home country and abroad and perform key downstream functions in the target market on behalf of focal firms, including advertising, sales, and customer service. They may organize transportation of goods and offer various logistics services such as warehousing and customer support. A worldwide survey by *McKinsey Quarterly* found that MNE executives are particularly concerned about the capabilities needed to manage global supply chains and distribution channels, as well as the recruitment and retention of skilled personnel in individual foreign markets.[13] These findings emphasize the importance of intermediaries in international business.

Intermediaries are of many different types, ranging from large international companies to small, highly specialized operations. Techdata (www.techdata.com) is a large distributor of laptops, peripherals, and other information technology products. Like typical wholesalers, the firm buys such goods from manufacturers and then resells them to retail stores. In 2010, Techdata distributed such products to thousands of retailers in 100 countries worldwide.

For most exporters, relying on an independent foreign distributor is a low-cost way to enter foreign markets. The intermediary's intimate knowledge, contacts, and services in the local market can provide a strong support system for exporters inexperienced in international business or too small to undertake market-based activities themselves. There are three major categories of intermediaries: those based in the foreign target market, those based in the home country, and those that operate via the Internet.

Intermediaries Based in the Foreign Market

Most intermediaries are based in the exporter's target market. They provide a multitude of services, including conducting market research, appointing local agents or commission representatives, exhibiting products at trade shows, arranging local transportation for cargo, and clearing products through customs. Intermediaries also orchestrate local marketing activities, including product adaptation, advertising, selling, and after-sales service. Many finance sales and extend credit, facilitating prompt payment to the exporter. In short, intermediaries based in the foreign market can function like the exporter's local partner, handling all needed local business functions.

A **foreign distributor** is a foreign market-based intermediary that works under contract for an exporter and takes title to and distributes the exporter's products in a national market or territory, often performing marketing functions such as sales, promotion, and after-sales service. Foreign distributors are essentially independent wholesalers that purchase merchandise from exporters (at a discount) and resell it after adding a profit margin. Because they take title to the goods, foreign distributors are often called *merchant distributors*. They promote, sell, and maintain an inventory of the exporter's products in the foreign market. They also typically maintain substantial physical resources and provide financing, technical support, and after-sales service for the product, relieving the exporter of these functions abroad. Distributors may carry a variety of noncompeting complementary products, such as home appliances and consumer electronics. For consumer goods, the distributor usually sells to retailers. For industrial goods, the distributor sells to other businesses and/or directly to end users. Distributors are a good choice for firms that seek a stable, committed presence in the target market. They typically have substantial knowledge of the exporter's products and of the local market.

Foreign distributor A foreign market-based intermediary that works under contract for an exporter, takes title to, and distributes the exporter's products in a national market or territory, often performing marketing functions such as sales, promotion, and after-sales service.

An **agent** is an intermediary (often an individual or a small firm) that handles orders to buy and sell commodities, products, and services in international business transactions for a commission. Also known as a *broker*, an agent may act for either the buyer or seller but does not assume title or ownership of the goods. The typical agent is compensated by commission, expressed as a percentage of the price of the product sold. In economic terms, the agent brings buyers and sellers together. Agents operate under contract for a definite period of time (often as little as one year), renewable by mutual agreement. The contract defines territory, terms of sale, compensation, and grounds and procedures for terminating the agreement.[14]

Agent An intermediary (often an individual or a small firm) that handles orders to buy and sell commodities, products, and services in international business transactions for a commission.

The function of the agent is especially important in markets made up of many small, widely dispersed buyers and sellers. For example, brokers on the London Metal Exchange (LME; www.lme.co.uk) deal in copper, silver, nickel, and other metals sourced

Logistics service providers move product shipments on behalf of manufacturers and intermediaries to destinations worldwide. Here cargo is offloaded from an aircraft owned by DHL, one of the largest transport providers in Europe and the Middle East.

Manufacturer's representative

An intermediary contracted by the exporter to represent and sell its merchandise or services in a designated country or territory.

from mining operations worldwide. The volume of metal buying and selling is huge—around $5 billion per year—and the suppliers are widely dispersed worldwide. The LME greatly increases the efficiency with which manufacturing firms access the metal ingredients they need to conduct manufacturing operations. Agents are common in the international trade of commodities, especially agricultural goods and base minerals. In the services sector, agents often transact sales of insurance and securities.

A **manufacturer's representative** is an intermediary contracted by the exporter to represent and sell its merchandise or services in a designated country or territory. Manufacturer's representatives go by various names, depending on the industry in which they work—agents, sales representatives, or service representatives. In essence, they act as contracted sales personnel in a designated target market on behalf of the exporter, but usually with broad powers and autonomy. Manufacturer's representatives may handle various noncompetitive, complementary lines of products or services. They do not take title to the goods they represent and are most often compensated by commission. With this type of representation, the exporter usually ships merchandise directly to the foreign customer or end user. Manufacturer's representatives do not maintain physical facilities, marketing, or customer support capabilities, so these functions must be handled primarily by the exporter.

In consumer markets, the foreign firm must get its products to end users through *retailers* located in the foreign market. A retailer represents the last link between distributors and end users. Some national retail chains have expanded abroad and are now providing retail services in multiple countries. For example, Tesco, Seibu, Carrefour, and Royal Ahold are major retail store chains based in Britain, Japan, France, and the Netherlands, respectively. Rolex and Ralph Lauren sell their products directly to these retailers. This type of transaction has emerged from the international growth of major retail chains. Often, a traveling sales representative facilitates such transactions. Large international retailers such as Carrefour and Walmart maintain purchasing offices abroad. Walmart and Toys "R" Us have opened hundreds of stores worldwide, especially in Mexico, Canada, Japan, China, and Europe. IKEA, a Swedish company, is the world's largest furniture retailer. Dealing directly with foreign-based retailers is efficient because it results in a much shorter distribution channel and reduced channel costs.

Intermediaries Based in the Home Country

Some intermediaries are domestically based. Wholesaler *importers* bring in products or commodities from foreign countries for sale in the home market, re-export, or use in the manufacture of finished products. Manufacturers also import a range of raw materials, parts, and components used in the production of higher value-added products. They may also import a complementary collection of products and services to supplement or augment their own product range. Retailers such as department stores, specialized stores, mail-order houses, and catalogue firms import many of the products they sell. A trip to retailers such as Best Buy, Canadian Tire, or Marks & Spencer reveals that most of their offerings are sourced from abroad, especially from low labor-cost countries.

Wholesalers import input goods that they in turn sell to manufacturers and retailers. A typical importer in this category is Capacitor Industries Inc. (www.capacitorindustries.com), an SME that imports low-cost electronic components from China and sells them to motor makers and other manufacturers in the United States and other countries. Capacitors are tiny devices that store electrical charges, keep motors running, and protect computers from surges. Capacitor Industries' strategy is simple—buy from a low-cost country and sell in an advanced economy at a profit. Importing from China and other low-cost suppliers means it can undercut the prices of domestic suppliers by up to 30 percent.

For exporting firms that prefer to minimize the complexity of selling internationally, a **trading company** serves as an intermediary that engages in import and export of a variety of commodities, products, and services. A trading company assumes the international marketing function on behalf of producers, especially those with limited international business experience. Large trading companies operate much like agents, coordinating sales of countless products in markets worldwide. Typically, they are high-volume, low-margin resellers compensated by adding profit margins to what they sell.

AJC International, based in Atlanta, Georgia, is a trading company dedicated to international business. Led by co-founders Eric Joiner (shown here) and Gerald Allison, this entrepreneurial firm is a world leader in marketing frozen and refrigerated food products, as well as in logistics and distribution services. Founded in 1972, it generates more than $1 billion annually in revenues, bringing together suppliers and customers in more than 140 countries on six continents. Its multicultural workforce represents 34 nationalities speaking 27 languages.

Trading companies are very common in commodities and agricultural goods such as grain. Companies such as Cargill (www.cargill.com) provide a useful service as international resellers of agricultural goods. With 160,000 employees in more than sixty countries and annual sales of more than $100 billion, Cargill is often listed as the largest private firm in the United States. It buys, sorts, ships, and sells a wide range of commodities, including coffee, sugar, cotton, oil, hemp, rubber, and livestock, controlling about 25 percent of U.S. grain exports and one-fifth of the U.S. meat market. Most of its profits come from turning commodities into value-added products, including oils, syrups, and flour. The company also processes the ingredients many food companies use to produce cereal, frozen dinners, and cake mixes.

Exhibit 3.7 provides a list of the largest trading companies in the world. What strikes you about these firms? First, they tend to be high-volume, low-margin resellers dealing largely in commodities such as grains, minerals, and metals. Second, note that five of the ten are based in Japan, where trading companies long have played a critical role in external trade. Being an island country with few natural resources, over time Japan became very good at importing parts and materials needed in manufacturing. Trading companies are also common in South Korea, India, and Europe.

In Japan, large trading companies are known as *sogo shosha*. The sogo shosha usually engage in both exporting and importing and are specialists in low-margin, high-volume trading. They may also supply a range of manufacturing, financial, and logistical services. To stay close to foreign markets, managers of the sogo shosha travel widely, employ extensive networks of local offices, participate in trade shows, and establish business relationships with agents and distributors worldwide.

The sogo shosha include giant firms that are little known in the West, such as Mitsui, Sumitomo, Itochu, and Marubeni, all firms on the *Fortune Global 500*. In the 1990s, total trade of the nine top sogo shosha averaged about 25 percent of Japan's total GDP. They typically have extensive global operations. For example, Marubeni (www.marubeni.com) has hundreds of subsidiaries in seventy countries. It is consistently ranked in the upper end of the *Global 500* and had recent annual sales of more than $25 billion.

In the United States, trading companies have had a relatively negligible impact on the volume of export activity. Although the U.S. Congress passed the Export Trading Company (ETC) Act in 1982, providing firms with incentives to engage in joint exporting through the formation of export trading companies, few were formed. One deterrent is the preference of U.S. firms to pursue international expansion independently of other firms.[15]

Trading company An intermediary that engages in import and export of a variety of commodities, products, and services.

Exhibit 3.7 World's
Largest Trading Companies

Rank Based on Annual Revenues	Company (Home Country)	Revenues (U.S.$ millions)	Profits (U.S.$ millions)	Profits as Percentage of Total Revenues
1	Mitsubishi (Japan)	$52,809	$4,052	7.7%
2	Mitsui (Japan)	50,252	3,591	7.1
3	Marubeni (Japan)	36,481	1,289	3.5
4	Sumitomo (Japan)	32,144	2,092	6.5
5	Sinochem (China)	30,204	644	2.1
6	Itochu (Japan)	25,054	1,914	7.6
7	Noble Group (China)	23,497	258	1.1
8	COFCO (China)	21,202	490	2.3
9	SHV Holdings (Netherlands)	20,867	779	3.7
10	Samsung (South Korea)	17,585	514	2.9

Export management company (EMC) A domestically based intermediary that acts as an export agent on behalf of a client company.

A domestically based intermediary is the **export management company (EMC)**, which acts as an export agent on behalf of a (usually inexperienced) client company. For example, Sharco is an EMC based in Chicago that assists manufacturers in the heating, ventilation, and refrigeration industries with exporting their products to Asia and the Middle East. In return for a commission, an EMC finds export customers on behalf of the client firm, negotiates terms of sale, and arranges for international shipping. While typically much smaller than a trading company, some EMCs have well-established networks of foreign distributors in place that allow exported products immediate access to foreign markets. EMCs are often supply-driven, visiting the manufacturer's facilities regularly to learn about new products and even to develop foreign-market strategies. But because of the indirect nature of the export sale, the manufacturer runs the risk of losing control over how its products are marketed abroad, with possible negative consequences for its international image.

Online Intermediaries

Some focal firms use the Internet to sell products directly to customers rather than going through traditional wholesale and retail channels. By eliminating traditional intermediaries, companies can sell their products more cheaply and faster. This benefits SMEs in particular because they usually lack the often substantial resources needed to undertake conventional international operations.

Countless online intermediaries broker transactions between buyers and sellers worldwide. Emergent technologies offer—and sometimes require—new roles that intermediaries have not taken previously. Many traditional retailers establish Web sites or link with online service providers to create an electronic presence. The electronic sites of retailers like Tesco (www.tesco.com) and Walmart (www.walmart.com) complement existing physical distribution infrastructure and bring more customers into physical outlets. Read more about Internet-based international intermediaries in the *Global Trend* feature.

GL🌐BAL TREND

Online Retailers: Contemporary Global Intermediaries

Online retailing is experiencing explosive growth. The leading online auctioneer, eBay, is attracting some 70 million buyers and sellers to its Web site in a typical month. Amazon.com is a leading online retailer with 40 million visitors. Offerings at eBay and Amazon resemble online versions of vast department stores. Amazon now sells more consumer electronics than books. The Web sites of conventional retailers—once considered stuck in the bricks-and-mortar era of retailing—are growing fast. The number of shoppers using Wal-Mart's Web site now exceeds those visiting Amazon. In the United Kingdom, popular e-retailers include Argos, a catalogue merchant, and Tesco, Britain's biggest supermarket chain. The hottest online products include toys, computer games, clothing, and jewelry.

Consumers like e-retailing because they can compare products and prices, and save time. For retailers, laws and restrictions that apply to retail stores are not as strict online, and selling online is cheap. Wal-Mart and Tesco use the Web to test the market for new products before offering them in their stores. Such advantages explain why traditional retailers have made the move to become major online sellers.

EBay's cross-border business is surging, with more than 30 sites straddling the globe, from Brazil to Germany. International transactions now generate half of eBay's overall trading revenues and are growing twice as fast as domestic operations. Roughly half of eBay's 125 million registered users are located outside the United States. EBay shoppers buy a soccer jersey every five minutes in Britain, a bottle of wine every three minutes in France, a garden gnome every six minutes in Germany, and a skincare product every 30 seconds in China. EBay has managed to rapidly transplant its business model around the world. Local managers adapt to local conditions without losing the core competencies at the heart of eBay. Germany is by far the biggest international site, generating roughly one-third the sales of the U.S. market. Germany boasts a far higher percentage of active users than any other country, with roughly three-quarters of registered users trading regularly.

The internationalization of online selling indicates an interesting trend: Most of the business of international online retailers occurs *within* individual countries. At eBay's Germany site, nearly all the products, information, and chat boards are created by local buyers and sellers. The site and conversations are nearly all in German, and virtually all the users are German citizens. The same is true for India and Italy. Only about 12 percent of eBay's total gross merchandise sales involve cross-border transactions. In most countries, eBay has acquired a strong local flavor as buyers and sellers create a local community. Each country is a self-contained marketplace.

Yet international online retailers must adapt to local conditions. A big challenge is getting global markets to accept online payment systems, such as PayPal. In much of Asia, electronic payment systems remain a mystery, and online deals often require face-to-face cash payments. Cultural differences play a role, too. Asians are typically reluctant to buy used goods. Even among siblings, it is uncommon to pass down clothing. Nevertheless, more and more Asians are acquiring online trading habits. With more than 90 million Internet users, China is a fast-growing market. Within a few years, more people will be surfing the Web in China than in the United States.

One challenge for online retailers is the fact that most of the world lacks access to the Internet. The success of international online retailers depends on the availability of IT infrastructure. Countries can be ranked in terms of *electronic readiness (e-readiness)*, the degree to which its citizens can participate in the advantages and opportunities of a knowledge-based economy. By this measure, Denmark is the most e-ready country in the world, followed by the United States, Sweden, Switzerland, the United Kingdom, Hong Kong, Finland, and the Netherlands. By contrast, countries such as Russia, China, Indonesia, and India score relatively low on e-readiness. In such places, online retailers can target only a small portion of the local population. In Africa and parts of South Asia, poverty is prevalent and the level of e-readiness is even lower.

SOURCES: *Economist.* (2005). "E-readiness," May 7, p. 98; *Economist.* (2005). "Clicks, Bricks and Bargains," December 3, pp. 57–58; Schonfeld, Erick. (2005). "The World According to eBay," *Business 2.0* (January/February): 77–84.

 Facilitators in International Business

The third category of participant in international business is facilitators, independent individuals or firms that assist the internationalization and foreign operations of focal firms and make it possible for transactions to occur efficiently, smoothly, and in a timely manner. Facilitators include banks, international trade lawyers, freight forwarders, customs brokers, and consultants. Their number and role have grown due to the complexity of international business operations, intense competition, and technological advances. Facilitators provide many useful services, from conducting market research to identifying potential business partners and providing legal advice. They rely heavily on information technology and the Internet to carry out their facilitating activities.

Some facilitators are supply-chain management specialists, responsible for physical distribution and logistics activities of their client companies. In the *Recent Grad in IB* feature, read about Cynthia Asoka, who is developing a career in global supply chain management.

Logistics service provider A transportation specialist that arranges for physical distribution and storage of products on behalf of focal firms, as well as controlling information between the point of origin and the point of consumption.

An important facilitator of international trade is the **logistics service provider**, a transportation specialist that arranges for physical distribution and storage of products on behalf of focal firms, as well as controlling information between the point of origin and the point of consumption. Companies such as DHL, FedEx, UPS, and TNT provide cost-effective means for delivering cargo anywhere in the world. They also offer traditional distributor functions such as warehousing, inventory management, and order tracking. FedEx, a leading express shipping company, delivers approximately 3.4 million packages and 11 million pounds of freight per day and offers supply-chain management services. It delivers to some 220 countries and territories, covering virtually the entire planet with its fleet of more than 670 aircraft and 43,000 cars, trucks, and trailers. FedEx's business in Brazil, China, and India has grown rapidly.

Red Wing, a U.S. shoe manufacturer, has taken advantage of UPS's supply chain services to bypass its own Salt Lake City distribution center, which is normally used to consolidate and repackage goods for shipment to retail stores. Red Wing produces some of its shoes in China and sorts and repackages them at a UPS facility in southern China. Shoes are then delivered directly to Red Wing retail stores around the United States. By using outside express delivery firms, Red Wing gets its product to market faster and at lower cost. To serve the international distribution needs of companies like Red Wing, UPS has built more than fifty warehouses in China.

Red Wing and countless other international manufacturers use *common carriers*, companies that own the ships, trucks, airplanes, and other transportation equipment they use to transport goods around the world. Common carriers play a vital role in international business and global trade. Maersk (www.maerskline.com) is a leading carrier, based in Denmark and operating some 500 ships that move containerized cargo around the world. You may have seen Maersk containers traveling down the highway, on the backs of trucks and lorries, on their way to being loaded on ocean-going ships. A *consolidator* is a type of shipping company that combines the cargo of more than one exporter into international shipping containers for shipment abroad.

Most exporters use the services of freight forwarders because they are a critical facilitator in international business. Usually based in major port cities, freight forwarders arrange international shipments for the focal firm to a foreign entry port, and even to the buyer's location in the target foreign market. They are experts on transportation methods and documentation for international trade, as well as the export rules and regulations of the home and foreign countries. They arrange for clearance of shipments through customs on the importing side of the transaction. Freight forwarders are an excellent source of advice on shipping requirements such as packing, containerization, and labeling.

Customs brokers Specialist enterprises that arrange clearance of products through customs on behalf of importing firms.

Governments typically charge tariffs and taxes and devise complex rules for the import of products into the countries they govern. **Customs brokers** (or *customs house brokers*) are specialist enterprises that arrange clearance of products through customs on behalf of importing firms. They are to importing what freight forwarders are to exporting. They prepare and process required documentation and get goods cleared through customs in the destination country. They understand the regulations of the national customs service and other government agencies that affect the import of products. Usually the freight forwarder, based in the home country, works with a customs house broker based in the destination country in handling importing operations.

Various players facilitate the financial operations of international business. *Commercial banks* make possible the exchange of foreign currencies and provide financing to buyers and

Recent Grad in IB

Cynthia's major: Business

Internships during College: GM auto plants in Argentina and Brazil

Jobs held since graduating:
- Volunteer, Peace Corps in the Dominican Republic
- Corporate Trainer, Samsung in South Korea
- Manager, Trade Promotion Organization (KOTRA) of South Korea, Chicago office
- Manager, IBM

Cynthia Asoka

While growing up in Detroit, you couldn't help but be aware of globalization while watching the local auto industry struggle to compete with imports from abroad. With hiring freezes at the "Big 3" automakers, area graduates often headed right back to school. After getting her undergraduate business degree from Oakland University with a minor in International Management, Cynthia Asoka did just that.

After a semester in Vienna, Austria as an exchange student piqued her interest in language learning, Cynthia began graduate language programs in Chinese and Spanish. She interrupted her studies to serve as a Peace Corps microenterprise development volunteer in the Dominican Republic, working on community projects funded by the Agency for International Development and teaching English in the evenings. She returned to graduate school to complete coursework in teaching English as a second language and then worked for Samsung in South Korea for two years as a corporate trainer.

Upon returning to the United States, Cynthia spent 18 months working for the Korean government's Trade Promotion Organization (KOTRA; www.kotra.or.kr) in its Chicago office, sourcing Korean products for U.S. importers and promoting U.S. exports to Korea. Hoping to sharpen her skills so she could open her own trading company one day, she returned to graduate school to pursue an MBA in Supply-Chain Management.

Following graduation, Cynthia was recruited by IBM (www.ibm.com) to join its Supply Chain Leadership Training program. After completing the two-year program, Cynthia sourced memory chips from Korean, German, and Taiwanese manufacturers and then managed buyers of information technology equipment and software.

Cynthia's Advice for an International Career

"Constantly seek out opportunities to learn new global skills. In multinational corporations, all solutions or processes you design should be applicable across many countries, forcing you to think and act globally, as well as work in teams (most often virtually) across the world. Although my dream was to open my own trading company, the skills and experience I acquired working at a multinational firm served as an education I could never have acquired on my own."

Success Factors

"Don't be afraid to be a trainee. As an intern at GM auto plants in Argentina and Brazil, I struggled to hold conversations in my mediocre Spanish and practically nonexistent Portuguese. After graduation the next year, I again spent two years as a trainee, moving every six months to work in different roles in various IBM plants across Canada and the United States. While your former classmates may already have become managers and directors at their companies, try to focus on skill acquisition rather than titles. Ultimately, a broad understanding of issues will help you identify better solutions and put global processes in place that will last."

sellers who usually require credit to finance transactions. The process of getting paid often takes longer in international than in domestic transactions, so a focal firm may need a loan from a commercial bank. Commercial banks can also transfer funds to individuals or banks abroad; provide introduction letters and letters of credit to travelers; supply credit information on potential representatives or foreign buyers; and collect foreign invoices, drafts, and other foreign receivables. Within each country, large banks in major cities maintain correspondent relationships with smaller banks spread around the nation or the world or operate their own foreign branches, thus providing a direct channel to foreign customers.

Commercial banks such as this one at the Mall of the Emirates in Dubai are key facilitators in international commercial transactions, providing financing, transferring funds, and exchanging foreign currencies. It is no wonder that banking is one of the most multinational of all business sectors.

Banking is one of the most multinational business sectors. Barclays, Citicorp, and Fuji Bank have as many international branches as any of the largest manufacturing MNEs. These banks frequently provide consultation and guidance free of charge to their clients, since they derive income from loans to the exporter and from fees for special services.

However, banks are often reluctant to extend credit to SMEs, as these smaller firms usually lack substantial collateral and they experience a higher failure rate than large MNEs. In the United States, smaller firms can turn to the *Export Import Bank* (Ex-IM Bank; www.exim .gov), a federal agency that assists exporters in financing sales of their products and services in foreign markets. The Ex-Im Bank provides direct loans, working capital loans, loan guarantees, and other financial products aimed at supporting the exporting activities of smaller firms.

In other countries, particularly in the developing world, governments provide financing at favorable rates even to foreign firms, often through public development banks and agencies, to finance the construction of infrastructure projects such as dams and power plants. Incoming investment usually results in new jobs, technology transfer, or substantial foreign exchange. Governments in Australia, Britain, Canada, Ireland, France, and numerous other countries similarly provide financing to MNEs for the construction of factories and other large-scale operations in their countries. In the United States, several state development agencies have provided loans to automakers like BMW, Honda, Mercedes, and Toyota to establish plants in individual states.

Focal firms and other participants also use the services of *international trade lawyers* to help navigate international legal environments. The best lawyers are knowledgeable about their client's industry, the laws and regulations of target nations, and the most appropriate means for international activity in the legal/regulatory context. Foreign lawyers are familiar with the obstacles to doing business in individual countries, including import licenses, trade barriers, intellectual property concerns, and government restrictions in specific industries.

Firms need international trade lawyers to negotiate contracts for the sales and distribution of goods and services to customers, intermediaries, or facilitators. Lawyers play a critical role when negotiating joint venture and strategic alliance agreements or for reaching agreement on international franchising and licensing. International trade lawyers also come into play when disputes arise with foreign business partners. A good lawyer can explain labor law and employment rights and responsibilities. Internationalizing firms often apply for patents for their products and register their trademarks in the countries where they do business, which requires the services of a patent attorney. In addition, lawyers can help to identify and optimize tax benefits that may be available from certain entry modes or within individual countries.

Insurance companies provide coverage against commercial and political risks. Losses tend to occur more often in international business because of the wide range of natural and human-made circumstances to which the firm's products are exposed as they make their way through the value chain. For example, goods shipped across the ocean are occasionally damaged in transit. Insurance helps to defray the losses that would otherwise result from such damage.

International business *consultants* advise internationalizing firms on various aspects of doing business abroad and alert them to foreign market opportunities. Consultants help companies improve their performance by analyzing existing business problems and helping management develop future plans. Particularly helpful are *tax accountants*, who can advise companies on minimizing tax obligations resulting from multicountry operations. *Market research firms* are a potential key resource for identifying and targeting foreign buyers. They possess or can gain access to information on markets, competitors, and the methods of international business.

Governments in International Business

Governments exist at the local, provincial, national, and supranational levels to make and enforce laws and regulations and provide essential economic security by devising fiscal and monetary policies. Recently, many governments have developed new legislation aimed at protecting the natural environment. For example, the U.S. and European governments are cooperating to develop policies to cut carbon dioxide emissions. Multilateral environmental regulations are deemed necessary to address climate change, which can lead to harmful cross-national events such as crop failures and business calamities.[16]

Increasingly, governments also regulate markets. During the recent global financial crisis, governments moved to stimulate national economies, through such programs as the Economic Stimulus Act in the United States, the European Union stimulus plan, and the Economic Stimulus Plan in China.[17] In some cases, important companies were nationalized. For example, the governments of Belgium, Luxembourg, and the Netherlands took control of Fortis, a large bank services company that faced financial ruin. In the United States, the U.S. Treasury took partial ownership of General Motors.

National finance ministers and central bank directors coordinated efforts aimed at restoring order following the global financial crisis. *Central banks* are the monetary authorities in each country that issue currency and regulate national money supplies. Australia, Canada, China, Indonesia, the United States, and numerous European countries cut bank interest rates and injected billions into national money supplies. The European Central Bank (www.ecb.int) devised new banking regulations with the goal of averting future crises.[18] At the G-20 Summit in London in 2009, heads of state announced a range of synchronized policy initiatives intended to revive the global economy, stimulate employment, reform national financial systems, and improve global institutions like the International Monetary Fund.[19] Officials from various countries coordinated efforts to restore international growth by providing more credit and liquidity in world banking systems. Several governments advocated creating a new, global currency to replace the U.S. dollar as the favored currency in international business.[20]

Governments participate in international business by investing in other economies. The trend is best exemplified by the **sovereign wealth funds** (SWFs), state-owned investment funds that undertake systematic, global investment activities[21] to generate income or to achieve policy objectives, such as reviving a collapsed economy. In 2007 China invested billions in Blackstone, a New York-based private-equity firm. In 2008, the governments of Singapore, Kuwait, and South Korea provided much of a $21 billion lifeline to Citigroup and Merrill Lynch, two banks that lost fortunes in the global financial crisis.

While SWFs have been around for decades, their numbers increased dramatically in the 2000s. Many are based in oil-producing countries and originate from massive commodity sales. For example, Kuwait's SWF derives from oil revenues and amounts to several hundred billion dollars. Some funds represent other types of assets, such as the SWF in Quebec, Canada, based on provincial pension funds. Holdings of some SWFs exceed the GDPs of the national economies of countries into which they invest. For example, the Abu Dhabi Investment Authority, the Government Pension Fund of Norway, and the China Investment Corporation each have several hundred billion dollars under management. Collectively, SWFs now amount to several trillion dollars.

Given their size, critics charge that SWFs substantially affect their investment targets, even to the point of endangering national interests. To address the potential harm of SWFs, some governments passed legislation to restrict inward SWF investments. In 2008, for example, Germany passed a law that requires parliamentary approval for foreign investments that acquire more than 25 percent of a German company. The United States has a similar law.

Some experts believe governments' role in the world economy should be curtailed and advocate capitalism and free trade as the best means for global economic success.[22] We discuss the role of government in international business more in later chapters.

Sovereign wealth fund (SWF)   A state-owned investment fund that undertakes systematic, global investment activities.

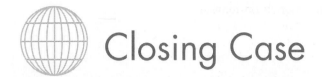

DHL, FedEx, and UPS: Shifting Fortunes in the Global Logistics Services Industry

In 2009, DHL ended its domestic air express service in the United States. In addition to requiring the abandonment of a massive sorting facility and dozens of brightly colored jumbo aircraft, the pullback put 9,500 U.S. employees out of work. DHL's troubles in the United States resulted from a declining market for express packages and inability to compete with rivals FedEx and UPS. Although DHL still offers U.S. customers international package services, its status as the world's largest logistics facilitator remains in doubt.

When Adrian Dalsey, Larry Hillbolm, and Robert Lynn founded DHL as a door-to-door delivery service between San Francisco and Honolulu in 1969, no one imagined the business would evolve into an international express delivery group linking 120,000 destinations in more than 200 countries. Now owned by the German company Deutsche Post World Net, DHL offers express services, international air and ocean freight, contract logistics, and various value-added services. Despite failing to maintain its solid U.S. presence, the firm remains the market leader for courier express delivery in Europe and Asia.

Global Supply-Chain and Logistics Industry

The supply-chain and logistics industry includes companies that move raw materials, finished goods, packages, and documents across the globe. Four major trends have changed it dramatically since the 1970s—globalization, deregulation, digitization, and outsourcing. The massive increase in international trade has increased the complexity of corporate supply chains. MNEs and other internationalizing firms require speed and efficiency in moving goods through supply chains around the world. To address this need, specialized logistics service providers like DHL, UPS, and FedEx organize, coordinate, and control supply chains through a global presence and skillful use of leading-edge technologies. These facilitating firms control thousands of trucks and aircraft, sophisticated information tracking systems, and global networks of offices and warehouses. Collectively, logistics service providers represent an industry unto themselves, generating over $800 billion in revenues in 2009.

Global Competitors

Globally, DHL competes with other large logistics companies such as UPS, FedEx, and TNT. Founded in 1907,

United Parcel Service (UPS) is one of the oldest competitors. Its primary business is delivering packages and documents worldwide. UPS also provides global supply chain services. FedEx oversees a vast empire, providing transportation, e-commerce, and business services in the United States and abroad. Although a relatively young firm, FedEx experienced rapid growth and is now one of the top three logistics providers worldwide. Founded in Australia, TNT began acquiring interests in other companies, which helped it grow into a large multinational firm. TNT acquired twenty-five companies in the nine years through 2008 alone.

Global Positioning

In the courier, express, and parcel market, DHL International is the leader in Europe, thanks to its efficient national express networks, served by company-owned vehicles. DHL is also the leader in China and Japan and holds 35 percent market share of the international express segment in the Asia Pacific region. In 2005, it acquired a controlling interest in the Indian express company, Blue Dart, strengthening its ability to serve customers in India and China. DHL is now the global leader in airfreight, offering those services in regions not covered by competitors via its extensive air and freight network. DHL is the leading provider of ocean freight and contract logistics.

But express delivery is a low-margin business, and logistics services providers increase profits by adding higher-value services such as door-to-door logistics management across networks of corporate value chains. DHL targets its services to industries with enormous global logistical needs, like the automotive, pharmaceutical, electronics, consumer goods, and fashion industries. When such contracts are signed, they are long term, on average three years in length. Recent investments have allowed DHL to provide warehousing and warehouse transportation services to clients as diverse as BMW, PepsiCo, Unisys, Electrolux, and Deutsche Telekom.

DHL's Experience in the United States

The United States represents 35 percent of the global logistics market. Over one-third of all global Fortune 500 companies are headquartered in the United States, and countless key decisions about global logistics and transport orders are made there. The market is intensely competitive and concentrated, with the top five competitors controlling nearly half of it. The largest sector is ground courier service, worth about $30 billion annually and dominated by the U.S. Postal Service.

DHL management badly wanted to conquer the United States but could not compete in a market thick with contenders. Despite performing well in Canada and Mexico, DHL won only a number-three position in the United States, following FedEx and UPS. Its strategy was to focus on small and medium-sized firms. To this end, the firm spent $1.1 billion to acquire Airborne Express, once the number-three U.S. express service. But because jet airliners consume so much fuel, rising petroleum prices shifted market demand toward ground transport. DHL's reliance on Airborne's air transport network hurt its ability to attract customers who increasingly preferred to send parcels overland.

DHL next sought to restructure itself, cutting operations and many services by one-third. But this move alienated customers, many of whom switched to FedEx or UPS. DHL's problems were further aggravated by the economic downturn that began in 2008. Squeezed by mounting losses, management decided to pull the plug on DHL's U.S. operations but maintain its U.S. Global Mail Division.

Case Questions

1. Describe the various services provided by logistics service providers. What is the role of these services in focal firms' value-chain activities?

2. Supply-chain management has evolved over time, largely due to globalization and technological advances. What does the future hold? Can you anticipate changes to the supply chain that would further alter the express and logistics industry?

3. What factors do focal firms consider when choosing one logistics service provider over another? In what ways do the global logistical and transportation needs of focal firms vary from one industry to another? Give some examples.

4. Given the importance of the U.S. market in the global express industry, should DHL reconsider its decision to withdraw from this segment? Lacking a significant presence in the United States, what should DHL management do to grow the firm and improve earnings?

An important lesson from DHL's U.S. experience is how difficult it is for a firm to grow in a slow market. It cannot be done without stealing market share from someone else. DHL's withdrawal leaves some 3 percent of the U.S. ground express market and 8 percent of the air parcel market—over $3 billion in business—up for grabs.

Challenges in the Global Recession and Financial Crisis

A slowing global economy portends declining profits for many firms. Already operating on slim margins, facilitators are vulnerable. Retailers are cutting inventories and pressuring facilitators to cut the cost of delivering goods. The collapse of such retailers as Circuit City, Woolworths, and Wise Stores imply tumbling revenues for logistics firms as well. In 2009, both FedEx and UPS reported sales declines and dramatic falls in international shipping, mostly in air freight. Economic challenges like these compel delivery and logistics firms to rethink internal processes, cut costs, and seek alternative revenue sources. Some are cutting services to certain geographic areas, laying off workers, and refocusing on value-added portions of the business. Global logistics providers are struggling to find the right balance between running lean operations during hard times and gearing up for new business as the global economy improves.

5. What strategies should facilitator companies such as DHL, UPS, and FedEx implement during an economic recession? What steps can they take to ensure their survival, while remaining prepared for the upsurge of new business once the economy improves? Have they overlooked the fast-growing emerging markets?

SOURCES: Corporate profile of Deutsche Post AG and DHL at Hoovers.com; Deutsche Post Worldwide Net, 2009, *Annual Report*, retrieved from http://www.dpwn.de; "DHL International Limited," June 2006, retrieved from http://www.datamonitor.com; J. Ewing, D. Foust, and M. Eidam, "DHL's American Adventure," *Business Week*, November 29, 2004, p. 126; T. Mucha, "Pouring It on to Compete with UPS and FedEx," *Business 2.0* 6, no. 2 (2005): 60; B. Barnard, "Deutsche Post Unveils New Strategy, New Name," *Journal of Commerce*, March 11, 2009, p. 6; D. Hannon, "DHL's Move Leaves Package Market Share Up For Grabs," *Purchasing*, January 15, 2009, p. 11; D. Hannon, "DHL to Exit US Express Shipping Market," *Purchasing*, March 26, 2008, p. 24; J. Ott, "Cargo Casualty," *Aviation Week and Space Technology*, February 2, 2009, p. 13; A. Roth, "UPS Woes Reflect Wide Economic Slump," *Wall Street Journal*, February 4, 2009, p. B6; A. Roth, "DHL Beats a Retreat from the US," *Wall Street Journal*, November 11, 2008, p. B1.

This case was written by Tracy González-Padrón, University of Colorado at Colorado Springs, and updated by Professor Carol Sánchez and Ashley Stickney, Grand Valley State University, Grand Rapids, MI.

CHAPTER ESSENTIALS

Key Terms

Summary

In this chapter, you learned about:

1. Four types of participants in international business

International business transactions require the participation of numerous focal firms, intermediaries, facilitators, and governments. A **focal firm** is the initiator of an international business transaction that conceives, designs, and produces the offerings for customers worldwide. A **distribution channel intermediary** is a specialist firm that provides a variety of logistics and marketing services for focal firms as part of the international supply chain, both in the home country and abroad. A **facilitator** is a firm or individual with special expertise such as legal advice, banking, and customs clearance that assists focal firms in the performance of international business transactions. *Governments* are increasingly important participants in international business.

2. Participants arranged by value-chain activity

Focal firms, intermediaries, and facilitators all make up participants in global value chains. The value chain is the complete business system of the focal firm, comprising all the focal firm's activities, including R&D, sourcing, production, marketing, and distribution. Channel intermediaries and facilitators support the focal firm by performing value-adding functions. In focal firms that export, most of the value chain is concentrated in the home country. In highly international firms, value-chain activities may be performed in various countries.

3. Focal firms in international business

Focal firms include **multinational enterprises (MNEs)**, large global corporations such as Sony and Ford. MNEs operate in multiple countries by setting up factories, marketing subsidiaries, and regional headquarters. **Small and medium-sized enterprises (SMEs)** now make up the majority of internationally active firms. They are flexible firms that emphasize exporting and leverage the help of intermediaries and facilitators to succeed in international business. **Born globals** are a category of international SMEs that internationalize at or near their founding.

4. International entry strategies of focal firms

Focal firms include a **licensor**, a firm that enters a contractual agreement with a foreign partner that allows the latter the right to use certain intellectual property for a specified period of time in exchange for royalties or other compensation. A **franchisor** is a firm that grants another the right to use an entire business system in exchange for fees, royalties, or other forms of compensation. A **turnkey contractor** is a focal firm or a consortium of firms that plans, finances, organizes, manages, and implements all phases of a project and then hands it over to a foreign customer. A **joint venture partner** is a focal firm that creates and jointly owns a new legal entity through equity investment or pooling of assets. **Project-based, nonequity venture partners** are focal firms that collaborate through a project with a relatively narrow scope and a well-defined timetable, without creating a new legal entity.

5. Distribution channel intermediaries in international business

Distribution channel intermediaries move products and services across national borders and eventually to end users. They perform key down-stream functions in the target market on behalf of focal firms, including marketing. A **foreign distributor** is a foreign market-based intermediary that works under contract for an exporter and takes title to and distributes the exporter's products in a market abroad, often performing marketing functions such as sales and after-sales service. An **agent** is an intermediary that handles orders to buy and sell commodities, products, and services in international transactions for a commission. A **manufacturer's representative** is an intermediary contracted by the exporter to represent and sell its offerings in a designated country or territory. A **trading company** is an intermediary that imports and exports various commodities, products, and services. An **export management company (EMC)** is an intermediary that acts as an export agent on behalf of client companies.

6. Facilitators in international business

Facilitators assist with international business transactions. A **logistics service provider** is a transportation specialist that arranges physical distribution and storage of products on behalf of focal firms, as well as controlling information between the point of origin and the point of consumption. A **freight forwarder** arranges international shipping on behalf of exporting firms, much like a travel agent for cargo. A **customs broker** is a specialist that arranges clearance of products through customs on behalf of importing firms. Other facilitators include *banks, lawyers, insurance companies, consultants,* and *market research firms.*

7. Governments in international business

Governments are increasingly active in international business. They make and enforce laws and regulations, and provide numerous other functions. Numerous national governments collaborated to address challenges that emerged in the global recession. Governments also invest in other economies, often through **sovereign wealth funds (SWFs)**, state-owned investment funds that undertake systematic global investment activities.

Test Your Comprehension

1. Identify and briefly define the three major categories of participants in international business.

2. In the stages of a typical international value chain, what role does each of the three categories of participants typically play?

3. What are the specific characteristics of focal firms? Distinguish the characteristics of international MNEs, SMEs, and born global firms.

4. What is unique about such focal firms as franchisors, licensors, and turnkey contractors?

5. What role do distribution channel intermediaries fulfill?

6. What are major distribution channel intermediaries based in the home country and those based abroad?

7. What are online intermediaries? How do focal firms use the Internet to carry out international activities?

8. What are the characteristics of facilitators? List and define the major types of facilitators.

9. What role do governments play in international business? What are the characteristics of sovereign wealth funds?

Apply Your Understanding AACSB: Reflective Thinking Skills, Communication Abilities, Ethical Understanding and Reasoning Abilities

1. Focal firms, distribution channel intermediaries, and facilitators each assume a different and critical role in the performance of international business transactions. Think about the degree of interdependency that exists among these groups. What would happen if distribution channel intermediaries could not provide competent services to the focal firm? What if adequate facilitators were not available to the focal firm? To what degree would the focal firm's international business performance be hampered? Under what circumstances would the focal firm choose to internalize its value-chain

activities in international business rather than delegate them to channel intermediaries and facilitators? What would be the consequences of retaining distribution and support activities within the firm?

2. Assume that after graduation you get a job at Kokanee Corporation, an SME that manufactures Italian tile, granite countertops, and other high-quality building materials for residential construction projects. Your boss, Eugenia Kimball, wants to begin exporting Kokanee's products to foreign markets. Prepare a memo for her in which you briefly describe the kinds of intermediaries and facilitators with whom Kokanee is likely to consult and work to maintain successful export operations.

3. *Ethical Dilemma:* You are Vice President of Manufacturing at MicroKey Company, a major producer of computer keyboards with factories in various countries that provide jobs to thousands of local residents. The firm imports many of the raw materials used to manufacture its keyboards abroad. At one of its factories in Russia, MicroKey has begun to experience problems getting parts and components processed through customs, resulting in delays that are hurting profits. Upon conferring with colleagues at the plant, you are advised the problem can be solved if MicroKey makes a payment to local officials, a common practice in the area. The bribe would expedite passage through customs. However, you strongly feel that bribery is unethical. Moreover, it is illegal in much of the world. For example, under laws of Canada, the United States, and most European countries, a manager can be prosecuted for offering bribes, even in countries where the practice is accepted. What should you do? Do you make the payment, realizing it reflects the way business is normally carried out in that part of the world?

globalEDGE Internet Exercises
(http://globalEDGE.msu.edu)

AACSB: Reflective Thinking Skills, Use of Information Technology

Refer to Chapter 1, page 62, for instructions on how to access and use globalEDGE™.

1. Visit the government agency or ministry in your country responsible for supporting international business. For example, in the United States, visit the Department of Commerce (www.doc.gov). In Canada, visit Industry Canada (www.ic.gc.ca). In Denmark, visit the Ministry of Economic and Business Affairs (www.oem.dk). Identify and describe the most important support functions that the agency provides to companies that do international business. One approach is to sketch out a typical value chain and then systematically identify the support services the agency offers. For example, for the distribution link in the value chain, numerous governments provide "matchmaker" services, trade missions, and commercial services that link manufacturing firms with appropriate distributors located abroad.

2. Visit the Whirlpool Corporation (www.whirlpool.com) and click on "International Sites". Whirlpool has a complex value chain. Based on the information provided at the Web site, address the following questions: What types of upstream (for example, R&D, sourcing, manufacturing) value-chain activities does Whirlpool perform? What types of downstream value-chain activities (for example, marketing, distribution, after-sales service) does Whirlpool perform? Identify the types of participants (mainly intermediaries and facilitators) that Whirlpool is likely to use at each stage of the value chain.

3. Your company is about to initiate export activities in a country of your choice. You will need to identify distribution channel intermediaries and freight forwarders to facilitate the distribution and delivery of your products to end users in this country. Visit the Resource Desk and Diagnostic Tools directories of globalEDGE™. What sources of information are especially helpful to you in identifying suitable foreign distributors and freight forwarders? What do you learn from these sources?

PART 2

CHAPTER 4

LEARNING OBJECTIVES In this chapter, you will learn about:

1. Culture and cross-cultural risk
2. Key concepts of culture
3. The role of culture in international business
4. Cultural metaphors, stereotypes, and idioms
5. Interpretations of culture
6. Subjective versus objective dimensions of culture
7. Language as a key dimension of culture
8. Contemporary issues in culture
9. Overcoming cross-cultural risk: Managerial guidelines

The Cultural Environment of International Business

American Football . . . in Europe?

There are few things more representative of U.S. culture than American football. It is an extravaganza, complete with exciting halftime shows and peppy cheerleaders. The game exemplifies national pride. The national anthem is played, flags are unfurled, and uniformed players charge up and down the field like an army in the throes of often violent conflict. The teams' huddles divide the game into small planning sessions for the next play.

In the United States, the National Football League (NFL) oversees the sport and, like any successful business, wants to score in new markets. The NFL first tackled Europe in 1991, with plans to establish American football there. After years of failed attempts, NFL Europe emerged as six teams, five of which were based in Germany (such as the Berlin Thunder, the Cologne Centurions, and the Hamburg Sea Devils). Earlier teams established in Spain had failed.

Why did American football triumph in Germany but fail in Spain? An excellent metaphor for Spanish culture is the bullfight, an ancient pursuit. In tradition-bound Spain, bullfights are often held in 2,000-year-old Roman amphitheaters. Rather than a competitive sport, bullfighting is a ritual and an art. It is the demonstration of style and courage by the matador, the hero who fights the bulls. If the matador has performed well, he receives a standing ovation by the crowds, who wave white handkerchiefs or throw hats and roses into the ring. The bullfight symbolizes Spanish culture by combining a passionate celebration of life with an elaborate system of rituals, a grandiose and artistic spectacle with blood, violence, and danger. In the hearts of the Spanish people, American football cannot attain such heights.

What accounts for American football's early success in Germany? For one, the sport strongly emphasizes the traditional German traits of rules and order. In Germany, rules are many and conformity is valued. For instance, German parks occasionally have sections marked by signs where you are "permitted" to throw a stick to your dog. Germans can also be very time conscious. They know how to allocate time efficiently, and frown upon tardiness. The tendency is similar to American football, where the stop-and-go pace is timed to the second.

A popular metaphor for German culture is the symphony. In fact, two of the most revered symphonic composers—Bach and Beethoven—were German. Germans are drawn to the symmetry and order of the symphony. A conductor brings together the distinctive talents of individual performers to produce a unified sound. Like a symphony, football depends on a strong leader—the quarterback—who unites the distinctive talents of the players so they perform as one. At halftime, the crowd is treated to the spectacle of a huge marching band and numerous other performers, all synchronized to the highest degree. Preparation, timing, precision, conformity, and an understanding of the individual's contribution to the "score" underlie both symphonic performances and American football.

The major reason for NFL's failure in Europe has been its inability to win over Europeans shaped by ancient cultures and wedded to soccer (called *football* in most of the world). Soccer is woven into the fabric of European society. It is an outlet for inter-European rivalries that in earlier times manifested as armed conflict. Although superstars such as David Beckham emerge, soccer emphasizes a group effort—unity aimed at achieving a common goal.

The United States is a mixture of many cultures that form a multifaceted collection of ethnic identities. By contrast, Europe is home to many more ethnicities that lack the integration of the United States. Europeans have made great strides toward creating an all-encompassing European culture, but the difficulties encountered with unification reveal how individual nations are unwilling to give up their cultural identities in favor of some larger European Union ideal. Thus, the appeal of American football has varied from country to country as a function of cultural differences. Most Europeans view the sport as a perversion of soccer. It represents the American headstrong attitude, with emphasis on violent conflict. From the perspective of many Europeans, the NFL tried to push an inferior product on a market long loyal to soccer. The NFL spent countless dollars promoting its teams, largely to no avail. In the end, national culture triumphed. In 2007, the NFL closed its European franchise.

SOURCES: Van Bottenburg, M. (2003). Thrown for a Loss: American Football and the European Sport Space. *American Behavioral Scientist* 46 (11): 1150–62; NFL Europe. Retrieved November 2005 from en.wikipedia.org/wiki/NFL_Europe; National Football League (NFL Europe). Retrieved November 2005 from www.nfleurope.com; White, E. (2003). "Is Europe Ready for Some Football?—NFL Drafts Dolls, Actors in $1.6 Million Campaign to Promote the Super Bowl." *Wall Street Journal,* Jan. 15, B4; Gannon, M. J., and Associates. (1994). *Understanding Global Cultures: Metaphorical Journeys Through 17 Countries.* Thousand Oaks, CA: Sage.

 ## Culture and Cross-Cultural Risk

Culture The learned, shared, and enduring orientation patterns in a society. People demonstrate their culture through values, ideas, attitudes, behaviors, and symbols.

Cross-cultural risk A situation or event in which a cultural misunderstanding puts some human value at stake.

Culture is the learned, shared, and enduring orientation patterns in a society. People demonstrate their culture through values, ideas, attitudes, behaviors, and symbols. In international business, we step into cultural environments characterized by unfamiliar languages and unique value systems, beliefs, behaviors, and norms. These differences influence all dimensions of international business. Often, they get in the way of straightforward communication, representing one of the four risks associated with international business that we introduced in Chapter 1. We highlight these risks in Exhibit 4.1. **Cross-cultural risk** is a situation or event in which a cultural misunderstanding puts some human value at stake.

Culture affects even simple rituals of daily life. Greeting ceremonies are a deeply embedded cultural marker and have evolved over many centuries. They specify such behaviors as whether to shake hands, what to say, and how far apart to stand. These cultural conventions may vary as a function of the age, gender, or status of the greeters. In China, friends express thoughtfulness by asking each other whether they have had their meal yet. In Turkey, a typical greeting is "What is new with you?" The Japanese, who follow elaborate greeting and parting rituals, routinely apologize to the other party just before ending a telephone conversation.

Unlike political, legal, and economic systems, culture has proven difficult to identify and analyze, but its effects on international business, as well as on interpersonal exchange, are profound and broad. Its effect on value-chain activities, such as product and service design, marketing, and sales, is substantial. Managers must design

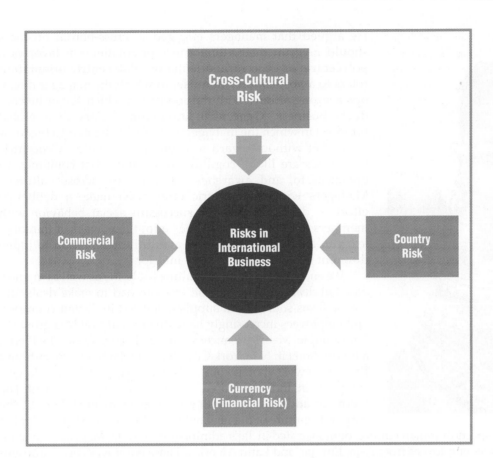

Exhibit 4.1 The Four Major Risks in International Business

products and packaging with culture in mind, even regarding color. While red may be beautiful to the Russians, it symbolizes mourning in South Africa. Items such as pens are universally acceptable as business gifts, but chrysanthemums are often associated with funerals and handkerchiefs may suggest sadness. In some cultures knives or scissors imply cutting off the relationship or other negative sentiments.

Companies want their employees to learn about other cultures and become cross-culturally proficient. In California's Silicon Valley, where many IT firms are concentrated, Intel offers a staff seminar called "Working with India" to help employees work more effectively with the estimated 400,000 Indian nationals in the valley. Several other Silicon Valley firms offer similar training. Another computer firm, AMD, flies IT workers from India to its facilities in Texas for a month of cultural training with U.S. managers. Workers role-play and study subjects like Indian movies, political history, and the differences between Hinduism and other Indian religions. Training includes lessons on assigning work (Indian workers often agree to aggressive timelines but may not inform a manager when falling behind, so managers should make sure timelines are reasonable), preparing food (to help those who practice Jainism, company cafeterias should clearly distinguish vegan from vegetarian food), and socializing (since it's polite to initially decline an invitation to a colleague's home, managers should offer more than once).[1]

Cross-cultural risk is exacerbated by **ethnocentric orientation**—using our own culture as the standard for judging other cultures. Most of us are raised in a single culture; we have a tendency to view the world primarily from our own perspective. Ethnocentric tendencies are widespread and entail the belief that one's own race, religion, or ethnic group is somehow superior to others. International business scholar Howard Perlmutter described ethnocentric views as "home-country orientation."[2]

Ethnocentric orientation Using our own culture as the standard for judging other cultures.

Limited interaction among societies, such as between Kenyans, Mexicans, and Russians, can magnify differences in values, behaviors, and symbols. In contrast, these differences are minimized with increased interaction.

Polycentric orientation   A host-country mind-set in which the manager develops a strong affinity with the country in which she or he conducts business.

Geocentric orientation   A global mind-set in which the manager is able to understand a business or market without regard to country boundaries.

He argued that managers engaged in cross-border business should give up their ethnocentric orientations in favor of a polycentric or geocentric orientation. **Polycentric orientation** refers to a host-country mind-set in which the manager develops a strong affinity with the country in which she or he conducts business. **Geocentric orientation** refers to a global mind-set in which the manager is able to understand a business or market without regard to country boundaries. Geocentric tendencies are like a cognitive orientation that combines an openness to, and awareness of, diversity across cultures.[3] Managers with a geocentric orientation make a deliberate effort to develop skills for successful social behavior with members of other cultures.[4] They adopt new ways of thinking, learn to analyze cultures, and avoid the temptation to judge different behavior as somehow inferior.[5]

We encounter unfamiliar cultures at home as well as in international dealings. Buyers visit from abroad to make deals, domestic firms source from suppliers located in distant countries, and employees increasingly have diverse cultural backgrounds. For example, Maurice Dancer is the head concierge at The Pierre, a luxury hotel in New York City. Recently, Taj Hotels Resorts and Palaces (www.tajhotels.com), a subsidiary of Tata, the largest company in India, acquired the management contract of The Pierre. In addition to adapting his management style to fit the corporate culture of the new owners, Maurice must also adapt to aspects of Indian culture, demonstrated in Taj's administrative style. Maurice also manages employees from Asia, Europe, and Latin America. These employees bring idiosyncrasies to their jobs characteristic of their home countries. For example, Asians tend to be reserved when dealing with customers. In the past, Maurice had to encourage Asian subordinates to be more outgoing. Finally, much of The Pierre's clientele is foreign-born. Without even leaving the United States, Maurice interacts with a wide variety of foreign cultures every day.

The cross-cultural integration of firms like The Pierre is yet another manifestation of globalization. Globalization is leading to convergence of cultural values as well. While people worldwide maintain traditional cultural values, common norms and expectations of behavior are gradually emerging, and many universal values apply to cross-cultural encounters.

Still, cultural differences remain a feature of international business. Cross-cultural misunderstandings can ruin business deals, hurt sales, or harm the corporate image. Today, developing an appreciation of, and sensitivity for, cultural differences has become an imperative for any manager. Those with cross-cultural savvy hold various advantages in managing employees, marketing products, and interacting with customers and business partners. Companies have much to gain from bridging the cultural divide.

Key Concepts of Culture

A broad definition of culture was offered by Herskovits as "the human made part of the environment."[6] Geert Hofstede, a well-known Dutch organizational anthropologist, views culture as a "collective mental programming" of people.[7] The "software of the mind," or how we think and reason, differentiates us from other groups. Such intangible orientations shape our behavior. Another scholar, Harry Triandis, views culture as an interplay of sameness and differences; all cultures are simultaneously very similar and very different.[8] While as human beings we share many commonalities and universals, as groups of people or societies we exhibit many differences. For example, some cultures are more complex than others. Some are more individualistic, while others are more collectivist. Some impose many norms, rules, and constraints on social behavior, while others impose very few.

Culture captures how the members of the society live—for instance, how they feed, clothe, and shelter themselves. It also explains how they behave toward each other and with other groups. Finally, it defines their beliefs and values and the way they perceive the meaning of life.

Cross-cultural encounters are increasingly common. Maurice Dancer (far right), head concierge at The Pierre hotel in New York, interacts with a wide variety of international cultures every day, without even leaving the United States.

What Culture Is *Not*

Now that you have an idea of what culture is, let us also define what it is *not*. Culture is:

■ *Not right or wrong.* Culture is relative; there is no cultural absolute. People of different nationalities simply perceive the world differently. Each culture has its own notions of acceptable and unacceptable behavior. For instance, in some Islamic cultures, a wife cannot divorce her husband. In many countries, nudity is entirely acceptable on TV. In Japan and Turkey, wearing shoes in the home is taboo.

■ *Not about individual behavior.* Culture is about groups. It refers to a collective phenomenon of shared values and meanings. Thus, while culture defines the collective behavior of each society, individuals often behave differently. For example, in most countries, men wear their hair short. But a few mavericks have very long hair and stand out among their peers. In numerous countries, some men wear makeup. But such behavior does not represent the cultural values of the larger population.

■ *Not inherited.* Culture is derived from the social environment. People are not born with a shared set of values and attitudes. Children gradually acquire specific ways of thinking and behaving as they are raised in a society. For example, in the United States, children usually acquire values of individualism and Christianity. But in China, children learn to depend on family members and acquire values based on Confucianism. Culture is passed from generation to generation by parents, teachers, mentors, peers, and leaders. Modern methods of communication, including transnational media, play an enormous role in transmitting culture.

Socialization and Acculturation

This process of learning the rules and behavioral patterns appropriate to one's society is called **socialization**. Socialization is cultural learning and provides the means to acquire cultural understandings and orientations shared by a particular society. It is a subtle process: We adapt our behavior unconsciously and unwittingly.

Acculturation is the process of adjusting and adapting to a culture *other than one's own*. It is commonly experienced by people who live in other countries for extended periods, such as expatriate workers.

The Many Dimensions of Culture

More than any other feature of human civilization, culture signals the differences among societies on the basis of language, habits, customs, and modes of thought. Yet most of us are not completely aware of how culture affects our behavior until we come into contact with people from other cultures.

Socialization The process of learning the rules and behavioral patterns appropriate to one's given society.

Acculturation The process of adjusting and adapting to a culture other than one's own.

Anthropologists use the iceberg metaphor to understand the many dimensions of culture, some subtle and some not so subtle. Above the surface certain characteristics are visible, but below, unseen to the observer, is a massive base of assumptions, attitudes, and values that strongly influence decision making, relationships, conflict, and other dimensions of international business. While we are conditioned by our own cultural idiosyncrasies, we are usually unaware of the nine-tenths of our cultural makeup that exists below the surface. In fact, we are often not aware of our own culture unless we come in contact with another one. Exhibit 4.2 illustrates the iceberg concept of culture using three layers of awareness: high culture, folk culture, and deep culture.

Exhibit 4.2 Culture as an Iceberg

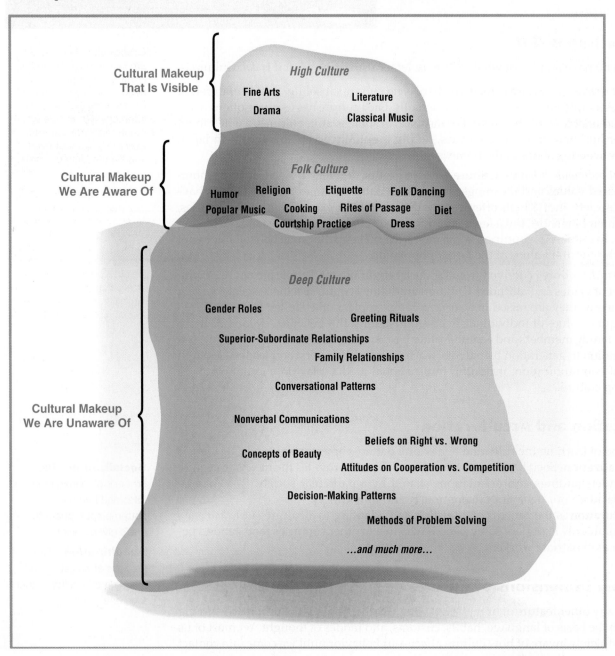

National, Professional, and Corporate Culture

While cultural idiosyncrasies influence international business, we cannot attribute all difficulties to differences in national culture. Exhibit 4.3 suggests that employees are socialized into three cultures: *national culture, professional culture*, and *corporate culture*.[9] Working effectively within these overlapping cultures is challenging. The influence of professional and corporate culture tends to grow as people are socialized into a profession and workplace.

Most companies have a distinctive set of norms, values, and modes of behavior that distinguish them from other organizations. Such differences are often as distinctive as national culture, so that two firms from the same country can have vastly different organizational cultures. For example, Lloyds (www.lloyds.com), a venerable large British insurance firm, has a conservative culture that may be slow to change. By contrast, Virgin (www.virgin.com), the much younger British music and travel provider, has an experimental, risk-taking culture.

These cultural layers present yet another challenge for the manager: To what extent is a particular behavior attributable to national culture? In companies with a strong organizational culture, it's hard to determine where the corporate influence begins and the national influence ends. For example, in the French cosmetics firm L'Oreal (www.loreal.com), the distinction between national and corporate cultures is not always clear. The French have a great deal of experience in the cosmetics and fashion industries, but L'Oreal is a global firm staffed by managers from around the world. Their influence, combined with management's receptiveness to world culture, has shaped L'Oreal into a unique organization distinctive within French culture. Thus, in international business, the tendency to attribute all differences to national culture is simplistic.

The edgy, risk-taking culture of companies under the Virgin brand owes much to the independent and flamboyant spirit of company founder Richard Branson and contrasts sharply with the conservative cultures of other British firms, despite sharing the same national culture.

Exhibit 4.3   National, Professional, and Corporate Culture

SOURCE: From Terpstra, David. *Cultural Environment of International Business*, 3E. © 1991 South-Western, a part of Cengage Learning, Inc. Reproduced by permission. http://www.cengage.com/permissions.

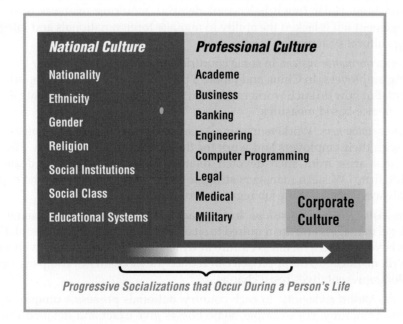

National Culture	Professional Culture	
Nationality	Academe	
Ethnicity	Business	
Gender	Banking	
Religion	Engineering	
Social Institutions	Computer Programming	
Social Class	Legal	
Educational Systems	Medical	**Corporate Culture**
	Military	

Progressive Socializations that Occur During a Person's Life

The Role of Culture in International Business

Effective handling of the cross-cultural interface is a critical source of a firm's competitive advantage. Managers not only need to develop empathy and tolerance toward cultural differences but also must acquire a sufficient degree of factual knowledge about the beliefs and values of foreign counterparts. Cross-cultural proficiency is paramount in many managerial tasks, including:

- Developing products and services
- Preparing advertising and promotional materials
- Preparing for overseas trade fairs and exhibitions
- Screening and selecting foreign distributors and other partners
- Communicating and interacting with foreign business partners
- Negotiating and structuring international business ventures
- Interacting with current and potential customers from abroad[10]

Let's consider specific examples of how cross-cultural differences may complicate company activities.[11]

Developing products and services. Cultural differences necessitate adapting marketing activities to suit the specific needs of target markets. In China, Burger King (www .burgerking.com/bkglobal) had to introduce the concept of all-beef hamburgers to local consumers. The Chinese prefer chicken, so the firm also added several chicken dishes to its menu. Meanwhile, on its menu in China, KFC offers "pumpkin porridge" and "Beijing chicken rolls" to accommodate local tastes.

Organizational structure. Some companies prefer to delegate authority to country managers, creating a decentralized organizational structure. Others are characterized by autocratic structures with power concentrated at regional or corporate headquarters. Firms may be bureaucratic or entrepreneurial. How do you deal with a bureaucratic partner or manage distantly located, decentralized subsidiaries?

Teamwork. Cooperating with partners and host-country nationals to achieve common organizational goals is critical to business success. But what should managers do if foreign and domestic nationals don't get along? The Chinese home appliance manufacturer Haier (www.haier.com) delayed acquiring overseas firms because management felt it lacked the ability to manage foreign nationals and integrate differing cultural systems.

Pay-for-performance system. In some countries, merit is not the primary basis for promoting employees. In China and Japan, a person's age is the most important determinant. But how do such workers perform when Western firms evaluate them using performance-based measures?

Lifetime employment. Workers in some Asian countries enjoy a paternalistic relationship with their employers and work for the same firm all their lives. The expectations that arise from such devoted relationships can complicate dealings with outside firms. Western managers struggle to motivate employees who expect they will always have the same job regardless of the quality of their work.

Union–management relationships. In Germany, union bosses hold the same status as top-level managers and are required to sit on corporate boards. In general, European firms have evolved a business culture in which workers enjoy a relatively equal status with managers. This approach can reduce the flexibility of company operations if union representatives resist change.

Attitudes toward ambiguity. In each country, nationals possess a unique capacity to tolerate ambiguity. For example, some bosses give exact and detailed instructions for work to be performed, while others give ambiguous and incomplete instructions. If you're not comfortable working with minimum guidance or taking independent action, then you may not fit well into some cultures.

To gain a more practical perspective on culture's role in business, consider doing business in Japan. In the West, "the customer is king," but in Japan, "the customer is God." Whenever customers enter retail stores in Japan, they are saluted with vigorous cries of "Welcome" and several choruses of "Thank you very much" when they leave. In some department stores, executives and clerks line up to bow to customers at the beginning of the business day. If customers have to wait in line—which is rare—they receive a sincere apology from store employees. Japanese firms value maintaining face, harmony, and good standing with customers and the business community. Culturally, the most important Japanese values are tradition, respect, politeness, hard work, cooperation, and group consensus.

Japan's orientation to customer service derives from its national culture. As reflected in the opening vignette, culture strongly influences the development of products and services. Good form, top product quality, and superior service are critical to success in Japan. For example, car dealers typically offer pickup and delivery for repair service and even make new-car sales calls to customers' homes. Nissan and Toyota use customer satisfaction surveys to evaluate their dealers. In the banking industry, personal bankers maintain relationships by calling on customers at their offices or by canvassing entire neighborhoods. They may help customers sell or buy homes, find outlets for merchandise sales, provide tax advice, or locate tenants for new buildings. Japanese taxi drivers spend spare moments shining their cabs and often wear white gloves. Trains are scheduled down to the second.

Japan is about the size of California, but with nearly half the population of the United States. Its densely populated and homogenous society has encouraged the development of a cohesive and polite culture. A focus on interpersonal relationships helps the Japanese avoid conflict and preserve harmony. Another key element of the Japanese culture is the emotional construct *amae*, roughly translated as "indulgent dependence," a critical part of child rearing in Japan. While Western mothers teach their children to be independent, Japanese mothers instill a sense of emotion-laden dependence in their children. Scholars believe that deeply felt amae guides social interactions in adulthood. The relationship between a senior and a junior is analogous to mother-child amae. Filial piety—respect for parents and elders—is the foundation of the Confucian ethic. Amae and the Confucian parent-child relationship provide the basis for all other relationships.

At the beginning of every work day, many Japanese firms have a group meeting intended to build harmony and team spirit, and employees even do calisthenics together. New employees are trained in groups, are evaluated collectively, and may even live together. The group discovers the sources of problems and fixes them as a team. Training is detailed. Stores provide instructions on how to greet people, what tone of voice to use, and how to handle complaints. They attach much weight to customer feedback and typically make a detailed report to the manufacturer on any product defects, returning the product to the manufacturer for careful analysis. Manufacturers and service suppliers design their offerings based on complaints and comments received from customers.[12]

Japan is slowly evolving. It increasingly operates according to values imported from abroad. Discount stores modeled on Carrefour, Toys "R" Us, and Walmart are beginning to displace department stores as the preferred shopping venues, especially

Culture strongly influences the development of products and services. Japan's Toto Company developed a line of toilets that fit the needs of Japanese culture, including purity and high technology.

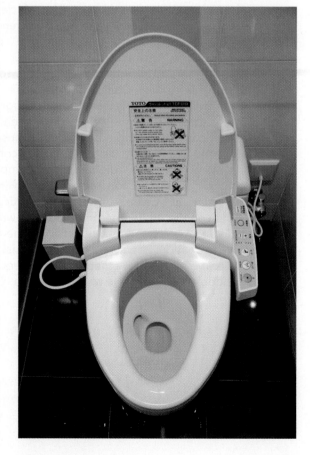

Recent Grad in IB

Lawrence's major: Supply-Chain Management

Objectives: Make a difference in the world. Get a career in international business. Work for Dell Computer.

Jobs held since graduating:
- Global Supply Manager, Dell Inc., Austin, Texas
- Logistics Program Manager, Dell Inc., Austin, Texas
- Notebook Master Scheduler, Dell Inc., Austin, Texas

Zhibo (Lawrence) Yu

Since opening to foreign investors, China's economy has grown rapidly. Lawrence Yu lived in China and witnessed amazing changes there as a teenager in the 1990s. He ate at McDonald's, wore Nike shoes, and watched NBA games. At sixteen, Lawrence came to the United States and eventually earned a bachelors degree in supply-chain management.

While in college, Lawrence undertook a study-abroad program in Mexico where he studied Spanish, lived with a Mexican family, and toured manufacturing firms. He got an internship at Whirlpool Corporation, where he created an asset-tracking system for the global procurement group and conducted market research in China. After Whirlpool, he completed another internship with Unilever North America.

After graduation, Lawrence worked at Dell Inc. as a master scheduler for notebook computers. He was primarily responsible for forecasting, planning, lead-time setting, and product transition management. One of Dell's key suppliers is located in Malaysia. Since Chinese was the first language of most of the Malaysian team members, Lawrence helped to increase communication quality and work efficiency. Management next sent Lawrence to Dell China to work with the procurement group in Shanghai.

After working as a master scheduler, Lawrence was recruited to Dell Global Logistics as a program manager, where his responsibilities included business reviews, financial analysis, contract negotiations, and process-improvement projects. With responsibility for overseeing eight U.S. logistics centers and a 100-truck fleet, Lawrence learned people-management skills and the ability to make decisions under pressure.

Subsequently, Lawrence was promoted to Global Supply Manager, helping administer Dell's $1 billion annual spending in semiconductor products. In this role, he negotiated prices with suppliers such as Samsung, Siemens, and Kingston.

Lawrence's Advice for an International Business Career

"While it was risky, I'm glad I did it. Language barriers, cultural differences, and being apart from family were all difficult. Language can be improved over time, and culture can be learned while you live in that culture. I got used to living alone pretty fast. In addition to going to class, by living, studying, and working in another country, I was naturally learning every day. The knowledge you gain from being in another country cannot be learned any other way. I now have greater confidence in whatever I pursue than I ever had before, thanks to my international experience!"

among younger shoppers. Given a choice between attentive personal service and the lowest possible prices, many Japanese citizens are making a new trade-off.

The *Recent Grad in IB* feature highlights the cross-cultural experiences of Chinese-born Lawrence Yu, who lived, studied, and worked in the United States. Having an inquiring mind and being open to new experiences helped Lawrence bridge cultural gaps.

Cultural Metaphors, Stereotypes, and Idioms

Scholars have offered several analytical approaches to gaining deeper insights into the role of culture in international business. In this section, we review three: cultural metaphors, stereotypes, and idioms.

Cultural Metaphors

Martin Gannon offered a particularly insightful analysis of cultural orientations.[13] In his view, a **cultural metaphor** refers to a distinctive tradition or institution strongly associated with a particular society. It is a guide to deciphering people's attitudes, values, and behavior.

Cultural metaphor A distinctive tradition or institution strongly associated with a particular society.

For example, American football is a cultural metaphor for traditions in the United States, such as being a team player and having a strong leader who moves an organization aggressively toward a desired goal. The Swedish *stuga* (cottage or summer home) is a cultural metaphor for Swedes' love of nature and desire for individualism through self-development. Other examples of cultural metaphors include the Japanese garden (tranquility), the Turkish coffeehouse (social interaction), the Israeli kibbutz (community), and the Spanish bullfight (ritual). The Brazilian concept of *jeito* or *jeitinho Brasileiro* refers to an ability to cope with the challenges of daily life through creative problem solving or manipulating the arduous bureaucracy of the country. In the Brazilian context, manipulation, smooth talking, and patronage are not necessarily viewed negatively, because individuals have to resort to these methods to conduct business.

Stereotypes

Stereotypes are generalizations about a group of people that may or may not be factual, often overlooking real, deeper differences. The so-called *mañana* syndrome (tomorrow syndrome) refers to the stereotype that Latin Americans tend to procrastinate. To a Latin American, *mañana* means an indefinite future. A business promise may be willingly made but not kept; after all, who knows what the future will bring? Many uncontrollable events may happen, so why fret over a promise?

Stereotype Generalization about a group of people that may or may not be factual, often overlooking real, deeper differences.

Stereotypes are often erroneous and lead to unjustified conclusions about others. But most people employ them, consciously or unconsciously, because they facilitate judging situations and people. Despite the harm stereotypes can cause, scholars believe there are real differences among groups and societies. We learn about these differences by examining descriptive rather than evaluative stereotypes.[14] For example, here is a sample of widely held stereotypes of people from the United States:

- Argumentative and aggressive relative to the Japanese, who tend to be reserved and humble
- Individualistic lovers of personal freedom relative to the Chinese, who tend to be group-oriented
- Informal and nonhierarchical relative to the Indians, who believe titles should be respected
- Entrepreneurial and risk-seeking relative to the Saudi Arabians, who tend to be conservative, employing time-honored methods for getting things done
- Direct and interested in immediate returns relative to the Latin Americans, who usually take time to be social and get to know their business partners

Country	Expression	Underlying Value
Japan	"The nail that sticks out gets hammered down."	Group conformity
Australia and New Zealand	"The tall poppy gets cut down." (Criticism of a person who is perceived as presumptuous, attention-seeking, or without merit.)	Egalitarianism
Sweden and other Scandinavian countries	*"Janteloven"* or *"Jante Law."* "Don't think you're anyone special or that you're better than us."	Modesty
Korea	"A tiger dies leaving its leather, a man dies leaving his name."	Honor
Turkey	"Steel that works, does not rust."	Hard work
United States	"Necessity is the mother of invention."	Resourcefulness
Thailand	"If you follow older people, dogs won't bite you."	Wisdom

Exhibit 4.4 Idioms that Symbolize Cultural Values

Idioms

Idiom An expression whose symbolic meaning is different from its literal meaning.

An **idiom** is an expression whose symbolic meaning is different from its literal meaning. It is a phrase you cannot understand by knowing only what the individual words in the phrase mean. For example, "to roll out the red carpet" is to extravagantly welcome a guest—no red carpet is actually used. The phrase is misunderstood when interpreted in a literal way. In Spanish, the idiom *"no está el horno para bolos"* literally means "the oven isn't ready for bread rolls." But the phrase is understood as "the time isn't right." In Japanese, the phrase *"uma ga au"* literally means "our horses meet," but the everyday meaning is "we get along with each other." Idioms exist in virtually every culture, and people often use them as a short way to express a larger concept. Managers can study national idioms to gain a better understanding of cultural values. Exhibit 4.4 offers several expressions that reveal cultural traits of different societies.

 ## Interpretations of Culture

Culture has been the subject of study by anthropologists and other social scientists for centuries. Two leading interpretations of national culture are those of E. T. Hall and Geert Hofstede. Hall's contribution was to make a distinction between high- and low-context cultures. Hofstede's seminal research led him to distinguish among four dimensions of culture.

High- and Low-Context Cultures

Low-context culture A culture that relies on elaborate verbal explanations, putting much emphasis on spoken words.

Renowned anthropologist Edward T. Hall made a distinction between cultures he characterized as "low context" and "high context."[15] **Low-context cultures** rely on elaborate verbal explanations, putting great emphasis on spoken words. As Exhibit 4.5 shows, the low-context countries tend to be in northern Europe and North America, which have long traditions of rhetoric, placing central importance on delivering verbal messages. The primary function of speech in such cultures is to express ideas and thoughts clearly, logically, and convincingly. Communication is direct and explicit, and meaning is straightforward. For example, in negotiations Americans typically come to the point and do not beat around the bush. Low-context cultures tend to value expertise and performance and conduct negotiations as efficiently as possible. These cultures use specific, legalistic contracts to conclude agreements.

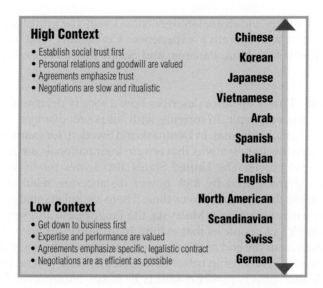

High Context

- Establish social trust first
- Personal relations and goodwill are valued
- Agreements emphasize trust
- Negotiations are slow and ritualistic

Chinese

Korean

Japanese

Vietnamese

Arab

Spanish

Italian

English

North American

Scandinavian

Swiss

German

Low Context

- Get down to business first
- Expertise and performance are valued
- Agreements emphasize specific, legalistic contract
- Negotiations are as efficient as possible

Exhibit 4.5 Hall's High- and Low-Context Typology of Cultures

SOURCE: From *Beyond Culture* by Edward T. Hall, copyright © 1976, 1981 by Edward T. Hall. Used by permission of Doubleday, a division of Random House, Inc. For on line information about other Random House, Inc. books and authors, see the Internet Web Site at http://www.randomhouse.com.

By contrast, **high-context cultures** such as Japan and China emphasize nonverbal messages and view communication as a means to promote smooth, harmonious relationships. They prefer an indirect and polite face-saving style that emphasizes a mutual sense of care and respect for others. They are on guard not to embarrass or offend others. This helps explain why Japanese people hesitate to say "no" when expressing disagreement. They are more likely to say "it is different," an ambiguous response. In East Asian cultures, showing impatience, frustration, irritation, or anger disrupts harmony and is considered rude and offensive. Asians tend to be soft-spoken, and people typically are sensitive to context and nonverbal cues (body language). At a business luncheon in Tokyo, for example, the boss is almost always the senior-looking individual seated farthest from the entrance to the room, because in Japan, superiors are given such favored seating to show respect. To succeed in Asian cultures, it is critical to have a keen eye for nonverbal signs and body language. Negotiations tend to be slow and ritualistic, and agreement is founded on trust.

Hall's work gained renewed importance because of the explosion of business between East Asia and the rest of the world. However, the notion of high- and low-context cultures plays a role even in communications between people who speak the same language. British managers sometimes complain that presentations by U.S. managers are too detailed. Everything is spelled out, even when meanings seem perfectly obvious.

Hofstede's Research on National Culture

Dutch anthropologist Geert Hofstede conducted one of the early empirical studies of national cultural traits. He collected data on the values and attitudes of 116,000 employees at IBM Corporation representing a diverse set of nationality, age, and gender. His investigation led Hofstede to delineate four independent dimensions of national culture, which we describe next.[16]

Individualism versus Collectivism   Individualism versus collectivism refers to whether a person functions primarily as an individual or as part of a group. In individualistic societies, ties among people are relatively loose, and each person tends to focus on his or her own self-interest. These societies prefer individualism over group conformity. Competition for resources is the norm, and those who compete best are rewarded financially. Australia, Canada, the United Kingdom, and the United States tend to be strongly individualistic societies. In collectivist societies, by contrast, ties among individuals are more important than individualism. Business is conducted in the context

High-context culture   A culture that emphasizes nonverbal messages and views communication as a means to promote smooth, harmonious relationships.

Individualism versus collectivism   Describes whether a person functions primarily as an individual or as part of a group.

of a group in which others' views are strongly considered. The group is all-important, as life is fundamentally a cooperative experience. Conformity and compromise help maintain group harmony. China, Panama, and South Korea are examples of strongly collectivist societies.

Power distance
Describes how a society deals with the inequalities in power that exist among people.

Power Distance   Power distance describes how a society deals with the inequalities in power that exist among people. In societies with *low* power distance, the gaps between the powerful and weak are minimal. In Denmark and Sweden, for example, governments institute tax and social welfare systems that ensure their nationals are relatively equal in terms of income and power. The United States also scores relatively low on power distance. Societies characterized by *high* power distance are relatively indifferent to inequalities and allow them to grow over time. There are substantial gaps between the powerful and the weak. Guatemala, Malaysia, the Philippines, and several Middle East countries are examples of countries that exhibit high power distance. The Apply Your Understanding exercise at the end of this chapter illustrates high power distance with an Ethical Dilemma on the relationship between an executive and a maid in Colombia.

Social stratification affects power distance. In Japan, almost everybody belongs to the middle class, while in India the upper stratum controls most of the decision making and buying power. In companies, the degree of centralization of authority and autocratic leadership determines power distance. In high power-distance firms, autocratic management styles focus power at the top and grant little autonomy to lower-level employees. In low power-distance firms, managers and subordinates are relatively equal and cooperate to achieve organizational goals.

Uncertainty avoidance   The extent to which people can tolerate risk and uncertainty in their lives.

Uncertainty Avoidance   Uncertainty avoidance refers to the extent to which people can tolerate risk and uncertainty in their lives. People in societies with *high* uncertainty avoidance create institutions that minimize risk and ensure financial security. Companies emphasize stable careers and produce many rules to regulate worker actions and minimize ambiguity. Managers may be slow to make decisions as they investigate the nature and potential outcomes of several options. Belgium, France, and Japan are countries that score high on uncertainty avoidance.

Societies that score low on uncertainty avoidance socialize their members to accept and become accustomed to uncertainty. Managers are entrepreneurial and relatively comfortable taking risks, and they make decisions relatively quickly. People accept each day as it comes and take their jobs in stride because they are less concerned about ensuring their future. They tend to tolerate behavior and opinions different from their own because they do not feel threatened by them. India, Ireland, Jamaica, and the United States are leading examples of countries with low uncertainty avoidance.

Masculinity versus femininity   Refers to a society's orientation based on traditional male and female values. Masculine cultures tend to value competitiveness, assertiveness, ambition, and the accumulation of wealth. Feminine cultures emphasize nurturing roles, interdependence among people, and taking care of less fortunate people.

Masculinity versus Femininity   Masculinity versus femininity refers to a society's orientation based on traditional male and female values. Masculine cultures tend to value competitiveness, assertiveness, ambition, and the accumulation of wealth. They are characterized by men and women who are assertive and focused on career and earning money and may care little for others. Typical examples include Australia and Japan. The United States is a moderately masculine society. Hispanic cultures are relatively masculine and display a zest for action, daring, and competitiveness. In business, the masculinity dimension manifests as self-confidence, proactiveness, and leadership. Conversely, in feminine cultures, such as the Scandinavian countries, both men and women emphasize nurturing roles, interdependence among people, and caring for less fortunate people. Welfare systems are highly developed and education is subsidized.

The Fifth Dimension: Long-Term versus Short-Term Orientation   The four dimensions of cultural orientation that Hofstede proposed have been widely accepted. They provide a tool to interpret cultural differences and a foundation for classifying countries. Yet, the Hofstede framework suffers from some limitations. First, the study is based on data collected from 1968 to 1972. Much has changed since then, including successive phases of globalization, widespread exposure to transnational media, technological advances, and changes in the role of women in the workforce. The framework fails to account for the convergence of cultural values that has occurred during the last several decades. Second, Hofstede's findings are based on the employees of a single company—IBM—in a single industry, making it difficult to generalize. Third, the data were collected using questionnaires, which is not effective for probing some of the deep issues that surround culture. Finally, Hofstede did not capture all potential dimensions of culture.

Partly in response to this last criticism, Hofstede eventually added a fifth dimension to his framework: **long-term versus short-term orientation.**[17] This refers to the degree to which people and organizations defer gratification to achieve long-term success. That is, firms and people in cultures with a long-term orientation tend to take the long view to planning and living. They focus on years and decades. The long-term dimension is best illustrated by the so-called Asian values—traditional cultural orientations of several Asian societies, including China, Japan, and Singapore. These values are partly based on the teachings of the Chinese philosopher Confucius (K'ung-fu-tzu), who lived about 2,500 years ago. In addition to long-term orientation, Confucius advocated other values that are still the basis for much of Asian culture today. These include discipline, loyalty, hard work, regard for education, esteem for family, focus on group harmony, and control over one's desires. Scholars credit these values for the *East Asian miracle*, the remarkable economic growth and modernization of East Asian nations during the last several decades.[18] By contrast, the United States and most other Western countries emphasize a short-term orientation.

The Hofstede framework should be viewed as only a general guide, useful for a deeper understanding in cross-national interactions with business partners, customers, and value-chain members.

Long-term versus short-term orientation Refers to the degree to which people and organizations defer gratification to achieve long-term success.

Subjective versus Objective Dimensions of Culture

We saw in Exhibit 4.2 that there are numerous dimensions of national culture. We can group them into two broad dimensions: subjective and objective. The *subjective dimension* of culture includes values and attitudes, manners and customs, deal versus relationship orientation, perceptions of time, perceptions of space, and religion. The *objective dimension* includes symbolic and material productions, such as the tools, architecture, and infrastructure unique to a society. In this section, we examine key examples of each dimension.

Values and Attitudes

Values represent a person's judgments about what is good or bad, acceptable or unacceptable, important or unimportant, and normal or abnormal.[19] Our values guide the development of our attitudes and preferences. *Attitudes* are similar to opinions but are often unconsciously held and may not have a rational basis. *Prejudices* are rigidly held attitudes, usually unfavorable and usually aimed at particular groups of people.[20] Typical values in North America, northern Europe, and Japan include hard work, punctuality, and the acquisition of wealth. People from such countries may misjudge those from developing economies who may not embrace such values.

Deal versus Relationship Orientation

In deal-oriented cultures, managers focus on the task at hand and prefer getting down to business. At the extreme, such managers may even avoid small talk and other preliminaries. They prefer to seal agreements with a legalistic contract, and take an impersonal approach to settling disputes. Leading examples of deal-oriented cultures include those of Australia, northern Europe, and North America. By contrast, in relationship-oriented

In Japan, bowing is the norm in both business and personal settings. Here, Japanese Foreign Minister Yoriko Kawaguchi and a U.S. Trade Representative (left) bow to each other before a meeting.

cultures, managers put more value on affiliations with people. To these managers, it is important to build trust and rapport and get to know the other party in business interactions. For example, it took nine years for Volkswagen to negotiate the opening of a car factory in China, a strongly relationship-oriented society. For the Chinese, Japanese, and many in Latin America, relationships are more important than the deal.[21] Trust is valued in business agreements. In China, the concept of *guanxi* (literally "connections") is deeply rooted in ancient Confucian philosophy, which values social hierarchy and reciprocal obligations. It stresses the importance of relationships within the family and between superiors and subordinates.

Manners and Customs

Manners and customs are ways of behaving and conducting oneself in public and business situations. Some countries are characterized by egalitarian, informal cultures, in which people are equal and work together cooperatively. In other countries people are more formal, and status, hierarchy, power, and respect are important. Customs that vary most worldwide are those related to eating habits and mealtimes, work hours and holidays, drinking and toasting, appropriate behavior at social gatherings, gift giving, and the role of women. Handshaking varies across the world: limp handshakes, firm handshakes, elbow-grasping handshakes, and no handshake at all. In much of the world, people greet by kissing each other on both cheeks. In some countries it is appropriate to kiss the other's hand. In Southeast Asia, greeting involves placing the palms together in front of the chest, as in praying. In Japan, bowing is the norm.[22] Gift giving is a complex ritual in much of the world. It is ingrained in Japanese culture, where it is usually a blunder to not offer a gift in initial meetings. The Middle East is characterized by generous gift giving.

Perceptions of Time

In business, time dictates expectations about planning, scheduling, profit streams, and promptness, or what constitutes lateness in arriving for work and meetings. Japanese managers tend to prepare strategic plans for extended periods, such as a decade. The planning horizon for Western companies is much shorter, typically a few years. Some societies are more oriented to the past, others to the present, and still others to the future. People in past-oriented cultures believe plans should be evaluated in terms of their fit with established traditions, customs, and wisdom. Innovation and change are infrequent and are justified to the extent they fit with past experience. Europeans are relatively past-oriented, insisting on the conservation of traditions and historical precedents.

By contrast, young countries like Australia, Canada, and the United States are relatively focused on the present. They can be characterized as having a **monochronic** orientation to time—a rigid orientation in which the individual is focused on schedules, punctuality, and time as a resource. People in these cultures view time as *linear*, like a river flowing into the future, carrying workers from one activity to the next. In such cultures, where people are highly focused on the clock, managers make commitments, set deadlines, and adhere to a strict schedule of meetings and activities. Punctuality is a virtue and time is money. Throughout the day, workers glance at their watches, their computer's clock, or the clock on the wall. Investors are impatient and want quick returns. Managers have a relatively short-term perspective when it comes to investments and making money; performance is measured on a quarterly basis. In this way, people in the United States have acquired a reputation for being hurried and impatient. Indeed, the word *business* was originally spelled *busyness*.

Monochronic   A rigid orientation to time, in which the individual is focused on schedules, punctuality, and time as a resource.

Some cultures have a **polychronic** perspective on time. In such societies, instead of performing single tasks serially, people are inclined to do many things at once. In this way, members of polychronic cultures are easily distracted. They can change plans often and easily, and long delays are sometimes needed before taking action. Punctuality per se is relatively unimportant, and managers consider time commitments flexible. They do not adhere strictly to the clock and schedules. They put more value on relationships and spending time with people.

Chinese and Japanese firms are future-oriented, focusing not on how the firm will perform next quarter, but on how it will perform a decade from now. Large Japanese firms offer lifetime employment and invest heavily in employee training, expecting workers to remain with the firm for 30 or 40 years. Latin Americans similarly have a flexible perception of time and are more inclined to arrive late for appointments than people from other cultures. In the Middle East, strict Muslims view destiny as the will of God ("Inshallah" or "God willing" is a frequently used phrase) and downplay the importance of future planning. They perceive appointments as relatively vague future obligations.

Polychronic A flexible, nonlinear orientation to time, whereby the individual takes a long-term perspective and emphasizes human relationships.

Perceptions of Space

Cultures also differ in their perceptions of physical space; we have our own sense of personal space and feel uncomfortable if others violate it. Conversational distance is closer in Latin America than in northern Europe or the United States. When a North American national interacts with a Latin American, he or she may unconsciously back up to maintain personal space. Those who live in crowded Japan or Belgium have smaller personal space requirements than those who live in land-rich Russia or the United States. In Japan, it is common for employee workspaces to be crowded together in the same room, desks pushed against each other. One large office space might accommodate fifty employees. North American firms partition individual workspaces and provide private offices for more important employees. In Islamic countries, close proximity may be discouraged between a man and a woman who are not married.

Religion

Religion is a system of common beliefs or attitudes concerning a being or a system of thought that people consider to be sacred, divine, or the highest truth. Religion also incorporates the moral codes, values, institutions, traditions, and rituals associated with this system. Almost every culture is underpinned by religious beliefs. Religion influences culture, and therefore business and consumer behavior, in various ways. Protestantism emphasizes hard work, individual achievement, and a sense that people can control their environment. The Protestant work ethic provided some of the basis for the development of capitalism.

In fundamentalist Islamic countries, Islam is the basis for government and legal systems as well as social and cultural order. Because people raised in Islamic cultures perceive God's will as the source of all outcomes, Muslims may be fatalistic and reactive. Islam's holy book, the Qur'an, prohibits drinking alcohol, gambling, usury, and immodest exposure. These prohibitions affect firms that deal in alcoholic beverages, resorts, entertainment, and women's clothing, as well as ad agencies and banks and other institutions that lend money. A growing number of businesses are reaching out to Muslim communities. Nokia launched a mobile phone that shows Muslims the direction toward Mecca, Islam's holiest site, when they pray. Heineken, the Dutch brewing giant, rolled out the nonalcoholic malt drink Fayrouz for the Islamic market.[23]

Exhibit 4.6 shows the dominant religions around the world. The major ones, based on number of adherents, are Christianity (2.1 billion), Islam (1.3 billion), Hinduism (900 million), Buddhism (376 million), and Judaism (14 million). Although the exhibit displays the most common religion in each location, most countries are home to people of various beliefs.

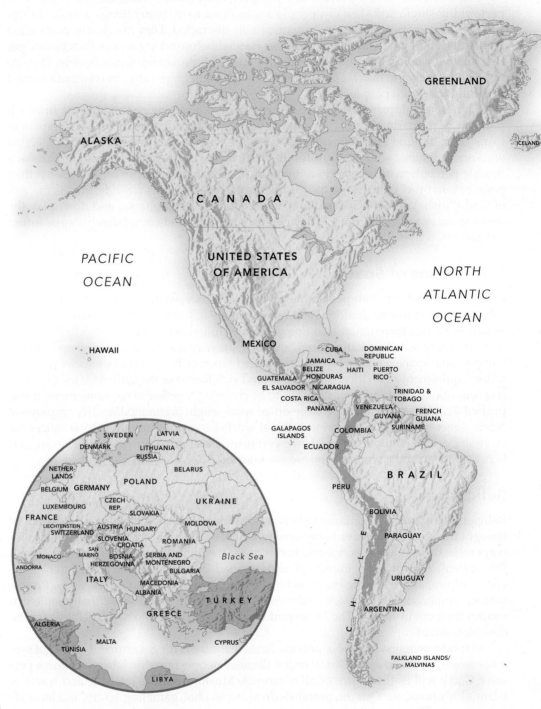

Exhibit 4.6 World Religions

SOURCES: http://www.godweb.org/religionsofworld.htm and http://www.mapsofworld.com/religion-map.htm

ARCTIC OCEAN

NORWAY
SWEDEN
FINLAND
ESTONIA
UNITED KINGDOM
IRELAND
DENMARK
LATVIA
LITHUANIA
RUSSIA
BELARUS
NETHER-LANDS
GERMANY
POLAND
BELGIUM
LUXEMBOURG
CZECH REP.
SLOVAKIA
UKRAINE
FRANCE
AUSTRIA
HUNGARY
MOLDOVA
LIECH.
SWITZ.
SLOVENIA
ROMANIA
MONACO
CROATIA
BOSNIA HERZEGOVINA
SERBIA AND MONTENEGRO
BULGARIA
ANDORRA
ITALY
MACEDONIA
ALBANIA
SPAIN
GREECE
TURKEY
PORTUGAL
CYPRUS
TUNISIA

RUSSIA

KAZAKHSTAN
MONGOLIA
GEORGIA
ARMENIA
AZERBAIJAN
UZBEKISTAN
TURKMENISTAN
KYRGYZSTAN
TAJIKISTAN
CHINA
NORTH KOREA
SOUTH KOREA
JAPAN

SYRIA
LEBANON
ISRAEL
JORDAN
IRAQ
KUWAIT
IRAN
AFGHANISTAN
PAKISTAN
NEPAL
BHUTAN
TAIWAN

MOROCCO
ALGERIA
LIBYA
EGYPT
QATAR
UNITED ARAB EMIRATES
SAUDI ARABIA
OMAN
INDIA
BANGLADESH
MYANMAR (BURMA)
LAOS

WESTERN SAHARA
MAURITANIA
MALI
NIGER
CHAD
SUDAN
YEMEN
ERITREA
DJIBOUTI
THAILAND
VIETNAM
CAMBODIA
PHILIPPINES

SENEGAL
GAMBIA
GUINEA-BISSAU
GUINEA
SIERRA LEONE
LIBERIA
BURKINA FASO
IVORY COAST
GHANA
TOGO
BENIN
NIGERIA
CAMEROON
CENTRAL AFRICAN REPUBLIC
ETHIOPIA
SOMALIA
SRI LANKA
MALAYSIA
BRUNEI

EQUATORIAL GUINEA
GABON
CONGO REPUBLIC
CONGO DEMOCRATIC REPUBLIC (ZAIRE)
UGANDA
RWANDA
BURUNDI
KENYA
TANZANIA
SINGAPORE
INDONESIA
PAPUA NEW GUINEA
SOLOMON ISLANDS

INDIAN OCEAN

PACIFIC OCEAN

SOUTH ATLANTIC OCEAN

ANGOLA
ZAMBIA
MALAWI
MOZAMBIQUE
MADAGASCAR
MAURITIUS
RÉUNION
VANUATU
FIJI

NAMIBIA
ZIMBABWE
BOTSWANA
SWAZILAND
LESOTHO
SOUTH AFRICA

AUSTRALIA

NEW CALEDONIA

NEW ZEALAND

Christianity   Buddhism

Judaism   Nature religion

Hinduism   Chinese religion

Islam   Other groups

141

Now that we have reviewed the subjective dimensions of culture, we turn to its objective dimensions—symbolic and material productions.

Symbolic Productions

A *symbol* can be letters, figures, colors, or other characters that communicate a meaning. For instance, the cross is the main symbol of Christianity. The red star was the symbol of the former Soviet Union. National symbols include flags, anthems, seals, monuments, and historical myths. These symbols represent nations and national values and help to unite people. Mathematicians and scientists use symbols as types of language. Businesses have many types of symbols, in the form of trademarks, logos, and brands. Can you easily identify popular company logos such as Nike's swoosh, Apple's apple, and Cadbury's unique lettering?

Material Productions and Creative Expressions of Culture

Material productions are artifacts, objects, and technological systems that people construct to cope with their environments. They are integral to human life and provide the means to accomplish objectives, as well as to communicate and conduct exchanges within and between societies. The most important technology-based material productions are the infrastructures that supply energy, transportation, and communications. Others include social infrastructure (systems that provide housing, education, and health care), financial infrastructure (systems for managing means of exchange in banks and other financial institutions), and marketing infrastructure (systems that support marketing-related activities, such as ad agencies).

Creative expressions of culture include arts, folklore, music, dance, theater, and high cuisine. Food is among the most interesting cultural markers. In Japan, pizza is often topped with fish and seaweed. In the United States, pizza can be piled high with meat. In France, it often comes with a variety of cheeses.

Language as a Key Dimension of Culture

Often described as the expression or *mirror* of culture, language is not only essential for communications, it also provides insights into culture. At present the world has nearly 7,000 active languages, including more than 2,000 each in Africa and Asia. But most of these languages have only a few thousand speakers.[24] Exhibit 4.7 highlights the major languages of the world. Note that while Arabic is listed in sixth place, it comprises fifteen major and often highly distinct language variants across forty-six countries. Linguistic proficiency is a great asset in international business because it facilitates cross-cultural understanding. Learning one or more of the frequently spoken languages can greatly enhance an international business career.

Language has both verbal and nonverbal characteristics. Much language is unspoken and entails facial expressions and gestures.[25] In fact, most verbal messages are accompanied by nonverbal ones. In this and other ways, language is extremely subtle.

Sometimes it is difficult to find words to convey the same meaning in a different language. For example, a one-word equivalent to "aftertaste" does not exist in many languages. There are also semantic gaps in languages. Even when a word can be translated well into other languages, its concept and meaning are not generally universal. The Japanese word *muzukashii* can be variously translated as "difficult," "delicate," or "I don't want to discuss it," but in business negotiations it usually means "out of the question."

National languages, dialects, and translation have a tendency to complicate straightforward communication. Ignorance can be embarrassing. Advertising themes often lose their original meaning in translation or convey unfavorable interpretations. Even people from different countries who speak the same language may experience communication problems because of unique colloquial words. The same word can convey different

Exhibit 4.7 The Most Common Primary Languages in the World

SOURCES: R. Gordon (ed.), *Ethnologue: Languages of the World,* 15 ed. (Dallas, TX: SIL International, 2005 at http://www.ethnologue.com), and CIA World Factbook, 2008, at http://www.cia.gov.

Rank	Language	Approximate Number of Native Speakers (Millions)	Countries With Substantial Number of Native Speakers
1	Mandarin Chinese	887	China, Singapore
2	Hindi	478	India
3	English	341	Britain, United States
4	Spanish	327	Argentina, Mexico, Spain
5	Bengali	249	Bangladesh, India
6	Arabic	209	Algeria, Egypt, Saudi Arabia
7	Portuguese	207	Brazil, Portugal
8	Russian	148	Russian Federation, Ukraine
9	Japanese	125	Japan
10	German	100	Germany, Austria
11	French	77	France, Belgium
12	Turkish	75	Turkey, Central Asia, Eastern Europe
13	Korean	72	South Korea, North Korea

meanings in the two countries. Exhibit 4.8 shows how the popular slogans of some languages translate into offensive phrases in other languages. Exhibit 4.9 shows how two English-speaking countries interpret the same word in very different ways. These exhibits demonstrate how easy it is for misinterpretations to get in the way of intended meaning.

Business jargon unique to a culture can also impede communication. For example, many words and expressions that have crept into U.S. business executives' jargon from sports or military terminology pose problems for non-U.S. businesspeople. Examples of English jargon that puzzle non-native speakers include: "the bottom line," "to beat around the bush," "shooting from the hip," "feather in your cap," and "get down to brass tacks." Imagine the difficulty professional interpreters encounter in translating such phrases!

Company and Location	Intended Ad Slogan	Literal Translation
Parker Pen Company in Latin America	"Use Parker Pen, avoid embarrassment!"	"Use Parker Pen, avoid pregnancy!"
Pepsi in Germany	"Come Alive with Pepsi"	"Come out of the grave with Pepsi."
Pepsi in Taiwan	"Come Alive with Pepsi"	"Pepsi brings your ancestors back from the dead."
Fisher Body (car exteriors) in Belgium	"Body by Fisher"	"Corpse by Fisher"
Salem cigarettes in Japan	"Salem—Feeling Free"	"Smoking Salem makes your mind feel free and empty."

Exhibit 4.8 Blunders in International Advertising

Exhibit 4.9 Examples of Differences in Meaning between Britain and the United States

Word	Meaning in U.S. English	Meaning in British English
Scheme	A somewhat devious plan	A plan
Redundant	Repetitive	Fired or laid off
Sharp	Smart	Conniving, unethical
To table	To put as issue on hold	To take up an issue
To bomb	To fail miserably	To succeed grandly
Windscreen	A screen that protects against wind	Automobile windshield

Contemporary Issues in Culture

We have seen that culture is relatively stable. However, the globalization of markets, transnational media, technological advances, and government regulations substantially influence culture, and culture is so powerful and pervasive that it influences these factors in turn. In this section, we explore the link between culture and key issues.

Culture and the Services Sector

In the most advanced economies, firms engaged in services like lodging and retailing account for a greater share of FDI than firms that manufacture products.[26] Contact-based services like architecture, consulting, and legal services bring providers into direct contact with foreign customers. Asset-based services include banks, restaurants, and retail stores.[27]

Cultural differences can create problems for service firms and lead to mishaps in the exchange process. The greater the cultural distance between the service provider and its customers, the more likely there will be cognitive and communication gaps. Imagine a Western lawyer who tries to establish a law office in China. Without a thorough knowledge of Chinese culture and language, the lawyer's efforts are largely futile. Imagine how much success a Western restaurant chain would have in Russia if it knew nothing of Russian food culture or the work habits of Russian workers!

Differences in language and national character have the same effect as trade barriers. Service firms that internationalize through FDI are vulnerable because each firm is shaped by both a national and an organizational culture.[28] A Chinese bank that establishes a branch in New York or London remains distinctly Chinese because the capabilities it brings with it are based on Chinese culture and the firm's own China-based corporate culture.[29]

To overcome these challenges, service firms seek to understand the cultures and languages of the countries where they do business. For example, at the global express company FedEx, management constantly seeks to hire, train, and motivate hundreds of sales representatives who speak different languages, represent different cultures, and serve different markets.[30] Without such efforts, service firms would not likely succeed at international business.

Technology, the Internet, and Culture

Technological advances are a key determinant of culture and cultural change. They have freed up leisure time and led to the proliferation of computers, multimedia, and communications systems that bring geographically separated cultures in closer contact than ever before. The *death of distance* refers to the demise of boundaries that once separated people, due to the integrating effects of communications, information, and transportation technologies. Just as distinctive cultures developed in the distant past because regions had limited contact with each other, today cultures are homogenizing due to increased contact among peoples of the world.

Ironically, technology also provides the means to promote individual cultures. Artistic traditions from Africa, Asia, and Latin America have received a big boost from the rise of world cinema and television. We can also choose our information sources. People usually prefer information in their native language that represents cultural traits similar to their own. Thus, Spanish speakers in the United States prefer mass media sources in Spanish, limiting the culturally homogenizing effect of English-speaking media. And the broadening of global communications allows ethnic groups scattered around the world to remain in touch with each other.[31]

The Internet also promotes the diffusion of culture. The number of Internet users is growing rapidly worldwide, and the potential for cultural blunders arising from international e-mail use is higher than ever. To help reduce such problems, managers can use software that instantly converts messages into any one of dozens of languages.[32]

Globalization's Effect on Culture: Are Cultures Converging?

There is little consensus about globalization's effects on culture. On the one hand, critics charge globalization is harmful to local cultures and their artistic expressions and sensibilities, replacing them with a homogeneous, often "Americanized" culture. Others argue that increased global communications is positive because it permits the free flow of cultural ideas, beliefs, and values. Clearly, globalization is a major factor in the emergence of a common worldwide culture.

People in many parts of the world consume the same Big Macs and Coca-Colas, watch the same movies, listen to the same music, drive the same cars, and stay in the same hotels. Although food often represents a distinct culture, hamburgers, tacos, and pizza are increasingly popular around the world.[33] Movies and TV shows promote the convergence of customs, fashions, and other manifestations of culture. Today, college students listen to much the same music and wear similar clothing worldwide. In Trinidad, the U.S. television series *The Young and the Restless* is so popular that in many places work effectively stops when it airs, and it has inspired calypso songs of the same name. *CSI Miami* and *Desperate Housewives* have ranked among the most popular TV series worldwide. The iconic Barbie doll has become a global phenomenon, even as the values it represents may not always agree with conservative cultures.[34]

In reality, however, the larger trend is more complex than these examples imply. As international business integrates the world's economies, it also increases the choices available to local people by making their countries culturally richer. Cultural homogeneity and heterogeneity are not mutually exclusive alternatives or substitutes; they may exist simultaneously. Cross-cultural exchange promotes innovation and creativity. Globalization brings a wider menu of choices to consumers and increases diversity within society.[35] Cultural flows originate in many places. Just as McDonald's hamburgers have become popular in Japan, so has Vietnamese food in the United States and Japanese sushi in Europe. Integration and the spread of ideas and images tend to provoke reactions and resistance to cultural homogenization, thereby spurring individual peoples to insist on their differences. While some past customs will disappear due to globalization, the process is also liberating people culturally by undermining the ideological conformity of nationalism.

 ## Overcoming Cross-Cultural Risk: Managerial Guidelines

Seasoned managers attest to the importance of a deep knowledge of culture and language in international business. Managers can achieve effective cross-cultural interaction by keeping an open mind, being inquisitive, and not rushing to conclusions about others' behaviors.

Even experienced managers undergo cultural training that emphasizes observational skills and human relations techniques. Skills are more important than pure information because skills can be transferred across countries, while information is often country-specific.

Cross-cultural proficiency increases the effectiveness of meetings and other encounters in international business.

Planning that combines informal mentoring from experienced managers and formal training through seminars, courses, and simulations abroad and at home can go far in helping managers meet cross-cultural challenges.

Although every culture is unique, certain basic guidelines are appropriate for consistent cross-cultural success. Let's review three guidelines managers can follow in preparing for successful cross-cultural encounters.

Guideline 1: Acquire factual and interpretive knowledge about the other culture, and try to speak the language. Successful managers acquire a base of knowledge about the values, attitudes, and lifestyles of the cultures with which they interact. Managers study the political and economic background of target countries—their history, current national affairs, and perceptions about other cultures. Such knowledge facilitates understanding about the partner's mind-set, organization, and objectives. Decisions and events become substantially easier to interpret. Sincere interest in the target culture helps establish trust and respect, laying the foundation for open and productive relationships. Even modest attempts to speak the local language are welcome. Higher levels of language proficiency pave the way for acquiring competitive advantages. In the long run, managers who can converse in multiple languages are more likely to negotiate successfully and have positive business interactions.

Guideline 2: Avoid cultural bias. Problems arise when managers make ethnocentric assumptions that foreigners think and behave just like the folks back home. Ethnocentric assumptions lead to poor business strategies in both planning and execution. Managers new to international business can find the behavior of a foreigner odd and perhaps improper. For example, it is easy to be offended when a foreign counterpart does not appreciate our food, history, entertainment, or everyday traditions. In this way, cultural bias can be a significant barrier to successful interpersonal communication.

A person's own culture conditions how he or she reacts to different values, behavior, or systems, so most people unconsciously assume those in other countries experience the world as they do. They view their own culture as the norm; everything else may seem strange. This is known as the **self-reference criterion**—the tendency to view other cultures through the lens of our own culture. Understanding the self-reference criterion is a critical first step to avoiding cultural bias and ethnocentric reactions.

Critical incident analysis (CIA) is a method that managers use to analyze awkward situations in cross-cultural encounters. CIA encourages a more effective approach to cultural differences by helping managers develop objectivity and empathy for other points of view. The *Global Trend* feature details how managers can avoid the self-reference criterion by using CIA.

Guideline 3: Develop cross-cultural skills. Working effectively with counterparts from other cultures requires you to make an investment in your professional development. Each culture has its own ways of conducting business transactions, negotiations, and dispute resolution. You're exposed to high levels of *ambiguity* regarding concepts and relationships that can be understood in a variety of ways.[36] To be successful in international business, you should strive for cross-cultural proficiency. Cross-cultural proficiency is characterized by four key personality traits:

- *Tolerance for ambiguity*—the ability to tolerate uncertainty and apparent lack of clarity in the thinking and actions of others.

Self-reference criterion The tendency to view other cultures through the lens of our own culture.

Critical incident analysis (CIA) A method for analyzing awkward situations in cross-cultural encounters by developing objectivity and empathy for other points of view.

GL🌐BAL TREND

Minimizing Cross-Cultural Bias with Critical Incident Analysis

To compete effectively, companies must continually improve ways to communicate with and manage customers and partners around the world. Global teams with members from a variety of cultural backgrounds enable firms to profit from knowledge amassed across the organization's worldwide operations. Such teams function best when the members engage in high-quality communications, minimizing miscommunications caused by differences in language and culture.

Nevertheless, inexperienced managers often misunderstand the behavior of foreign counterparts, which hinders the effectiveness of cross-cultural meetings. One way to minimize such problems is *critical incident analysis (CIA)*.

Consider the following scenario: Working on a joint product design, engineers from Ford (United States) and Mazda (Japan) interact intensively with each other. Ford wants to share its engineering studies and critical materials with its Japanese counterpart. After a week of interaction, the Ford team has grown uncomfortable because the Japanese appear strangely indifferent and do not exhibit much reaction. When the teams meet, the Japanese appear to keep conversation among themselves and offer little feedback. Eventually, the Ford team's surprise turns to frustration

and anger. They now believe the Japanese are arrogant, indifferent about Ford's designs, and uninterested in collaboration.

In reality, the Ford team has jumped to conclusions and judged the Japanese with its own culturally bound expectations. An expert on Japanese business culture could have provided alternative explanations. For one, the Japanese engineers may not be proficient in English. They are unable to explain themselves easily or to understand the Ford team's briefings, which all occur in English. Japanese are generally thoughtful and typically show respect for counterparts by listening intently while remaining quiet. Furthermore, before their team meets in private and reaches consensus, Japanese usually refrain from speaking out. These and other explanations are all plausible in the context of Japanese culture.

What should you do when confronted with an awkward or uncomfortable situation in a cross-cultural interaction? CIA involves the following steps:

1. Identify the situations where you need to be culturally aware to interact effectively with people from another culture. These may include socializing, working in groups,

negotiating, and reaching agreement.

2. When confronted with seemingly strange behavior, discipline yourself to avoid making hasty judgments. Instead, try to view the situation or the problem in terms of the unfamiliar culture. Make observations and gather objective information from native citizens or secondary sources. In this way, you can isolate the self-reference criterion that led to your possibly inaccurate conclusion.

3. Learn to make a variety of interpretations of others' behavior, to select the most likely one in the cultural context, and only then to formulate your own response. In this way, you can avoid the self-reference criterion and likely make a better decision.

4. Learn from this process and continuously improve.

SOURCES: Robert Keller, Christoph Senn, and Axel Thoma, "Worldly Wise: Attracting and Managing Customers Isn't the Same When Business Goes Global," *Wall Street Journal*, March 3, 2007, p. R5; "Cross-Functional Project Groups in Research and New Product Development," *Academy of Management Journal* 44, no. 3 (2001): 547–55; C. Solomon, "Building Teams Across Borders," *Workforce* 52, no. 4 (1998): 12–17.

- *Perceptiveness*—the ability to closely observe and appreciate subtle information in the speech and behavior of others.

- *Valuing personal relationships*—the ability to recognize the importance of interpersonal relationships, which is often much more important than achieving one-time goals or winning arguments.

- *Flexibility and adaptability*—the ability to be creative in devising innovative solutions, to be open-minded about outcomes, and to show grace under pressure.

Managers with a geocentric view of the world are generally better at understanding and accommodating similarities and differences among cultures. Successful multinational firms seek to instill a geocentric cultural mind-set in their employees and use a geocentric staffing policy to hire the best people for each position, regardless of national origin. Over time, such firms develop a core group of managers who are comfortable in any cultural context.

One way for managers to determine the skills they need to approach cultural issues is to measure their cultural intelligence.[37] *Cultural intelligence (CQ)* is a person's capability to function effectively in situations characterized by cultural diversity. It focuses on specific capabilities important for high-quality personal relationships and effectiveness in culturally diverse settings and work groups.

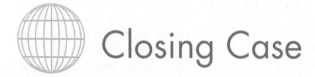

Closing Case

Hollywood's Influence on Global Culture

The most commercially successful filmmaker of all time, Steven Spielberg, is synonymous with U.S. cinema. He has directed and produced international blockbusters like *Jurassic Park*, *War of the Worlds*, and the Indiana Jones movies. As U.S. dominance of the international film industry grows, Spielberg also has been the target of complaints about how Hollywood is changing world cultures. The values represented in his films are often viewed as part of the larger trend of the homogenization or, worse, Americanization of global values and beliefs.

Jurassic Park ignited a storm of protest. Film critics and cultural ministries around the globe found it to be a brainless film, lacking plot and succeeding wholly through special effects and big-budget bells and whistles. French officials labeled the film a threat to their national identity. Three leading filmmakers—Pedro Almodóvar, Bernardo Bertolucci, and Wim Wenders—wrote Spielberg to reprimand him for the poor quality of the film, calling him personally responsible for undermining their efforts to keep culturally rich European cinema afloat.

Another popular U.S. movie, *Lost in Translation*, came under fire from Los Angeles to Tokyo. Set in Japan's capital and starring Bill Murray, the film was nominated for four Academy Awards and won for best screenplay. It also won three Golden Globes. But it was criticized for its portrayal of Japanese people as robotic caricatures who mix up their Ls and Rs. The image-conscious Japanese were disappointed by their depiction as comic relief. In a scene where Bill Murray's character is taking a shower in what is meant to be a five-star hotel, he has to bend and contort to get his head under the shower head.

In reality there isn't a five-star hotel in Tokyo that hasn't accounted for the varying heights of its potential guests. Another scene, in which Murray is shown towering at least a foot above an elevator full of local businessmen, mocks the smaller physique of the Japanese. The film was seen to reinforce negative stereotypes about the Japanese.

Is the U.S. film industry overwhelming the cultures of the world? And if so, can the world really blame Hollywood? American studios produce 80 percent of the films viewed internationally. The European film industry is now about one-ninth the size it was in 1945. After aerospace, Hollywood is often the United States' largest net export. The copyright-based industries, which also include software, books, music, and TV, contributed more to the U.S. economy in the 2000s than any single manufacturing sector. While the United States imports few foreign films, Hollywood's output remains in high demand worldwide. Today, foreign films hold less than 1 percent of the U.S. market.

Distorting History and Religious Values

Under attack since their origin, Hollywood war films are widely accused of presenting biased accounts of history. War movies portray U.S. soldiers as patriotic heroes, protecting all that is good from all that is evil. *Apocalypse Now* painted an ethnocentric view of the Vietnam War, focusing on the U.S. tragedy while ignoring that of the Vietnamese.

Mel Gibson's controversial film *The Passion of the Christ* enraged religious groups and governments in various countries. The government of Malaysia found it inappropriate for its largely Muslim population and banned its initial release in the country. (Christians were later allowed to view it.) International organizations and individuals also attacked *The Passion of the Christ* as anti-Semitic. Other nations with deep religious values were offended by *Brokeback Mountain*, which portrayed a homosexual relationship between two cowboys in the United States.

Crucial to U.S. dominance of world cinema is widespread acceptance of the cultural associations inherent in Hollywood films, an obstacle competitors must overcome. U.S. stars and Hollywood directors are well established in the international movie scene, and their drawing power transcends national boundaries. The CEO of Time Warner attributed Hollywood's global success to the association of "American style with a way of existence that to one degree or another [people] wish to share in."

Movies and Comparative Advantage

According to the theory of comparative advantage, countries should specialize in producing what they do best and import the rest. Economists argue this theory applies to films as much as to any industry. Movies are like any other commodity, they say, and the United States has advantages in producing entertainment and exporting it to the rest of the world. However, critics suggest such an assertion ignores the fact that movies influence national culture and social development. The motion picture industry is a venue for enhancing cultural identity. As a former Canadian Prime Minister remarked, "Movies are culture incarnate. It is mistaken to view culture as a commodity. . . . Cultural industries, aside from their economic impact, create products that are fundamental to the survival of Canada as a society."

This view highlights why governments often engage in *cultural protectionism*—a systematic effort to prevent local film industries from being swamped by U.S. imports. This effort includes erecting legal and bureaucratic trade barriers to prevent the import of foreign films,

especially from the United States. Governments may also subsidize domestic filmmakers to ensure the survival and growth of the home-country film industry. *Quotas* restrict the number of foreign films that can be imported or require that a minimum number of movies be produced domestically.

However, subsidies can weaken film industries by insulating them from competitive pressures and reducing their ability to create globally viable films. Quotas may prevent movie-goers from seeing the films they want to see. Cultural protectionism can result in the local production of films simply to fulfill government mandates. At one time France had its own booming film industry. But a complex system of quotas and subsidies has done little to slow its gradual demise. Meanwhile, the proportion of Hollywood revenues generated from abroad continues to grow.

A Cultural Dilemma

Despite plenty of arguments on both sides of this ongoing debate, many big-budget Hollywood movies these days are in fact multinational creations. The James Bond thriller *Quantum of Solace*, with its German-Swiss director and stars hailing from Britain, Ukraine, and France, was filmed in Britain, Panama, Chile, Italy, and Austria. Russell Crowe, Charlize Theron, Penelope Cruz, Nicole Kidman, and Daniel Craig are just a few of the many global stars not from the United States. Two of the seven major film companies collectively known as Hollywood aren't even U.S. firms. Hollywood is not as "American" as it once was.

As the lines connecting Hollywood with the United States are increasingly blurred, protectionists should not abandon their quest to salvage the intellectual and artistic quality of films. In an interview with *The New York Times*, French director Eric Rohmer stated that his countrymen should fight back with high-quality movies, not protection. "I am a commercial film maker. I am for free competition and am not supported by the state."

AACSB: **Reflective Thinking Skills**

Case Questions

1. Most aspects of foreign culture, like language, religion, gender roles, and problem-solving strategies, are hard for the casual observer to understand. In what ways do Hollywood movies affect national culture outside the United States? What aspects of U.S. culture do Hollywood films promote around the world? Can you observe any positive effects of Hollywood movies on world cultures?

2. Culture plays a key role in business. In what ways have movies influenced managerial tasks, company

activities, and other ways of doing business around the world? Can watching foreign films be an effective way of learning how to do business abroad? Justify your answer.

3. Hollywood movies are very popular abroad, but foreign films are little viewed in the United States. What factors determine the high demand for Hollywood films? Why are they so popular in Europe, Japan, Latin America, and elsewhere? Why are foreign films so little demanded in the United States? What can

foreign filmmakers do to increase demand for their movies in the United States?

4. Worldwide, protectionism of most goods is declining. Do movies constitute a separate category, or should they be treated like any other good? Given the nature of movies, should a country shield and support its own film industry via protectionism? Are there better ways to maintain and enhance a home-grown film industry? Justify your answer.

SOURCES: K. Lee, "'The Little State Department': Hollywood and the MPAA's Influence." *Northwestern Journal of International Law & Business* 28, no. 2 (2008): 371–83. "Moreover: Culture Wars," *Economist*, September 12, 1998, pp. 97–100; K. Day, "Totally Lost in Translation," *The Guardian*, January 24, 2004; J. Delacroix and J. Bornon, "Can Protectionism Ever Be Respectable?" *The Independent Review* 9, no. 3 (2005): 353–65; A. Marvasti and E. Canterbery, "Cultural and Other Barriers to Motion Picture Trade," *Economic Inquiry*, January 2005, pp. 39–55; T. Teachout, "Cultural Protectionism," *Wall Street Journal*, July 10, 1998, p. W11.

NOTE: This case was written by Sonia Prusaitis, under the supervision of Dr. Gary Knight.

CHAPTER ESSENTIALS

Key Terms

acculturation, p. 127
critical incident analysis (CIA),
    p. 146
cross-cultural risk, p. 124
cultural metaphor, p. 133
culture, p. 124
ethnocentric orientation, p. 125
geocentric orientation, p. 126
high-context culture, p. 135

idiom, p. 134
individualism versus collectivism,
    p. 135
long-term versus short-term
    orientation, p. 137
low-context culture, p. 134
masculinity versus femininity,
    p. 136
monochronic, p. 138

polycentric orientation, p. 126
polychronic, p. 139
power distance, p. 136
self-reference criterion, p. 146
socialization, p. 127
stereotype, p. 133
uncertainty avoidance, p. 136

Summary

In this chapter, you learned about:

1. Culture and cross-cultural risk

In international business, we step into different cultural environments characterized by unfamiliar languages, distinctive motivations, and different values. **Culture** is the learned, shared, and enduring orientations of a society, expressed in values, ideas, attitudes, behaviors, and other meaningful symbols and artifacts. **Cross-cultural risk** arises from a situation or event in which a cultural misunderstanding puts some human value at stake. **Ethnocentric orientation** refers to using our own culture as the standard for judging other cultures. **Polycentric orientation** refers to a host country mind-set that gives the manager greater affinity with the country in which she or he conducts business. **Geocentric orientation** refers to a global mind-set with which the manager is able to understand a business or market without regard to country boundaries.

2. Key concepts of culture

National culture influences consumer behavior, managerial effectiveness, and the range of value-chain operations, such as product and service design, marketing, and sales. The influence of professional and corporate cultures grows as people are socialized into a profession and their workplace. Most corporations exhibit a distinctive set of norms, values, and beliefs that distinguish them from other organizations. Managers can misinterpret the extent to which a counterpart's behavior is attributable to national, professional, or corporate culture.

3. The role of culture in international business

Culture matters in international business in areas such as developing products and services, interacting with foreign business partners, selecting foreign distributors, negotiating, dealing with customers, preparing for trade fairs, and preparing promotional materials. Cross-cultural differences complicate workplace issues such as teamwork, employment, pay-for-performance systems, organizational structures, union-management relationships, and attitudes toward ambiguity. Managers need to develop understanding and skills in dealing with other cultures.

4. Cultural metaphors, stereotypes, and idioms

Culture can be interpreted through **cultural metaphors,** distinctive traditions or institutions that serve as a guide or map for deciphering attitudes, values, and behavior. **Stereotypes** are generalizations about a group of people that may or may not be factual. An **idiom** is an expression whose symbolic meaning is different from its literal meaning.

5. Interpretations of culture

Low-context cultures rely on elaborated verbal explanations, putting much emphasis on spoken words. **High-context cultures** emphasize nonverbal communications and a more holistic approach to communication that promotes harmonious relationships. Hofstede's typology of cultural dimensions consists of **individualism versus collectivism, power distance, uncertainty avoidance, masculinity versus femininity,** and **long-term versus short-term orientation**.

6. Subjective versus objective dimensions of culture

Values and attitudes are shared beliefs or norms that individuals have internalized. **Monochronic** cultures exhibit a rigid orientation to time in which the individual is focused on schedules, punctuality, and time as a resource. **Polychronic** cultures have a flexible, nonlinear orientation to time in which the individual takes a long-term perspective. Religion provides meaning and motivation that define people's ideals and values. Symbolic and material productions refer to the intangible and tangible meanings, institutions, and structures that cultures construct for themselves.

7. Language as a key dimension of culture

There are nearly 7,000 active languages in the world, but most have only a few thousand speakers. The major languages include Mandarin Chinese, Hindi, English, Spanish, and Arabic. Language has both verbal and nonverbal characteristics and is conditioned by our environment. Sometimes it is hard to find words to convey the same meaning in two different languages.

8. Contemporary issues in culture

While culture is relatively stable, it is influenced by contemporary issues. In contact-based services, providers interact directly with foreign nationals in culture-laden transactions. Cultural differences may lead to mishaps in the exchange process. Technological advances are a key determinant of culture and cultural change. Improved transportation and communications technologies have removed the boundaries that once separated nations. Technology also promotes culture. The Internet emphasizes the role of language in communications. Globalization promotes common culture and the consumption of similar products and services worldwide.

9. Overcoming cross-cultural risk: Managerial guidelines

Managerial guidelines include the need to acquire factual and interpretive knowledge about the other culture, and to try to speak the language. Managers should avoid cultural bias and engage in **critical incident analysis** to avoid the **self-reference criterion**. Critical incident analysis requires being culturally aware, not making value judgments, and selecting the most likely interpretation of foreign behaviors. Experienced managers develop cross-cultural skills, including tolerating ambiguity, developing perceptiveness, valuing personal relationships, and being flexible and adaptable. Cultural intelligence is the ability to function effectively in culturally diverse situations.

Test Your Comprehension

1. Describe culture and cross-cultural risk.

2. Distinguish between socialization and acculturation.

3. Explain why culture matters in international business. In what types of contexts can cross-cultural differences cause concerns for managers?

4. Distinguish the three layers of culture. What are the major elements of country-level and professional culture?

5. How does a manager with a deal orientation differ from a manager with a relationship orientation?

6. What are the two major perceptions of time, and how does each affect international business?

7. What are the five dimensions that make up Hofstede's model of culture?

8. Distinguish between cultural metaphors and stereotypes.

9. Summarize the three major guidelines for success in cross-cultural settings.

Apply Your Understanding AACSB: Communication Abilities, Reflective Thinking Skills, Ethical Understanding and Reasoning Abilities, Multicultural and Diversity Understanding

1. Suppose you get a job at Kismet Indemnity, a life insurance company. In its 45-year history, Kismet has never done any international business. Now its president, Randall Fraser, wants to expand abroad. You have noted in meetings that he seems to lack much awareness of the role of culture. Write a memo to him in which you explain why culture matters in international business. Be sure to speculate on the effects of various dimensions of culture on sales of life insurance.

2. People tend to see other cultures from their own point of view. They accept their own culture and its ways as the norm—everything else seems foreign, or even mysterious. This chapter described a technique called critical incident analysis (CIA) that encourages an objective reaction to cultural differences by helping managers develop empathy for other points of view. Using the CIA approach, define a situation that you or someone else has experienced that led to a cross-cultural misunderstanding—perhaps an interaction with a fellow student, a visit to a store in your town, or an experience you had while traveling abroad. Explain what actually happened and how a more culturally sensitive response might have been possible if you or your fellow student had used CIA.

3. *Ethical Dilemma*: Suppose you work for a multinational firm and are posted to Bogota, Colombia. After renting a house in a posh neighborhood, you hire a full-time maid to perform household chores, a common practice among wealthy Colombians. A colleague at work tells you local maids are typically poor women who live in Bogota's slums and earn about $200 a month. As an executive, you feel guilty about paying such a cheap wage when you can afford much more. But for cultural and socioeconomic reasons, your colleague insists you cannot pay more than the going rate. Doing so might embarrass your maid and risk upsetting the economic balance in her community. Analyze this dilemma. Do you pay your maid the customary local rate or a higher wage? Justify your decision. Can you think of any creative solutions to this dilemma?

globalEDGE Internet Exercises
(http://globalEDGE.msu.edu)

AACSB: Reflective Thinking Skills

Refer to Chapter 1, page 62, for instructions on how to access and use globalEDGE™.

1. Ethnologue (www.ethnologue.com/web.asp) is a site that lists the world's known languages. It is an excellent resource for scholars and others with language interests and contains statistical summaries of the number of language speakers by language size, family, and country. Using Ethnologue, try the following:

   a. Visit the "Languages of China" site. What is the population of China? Of the country's more than 200 languages, which has the largest number of speakers? Which has the second-most speakers? How do these figures compare to the total number of English speakers in the English-speaking countries of Australia, Britain, Canada, New Zealand, and the United States?

   b. Visit the "Languages of Spain" site. How many people live in Spain? How many native Spanish speakers are in Spain? How many languages altogether are spoken in Spain?

   c. Switzerland is one of the smallest European countries. What are the major languages of Switzerland, and how many speakers does each have?

   d. Find the table "Linguistic Diversity of Countries," which shows the population for each language as a proportion of the total population for most countries. What are the most linguistically diversified countries in the world? What are the least diversified countries?

2. Cultural intelligence is a person's ability to function effectively in situations characterized by cultural diversity. globalEDGE™ and other online resources feature *cultural intelligence* scales. What are the components of cultural intelligence? Answer the questions on this scale and calculate your score on cultural intelligence. Compare your score to those of your classmates.

3. Various Web sites list cultural blunders or *faux pas* (false steps) people make in their international interactions. Neglecting to develop relationships (as in "Just sign the contract, I'm in a hurry!") and making too-casual use of first names (as in "Just call me Bill!") are examples of such blunders. Research online sources such as International Education Systems (www.marybosrock.com), or simply by entering "cultural blunders" in an Internet search engine, to identify examples of improper cultural behaviors. How can managers avoid these errors?

CHAPTER 5

LEARNING OBJECTIVES In this chapter, you will learn about:

1. Ethics in international business
2. Corporate social responsibility
3. The role of sustainability in international operations
4. Corporate governance and Its implications for managers
5. A framework for making ethical decisions

Ethics and International Business

The Challenge of Corruption Around the World

Corruption is the abuse of power to achieve illegitimate personal gain. Bribery and corruption are extreme forms of unethical behavior. Standards of ethical behavior vary around the world. It is estimated that every year more than $1 trillion in bribes are paid worldwide to gain access to important markets and achieve other business objectives. For example, roughly 10 percent of the $4 trillion spent annually on global construction procurement is wasted through bribery and corruption. The Yacyretá hydroelectric dam was built on the border of Argentina and Paraguay, with support from the World Bank. Much of the $1.87 billion spent on the project was used fraudulently by firms engaged in its construction.

In 2009, the oil field services company Halliburton agreed to pay a $559 million fine to settle charges that one of its former units bribed Nigerian officials during the construction of a gas plant in Nigeria. As part of the investigation, a top Halliburton executive pleaded guilty to orchestrating more than $180 million in bribes and faced seven years in prison and a $10 million restitution payment.

Various bodies have issued international conventions against bribery and corruption. Numerous countries have signed the antibribery convention developed by the Organisation for Economic Co-operation and Development (OECD). The United Nations issued a declaration against corruption in international transactions. The U.S. Foreign Corrupt Practices Act (FCPA) makes it illegal for U.S. firms to offer bribes to foreign parties to secure or retain business. Under the FCPA, firms can be fined $2 million and managers can be imprisoned for up to five years.

Corruption is less prevalent in countries that have transparent accounting systems, consistently enforced anticorruption laws, governments committed to above-the-board practices, and ties to the global economy. Widespread corruption hinders economic development. This relationship points to an important dilemma: Trade and investment can help reduce poverty; yet MNEs are reluctant to do business with countries that have high levels of corruption. Corruption harms the poorest in societies, those forced to pay bribes to gain access to needed products and services, such as water, electricity, and phone service.

Corruption is frequently cited as a key contributor to poverty in Africa. Numerous African countries have been characterized by military dictatorships or other tyrannical governments. Although some rulers seek to improve conditions for their citizens, others use power for their own benefit. Among the most notorious was Mobuto Sese Seko of Zaire, whose regime looted billions from the nation's treasury. Such corruption discourages foreign MNEs from doing business in such countries.

SOURCES: Larry Beer, *Business Ethics for the Global Business and the Global Manager: A Strategic Approach* (New York: Business Expert Press, 2010); Russell Gold, "Halliburton Ex-Official Pleads Guilty in Bribe Case," *Wall Street Journal*, September 4, 2008, p. A1; Russell Gold, "Halliburton to Pay $559 Million to Settle Bribery Investigation," *Wall Street Journal*, January 27, 2009, p. B3; John Sullivan, *The Moral Compass of Companies: Business Ethics and Corporate Governance as Anti-Corruption Tools* (Washington, DC: International Finance Corporation, World Bank, 2009); Transparency International, *Progress Report: OECD Anti-Bribery Convention 2009*, retrieved from http://www.transparency.org; Transparency International, "Promoting Good Governance in Africa,"

March 5, 2009, retrieved from http://www.transparency.org; N. Watson, "Bribery Charge Hits Halliburton Profits," *Petroleum Economist*, May 2009, p. 2; John Zhao, Seung Kim, and Jianjun Du, "The Impact of Corruption and Transparency on Foreign Direct Investment: An Empirical Analysis," *Management International Review* 43, no. 1 (2003): 41–62; David Zussman, "Fighting Corruption Is a Global Concern," *Ottawa Citizen*, October 11, 2005, A15.

nappropriate corporate conduct abroad has always been a concern in international business.[1] For example, firms may:

- Falsify or misrepresent contracts or financial statements;
- Pay or accept bribes, kickbacks, or inappropriate gifts;
- Tolerate sweatshop conditions or otherwise abuse employees;
- Undertake false advertising and other deceptive marketing practices;
- Engage in deceptive, discriminatory, or predatory pricing;
- Deceive or abuse intermediaries in international channels; and
- Engage in activities that harm the natural environment.[2]

The opening vignette reveals how managers may be faced with ethical dilemmas and corruption. **Ethics** are moral principles and values that govern the behavior of people, firms, and governments regarding right and wrong.[3] **Corruption** is the abuse of power to achieve illegitimate personal gain. More than 30 percent of MNEs believe corruption is a major or severe concern in their activities worldwide.[4]

Ethics and appropriate behavior transcend all international business activities and figure prominently in management decisions about financial performance and competitive advantage. However, corruption and paying bribes are commonplace in many countries, particularly those that lack transparent business systems. Bribery frequently takes the form of *grease payments*, relatively small inducements intended to expedite decisions and transactions, or otherwise gain favors. In many countries, such facilitating payments are both legal and acceptable.

To assess the level of corruption worldwide, Transparency International (www .transparency.org) surveys business executives every year regarding their perceptions of bribery, embezzlement, and other illicit behavior in the public sector in 180 countries. The result is the Corruption Perceptions Index, shown in Exhibit 5.1. Countries with the highest scores have the lowest levels of corruption, such as Canada, Denmark, Finland, and New Zealand. Countries with the highest corruption levels include many nations in Africa and the former Soviet Union states.

Simply obeying the law is usually insufficient to ensure against violating fundamental standards of ethical behavior. This results because such standards vary around the world, which makes ethics a complex issue in international business.

Most companies seek to ensure ethical practices in their international operations. The most advanced firms proactively emphasize not just ethical behavior, but also corporate social responsibility and sustainability. **Corporate social responsibility (CSR)** means operating a business in a manner that meets or exceeds the ethical, legal, and commercial expectations of all stakeholders, including customers, shareholders, employees, and the communities where the firm does business. **Sustainability** means meeting humanity's needs without harming future generations.

An integrated, strategic approach to ethical, sustainable, and socially responsible behavior provides firms with competitive advantages, including stronger relationships

Ethics Moral principles and values that govern the behavior of people, firms, and governments regarding right and wrong.

Corruption The abuse of power to achieve illegitimate personal gain

Corporate social responsibility (CSR) A manner of operating a business that meets or exceeds the ethical, legal, commercial, and public expectations of stakeholders, including customers, shareholders, employees, and communities.

Sustainability Meeting humanity's needs without harming future generations.

with customers, employees, shareholders, suppliers, and the communities where they do business. Let's begin by discussing the critical role of ethical conduct in international business.

Ethics in International Business

Wherever they do business around the world, managers must not only avoid breaking the law, they should follow high ethical standards. Companies encounter ethical challenges in a range of international activities. One is global sourcing, the procurement of products or services from suppliers located abroad. In a typical scenario, the focal firm buys parts and components from foreign companies that manufacture such goods, or the firm may establish its own factories abroad. Global sourcing raises public debate about protecting the environment and ensuring human rights. For example, some companies operate sweatshops, factories in which employees may work long hours for very low wages, often in harsh conditions.[5] Sweatshops may also employ child labor, which is illegal in much of the world. In other cases, firms operate factories that pollute the air, water, or land.

Some firms engage in deceptive marketing practices in advertising and selling to induce people to buy their products. Others offer defective or harmful products or packaging that can lead to disastrous outcomes for public health and safety or for natural environments. For example, countless cell phones, computers, and other electronic products are discarded every year, not because they are broken but because better versions become available. Products that could be recycled instead end up in landfills.

Easy accessibility of the Internet has led shady online marketers to harm unsuspecting consumers. For example, in developing economies, the majority of online drug stores operate illegally. [6] The drugs offered by such outlets are often fake and may harm users. Phony Viagra made in Thailand was found to contain vodka; bogus Tamiflu has been manufactured with vitamin C and lactose, and some fake medications contain lethal amounts of dangerous chemicals. Although the pharmaceutical industry and governments pursue such firms, they are often elusive and beyond the reach of authorities.

Illicit use of intellectual property represents yet another ethical violation, especially common in international business. **Intellectual property** refers to ideas or works created by individuals or firms and includes a variety of proprietary, intangible assets: discoveries and inventions; artistic, musical, and literary works; and words, phrases, symbols, and designs.

Intellectual property may be stolen or copied illicitly. In Russia, for example, software and movies produced by such firms as Microsoft and Disney often fall prey to *counterfeiting;* the assets are reproduced without compensating those who originally created them. Widely recognized global brands—Rolex, Louis Vuitton, and Tommy Hilfiger, among others—often fall victim to counterfeiting, eroding firms' competitive advantages and brand equity.

Trademarks, copyrights, and patents are examples of **intellectual property rights**, the legal claim through which proprietary assets are protected from unauthorized use by other parties.

Intellectual property Ideas or works created by individuals or firms, including discoveries and inventions; artistic, musical, and literary works; and words, phrases, symbols, and designs.

Intellectual property rights The legal claim through which the proprietary assets of firms and individuals are protected from unauthorized use by other parties.

Workers at a Nike factory in Vietnam, where Nike is the largest private employer. Following charges that its foreign contract factories were run like "sweatshops," Nike took steps to improve working conditions.

GREENLAND

ICELAND

ALASKA

CANADA

PACIFIC
OCEAN

UNITED STATES
OF AMERICA

NORTH
ATLANTIC
OCEAN

MEXICO

CUBA

DOMINICAN
REPUBLIC

JAMAICA
BELIZE
HONDURAS   HAITI   PUERTO
                             RICO

GUATEMALA
EL SALVADOR   NICARAGUA   St. LUCIA
         COSTA RICA   TRINIDAD &
                  PANAMA   TOBAGO
                          VENEZUELA
GALAPAGOS   GUYANA   FRENCH
ISLANDS   COLOMBIA   SURINAME GUIANA

ECUADOR

B R A Z I L

PERU

TONGA   BOLIVIA

                      PARAGUAY

                 C
                 H
                 I
                 L   URUGUAY
                 E
                ARGENTINA

FALKLAND ISLANDS/
MALVINAS

Exhibit 5.1 Corruption Perceptions Index 2009

ARCTIC OCEAN

NORWAY
SWEDEN
FINLAND

ESTONIA
LATVIA
LITHUANIA
RUSSIA
BELARUS

UNITED
KINGDOM
DENMARK
IRELAND
NETHERLANDS
POLAND
BELGIUM
CZECH
GERMANY
REP.
LUXEMBOURG
SLOVAKIA
UKRAINE
FRANCE
LIECH. AUSTRIA
HUNGARY
MOLDOVA
SWITZ.
SLOVENIA
ROMANIA
CROATIA
MONACO
BOSNIA AND
SERBIA AND
HERZEGOVINA
MONTENEGRO
BULGARIA
SPAIN
ANDORRA
ITALY
MACEDONIA
PORTUGAL
ALBANIA
GREECE
TURKEY
CYPRUS

RUSSIA

KAZAKHSTAN

MONGOLIA

NORTH
KOREA
SOUTH
KOREA
JAPAN

GEORGIA
AZERBAIJAN
UZBEKISTAN
KYRGYZSTAN
ARMENIA
TURKMENISTAN
TAJIKISTAN
SYRIA
LEBANON
AFGHANISTAN
ISRAEL
IRAQ
IRAN
JORDAN
KUWAIT
PAKISTAN
CHINA

TUNISIA

MOROCCO
QATAR
UNITED ARAB
EMIRATES
NEPAL
BHUTAN
ALGERIA
LIBYA
EGYPT
SAUDI
ARABIA
OMAN
INDIA
BANGLADESH
MYANMAR
(BURMA)
TAIWAN
HONG KONG
PACIFIC
OCEAN

WESTERN
SAHARA
LAOS
MAURITANIA
MALI
NIGER
CHAD
ERITREA
YEMEN
THAILAND
VIETNAM
SENEGAL
SUDAN
DJIBOUTI
CAMBODIA
GAMBIA
BURKINA
FASO
GUINEA-BISSAU
GUINEA
NIGERIA
SOMALIA
PHILIPPINES
SIERRA LEONE
IVORY
COAST
GHANA
TOGO
BENIN
CENTRAL AFRICAN
REPUBLIC
ETHIOPIA
SRI
LANKA
LIBERIA
CAMEROON
BRUNEI
EQUATORIAL
GUINEA
CONGO
REPUBLIC
UGANDA
KENYA
MALAYSIA
SINGAPORE
GABON
CONGO
DEMOCRATIC
REPUBLIC
(ZAIRE)
RWANDA
BURUNDI
INDONESIA
PAPUA
NEW
GUINEA
SOLOMON
ISLANDS
TANZANIA
INDIAN
OCEAN

SOUTH
ATLANTIC
OCEAN

ANGOLA
ZAMBIA
MALAWI
MOZAMBIQUE
VANUATU
FIJI
NAMIBIA
ZIMBABWE
MADAGASCAR
MAURITIUS
RÉUNION
BOTSWANA
NEW
CALEDONIA
SWAZILAND
AUSTRALIA
SOUTH
AFRICA
LESOTHO

NEW
ZEALAND

CPI 2009

● 9.0 to 10.0	● 4.0 to 4.9
● 8.0 to 8.9	● 3.0 to 3.9
● 7.0 to 7.9	● 2.0 to 2.9
● 6.0 to 6.9	● 1.0 to 1.9
● 5.0 to 5.9	○ no data available

Trademarks are distinctive signs and indicators that firms use to identify their products and services. *Copyrights* grant protections to the creators of art, music, books, software, movies, and TV shows. *Patents* confer the exclusive right to manufacture, use, and sell products or processes. Intellectual property rights are not guaranteed in much of the world. Laws enacted in one country are enforceable only in that country and confer no protection abroad. [7]

Exhibit 5.2 documents losses from piracy, or the illicit use of copyrighted assets from around the world. For example, Disney has struggled to launch its DVD movie business in China, due to rampant local piracy. Legitimate Disney DVDs of films like *Finding Nemo* and *The Lion King* cost up to ten times as much as knockoffs, restricting sales to a trickle.[8] In Russia, illicit Web sites sell popular music downloads for as little as 5 cents apiece, or less than one U.S. dollar for an entire CD. Russia's laws regarding counterfeiting are often insufficient to thwart such crimes, and enforcement is weak.[9]

Suppose you work for a small online retailer that decides to offer pirated music via the company Web site to potential buyers in Russia and other emerging markets with weak intellectual property laws. How should you respond to this dilemma? Later in this chapter, we present a framework for ethical conduct that you can use to analyze this problem and identify an appropriate course of action.

The Value of Ethical Behavior

Behaving ethically is important for several reasons. First, ethical behavior is simply the right thing to do. Second, it is often prescribed within laws and regulations. Violating laws and regulations has obvious legal consequences. Third, ethical behavior is demanded by customers, governments, and the news media. Firms that commit ethical blunders attract unwanted attention from opinion leaders. Finally, ethical behavior is good business, leading to enhanced corporate image and selling prospects. The firm with a reputation for high ethical standards gains advantages in hiring, motivating employees, partnering, and dealing with foreign governments. Firms that behave unethically run the risk of facing criminal or civil prosecution, hurting their own reputations, harming employee morale and recruitment efforts, and/or exposing themselves to blackmailers or other unscrupulous parties.[10] For all these reasons, companies incorporate ethical considerations into their international activities. The major challenge is that ethical standards vary greatly around the world.

Variation in Ethical Standards among Countries

Appropriate behavior in one culture may be viewed as unethical behavior elsewhere.[11] In China, counterfeiters frequently publish translated versions of imported books without compensating the original publisher or authors, an illegal practice in most of the world. In parts of Africa, accepting expensive gifts from suppliers is acceptable, even if inappropriate elsewhere. In the United States, some CEOs receive compensation hundreds of times greater than that of their most junior employees, a practice widely considered unacceptable. Ethical standards also change over time. Although slavery is no longer tolerated, some multinational firms today tolerate working conditions that are akin to it.

Relativism The belief that ethical truths are not absolute but differ from group to group.

Scholars and managers examine ethics from two different perspectives.[12] **Relativism** is the belief that ethical truths are not absolute but differ from group to group; according to this perspective, a good rule is, "When in Rome, do as the Romans do." Thus, a Japanese multinational firm adhering to the position that bribery is wrong might nevertheless pay bribes in countries where the practice is customary and culturally acceptable.

Country	Books	Records & Music		Business Software	
	Losses	Losses	Levels	Losses	Levels
Brazil	$18	$117.1	48%	$905	58%
China	52	564	90	3,005	80
India	38	36.2	55	1,384	68
Italy	20	350	25	1,137	48
Malaysia	9	26.2	60	184	59
Mexico	41	419.7	80	453	59
Poland	NA	100	27	389	56
Russia	42	NA	NA	2,318	68
Spain	NA	13.4	20	617	42
Thailand	37	17.8	65	335	76

Exhibit 5.2 2008 Estimated Trade Losses Due to Copyright Piracy (in Millions of U.S. Dollars) and 2008 Estimated Levels of Copyright Piracy in Selected Countries

SOURCE: Copyright © International Intellectual Property Alliance. Reprinted with permission.

Relativists opt for passive acceptance of the values, behaviors, and practices that prevail in each of the countries where they do business.

By contrast, **normativism** is a belief that ethical behavioral standards are universal, and firms and individuals should seek to uphold them consistently around the world. According to this view, managers of the Japanese multinational firm who believe bribery is wrong will enforce this standard everywhere in the world. The United Nations and other ethics proponents encourage companies to follow a normative approach in their international dealings. Progressive firms attempt to correct unethical practices that arise in their ongoing business dealings around the world.[13]

Normativism The belief that ethical behavioral standards are universal, and firms and individuals should seek to uphold them around the world.

Most firms apply a combination of relativism and normativism abroad. Rightly or wrongly, they strike a balance between corporate values developed in the home country and local standards. However, this approach puts them at risk of violating norms that are increasingly universal. In countries with questionable ethical norms, it is usually best to maintain ethical standards *superior* to what is required by local laws and values. This strategy helps garner goodwill in the local market and averts potentially damaging publicity in the firm's other markets.

In host countries, companies are under continuous public scrutiny. Firms with iconic global brands, such as Coca-Cola, Microsoft, and Volkswagen, are especially conspicuous to consumers and can become targets of public protest. Governments are increasingly insistent about ensuring that companies behave in ways that serve the public interest. The European Union restricts the use of lead, mercury, and other harmful substances in manufacturing, and requires firms to collect and recycle unwanted electronic products. In Australia, the government has increased efforts to root out corruption. A new legislative framework aims to eliminate money laundering and other illicit activities. Canada has well-developed complaint procedures for dealing with bribery, including liaison officers

Global companies with well-known brands like McDonald's are especially conspicuous to consumers and need strong ethical values to thrive under public scrutiny. This airport restaurant is in Madrid, Spain.

in twenty-five countries and a Web site (www .recol.ca) through which anyone can make complaints about possible corruption cases.[14]

An Ethical Dilemma

Most firms attempt to satisfy ethical standards wherever they do business. However, deciding what is right and wrong is not always clear. Ethical problems arise when requirements are ambiguous, inconsistent, or based on multiple legal or cultural norms. Even when a country has a sound legal system, or even when the firm has a strong code of ethics, managers regularly face the challenge of determining appropriate behavior.

An *ethical dilemma* is a predicament with major conflicts among different interests and in which determining the most appropriate course of action is confounded by a set of solutions that are equally justifiable, and often equally imperfect. Possible actions may be mutually exclusive: The choice of one automatically negates the other(s).[15]

Imagine you are a manager and visit a factory owned by an affiliate in Colombia, only to discover the use of child labor in the plant. You are told that without the children's income, their families might go hungry. If the children are dismissed from the plant, they will likely turn to other income sources, including prostitution or street crime. What should you do? Do you make a fuss about the immorality of child labor, or do you look the other way?

This example is typical of the type of ethical dilemmas that employees frequently encounter in international business. Managers embedded in host countries may be most exposed because they are caught between home country ethical norms and those encountered in the foreign country.

Linking Ethics, Corruption, and Responsible Behavior

In a world of seemingly endless ethical challenges, how should managers and companies respond? Consider the framework in Exhibit 5.3. After complying with local law (the bottom of the pyramid), management should ensure that company activities follow high ethical standards (the middle). As they expand abroad, most firms believe it is sufficient to comply with laws, regulations, and basic ethical standards. However, in addition, progressive MNEs now emphasize socially responsible behavior (the top of the pyramid). Let's examine this notion in more detail.

Exhibit 5.3 The Pyramid of Ethical Behavior

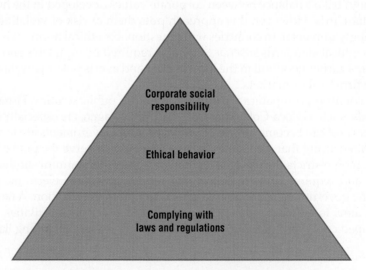

Corporate Social Responsibility

Adhering to principles of CSR implies a *proactive* approach to ethical behavior in which firms not only seek to maximize profits, but also to benefit society and the environment. Core CSR values include avoiding human rights abuses, upholding the right to join or form labor unions, eliminating compulsory and child labor, avoiding workplace discrimination, protecting the natural environment, guarding against corruption, and undertaking philanthropic efforts.[16] CSR is about business giving back to society. However, numerous firms and industries have been slow to adopt CSR.

Cigarette sales raise potential CSR concerns because more than five million people die annually from lung cancer and other ailments related to smoking. Smoking also harms national GDPs because it incurs billions in tax-funded health care costs. The average price of a pack of cigarettes is high in many countries, relative to local incomes. As cigarette sales have declined in the advanced economies, British American Tobacco, Philip Morris International, and other cigarette companies increasingly target emerging markets. In China, a pack typically sells for the equivalent of $2, but smokers earn only a few thousand dollars per year. The proportion of Chinese men who smoke is 60 percent, making crowded China home to the largest number of smokers. In the Ukraine, the average smoker consumes more than 2,500 cigarettes per year. Russia has the highest density of smokers, where 70 percent of men smoke, but average life expectancy is under 60 years, partly due to high cigarette consumption. In emerging markets, tobacco firms target cigarette sales to women, a largely untapped market, and to young people with rising incomes. Advertising portrays cigarette smoking as "hip" and "liberating."[17]

Failure to adopt CSR behaviors can have adverse, even ruinous, consequences. Efforts by the China National Petroleum Company (CNPC) to raise money on the New York Stock Exchange in 2000 were partly depressed by the firm's activities in Sudan, which human rights groups had criticized. The Shell Oil Company has experienced protests and lost revenues due to opposition of its oil-drilling activities in Nigeria, which some view as harming community interests and generating excessive pollution. In India, Walmart experienced lost sales and massive protests because of concerns the firm's market entry would hurt small retailers in the region.[18]

In contrast, numerous firms have improved their performance by adopting CSR. Petrobras (www.petrobras.com) is a Brazilian oil company that developed CSR programs aimed at reducing poverty and child labor, as well as promoting youth education and rights for people with disabilities. In Africa, Petrobras has built hospitals, schools, and day-care centers. In Colombia, it developed a program to train community health agents. In Nigeria, Petrobras cooperates with a local non-governmental organization to provide HIV/AIDS prevention education.[19]

Efficient telecommunications promote productivity and raise GDP. Motorola (www.motorola.com) has delivered more than 16 million low-cost mobile phones to people in fifty developing countries. It developed a mobile phone system for disease management in Africa, through which field health workers file patient reports and check drug supplies. Cellular connectivity helps professionals in poor areas deal more effectively with disease outbreaks, medicine shortages, and health maintenance.[20]

Exhibit 5.4 summarizes additional CSR initiatives undertaken by firms worldwide.

Environmentally friendly policies are an important part of most corporate social responsibility programs. Accepting computers and parts for recycling is an example of Dell Computer's CSR initiatives.

Company	Industry	Sample Accomplishments
ABN AMRO (Netherlands)	Financial services	Finances various socially responsible projects, including biomass fuels and micro enterprises. Involved in carbon-emissions trading.
Dell (United States)	Computers	Accepts old computers from customers for recycling, free of charge.
GlaxoSmithKline (Britain)	Pharmaceuticals	Devotes substantial R&D to poor-country ailments, such as malaria and tuberculosis. Was first to offer AIDS medication at cost.
Marks & Spencer (Britain)	Retailing	Sources locally in order to cut fuel use and transportation costs. Provides good wages and benefits to retain staff.
Nokia (Finland)	Telecommunications	Makes telephones for low-income consumers. Has been a leader in environmental practices, such as phasing out toxic materials.
Norsk Hydro (Norway)	Oil and gas	Cut greenhouse gas emissions by 32 percent. Consistently measures the social and environmental impact of its projects.
Philips Electronics (Netherlands)	Consumer electronics	Top innovator of energy-saving appliances and lighting products, as well as medical devices for developing economies.
Scottish & Southern (Scotland)	Utilities	Proactively discloses the environmental risk, including air pollution and climate change, posed by its services.
Toyota (Japan)	Automobiles	The world leader in developing efficient gas-electric vehicles, such as the top-selling Prius.

Exhibit 5.4   Corporate Social Responsibility: A Sampling of MNE Accomplishments

SOURCE: Engardio, Pete. "Beyond the Green Corporation," *Business Week*, January 29, 2007, pp. 50–64.

The Value of CSR

As with ethical behavior, there is a strong business case for CSR.[21] First, as with ethical behavior, CSR is simply the right thing to do. Second, it helps the firm recruit and retain high-quality employees. It also improves employee perceptions of the firm, which in turn enhances their loyalty and focus on company goals. Third, strong CSR can help the firm differentiate itself in the marketplace and enhance its brand, which is particularly useful in foreign markets where the entrant may be unknown or struggling against local competitors. Fourth, CSR is a factor in cutting the cost of doing business. For example, firms save money and other resources when they take steps to minimize packaging, recycle materials, economize on energy usage, and reduce waste in their operations. Finally, CSR helps the firm avoid increased taxation, regulation, or other legal actions by local government authorities. In 2009, Denmark enacted a law that requires companies to incorporate CSR activities and report on them in their financial reports.

Consumers, other stakeholders, and the media increasingly look to companies to be socially and environmentally responsible. Communications technology allows them to learn quickly about the misdeeds of any firm with which they do business. Over time

GL○BAL TREND

Global Corporate Social Responsibility Rises to the Top of the MNE Agenda

As companies internationalize, they increasingly confront the question of how to be good global citizens. Global corporate social responsibility addresses issues such as workers' rights, workers' pay compared to a reasonable living standard, company activities that disrupt traditional communities and lifestyles, and environmental damage. A study by McKinsey & Co. found executives worldwide overwhelmingly embrace the idea that firms have societal and environmental obligations in addition to ensuring profitability.

IKEA (www.ikea.com) proactively promotes social and environmental responsibility. The firm employs its own specially trained auditors and environmental coordinators. Its products must be manufactured under acceptable working conditions by suppliers who take responsibility for the environment. All must meet the standards of the Forest Stewardship Council. IKEA and its suppliers work closely with UNICEF, Save the Children, and the World Wildlife Fund to prevent child labor and support responsible forestry. All work is in conjunction with the UN Convention on the Rights of the Child (1989). The IKEA Foundation supports various charitable causes through generous contributions.

Governments and stakeholders have expectations of how multinational firms should fulfill their global social responsibilities. Appropriate actions include contributing to a region's employment opportunities, protecting workers and communities from physical harm, providing good working conditions, avoiding discriminatory hiring and work practices, maintaining transparency and avoiding corruption, reducing poverty and injustice, and improving access to quality health care and education.

Accepting social and environmental accountability is increasingly part of how international business gets done. The task is complex, because when companies step onto the global stage, they encounter a wide variety of stakeholders whose expectations often appear overwhelming or even contradictory. Social and environmental problems can appear baffling to headquarters managers, who may lack international experience. Thus, country managers often decide what issues are important and how to address them.

SOURCES: McKinsey & Co., "From Risk to Opportunity: How Global Executives View Sociopolitical Issues: The McKinsey Quarterly Survey on the Role of Business in Society," 2006, retrieved from http://www.mckinseyquarterly.com; L. Kaufmann, F. Reimann, M. Ehrgott, and J. Rauer, "Sustainable Success," *Wall Street Journal*, June 22, 2009, retrieved from http://www.wsj.com; Center for Corporate Citizenship, *Going Global: Managers' Experiences Working with Worldwide Stakeholders* (Boston: Boston College, 2005).

many consumers tend to choose products made by firms with strong CSR. The *Global Trend* feature elaborates on the role of corporate social responsibility in the multinational firm.

In addition to profit-seeking focal firms, more non-governmental organizations (NGOs) are undertaking international CSR initiatives, often in conjunction with multinational firms. For example, such NGOs as CARE, Médecins Sans Frontières, and the Bangladesh Rural Advancement Committee work to reduce global poverty and frequently partner with private companies to provide vital products and services.[22]

 ## The Role of Sustainability in International Operations

In a world of increasing population and finite resources, ever-expanding trade and investment have important implications for Earth and the future of humankind. Sustainability is an ideal endorsed by economic development experts, environmentalists, and human rights activists. Companies also increasingly embrace sustainability issues. The Canadian aluminum giant Alcan (www.alcan.com) has invested huge sums to develop clean, fuel-efficient manufacturing technologies. By emphasizing sustainability, Alcan reduced its greenhouse gas output by one-quarter, while increasing production by 40 percent. Alcan is in the process of installing additional technology that will further reduce toxic emissions, while increasing energy efficiency in its smelting plants.[23]

The supermarket chain Tesco (www.tesco.com) uses wind power to provide electricity for many of its U.K. stores and has installed massive solar panels on its U.S. facilities. The firm has substantially cut energy usage in its warehouses and operates low-pollution transportation in its supply chains. It attempts to measure the "carbon costs" of each item it sells to reduce the pollution burden of serving customer needs. Customers are rewarded for bringing reusable shopping bags to stores, instead of using disposable plastic. Senior managers' bonuses are partly based on their meeting energy- and waste-reduction targets.[24]

A sustainable business simultaneously pursues three types of interests:[25]

1. *Economic interests* refer to the firm's economic impact on the localities where it does business. Management considers the effect of the firm's activities on such local concerns as job creation, wages, tax flows, disadvantaged communities, public works, and other areas where the firm can contribute positively to local economic interests.

2. *Social interests* refer to how the firm performs relative to societies and social justice, often termed *social impact*. The firm with a strong social interest aims to optimize work conditions and diversity in hiring. It avoids using sweatshops, child labor, and other practices that harm workers. Instead, the sustainable firm provides safe work environments, health insurance, retirement benefits, and educational opportunities for employees.

3. *Environmental interests* refer to the extent of the firm's contribution to preserving environmental quality, commonly known as *environmental impact*. This concept refers to reducing the effect of the firm's value-chain activities on the natural environment. The sustainable firm maximizes its use of recycled or renewable raw materials and environmentally friendly energy. It minimizes pollutants, designs production lines to use water and energy efficiently, and constantly seeks ways to reduce waste. Many firms establish a green purchasing policy, through which they source inputs that support environmental interests.

The most advanced companies monitor suppliers to ensure that they use sustainable practices. For example, following charges that some of its Indian subcontractors were using forced child labor, GAP withdrew a line of children's wear from its clothing stores worldwide. Sustainable firms usually opt for local suppliers to reduce the pollution caused by transporting goods long distances.

Like CSR, sustainable practices pay off in various ways, such as promoting a strong corporate reputation, the ability to hire and retain superior employees, cost savings from more efficient production, better linkages with suppliers, and smoother relations with foreign governments.

Achieving sustainability often requires the firm to be flexible and creative. A good example is Coca-Cola, which had to deal with water sustainability challenges. As water resources dwindled in some countries, Coke began to experience conflicts with communities and other water users, especially in India. To address such challenges, Coke developed a water sustainability program that goes well beyond efficiency and legal compliance needs alone. Management devised global projects that protect water resources and ensure access to clean drinking water. Coke mobilized the international community to anticipate and deal with ever-severe water crises worldwide.[26]

As water grows scarce in many parts of the world, some multinational firms are taking a closer look at their use of this critical resource. Coca-Cola, a major consumer of water, conducts a water sustainability program in India, where conflict over water use had begun to grow.

Corporate Governance and Its Implications for Managers

The challenge for management is to increase awareness of ethical, CSR, and sustainability issues throughout the firm and to view them not just as added costs, but as opportunities for improving society, the environment, and company performance. The level of managers' commitment to appropriate behavior is critical to fostering ethics and CSR in international operations.[27] **Corporate governance** is the system of procedures and processes by which corporations are managed, directed, and controlled. It provides the means through which firms undertake ethical behaviors, CSR, and sustainability.

How does corporate governance help firms support ethical behaviors, CSR, and sustainability? First, individual employees must learn to recognize and manage the ethical problems that confront the firm. Let's explore this issue in detail.

Scholars have devised five standards that managers can use to examine ethical dilemmas.[28] According to the *utilitarian approach*, the best ethical action is the one that provides the most good or does the least harm or, stated differently, produces the greatest balance of good over harm to customers, employees, shareholders, the community, and the natural environment.

In the *rights approach*, the decision maker chooses the action that best protects and respects the moral rights of everyone involved. It is based on the belief that, regardless of how you deal with an ethical dilemma, human dignity must be preserved. Accordingly, humans are entitled to certain moral rights, including the right to live life as one desires, to be free from harm, to pursue happiness, and so forth.

The *fairness approach* suggests that everyone should be treated equally and fairly. Workers should be paid a fair wage that provides a decent standard of living, and colleagues and customers should be treated as we would like to be treated.

The *common good approach* suggests that actions should be based on the welfare of the entire community or nation. It asks which action contributes most to the quality of life of all affected people. The interlocking relationships of society are the basis of ethical reasoning in this view. Respect and compassion for all, especially the vulnerable, should be the basis for decision making.

Finally, the *virtue approach* argues that ethical actions should be consistent with certain ideal virtues that provide for the full development of our humanity. The most important virtues are truth, courage, compassion, generosity, tolerance, love, integrity, and prudence.

Using these five approaches to analyze ethical dilemmas can be challenging because they occasionally conflict with each other, and not everyone agrees on which standard to use in all situations. Different cultures adhere to differing norms of morality and human rights and basic standards of right and wrong. Moreover, many ethical dilemmas are complex and proposed approaches may not provide adequate guidance in determining the best course of action. Nevertheless, each standard is useful because it helps guide ethical behavior in almost any predicament. More often than not, they lead to similar solutions.

How should you decide what constitutes ethical behavior? First, be sensitive to the existence of ethical problems. Before entering a country and throughout the life of the firm's operations there, management must be alert to the various ethical challenges that may confront the firm. Management should scan the country and potential partners for the possibility of ethical abuses. Such scanning is an ongoing process. Managers need to acquire a vigilance that they apply to current and potential company activities on a continuous basis. The process is challenging due to the substantial unknowns present in most foreign settings. However, with enough practice, management creates a systematic approach to scanning and a culture within the firm that supports alertness and ongoing analysis of potential ethical concerns. Management should focus not only on specific national environments but also on proposed and existing value-chain activities, which often take place in multiple countries. In each country and venture, areas that merit particular attention encompass commercial environments, labor conditions, partner

Corporate governance
The system of procedures and processes by which corporations are managed, directed, and controlled.

firms, customers, accounting practices, and conditions regarding the natural environment, as well as the range of the firm's potential or existing value-chain activities, including sourcing, production, marketing, and distribution.

Once management possesses this ongoing awareness of potential ethical abuses, the next step is to systematically explore the ethical aspects of each decision the firm may make regarding its current and potential activities. In helping identify ethical problems, the firm should develop a cogent and practicable *code of ethics*, a formal statement that describes what management expects of employees in the face of ethical challenges.[29] In international business, the code should be designed to function like a moral compass for the firm's operations worldwide. Like a mission statement, it should guide employee behavior in all situations, so the firm avoids behaviors that compromise corporate ethical standards wherever it does business. The code is not a cure-all, but it can help employees deal with ethical dilemmas by prescribing or limiting specific activities.

To further clarify the process of scanning for and analyzing potential ethical concerns, we provide a framework for making ethical decisions in the shaded exhibit.

A Framework for Making Ethical Decisions

Scholars suggest that managers follow a systematic approach to resolving ethical dilemmas. With practice, it can become second nature. Here is a four-step framework for arriving at ethical decisions: [30]

1. *Recognize an ethical problem.* The first step is to acknowledge the presence of an ethical problem. Ask questions such as: Is there something wrong? Is an ethical dilemma present? Is there a situation that might harm personnel, customers, the community, or the nation? In international business, recognizing the issue can be tricky because subtleties of the situation may be outside your knowledge or experience. Often, it is best to rely on your instincts: If some action feels wrong, it probably is.

2. *Get the facts.* Determine the nature and dimensions of the situation. Have all the relevant persons and groups been consulted? What individuals or groups have a stake in the outcome? How much weight should be given to the interests of each? Do some parties have a greater stake because they are disadvantaged or have a special need?

3. *Evaluate alternative courses of action.* Identify potential courses of action and evaluate each. Initially, consistent with the pyramid of ethical behavior, review any proposed action to ensure it is legal. If it violates host or home country laws or international treaties, it should be rejected. Next, review any proposed action to ensure it is acceptable according to company policy, the firm's code of conduct, and/or its code of ethics. If discrepancies are found, the action should be rejected. Finally, evaluate each proposed action to assess its consistency with accepted ethical standards, using the approaches described earlier:

   - Utilitarian—which action results in the most good and least harm?

   - Rights—which action respects the rights of everyone involved?

   - Fairness—which action treats people most fairly?

   - Common good—which action contributes most to the overall quality of life of the people affected?

   - Virtue—which action embodies the character strengths you value?

The goal is to arrive at the best decision or most appropriate course of action. It may be useful to enlist the aid of local colleagues familiar with the situation, to provide insights and help generate options. Assess the consequences of each action from the perspective of all parties who will be affected by it. Any decision should be tested by asking if you would feel comfortable explaining it to your mother, a colleague you respect, or a valued mentor. If you had to defend the decision on television, would you be comfortable doing so?

4. *Implement and evaluate your decision.* Implement your decision. Then evaluate it to see how effective it was. How did it turn out? If you had it to do again, would you do anything differently?

The steps in this framework will help you arrive at appropriate solutions to ethical dilemmas. To briefly illustrate, let's revisit the example of you as a manager visiting a company factory in Colombia, where you discover child labor. Without the children's income, their families may go hungry, or the children may turn to illicit activity, such as street crime. Having recognized the problem, you obtain more facts by consulting colleagues both at the plant and headquarters. You seek information on the status of the employed children, as well as local law and customs on child labor. You then evaluate possible solutions, ensuring they are legal and consistent with company policy. Keeping the five ethical standards in mind, you evaluate each proposed action. Finally, you choose the best one and act on it.

Embracing CSR and Sustainability

In a world ever sensitive to social and environmental issues, managers increasingly undertake the following types of activities:

- Develop closer relations with foreign stakeholders to better understand their needs and jointly work toward solutions
- Build internal and external capabilities to enhance the firm's contribution to the local community and global environment
- Ensure diverse voices are heard by creating organizational structures that employ managers and workers from around the world
- Develop global CSR standards and objectives that are communicated and implemented across the firm worldwide
- Train managers in global CSR principles and integrate these into managerial responsibilities

Ethical behavior and CSR must become a key part of managers' day-to-day pursuits. MNE activities generate environmental harm and bring firms into contact with various activities—from R&D to manufacturing to marketing—that can pose various ethical dilemmas. Business executives should balance their obligation to shareholders with explicit contributions to the broader public good. Most executives agree that generating high returns for investors should be accompanied by a focus on providing good jobs, supporting social causes in local communities, and going beyond legal requirements to minimize pollution and other negative effects of business.

A Global Consensus

Incorporating ethics, CSR, and sustainability into global operations is a path to long-term superior performance. Various resources are available to assist managers. International organizations such as the United Nations, the World Bank, and the International Monetary Fund have launched programs to combat international corruption. The International Chamber of Commerce has adopted "Rules of Conduct to Combat Extortion and Bribery," and the United Nations issued a "Declaration against Corruption and Bribery in International Commercial Transactions." The Organisation for Economic Cooperation and Development (OECD) has developed an antibribery agreement, which was signed by its thirty member nations (essentially, all the advanced economies) plus several Latin American countries.[31]

The *United Nations Global Compact* (see www.unglobalcompact.org) is a policy platform and practical framework for companies committed to sustainability and responsible business practices. It seeks to align business operations and strategies with universally accepted principles in the areas of human rights, labor, corruption, and the natural environment. It is the world's largest voluntary corporate citizenship initiative, representing thousands of businesses in more than 135 countries.

The *Global Reporting Initiative* (www.globalreporting.org) pioneered the development of the most widely used sustainability reporting framework. The framework sets out the principles and indicators that organizations can use to measure and report their economic, environmental, and social performance. Today, most large MNEs produce sustainability reports, many following the GRI guidelines.

Ultimately, CSR and sustainability require the firm to go "deep, wide, and local." *Going deep* means institutionalizing appropriate behavior into the organization's culture so it becomes part and parcel of strategy. *Going wide* implies a continuous effort to understand how CSR and sustainability affect every aspect of the firm's operations worldwide. *Going local* goes hand-in-hand with globalization. It requires the firm to examine its global operations to identify and improve specific local issues that affect customers, competitive position, reputation, and any other dimension that affects the firm's operations worldwide.[32]

To make ethical practices, CSR, and sustainability succeed in the firm, it is important to undertake a systematic and ongoing process of education for employees, suppliers, and intermediaries alike. As the firm builds a track record of changes and successes, it will begin to build a culture of appropriate behavior in its operations worldwide.

Ethics, CSR, and Sustainability in Practice

Developing and implementing appropriate conduct pose various challenges for the multinational firm.[33] For companies that operate in dozens of countries, deciding which laws and regulations to follow is often ambiguous. At minimum, the firm must adhere to the law of the country where it does business. But occasionally such laws conflict with, or fall short of, home-country laws. For example, in the United States, the Occupational Safety and Health Administration (OSHA) specifies numerous regulations regarding labor and employment conditions. When operating abroad, should the U.S. firm adhere only to local regulations, or should it follow OSHA standards as well? Should management decide which regulations are best and then follow them? If the host country has no laws or agencies controlling the matter, where should management turn for guidance?

In many industries (e.g., oil, minerals, agriculture, textiles), MNEs operate in countries characterized by governments that repress human rights. Some of the world's richest and most important resources are found in countries with such regimes. What is management's responsibility when considering entry and operations in such countries? Activists argue that firms should avoid operating in repressive regimes. Others say promoting economic development through commerce helps reduce despotism and improves peoples' lives. Which approach is best?

Another issue is the use of third-party suppliers and contractors, many of whose activities offend ethical values. In the shoe industry, for example, several well-known firms have contracted factories abroad with sweatshop conditions. A key question centers on the MNE's responsibility for knowing about and taking steps to improve such conditions. Activists argue that before partnering with another firm, management should: (a) investigate its workplace and operating methods; (b) hold it to appropriate ethical conduct; and (c) monitor its activities to ensure compliance with accepted norms. But such thoroughness is costly and takes time. Many firms, especially SMEs, lack the resources to ensure partner operations are consistently ethical. How then does the MNE with numerous partners strike the right balance between assuring ethical behavior and the costs of such assurance? The issue is particularly challenging for international firms like Nike, Sony, or Philips, with thousands of partners operating in various cultures and belief systems worldwide.

More and more firms recognize the need to incorporate ethics and CSR into their mission and strategic planning. Managers increasingly account for ethical behavior and responsible practices in the development of planning, strategy and everyday operations. Such matters no longer can be relegated to the "back burner" in global firms. Responsible global leadership must incorporate such components alongside traditional business disciplines that facilitate management in the global enterprise. As they ply the waters of international business, addressing the moral integrity of strategic and daily operational decisions is a prime consideration for companies today.[34]

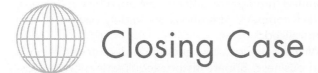 # Closing Case

Corruption at Siemens

One day in 2004, a senior executive at Siemens Company said he received a disturbing phone call from a Saudi Arabian businessman. The caller said he represented a Saudi consulting firm that had been a business partner of Siemens. He wanted $910 million in U.S. currency in payments and if Siemens didn't pay up, he would forward documents to government authorities detailing bribes paid on Siemens' behalf to win telecommunications contracts in Saudi Arabia. The incident was the beginning of a series of events—police raids, forensic investigations, and arrests of top executives—that became one of the biggest corruption cases in corporate history.

Based in Germany, Siemens is one of the world's largest electronics and industrial engineering firms. It produces industrial controls, lighting products, power generation equipment, and transportation systems. Siemens operates in 190 countries and recently generated annual revenues exceeding $100 billion.

A Culture of Corruption?

Since the 1970s, Siemens has been stung by a series of scandals, many of them including accusations of bribery brought by governments in numerous countries, the European Union, and the United Nations. One former executive was accused of handling $77 million in bribes. Another admitted to bribing a labor union. A court found that in 2007 Siemens had paid millions to bribe government officials in Libya, Nigeria, and Russia.

Investigators alleged there was a culture at Siemens, endorsed by senior managers, to use bribes and slush funds to win contracts, especially in its communications and power-generation divisions. Millions of dollars were regularly dispensed, the money carted off to foreign destinations in suitcases by managers who often felt confident they were doing "business as usual."

Reckoning and Deliverance

In the end, bribery caught up with Siemens. In a ruling under the Foreign Corrupt Practices Act, U.S. authorities ordered the company to pay $800 million in fines. The United States found that, in order to win infrastructure contracts, Siemens allegedly spent more than $1 billion bribing government officials around the world, including the former President of Argentina. The U.S. Securities and Exchange Commission (SEC) claimed that Siemens made more than 4,000 bribe payments over seven years. Payments were intended to obtain contracts to supply medical devices in Russia, transmission lines in China, transit systems in Venezuela, medical equipment in Vietnam, power equipment in Iraq, and telecommunications equipment in Bangladesh. In 2006, a U.S. grand jury indicted Siemens and two of its employees in a fraud scheme to pay $500,000 to win a $49 million contract. In 2007, two former Siemens officials were convicted of bribery for their involvement in multimillion-dollar payments to officials of a power utility in Italy.

In response to the scandals, some Siemens customers indicated they would delay ordering telecommunications equipment from the firm, and Nokia Corporation announced it would postpone a planned joint venture. In 2008, Siemens' profits declined, partly due to the creation of a fund for expenses related to bribery investigations. In 2009, the World Bank required Siemens to pay $100 million to help global anticorruption efforts and to forego bidding on World Bank development projects for two years. In the end, Siemens' two top executives, the chairman and the CEO, were forced to resign.

In Germany, Siemens executives indicted in the scandal received only suspended prison sentences. A German court ordered Siemens to pay $284 million, a modest fine for a firm that usually generates billions in annual net profits.

Germany is the world's leading exporter, and bribery cases often include efforts to generate foreign business, especially in developing economies. Until 1999, German firms were permitted to write off such bribes as business expenses. Many European countries did not outlaw paying bribes overseas until the late 1990s.

Remedial Actions

In the wake of the scandal, Siemens management took steps to prevent further bribery. The company appointed a law firm to conduct an independent review of its compliance system and uncover possible improprieties. Sixty-five countries were flagged for scrutiny. Siemens' own internal investigation identified more than $1.5 billion in suspicious transactions worldwide between 2000 and 2006. Management remarked on the difficulty of closely monitoring activities of the firm's 430,000 employees in 190 countries and bank accounts that once numbered 5,000 and handled up to 50 million transactions a day. International subsidiaries were free to act with substantial autonomy.

Siemens hired an independent ombudsman, strengthened its business-conduct code, and established a task force to improve internal controls over international funds transfers, reduce the number of bank accounts, and supervise the opening and maintaining of bank accounts. Subsidiaries were required to provide comprehensive details of all transactions. The German government tightened standards for managers, seeking to ensure that those at all large firms report regularly to supervisory boards regarding compliance with ethics codes.

Conclusion

In the United States, the number of companies reporting foreign corruption investigations into their activities abroad is up sharply. Foreign companies that do business in the U.S. are attracting greater scrutiny as well. In most countries, however, antibribery laws are weak or poorly enforced. Bribery is difficult to detect when funds are channeled through consultants and other intermediaries, or when company operations are widely dispersed and decentralized.

Why should firms care about bribery? For one thing, it is bad business. Bribery distorts legitimate efforts to sustain and enhance company performance. Where corruption becomes a pattern, eventually the firm is caught and its reputation tarnished. Corruption also inhibits development in poor countries and is at the root of persistent poverty in many. It sustains repressive governments and can lead to the failure of societies and national economies.

The best firms create a culture in which ethical conduct is valued as highly as efforts to maximize sales and profits. It is insufficient to merely publicize the need for integrity; managers must lead through ongoing actions that demonstrate adherence to ethical standards. They should establish transparency and compliance processes that ensure senior executives know what is going on throughout the firm.

AACSB: Reflective Thinking Skills, Multicultural and Diversity Understanding, Ethical Understanding and Reasoning Abilities

Case Questions

1. What does the case suggest is the value of ethical behavior? What did Siemens gain by introducing controls to minimize the likelihood of corruption?

2. Most countries lack adequate laws or enforcement to deal with bribery and other forms of corruption. Why is this? How do countries benefit from a strong rule of law that minimizes corruption?

3. Do you think Siemens was penalized enough for its corruption? Why or why not? What can governments or other organizations do to discourage firms and others from engaging in corrupt behavior?

4. Some argue that because ethical standards are lax in many countries, Siemens and other firms must pay bribes to obtain new business. Do you agree with this view? Stated differently, when doing business around the world, is it generally better to emphasize normativism or relativism? Justify your answer.

SOURCES: M. Esterl, "Corruption Probes Threaten Germany's Image," *Wall Street Journal*, November 24, 2006, p. A3; M. Esterl and D. Crawford, "Siemens to Pay Huge Fine in Bribery Inquiry," *Wall Street Journal*, December 15, 2008, p. B1; "Siemens to Tighten Controls on Money," *Financial Times*, April 18, 2007, p. 16; "Action against Bribery Requires Political Will," *Financial Times*, April 10, 2007, p. 14; V. Fuhrmans, "Siemens Settles with World Bank on Bribes," *Wall Street Journal*, July 3, 2009, p. B1; M. Hamblen, "Selloff Plans, Fraud Probe Put Spotlight on Siemens," *Computerworld*, December 18, 2006, p. 12; R. Minder, "Siemens Bows to Pressure for Transparency," *Financial Times*, December 12, 2006, p. 24; A. Preuschat, "Siemens Posts Loss Due to Charges But Says Its Orders Remain Strong," *Wall Street Journal*, November 14, 2008, p. B3; C. Verschoor, "Siemens AG Is Latest Fallen Ethics Idol," *Strategic Finance* 89 no. 5 (2007): 11–13; "Two Siemens Ex-Officials Convicted in Bribery Case," *Wall Street Journal*, May 15, 2007, p. C6; D. Crawford and M. Esterl, "Siemens Fine Ends a Bribery Probe," *Wall Street Journal*, October 5, 2007, p. A2; D. Crawford and M. Esterl, "Siemens Probe Spotlights Murky Role of Consultants," *Wall Street Journal*, April 20, 2007, p. A1; D. Crawford and M. Esterl, "Widening Scandal: At Siemens, Witnesses Cite Pattern of Bribery," *Wall Street Journal*, January 31, 2007, p. A1; M. Esterl, "Ethics Hurdle: Corruption Scandal at Siemens May Derail Restructuring Drive," *Wall Street Journal*, December 18, 2006, p. A1; M. Esterl, "Siemens CEO Hopes New Audit Cuts Scope of Suspected Fraud," *Wall Street Journal*, December 22, 2006, p. B.4; R. Milne, "Siemens 'Had a System for Paying Bribes,'" *Financial Times*, March 14, 2007, p. 27; R. Milne and M. Scheele, "Probe Finds 'General Practice' of Alleged Bribery at Siemens," *Financial Times*, May 7, 2007, p. 1; D. Crawford and M. Esterl, "Siemens Ruling Details Bribery Across the Globe," *Wall Street Journal*, November 16, 2007, p. A1; D. Crawford and M. Esterl, "Inside Bribery Probe of Siemens," *Wall Street Journal*, December 28, 2007, p. A4; M. Esterl and D. Crawford, "Ex-Siemens Manager Sentenced," *Wall Street Journal*, November 25, 2008, p. B.2; M. Esterl and D. Crawford, "At Siemens, A Conviction Could Trigger More Cases," *Wall Street Journal*, July 29, 2008, p. B1; "Stopping the Rot; Face Value," *The Economist*, March 8, 2008, p. 89; "Bavarian Baksheesh; The Siemens Scandal," *The Economist*, December 20, 2008, p. 112.

CHAPTER ESSENTIALS

Key Terms

corporate governance, p. 167
corporate social responsibility (CSR),
   p. 156
corruption, p. 156

ethics, p. 156
intellectual property, p. 157
intellectual property rights, p. 157
normativism, p. 161

relativism, p. 160
sustainability, p. 156

Summary

In this chapter, you learned about:

1. Ethics in international business

Ethics are the moral principles and values that govern the behavior of people, firms, and governments. Ethical standards vary around the world. **Relativism** is the belief that ethical truths are not absolute but differ from group to group. **Normativism** holds that ethical standards are universal, and firms and individuals should seek to uphold them consistently around the world. An *ethical dilemma* is a predicament with major conflicts among different interests. Determining the best course of action is confounded by several possible solutions that may be equally justifiable. Governments aim to protect **intellectual property**. However, protection is not guaranteed in much of the world. Maintaining **corporate social responsibility (CSR)** means operating a business in a manner that meets or exceeds the ethical, legal, commercial, and public expectations of stakeholders. **Sustainability** refers to meeting humanity's needs without harming future generations.

2. Corporate social responsibility

In addition to complying with laws, regulations, and basic ethical standards, prudent MNEs emphasize corporate social responsibility in their activities. A strong business rationale for CSR includes the firm's ability to motivate employees and develop superior strategy. Failure to develop a CSR has important negative consequences for the firm.

3. The role of sustainability in international operations

Sustainable businesses simultaneously pursue three types of interests: economic, social, and environmental. They maximize the use of recycled or renewable materials and environmentally friendly energy. They reduce waste in manufacturing and minimize harmful air and water pollution. They provide health insurance and training and care for employees in various other ways. They are active in the local community with initiatives in education, health care, and environmental protection. Sustainable firms choose and work with suppliers that adhere to high social and environmental standards.

4. Corporate governance and its implications for managers

A focus on ethics, CSR, and sustainability is in the firm's best interests, in terms of business strategy and organizational performance. Scholars have devised five standards managers can use to examine ethical dilemmas, based on utilitarianism, rights, fairness, common good, and virtue. Senior managers should develop a *code of ethics* that describes what the firm expects of its employees when facing ethical dilemmas.

5. A framework for making ethical decisions

Scholars have devised a four-step framework for making ethical decisions. Initially, the manager should recognize the existence of an ethical problem. The next steps are to get the facts, evaluate alternative courses of action, and then implement and evaluate the decision made. Ethical behavior and CSR must be part of managers' day-to-day pursuits. Various resources are available to assist managers, such as the United Nations and the World Bank.

Test Your Comprehension AACSB: Reflective Thinking Skills, Analytic Skills, Ethical Understanding and Reasoning Abilities

1. Distinguish between ethics and corruption in international business.

2. What is the Corruption Perceptions Index, and how can a manager use it to assess international risk?

3. Describe typical ethical problems that firms encounter in international business.

4. What is intellectual property? What industries are most affected by threats to intellectual property?

5. What advantages do firms gain from behaving according to high ethical standards?

6. Distinguish relativism and normativism. Which one should the firm apply in its activities?

7. What is an ethical dilemma? Give an example of an ethical dilemma that MNEs encounter abroad.

8. What is corporate social responsibility (CSR)? How does it differ from general ethical behavior?

9. Why is CSR important to the internationalizing firm?

10. What is sustainability? How might the firm undertake sustainability in its value-chain activities?

11. Describe the five standards managers can use to examine ethical dilemmas.

12. Describe the steps in the framework for ethical conduct.

13. What steps can the firm take to develop its orientation to CSR and sustainability in international operations?

Apply Your Understanding AACSB: Reflective Thinking Skills, Analytic Skills, Communication Abilities, Ethical Understanding and Reasoning Abilities

1. *Ethical Dilemma:* You were recently hired by ThunderCat Corporation, a major aircraft producer with a manufacturing presence in numerous countries. ThunderCat's sales personnel constantly travel the world, selling fighter jets and commercial aircraft to airlines and foreign governments. You are keenly aware that countries vary enormously in terms of culture, laws, and political systems. Top management has asked you to develop a code of ethics to guide ThunderCat employees in their interactions anywhere in the world. Given the diversity of countries where ThunderCat operates, what sort of code will you develop? What issues should you consider? Given the diversity of countries around the world, is it possible to develop a code that guides ethical behavior everywhere?

2. *Ethical Dilemma:* Royal Dutch Shell has been doing business in Nigeria since the 1920s and has announced new plans to develop oil and gas projects there. However, over the years Shell has experienced a series of complex issues. Its operations are centered in Nigeria's Ogoni region, where the local citizens have protested Shell's drilling and refining activities, which harm the natural environment and reduce the amount of available farmland. Protestors also accuse Shell of extracting wealth from the region without adequately compensating local residents. Following sabotage of its facilities, the firm suspended some of its Nigerian operations. It then came under pressure to divest its Nigerian operations and pay reparations to the local people. Despite these problems, Shell has persisted in Nigeria. Management instituted various community development programs in the region, budgeted at $50 million per year. Using the ethical framework in this chapter, identify steps Shell can take to be a better corporate citizen in Nigeria.

3. *Ethical Dilemma:* The American International Group (AIG) is the largest insurance company in the United States. In the recent global financial crisis, AIG faced financial ruin. Thus, the U.S. government used taxpayer money to loan AIG more than $170 billion in exchange for an 80 percent stake in the firm. A few months later, it was revealed that AIG had used part of the money (at least $30 billion) to pay off banks in Europe, largely for debt obligations it incurred in foreign transactions. U.S. government officials were furious. The furor intensified when AIG tried to renegotiate loans with some of its U.S. creditors, implying they were less important than the European banks. Suppose you were the Chief Financial Officer at AIG. What would you have done? How would you handle this predicament? Use the ethical framework in this chapter to analyze how AIG might have better handled the situation.

globalEDGE Internet Exercises
(http://globalEDGE.msu.edu)

AACSB: Analytic Skills, Use of Information Technology, Ethical Understanding and Reasoning Abilities

Refer to Chapter 1, page 62, for instructions on how to access and use globalEDGE™.

1. Various organizations have devised international standards for ethical corporate behavior. These include the United Nations "Universal Declaration for Human Rights" (available at www.un.org), the OECD's "Guidelines for Multinational Enterprise" (www.oecd.org), the International Labour Organization's "Minimum Labor Standards" (www.ilo.org), and the U.S. Department of Commerce's "Model Business Principles" (www.commerce.gov). Visit these online portals and prepare a set of guidelines firms can follow in pursuing acceptable ethical standards in international business.

2. Transparency International (www.transparency.org) publishes information about the nature of corruption around the world. Suppose you worked at a firm that makes computer software and wanted to begin doing business in Brazil and Russia. Your task is to examine reports and indices on these countries at the Transparency International site and write a brief report explaining how your firm should conduct business in these countries, with a view to avoiding problems associated with corruption. Key issues to consider include bribery and threats to intellectual property.

3. The Web sites for Lenovo (China; www.lenovo.com), Nokia (Finland; www.nokia.com), and Banco do Brasil (Brazil; www.bb.com.br, click on 'English') contain substantial information about how these firms undertake corporate social responsibility (CSR). Visit each Web site and write a report in which you compare and contrast each firm's CSR. Which firm appears most effective in CSR? How does the CSR of a bank differ from that of manufacturing firms such as Lenovo and Nokia? Lenovo and Banco do Brasil are based in emerging markets, while Nokia is in an advanced economy. What differences in the firms' CSR orientations can you detect based on this distinction? Justify your answer.

CHAPTER 6

LEARNING OBJECTIVES In this chapter, you will learn about:

1. Theories of international trade and investment
2. Why do nations trade?
3. How can nations enhance their competitive advantage?
4. Why and how do firms internationalize?
5. How can internationalizing firms gain and sustain competitive advantage?

Theories of International Trade and Investment

Dubai: The Path to Creating a Knowledge-Based Economy

The Persian Gulf enjoys a *comparative advantage* in oil because this natural resource is abundant in the region, compared to other areas. One of the Gulf's most intriguing locales is Dubai, a city-state on the southern Arabian Peninsula and one of the seven emirates that make up the United Arab Emirates.

Home to more than one million people, Dubai has a per-capita GDP of about US $37,000. Oil revenues have allowed it to finance the development of non-oil economic sectors. Beginning in the 1980s, local government began collaborating with private businesses to reposition Dubai as a major commercial hub, a center for international trade, finance, tourism, and e-commerce.

The public-private partnership allowed Dubai to develop a national comparative advantage in specific industrial sectors—advantages that are difficult for other states to replicate. Dubai's ambitious initiatives included the following:

- *State-of-the-art commercial infrastructure.* Dubai built the world's biggest artificial harbor to accommodate international trade and cruise ships. Every year, millions of passengers pass through Dubai's modern international airport, which serves more than 120 airlines. The country created the Jebel Ali Free Trade Zone, a massive business center that hosts and provides tax incentives to more than 2,000 firms, such as Microsoft and AT&T.
- *State-of-the-art infrastructure in information and communications technology (ICT).* Dubai created an ICT

industrial cluster, an oasis for firms in software development, business services, and e-commerce. Dubai Internet City offers foreign companies like Canon, IBM, and Siemens minimal bureaucracy, no income tax, and other incentives. Because few other countries have such cutting-edge ICT infrastructure, Dubai has a *monopolistic advantage*, leading to superior performance for its companies.

- *State-of-the-art financial infrastructure.* To nurture new business, the partnership developed the "Dubai Ideas Oasis," a community of entrepreneurs and venture capitalists. It also established the Dubai International Financial Center, home to dozens of global banks and financial services firms.
- *Attractive urban environment.* The partnership developed Burj al Arab, a stunning hotel and a landmark recognized worldwide, and the Creek, an eight-mile waterway lined with dazzling buildings, monuments, restaurants, and retail stores.
- *Educational infrastructure.* The country launched The Dubai Knowledge Village, inviting foreign universities and training institutes to offer their services. Other educational initiatives ensure a pool of trained knowledge workers. English is the official language in most Dubai schools.
- *Progressive labor laws.* The government devised labor laws to ensure that industry needs for part-time and temporary workers are quickly met. A fast-track immigration process and 24-hour visa service guarantee quick access to needed international talent.

The Emirate of Dubai is a leading example of countries that have successfully repositioned themselves to create comparative advantages. Its transformation into a knowledge-based economy has been remarkable. Oil and gas production now contribute only 6 percent of GDP. It is all part of a plan to transform the nation into what might be termed "Dubai Inc." Beginning in late 2008, however, Dubai was hit hard by the global recession and financial crisis. The cause of the crisis was collapsing real estate values. As in much of the world, Dubai's assets were concentrated in major property developments, a collection of construction projects ostentatious in design and price. Problems arose when tightening credit collided with the global recession to scare away international investors who had fanned years of rising real estate prices.

By 2009, the collapse of global real estate values had transformed central Dubai into a collection of half-finished skyscrapers. Dozens of high-profile projects, such as Nakheel's Harbour and Tower project (valued at US $38 billion) and Tatweer's 6,500-room

Asia-Asia Hotel ($3.3 billion), fell into financial trouble. In all, Dubai's companies racked up some $70 billion in debt, almost as big as the Emirate's annual GDP. The crisis was especially hard for the region's 1.2 million migrant workers, many of whom lost their jobs and returned home to Bangladesh, Pakistan, and other poor countries.

By 2011, the global financial system was improving. The Emirate is the region's main trading hub, with ports and other infrastructure unmatched in the Gulf. Tourism is recovering and Dubai likely will remain a favorite base for global finance in the Middle East. To fully recover, it needs to attract more inward investment and focus on sensible, self-sustaining development.

SOURCES: Central Intelligence Agency, *CIA World Factbook,* 2009, retrieved from http://www.cia.gov/cia; Dubai Internet City Web site, http://www.dubaiinternetcity.com; "The outstretched palm: Dubai's bail-out," *Economist,* February 28, 2009, p. 78; International Monetary Fund, *United Arab Emirates: Statistical Appendix.* IMF Country Report No. 07/348, October 2007, retrieved from http://www.imf.org; Hugh Pope, "Why Is the Tech Set Putting Down Roots in the Desert?" *Wall Street Journal,* January 23, 2001, p. A18; R. Priyadarshini, "Crisis in the Desert," *Business Today,* April 19, 2009.

In this chapter, we explain why nations and firms trade and invest internationally.[1] We explain why such participation allows nations to acquire and sustain comparative advantage and why it enables firms to acquire and sustain competitive advantage in the global marketplace. We review leading theories of why nations and firms undertake international activities. We address such questions as:

- What is the underlying economic rationale for international business activity?
- Why does trade take place?
- What are the gains from trade and investment?

To illustrate the theories, we will refer to Sony Corporation (www.sony.com) and other companies throughout this chapter. Sony has annual revenues exceeding USD $100 billion and is a world leader in consumer electronics products like PlayStation. Sony's wide-ranging experience since its founding in 1946 is useful for explaining the why and how of international business.

Comparative advantage
Superior features of a country that provide unique benefits in global competition, typically derived from either natural endowments or deliberate national policies.

 Theories of International Trade and Investment

For centuries, scholars have offered theories and economic rationales for international trade and investment. They have debated why nations should promote trade and investment with other nations, and how they create and sustain comparative advantage. **Comparative advantage** describes superior features of a country that provide unique benefits in global competition, typically derived from either natural endowments or deliberate national policies. Also known as *country-specific advantage*, comparative advantage includes inherited resources, such as labor, climate, arable land, and petroleum reserves, such as those enjoyed by the Gulf nations. Other types of comparative advantages are acquired over time, such as entrepreneurial orientation, availability of venture capital, and innovative capacity.

Over time, to understand why companies engage in cross-border business, the focus of research shifted from the nation to the individual firm. This work produced the concept of **competitive advantage**, which describes organizational assets and competencies that are difficult for competitors to imitate and thus help firms enter and succeed in foreign markets. These competencies take various forms, such as specific knowledge, capabilities, innovativeness, superior strategies, or close relationships with suppliers. Competitive advantage is also known as *firm-specific advantage*.

In recent years business executives and academics such as Michael Porter have used *competitive advantage* to refer to the advantages possessed by both nations *and* individual firms in international trade and investment. To be consistent with the recent literature, we adopt this convention as well.

Exhibit 6.1 categorizes leading theories of international trade and investment into two broad groups. The first group includes nation-level theories. These are classical

Competitive advantage
Distinctive assets or competencies of a firm that are difficult for competitors to imitate and are typically derived from specific knowledge, capabilities, skills, or superior strategies.

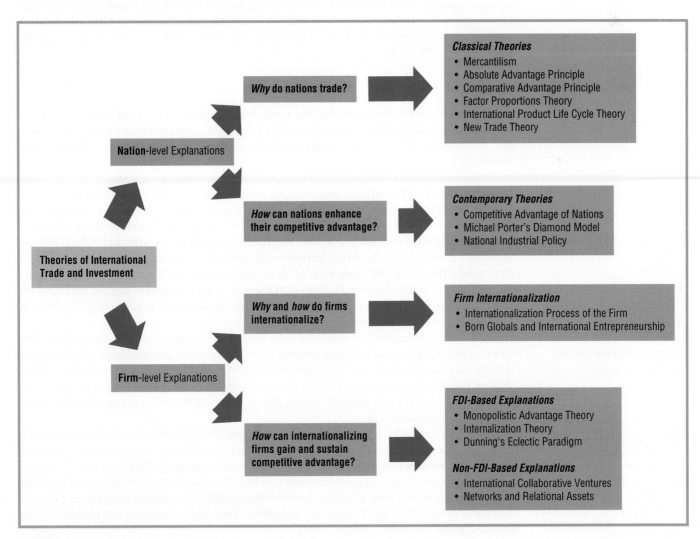

Exhibit 6.1 Theories of International Trade and Investment

theories that have been advocated since the sixteenth century. They address two questions: (1) *Why* do nations trade? (2) *How* can nations enhance their competitive advantage?

The second group includes firm-level theories. These are more contemporary theories of how firms can create and sustain superior organizational performance. Firm-level explanations address two additional questions: (3) *Why* and *how* do firms internationalize? and (4) *How* can internationalizing firms gain and sustain competitive advantage?

We organize the remainder of our discussion according to the four fundamental questions.

Why Do Nations Trade?

Why do nations trade with one another? The short answer is that trade allows countries to use their national resources more efficiently through *specialization*. Trade allows industries and workers to be more productive. It also allows countries to achieve higher living standards and keep the cost of many everyday products low. Without international trade, most nations would be unable to feed, clothe, and house their citizens at current levels. Even resource-rich countries like the United States would suffer immensely without trade. Some types of food would become unavailable or very expensive. Coffee and sugar would be luxury items. Petroleum-based energy sources would dwindle. Vehicles would stop running, freight would go undelivered, and people would not be able to heat their homes in winter. In short, not only do nations, companies, and citizens benefit from international trade, but modern life is virtually impossible without it.

Classical Theories

Six classical perspectives explain the underlying rationale for trade among nations: the mercantilist view, absolute advantage principle, comparative advantage principle, factor proportions theory, international product life cycle theory, and new trade theory.

Mercantilism   The earliest explanations of international business emerged with the rise of European nation states in the 1500s, when gold and silver were the most important sources of wealth, and nations sought to amass as much of these treasures, particularly gold, as possible. Nations received payment for exports in gold, so exports increased their gold stock, while imports reduced it because they paid for imports with their gold. Thus, exports were seen as good and imports as bad. Because the nation's power and strength increase as its wealth increases, **mercantilism** argues that national prosperity results from a positive balance of trade achieved by maximizing exports and minimizing or even impeding imports.

In essence, mercantilism explains why nations attempt to run a *trade surplus*—that is, to export more goods than they import. Even today many people believe that running a trade surplus is beneficial. They subscribe to a view known as *neo-mercantilism*. Labor unions (which seek to protect home-country jobs), farmers (who want to keep crop prices high), and certain manufacturers (those that rely heavily on exports) all tend to support neo-mercantilism.

On the other hand, mercantilism tends to harm the interests of firms that import, especially those that import raw materials and parts used in the manufacture of finished products. Mercantilism also harms the interests of consumers, because restricting imports reduces the choice of products they can buy. Product shortages that result from import restrictions may lead to higher prices—that is, inflation. When taken to an extreme, mercantilism may invite "beggar thy neighbor" policies, promoting the benefits of one country at the expense of others.

Mercantilism   The belief that national prosperity is the result of a positive balance of trade, achieved by maximizing exports and minimizing imports.

By contrast, **free trade**—the relative absence of restrictions to the flow of goods and services between nations—is a generally superior approach and should produce the following outcomes:

- Consumers and firms can more readily buy the products they want.

- Imported products tend to be cheaper than domestically produced products (because access to world-scale supplies forces prices down, mainly from increased competition, or because the goods are produced in lower-cost countries).

- Lower-cost imports help reduce the expenses of firms, thereby raising their profits (which may be passed on to workers in the form of higher wages).

- Lower-cost imports help reduce the expenses of consumers, thereby increasing their living standards.

- Unrestricted international trade generally increases the overall prosperity of poor countries.

Free trade Relative absence of restrictions to the flow of goods and services between nations.

Absolute Advantage Principle In *An Inquiry into the Nature and Causes of the Wealth of Nations*, a landmark book published in 1776, Scottish political economist Adam Smith attacked the mercantilist view by suggesting that nations benefit most from free trade. Smith argued that mercantilism robs individuals of the ability to trade freely and to benefit from voluntary exchanges. By trying to minimize imports, a country wastes much of its national resources in the production of goods it is not suited to produce efficiently. The inefficiencies of mercantilism end up reducing the wealth of the nation as a whole while enriching a limited number of individuals and interest groups. Relative to others, each country is more efficient in the production of some products and less efficient in the production of other products. Smith's **absolute advantage principle** states that a country benefits by producing primarily those products in which it has an absolute advantage or that it can produce using fewer resources than another country. Each country thus increases its welfare by specializing in the production of certain products, exporting them, and importing others. This approach allows the nation to consume more than it otherwise could, generally at lower cost.

Absolute advantage principle A country benefits by producing only those products in which it has absolute advantage or that it can produce using fewer resources than another country.

Exhibit 6.2 illustrates how the absolute advantage principle works in practice. Consider two nations, France and Germany, engaged in a trading relationship. France has an absolute advantage in the production of cloth, and Germany has an absolute advantage in the production of wheat. Assume labor is the only factor of production used in making both goods. (Firms employ *factors of production*—for example, labor, capital, entrepreneurship, and technology—to generate goods and services.) In Exhibit 6.2, it takes an average worker in France 30 days to produce one ton of cloth and 40 days to produce one ton of wheat. It takes an average worker in Germany 100 days to produce one ton of cloth and 20 days to produce one ton of wheat.

France has an absolute advantage in the production of cloth, since it takes only 30 days of labor to produce one ton compared to 100 days for Germany. Germany has an absolute advantage in the production of wheat, since it takes only 20 days to produce one ton compared to 40 days for France. If both France and Germany were to specialize, exchanging cloth and wheat at a ratio of one-to-one, France could employ more of its resources to produce cloth and Germany could employ more of its resources

Scottish political economist Adam Smith was among the first to articulate advantages of international trade.

| | One Ton of | |
	Cloth	Wheat
France	30	40
Germany	100	20

Exhibit 6.2 Example of Absolute Advantage (Labor Cost in Days of Production for One Ton)

Comparative advantage principle It can be beneficial for two countries to trade without barriers as long as one is relatively more efficient at producing goods or services needed by the other. What matters is not the absolute cost of production but rather the relative efficiency with which a country can produce the product.

to produce wheat. According to Exhibit 6.2, France can import one ton of wheat in exchange for one ton of cloth, thereby "paying" only 30 labor-days for one ton of wheat. If France had produced the wheat itself, it would have used 40 labor-days, so it gains 10 labor-days from the trade. In a similar way, Germany gains from trade with France.

Each country benefits by specializing in producing the product in which it has an absolute advantage and securing the other product through trade. Each then employs its labor and other resources with maximum efficiency and, as a result, increases its standard of living. To employ a more contemporary example, Japan has no natural holdings of oil, but it manufactures some of the world's best automobiles. Saudi Arabia produces much oil, but lacks a substantial car industry. Given this state of resources, it is wasteful for each country to attempt to produce both oil and cars. By trading with each other, Japan and Saudi Arabia employ their respective resources more efficiently in a mutually beneficial relationship. Japan gets oil that it refines to power cars, and Saudi Arabia gets the cars its citizens need. By extending this example we see that freely trading countries achieve substantial gains from trade. Brazil can produce coffee more cheaply than Germany; Australia can produce wool more cheaply than Switzerland; Britain can provide financial services more cheaply than Zimbabwe; and so forth.

While the concept of absolute advantage provided perhaps the earliest sound rationale for international trade, it accounted only for the *absolute* advantages possessed by nations and failed to consider more subtle advantages they may enjoy. Later studies revealed that a country benefits from international trade even when it lacks an *absolute* advantage. This line of thinking led to the principle of *comparative advantage*.

Comparative Advantage Principle In his 1817 book *The Principles of Political Economy and Taxation*, British political economist David Ricardo explained why it is beneficial for two countries to trade even though one of them may have absolute advantage in the production of all products. Ricardo demonstrated that what matters is not the absolute cost of production, but rather the *relative efficiency* with which the two countries can produce the products. Hence, the **comparative advantage principle** states that it can be beneficial for two countries to trade without barriers as long as one is *relatively* more efficient at producing goods or services needed by the other. The principle of comparative advantage is the foundation and overriding justification for international trade.

To illustrate, let's modify the example of France and Germany. As shown in Exhibit 6.3, suppose now that Germany has an absolute advantage in the production of both cloth and wheat. That is, in labor-per-day terms, Germany can produce *both* cloth and wheat in fewer days than France. Based on this new scenario, you might initially conclude that Germany should produce all the wheat and cloth it needs and not trade with France at all. However, even though Germany can produce both items more cheaply than France, it is still beneficial for Germany to trade with France.

How can this be true? The answer is that rather than the absolute cost of production, it is the *ratio of production costs* between the two countries that matters. In Exhibit 6.3, Germany is comparatively more efficient at producing cloth than wheat: It can produce three times as much cloth as France (30/10), but only two times as much wheat (40/20). Thus, Germany should

It would be wasteful for Saudi Arabia to attempt to produce both oil and cars. Instead, it can focus on extracting and refining petroleum while procuring cars from Japan, which has no natural holdings of oil but manufactures some of the best automobiles in the world.

devote all its resources to producing cloth and import all the wheat it needs from France. France should specialize in producing wheat and import all its cloth from Germany. Both countries then can each produce and consume relatively more of the goods they desire for a given level of labor cost.

	One Ton of	
	Cloth	Wheat
France	30	40
Germany	10	20

Exhibit 6.3 Example of Comparative Advantage (Labor Cost in Days of Production for One Ton)

Another way to understand comparative advantage is to consider *opportunity cost*, the value of a foregone alternative activity. In Exhibit 6.3, if Germany produces 1 ton of wheat, it forgoes 2 tons of cloth. However, if France produces 1 ton of wheat, it forgoes only 1.33 tons of cloth. Thus, France should specialize in wheat. Similarly, if France produces 1 ton of cloth, it forgoes 0.75 ton of wheat. But if Germany produces 1 ton of cloth, it forgoes only 0.5 ton of wheat. Thus, Germany should specialize in cloth. The opportunity cost of producing wheat is lower in France, and the opportunity cost of producing cloth is lower in Germany.

In an example provided by Ricardo:

> Two men can make both shoes and hats, and one is superior to the other in both employments, but in making hats he can only exceed his competitor by 20 percent, and in making shoes he can excel him by 33 percent; will it not be for the interest of both that the superior man should employ himself exclusively in making shoes and the inferior man in making hats?[2]

While a nation might conceivably have a sufficient variety of production factors to provide every kind of product and service, it cannot produce each with equal facility. The United States could produce all the car batteries its citizens need, but only at high cost. This occurs because batteries require much labor to produce, and wages in the United States are relatively high. By contrast, producing car batteries is a reasonable activity in China, where wages are lower than in the United States. It is advantageous, therefore, for the United States to specialize in a product such as patented medications, the production of which more efficiently employs the country's abundant supply of knowledge workers and technology in the pharmaceutical industry. The United States is better off exporting medications and importing car batteries from China. The comparative advantage view is optimistic because it implies that a nation need not be the first-, second-, or even third-best producer of particular products to benefit from international trade. Indeed, it is generally advantageous for all countries to participate in international trade.

Initially, adherents of the comparative advantage principle focused on the importance of *inherited* or *natural resource advantages*, such as fertile land, abundant minerals, and favorable climate. Thus, because South Africa has extensive mineral deposits, it produces and exports diamonds. Because Argentina has much agricultural land and a suitable climate, it grows and exports wheat. Because Russia has vast forests, it makes and exports wood products. Over time, however, it has become clear that countries can also *create* or *acquire* comparative advantages.

Consider the case of Japan. In the years following World War II, Japan systematically acquired a collection of advantages that benefited its consumer electronics industry. The investments made by Japan's government, banks, and manufacturing firms paid off enormously. Companies like Hitachi, Panasonic, and Sony invested massive resources to acquire the knowledge and skills needed to become the world leader in consumer electronics. Today Japan accounts for approximately half of the industry's total world production, including digital cameras, flat panel TVs, and personal computers. More recently, South Korea made similar investments,

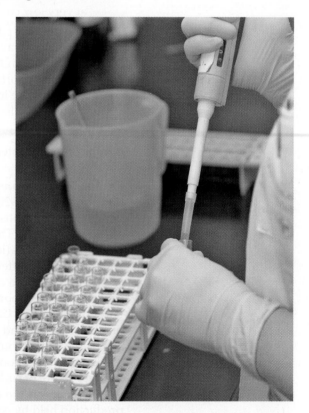

The United States could produce all the car batteries its citizens need, but only at a high cost. However, China is relatively more efficient in producing car batteries, and the United States is relatively more efficient at producing pharmaceutical medications. Thus, the United States is better off exporting pharmaceuticals and importing car batteries from China.

giving rise to leading-edge firms like LG and Samsung. We elaborate on the *acquired advantages* of countries later in the chapter.

Limitations of Early Trade Theories While the concepts of absolute advantage and comparative advantage provide the rationale for international trade, they fail to account for factors that make contemporary trade complex, including:

- Traded products are not just commodities anymore, such as wheat and cloth. To-day, many traded goods are characterized by strong branding and differentiated features.

- International transportation, critical for cross-border trade to take place, is often costly.

- Government restrictions such as tariffs (taxes on imports), import barriers, and regulations can hamper international trade.

- Large-scale production in certain industries may bring about scale economies, and therefore lower prices, that can help offset weak national comparative advantage.

- Just as Japan did after World War II, governments may target and invest in certain industries, build infrastructure, or provide subsidies, all to boost the competitive advantages of home-country firms.

- Many services, such as banking and retailing, cannot be traded in the usual sense and must be internationalized via foreign direct investment.

- Modern telecommunications and the Internet facilitate global trade in many services at very low cost.

- The primary participants in international trade are individual firms that differ in significant ways. Far from being homogenous enterprises, many are highly entrepreneurial and innovative or have access to exceptional human talent, all of which support international business success. In other cases, some firms may need to trade internationally if their home markets are too small to support their growth or sales objectives.

In the following sections, we discuss additional theories that have been introduced in view of these contemporary trends.

Factor Proportions Theory A significant contribution to explaining international trade came in the 1920s, when two Swedish economists, Eli Heckscher and his student, Bertil Ohlin, proposed the *factor proportions theory*, sometimes called the *factor endowments theory*.[3] This view rests on two premises: (1) products differ in the types and quantities of factors (labor, natural resources, and capital) required for their production; and (2) countries differ in the type and quantity of production factors they possess. Thus, each country should export products that intensively use relatively abundant factors of production and import goods that intensively use relatively scarce factors of production. For example, the U.S. produces and exports capital-intensive products, such as pharmaceuticals and commercial aircraft, while Argentina produces land-intensive products, such as wine and sunflower seeds.

Factor proportions theory differs somewhat from earlier theories by emphasizing the importance of each nation's factors of production. The theory states that, in addition to differences in the *efficiency* of production, differences in the *quantity* of factors of production held by countries also determine international trade patterns. This leads to a *per-unit-cost advantage* due to the abundance of a given factor of production, say labor, over another, say land, which is not in as much supply. Originally, labor was the most important factor of production. This explains why, for example, countries like China and India have become popular manufacturing bases.

In the 1950s, Russian-born economist Wassily Leontief pointed to empirical findings that seemed to contradict the factor proportions theory. The theory suggests that because the United States has abundant capital, it should be an exporter of capital-intensive products. However, Leontief's analysis, termed the *Leontief paradox,* revealed that the United States often exported labor-intensive goods and imported more capital-intensive goods than the theory would ordinarily predict. What accounts for the inconsistency? One explanation is that numerous factors determine the composition of a country's exports and imports. Another is that, in Leontief's time, U.S. labor was relatively more productive than labor elsewhere in the world.

Perhaps the main contribution of the Leontief paradox is its suggestion that international trade is complex and cannot be fully explained by a single theory. Subsequent refinements of factor proportions theory suggested that other country-level assets—knowledge, technology, and capital—are instrumental in explaining each nation's international trade prowess. Taiwan, for example, is very strong in information technology and is home to a sizable population of knowledge workers in the IT sector. These factors helped make Taiwan a leader in the global computer industry.

Factor proportions theory describes how abundant production factors give rise to national advantages. For example, Brazil has an abundance of workers in various industries. Here, workers at the Accessorios Para Panela de Pressao in São Paulo assemble parts for pressure cookers.

International Product Life Cycle Theory   In a 1966 article, Harvard Professor Raymond Vernon sought to explain international trade based on the evolutionary process that occurs in the development and diffusion of products to markets around the world.[4] In his *International Product Life Cycle* (IPLC) *Theory,* Vernon observed that each product and its manufacturing technologies go through three stages of evolution: introduction, maturity, and standardization. This is illustrated in Exhibit 6.4.

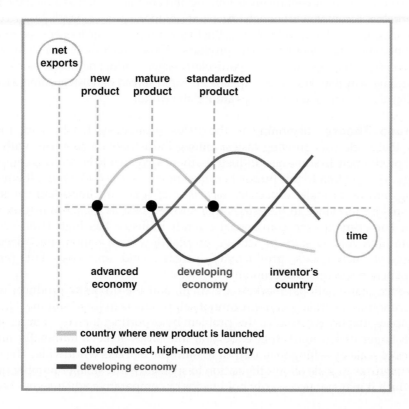

Exhibit 6.4   Illustration of Vernon's International Product Life Cycle

SOURCE: http://www.provenmodels.com/583/international-product-life-cycle/raymond-vernon

In the introduction stage, a new product typically originates in an advanced economy, such as the United States. Such countries possess abundant capital and R&D capabilities, providing key advantages in the development of new goods. Advanced economies also have abundant, high-income consumers who are willing to try new products, which are often expensive. During the introduction stage, the new product is produced in the home country, which enjoys a temporary monopoly.

As the product enters the maturity phase, the product's inventors mass-produce it and seek to export it to other advanced economies. Gradually, however, the product's manufacturing becomes more routine and foreign firms begin producing alternative versions, ending the inventor's monopoly power. At this stage, as competition intensifies and export orders begin to come from lower-income countries, the inventor may earn only a narrow profit margin.

In the standardization phase, knowledge about how to produce the product is widespread and manufacturing has become straightforward. Early in the product's evolution, production required specialized workers skilled in R&D and manufacturing. Once standardized, however, mass production is the dominant activity and can be accomplished using cheaper inputs and low-cost labor. Consequently, production shifts to low-income countries where competitors enjoy low-cost advantages and can economically serve export markets worldwide. Eventually, the country that invented the product becomes a net importer. It and other advanced economies become saturated with imports of the good from developing economies. In effect, exporting the product has caused its underlying technology to become widely known and standardized around the world.

As an example, consider the evolution of television sets. The base technology was invented in the United States, and U.S. firms began producing TVs there in the 1940s. U.S. sales grew rapidly for many years. However, once TVs became a standardized product, production shifted to China, Mexico, and other countries that offer lower-cost production. Today the United States imports nearly all its TVs from such countries.

The IPLC illustrates that national advantages are dynamic; they do not last forever. Firms worldwide are continuously creating new products, and others are constantly imitating them. The product cycle is continually beginning and ending. Vernon assumed the product diffusion process occurs slowly enough to generate temporary differences between countries in their access and use of new technologies. But this assumption is no longer valid today: The IPLC has become much shorter as new products diffuse much more quickly around the world. Buyers in emerging markets are particularly eager to adopt new technologies as soon as they become available. This trend explains the rapid spread of new consumer electronics such as digital assistants and cell phones around the world.

New Trade Theory Beginning in the 1970s, economists led by Paul Krugman observed that trade was growing fastest among industrialized countries with similar factors of production. In some new industries, there appeared to be no clear comparative advantage. The solution to this puzzle became known as *new trade theory*. It argues that increasing returns to scale, especially *economies of scale*, are important for superior international performance in industries that succeed best as their production volume increases. For example, the commercial aircraft industry has high fixed costs that necessitate high-volume sales to achieve profitability. As a nation specializes in the production of such goods, productivity increases and unit costs fall, providing significant benefits to the local economy.

However, many national markets are small, and the domestic producer may not achieve economies of scale because it cannot sell products in large volume. New trade theory implies that firms can solve this problem by exporting, thereby gaining access to the much larger global marketplace. Several industries achieve minimally profitable economies of scale by selling their output in multiple markets worldwide. The effect of increasing returns to scale allows the nation to specialize in a smaller number of industries in which it may not necessarily hold factor or comparative advantages. According to new trade theory, trade is thus beneficial even for countries that produce only a limited variety of products.

 ## How Can Nations Enhance Their Competitive Advantage?

The globalization of markets has fostered a new type of competition—a race among nations to reposition themselves as attractive places in which to invest and do business. The most advantaged nations today possess national competitive advantage, maximized when numerous industries collectively possess firm-level competitive advantages *and* the nation itself has comparative advantages that benefit those particular industries. This notion is illustrated in Exhibit 6.5.

Many governments create policies designed to encourage competitive advantage, often by developing world-class economic sectors and prosperous geographic regions. These policies aim to assist firms to develop acquired advantages.

Contemporary Theories

Three key modern perspectives that help explain the development of national competitive advantage are the competitive advantage of nations, Michael Porter's diamond model, and national industrial policy.

The Competitive Advantage of Nations   Just as scholars recognized that international business is good for individual nations, they increasingly sought to explain how nations can position themselves for international business success. An important

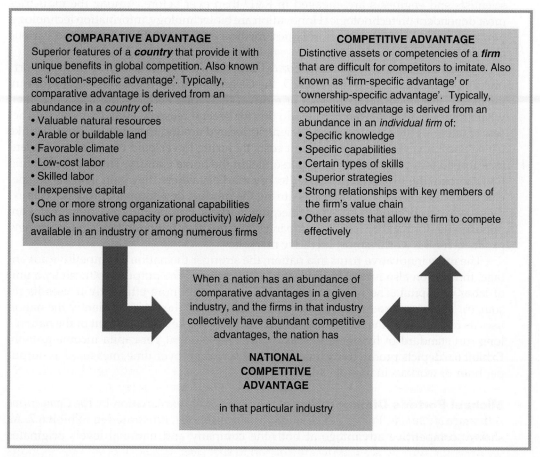

Exhibit 6.5   Comparative Advantage and Competitive Advantage

contribution came from Professor Michael Porter in his 1990 book, *The Competitive Advantage of Nations*.[5] According to Porter, the competitive advantage of a nation depends on the collective competitive advantages of the nation's firms. Over time, this relationship is reciprocal: The competitive advantages held by the nation tend to drive the development of new firms and industries with these same competitive advantages.

For example, Britain achieved a substantial national competitive advantage in the prescription drug industry due to its first-rate pharmaceutical firms, including Glaxo-SmithKline and AstraZeneca. The United States has a national competitive advantage in service industries because of many leading firms, such as Goldman Sachs (investment banking), Marsh & McLennan (insurance), and Booz & Company (consulting). The presence of these and numerous other strong services firms, in turn, has engendered overall national competencies in the global services sector.

At both the firm and national levels, competitive advantage and technological advances grow out of *innovation*.[6] Companies innovate in various ways: They develop new product designs, new production processes, new approaches to marketing, new ways of organizing or training, and so forth. Firms sustain innovation (and by extension, competitive advantage) by continually finding better products, services, and ways of doing things.[7] For example, Australia's Vix ERG (www.vix-erg.com) is a world leader in fare collection equipment and software systems for the transit industry. The firm has installed systems in subways, bus networks, and other mass transit systems in major cities like Melbourne, Rome, San Francisco, Stockholm, and Singapore. It has won numerous awards for its innovative products, which have allowed the firm to internationalize quickly. Vix ERG's investment in R&D has been significant, running as high as 23 percent of the firm's revenue.

Innovation results primarily from research and development. Worldwide, more scientists and engineers are engaged in R&D than ever before. Among the industries most dependent on technological innovation are biotechnology, information technology, new materials, pharmaceuticals, robotics, medical equipment, fiber optics, and various electronics-based industries.

The management consultancy Booz & Company (www.booz.com) annually reports on MNEs that spend the most on R&D, the *Global Innovation 1000*. Most top European, Japanese, and U.S. firms spend half or more of their total R&D in countries other than where they are headquartered. They do this for several reasons. First, they can gain access to talent—gifted engineers and scientists located around the world in countries like China and India. Second, they can cut costs by hiring lower-paid engineers and scientists abroad to replace higher-paid personnel in the home country. Third, by relocating R&D abroad, the firms can get closer to key markets, where they gain insights on specific characteristics of target markets during the product development process.[8] This explains why, in addition to low-cost emerging markets, Europe and the United States are popular sites for R&D by foreign companies, as firms seek to understand and create new products for the world's most lucrative markets.

The more innovative firms in a nation, the stronger the nation's competitive advantage. Innovation also promotes *productivity*, the value of the output produced by a unit of labor or capital. The more productive a firm is, the more efficiently it uses its resources. The more productive the firms in a nation are, the more efficiently the nation uses its resources. At the national level, productivity is a key determinant of the nation's long-run standard of living and a basic source of national per-capita income growth. Exhibit 6.6 depicts productivity levels in various nations over time, measured as output per hour of workers in manufacturing.

Michael Porter's Diamond Model As part of his explanation in *The Competitive Advantage of Nations*, Porter developed the *diamond model*, illustrated in Exhibit 6.7. As shown, competitive advantage at both the company and national levels originates

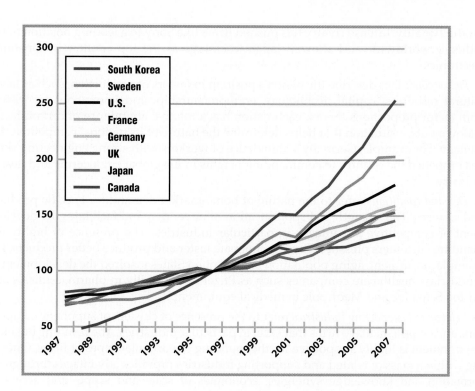

Exhibit 6.6 Productivity Levels in Selected Countries: Output per Hour in Manufacturing, 1987–2008, where 1996 = 100

SOURCE: U.S. Department of Labor, Bureau of Labor Statistics, 2009.

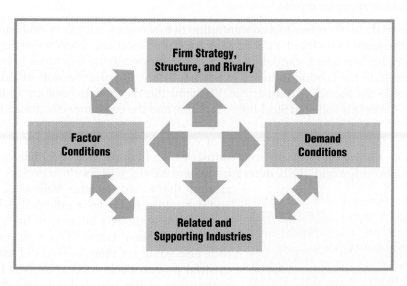

Exhibit 6.7 Porter's Diamond Model

SOURCE: Reprinted with the permission of The Free Press, a Division of Simon & Schuster, Inc., from *The Competative Advantage of Nations* by Michael E. Porter. Copyright © 1990, 1998 by Michael E. Porter. All rights reserved.

from the presence and quality in the country of four major elements, which we review next.

1. *Firm strategy, structure, and rivalry* refer to the nature of domestic rivalry and conditions in a nation that determine how firms are created, organized, and managed. The presence of strong competitors in a nation helps create and maintain national competitive advantage. Japan has the world's most competitive consumer electronics industry, with major players like Nintendo, NEC, Sharp, and Sony producing semiconductors, computers, video games, and liquid crystal displays. Vigorous competitive rivalry puts these firms under continual pressure to innovate and improve. They compete not only for market share, but also for human talent, technical leadership, and superior product quality. Intense rivalry has pushed firms like Sony to a leading position in the industry worldwide and allowed Japan to emerge as the top country in consumer electronics.[9]

2. *Factor conditions* describe the nation's position in factors of production, such as labor, natural resources, capital, technology, entrepreneurship, and know-how. Consistent with factor proportions theory, each nation has a relative abundance of certain factor endowments, a situation that helps determine the nature of its national competitive advantage. For example, Germany's abundance of workers with strong engineering skills has propelled the country to commanding heights in the global engineering and design industry.

3. *Demand conditions* refer to the nature of home-market demand for specific products and services. The strength and sophistication of buyer demand facilitates the development of competitive advantages in particular industries. The presence of highly demanding customers pressures firms to innovate faster and produce better products. For example, an affluent, aging population in the United States inspired the development of world-class health care companies such as Pfizer and Eli Lilly in pharmaceuticals and Boston Scientific and Medtronic in medical equipment.

4. *Related and supporting industries* refer to the presence of clusters of suppliers, competitors, and complementary firms that excel in particular industries. The resulting business environment is highly supportive for the founding of particular types of firms. Operating within a mass of related and supporting industries provides advantages through information and knowledge synergies, economies of scale and scope, and access to appropriate or superior inputs.

Industrial cluster
A concentration of businesses, suppliers, and supporting firms in the same industry at a particular location, characterized by a critical mass of human talent, capital, or other factor endowments.

Industrial cluster refers to a concentration of businesses, suppliers, and supporting firms in the same industry at a particular geographic location, characterized by a critical mass of human talent, capital, or other factor endowments. Examples of industrial clusters include the fashion industry in northern Italy; the pharmaceutical industry in Switzerland; the footwear industry in Vietnam; the medical technology industry in Singapore; Wireless Valley in Stockholm, Sweden; and the consumer electronics industry in Japan.

Today, the most important sources of national advantage are the *knowledge and skills* possessed by individual firms, industries, and countries. More than any other factors, knowledge and skills determine where MNEs will locate economic activity around the world. Silicon Valley, California, and Bangalore, India, have emerged as leading-edge business clusters because of the availability of specialized talent. These regions have little else going for them in terms of natural industrial power. Their success derives from the knowledge of the people employed there, so-called knowledge workers. Some even argue that knowledge is now the only source of sustainable long-run competitive advantage. If correct, then future national wealth will go to those countries that invest the most in R&D, education, and infrastructure that support knowledge-intensive industries.

Visionary national industrial policy is transforming Dubai into a high value-adding economy based on IT, biotechnology, financial services, and other knowledge-intensive industries.

National Industrial Policy Perhaps the greatest contribution of Porter's work has been to underscore the notion that national competitive advantage does not derive entirely from the store of natural resources each country holds. Inherited national factor endowments are relatively less important than in the past. Rather, as Porter emphasized, countries can successfully *create* new advantages and develop factor conditions they deem important for their success. The government can devote resources to improve national infrastructure, education systems, and capital formation. In short, Porter's diamond model implies that any country, regardless of its initial circumstances, can attain economic prosperity by systematically cultivating new and superior factor endowments.

Nations can develop these endowments through proactive **national industrial policy**. Such a policy encourages economic development, often in collaboration with the private sector, to develop or support high value-adding industries that generate superior corporate profits, higher worker wages, and tax revenues. As illustrated in the chapter opening vignette, Dubai is pursuing a national industrial policy to become an international commercial center in the information and communications technology (ICT) sector. Historically, nations have favored more traditional industries, including automobiles, shipbuilding, and heavy machinery—all with long value chains that generate substantial added value. As the Dubai example illustrates, progressive nations increasingly favor high value-adding, knowledge-intensive industries such as IT, biotechnology, medical technology, and financial services. Not only do these industries provide substantial revenues to the nation, they also lead to the development of supplier and support companies that further enhance national prosperity.

National industrial policies designed to build new capabilities and encourage the emergence of new industries typically include these specifics:

- Tax incentives to encourage citizens to save and invest, which provides capital for public and private investment in R&D, plant, equipment, and worker skills
- Monetary and fiscal policies, such as low-interest loans, that provide a stable supply of capital for company investment needs
- Rigorous educational systems at the precollege and university levels that ensure a steady stream of competent workers who support high technology or high value-adding industries in the sciences, engineering, and business administration
- Development and maintenance of strong national infrastructure in areas such as IT, communication systems, and transportation
- Creation of strong legal and regulatory systems to ensure that citizens are confident about the soundness and stability of the national economy[10]

National Industrial Policy in Practice: An Example
How well does national industrial policy work in practice? Let's examine Ireland and the outcomes of its repositioning, implemented through collaboration between the nation's public and private sectors.

For much of the early twentieth century, government policies had limited Ireland's ability to trade with the rest of the world. Living standards were low, young people were fleeing the country, and many wondered whether Ireland had a future. Then, in the 1980s, the Irish government undertook protrade policies in cooperation with the private sector that led to the development of national advantages, helping Ireland's economy to

National industrial policy A proactive economic development plan initiated by the government, often in collaboration with the private sector, that aims to develop or support particular industries within the nation.

Following many years of poor economic performance, the government of Ireland implemented various national industrial policies that succeeded in elevating several key economic indicators, thus raising living standards for the Irish people.

Statistic	Ireland in 1988	Ireland in 2008
GDP per capita	69% of the average of Europe	142% of the average of Europe
Unemployment rate	17%	6%
National debt	112% of the nation's GDP	32% of the nation's GDP

Exhibit 6.8   Transformation of Ireland's Economy, 1988 to 2008

grow rapidly and achieve high living standards. The magnitude of Ireland's accomplishment becomes clear in Exhibit 6.8, which compares the country's changing economic conditions from 1988 to 2008.

Annual GDP growth averaged nearly 7 percent throughout the 1990s—a fast pace. Ireland's rejuvenation was so successful that officials from around the world visited the country to learn how it transformed from one of Europe's stagnant economies to one of its most dynamic. Ireland's success resulted from a combination of efforts:

- *Fiscal, monetary, and tax consolidation.* The Irish government lowered the basic corporate tax rate to zero, helping foster entrepreneurship and increasing the nation's attractiveness for inward investment from foreign MNEs. Personal taxes were reduced, boosting consumer spending. The government cut spending and borrowing, leading to lower interest rates and stimulating the economy.

- *Social partnership.* The government initiated earnest dialogue with labor unions. Increased coordination between government and industry improved the quality of the workforce and strengthened the Irish labor pool.

- *Emphasis on high value-adding industries.* Ireland created a national infrastructure and investment climate that fostered the development of industries in pharmaceuticals, biochemistry, and IT.

- *Membership in the European Union.* Emergence of the European single market and resulting fall of trade barriers provided Ireland with a huge new market for its exports consisting of 400 million consumers.

- *Subsidies.* Ireland received subsidies from the European Union that allowed it to offset debt, invest in infrastructure projects, and develop a range of key industries, particularly in the IT sector.

- *Education.* The country invested heavily in education, providing a steady supply of skilled workers, including scientists, engineers, and business school graduates.

Attracted by these positive developments, many foreign MNEs began investing in the country. Thanks to its national industrial policy, Ireland became a major player in world trade and now hosts some 1,000 foreign firms. International trade, inward FDI, and economic development dramatically raised living standards for its citizens.[11]

In the recent global financial crisis, economic activity fell and Ireland experienced a recession for the first time in many years. As in much of the world, the main problem was declining real estate markets. Fundamentally, however, Ireland's economy remains strong, with one of the world's highest per-capita income levels.[12]

Read the *Global Trend* feature for more examples of proactive nation repositioning to create new comparative advantages.

GL⊕BAL TREND

Moving from Comparative to National Competitive Advantages

The principle of comparative advantage and factor endowment theory imply that nations should nurture industries that use inputs inherent or abundant in their environment. Today, however, numerous countries with few natural or other resources have created their own competitive advantages through skillful application of national industrial policies. In most cases, these acquired advantages have become more critical than natural endowments. Here are some examples:

Singapore is a free market economy with high per-capita GDP. Beginning in the 1960s, the government adopted pro-business, pro-investment, export-oriented policies, combined with state-directed investments in strategic corporations. The approach stimulated economic growth that averaged 8 percent from 1960 to 1999. Singapore cut taxes and government spending and encouraged massive inward investment in high-value industries such as electronics, engineering, and chemicals. The country boasts a highly educated labor force, state-of-the-art telecommunications facilities, and excellent infrastructure—its airport and seaport are among the best in the world.

New Zealand's government, beginning in 1984, systematically transformed the country from an agrarian, protectionist, highly regulated economy to an industrialized free-market economy that competes globally. The government privatized a number of former state-owned enterprises, joined various international free trade agreements, and focused on building a knowledge economy. Dynamic growth has boosted real incomes and deepened technological capabilities.

India positioned *Bangalore*, the country's third largest city, as a center of IT and business support services. Cooperating with private interests, India reduced restrictions on trade and investment, resulting in a big influx of foreign FDI. The public-private partnership also emphasized high-value industries such as biotechnology and business consulting and capitalized on Bangalore's large, well-educated, English-speaking workforce.

In the *Czech Republic*, economic reforms and exports to the European Union (EU) led to economic prosperity. The Czech government harmonized its laws and regulations with those of the EU by reforming its judicial system, financial markets regulation, intellectual property rights protection, and other areas important to investors. It also privatized state-owned companies. Government FDI incentives attracted firms like Toyota, ING, Siemens, Daewoo, DHL, and South African Breweries.

Vietnam's government privatized state enterprises and modernized the economy, emphasizing competitive, export-driven industries. It ramped up the country's exports of everything from shoes to ships, modernized its intellectual property regime, entered several free trade agreements, and revamped its educational system to provide a constant stream of skilled workers. The government also built infrastructure, including roads, railways, and power stations. Reforms have attracted much inward FDI from firms like Intel. The national savings rate increased several-fold. Economic repositioning dramatically reduced Vietnam's poverty rate.

 ## Why and How Do Firms Internationalize?

Firm Internationalization

Earlier theories of international trade focused on why and how cross-national business occurs. However, in the 1960s scholars began to develop theories about the managerial and organizational aspects of firm internationalization.

Internationalization Process of the Firm   The *internationalization process model* was developed in the 1970s to describe how companies expand abroad. According to this model, internationalization takes place in incremental stages over a long time.[13]

Exhibit 6.9 Stages in the Internationalization Process of the Firm

Typically, firms start without much analysis or planning and begin to export, the simplest form of international activity, and progress to FDI, the most complex. The gradual and incremental nature of internationalization often results from managers' uncertainty and uneasiness about how to proceed, because they lack information about foreign markets and experience with cross-border transactions.

A simplified illustration of the internationalization process model appears in Exhibit 6.9. A firm starts out in a *domestic focus* phase and is preoccupied with acquiring business in the home market. Management may be unable or unwilling to get started in international business because of concerns over its readiness or perceived obstacles in foreign markets. Eventually, the firm advances to the *pre-export* stage, often because it receives unsolicited product orders from abroad. In this stage, management investigates the feasibility of undertaking international business. Subsequently, the firm advances to the *experimental involvement* stage by initiating limited international activity, typically in the form of basic exporting. As managers begin to view foreign expansion more favorably, they eventually undertake *active involvement* in international business through systematic exploration of international options and the commitment of managerial time and resources to achieving international success. Ultimately management may advance to the *committed involvement stage*, characterized by genuine interest and commitment of resources to making international business a key part of the firm's profit-making and value-chain activities. In this stage, the firm targets numerous foreign markets via various entry modes, especially FDI.[14]

To illustrate, let's revisit Sony Corporation. In the 1950s, Sony began exporting transistor radios and other products to Australia, Europe, and North America. In the 1960s, it entered joint ventures with various partners abroad, including CBS and Texas Instruments. Around the same time, Sony used FDI to establish sales offices in Hong Kong, Switzerland, and the United States. Later, the firm set up factories in numerous countries to manufacture the consumer electronics that made it famous. Sony established its first television factory in the United States in San Diego in 1972. Today it has joint ventures and wholly-owned operations in hundreds of locations worldwide, including five R&D centers and nine plants in Europe that produce computers, game consoles, personal navigation devices, and portable audio players. Sony's experience illustrates the internationalization process well.[15]

Born Globals and International Entrepreneurship Because international business has long been the domain of large, resource-rich MNEs, earlier theories tended to focus on them. But recently scholars have begun to question the slow and gradual process proposed by the internationalization process model.[16] Despite the scarcity of financial, human, and tangible resources that characterize most new businesses, *born global firms* internationalize early in their evolution. Among the reasons are the growing intensity of international competition, the integration of world economies under globalization, and advances in communication and transportation technologies that reduce the cost of venturing abroad and make it easier to internationalize earlier and faster than ever before. The born global phenomenon has given rise to a new field of scholarly inquiry, *international entrepreneurship*.[17] Current trends suggest that early internationalizing firms will gradually become the norm in international business.

How Can Internationalizing Firms Gain and Sustain Competitive Advantage?

So far we have focused on the internationalization processes of individual firms, including smaller firms or those new to international business. Since the 1950s, MNEs such as Nestlé, Unilever, Sony, Coca-Cola, and Caterpillar have expanded abroad on a massive scale, shaping international patterns of trade, investment, and technology flows. Over time, the aggregate activities of these firms became a key driving force of globalization and ongoing integration of world economies. So important is the rise of the MNE that it ranks with the development of electric power or the invention of the aircraft as one of the major events of modern history. Let's examine MNEs and their internationalization processes in more detail.

As explained in Chapter 1, an MNE is a large, resource-rich company whose business activities are performed by a network of subsidiaries in numerous countries. The typical MNE establishes worldwide production facilities, marketing subsidiaries, regional headquarters, and other physical facilities directly in the countries where it does business and has value chains that span multiple countries. MNEs leverage leading-edge technologies, talented managers, large capital bases, and other advantages to succeed around the world, using global capital markets and local resources in the countries where they operate. They are the foremost agents in disseminating new products, new technologies, and business practices worldwide, contributing to ongoing globalization of markets.

Sony has 170,000 employees and hundreds of subsidiaries and affiliates around the world that perform the widest range of value-chain activities. Its PlayStation dominates the game console market with about 50 percent of global sales. Its Vaio computers, digital cameras, Walkman stereos, and semiconductors are popular worldwide. Sony is headquartered in Tokyo, but Japan accounts for only a quarter of its roughly $100 billion in worldwide sales. It conducts business in emerging markets such as Argentina, Brazil, China, Turkey, Indonesia, Vietnam, and the Philippines. In short, Sony is a borderless MNE that locates its activities wherever it can maximize competitive advantages.

FDI-Based Explanations

FDI stock refers to the total value of assets that MNEs own abroad via their investment activities. Exhibit 6.10 shows the stock of inward FDI, and Exhibit 6.11 shows the stock of outward FDI. MNEs invest millions abroad every year to establish and expand factories and other facilities. Total inward FDI stock now constitutes about 30 percent of global GDP, a huge amount. While historically most of the world's FDI was invested both by and in Western Europe, the United States, and Japan, in recent years MNEs have invested heavily in emerging markets, such as China, Mexico, Brazil, and Eastern Europe.[18]

FDI is such an important entry strategy that scholars provide three alternative theories of how firms can use it to gain and sustain competitive advantage: the monopolistic advantage theory, internalization theory, and Dunning's eclectic paradigm. These theoretical perspectives are summarized in Exhibit 6.12 and described in the following sections.

Monopolistic Advantage Theory   A monopolistic advantage is one or more resources or capabilities a company possesses that few other firms have and that it leverages to generate profits and other returns. Monopolistic advantage theory suggests that firms which use FDI as an internationalization strategy must own or control certain resources and capabilities not easily available to competitors, that give them a degree of monopoly power over local firms in foreign markets. This monopolistic advantage should be specific to the MNE itself, such as a proprietary technology or a brand name, rather than to the locations where it does business. This theory argues that at least two

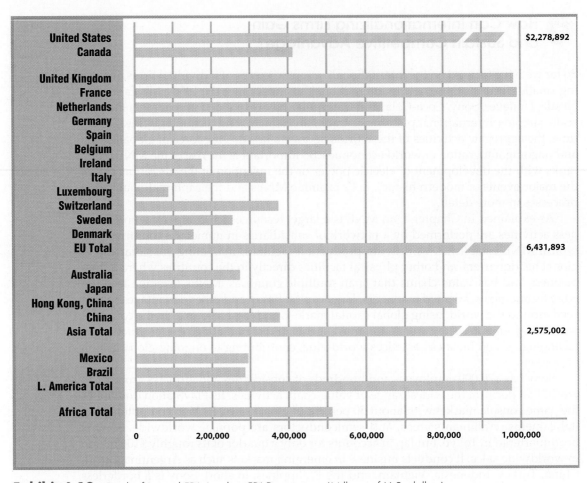

Exhibit 6.10 Stock of Inward FDI: Leading FDI Destinations (Millions of U.S. dollars)

SOURCES: UNCTAD, *World Investment Report 2009* (New York: United Nations, 2009, p. 251, "Annex table B.2. FDI stock, by region and economy, 1999, 2000, 2010"), accessed June 4, 2010 at http://unctad.org/en/docs/wir2009_en.pdf.

conditions should be present for a firm to prefer targeting a foreign market rather than its home market. First, returns obtainable in the foreign market should be superior to those available in the home market. This would provide the firm with incentives to expand abroad to take advantage of its monopoly power. Second, returns obtainable in the foreign market should be superior to those earned by its domestic competitors in its industry in the foreign market. This would give the firm an opportunity to make monopoly profits that domestic companies in the foreign market cannot imitate.

To illustrate, let's revisit Sony Corporation. By being on the leading edge of innovation, Sony established numerous pioneering standards in the consumer electronics industry. Over the course of several decades, Sony's superior R&D and internal control mechanisms allowed the firm to acquire and maintain a large body of relatively unique knowledge. This unique knowledge provided the firm with various monopolistic advantages. Sony invented numerous popular products that were, for a time at least, relatively unique. Continuous innovation within the firm allowed Sony to maintain this uniqueness for many years. Sony used its superior innovativeness to develop monopoly power and dominate world markets in such products as the PlayStation and Blu-ray disc format. As the Sony example implies, the most important monopolistic advantages are superior knowledge and intangible skills. Superior, proprietary knowledge has allowed Sony to create differentiated products that provide unique value to customers.[19]

Internalization Theory Numerous scholars have investigated the specific benefits that MNEs derive from FDI-based entry. For example, when Procter & Gamble entered

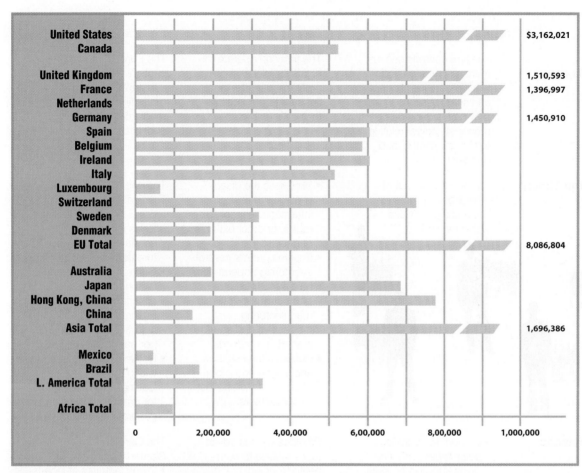

Exhibit 6.11   Stock of Outward FDI: Top Sources of Outward FDI (Millions of U.S. dollars)

SOURCE: UNCTAD, *World Investment Report 2009* (New York: United Nations, 2009, p. 251 "Annex table B.2. FDI stock, by region and economy, 1990, 2000, 2010"), accessed June 4, 2010 at http://unctad.org/en/docs/wir2009_en.pdf

Japan, management initially considered exporting and FDI. With exporting, P&G would have had to contract with an independent Japanese distributor to handle warehousing and marketing of its soap, diapers, and other products. However, because of trade barriers imposed by the Japanese government, the strong market power of local Japanese firms, and the risk of losing control over its proprietary knowledge, P&G chose instead to enter Japan via FDI. It established its own marketing subsidiary and, eventually, national headquarters in Tokyo. This arrangement provided various benefits P&G would not have received had it entered Japan by contracting with Japanese distributors it did not own.

Internalization theory explains the process by which firms acquire and retain one or more value-chain activities inside the firm, as P&G did in Japan. Internalizing value-chain activities helps minimize the disadvantages of dealing with external partners for performing arms-length activities such as exporting and licensing. Internalization also gives the firm greater control over its foreign operations.

For example, the MNE might internalize the supplier function by acquiring or establishing its own plant in the foreign market to produce needed inputs itself instead of buying them from a foreign, independent supplier. Or it might internalize the marketing function by establishing its own distribution subsidiary abroad, instead of contracting with an independent foreign distributor to handle its marketing in the foreign market. The MNE is ultimately a vehicle for bypassing the bottlenecks and costs of the international, inter-firm exchange of goods, materials, and workers. In this way, the firm

Internalization theory
An explanation of the process by which firms acquire and retain one or more value-chain activities inside the firm, minimizing the disadvantages of dealing with external partners and allowing for greater control over foreign operations.

Theory	Key Characteristics	Benefits	Examples
Monopolistic Advantage Theory	The firm controls one or more resources, or offers relatively unique products and services that provide it a degree of monopoly power relative to foreign markets and competitors.	The firm can operate foreign subsidiaries more profitably than the local firms that compete in their own markets.	The European pharmaceutical Novartis earns substantial profits by marketing various patent medications through its subsidiaries worldwide.
Internalization Theory	The firm acquires and retains one or more value-chain activities within the firm.	• Minimizes the disadvantages of relying on intermediaries, collaborators, or other external partners. • Ensures greater control over foreign operations, helping to maximize product quality, reliable manufacturing processes, and sound marketing practices. • Reduces the risk that knowledge and proprietary assets will be lost to competitors.	The Japanese MNE Toshiba: • Owns and operates factories in dozens of countries to manufacture laptop computers. • Controls its own manufacturing processes, ensuring quality output. • Ensures its marketing activities are carried out per headquarters' plan. • Retains key assets within the firm, such as leading-edge knowledge for producing the next generation of laptops.
Dunning's Eclectic Paradigm	• *Ownership-specific advantages*: The firm owns knowledge, skills, capabilities, processes, or physical assets. • *Location-specific advantages*: Factors in individual countries provide specific benefits, such as natural resources, skilled labor, low-cost labor, and inexpensive capital. • *Internalization advantages*: The firm benefits from internalizing foreign manufacturing, distribution, or other value-chain activities.	Provides various advantages relative to competitors, including the ability to own, control, and optimize value-chain activities—R&D, production, marketing, sales distribution, after-sales service, as well as relationships with customers and key contacts—performed at the most beneficial locations worldwide.	The German MNE Siemens: • Owns factories at locations worldwide that provide optimal access to natural resources, as well as skilled and low-cost labor. • Leverages the knowledge base of its employees in 190 countries. • Internalizes a wide range of manufacturing activities in categories such as lighting, medical equipment, and transportation machinery.

Exhibit 6.12 Theoretical Perspectives on Why Firms Choose FDI

replaces business activities performed by independent suppliers in external markets with business activities it performs itself.

In the 1950s, for example, Sony followed a policy of exporting its products to Europe and North America. However, management soon realized it could accelerate and improve the performance of international operations by creating its own sales and production facilities in strategic markets abroad. Thus, in the 1960s, Sony internalized much of its global production and distribution channels by establishing company-owned subsidiaries in Europe, the United States, and other key markets. To ensure product quality,

Sony internalized production of semiconductors and circuit boards for use in making cell phones and PlayStations. Recently, Sony transferred production of camcorders from a plant run by a joint venture partner in China to a wholly owned Sony plant in Japan. The move allowed Sony to improve supply-chain management and manufacturing of camcorders.

In addition to consumer electronics, Sony has long been a major player in the movie industry, through its subsidiary Sony Pictures Entertainment (SPE). Acquiring the Loews chain of movie theaters in the United States allowed SPE to internalize a substantial portion of the distribution channel for its film business, ensuring its movies would be supplied to thousands of movie screens. Since its founding, Sony has consistently internalized key units to maintain control over the most important links in its global value chains.

Another key reason companies internalize certain value-chain functions is to control proprietary knowledge critical to the development, production, and sale of their products and services. Because independent foreign companies are outside the MNE's direct control, they can acquire and use the knowledge to their own advantage, perhaps becoming competitors in the process. FDI allows the MNE to control and optimally use its knowledge in foreign markets.[20]

Dunning's Eclectic Paradigm   Professor John Dunning proposed the eclectic *paradigm* as a framework for determining the extent and pattern of the value-chain operations that companies own abroad. He drew from various theoretical perspectives, including comparative advantage, factor proportions, monopolistic advantage, and internalization advantage. Thus, the eclectic paradigm is often viewed as the most comprehensive of FDI theories. The eclectic paradigm specifies three conditions that determine whether a company will internationalize via FDI: ownership-specific advantages, location-specific advantages, and internalization advantages.

To successfully enter and conduct business in a foreign market, the MNE must possess *ownership-specific advantages* relative to other firms already doing business in the market. That is, it should hold knowledge, skills, capabilities, key relationships, and other assets that allow it to compete effectively in foreign markets. These assets amount to the firm's competitive advantages. To ensure international success, the advantages must be substantial enough to offset the costs the firm incurs in establishing and operating foreign operations. The advantages should also be specific to the MNE that possesses them and not readily transferable to other firms, such as proprietary technology, managerial skills, trademarks or brand names, economies of scale, and access to substantial financial resources. The more valuable the firm's ownership-specific advantages, the more likely it is to internationalize via FDI.[21]

Let's use Alcoa, the Aluminum Corporation of America (www.alcoa.com), to illustrate. Alcoa has more than 70,000 employees in thirty-five countries. The company's integrated operations include bauxite mining and aluminum refining. Its products include primary aluminum (which it refines from bauxite), automotive components, and sheet aluminum for beverage cans and Reynolds Wrap®.

One of Alcoa's most important ownership-specific advantages is the proprietary technology it has acquired through its R&D activities. It has also acquired special managerial and marketing skills in the production and marketing of refined aluminum. The firm has a well-known brand name that helps increase sales. As a large firm, Alcoa also profits from economies of scale and the ability to finance expensive projects. These advantages have allowed Alcoa to generate maximal profits from its international operations.

The second condition that determines whether a firm will internationalize via FDI is the presence of *location-specific advantages,* the comparative advantages available in individual foreign countries, such as natural resources, skilled labor, low-cost labor, and inexpensive capital. For example, Alcoa located refineries in Brazil because of that country's huge deposits of bauxite, a mineral found in relatively few other locations worldwide. The Amazon and other major rivers in Brazil generate huge amounts of hydroelectric power, a critical ingredient in electricity-intensive aluminum refining. Alcoa also benefits from Brazil's low-cost, relatively well-educated laborers who work in the firm's refineries. The presence of these location-specific advantages helped persuade Alcoa to locate in Brazil through FDI.

The third condition that determines FDI-based internationalization is the presence of *internalization advantages,* benefits that the firm derives from internalizing foreign-based manufacturing, distribution, or other stages in its value chain. When profitable, the firm will transfer its ownership-specific advantages across national borders *within* its own organization rather than dissipating them to independent, foreign entities. The FDI decision depends on which is the best option—internalization versus utilizing external partners, whether they are licensees, distributors, or suppliers. Internalization advantages include the ability to control how the firm's products are produced or marketed, the ability to prevent unintended dissemination of the firm's proprietary knowledge, and the ability to reduce buyer uncertainty about the value of products the firm offers.[22]

Alcoa had five reasons to internalize many of its operations instead of letting external suppliers handle them. First, its management wants to minimize dissemination of knowledge about its aluminum refining operations—knowledge the firm acquired at great expense. Second, internalization provides the best net return, allowing Alcoa to minimize the cost of operations. Third, Alcoa needs to control sales of its aluminum products to avoid depressing world aluminum prices through oversupply. Fourth, the firm wants to be able to apply a differential pricing strategy, charging different prices to different customers, a strategy it could not follow very effectively without the control over distribution that internalization provides. Finally, aluminum refining is a complex business, and Alcoa wants to control it to maintain the quality of its products.

Non-FDI-Based Explanations

FDI became a popular entry mode with the rise of the MNE in the 1960s and 1970s. In the 1980s, firms began to recognize the importance of collaborative ventures and other flexible entry strategies.

International Collaborative Ventures   A collaborative venture is a form of cooperation between two or more firms. There are two major types: (1) equity-based *joint ventures* that result in the formation of a new legal entity; and (2) non-equity-based *strategic alliances* in which firms partner temporarily to work on projects related to R&D, design, manufacturing, or any other value-adding activity. In both cases, collaborating firms pool resources and capabilities and generate synergy. In other words, collaboration allows the partners to carry out activities that each might be unable to perform on its own. Collaborating firms share the risk of their joint efforts, which reduces vulnerability for any one partner.

Collaboration is a critical activity in international business. A firm sometimes has no choice but to partner with other companies in order to use resources and capabilities unavailable within its own organization. In addition, occasionally a government will restrict companies from entering its national market via wholly owned FDI. For example, the Mexican government prohibits foreign firms from attaining full ownership of ventures in its domestic oil industry because oil is critical to Mexico's economy. Where such restrictions exist, the firm may have no choice but to collaborate with a foreign partner to enter the market.[23]

A collaborative venture can give a company access to foreign partners' know-how, capital, distribution channels, marketing assets, or the ability to overcome government-imposed obstacles. By collaborating, the firm can position itself better to create new products and enter new markets. Starbucks now boasts more than 700 coffee shops in Japan, thanks to a joint venture with its local partner, Sazaby League, Ltd. The venture allowed Starbucks to internationalize and to navigate the marketplace with the help of a knowledgeable local partner.[24]

Networks and Relational Assets   Networks and relational assets represent the economically beneficial long-term *relationships* the firm undertakes with other business entities, such as manufacturers, distributors, suppliers, retailers, consultants, banks, transportation suppliers, governments, and any other organization that can provide needed capabilities. Firm-level relational assets represent a distinct competitive advantage in international business. Japanese *keiretsu*, complex groupings of firms with interlinked ownership and trading relationships that foster inter-firm organizational learning, are their predecessors.[25] Like the keiretsu, networks are neither formal organizations with clearly defined hierarchical structures nor impersonal, decentralized markets.

The International Marketing and Purchasing (IMP) research consortium in Europe (www.impgroup.org) has driven much of the theory development on networks.[26] *Network theory* was proposed to compensate for the inability of traditional organizational theories to account for much that goes on in business markets.[27] In networks, buyers and sellers become bound to one another through ongoing exchanges and linkages of products, services, finance, technology, and know-how. Continued interaction among the partners results in stable relationships based on cooperation and creates value and competitive advantage even among competitors. Network linkages represent a key route by which many companies expand their business abroad, develop new markets, and develop new products. In international business, mutually beneficial and enduring strategic relationships provide real advantages to partners and reduce uncertainty and transaction costs.

Sony Corporation has countless network connections that provide substantial benefits. It has done extensive joint R&D with the Dutch electronics giant Philips and is well connected in the Japanese financial sector, where it launched Sony Bank, Sony Life Insurance, and Sony Bank Securities. These allied companies provide Sony with much of the financing it needs to conduct R&D and perform other key value-chain activities. In short, Sony's network and relational assets have been critical to its success.

As we'll see later in this book, in the contemporary global economy, firms have increasingly shied away from making permanent, direct investments in host countries. Instead, many firms now opt for more flexible collaborative ventures or other relationships with independent business partners abroad.

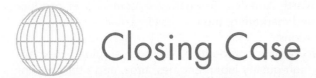 Closing Case

Hyundai: Leading the Way in the Global Auto Industry

The global automotive industry is one of the largest and most internationalized business sectors. There are seventeen major global automotive companies producing more than one million cars a year. Hyundai Motor Company is South Korea's number one carmaker and the tenth largest in the world. It sells vehicles in over 190 countries, producing about a dozen car and minivan models, plus trucks, buses, and other commercial vehicles. Popular models in the United States are the Accent and Sonata, while exports to Europe and Asia include the GRD and Equus. In 2008, during the global financial crisis, Hyundai earned a profit of $1.3 billion—among the best in the global auto industry.

The Industry

During the recent global financial crisis, global automotive sales declined to near-record lows. Automotive industry profits suffered due to significant excess production capacity. Although there is capacity to produce 80 million cars worldwide, total global demand fell to only about 60 million a year. This led to consolidations and divestitures, including those between Ford and Land Rover; Jaguar and Volvo; Fiat and Chrysler; and General Motors and Opel, among others. Consistent with new trade theory, the requisite scale compels automakers to target world markets, where they can achieve economies of scale and maximize sales.

The Industry in South Korea

Despite its large size, the car market in South Korea (Korea) is insufficient to sustain indigenous automakers like Hyundai and Kia. Korea holds numerous competitive advantages in the car industry. The country is a world center of new technology development. Korea has abundant, cost-effective knowledge workers who drive innovations in design, features, production, and product quality. The country also has a high savings rate, with massive inward FDI, which ensures a ready supply of capital for carmakers to fund R&D and other ventures. Collectively, Korea's abundance of production factors in cost-effective labor, knowledge workers, high technology, and capital represent key location-specific advantages.

Korean consumers are demanding, so carmakers take great pains to produce high quality automobiles. Intense rivalry in the domestic auto industry ensures that carmakers and auto parts producers improve products continuously.

The Korean economy is dominated by several conglomerates, called *chaebols*. They include Hyundai, Samsung, LG, and SK and account for about 40 percent of Korea's GDP and exports.

In recent years, the Korean government imposed stringent accounting controls on many of these firms. The government cooperates closely with the business sector, protecting some industries, ensuring funds for others, and sponsoring still others. The government promoted imports of raw materials and technology at the expense of consumer goods and encouraged savings and investment over consumption. Partly due to these efforts, Korea is home to a substantial industrial cluster for the production of cars and car parts. The nation benefits from the presence of numerous suppliers and manufacturers in the global automotive industry.

In past years, Hyundai also benefited from a weak Korean *won* (Korea's currency), making prices for Hyundai cars cheaper for customers in Europe and the United States who buy imported cars in their local currencies. Hyundai owes much of its success to favorable international exchange rates.

Background on Hyundai

Hyundai was founded in 1947 by Chung Ju-yung, a visionary entrepreneur from a peasant background. By the 1970s, the firm had begun an aggressive effort to develop engineering capabilities and new designs in the auto industry. In the 1980s, Hyundai began exporting the Excel, an economy car priced at $4,995, to the United States. An instant success, Excel exports grew to 250,000 units per year. But the Excel suffered from quality issues and a weak dealer network. Buyer confidence waned in the late 1990s and Hyundai's brand equity weakened. In response to complaints, Hyundai initiated major quality improvement programs and introduced a 10-year powertrain warranty program, unprecedented in the auto industry. The strategy was a major turning point for the firm.

Geographic Diversification

In 1997, Hyundai built a car factory in Turkey, giving the firm convenient access to key markets in the Middle East and Europe. Next, Hyundai opened a plant in India and within a few years became the country's best selling brand of imported car. In 2002, Hyundai launched a factory in China, doubling production, and is aiming for 20 percent share of the Chinese car market. The firm also partnered with Guangzhou Motor Group, winning entry to China's huge commercial-vehicle market. In addition to gaining access to low-cost, high-quality labor in emerging markets, Hyundai hopes its presence in local showrooms will improve consumer awareness and drive new sales.

Hyundai uses FDI to develop key operations around the world. Management chooses locations based on the advantages they bring to the firm. By 2006, Hyundai established plants in Iran, Sudan, Taiwan, Vietnam, Venezuela, and numerous other countries. Recently, the firm opened plants in the U.S. states of Alabama and Georgia. Hyundai also has R&D centers in Europe, Japan, and North America. It has distribution centers and marketing subsidiaries at various locations that deliver parts to its expanding base of car dealers worldwide. Hyundai also has regional headquarters in Asia, Europe, and North America. To guarantee control over production and marketing, the firm has internalized many of its operations.

To remain competitive, Hyundai employs inexpensive, high-quality labor. Engines, tires, and other key inputs are sourced from low-cost suppliers. The firm has entered various collaborative ventures to cooperate in R&D, design, manufacturing, and other value-adding activities. These allow Hyundai access to foreign partners' know-how, capital, distribution channels, marketing assets, and the ability to overcome government-imposed obstacles. For example, Hyundai partnered with Daimler-Chrysler to develop new technologies and improve supply- chain management. Compared to Japanese or Western rivals, Hyundai has superior cost advantages in the acquisition of high-quality inputs.

While Japanese auto giants such as Toyota and Honda rely heavily on U.S. sales for their profits, Hyundai is more diversified. In 2008, the U.S. market accounted for only 14 percent of Hyundai's total sales, while China,

India, Russia, and Latin America represented a combined 35 percent of sales.

Hyundai recently launched its first luxury model, the Genesis. It was named the North American Car of the Year at the 2009 Detroit Auto Show, trumping industry favorites like the Audi A4, Jaguar XF, and Cadillac CTS-V.

A recent marketing innovation is the "Assurance Program" under which buyers can return recently purchased cars if they lose their job within one year of purchase. The program even pays the customer's lease payments for up to 90 days while the customer searches for a new job. Owners who elect to keep their cars are not required to reimburse Hyundai.

Recent Events

Like other carmakers, Hyundai has problems with excess capacity. In 2009, due to unwanted inventory, the firm slowed production at its Alabama plant and laid off hundreds of employees at regional headquarters in the United States. Hyundai cut production by some 25 percent at plants in Korea.

But the firm continues to launch new marketing campaigns and replaced General Motors as the official automotive sponsor of the Academy Awards.

Hyundai has pursued internationalization aggressively. While many global firms struggle to stay afloat during a crisis, Hyundai is seeking to expand. Hyundai sees the crisis as an opportunity, with plans to emerge even stronger. Hyundai has improved quality and increased sales against all odds. Given its focus on quality, energy efficiency, cost control, and customer satisfaction, perhaps Hyundai is the new standard bearer in the global auto industry.

AACSB: Reflective Thinking Skills, Analytic Skills, Multiculturalism and Diversity

Case Questions

1. What are the roles of comparative and competitive advantages in Hyundai's success? Illustrate your answers by providing specific examples of natural and acquired advantages that Hyundai employs to succeed in the global car industry.

2. In terms of factor proportions theory, what abundant factors does Hyundai leverage in its worldwide operations? Provide examples and explain how Hyundai exemplifies the theory. In what ways does Hyundai's success contradict the theory? Justify your answer.

3. Discuss Hyundai and its position in the global car industry in terms of Porter's diamond model. What is the role of firm strategy, structure, and rivalry; factor conditions; demand conditions; and related and supporting industries to Hyundai's international success?

4. The Korean government has been instrumental to Hyundai's success. In terms of national industrial policy, what has the government done to support Hyundai? What can the government do to encourage future success at Hyundai? What can the government in your country do to support development or maintenance of a strong auto industry?

5. Consistent with Dunning's Eclectic Paradigm, describe the ownership-specific advantages, location-specific advantages, and internalization advantages held by Hyundai. Which of these advantages do you believe has been most instrumental to the firm's success? Justify your answer.

SOURCES: "Hyundai Floors It in the US," *Business Week*, February 23, 2009, p. 30; M. Ihlwan, D. Kiley, and I. Rowley, "No Crisis for Samsung, Hyundai, and LG," *Business Week*, September 19, 2008, retrieved from http://www.businessweek .com; "Business: Sui Genesis; Hyundai's Surprising Success," *Economist*, March 7, 2009, retrieved from http://www.economist.com; M. Ihlwan, "Hyundai's Halo: Car of the Year Award," *Business Week*, January 12, 2009, retrieved from http://www .businessweek.com; "Hyundai Motor Company," *Hoover's Company Records*, February 17, 2009, retrieved from http://www.hoovers.com; M. Ihlwan, "Weak Currency Eases Pain for Korean Exporters," *Business Week*, January 23, 2009, retrieved from http://www.hoovers.com; T. Murphy, "Hyundai Ratchets Up Momentum," *Ward's Auto World*, March 2010, p. 28; "2009 Production Statistics," *OICA*, 2010, retrieved from http://oica.net; "Survey: Driving Change," *Economist*, September 2, 2004, pp. 15-24; "The Quick and the Dead," *Economist*, January 27, 2005, retrieved from http://www.economist.com; R. M. Steers, *Made in Korea* (New York: Routledge, 1999); M. Schuman, "Hyundai Revs Up," *Time*, April 25, 2005, pp. 27–30; "Special Report: The Car Company in Front – Toyota," *Economist*, January 29, 2005, pp. 73-77.

NOTE: This case was written by Professor Nukhet Vardar, Yeditepe University, Istanbul, Turkey, and updated in 2009 by Professor Carol Sánchez and Claire Liang, Grand Valley State University, Grand Rapids, Michigan.

CHAPTER ESSENTIALS

Key Terms

absolute advantage principle, p. 181
comparative advantage,   p. 178
comparative advantage principle,
   p. 182

competitive advantage,   p. 179
free trade,   p. 181
industrial cluster,   p. 190

internalization theory,   p. 197
mercantilism,   p. 180
national industrial policy,   p. 191

Summary

In this chapter, you learned about:

1. **Theories of international trade and investment**

   The basis for trade is specialization. Each nation specializes in producing certain goods and services and then trades with other nations to acquire those goods and services in which it is not specialized. Life as we know it would be impossible without international trade.

2. **Why do nations trade?**

   Classical explanations of international trade began with **mercantilism**, which argued that nations should seek to maximize their wealth by exporting more than they import. The **absolute advantage principle** argues that a country benefits by producing only those products in which it has absolute advantage or can produce using fewer resources than another country. The principle of **comparative advantage** contends that countries should specialize and export those goods in which they have a relative advantage compared to other countries. Nations benefit by trading with one another. Comparative advantage is based on *natural advantages* and *acquired advantages*. **Competitive advantage** derives from distinctive assets or competencies of a firm, such as cost, size, or innovation strengths, which are difficult for competitors to replicate or imitate. The

   collective competitive advantages of many firms give rise to competitive advantage in the nation as a whole. *Factor proportions theory* holds that nations specialize in the production of goods and services whose factors of production they hold in abundance. *International product life cycle theory* describes how a product may be invented in one country and eventually mass-produced in other countries, with the innovating country losing its initial competitive advantage. *New trade theory* argues that increasing economies of scale determine superior performance in some industries.

3. **How can nations enhance their competitive advantage?**

   A major recent contribution to trade theory is *Porter's diamond model*, which specifies the four conditions in each nation that give rise to national competitive advantages: *firm strategy, structure, and rivalry; factor conditions; demand conditions;* and *related and supporting industries.* An **industrial cluster** is a concentration of companies in the same industry in a given location that interact closely with one another, gaining mutual competitive advantage. Competitive advantage of nations describes how nations acquire international trade advantages by developing specific skills, technologies, and industries.

National industrial policy refers to efforts by governments to direct national resources to developing expertise in specific industries.

4. Why and how do firms internationalize?

The *internationalization process model* describes how companies expand into international business gradually, usually going from simple exporting to the most committed stage, FDI. Born global firms internationalize at or near their founding and are part of the emergent field of international entrepreneurship.

5. How can internationalizing firms gain and sustain competitive advantage?

MNEs have value chains that span geographic locations worldwide. Foreign direct investment means that firms invest at various locations to establish factories, marketing subsidiaries, or regional headquarters. *Monopolistic advantage theory* describes how companies succeed internationally by developing resources and capabilities that few other firms possess. Internalization is the process of acquiring and maintaining one or more value-chain activities inside the firm to minimize the disadvantages of subcontracting these activities to external firms. **Internalization theory** explains the tendency of MNEs to internalize value-chain stages when it is to their advantage. The *eclectic paradigm* specifies that the international firm should possess certain internal competitive advantages, called *ownership-specific advantages, location-specific advantages,* and *internalization advantages.* Many companies engage in international *collaborative ventures,* interfirm partnerships that give them access to assets and other advantages held by foreign partners. MNEs also develop extensive networks of supportive companies such as other manufacturers, distributors, suppliers, retailers, banks, and transportation suppliers.

Test Your Comprehension AACSB: Reflective Thinking Skills, Analytic Skills

1. Why do nations engage in international business? That is, what are the benefits of international trade and investment?

2. Describe the classical theories of international trade. Which theories do you believe are relevant today?

3. What is the difference between the concepts of absolute advantage and comparative advantage?

4. Summarize factor proportions theory. What factors are most abundant in the following countries: China, Japan, Germany, Saudi Arabia, and the United States? Visit globalEDGE™ for helpful information.

5. Summarize the international product life cycle theory. Use the theory to explain the international evolution of automobiles and laptop computers.

6. What are the main sources of national competitive advantage? Think about a successful product in your country; what are the sources of competitive advantage that explain its success?

7. Do you believe your country should adopt a national industrial policy? Why or why not?

8. Describe the internationalization process of the firm. Review the background of major MNEs by visiting their Web sites. What is the nature of internationalization in these firms? What is the nature of internationalization in born global firms?

9. FDI-based explanations of international business evolved over time. Describe the evolution of these explanations from monopolistic advantage theory, through internalization theory, to the eclectic paradigm.

10. What are ownership-specific advantages, location-specific advantages, and internalization advantages?

Apply Your Understanding AACSB: Reflective Thinking Skills, Analytic Skills, Communication Abilities, Ethical Understanding and Reasoning Abilities

1. South Africa is home to huge reserves of coal, gold, diamonds, and natural gas. In addition to their intrinsic value, gold and diamonds have many industrial uses in which South Africa is the world leader. Mining precious minerals has transformed South Africa into a major industrial state and financed modern transportation and communications systems. To handle international shipping, the government developed major ports that connect South Africa to markets around the world. South Africa is also home to a large pool of low-cost workers in mining and related industries. The government has devised a collection of plans that support specific industries, especially mining. These developments support a cluster of highly specialized firms in the mining and extractive industries. Some of the world's most knowledgeable firms in these industries are concentrated in South Africa, especially De Beers SA (www.debeers.com). De Beers has substantial capabilities in marketing and international strategy and a near-monopoly in the global diamond industry. The firm partners with MNEs that hold major financial resources. Use the theories discussed in this chapter to explain the advantages held by South Africa and De Beers. What insights emerge from these theories that shed light on South Africa and De Beers?

2. Economist Lester Thurow once posed the following question: "If you were the president of your own country and could choose one of two industries in which to specialize, computer chips or potato chips, which would you choose?" When faced with this question, many people choose potato chips, because "everybody can use potato chips, but not everybody can use computer chips." But the answer is much more complex. Whether to choose computer chips or potato chips depends on such factors as the relationship between national wealth and the amount of value added in manufacturing products, the possibility that the country can benefit from monopoly power (few countries can make computer chips), and the likelihood of spin-off industries (computer chip technology gives rise to other technologies, such as computers). In light of these and other possible considerations, which would you choose: computer chips or potato chips? Justify your answer.

3. *Ethical Dilemma:* To reduce poverty in Africa, government officials want to increase African exports to Europe. Africa's top exports include agricultural products, such as meat, coffee, peanuts, and fruit. However, the European Union (EU) imposes high trade barriers on the import of agricultural products. There are various reasons for the barriers. For one, Europeans are concerned about food quality, and the EU has adopted rigorous agricultural safety standards. But the tough food regulations hurt African countries, which have experienced problems with food toxins, avian flu, and bovine diseases. In addition, the agricultural lobby in Europe is powerful, and farmers are heavily subsidized by the EU. Many European politicians do not want to risk angering Europe's farm lobby by supporting free international trade in agricultural products. Suppose you are part of an EU government task force that is investigating trade barriers on African agricultural imports. Using the ethical framework in Chapter 5, analyze the arguments for and against agricultural trade with Africa. What should the EU do? Justify your answer.

globalEDGE Internet Exercises
(http://globalEDGE.msu.edu)

AACSB: Analytic Skills, Use of Information Technology

Refer to Chapter 1, page 62, for instructions on how to access and use globalEDGE™.

1. Your company is interested in importing wines from Argentina. In analyzing this opportunity, you want to identify the strengths and weaknesses of the Argentine wine industry. What are the conditions that make Argentina a favorable location for wine cultivation? Provide a short description of the current status of Argentina's wine exports and a list of the top importing countries of Argentine wines. In addition to globalEDGE™, some useful Web sites for this research include www.winesofchile.org and www.ita.doc.gov.

2. Volvo (www.volvo.com) and Pilkington (www.pilkington.com) are major multinational firms with operations that span the globe. Investigate these firms by visiting their Web sites, as well as www.hoovers.com (a site that provides specific company information) and globalEDGE™. For each company, describe its ownership-specific advantages, location-specific advantages, and internalization advantages.

3. The World Bank works to alleviate world poverty. The Bank provides information about conditions in developing countries, which it uses to measure progress in economic and social development. World Development Indicators (www.worldbank.org/data) is the Bank's premier source for data on international development. The Bank measures more than 800 indicators of national conditions regarding people, environment, and economy. Consult the Web site, click on World Development Indicators, and answer the following questions: (a) In countries with developing economies, what indicators are most associated with poverty? (b) What types of industries are most typically found in poor countries? (c) Based on comparing development indicators in poor and affluent countries, speculate on what types of actions governments in developing countries can take to help spur economic development and alleviate poverty.

CHAPTER 7

LEARNING OBJECTIVES In this chapter, you will learn about:

1. The nature of country risk
2. Political and legal environments in international business
3. Political systems
4. Legal systems
5. Participants in political and legal systems
6. Types of country risk produced by political systems
7. Types of country risk produced by legal systems
8. Managing country risk

Political and Legal Systems in National Environments

The Political and Legal Realities of Doing Business in Russia

Paying bribes to gain favors, whether small or large amounts, is commonplace in many countries. In Russia, it is not unusual for business people to make payments to facilitate business, and some bribes exceed US $100,000, enough to buy a small flat in Moscow. Survey data suggest that most Russians consider paying bribes a normal cost of doing business.

Counterfeiting is also a problem. Take a walk through the open-air markets in Moscow, and you will likely find vendors selling pirated software, music, and movies. Russian police are aware of these products but usually do not issue fines or arrest the sellers. Some corrupt officers even get a cut of the vendors' total sales.

In the corruption index compiled by Transparency International, Russia ranks high among countries where kickbacks and questionable business practices exist. Because of a weak legal environment, the country is a tough place to do business. Prime Minister Vladimir Putin even remarked that anyone who successfully registers a business in Russia deserves a medal. Vague and overlapping regulations enrich a host of public officials. Any new venture may necessitate dozens of government licenses, and each license may require paying a bribe.

There are also countless incidents of strong-handed government interference in the private sector. Criminal raiders, sometimes in collaboration with government officials, seize independently operating businesses. One well-known example is Yukos, an oil company once controlled by the Russian industrialist Mikhail Khodorkovsky, who has been imprisoned by the government for alleged tax evasion. Claiming that Yukos owed back taxes, Russia's government sold part of the firm and kept the $9.3 billion in proceeds.

Organized crime is also part of the difficult landscape. In 2006, the deputy chairman of Russia's central bank was shot dead in Moscow. He was trying to reform a corrupt banking system and had closed dozens of banks linked to organized crime, making enemies in the process. Numerous other contract killings have occurred, as criminal organizations attempt to maintain their stronghold on much of Russia's economy. Criminal groups are believed to control some large Russian firms. Foreign MNEs routinely perform background checks on employees and contractors in an effort to identify people linked to organized crime. Foreign companies also attempt to provide for the security of staff and facilities.

One consequence of these challenges is that direct investors are often hesitant to do business in Russia. Indeed, some have pulled out altogether, taking tens of billions of dollars with them. Corruption and crime have raised doubts about Russia's evolving legal system and its commitment to market economics. Things have gotten so bad that the country's bid to join the World Trade Organization (WTO) was temporarily abandoned.

Russia is transitioning from a command economy to a market economy. The shift has created much uncertainty for foreign firms doing business there. Ambiguous regulations, inadequate laws, capricious enforcement, a rudimentary court system, and a formerly totalitarian government all pose numerous difficulties. Managers must be mindful of the political and legal environments that characterize transition economies. Although they can take precautionary measures to minimize risk, not all risk is avoidable. Numerous firms, from Boeing to IKEA, have invested billions in Russia. Potential rewards are promising for firms that plan ahead and protect their assets, but operating there poses many challenges.

SOURCES: D. Dombey, "Russia's WTO Bid on Ice, Say Diplomats," *Financial Times*, August 27, 2008, p. 6; "Russia Economy: Grease my Palm," *EIU ViewsWire*, November 28, 2008, p. 1; "RUSSIA: Corporate Raiding Challenges Investors." *Oxford Analytica Daily Brief Service*, August 21, 2008, p. 1; G. Chazan, "Russian Trial Opens Messy Chapter," *Wall Street Journal*, June 16, 2004; "Business: The Reluctant Briber," *Economist*, November 4, 2006, p. 79; A. Kouznetsov and M. Dass, "Areas of Corruption in the Distribution of Foreign-Made Goods Where a Firm's Size and Origin Play a Role: The Russian Experience," *Journal of East-West Business*, Vol. 16, No. 1, 2010, pp. 24-44 ; V. Kvint, "The Scary Business of Russia," *Forbes*, May 23, 2005, p. 42; C. Matlack and M. Elder, "The Peril and Promise of Investing in Russia," *Business Week*, October 5, 2009, pp. 48–52.

 ## The Nature of Country Risk

Most of us expect a familiar business landscape when we conduct business at home. But foreign markets frequently differ in terms of political and legal systems, as well as business norms. As illustrated by the opening vignette, foreign markets often pose major challenges and create vulnerabilities for the firm. Managers must be able to navigate difficult regulations and practices and avoid unethical or questionable conduct.

At the same time, the political and legal context may also present opportunities for companies. Preferential subsidies, government incentives, and protection from competition reduce business costs and influence strategic decision making. Many governments encourage domestic investment from foreign MNEs by offering tax holidays and cash incentives to employ local workers.

Country risk Exposure to potential loss or adverse effects on company operations and profitability caused by developments in a country's political and/or legal environments.

Country risk is exposure to potential loss or adverse effects on company operations and profitability caused by developments in a country's political and/or legal environments. Also referred to as *political risk,* it is one of four major types of international business risks introduced in Chapter 1. While the immediate cause of country risk is a political or legal factor, underlying such factors may be economic, social, or technological developments. Exhibit 7.1 identifies dimensions of country risk prevalent in international business. We address most of them in this chapter. Government intervention, protectionism, and barriers to trade and investment are particularly notable in international business. Mismanagement or failure of the national economy can lead to financial crises, recessions, market downturns, currency crises, and inflation. Such events usually arise from business cycles, poor monetary or fiscal policies, a defective regulatory environment, or imbalances in the underlying economic fundamentals of the host country.

Political or legislative actions can inadvertently harm business interests, such as laws that are unexpectedly strict or result in unintended consequences. Many laws favor host-country interests—that is, interests in foreign countries where the firm has direct operations. For example, Coca-Cola's business suffered in Germany after the government enacted a recycling plan that required consumers to return non-reusable soda containers to stores for a refund of 0.25 euros. Rather than coping with unwanted returns, big supermarket chains responded by yanking Coke from their shelves and pushing their own store brands instead.[1] In China, the government censors material that is critical of its actions and policies. Yahoo must monitor the information that appears on its Web sites to prevent the Chinese government from closing its China operations. In

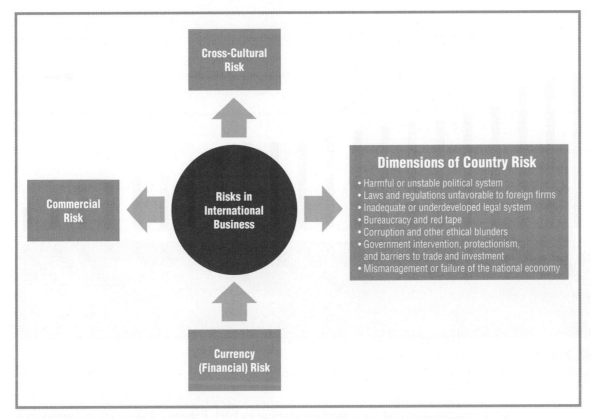

Exhibit 7.1   Country Risk as One of Four Major Risks in International Business

2010, Google took a censorship stand against the Chinese government when it moved its search engine to Hong Kong. Google's action was bold but could potentially cost the company advertising revenue and customers.

How Prevalent Is Country Risk?

Exhibit 7.2 presents the level of country risk in various countries measured in terms of political stability, legal environment, economic indicators, and tax policy. Iraq is one of the riskiest countries in the wake of war and the emergence of a new political regime. Zimbabwe is risky because of ongoing bribery, fraud, and political turmoil. Canada, Ireland, and Singapore are among the most politically stable countries.[2] For the complete list of countries ranked by risk, visit the Risk Briefing site at the Economist Intelligence Unit (viewswire.eiu.com).

Country risk may affect all firms in a country equally or only a subset. Civil war in the former Yugoslavia in the 1990s tended to affect all firms. By contrast, the Russian government targeted only Yukos with politically motivated persecution, despite the presence of several competitors in Russia like ConocoPhillips and Royal Dutch Shell.[3]

India is often characterized by high country risk. Hindu nationalists who came to political power in 1996 openly opposed foreign investment and influence on Indian society and enacted laws that targeted foreign firms for harassment. The KFC restaurant chain was forced to step up security after threats by local political groups to destroy the firm's fast-food outlets. About one hundred farmers ransacked a KFC restaurant in Bangalore. In an earlier incident, the same restaurant was forced to close after health officials said its chicken contained excessive levels of monosodium glutamate, a common flavor enhancer.[4]

As countries develop economic ties with foreign trading partners and integrate themselves with the global economy, they tend to liberalize their markets and reduce restrictions on foreign business. This happened in India as well, with the introduction of

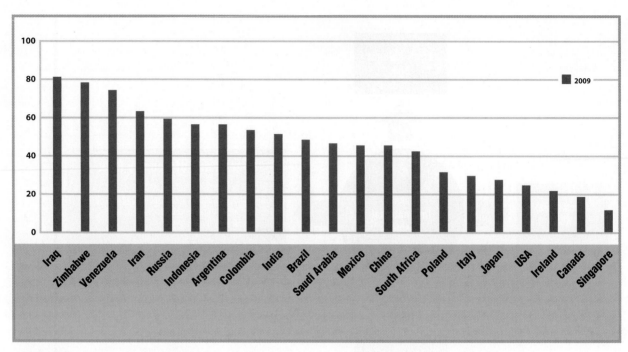

Exhibit 7.2 Country Risk in Selected Countries

SOURCE: *Economist Intelligence Unit* (2009), "Risk Briefing", viewswire.eiu.com, accessed August 2, 2009.

economic reforms and open markets starting in 1991. Exhibit 7.2 shows that country risk tends to be lower in countries with a favorable legal climate and political stability and higher in countries with excessive regulatory burdens and political instability. Many of the riskiest locations are poor countries that would benefit enormously from direct investment and integration into the global economy.

 ## Political and Legal Environments in International Business

Political system A set of formal institutions that constitute a government.

A **political system** is a set of formal institutions that constitute a government. It includes legislative bodies, political parties, lobbying groups, and trade unions. The principal functions of a political system are to provide protection from external threats, establish stability based on laws, and govern the allocation of valued resources among the members of a society. A political system also defines how these groups interact with each other.

Each country's political system is unique, having evolved within a particular historical, economic, and cultural context. Political systems are also constantly evolving in response to constituent demands and the evolution of the national and international environment. *Constituents* are the people and organizations that support the political system and receive government resources.

Legal system A system for interpreting and enforcing laws.

A **legal system** is a system for interpreting and enforcing laws. The laws, regulations, and rules establish norms for conduct. A legal system incorporates institutions and procedures for ensuring order and resolving disputes in commercial activities, as well as taxing economic output and protecting intellectual property and other company assets.

Exhibit 7.3 identifies the aspects of political and legal systems that contribute to country risk. Political and legal systems are dynamic and constantly changing. The two systems are interdependent—changes in one affect the other. Adverse developments in political and legal systems give rise to country risk. They can result from installation of a new government, shifting values or priorities in political parties, initiatives developed by special interest groups, and the creation of new laws or regulations. Gradual change is easier for the firm to accommodate, while sudden change is harder to deal with and poses greater risk to the firm.

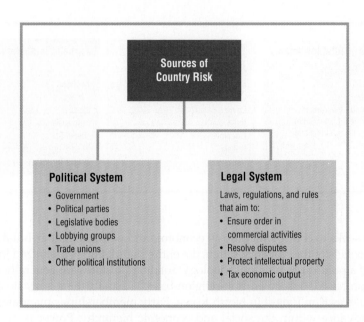

Exhibit 7.3   Sources of Country Risk

Unfavorable developments give rise to new conditions that may threaten the firm's products, services, or business activities. For example, a new import tariff may increase the cost of a key component used to manufacture a product. A modification in labor law may alter the hours the firm's employees are allowed to work. The installation of a new political leader may lead to government takeover of corporate assets.

Country risk is *always* present, but its nature and intensity vary over time and from country to country. In China, for example, the government is currently overhauling the national legal system, making it increasingly more consistent with Western systems. Some new regulations have been poorly formulated or are confusing or contradictory. For example, at one point the Beijing government announced that foreign investments in China's Internet industry were illegal. By this time Western firms had already invested millions in the Chinese dot.com sector, without any indication that the investments were inappropriate. In disputes between local and foreign firms, governments are often inclined to protect local interests. Even where Western firms obtain favorable judgments in the courts, they may not be enforced. Let's delve into political and legal systems in greater detail.

 ## Political Systems

Recent history has witnessed three major types of political systems: totalitarianism, socialism, and democracy. Exhibit 7.4 highlights countries that exemplify these systems. However, these categories are not mutually exclusive. Most democracies also include some elements of socialism. Most former totalitarian regimes now embrace a mix of socialism and democracy.

To control the recent global financial crisis, governments in Europe and the United States implemented relatively socialistic policies, such as nationalizing firms in the banking and automotive industries. China applied more democratic approaches, such as land reforms and open markets, to stimulate commercial activity. Worldwide, political systems are evolving as governments experiment with ways to fight recession and avert financial crisis.

Totalitarianism

Well-known totalitarian states from the past include Nazi Germany (1933–1945), Spain (1939–1975), China (1949–1980s), and the Soviet Union (1918–1991). Under totalitarianism, the state attempts to regulate most aspects of public and private behavior. A totalitarian

Exhibit 7.4 Examples of Countries under Various Political Systems

Elements of Totalitarianism Found in	Elements of Socialism Found in	Largely Democratic
Cuba North Korea Several countries in Africa (such as Eritrea, Libya, Sudan, Equatorial Guinea, Zimbabwe)	Bolivia China Egypt India Romania Russia Venezuela	Australia Canada Japan New Zealand United States Most European countries Most Latin American countries

government seeks to control not only all economic and political matters but the attitudes, values, and beliefs of the citizenry. Often, the entire population is mobilized in support of the state and a political or religious ideology. Totalitarian states are generally either theocratic (religion-based) or secular (non-religion-based). Usually there is a state party led by a dictator, such as Kim Jong-il in North Korea. Party membership is mandatory for those seeking to advance within the social and economic hierarchy. Power is maintained by means of secret police, propaganda disseminated through state-controlled mass media, regulation of free discussion and criticism, and the use of terror tactics. Totalitarian states usually do not tolerate activities by individuals or groups such as churches, labor unions, or political parties that are not directed toward the state's goals.[5]

Over time, many of the world's totalitarian states have either disappeared or shifted their political and economic systems toward democracy and capitalism. China initiated major reforms in the 1980s, and the Soviet Union collapsed in 1991. Agricultural land and state enterprises were sold to private interests and entrepreneurs gained the right to establish their own businesses. The transition has not been easy, and former totalitarian states continue to maintain political control, including government intervention in business (as in Russia in the opening vignette). Former Soviet Union states and China are still characterized by red tape that hinders the founding of new firms, bureaucratic accounting and tax regulations, inadequate legal systems to protect business interests, and weak infrastructure in transportation, communications, and information technology (for example, see the World Bank's www.doingbusiness.org). Today, numerous states exhibit elements of totalitarianism, particularly in Africa, Asia, and the Middle East. Several countries are controlled by individuals with substantial dictatorial powers, such as Muammar al-Qaddafi in Libya, Hugo Chavez in Venezuela, and Robert Mugabe in Zimbabwe.

Socialism

Socialism's fundamental tenet is that capital and wealth should be vested in the state and used primarily as a means of production rather than for profit. Socialism is based on a collectivist ideology in which the collective welfare of people is believed to outweigh the welfare of the individual. Socialists argue that capitalists receive a disproportionate amount of society's wealth relative to workers. They believe that in a capitalist society, the pay of workers does not represent the full value of their labor, and thus government should control the basic means of production, distribution, and commercial activity.

Socialism has manifested itself in much of the world as *social democracy* and has been most successful in western Europe. It has also played a major role in the political systems of large countries such as Brazil and India, and today it remains a viable system in much of the world. In social democratic regimes, such as Italy and Norway, government frequently intervenes in the private sector and in business activities. Corporate income tax rates are often relatively high, as in France and Sweden. Even robust economies like Germany have experienced net outflows of FDI as businesses seek to escape extensive regulation.

Democracy

Democracy has become the prevailing political system in many of the world's advanced economies. It is characterized by two key features:

- *Private property rights,* or the ability to own property and assets and to increase one's asset base by accumulating private wealth. *Property* includes tangibles, such as land and buildings, as well as intangibles, such as stocks, contracts, patent rights, and intellectual assets. Democratic governments devise laws that protect property rights. People and firms can acquire property, use it, buy or sell it, and bequeath it to whomever they want. These rights are important because they encourage individual initiative, ambition, and innovation, as well as thrift and the desire to accumulate wealth. People are less likely to have these qualities if there is any uncertainty about whether they can control their property or profit from it.

- *Limited government.* The government performs only essential functions that serve all citizens, such as conducting national defense, maintaining law and order and diplomatic relations, and constructing and maintaining infrastructure such as roads, schools, and public works. State control and intervention in the economic activities of private individuals or firms is minimal. By allowing market forces to determine economic activity, the government ensures resources are allocated with maximal efficiency.[6]

Under democracy, the individual pursuits of people and firms are sometimes at odds with equality and justice. Because people have differing levels of personal and financial resources, each performs with varying degrees of success, leading to inequalities. Critics of pure democracy argue that when these inequalities become excessive, government should step in to correct them. Each society balances individual freedom with broader social goals. In democracies such as Japan and Sweden, the rights and freedoms associated with democracy are construed in larger societal terms rather than on behalf of individuals.

Virtually all democracies include elements of socialism, such as government intervention in the affairs of individuals and firms. Socialistic tendencies emerge because of abuses or negative externalities that occur in purely democratic systems. For example, Japan has been striving to achieve the right balance between democracy and socialism. In the 1990s, poor management practices and an economic recession led to the bankruptcy of thousands of Japanese firms. To maintain jobs and economic stability, the Japanese government intervened to support numerous large firms and banks that, in a pure democracy, would have failed. But such policies have led to inflexibility in the Japanese economy and a delay of needed structural improvements.

By protecting private property rights, democracies promote entrepreneurship. These women in Chetumal, Mexico, make tortillas in their small business and are able to enjoy its profits.

Many countries, including Australia, Canada, the United States, and those in Europe, are best described as having a *mixed* political system—characterized by a strong private sector *and* a strong public sector, with considerable government regulation and control.

Democracy's Link to Economic Freedom and Openness

Compared to totalitarianism and socialism, democracy is associated with greater economic freedom and, usually, higher living standards. Economic freedom flourishes when governments support the institutions necessary for that freedom, such as freely operating markets and

DGR83357000   Chetumal, Mexico: Mayan women who are small business owners making tortillas. 1998 ©Jeff Greenberg / The Image Works   NOTE: The copyright notice must include "The Image Works" DO NOT SHORTEN THE NAME OF THE COMPANY

Exhibit 7.5

Relationship between
Political Freedom and
Economic Freedom for a
Sample of Countries

SOURCE: Freedom House, 2008.
Accessed at http://www.freedomhouse.org

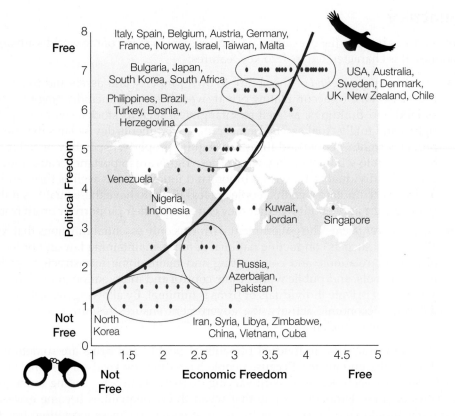

rule of law. Exhibit 7.5 reveals that the more political freedom in a nation, the more economic freedom its citizens enjoy. Political freedom is characterized by free and fair elections; the right to form political parties; fair electoral laws; existence of a parliament or other legislative body; freedom from domination by the military, foreign powers, or religious hierarchies; and self-determination for cultural, ethnic, and religious minorities. Economic freedom is related to the extent of government interference in business, the strictness of the regulatory environment, and the ease with which commercial activity is carried out according to market forces. Visit Freedom House (www.freedomhouse.org) to view the latest information on political and economic freedom around the world.

Democracy is closely associated with *openness*, or lack of regulation or barriers to the entry of firms in foreign markets. The greater the openness, the fewer the constraints placed on foreign firms. Absence of excessive regulations also benefits buyers because openness increases the quantity and variety of products available. Competition also helps improve quality standards for products on the market. Increased efficiency and lower prices may follow. For example, since the 1980s the government of India has steadily lowered entry barriers in the Indian automobile market. Foreign automakers have steadily entered the market, greatly increasing the number of models available for sale, raising the quality of available cars, and lowering prices. A similar phenomenon can be observed in the mobile telephone market in China.[7]

The Relationship between Political Systems and Economic Systems

Each political system tends to be associated with a particular type of economic system. Generally speaking, totalitarianism is associated with command economies, democracy with market economies, and socialism with mixed economies. Let's review these economic systems.

Command Economy   Also known as a centrally planned economy, a command economy makes the state a dominant force in the production and distribution of goods and services. Central planners make resource allocation decisions, and the state owns major sectors of the economy. In command economies, sizable bureaucracy thrives, and central planning tends to be less efficient than market forces in synchronizing supply and demand. For example, goods shortages were so common in the Soviet Union that people often waited in lines for hours to buy basic necessities like sugar and bread. Today, countries such as China and Russia still exhibit some characteristics of command economies. However, the system is gradually dying out in favor of market economies and mixed economies.

Market Economy   In a market economy, market forces—the interaction of supply and demand—determine prices. Government intervention in the marketplace is limited, and economic decisions are left to individuals and firms. Market economies are closely associated with capitalism, in which the means of production are privately owned and operated. Participants typically exhibit a market-oriented mentality and entrepreneurial spirit. The task of the state is to establish a legal system that protects private property and contractual agreements. However, the government may also intervene to address the inequalities that market economies sometimes produce.

Mixed Economy   A mixed economy exhibits the features of both a market economy and a command economy. It combines state intervention and market mechanisms for organizing production and distribution. Most industries are under private ownership, and entrepreneurs freely establish, own, and operate corporations. But the government also controls certain functions, such as pension programs, labor regulation, minimum wage levels, and environmental regulation. State-owned enterprises operate in key sectors such as transportation, telecommunications, and energy. In France, for example, the government owns key banks and some key industries, such as aluminum refining. One car company, Renault, is partially state owned, but another, Peugeot, is not. In Germany, Japan, Norway, Singapore, and Sweden, the government often works closely with business and labor groups to determine industrial policy, regulate wage rates, and/or provide subsidies to support specific industries.

The last century saw a substantial increase in the number of mixed economies and a concurrent rise in government involvement in economic matters. For example, in the United States, combined government spending increased from about 3 percent of GDP in the 1930s to roughly 20 percent by the 1980s. During the same period in most other developed economies, average government spending as a percent of GDP rose from 8 percent to more than 40 percent. Governments in Europe, Japan, and North America imposed many new regulations on private firms, especially after the most recent global financial crisis.[8] Regulations were adopted that covered workplace safety, minimum wages, pension benefits, and environmental protection.

 Legal Systems

Legal systems provide a framework of rules and norms of conduct that mandate, limit, or permit specified relationships among people and organizations and provide punishments for those who violate these rules and norms. Laws require or limit specific actions while empowering citizens to engage in others, such as entering into contracts and seeking remedies for contract violations. Legal systems are dynamic—they evolve over time to represent each nation's changing social values and the evolution of their social, political, economic, and technological environments.

Prevailing political systems—totalitarianism, socialism, and democracy—tend to influence their respective legal systems as well. Democracies tend to encourage market forces and free trade. In well-developed legal systems, such as in Australia, Canada,

Rule of law A legal system in which rules are clear, publicly disclosed, fairly enforced, and widely respected by individuals, organizations, and the government.

Japan, the United States, and most European countries, laws are widely known and understood. They are effective and legitimate because they are applied to all citizens equally, issued by means of formal procedures by recognized government authorities, and enforced systematically and fairly by police forces and formally organized judicial bodies.

In these countries, a culture of law exists in which citizens consistently respect and follow the rule of law. **Rule of law** refers to a legal system in which rules are clear, publicly disclosed, fairly enforced, and widely respected by individuals, organizations, and the government. International business flourishes in societies where the rule of law prevails. For example, in the United States, the Securities and Exchange Act encourages confidence in business transactions by requiring public companies to frequently disclose their financial indicators to investors. Legal systems can be eroded by declining respect for the law, weak government authority, or burdensome restrictions that attempt to forbid behavior prevalent in the society. In the absence of the rule of law, firms must contend with great uncertainty and economic activity may be impeded.

We can characterize nations as having one of four basic legal systems: common law, civil law, religious law, and mixed. These legal systems are the foundation for laws and regulations. Exhibit 7.6 provides examples of countries where these legal systems tend to prevail.

Common Law

Also known as case law, common law is a legal system that originated in England and spread to Australia, Canada, the United States, and former members of the British Commonwealth. The basis of common law is tradition, previous cases, and legal precedents set by the nation's courts through interpretation of statutes, legislation, and past rulings. The national legislature in common-law countries (such as Parliament in Britain and Congress in the United States) holds ultimate power to pass or amend laws. In the United States, because the constitution is difficult to amend, the Supreme Court and even lower courts have much flexibility to interpret the law. Because common law is more open to interpretation by courts, it is more flexible than other legal systems. Thus, judges in a common-law system have substantial power to interpret laws based on the unique circumstances of individual cases, including commercial disputes and other business situations.

Civil Law

Also known as code law, civil law is found in France, Germany, Italy, Japan, Turkey, and Latin America. Its origins go back to Roman law and the Napoleonic Code. Civil law is

Primarily Common Law	Primarily Civil Law	Primarily Religious Law	Mixed Systems
Australia	Much of western	Much of the	Bangladesh
Canada	Europe and Latin	Middle East and	India
Ireland	America	North Africa	Indonesia
New Zealand	Japan	Afghanistan	Israel
United Kingdom	Russia	Mauritania	Kenya
United States	South Korea	Pakistan	Malaysia
		Sudan	Philippines

Exhibit 7.6 Dominant Legal Systems in Selected Countries

SOURCE: World Legal Systems at www.juriglobe.ca

based on an all-inclusive system of laws that have been "codified"; the laws are clearly written and accessible. It is divided into three separate codes: commercial, civil, and criminal. Civil law is considered complete as a result of catch-all provisions found within the law. Rules and principles form the starting point for legal reasoning and administering justice. The codified rules emerge as specific laws and codes of conduct produced by a legislative body or some other supreme authority.

Both common law and civil law systems originated in western Europe and represent the common values of western Europeans. A key difference between the two systems is that common law is primarily judicial in origin and based on court decisions, whereas civil law is primarily legislative in origin and based on laws passed by national and local legislatures. Common law and civil law pose various differences for international business. These are highlighted in Exhibit 7.7. In reality, common-law systems generally contain elements of civil law and vice versa. The two systems complement each other, and countries that employ one also tend to employ some elements of the other.

Religious Law

This legal system is strongly influenced by religious beliefs, ethical codes, and moral values viewed as mandated by a supreme being. The most important religious legal systems are based on Hindu, Jewish, and Islamic law. Among these, the most widespread is Islamic law, found mainly in the Middle East and North Africa. In addition to these areas, other countries with substantial populations of Muslims (followers of Islam) include India (about 161 million Muslims), Indonesia (202 million), Nigeria (78 million), and Pakistan (174 million). Islamic law, also known as the *shariah*, is based on the Qur'an, the holy book of Muslims, and the teachings of the Prophet Mohammed. Adherents generally do not differentiate between religious and secular life. Islamic law governs relationships among people, between people and the state, and between people and a supreme being. It spells out norms of behavior regarding politics, economics, banking, contracts, marriage, and many other social issues. Thus, Islamic law might be said to encompass all possible human relationships. Because it is seen as divinely ordained, it is relatively static and absolute. Unlike other legal systems, it evolves very little over time.

Legal Issues	Civil Law	Common Law
Ownership of intellectual property	Determined by registration.	Determined by prior use.
Enforcing agreements	Commercial agreements become enforceable only if properly notarized or registered.	Proof of agreement is sufficient for enforcing contracts.
Specificity of contracts	Contracts tend to be brief because many potential problems are already covered in the civil code.	Contracts tend to be very detailed, with all possible contingencies spelled out. Usually more costly to draft a contract.
Compliance with contracts	Noncompliance is extended to include unforeseeable human acts such as labor strikes and riots.	Acts of God (floods, lightning, hurricanes, etc.) are the only justifiable excuses for noncompliance with the provisions of contracts.

Exhibit 7.7 Examples of Differences between Common Law and Civil Law

Iranian women with Iran's flag attend a football match in Tehran after the Iranian government rescinded a quarter-century ban that had prohibited women from going to stadiums for sports events.

Most Muslim countries currently maintain a dual system, wherein both religious and secular courts coexist. Other countries with large Muslim populations, such as Indonesia, Bangladesh, and Pakistan, now have secular constitutions and laws. Turkey, another country with a majority Muslim population, has a strongly secular constitution. Saudi Arabia and Iran are unusual in that religious courts have authority over all aspects of jurisprudence.

Modern liberal movements within Islam oppose traditional views of religious law. For example, strict interpretation of Islamic law prohibits the giving and receiving of interest on loans or investments. To comply with Islamic law, financial institutions employ a variant of international banking known as "Islamic finance," based on the principles of shariah law. Many Western banks—for example, JP Morgan and Deutsche Bank—have subsidiaries in Muslim countries that comply with shariah laws. Instead of requiring interest payments, they charge administrative fees or take equity positions in the projects they finance. Many issue *sukuks*, Islamic-compliant bonds that offer revenue from an asset, such as a rental property, rather than interest. The global market for Shariah-compliant financial instruments now exceeds $1 trillion worldwide.[9]

Mixed Systems

Mixed systems consist of two or more legal systems operating together. In most countries, legal systems evolve over time, adopting elements of one system or another that reflect their unique needs. The contrast between civil law and common law has become blurred as many countries combine them. For example, legal systems in South Africa and the Philippines mix elements of civil law and common law. Legal systems in Indonesia and most Middle East countries share elements of civil law and Islamic law.

Historically, socialist law was a legal system found in the former Soviet Union, China, and a few states in Africa. It was based on civil law, with elements of socialist principles that emphasized state ownership of property. The rights of the state dominated those of the individual. When the Soviet Union collapsed and China began transitioning to capitalism, socialist law gave way to other legal systems, especially civil law.

Participants in Political and Legal Systems

Political and legal systems evolve from the interplay among various societal institutions, at both the national and international levels. Five types of participants are active in transforming political and legal systems.

Government

The government, or the public sector, is the most important actor, operating at national, state, and local levels. Governments have the power to enact and enforce laws. They strongly influence how firms enter host countries and how they conduct business there. Governments regulate international business activity through a complex system of institutions, agencies, and public officials. Agencies that possess such powers in the

United States include the U.S. Trade Representative and the International Trade Administration (www.ita.doc.gov). In Canada, such functions are handled by the Ministry of Foreign Affairs (www.international.gc.ca), the Ministry of Finance, and the Export and Import Controls Bureau. Similar agencies operate in Australia, Britain, and virtually all other countries.

International Organizations

Supranational agencies such as the World Trade Organization (www.wto.org), the United Nations (www.un.org), and the World Bank (www.worldbank.org) strongly influence international business. For example, the United Nations Conference on Trade and Development (UNCTAD, www.unctad.org) helps oversee international trade and development in the areas of investment, finance, technology, and enterprise development. Such organizations facilitate free and fair trade by providing administrative guidance, governing frameworks, and, occasionally, financial support.

Regional Economic Blocs

Regional trade organizations, such as the European Union (EU), the North American Free Trade Agreement (NAFTA), and the Association of Southeast Asian Nations (ASEAN), aim to advance the economic and political interests of their members. The EU is especially well developed, with its own executive, legislative, and bureaucratic bodies. It enacts and enforces laws and regulations that directly affect business. For example, following new regulations forced by Lithuania's entry into the EU, the supermarket chain IKI had to spend millions to build separate entrances for fresh meat delivery in each of its 136 stores.[10] Given their importance in international business, we devote Chapter 9 to regional economic blocs.

Special Interest Groups

Special interest groups serve the interests of particular countries, industries, or causes. For example, the Organisation for Economic Co-operation and Development (OECD, www.oecd.org) supports the economic developmental and business goals of advanced economies. The Organization of Petroleum Exporting Countries (OPEC, www.opec.org) is a powerful cartel that controls global oil prices, which, in turn, affect consumer prices and everyone's cost of doing business. OPEC emerged in the 1970s as a powerful voice for oil-producing countries, including Saudi Arabia, Iran, Venezuela, Nigeria, and Indonesia. Other groups exercise similar control over the production and allocation of commodities such as sugar, coffee, and iron ore.

Special interest groups engage in political activity to advance specific causes, ranging from labor rights to environmental protection. They often influence national political processes and produce outcomes with far-reaching consequences for business. Many target particular industries and affect individual firms accordingly. Special interest groups operate not only in host countries but also in the home country. For example, well-orchestrated U.S. interest groups forced U.S.-owned firms to reduce their investments in South Africa when its apartheid policies were in force.[11] Greenpeace (www.greenpeace.org) and the Save the Waves Coalition are environmental groups that opposed the plan of Sempra Energy, a California energy utility, to build a natural gas terminal and pipeline in Mexico. They believe Sempra's planned facility will pollute the ocean and wipe out lobster and tuna stocks. Protestors disrupted Sempra's construction progress.[12] Greenpeace also has been successful in pressuring appliance manufacturers from China to Germany to produce environmentally friendly refrigerators.[13] Exhibit 7.8 provides a sample of interest groups and their likely stance toward various business issues.

Exhibit 7.8 Issues of Concern to Special Interest Groups

Group	Typical Issue	Example
Labor unions	Oppose imported goods and global sourcing	U.S. united steelworkers union opposed imports of steel from China
Competing businesses	Dislike competition from foreign firms	Japanese rice producers opposed imports of rice from the United States
Customers	May avoid foreign-made products. Dislike improper marketing practices.	Motorists in Australia accused BP of unfair pricing of petroleum products
Conservationists	Fight against wildlife loss and destruction of the natural environment	Environmentalists oppose lumber imports from countries with tropical rain forests

Competing Firms

Rival domestic firms with a strong presence in the host country naturally have an interest in opposing the entry of foreign firms into the local market and may lobby their government for protection. For example, host-country competitors often complain when foreign firms receive financial support from the parent or host-country governments. Asterix, a French theme park, opposed French government support for the U.S.-based Disney when the latter established Disneyland Paris. Similarly, U.S. automakers in Detroit opposed BMW's construction of a factory in South Carolina. However, the state government of South Carolina supported the BMW facility on the grounds that it would generate jobs and increase tax revenues.

Types of Country Risk Produced by Political Systems

How do political systems create challenges for firms engaged in international business? Let's examine the specific risks brought about by political systems next.

Government Takeover of Corporate Assets

Governments seize corporate assets in two major ways: confiscation and expropriation. *Confiscation* is the seizure of corporate assets *without* compensation. *Expropriation* is seizure *with* compensation. The industry sectors most frequently targeted by such events are natural resources (for example, mining and petroleum), utilities, and manufacturing.

In Venezuela, ExxonMobil and ConocoPhillips were forced to abandon multibillion-dollar investments in the local oil industry. Recently, Venezuela President Hugo Chavez ordered troops to seize two plants owned by Mexico's Cemex, the country's largest cement producer. In 2008, gradual yet persistent pressure from the Russian government led TNK-BP, a Russian subsidiary of British energy giant BP, to sell a major stake in its oil business to the national gas monopoly Gazprom.[14]

A third category of takeover, *nationalization*, describes government's seizing not a firm but an entire industry, with or without compensation. In 2006, the government of Bolivia nationalized much of the oil and gas industry in that country.[15] Nationalization occurs in advanced economies as well. Following the recent global financial crisis, the federal government of the Netherlands nationalized part of the financial-services company Fortis NV, and Britain nationalized the Royal Bank of Scotland.[16]

In the decades following World War II, confiscation and expropriation were the main country risk confronting firms with extensive international operations, particularly in developing economies. In the 1960s and 1970s, Egypt, Nigeria, Peru, and other countries with nationalist and leftist host governments undertook numerous nationalizations. A wave of confiscations occurred under revolutionary regimes in Cuba, Iran, and Nicaragua.[17] Such events have become less common in recent years as governments in developing countries have adopted institutional reforms that aim to attract FDI from abroad and foster economic growth.

More common today is so-called "creeping expropriation," a subtle form of country risk in which governments modify laws and regulations after foreign MNEs have made substantial local investments in property and plants.[18] Examples include abrupt termination of contracts and the creation of new laws that favor local firms. As reported in the opening vignette, corporate raiders and government officials in Russia occasionally raid the offices of competitors and subject them to baseless criminal investigations. Such tactics occasionally force foreign MNEs to cede control of their operations to local interests.[19] Governments in Bolivia, Kazakhstan, Russia, and Venezuela have modified tax regimes to extract revenues from foreign coal, oil, and gas companies. Troops stormed the Kazakhstan offices of U.S. mining company AES to enforce an alleged tax fine amounting to some $200 million. One of the country's largest providers of electricity, AES reduced its operations in Kazakhstan in the wake of persistent abuse by the Kazakh government.[20] Subtle or devious approaches to government takeover make country risk harder to predict.

French farmers block the main entrance of a McDonald's fast-food restaurant in Auch, southwestern France, during a protest. The banner translates, "No to American Orders."

Embargoes and Sanctions

Most countries are signatories to international treaties and agreements that specify rules, principles, and standards of behavior in international business. Nevertheless, governments may unilaterally resort to sanctions and embargoes to respond to offensive activities of foreign countries. A *sanction* is a type of trade penalty imposed on one or more countries by one or more other countries. Sanctions typically take the form of tariffs, trade barriers, import duties, and import or export quotas. They generally arise in the context of an unresolved trade or policy dispute, such as a disagreement about the fairness of some international trade practice. There is much evidence to suggest that sanctions often do not achieve desired outcomes.

An *embargo* is an official ban on exports to or imports from a particular country, in order to isolate it and punish its government. It is generally more serious than a sanction and is used as a political punishment for some disapproved policies or acts. For example, the United States has enforced embargoes against Iran and North Korea, at times labeled as state sponsors of terrorism. The European Union has enacted embargoes against Belarus, Sudan, and China in certain areas, such as foreign travel, to protest human rights and weapon-trading violations.

Boycotts against Firms or Nations

Consumers and special interest groups occasionally target particular firms perceived to have harmed local interests. Consumers may refuse to patronize firms that behave inappropriately. A *boycott* is a voluntary refusal to engage in commercial dealings with a nation or a company. Boycotts and public protests result in lost sales and increased costs (for public relations activities needed to restore the firm's image). Disneyland Paris and McDonald's have been the targets of boycotts by French farmers, who believe these firms represent U.S. agricultural policies and globalization, which many French citizens abhor. Many U.S. citizens boycotted French products following France's decision not to support the U.S.-led invasion of Iraq in the early 2000s.

War, Insurrection, and Violence

War, insurrection, and other forms of violence pose significant problems for business operations. While such events usually do not affect companies directly, their indirect effects can be disastrous. Violent conflict among drug cartels and security services along the U.S.-Mexico border has led some firms and financiers to withdraw investments from Mexico because of perceived heightened risks and political instability. In India, Tata Motors (www.tatamotors.com) had to shift the location of a major new factory due to violent protests by local farmers who feared the loss of their livelihood. Although the plant would have created thousands of jobs, nearly 700 million people in India live off the land, which leaves little acreage for new factories.[21] To minimize losses from violent acts, firms can purchase risk insurance.

Terrorism

Terrorism is the threat or actual use of force or violence to attain a political goal through fear, coercion, or intimidation.[22] It is sometimes sponsored by national governments. Terrorism has escalated in much of the world, as exemplified by the September 11, 2001, attacks in the United States and the 2008 terrorist attacks in Mumbai, India, which killed 173 people and injured hundreds more. Since 1993, more than 29,000 Indians have died in other terrorist attacks.[23] In addition to causing loss of life, terrorism can severely damage commercial infrastructure and disrupt the business activities of countless firms. It induces fear in consumers, who reduce their purchasing, potentially leading to economic recession. The hospitality, aviation, entertainment, and retailing industries can be particularly affected. Terrorism also affects financial markets. In the days following the 9/11 attacks, the value of the U.S. stock market dropped some 14 percent.[24]

 Types of Country Risk Produced by Legal Systems

Country risk also arises due to peculiarities of national legal systems. Particularly relevant to international business are *commercial law*, which specifically covers business transactions, and *private law*, which regulates relationships between persons and organizations, including contracts, and liabilities that may arise due to negligent behavior. In many countries, the legal system favors home-country nationals. Laws are designed to promote the interests of local businesses and the local economy.

Legal systems in both the host country and the home country pose various challenges to firms.

Country Risk Arising from the Host Country Legal Environment

Governments in host countries can impose a variety of legal stipulations on foreign companies doing business there.

Foreign Investment Laws   These laws affect the type of entry strategy firms choose, as well as their operations and performance. Many nations impose restrictions on inward FDI. For example, Japan's *daitenhoo* (large retail store law) restricted foreigners from opening warehouse-style stores such as Walmart or Toys "R" Us. The law protected smaller shops by requiring large-scale retailers to obtain the approval of local retailers, a painstaking and time-consuming process. In Malaysia, firms wishing to invest in local businesses must obtain permission from the Malaysian Industrial Development Authority, which screens proposed investments to ensure they fit national policy goals. The United States restricts foreign investments that are seen to affect national security. Major investments may be reviewed by the U.S. Committee on Investments. In 2006, the U.S. Congress opposed a pending deal granting operational control at several U.S. ports to Dubai Ports World, a firm based in the United Arab Emirates. Under opposition from the U.S. public and Congress, the firm abandoned its investment plans.

In Japan, foreign-owned large retail stores such as Walmart face restrictive laws designed to protect smaller shops.

Controls on Operating Forms and Practices Governments impose laws and regulations on how firms can conduct production, marketing, and distribution activities within their borders. Such restrictions may reduce firms' efficiency, effectiveness, or both. For example, host countries may require companies to obtain permits to import or export. They may devise complex regulations that complicate transportation and logistical activities or limit the options for entry strategies. In China's huge telecommunications market, the government requires foreign investors to seek joint ventures with local firms; local operations cannot be wholly owned by foreigners. The government's goal is to ensure that China maintains control of its telecommunications industry and obtains inward transfer of technology, knowledge, and capital.

Marketing and Distribution Laws These laws determine which practices are allowed in advertising, promotion, and distribution. For example, Finland, France, Norway, and New Zealand prohibit cigarette advertising on television. Germany largely prohibits comparative advertising, in which a product is touted as superior to a competing brand. Many countries cap the pricing of critical goods and services, such as food and health care. Such constraints affect firms' marketing and profitability. Product safety and liability laws hold manufacturers and sellers responsible for damage, injury, or death caused by defective products. In the case of violations, firms and company executives are subject to legal penalties such as fines or imprisonment, as well as civil lawsuits. In contrast to the case in advanced economies, product liability laws in developing countries are generally weak. Some firms take advantage of these weaknesses. For example, as litigants pursued tobacco companies in Europe and the United States, these companies shifted much of their marketing of cigarettes to developing countries.

Laws on Income Repatriation MNEs earn profits in various countries and typically seek ways to transfer these funds back to their home country. However, in some countries, governments devise laws that restrict such transfers. The action is often taken to preserve hard currencies, such as euros, U.S. dollars, or Japanese yen. Repatriation restrictions limit the amount of net income or dividends that firms can remit to their home-country headquarters. While such constraints often discourage inward FDI, they are common in countries experiencing a shortage of hard currencies.

Environmental Laws Governments also enact laws to preserve natural resources; to combat pollution and the abuse of air, earth, and water resources; and to ensure health and safety. In Germany, for example, companies must follow strict recycling regulations, and the burden of recycling product packaging is placed on manufacturers and distributors. Nevertheless, governments attempt to balance environmental laws against the impact such regulations may have on employment, entrepreneurship, and economic development. For example, environmental standards in Mexico are looser or less well enforced than in other countries, but the Mexican government is reluctant to strengthen them for fear that foreign MNEs will reduce their investments.

Contract Laws   International contracts attach rights, duties, and obligations to the contracting parties. Contracts are used in five main types of business transactions: (1) sale of goods or services, especially large sales; (2) distribution of the firm's products through foreign distributors; (3) licensing and franchising—that is, a contractual relationship that allows a firm to use another company's intellectual property, marketing tools, or other assets for a fee; (4) FDI, especially in collaboration with a foreign entity, in order to create and operate a foreign subsidiary; and (5) joint ventures and other types of cross-border collaborations.

Convergence toward an international standard for international sales contracts is occurring. In 1980, the United Nations instituted the Convention on Contracts for the International Sale of Goods (CISG), a uniform text of law for international sales contracts. More than seventy countries are now party to the CISG, covering about three-quarters of all world trade. Unless excluded by the express terms of a contract, the CISG is deemed to supersede any otherwise applicable domestic law(s) regarding an international sales transaction.

Internet and E-Commerce Regulations   Internet and e-commerce regulations are the new frontier in legal systems. As highlighted in the *Global Trend*, these laws are still evolving. Firms that undertake e-commerce in countries with weak laws face considerable risk. In China, for example, the government has developed legislation to ensure security and privacy due to the rapid spread of the Internet and e-commerce. Many consumer-privacy laws have yet to be enacted, and progress has been delayed on the development of methods to protect private data from criminal or competitive eyes. Protections for online contracting methods have been implemented with the recent adoption of e-signature laws. However, enforcement of e-commerce laws in China remains inconsistent.

Inadequate or Underdeveloped Legal Systems   Just as laws and regulations can lead to country risk, an underdeveloped regulatory environment or poor enforcement of existing laws can pose challenges for the firm. Safeguards for intellectual property are often inadequate. Regulations to protect intellectual property may exist on paper but not be adequately enforced. When an innovator invents a new product, develops new computer software, or produces some other type of intellectual property, another party can copy and sell the innovation without acknowledging or paying the inventor. As reported in the opening vignette, Russia's legal framework is relatively weak and inconsistent. Russian courts lack substantial experience ruling on commercial and international affairs. Due to the unpredictable and potentially harmful legal environment, Western firms frequently abandon joint ventures and other business initiatives in Russia.[25]

Inadequate legal protection is most common in developing economies, but it can be a factor in developed economies as well. The most recent global financial crisis was precipitated, in part, by insufficient regulation in the financial and banking sectors of the United States, Europe, and other areas. Government authorities have been considering how regulatory structures can be revamped to provide a sounder footing for connecting global savers and investors, as well as a reliable method for dealing with financial instability. Regulators seek to expand the reach of regulation, provide new means to increase transparency and information flows, and find ways to harmonize regulatory policies and legal frameworks across national borders. Banks and other financial institutions are revising disclosure rules to make information more specific and consistent. Some experts suggest the financial crisis is not proof that more regulation is needed. Rather, they argue for more intelligent regulation, better enforcement of existing regulation, and better supervision of national financial institutions.[26]

Country Risk Arising from the Home Country Legal Environment

Does country risk arise only due to the host country's legal environment? Home country legal systems are just as relevant. **Extraterritoriality** refers to the application of home country laws to persons or conduct outside national borders. In most cases, such laws are intended to prosecute individuals or firms located abroad for some type of wrongdoing.

Extraterritoriality
Application of home country laws to persons or conduct outside national borders.

Examples of extraterritoriality in international business abound. A French court ordered Yahoo! to bar access to Nazi-related items on its Web site in France and to remove related messages and images from its sites accessible in the United States.[27] In 2001, the United States enacted the Patriot Act, which authorized the U.S. government to seize funds held by non-U.S. banks in the United States. The European Union pursued the U.S. firm Microsoft for perceived monopolistic practices in the marketing of its operating system software. Monopolies are considered harmful because they can unfairly restrain trade. Businesses generally oppose extraterritoriality because it adds to the compliance and regulatory costs and causes considerable uncertainty.

The Foreign Corrupt Practices Act (FCPA)   Passed by the U.S. government in 1977, the Foreign Corrupt Practices Act (FCPA) makes it illegal for a firm to offer bribes to foreign parties for the purpose of securing or retaining business. The FCPA came about in an era when more than 400 U.S. companies admitted paying bribes to foreign government officials and politicians. The Act was strengthened in 1998 to cover foreign firms and managers who act in furtherance of corrupt payments while in the United States. The FCPA also requires firms with securities listed in the United States to meet U.S. accounting provisions. Such firms must devise and maintain accounting systems that control and record all company expenditures.[28] One problem with the FCPA is that a "bribe" is not clearly defined. For example, the Act draws a distinction between bribery and "facilitation" payments; the latter may be permissible if making such payments does not violate local laws.[29]

Many countries do not have antibribery laws for international transactions. Some U.S. managers argue the FCPA harms their interests because foreign competitors often are not constrained by such laws. FCPA criminal and civil penalties have become increasingly harsh. Firms can be fined up to $2 million, while individuals can be fined up to $100,000 and face imprisonment. Recently, the U.S. Justice Department stepped up FCPA prosecutions against smaller companies and non-U.S. firms that do business in the United States. In 2010, the United States settled allegations against Panalpina, a Switzerland-based logistics company, regarding claims it had violated the FCPA in Nigeria to secure energy contracts. The OECD recently called for a ban on "grease payments," small-scale bribes intended to speed up telephone hookups, government paperwork, and other everyday matters in international commerce.[30]

Antiboycott Regulations   Antiboycott regulations prevent companies from participating in restrictive trade practices or boycotts imposed by foreign countries against other countries. Firms are not allowed to participate in boycotts to the extent they discriminate against others on the basis of race, religion, gender, or national origin. For example, some Arab nations have long boycotted Israel because of political disagreements and made it a requirement for any foreign company that wishes to do business with the Arab countries to also observe this boycott. The antiboycott regulations passed by the U.S. Congress in 1977 effectively prohibit U.S. firms from participating in the boycott of Israel when operating in these Arab nations.

GL BAL TREND
Evolving Legal Aspects of E-Commerce

While still a small fraction of world trade, international e-commerce is growing fast, operating in an electronic space not bound by geography or national borders. E-commerce reduces traditional barriers of distance from markets and the lack of information about market opportunities.

The World Wide Web remains a "wild west" of international business, as most countries lack adequate legal protections, leaving e-commerce fraught with thorny issues. For example, individuals or firms that place information, photographs, or music online may be violating the intellectual property laws of some nations but not others. Although electronic contracts are in digital format, existing contract law typically covers only paper documents. Consumers who use the Internet to make purchases with credit cards may risk identity theft and fraud.

Taxation of international e-commerce is complex because of the difficulty of defining merchandise sold online. Do software, books, and music constitute products—or services? For tax purposes, the two categories are usually treated differently. E-commerce can also circumvent tariffs and other trade barriers. Most e-commerce is free of customs duties because it is too difficult to apply them. A related problem is identifying the location of a sale. When

a customer in Japan buys software from Microsoft's Web site, which is based in the United States, does the sale originate in Japan or the United States? Such questions affect not only taxation but also legal jurisdiction in the event of disputes between buyers and sellers.

Inadequate legal frameworks are hindering the growth of global e-commerce, and therefore international organizations are driving efforts to devise internationally appropriate laws. For example, the *United Nations Commission on International Trade Law (UNCITRAL)* developed the Model Law on Electronic Commerce to ensure that online transactions and legal documents are legally recognized and that a course of action is available to enforce them. The UNCITRAL model is only a guide, and national governments are not bound by it.

E-commerce laws are evolving differently in different countries and represent the distinct values and approaches of each locale. The resulting inconsistency creates conflicts between national jurisdictions. When creating e-commerce law, some governments favor strong control and regulation. Others opt for a liberal, hands-off approach. Those who favor government intervention argue, for example, that the Internet exposes their citizens to pornography, gambling, or fraud. Many want to tax

e-commerce and impose international trade controls. Those who favor a more liberal approach argue the Internet has the potential to transform national economies and ease global poverty. They oppose strong government intervention because it can slow the pace of global e-commerce and economic development.

Strong legal frameworks are needed to ensure trust between buyers and sellers. Experts argue that evolving regulatory frameworks should be governed by consistent principles that lead to predictable results, regardless of where buyers and sellers reside. Law enforcement authorities need to cooperate cross-nationally to reduce online crime. Governments must devise frameworks that ensure the security of electronic payment systems and the privacy of online data but are not so restrictive as to hinder the promise of international e-commerce.

SOURCES: Ling Zhu and Sherry Thatcher, "National Information Ecology: A New Institutional Economics Perspective on Global E-Commerce Adoption," *Journal of Electronic Commerce Research* 11, no. 1 (2010): 53–72; C. Primo Braga, "E-Commerce Regulation: New Game, New Rules?," *Quarterly Review of Economics and Finance* 45, no. 2/3 (2005): 541–58; George Takach, "E-Procurement E-Performance," *Summit*, May/June 2008, pp. 16–17; UNCITRAL Model Law on Electronic Commerce Guide to Enactment, retrieved from United Nations Web site at http://www.un.org.

Accounting and Reporting Laws Accounting practices and standards differ greatly around the world. Such differences pose difficulties for firms, but can create opportunities as well. For example, when assigning value to stocks and other securities, most countries use the lower of cost or market value. However, Brazil encourages firms to adjust portfolio valuations because of historically high inflation there. When valuing physical assets such as plant and equipment, Canada uses historical costs, but some Latin American countries use inflation-adjusted market value. While firms can write off uncollectible accounts in the United States, the allowance is not permitted in France, Spain, and South Africa. Research and development costs are expensed as incurred in most of the world but capitalized in South Korea and Spain. Belgium, Malaysia, and Italy use both conventions.

Transparency in Financial Reporting   The timing and transparency of financial reporting vary widely around the world. **Transparency** is the degree to which firms regularly reveal substantial information about their financial condition and accounting practices. In the United States, public firms are required to report financial results to stockholders and to the Securities and Exchange Commission every quarter. In much of the world, however, financial statements may come out once a year or less often, and they often lack transparency. Not only does greater transparency improve the environment for business decision making, it also improves the ability of citizens to hold companies accountable.

> **Transparency** The degree to which companies regularly reveal substantial information about their financial condition and accounting practices.

In an effort to curb corruption, the U.S. Congress passed the 2002 Sarbanes-Oxley Act to promote greater transparency in accounting practices and enhance corporate responsibility. The Act aims to deter accounting and managerial abuses by making corporate CEOs and CFOs personally responsible for accuracy in annual reports and other financial data. Foreign affiliates of U.S. firms, and foreign firms with significant U.S. operations, also must comply with the Act's provisions. European firms like Royal Ahold (Netherlands), Parmalat (Italy), and Vivendi (France) have also been accused of managerial and accounting irregularities in recent years.

However, a drawback of the Sarbanes-Oxley reforms is the cost of compliance—estimated at tens of billions of dollars and millions of work-hours—to develop sophisticated internal accounting controls. In an effort to avoid these rigid financial requirements, some European firms are reducing their business investments in the United States, and several have deregistered from U.S. stock markets.[31] In the meantime, some governments in Europe have called for stricter standards in European accounting practices. The Act tends to discriminate against companies with extensive international operations because of the higher compliance costs for decentralized companies with multiple or widely dispersed operations.

 ## Managing Country Risk

How should managers respond to country risk in a proactive manner? In the discussion that follows, we highlight five specific strategies managers can employ to manage country risk.

Proactive Environmental Scanning

Anticipating country risk requires advance research. Initially, managers develop a comprehensive understanding of the political and legal environment in target countries. They then engage in *scanning* to assess potential risks and threats to the firm. Scanning allows the firm to improve practices in ways that conform with local laws and political realities and to create a positive environment for business success.

One of the best sources of intelligence in the scanning process is employees working in the host country. They are knowledgeable about evolving events and can evaluate them in the context of local history, culture, and politics. Embassy and trade association officials regularly develop and analyze intelligence on the local political scene. Some consulting firms, such as PRS Group (www.prsgroup.com) and Business Entrepreneurial Risk Intelligence (www.beri.com), specialize in country-risk assessment and provide guidelines for appropriate strategic responses. Once the firm has researched the political climate and contingencies of the target environment, it develops and implements strategies to facilitate effective management of relations with policymakers and other helpful contacts in the host country. The firm then takes steps to minimize its exposure to country risks that threaten its performance.

Strict Adherence to Ethical Standards

Ethical behavior is important not only for its own sake but also because it helps insulate the firm from some country risks that less-conscientious firms encounter. Those companies that engage in questionable practices or operate outside the law naturally invite redress from the governments of the host countries where they do business.

Alliances with Qualified Local Partners

A practical approach to reducing country risk is to enter target markets in collaboration with a knowledgeable and reliable local partner. Qualified local partners are better informed about local conditions and better situated to establish stable relations with the local government. For instance, because of various challenges in China and Russia, Western firms often enter these countries by partnering with local firms that assist in navigating complex legal and political landscapes.

Protection through Legal Contracts

A legal contract spells out the rights and obligations of each party and is especially important when relationships go awry. Contract law varies widely from country to country, and firms must adhere to local standards. For example, a Canadian firm doing business in Belgium generally must comply with the laws of both Belgium and Canada, as well as with the evolving laws of the European Union, some of which may override Belgian law.

International contractual disputes arise from time to time, and firms generally employ any of three approaches for resolving them: conciliation, arbitration, and litigation. *Conciliation* is the least adversarial method. It is a formal process of negotiation with the objective to resolve differences in a friendly manner. The parties in a dispute employ a conciliator, who meets separately with each in an attempt to resolve their differences. Parties can also employ mediation committees—groups of informed citizens—to resolve civil disputes. *Arbitration* is a process in which a neutral third party hears both sides of a case and decides in favor of one party or the other, based on an objective assessment of the facts. Compared to litigation, arbitration saves time and expense, while maintaining the confidentiality of proceedings. Arbitration is often handled by supranational organizations, such as the International Chamber of Commerce in Paris or the Stockholm Chamber of Commerce. *Litigation* is the most adversarial approach and occurs when one party files a lawsuit against another in order to achieve desired ends. Litigation is most common in the United States; most other countries favor arbitration or conciliation.

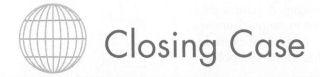 Closing Case

Political, Legal, and Ethical Dilemmas in the Global Pharmaceutical Industry

The $600 billion global pharmaceutical industry is dominated by about ten firms; five are headquartered in Europe and five in the United States. Examples include Glaxo-SmithKline (United Kingdom, www.gsk.com), Novartis AG (Switzerland, www.novartis.com), Sanofi Aventis (France, www.sanofi-aventis.com), Merck (United States, www.merck.com), and Pfizer (United States, www.pfizer.com). Europe and the United States account for roughly 25 percent and 50 percent of worldwide pharmaceutical sales, respectively. The industry is confronted with several major challenges.

High Cost of Research and Development

Pharmaceutical firms engage in large-scale, intensive R&D to create and market drugs meant to treat everything from cancer to hair loss. Thousands of pharmaceutical drugs allow people to live longer and healthier lives. Europe and the United States are home to the major pharmaceutical firms and to industry R&D. They benefit from strong patent protection laws and abundant investment capital. According to industry statistics, it takes 12 to 15 years, and more than $800 million in R&D expense, to successfully bring a new pharmaceutical compound to market. Only 1 in 10,000 investigated and tested compounds is approved for patient use. Only three out of every ten new, approved compounds are successful enough to recover their R&D costs. For their successful products, pharmaceutical firms must charge prices high enough to recover not only the high costs of product development, but also to recover the cost of products that never achieve profitability.

Limited Protection for Intellectual Property

Governments grant patents and provide other types of protections for intellectual property. In practice, such protection is frequently inadequate, especially in developing countries. For example, India has a history of weak intellectual property protection, which has discouraged R&D and innovation. It is one of the world's poorest countries, and very few of its citizens can afford health care or medications. In 1972, a major revision to the Indian Patent Act revoked all patents for medicines. Following this dramatic shift, foreign-branded pharmaceutical manufacturers abandoned India, and numerous pharmaceutical "chop shops" emerged. The new firms freely infringed on drug patents and engaged in a selling "free-for-all" in the huge Indian pharmaceutical market. They reverse-engineered patented compounds developed by European and U.S. companies and began selling the pirated generics at drastically lower prices. The foreign pharmaceuticals launched legal actions against these violations but, in the absence of strict patent protection and with little local competition, India's generic drug manufacturers flourished.

The Challenge from Generic Brands

Under World Trade Organization (WTO) rules, a patent protects a drug inventor from competition for up to 20 years. In reality, when the lengthy testing and approval phase is factored in, the effective life of a drug patent is often less than 12 years. The manufacturer typically has only 5 to 8 years of patent protection in which to recover its investment before generic manufacturers can legally enter the market. Once a patent expires, generic manufacturers have the right to produce medications originally invented by major pharmaceuticals. Generic manufacturers typically sell the medications that they produce at very low prices. Patent protections are important because they encourage innovation by allowing inventors a limited opportunity to recover their R&D investments. However, patent protection laws governing pharmaceuticals differ substantially around the world.

A *branded compound* is produced under patent protection by a pharmaceutical manufacturer that has undertaken expensive R&D to invent the drug. Each year, pharmaceutical firms typically invest some 20 percent of revenues into R&D to invent new compounds. "Approved generic compounds," manufactured in countries with strict bio-equivalency regulations, are comparable to branded compounds in safety, efficacy, and intended use. The main reason that generic manufacturers can charge lower prices is that they do not incur the high costs of R&D to develop new drugs. Because the medications are already established in the marketplace, generic manufacturers also incur substantially lower marketing and sales expenses.

In the world of generic drugs, Israel-based Teva is the largest manufacturer with 2009 global sales of $13.9 billion. Teva and other generic producers have greatly increased their world market share in recent years due to the patent expiration of leading medications and rising demand for medications in developing economies and countries with weak patent protection. In the United States alone, generic medications now account for over half of all dispensed prescriptions. Once a branded compound's patent expires, generic manufacturers, after receiving government approval, begin producing generic versions almost immediately. Retail prices for the compound can fall by as much as 90 percent within 12–18 months.

Counterfeit Drugs

Many governments fail to ensure the quality of imported medicines. As a result, a growing industry of counterfeit and bio-inequivalent medications has emerged worldwide. In 2007, a counterfeit ring from China supplied one million fake OneTouch Test Strips (used to treat diabetes) to hundreds of pharmacies in Canada, India, the United States, and numerous other countries. A healthy 22-year-old woman in Argentina died from liver failure after receiving iron injections to treat mild anemia. The medicine she received was a highly toxic counterfeit. In Niger, some 2,500 people died after receiving fake vaccines for meningitis. Recently, European Union officials seized more than 35 million fake pills at ports around Europe, including drugs intended to treat malaria, cancer, cholesterol, and pain.

The United Nations estimates that sales of counterfeit pharmaceuticals now exceeds $500 billion annually. Counterfeiting is greatest in countries where regulatory oversight is weakest. The WHO estimates that up to 30 percent of medicines sold in developing countries may be counterfeit. It is estimated that between 200,000 and 300,000 people die each year in China due to counterfeit or substandard medicine.

Internet-based pharmacies are especially dubious. In 2006, a woman in Canada died of metal poisoning after taking a tainted prescription medicine obtained from an Internet pharmacy. MarkMonitor, an industry watchdog, found that only a tiny fraction of the 3,160 online pharmacies it examined were legitimate. Many of the pharmacies claiming to be based in Canada and the United States were in fact traced to China, Russia, and India. It is estimated that over 50 percent of medicines sold through the Internet are fake—often containing no or too little of the active ingredient.

Because of the threats posed by counterfeit manufacturers, branded pharmaceutical firms spend significant resources to protect their patents and intellectual property around the world. Branded pharmaceutical manufacturers have pursued legal actions at the WTO and against individual nations. In 1995, the WTO's agreement on Trade-Related Aspects of Intellectual Property Rights (TRIPS) was approved by approximately 150 WTO member countries.

Neglected Therapeutic Areas

A large portion of pharmaceutical research is focused on developing treatments for diseases that can return the cost of capital and generate profits. For these reasons, pharmaceutical firms tend to target the most attractive markets. For example, these firms are much more likely to develop a drug for cancer and central nervous system diseases (such as psychiatric ailments) than for ailments common to poor countries (such as tuberculosis). Some in the pharmaceutical industry believe that R&D is too costly and risky to invest in diseases common to poor countries.

At the same time, governmental and private initiatives have begun to address these market realities by providing incentive packages and public-private partnerships. For example, the Bill and Melinda Gates Foundation (www.gatesfoundation.org) is investing billions of dollars to fight AIDS, tuberculosis, and various infectious diseases that affect developing countries.

Public Scrutiny

The pharmaceutical industry's actions are often subject to public scrutiny. For example, the government of South Africa got into a tussle with several manufacturers of branded AIDS drugs. Because of high prices, the government sanctioned the importation of nonapproved generics. The reaction from branded pharmaceutical manufacturers was to sue South Africa, which created an international backlash against the firms. Not only did the episode generate much negative publicity for the branded

pharmaceutical firms, it made people more aware of the generic drug industry and its potential for helping those affected by the AIDS pandemic. In the wake of the South African debacle, Brazil and several other countries threatened to break patents if pharmaceutical firms did not make their drugs more affordable. In the interest of good public relations, several branded pharmaceutical firms began to offer their AIDS drugs at lower prices in Africa. In all, the pharmaceutical firms have developed at least eighty-eight medicines to treat AIDS and related conditions. The United States and various European governments have provided billions of dollars in subsidies to support AIDS treatment in Africa.

The Future

Without adequate intellectual property protection, the pharmaceutical industry has fewer incentives to invent new drugs. At the same time, consumers in poor countries need access to drugs but can't afford them. Lax intellectual property laws facilitate the production of cheap generic drugs, but without these protections, major pharmaceutical firms have fewer incentives to fund the R&D that results in new treatments for the diseases that plague the world.

Case Questions

1. Specify the types of country risks that pharmaceutical firms face in international business. How do the political and legal systems of countries affect the global pharmaceutical industry?

2. People need medications, but the poor often cannot afford them. Governments may not provide subsidies for health care and medications. Meanwhile, pharmaceutical firms focus their R&D on compounds likely to provide the best returns. What is the proper role of the following groups in addressing these dilemmas: national governments, branded pharmaceutical firms, and generic manufacturers?

3. Consult www.phrma.org, The Pharmaceutical Research and Manufacturers of America. What steps is the branded industry taking to address the various ethical issues it faces, such as providing affordable drugs to poor countries?

4. Consult the TRIPS agreement at the WTO portal (www.wto.org). What are the latest developments regarding this treaty? What types of protection does this treaty provide to pharmaceutical firms? What enforcement mechanisms does TRIPS provide for ensuring that these protections will be carried out?

5. Recommend a strategy that management at a large pharmaceutical firm should employ to reduce the likelihood of political and legal risks that such firms face. What steps should management take to minimize its exposure to such risks?

SOURCES: Chris Enyinda, Chris Mbah, and Alphonso Ogbuehi, "An Empirical Analysis of Risk Mitigation in the Pharmaceutical Industry Supply Chain: A Developing-Country Perspective," *Thunderbird International Business Review* 52, no. 1 (2010): 54–69; Sarah Houlton, "Cracking Down on Counterfeit Drugs," *Pharmaceutical Executive*, February 2009, p. 18; Nancy Shute, "Fake Medications Are a Growing Threat," *US News and World Report*, August 21, 2007, retrieved from http://health.usnews.com; P. Trouiller et al., "Drug Development for Neglected Diseases," *Lancet* 359 (June 2002): 2188–94; H. Lofgren and P. Malhotra, "India's Pharmaceutical Industry: Hype or High Tech Take-Off," *Australian Health Review* 28, no. 2 (2004): 182–93; G. Glass, "Patent Attack," *Pharmaceutical Executive* 25, no. 4 (2005): 76–81; "Survey: Prescription for Change," *Economist*, June 18, 2005; "Business: Big Generic Pharma; Pharmaceuticals," *Economist*, July 30, 2005; "Business: Corrupted; Medications and Intellectual Property." *Economist*, July 23, 2005; World Trade Organization, "Agreement on Trade-Related Aspects of Intellectual Property Rights," 1994, retrieved from http://www.wto.org; Pharmaceutical Research and Manufacturers Association of America, "What Goes Into the Cost of Prescription Drugs?," June, 2005, retrieved from http://www.phrma.org; World Health Organization, "Counterfeit Medicines," Fact Sheet No. 275, November 14, 2006, retrieved from http://www.wto.int; Peter Pitts, "Counterfeit Drugs and China," 2009, retrieved from the Center for Medicine in the Public Interest Web site http://www.cmpi.org; U.S. Food and Drug Administration, "Counterfeit Drugs," 2009, retrieved from http://www.fda.gov/counterfeit/.

NOTE: Kevin McGarry assisted in the development of this case.

CHAPTER ESSENTIALS

Key Terms

country risk, p. 210

extraterritoriality, p. 227

legal system, p. 212

political system, p. 212

rule of law, p. 218

transparency, p. 229

Summary

In this chapter, you learned about:

1. The nature of country risk

International business is influenced by political and legal systems. **Country risk** refers to exposure to potential loss or to adverse effects on company operations and profitability caused by developments in national political and legal environments.

2. Political and legal environments in international business

A **political system** is a set of formal institutions that constitute a government. A **legal system** is a system for interpreting and enforcing laws. Adverse developments in political and legal systems increase country risk. These can result from events such as a change in government or the creation of new laws or regulations.

3. Political systems

The three major political systems are totalitarianism, socialism, and democracy. They provide frameworks within which laws are established and nations are governed. Democracy is characterized by private property rights and limited government. Socialism occurs mainly as *social democracy*. Today, most governments combine elements of socialism and democracy. Totalitarianism is associated with command economies, socialism with mixed economies, and democracy with market economies.

4. Legal systems

There are four major legal systems: common law, civil law, religious law, and mixed systems. The **rule of law** implies a legal system in which laws are clear, understood, respected, and fairly enforced.

5. Participants in political and legal systems

Actors include government, which exists at the national, state, and municipal levels. The World Trade Organization and the United Nations are typical of international organizations that influence international business. Special interest groups serve specific industries or country groupings and include labor unions, environmental organizations, and consumers that promote particular viewpoints. Companies deal with competing firms in foreign markets, which may undertake political activities aimed at influencing market entry and firm performance.

6. Types of country risk produced by political systems

Governments impose constraints on corporate operating methods in areas such as production, marketing, and distribution. Governments may expropriate or confiscate the assets of foreign firms. Governments or groups of countries also impose embargoes and sanctions that restrict trade with certain countries. Boycotts are an attempt to halt trade or prevent business activities and are usually pursued for political reasons. War and revolution have serious consequences for international firms. Terrorism has become more salient recently.

7. Types of country risk produced by legal systems

Foreign investment laws restrict FDI in various ways. Such laws include controls on operating forms and practices, regulations affecting marketing and distribution, restrictions on income repatriation, environmental laws, and Internet and e-commerce regulations. **Extraterritoriality** is the application of home country laws to conduct outside of national borders. Antiboycott regulations prevent companies from participating in restrictive trade practices. Accounting and reporting laws vary around the world. **Transparency** is the degree to which firms reveal substantial and regular information about their financial condition and accounting practices.

8. Managing country risk

Successful management requires developing an understanding of the political and legal context abroad. The firm should scan the environment proactively. It should strictly adhere to ethical standards. Country risk is also managed by allying with qualified local partners abroad. The firm should seek protection through legal contracts.

Test Your Comprehension AACSB: Reflective Thinking Skills

1. What are the components of political systems? What are the components of legal systems? How do these systems lead to country risk?

2. Distinguish between totalitarianism, socialism, and democracy. What are the implications of each for internationalizing firms?

3. What are the specific characteristics of democracy? How do these characteristics facilitate international business?

4. What is the relationship between political freedom and economic freedom?

5. Describe the major types of legal systems. Which systems are most widely encountered?

6. Who are the major actors in political and legal systems? Which participant do you believe is most influential in international business?

7. Summarize how political and legal systems affect international business.

8. Describe proactive actions that firms can take to minimize country risk.

Apply Your Understanding AACSB: Reflective Thinking Skills, Communication Abilities, Ethical Understanding and Reasoning Abilities

1. For business enterprises to thrive, some minimum conditions must be present, including recognition of private property rights and limited government intervention. To what extent may totalitarianism, socialism, and democracy interfere with the ideal commercial environment for firms?

2. Suppose you get a job at Aoki Corporation, a firm that manufactures glass for industrial and consumer markets. Aoki is a large firm but has little international experience. Senior managers are considering a plan to move Aoki's manufacturing to China, Mexico, or Eastern Europe and to begin selling its glass in Latin America and Europe. However, they know little about the country risks that Aoki may encounter. Describe how each of the following factors might contribute to country risk as Aoki ventures abroad: foreign investment laws, controls on operating forms and practices, and laws regarding repatriation of income, environment, and contracts.

3. *Ethical Dilemma:* The United States imposed a trade and investment embargo on Iran. U.S. citizens were barred from doing business with Iran. Proponents argue the embargo is justified because Iran has supported terrorism and is developing nuclear weapons. However, critics condemn the trade sanctions. First, they argue the sanctions represent a "double standard," as the United States supports other countries that have engaged in terrorism and

other bad behaviors. Second, the best way to nurture healthy dissent and civil society in Iran may be to engage the country, rather than restrict economic relationships. Third, the sanctions harm the Iranian people, who are deprived of the benefits of trade with the United States. Fourth, the sanctions are largely ineffective, since other countries supply Iran with products it needs. Finally, the sanctions harm

U.S. companies, especially oil and gas firms, which cannot do business with Iran. What is your view? Using the Ethical Framework in Chapter 5, analyze the arguments for and against trade with Iran. Can the United States, acting alone, compel desired changes in Iran by imposing sanctions? Justify your answer.

globalEDGE Internet Exercises
(http://globalEDGE.msu.edu)

AACSB: Reflective Thinking Skills, Communication Abilities, Use of Information Technology, Ethical Understanding and Reasoning Abilities

Refer to Chapter 1, page 62, for instructions on how to access and use globalEDGE™.

1. Supranational organizations such as the World Bank (www.worldbank.org) and the World Trade Organization (www.wto.org) oversee much of the legal framework within which the world trading system operates. Political frameworks for industries or country groupings are influenced by organizations such as the Organization of Petroleum Exporting Countries (www.opec.org) and the Organisation for Economic Co-operation and Development (www.oecd.org). Using globalEDGE™ and the online portals cited here, address the following question: What is the goal of each organization, and how does it go about achieving its goal? By viewing the news and press releases at each Web site, summarize the latest initiatives of each organization.

2. When companies venture abroad, managers seek information on the legal and political environments in each country. This information is available from various Web sources, as illustrated in the following exercises. (I) Suppose you want to sign up distributors in the European Union and want to learn about EU contract law. What should you do? Consult the globalEDGE™ portal to learn about EU trade and contract laws. Try the following: From the globalEDGE™ Resource Desk, click on Trade Law. Describe the resources there for learning about contract law in Europe. (II) The Central Intelligence Agency's portal provides up-to-date information about national governments and political environments. Go to www.cia.gov, click on "The World Factbook," and summarize the political environment in China, Colombia, France, and Russia.

3. Freedom House is a nonprofit organization that monitors the state of freedom worldwide. It conducts an annual "Freedom in the World Survey," which you can view at www.freedomhouse.org. The survey compares the state of political rights and civil liberties in nearly 200 countries over time. Visit the site and answer the following questions: (a) What is the role of political rights and civil liberties in the Freedom House rankings? (b) What can governments in these countries do to facilitate more rapid social and political development? (c) What are the implications of the rankings for companies doing international business?

CHAPTER 8

LEARNING OBJECTIVES In this chapter, you will learn about:

1. The nature of government intervention
2. Rationale for government intervention
3. Instruments of government intervention
4. Consequences of government intervention
5. Evolution of government intervention
6. Intervention and the global financial crisis
7. How firms can respond to government intervention

Government Intervention in International Business

India's Transition to a Liberal Economy

India is a study in contrasts. On the one hand, it is the world's leading emerging economy in information technology and e-business. On the other hand, it is awash in trade barriers, business regulations, and a powerful bureaucracy. Not only does the Indian federal government impose countless regulations, standards, and administrative hurdles on businesses, each of India's twenty-eight states also imposes its own local bureaucracy and red tape. Import taxes and controls on foreign investment are substantial, with tariffs averaging over 25 percent on many products, compared to less than 12 percent in Europe, Japan, and the United States. Hundreds of commodities, from cement to household appliances, can be imported only after receiving government approval. Licensing fees, testing procedures, and other hurdles can be costly to importers.

Since the early 1980s, however, India's government has been liberalizing the nation's regulatory regime. The government has abolished many import licenses and reduced tariffs substantially. It has also implemented numerous reforms to free the economy from state control by selling off many state enterprises to the private sector and to foreign investors.

India has always had a huge sector of small retailers. The country is home to 10 million "mom-and-pop" shops scattered across 500,000 cities and villages. The arrival of big-box retailers triggered a storm of controversy, sparking widespread protests from small merchants. Although Walmart (www.walmart.com) opened its first Indian branch in 2009, the store cannot sell directly to consumers and is restricted to wholesaling merchandise only to licensed small retailers, hospitals, hotels, and other institutions. In a joint venture with the Indian firm Bharti Enterprises, Walmart plans to open numerous stores nationwide in coming years.

India's economic revolution is unleashing the country's entrepreneurial potential. The government is establishing Special Economic Zones (SEZs), virtual foreign territories that offer foreign firms the benefits of India's low-cost, high-skilled labor. In a typical SEZ, firms are exempt from trade barriers, sales and income taxes, licensing requirements, FDI restrictions, and customs clearance procedures. Mahindra City is home to an 840-acre SEZ that boasts a $277 million software development center built by Infosys Technologies, India's leading IT firm.

In Europe and the United States, the outsourcing of jobs to India has generated calls for *protectionism*—trade barriers and defensive measures intended to minimize the export of jobs abroad. U.S. and European trade unions host numerous Web sites that denounce outsourcing and offshoring. Trade barriers and government bureaucracy in India, as well as calls for protectionism in Europe and the United States, exemplify the complex world of government intervention.

SOURCES: E. Bellman, "Wal-Mart Exports Big-Box Concept to India," *Wall Street Journal*, May 29, 2009, p. A4; J. Lamont, "Strike-hit India Eyes Fuel Price Cuts," *Financial Times*, January 8, 2009, retrieved from http://www.ft.com; "India Plays Catch Up," *Asiamoney*, April 2005, p. 1; Central Intelligence Agency, *World Factbook*, 2006, retrieved from http://www.cia.gov/cia/publications/factbook; "Survey: A World of Opportunity," *Economist*, November 13, 2004, p. 15; Oxford Analytica Daily Brief Service, "India: Civil Service Flaws Obstruct Development," January 28, 2010, p. 1; United States Trade Representative, *National Trade Estimate Report on Foreign Trade Barriers: India*, 2009, retrieved from http://www.ustr.gov.

As we learned in Chapter 6, economists have long used trade theories to make the case for *free trade*, the unrestricted flow of products, services, and physical and intellectual capital across national borders. Trade theorists argue that countries should trade with each other to make optimal use of national resources and to increase living standards. FDI-based explanations reveal how firms obtain advantages by locating factories and subsidiaries in attractive locations abroad. In short, contemporary economic theory argues that international trade and investment are good for the world.

There is much empirical evidence to support free trade. One study that examined more than one hundred countries in the 50 years after 1945 found a strong association between market openness—that is, unimpeded free trade—and economic growth. Countries with an open economy enjoyed average annual per-capita GDP growth of 4.49 percent, while relatively closed countries—those with less-free trade—grew at only 0.69 percent per year.[1] Other studies confirm that market liberalization and free trade are best for supporting economic growth and national living standards.[2]

In reality, however, there is no such thing as unimpeded free trade. Well before economists recognized the value of free trade, governments began intervening in business and the international marketplace in ways that obstruct the free flow of trade and investment. Intervention can take many forms. The government may impose tariffs and quotas, restrictions on international investment, bureaucratic procedures and red tape, and regulations that restrict types of business and value-chain activities. In addition, the government may provide subsidies and financial incentives intended to sustain domestic firms and industries in ways that hamper the internationalization efforts of foreign firms.

 ## The Nature of Government Intervention

Governments intervene in trade and investment to achieve political, social, or economic objectives. They often create trade barriers that benefit specific interest groups, such as domestic firms, industries, and labor unions. A key rationale is to create jobs by protecting industries from foreign competition. Governments may also intervene to support home-grown industries or firms. In various ways, government intervention alters the competitive position of companies and industries and the status of citizens. As highlighted in Exhibit 8.1, intervention is an important dimension of *country risk*.

Government intervention is often motivated by **protectionism**, which refers to national economic policies designed to restrict free trade and protect domestic industries from foreign competition. Protectionism is typically manifested by tariffs, nontariff barriers such as quotas, and arbitrary administrative rules designed to discourage imports. A **tariff** (also known as a *duty*) is a tax imposed by a government on imported products, effectively increasing the cost of acquisition for the customer. A **nontariff trade barrier** is a government policy, regulation, or procedure that impedes trade through means other than explicit tariffs. Trade barriers are enforced as products pass through **customs**, the checkpoints at the ports of entry in each country where government officials inspect imported products and levy tariffs. An often-used form of nontariff trade barrier is a **quota**, a quantitative restriction placed on imports of a specific product over a specified period of time. Government intervention may also target FDI flows through *investment barriers* that restrict the operations of foreign firms.

Government intervention affects the normal operation of economic activity in a nation by hindering or helping the ability of its indigenous firms to compete internationally. Often companies, labor unions, and other special interest groups convince governments to adopt policies that benefit them. For example, in the early 2000s, the Bush administration imposed tariffs on the import of foreign steel into the United States. The rationale was to give the U.S. steel industry time to restructure and revive itself following years of

Protectionism National economic policies designed to restrict free trade and protect domestic industries from foreign competition.

Tariff A tax imposed on imported products, effectively increasing the cost of acquisition for the customer.

Nontariff trade barrier A government policy, regulation, or procedure that impedes trade through means other than explicit tariffs.

Customs Checkpoints at the ports of entry in each country where government officials inspect imported products and levy tariffs.

Quota A quantitative restriction placed on imports of a specific product over a specified period of time.

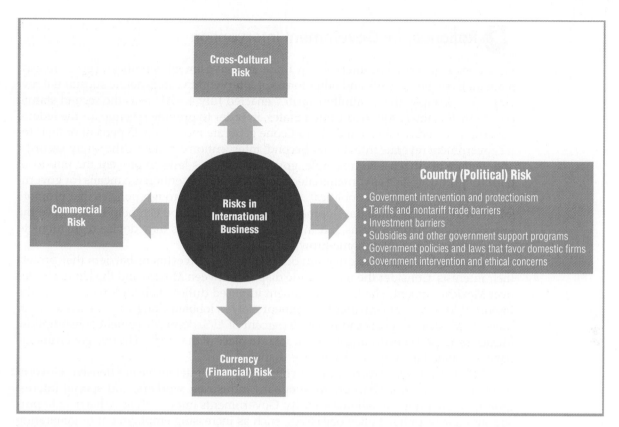

Exhibit 8.1   Government Intervention as a Component of Country Risk

decline due to tough competition from foreign steel manufacturers. The action may have saved hundreds of U.S. jobs. On the downside, however, the tariffs also increased production costs for firms that use steel, such as Ford, Whirlpool, and General Electric. Higher material cost made these firms less competitive and reduced prospects for selling their products in world markets.[3] The steel tariffs were removed within two years, but in the process of attempting to do good, the government also did some harm.

Another example of intervention was the U.S. government's response to the growing threat of Japanese car imports in the 1980s, when it established "voluntary export restraints" on the number of Japanese vehicles that could be imported into the United States. This move helped insulate the U.S. auto industry for several years. In a protected environment, however, Detroit automakers had less incentive to improve quality, design, and overall product appeal. Much like the athlete who performs best when faced with formidable opponents, companies fight harder to succeed when confronted with stiff competition. Thus, government intervention motivated by protectionism has been one of several factors that, over time, weakened Detroit's ability to compete in the global auto industry.

Protectionist policies may also lead to price inflation because tariffs can restrict the supply of a particular product. Tariffs may also reduce the choices available to buyers by restricting the variety of products available for sale.

These examples illustrate that government intervention often leads to adverse *unintended consequences*—unfavorable outcomes of policies or laws. In a complex world, legislators and policymakers cannot foresee all possible outcomes. The problem of unintended consequences suggests that government intervention should be planned and implemented with great care.

Rationale for Government Intervention

Why does a government intervene in trade and investment activities? There are four main motives. First, tariffs and other forms of intervention can generate substantial revenue. For example, the "Hamilton Tariff," enacted July 4, 1789, was the second statute passed by the newly founded United States, in order to provide revenue for the federal government. Today, Ghana and Sierra Leone generate more than 25 percent of their total government revenue from tariffs. Second, intervention can ensure the safety, security, and welfare of citizens. For example, governments pass laws to prevent the import of harmful products such as contaminated food. Third, intervention is a means for governments to pursue economic, political, or social objectives through policies that promote job growth and economic development. Fourth, intervention can help better serve the interests of the nation's firms and industries. Governments may devise regulations to stimulate development of home-grown industries.

Special interest groups often advocate trade and investment barriers that protect their interests. Consider the recent trade dispute between Mexico and the United States over Mexican cement. The U.S. government imposed duties of about $50 per ton on the import of Mexican cement after U.S. cement makers lobbied Congress. The stakes were huge, as Mexican imports can reach 10 percent of U.S. domestic cement consumption. Mexico proposed substituting import quotas in place of the tariffs. The two governments have negotiated for years to resolve the dispute.[4]

Trade and investment barriers can be considered either defensive or offensive. Governments impose *defensive* barriers to safeguard industries, workers, and special interest groups and to promote national security. Governments impose *offensive* barriers to pursue strategic or public policy objectives, such as increasing employment or generating tax revenues. Let's review the specific rationale for government intervention.

Defensive Rationale

Four major defensive motives are particularly relevant: protection of the nation's economy, protection of an infant industry, national security, and national culture and identity.

Protection of the National Economy Proponents argue that firms in advanced economies cannot compete with those in developing countries that employ low-cost labor. In the opening vignette, labor activists called for government intervention to prevent the outsourcing of jobs from Europe and the United States to India. Activists call for trade barriers to curtail the import of low-priced products, fearing that advanced-economy manufacturers will be undersold, wages will fall, and home country jobs will be lost. Accordingly, activists urge governments to impose trade barriers that block imports.

In response, critics counter that protectionism is at odds with the theory of comparative advantage, according to which nations should engage in *more* international trade, not less. Trade barriers interfere with country-specific specialization of labor. When countries specialize in the products they can produce best and then trade for the rest, they perform better in the long run, delivering superior living standards to their citizens. Critics also charge that blocking imports reduces the availability and increases the cost of products sold in the home market. Industries cannot access all the input products they need. Finally, protection can trigger retaliation, resulting in foreign governments imposing their own trade barriers, which reduces sales prospects for exporters.

Protection of an Infant Industry In an emerging industry, companies are often inexperienced and lack the latest technologies and know-how. They may also lack the scale typical of larger competitors in established industries abroad. An infant industry may need temporary protection from foreign competitors. Governments can impose temporary trade barriers on foreign imports to ensure that young firms gain a large share of the domestic market. Protecting infant industries has allowed some countries to develop a modern industrial sector. For example, government intervention allowed Japan and South Korea to become dominant players in the global automobile and consumer electronics industries.

Once in place, however, such protection may be hard to remove. Industry owners and workers tend to lobby to preserve government protection. Infant industries in many countries (especially in Latin America, South Asia, and Eastern Europe) have shown a tendency to remain dependent on government protection for many years. Industries become inefficient, costing the nation's citizens higher taxes and higher prices for the products produced by the protected industry.[5]

National Security Countries impose trade restrictions on products viewed as critical to national defense and security, such as military technology and computers that help maintain domestic production in security-related products. For example, Russia blocked a bid by German engineering giant Siemens to purchase the Russian turbine manufacturer OAO Power Machines, on grounds of national security. The Russian government has strict legislation that limits foreign investment in sectors considered vital to Russia's national interests.[6] Countries may also impose **export controls**, government measures intended to manage or prevent the export of certain products or trade with certain countries. For example, many countries prohibit exports of plutonium to North Korea because it can be used to make nuclear weapons. The United States generally blocks exports of nuclear and military technology to countries it deems state sponsors of terrorism, such as Iran, Libya, and Syria.

Export control A government measure intended to manage or prevent the export of certain products or trade with certain countries.

National Culture and Identity Should foreign entities, say the Japanese or the Saudis, be allowed to purchase national landmarks such as the Empire State Building or the Rockefeller Center in New York? In most countries, certain occupations, industries, and public assets are seen as central to national culture and identity. Governments may impose trade barriers to restrict imports of products or services seen to threaten such national assets. Switzerland has imposed trade barriers to preserve its long-established tradition in watchmaking. In the United States, authorities opposed Japanese investors' purchase of the Pebble Beach golf course in California and the Seattle Mariners baseball team, because these assets are viewed as part of the national heritage. France does not allow significant foreign ownership of its TV stations because of concerns about foreign influence on French culture.

To safeguard its national culture, the French government makes it difficult for foreign companies to own television stations in France. This television crew is shooting footage in Paris.

Offensive Rationale

Offensive rationales for government intervention fall into two categories: national strategic priorities and increasing employment.

National Strategic Priorities Government intervention sometimes aims to encourage the development of industries that bolster the nation's economy. It is a *proactive* variation of the infant industry rationale and related to national industrial policy. Countries with many high-tech or high-value-adding industries, such as information technology, pharmaceuticals, car manufacturing, or financial services, create better jobs and higher tax revenues than economies based on low-value-adding industries, such as agriculture, textile manufacturing, or discount

retailing. Accordingly, governments in Germany, Japan, Norway, South Korea, and numerous other countries have devised policies that promote the development of relatively desirable industries. The government may provide financing for investment in high-tech or high-value-adding industries, encourage citizens to save money to ensure a steady supply of loanable funds for industrial investment, and fund public education to provide citizens the skills and flexibility they need to perform in key industries.[7]

Increasing Employment   Governments often impose import barriers to protect employment in designated industries. Insulating domestic firms from foreign competition stimulates national output, leading to more jobs in the protected industries. The effect is usually strongest in import-intensive industries that employ much labor. For example, the Chinese government has traditionally required foreign companies to enter its huge markets through joint ventures with local Chinese firms. This policy creates jobs for Chinese workers. For example, a joint venture between Shanghai Automotive Industry Corporation (SAIC) and Volkswagen created jobs in China.

 ## Instruments of Government Intervention

Principal instruments of trade intervention and the traditional forms of protectionism are tariffs and nontariff trade barriers. Individual countries or groups of countries, such as the European Union (http://europa.eu), can impose these barriers. In aggregate, barriers constitute a serious impediment to cross-border business. The United Nations estimated that trade barriers alone cost developing countries more than $100 billion in lost trading opportunities with developed countries every year.[8] Exhibit 8.2 highlights the most common forms of government intervention and their effects.

Intervention Type	Definition	Practical Effect on Customers, Firms, or Government	Contemporary Examples
Tariff	Tax imposed on imported products.	Increases cost to the importer, exporter, and usually the buyer of the product. Discourages imports of products. Generates government revenue.	Switzerland charges a tariff of 44% on agricultural product imports. Cote d'Ivoire charges a tariff on most finished products.
Quota	Quantitative restriction on imports of a product during a specified period of time.	Benefits early importers, giving them monopoly power and the ability to charge higher prices. Harms late importers, who may be unable to obtain desired products. Usually results in higher prices to the buyer.	Brazil has imposed a quota on the number of foreign films that can be imported for theatrical screening and home video distribution.
Local content requirements	Requirement that a manufacturer include a minimum percentage of added value that is derived from local sources.	Discourages imports of raw materials, parts, components, and supplies, thereby reducing sourcing options available to manufacturers. May result in higher costs and lower product quality for importers and buyers.	The Nigerian government requires that products and services used by foreign firms in the oil industry in Nigeria must contain over 50% Nigerian content.

Exhibit 8.2   Types and Effects of Government Intervention

SOURCE: Adapted from the Office of the United States Trade Representative, retrieved from http://www.ustr.gov.

Intervention Type	Definition	Practical Effect on Customers, Firms, or Government	Contemporary Examples
Regulations and technical standards	Safety, health, or technical regulations; labeling requirements.	May delay or block the entry of imported products; and reduce the quantity of available products, resulting in higher costs to importers and buyers.	Saudi Arabia bans importation of firearms and used clothing. The European Union requires extensive testing on thousands of different imported chemicals.
Administrative and bureaucratic procedures	Complex procedures or requirements imposed on importers or foreign investors that hinder their trade or investment activities.	Slows the import of products or services. Hinders or delays firms' investment activities.	Russia imposes a series of inspections and bureaucratic procedures for the import of alcoholic beverages.
FDI and ownership restrictions	Rules that limit the ability of foreign firms to invest in certain industries or acquire local firms.	Reduces the amount of money that a foreigner can invest in a country, and/or the proportion of ownership that a foreigner can hold in an existing or new firm in the country. May require a foreign firm to invest in the country in order to do business there.	Switzerland requires foreign firms seeking to sell insurance there to do so by establishing a local subsidiary or branch office, via FDI. Brazil restricts foreign investment in its media industry and certain transportation industries.
Subsidy	Financing or other resources that a government grants to a firm or group of firms, intended to ensure their survival or success.	Increases the competitive advantage of the grantee, while diminishing the competitive advantages of those that do not receive the subsidy.	Turkey grants an export subsidy of up to 20% for local producers of wheat and sugar.
Countervailing duty	Increased duties imposed on products imported into a country to offset subsidies given to producers or exporters in the exporting country.	Reduces or eliminates the competitive advantages provided by subsidies.	India imposes countervailing duties on the import of numerous products.
Antidumping duty	Tax charged on an imported product whose price is below usual prices in the local market or below the cost of making the product	Reduces or eliminates the competitive advantage of imported products priced at abnormally low levels.	The United States has imposed antidumping duties on the import of low-cost steel, in order to support U.S.-based steel manufacturers.

Tariffs

Some countries impose *export tariffs,* taxes on products exported by their own companies. For example, Russia charges a duty on its oil exports with the intention of generating government revenue and maintaining high oil stocks within Russia. The most common type of tariff, however, is the *import tariff,* a tax levied on imported products.

Import tariffs are usually *ad valorem*—that is, they are assessed as a percentage of the value of the imported product. Or a government may impose a *specific tariff*—a flat fee or fixed amount per unit of the imported product—based on weight, volume, or surface area, such as barrels of oil or square meters of fabric. A *revenue tariff* is intended to raise money for the government. A tariff on cigarette imports, for example, produces a steady flow of revenue. A *protective tariff* aims to protect domestic industries from foreign competition. A *prohibitive tariff* is one so high that no one can import any of the items.

The amount of a tariff is determined by examining a product's *harmonized code*. Products are classified under about 8,000 different unique codes in the *harmonized tariff* or *harmonized code* schedule, a standardized system used worldwide. Without this system, firms and governments might have differing opinions on product definitions and the tariffs charged.

Import tariffs can generate substantial revenue for national governments. This helps explain why they are common in developing economies. Even in advanced economies, tariffs provide a significant source of revenue for the government. The United States charges tariffs on many consumer, agricultural, and labor-intensive products. Interestingly, the United States typically collects as much tariff revenue on shoes as on cars—about $1.9 billion in 2008. The European Union applies tariffs of up to 215 percent on meat, 116 percent on cereals, and 133 percent on sugar and confectionary products.[9]

Exhibit 8.3 provides a sample of import tariffs in selected countries. Despite its reputation as a challenging market to enter, Japan maintains average tariffs for nonagricultural products at low levels. Under the North American Free Trade Agreement (NAFTA), Mexico eliminated nearly all tariffs on product imports from the United States. However, it maintains significant tariffs with the rest of the world—39.8 percent for agricultural products and 9.1 percent for nonagricultural products. India's tariffs are relatively high, especially in agriculture, where the rate is 41.9 percent. India's tariff system lacks transparency, and officially published tariff information is sometimes hard to find. China has reduced its tariffs since joining the World Trade Organization (WTO, www.wto.org) in 2001, but trade barriers remain high in some areas.

In Africa, over half of all workers are employed in agriculture. Significant tariffs and other trade barriers in the advanced economies hinder imports of agricultural goods from Africa, which worsens already-severe poverty in many African countries.

Because high tariffs inhibit free trade and economic growth, governments have tended to reduce them over time. This was the primary goal of the General Agreement on Tariffs and Trade (GATT; now the WTO). Countries as diverse as Chile, Hungary, Turkey, and South Korea have liberalized their previously protected markets, lowering trade barriers and subjecting themselves to greater competition from abroad. Exhibit 8.4 illustrates trends in average world tariff rates over time. Notice that developing economies have been lowering their tariff rates since the early 1980s. Continued reductions represent a major driver of market globalization.

Nontariff Trade Barriers

Nontariff trade barriers are government policies or measures that restrict trade without imposing a direct tax or duty. They include quotas, import licenses, local content requirements, government regulations, and administrative or bureaucratic procedures. The use of nontariff barriers has grown substantially in recent decades. Governments sometimes prefer them because they are easier to conceal from the WTO and other organizations that monitor international trade.

Exhibit 8.3 A Sampling of Import Tariffs

SOURCES: World Trade Organization statistics database, retrieved from http://stat.wto.org; United States Trade Representative reports, retrieved from http://www.ustr.org.

Country/Region	Average Import Tariff	
	Agricultural Products	Nonagricultural Products
Australia	2.8	5.6
Canada	10.8	2.9
China	16.0	9.1
European Union	11.8	2.4
India	41.9	5.5
Japan	10.1	1.3
Mexico	39.8	9.1
United States	5.3	2.0

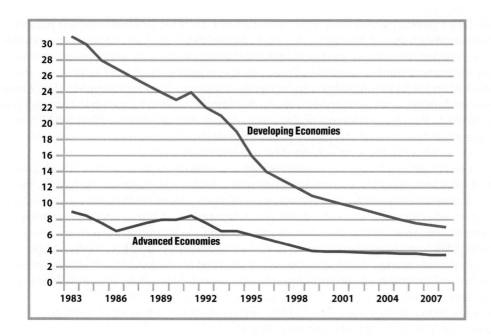

Exhibit 8.4 Trends in Average Tariff Rates (Percentages)

SOURCES: International Monetary Fund, "World Economic Outlook," April 2009, retrieved from http://www.imf.org; United Nations Conference on Trade and Development, *UNCTAD Handbook of Statistics 2008.*

Quotas restrict the physical volume or value of products that firms can import into a country. In a classic type of quota, the U.S. government imposed an upper limit of roughly two million pounds on the total amount of sugar that can be imported into the United States each year. Sugar imports that exceed this level face a tariff of several cents per pound. The upside is that U.S. sugar producers are protected from cheaper imports, giving them a competitive edge over foreign sugar producers. The downside is that U.S. consumers and producers of certain types of products, such as Hershey's and Coca-Cola, pay more for sugar. It also means companies that manufacture products containing sugar may save money by moving production to countries that do not impose quotas or tariffs on sugar.

Governments can impose voluntary quotas, under which firms agree to limit exports of certain products. These are also known as *voluntary export restraints*, or *VERs*. For example, in 2005, import quotas in the European Union led to an impasse in which millions of Chinese-made garments piled up at ports and borders in Europe. The EU impounded the clothing because China had exceeded the voluntary import quotas it had negotiated with the EU. The action created hardship for European retailers, who had ordered their clothing stocks several months in advance.[10]

Governments occasionally require importing firms to obtain an **import license**, a formal permission to import, which restricts imports in a way that is similar to quotas. Do not confuse import licenses with "licensing," a strategy for entering foreign markets in which one firm allows another the right to use its intellectual property in return for a fee. Governments sell import licenses to companies on a competitive basis or grant the licenses on a first-come, first-served basis. This tends to discriminate against smaller firms, which typically lack the resources to purchase them. Obtaining a license can be costly and complicated. In some countries, importers must pay hefty fees to government authorities. In other countries, they must deal with bureaucratic red tape. In Russia a complex web of licensing requirements limits imports of alcoholic beverages. Until the 1990s, the government of India imposed the "license raj," an especially elaborate system of licenses that regulated establishing and running businesses in the country.

Local content requirements require manufacturers to include a minimum of local value added—that is, production that takes place locally. Local content requirements are usually imposed in countries that are members of an economic bloc, such as the EU and NAFTA. The so-called *rules of origin requirement* specifies that a certain proportion of products and supplies, or of intermediate goods used in local manufacturing, must be

Import license
Government authorization granted to a firm for importing a product.

produced within the bloc. For a car manufacturer, the tires or windshields it purchases from another firm are intermediate goods. When the firm does not meet this requirement, the products become subject to trade barriers that member governments normally impose on nonmember countries. Thus, producers within the NAFTA zone of Canada, Mexico, and the United States pay no tariffs on the products and supplies they obtain from each other, unlike countries such as China or the United Kingdom that are not part of NAFTA. Roughly 60 percent of the value of a car manufactured within NAFTA must originate within the NAFTA member countries. If this condition is not met, the product becomes subject to the tariffs charged to non-NAFTA countries.

Government regulations and technical standards are another type of nontariff trade barrier. Examples include safety regulations for motor vehicles and electrical equipment, health regulations for hygienic food preparation, labeling requirements that indicate a product's country of origin, technical standards for computers, and bureaucratic procedures for customs clearance, including excessive red tape and slow approval processes. The European Union strictly regulates food that has been genetically modified (GM), a policy that blocks some food imports into Europe from the United States. In China, the government requires foreign firms to obtain special permits to import GM foods. In 2010, the Chinese government clashed with Google over the latter's refusal to censor its Web search and news services in mainland China. The Chinese government has a history of regulating online news and other content that it considers illegal.[11]

Governments may impose *administrative or bureaucratic procedures* that hinder the activities of importers or foreign firms. For example, the opening vignette revealed how India's business sector is burdened by countless regulations, standards, and administrative hurdles at the state and federal levels. In Mexico, government-imposed bureaucratic procedures led United Parcel Service to temporarily suspend its ground delivery service across the U.S.-Mexican border. Similarly, the United States barred Mexican trucks from entering the United States on the grounds that they were unsafe. Business regulations vary worldwide. Many countries in Africa and Latin America impose countless bureaucratic procedures that hinder commercial activities and business start-ups. By contrast, Australia, Britain, Canada, Ireland, New Zealand, and Singapore impose relatively few such procedures.[12]

Saudi Arabia is home to various restrictive practices that hinder international trade. Every foreign business traveler to the Arab kingdom must hold an entry visa that can be obtained only by securing the support of a sponsor—a Saudi citizen or organization who vouches for the visitor's actions. Because few Saudis are willing to assume such responsibility, foreigners who want to do business in Saudi Arabia face great difficulty.[13]

Convoluted administrative procedures are widespread in national customs agencies. The revenue generated by tariffs depends on how customs authorities classify imported products. Products often appear to fit two or more tariff categories. For example, a sport utility vehicle could be classified as a truck, a car, or a van. Each of these categories can entail a different tariff. Depending on the judgment of the customs agent, the applicable tariff might end up being high or low. Because thousands of categories exist for customs classification, a product and its corresponding tariff can be easily misclassified, by accident or intent.

Investment Barriers

As we saw in the opening vignette on India, countries also impose restrictions on FDI and ownership that restrict the ability of foreign firms to invest in some industry sectors or acquire local firms. Excessive restrictions in India prevent the approval of countless investment proposals that could produce billions of dollars in revenue to the local economy and government. Around the world, FDI and ownership restrictions are particularly common in such industries as broadcasting, utilities, air transportation, military technology, and financial services, as well as industries in which the government has major holdings, such as oil and key minerals. The Mexican government restricts FDI by foreign investors to protect its oil industry, which is deemed critical to the nation's security. The Canadian government restricts foreign ownership of local movie studios and TV networks to protect its indigenous film and TV industries from excessive foreign influence. FDI and ownership restrictions are particularly burdensome in the services sector because services usually cannot be exported and providers must establish a physical presence in target markets to conduct business there. Occasionally, governments impose investment barriers aimed at protecting home country industries and jobs.

Currency controls restrict the outflow of widely used currencies, such as the dollar, euro, and yen, and occasionally the inflow of foreign currencies. Controls can help conserve especially valuable currency or reduce the risk of capital flight. They are particularly common in developing economies. Some countries employ a system of dual official exchange rates, offering exporters a relatively favorable rate to encourage exports, while importers receive a relatively unfavorable rate to discourage imports.

State-owned oil company PEMEX (Petroleos de Mexico) benefits from Mexico's investment barriers.

Currency control
Restrictions on the outflow of hard currency from a country or the inflow of foreign currencies.

Currency controls both help and harm firms that establish foreign subsidiaries through FDI. They favor companies when they export their products from the host country but harm those that rely heavily on imported parts and components. Controls also restrict the ability of MNEs to *repatriate* their profits—that is, transfer revenues from profitable operations back to the home country.

As an example, in Colombia, international investors who wish to buy stocks and bonds must make a refundable deposit of 40 percent of their total investment with the Banco de la Republica (www.banrep.gov.co), the central bank of Colombia, for a minimum of six months. The policy lets monetary authorities monitor the inflow and outflow of foreign investments and helps ensure foreign funds will not be used for speculative activities.

Subsidies and Other Government Support Programs

Subsidies are monetary or other resources that a government grants to a firm or group of firms, intended either to encourage exports or simply to facilitate the production and marketing of products at reduced prices, to help ensure the involved companies prosper. Subsidies come in the form of outright cash disbursements, material inputs, services, tax breaks, the construction of infrastructure, and government contracts at inflated prices. For example, the French government has provided large subsidies to Air France, the national airline.

The *Closing Case* focuses on European government support of Airbus, the leading European manufacturer of commercial aircraft. Perhaps the ultimate examples of subsidized firms are in China. Several leading corporations, such as China Minmetals ($12 billion annual sales) and Shanghai Automotive ($12 billion annual sales), are in fact state enterprises wholly or partly owned by the Chinese government, which provides them with huge financial resources.[14]

Critics argue that subsidies confer unfair advantages on recipients by reducing their cost of doing business. In India, the government provides massive subsidies to state-owned oil companies, which allows them to offer gasoline at very low prices. Foreign MNEs such as Royal Dutch Shell cannot operate profitably at such prices and consequently avoid doing business in the market.[15] The WTO prohibits subsidies when it can be proven that they hinder free trade. Subsidies, however, are hard to define. For example, when a government provides land, infrastructure, telecommunications systems, or utilities to the firms in a corporate park, this is technically a subsidy. Yet many view this type of support as an appropriate public function.

In Europe and the United States, governments frequently provide agricultural subsidies to supplement the income of farmers and help manage the supply of agricultural commodities. The U.S. government grants subsidies for more than two dozen

Subsidy Monetary or other resources that a government grants to a firm or group of firms, usually intended to encourage exports or to facilitate the production and marketing of products at reduced prices, to ensure the involved firms prosper.

Agencies such as Canada's Department of Foreign Affairs and International Trade work to facilitate international activities.

Countervailing duty

Tariff imposed on products imported into a country to offset subsidies given to producers or exporters in the exporting country.

Dumping   Pricing exported products at less than their normal value, generally less than their price in the domestic or third-country markets, or at less than production cost.

Antidumping duty   A tax imposed on products deemed to be dumped and causing injury to producers of competing products in the importing country.

Investment incentive

Transfer payment or tax concession made directly to foreign firms to entice them to invest in the country.

commodities, including wheat, barley, cotton, milk, rice, peanuts, sugar, tobacco, and soybeans. In Europe, the Common Agricultural Policy (CAP) is a system of subsidies that represents about 40 percent of the EU's budget, amounting to tens of billions of euros annually. The CAP and U.S. subsidies have been criticized for promoting unfair competition and high prices because they tend to prevent developing economies from exporting their agricultural goods to Europe and the United States. Subsidies encourage overproduction and therefore lower food prices at home, making agricultural imports from developing countries less competitive.

Governments sometimes retaliate against subsidies by imposing **countervailing duties**, tariffs on products imported into a country to offset subsidies given to producers or exporters in the exporting country. In this way, the duty serves to cancel out the effect of the subsidy by converting it into a direct income transfer by the exporting country to the rest of the world.

Subsidies may allow a manufacturer to practice **dumping**— that is, to charge an unusually low price for exported products, typically lower than that for domestic or third-country customers, or even lower than manufacturing cost.[16] The European Union has provided billions of euros in subsidies every year to EU sugar producers, which allowed Europe to become one of the world's largest sugar exporters at artificially low prices. Without the subsidies Europe would be one of the world's biggest sugar *importers*.

While dumping is hard to prove because firms usually do not reveal data on their cost structures, it is against WTO rules because it amounts to unfair competition. A large MNE that charges very low prices could conceivably drive competitors out of a foreign market, achieving a monopoly, with the ability to raise prices later. Governments in the importing country often respond to dumping by imposing an **antidumping duty**—a tax imposed on products deemed to be dumped and thereby causing injury to producers of competing products in the importing country. The WTO allows this practice.[17] The duties are generally equal to the difference between the product's export price and their normal value.

Government subsidies are not always direct or overt. For example, governments may support home country businesses by funding R&D, granting tax exemptions, and offering business development services such as market information, trade missions, and privileged access to key foreign contacts. Most countries have agencies and ministries that provide such services to facilitate the international activities of their own firms. Examples include the Department of Foreign Affairs and International Trade in Canada (www.dfait-maeci.gc.ca), U.K. Trade & Investment in Britain (www.uktradeinvest.gov.uk), and the International Trade Administration of the U.S. Department of Commerce (www.doc.gov).

Related to subsidies are governmental **investment incentives**, transfer payments or tax concessions made directly to individual foreign firms to entice them to invest in the country. Hong Kong's government put up most of the cash to build the Hong Kong Disney park (park.hongkongdisneyland.com). While the park and facilities cost about $1.81 billion, the government provided Disney an investment of $1.74 billion to develop the site.

Recently, Austin, Texas, and Albany, New York, competed for the chance to have the Korean manufacturer Samsung Electronics (www.samsung.com) build a semiconductor plant in their regions. Austin offered $225 million worth of tax relief and other concessions in its successful bid to attract Samsung's $300 million plant, estimated to create nearly 1,000 new jobs locally. To entice MNEs to establish local production facilities, the country of Macedonia offers such incentives as low corporate taxes, immediate access to utilities and transportation, and financial support for training workers (see www.investinmacedonia.com).

Such incentives often help the economic development in a particular region or community. In the 1990s, Germany encouraged foreign companies to invest in the economically disadvantaged East German states by providing tax and investment incentives. The government of Ireland has undertaken various initiatives aimed at promoting Ireland as a place to do business. It targeted foreign companies in the high-tech sector—including medical instruments, pharmaceuticals, and computer software—and offered preferential corporate tax rates of 12 percent. These targeted efforts paid dividends by creating substantial new employment and helping diversify the Irish economy away from agricultural activities.

Governments also support domestic industries by adopting *procurement policies* that restrict purchases to home country suppliers. Several governments require that air travel purchased with government funds be booked with home country carriers. Such policies are especially common in countries with large public sectors, such as China and Russia. In the United States, government agencies favor domestic suppliers unless their prices are high compared to foreign suppliers. In Japan, government agencies often do not even consider foreign bids, regardless of pricing. Public procurement agencies may impose requirements that effectively exclude foreign suppliers.

Consequences of Government Intervention

As illustrated in Exhibit 8.4, average tariffs have declined over time. Simultaneously, as shown in Exhibit 8.5, world GDP and especially world trade have flourished. Decreasing trade barriers are a major factor in the growth of global commerce and consequently in rising incomes around the world. Firms that participate actively in international trade and investment not only improve their performance but also contribute to reducing global poverty.[18]

One way of evaluating the effects of government intervention is to examine each nation's level of *economic freedom*, defined as the "absence of government coercion or constraint on the production, distribution, or consumption of goods and services beyond the extent necessary for citizens to protect and maintain liberty itself. In other words, people are free to work, produce, consume, and invest in the ways they feel are most productive."[19] An *Index of Economic Freedom* is published annually by the Heritage Foundation (www.heritage.org) that measures economic freedom in 161 countries.

Exhibit 8.6 shows the degree of economic freedom for each country in the Index for 2009, based on criteria such as the level of trade barriers, rule of law, level of business

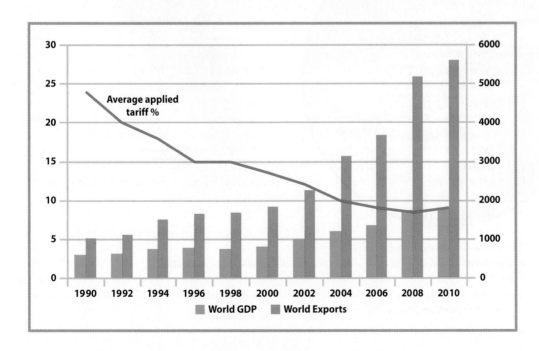

Exhibit 8.5

Relationship between Tariffs, World GDP, and the Volume of World Trade

SOURCE: Based on "World Trade: Barriers to Entry" © *The Economist* Newspaper Limited, London (December 18, 2008).

Exhibit 8.6 Countries Ranked by Level of Economic Freedom, 2010

SOURCES: *2010 Index of Economic Freedom*, The Heritage Foundation, Washington DC, and the *Wall Street Journal*, New York, accessed at http://www.heritage.org

ARCTIC OCEAN

Norway
Sweden
Finland
Estonia

United
Kingdom
Ireland

Denmark
Russia
Latvia
Lithuania
Belarus

Netherlands
Belgium
Luxembourg
Germany
France
Switz.
Liech.
Austria
Slovenia
Croatia
Monaco
Andorra
Italy
Bosnia-
Herzegovina
Montenegro
Macedonia
Albania
Greece
Tunisia
Malta
Cyprus
Lebanon
Israel
Jordan

Czech
Rep.
Slovakia
Hungary
Poland
Ukraine
Moldova
Romania
Serbia
Bulgaria
Turkey

Portugal
Spain

Morocco

Western
Sahara

Mauritania
Mali

Senegal
Gambia
Guinea-bissau
Guinea
Sierra Leone
Liberia
Ivory
Coast
Ghana
Togo
Benin
Nigeria

Burkina
Faso

Algeria
Libya
Egypt

Niger
Chad
Sudan
Eritrea

Cameroon
Central
African
Republic
Equatorial
Guinea
Gabon
Congo
Republic
Congo
Democratic
Republic
(Zaire)
Uganda
Rwanda
Burundi
Tanzania
Kenya
Ethiopia
Djibouti
Somalia

Angola
Zambia
Malawi
Mozambique
Zimbabwe
Namibia
Botswana
Madagascar
Swaziland
South
Africa
Lesotho

Comoros
Mauritius
Réunion

Seychelles

Maldives

Sri
Lanka

INDIAN
OCEAN

Russia

Kazakhstan

Mongolia

Georgia
Armenia
Azerbaijan
Uzbekistan
Turkmenistan
Kyrgyzstan
Tajikistan
Afghanistan
Pakistan

Syria
Iraq
Iran

Kuwait
Bahrain
Qatar
United
Arab
Emirates
Oman
Saudi
Arabia
Yemen

Nepal
Bhutan
India
Bangladesh
Myanmar
(Burma)
Laos
Thailand
Cambodia
Vietnam

China

North
Korea
South
Korea
Japan

Macau
Hong
Kong
Taiwan

Philippines

Brunei
Malaysia
Singapore

Indonesia

Timor-leste

Papua
New
Guinea

Solomon
Islands

Micronesia

PACIFIC
OCEAN

Samoa

Vanuatu
Fiji

New
Caledonia
Tonga

Australia

New
Zealand

SOUTH
ATLANTIC
OCEAN

Level of economic freedom

- 80-100% free
- 70-79.9% free
- 60-69.9% free
- 50-59.9% free
- 0-49.9% free
- Not ranked
- Others

regulation, and protection of intellectual property rights.[20] The Index classifies virtually all the advanced economies as "free," all the emerging markets as either "free" or "mostly free," and all the developing economies as "mostly unfree" or "repressed," underscoring the close relationship between limited government intervention and economic freedom.

Economic freedom flourishes when government supports the institutions necessary for that freedom and provides an appropriate level of intervention and regulation. In 2010 for the first time, the United States fell into the second highest category, due to increased U.S. federal government intervention in that nation's economy, following the recent global financial crisis.

Government intervention and trade barriers raise ethical concerns for developing economies. For example, United States import tariffs on clothing and shoes often exceed 20 percent. In 2008, duties on imported clothing alone produced $10 billion in revenue for the U.S. government. The tariffs hurt poor countries like Bangladesh, Pakistan, India, and several nations in Africa, where clothing and shoe exporters are concentrated. The tariffs that confront such nations are often several times those faced by the richest countries.[21]

Government intervention can also offset harmful effects. For example, trade barriers can create or protect jobs. Subsidies can help counterbalance harmful consequences that disproportionately affect the poor. In Denmark, for example, globalization has affected thousands of workers whose jobs have been shifted to other countries with lower labor costs. The Danish government provides generous subsidies to the unemployed, aimed at retraining workers to upgrade their job skills or find work in other fields.[22]

Evolution of Government Intervention

A century ago, trade barriers worldwide were relatively high. The trading environment worsened through two world wars and the Great Depression. In 1938, the United States passed the Smoot-Hawley Tariff Act, which raised U.S. tariffs to near-record highs of more than 50 percent, compared to only about 3 percent today. Tariffs that other countries imposed to retaliate against Smoot-Hawley choked off foreign markets for U.S. agricultural products, leading to plummeting farm prices and many bank failures. In an effort to revive trade, the U.S. government began to reduce restrictive tariffs. By the late 1940s, prudent policy-making had led to substantial tariff reductions worldwide.

In 1947, twenty-three nations signed the General Agreement on Tariffs and Trade (GATT), the first major effort to systematically reduce trade barriers worldwide. The GATT created: (1) a process to reduce tariffs through continuous negotiations among member nations, (2) an agency to serve as watchdog over world trade, and (3) a forum for resolving trade disputes. The GATT introduced the concept of *most favored nation* (renamed *normal trade relations* in 1998), according to which each signatory nation agreed to extend the tariff reductions covered in a trade agreement with a trading partner to all other countries. Thus, a concession to one country became a concession to all. Eventually, the GATT was superseded by the WTO in 1995 and grew to include about 150 member nations. The organization proved extremely effective and resulted in the greatest global decline in trade barriers in history. The *Global Trend* feature highlights the founding and current progress of the WTO.

In the 1950s, Latin America and other developing nations adopted protectionist policies aimed at industrialization and economic development. Governments imposed high tariffs and quotas on imports from the developed world, established government-supported enterprises to make the products they formerly imported, and sought to substitute local production for imports. Known as *import substitution*, the approach did not succeed. Quasi-public-private enterprises lived behind high quotas and tariffs and enjoyed big government subsidies. However, these enterprises never became competitive in world markets or raised living standards to the levels of free-trading countries.

GL BAL TREND

The World Trade Organization and Collapse of the Doha Round

Based in Geneva, Switzerland, the World Trade Organization (www.wto.org) is the main watchdog for world trade and counts some 150 countries as its members. The WTO works to ensure world trade operates smoothly, fairly, and with as few restrictions as possible. Since joining the WTO in 2001, for example, China has gradually reduced import tariffs and quotas. Most recently, the WTO has been working to reduce trade barriers in the agricultural and services sectors.

Services like the expertise of a lawyer or an accountant are intangible. Consequently, as they do not pass through ports or customs stations, governments usually cannot impose tariffs on them. Thus, services are subject to various *nontariff* trade barriers. For example, some countries in Europe refuse to license foreign insurance companies. In transportation, the United States and numerous other nations require their own merchandise fleets to carry their country's cargo, creating a barrier to foreign-based cargo handlers.

Governments also restrict services by setting licensing and professional standards that may be difficult for foreigners to meet. Regulations usually ensure that law, medicine, accounting, and other professions are undertaken by people who are educated locally, speak the national language, and are socialized according to local standards and norms. Standards in one country are usually not recognized by other countries. Thus, lawyers, doctors, accountants, and many other professionals face restrictions when attempting to do business abroad.

The Doha Development Agenda was a round of WTO negotiations launched in Qatar in November 2001 that sought to reduce barriers in the services sector. The WTO wants to ensure that banks, hotel chains, insurance firms, tour operators, transport companies, and other service firms enjoy the same trade and investment freedoms that apply to goods producers. The Doha Agenda also sought freer trade in agricultural goods, where restraints are particularly burdensome to developing countries. Free global trade in agricultural products is the best way to ensure widespread access and lower prices for food.

Doha was the first round of WTO negotiations in which big emerging markets, especially Brazil, China, and India, played a strong role. The unique circumstances of such countries have increased the complexity of negotiations.

Unfortunately, the talks collapsed in 2008 when trade negotiators were unable to reach agreement. The main reason was that, under WTO rules, all nations were required to agree to all parts of the final deal. This proved impossible for various reasons. For example, China and India insisted on protecting the agricultural sectors in their countries. India alone has more than 200 million farmers, and the Indian government is reluctant to expose them to international competition. In the wake of Doha's collapse, many nations are choosing to concentrate on negotiating bilateral (two-country) and regional trade deals instead.

SOURCES: P. Coy, "Free Trade: After the Impasse," *Business Week*, August 11, 2008, p. 29; "Beyond Doha," *Economist*, October 11, 2008, pp. 30–33; Oxford Analytica Daily Brief Service, "International: Stalled Doha Spurs Trade Discrimination," February 12, 2010, p. 1; United States Trade Representative, "National Trade Estimate Report," 2009, retrieved from http://www.ustr.gov; U.S. and Foreign Commercial Service and U.S. Department of State, *Doing Business in Japan: A Country Commercial Guide for U.S. Companies* (Washington, DC: Government Printing Office, 2007); World Trade Organization, 2007, retrieved from http://www.wto.org.

Meanwhile, the protected industries required ongoing subsidies. Most countries that experimented with import substitution eventually rejected it.

By contrast, from the 1970s onward, Singapore, Hong Kong, Taiwan, and South Korea achieved rapid economic growth by encouraging the development of export-intensive industries. Their model, known as *export-led development*, proved much more successful than import substitution. These countries, along with others in East Asia, such as Malaysia, Thailand, and Indonesia, substantially increased living standards and gained strong international trading links. A rising middle class helped transform these countries into competitive economies.

Elsewhere in Asia, Japan had already launched an ambitious program of industrialization and export-led development following World War II. The country's rise from

Bangladesh is a major clothing exporter that faces high tariffs. Here, women work at Dhaka, the Bangladesh capital and a center of garment manufacturing.

poverty in the 1940s to one of the world's wealthiest countries by the 1980s has been called the *Japanese miracle*. The feat was achieved with the help of national strategic policies, including tariffs that fostered and protected Japan's infant industries such as automobiles, shipbuilding, and consumer electronics.

Since gaining independence from Britain in 1947, India adopted a quasi-socialist model of isolationism and strict government control. High trade and investment barriers, state intervention in labor and financial markets, a large public sector, heavy regulation of business, and central planning all contributed to the nation's poor economic performance over several decades. Beginning in the early 1990s, India began to open its markets to foreign trade and investment. Free-trade reforms, combined with privatization of state enterprises, have progressed slowly. Protectionism has declined, but FDI limitations and high tariffs (more than 40 percent in agricultural products) are still in place.

After establishing a communist government in 1949, China relied on centralized economic planning, and agriculture and manufacturing were controlled by inefficient state-run industries. The country remained relatively closed to international trade until the 1980s, when it began to liberalize its economy. In 1992, China joined Asia-Pacific Economic Cooperation (APEC), a free-trade organization similar to the European Union. In 2001, it joined the WTO and committed to reducing trade barriers and increasing intellectual property protection. Trade has stimulated the Chinese economy. By 2008, its GDP was more than ten times the 1978 level, and the value of exports had reached $1.5 trillion. China has become a leading exporter of manufactured products and home to numerous large MNEs that compete with Western firms.

Intervention and the Global Financial Crisis

The recent global recession and financial crisis have raised new questions about government's role in business and the world economy. The crisis arose largely from inadequate regulation and enforcement of current regulations in the banking and finance sectors. In response, governments around the world are increasing regulation and examining ways to improve enforcement. For example, the U.S. government has increased the power of its Treasury Department, Federal Reserve System, and Federal Deposit Insurance Corporation (FDIC). The European Central Bank is creating a new agency that aims to take aggressive action in needed areas. The European Union is increasing oversight of multinational banks and supervision of financial institutions. The United Nations has called for greater transparency in financial activities and closure of loopholes that allow excessive speculation in global finance.[23]

Some governments are also increasing protectionism in an effort to safeguard jobs and wage levels. In 2009, for example, Argentina and Brazil increased import tariffs on numerous products. Russia raised tariffs on dozens of goods, including cars and combine harvesters. The United States sought to include a clause in the 2009 stimulus package requiring the use of U.S. goods in public works projects.[24]

Hoping to jumpstart economic growth, governments have also increased subsidies to their own industries. The EU granted more than $50 billion in aid to Daimler (Germany), Skoda (Czech Republic), and other struggling carmakers in Europe. The U.S. government provided billions to banks and carmakers in the United States. China has pumped hundreds of billions of dollars into its own economy.[25]

In addition to the harmful fallout of the recession and financial crisis, rising protectionism is impacting international commerce. Ripple effects of government reforms are extending beyond the banking and financial areas.[26]

 How Firms Can Respond to Government Intervention

Although a manager's first inclination might be to avoid markets with high trade and investment barriers or excessive government intervention, this course is not usually practical. Depending on the industry and country, firms generally must cope with protectionism and other forms of intervention. For example, in extractive industries such as aluminum and petroleum, foreign firms seek to do business in nations that impose formidable barriers. The food-processing, biotechnology, and pharmaceutical industries also encounter countless laws and regulations abroad.

Strategies for Managers

We've seen that China, India, and numerous other countries in Africa, Asia, Latin America, and Eastern and Central Europe feature extensive trade barriers and government involvement. Yet many firms seek to target emerging markets and developing economies because of the huge long-term potential they offer.[27] Firms devise various strategies to manage harmful government intervention.

Research to Gather Knowledge and Intelligence Experienced managers continually scan the business environment to identify the nature of government intervention and to plan market-entry strategies and host country operations. They review their return-on-investment criteria to account for the increased cost and risk of trade and investment barriers. For example, the EU is devising new guidelines that affect company operations in areas ranging from product liability laws to standards for investment in European industries.

Choose the Most Appropriate Entry Strategies Tariffs and most nontariff trade barriers apply to exporting, whereas investment barriers apply to FDI. Most firms choose exporting as their initial entry strategy. However, if high tariffs are present, managers should consider other strategies, such as FDI, licensing, and joint ventures that allow the firm to operate directly in the target market, avoiding import barriers. For example, Japan's Fuji Company had long exported camera film to the United States. Subsequently, Fuji built a factory in South Carolina to manufacture film, which allowed it to avoid U.S. tariffs and deflect claims that it was unfairly dumping Japanese-made film there.

However, even investment-based entry is affected by tariffs if it requires importing raw materials and parts to manufacture finished products in the host country. Tariffs often vary with the *form* of an imported product. Food processor Conagra (www.conagrafoods .com) imports bulk tuna into the United States, which it then separates and cans there under the Bumble Bee brand. Conagra could can the tuna abroad, but the tariff on canned tuna is higher than the tariff on bulk tuna. By canning in the United States, Conagra avoids paying import tariffs.[28] Companies often ship manufactured products "knocked-down" and assemble them in the target market. In countries with relatively high tariffs on imported personal computers, importers often bring in the parts and assemble the computers locally.

Take Advantage of Foreign Trade Zones In an effort to create jobs and stimulate local economic development, governments establish foreign trade zones (also known as *free trade zones* or *free ports*). A **foreign trade zone (FTZ)** is an area within a country that receives imported goods for assembly or other processing and subsequent re-export.[29] Products brought into an FTZ are not subject to duties, taxes, or quotas until they, or the products made from them, enter into the non-FTZ commercial territory of the country where the FTZ is located. Firms use FTZs to assemble foreign dutiable materials and

Foreign trade zone (FTZ) An area within a country that receives imported goods for assembly or other processing and re-export. For customs purposes the FTZ is treated as if it is outside the country's borders.

components into finished products, which are then re-exported. Alternatively, firms may use FTZs to manage inventory of parts, components, or finished products that the firm will eventually need at some other location. In the United States, for example, Japanese carmakers store vehicles at the port of Jacksonville, Florida, without having to pay duties until the cars are shipped to U.S. dealerships.

FTZs exist in more than seventy-five countries, usually near seaports or airports. They can be as small as a factory or as large as an entire country. The United States is home to several hundred FTZs used by thousands of firms. Located on the Atlantic side of the Panama Canal, the Colon Free Zone (www.colonfreezone.com) is an enormous FTZ where products are imported, stored, modified, repacked, and re-exported without being subject to tariffs or customs regulations. The many private firms and wholesalers that set up shop inside the huge zone transship their merchandise from Panama to other parts of the Western Hemisphere and Europe. Some firms obtain FTZ status within their own physical facilities.

Maquiladoras Export-assembly plants in northern Mexico along the U.S. border that produce components and typically finished products destined for the United States on a tariff-free basis.

A successful experiment with FTZs has been **maquiladoras**—export-assembly plants in northern Mexico along the U.S. border that produce components and finished products, usually destined for the United States. Since the 1960s, "maquilas" have imported materials and equipment on a tariff-free basis for assembly or manufacturing and then re-exported the assembled products. Today under NAFTA, maquiladoras employ millions of Mexicans who assemble clothing, furniture, car parts, electronics, and other goods. The arrangement enables firms from the United States, Asia, and Europe to tap low-cost labor, favorable duties, and government incentives while serving the U.S. market. Maquilas account for about half of Mexico's exports.

Seek Favorable Customs Classifications for Exported Products One approach for reducing exposure to trade barriers is to have exported products classified in the appropriate harmonized product code. As noted earlier in this chapter, many products can be classified within two or more categories, each of which may imply a different tariff. For example, some telecommunications equipment can be classified as electric machinery, electronics, or measuring devices. The manufacturer should analyze the trade barriers on differing categories to ensure exported products are classified under the lowest tariff code. Or the manufacturer may be able to modify the exported product in a way that helps minimize trade barriers. South Korea faced a quota on the export of nonrubber footwear to the United States. By shifting manufacturing to rubber-soled shoes, Korean firms greatly increased their footwear exports.

Take Advantage of Investment Incentives and Other Government Support Programs Obtaining economic development incentives from host or home country governments is another strategy to reduce the cost of trade and investment barriers. When Mercedes built a factory in Alabama, it benefitted from reduced taxes and direct subsidies provided by the Alabama state government. When Siemens built a semiconductor plant in Portugal, it received subsidies from the Portuguese government and the EU. Incentives cover nearly 40 percent of Siemens's investment and training costs. Governments in Europe, Japan, and the United States increasingly provide incentives to companies that set up shop within their borders. Incentives can also include reduced utility rates, employee training programs, tax holidays, and construction of new roads and communications infrastructure.

Lobby for Freer Trade and Investment More nations are liberalizing markets to create jobs and increase tax revenues. The trend results partly from the efforts of firms to lobby domestic and foreign governments to lower their trade and investment barriers. The Japanese have achieved much success in reducing trade barriers by lobbying U.S. and European governments. In China, domestic and foreign firms lobby the government to relax protectionist policies and regulations that make China a difficult place to do business. Foreign firms often hire former Chinese government officials to help lobby their former colleagues.[30] European automakers have obtained various concessions by lobbying individual state governments in the United States. BMW leased its 1,039-acre factory site in South Carolina at an annual rent of one dollar. The private sector lobbies federal authorities to undertake government-to-government trade negotiations, aimed at lowering barriers. Private firms bring complaints to world bodies, especially the WTO, to address unfair trading practices of key international markets.

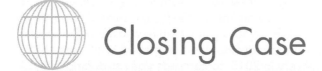 # Closing Case

Government Intervention at Airbus and Boeing

In the 1960s, United States companies such as Boeing (www.boeing.com) and McDonnell Douglas were the dominant players in global aircraft manufacturing. Boeing was founded in 1916 in Seattle, and had many years to develop the critical mass necessary to become the world's leading aerospace manufacturer. During World War II and the subsequent Cold War years, Boeing was the recipient of many lucrative contracts from the U.S. Department of Defense.

In Europe, no single country possessed the means to launch an aerospace company capable of challenging Boeing. Manufacturing commercial aircraft is complex and capital-intensive and necessitates a highly skilled workforce. In 1970, the governments of France and Germany formed an alliance, supported with massive government subsidies, to create Airbus S.A.S. (www.airbus .com). The governments of Spain and Britain joined Airbus later. By 1981, the four-country alliance succeeded in becoming the world's number-two civil aircraft manufacturer. Airbus launched the A300, among the best-selling commercial aircraft of all time. Airbus also created the A320, receiving more than 400 orders before its first flight and becoming the fastest-selling large passenger jet in aviation history. By 1992, Airbus had captured roughly one-third of the global commercial aircraft market.

Government Support for Airbus

Since the 1940s, European governments have pursued public policies based on democratic socialism. Under this system, the government plays a strong role in the national economy and provides key services such as health care, mass transit, and sometimes banking and housing. Most Europeans are accustomed to government playing a significant role in guiding the national economy.

In this context, Airbus has benefited enormously from the support of various governments. The firm has received tens of billions of euros of subsidies and soft loans from the four founding country governments and the EU. Airbus must repay the loans only if it achieves profitability. Government aid has financed, in whole or part, every major Airbus aircraft model. European governments have forgiven Airbus's debt, provided huge equity infusions, dedicated infrastructure support, and financed R&D for civil aircraft projects.

Airbus is currently a stock-held company jointly owned by the British, Germans, French, and Spanish. It is based in Toulouse, France, but has R&D and production operations scattered throughout Europe. European governments justify their financial aid to Airbus on several grounds. First, Airbus R&D activities result in new technologies of considerable value to the EU. Second, Airbus provides jobs to some 53,000 skilled and semiskilled Europeans. Third, its value-chain activities attract massive amounts of capital into Europe. Finally, Airbus generates enormous tax revenues.

Complaints about Unfair Government Intervention

Boeing and the U.S. government have long complained about the massive subsidies and soft loans that were responsible not only for Airbus's birth, but also for its ongoing success. The outcry became louder in the 2000s, when Airbus surpassed Boeing in annual sales, becoming the world's leading commercial aircraft manufacturer. Boeing has argued that Airbus never would have gotten this far without government support.

In 2005, the U.S. Trade Representative brought its case to the WTO. The case arose because EU member states approved $3.7 billion in new subsidies and soft loans to Airbus. The case alleged that financial aid for the A350, A380, and earlier Airbus aircraft qualified as subsidies under the WTO's Agreement on Subsidies and Countervailing Measures (ASCM) and that the subsidies were actionable because they caused adverse effects to international trade. Under the ASCM, subsidies to specific firms or industries from a government or other public bodies are prohibited. Airbus confirmed that it had applied to the governments of Britain, France, Germany, and Spain for launch aid for its model A350. In 2010, the WTO ruled that EU aid to Airbus was illegal. In total, the WTO found that Airbus had received some $20 million in preferential subsidies from the European governments.

EU officials have argued that government subsidies to Airbus were permissible and that it was up to individual EU countries to decide whether to provide them.

Government Support for Boeing

The EU argues the United States government has indirectly subsidized Boeing through massive defense contracts paid via tax dollars. The U.S. government gave Boeing more than $23 billion in indirect government subsidies by means of R&D funding and other indirect support from the Pentagon and NASA, the nation's space agency. Boeing is at liberty to use the knowledge acquired from such projects to produce civilian aircraft. The state of Washington, Boeing's primary manufacturing and assembly location, has provided the firm with tax breaks, infrastructure support, and other incentives totaling billions of dollars.

The EU also has a case at the WTO regarding Boeing's relations with its Japanese business partners. The new Boeing 787 Dreamliner is built in an alliance with the heavy-industry divisions of Japanese MNEs like Mitsubishi, Kawasaki, and Fuji. They have provided more than $1.5 billion in soft loans, repayable only if the aircraft is a commercial success.

New Aircraft from Airbus and Boeing

In 2007, Airbus launched the A380, an innovative airplane with an upper deck extending the entire length of the fuselage and a cabin that provides 50 percent more floor space than Boeing's largest aircraft. The A380 can seat between 555 and 853 passengers, depending on the seating configuration. It has a maximum range of 15,000 kilometers (8,000 nautical miles). The total cost of developing and launching the A380 reached 15 billion euros (USD $21 billion), partly supported by funding from European governments.

Boeing successfully launched a test version of its Boeing 787 Dreamliner in 2007 and is several years ahead of Airbus in launching innovative and fuel-efficient aircraft. Airbus is developing a mid-sized A350 model, due for delivery in 2013, to compete against Boeing's 787.

In 2008, the government of China established a company to make passenger jumbo jets, part of its quest to challenge Boeing and Airbus in the global aircraft industry. China Commercial Aircraft Co. was established in Shanghai amid forecasts that China's domestic market for commercial aircraft will increase fivefold by 2026.

Global Financial Crisis

The recent global financial crisis has adversely impacted Airbus and Boeing. Both companies were forced to reduce output and laid off more than 10,000 workers each. Following sharp drops in passenger traffic, airlines grounded planes and cut routes. Many airlines cancelled or postponed new aircraft orders. Following cuts in U.S. military spending, orders for military hardware also declined. Longer term, Airbus is reorganizing its global operations, outsourcing more manufacturing, and selling all or part of six factories. Airbus and Boeing are generating new business from emerging markets. Recently, India signed a $2.1 billion deal with Boeing to purchase military aircraft.

AACSB: Reflective Thinking Skills, Ethical Understanding and Reasoning Abilities

Case Questions

1. Where do you stand? Do you think EU subsidies and soft loans to Airbus are fair? Why or why not? What advantages does Airbus gain from free financial support from the EU governments? Are complaints about EU subsidies fair in light of Europe's history of democratic socialism?

2. Do you believe U.S. military contracts with Boeing amount to subsidies? Have these types of payments provided Boeing with unfair advantages? Justify your answer.

3. Assuming that Airbus cannot compete without subsidies and loans, is it likely that the EU will discontinue its financial support of Airbus? Is it in the EU's interests to continue supporting Airbus? Justify your answer.

4. Visit the Web site of the WTO (www.wto.org) and enter the keywords *aircraft* or *civil aircraft* in the search engine. Summarize the current status of the dispute before the WTO between Airbus and Boeing.

5. In the event the WTO rules against Airbus and tells it to stop accepting subsidies and soft loans, how should Airbus management respond? What new approaches can management pursue to maintain Airbus's lead in the global commercial aircraft industry?

SOURCES: Corporate profiles of Airbus and Boeing at http://www.hoovers.com; K. Epstein & J. Crown, "Globalization Bites Boeing," *Business Week*, March 24, 2008, p. 32; D. Gauthier-Villars & D. Michaels, "Airbus Buyers Get French Aid," *Wall Street Journal*, January 27, 2009, p. B4; N. Luthra, "Boeing to Sell India $2.1 Billion in Planes," *Wall Street Journal*, January 6, 2009, p. B4; D. Michaels, "Airbus Trims Jumbo Output as Carriers Defer Orders," *Wall Street Journal*, May 7, 2009, p. B1; "China to Make Jumbo Jetliners, Trim Roles of Boeing, Airbus," *Wall Street Journal*, May 12, 2008, p. B4; "How Airbus Flew Past Its American Rival," *Financial Times*, March 17, 2005, p. 6; "Airbus versus Boeing: The Super-jumbo of All Gambles," *Economist*, January 22, 2005, pp. 55–56; J. Lunsford and D. Michaels, "Bet on Huge Plane Trips Up Airbus," *Wall Street Journal*, June 15, 2006, p. A1; S. Malveaux, "U.S. Takes Airbus Dispute to WTO," *CNN*, May 31, 2005, retrieved from http://edition.cnn.com; J. Miller and M. Dalton, "WTO Finds EU Aid to Airbus Is Illegal," *Wall Street Journal*, March 24, 2010, p. A10; X. Vives, "Airbus and the Damage Done by Economic Patriotism," *Financial Times*, March 7, 2007, p. 17.

NOTE: The authors acknowledge the assistance of Stephanie Regales with this case.

CHAPTER ESSENTIALS

Key Terms

antidumping duty, p. 248
countervailing duty, p. 248
currency control, p. 247
customs, p. 238
dumping, p. 248

export control, p. 241
foreign trade zone (FTZ), p. 255
import license, p. 245
investment incentive, p. 248
maquiladoras, p. 256

nontariff trade barrier, p. 238
protectionism, p. 238
quota, p. 238
subsidy, p. 247
tariff, p. 238

Summary

In this chapter, you learned about:

1. The nature of government intervention

Despite the value of free trade, governments often intervene in international business. **Protectionism** refers to national economic policies designed to restrict free trade and protect domestic industries from foreign competition. Government intervention arises typically in the form of tariffs, nontariff trade barriers, and investment barriers. **Tariffs** are taxes on imported products, imposed mainly to collect government revenue and protect domestic industries from foreign competition. **Nontariff trade barriers** consist of policies that restrict trade without directly imposing a tax. An example of a nontariff trade barrier is a **quota,** a quantitative restriction on imports. Managers find out what tariffs apply to their products by consulting *harmonized code schedules,* available from government agencies.

2. Rationale for government intervention

Governments impose trade and investment barriers to achieve political, social, or economic objectives. Such barriers are either defensive or offensive. A key rationale is the protection of the nation's economy, its industries, and its workers. **Export controls** limit trade in sensitive products deemed critical to national security. Governments also impose barriers to protect infant industries.

3. Instruments of government intervention

Governments also impose regulations and technical standards, as well as administrative and bureaucratic procedures. Countries may also impose **currency controls** to minimize international withdrawal of national currency. FDI and ownership restrictions ensure that the nation maintains partial or full ownership of firms within its national borders. Governments also provide **subsidies**, a form of payment or other material support. Foreign governments may offset foreign subsidies by imposing **countervailing duties**. With **dumping**, a firm charges abnormally low prices abroad. A government may respond to dumping by imposing an **antidumping duty**. Governments support homegrown firms by providing **investment incentives** and biased government procurement policies.

4. Consequences of government intervention

Economic freedom refers to the extent of government intervention in the national economy. Government intervention and trade barriers can raise ethical concerns that affect developing economies and low-income consumers. However, government intervention also can be used to offset such harmful effects.

5. Evolution of government intervention

Intervention has a long history. In the late 1800s, many countries imposed substantial protectionism. From the 1930s onward, countries reduced trade barriers worldwide. The nature and outcomes of government intervention have varied across Latin America, Japan, India, and China. The most important development for reducing trade barriers was the General Agreement on Tariffs and Trade (GATT), replaced in 1995 by the World Trade Organization (WTO). The 150 members of the WTO account for nearly all world trade.

6. Intervention and the global financial crisis

The crisis arose from inadequate regulation in the banking and finance sectors. In response, governments are implementing new regulations. Governments are also increasing protectionism, to safeguard jobs and wage levels, and providing new subsidies to their countries' industries. Government reforms are having ripple effects that extend beyond the banking and financial areas.

7. How firms can respond to government intervention

Firms should conduct research to understand the extent and nature of trade and investment barriers abroad. When trade barriers are substantial, FDI or joint ventures are often the most appropriate entry strategies. Where importing is essential, the firm can take advantage of **foreign trade zones**, areas where imports receive preferential tariff treatment. Government assistance in the form of subsidies and incentives helps reduce the impact of protectionism. Firms sometimes lobby the home and foreign governments for freer trade and investment.

Test Your Comprehension AACSB: Reflective Thinking Skills

1. Discuss the relationship between government intervention and protectionism.

2. Distinguish among tariffs, nontariff trade barriers, investment barriers, and government subsidies.

3. What are the major types of nontariff trade barriers? Suggest business strategies for minimizing the effect of nontariff trade barriers.

4. Distinguish between countervailing duties and antidumping duties.

5. In what ways do government subsidies and procurement policies amount to protectionism?

6. What is the rationale for intervention? Why do governments engage in protectionism?

7. How did government intervention evolve between the first and second halves of the twentieth century?

8. How has government intervention evolved during the global financial crisis?

9. Describe various company strategies to manage government intervention.

10. What is the role of FDI, licensing, and joint ventures in reducing the impact of import tariffs?

Apply Your Understanding AACSB: Ethical Understanding and Reasoning Abilities, Reflective Thinking Skills, Communication Abilities

1. TelComm Corporation is a manufacturer of components for the cell phone industry. TelComm's founder, Mr. Alex Bell, is interested in exporting the firm's products to China. He heard that China has the world's largest population of cell phone users and wants to enter the market. But TelComm has little international experience. Mr. Bell is unaware of the various types of nontariff trade barriers that TelComm might face in China and other foreign markets. Please summarize major nontariff trade barriers to Mr. Bell. What types of investment barriers might TelComm face in the event management decides to establish a factory in China to manufacture cell phone components? What can TelComm management do to minimize the threat of these nontariff trade and investment barriers?

2. *Ethical Dilemma:* The United States steel industry, once the world leader, now produces less steel than either China or Japan. American steel producers are threatened by price-competitive suppliers in Brazil, Russia, and other emerging markets. The U.S. steel industry dealt with this threat by launching a lobbying campaign to persuade the U.S. government to impose barriers on the import of foreign steel. The following is an advertisement used by the steel industry in this effort:

> In recent years, the United States has lost millions of manufacturing jobs because domestic factories have shifted their operations to low-wage countries. Manufacturing assures our national defense, our global leadership, and the living standards of more than 17 million workers. Other nations subsidize their domestic steel industries. Longer-term, subsidized imports will destroy a vital American industry and U.S. jobs. In an uncertain and dangerous world, does America really want to become dependent on Russia, Japan, China, Brazil and developing countries for something so basic as steel?

Evaluate this statement. How valid is the argument? Using the Ethical Framework in Chapter 5, analyze the arguments for and against imposing trade barriers on the import of steel from abroad. Should the U.S. government impose trade barriers? What is the effect of barriers on (a) U.S. steel producers, (b) U.S. firms that use a lot of steel to manufacture finished products, and (c) consumers of products made with U.S. steel. Recall that Brazil, China, and Russia are emerging markets with substantial poverty. What is the effect of the barriers on these countries?

3. *Ethical Dilemma:* You are Vice President for International Sales at AgriCorp, a large trading company that exports processed foods to Africa. You are often frustrated that African countries impose high tariffs (typically 75 percent) on processed food imports. These barriers raise AgriCorp's cost of doing business and make your prices less competitive in African markets. But Africa suffers from widespread poverty and African governments use tariffs to raise needed revenues and achieve policy objectives. Using the concepts in this chapter and the Ethical Framework in Chapter 5, analyze the arguments for and against high agricultural tariffs in Africa. What ethical concerns do you perceive in Africa's use of high tariffs on agricultural goods? What ethical concerns do you perceive in AgriCorp's efforts to avoid the tariffs? How should AgriCorp respond to the tariffs?

globalEDGE Internet Exercises
(http://globalEDGE.msu.edu)

AACSB: Reflective Thinking Skills, Analytic Skills, Ethical Understanding and Reasoning Abilities

Refer to Chapter 1, page 62, for instructions on how to access and use globalEDGE™.

1. Your firm is considering exporting to two countries: Kenya and Vietnam. However, management's knowledge about the trade policies of these countries is limited. Conduct a search at globalEDGE™ to identify the current import policies, tariffs, and restrictions in these countries. Prepare a brief report on your findings. In addition to globalEDGE™, other useful sites include UNCTAD Trains (www.unctad.org/trains, once there, click on Country Notes) and the U.S. Commercial Service (www.buyusa.gov).

2. The Office of the U.S. Trade Representative (USTR) is responsible for developing and coordinating United States international trade and investment policies. Visit the USTR Web site from globalEDGE™ or directly (www.ustr.gov). Search for "National Trade Estimate Report" for the latest year. This document summarizes trade barriers around the world. See the reports for the country of your choice. What are the country's import policies and practices? What are its nontariff trade barriers? What about barriers in the services sector? Are there any sectors that seem to be particularly protected (for example, aviation, energy, telecommunications)? What is the nature of government restrictions on e-commerce? If you were a manager in a firm that wanted to export its products to the country, how would you use the USTR report to develop international business strategies?

3. Visit the following web portals and review their perspectives on the debate about free trade and government policies on trade barriers. Given the inherent conflict between national interests, special interests, asymmetries in world wage rates, and other economic conditions, what is the best path forward for national governments? That is, should governments generally favor free trade, or should they intervene to protect national interests?

http://www.heritage.org/issues

http://www.wto.org

http://www.citizen.org/trade/

http://www.aflcio.org/globaleconomy/

http://www.sierraclub.org/trade/

CHAPTER 9

Regional Economic Integration

Evolution of the European Union

Europe was economically and physically devastated at the end of World War II, with much of its industry and infrastructure destroyed. At the onset of the Cold War between the United States and the Soviet Union, the continent was also physically and politically divided between Western and Eastern Europe.

To help address these issues and promote peace and harmony in Europe, six countries—Belgium, France, Italy, Luxembourg, the Netherlands, and West Germany—formed an alliance in 1957 called the European Economic Community (EEC). Its successor is today's European Union (EU), which was established in 1992 and now includes twenty-seven countries from both Eastern and Western Europe with a total of twenty-three official languages among them. The EU is the world's most advanced and largest regional economic bloc, with a half-billion people and about $16 trillion in annual GDP. A regional economic bloc (or economic bloc) is an alliance of two or more countries that agree to eliminate tariffs and other restrictions to the cross-border flow of products, services, capital, and, occasionally, labor.

Trade and investment within Europe have become much easier since the 1950s. The member states allow investors from other member countries to freely establish and conduct business and transfer capital. Gradual elimination of bureaucracy at Europe's national borders cut delivery times and reduced transportation costs. The EU eliminated the need to use most customs clearance documents. Sixteen EU countries have adopted the euro as their common currency, helping to lower business transaction costs and increase the transparency of pricing throughout the continent.

The EU is home to the headquarters of some of the world's most important firms. Allianz, an insurance company founded in Germany, offers a variety of life, health, and casualty insurance. While previously its management viewed Europe as a collection of disparate countries, Allianz treats Europe increasingly as one large marketplace. In strategy-making, management emphasizes a pan-European approach, which cuts costs and increases the efficiency of Allianz's operations throughout Europe.

Development of the EU has allowed Allianz to internationalize faster than other insurers. The firm is present in all the new EU countries, such as Poland, Hungary, and the Czech Republic, which are proving to be among Allianz's most profitable markets. In 2006, Allianz changed its legal status from a German company to a *Societas Europaea (SE)*, a European company based in and regulated by the EU as a whole. SE status allows such firms to operate seamlessly across all twenty-seven EU countries.

The EU is at a crossroads today. Member countries aim to develop a European constitution to clarify distribution of powers and legitimize the EU's federal authority, in much the same way the U.S. Constitution does for the United States. The EU economy has been sluggish for more than a decade; GDP growth and productivity stagnated and unemployment has hovered between 8 and 12 percent. The situation worsened during the recent global recession. In 2010, the EU sought to rescue member countries fiscally weakened during the global crisis. Greece's economy faced collapse due to massive government debt. Greece's financial travails forced the euro-zone countries further along a path to greater economic coordination.

Economic blocs are a fixture of the emerging landscape of international trade and investment. The challenges facing the EU today may be typical of those faced by economic blocs in the most advanced stages of development. Such alliances represent a long-term trend and may be a stepping-stone to the emergence of worldwide free trade.

SOURCES: "Retake the Reins: The European Union Must Harmonise Financial Regulation," *Financial Times,* January 23, 2009, p. 8; "Fit at 50? A Special Report on the European Union," *Economist,* March 17, 2007; European Commission, "The Internal Market—Ten Years without Frontiers," retrieved from http://www.ec.europa.eu; C. Forelle and M. Walker, "Europeans Agree on Bailout for Greece," *Wall Street Journal,* March 26, 2010, p. A1; Corporate profile of Allianz at http://www.hoovers.com; U.S. Commercial Service, *Doing Business in the European Union* (Washington, DC: U.S. and Foreign Commercial Service and U.S. Department of State, 2008).

 ## Regional Integration and Economic Blocs

Regional economic integration The growing economic interdependence that results when two or more countries within a geographic region form an alliance aimed at reducing barriers to trade and investment.

The opening vignette highlights one of the most remarkable features of contemporary international business: the worldwide trend toward **regional economic integration.** Also known as *regional integration,* regional economic integration refers to the growing economic interdependence that results when two or more countries within a geographic region form an alliance aimed at reducing barriers to trade and investment. Since the end of World War II, most nations have sought to cooperate, with the aim of achieving some degree of economic integration. More than 50 percent of world trade today takes place under some form of preferential trade agreement signed by groups of countries. The trend is based on the premise that, by cooperating, nations within a common geographic region connected by historical, cultural, linguistic, economic, or political factors can gain mutual advantages.[1] The free trade that results from economic integration helps nations attain higher living standards by encouraging specialization, lower prices, greater choices, increased productivity, and more efficient use of resources.

To better understand regional integration, think of international business as existing along a continuum where, at one extreme, the world operates as one large free-trade area in which there are no tariffs or quotas, all countries use the same currency, and products, services, capital, and workers can move freely among nations without restriction. At the other extreme of this continuum is a world of prohibitive barriers to trade and investment where countries have separate currencies and very little commercial interaction with each other. Regional integration represents a compromise, a middle-ground within this continuum. Two of the best-known examples are the European Union (EU) and the North American Free Trade Agreement (NAFTA). NAFTA consists of Canada, Mexico, and the United States.

Regional economic integration bloc
A geographic area consisting of two or more countries that have agreed to pursue economic integration by reducing barriers to the cross-border flow of products, services, capital, and, in more advanced states, labor.

Free trade agreement
A formal arrangement between two or more countries to reduce or eliminate tariffs, quotas, and barriers to trade in products and services.

Regional integration results from the formation of a **regional economic integration bloc** or, simply, an economic bloc. This refers to a geographic area that consists of two or more countries that agree to pursue economic integration by reducing tariffs and other restrictions to the cross-border flow of products, services, capital, and, in more advanced stages, labor. (In this text, following convention, we use the French term *bloc* instead of *block.*) At a minimum, the countries in an economic bloc become parties to a **free trade agreement,** a formal arrangement between two or more countries to reduce or eliminate tariffs, quotas, and other barriers to trade in products and services. The member nations also undertake cross-border investments within the bloc.

More advanced economic blocs, such as the EU, permit the free flow of capital, labor, and technology among their member countries. The EU is also harmonizing monetary policy (to manage the money supply and currency values) and fiscal policy (to manage government finances, especially tax revenues) and gradually integrating the economies of its member nations. In recent years, cross-border merger and acquisition deals have increased markedly among firms from Austria, Britain, France, and other member countries.

Why would a nation opt to be a member of an economic bloc instead of working toward a system of worldwide free trade? The main reason is that reaching agreement on free trade is much easier in negotiations among a handful of countries than among all the nations in the world. This helps explain why there are hundreds of regional trade integration blocs around the world today. They present both opportunities and challenges to internationalizing firms.

Since 1947, the General Agreement on Tariffs and Trade (GATT) and later the World Trade Organization (WTO) have achieved great success in fostering economic integration on a *global* scale. In addition, the WTO recognizes regional integration can play an important role in liberalizing trade and fostering economic development. However, regional economic blocs are powerful and the WTO has encountered various challenges in dealing with them. Slow progress in liberalizing trade, especially for agricultural products, has prompted many developing countries to seek alternatives to the global trading system favored by the WTO. The WTO is continuing negotiations with economic blocs, with the aim of exercising better control over their evolution and of minimizing risks associated with regional economic integration.[2]

 ## Levels of Regional Integration

Regional integration allows distinct national economies to become economically linked and interdependent through greater cross-national movement of products, services, and factors of production. It also allows member states to use resources more productively. The total output of the integrated area becomes greater than that achievable by individual states.

Exhibit 9.1 identifies five possible levels of regional integration. We can think of these levels as a continuum, with economic interconnectedness progressing from a low level of integration—the free trade area—through higher levels to the most advanced form of integration—the political union. The *political union* represents the ultimate degree of integration among countries, which no countries have yet achieved.

The **free trade area** is the simplest and most common arrangement, in which member countries agree to gradually eliminate formal barriers to trade in products and services within the bloc, while each member country maintains an independent international trade policy with countries outside the bloc. NAFTA is an example. The free trade area emphasizes the pursuit of comparative advantage for a group of countries rather than for individual states. Governments may impose local content requirements, which specify that producers located within the member countries provide a certain proportion of products and supplies used in local manufacturing. If the content requirement is not met, the product becomes subject to the tariffs that member governments normally impose on nonmember countries.

The **customs union** is the second level of regional integration, similar to a free trade area except that member states harmonize their external trade policies and adopt *common* tariff and nontariff barriers on imports from nonmember countries. MERCOSUR, an economic bloc in Latin America, is an example of this type of arrangement. The adoption of a common tariff system means that an exporter outside MERCOSUR faces the *same* tariffs and nontariff barriers when trading with *any* MERCOSUR member country. Determining the most appropriate common external tariff is challenging, because member countries must agree on the level and on how to distribute proceeds from the tariff among the member countries.

Free trade area
A stage of regional integration in which member countries agree to eliminate tariffs and other barriers to trade in products and services within the bloc.

Customs union
A stage of regional integration in which the member countries agree to adopt common tariff and nontariff barriers on imports from nonmember countries.

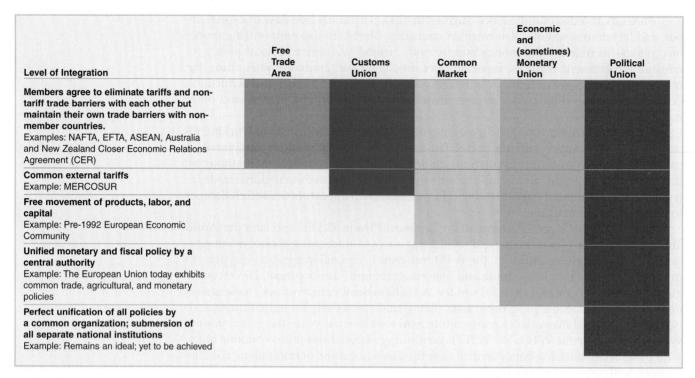

Level of Integration	Free Trade Area	Customs Union	Common Market	Economic and (sometimes) Monetary Union	Political Union
Members agree to eliminate tariffs and non-tariff trade barriers with each other but maintain their own trade barriers with non-member countries. Examples: NAFTA, EFTA, ASEAN, Australia and New Zealand Closer Economic Relations Agreement (CER)					
Common external tariffs Example: MERCOSUR					
Free movement of products, labor, and capital Example: Pre-1992 European Economic Community					
Unified monetary and fiscal policy by a central authority Example: The European Union today exhibits common trade, agricultural, and monetary policies					
Perfect unification of all policies by a common organization; submersion of all separate national institutions Example: Remains an ideal; yet to be achieved					

Exhibit 9.1 Five Potential Levels of Regional Integration among Nations (For example, a customs union has the features of a free trade area, plus common external tariffs)

SOURCE: Bela Balassa, *The Theory of Economic Integration* (Santa Barbara, CA: Greenwood Press Reprint, 1982).

Common market

A stage of regional integration in which trade barriers are reduced or removed, common external barriers are established, and products, services, and *factors of production* are allowed to move freely among the member countries.

In the third stage of regional integration, member countries establish a **common market** (also known as a single market), in which trade barriers are reduced or removed, common external barriers are established, and products, services, and *factors of production* such as capital, labor, and technology are allowed to move freely among the member countries. Like a customs union, a common market also establishes a common trade policy with nonmember countries. The EU is a common market. It has gradually reduced or eliminated restrictions on immigration and the cross-border flow of capital. A worker from an EU country has the right to work in other EU countries, and EU firms can freely transfer funds among their subsidiaries within the bloc.

Common markets are hard to create because they require substantial cooperation on labor and economic policies. Since labor and capital can flow freely inside the bloc, benefits to individual members vary; skilled labor may move to countries where wages are higher, and investment capital may flow to countries where returns are greater. In the EU, for example, Germany has seen an influx of workers from Poland and the Czech Republic, because these workers can earn substantially higher wages in Germany than they can at home.

Economic union

A stage of regional integration in which member countries enjoy all the advantages of early stages, but also strive to have common fiscal and monetary policies.

An **economic union** is the fourth stage of regional integration, in which member countries enjoy all the advantages of early stages but also strive to have common fiscal and monetary policies. At the extreme, each member country adopts identical tax rates. The bloc aims for standardized monetary policy, which requires establishing fixed exchange rates and free convertibility of currencies among the member states, in addition to allowing the free movement of capital. This standardization helps eliminate discriminatory practices that might favor one member state over another. Through greater mobility of products, services, and production factors, an economic union enables firms within the bloc to locate productive activities in member states with the most favorable economic policies.

The EU has made great strides toward achieving an economic union. For example, sixteen EU countries have established a *monetary union* in which a single currency, the euro, is now in circulation. Monetary union and the euro have greatly increased the ease with which European financial institutions establish branches across the EU and offer banking services, insurance, and savings products. The single currency also makes trading and investment easier for European firms doing business within the union.

To achieve greater economic integration, economic union member countries strive to eliminate border controls, harmonize product and labeling standards, and establish region-wide policies for energy, agriculture, and social services. An economic union also requires its members to standardize laws and regulations regarding competition, mergers, and other corporate behaviors. To facilitate free trade in services, member countries harmonize procedures for licensing of professionals so that a doctor or lawyer qualified in one country can practice in any other country.

The United States provides a good analogy for an economic union. Imagine each state is like an individual country, but all are joined together in a union. The members have a common currency and a single central bank with a uniform monetary policy. Trade among the members takes place unobstructed, and both labor and capital move freely among them. The federal government applies a uniform tax and fiscal policy. Just as would occur in an economic union, the individual U.S. states also govern themselves in such areas as education, police protection, and local taxes. This analogy only goes so far, of course. The United States is a country and, unlike members of a real economic union, the states cannot withdraw.

The Leading Economic Blocs

Examples of regional integration can be found on all continents. In this section, we discuss notable blocs in Europe, the Americas, Asia, the Middle East, and Africa. The leading economic blocs are illustrated in Exhibit 9.2.

Europe has the longest experience with regional integration and is home to several economic blocs. The most important of these are the EU and the European Free Trade Association. Exhibit 9.3 shows these two blocs in detail.

The European Union (EU)

Exhibit 9.4 highlights notable features of the member countries in the EU, the world's most integrated economic bloc. "PPP terms" in the exhibit refers to *purchasing power parity* (PPP), which means per-capita GDP figures have been adjusted for price differences. The PPP concept suggests that, in the long run, exchange rates should move toward levels that would equalize the prices of an identical basket of goods and services in any two countries. Since prices vary greatly among countries, economists adjust ordinary GDP figures for differences in purchasing power. Adjusted per-capita GDP more accurately represents the amount of products that consumers in a given country can buy, using their own currency and remaining consistent with their standard of living.

Over time, the EU has taken the following steps on its path to becoming a full-fledged economic union:

- *Market access.* Tariffs and most nontariff barriers have been eliminated for trade in products and services, and rules of origin favor manufacturing using parts and other inputs produced in the EU.

- *Common market.* Barriers to the cross-national movement of production factors—labor, capital, and technology—have been removed. For example, an Italian worker now has the right to get a job in Ireland, and a French company can invest freely in Spain.

Exhibit 9.2 The Most Active Economic Blocs

ARCTIC OCEAN

NORWAY
SWEDEN
FINLAND
ESTONIA
UNITED KINGDOM
DENMARK
LATVIA
LITHUANIA
RUSSIA
BELARUS
IRELAND
NETHERLANDS
POLAND
BELGIUM
GERMANY
CZECH REP.
SLOVAKIA
LUXEMBOURG
FRANCE
LIECH.
AUSTRIA
HUNGARY
SWITZ.
SLOVENIA
CROATIA
MOLDOVA
MONACO
BOSNIA
HERZEGOVINA
SERBIA AND MONTENEGRO
ROMANIA
ANDORRA
ITALY
MACEDONIA
BULGARIA
SPAIN
ALBANIA
GEORGIA
PORTUGAL
GREECE
TURKEY
AZERBAIJAN
ARMENIA
TUNISIA
CYPRUS
SYRIA
LEBANON
ISRAEL
IRAQ
JORDAN
MOROCCO
ALGERIA
LIBYA
EGYPT
KUWAIT
IRAN
QATAR
SAUDI ARABIA
UNITED ARAB EMIRATES
OMAN

RUSSIA

KAZAKHSTAN
UZBEKISTAN
KYRGYZSTAN
TURKMENISTAN
TAJIKISTAN
MONGOLIA
AFGHANISTAN
PAKISTAN
CHINA
NORTH KOREA
SOUTH KOREA
JAPAN

PACIFIC OCEAN

WESTERN SAHARA
MAURITANIA
MALI
NIGER
CHAD
SENEGAL
GAMBIA
GUINEA-BISSAU
BURKINA FASO
GUINEA
SIERRA LEONE
IVORY COAST
GHANA
TOGO
BENIN
LIBERIA
NIGERIA
SUDAN
CAMEROON
EQUATORIAL GUINEA
CONGO REPUBLIC
GABON
CONGO DEMOCRATIC REPUBLIC (ZAIRE)
CENTRAL AFRICAN REPUBLIC
ETHIOPIA
ERITREA
YEMEN
DJIBOUTI
SOMALIA
UGANDA
KENYA
RWANDA
BURUNDI
TANZANIA
NEPAL
BHUTAN
INDIA
BANGLADESH
MYANMAR (BURMA)
LAOS
THAILAND
VIETNAM
CAMBODIA
PHILIPPINES
SRI LANKA
BRUNEI
MALAYSIA
SINGAPORE
TAIWAN

INDIAN OCEAN

SOUTH ATLANTIC OCEAN

ANGOLA
ZAMBIA
MALAWI
MOZAMBIQUE
NAMIBIA
ZIMBABWE
BOTSWANA
MADAGASCAR
MAURITIUS
RÉUNION
SWAZILAND
SOUTH AFRICA
LESOTHO

INDONESIA
PAPUA NEW GUINEA
SOLOMON ISLANDS
VANUATU
FIJI
NEW CALEDONIA
AUSTRALIA
NEW ZEALAND

The most active economic blocs

EU   MERCOSUR   ASEAN
EFTA   CARICOM   APEC
NAFTA   CAN   CER

Exhibit 9.3 Economic Integration in Europe

- *Trade rules.* The member countries have largely eliminated customs procedures and regulations, which streamlines transportation and logistics within Europe.

- *Standards harmonization.* The EU is harmonizing technical standards, regulations, and enforcement procedures that relate to products, services, and commercial activities. Where British firms once used the imperial measurement system (pounds, ounces, and inches), they have converted to the metric system used by all EU countries. Where German food merchants once had their own standard for handling meat and produce, they now follow procedures prescribed by the EU.

In the long run, the EU is seeking to adopt common fiscal, monetary, taxation, and social welfare policies. The 2002 introduction of the euro—the EU's common currency and now one of the world's leading currencies—simplified the process of cross-border

Members	Population (millions)	GDP (U.S.$, billions, PPP terms)	GDP per Capita (U.S.$; PPP terms)	Exports as a Percentage of GDP
Austria	8	$329	$39,647	29%
Belgium	11	390	36,322	52
Bulgaria	8	94	12,900	24
Cyprus	1	23	28,381	7
Czech Republic	10	266	25,754	44
Denmark	5	210	38,208	26
Estonia	1	28	20,754	36
Finland	5	194	36,844	29
France	63	2,125	34,262	17
Germany	83	2,919	35,552	26
Greece	11	343	30,661	3
Hungary	10	199	19,900	42
Ireland	4	189	42,780	53
Italy	57	1,821	30,705	17
Latvia	2	40	17,800	21
Lithuania	3	64	18,855	36
Luxembourg	0.5	40	81,730	28
Malta	0.4	10	23,908	44
The Netherlands	17	675	40,434	44
Poland	38	669	17,560	24
Portugal	11	236	22,264	18
Romania	22	272	12,200	22
Slovakia	5	120	22,242	51
Slovenia	2	58	29,894	38
Spain	45	1,400	30,757	16
Sweden	9	346	37,526	30
United Kingdom	61	2,231	36,570	14
Total	**493**	**$15,291**		

Exhibit 9.4   Key Features of the European Union Member Countries, 2009

SOURCES: International Monetary Fund at http://www.imf.org and European Union at http://europa.eu.

trade and enhanced Europe's international competitiveness. Its introduction eliminated exchange rate risk in much of the bloc and forced member countries to improve their fiscal and monetary policies. The single currency allows consumers and businesses to think of Europe as a single national entity. However, national governments had to cede monetary power to the European Central Bank, which is based in Luxembourg and oversees EU monetary functions.

The EU has four additional institutions that perform its executive, administrative, legislative, and judicial functions. The *Council of the European Union*, based in Brussels, is the main decision-making body. Composed of representatives from each member country, it makes decisions regarding economic policy, budgets, foreign policy, and admission of new member countries. The *European Commission*, also based in Brussels, is similarly composed of delegates from each member state and represents the interests of the EU as a whole. It proposes legislation and policies and is responsible for implementing the decisions of the *European Parliament* and the Council of the EU. The European

Parliament consists of elected representatives that hold joint sessions each month. By common agreement, the Parliament meets in three different cities (Brussels, Luxembourg, and Strasbourg, France) and can have up to 785 total representatives. The Parliament has three main functions: (1) form EU legislation, (2) supervise EU institutions, and (3) make decisions about the EU budget. Finally, the *European Court of Justice*, based in Luxembourg, interprets and enforces EU laws and settles legal disputes between member states.[3]

The *Global Trend* feature discusses the specific challenges of integrating new member states into the EU. Since 2004, twelve new states have joined, and the recent addition of Bulgaria and Romania brings the total number of member countries to twenty-seven. The new members are important, low-cost manufacturing sites for EU firms.[4] Peugeot and Citroën now produce cars at a plant in the Czech Republic that, at full capacity, can turn out 320,000 vehicles per year. South Korea's Hyundai now produces the Kia brand of cars at a plant in Slovakia, while Japan's Suzuki makes cars in Hungary. Output of automobiles in the eastern region is growing rapidly.[5] Most of the newest EU entrants are one-time satellites of the former Soviet Union and have economic growth rates higher than their fifteen Western European counterparts. They are poised to achieve per-capita income levels similar to those of the EU's wealthier countries within several years. However, their ascension poses special challenges. Less-developed economies such as Romania, Bulgaria, and Lithuania will require years of developmental aid to catch up.[6]

The EU faces other challenges as well, including the tension between the forces for regional integration and the forces for retaining national identity. EU countries recognize that relinquishing autonomy in certain key areas and combining resources across national borders are necessary steps. However, some, particularly Britain, are reluctant to surrender certain sovereign rights. They insist on maintaining their ability to set their own monetary and fiscal policies and to undertake their own national military defense.

The Common Agricultural Policy (CAP) has long been a fixture of the European bloc. The CAP is a system of agricultural subsidies and programs that guarantees a minimum price to EU farmers and ranchers. Its original goals were to provide a fair living standard for agricultural producers and food at reasonable prices. In reality, however, the CAP has increased food prices in Europe and consumes almost half the EU's annual budget while complicating negotiations with the WTO for reducing global trade barriers. The CAP's high import tariffs also affect exporters in developing economies, such as Africa, that rely heavily on agricultural production. The EU is working to reform the CAP, but progress has been slow.

European Free Trade Association (EFTA)

The second-largest free trade area in Europe is the EFTA (www.efta.int), established in 1960 by Austria, Britain, Denmark, Norway, Portugal, Sweden, and Switzerland. Most of these countries eventually left EFTA to join the EU; current EFTA members are Iceland, Liechtenstein, Norway, and Switzerland. The bloc promotes free trade and strengthens economic relations with other European countries and the world. The EFTA Secretariat, headquartered in Geneva, has negotiated trade agreements with several non-European countries. EFTA members cooperate with the EU via bilateral free trade agreements and, since 1994, through the European Economic Area arrangement, which allows for free movement of people, products, services, and capital throughout the combined area of the EFTA and the EU.

North American Free Trade Agreement (NAFTA)

Consisting of Canada, Mexico, and the United States, NAFTA launched in 1994. It is the most significant economic bloc in the Americas and comparable to the EU in size (see www.nafta-sec-alena.org). Exhibit 9.5 highlights key features of the NAFTA countries. Its passage was smoothed by the existence, since the 1960s, of the *maquiladora* program.

GL🌐BAL TREND

Integrating Eastern Europe and Turkey into the EU

While per-capita GDP in Germany is $34,200, it is only $11,500 in Romania, $12,600 in Bulgaria, and $17,800 in Poland. Firms from Western Europe and elsewhere often locate their manufacturing in Eastern Europe countries to take advantage of the low-cost labor there. But as firms increasingly shift production and other value-chain activities to Eastern Europe, long-established EU members like Germany and France fear the resulting loss of jobs and investments in their own countries. This helps explain why officials in Western Europe are often reluctant to allow other low-wage countries, like Turkey and Ukraine, join the EU.

Turkey has a per-capita GDP of $11,200. Its population of 77 million people is equivalent to the twelve Eastern European countries that joined the EU since 2004. Turkey has long sought to join the EU, partly because of the economic benefits that membership would bring. But many Western Europeans oppose this move because they regard Turkey, an Islamic country, as too remote from current EU countries in religious, cultural, and economic terms.

Proponents of EU enlargement are optimistic. They argue that low wages in the bloc's newest members are more an opportunity than a threat. Why? One reason is that Poland, Hungary, and other recent entrants are attracting substantial business investment that might otherwise go to China and other low-wage countries on the opposite side of the world.

The Eastern European countries will not maintain their low-cost labor advantages forever. These satellites of the former Soviet Union are much richer today than they were after the collapse of communism in 1989, when Poland's per-capita GDP was just $2,000. Starting from a much lower income level, the countries are growing their economies far faster than their affluent Western EU neighbors. The reason relates partly to the incremental value of inward investment in poorer countries. Additional capital or better technology is more profitable in an emerging market like Poland than in an already high-income country like Germany. While replacing an existing computer with a new, faster one has a relatively small payoff for a German firm, installing a new computer in a Polish firm where records are kept by hand has an enormous payoff.

Rapid economic growth spurred by affiliation with the European Union implies that the newest EU members may reach economic parity with the rest of Europe within a few decades, a short span in the life of a nation. When that day arrives, Germans, French, British, and other venerable members of the EU bloc will no longer worry about the competitive threat of their new low-wage neighbors.

SOURCES: M. Champion and F. Fassihi, "Obama Urges EU to Accept Turkey, But Member Nations Remain Cool," *Wall Street Journal*, April 6, 2009, p. A7; "Out of Sight, Out of Mind; Britain's Relationship with Europe," *Economist*, May 30, 2009, p. 57; "Transformed: EU Membership Has Worked Magic in Central Europe," *Economist*, June 25, 2005, pp. 6–8; "The Impossibility of Saying No," *Economist*, September 18, 2004, pp. 30–32; "Why Turks Are Changing Tack on Foreign Ownership," *Financial Times*, June 28, 2005; S. Wagstyl, "Fifth Anniversary Fails to Assuage Public Concerns," *Financial Times*, May 5, 2009, p. 6.

Members	Population (millions)	GDP (U.S.$ billions, PPP terms)	GDP per Capita (U.S.$; PPP terms)	Exports as a Percentage of GDP
Canada	33	1,229	36,589	33%
Mexico	106	827	7,703	19
United States	304	14,003	45,550	7
Total	**443**	**16,059**		

Exhibit 9.5 North American Free Trade Agreement (NAFTA), 2009

SOURCE: International Monetary Fund at http://www.imf.org

Under this program, U.S. firms were allowed to locate manufacturing facilities in an area just south of the U.S. border and access low-cost labor and other advantages in Mexico without having to pay significant tariffs.

What has NAFTA accomplished for its members? Initially, the accord increased market access between Canada, Mexico, and the United States. It eliminated tariffs and most nontariff barriers for products and services traded in the bloc and made it possible for member-country firms to bid for government contracts in all three countries. NAFTA also established trade rules and uniform customs procedures and regulations, while prohibiting the use of standards and technical regulations as trade barriers. The members agreed to rules for investment and intellectual property rights. NAFTA also provides for dispute settlement in such areas as investment, unfair pricing, labor issues, and the environment.

Since the bloc's inception, trade among its three members has more than tripled and now exceeds $1 trillion per year. In the early 1980s, Mexico's tariffs averaged 100 percent and gradually decreased over time, eventually disappearing under NAFTA. U.S. exports to Mexico grew from about $40 billion in 1994 to more than $150 billion in 2008. Over the same time, U.S. exports to Canada more than doubled, to over $260 billion. Canada's exports to Mexico and the United States have also more than doubled. In 1994, Mexican exports to the United States averaged about $50 billion per year, compared to more than $215 billion in 2008.[7]

Access to Canada and the United States helped launch numerous Mexican firms in industries such as electronics, automobiles, textiles, medical products, and services. For example, Mexico developed a $100 million-per-year dental supply industry in which entrepreneurs export to the United States labor-intensive products such as braces, dental wax, and instruments. Annual NAFTA foreign investment in Mexico rose from $4 billion in 1993 to more than $20 billion by 2008 as U.S. and Canadian firms invested in their southern neighbor. Following NAFTA's passage, Mexico's per-capita income has risen substantially, making Mexico into Latin America's wealthiest country in per-capita income terms.[8]

Both Canada and Mexico conduct approximately 80 percent of their trade with, and have 60 percent of their FDI stocks in, the United States.[9] Given Mexico's attractiveness as a manufacturing location, firms like Gap and Liz Claiborne moved their factories from Asia to Mexico during the 1990s. IBM shifted manufacturing of many computer parts from Singapore to Mexico.

NAFTA stimulated restructuring of the labor market in North America. Falling trade barriers triggered job losses in the North as factories were "exported" to Mexico to profit from its low-cost labor. Increased purchasing power of Mexican consumers meant they could afford to buy U.S. and Canadian imports. As part of the accord, the member countries were also required to strengthen their labor standards, which helped improve working conditions and compliance with labor laws. NAFTA also includes provisions that promote sustainable development and environmental protection. In a recent development, Quebec is easing commerce and labor barriers with France, and Canada is in negotiations to join the EU.[10]

Compared to the EU or NAFTA, some economic blocs are less stable and have been less successful. These blocs, which we examine next, are located in Latin America, Asia, the Middle East, and Africa.

El Mercado Comun del Sur (MERCOSUR)

Established in 1991, MERCOSUR, or the *El Mercado Comun del Sur* (the Southern Common Market), is the strongest economic bloc in South America (see www.mercosur.int). Exhibit 9.6 lists its membership and key features. Within its borders, MERCOSUR established the free movement of products and services, a common external tariff and trade policy, and coordinated monetary and fiscal policies. An additional priority is the construction of reliable infrastructure—roads, electricity grids, and gas pipelines—across a landmass larger than Mexico and the United States combined. MERCOSUR eventually aims to become an economic union.

MERCOSUR's early progress was impressive. It attracted much investment from nonmember countries, especially in the auto industry. During its first six years, trade

Members	Population (millions)	GDP (U.S.$ billions, PPP terms)	GDP per Capita (U.S.$; PPP terms)	Exports as a Percentage of GDP
Argentina	40	$569	$14,200	13%
Brazil	194	1,974	10,100	10
Paraguay	6	29	4,800	24
Uruguay	3	41	12,200	15
Venezuela	29	354	12,933	18
Bolivia *	10	45	4,500	13
Chile *	17	246	14,900	28
Colombia *	49	400	8,900	10
Ecuador *	14	106	7,500	19
Peru *	29	257	6,609	13
Total	**391**	**4,021**		

*Associate members.

Exhibit 9.6   El Mercado Comun del Sur (MERCOSUR), 2009

SOURCE: International Monetary Fund at http://www.imf.org

among the member countries tripled.[11] In addition to its regular members, MERCOSUR also has five associate members, which have access to preferential trade but not to the tariff benefits of full members. MERCOSUR also has trade agreements with nations outside the bloc. In the future, it may become integrated with NAFTA and the Dominican Republic–Central American Free Trade Agreement (DR-CAFTA) as part of a proposed Free Trade Area of the Americas (FTAA), bringing free trade to the entire western hemisphere.

The Caribbean Community (CARICOM)

Composed of roughly twenty-five member and associate member states around the Caribbean Sea, CARICOM was established in 1973 to lower trade barriers and institute a common external tariff (see www.caricom.org). The bloc has met with little success in stimulating economic development, however, due to economic difficulties of the individual members and their inability to agree on basic issues. The bloc is progressing toward establishing the Caribbean Single Market, a common market that allows for a greater degree of free movement for products, services, capital, and labor and gives citizens of all CARICOM countries the right to establish businesses throughout the region.

Comunidad Andina de Naciones (CAN)

Long called the Andean Pact, the Comunidad Andina de Naciones (CAN) was established in 1969. Its main members are Bolivia, Colombia, Ecuador, and Peru (see www.comunidadandina.org). CAN is expected to merge with MERCOSUR to form a new economic bloc that encompasses all of South America. The pact achieved little progress in its first twenty years, with intrabloc trade reaching only 5 percent of the bloc members' total trade.[12] This low trade rate is partially due to geography: The Andes mountain range makes cross-border land transportation costly and cumbersome.

Association of Southeast Asian Nations (ASEAN)

ASEAN, the Association of Southeast Asian Nations, was created in 1967 with the goal of maintaining political stability and promoting regional economic and social development among its members, shown in Exhibit 9.7 (see www.aseansec.org). ASEAN created a free trade area in which many tariffs were reduced to less than 5 percent. Further regional integration has been slowed by large economic differences among the member

Members	Population (millions)	GDP (U.S.$ billions, PPP terms)	GDP per Capita (U.S.$; PPP terms)	Exports as a Percentage of GDP
Brunei	0.4	$20	$48,714	52%
Cambodia	14	30	2,084	6
Indonesia	235	1,027	4,380	8
Laos	6	11	1,700	3
Malaysia	28	403	14,275	47
Myanmar (Burma)	61	76	1,244	3
Philippines	94	339	3,603	9
Singapore	5	255	52,840	130
Thailand	67	574	8,479	16
Vietnam	88	274	3,104	10
Total	**598**	**3,009**		

Exhibit 9.7   Association of Southeast Asian Nations (ASEAN), 2010

SOURCE: International Monetary Fund at http://www.imf.org.

countries. For example, oil-rich Brunei has a per-capita income of nearly $50,000, while Vietnam's is only about $3,000. Were ASEAN to become a common market or economic union, millions of job seekers from poor member countries would probably migrate to wealthier member countries, potentially disrupting the economies of these latter nations. Consequently, ASEAN is unlikely to advance beyond its free trade area status for decades to come. In the long run, ASEAN aims to incorporate international trading powerhouses like Japan and China, whose membership would accelerate the development of extensive trade relationships.

Asia Pacific Economic Cooperation (APEC)

Originally suggested by Australia, APEC, or Asia Pacific Economic Cooperation, aims for greater free trade and economic integration of the Pacific Rim countries. It incorporates twenty-one nations on both sides of the Pacific, including Australia, Canada, Chile, China, Japan, Mexico, Russia, and the United States (see www.apec.org). Its members account for 85 percent of total regional trade, as well as one-third of the world's population and over half its GDP. APEC aspires to remove trade and investment barriers by 2020. Progress has been slowed by economic and political turmoil in some member countries, as well as failure to agree on foundational issues. Members also have varying national economic priorities, and the inclusion of less-affluent Asian countries alongside strong international traders like Australia, Japan, and the United States complicates agreement on a range of issues.

Australia and New Zealand Closer Economic Relations Agreement (CER)

In 1966, Australia and New Zealand reached a free trade agreement that removed 80 percent of tariffs and quotas between the two nations, but it was relatively complex and bureaucratic. In 1983, the Closer Economic Relations Agreement (CER) sought to accelerate free trade, leading to further economic integration of the two nations. The CER gained importance when Australia and New Zealand lost their privileged status in the British market as Britain joined the EU. Many believe the CER has been one of the world's most successful economic blocs. In 2009, its members concluded important negotiations on creating a free trade agreement with the ASEAN countries.

Economic Integration in the Middle East and Africa

The Middle East and North Africa are home to primarily Islamic countries in which oil is often the driving economic force. The Middle East's main regional organization is the Gulf Cooperation Council (GCC; see www.gcc-sg.org.htm). Established in 1981 to coordinate economic, social, and cultural affairs, the GCC consists of Bahrain, Kuwait, Oman, Qatar, Saudi Arabia, and the United Arab Emirates. Specific GCC initiatives include coordination of the petroleum industry, abolition of certain tariffs, and liberalization of investment, as well as harmonization of banking, financial, and monetary policies. In 2008, the GCC established a common market among all its member countries.

These workers harvest table grapes growing in Robertson, South Africa. External tariffs of NAFTA and the EU hinder African agricultural exports to Europe and North America.

Elsewhere in the Middle East, efforts toward regional economic integration include the Arab Maghreb Union (composed of Algeria, Libya, Mauritania, Morocco, and Tunisia), which is still struggling to become a viable economic bloc. The Economic Cooperation Organization (ECO) is an international organization that now includes ten Middle Eastern and Asian countries seeking to promote trade and investment opportunities in the region. Such groups are very early attempts at regional integration that may foster the development of inter-Arab trade and investment. Another grouping, the Arab League, is a longstanding political organization with twenty-two member states that promotes unity and nationalism in the Middle East. It has been relatively unsuccessful in fostering regional economic development.

African countries want better access to Europe and North America for sales of their farm and textile products. To increase their bargaining power, they have established at least nine economic blocs. Most notable are the Southern African Development Community, the Economic Community of West African States, and the Economic Community of Central African States. These groups have not had much impact on regional trade, due in part to political turmoil and misunderstandings about free trade as well as underdeveloped economic and transportation systems, political instability, civil unrest, and war, in the region.

 ## Advantages of Regional Integration

Regional integration contributes to corporate and industrial growth and hence to better living standards, higher tax revenues, and national economic growth for the member countries. Nations seek at least four objectives in pursuing regional integration.[13]

Expand market size. Regional integration greatly increases the scale of the marketplace for firms inside the economic bloc. For example, while Belgium has a population of just 10 million, the absence of trade barriers with other countries in the EU gives Belgian firms easier access to a total market of roughly 500 million EU buyers. In a similar way, management at Allianz, the German insurance firm featured in the opening vignette, has come to view Europe as one large marketplace. When NAFTA was formed, Canadian firms gained access to the much larger markets of Mexico and the United States, and consumers in all three countries access a wider selection of products and services.

Achieve scale economies and enhanced productivity. Expansion of market size within an economic bloc gives member country firms the opportunity to increase the scale of

MERCOSUR includes Argentina, Brazil, Paraguay, and Uruguay. The bloc aims to expand market size, achieve scale economies, attract foreign direct investment, and build defensive and political posture. Shown is the Mercosur headquarters in Montevideo, Uruguay.

operations in both production and marketing, gaining greater concentration and increased efficiency. While a German firm may be only moderately efficient when producing 10,000 units of product for Germany, it greatly increases its efficiency by producing 50,000 units for the much larger EU market. Internationalization inside the bloc helps firms learn to compete outside the bloc as well. The firms enjoy additional benefits through increased access to factors of production that now flow freely across national borders within the bloc. Labor and other inputs are allocated more efficiently among the member countries. More efficient resource usage leads to lower prices for consumers.

Attract direct investment from outside the bloc. Foreign firms prefer to invest in countries that are part of an economic bloc because factories they build there receive preferential treatment for exports to all member countries within the bloc. For example, many non-European firms—including General Mills, Samsung, and Tata—invested heavily in the EU to take advantage of Europe's economic integration. By establishing operations in a single EU country, these firms gain free trade access to the entire EU market.

Acquire stronger defensive and political posture. One goal of regional integration is to strengthen member countries relative to other nations and world regions. This was one of the motives for creating the European Community (the precursor to the EU), whose members sought to strengthen their mutual defense against the expanding influence of the former Soviet Union. Today, the EU is one way Europe counterbalances the power and international influence of the United States. Forming an economic bloc also helps countries gain bargaining and political power in world affairs. For example, the EU enjoys greater influence with the WTO in trade negotiations than any individual member country. Broadly speaking, countries are more powerful when they cooperate than when they operate alone.

Success Factors for Regional Integration

Experience with regional economic integration suggests that the most successful economic blocs tend to possess the following characteristics.

Economic similarity. The more similar the economies of the member countries, the more likely the economic bloc will succeed. Significant wage rate differences mean workers in lower-wage countries will migrate to higher-wage countries. Significant economic instability in one member country can quickly spread and harm the economies of the other members. Compatibility of economic characteristics is so important that the EU requires its current and prospective members to meet strict membership conditions, ideally low inflation, low unemployment, reasonable wages, and stable economic conditions.

Political similarity. Similarity in political systems enhances prospects for a successful bloc. Countries that seek to integrate regionally should share similar aspirations and a willingness to surrender national autonomy for the larger goals of the proposed union. For example, most of the existing EU members are characterized by a long history of stable, socially democratic forms of government. By contrast, many Europeans have been reluctant to allow Ukraine to enter the EU, partly due to the country's history of socialism and political turmoil.[14]

Similarity of culture and language. Cultural and linguistic similarity among the countries in an economic bloc provides the basis for mutual understanding and cooperation. The MERCOSUR bloc enjoys advantages because its members share many cultural and linguistic similarities. Under NAFTA, it was easier for Canadian firms to establish trade and investment relationships in the United States than in Mexico because of the similarities between the two northern countries.

Geographic proximity. Most economic blocs are formed by countries within the same geographic region. Close geographic proximity facilitates transportation of products, labor, and other factors of production. Neighboring countries also tend to share culture and language.

While all four types of similarities enhance the potential for successful regional integration, economic interests are often most important. Dissimilarity in one area can be overcome by similarity in the other areas. This was demonstrated in the EU, whose member countries, despite strong cultural and linguistic differences, achieved common goals based on pure economic interests.

Ethical Dilemmas and Drawbacks of Regional Integration

Regional integration is not a uniformly positive trend; it can give rise to ethical and moral concerns. These include:

Trade diversion. At least in the short run, regional integration gives rise to both trade creation and trade diversion. *Trade creation* means trade is generated among the countries inside the economic bloc because, as barriers fall, each member country tends to begin trading more with members than with nonmembers. As this occurs, members begin trading less with countries outside the bloc, leading to *trade diversion*. In this way, national trade patterns are altered: More trade takes place inside the bloc, and less with countries outside the bloc.

Suppose that before the formation of NAFTA, Canada's government had imposed a tariff of 100 percent on imports of wine from the United States and a tariff of 50 percent on wine imports from France. Further assume Canada had always imported its wine from France because the lower tariff made French wine cheaper than U.S. wine. Subsequently, however, NAFTA eliminated the U.S. tariff and made U.S. wine cheaper than French wine. Under this new tariff regime, suppose Canada reduced its wine imports from France and began importing wine from the United States. This exemplifies trade diversion (stopping wine imports from France) and trade creation (starting wine imports from the United States). Such outcomes suggest the EU, NAFTA, and other economic blocs may become "economic fortresses," resulting in a decline in trade between blocs that exceeds the gains from trade within the blocs.

Reduced global free trade. In more advanced stages, regional integration can give rise to two opposing tendencies. On the one hand, a country that reduces trade barriers is moving toward free trade. On the other hand, an economic bloc that imposes external trade barriers is moving *away* from *worldwide* free trade.

For example, countries that form a customs union impose common external trade barriers, and some member countries' external tariffs may actually rise. Suppose Germany, the EU's largest member, once had a 10 percent tariff on imported footwear. Assume that in the process of developing a common market, the EU countries collectively imposed a 20 percent tariff on footwear imports. In effect, Germany's external tariff on footwear has increased. In this way, regional integration can result in *higher* tariffs, making buyers inside the bloc worse off because they must pay higher prices for the products they want to consume. Tariffs also counteract comparative advantages and interfere with trade flows that should be dictated by national endowments. All told, external trade barriers imposed by economic blocs result in a net loss in well-being to all members in the bloc.

Some nations fear regional integration triggers cross-border assimilation, diminishing the distinctiveness of individual member countries. Pictured here is France's Minister of Immigration, Integration, and National Identity, Eric Besson, in 2010.

Finally, because foreign firms sell less into a bloc that imposes restrictions, they are harmed as well. When external suppliers are based in developing economies, the consequences are significant. By limiting imports from such countries, trade barriers imposed by economic blocs threaten the ability of producers in these countries to improve their living conditions. Agricultural tariffs imposed by the EU and NAFTA blocs, for instance, do the most harm to farmers in Africa, South America, and other areas characterized by substantial poverty. Suppose you were a government trade official in Europe or North America. Use the Ethical Framework in Chapter 5 to analyze the pros and cons of advanced-economy nations imposing high trade barriers on imports of agricultural goods from Africa and other poor regions.

Loss of national identity. When nations join in an economic bloc, increased cross-border contact has a homogenizing effect; national cultural identity is diluted as the members become more similar to each other. For this reason, member countries typically retain the right to protect certain industries vital to national heritage or security. For instance, because Canada fears its indigenous culture will be diluted by an invasion of U.S. movie and television programming, it restricts the ability of U.S. movie and TV producers to invest in its film market. By enacting specific exclusions in the NAFTA accord, Canada has ensured that Canadian TV and movie interests remain largely in the hands of Canadians.

Sacrifice of autonomy. Later stages of regional integration require member countries to establish a central authority to manage the bloc's affairs. Each participating country must sacrifice some of its autonomy, such as control over its own economy. In this way, nations that join an economic bloc risk losing some of their national sovereignty. Concerns about national sovereignty have been a stumbling block in the development of the EU. In Britain, critics see the passage of many new laws and regulations by centralized EU authorities as a direct threat to British self-governance.[15] The British have resisted joining the European Monetary Union because such a move would reduce the power they currently hold over their own currency, economy, and monetary regime.

Transfer of power to advantaged firms. Regional integration can concentrate economic power in the hands of fewer, more advantaged firms. Development of the regional marketplace attracts new competitors from other bloc countries or from outside the bloc into formerly protected national markets. Foreign invaders that are larger, have stronger brands, or enjoy other advantages can overwhelm local firms in their home markets. Over time, economic power gravitates toward the most advantaged firms in the bloc. Regional integration also encourages mergers and acquisitions within the bloc, leading to the creation of larger rivals that can come to dominate smaller firms. For example, critics charged that as the DR-CAFTA accord eliminated trade barriers that had protected Central American economies, U.S. firms entered these countries to manufacture and sell products. Because U.S. firms often enjoy advantages such as large size and better resources, some have come to dominate industries in Central America.

Failure of small or weak firms. As trade and investment barriers decline, protections are eliminated that previously shielded smaller or weaker firms from foreign competition. Companies typically find themselves battling new, often better-resourced rivals. New competitive pressures particularly threaten smaller firms. The risk can be substantial for companies in smaller bloc countries or in industries that lack comparative advantages. Under NAFTA, many U.S. companies in industries covered by the accord relocated their production to Mexico, which has low wage rates. As a result, numerous firms in the U.S. tomato-growing industry went out of business as that industry shifted south to Mexico.

Corporate restructuring and job loss. Many firms must restructure to meet the competitive challenges posed in the new, enlarged marketplace of regional integration. Increased competitive pressures and corporate restructuring may lead to worker layoffs or reassignments to distant locations. MERCOSUR was a factor in the layoff of thousands of workers in Argentina's auto parts manufacturing sector. Low-priced auto parts from Brazil flowed into the MERCOSUR countries following implementation of the accord. The intense competition forced parts manufacturers in Argentina to cut costs, leading to worker layoffs. When they negotiate regional integration agreements, national governments have a responsibility to reduce harmful effects such as job losses and the failure of small or weak firms. NAFTA included various clauses aimed at softening the effects of economic restructuring, maintaining or improving labor conditions for workers in the member countries, and retraining workers who lost their jobs due to NAFTA.

The advantages and drawbacks of regional integration mean that passing such accords entails significant controversy. Critics suggest NAFTA has disproportionately helped some and harmed others. Increased industrialization has led to substantial pollution in Mexico. Thousands of Canadian firms faced bankruptcy or were taken over by foreigners. In Europe, EU-imposed standards have forced firms to substantially revise manufacturing practices, packaging, and other value-chain activities. The European Central Bank encountered substantial complexity in devising monetary policy suitable for all the euro zone countries. Mass migration of workers into high-income countries has triggered increased social problems. Despite such controversies, however, most governments regard regional integration as relatively advantageous. Thus, nations worldwide continue to pursue free trade and economic interdependence within their regions.

Management Implications of Regional Integration

Many firms modify their strategies to take advantage of new opportunities in the marketplace enlarged by economic integration or to safeguard their positions against potential threats. The choice of strategies depends largely on the characteristics of the firm's industry, the firm's current position in the regional market, and the market's particular rules and regulations. Regional economic integration suggests at least five implications for management.

Internationalization by firms inside the economic bloc. Initially, regional integration pressures or encourages companies to internationalize into neighboring countries within the bloc. The elimination of trade and investment barriers also presents new opportunities to source input goods from foreign suppliers within the bloc. Internationalizing into neighboring, familiar countries also provides the firm with the skills and confidence to further internationalize to markets outside the bloc. For example, after the formation of NAFTA, many U.S. companies entered Canada and gained valuable international experience that inspired them to launch ventures into Asia and Europe.

Rationalization of operations. The creation of an economic bloc decreases the importance of national boundaries. Instead of viewing the bloc as a collection of disparate countries, firms begin to view the bloc as a unified whole. Managers develop strategies and value-chain activities suited to the region as a whole, rather than to individual countries. *Rationalization* is the process of restructuring and consolidating company operations following regional integration to reduce redundancy and costs and increase the efficiency of operations. Management may combine two or more factories into a single factory, eliminating duplication and increasing economies of scale. In this way, the firm that formerly operated factories in each of several countries benefits by consolidating the factories into a single, central location inside the economic bloc.

Caterpillar, the U.S. manufacturer of earth-moving equipment, was one of many firms that shifted its focus from serving individual European countries to serving the EU region. Caterpillar undertook a massive program of rationalization and modernization

A Home Depot store in Mexico. Regional integration arrangements have induced countless firms to internationalize within economic blocs like NAFTA. Expansion into neighboring countries provides valuable experience, prompting further internationalization to markets around the world.

at its EU plants to streamline production, reduce inventories, increase economies of scale, and lower operating costs.

Companies can apply rationalization to other value-chain functions such as distribution, logistics, purchasing, and R&D. Formation of the EU and subsequent elimination of trade barriers, customs checkpoints, and country-specific transportation regulations allowed U.S. firms to restructure their EU distribution channels to make them better suited to the greatly enlarged EU marketplace. Creation of the economic bloc eliminated the need for separate distribution strategies in individual countries. Instead, the firms were able to employ a *global* approach for the larger marketplace, generating economies of scale in distribution.

Mergers and acquisitions. The formation of economic blocs also leads to mergers and acquisitions (M&A), sometimes due to rationalization. Two giant engineering firms, Asea AB of Sweden and Brown, Boveri & Co. of Switzerland, merged to form Asea Brown Boveri (ABB), facilitated by development of the EU. The merger allowed the new firm to increase its R&D activities and pool greater capital funding for major projects, such as construction of power plants and large-scale industrial equipment.

Regional products and marketing strategy. It is easier and much less costly to make and sell a few product models rather than dozens. An economic bloc facilitates the standardization of products and streamlining of marketing activities because, in more advanced stages of regional integration, the member countries tend to harmonize product standards and commercial regulations.[16] For instance, J. I. Case Company once produced seventeen versions of its Magnum model of farm tractors to comply with varying national regulations regarding the placement of lights, brakes, and other specifications. The harmonization of EU product standards allowed the firm to standardize its tractor and produce only a handful of models appropriate for serving the whole EU market.[17]

Internationalization by firms from outside the bloc. The most effective way for a foreign firm to enter an economic bloc is to establish a physical presence there via foreign direct investment (FDI). By building a production facility, marketing subsidiary, or regional headquarters anywhere inside a bloc, the outsider gains access to the entire bloc and to advantages enjoyed by local firms based inside the bloc. Since formation of the EU, Britain has become the largest recipient of FDI from the United States. Many U.S. firms choose Britain as the beachhead to gain access to the massive EU market. Many European firms likewise have established factories in Mexico to access countries in the NAFTA bloc.

In 1990, there were approximately fifty regional economic integration agreements worldwide. Today, some 400 are in various stages of development, and many nations belong to more than one. Since the Doha round of global trade negotiations collapsed in 2008, countries have been putting more emphasis on developing regional trade agreements.[18] Economic blocs are joining with other blocs around the world. Several countries, including Canada and India, are negotiating free trade agreements with the EU.[19] Other intercontinental blocs are underway. Meanwhile, evidence suggests that regional economic integration is not slowing the progress of global free trade. Rather, global free trade will tend to emerge as economic blocs link up with each other over time. The evidence suggests regional economic integration is gradually giving way to a system of free trade worldwide.

 Closing Case

Russell Corporation: Choosing between Global and Regional Free Trade

Russell Corporation is a leading manufacturer of sportswear, including sweatshirts, sweatpants, and T-shirts. Owned by Berkshire Hathaway, Russell is based in Atlanta, Georgia. Its main competitors include Adidas, Nike, Benetton, and Zara. Russell runs every step of the manufacturing process, from weaving raw yarn into fabric, to dyeing, cutting, and sewing, to selling garments through retailers. Russell's brands include JERZEES, American Athletic, Brooks, Cross Creek, Huffy Sports, Russell Athletic, and Spalding. The firm sells through mass merchandisers, department stores such as Walmart, and golf pro shops. Russell sells its apparel in about one hundred countries. Recently, the firm contracted with Kangwei, one of China's largest sports brands, to manufacture and market athletic apparel there. Kangwei runs more than 1,000 retail stores in China and plans to open several hundred more to offer Spalding apparel.

Unlike Nike and Adidas, Russell does not enjoy much brand loyalty, which prevents the firm from charging premium prices. To cut costs, Russell needs to manufacture its products in low-cost countries. Management was pleased with passage of the Dominican Republic–Central American Free Trade Agreement (DR-CAFTA) in 2005. The pact eliminated trade barriers between the United States and six Latin American countries: Guatemala, Honduras, El Salvador, Nicaragua, Costa Rica, and the Dominican Republic. Following DR-CAFTA's passage, Central American countries experienced a significant rise in FDI from abroad. The apparel and clothing sector, consisting of firms like Russell, were among the biggest beneficiaries.

Prior to DR-CAFTA, many North American apparel companies sourced from China and other Asian nations, where production costs are low. DR-CAFTA virtually eliminated tariffs on trade between the United States, Central America, and the Dominican Republic. Now Russell can cost-effectively source raw materials in Central America, manufacture fabric in the United States, then send the fabric to its factories in Honduras for assembly. Once the garments are completed, they are re-exported to the United States for distribution. Without DR-CAFTA, it would not have been cost effective to make fabric in the United States, export it to Asia, and have the products manufactured there and then re-exported back.

Under that scenario, Russell would have shifted all its manufacturing to China.

Background on DR-CAFTA

In the past, Latin American countries were shielded from international competition in the textiles sector by the protectionist Multi-Fibre Agreement (MFA), which imposed strict import quotas. When the MFA expired in 2005, many countries became exposed to the full force of cheap imports from low-cost producers in Asia. China dramatically increased its apparel exports to the United States, to the detriment of U.S. and Central American producers that long had supplied Western markets. For example, Alabama was once the world center of sock manufacturing. When the MFA expired, the sock capital shifted to Datang, China. Alabama sock workers received an average of $10 an hour, compared to 75 cents an hour in Datang.

Since the expiration of the MFA, China has been flooding the United States with apparel. In recent years, China's share of finished clothing exports to the United States, once less than 20 percent, has leaped past 50 percent in some segments. To protect its home-grown apparel industry, the United States reimposed some trade barriers against Chinese imports. The U.S. government justified this action in part because China's currency, the yuan, is considered undervalued, which makes Chinese exports artificially cheap. Such protection of the U.S. apparel industry is only temporary. WTO rules require the U.S. government to remove the trade barriers, at which time Chinese exports to the United States will increase.

Many in the U.S. apparel industry see DR-CAFTA as perhaps the only way to compete with China. DR-CAFTA helps maintain much apparel production in the Western hemisphere by creating a bigger apparel market in the region and granting favorable trade status to apparel producers who manufacture their products using raw material from the DR-CAFTA region.

The United States is the biggest apparel market, importing more than $9 billion worth of apparel from the DR-CAFTA countries in each of 2006, 2007, and 2008. As the biggest shipper in dollar value, Honduras exported products such as cotton blouses, shirts, and underwear. Meanwhile, DR-CAFTA gave U.S. producers an equal footing to sell their products to Central America. The region is the second largest market for U.S. textiles and yarn, which Central American manufacturers use to produce finished apparel.

The Situation in Honduras

Russell manufactures much of its garments in Honduras, a poor Central American country with seven million people, one-quarter of whom are illiterate. Honduras has an annual per-capita GDP of about $4,500. In 2008, the country's unemployment rate was 28 percent. Growth remains dependent on the U.S. economy, its largest trading partner. Honduras sends more than two-thirds of its exported goods to the United States and receives about 50 percent of its imports from that country. The Honduran government is counting on the DR-CAFTA agreement to increase trade with the United States and the Central American region.

Honduras's apparel sector employs more than 110,000 people, or 30 percent of the country's total industrial employment. The Honduran government used incentives to create a large cluster of apparel firms. In addition to low-cost labor, Honduras offers a generous tax package: Firms pay no income tax, value-added tax, or duties. Honduran apparel manufacturers can truck their merchandise to Puerto Cortes, Central America's biggest port, in just 30 minutes. From there, it takes only 22 hours to reach Miami by container ship. By comparison, it takes up to a month to make similar shipments from China. Honduras is investing to improve Puerto Cortes and create a "Textiles and Apparel University" to train future managers and supervisors. To counter Chinese competition, the apparel industry in Honduras has begun to offer the "total package"—buying fabric, and sometimes even designing the garments, as well as final assembly.

In 2007, the stock of U.S. FDI in Honduras was $968 million, up sharply from only $262 million in 2003.

Russell's Dilemmas

Russell management must decide whether to keep its manufacturing in Honduras or move everything to China. Another possibility is to establish production in Eastern Europe to gain access to the huge EU market. Adidas and Nike are pursuing markets in China and other Asian countries. Labor costs for manufacturing apparel are similar in Central America and China. In both locations, workers earn around a dollar per hour and can produce more than one hundred garments per day from precut cloth. Labor costs are roughly $2 an hour in Eastern Europe, but producers are advantaged by being so close to the 500 million consumers in the EU.

Management at Russell is keeping an eye on the proposed FTAA, which would widen access to the Latin American marketplace with its 500 million consumers. Maintaining a presence in Latin America would give Russell a favorable position for targeting new markets there. In 2009, growth prospects in several Central American countries declined, partly due to their heavy dependence on trade with the United States and other advanced economies, which reduced their imports from the region during the recent global recession.

AACSB: **Reflective Thinking Skills, Ethical Understanding and Reasoning Abilities**

Case Questions

1. China has the most comparative advantages in producing apparel. Free trade theory implies that retailers should import clothing from the most efficient country. Given this, and potential drawbacks of regional integration, would it be better to allow free trade to take its natural course? That is, should DR-CAFTA be rescinded and apparel retailers allowed to import from the most cost-effective suppliers, wherever they are located worldwide?

2. What are the advantages and disadvantages of DR-CAFTA to Honduran firms? To Honduras as a nation? Should free trade be extended throughout Latin America via the proposed Free Trade Area of the Americas (FTAA)?

3. Honduras is a poor country that faces job losses in its apparel sector from growing foreign competition. What can the Honduran government do to help keep jobs in Honduras? Should the government try to attract more foreign investment into Honduras? What steps could the government take to attract more FDI?

4. Russell Corporation is smaller than Adidas and Nike. What should Russell do to counter these firms? What should Russell do to counter the flood of low-cost athletic apparel now entering the United States from China? What can Russell do to ensure its future survival and success?

SOURCES: D. Clark, "Adjustment Problems in Developing Countries and the U.S.-Central America-Dominican Republic Free Trade Agreement," *The International Trade Journal*, January 2009, pp. 31–37; R. Knee and S. Nall, "The CAFTA Effect," *Journal of Commerce*, Sept. 15, 2008, p. 3; J. Authers, "Employment Shrinks in the Textile Sector," *Financial Times*, March 10, 2006, p. 5; J. Borneman, "Regional Support in a Global Fight," *Textile World*, May/June 2006, pp. 26–32; Central Intelligence Agency, *CIA World Factbook*, entry on Honduras, 2009; G. Colvin, "Saving America's Socks," *Fortune*, August 22, 2005, p. 38; "Textiles: Losing Their Shirts," October 16, 2004, pp. 59–60; Corporate profiles of Russell, Nike, and Adidas, retrieved from http://www.hoovers.com; R. Lapper, "Textile Groups in a Bind if U.S. Unravels CAFTA Treaty," *Financial Times*, June 7, 2005, p.18; E. Morphy, "Trade Watch: CAFTA—The Rocky Path to Regional Free Trade, *Foreign Direct Investment*, October 1, 2005, p. 1.

CHAPTER ESSENTIALS

Key Terms

common market, p. 266
customs union, p. 265
economic union, p. 266

free trade agreement, p. 264
free trade area, p. 265
regional economic integration, p. 264

regional economic integration
bloc, p. 264

Summary

In this chapter, you learned about:

1. **Regional integration and economic blocs**

   Under **regional economic integration**, groups of countries form alliances to promote free trade, cross-national investment, and other mutual goals. This integration results from **regional economic integration blocs** (or economic blocs), in which member countries agree to eliminate tariffs and other restrictions on the cross-national flow of products, services, capital, and, in more advanced stages, labor within the bloc. At minimum, the countries in an economic bloc become parties to a **free trade agreement**, which eliminates tariffs, quotas, and other trade barriers.

2. **Levels of regional integration**

   For countries that become members of an economic bloc, there are various stages of regional integration. First is the **free trade area**, which eliminates tariffs and other trade barriers. Second is the **customs union**, a free trade area in which common trade barriers are imposed on nonmember countries. Third is the **common market**, a customs union in which factors of production move freely among the members. Fourth is the **economic union**, a common market in which some important economic policies are harmonized among the member states. A true *political union* does not yet exist.

3. **The leading economic blocs**

   There are hundreds of economic integration agreements in the world. The European Union (EU) is the most advanced, comprising twenty-seven countries in Europe. It has increased market access, improved trade rules, and harmonized standards among its members. Europe is also home to the European Free Trade Association. In the Americas, the most notable bloc is the North American Free Trade Agreement (NAFTA), consisting of Canada, Mexico, and the United States. NAFTA has reached only the free-trade-area stage of regional integration. Other

economic blocs in the Americas include MERCOSUR, CARICOM, and CAN. In the Asia/Pacific region, ASEAN, APEC, and the Australia and New Zealand Closer Economic Relations Agreement (CER) are the leading blocs. Economic blocs in Africa and the Middle East have experienced only limited success.

4. **Advantages of regional integration**

   Regional integration contributes to corporate and industrial growth and hence to economic growth, better living standards, and higher tax revenues for the member countries. It increases market size by integrating the economies within a region. It increases economies of scale and factor productivity among firms in the member countries and attracts foreign investors to the bloc. Regional integration also increases competition and economic dynamism within the bloc and increases the bloc's political power.

5. **Success factors for regional integration**

   The most successful blocs consist of countries that are relatively similar in terms of culture, language, and economic and political structures. Members also are usually close to each other geographically. They can overcome major differences in any one of these factors if there are strong similarities in all the other factors.

6. **Ethical dilemmas and drawbacks of regional integration**

   Regional integration simultaneously leads to trade creation, whereby new trade is generated among the countries inside the bloc, and trade diversion, in which member countries reduce trade with countries outside the bloc. Regional integration entails specific disadvantages. It can reduce global free trade, particularly when member countries form a customs union that results in substantial trade barriers to countries outside the bloc. When economic blocs involve many countries of various sizes, regional integration can concentrate power into large firms and large nations inside the bloc. Regional integration results in economic restructuring, which may harm particular industries and firms. When a country joins an economic bloc, it must relinquish some of its autonomy and national power to the bloc's central authority. Individual countries risk losing some of their national identity.

7. **Management implications of regional integration**

    Regional integration leads to increased internationalization by firms inside their economic bloc. Firms reconfigure and rationalize their operations in line with the larger internal market. Management reconfigures value-chain activities on a pan-regional basis. The formation of economic blocs also leads to mergers and acquisitions because the emergence of a new, larger market favors the creation of larger firms. Managers revise marketing strategies by standardizing products and developing regional brands. Regional integration also leads firms from outside the bloc to expand into the bloc, often via direct investment. However, regional integration leads to competitive pressures and other challenges to firms inside the bloc, some of which may lay off workers or go out of business.

Test Your Comprehension AACSB: Ethical Understanding and Reasoning Abilities, Reflective Thinking Skills

1. What is a regional economic integration bloc (also called an economic bloc)?

2. What is the role of free trade agreements in the formation of economic blocs?

3. Distinguish the different levels of economic integration.

4. Differentiate between a free trade area and a customs union. Differentiate between a customs union and a common market.

5. What are the world's leading economic blocs? Which blocs are most advanced in terms of regional integration?

6. Describe the major characteristics of the EU and NAFTA.

7. Why do nations seek to join or form economic blocs? What are the advantages of such arrangements?

8. What national conditions contribute to the success of economic integration?

9. Explain the drawbacks and ethical dilemmas of regional integration for nations. Explain the drawbacks and ethical dilemmas for firms.

10. Distinguish between trade creation and trade diversion.

11. What strategies should companies employ to maximize the benefits of regional integration?

Apply Your Understanding AACSB: Ethical Understanding and Reasoning Abilities, Reflective Thinking Skills, Communication Abilities

1. There are some 200 economic integration agreements in effect around the world already, far more than even a few years ago. Virtually every country is now party to one or more free trade agreements. Supporters argue that free trade is good for nations. What is the basis for their support? That is, what are the specific benefits that countries seek by joining an economic bloc? What is the main economic bloc for your country? From your perspective, what advantages has bloc membership brought to your country? What disadvantages has bloc membership produced?

2. Following implementation of free trade agreements, trade has grown *within* each of the CARICOM and CAN economic blocs. The growth of within-bloc trade implies that exports from your country to these blocs may be declining over time. Discuss strategies for counteracting such a shift. What recommendations would you make to a company for pursuing opportunities within these blocs? What is the role of international business research, market entry strategy, foreign direct investment, marketing strategy, and collaboration for maintaining or augmenting commerce with these blocs?

3. *Ethical Dilemma:* You are a member of a government task force evaluating the future of NAFTA between Canada, Mexico, and the United States. Proponents want to transform NAFTA into a common market by removing barriers to the movement of labor. The goal is to reduce poverty in Mexico by allowing Mexican citizens to work freely in Canada and the United States. Per-capita income in Mexico is less than $10,000, compared to more than $35,000 in both Canada and the United States. Critics oppose the common market because of the huge income difference. They argue an open border would induce millions of Mexicans to migrate northward seeking work and threaten the jobs and wages of millions of Americans and Canadians. Proponents argue that, as economic integration progressed under a common market, average wages in the three countries would equalize and eliminate pressures on northern job markets. Analyze this situation using the Ethical Framework in Chapter 5. Should the task force recommend the common market? Or is the potential harm too great for Canada and the United States? If NAFTA became a common market, what could U.S. and Canadian firms do to maintain their competitiveness relative to Mexican firms, given Mexico's advantage in low wages?

globalEDGE Internet Exercises
(http://globalEDGE.msu.edu)

AACSB: Reflective Thinking Skills, Analytic Skills, Ethical Understanding and Reasoning Abilities

Refer to Chapter 1, page 62, for instructions on how to access and use globalEDGE™.

1. There has been much opposition to the Free Trade Area of the Americas (FTAA). For a sampling of arguments against this proposed pact, visit www.globalexchange.org, www.citizenstrade.org, and www.corpwatch.org. Also visit the official site of the FTAA at www.ftaa-alca.org, or obtain information on the proposed pact from globalEDGE™. Based on your reading of the chapter, evaluate the arguments against the FTAA. Do you agree or disagree with arguments made by the critics? Why or why not? Do you think the proposed FTAA would harm small Latin American countries? Would it be a boon only to large countries such as Brazil, Canada, and the United States?

2. Visit the Web sites of three major economic blocs. One way to do this is to enter the acronyms for each bloc into a globalEDGE™ search. Using the "Success Factors for Regional Integration" framework highlighted in this chapter, discuss the likely long-term prospects for success in each of these blocs. For each bloc, which of the success factors are strongest, and which are weakest? Which bloc seems to have the best chances for long-term success? Why?

3. NAFTA is a free trade area, and the EU is a common market. Visit the Web sites of these two economic blocs, www.nafta-sec-alena.org and europa.eu, and explain the business strategy implications of each type of economic bloc. Small and medium-sized enterprises (SMEs) tend to be disadvantaged when it comes to competing against large corporations in regional economic blocs. What steps can SMEs, in particular, take to maximize prospects for success when doing business in a free trade area? What steps can SMEs take when doing business in a common market?

CHAPTER 10

LEARNING OBJECTIVES In this chapter, you will learn about:

1. Emerging markets, developing economies, advanced economies
2. What makes emerging markets attractive for international business
3. Assessing the true potential of emerging markets
4. Risks and challenges of emerging markets
5. Strategies for emerging markets
6. Corporate social responsibility in emerging markets and developing economies
7. The special case of Africa

Emerging Markets, Developing Economies, and Advanced Economies

The New Global Challengers: MNEs from Emerging Markets

Emerging markets are countries such as China, India, Mexico, and Turkey that, in contrast to already advanced economies, are now experiencing rapid industrialization, modernization, and economic growth. They represent attractive markets and low-cost manufacturing bases but also high-risk business environments with evolving commercial infrastructure and legal systems. Despite their drawbacks, emerging markets have begun to produce *new global challengers,* top firms that are fast becoming key contenders in world markets. They increasingly pose competitive challenges to companies from advanced economies such as Europe, Japan, and North America.

In a recent study, the Boston Consulting Group identified the top 100 challengers. Many are from China and India. Mexico's Cemex is one of the world's largest cement producers and Russia's Lukoil has big ambitions in global energy. In Turkey, diversified conglomerate Koc Holding owns Arcelik, a giant home appliance producer.

The Brazilian food processors Sadia and Perdigao exemplify challengers' international entrepreneurship. These firms, which recently completed a merger, operate farms and market processed foods and ready-to-eat meals; each is a $4 billion enterprise that exports over half its annual production. Abundant production resources for pork, poultry, and grains and ideal growing conditions for animal feed provide superior advantages.

Both firms built world-class distribution and supply-chain management systems.

In their home countries, challengers leverage low-cost labor, as well as engineering and managerial talent often superior to that of competitors in the advanced economies. Many challengers are family-owned or family-run businesses (family conglomerates), which means they can make important business decisions quickly. They can often access low-interest loans from home-country, government-owned banks. Many are growing internationally by taking their established brands to global markets. China's Hisense sells its branded televisions and air conditioners in more than 40 countries, including the best-selling brand of flat-panel TV in France. Hisense also makes stylish consumer electronics at low prices.

Many challengers leverage superior engineering capability. Hong Kong's Johnson Electric is the world leader in small electric motors for automotive and consumer applications. Brazil's Embraer taps the large pool of experienced but low-cost engineers in that country to build innovative small jets. It has zipped past Canada's Bombardier to become the world's largest producer of regional jet aircraft.

Other challengers benefit from local bases of ample natural resources. Russia's Rusal is extracting the country's rich reserves of bauxite to produce aluminum for international markets. The majority of the world's natural resources are located in developing economies, and a growing number of challengers use these to their advantage. China's CNOOC, for example, has been buying into oil and gas reserves in Asia and Africa.

Today, many more emerging market firms are active on the world stage. They possess distinct advantages and are becoming key competitors to MNEs from advanced economies. Their success suggests the character of international trade and investment is changing. The challengers identified in the Boston Consulting Group study are just the tip of the iceberg; thousands of firms from emerging markets have big global dreams and are rapidly expanding worldwide.

SOURCES: G. Adolph and J. Pettit, "The Rise of the New Blue Chips," *Strategy and Business,* Autumn 2008, pp. 8–10; A. Bhattacharya and D. Michael, "How Local Companies Keep Multinationals at Bay," *Harvard Business Review,* March 2008, pp. 85–95; Boston Consulting Group, *The New Global Challengers* (Boston: Boston Consulting Group, 2006); Boston Consulting Group, *The 2009 BCG 100 New Global Challengers* (Boston: Boston Consulting Group, 2009); "Emerging-Market Multinationals: The Challengers," *Economist,* January 12, 2008, pp. 62–63; N. Kumar, "India Unleashed," *Business Strategy Review* 20, no. 1 (2009): 4; H. Sirkin, "Global Leaders in Waiting," *Global Finance* 24, no. 1 (2010): 20–22.

In this chapter we discuss emerging market economies and contrast them with developing and advanced economies. Each country group poses distinctive opportunities and risks. By analyzing a country in terms of its stage of economic development, the manager can gain insights into at least three important characteristics: the purchasing power of its citizens, the sophistication of its business sector, and the adequacy of its commercial infrastructure in such areas as communications, transportation, and energy generation. Let's explore the country groups in detail.

 ## Advanced Economies, Developing Economies, and Emerging Markets

Exhibit 10.1 highlights the advanced economies, developing economies, and emerging markets differentiated by degree of economic development and per-capita income. **Advanced economies** are post-industrial countries characterized by high per-capita income, highly competitive industries, and well-developed commercial infrastructures. They are the world's richest nations and include Australia, Canada, Japan, New Zealand, the United States, and most European countries. **Developing economies** are low-income countries characterized by limited industrialization and stagnant economies. They make up the largest group of countries and include Bangladesh, Nicaragua, and Zaire. Emerging market economies or **emerging markets** are former developing economies that have achieved substantial industrialization, modernization, and rapid economic growth since the 1980s. Currently, some twenty-seven countries are considered emerging markets and are found mainly in Asia, Latin America, and Eastern Europe. The largest are Brazil, Russia, India, and China (sometimes abbreviated 'BRIC').

One way to visualize the three groups of countries is to examine a map of the world at night, shown in Exhibit 10.2. The advanced economies are the most visible areas because, with the highest levels of industrialization, they are generally the most brightly lit. However, the map also suggests significant economic activity in the emerging market countries. Finally, it reveals very low levels of industrialization across large stretches of Africa, central Asia, eastern Russia, and major parts of Latin America. These represent developing economies and other areas with little or no industrialization and limited economic development. Note how areas of advanced industrialization tend to consume the most energy. Widespread industrialization and resource consumption release various pollutants into the natural environment. Increasingly, nations must consider how economic development can be achieved without excessive ecological harm.

Advanced economies
Post-industrial countries characterized by high per-capita income, highly competitive industries, and well-developed commercial infrastructure.

Developing economies
Low-income countries characterized by limited industrialization and stagnant economies.

Emerging markets
Former developing economies that have achieved substantial industrialization, modernization, and rapid economic growth since the 1980s.

Exhibit 10.3 provides an overview of the key differences among the three groups of countries.

Advanced Economies

Having reached a mature state of industrial development, advanced economies have largely evolved from manufacturing economies into service-based economies. Home to only about 14 percent of the world's population, they have long dominated international business. They account for about half of the world's GDP, over half of world trade in products, and three-quarters of world trade in services.

Advanced economies have democratic, multiparty systems of government. Their economic systems are usually based on capitalism. They have tremendous purchasing power, with few restrictions on international trade and investment. They host the world's largest MNEs. A leading example is Ireland, which has one of the world's best-performing economies and per-capita income higher than many of its European neighbors. Ireland emphasizes strict fiscal and monetary policies. The government cut federal spending, taxes, and borrowing. Such policies gave rise to lower interest rates and more available capital and attracted much FDI from foreign manufacturers in high-tech industries, such as Dell and Gateway. Over time, Ireland has built up a strong educational system, producing a steady supply of skilled workers, scientists, engineers, and managers.[1]

Developing Economies

Consumers in developing economies have low discretionary incomes; the proportion of personal income they spend on purchases other than food, clothing, and housing is very limited. Approximately 17 percent of citizens in developing economies live on less than $1 per day; around 40 percent live on less than $2 per day.[2] The combination of low income and generally high birth rates tends to perpetuate poverty in these countries. Developing economies are sometimes called *underdeveloped countries* or *third-world countries*; however, these terms are imprecise and often offensive to citizens of such countries because, despite poor economic conditions, they tend to be highly developed in historical and cultural terms.

Developing economies are hindered by high infant mortality, malnutrition, short life expectancy, illiteracy, and poor education systems. For example, the proportion of children who finish primary school in most African countries is less than 50 percent.[3] Because education is strongly correlated with economic development, poverty tends to persist. Lack of adequate health care is a big concern. Some 95 percent of the world's AIDS victims are found in developing economies, an additional hardship that hampers their development. Ailing adults cannot work or care for their children and require much medical care. As a result, productivity is stagnant, which means living standards deteriorate. Orphaned children are unlikely to get an education, and the vicious cycle of poverty persists.

Governments in developing economies are often severely indebted. In fact, some countries in Africa, Latin America, and South Asia have debt levels that approach or exceed their annual gross domestic product. This means it would cost a year's worth of national productive output just to pay off the national debt. Much of Africa's poverty is the result of government policies that discourage entrepreneurship, trade, and investment. For example, starting a new business in sub-Saharan countries in Africa requires an average of eleven different approvals and takes 62 days to complete. In the advanced economies, by contrast, starting a new business takes an average of six approvals and 17 days.[4] Bureaucracy and red tape in developing economies deter firms from these countries from participating in the global economy.

International trade and investment help to stimulate economic growth, create jobs, raise incomes, and lower prices for the products and services demanded by consumers

Exhibit 10.1 Advanced Economies, Developing Economies, and Emerging Markets

ARCTIC OCEAN

NORWAY
SWEDEN
FINLAND
ESTONIA
NETHERLANDS
LATVIA
DENMARK
LITHUANIA
IRELAND
BELGIUM
RUSSIA
BELARUS
UNITED
KINGDOM
GERMANY
POLAND
LUXEMBOURG
CZECH
REP.
SLOVAKIA
UKRAINE
FRANCE
LIECH.
AUSTRIA
HUNGARY
MOLDOVA
SWITZ.
SLOVENIA
ROMANIA
MONACO
CROATIA
BOSNIA
HERZEGOVINA
ANDORRA
ITALY
YUGOSLAVIA
BULGARIA
SPAIN
ALBANIA
MACEDONIA
GEORGIA
PORTUGAL
GREECE
TURKEY
ARMENIA
AZERBAIJAN
UZBEKISTAN
KYRGYZSTAN
TUNISIA
CYPRUS
SYRIA
TURKMENISTAN
TAJIKISTAN
MOROCCO
ISRAEL
LEBANON
IRAQ
AFGHANISTAN
JORDAN
IRAN
ALGERIA
LIBYA
EGYPT
KUWAIT
PAKISTAN
WESTERN
SAHARA
QATAR
UNITED ARAB
EMIRATES
NEPAL
BHUTAN
URITANIA
MALI
NIGER
CHAD
SAUDI
ARABIA
OMAN
INDIA
BANGLADESH
MYANMAR
(BURMA)
LAOS
EGAL
BIA
BURKINA
FASO
ERITREA
YEMEN
THAILAND
VIETNAM
EA-BISSAU
GUINEA
NIGERIA
SUDAN
DJIBOUTI
CAMBODIA
A LEONE
IVORY
COAST
GHANA
TOGO
BENIN
SRI
LANKA
PHILIPPINES
LIBERIA
CENTRAL AFRICAN
REPUBLIC
CAMEROON
ETHIOPIA
SOMALIA
EQUATORIAL
GUINEA
CONGO
REPUBLIC
GABON
UGANDA
KENYA
BRUNEI
CONGO
DEMOCRATIC
REPUBLIC
(ZAIRE)
RWANDA
BURUNDI
MALAYSIA
SINGAPORE
TANZANIA
ANGOLA
ZAMBIA
MALAWI
MOZAMBIQUE
NAMIBIA
ZIMBABWE
MADAGASCAR
MAURITIUS
BOTSWANA
RÉUNION
SWAZILAND
SOUTH
AFRICA
LESOTHO

RUSSIA
KAZAKHSTAN
MONGOLIA
NORTH
KOREA
SOUTH
KOREA
CHINA
JAPAN
TAIWAN
INDONESIA
PAPUA
NEW
GUINEA
SOLOMON
ISLANDS
VANUATU
FIJI
NEW
CALEDONIA
AUSTRALIA
NEW
ZEALAND

PACIFIC
OCEAN

INDIAN
OCEAN

SOUTH
ATLANTIC
OCEAN

- **Advanced Economies** - Post-industrial countries characterized by high per-capita income, highly competitive industries, and well-developed commercial infrastructure.

- **Emerging Markets** - Former developing economies that have achieved substantial industrialization, modernization, and rapid economic growth since the 1980s.

- **Developing Economies** - Low-income countries characterized by limited industrialization and stagnant economies.

Exhibit 10.2 The World at Night, Showing Varying Areas of Industrialization

SOURCE: C. Mayhew & R. Simmon (NASA/GSFC), NOAA/ NGDC, DMSP Digital Archive

Dimension	Advanced Economies	Developing Economies	Emerging Markets
Representative countries	Canada, France, Japan, United Kingdom, United States	Angola, Bolivia, Nigeria, Bangladesh	Brazil, China, India, Indonesia, Turkey
Approximate number of countries	30	150	27
Population (% of world)	14%	24%	62%
Approximate average per-capita income (U.S. dollars; PPP basis)	$33,750	$4,968	$13,620
Approximate share of world GDP (PPP basis)	48%	9%	43%
Population (millions)	896	1,971	3,912
Telephone lines per 1,000 people (fixed and mobile)	1,369	355	724
Personal computers per 1,000 people	1,473	355	810
Internet users per 1,000 people	726	148	400

Exhibit 10.3 Key Differences among the Three Major Country Groups

SOURCES: World Bank at http://www.worldbank.org; International Monetary Fund at http://www.imf.org.

and companies. When countries are cut off from the global economy, the result is increased poverty and unemployment—conditions that can give rise to revolution, terrorism, and war. By contrast, nations that participate actively in the global economy enjoy economic stability and better living standards. As Exhibit 10.4 illustrates, there are substantial differences in critical trade conditions across the three country groups.

Emerging Market Economies

Emerging markets are found in East and South Asia, Eastern Europe, Southern Africa, Latin America, and the Middle East. Perhaps their most distinguishing characteristic is rapidly improving living standards and a growing middle class with rising economic as-

Trade Condition	Advanced Economies	Developing Economies	Emerging Markets
Industry	Highly developed	Poor	Rapidly improving
Competition	Substantial	Limited	Moderate but increasing
Trade barriers	Minimal	Moderate to high	Rapidly liberalizing
Trade volume	High	Low	High
Inward FDI	High	Low	Moderate to high

Exhibit 10.4 Trade Conditions with Major Country Groups

SOURCES: International Monetary Fund at http://www.imf.org, World Bank, 2010 at http://www.worldbank.org, and Central Intelligence Agency, *CIA World Factbook 2009* at http://www.cia.gov/cia/publications/factbook.

pirations. As a result, their attractiveness as destinations for exports, FDI, and sourcing is increasing.

Because their economies are changing so dynamically, it can be argued that Hong Kong, Israel, Singapore, South Korea, and Taiwan have developed beyond the emerging market stage. Several emerging markets will join the group of wealthy nations in the not-too-distant future. Recently, Bulgaria and Romania received a boost when they became members of the European Union and adopted stable monetary and trade policies. They leverage their low-cost labor to attract investment from Western Europe, thereby boosting their economies.

Similarly, some countries currently classified as developing economies have the potential to become emerging markets in the near future. These "frontier economies" include the European countries of Estonia, Latvia, Lithuania, Slovakia; the Latin American countries of Costa Rica, Panama, and Uruguay; and Kazakhstan, Nigeria, and the United Arab Emirates.

Finally, economic prosperity often varies *within* emerging markets. In these countries, there are usually two parallel economies—those in urban areas and those in rural areas. Urban areas tend to have more developed economic infrastructure and consumers with greater discretionary income in comparison to rural areas.

Certain emerging markets that have evolved from centrally planned economies to liberalized markets—specifically China, Russia, and several countries in Eastern Europe—are called **transition economies**. These countries were once socialist states but have been largely transformed into capitalism-based systems, partly via a process of **privatization**—the transfer of state-owned industries to private concerns. Privatization and the promotion of new, privately owned businesses have allowed the transition economies to attract substantial direct investment from abroad. Long burdened by excessive regulation and entrenched government bureaucracy, they are gradually introducing legal frameworks to protect business and consumer interests and ensure intellectual property rights. They hold much potential.[5]

Privatization provided many opportunities for foreign firms to enter transition economies by purchasing former state enterprises. In Eastern Europe, Western companies are leveraging inexpensive labor and other advantages in the region to manufacture products bound for export markets. Poland, the Czech Republic, Hungary, and other former East Bloc countries have made great strides in political and economic restructuring. These countries are well on their way to more advanced stages of economic development.

Exhibit 10.5 contrasts the national characteristics of emerging markets with the other two country groups. Exhibit 10.6 shows that emerging markets account for more than 40 percent of world GDP. Similarly, they represent more than 30 percent of exports and receive more than 20 percent of FDI.

In the mid-2000s, the emerging markets collectively enjoyed an average annual GDP growth rate of around 7 percent, a remarkable feat. While the economies of most emerging

Transition economies A subset of emerging markets that evolved from centrally planned economies into liberalized markets.

Privatization Transfer of state-owned industries to private concerns.

Characteristic	Advanced Economies	Developing Economies	Emerging Markets
Median age of citizens	40 years	26 years	34 years
Major sector focus products	Services, branded commodities	Agriculture, services	Manufacturing, some
Education level	High	Low	Medium
Economic and political freedom	Free or mostly free	Mostly repressed	Moderately free or mostly not free
Economic / political system	Capitalist	Authoritarian, socialist, or communist	Rapidly transitioning to capitalism
Regulatory environment	Minimal regulations	Highly regulated, burdensome	Achieved much economic liberalization
Country risk	Low	Moderate to high	Variable
Intellectual property protection	Strong	Weak	Moderate and improving
Infrastructure	Well-developed	Inadequate	Moderate but improving

Exhibit 10.5 National Characteristics of Major Country Groups

SOURCES: International Monetary Fund at http://www.imf.org, World Bank at http://www.worldbank.org, and Central Intelligence Agency, *CIA World Factbook 2010* at http://www.cia.gov/cia/publications/factbook.

Exhibit 10.6 Why They Matter: Emerging Markets as a Percent of World Total

SOURCES: "The New Titans," *Economist,* September 14, 2006, survey section; International Monetary Fund at http://www.imf.org; Central Intelligence Agency, *CIA World Factbook,* 2008, at http://www.cia.gov/cia/publications/factbook; World Bank at http://www.worldbank.org.

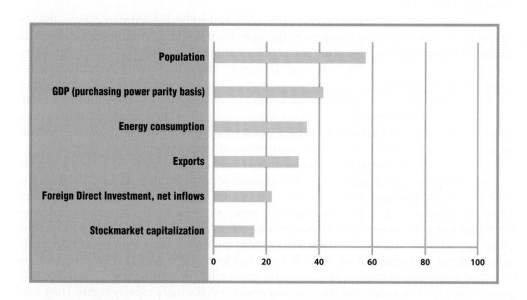

markets were disrupted by the global recession and financial crisis, their average growth rates have remained strongly positive. As Exhibit 10.7 shows, emerging markets have been growing much faster than advanced economies.

Emerging markets possess numerous advantages that have fostered their rise. The presence of low-cost labor, knowledge workers, government support, low-cost capital, and powerful, highly networked conglomerates have helped make these countries formidable challengers in the global marketplace. As highlighted in the opening vignette, **new global challengers** are top firms from emerging markets that are fast becoming key contenders in world markets. One is Orascom Telecom (www.orascomtelecom.com), an Egyptian mobile telecommunications provider that has leveraged managerial skills, superior technology, and rapid growth to become an industry leader in Africa and the Mid-

New global challengers
Top firms from emerging markets that are fast becoming key contenders in world markets.

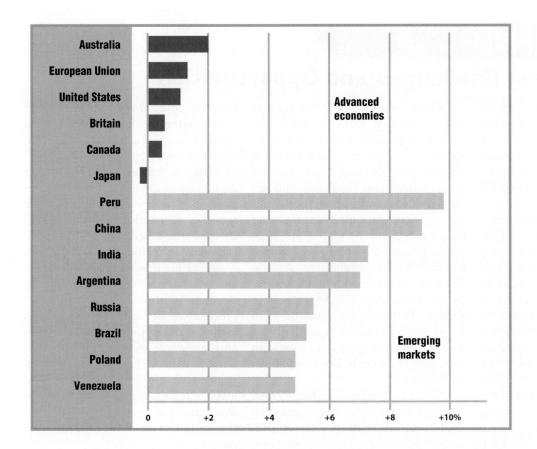

Exhibit 10.7 GDP Growth Rates in Advanced Economies and Emerging Markets

SOURCE: International Monetary Fund (2009), *World Economic Outlook Database*, at http://www.imf.org.

dle East. Starting in 1997, management strung together a telecom empire of more than 80 million subscribers, stretching from North Africa to Bangladesh. Operating expenses in Egypt are much lower than in Europe, because engineers and salespeople work for less. Orascom's advantage is growth, which provides a continuous stream of capital to fund expansion plans. Management has excelled at local branding and tailoring telephone products and services to local pocketbooks.[6]

Each year, *Forbes* magazine catalogs the top 2,000 global firms. Its analysis revealed that between 2004 and 2008 a total of 117 MNEs entered the list from such emerging markets as China, India, Brazil, and Russia. Meanwhile, in the same period, 233 firms from the United States, Japan, and Britain *fell off* the Forbes list. In 1990, only nineteen companies from low-income countries were among the *Fortune* Global 500 listing of the world's largest MNEs. By 2010, China alone had fifty-four companies in the Global 500. These statistics reveal how new global challengers are displacing traditional MNEs from the advanced economies and becoming key competitors in world markets. Managers need to devise innovative strategies to compete with them effectively.[7]

China is the largest emerging market, with a population of 1.3 billion people, one-fifth of the world's total. Its economy continues to grow at an impressive rate, and its role in international business is expanding rapidly. The country has already produced numerous new global challengers, such as Shanghai Automotive (China's top automaker), Sinopec (a large oil company), and Shanghai Baosteel (a steel manufacturer). Since 1993, the share of world merchandise exports from Japan, the United States, and most European countries has declined. In the same period, the proportion of goods produced and shipped from China has risen sharply; it now accounts for more than 10 percent of total world merchandise exports. The figure is impressive given that most of the world's 200 or so countries engage in product exporting.[8] The *Global Trend* feature highlights China's growing role in international business.

GL🌐BAL TREND

China's Evolving Challenges and Opportunities

Since pursuing market reforms in the late 1970s, China has achieved explosive economic growth, often 10 percent or more per year. Although income per person is still modest at around $6,500, in 2009 China stood as the second-largest economy in the world (after the United States). After joining the WTO, it expanded its role as a global manufacturing site, and intensified its massive exports to countries worldwide. Investment poured in from MNEs that perceive a bright future for China as both a manufacturing platform and a huge consumer market. The country attracted an impressive $92 billion in FDI in 2008. China buys roughly 20 percent of the world's aluminum, copper, washing machines, soybeans, poultry, and ice cream. It consumes roughly one-third of the world's coal, cotton, fish, rice, and cigarettes, one-quarter of the world's steel, and one-half its pork.

But success in China has come slowly for most foreign firms. A big challenge is low per-capita income. About one-third of China's population (roughly 400 million people) lives on less than $2 per day. Of a total population of 1.3 billion, the realistic target consumer segment is the 250 million residents of urban areas, largely in the developed eastern regions. Other challenges include regional differences in language, autonomous local governments, and inadequate infrastructure. Yet many companies have succeeded in China, including Airbus, Coca-Cola, Motorola, and Volkswagen.

China was severely hit by the global financial crisis in 2009. Although economic growth remained strong by Western standards, it slowed considerably, and exports sharply declined. Factories laid off tens of thousands of workers, and the country struggled to maintain jobs for millions more. The fast economic growth of earlier years cannot be maintained indefinitely. As the Chinese government seeks to improve local labor conditions, some foreign firms whose operations in China were based on exploiting low wages are moving to countries with still-lower labor costs, like Bangladesh and Vietnam.

China's growth has also strained world resources, leading to higher commodity prices. Rapid, under-regulated industrialization has produced much environmental degra-dation. China is home to eight of the 10 most polluted cities worldwide. China emits more carbon dioxide than any other country (although the United States is highest in per-capita terms). More than one million Chinese are thought to die every year from pollution-related causes. Most power is generated in low-tech coal plants, which are major polluters. There are also serious problems of water pollution, deforestation, desertification, and soil deterioration. Because of the weak regulatory environment, factories in China are required to follow only minimal pollution control standards, which further harms the natural environment. Firms from

Europe, the United States, and other economically advanced areas must follow much tougher standards in their home countries.

The Chinese government is beginning to develop clean technologies and new industries based on growing demand for products and services that support the natural environment. In 2009, China set about investing hundreds of billions of dollars in wastewater treatment infrastructure and energy-saving power production. China is already a world leader in developing green industries and renewable energy. It has become a major manufacturer of solar photovoltaic technology and wind turbines, much of it for export. Due to an extensive system of rivers, China has massive potential to install hydroelectric power.

China is home to numerous challenges and opportunities. For Western firms, success requires a deep understanding of the market and long-term commitment.

SOURCES: F. Balfour, "The Surprising Strength of Southeast Asia," *Business Week*, June 8, 2009, p. 34; Central Intelligence Agency, *World Factbook*, 2009, at http://www.cia.gov/cia/publications/factbook; "What China Eats (and Drinks and. . .)," *Fortune*, October 4, 2004, pp. 151–53; Y. Ma, "China's View of Climate Change," *Policy Review*, June/July, 2010, pp. 27-44; B. Powell, "China's Hard Landing," *Fortune*, March 16, 2009, pp. 114–16; A. Wahl, "Clean and Green China," *Canadian Business*, Summer 2009, pp. 103–104; J. Warren, "China's Green Future," *Far Eastern Economic Review*, December 2008, pp. 53–57; Alex Wang, "The Downside of Growth: Law, Policy and China's Environmental Crisis," *Perspectives* 2 (2000), retrieved from the Web site of the Overseas Young Chinese Forum at http://www.oycf.org.

 What Makes Emerging Markets Attractive for International Business

Emerging markets are attractive to internationalizing firms as target markets, manufacturing bases, and sourcing destinations.

Emerging Markets as Target Markets

Emerging markets have become important target markets for a wide variety of products and services. The largest ones have doubled their share of world imports in the last few years. Exports to such countries account for one-third of total merchandise exports from the United States. The growing middle class in emerging markets implies rising demand for various consumer products, such as electronics and automobiles, and services such as health care.[9] Roughly a quarter of Mexico's 105 million people enjoy affluence equivalent to that of the middle class in the United States. In some product categories, demand is growing fastest in emerging markets. For example, the fastest-growing markets for power tool companies like Black & Decker and Robert Bosch are in Asia, Latin America, Africa, and the Middle East.[10] Even during the global recession, technology firms such as Cisco, Hewlett-Packard, and Intel were generating a large and growing proportion of their revenues from sales to such countries.[11]

In 2008, firms in the global pharmaceutical companies such as Pfizer and Glaxo-SmithKline increased their emphasis on developing and marketing drugs in emerging markets. Industry insiders forecast that medication sales in the biggest emerging markets will hit $300 billion by 2017, equal to today's sales in the top five European markets and the United States combined. Already Merck and Pfizer have launched popular drugs in India, using innovative pricing strategies that make once-expensive medications affordable for millions of low-income consumers.[12]

Businesses in emerging markets are important targets for machinery and equipment sales. In this category, markets are huge for textile machinery in India, for agricultural equipment in China, and for oil and gas exploration technology in Russia. In a similar way, governments and state enterprises in emerging markets are major targets for sales of infrastructure-related products and services such as machinery, power transmission equipment, transportation equipment, high-technology products, and other products that countries in the middle stage of development typically need.

Emerging Markets as Manufacturing Bases

Firms from Japan, Europe, the United States, and other advanced economies have invested vast sums to develop manufacturing facilities in emerging markets. These markets are home to low-wage, high-quality labor for manufacturing and assembly operations. In addition, some emerging markets have large reserves of raw materials and natural resources. Mexico and China are important production platforms for manufacturing cars and consumer electronics. South Africa is a key source for industrial diamonds. Brazil is a center for mining bauxite, the main ingredient in aluminum. Thailand has become an important manufacturing location for Japanese MNEs such as Sony and Sharp. Motorola, Intel, and Philips manufacture semiconductors in Malaysia and Taiwan.

These workers are assembling Audi car engines in Hungary. Emerging markets are excellent locations for global sourcing.

Emerging markets also enjoy considerable success in certain industries, such as Brazil in iron ore and processed foods, Taiwan and Malaysia in personal computers, and South Africa in mining. Individual firms, including those highlighted in the opening vignette, have also become world-class companies. Did you know, for example, that the world's number three and four top-selling beer brands are produced by new global challengers based in Brazil (Skol, made by InBev) and China (Snow, made by China Resources Snow Breweries)? Together, these firms produce more than 50 million barrels of beer annually. South Korea's Samsung is the world's largest electronics company and the leading producer of semiconductors and flat screen TVs. It has displaced Sony (Japan) and Motorola (USA) in these industries.

Emerging Markets as Sourcing Destinations

Outsourcing The procurement of selected value-adding activities, including production of intermediate goods or finished products, from independent suppliers.

Global sourcing The procurement of products or services from independent suppliers or company-owned subsidiaries located abroad for consumption in the home country or a third country.

In recent years, companies sought ways of transferring or delegating non-core tasks or operations from in-house groups to specialized contractors. This business trend is known as **outsourcing**—the procurement of selected value-adding activities, including production of intermediate goods or finished products, from independent suppliers or company-owned subsidiaries. Outsourcing helps foreign firms become more efficient, concentrate on their core competencies, and obtain competitive advantages. When sourcing relies on foreign suppliers or production bases, it is known as **global sourcing** or *offshoring*. We dedicate Chapter 17 to global sourcing topics.

Emerging markets have served as excellent platforms for sourcing. Numerous MNEs have established call centers in Eastern Europe, India, and the Philippines. Firms in the IT industry such as Dell and IBM reap substantial benefits from their ability to outsource certain technological functions to knowledge workers in India. Intel and Microsoft have many of their programming activities performed in Bangalore, India. Investments from abroad benefit emerging markets as they lead to new jobs and production capacity, transfer of technology and know-how, and linkages to the global marketplace.

 ## Assessing the True Potential of Emerging Markets

Unique country conditions such as limited data, unreliable information, or the high cost of carrying out market research can make it challenging for Western firms to estimate the true market potential of emerging markets. Often firms may have to improvise.[13] To overcome these challenges, in the early stages of market research, managers examine three important statistics to estimate market potential: per-capita income, size of the middle class, and market potential indicators.

Per-Capita Income as an Indicator of Market Potential

When evaluating the potential of individual markets, managers often start by examining aggregate country data, such as gross national income (GNI) or per-capita GDP, expressed in terms of a reference currency such as the U.S. dollar. The second column in Exhibit 10.8 provides per-capita GDP for a sample of emerging markets and the United States, for comparison purposes. For example, in 2009 China's per-capita GDP converted at market exchange rates was $3,180, while that of the United States was $47,025.

However, per-capita GDP converted at market exchange rates paints an inaccurate picture of market potential because it overlooks the substantial price differences between advanced economies and emerging markets. Prices are usually lower for a wide variety of products and services in emerging markets. A U.S. dollar exchanged and spent in China will buy much more than a dollar spent in the United States, for instance.

Purchasing power parity (PPP) An adjustment for prices that reflects the amount of goods that consumers can buy in their home country, using their own currency and consistent with their own standard of living.

What should managers do to accurately estimate market potential? The answer lies in using per-capita GDP figures *adjusted* for price differences. Economists estimate real buying power by calculating GDP statistics based on **purchasing power parity (PPP)**. The PPP concept suggests that, in the long run, exchange rates should move toward levels that would equalize the prices of an identical basket of goods and services in any two countries. Since prices vary greatly among countries, economists adjust ordinary GDP figures for differences in purchasing power. Adjusted per-capita GDP more accurately represents the amount of products consumers can buy in a given country, using *their own currency* and consistent with *their own standard of living*.

Country	Per-Capita GDP, Converted using Market Exchange Rates (US$)	Per-Capita GDP, Converted using PPP Exchange Rates (US$)
Argentina	$ 8,522	$14,354
Brazil	8,676	10,298
Bulgaria	6,849	12,372
China	3,180	5,943
Hungary	16,343	19,829
South Korea	19,637	26,340
Mexico	10,747	14,581
Russia	12,579	16,161
Turkey	11,468	13,447
United States	**47,025**	**47,025**

Exhibit 10.8

Difference in Per Capita GDP, in Conventional and Purchasing Power Parity (PPP) Terms, 2009

SOURCE: International Monetary Fund, *World Economic Outlook Database,* 2009, at http://www.imf.org

Now examine per-capita GDP, adjusted for purchasing power parity, for the same sample of countries in the third column in Exhibit 10.8. Note that a more accurate estimate of China's per-capita GDP is $5,943—nearly double the per-capita GDP at market exchange rates. Compare the two figures for other countries as well. These adjusted estimates help explain why firms increasingly target emerging markets despite the seemingly low income levels in conventional income statistics.

Another way to illustrate the PPP concept is to examine the Big Mac Index developed by *The Economist* (www.economist.com). The Index first gathers information about the price of hamburgers at McDonald's restaurants worldwide. It then compares the prices based on actual exchange rates to those based on the PPP price of Big Macs to assess whether a nation's currency is under- or overvalued. Exhibit 10.9 presents the Big Mac Index for the most recent year. It reveals that the currencies of most European countries (mainly the euro) are overvalued, while those of most developing economies or emerging markets are undervalued. The Big Mac Index also implies the Chinese yuan is undervalued. It suggests the yuan is 49 percent below its fair-value benchmark with the dollar.[14]

Even when per-capita income is adjusted for purchasing power parity, managers should exercise caution in relying on it as an indicator of market potential in an emerging or developing economy. There are four reasons for this caution.

First, official data do not account for the existence of an *informal economy,* where economic transactions occur that are not officially recorded and are therefore left out of government calculations of a nation's GDP. In developing economies, the informal economy is often as large as the formal economy, but countries typically lack sophisticated taxation systems for detecting and reporting its operation, and individuals and businesses often underreport income to minimize tax obligations. Nor are barter exchanges in which no money changes hands captured by national estimates of GDP.

Second, the great majority of the population is on the low end of the income scale in emerging markets and developing economies. As you may recall from your statistics training, "mean" or "average" does not accurately represent a non-normal distribution; often, median income provides a more accurate depiction of purchasing power.

Third, *household* income is substantially larger than per-capita income because of multiple wage earners within individual households in these countries. Multiple-income households naturally have much greater spending power than individuals, a fact overlooked by statistics that emphasize per-capita GDP. Fourth, governments in these countries may underreport national income so they can qualify for low-interest loans and grants from international aid agencies and development banks.

Exhibit 10.9 The Big Mac Index

SOURCE: Re-created "Our Big Mac Index Shows the Chinese Yuan Is Still Undervalued," Mar 17th 2010. From *The Economist* online.

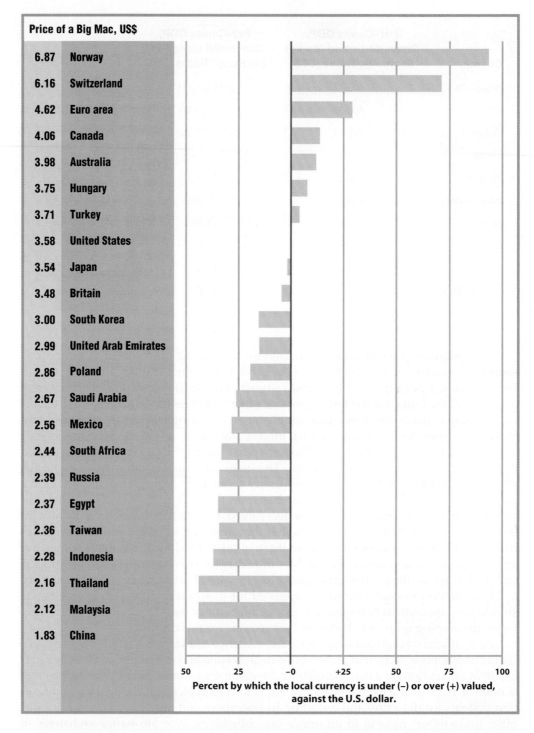

Price of a Big Mac, US$	
6.87	Norway
6.16	Switzerland
4.62	Euro area
4.06	Canada
3.98	Australia
3.75	Hungary
3.71	Turkey
3.58	United States
3.54	Japan
3.48	Britain
3.00	South Korea
2.99	United Arab Emirates
2.86	Poland
2.67	Saudi Arabia
2.56	Mexico
2.44	South Africa
2.39	Russia
2.37	Egypt
2.36	Taiwan
2.28	Indonesia
2.16	Thailand
2.12	Malaysia
1.83	China

Percent by which the local currency is under (−) or over (+) valued, against the U.S. dollar.

In addition to per-capita GDP, managers should examine other market potential indicators, including GDP growth rate, income distribution, commercial infrastructure, the rate of urbanization, consumer expenditures for discretionary items, and unemployment rate. Managers will also find the size and growth rate of the middle class to be revealing. Let's explore this next.

Middle Class as an Indicator of Market Potential

In every country, the middle class represents the segment of people between wealthy and poor. They have economic independence; work in businesses, education, government, and hourly jobs; and consume many discretionary items, including electronics,

Country	Middle-Class Population (millions)	Percent of Income Held by Middle Class	Per-Capita GDP, (PPP, U.S.$)
Brazil	65	35%	$10,456
China	587	45	6,546
India	534	49	2,932
Indonesia	105	48	4,149
Mexico	42	41	13,542
Russia	67	47	15,039
South Korea	26	55	25,403
Thailand	28	45	7,998
Turkey	32	45	12,339

Exhibit 10.10 Size of Middle-Class Population for a Sample of Emerging Markets, 2009

SOURCES: International Monetary Fund at http://www.imf.org, World Bank at http://www.worldbank.org, and globalEDGE™ at http://globalEDGE.msu.edu.

furniture, automobiles, and entertainment. Middle-class households make up the largest proportion of households in advanced economies. In emerging markets, the size and growth rate of the middle class serve as signals of a dynamic market economy.

Exhibit 10.10 provides data for a sample of emerging markets with relatively sizable middle-class populations.[15] For marketers of products and services, these countries are prime prospects. India and Indonesia rank at the very top, given their large populations. Note, however, the trade-off between various indicators. While India and Indonesia feature large middle-class populations in absolute terms, per-capita GDP in these countries is rather modest, especially when compared to South Korea, China, Russia, and Mexico. However, the percentage of income held by the middle class in India and Indonesia is relatively high, at 49 and 48 percent, respectively. Contrast this to Brazil where the middle class controls only about 35 percent of national income. Demographic trends indicate that, in the coming two decades, the proportion of middle-class households in emerging markets will become much bigger, acquiring enormous spending power.[16] As incomes increase, spending patterns will evolve, fueling growth across various product and service categories.

 ## Risks and Challenges of Emerging Markets

Emerging markets exhibit certain risks that affect their viability for international business. Let's review the most common, and the most harmful, of these risks.

Political Instability

The absence of reliable or consistent governance from recognized government authorities adds to business costs, increases risks, and reduces managers' ability to forecast business conditions. Political instability is associated with corruption and weak legal frameworks that discourage inward investment and the development of a reliable business environment. In Russia, for example, evolving political conditions threaten the business activities of foreign firms. Bureaucratic practices favor well-connected, home-grown firms. Western oil companies have been denied access to Russia's energy resources. In the 2010 *Ease of Doing Business* rankings of the World Bank, the Russian Federation received an overall ranking of 120 out of 183 countries (with first being the best). It ranked 182nd in dealing with construction permits; 103rd in paying taxes; and 162nd in trading across borders procedures (www.doingbusiness.org). These conditions have harmed foreign investor confidence.[17]

Weak Intellectual Property Protection

Even when they exist, laws that safeguard intellectual property rights may not be enforced, or the judicial process may be painfully slow. In Argentina, for example, enforcement of copyrights on recorded music, videos, books, and computer software is inconsistent. Authorities attempt to stop shipments of pirated merchandise, but inadequate resources and slow court procedures hamper enforcement. Laws against Internet piracy are weak and ineffective.[18] Counterfeiting—unauthorized copying and production of a product—is common in China, Indonesia, and Russia, especially of software, DVDs, and CDs. In India, weak patent laws often discourage investment by foreign firms.

Bureaucracy, Red Tape, and Lack of Transparency

Burdensome administrative rules and excessive requirements for licenses, approvals, and paperwork all delay business activities. Canamo is a Venezuelan company that was eager to export its products to the United States. However, it first had to obtain numerous certificates and licenses from various government authorities in Venezuela, a jumble of paperwork that can take two to six months to complete. Faced with this long and unpredictable process, Canamo all but abandoned hope of entering the U.S. market.[19] In China, getting a bank loan is arduous, especially for smaller firms. There are many government forms to complete, and it can take several months to register collateral with the appropriate authorities. As a result, many firms cannot obtain bank loans in a timely manner, delaying their ability to grow and flourish. While smaller businesses contribute some 60 percent of China's GDP, they account for only 15 percent of outstanding bank loans.[20]

Excessive bureaucracy is usually associated with lack of transparency, suggesting that legal and political systems may not be open and accountable to the public. Bribery, kickbacks, and extortion, especially in the public sector, cause difficulty for managers. Where anti-corruption laws are weak, managers may be tempted to offer bribes to ensure the success of business deals. In *Transparency International's* ranking of the most corrupt countries (www.transparency.org), emerging markets such as Russia, Venezuela, and the Philippines are among those with substantial corruption.[21]

Poor Physical Infrastructure

In advanced economies, high-quality roads, drainage systems, sewers, and electrical utilities are taken for granted. However, in emerging markets, such basic infrastructure is often sorely lacking. In India, many still do not have access to toilets and sewage treatment systems. Poor sanitation gives rise to widespread illness, and thousands of Indian children die every week from diarrheal illness. India's ports, roads, railways, and airports are insufficient to handle the massive volumes of cargo that enter and leave the country every day. Industrial cities like Bangalore and Pune regularly experience power outages that can last 24 hours or more.[22] The government is working to improve infrastructure, but MNEs often must build their own systems and employ creative solutions to support value-chain activities. In much of the world, firms find themselves building roads, installing localized energy sources, and developing other such systems in order to conduct business. A subsidiary of Tata Chemicals, part of India's giant Tata conglomerate, had to build its own road and railway infrastructure in Africa to support the firm's operations there.[23]

Partner Availability and Qualifications

Foreign firms should seek alliances with well-qualified local companies in countries characterized by inadequate legal and political frameworks. Through such partners, foreign firms can access local market knowledge, establish supplier and distributor networks, and develop key government contacts. However, partners that can provide these advantages are not always readily available in emerging markets, especially smaller ones.

Dominance of Family Conglomerates

Many emerging market economies are dominated by family-owned rather than publicly owned businesses. A **family conglomerate** (FC) is a large, highly diversified company that is privately owned. FCs operate in industries ranging from banking to construction to manufacturing. They control the majority of economic activity and employment in emerging markets like South Korea, where they are called *chaebols;* in India, where they are called *business houses;* in Latin America, where they are called *grupos;* and in Turkey, where they are called *holding companies.* Exhibit 10.11 illustrates some of the world's leading FCs.

A typical FC may hold the largest market share in each of several industries in its home country. In South Korea, the top thirty FCs account for nearly half the economy's assets and industry revenues. Samsung is perhaps the most famous Korean FC. In

Family conglomerate
A large, highly diversified company that is privately owned.

Family Conglomerate	Home Country	Primary Sectors	Distinction
ALFA	Mexico	Petrochemicals, machinery, foods, electronics, telecommunications	One of the world's largest producers of engine blocks and petrochemicals
Astra	Indonesia	Motor vehicles, financial services, heavy equipment, agribusiness, information technology	Largest distributor of automobiles and motorcycles in Indonesia
Ayala	Philippines	Real estate, financial services, utilities, telecommunications, electronics	The oldest and largest conglomerate in the Philippines
Hyundai	South Korea	Automobiles, shipbuilding	A truly global car company, selling Sonatas, Elantras, and other models in nearly 200 countries
Reliance Industries	India	Petroleum products, retailing, chemicals, textiles, solar energy systems	Named on Forbes, list as one of the "World's 100 Most Respected Companies"
Russian Standard	Russia	Alcoholic beverages, banking, life insurance	The leading premium producer of vodka in Russia
Sabanci Holding	Turkey	Cars, cement, energy, retailing, insurance, telecom, tires, plastic, hotels, paper, tobacco	Controls about seventy companies, which include Turkey's largest bank, Akbank
Tatung	Taiwan	Computers, liquid crystal display televisions, network devices, media players, home appliances	OEM manufacturer for HP, Acer, and Dell. World's largest producer of flat panels for the TV industry
Votorantim Group	Brazil	Finance, energy, agribusiness, mining, steel, paper	One of the largest industrial conglomerates in Latin America

Exhibit 10.11   A Sample of Leading Family Conglomerates

Turkey, the Koc Group accounts for about 20 percent of trading on the Istanbul Stock Exchange, and Sabanci provides more than 5 percent of Turkey's national tax revenue. FCs enjoy various competitive advantages in their home countries, such as government protection and support, extensive networks in various industries, superior market knowledge, and access to capital. Hyundai Group was an early mover in South Korea's auto industry and now holds the largest share of that country's car market. When foreign automakers tried to enter the market, they found Hyundai's advantages overwhelming.

An FC's origins and growth often derive from a special relationship with the government, which protects it by providing subsidies, loans, and tax incentives and setting up market-entry barriers to competitors. In some cases, the government may even launch the FC, just as the Siam Cement Group was launched by the government of Thailand. One of the largest FCs in Indonesia, the Bimantara Citra Group, got its start by selling its foreign oil allocations to the state-owned oil monopoly. The Group has long enjoyed a close relationship with the Indonesian government and secured numerous lucrative contracts. When the Hyundai Group in South Korea experienced a financial crisis, the Korean government and Hyundai's major creditors provided more than $300 million in assistance, including credit extension and short-term loans.[24]

FCs provide huge tax revenues and facilitate national economic development, which helps explain why governments eagerly support them. The fact that they dominate the commercial landscape in many emerging markets suggests they will be either formidable competitors or capable partners, possibly with much bargaining power. We return to this issue in the next section.

Strategies for Emerging Markets

The "cookie-cutter" strategies that MNEs developed decades ago and refined in mature advanced-economy markets are often inappropriate for the unique circumstances in emerging markets. Foreign firms must devise creative strategies to succeed.[25] For example, Toyota developed a line of inexpensive cars, costing about $7,000, for low-income countries. In India, it built a large factory to boost its share of the Indian car market to 10 percent.[26] Meanwhile, Renault and Volkswagen are building low-cost cars targeted to emerging markets such as China, India, and Russia.[27] In this section, we discuss three strategies that firms employ to succeed in emerging markets.

Customize Offerings to Unique Emerging Market Needs

Successful firms develop a deep understanding of the distinctive characteristics of buyers, local suppliers, and distribution channels in emerging markets. They build good relationships with the communities in which they operate, partly to better understand local conditions and partly to earn customer respect and loyalty. The ability to customize offerings and devise innovative business models depends largely on the firm's *flexibility* and entrepreneurial orientation. In emerging markets, many people are illiterate and fewer than one in four have regular access to the Internet and other computer-based systems.[28] Consequently, MNEs employ creative approaches to promote their offerings in local markets. Where suppliers and distribution channels are lacking, they develop their own infrastructure to obtain requisite raw materials and components or move finished goods to local buyers.[29]

Successful MNEs set prices appropriate for local conditions. In China, consumers favor text messaging on mobile phones, largely to keep communication costs low. Local competitor Tencent developed a free messenger service that captured most of the local market. In India, General Electric subsidiary GE Healthcare developed a superlightweight electrocardiograph machine that sells for just $1,500. The machine is targeted to doctors and clinics in poor areas. Low pricing allows health care providers to treat heart patients for a fraction of the cost required by earlier technologies. In Brazil, local airliner Gol Linhas Aereas Inteligentes (www.voegol.com.br) dominates the market for air travel. Gol succeeded by emphasizing smaller, newer aircraft that have lower operating and maintenance costs and by leveraging information technology to issue e-tickets and promote Internet-based sales. In Brazil, Gol has developed a deep understanding of the special needs of its customers, including lower income levels, simple travel requirements, and destinations in remote locations that hold limited interest for larger airlines.[30] Read the *Recent Grads in IB* feature on Andrew and Jamie Waskey, who learned to adapt themselves to life and work in various emerging markets.

Partner with Family Conglomerates

Family conglomerates are key players in their respective economies and have much capital to invest in new ventures. For example, most major FCs in Korea, as well as Koc and Sabanci in Turkey, Vitro in Mexico, and Astra in Indonesia, own their own financing operations in the form of insurance companies, banks, and securities brokers. Many FCs possess extensive distribution channels throughout their home countries. They have a deep understanding of local markets and customers.

For foreign firms that want to do business in emerging markets, FCs can make valuable venture partners.[31] By collaborating with an FC, the foreign firm can: (a) reduce the risks, time, and capital requirements of entering the market; (b) develop helpful relationships with governments and other key, local players; (c) target market opportunities more rapidly and effectively; (d) overcome infrastructure-related hurdles; and (e) leverage FC resources and local contacts.

There are many examples of successful FC partnering. Ford partnered with Kia to introduce the Sable line of cars in South Korea and benefited from Kia's strong distribution and after-service network. Digital Equipment Corporation (DEC) designated Tatung, a Taiwanese FC, as the main distributor of its workstations and client-server products in Taiwan. DEC benefited from Tatung's local experience and distribution network. In Turkey, Sabanci entered a joint venture with Danone, the French yogurt producer and owner of the Evian brand of bottled water. Danone brought ample technical knowledge in packaging and bottling and a reputation for healthy and environmentally friendly products, but it lacked information about the local market. As the Turkish market leader, Sabanci knew the market, retailers, and distributors. The collaboration helped make Danone the most popular bottled water in the first year.

Tenders Formal offers made by a buyer to purchase certain products or services.

Target Governments in Emerging Markets

In emerging markets and developing economies, government agencies and state-owned enterprises are an important customer group for three reasons. First, governments buy enormous quantities of products (such as computers, furniture, office supplies, motor vehicles) and services (such as architectural, legal, and consulting services). Second, state enterprises in areas like railways, airlines, banking, oil, chemicals, and steel buy goods and services from foreign companies. Third, the public sector influences the procurement activities of various private or semi-private corporations. In India the government works directly in planning housing projects. Construction firms lobby the government to gain access to promising deals to build apartments and houses for local dwellers.

Emerging market governments regularly announce **tenders**—formal offers made by a buyer to purchase certain products or services. A tender is also known as a *request for proposals (RFPs)*. Government agencies seek bids from suppliers

Emerging market governments are important potential customers for various products and services. Pictured here is a railway station in India.

Recent Grads in IB

Andrew & Jamie Waskey

Andrew's majors: Master of International Business (MIB), Master of Business Administration (MBA), Bachelor's in Spanish

Jamie's majors: Master of International Business (MIB), Bachelor's in International Affairs and Modern Language

Andrew's jobs since graduation: Various positions in international logistics at DHL and other firms; Marketing Intern at U.S. Department of Commerce (Shanghai, China)

Jamie's jobs since graduation: Research Manager at YouGov (Dubai, United Arab Emirates); Market Research Analyst at Delta Air Lines (Atlanta, GA); Market Research Intern at U.S. Department of Commerce (Buenos Aires, Argentina)

Objectives: Leverage and grow our international expertise while accelerating the global positioning of our firms and creating a life filled with adventure.

Andrew and Jamie Waskey met during their Masters of International Business (MIB) Program at Georgia State University. As undergraduates, both majored in international studies and Spanish. They enjoy traveling and learning languages, especially in emerging markets in Latin America. After completing college, Andrew worked for DHL, the international logistics company. His company funded his MIB degree, which provided an internship with DHL and the U.S. Department of Commerce office in Shanghai, China.

After completing her undergrad degree, Jamie worked for a non-profit organization. Desiring a career in international market research, she attended an MIB program. In her last semester, she completed an internship in Buenos Aires, Argentina, performing market research for the U.S. Department of Commerce there.

Andrew and Jamie got married after earning their MIB degrees and quickly secured international jobs in Atlanta with Delta Airlines and BlueLinx Corporation. Networking was key to obtaining these jobs and those that followed. Ultimately, they were both committed to living and working abroad. After sending his résumé to a firm in Dubai, Andrew obtained a position with MKM Holdings/The Wafi Group, in the firm's transportation division. In Dubai, he works as an internal consultant and also as a marketing and sales man-

ager. The highlight of the job is working with multicultural teams, overcoming communication challenges, and bringing positive results to the business units where he works.

Meanwhile, Jamie leveraged her contacts to secure a position with a UK-based market research consultancy in Dubai, YouGov. Jamie's favorite part of the job is the channel it provides for learning about and understanding the region's various cultures. She also gets to travel around the Middle East to places like Saudi Arabia.

Success Factors

- Set goals and be persistent in working toward them. If you want to work abroad, pursue your goal actively and remain fully committed.

- Know what you want to do. A clear professional path will facilitate your career search.

- Leverage contacts. Network with key people; leverage friends and other contacts in your field. Building a personal network is one of the most important factors in securing an international position.

Advice for an International Career

- Adopt a patient, flexible, and lighthearted outlook. The ability to maintain a positive atti-

tude and place challenges into perspective will facilitate and enrich your life abroad.

- Keep an open mind. In new environments where people do things differently, having an open mind helps you survive and thrive.

- Be curious about everything. Immersing yourself in the local culture will allow you to adapt easily and acquire a different lens for viewing the world.

Challenges

- Mastering cross-cultural communication and differing management structures
- Adapting to different living situations
- Making friends
- Striking a healthy work–life balance

What's Ahead

"For us, Dubai is just the start of a new lifestyle. We see ourselves as international citizens and expect to live in many places, with lots of adventure and unique challenges throughout our lives. We plan to have and raise our future children overseas so they will have a truly enriched upbringing and a natural global perspective. After Dubai, we want live in Shanghai, Singapore, Sydney, and beyond!"

to procure bulk commodities, equipment, and technology or to build power plants, highways, dams, and public housing. Vendors submit bids to the government to work on these projects.

Governments in emerging markets as well as developing countries often formulate economic development plans and annual programs to build or improve national infrastructure. To find vendors, the government follows specific buying procedures that lead to large, lucrative sales to international vendors. Securing major government contracts usually requires substantial competencies and resources. Firms competing for such projects assemble a team of managers and technical experts, especially when pursuing large deals. Governments prefer dealing with vendors that offer complete sales and service packages. The most successful vendors also offer financing for major sales, in the form of low-interest loans or grants. Governments are attracted by deals that create local jobs, employ local resources, reduce import dependence, and provide other country-level advantages.

Bechtel, Siemens, General Electric, Hitachi, and other major vendors regularly participate in bidding for global tenders from emerging market governments. Some of the largest construction projects include the Panama Canal expansion and the Channel tunnel between Britain and France. Another mega project, the Three Gorges Dam (www.ctgpc.com) on the Yangtze River in China, is expected to cost about $25 billion when completed. It will be the largest hydroelectric dam in the world. Numerous global contractors worked on the project, including ABB, Kvaerner, Voith, Siemens, and General Electric. In addition, the central government in China is spending nearly $250 billion through 2020 to lay 75,000 miles of new track for the country's crowded rail system. The project will increase China's existing rail network, which carries about one-quarter of the world's train cargo, by 150 percent. The mega-project is attracting interest from MNEs around the world.

Skillfully Challenge Emerging Market Competitors

As the opening vignette shows, the new global challengers possess various strengths that make them formidable competitors, such as low-cost labor, skilled workforces, government support, and family conglomerates. The global farm equipment industry was long dominated by venerable names such as John Deere and Komatsu. Recently, however, India's Mahindra & Mahindra (www.Mahindra.com) has been grabbing market share with brands such as the Mahindra 5500, a powerful, high-quality tractor that sells for far less than competing models. One dealership in the state of Mississippi, a market long dominated by John Deere, sold more than 300 Mahindras in just four months.[32]

Advanced-economy firms can counter in various ways. Initially, managers must conduct research to develop an understanding of the new challengers. It is critical to analyze the advantages of the emergent firms and how they are transforming the industry of the incumbent firm, which might have long enjoyed superior advantages in its industry in the target market. The next step is to acquire new capabilities that improve the firm's competitive advantages. For example, many incumbents are boosting their R&D to invent new, superior products. Others are partnering with competitors to pool resources against emerging market rivals. Incumbent firms can also match new global challengers at their own game by leveraging low-cost labor

Investing in emerging markets helps foster economic development and the creation of critical infrastructure, such as this freeway in Brazil.

and skilled workers in locations such as China, Mexico, and Eastern Europe. Many advanced economy firms partner with family conglomerates and others in emerging markets on critical value-chain activities such as R&D, manufacturing, and technical support.

 ## Corporate Social Responsibility in Emerging Markets and Developing Economies

Internationalizing firms increasingly facilitate economic development in emerging markets and developing economies. The most important trends here are fostering economic development with profitable modernization projects and facilitating entrepreneurship through small-scale loans. Such efforts are a form of corporate social responsibility because they help developing economies grow. In most cases they make good business sense, too. Let's examine these trends.

Foster Economic Development with Profitable Projects

Historically, few firms targeted poor countries because managers assumed there were few profitable opportunities. In reality, if firms market appropriate products and employ suitable strategies, they can earn substantial profits in emerging markets and developing economies. Unilever and P&G sell Sunsilk and Pantene shampoo for less than 2 cents per mini-sachet in India. Narayana Hrudayalaya is an insurance company that sells health insurance for less than 20 cents per person per month and has millions of customers. Amul, one of India's largest foodstuff firms, sells a wide range of food products to millions of poor people. To succeed, such firms had to devise new business models in manufacturing, packaging, distribution, and market reach.[33]

Every day in India, some 20 million people travel long distances for work or pleasure. Hotel accommodations generally fall into two categories: dirty, low-quality lodgings for the poor, or $350-per-night luxury hotels for the rich. To address the shortage of accommodations for middle-class travelers, Tata launched the Ginger chain of medium-priced hotels ($20–$40 per night; www.gingerhotels.com). To keep costs low, the hotels have minimal staff and few furnishings, but the rooms are clean and offer broadband Internet, flat-screen TV, and a work space. By devising an innovative business model, Tata captured a major, lucrative market in a poor country and simultaneously addressed an important need of lower-income travelers.[34]

Africans are using cell phones to leapfrog landline-based telecom technologies. Newly installed cellular networks promote economic development by facilitating dramatic gains in productivity. Here a Berber uses a cell phone in Morocco.

The Swedish telecommunications company Ericsson (www.ericsson.com) helped modernize the telecom infrastructure in rural parts of Tanzania by installing phone lines and cellular systems that meet the communication needs of households, companies, and aid agencies.[35] The emergence of a significant cell phone market in Africa led to the development of related industries and the launch of local firms that produce accessories, such as devices for recharging cell phone batteries. Ericsson's experience suggests that market-based solutions not only contribute to social and economic transformation but can be profitable as well. In India, Ericsson produces optical fiber cables for local markets. In Vietnam, it leveraged financing from the World Bank to expand the country's telecommunications network.

Advanced-economy firms that invest in developing economies and emerging markets support the development of infrastructure in transportation, communications, and energy systems. Firms create jobs and contribute to regional and sector development. Investment generates local tax revenues, which can be spent to improve living standards among the poor. Transferring technology and know-how promotes local innovation and enterprise. Many firms develop community-oriented social programs that foster economic and social development.

Microfinance to Facilitate Entrepreneurship

Microfinance provides small-scale financial services, such as "microcredit" and "microloans," that assist entrepreneurs to start businesses in poor countries. By taking small loans, frequently less than $100, small-scale entrepreneurs accumulate sufficient capital to launch successful businesses. This realization led economics professor Muhammad Yunus to found the Grameen Bank (www.grameen-info.org) in Bangladesh in 1974. Since then, millions of Grameen borrowers in Bangladesh have emerged from acute poverty. Aspiring entrepreneurs use the small loans to buy everything from cows that produce milk to sell in markets, to mobile phones that villagers can rent to make calls. Today, thousands of microfinance institutions provide loans to millions of poor people in developing economies worldwide.[36] The Grameen Bank now has more than 2,500 branches and has inspired similar poverty-reducing efforts, often sponsored by philanthropic organizations such as the Omidyar Network and the Bill and Melinda Gates Foundation.[37] For his efforts, Yunus was awarded the 2006 Nobel Peace Prize.

Historically, ordinary banks did not loan money to start-up entrepreneurs because such individuals lack collateral, steady employment, and a verifiable credit history. But because a small amount of money can have a dynamic, ripple effect on many lives in a village, microfinance holds the potential to improve the lives of millions. Recently, mainstream banks have begun to view microfinance as a source of future growth. Various institutions now offer small-scale insurance, mortgage lending, and other financial services in poor countries worldwide. In Mexico, Cemex's *Patrimonio Hoy* program (www.cemexmexico.com) has widened access to cement and other building materials by organizing low-income customers into groups of three families that monitor each other's progress in constructing their own homes and collectively paying off debts at regular intervals. Patrimonio Hoy and other Cemex programs have made home ownership a reality for tens of thousands of low-income Mexican families.[38]

The Special Case of Africa

The economies of China and India have grown rapidly and Latin America has experienced at least moderate growth, lifting millions above subsistence living. By contrast, much of Africa has stagnated and even regressed in terms of trade, investment, and per-capita income. Indeed, Africa's GDP has improved little since the 1960s. Africa is afflicted by illiteracy, malnutrition, and inadequate sanitation and water supply. Unemployment is stubbornly high in many areas.[39]

Despite these tendencies, however, Africa is beginning to transform itself. Several African countries have begun to experience economic success, with annual GDP growth now approaching 5 percent per year. Ghana is becoming a regional hub for financial and technological services. Nigeria is enjoying a boom in oil and banking. Zambia is developing strengths in mining and agriculture. Tanzania is investing in major power generation projects. Kenya has developed a large and diversified economy. Stock markets in Botswana, Nigeria, and Zambia are enjoying record levels of investment.[40] Botswana's diamond trade is experiencing a boom, thanks to investments from South Africa's De Beers company. De Beers is the world's largest diamond producer and recently entered a 50-50 joint venture with Botswana interests to develop the country's mining industry. In the course of this effort, De Beers built roads and schools, helped devise solutions for preventing and treating HIV/AIDS, and supported numerous programs to develop the economy in Botswana.[41]

Improving conditions in Africa are supported by two major trends. First, compared to earlier times, African governments are doing a better job of managing their national economies. Policy reforms in various countries, including Botswana, Ghana, Kenya, Mozambique, Nigeria, Tanzania, Uganda, and Zambia, emphasize economic and political freedom. In these countries, better governance is helping drive economic success. Second, much of Africa has begun to receive a steady inflow of direct investment from abroad. China, India, and other emerging market firms are investing billions in Africa to manufacture and market various products and services. Inspired by such activity, more firms from Europe, Japan, and the United States are exploring Africa for business and investment opportunities. All told, annual inflows of FDI and loans now exceed $50 billion per year. Much of this stems from the commodities boom, in which foreign firms are investing in Africa's oil industry.

Without reliable phone service, workers cannot find jobs and firms cannot operate efficiently. While Africa long lacked substantial landline telephony, cell phones are proving vital to the continent's development. Africans are using cell phones to leapfrog landline-based telecom technologies. Newly installed cellular networks promote economic development by facilitating dramatic gains in worker and company productivity. A study by the business consultancy McKinsey found that the economic impact of cellular telephony in poor countries is up to four times the value of the wireless operators alone.[42] Orascom, Millicom, and other telecom firms are establishing cell phone operations from Egypt to South Africa, applying business models that allow them to earn profits even in countries where people live on less than $2 per day.

Another factor in Africa's recent success is microfinance. Small African entrepreneurs can increasingly access small-scale loans to develop businesses ranging from cotton plantations to major construction projects. South Africa-based Blue Financial Services has more than 170 branches throughout Africa, offering small loans that local entrepreneurs use to develop new businesses.[43]

One promising investment target in Africa is the food processing sector. Firms are investing to profit from the region's abundant agricultural sector and food-producing potential. Companies are also beginning to address Africa's massive health care needs. Worldwide, Africa bears the burden of about one-quarter of all disease, yet has only 3 percent of the health care workers. Most Africans cannot obtain adequate medical care. Every day, thousands die from treatable or preventable ailments such as malaria, tuberculosis, and HIV/AIDS. Governments and international agencies cannot provide for all Africa's health care needs. However, MNEs are finding market opportunities in the private sector. By employing innovative business models adapted to local conditions, they play a key role in addressing the continent's medical needs and generate profits as well. For example, establishing chains of low-cost clinics would go far in addressing Africa's health care needs.[44]

The application of business models such as local entrepreneurship, microfinance, targeted marketing, and MNE direct investing holds enormous potential for addressing poverty in Africa.[45] In addition to telecommunications, agriculture, and health care, private firms have an important role to play in Africa by finding profitable ways to address needs in education, banking, electricity, and infrastructure development. As improvements are made in these areas, further investment to develop African economies will surely follow.

Critics charge that MNEs do much harm in Africa, such as exploiting local resources, operating sweatshops, and generating pollution. Where do you stand? Can MNEs successfully address poverty and other problems in Africa, or do such firms do more harm than good? Use the Ethical Framework in Chapter 5 to analyze this question.

Tata Group: India's New Global Challenger

Tata, India's largest company, operates in seven distinct business sectors, including automobiles, chemicals, IT, consumer products, engineering, and consulting. Altogether, Tata comprises more than 90 separate firms. The chairman of Tata Group is Ratan Tata, the charismatic descendent of the company founder. Now in his seventies, he has emerged as a popular and respected corporate titan, known around the world. An avid aviator, he often flies his own Falcon 2000 jet to meetings around India.

As the group's chief visionary and dealmaker, Mr. Tata has been aggressively expanding the Tata Group into world markets. For example, one of the group subsidiaries, Tata Steel, recently purchased the Dutch-British steel giant Corus Group, for $13 billion. The move boosted the firm's steel-making capacity fivefold. In 2008, another group subsidiary, Tata Motors, became the focus of world attention when it acquired Jaguar and Land Rover from Ford for $2.3 billion. Tata Motors launched the Nano in 2009 which, at approximately $2,500, is the world's cheapest car. The Nano addresses a longtime dream of Ratan Tata to develop reliable but supercheap automobiles, revolutionize the global auto industry, and make India a major economic power. "Nano" means "small" in Gujarati, the language of Tata's founders.

Background on the Tata Group

Founded in 1868 in Bombay as a textile trading company, Tata gradually expanded into hotels, power plants, chemicals, steel production, and several other industries. The government of India long discouraged international trade by imposing high trade barriers and bureaucracy. As these restrictions loosened in the 1990s, Tata's international operations flourished. Tata Motors began producing cars in joint ventures with Fiat and Daimler-Benz. Tata bought 30 percent of the coal subsidiaries of an Indonesian mining company to supply coal for Tata's power plant in India. Altogether, the Tata Group has factories in numerous emerging markets, including Kenya, South Korea, Malaysia, Russia, and Thailand.

As India's biggest firm, Tata has many competitive advantages, including vast financial resources and access to capital on favorable terms; strong corporate image; connections with countless high-quality business partners; competitive cost structure, thanks to the huge, low-cost Indian labor pool; and long-standing relationships with national and state governments in India. In the auto industry, Tata Motors' reputation is growing. It counts on sister subsidiary Tata Steel to continuously provide steel to manufacture Nanos and other cars, a key advantage. The purchase of Corus Group, in addition to increasing steel capacity, also greatly expanded Tata's access to automakers across Europe and the United States.

Tata is arguably the most important of the new global challenger firms charging out of big emerging markets such as China, Brazil, India, and Russia. The emerging giants tap abundant low-cost labor, tech talent, and mineral resources to increasingly target the world's biggest growth markets. Brimming with cash and confidence, they export innovative business models honed in some of the world's most challenging markets. Governments and state-owned enterprises influence the procurement activities of corporations. Tata capitalizes on its family conglomerate networks to enhance its position as government supplier in numerous business sectors.

Tata Motors

Today Tata Motors, or "Tamo," is one of India's largest motor vehicle companies. At present, Tamo's main market is India, but the firm also operates in other countries, especially in Asia. In 2008, Tamo unveiled the Nano, the world's cheapest car. Manufactured in India, the Nano seats up to five people and gets extremely good gas mileage. Initially, the car was targeted to India's middle class, the approximately 200 million people who earn $20,000 or more per year.

About one-quarter of all cars and trucks sold in India bear the Tamo brand. The firm's next logical target will be countries outside India, especially emerging markets that provide key growth opportunities. Tamo aims to transfer its vast experience in India to markets in Africa, Latin America, and the Middle East. In Asia, the countries of Indonesia, Thailand, and Vietnam appear ripe for sales of a cheap car. Millions of low-income consumers worldwide would love to own a car, but until the launch of the Nano, they have had few or no alternatives. The acquisition of Jaguar and Land Rover has increased Tamo's visibility through globally recognized brands and provided an entree to Europe and the United States.

Challenges

Tamo faces numerous challenges in making the Nano a success. For one, despite its very low price tag, management needs to market the Nano as an aspirational status symbol. Tamo will need to provide attractive financing packages for potential owners. The Nano has numerous other challenges, including growing competition and the global recession.

In India, 70 percent of the population still lives in the countryside, and the transition of land from agrarian to industrial use often meets with angry protest. In 2008, Tamo was forced to abandon construction of a factory in West Bengal, India, intended to manufacture the Nano. Protesters surrounded the new Nano plant and blocked roads to prevent workers or deliveries from reaching the facility. In Calcutta, activists burned the Nano in effigy. Violence and threats to worker safety ensued for months during construction of the plant. West Bengal politicos encouraged labor unrest, leading to capital flight and making the region unfriendly to business. Despite being 80 percent complete and costing $350 million, Tamo had to abandon the plant due to violent protests from farmers and political activists. Production of the Nano was moved to another location in India.

Throughout India, Tamo works continuously to satisfy government authorities. India has a reputation for "suffocating bureaucracy" and its civil servants are among the least efficient in Asia. The country is awash in trade barriers, business regulations, and administrative hurdles. Many commodities can be imported only after receiving government approval. Import tariffs on parts and components can be substantial, often exceeding 25 percent. Licensing fees, testing procedures, and other hurdles are expensive and time-consuming. The commercial environment in India is still evolving and poses numerous hurdles for firms that do business there.

Pollution and Overcrowding in India

Growing car ownership is severely straining India's already congested urban infrastructure. If the Nano proves a big success, India's road network seems unable to absorb millions of new cars. Burgeoning car ownership in India and China are straining the world's already self-destructive carbon footprint. India suffers from severe pollution. Throughout southern Asia, a thick brown cloud of particulate continually blocks the sun, altering weather patterns and causing health problems. The cloud is a by-product of emissions from coal-fired power plants, cars and trucks, and wood-burning stoves. As India industrializes, the country's water, air, and soil are under increasing environmental pressure. Most Indians make their living from farming, and pollution has reduced growth yields of rice, wheat, maize, and sorghum.

Competitors

In addition to Tamo, several automakers have plans to enter the cheap car market in India. For example, Renault, Nissan, and India's Bajaj Motors plan to jointly build a $2,500 car. Nissan CEO Carlos Ghosn aims to make emerging markets a cornerstone of his firm's plans for global growth. Ford, Hyundai, Toyota, and General Motors are all developing inexpensive, small cars for

emerging markets. Several Chinese companies already manufacture various car models, both for export and domestic consumption, and a few firms are exploring ultra-cheap options. Japan's Suzuki sells the Maruti 800 in India, retailing for about $4,500.

Global Financial Crisis and Opportunities for Emerging Global Giants

Just as automotive sales declined in recent years, many automakers have launched new models, which boosted global competition. Tamo is well positioned to weather the recent global financial crisis. First, it enjoys low-cost production capacity, partly based on employing inexpensive labor in India. Second, the firm has significant experience in emerging markets, which are growing rapidly. By contrast, advanced-economy markets are largely saturated. Third, as the global financial crisis unfolded, many advanced-economy MNEs retrenched and focused more heavily on their home markets, especially in Europe and North America. For example, bankruptcy and restructuring led General Motors to refocus on the United States.

Corporate Social Responsibility

For decades Tata has promoted good works in India. Tata Steel spends millions every year on education, health, and agricultural development projects. It has developed irrigation systems that allow Indian farmers to grow cash crops. The firm has built schools, hospitals, and electrical plants and undertaken countless other socially responsible projects throughout India.

Similarly, Tamo undertakes various charitable activities in the communities where it operates. In 2008 Tamo acquired a major stake in Miljo Grenland/Innovasjon, a Norwegian electric car producer. Tamo is leveraging Miljo's know-how to launch a new electric vehicle, the Indica.

Another group company, Tata BP Solar, makes rooftop solar-electric systems for buildings. The firm offers low-cost, solar-powered water pumps, refrigerators, and lanterns for areas that normally lack electricity. It has fitted 50,000 homes with $300 systems that can power lights, hot plates, and TV sets.

Conclusion

In emerging markets and developing economies, family conglomerates are leveraging various advantages to dominate home-country markets. Today, the conglomerates are applying these same advantages to extend their reach to markets worldwide. Tata's numerous home country resources provide the firm with substantial competitive advantages and should allow it to perform well and capture market share from incumbent players in markets around the world.

AACSB: Reflective Thinking Skills, Ethical Understanding and Reasoning Abilities

Case Questions

1. Describe the various advantages that firms like Tata employ to become large industrial conglomerates. How can Tata use these same advantages to succeed in foreign markets?

2. What makes emerging markets attractive for international business? Discuss emerging markets as target markets, as platforms for manufacturing, and as sourcing destinations.

3. What is the relationship between trade barriers, bureaucracy, country risk, and the emergence of Tata as a major player in world trade? What is the role of declining government intervention in Tata's success in India and its ability to internationalize? What should Tata do to manage country risk in India and other emerging markets?

4. Given growth rates and other characteristics of emerging markets, what markets should Tamo target for sales of Nano cars? What country-level factors should Tamo consider as it evaluates the potential of various emerging markets?

5. As it prepares to expand abroad, how can Tamo improve its corporate social responsibility toward future customers in emerging markets? What can Tamo do to minimize the impact of its operations on the natural environment in Asia and elsewhere?

SOURCES: M. Aguiar et al., *The 2009 BCG 100 New Global Challengers*, Boston Consulting Group, retrieved from http://www.bcg.com; B. Coffin, "Cheap Cars, Costly Protests," *Risk Management*, December 2008, pp. 14–15; "Up to Their Necks in It," *Economist*, July 17, 2008, p. 42; "World Business: Emerging-Market Multinationals: Not So Nano," *Economist*, March 27, 2009, retrieved from http://www.economist.com; "The Big Chill: The Car Industry," *Economist*, January 16, 2009, p. 68; Corporate profiles on various Tata group companies from http://www.hoovers.com; D. Jain, "Tata Motors: Smooth Ride with a Few Bumps," *Macquarie Research Equities*, August 9, 2007; A. Kazmin, "Tata Reroutes 'People's Car' to the Safety of Gujarat," *Financial Times*, October 8, 2008, p. 31; V. Nair, "Tata Nano, World's Cheapest Car, Won't Help Pay Debt," 2009, retrieved from http://www.bloomberg.com; A. Revkin, "On the Road toward One Billion Cars," *New York Times*, January 10, 2008, p. 9; S. Sen, "Tata Group: Transforming the Sleeping Giant," *The ICFAI Journal of Business Strategy* 6, no. 1 (2009): 31–45; C. Squatriglia, "Does a $2,500 Tata Nano in India Mean Higher Gas Prices and More CO2 Everywhere Else?" *Autopia*, February 6, 2008, retrieved from http://www.wired.com/autopia/2008/02/2500-cars-in-in/; Tata, various annual reports and filings on Tata group companies, from http://www.tata.com, http://www.sec.gov, and http://www.tatanano.com; Thomson Financial, various summaries on the Tata group, 2008.

NOTE: This case was authored by Marta Szabo White, Ph.D., Georgia State University.

CHAPTER ESSENTIALS

Key Terms

advanced economies, p. 290
developing economies, p. 290
emerging markets, p. 290
family conglomerate, p. 305

global sourcing, p. 300
new global challengers, p. 296
outsourcing, p. 300
privatization, p. 295

purchasing power parity (PPP), p. 300
tenders, p. 307
transition economies, p. 295

Summary

In this chapter, you learned about:

1. Emerging markets, developing economies and advanced economies

Advanced economies are post-industrial countries characterized by high per-capita income, highly competitive industries, and well-developed commercial infrastructure. They consist mainly of post-industrial societies of Western Europe, Japan, the United States, Canada, Australia, and New Zealand. The **developing economies** are low-income countries that have not yet industrialized. Due to low buying power and limited resources, their participation in international business is limited. The **emerging markets** are former developing economies on their way to becoming advanced economies. Located mainly in Asia, Eastern Europe, and Latin America, emerging markets are transforming themselves into market-driven economies by liberalizing trade and investment policies, privatizing industries, and forming economic blocs. Brazil, Russia, India, and China are leading exemplars.

2. What makes emerging markets attractive for international business

Emerging markets represent promising export markets for products and services. They are ideal bases for manufacturing activities. They are popular destinations for **global sourcing**—procurement of products and services from foreign locations.

3. **Assessing the true potential of emerging markets**

    In the early stages of market research, to reliably estimate demand in emerging markets, managers examine three important statistics: per-capita income, size of the middle class, and market potential indicators. Income should be adjusted for **purchasing power parity**.

4. **Risks and challenges of emerging markets**

    Emerging markets pose various risks, including political instability, inadequate legal and institutional frameworks, lack of transparency, and inadequate intellectual property protection. **Family conglomerates** are large, diversified, family-owned businesses that dominate many emerging markets and represent formidable rivals and attractive choices for partnerships.

5. **Strategies for emerging markets**

    Firms should adapt strategies and tactics to suit unique, local conditions. Some firms succeed by partnering with family conglomerates. Governments are often major buyers, but require specific strategies. Successful advanced-economy firms conduct research and acquire capabilities specific to target markets and leverage advantages available in emerging markets, such as low-cost labor.

6. **Corporate social responsibility in emerging markets and developing economies**

    In emerging markets and developing economies, leading firms undertake activities that facilitate economic development. They can serve low-income countries with inexpensive, specifically designed products and services, and community involvement. Microfinance, availability of small-scale loans to emerging-market entrepreneurs, is promoting entrepreneurial initiatives.

7. **The special case of Africa**

    Although Africa long stagnated in terms of income, trade, and investment, several African countries are beginning to experience economic success. Much of the continent has begun to receive substantial investment from abroad. Africa is benefiting from microfinance and widespread diffusion of mobile telephones. For MNEs, agriculture, health care, and several other industries are promising investment targets. Firms can succeed by applying innovative business models.

Test Your Comprehension AACSB: Reflective Thinking Skills, Ethical Understanding and Reasoning Abilities

1. What are advanced economies, developing economies, and emerging markets? What are the major distinctions among these three country groups?

2. Explain why firms want to do business in emerging markets. What makes these markets attractive?

3. How can managers estimate the true market potential of emerging markets?

4. Describe the various risks and challenges encountered in emerging markets.

5. What is a family conglomerate (FC)? How do FCs differ from publicly owned companies? What role do FCs play in emerging markets?

6. Describe the process for selling to foreign governments and state enterprises.

7. Doing business in emerging markets involves strategies that are often distinct from those of other international venues. What types of business approaches can firms use when doing business in emerging markets?

8. How can firms show corporate social responsibility in emerging markets and developing economies?

9. How is Africa evolving? What can businesses do to support the development of Africa?

Apply Your Understanding AACSB: Communication Abilities, Reflective Thinking Skills

1. Suppose you work at Microsoft in their Xbox video game console division. Microsoft has long targeted Xbox to the advanced economies, especially in North America and Europe. Management would like to sell more Xbox 360s to emerging markets. What characteristics of emerging markets might make them attractive for sales of the Xbox? Identify the major risks and challenges that Microsoft might encounter in selling the Xbox 360 to emerging markets.

2. CBKing has been trying to export its products to various emerging markets and has enjoyed little success so far. You know a lot about emerging markets and have been anxious to share your views with CBKing's president, Mr. Roger Wilko. What strategies would you recommend Roger pursue in doing business with emerging markets? You conclude there is substantial demand among military and government agencies. Explain how your firm should go about selling to emerging market customers.

3. *Ethical Dilemma:* One mission of the International Monetary Fund (IMF) is to help poor countries overcome economic crises by providing loans and policy advice. During the global financial crisis, many countries suffered corporate bankruptcies, collapsing economies, and political turmoil. These effects particularly hurt Ukraine, which requested massive loans and other financial assistance from the IMF. Note, however, that taxpayers in advanced economies generally foot the bill for IMF activities, which often run to billions of dollars. Critics argue the IMF rescues countries that fail to put in place robust regulatory systems and responsible fiscal and monetary policies. The critics assert that economic prosperity is best determined by market forces and free enterprise. They claim that reviving poor countries is too costly and discourages responsible behavior because, if local officials know they can count on bailouts from wealthy countries, they are less likely to enact policies that ensure stable economic growth. Suppose you are a financial officer at the IMF. Where do you stand? Using the Ethical Framework in Chapter 5, decide if the IMF should bail out Ukraine.

globalEDGE Internet Exercises

(http://globalEDGE.msu.edu)

AACSB: Analytic Skills, Reflective Thinking Skills, Ethical Understanding and Reasoning Abilities

Refer to Chapter 1, page 62, for instructions on how to access and use globalEDGE™.

1. The World Bank sponsors the Doing Business database (www.doingbusiness.org), which provides measures of business regulations and their enforcement in 175 countries. Firms can use these measures to analyze specific regulations that enhance or constrain investment, productivity, and growth. Visit the site and choose two emerging markets. Then answer the following questions: (a) How well does each country rank in terms of ease of starting a business, employing workers, and trading across borders? (b) How long does it take to start a business? (c) How much time does it take to pay taxes? (d) Review other statistics and identify which country is most friendly for doing business.

2. Using globalEDGE™, find the "country commercial guide" for two emerging markets of your choice. Compare the two countries on the following dimensions: "leading sectors for exports and investment" and "marketing products and services." (a) Which of the two countries is more promising for marketing laptop computers? (b) Which of the two countries is more promising for sales of portable electrical power generators? (c) Which of the two countries is more promising for sales of telecommunications equipment? Be sure to justify your answers.

3. The three groups of countries described in this chapter can be contrasted in terms of degree of economic freedom. Economic freedom refers to the extent to which economic activities in a nation can take place freely and without government restrictions. The Heritage Foundation provides an *Index of Economic Freedom* (www.heritage.org) that considers such factors as trade policies, extent of government intervention, monetary and fiscal policies, inward foreign direct investment, property rights, and infrastructure for banking and finance. Countries are classified into categories such as free, mostly free, mostly unfree, and repressed. How are emerging market and developing economies classified? What is the relationship between market liberalization and economic development? How might market liberalization contribute to reducing poverty in developing economies?

CHAPTER 11

The International Monetary and Financial Environment

The Complex Monetary and Financial Relationship between China and the United States

China and the United States are large economies, providing nearly half the world's economic growth in recent years. The two countries represent the world's most important bilateral economic and trading relationship. Each has a distinct role: China is the world's leading product manufacturer, and the United States is one of the wealthiest consumer and industrial markets.

China owes much of its international trading success to the value of the renminbi, its national currency (also called the yuan). For years the renminbi has been cheap by world standards, making Chinese products inexpensive to foreign importers. The value of the renminbi is set at a fixed exchange rate to the U.S. dollar and other world currencies. The Chinese government intervenes regularly in currency markets to ensure that this fixed rate is maintained. The relatively low value of the renminbi has stimulated huge demand for Chinese-made products, a major cause of the United States' persistent trade deficit with China.

Large-scale exporting has led to massive capital inflows, making China the world's biggest holder of "foreign exchange reserves" (money that nations receive from their international transactions, such as exporting). China has used much of these reserves to invest in U.S. government securities, helping to finance the United

States' huge government budget deficits. In 2006, China purchased nearly half the issues of U.S. Treasury securities, totaling $87 billion and making China the world's largest investor in U.S. government debt. The United States needs Chinese capital to finance its trade and budget deficits. Simultaneously, China needs the United States to buy the exports responsible for much of China's wealth.

China's fixed exchange-rate policy is one of the hottest topics in international finance. Some economists argue that the system has been good for China, stabilizing its currency and giving foreign investors the confidence to build factories in China. But other economists have argued that China's fixed rate distorts trade and investment flows. They believe China should allow its currency to float freely in response to market forces. Partly because of pressure from the United States and other countries, China revalued the renminbi slightly in 2005 to make it more expensive relative to the dollar.

When the Chinese government increased the renminbi's value, its products became more expensive to foreigners, reducing world demand for Chinese exports. Currency revaluations of this sort can lower a country's earnings and trigger an economic recession. Because China is highly integrated into the world economy, a

Chinese recession could trigger economic problems in the United States and other countries. A slowing Chinese economy could also reduce China's appetite for U.S. imports. The effect could be substantial—China is the world's biggest consumer of pork, cotton, coal, aluminum, steel, washing machines, cell phones, and a host of other products.

China and the United States are inextricably linked in a complex relationship, critical to the economic health of both countries. How this relationship evolves over time will determine, to a great extent, the future prosperity of the world economy.

SOURCES: Areddy, James. (2007). "China's Rate Boost Shows Economy's Vigor," *Wall Street Journal*, March 19, p. A2; Batson, Andrew. (2007). "China Says It Won't Rattle Markets," *Wall Street Journal*, March 17–18, p. A10; *Economist*, (2004). "A Survey of the World Economy: The Dragon and the Eagle," October 2, special section; Field, Alan. (2005). "China Revalues Yuan," *Journal of Commerce*, July 21, p. 1; Morici, Peter. (2005). "Why China Should Revalue the Yuan," *Journal of Commerce*, July 4, p. 1; Norris, Floyd. (2007). "Washington Dares to Challenge the Lender It Depends Upon," *New York Times*, April 14, p. C3; *Wall Street Journal* (2005). "China's Currency Bow," July 22, p. A12.

International business transactions take place within the global monetary and financial systems. When people think of international trade, they invariably think of trade in products and services. However, the markets for foreign exchange and capital are much larger. Firms regularly trade the U.S. dollar, European euro, Japanese yen, and other leading currencies to meet their international business obligations. In this chapter, we explore the monetary and financial structure that makes trade and investment possible. We explain the nature, organization, and functions of the foreign exchange market and the monetary and financial issues that confront internationalizing firms.

Exchange Rates and Currencies in International Business

There are more than 150 currencies in use around the world today. Cross-border transactions occur through an exchange of these currencies between buyers and sellers. A currency is a form of money and a unit of exchange. The tendency of each country to prefer to use its own unique currency complicates international business transactions. When buying a product or service from a Mexican supplier, for example, you must convert your own currency into Mexican pesos to pay the supplier. The currency regime is being simplified in some locations, however. As we saw in the opening vignette, numerous countries in Europe use the euro. Other countries, such as Ecuador, Panama, and East Timor, have adopted the U.S. dollar as their currency, in a process known as "dollarization."

Exchange rate The price of one currency expressed in terms of another; the number of units of one currency that can be exchanged for another.

The **exchange rate**—the price of one currency expressed in terms of another—varies over time. It links different national currencies so that buyers and sellers can make international price and cost comparisons. Exhibit 11.1 provides the exchange rates for the U.S. dollar and a sample of other currencies on a recent day. The values of these national currencies, and thus their exchange rates, fluctuate constantly. This fluctuation means managers must keep three things in mind: (1) the prices the firm charges can be quoted in the firm's currency or in the currencies of its foreign customers; (2) the firm and its customers can use the exchange rate as it stands on the date of each transaction, or they can agree to use a specific exchange rate; and (3) because several months can pass between placement and delivery of an order, fluctuations in the exchange rate during that time can cost or earn the firm money.

Currency risk Potential harm that arises from changes in the price of one currency relative to another.

These and similar complications in international transactions create **currency risk**, the potential harm that can arise from changes in the price of one currency relative to another. It is one of the four types of international business risk we illustrated in Exhibit 1.6 on page 47. If you buy from a supplier whose currency is appreciating against yours,

	Currency per One U.S. Dollar	U.S. Dollars per Unit of Currency
Australian dollar	1.083	0.924
Brazilian real	1.786	0.560
British pound	0.658	1.520
Canadian dollar	1.008	0.992
Chinese yuan	6.825	0.147
European euro	0.752	1.330
Indian rupee	44.472	0.022
Japanese yen	93.082	0.011
Mexican peso	12.322	0.081
New Zealand dollar	1.424	0.702
Norwegian kroner	5.980	0.167
Saudi riyal	3.750	0.267
Singapore dollar	1.396	0.716
South African rand	7.342	0.136
South Korean won	1,123.290	0.001
Turkish lira	1.505	0.665

Exhibit 11.1 U.S. Dollar Exchange Rates for a Sample of Currencies as of April 9, 2010

SOURCE: x-rates.com

you may need to pay a larger amount of your currency to complete the purchase. If you expect payment from a customer whose currency is depreciating against your own, currency risk also arises, because you may receive a smaller amount of your currency if the sale price was expressed in the currency of the customer. Of course, if the foreign currency fluctuates in your favor, you may gain a windfall. Exporters or importers usually are not in the business of making money from currency speculation; rather, they worry about *losses* that arise from currency fluctuations.

Exporters and licensors also face risk because foreign buyers must either pay in a foreign currency or convert their currency into that of the vendor. Foreign direct investors face currency risk because they both receive payments and incur obligations in foreign currencies.

Convertible and Nonconvertible Currencies

A *convertible currency* can be readily exchanged for other currencies. The most readily convertible are called *hard currencies*. These are strong, stable currencies that are universally accepted and used most often for international transactions, such as the U.S. dollar, Japanese yen, Canadian dollar, British pound, and European euro. Nations prefer to hold hard currencies as reserves because of their strength and stability in comparison to other currencies.

A currency is *nonconvertible* when it is not acceptable for international transactions. Some governments may not allow their currency to be converted into a foreign currency in order to preserve their supply of hard currencies, such as the U.S. dollar or the euro, or to avoid the problem of capital flight. **Capital flight** is the rapid sell-off by residents or foreigners of their holdings in a nation's currency or other assets, usually in response to a domestic crisis that causes them to lose confidence in the country's economy. The investors exchange their holdings in the weakening currency for those of another, often a hard currency. Capital flight from a country diminishes its ability to service debt and pay for imports.

Capital flight The rapid sell-off by residents or foreigners of their holdings in a nation's currency or other assets, usually in response to a domestic crisis that causes investors to lose confidence in the country's economy.

As national economies have become more integrated in recent years, capital flight has become a relatively common occurrence. For example, at least $40 billion in roubles were reportedly withdrawn from Russia as foreign investors lost confidence in the Russian economy in the mid-2000s. Since coming to power in Venezuela, President Hugo Chavez has confiscated foreign company assets and engaged in questionable financial deals. Dubious governance, depreciating currency, and other economic problems have panicked foreign investors and Venezuela's wealthier citizens, who have withdrawn their liquid assets from the country's economy.[1] In some developing economies, currency convertibility is so strict that firms may avoid using currencies altogether and receive payments in goods; in other words, they engage in barter.

Foreign Exchange Markets

A critical function of money is to facilitate payment for the products and services the firm sells. Getting paid in your own country is straightforward: The U.S. dollar is accepted throughout the United States, the euro is widely used in Europe, and the Japanese need only yen when transacting with each other. But suppose a Canadian needs to pay a Japanese, or a Japanese needs to pay an Italian, or an Italian needs to pay a Canadian. What then? The Canadian wants to be paid in Canadian dollars, the Japanese wants to be paid in yen, and the Italian wants to be paid in euros. All these currencies are known as *foreign exchange*. **Foreign exchange** represents all forms of money that are traded internationally, including foreign currencies, bank deposits, checks, and electronic transfers. Foreign exchange resolves the problem of making international payments and facilitates international investment and borrowing among firms, banks, and governments.

Currencies such as the U.S. dollar, yen, and euro are traded on the **foreign exchange market**, the global marketplace for buying and selling national currencies. The market has no fixed location. Rather, trading occurs through continuous buying and selling among banks, currency traders, governments, and other exchange agents located worldwide. International business would be impossible without foreign exchange and the foreign exchange market.

Foreign exchange All forms of money that are traded internationally, including foreign currencies, bank deposits, checks, and electronic transfers.

Foreign exchange market The global marketplace for buying and selling national currencies.

Exchange Rates Fluctuate Constantly

In 1999, eleven EU countries switched to the euro, eliminating the problem of exchange rate fluctuations in trade and investment with each other. By 2010, sixteen member states were participating in the euro zone. Other countries in Latin America, the Caribbean, and the Middle East have opted to use a regional or hard currency. The challenges posed by fluctuating exchange rates motivate countries to coordinate their monetary policies, at regular meetings of the Bank for International Settlements, the G8 (the group of eight major industrial countries), and other such entities. Governments attempt to manage exchange rates by buying and selling hard currencies and by keeping inflation in check. However, the foreign exchange market has become so huge and its shifts so fluid that even major governments have difficulty controlling exchange rate movements.

Sometimes exchange rate fluctuations between the U.S. dollar, the euro, and other currencies are dramatic, as illustrated in Exhibit 11.2. In 2008, the Indian rupee was trading at 40 rupees to the U.S. dollar. By mid-2010, the rate had fluctuated to 48 rupees to the dollar, a depreciation of nearly 25 percent. More rupees to the dollar means the rupee is worth less in terms of the dollar; hence the rupee had depreciated in value. Implications for international business with India were substantial. In the span of only 18 months, Indian firms perceived a significant upturn in their exports, as Indian products became less expensive in dollar terms. Meanwhile, as rupee-buying power for dollars decreased, U.S. firms experienced a decline in their exports to India.[2] Exhibit 11.2 also shows that the French franc is one of the euro zone-country currencies that was taken out of circulation and replaced by the euro.

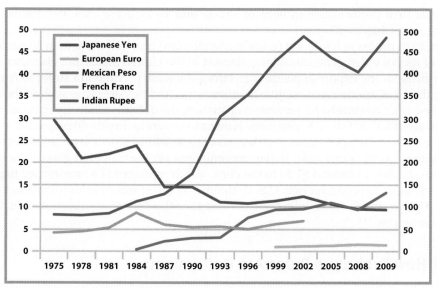

Exhibit 11.2 Selected Exchange Rates against the U.S. Dollar over Time
SOURCES: IMF and World Bank data.

NOTE: Right-hand scale is for Japanese yen; left-hand scale is for all other currencies. For example, in 2008, the Mexican peso was trading at 10 pesos per one U.S. dollar. The euro became the common currency of various countries in the European Union in 1999, replacing the French franc and other European currencies. The Mexican peso was revalued by government action in 1983.

Fluctuating exchange rates affect both firms and customers. Suppose today the euro/dollar exchange rate is €1 = $1; that is, for a European to buy one U.S. dollar, she or he must pay one euro. Next, suppose that during the coming year the exchange rate goes to €1.50 = $1. Now the dollar is much more expensive to European firms and consumers than before—it costs 50 percent more to acquire a dollar. Let's examine the effect of this change on Europeans.[3]

Effect on European Firms

- European firms must pay more for inputs from the United States, such as raw materials, components, and support services they use to produce finished products and services.

- Higher input costs reduce profitability and may force firms to raise prices to final customers; these higher prices lower customer demand for goods and services.

- Because the euro has become less expensive for U.S. consumers, firms can increase their exports to the United States. Firms can even raise their export prices and remain competitive in the U.S. market.

- Increased exports to the United States generate higher revenues and higher profits.

Effect on European Consumers

- Because U.S. products and services now cost more, European consumers demand fewer of them.

- The cost of living rises for those Europeans who consume many dollar-denominated imports.

- Fewer European tourists can afford to visit the United States. Fewer European students study at U.S. universities.

Now, suppose the euro/dollar exchange rate goes to €0.50 = $1. What are the effects on European firms and consumers? They are essentially the opposite of those summarized previously: European firms pay less for inputs from the United States, which means they can drop their prices on goods and services. Because U.S. products and services now cost less, consumers demand more of them.

As you can see, a fluctuating exchange rate affects both sides of international transactions. Management must monitor exchange rates constantly and devise strategies to optimize firm performance in light of strong and weak currencies. We discuss these strategies in Chapter 20.

In 2009, profits at Nintendo (www.nintendo.com) plunged more than 50 percent as sales of its Wii video game consoles collapsed in the United States and elsewhere. Like many firms in the export-dependent electronics industry, Nintendo suffered from the strength of the Japanese yen relative to other major trading currencies such as the dollar and the euro. Conversely, for Japanese consumers, the dollar is relatively cheaper, which encourages them to buy U.S. products. Nintendo generates nearly 90 percent of its sales outside Japan. The type of currency risk it faces is a natural outcome of its multi-country operations.[4] At the same time, dollar-denominated products offered good value to Europeans, trading at around $1.50 to the euro, which represented a near-record high. On eBay, the online auction service, U.S. companies enjoyed record sales to buyers in Australia, Britain, and Canada, who took advantage of the dollar's weaker value relative to their currencies.[5]

How Exchange Rates Are Determined

In a free market, the "price" of any currency—that is, its rate of exchange—is determined by supply and demand. The levels of supply and demand for a currency vary inversely with its price. Thus, all else being equal:

- The greater the supply of a currency, the lower its price.
- The lower the supply of a currency, the higher its price.
- The greater the demand for a currency, the higher its price.
- The lower the demand for a currency, the lower its price.

Suppose a U.S. consumer wants to buy a BMW, sourced from Germany and priced at the nominal price of 25,000 euros. Assume further that the euro/dollar exchange rate is €1=$1.25. Now suppose the consumer delays six months, during which the exchange rate shifts, becoming €1=$1.50. That is, due to increased demand for and/or decreased supply of euros, the euro has become more expensive to U.S. customers. Assuming the euro price of the BMW remains unchanged, the car will now cost more in U.S. dollars, making the consumer less inclined to buy the BMW. By contrast, if, during the six-month period, the euro becomes cheaper (with, say, an exchange rate of €1=$1), the U.S. consumer will be more inclined to buy the BMW. As this example implies, the greater the demand for a country's products and services, the greater the demand for its currency.

Four main factors influence the supply and demand for a currency: economic growth, interest rates and inflation, market psychology, and government action. Let's review each of these next.

Economic Growth

Economic growth is the increase in value of the goods and services produced by an economy. To ensure accuracy, we usually measure economic growth as the annual increase in real GDP, in which the inflation rate is subtracted from the growth rate. Economic growth results from continual economic activities, including innovation and entrepreneurship. It implies a continued increase in business activities and a corresponding increase in consumer need for money to facilitate more economic transactions.

Central bank The monetary authority in each nation that regulates the money supply and credit, issues currency, and manages the exchange rate of the nation's currency.

To accommodate economic growth, the **central bank** increases the nation's money supply. The central bank is the monetary authority in each country that regulates the money supply, issues currency, and manages the exchange rate of the nation's currency relative to other currencies. Economic growth is associated with an increase in the supply and demand of the nation's money supply and, by extension, the nation's currency. Thus, it has a strong influence on the supply and demand for national currencies. For example, recent rapid economic growth in several East Asian countries has stimulated increased demand for their currencies by firms and individuals, both domestic and foreign.

Inflation and Interest Rates

Inflation is an increase in the price of goods and services, so that money buys less than in preceding years. Exhibit 11.3 shows that inflation rates can reach high levels in some countries over time. Argentina, Zimbabwe, and some other countries have had prolonged periods of *hyperinflation*—persistent annual double-digit and sometimes triple-digit rates of price increases. A practical effect of hyperinflation is the need, say, for a restaurant owner to change the menu every few days in order to list the most recent prices. In a high-inflation environment, the purchasing power of the currency is constantly falling. Interest rates and inflation are closely related. In countries with high inflation, interest rates tend to be high because investors expect to be compensated for the inflation-induced decline in the value of their money. If inflation is running at 10 percent, for example, banks must pay *more* than 10 percent interest to attract customers to open savings accounts.

Inflation occurs when (1) demand for money grows more rapidly than supply, or (2) the central bank increases the nation's money supply faster than output. For instance, triggered by sizable increases in the national money supply, inflation ran to more than 400 percent per year in Brazil in the mid-1990s. Imagine the difficulty to both buyers and sellers of adjusting to a constant decline of the currency's value and ever-rising prices! Inflation is a common challenge for developing economies and emerging markets.

Inflation directly affects the value of the nation's currency. If it results from an excessive increase in the money supply, all else being equal, the price of that money (expressed in terms of foreign currencies) will fall.

The link between interest rates and inflation, and between inflation and the value of currency, implies there is a relationship between real interest rates and the value of currency. For example, when interest rates in Japan are high, foreigners seek profits by buying Japan's interest-bearing investment opportunities, such as bonds and deposit certificates. Investment from abroad will have the effect of increasing demand for the Japanese yen.

Market Psychology

Exchange rates are often affected by *market psychology,* the unpredictable behavior of investors. *Herding* is the tendency of investors to mimic each others' actions. *Momentum trading* occurs when investors buy stocks whose prices have been rising and sell stocks

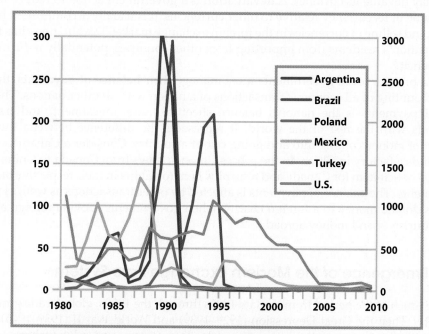

Exhibit 11.3 Inflation in Selected Countries, 1980–2005

SOURCE: International Monetary Fund (http://www.imf.org)

NOTE: Chart shows annual percentage rate of inflation. Right-hand scale is for Argentina, Brazil, and Poland; left-hand scale is for all the other countries.

whose prices have been falling. It is usually carried out using computers set up to do massive buying or selling when asset prices reach certain levels. Herding and momentum trading tend to occur in the wake of financial crises. A case in point is Pakistan, which recently experienced a massive flight of portfolio investment amid concerns about its homeland security, untenable budgetary deficits, and high inflation (above 20 percent in 2008). Foreign investors panicked and many deserted the country.[6]

Government Action

The pricing of currencies affects company performance. When a nation's currency is expensive to foreigners, its exports are likely to fall.[7] When a nation's currency is cheap to foreigners, exports increase. When the value of a nation's currency depreciates over a prolonged period, consumer and investor confidence can be undermined. A steep currency depreciation weakens the nation's ability to pay foreign lenders, possibly leading to economic and political crisis.

To minimize these effects, governments often act to influence the value of their own currencies. The Chinese government regularly intervenes in the foreign exchange market to keep the renminbi undervalued, helping to ensure that Chinese exports remain strong.

Trade surplus
A condition in which a nation's exports exceed its imports for a specific period of time.

An undervalued national currency can result in a **trade surplus**, which arises when a nation's exports exceed its imports for a specific period of time, causing a net inflow of foreign exchange. By contrast, a **trade deficit** results when a nation's imports exceed its exports for a specific period of time, causing a net outflow of foreign exchange. The *balance of trade* is the difference between the monetary value of a nation's exports and its imports over the course of a year. For example, if Germany exports cars to Kenya, money flows out of Kenya and into Germany, because the car importer in Kenya pays the exporter in Germany. This results in a surplus item in Germany's balance of trade and a deficit item in Kenya's balance of trade. If the total value of Kenya's imports from Germany becomes greater than the total value of Kenya's exports to Germany, Kenya will have a trade deficit with Germany. Factors that affect the balance of trade include the prices of goods manufactured at home, exchange rates, trade barriers, and the method the government uses to measure the trade balance.

Trade deficit A condition in which a nation's imports exceed its exports for a specific period of time.

Many economists believe a persistent trade deficit is harmful to the national economy. When a trade deficit becomes severe or persists for a long time, the nation's central bank may devalue its currency. A **devaluation** is a government action to reduce the official value of its currency relative to other currencies. It is usually accomplished by the buying and selling of currencies in the foreign exchange market. Devaluation aims to deter the nation's residents from importing from other countries, potentially reducing the trade deficit.[8]

Devaluation Government action to reduce the official value of its currency, relative to other currencies.

At a broader level, governments must manage their **balance of payments**, the annual accounting of all economic transactions of a nation with all other nations. The balance of payments is the nation's balance sheet of trade, investment, and transfer payments with the rest of the world. It represents the difference between the *total* amount of money coming into and going out of a country. Consider a Canadian MNE that builds a factory in China. In the process, money flows from Canada to China, generating a deficit item for Canada and a surplus item for China in their respective balance of payments. The balance of payments is affected by other transactions as well, as when citizens donate money to a foreign charity, when governments provide foreign aid, or when tourists spend money abroad.

Balance of payments
The annual accounting of all economic transactions of a nation with *all* other nations.

Emergence of the Modern Exchange Rate System

During much of the period from the late 1800s through the 1920s, global trade grew significantly. Then the Great Depression (1929–1939) and World War II (1939–1945) coincided with a collapse of the international trading system and relationships among nations. Following the war, several countries came together to energize international commerce and devise a framework for stability in the international monetary and financial systems. In 1944, the governments of forty-four countries negotiated and signed the Bretton Woods Agreement.

The Bretton Woods Agreement

This agreement pegged the value of the U.S. dollar to an established value of gold, at a rate of $35 per ounce. The U.S. government agreed to buy and sell unlimited amounts of gold in order to maintain this fixed rate. Each of Bretton Woods' other signatory countries agreed to establish a par value of its currency in terms of the U.S. dollar and to maintain this pegged value through central bank intervention. In this way, the Bretton Woods system kept exchange rates of major currencies fixed at a prescribed level relative to the U.S. dollar and, therefore, to each other.

The demise of the Bretton Woods agreement began in the late 1960s when the U.S. government used deficit spending to finance both the Vietnam War and expensive government programs. Rising government spending stimulated the economy and U.S. citizens began buying more imported goods. This aggravated the U.S. balance of payments, and the United States began to experience trade deficits with Japan, Germany, and other European countries. Over time, demand for U.S. dollars so exceeded supply that the U.S. government could no longer maintain an adequate stock of gold. This situation put pressure on governments in Europe, Japan, and the United States to revalue their currencies. As a result, the link between the U.S. dollar and gold was suspended in 1971, and the promise to exchange gold for U.S. dollars was withdrawn. This action brought an end to the Bretton Woods system.

IMF and the World Bank

Bretton Woods left a legacy of principles and institutions that remain in use today. First is the concept of international monetary cooperation, especially among the central banks of leading nations. Second, Bretton Woods established the notion of fixing exchange rates within an international regime to minimize currency risk. Third, it created the **International Monetary Fund (IMF**; www.imf.org) and the **World Bank** (www.worldbank.org). The IMF is an international agency that attempts to stabilize currencies by monitoring the foreign exchange systems of member countries and lending money to developing economies. The World Bank is an international agency that provides loans and technical assistance to low- and middle-income countries, with the goal of reducing poverty. Finally, Bretton Woods established the importance of currency convertibility, in which countries agree not to impose restrictions on currency trading and to avoid discriminatory currency arrangements.

In 1999, following the 1997 Asian financial crisis, finance ministers and central bank heads from twenty advanced and emerging market economies established the Group of Twenty (G-20), an international organization that aims to bring greater stability to the global financial system. Representing about 90 percent of the world economy, the members have met annually to develop measures that promote economic growth and strong financial systems. They have held meetings in Britain, Canada, South Korea, and the United States. The members were instrumental in devising new policies to address the financial and economic crisis that began in 2008, which included increasing financial resources, coordinating expansionary macroeconomic policies, and enhancing national financial regulations. The G-20 cooperates closely with the IMF and World Bank.

International Monetary Fund (IMF) An international agency that aims to stabilize currencies by monitoring the foreign exchange systems of member countries and lending money to developing economies.

World Bank An international agency that provides loans and technical assistance to low- and middle-income countries with the goal of reducing poverty.

The Modern Exchange Rate System

Today most major currencies are traded freely, with their value floating according to the forces of supply and demand. The official price of gold was formally abolished, and governments became free to choose the type of exchange rate system that best suited their individual needs. Fixed exchange rate systems were given equal status with floating exchange rate systems, and countries were no longer compelled to maintain specific pegged values for their currency. Instead, they were urged to pursue domestic economic policies that would support the stability of their currency relative to others. The exchange rate system today consists of two main types of foreign exchange management: the floating system and the fixed system.

The Floating Exchange Rate System   Most advanced economies use the floating exchange rate system, in which governments refrain from systematic intervention, and each nation's currency floats independently, according to market forces. Major world currencies—including the Canadian dollar, the British pound, the euro, the U.S. dollar, and the Japanese yen—float independently on world exchange markets, their exchange rates determined daily by supply and demand. The floating system gives governments the latitude to modify monetary policy to fit the circumstances they face at any time. If a country is running a trade deficit, the floating rate system allows it to be corrected more naturally than if the country uses a fixed exchange rate regime.

The Fixed Exchange Rate System   This approach is similar to the system used under the Bretton Woods agreement and is sometimes called a *pegged* exchange rate system. In it, the value of a currency is set relative to the value of another (or to the value of a basket of currencies) at a specified rate. As this "reference value" rises and falls, so does the currency pegged to it. In the past, some currencies were also fixed to some set value of gold.

Many developing economies and some emerging markets use the fixed system today. China pegs its currency to the value of a basket of currencies. Belize pegs its currency to the U.S. dollar. To maintain the peg, the governments of China and Belize, for instance, will intervene in currency markets to buy and sell dollars and other currencies, to maintain the exchange rate at a fixed, preset level. A fixed regime promotes greater stability and predictability of exchange rate movements and helps stabilize a nation's economy. The central bank must stand ready to fill any gaps between supply and demand for its currency.

Many economists believe floating exchange rates are preferable to fixed because floating rates more naturally respond to, and represent, the supply and demand for currencies in the foreign exchange market. In some situations, however, fixed exchange rates may be preferable for their greater stability. For example, the recent global financial crisis was contained in part because of some countries' adherence to fixed exchange regimes. A fixed regime provided much stability to world currencies under the Bretton Woods system in the years following World War II.

At times, countries adhere to neither a purely fixed nor a floating exchange rate system. Rather, they try to hold the value of their currency within some *range* against the U.S. dollar or other important reference currency, in a system often referred to as *dirty float*. That is, the value of the currency is determined by market forces, but the central bank intervenes occasionally in the foreign exchange market to maintain the value of its currency within acceptable limits relative to a major reference currency. Many Western countries resort to this type of intervention from time to time.

The Monetary and Financial Systems

We've seen how currencies facilitate international transactions and how exchange rates affect the amount of international trade. Let's now examine the two systems that determine exchange rates: the international monetary system and the global financial system.

International Monetary System

International monetary system Institutional framework, rules, and procedures by which national currencies are exchanged for one another.

Firms seek to get paid for the products and services they sell abroad. Portfolio investors seek to invest in stocks and other liquid assets around the world. The resulting monetary flows take the form of various currencies traded among nations. Accordingly, the **international monetary system** consists of the institutional frameworks, rules, and procedures that govern how national currencies are exchanged for one another. By providing a framework for the monetary and foreign exchange activities of firms and governments worldwide, the system facilitates international trade and investment. To function well, national governments and international agencies have focused on creating a system that inspires confidence and ensures liquidity in monetary and financial holdings.

Global Financial System

The **global financial system** consists of the collective financial institutions that facilitate and regulate flows of investment and capital funds worldwide. Key players in the system include finance ministries, national stock exchanges, commercial banks, central banks, the Bank for International Settlements, the World Bank, and the International Monetary Fund. Thus, the system incorporates the national and international banking systems, the international bond market, the collective of national stock markets, and the market for bank deposits denominated in foreign currencies.

The global financial system is built on the activities of firms, banks, and financial institutions engaged in ongoing international financial activity. It also has many linkages with national financial markets. Since the 1960s, the global financial system has grown substantially in volume and structure, becoming increasingly more efficient, competitive, and stable.

Today, the global financial system can accommodate massive cross-national flows of money and the huge foreign exchange markets these transactions have engendered. Initially triggered by the rapid growth in world trade and investment, the globalization of finance accelerated in the 1990s with the opening of the former Soviet Union and China to international business. More recently, very large flows of capital—mostly in the form of pension funds, mutual funds, and life insurance investments—have been pouring into stock markets worldwide. Firms can increasingly access a range of capital markets and financial instruments around the world.[9]

Money flowing abroad as portfolio investments is a relatively new trend. The volume of these flows is enormous. In 2008, for example, foreign residents held about 18 percent of total outstanding U.S. long-term securities.[10] In developing economies, inward investment increases foreign exchange reserves, reduces the cost of capital, and stimulates local development of financial markets.

The growing integration of financial and monetary activity worldwide has several causes, including:

- The evolution of monetary and financial regulations worldwide
- The development of new technologies and payment systems and the use of the Internet in global financial activities
- Increased global and regional interdependence of financial markets
- The growing role of single-currency systems, such as the euro

Capital flows are much more volatile than FDI-type investments, because it is much easier for investors to withdraw and reallocate liquid capital funds than FDI funds, which are directly tied to factories and other permanent operations that firms establish abroad.[11]

The globalization of financial flows has yielded many benefits, but it is also associated with increased risk. Economic difficulties in one country can quickly spread to other countries, like a contagion. Financial instability is worsened when governments fail to adequately regulate and monitor their banking and financial sectors.[12] The *Global Trend* feature explains the global financial crisis that began in 2008.

Let's discuss various organizations that attempt to reduce capital flight and manage other challenges in the global monetary and financial systems.

The international monetary system provides the framework within which national currencies, including the U.S. dollar, British pound, and euro, are exchanged for one another.

Global financial system The collective of financial institutions that facilitate and regulate investment and capital flows worldwide, such as central banks, commercial banks, and national stock exchanges.

GLOBAL TREND

Global Financial Crisis

In 2008 a major crisis emerged in the global financial and monetary systems. It was triggered in the United States, where investors lost confidence in the value of home mortgages. As commercial banks, mortgage lenders, and insurance companies entered a period of high volatility, stock markets crashed around the world, and many national economies sank into a deep recession. In the ensuing months, much of the world experienced sharp declines in consumer wealth, economic activity, and international trade.

A key factor in the crisis was the widespread availability of "easy money." For several years the U.S. central bank, the Federal Reserve Bank (www.federalreserve.gov), had pursued a policy of low interest rates, generating surplus capital in the United States and abroad. Simultaneously, China and other emerging markets had been investing enormous sums in treasury bonds and other securities in the United States. These trends led to the build-up of a vast global money supply—easy money that facilitated the excessive demand for housing and commodities such as oil and food and led to soaring price inflation in these goods.

Much of the money was used to finance the huge U.S. trade deficit, which had arisen from massive imports of consumer and industrial goods into the United States. In addition, U.S. banks and mortgage companies had granted billions of dollars in loans to individuals who spent excessively on homes and other consumer goods. Many of the loans were "securitized," or bundled into investment assets that were sold in financial markets worldwide. Over time, however, investors realized that many of the loans were high risk and unlikely to be repaid. As the overheated U.S. mortgage market cooled, the value of homes and securitized mortgages crashed, and the U.S. financial system fell into crisis.

Like a contagion, the crisis spread quickly to Europe and beyond. Countries not directly affected were caught up in a global recession triggered by the financial crisis. As the global economy slowed, demand for exports shrank, and export-dependent countries such as Japan and Mexico floundered. In some countries, central banks devalued their currencies. In several emerging markets, a currency crisis arose as foreign financiers quickly sold the investments they had made in local markets, which they perceived as too risky. Eastern Europe and Russia suffered capital flight as investors withdrew billions from local economies. Ireland, Spain, and several other advanced economies experienced negative GDP growth. Huge declines in industrial output occurred in many nations. In Iceland, all three of the country's major banks collapsed, the national currency fell sharply, and the total value of shares in the Icelandic stock exchange fell by more than 90 percent.

In subsequent months governments took corrective measures, such as injecting massive sums into their national economies and launching aid packages. Numerous emerging markets obtained loans from the International Monetary Fund and World Bank. Others imposed trade and investment barriers. Gradually, governments began to cooperate in financial matters. Several have sought to create new regulations appropriate for the globalization of finance and a host of new investment approaches and opportunities. The crisis highlights the importance of strong regulation, transparency, and supervision of institutions in the global financial system.

All three of Iceland's major banks collapsed in the wake of the recent global financial crisis. Relative to the size of its economy, Iceland's banking collapse was the largest suffered by any country in economic history. Here, protestors gather outside the Icelandic parliament in Reykjavik.

SOURCES: "When Fortune Frowned," *Economist*, October 11, 2008, pp. 3–5; P. Engardio, "Look Who's Swimming in Cash," *Business Week*, October 13, 2008, p. 26; International Monetary Fund, *Note on the Group of Twenty Meeting of the Deputies*, January 31–February 1, 2009, London; Carol Matlack and Mark Scott, "Emerging-Market Time Bombs," *Business Week*, November 3, 2008, pp. 40–41; Ilian Mihov, "Keeping the Global Economy Afloat," *Financial Times*, January 22, 2009, pp. 1–2; Gideon Rachman, "When Globalisation Goes into Reverse," *Financial Times*, February 2, 2009, p. 12; United Nations Conference on Trade and Development, *The Global Economic Crisis* (New York: United Nations, 2009).

Key Players in the Monetary and Financial Systems

A variety of national, international, private, and government players make up the international monetary system and the global financial system. Exhibit 11.4 highlights the major players and the relationships among them. These players operate at the levels of the firm, the nation, and the world.

The Firm

As companies engage in international trade and are paid by their customers abroad, they typically acquire large quantities of foreign exchange and must convert them into the currency of the home country. Firms also engage in investment, franchising, and licensing activities abroad that generate revenues they must exchange into their home currency. For example, Jim Moran Enterprises in Florida, the largest importer of Toyota cars in the United States, imports thousands of cars every year and must ultimately pay for them in Japanese yen. Moran deals with the foreign exchange market to convert U.S. dollars to yen.

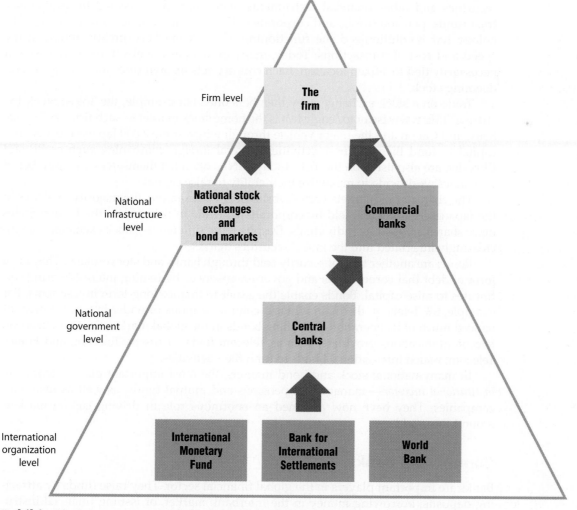

Exhibit 11.4   Key Participants and Relationships in the Global Monetary and Financial Systems

Some MNEs with spare cash acquire foreign currencies for speculative purposes. Effectively, they invest in currencies with the intention of profiting from exchange rate fluctuations. Other firms may acquire foreign currency to invest in foreign stock markets and other foreign investment vehicles for short-term gains.

Other private-sector players in the international monetary and financial systems include life insurance companies, savings and loan associations, and stockbrokers that manage pensions and mutual funds. Some large MNEs have in-house finance departments that manage their foreign exchange and financial transactions. Nontraditional financial institutions play a key role in international funds transfers. In 2007, foreign residents in the United States used wire-transfer specialists such as Western Union to wire billions of dollars to family members in India ($13 billion) and Mexico ($26 billion), where the funds were converted into local currencies. Remittances from Africans living abroad have been a major factor in helping sustain Africa's poorest countries. Indeed, some nations receive more foreign income from remittances than from either foreign aid or inward FDI.[13] Read this chapter's *Recent Grad in IB* feature, which highlights Maria Keeley, who works in finance for a major multinational firm.

National Stock Exchanges and Bond Markets

Selling stock (shares of ownership) is an important way for firms to raise the funds they need to engage in international business. A *stock exchange* is a facility for trading securities and other financial instruments, including shares issued by companies, trust funds, pension funds, and corporate and government bonds. Information technology has revolutionized the functioning of stock markets, greatly reducing the speed and cost of transactions. Today, many exchanges are electronic networks not necessarily tied to a fixed location. Each country sets its own rules for issuing and redeeming stock.

Trade on a stock exchange is by members only. For example, the Tokyo Stock Exchange (TSE; www.tse.or.jp/english/) is the home stock market to such firms as Toyota, Sony, and Canon and the major vehicle through which some 2,000 Japanese firms raise capital to fund their business activities. Several foreign companies, such as BP and Chrysler, are also listed on the TSE. Today, MNEs often list themselves on a number of exchanges worldwide to maximize their ability to raise capital.

The character of markets varies worldwide. For example, the majority of shares in the Japanese market are held by corporations, while in Britain and the United States more shares are held by individuals. Despite these differences, stock exchanges are increasingly integrated into the global securities market.

Bonds are another type of security sold through banks and stockbrokers. They are a form of debt that corporations and governments incur by issuing interest-bearing certificates to raise capital. Bonds enable the issuer to finance long-term investments. For example, SK Telekom, the main wireless communications provider in South Korea, financed much of its operations by selling bonds in the global market. Several European telecommunications providers, such as Telecom Italia, Deutsche Telecom, and France Telecom, issued international bonds to fund their activities.[14]

In many national stock and bond markets, the most important players today are *institutional investors*—managers of pensions and mutual funds, as well as insurance companies. They have now assumed an enormous role in driving capital markets around the world.

Commercial Banks

Banks are important players in the global financial sector. They raise funds by attracting deposits, borrowing money in the interbank market, or issuing financial instruments in the global money market or securities markets. Commercial banks—Bank of

Recent Grad in IB

Chip's majors: Bachelor's degree in Finance with a minor in Spanish

Objectives: Adventure, international perspective, career growth, self-understanding, and the opportunity to learn foreign languages

Internships during college: Merrill Lynch investment broker

Jobs held since graduating:
- A major bank in London
- A new investment firm in London

Chip Besse

Chip Besse is a natural entrepreneur who started a waste management company while in college. He realized early that he wanted a career in finance, so in his junior year he obtained a 10-month internship with Merrill Lynch, the investment broker, where he assisted with quarterly reports on restructuring client portfolios. Chip studied on his own and became well versed in insurance sales and variable investment annuities.

In his senior year, Chip studied in Valencia, Spain. The experience opened his eyes to the possibilities of an international career. A campus visit from an international bank executive motivated Chip further. He contacted the banker via e-mail and telephone for several months until, impressed by his persistence, she offered him an internship at the large international bank where she worked in London.

Chip's hard work so impressed his superiors that they enrolled him in the bank's Graduate Training Program, where he learned how to build financial models for managed buy-outs (MBOs) and leveraged buy-outs (LBOs), as well as mergers and acquisitions. Chip's work involved him in deals to buy companies, make them more profitable, then sell them. He worked with a team that closed deals throughout Europe and the Middle East, accumulating experience as he assisted in soliciting funds from equity investors and banks, and he made presentations to credit committees and transaction management teams. He also researched financial data on acquisition targets in various sectors and devised a system for monitoring budget variances on ongoing investments.

Chip's group acquired underperforming firms and restructured their strategies to make them leading industry players. To refocus a family-run Scandinavian firm that was losing money, Chip and his group cut costs and devised new growth strategies. Through the team's efforts, the firm brought in proceeds from divestment of nearly $150 million and increased its profit margin from 2 to 9 percent.

In Britain, Chip worked on the LBO of a movie-theatre chain worth over $800 million. His assignments included financial modeling of the acquisition, refinancing, and optimizing the firm's capital structure. Chip negotiated with lawyers, accountants, and trade partners. In Central America, he negotiated an LBO for a solid-waste removal firm. He worked on a $30 million debt and equity fund-raising deal for an Eastern European startup, also in the waste management business, and a $600 million acquisition of a European sporting firm. In his spare time, Chip obtained certification in advanced financial modeling, corporate valuations, and analysis of financial statements.

Success Factors for a Career in International Business

"I enjoy learning about new cultures and assessing investment opportunities where the common variables change drastically. My work requires an eclectic skill base. We often deal with political risk, currency risk, and cultural risk. We try to mitigate most of the risks by doing our homework, talking to local people, immersing ourselves in the culture, and being really diligent by visiting all the locations. There is no 'normal' day at the office."

Challenges

"I recommend a career in international business even though doing business in another country and living away from your family and friends is not easy. It takes an open mind, much hard work, and persistence."

America, Mizuho Bank in Japan, and BBVA in Spain—are the foot soldiers of the international monetary system. They circulate money and engage in a wide range of international financial transactions. Banks are regulated by national and local governments, which have a strong interest in ensuring the solvency of their national banking system.

The many types of banks and their primary activities include the following:

- *Investment banks* underwrite (guarantee the sale of) stock and bond issues and advise on mergers, such as the merger of Goldman Sachs in the United States and Nomura Securities in Japan.

- *Merchant banks* provide capital to firms in the form of shares rather than loans. They are essentially investment banks that specialize in international operations. The Arab-Malaysian Merchant Bank is an example.

- *Private banks* manage the assets of the very rich. Union Bank in Switzerland (UBS) and ABN AMRO Private Banking in Luxembourg are examples.

- *Offshore banks* are located in jurisdictions with low taxation and regulation, such as Switzerland or Bermuda. Banco General in Panama and Bank of Nova Scotia in the British Virgin Islands are examples.

- *Commercial banks* deal mainly with corporations or large businesses. Credit Lyonnais in France and Bank of America are examples.

For firms, the most important functions of banks are to lend money to finance business activity, exchange foreign currencies, and facilitate adjustments in national money supplies. The major world banking centers are London, New York, Tokyo, Frankfurt, and Singapore, with London having the world's greatest concentration of international banks. Many banks are MNEs themselves, such as Citibank, Britain's HSBC, and Spain's BBVA. Smaller banks participate in international business by interacting with larger, *correspondent* banks abroad. A correspondent bank is a large bank that maintains relationships with other banks worldwide to facilitate international banking transactions.

Banking practices vary widely. In some countries, banks are owned by the state and are extensions of government. In other countries, they face little regulation and may lack safety nets that might prevent their failure. In developing economies, private banks are usually subject to substantial government regulation.

The density of banks varies cross-nationally. Consider Canada, Sweden, and the Netherlands. Just five banks in each country control more than 80 percent of all banking assets. In Germany, Italy, and the United States, by contrast, the top five banks control less than 30 percent of all banking assets. Banks also charge different rates for their services. For a typical customer, the annual price of core banking services in Italy is over $300; in the United States it is $150, and in China and the Netherlands it is only $50.[15]

In Africa, banking has long been problematic. Egypt and South Africa are among the few African countries that possess a thriving, home-grown banking sector. In the rest of Africa, industry and governments have tended to rely on international banks because local banks are often unstable and corrupt. In the past, heavy restrictions on foreign banks reduced competition, which delayed the development of a strong indigenous banking sector. Recently, however, globalization of the financial industry has contributed substantially to the development of efficient markets and financial institutions. Foreign banks have brought technology, managerial expertise, and new product ideas to Africa. Tough foreign competition has put pressure on indigenous banks to be more innovative. In addition, some innovative banks are using widespread mobile telephone technology to offer various banking services in Africa.[16]

In late 2006, nine foreign banks took a key step toward entering the Chinese retail banking industry, receiving permission to become the first international lenders to incorporate in China under World Trade Organization market-opening pledges. Here, Citibank of the United States is pictured in Shanghai.

Central Banks

As the official national bank of each country, the central bank regulates the money supply and credit, issues currency, and manages the rate of exchange. The bank also seeks to ensure the safety and soundness of the national financial system, by supervising and regulating the nation's banking system. A key goal is to keep price inflation low. The central bank regulates the nation's money supply and credit by (1) buying and selling money in the banking system, (2) increasing or decreasing interest rates on funds loaned to commercial banks, or (3) buying and selling government securities, such as treasury bills and bonds. Many central banks also buy and sell government securities to finance government programs and activities.

Monetary intervention describes how central banks manipulate currency rates, usually with the aim of maintaining stable or orderly exchange rates. Such intervention is achieved by buying or selling currencies in the foreign exchange market. For example, if the central bank of the United States (called the Federal Reserve Bank) wants to support the value of the U.S. dollar, it might buy dollars in the foreign exchange market. By so doing, the supply of dollars is reduced, which increases the value of dollars still in circulation.

Other central banks include the Reserve Bank of India, the Bank of England, the Banque de France, and the Bank of Japan. They work with the International Monetary Fund, the Bank for International Settlements, the Organisation for Economic Co-operation and Development (OECD), and other international agencies to ensure sound international monetary and financial policies in global markets.

Monetary intervention
The buying and selling of currencies by a central bank to maintain the exchange rate of a country's currency at some acceptable level.

The Bank for International Settlements

Based in Basel, Switzerland, the Bank for International Settlements (www.bis.org) is an international organization that fosters cooperation among central banks and other governmental agencies. It provides banking services to central banks and assists them in devising sound monetary policy. It seeks to support stability in the global monetary and financial systems and help governments avoid becoming too indebted. It also attempts to ensure that central banks maintain reserve assets and capital/asset ratios above prescribed international minimums. Maintaining adequate capital is prescribed by the Basel Capital Accord, a set of recommendations on how central banks should structure their banking laws and regulations.[17]

The global crisis that emerged in 2008 generated much turmoil in the world financial sector. Central banks in nations worldwide increased money supplies, and international agencies like the IMF and World Bank provided emergency loans to numerous developing economies.

International Monetary Fund

Headquartered in Washington, D.C., the IMF provides the framework of and determines the code of behavior for the international monetary system. The agency promotes international monetary cooperation, exchange rate stability, and orderly exchange arrangements and encourages countries to adopt sound economic policies. These functions are critical because economic crises can destroy jobs, slash incomes, and cause human suffering.

Governed today by 186 countries, the IMF stands ready to provide financial assistance in the form of loans and grants to support policy programs intended to correct macroeconomic problems. During the recent global financial crisis, the IMF pledged several billion dollars to assist Romania, Hungary, Ukraine, Turkey, and Pakistan, whose economies were impacted in the event.[18]

Special Drawing Right (SDR) A unit of account or a reserve asset, a type of currency used by central banks to supplement their existing reserves in transactions with the IMF.

To help manage currency valuation worldwide, the IMF established a type of international reserve known as the **Special Drawing Right (SDR)**. The SDR is a unit of account or a reserve asset, a type of currency used by central banks to supplement their existing reserves in transactions with the IMF and to manage international exchange rates. For example, a central bank might use SDRs to purchase foreign currencies to manage the value of its currency on world markets. The value of the SDR is very stable because it is based on a basket of currencies: the euro, the Japanese yen, the U.K. pound, and the U.S. dollar.

The IMF plays an important role in addressing financial and monetary crises faced by nations around the world. Typical crises fall into three major categories.

A *currency crisis* results when the value of a nation's currency depreciates sharply or when its central bank must expend substantial reserves to defend the value of its currency, thereby pushing up interest rates. Currency crises occur more commonly in smaller countries and are sometimes the result of a sudden loss of confidence in the national economy or speculative buying and selling of the nation's currency.

A *banking crisis* results when domestic and foreign investors lose confidence in a nation's banking system, leading to widespread withdrawals of funds from banks and other financial institutions. This situation arose in the United States in the 1930s when, during the Great Depression, millions of people panicked about their savings and rushed to withdraw funds from their bank accounts. The crisis led to the failure of numerous banks. Banking crises tend to occur in developing economies with inadequate regulatory and institutional frameworks. These crises can lead to other problems, such as exchange rate fluctuations, inflation, abrupt withdrawal of FDI funds, and general economic instability.

A *foreign debt crisis* arises when a national government borrows an excessive amount of money, either from banks or from the sale of government bonds. For example, China's total foreign debt now exceeds $200 billion. However, the debt is manageable because China has a huge reserve of foreign exchange. By contrast, Argentina's foreign debt has reached roughly 150 percent of the country's GDP. In an effort to pay its debt, Argentina must use financial resources that it might have invested instead in important national priorities. Indebted governments draw huge sums out of their national money supply, reducing the availability of these funds to consumers and to firms attempting to finance business activities.

The IMF assists countries in resolving crises by offering technical assistance and training. It provides assistance by setting fiscal policy, devising monetary and exchange rate policies, and supervising and regulating banking and financial systems. It also provides loans to help distressed countries in recovery. However, the agency has been criticized because its prescriptions often require national governments to undertake painful reforms. For example, the IMF may recommend that a government downsize state-owned enterprises or give up subsidies or price supports for basic commodities. Some critics charge the IMF harms countries by imposing too much austerity in times of financial distress. The IMF argues that any country in an economic crisis usually must undergo substantial restructuring, such as the deregulation of national industries or privatization of state enterprises. However, it is sometimes difficult to pinpoint whether IMF prescriptions cause more harm than good. At the 2009 G-20 summit, responding to the global financial crisis, the G-20 members pledged to increase the IMF's financial resources and increase its lending capacity substantially.

The World Bank

Originally known as the International Bank for Reconstruction and Development, the World Bank (www.worldbank.org) was founded to fund reconstruction of Japan and Europe after World War II. Today it aims to reduce world poverty and is active in various development projects to bring water, electricity, and transportation infrastructure to poor countries. Headquartered in Washington, D.C., the bank is a specialized agency of the United Nations, with more than one hundred offices worldwide. It is supported by some 184 member countries that are jointly responsible for how the institution is financed and how its money is spent.

The World Bank's collection of subagencies oversees various international development activities. The International Development Association loans billions of dollars each year to the world's poorest countries. The International Finance Corporation works with the private sector to promote economic development. It invests in sustainable private enterprises in developing countries and provides equity, loans, loan guarantees, risk management products, and advisory services to clients in need. The Multilateral Investment Guarantee Agency aims to encourage FDI to developing countries by providing guarantees to foreign investors against losses caused by noncommercial risks.

The IMF and the World Bank often work together. While the IMF focuses on countries' economic performance, the World Bank emphasizes longer-term development and the reduction of poverty. The IMF makes short-term loans to help stabilize foreign exchange, and the World Bank makes long-term loans to promote economic development.

 Closing Case

AIG and Global Financial Contagion

Growing integration of financial and monetary sectors of the world's economies is yet another facet of globalization. Globalization of finance is typified by massive cross-national flows of money and capital and the development of a giant foreign exchange market. Every day around the world, firms access global capital markets. Banks and brokers move huge sums across national borders via pensions, mutual funds, life insurance, and other investments. In short, national financial markets are increasingly interdependent. Among numerous benefits, financial globalization increases savings and reduces capital costs in developing economies.

The globalization of finance is driven mainly by falling investment barriers and the emergence of information and communications technologies. But capital flows are volatile: Investors can quickly withdraw and reallocate capital funds. Economic problems that arise in one country can spread quickly to other countries like a rampaging virus—thus the term *contagion*. Financial instability is worsened when governments fail to adequately regulate and monitor their banking and financial sectors.

American International Group

When the financial crisis began in the United States in late 2008, many hoped other economies would escape its harmful effects. Analysts argued that rapid GDP growth in such emerging markets as Brazil, China, and India would continue, helping to lift sinking financial boats worldwide. But many nations could not avoid contagion and its pernicious effects.

In the United States, a notable casualty was American International Group (AIG; www.aig.com), the giant insurance company. AIG was founded in 1919 in China and today is headquartered in New York City. Through its many subsidiaries, AIG offers insurance, pension plans, asset management, and financial services in more than 130 countries.

In September 2008, the U.S. government provided AIG a bailout of USD $85 billion in exchange for an 80 percent ownership stake in the firm. AIG's near collapse was symptomatic of contagion that spread throughout the global financial system. In an effort to prevent the crisis from spreading worldwide, the U.S. government provided an additional $170 billion in bailout funds, with $44 billion going to U.S. financial institutions and other domestic interests and $58 billion going to non-U.S. financial institutions.

The Collapse of AIG

In its prime, AIG was the world's biggest insurer, trusted for stability and for the financial protection it offered. AIG exemplified how a financial services firm could multiply its success through global expansion. AIG Financial Products (AIGFP), one of numerous subsidiaries, was the source of AIG's collapse. In 2008, AIGFP reported assets of $860 billion, 116,000 employees, and average sales of more than $7 million per employee. Under pressure to increase revenues and profits in the late 1990s, AIGFP's London office began insuring bundles of debt, known as collateralized debt obligations (CDOs). A CDO is a type of security that derives its value from a portfolio of fixed-income assets. CDOs lump various types of debt—from the very safe to the very risky—into one bundle. Interest and principal payments are made based on the level of risk, with riskier vehicles offering higher coupon payments, higher interest rates, or lower prices to compensate the risk.

From there, AIGFP created an instrument to insure CDOs, called a credit default swap (CDS). A CDS is a contract in which the buyer makes periodic payments to the seller and in return receives a payoff if the underlying credit instrument—in this case, the CDO—defaults. CDS contracts are similar to insurance, because the buyer pays a premium and, in return, receives a payoff if the credit instrument, typically a bond or loan, fails to pay. However, unlike insurance, CDS sellers were not required to maintain any reserves to pay off buyers. AIGFP sold countless CDSs, generating revenues of more than $3 billion, or nearly 18 percent of AIG's business. Because most CDS bundles were relatively diversified, AIG management believed the risk of having to make payouts was low. In reality, however, many CDO bundles were stuffed with risky subprime mortgage loans.

Simultaneously, as real estate values crashed in the subprime mortgage crisis, homeowners were left with mortgage debt greater than the value of their homes. Thousands of mortgages had been "securitized"—that is, sold as investment vehicles such as the CDO bundles sold by AIG. When foreclosure rates escalated in mid-2008, AIGFP and its parent company faced enormous obligations they had not expected to pay. As AIGFP incurred massive losses, AIG's stock price plummeted. AIG's credit rating fell and the firm faced financial ruin.

Global Connections

AIG was at the forefront of the globalization of finance. The firm's network of operations involved investments—mutual funds, pension funds, and other financial instruments—with banks and financial institutions worldwide. The effects of AIG's failure were felt in such banking institutions as Societe Generale in France, Deutsche Bank in Germany, and Barclay's in England, which were heavily invested in AIG or insured by it. As the insurance giant fell into ruin, the fortunes of many non-U.S. financial institutions declined as well.

AIG's bailout occurred just as individual homeowners found themselves unable to repay debt and national economies fell into recession. At the same time, many Americans resented how their tax dollars were used on a massive scale to rescue AIG. Further controversy arose when AIG used nearly $60 billion of the bailout to pay off banks in Europe, much of it representing obligations that AIG incurred in its global transactions. In comparison, U.S. institutions received roughly $44 billion. The furor intensified when AIG tried to renegotiate loans with some of its American creditors, implying they were less important than European banks.

In the wake of the crisis, governments in various countries increased efforts to regulate the banking and finance sector. But regulation varies by nation, and multinational firms often prefer doing business in countries with minimal regulatory constraints. Overseas locations provide Wall Street banks with opportunities for "regulatory arbitrage"—that is, finding the most beneficial legal environments in which to do business. For example, before going bankrupt, Lehman Brothers established a subsidiary in the Netherlands that sold complex bonds valued at $35 billion. Resolving investor claims against Lehman's Dutch subsidiary was complicated because the notes were governed by a hodgepodge of laws in Britain and the Netherlands, as well as at the state and federal levels in the United States.

The Crisis in Emerging Markets

Eastern Europe is often characterized by a dangerous combination of devalued local currencies and mounting foreign currency debt. This occurs because, as they participate in the global economy, such countries as Hungary, Poland, and the Czech Republic must use "hard currencies," or widely recognized foreign exchange. Many homeowners in Poland pay their monthly mortgages in *zlotys* (Poland's national currency), but because the loans often originate in Britain, Germany, or the United States, they ultimately must be paid in pounds, euros, or dollars. As currencies in Eastern Europe lose value, nations in the region struggle to pay their foreign debt.

Part of the problem stems from an earlier time when Eastern European currencies appreciated in value, making loans denominated in British pounds and Swiss francs more attractive. For example, most home mortgages in Hungary were originally negotiated in Swiss francs. In mid-2008, meanwhile, the value of Eastern European currencies declined as much as 30 percent. In addition, the region depends heavily on exports to advanced economies, especially in Western Europe. As these latter countries fell into recession, exports from Eastern Europe fell, reducing their foreign exchange revenues. Countries also experienced sharp declines in foreign direct investment, further reducing national income levels.

At the same time, however, emerging markets have remained relatively strong. While financial crisis and recession afflicted the advanced economies, most emerging markets continued to grow their GDPs at rates often exceeding 6 percent. Emerging markets will not fully compensate for slow growth in Europe, Japan, and the United States. But it is ironic that countries once considered "less developed" may keep the world from reeling completely out of control.

The IMF and the World Bank

In the wake of the financial crisis, the International Monetary Fund stepped up efforts to foster cooperation, stability, and economic growth around the world. In 2009, the IMF provided more than $100 billion in loans and credit to emerging countries hit by falling demand for their exports, collapsing financial markets, and wary consumers. For example, the IMF committed lending to

Hungary, Iceland, Poland, and Ukraine. In 2009, Mexico was granted a credit line worth $47 billion. Similarly, the World Bank provided financial aid and technical assistance to numerous developing economies. The Bank provides grants and low-interest loans to poor countries for investments in education, health, infrastructure, and private sector development. For example, the Bank loaned millions to El Salvador and other Latin American countries to buffer against the global financial crisis. In Africa, the Bank provided millions to finance highway construction and other infrastructure development. At the same time, however, while IMF and World Bank loans help struggling economies, they are yet another form of debt in a debt-fueled crisis and a debt-ridden world.

NOTE: For background on this case, see the Global Trend feature in this chapter.

Case Questions

1. Explain the advantages and disadvantages of the globalization of finance. How did it contribute to the global financial crisis?

2. Describe how the fall of AIG exemplifies contagion. How did the U.S. government bailout of AIG benefit foreign as well as U.S. firms and investors? Experts are advocating increased regulation to prevent con-tagion. At the national and international levels, what types of regulation might prevent future crises?

3. Several European countries have adopted a single currency, the euro. Describe how adopting the euro might benefit countries in Eastern Europe. What are the advantages and disadvantages of a single currency regime in international financial transactions?

4. As the world emerges from the global financial crisis, what is the potential role of each of the following: firms, banks, central banks, national governments, the International Monetary Fund, and the World Bank? What is the role of national governments in stimulating national economic growth?

SOURCES: D. Dickson, "IMF Role Grows with Crisis," *The Washington Times*, April 27, 2009; G. Gethard, "Falling Giant: A Case Study of AIG," 2009, *Investopedia.com*; Hoovers, Inc., Company Profile: American International Group Inc., 2010, retrieved from http://www.hoovers.com; P. Gumbel, "Global Break-down," *Fortune*, October 13, 2008, p. 26; D. Henry and M. Goldstein, "The Perils of Global Banking," *Business Week*, May 18, 2009; M. Mandel, "German and French Banks got $36 Billion from AIG Bailout," Unstructured Finance, *Business Week's* Wall Street News Blog, March 15, 2009, retrieved from http://www.businessweek .com/investing/wall_street_news_blog/; R. Samuelson, "A Global Free-For-All?" *Newsweek*, April 13, 2009; Trading Economics, Russia, Argentina, Brazil, China, India, 2009, retrieved from http://www.tradingeconomics.com/default.aspx; C. Whittall, "History Repeating," *Risk*, April 2009, p. 70.

This case was written by Professor Carol Sánchez and Jeffrey Sayers, of Grand Valley State University, Grand Rapids, Michigan.

CHAPTER ESSENTIALS

Key Terms

balance of payments, p. 326
capital flight, p. 321
central bank, p. 324
currency risk, p. 320
devaluation, p. 326
exchange rate, p. 320

foreign exchange, p. 322
foreign exchange market, p. 322
global financial system, p. 329
International Monetary Fund (IMF), p. 327
international monetary system, p. 328

monetary intervention, p. 335
Special Drawing Right (SDR), p. 336
trade surplus, p. 326
trade deficit, p. 326
World Bank, p. 327

Summary

In this chapter, you learned about:

1. **Exchange rates and currencies in international business**

   Much of international trade requires the exchange of currencies, such as the dollar, euro, and yen. An **exchange rate** is the price of one currency expressed in terms of another. **Currency risk** arises from

changes in exchange rates, and affects firms' international business prospects. A *convertible currency* is one that can be readily exchanged for other currencies. Some currencies are nonconvertible and not readily exchangeable. **Foreign exchange** refers to all forms of money that are traded internationally, including foreign currencies, bank deposits, checks, and electronic transfers. **Capital flight** refers to the tendency of international investors to drastically reduce their investments in a troubled currency or other assets. Currencies are exchanged in the **foreign exchange market**—the global marketplace for buying and selling currencies—mainly by banks and governments.

2. How exchange rates are determined

Currency values are determined by various factors, including *economic growth, inflation, market psychology*, and *government action*. As inflation rises, so do interest rates, usually accompanied by a decrease in currency value. **Trade deficit** refers to the amount by which a nation's imports exceed its exports for a specific time period. **Trade surplus** is the amount by which a nation's exports exceed its imports for a specific time period. Government action to influence exchange rates is broadly termed **monetary intervention**. When the goal is **devaluation**, the government acts to reduce the official value of its currency, relative to other currencies. The **balance of payments** is the annual accounting of *all* economic transactions of a nation with all other nations.

3. Emergence of the modern exchange rate system

The Bretton Woods agreement of 1944 aimed to stabilize exchange rates worldwide. But the system collapsed in 1971 as currency values began floating according to market forces. Today, currency values are determined in some countries by a *floating exchange rate system*, according to market forces, and in developing economies by a *fixed exchange rate system*, controlled via government intervention. The **International Monetary Fund** (IMF) is a key international agency that aims to stabilize currencies by monitoring the foreign exchange systems of member countries and lending money to developing

economies. The **World Bank** is an international agency that provides loans and technical assistance to low- and middle-income countries with the goal of reducing poverty.

4. The monetary and financial systems

The **international monetary system** is the institutional framework, rules, and procedures by which national currencies are exchanged for each other. It includes institutional arrangements that countries put in place to govern exchange rates. The **global financial system** is the collective of financial institutions that facilitate and regulate investment and capital flows, and make possible massive trading of currencies and financial assets. It reflects the activities of companies, banks, and financial institutions, all engaged in ongoing financial activity.

5. Key players in the monetary and financial systems

Key participants include firms that generate revenues and acquire foreign exchange in the course of international business, invest abroad, and inject money into the financial system. Trading of securities and bonds takes place in *national stock exchanges* and *bond markets*. Each country has a **central bank,** the monetary authority that regulates the money supply and credit, issues currency, manages the rate of exchange, and acts as lender of last resort. The IMF employs **Special Drawing Rights**, a type of international reserve, to help manage currency valuation worldwide. A *currency crisis* results when the value of the nation's currency depreciates sharply. A *banking crisis* results when investors lose confidence in a nation's banking system and massively withdraw funds. Excessive *foreign debt* can harm the stability of national financial systems.

Test Your Comprehension AACSB: Reflective Thinking Skills

1. Distinguish between *exchange rate* and *foreign exchange*. What does each term mean?

2. Distinguish between convertible and nonconvertible currencies.

3. Exchange rates fluctuate constantly. What is the effect of this fluctuation on firms engaged in international business?

4. Summarize the four major factors that determine exchange rates.

5. What is the relationship between inflation, interest rates, and currency values?

6. What was the Bretton Woods agreement, and what is its legacy today?

7. Distinguish the two systems that make up the exchange rate system today.

8. What is the difference between the international monetary system and the global financial system?

9. What are the key players in the international monetary and financial systems?

10. What are the aims of the World Bank and the International Monetary Fund?

Strategy and Organization in the International Firm

IKEA's Global Strategy

IKEA is a Swedish furniture retailer that transformed into a global player. Ingvar Kamprad founded the firm in Sweden in 1943. IKEA originally sold pens, picture frames, jewelry, and nylon stockings—anything Kamprad could sell at a low price. In 1950, IKEA began selling furniture and housewares. In the 1970s, the firm expanded into Europe and North America and began to grow rapidly. Total sales in 2009 exceeded 22 billion euros, making IKEA the world's largest furniture retailer. Its stores, usually located in major cities, are huge warehouse-style outlets that stock some 9,500 items, including everything for the home—from sofas to plants to kitchen utensils.

IKEA's philosophy is to offer high-quality, well-designed furnishings at low prices. Its functional, utilitarian, and space-saving pieces have a distinctive Scandinavian style and are "knock-down" furniture, which the customer assembles at home.

IKEA is owned by the Kamprad family, with corporate offices in the Netherlands, Sweden, and Belgium. Product development, purchasing, and warehousing are concentrated in Sweden. Its headquarters designs and develops IKEA's global branding and product line, often collaborating closely with external suppliers. About 30 percent of the merchandise is made in Asia and two-thirds in Europe. A few items are sourced in North America to address the specific needs of that market, but 90 percent of the product line is identical worldwide. Store managers constantly feed market research back to headquarters on sales and customer preferences.

IKEA targets moderate-income households with limited living space. The preferred market segment is progressive, well-educated people, including college students, who care little about status. Targeting a global customer segment allows IKEA to offer standardized products at uniform prices, a strategy that minimizes the costs of international operations. IKEA seeks scale economies by consolidating worldwide design, purchasing, and manufacturing. It distinguishes itself from conventional furniture makers that serve fragmented markets.

Each IKEA store follows a centrally developed advertising strategy in which the catalogue is the most important marketing tool. In 2008, about 200 million copies were printed in twenty-seven languages, representing the largest circulation of a free publication in the world. Also available online (www.ikea.com), the catalogue is prepared in Sweden to ensure conformity with IKEA's cosmopolitan style. Each product has a unique proper name. IKEA uses Scandinavian rivers or cities for sofas (Henriksberg, Falkenberg), women's names for fabric (Linne, Mimmi, Adel), and men's names for wall units (Billy, Niklas, Ivar).

IKEA employees ("co-workers") worldwide are widely acknowledged to be the basis for the firm's success.

Corporate culture is informal. There are few titles, no executive parking spaces, and no corporate dining rooms. Managers fly economy class and stay in inexpensive hotels. Most initiatives are developed at headquarters in Sweden and communicated to all stores worldwide. This speeds decision making and ensures the IKEA culture is easily globalized. Management in each store is required to speak either English or Swedish to ensure efficient communications with headquarters.

IKEA organizes an "anti-bureaucratic week" each year in which managers wear sales clerks' uniforms and do everything from operating cash registers to driving forklifts. The system keeps managers in touch with all IKEA operations and close to suppliers, customers, and sales staff. The firm's culture, emphasizing consensus-based decision making and problem solving, lets managers share their knowledge and skills with co-workers and helps employees and suppliers feel they are an important part of a global organization. The strong appeal of its global culture supports IKEA's continued growth.

It is challenging to manage operations across forty countries, 295 stores, twenty franchises, 125,000 employees, twenty-seven distribution centers, and 1,400 suppliers in fifty-four countries. IKEA chooses its target markets strategically. In 2009, it suspended further investment in Russia because of burdensome government intervention there. Elsewhere, it faces much complexity in adapting to national markets regarding employment, operations, supplier relationships, and customer preferences. Among other challenges, IKEA must figure out how to:

- Incorporate customer feedback and design preferences from diverse markets into decision making at headquarters
- Reward employees and motivate suppliers despite varying business customs and expectations from country to country
- Achieve the real benefits of international operations—efficiency on a global scale and learning—while remaining responsive to local needs
- Keep designs standardized across markets yet respond to local preferences and trends
- Delegate adequate autonomy to local store managers while retaining central control

IKEA fared well during the recent global recession. Its value-oriented furniture and housewares appeal to customers during tough economic times.

SOURCES: J. Bush and K. Capell, "IKEA in Russia: Enough Is Enough," *Business Week*, July 13, 2009, p. 33; "IKEA: How the Swedish Retailer Became a Global Cult Brand," *Business Week*, November 14, 2005, retrieved from http://www.businessweek.com; "Online Extra: IKEA's Design for Growth," *Business Week*, June 6, 2005, retrieved from http://www.businessweek.com; M. Duff, "IKEA Eyes Aggressive Growth," *DSN Retailing Today*, January 27, 2003, p. 23; M. Lloyd, "IKEA Sees Opportunity During Hard Times," *Wall Street Journal*, February 18, 2009, p. B1; IKEA corporate Web site at http://www.IKEA-group.IKEA.com; IKEA company profile at http://www.hoovers.com.

A s the IKEA vignette shows, managers strive to coordinate sourcing, manufacturing, marketing, and other value-adding activities on a worldwide basis. They adopt organization-wide standards and common processes. They seek to develop products that appeal to the broadest base of customers worldwide. Organizing the firm on a global scale is challenging. It requires skillfully configuring activities across diverse settings, integrating and coordinating these activities, and implementing common processes to ensure the activities are performed optimally. In addition, the firm must simultaneously respond to the specific needs and conditions that characterize the individual locations where it does business. In this chapter, we discuss the role of strategy and organization, and the various company attributes that support them, in building the successful international firm.

Strategy in International Business

Strategy is a planned set of actions that managers employ to make best use of the firm's resources and core competencies to gain competitive advantage. When developing strategies, managers start by examining the firm's specific strengths and weaknesses. They then analyze the particular opportunities and challenges that confront the firm. Once they understand the firm's strengths, weaknesses, opportunities, and challenges, they decide which customers to target, what product lines to offer, how best to contend with competitors, and how generally to configure and coordinate the firm's activities around the world.

International strategy is strategy carried out in two or more countries. Managers in experienced MNEs develop international strategies to help the firm allocate scarce resources and configure value-adding activities on a worldwide scale, participate in major markets, implement valuable partnerships abroad, and engage in competitive moves in response to foreign rivals.[1]

Managers devise strategies that develop and ensure the firm's competitive advantages. The most widely accepted prescription for building sustainable, competitive advantage in international business is that of Bartlett and Ghoshal.[2] These scholars argued the firm should strive to develop: "global-scale efficiency in its existing activities; multinational flexibility to manage diverse country-specific risks and opportunities; and learn from international exposure and exploit that learning on a worldwide basis."[3] Accordingly, firms aspiring to become globally competitive must seek simultaneously three strategic objectives—efficiency, flexibility, and learning.[4] Let's review each objective.

Efficiency *The firm must build efficient international value chains.* Efficiency refers to lowering the cost of the firm's operations and activities on a global scale. MNEs with multiple value chains must pay special attention to how they organize their R&D, manufacturing, product sourcing, marketing, and customer service activities. Automotive companies strive to achieve scale economies by concentrating manufacturing and sourcing activities in a limited number of locations. For Toyota (www.toyota.com), this means manufacturing in low-cost countries like China and in major markets like the United States. Toyota works with its suppliers to ensure they provide low-cost parts and components while maintaining quality. Its logistical operations for shipping its cars around the world are efficient and cost-effective.

Flexibility *The firm must develop worldwide flexibility to accommodate diverse country-specific risks and opportunities.* The diversity and volatility of the international environment are especially challenging for managers, making the firm's ability to tap local resources and exploit local opportunities critical. Managers may opt for contractual relationships with independent suppliers and distributors in one country, while engaging in direct investment in another. They may adapt their marketing and human resource practices to suit unique country conditions. Exchange rate fluctuations may prompt managers to switch to local sourcing or to adjust prices. The firm structures its operations to ensure it can respond to specific customer needs in individual markets, especially those critical to company performance.[5]

Learning *The firm must create the ability to learn from operating in international environments and exploit this learning on a worldwide basis.* The diversity of the international environment presents the internationalizing firm with unique learning opportunities. By operating in various countries, the MNE can acquire new technical and managerial know-how, new product ideas, improved R&D capabilities, partnering skills, and survival capabilities in unfamiliar environments. The firm's partners or subsidiaries capture and disseminate this learning throughout their corporate network. Although Procter & Gamble (www.pg.com) is based in the United States, the firm's research center

Strategy A planned set of actions that managers employ to make best use of the firm's resources and core competencies to gain competitive advantage.

in Belgium developed a special water-softening technology to deal with Europe's hard water. P&G's subsidiary in Japan formulated a detergent that works well in cold water, to adapt to Japanese customers' preference for cold-water clothes washing. P&G incorporated these inventions into its knowledge base and applied the knowledge to the development of products for other markets around the world.

International business success is determined in the end by the degree to which the firm achieves all three skills—efficiency, flexibility, and learning. But it is often difficult to excel in all three simultaneously. One firm may be highly efficient, while another excels at flexibility and a third at learning. Many Japanese firms achieved international success by developing highly efficient and centralized manufacturing systems. In Europe, numerous firms succeeded internationally by being locally responsive, despite sometimes failing to achieve substantial efficiency or technological leadership. Many MNEs from the United States have struggled to adapt their activities to the cultural and political diversity of national environments and instead have proven adept at achieving efficiency via economies of scale. During the global financial crisis that began in 2008, efficiency and flexibility became particularly important to the success of multinational firms.[6]

 ## Building the Global Firm

Exhibit 12.1 illustrates the requisite dimensions of the successful international firm. Truly global firms are characterized by visionary leadership, strong organizational culture, and superior organizational processes, as well as an appropriate organizational structure and strategies that optimize international operations.[7] We examine these key dimensions next.

Visionary leadership
A quality of senior management that provides superior strategic guidance for managing efficiency, flexibility, and learning.

Visionary Leadership

Visionary leadership is a quality of senior management that provides superior strategic guidance for managing efficiency, flexibility, and learning.[8] Leadership is more complex in firms that operate in international than in domestic settings because valuable organizational assets, such as productive capabilities, brands, and human resources, may be

Exhibit 12.1 Key Dimensions of Successful International Firms

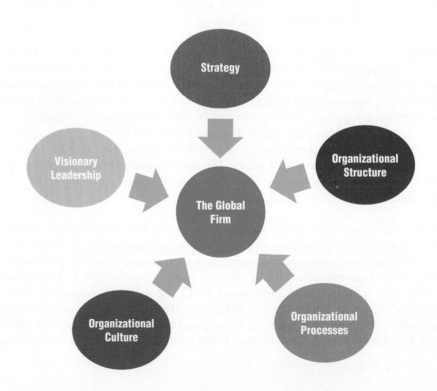

employed in many different countries and diverse business environments. Visionary leadership is vital in firms with complex international operations.

How do leaders differ from managers? The main difference is that managers are relatively focused on directing the firm's day-to-day operations. By contrast, leaders are visionary and hold a long-term perspective on the challenges and opportunities that confront the firm. Leaders are exceptionally skilled at motivating people and at setting the tone for how the firm will pursue its goals and objectives.

Consider Peter Brabeck, former Chief Executive Officer (CEO) of Nestlé (www.nestle.com). From headquarters in Switzerland, Brabeck led Nestlé into the worldwide market for products that meet consumers' growing interest in health and nutrition. To pursue this market, Nestlé purchased Jenny Craig, the U.S. weight management and food-products company. In Germany, Nestlé launched an institute to advise consumers on dietary issues, dispensing nutritional advice to more than 300,000 customers per month. In France, Brabeck created a nutritional home-care service, providing for patients with special dietary needs. These initiatives position Nestlé in a growing global market and generate global brand loyalty for the firm's line of healthy food products.[9] Visionary leaders such as Peter Brabeck are characterized by four major traits:

- *International mind-set and cosmopolitan values.* Visionary leadership requires managers to acquire an international mind-set—an openness to, and awareness of, diversity across cultures.[10] Dogmatic, close-minded managers who lack vision and have difficulty adapting to other cultures are likely to fail. Those who are open minded, committed to internationalization, and ready to adapt to other cultures are likely to succeed.[11]

- *Willingness to commit resources.* The complexities of foreign markets imply that international ventures take more time than domestic ones to become profitable. Visionary leaders commit to them and unswervingly believe the firm will eventually succeed. Commitment drives them to develop the financial, human, and other resources their firms need to achieve their international goals. Highly committed firms engage in systematic international market expansion, allocate necessary resources, and empower structures and processes that ensure ultimate success.

- *Strategic vision.* Visionary leaders articulate a *strategic vision*— what the firm wants to be in the future and how it will get there. As they develop strategic vision, senior managers focus on the ideal picture of what the firm should become. The picture is a central rallying point for all plans, employees, and employee actions.[12] For example, by 2015, one in four Japanese—about 30 million people—will be over age 65. Synclayer (www.synclayer.com) is a Japanese SME whose managers anticipate a large and growing market for new products for the elderly. Their vision of achieving worldwide leadership in this market led Synclayer to develop, among other products, a system that allows homebound seniors to measure their blood pressure, temperature, and other vital signs, and send them to a health care service that can dispatch an ambulance if problems are detected. Synclayer's vision is to develop the products in Japan and then launch them in other countries with sizable elderly populations.[13]

- *Willingness to invest in human assets.* Visionary leaders must nurture the most critical asset of any organization—human capital. In global firms, senior leaders adopt such human resource practices as hiring foreign nationals, promoting multicountry careers, and providing cross-cultural and language training to develop international supermanagers.[14]

Ratan Tata is chairman of India's Tata group. Tata transformed the giant Indian conglomerate into a transnational organization, with operations throughout the world.

Ratan Tata is chairperson of the Tata Group in India and oversees a $63 billion family conglomerate whose companies market a range of products from cars to watches. His group has made numerous international acquisitions (from Tetley Tea to the Anglo-Dutch steel firm Corus), reflecting a change in strategic vision from local to global. In its latest venture, Tata developed a $2,500 car, the Nano, targeted to emerging markets worldwide. Another visionary leader is Fujio Cho, who led Toyota to record sales in the intensely competitive global car industry. His leadership style emphasized innovation, continuous improvement, and an ability to spot future-oriented opportunities, including the Prius hybrid and the youth-oriented Scion brands of Toyota cars. Toyota's main sales focus now is emerging markets, especially China and India.[15]

Organizational Culture

Organizational culture
The pattern of shared values, behavioral norms, systems, policies, and procedures that employees learn and adopt.

Organizational culture is the pattern of shared values, behavioral norms, systems, policies, and procedures that employees learn and adopt. It spells out the correct way for employees to perceive, think, and behave in relation to new problems and opportunities that confront the firm.[16] As the opening vignette about IKEA showed, organizational culture usually derives from the influence of founders and visionary leaders or some unique history of the firm.

At the Japanese electronics giant Canon (www.canon.com), CEO Fujio Mitarai has developed an organizational culture that emphasizes science and technology. Canon invests billions in R&D and is the world's second-largest recipient of new U.S. patents. Its technology focus extends from product development to the way goods are made on the factory floor; this focus has allowed Canon to become the world leader in digital cameras, copiers, printers, and flat-screen TVs.[17] Recent innovations have slashed production time and costs.

Similarly, focus on product quality is a pillar of the organizational culture at the South Korean firm Hyundai. The firm's leaders have set a goal of becoming the world quality leader in the auto industry. A stringent quality approval system is enforced at each value-chain stage, including sourcing, procurement, manufacturing, marketing, and sales. Top managers hold quality oversight meetings every two weeks. In 2010, a survey of 60,000 new car buyers ranked Hyundai third in overall quality, behind only Porsche and Lexus.[18]

Today, management at firms like Canon and Hyundai seek to build a *global* organizational culture—an organizational environment that plays a key role in the development and execution of corporate global strategy. Companies that proactively build a global organizational culture:[19]

- Value and promote a global perspective in all major initiatives
- Value global competence and cross-cultural skills among their employees
- Adopt a single corporate language for business communications
- Promote interdependency between headquarters and subsidiaries
- Subscribe to globally accepted ethical standards

Firms aspiring to become truly global seek to maintain strong ethical standards in all the markets where they do business. Ultimately, management should cultivate a culture that welcomes social responsibility and is deliberate about fulfilling its role.

Visionary leadership with organizational culture needs to be supplemented with processes that define how managers will carry out day-to-day activities to achieve company goals. Let's examine these organizational processes next.

Organizational processes Managerial routines, behaviors, and mechanisms that allow the firm to function as intended.

Organizational Processes

Organizational processes are the managerial routines, behaviors, and mechanisms that allow the firm to function as intended. Typical processes include mechanisms for collecting strategic information, ensuring quality control in manufacturing, and maintaining efficient payment systems for international sales. General Electric has gained substantial competitive advantage by emphasizing and refining the countless processes that comprise its value chains. For instance, GE digitizes all key documents and uses intranets and the Internet to automate many activities and reduce operating costs.

Managers attempt to achieve global coordination and integration not just by subscribing to a particular organizational design, but also by implementing common processes or *globalizing mechanisms*. These common processes provide substantial interconnectedness within the MNE network and allow for meaningful cross-fertilization and knowledge. Globalizing mechanisms include *global teams* and *global information systems*.

Global teams are charged with problem solving and best-practice development within the firm.[20] A **global team** is an internationally distributed group of employees charged with a specific problem-solving or best-practice mandate that affects the entire organization.[21] Team members are drawn from geographically diverse units of the MNE and may interact via in-person meetings, corporate intranets, and video conferencing. In this way, a global team brings together employees with the experience, knowledge, and skills to resolve common challenges.

Tasks of global teams vary. *Strategic global teams* identify or implement initiatives that enhance the long-term direction of the firm in its global industry. *Operational global teams* focus on the efficient and effective operation of the business across the whole network.[22] The most successful teams are flexible, responsive, and innovative. To develop global strategies, the team should include culturally diverse managers whose business activities span the globe. Culturally diverse teams have three valuable roles: create a global view inside the firm while remaining in touch with local realities; generate creative ideas and make fully informed decisions about the firm's global operations; and ensure team decisions are implemented throughout the firm's global operations.

Top managers' desire to create a globally coordinated company is motivated by the need for world-scale efficiency and minimal redundancy. In the past, geographic distance and cross-cultural differences were impediments. Today, *global information systems*—global IT infrastructure and tools such as intranets, the Internet, and electronic data interchange—ensure that distant parts of the global network share knowledge and learn from each other.

When General Motors developed the Equinox, a sport utility vehicle to compete with Toyota's RAV4 and Honda's CR-V, it leveraged global information systems to tap GM capabilities around the world. The Equinox's V6 engine was built in China, with cooperation from engineers in Canada, China, Japan, and the United States. From a room in Toronto, engineers teleconferenced almost daily with their counterparts from Shanghai, Tokyo, and Ohio. They exchanged virtual-reality renderings of the vehicle and collaborated on styling of exteriors and component design.

In later sections, we explain two especially critical dimensions of internationalizing firms: strategy and organizational structure. First, however, let's lay the foundation for these key concepts by distinguishing between multidomestic and global industries and by introducing the global integration–local responsiveness framework.

The Distinction between Multidomestic and Global Industries

Companies that specialize in particular industries, such as processed food, beverages, consumer products, fashion, retailing, and publishing, have long approached international business by catering to the specific needs and tastes of each of the countries where they do business. For example, the British publisher Bloomsbury translates each volume of its Harry Potter series into the local language in every country where the book is sold. Coca-Cola varies the formula of its beverages to suit differing conditions abroad. Industries such as this, in which the firm must adapt its offerings to suit the culture, laws, income level, and other specific characteristics of each country, are known as **multidomestic industries**. In such industries, each country tends to have a unique set of competitors. Accordingly, a multidomestic industry is one in which competition takes place on a *country-by-country* basis.

By contrast, in other types of industries, such as aerospace, automobiles, metals, computers, chemicals, and industrial equipment, firms generally approach international

Global team An internationally distributed group of employees charged with a specific problem-solving or best-practice mandate that affects the entire organization.

Multidomestic industry An industry in which competition takes place on a country-by-country basis.

Global industry An industry in which competition is on a regional or worldwide scale.

business by catering to the needs and tastes of customers on a regional or global scale. For example, Dupont sells essentially the same chemicals around the world. Subaru markets very similar cars in most of the countries where it does business. Industries such as this, in which competition takes place on a *regional or worldwide* basis, are known as **global industries**. Most global industries are characterized by a handful of major players that compete head-on in multiple markets. Kodak must contend with the same rivals—Japan's Fuji and Europe's Agfa-Gevaert—around the world. In the earth-moving equipment industry, Caterpillar and Komatsu compete head-on in all major world markets.

The Integration-Responsiveness Framework

Global integration Coordination of the firm's value-chain activities across countries to achieve worldwide efficiency, synergy, and cross-fertilization in order to take maximum advantage of similarities between countries.

Global integration is the *coordination* of the firm's value-chain activities across multiple countries to achieve worldwide efficiency, synergy, and cross-fertilization in order to take advantage of similarities between countries. Firms that emphasize global integration make and sell products and services that are relatively standardized—that is, uniform or with minimal adaptation—to capitalize on converging customer needs and tastes worldwide. Such firms compete on a *regional or worldwide* basis. They seek to minimize operating costs by centralizing value-chain activities and emphasizing economies of scale.[23]

Local responsiveness Management of the firm's value-chain activities on a country-by-country basis to address diverse opportunities and risks.

In contrast to global integration, many companies seek to respond to specific conditions in individual countries. Accordingly, **local responsiveness** refers to managing the firm's value-chain activities, and addressing diverse opportunities and risks, on a *country-by-country* basis. It emphasizes meeting the specific needs of customers in individual markets.

When they operate internationally, firms try to strike the right balance between the objectives of global integration and local responsiveness. The *integration-responsiveness (IR) framework* (Exhibit 12.2) illustrates the pressures they face in attempting to achieve these often-conflicting objectives.[24] It was developed to help managers better understand the trade-offs common in international business.

The primary goal of firms that emphasize global integration is to maximize the efficiency of their value-chain activities on a worldwide scale. They seek to reduce redundancy

Exhibit 12.2
Integration-Responsiveness Framework: Competing Pressures on the Internationalizing Firm

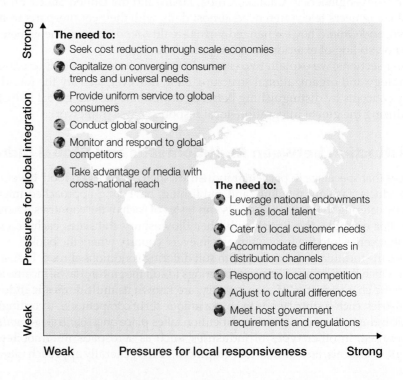

Pressures for global integration (Weak → Strong)

The need to:
- Seek cost reduction through scale economies
- Capitalize on converging consumer trends and universal needs
- Provide uniform service to global consumers
- Conduct global sourcing
- Monitor and respond to global competitors
- Take advantage of media with cross-national reach

The need to:
- Leverage national endowments such as local talent
- Cater to local customer needs
- Accommodate differences in distribution channels
- Respond to local competition
- Adjust to cultural differences
- Meet host government requirements and regulations

Weak   Pressures for local responsiveness   Strong in their operations. They acknowledge that designing numerous variations of the same product for individual markets is costly, and they minimize it. They also promote learning and cross-fertilization of knowledge within their global network in order to enhance innovation and gain competitive advantages. Senior management justifies global integration by citing converging buyer demand, spread of global brands, diffusion of uniform technology, availability of pan-regional media, and the need to monitor competitors on a global basis. Firms that emphasize global integration are typically found in *global industries.*

By contrast, companies that emphasize local responsiveness adjust the firm's practices to suit distinctive needs and conditions in each country. They adapt to local customer requirements, language, culture, regulation, the competitive environment, and the local distribution structure. They are typically found in *multidomestic* industries. For example, in Mexico, Walmart adjusts its store hours, employee training, compensation, product line, and promotional tools to suit local conditions.

Pressures for Global Integration

Let's examine the specific factors that compel companies to globally integrate their activities:[25]

- *Seek cost reduction through scale economies.* Some industries profit from manufacturing in a few select locations, where firms can take advantage of economies of scale in production. Concentrating production also makes it easier to control the quality, speed, and cost of manufacturing.

- *Capitalize on converging consumer trends and universal needs.* Making and selling products that are standardized is more cost effective than adapting products for each market. For example, firms that make computer chips and electronic components can generally sell similar offerings worldwide. Standardization has become possible as buyer needs and tastes have become increasingly similar worldwide.

- *Provide uniform service to global customers.* Services are easiest to standardize when firms can centralize their creation and delivery. MNEs with operations in numerous countries particularly value service inputs that are consistent worldwide.

- *Conduct global sourcing of raw materials, components, energy, and labor.* Firms face ongoing pressure to procure high-quality input goods cost effectively. Sourcing inputs from large-scale, centralized suppliers allows firms to obtain economies of scale, more consistent quality, lower costs, and generally more efficient operations.

- *Monitor and respond to global competitors.* Foreign rivals that compete on a global basis are usually more threatening than those that compete only locally. Thus, it is generally best to formulate strategies that challenge competitors on an integrated, global basis.

- *Take advantage of media that reaches buyers in multiple markets.* The availability of cost-effective, global media makes it possible for firms to design advertising and other promotional activities that target multiple countries simultaneously.

Pressures for Local Responsiveness

On the other hand, the following pressures compel companies to be locally responsive in individual countries:

- *Leverage natural endowments available to the firm.* Each country has distinctive resources such as raw materials and skilled knowledge workers that provide foreign firms with competitive advantages.

- *Cater to local customer needs.* Particularly in multidomestic industries, buyer needs vary from country to country. The internationalizing firm must adapt its products to meet diverse cross-national needs.

■ *Accommodate differences in distribution channels.* Channels can vary from market to market and may increase the need for local responsiveness. In Latin America, small stores are the most common type of retailer. Foreign firms that ordinarily distribute their goods via large stores must adapt their approach when doing business there.

■ *Respond to local competition.* Foreign firms are disadvantaged in markets that have numerous local competitors. To outdo local rivals, successful MNEs must devise offerings that best meet local demand.

■ *Adjust to cultural differences.* Culture's influence on business activities can be substantial, depending on the market and the product. Where cultural differences are important, such as in sales of food and clothing, the firm must adapt its products and marketing activities accordingly.

■ *Meet host government requirements and regulations.* To protect local firms, governments sometimes impose trade barriers or other restrictions that hinder foreign firms. The MNE can overcome such obstacles by establishing local operations to attain the status of a local firm.

Strategies Based on the Integration-Responsiveness Framework

The integration-responsiveness framework is associated with four distinct strategies, summarized in Exhibit 12.3. Internationalizing firms pursue one or a combination of these.

In the **home replication strategy**, the firm views international business as separate from, and secondary to, its domestic business. Expanding abroad is viewed as an opportunity to generate additional sales for domestic product lines. Thus, the firm designs products with domestic customers in mind and pursues international business in order to extend product life cycles and replicate home-market success. Such a firm expects little useful knowledge to flow from its foreign operations.[26] Firms that make and sell commodities (such as raw materials and basic parts) sometimes use the home replication strategy because such products often do not require a sophisticated internationalization approach. The strategy can also succeed when the firm targets only markets that are similar to the home market.

Home replication strategy An approach in which the firm views international business as separate from, and secondary to, its domestic business.

Exhibit 12.3 Four Distinct Strategies Emerging from the Integration-Responsiveness Framework

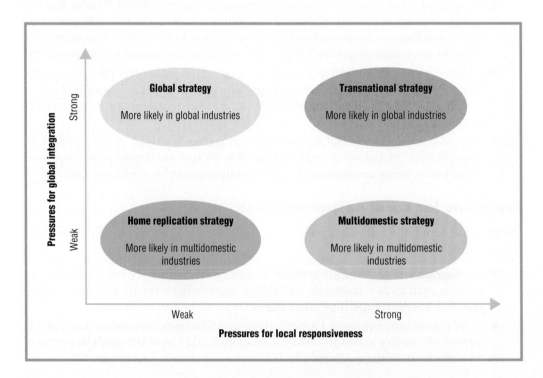

Home replication strategy is typically employed by the smaller firm with products it wants to sell abroad to generate additional sales. It contracts with an intermediary in each of several foreign markets to import and distribute the product and generally does not adapt it for foreign customers. Because management knows little about international business and has limited human and financial resources, the firm relies heavily on its foreign intermediaries. A key consequence is that it maintains little control over how its products are marketed abroad. Replicating abroad what the firm normally does at home provides few competitive advantages in foreign markets. Consequently, for most internationalizing firms, home replication is usually an initial, temporary approach rather than a long-term strategy.

A second, more advanced approach is **multidomestic strategy** (sometimes called *multilocal strategy*), in which the internationalizing firm develops subsidiaries or affiliates in each of numerous foreign markets. The firm delegates much autonomy to managers in each foreign unit, allowing them to operate independently and pursue local responsiveness. Using this strategy, headquarters recognizes and emphasizes differences between national markets. As a result, the firm allows subsidiaries to vary product and management practices by country. Country managers are often nationals of the host country and tend to function independently, with little incentive to share knowledge and experience with managers in other countries. Products and services are carefully adapted to suit the unique needs of each country.[27]

The food and beverage giant Nestlé (www.nestle.com) applies a multidomestic strategy. In each of its country subsidiaries, the firm employs highly autonomous nationals who adapt corporate strategic guidelines to meet specific local needs and conditions. Because of this approach, Nestlé is often perceived as a local firm in each of its markets. For example, the firm varies the taste of its Nescafé brand instant coffees. In Spain, the coffee has an intense, full-bodied flavor. In Northern Europe, it is mild and aromatic. Depending on the country, Nestlé sells its products through various channels, including supermarkets, small shops, market stalls, vending machines, mobile vendors, and even door-to-door. In Nigeria, it built a network of small warehouses and ships goods via pickup trucks. In China, the firm created a system of simple distribution links among villages that facilitate direct delivery by local vendors, often by bicycle. Nestlé also adapts its marketing. In patriotic Russia, advertising emphasizes Russian history and literature. In Africa, the firm hired local singers to visit villages and offer a mix of entertainment and product demonstrations. Nestlé also charges lower prices for its products in markets such as Brazil and China, to suit lower local buying power.[28]

The multidomestic approach has several advantages. If the foreign subsidiary includes a factory, locally produced products can be better adapted to the local market. There is minimal pressure on headquarters staff because local operations are managed by individual managers in each country. Firms with limited international experience find multidomestic strategy an easy option, as they can delegate many tasks to their country managers (or to foreign distributors, franchisees, or licensees, where they are used).

Multidomestic strategy has some disadvantages. Each foreign subsidiary manager tends to develop a local strategic plan, organizational culture, and business processes that can differ substantially from those of headquarters. Subsidiaries have little incentive to share their knowledge and experience with managers in the firm's other country markets. This may lead to reduced economies of scale. Limited information sharing also reduces the possibility of developing a knowledge-based competitive advantage.[29] While multidomestic strategy is more responsive to individual markets, it may lead to inefficient manufacturing, redundant operations, a proliferation of over-adapted products, and higher operating costs.[30]

These disadvantages may eventually lead management to abandon a multidomestic strategy in favor of a third approach—**global strategy**. With global strategy, headquarters seeks substantial control over its country operations in order to minimize redundancy and achieve maximum efficiency, learning, and integration worldwide. In the extreme, global strategy asks, "Why not make the same thing, the same way, everywhere?" Thus,

Multidomestic strategy An approach to firm internationalization in which headquarters delegates considerable autonomy to each country manager, allowing him or her to operate independently and pursue local responsiveness.

Global strategy An approach in which headquarters seeks substantial control over its country operations in order to minimize redundancy and maximize efficiency, learning, and integration worldwide.

Whirlpool's global strategy emphasizes relying on a handful of first-rate suppliers around the world and manufacturing in low-cost countries. This Whirlpool factory is in Shanghai, China.

global strategy emphasizes central coordination and control of international operations. Headquarters managers are often largely responsible for the firm's operations worldwide. Activities such as R&D and manufacturing are centralized at headquarters, and management tends to view the world as one large marketplace.[31]

An example of global strategy is Whirlpool Corporation (www.whirlpool.com), the home appliance firm. Once a disjointed collection of autonomous national subsidiaries, the firm now manages its global activities from company headquarters. Its integrated value chains mean Whirlpool's most advanced expertise in appliance technology, production, and distribution are continuously shared among all the firm's business units worldwide. Its engineers continuously seek the most cost-effective ways to produce leading-edge products based on common parts and components. Whirlpool R&D personnel from Asia, Europe, and the Americas work in global teams to develop appliances based on standardized platforms, with little cross-national variation. For example, the firm developed the "World Washer," a single washing machine that can be sold anywhere. In a typical Whirlpool refrigerator, the compressor, casing, and door are identical wherever the product is sold. Only basic controls and position of the freezer cabinet are varied, to suit differing national preferences. The company intranet allows R&D teams to access ideas and specifications on how to create inputs that can be integrated into Whirlpool products, wherever they are made.

Parts and components are sourced from a limited number of top suppliers worldwide, who operate globally to deliver to as many of Whirlpool's factories as possible. Whirlpool does much of its manufacturing in China, Mexico, and other emerging markets to keep costs low. In total, it makes its appliances in just twelve countries and sells them in 170. Marketing activities are standardized and focus on making Whirlpool a globally recognized brand. By emphasizing global strategy, Whirlpool optimizes its value chains and enjoys superior performance around the world.[32]

Global strategy offers many advantages. It provides a substantial ability to respond to worldwide opportunities. It increases opportunities for cross-national learning and cross-fertilization of the firm's knowledge among all its subsidiaries. It creates economies of scale, which result in lower operational costs. Global strategy can also improve the quality of products and processes, primarily by simplifying manufacturing and other processes. High-quality products give rise to global brand recognition, increased consumer preference, and efficient international marketing programs.

Many factors make it easier to pursue global strategy, including converging buyer characteristics worldwide, growing acceptance of global brands, increased diffusion of uniform technology (especially in industrial markets), the spread of international collaborative ventures, and the integrating effects of globalization and advanced communications technologies.

Transnational strategy
A coordinated approach to internationalization in which the firm strives to be relatively responsive to local needs while retaining sufficient central control of operations to ensure efficiency and learning.

Like other approaches, global strategy has limitations. It is challenging for management to closely coordinate the activities of widely dispersed international operations. The firm must maintain ongoing communications between headquarters and its subsidiaries, as well as between the subsidiaries. When carried to an extreme, global strategy results in a loss of responsiveness and flexibility in local markets.

A final alternative is **transnational strategy**, a coordinated approach to internationalization in which the firm strives to be relatively responsive to local needs while retaining sufficient central control of operations to ensure efficiency and learning. Transnational strategy combines the major advantages of multidomestic and global strategies while minimizing their disadvantages.[33] It is a flexible approach: *standardize where feasible; adapt where appropriate.* To implement transnational strategy, the firm should:

- Exploit scale economies by sourcing from a reduced set of global suppliers and concentrate manufacturing in relatively few locations where competitive advantages can be maximized
- Organize production, marketing, and other value-chain activities on a global scale
- Optimize local responsiveness and flexibility
- Facilitate global learning and knowledge transfer
- Coordinate global *competitive moves*—that is, rather than following a country-by-country approach, deal with competitors on a global, integrated basis[34]

China computer firm Lenovo follows a transnational strategy. The basic laptops that Lenovo sells are similar worldwide except the keyboards and internal software, which are adapted for individual markets due to language differences. The firm's retailing Web sites, which look identical across the world, are also adapted for language. Pictured is a Lenovo store in Beijing.

One example of transnational strategy is Lenovo (www.lenovo.com), the Chinese producer of personal computers and laptops. Lenovo went global when it bought the PC arm of IBM, gaining a global sales force and strong global brands, such as the Thinkpad line. The firm rotates its headquarters between China and the United States; its official language is English. Planning and design are done in the United States, while manufacturing is done in China (for Asian markets), Mexico (for the Americas), and Poland (for Europe). Lenovo concentrates production in these low-cost countries to generate the greatest cost efficiencies and economies of scale.

Lenovo's basic computers are the same, but the keyboards and internal software are adapted for each market to accommodate differences in language. The firm's retailing Web sites look identical worldwide, but are adapted for language. Marketing operations, centralized to Bangalore, India, include global campaigns designed to sell computers in more than sixty countries with ads that can air in multiple regions. In short, Lenovo strikes a balance between pursuing global strategy and adapting its offerings and approaches, as needed, to suit individual markets.[35]

Given the difficulty of balancing central control and local responsiveness, most MNEs find it difficult to implement transnational strategy. In the long run, almost all need to include some elements of localized decision making, because each country has idiosyncratic characteristics.

Having discussed distinct strategies that firms pursue in international expansion, let's now explore the related topic of organizational structure. While a strategy is the blueprint for action, a firm needs a structure with people, resources, and processes to implement it.

Organizational Structure

Organizational structure describes the reporting relationships inside the firm or the "boxes and lines" that specify the links between people, functions, and processes that allow the firm to carry out its operations. Organizational structure dictates the reporting relationships through which the firm's vision and strategies are implemented. In the large, experienced MNE, these linkages are extensive and include the firm's subsidiaries and affiliates. A fundamental issue in organizational structure is how much decision-making responsibility the firm should retain at headquarters and how much it should delegate to foreign subsidiaries and affiliates. This is the choice between *centralization* and *decentralization*. Let's examine these options in more detail.

Organizational structure Reporting relationships inside the firm that specify the links between people, functions, and processes.

A worker inspects production of Coca-Cola beverages in a plant in Africa. While Coca-Cola headquarters provides global brand support and broad marketing guidance to its bottlers in individual countries, the local bottler assumes responsibility for meeting local government requirements, local customer research, local sales promotion, and retailer support.

Centralized or Decentralized Structure?

A *centralized approach* gives headquarters considerable authority and control over the firm's activities worldwide. A *decentralized approach* means substantial autonomy and decision-making authority are delegated to the firm's subsidiaries around the world. In every company, management tends to devise a structure consistent with its vision and strategies. Thus, MNEs that emphasize global integration tend to have a centralized structure. Those that emphasize local responsiveness generally are decentralized.

Exhibit 12.4 identifies the typical contributions of headquarters and subsidiaries. Whether headquarters or the subsidiary will make decisions about the firm's value-chain activities depends on the firm's products, the size of its markets, the nature of competitor operations, and the size and strategic importance of each foreign venture. Generally, the larger the financial outlay or the riskier the anticipated result, the more headquarters will contribute to decision making. For example, decisions about developing new products or building factories abroad tend to be centralized to headquarters. Decisions that affect two or more countries are best left to headquarters managers who have a regional or global perspective.[36] Decisions about local products that will be sold in only one country, however, are typically the joint responsibility of corporate and country-level managers, with the latter taking the lead role. Decisions on day-to-day human resource issues in individual subsidiaries are generally left to local managers.

Generally, it is neither beneficial nor feasible for the firm to centralize all its operations. Retaining some local autonomy is both desirable and necessary. Companies must strike the right balance between centralization and local autonomy. The challenge for managers is to achieve these goals simultaneously.[37] The phrase "Think globally, act locally" oversimplifies the true complexities of today's global competition; "Think globally *and* locally *and act appropriately*" better describes the reality faced by MNEs today.[38]

Planning shared by managers at headquarters and at subsidiaries, with negotiation and give-and-take on both sides, is vital to the design of effective strategies. Highly centralized, top-down decision making ignores subsidiary managers' intimate knowledge of host countries. Highly decentralized, bottom-up decision making by autonomous subsidiary

A subsidiary is the primary contributor to these activities:	Headquarters is the primary contributor to these activities:	Shared responsibility of subsidiary and headquarters:
• Sales • Marketing • Local market research • Human resource management • Compliance with local laws and regulations	• Capital planning • Transfer pricing • Global profitability	**With the subsidiary's lead:** • Geographic strategy • Local product and service development • Technical support and customer service • Local procurement **With the headquarters' lead:** • Broad corporate strategy • Global product development • Basic research and development • Global product sourcing • Development of global managers

Exhibit 12.4 Subsidiary and Headquarters Contributions

managers ignores the big-picture knowledge of headquarters managers and fails to integrate strategies across countries and regions. Ultimately, however, most decisions are subject to headquarters approval. Headquarters management should promote positive, open-minded, collaborative relationships with country managers. Specifically, they should:

- Encourage local managers to identify with broad, corporate objectives
- Visit subsidiaries periodically to instill corporate values and priorities
- Rotate employees within the corporate network to promote development of a global perspective
- Encourage country managers to interact and share experiences with each other through regional and global meetings
- Provide incentives and penalties to promote compliance with headquarters' goals

Organizational Structures for International Operations

As a general rule, "structure follows strategy." That is, we can think of organizational structure as a *tool* that facilitates the implementation of strategy and ultimately the firm's strategic vision.[39] Moreover, the organizational structure senior managers choose is largely the result of how important they consider international business and whether they prefer centralized or decentralized decision making. Organizational structures tend to evolve over time: As the firm's involvement in international business increases, it adopts increasingly complex organizational structures.

Exhibit 12.5 describes the advantages and disadvantages of each structure. Let's explore the major types of organizational structures in detail.

Export Department

For manufacturing firms, exporting is usually the first foreign market entry strategy. It rarely requires much organizational structure until export sales reach a critical point. Initially, the firm will channel exports through an outside intermediary, such as a foreign distributor. When export sales reach a substantial proportion of total sales, the firm will usually establish a separate **export department** charged with managing export operations. The approach is most closely associated with home replication strategy. Exhibit 12.6 illustrates the export department structure.

Export department A unit within the firm charged with managing the firm's export operations.

International Division Structure

Over time, as the firm undertakes more advanced activities abroad, management will typically create an **international division structure**, making a separate unit within the firm dedicated to managing its international operations. Exhibit 12.7 illustrates this structure. The decision to create a separate division is usually accompanied by a significant shift in resource allocation and an increased focus on international business.[40] Typically, a vice president of international operations is appointed, who reports directly to the corporate CEO. Division managers oversee the development and maintenance of relationships with foreign suppliers, distributors, and other value-chain partners. Over time, the division typically undertakes more advanced internationalization options, such as licensing and small-scale foreign direct investment. In the early stages, the structure is most closely associated with home replication strategy. However, with time, management may advance toward multidomestic or global strategies.

International division structure An organizational design in which all international activities are centralized within one division in the firm, separate from domestic units.

The international division structure offers several advantages. It centralizes management and coordination of international operations. It is staffed with international experts who focus on developing new business opportunities abroad and offering assistance and training for foreign operations. Its creation signals that management is committed to international operations.

Structure	Advantages	Disadvantages
Export Department A unit within the firm charged with managing the firm's export operations	• Export activities unified under one department • Efficiencies in selling, distribution, and shipping • Small resource commitment	• Focus on the domestic market • Minimal learning about foreign markets • Minimal control of international operations. Potential to rely excessively on foreign intermediaries
International Division All international activities are centralized within one division in the firm, separate from domestic units	• Greater focus on internationalization • Concentration and development of international expertise • Increased commitment to, and coordination and management of, international operations	• Potential for fierce competition between domestic and international units for company resources • Limited knowledge sharing among the foreign units and with headquarters • R&D and future-oriented planning activities are separate for foreign operations and headquarters • Possibility that corporate management may favor domestic over international operations because most will have advanced through the domestic organization
Geographic Area Structure Management and control are decentralized to individual geographic regions, whose managers are responsible for operations within their region	• Greater responsiveness to customer needs and wants in each regional/local market • Better balance between global integration and local adaptation • Improved communications and co-or-dination among the subsidiaries within each geographic region	• Geographic area managers' lack of *global* orientation for developing and managing products • Limited communications, coordination, and knowledge sharing with other geographic units and with headquarters • Limited economies of scale among the far-flung geographic regional units
Product Structure Management of international operations is organized by major product line	• Development of expertise with specific products, on a global basis • Individual product lines are coordinated and managed globally • Scale economies and sharing of product knowledge among units worldwide	• Duplication of corporate support functions for each product division • Possibility that headquarters may favor subsidiaries offering fastest returns • Potential for excessive focus on products and too little on developments in the firm's markets
Functional Structure Management of international operations is organized by functional activity	• Small central staff that provides strong central control and coordination • United, focused global strategy with a high degree of functional expertise	• Headquarters may lack expertise in coordinating functions in diverse geographic locations • Coordination becomes unwieldy when the firm has numerous product lines • May not respond well to specific customer needs in individual markets
Global Matrix Structure Blends product, geographic area, and functional structures to leverage the benefits of global strategy and local responsiveness	• Leverages the benefits of global strategy while responding to local needs • Aims to combine the best elements of the geographic area, product, and functional structures • Emphasizes interorganizational learning and knowledge sharing among the firm's units worldwide	• Dual reporting chain of command with risk of employees receiving contradictory instructions from multiple managers • Can result in conflicts • Difficulties managing many subsidiaries or products, or operations in many foreign markets

Exhibit 12.5 Advantages and Disadvantages of International Organizational Structures

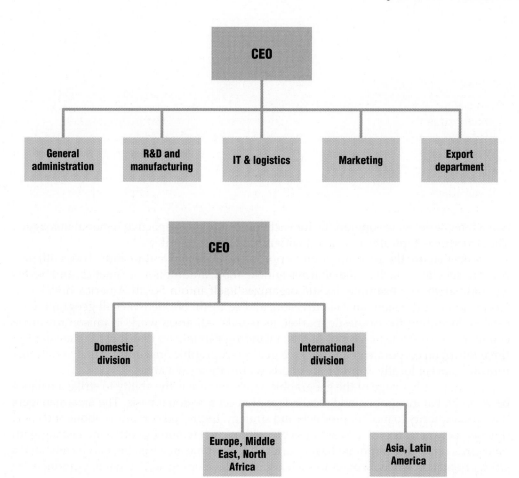

Exhibit 12.6
The Export Department
Structure

Exhibit 12.7
The International Division
Structure

However, initially, this structure can lead to a domestic versus international power struggle over, for example, control of financial and human resources. There is likely to be little sharing of knowledge between the foreign units and domestic operations or among the foreign units themselves. R&D and future-oriented planning activities tend to remain separate and may be domestically focused. Products continue to be developed for the domestic market, with international needs considered only after domestic needs have been addressed. Given these problems, many companies eventually evolve out of the international division structure.[41]

Firms at advanced stages of internationalization establish more complex organizational structures. A major rationale is to reap the benefits of economies of scale and scope—that is, high-volume manufacturing and more efficient use of marketing and other strategic resources over a wider range of products and markets. There is greater emphasis on innovative potential through learning effects, pooling of resources, and know-how.

More advanced organizational structures emphasize a decentralized structure, typically organized around geographic areas, or a centralized structure, organized around product or functional lines. We describe these structures next.

Geographic Area Structure (Decentralized Structure)

Geographic area structure is an organizational arrangement in which management and control are highly decentralized to the level of individual geographic regions, where local managers are responsible for operations within their own regions. Exhibit 12.8 illustrates this type of organizational design. Firms that organize their operations geographically tend to market products that are relatively standardized across entire regions or groupings of countries. The structure is decentralized because headquarters

Geographic area structure An organizational design in which management and control are decentralized to the level of individual geographic regions.

Exhibit 12.8
The Geographic Area
Structure

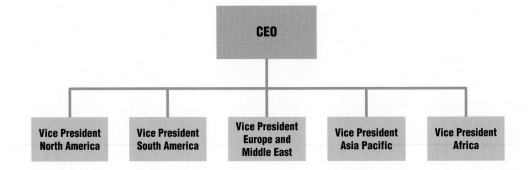

management delegates operations for each locality to the respective regional managers. The structure is typically associated with multidomestic strategy.

Firms that use the geographic area approach are often in mature industries with narrow product lines, such as the pharmaceutical, food, automotive, cosmetics, and beverage industries. For example, Nestlé organizes itself into a South America division, a North America division, an Asia division, and so forth. Nestlé treats all geographic locations, including the domestic market, as equals. All areas work in unison toward a common global strategic vision. Assets, including capital, are distributed to ensure optimal return on corporate goals, not area goals. Geographic area units usually manufacture and market locally appropriate goods within their own areas.

The main advantage of the geographic area structure is the ability to strike a balance between global integration and local adaptation on a regional basis. The area managers have the authority to modify products and strategy. Improved communications and coordination between subsidiaries are possible within each region but often are lacking with other area units and corporate headquarters. Geographic area managers typically lack a *global* orientation when it comes to such issues as developing and managing products.[42]

Product Structure (Centralized Structure)

Product structure
An arrangement in which management of international operations is organized by major product line.

Under the **product structure** arrangement, the firm organizes its international operations by major product line. Each product division is responsible for producing and marketing a specific group of products worldwide. For example, product categories for Motorola's international operations include mobile phones and network solutions. Apple's product categories include the iPad, iPod, iPhone, and personal computers.

Exhibit 12.9 illustrates such an organization. Each international product division operates as a stand-alone profit center with substantial autonomy. The goal is to achieve a high degree of worldwide coordination within each product category. Increased coordination facilitates economies of scale and sharing of technology and product knowledge among the firm's operations worldwide. Thus, the product division structure is highly centralized and typically associated with global strategy.

The advantage of the product division structure is that all support functions, such as R&D, marketing, and manufacturing, are focused on the product. At the same time, products are easier to

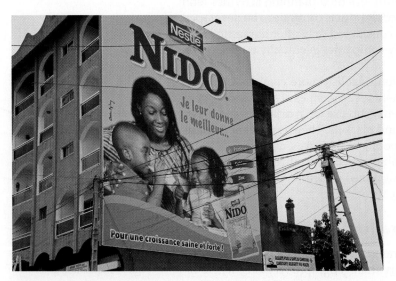

Nestlé uses a geographic area structure for organizing its international operations. In Africa, Nestlé conducts advertising in local languages. Pictured is a large-scale ad for Nido milk powder in Cameroon.

tailor for individual markets to meet specific buyer needs. The product division structure may also lead to duplication of corporate support functions for each product division and a tendency for managers to focus their efforts on subsidiaries with the greatest potential for quick returns.[43]

Functional Structure (Centralized Structure)

In the **functional structure**, management of the firm's international operations is organized by functional activities, such as production and marketing. Exhibit 12.10 illustrates such an arrangement. For example, oil companies tend to organize their worldwide operations along two major functional lines—*production* and *marketing* of petroleum products. Some cruise ship lines engage in both shipbuilding and cruise marketing, two distinctive functions that require separate departments. The advantages of functional division are a small central staff, which provides strong centralized control and coordination, and a united, focused global strategy with a high degree of functional expertise. However, the functional approach may falter if headquarters lacks expertise in coordinating manufacturing, marketing, and other functions in diverse geographic locations. In addition, when the firm deals with numerous product lines, coordination can become unwieldy.[44]

Functional structure
An arrangement in which management of the firm's international operations is organized by functional activity, such as production and marketing.

Global Matrix Structure

The experience of MNEs in the 1970s and 1980s highlighted the strengths and weaknesses of the previously described organizational structures. The geographic area structure proved effective for responding to local needs but did little to enhance worldwide economies of scale and knowledge sharing among far-flung geographic units. The product structure overcame these shortcomings but was weak in responding to local needs. In the 1980s, conditions began to evolve quickly toward a more globally oriented world economy. At the same time, in some markets, customers showed a renewed preference

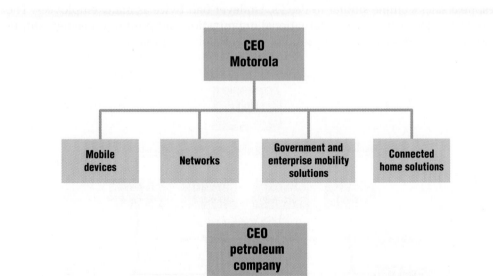

Exhibit 12.9
The Product Structure

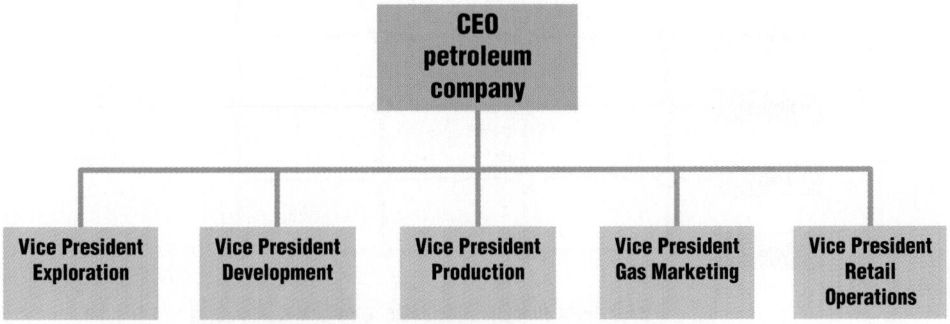

Exhibit 12.10
The Functional Structure

Global matrix structure
An arrangement that blends the geographic area, product, and functional structures to leverage the benefits of a purely global strategy while keeping the firm responsive to local needs.

for local brands. Gradually, MNE managers realized that such trends increasingly required them to address global and local needs *simultaneously*.

This new understanding led to the creation of the **global matrix structure**, an arrangement that seeks to leverage the benefits of global strategy *and* responsiveness to local needs. Specifically, the global matrix structure is a combination of the geographic area, product, and functional structures. It aims to reap the advantages of each while minimizing their disadvantages. Exhibit 12.11 shows such a structure. To make it work, headquarters management should simultaneously: (1) coordinate and control international operations; (2) respond to needs in individual countries; and (3) maximize interorganizational learning and knowledge sharing among the firm's units worldwide.[45]

The global matrix structure is closely associated with transnational strategy. Managerial responsibility for each product is shared by each product unit and the particular geographic areas of the firm. Thus, firms develop a dual reporting system in which, for example, an employee in a foreign subsidiary reports to two managers—the local subsidiary general manager and the corporate product division manager. Often the country manager is superior in authority, with responsibility for appraisal. Global matrix structure recognizes the importance of flexible and responsive country-level operations and shows firms how to link those operations to optimize operational efficiency and competitive effectiveness. The manager working in this structure shares decision making with other managers, wherever they may be, to achieve best practice for the firm's operations worldwide.

Unilever, the $57 billion European producer of food, beverage, household, and personal care products, successfully applied the global matrix structure. Originally a merger between British and Dutch firms, Unilever (www.unilever.com) long pursued a multidomestic approach to international business. In the 1990s, for example, in order to manufacture ice cream, it regularly sourced more than thirty different types of vanilla. Its Rexona deodorant had thirty different packages and forty-eight distinctive formulations. Advertising and branding were handled locally and often amateurishly. Competitors with more centralized operations were able to respond faster to changing consumer tastes. They were better at coordinating their international units and had captured efficiencies by striking supplier contracts for many countries simultaneously. Despite a sales volume similar to P&G's, Unilever had twice as many employees. The decentralized structure of its international organization had produced needless duplication and countless obstacles to a more efficient global approach.

Exhibit 12.11
The Global Matrix Structure

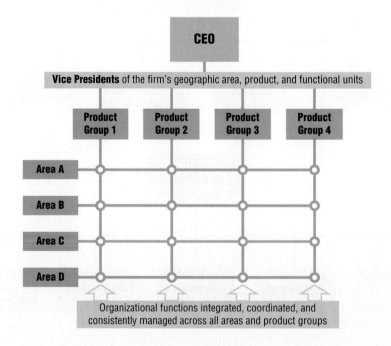

To address such problems, Unilever implemented a massive reorganization plan to centralize authority, reduce the autonomy of local subsidiaries, and create a global employee culture. The firm divested hundreds of businesses, cut 55,000 jobs, closed 145 factories, and discontinued 1,200 brands, retaining about 400. Today, the firm develops new products using global teams that emphasize the *commonalities* among major-country markets. Local managers are not allowed to tinker with packaging, formulation, or advertising of global brands such as Dove soap. Unilever is well on the road to implementing a more balanced matrix approach to its global operations.[46]

The multinational firm Unilever, headquartered in the Netherlands, owns many global brands such as Lipton tea, Hellman's spreads, Slimfast, and Dove personal care products. Management must balance global integration with local adaptation to such practices as retail distribution strategy, labeling requirements, and consumer incentives. In this Malaysian supermarket, a label identifies Dove products from the Netherlands.

Philips, the Dutch producer of electronics products, has long sought to apply a global matrix structure. Philips operates in more than one hundred countries worldwide. Management has structured the firm so that its product groups are integrated across all its major country markets, and, in turn, its organizational functions are integrated and coordinated across all areas and product groups. To streamline its matrix organization, Philips reorganized itself around three product core units: consumer electronics, health care, and lighting products. The matrix structure assigns various roles to regional executives: They hold responsibility for their respective regions, for the firm's core product units, and for the functions associated with the product units.[47]

Like the other organizational structures, the global matrix structure has shortcomings. The chain of command from superiors to subordinates can become muddled. Employees may receive contradictory instructions from multiple managers who may be located far apart and come from different cultural and business backgrounds. The matrix structure can waste managerial time and result in conflicts and organizational chaos. Potential limitations tend to emerge as the firm's international operations become more complex over time. For this reason, many firms that experimented with the global matrix structure eventually returned to simpler organizational arrangements.[48]

 Closing Case

Carlos Ghosn: Leading for Global Success at Renault-Nissan

Nissan Motor Co. (www.nissan-global.com), based in Tokyo, is Japan's number-two automobile manufacturer. Sales in 2009 were nearly $90 billion, and management is planning to launch forty-eight new car models. A few years ago, Nissan, with 160,000 employees, was on the verge of bankruptcy. The French automaker Renault stepped in, took a 44 percent stake, and installed Carlos Ghosn as

Nissan's CEO. In a dramatic turnaround, Ghosn (hard G, rhymes with "stone") returned Nissan to profitability and became a celebrity in Japan. Born in Brazil, raised in Lebanon, and educated in France, he is a charismatic leader who speaks four languages. Smooth in public, he works constantly and is committed to organizational goals. He is featured in Japanese comic books, mobbed for autographs during factory tours, and idolized for saving one of the world's premier car companies.

Ghosn closed inefficient factories, reduced Nissan's workforce, curbed purchasing costs, shared operations with Renault, and introduced new products. Under his watchful eye, Nissan evolved from a troubled carmaker to a corporate success story in just a few years. How did Ghosn do it?

Nissan's Organizational Culture

One of Ghosn's biggest tests was overcoming the denial inside Nissan about the firm's perilous condition. Ghosn cut through antiquated thinking, defying Japan's often bureaucratic and clubby business culture by, for example, reducing Nissan's steel suppliers from five to three. The CEO of NKK Steel protested that "Toyota would never act in such a way."

Corporate Japan often moves slowly and reactively. Ghosn introduced a proactive style, with fast decision making and a culture of anticipating problems and eliminating them before they happen. Senior management at Nissan now operates with a sense of urgency, even when the firm is not in crisis. Ghosn is always in a rush, relying on decisiveness and delegation—but yielding to consensus when it is passionate. He dislikes long meetings. Instead of squandering time analyzing and discussing, he prefers action. At Nissan, he pushes staff to meet tough sales targets and once publicly promised the management team would resign if it didn't meet them. He inspires the workforce, regularly visiting them on the factory floor. Even the most mundane events are handled like big media shows. One Nissan earnings news conference opened with loud music and dazzling video shots of zooming cars.

Ghosn's Global Orientation

In the style of a true globalist, Ghosn states, "It's irrelevant where you are headquartered . . . the keys are where the jobs are located and where the profits go." To reinforce his global aspirations, Ghosn made English, not Japanese, the official language of Nissan. Managers who learn English advance faster than those who speak only Japanese. The move proclaimed Ghosn's intention to reorganize Nissan as a global firm.

Ghosn took over as CEO of Renault in 2005. He now runs both companies, commuting between Paris and Tokyo in his Gulfstream jet. The unusual arrangement underscores the demand for proven leaders in the global auto industry, which suffers from oversupply and intense competition. In a typical month, Ghosn might spend the first week in Paris, focusing solely on Renault, and the third week in Japan, focusing on Nissan. He carries two agendas: one for Nissan and one for Renault. He personally oversees Nissan's North American business, where half of Nissan's profits are earned.

The Role of Innovation

Nissan constantly invests in R&D for breakthrough technologies and innovative products. Roughly 5 percent of net sales are reinvested in new technologies. At its new Mississippi plant in the United States, Nissan launched four models in less than eight months, rolling out a small car (the "Versa"), a re-engineered Altima midsize sedan, a heavily redesigned Nissan Quest minivan, and a redesigned Infiniti G35. It established a design subsidiary in Shanghai, China, to produce cars that fit that country's growing market.

In green technology, Nissan is stressing all-electric vehicles. In 2009, Ghosn unveiled the Nissan LEAF, the world's first affordable, zero-emission car, based on lithium-ion battery technology. The LEAF is a medium-size hatchback with a range of more than 160 km (100 miles). In 2010, it was launched in Japan, Europe, and the United States.

Global Production

Renault-Nissan has factories in Britain, France, and the United States, to be close to key markets. It also manufactures in China, Taiwan, and the Philippines to leverage low-cost, high-quality labor. Nissan uses modular architecture: Suppliers manufacture single modules, which are then bolted into a car or truck body rolling down the assembly line. The modular approach minimizes the total cost of manufacturing cars.

Nissan consolidated its U.S. manufacturing operations, moving thousands of jobs from southern California to its new plant in Tennessee. The move centralized manufacturing and made it easier for senior management to keep tabs on U.S. operations. The Tennessee plant is Nissan's most productive factory in North America, producing a car in under 16 labor hours, several hours fewer than rival carmakers.

Additional Global Strategy Elements

The integration of Nissan with Renault has gone smoothly. Renault-Nissan's board of directors consists of four members from each organization. The combined firm is globalizing engineering, production, and purchasing operations. Management established a joint design center in Amsterdam—Renault-Nissan BV—that provides a neutral forum to map out common strategy for product development and engineering. A $45 million engineering center near Tokyo consolidates global production and engineering.

Renault-Nissan minimizes the number of platforms (chassis) used in manufacturing. Every shared platform saves $500 million annually for each carmaker. Renault shares eight engine designs with Nissan. Roughly three-quarters of the parts used by the two automakers are sourced jointly, generating economies of scale. Common parts, such as door handles, windshield wipers, and seat belts, are shared among different models. Such moves have allowed both firms to slash purchasing costs and shave months off the development time of new vehicles. One result is the world's most global car, called the Nissan Versa in the United States, the Renault Clio in Europe, the Nissan Tiida in Asia, and the Renault Logan in the Middle East. In total, Nissan offers seven different vehicles based on the underpinnings that go into the Versa, creating scale economies that improve profits.

Nissan has a presence in the most important markets worldwide. While the United States is a relatively expensive place to make cars, it is also the world's biggest market. Thus, Nissan has a major manufacturing and marketing presence there. It now exports its U.S.-made Quest minivans to China, considered the next big market. It exports other U.S.-made models—the Altima sedan and Infiniti QX56 SUV—to the Middle East and Latin America.

Emerging Markets: The Next Big Target

In the coming decade, millions of consumers in Brazil, China, India, and other emerging markets will join the middle class. Many dream of owning a car. Estimates indicate the market for automobiles priced under $10,000 will soon grow to roughly 20 million cars. India's car market will double to 3.3 million cars by 2014, and China's demand will grow 140 percent, to 16.5 million cars in the same period. In 2009, India's Tata Motors launched a new car, the Nano, priced at around $2,500. The Chinese have launched a similar car. Automakers in China and India leverage low wages in their countries to squeeze down manufacturing costs.

Ghosn is making emerging markets a cornerstone of Nissan's global strategy. Renault-Nissan launched the Logan, built in Romania, with a base price around $7,500. The company is building a low-cost pickup truck based on the Logan for sale in Southeast Asia, South Africa, and the Middle East. Demand is high because of the high quality and low price. Nissan-Renault teamed with India's Bajaj Motors to build a $2,500 car to compete with Tata's Nano. The ULC (for "ultra low-cost") was launched in India and is being targeted to other emerging markets as well.

Renault acquired full control of Samsung Motors, making South Korea an important base for Renault-Nissan. Nissan launched a midsize sedan in China. The Bluebird sedan is produced in a 50-50 joint venture with a local Chinese firm. The Nissan Tsuru subcompact is the top-selling car in Mexico, accounting for 20 percent of new-car sales. It is increasing its presence in other emerging markets, such as Russia and India.

Global Recession

Like other automakers, Nissan hit a downturn in 2009, leading the firm to post its first loss in a decade. The firm attributed the loss to the global financial crisis, the negative impact of a strong yen, and the loss of consumer confidence around the world. In response, Ghosn moved quickly to cut production at several plants in Japan and Europe, especially those that make vehicles for advanced economies. Nissan also reduced its worldwide workforce by some 20,000 employees. Nissan is increasing its presence in China, Russia, and India, and further shifting engineering, production, and purchasing to low-cost countries. The firm will source more parts and components outside Japan, in emerging markets.

AACSB: Reflective Thinking Skills

Case Questions

1. In what ways is Carlos Ghosn a visionary leader? What traits does he possess that are typical of a visionary leader?

2. What is the nature of Nissan's international strategy? Is the firm's strategy primarily multidomestic or global? Justify your answer. What advantages does Nissan derive from the particular strategy(s) that it pursues? In what ways does Nissan demonstrate efficiency, flexibility, and learning?

3. Describe Nissan's organizational culture. What are the characteristics of Nissan's culture? In what ways has Carlos Ghosn contributed to Nissan's culture? Elaborate.

4. Global firms pursue a relatively centralized approach to international operations. What are the characteristics of the trend toward global integration of company operations? How does Nissan demonstrate these characteristics?

5. Examine Nissan in terms of the integration-responsiveness framework. What are the pressures that Nissan faces for local responsiveness? What are the pressures that Nissan faces for global integration? What advantages do local responsiveness and global integration each bring to Nissan?

SOURCES: C. Ghosn and P. Ries, *Shift: Inside Nissan's Historic Revival* (New York: Currency/Doubleday, 2005); Profile of Nissan at http://www.hoovers.com; "Nissan: 2009 Company Profile Edition 2," *Just-Auto*, September 2009; David Kiley, Ian Rowley, and Carol Matlack, "Ghosn Hits the Accelerator," *Business Week*, May 12, 2008, p. 48; J. Muller, "The Impatient Mr. Ghosn," *Forbes*, May 22, 2006, pp. 104–107; John Murphy, "Nissan Reports Its First Annual Loss under Ghosn," *Wall Street Journal*, May 13, 2009, p. B3; John Reed and Amy Yee, "Renault and Nissan to Launch Low-Cost Car," *FT.com*, May 12, 2008; N. Shirouzu, "Ghosn's Goal for Renault: Go Global," *Wall Street Journal*, June 21, 2006, p. B3; J. Wrighton and J. Sapsford, "Split Shift: For Nissan's Rescuer, Ghosn, New Road Rules Await at Renault," *Wall Street Journal*, April 26, 2005, p. A.1; "Putting Ford in the Rearview Mirror," *Business Week*, February 12, 2007, retrieved from http://www.businessweek.com; "The Race to Build Really Cheap Cars," *Business Week*, April 23, 2007, retrieved from http://www.businessweek.com; Nissan corporate Web site at http://www.nissan-global.com.

CHAPTER ESSENTIALS

Key Terms

Summary

In this chapter, you learned about:

1. Strategy in international business

Strategy is a planned set of actions that managers employ to make best use of the firm's resources and core competencies, in order to gain a competitive advantage. The firm that aspires to become globally competitive must simultaneously seek three key strategic objectives—efficiency, flexibility, and learning.

2. Building the global firm

Managers who exhibit **visionary leadership** possess an international mind-set, cosmopolitan values, and a globally strategic vision. They engage in strategic thinking, committing resources and human assets to realizing a global approach to business. Advanced international firms value global competence and cross-cultural skills, adopt a single language, and promote interdependency among headquarters and the firm's subsidiaries. They adopt an international **organizational culture**. They subscribe to globally accepted ethical standards and responsible citizenship. International **organizational processes** include **global teams** and global information systems.

3. The integration-responsiveness framework

The integration-responsiveness (IR) framework describes how internationalizing firms simultaneously seek global integration and local responsiveness. **Local responsiveness** refers to managing the firm's value-chain activities, and addressing diverse opportunities and risks, on a country-by-country basis. **Global integration** describes efforts to coordinate the firm's value-chain activities cross-nationally to achieve worldwide efficiency, synergy, and cross-fertilization to take maximum advantage of similarities across countries.

4. Strategies based on the integration-responsiveness framework

The IR framework presents four alternative strategies. Using **home replication strategy**, the firm views international business as separate from, and secondary to, its domestic business. Products are designed with domestic consumers in mind, and the firm is essentially a domestic company, with some foreign activities. **Multidomestic strategy** is a more committed approach, in which managers recognize and emphasize differences among national markets. They treat individual markets on a stand-alone basis, with little cross-national integration of company efforts. **Global strategy** aims to integrate the firm's major objectives, policies, and activities into a cohesive whole, targeted primarily to the global marketplace. Top management performs sourcing, resource allocation, market participation, and competitive moves on a global scale. Using **transnational strategy**, the firm strives to be more responsive to local needs while simultaneously retaining maximum global efficiency and emphasizing global learning and knowledge transfer. The strategy aims to combine the major benefits of both multidomestic and global strategies while minimizing their disadvantages.

5. Organizational structure

Organizational structure consists of the reporting relationships in the firm between people, functions, and processes that facilitate carrying out international operations. It determines where key decisions are made, the relationship between headquarters and subsidiaries, and the nature of international staffing. It also determines the degree of *centralization* and *decentralization* in decision making and value-chain activities in the firm's operations worldwide. The main role for headquarters managers is to provide broad leadership, while subsidiary managers are best at dealing with customers, handling employee issues, and initiating action in the field.

6. **Organizational structures for international operations**

The **export department** is the simplest organizational structure, in which a unit within the firm manages all export operations. Slightly more advanced is the **international division structure**, in which all international activities are centralized within one organizational unit, separate from the firm's domestic units. The **geographic area structure** features control and decision making that are decentralized to the level of individual geographic regions. Using the **product structure**, decision making and management of international operations are centralized and organized by major product line. The **functional structure** organizes decision making by functional activity, such as production and marketing. The **global matrix structure** blends the geographic area, product, and functional structures in an attempt to leverage the benefits of a purely global strategy and maximize global organizational learning while keeping the firm responsive to local needs.

Test Your Comprehension AACSB: Reflective Thinking Skills

1. What are the primary strategic objectives in international business?

2. Describe the requisite dimensions that characterize truly successful, contemporary international firms.

3. Define visionary leadership. What are the traits of a manager who has visionary leadership?

4. Describe the distinction between multidomestic and global industries.

5. Describe the integration-responsiveness framework. What are the specific pressures for local responsiveness and for global integration?

6. What is the difference between global strategy and multidomestic strategy? Visit the Web site of Dell Computer (www.dell.com). Does Dell generally apply a global strategy or a multidomestic strategy? How can you tell?

7. Define transnational strategy. Give examples of firms that apply a transnational strategy.

8. What is the difference between a centralized and a decentralized organizational structure? Why do firms often prefer to have a centralized structure?

9. What are the different organizational structures for international operations? Which structure(s) is most associated with global strategy?

10. What is the global matrix structure? What are the advantages and disadvantages of this approach?

Apply Your Understanding AACSB: Communication Abilities, Reflective Thinking Skills, Ethical Understanding and Reasoning Abilities

1. AlumCo is a large producer of aluminum products. AlumCo now handles international operations through its export department. However, management believes this arrangement is no longer suited to the firm's growing international activities and wants to adopt a more sophisticated approach. What alternative organizational structures (international division, geographic area structure, etc.) should the firm consider? Make a recommendation to management regarding the most appropriate international structure that AlumCo should employ. For reference, check out the Web site of Alcan, the well-known Canadian aluminum firm, at www.alcan.com.

2. Firms with a global organizational culture have several common characteristics. They seek a global identity, value a global perspective in all undertakings, adopt a common language, promote interdependency between headquarters and subsidiaries, value input from foreign units, and subscribe to globally accepted ethical standards. Recall the opening vignette in this chapter on IKEA, the giant furniture retailer. Based on your reading, outline the various ways that IKEA exhibits these characteristics.

3. *Ethical Dilemma:* You were recently hired as a manager for international operations of Despoyle Chemical Corporation, a major manufacturer of dyes, fertilizers, and other industrial chemicals. Despoyle has chemical production plants in twenty-eight countries, including many developing economies. Despoyle has a decentralized organizational structure,

and managers in individual countries operate their plants independently of headquarters. After visiting various Despoyle plants, you find the firm follows distinct environmental protection standards in different countries. In India, for example, Despoyle allows pollutants to flow freely into local rivers. In Mexico, Despoyle generates much pollution in local landfills and production sites. In Nigeria, Despoyle's factory emits air pollution that greatly exceeds levels acceptable in more advanced countries. As a new manager, you are shocked by the firm's lax environmental practices around the world. What should you do? Do you complain to top management and risk angering your superiors? Should you "blow the whistle" on Despoyle's global practices to environmental groups and the media? What solution, if any, do you undertake to address Despoyle's environmental practices around the world? Use the Ethical Framework in Chapter 5 to formulate your answer.

globalEDGE Internet Exercises
(http://globalEDGE.msu.edu)

AACSB: Reflective Thinking Skills, Analytic Skills, Use of Information Technology

Refer to Chapter 1, page 62, for instructions on how to access and use globalEDGE™.

1. Visit the Web sites for Toyota (www.toyota.com) and Procter & Gamble (www.pg.com). From what you can gather, how do these two firms organize their international activities? Do they seem to be applying multidomestic strategy or global strategy in their sourcing, manufacturing, product development, and marketing activities? How and why might an internationalizing firm evolve its approaches to internationalization over time?

2. Multinational firms play a key role in globalization. Various news organizations prepare classifications and rankings of MNEs (e.g., *Financial Times*, *Business Week*, *Forbes*, *Fortune*). Find two such rankings and identify the criteria used to rank the top global firms. What countries are home to the great majority of MNEs on these lists? For each list, how "global" are the top three firms? That is, in what countries do they operate? Conduct a search for "rankings."

3. You work for an MNE that makes and markets cellular telephones. Senior managers want to begin selling the phones in Latin America. To pursue a transnational strategy, management wants to minimize adaptation of the phones. They have asked you for a briefing. Focusing on three Latin American countries, prepare a brief report that identifies the common features of Latin American markets that management should consider when developing the cell phones the firm will sell there. For example, what language should be used in the cell phones? What pricing should management use? You may wish to consult the country commercial guides, Country Insights, and market research reports available through globalEDGE™. In addition, the U.S. Department of Commerce (www.export.gov) is a useful resource.

CHAPTER 13

LEARNING OBJECTIVES In this chapter, you will learn about:

1. Assessing global market opportunities
2. Analyzing organizational readiness to internationalize
3. Assessing the suitability of products and services for foreign markets
4. Screening countries to identify target markets
5. Assessing industry market potential
6. Choosing foreign business partners
7. Estimating company sales potential

Global Market Opportunity Assessment

Estimating Demand in Emerging Markets

Estimating the demand for products or services in emerging markets and developing economies is a challenging task for managers. These countries have unique commercial environments and may be limited in terms of reliable data, market research firms, and trained interviewers. Consumers in some of these countries may consider surveys an invasion of privacy. Survey respondents may try to please researchers by telling them what they want to hear rather than providing honest answers to their questions.

Three of the largest emerging markets—China, India, and Brazil—have a combined GDP of more than $15 trillion, surpassing that of the United States. Africa is among the biggest markets for mobile phone sales, growing to more than 100 million users in just a few years. Automakers are doing substantial business selling economy cars throughout Latin America, South Asia, and Eastern Europe. In short, emerging markets and developing economies are huge markets for products and services.

Estimating demand in such countries requires managers to use innovative research methods for gaining insights or data. Let's consider two firms trying to estimate the demand for wallpaper and adhesive bandages in Morocco.

In Morocco, wealthy people tend to live in villas or condominiums, potential target markets for sales of wallpaper. Import statistics are often not helpful, because the government usually records wallpaper imports by weight

and value. Companies sell wallpaper by the roll, and different qualities and designs will have different weights. Such information is of little use in estimating the number of households likely to buy wallpaper.

One wallpaper company examined data from various sources to estimate demand. First, managers reviewed a recent study of the number of water heaters purchased in Morocco. From past experience, they knew that if households purchased this important "modern" convenience, they also would likely buy wallpaper. Second, managers reviewed government statistics on the level of domestic wallpaper sales, discretionary income by type of household, and home construction data. Third, they studied the lifestyle of a sample of local consumers and found that Moroccans typically shop for wallpaper to complement wall-to-wall carpets. Among married couples, the wife usually decides on decorations for the home. Customers tend to be well-to-do; they include professionals, merchants, and high-ranking administrators. By triangulating data from these sources and blending their own judgment into the findings, the wallpaper company ultimately arrived at a reasonably reliable estimate of demand for wallpaper.

In the case of adhesive bandages, available data revealed that 70 percent of demand for pharmaceutical items, including bandages, was met by wholesalers concentrated in Casablanca, Morocco's capital city. The country imported all its adhesive bandages. Demand was growing quickly, due to rapid population growth, free hospitalization and medication for the needy, and reimbursement programs for medical and drug expenses. Although the government published import statistics, the information was confusing, because data on bandage imports was mixed together with data on other types of adhesives. Further, the bandage data was superficial and incomplete, and widespread smuggling and gray marketing of adhesive bandages through unofficial distribution channels complicated estimates of demand.

To gather more information, researchers interviewed bandage salespeople from firms such as Johnson & Johnson and Curad and visited retail stores to ask about sales, prevailing prices, competitive brands, and consumer attitudes. They found that consumers tend to be price-sensitive when buying bandages and rely on doctors and pharmacists to recommend well-known

brands. Researchers also tallied statistics from the United Nations Development Program and other aid agencies that donate medical supplies to developing countries. They eventually arrived at a reasonable estimate of bandage sales by assimilating data from these various sources.

As you can see, estimating demand in foreign markets is often complicated, and managers must meet the challenge through creative use of market research.

SOURCES: "Morocco Economy: Demographic Profile," *EIU ViewsWire*, June 15, 2009; Sonya Misquitta, "Cadbury Redefines Cheap Luxury," *Wall Street Journal*, June 8, 2009, p. B4; Lyn Amine and S. Tamer Cavusgil, "Demand Estimation in a Developing Country Environment: Difficulties, Techniques, and Examples," *Journal of the Market Research Society* 28, no. 1 (1986): 43–65; V. Wilkes, "Marketing and Market Development: Dealing with a Global Issue: Contributing to Poverty Alleviation," *Corporate Governance* 5, no. 3 (2005): 61–69; U.S. Commercial Service and the U.S. Department of State, *Country Commercial Guide Morocco Fiscal Year 2005*, retrieved from http://www.buyusainfo.net.

 ## Assessing Global Market Opportunities

Managers' choices determine the future of the firm. Making good choices depends on having objective evidence and hard data about what products and services to offer and where to offer them. The more managers know about an opportunity, the better equipped they will be to exploit it. This is particularly true in international business, which usually entails greater uncertainty and unknowns than domestic business.[1] To skillfully navigate international markets, managers require substantial information on potential threats and opportunities and how to conduct business abroad.[2] Managers devise strategies as part of planned actions to optimize the firm's competitive advantages. Planning involves estimating, forecasting, and problem solving and therefore requires substantial information inputs.

Central to a firm's research is identifying and defining the best business opportunities in the global marketplace. A **global market opportunity** is a favorable combination of circumstances, locations, and timing that offers prospects for exporting, investing, sourcing, or partnering in foreign markets. In such locations, the firm may perceive opportunities to sell its products and services; establish factories or other production facilities to produce its offerings cheaper or more competently; procure raw materials, components, or services of lower cost or superior quality; or enter beneficial collaborations with foreign partners. Global market opportunities can enhance company performance, often far beyond what the firm can normally achieve in its home market. For example, John Deere & Company saw an opportunity to sell small tractors to India's 300 million small farmers. After conducting extensive research, the firm developed four small tractor models for the new market and is now doing considerable business there.[3]

In this chapter, we discuss six key tasks the manager should perform to define and pursue global market opportunities. Exhibit 13.1 illustrates the objectives, outcomes,

Global market opportunity Favorable combination of circumstances, locations, and timing that offers prospects for exporting, investing, sourcing, or partnering in foreign markets.

Task	Objective	Procedure
1. Analyze organizational readiness to internationalize	To provide an objective assessment of the company's preparedness to engage in international business activity.	• Examine company strengths and weaknesses, relative to international business, by evaluating the availability in the firm of key factors, such as: — appropriate financial and tangible resources — relevant skills and competencies — commitment by senior management to international expansion • Take action to eliminate deficiencies in the firm that hinder achieving company goals.
2. Assess the suitability of the firm's products and services for foreign markets	To conduct a systematic assessment of the suitability of the firm's products and services for international customers; to evaluate the degree of fit between the product or service and foreign customer needs.	• For each possible target market, identify those factors that may hinder market potential. Determine how the product or service may need to be adapted for each market. Specifically, for each potential market, assess the firm's products and services with regard to such factors as: — foreign customer characteristics and preferences — relevant laws and regulations — requirements of channel intermediaries — characteristics of competitors' offerings
3. Screen countries to identify target markets	To reduce the number of countries that warrant in-depth investigation as potential target markets to a manageable few.	• Identify the five or six country markets that hold the best potential for the firm by assessing each candidate country market with regard to such criteria as: — size and growth rate — 'market intensity' (customers' buying power) — 'consumption capacity' (size and growth rate of the middle class) — receptivity to imports — infrastructure for doing business — degree of economic freedom — country risk
4. Assess industry market potential	To estimate the most likely share of industry sales within each target country; to investigate and evaluate any potential barriers to market entry.	• Develop 3- to 5-year forecast of industry sales for each target market. Specifically, assess industry market potential in each market by examining such criteria as: — market size and growth rate — relevant trends in the industry — degree of competitive intensity — tariff and nontariff trade barriers — relevant standards and regulations — availability and sophistication of local distribution intermediaries — specific customer requirements and preferences — industry-specific market potential indicators — industry-specific market entry barriers

(continues)

Exhibit 13.1   Key Tasks in Global Market Opportunity Assessment

and selection criteria associated with each task. Such a formal process is especially appropriate for pursuing marketing or collaborative venture opportunities abroad. The six tasks are:

1. Analyze organizational readiness to internationalize.
2. Assess the suitability of the firm's products and services for foreign markets.
3. Screen countries to identify attractive target markets.

5. Choose foreign business partners	To decide on the type of foreign business partner, clarify ideal partner qualifications, and determine appropriate market entry strategy.	• Determine what value-adding activities must be performed by foreign business partners. • Based on needed value-adding activities, determine the most desirable attributes in foreign business partners. • Assess and select foreign business partners. That is, evaluate each potential business partner based on criteria such as: — specific industry expertise — commitment to the international venture — access to local distribution channels — financial strength — technical expertise — quality of staff — appropriate facilities and infrastructure
6. Estimate company sales potential	To estimate the most likely share of industry sales the company can achieve, over a period of time, for each target market.	• Develop 3- to 5-year forecast of company sales in each target market. Estimate the potential to sell the firm's product or service, based on criteria such as: — capabilities of partners — access to distribution — competitive intensity — pricing and financing — market penetration timetable of the firm — risk tolerance of senior managers • Determine the factors that will influence company sales potential

Exhibit 13.1 *(continued)*

4. Assess the industry market potential, or the market demand, for the product(s) or service(s) in selected target markets.

5. Choose qualified business partners, such as distributors or suppliers.

6. Estimate company sales potential for each target market.

In carrying out this systematic process, the manager will need to employ objective *selection criteria* by which to make choices, as listed in the final column of Exhibit 13.1. Let's examine each task in detail.

Task One: Analyze Organizational Readiness to Internationalize

Before undertaking an international venture, whether launching a product abroad or sourcing from a foreign supplier, the firm should conduct a formal assessment of its readiness to internationalize. An evaluation of organizational capabilities is useful for both firms new to international business and those with considerable experience. Such a self-audit is similar to a SWOT analysis—that is, an evaluation of the firm's strengths, weaknesses, opportunities, and threats.

When assessing the firm's readiness to internationalize, managers peer into their organization to determine the degree to which it has the motivation, resources, and skills necessary to successfully engage in international business. They measure the firm's degree of international experience; the goals and objectives it envisions for internationalization; the quantity and quality of skills, capabilities, and resources available for internationalization; and the actual and potential support provided by the firm's network of relationships. If one or more key resources is lacking, management must acquire or develop them *before* allowing the contemplated venture to go forward. Organizational culture plays an important role, because key employees should possess the motivation and commitment to expand the firm's activities into foreign markets.

Managers also examine conditions in the *external* business environment by studying opportunities and threats in the markets where the firm seeks to do business. They research the specific needs and preferences of buyers, as well as the nature of competing products and the risks inherent in foreign markets.

Consider Home Instead, Inc. (www.homeinstead.com), a small U.S. firm that provides services for the elderly who choose to live independently at home but require companionship, assistance with meal preparation, and help with shopping and housekeeping. Following an assessment of its readiness to internationalize, management perceived substantial international opportunities, particularly in Japan, but also recognized deficiencies in certain key capabilities. The firm hired Yoshino Nakajima, who is fluent in Japanese and an expert on the Japanese market, to be vice president for international development. She launched the franchise in Japan, which captured substantial market share. Next, management tapped into the global network of 1,700 trade specialists of the United States Commercial Service, a government agency that provided the firm with leads and contacts in countries it had identified as the best target markets. Today, Home Instead has numerous franchises in Australia, Canada, Ireland, and Portugal. Its international operations are thriving.[4]

A formal analysis of organizational readiness to internationalize requires managers to address the following questions:

- *What do we hope to gain from international business?* Objectives might include increasing sales or profits, following key customers who locate abroad, challenging competitors in their home markets, or pursuing a global strategy of establishing production and marketing operations at various locations worldwide.

- *Is international expansion consistent with other firm goals, now or in the future?* The firm should evaluate and manage internationalization in the context of its mission and business plan to ensure it represents the best use of company resources.

- *What demands will internationalization place on firm resources, such as management, human resources, and finance, as well as production and marketing capacity?* How will the firm meet such demands? Management must ensure the firm has enough production and marketing capacity to serve foreign markets. It is frustrating to channel members—and management—when insufficient capacity prevents the firm from fulfilling customer orders from abroad. Because people are critical for carrying out company plans, it is critical to have the appropriate personnel on board.

- *What is the basis of the firm's competitive advantage?* Companies seek competitive advantages by doing things better than their competitors. Competitive advantage can be based on strong R&D, superior input goods, cost-effective or innovative manufacturing capacity, skillful marketing, highly effective distribution channels, or other capabilities.

Diagnostic tools help managers audit the firm's readiness to internationalize. One of the best known is CORE (COmpany Readiness to Export, developed by Tamer Cavusgil in the early 1990s; see globalEDGE.msu.edu). CORE has been widely adopted by individual enterprises, consultants, and the U.S. Department of Commerce. Since it was developed

Levi makes tight-fit jeans to accommodate the Japanese physique and loose-fitting jeans to accommodate tastes in Islamic countries.

from extensive research on the factors that contribute to successful exporting, it also serves as an ideal tutorial for self-learning and training.

CORE asks managers questions about their organizational resources, skills, and motivation to arrive at an objective assessment of the firm's readiness to successfully engage in exporting. It generates assessments of both organizational and product readiness to identify the useful assets managers have and the additional ones they need to make internationalization succeed. The assessment emphasizes exporting, since it is the typical entry mode for most newly internationalizing firms.

Assessing organizational readiness to internationalize is an ongoing process. Managers need to continuously verify the firm's ability to modify its products to suit conditions, needs, and tastes in foreign markets. In marketing its denim jeans, for example, Levi Strauss (www.levi.com; click on "global sites") assessed its ability to adapt its products for various markets. In evaluating entry into Islamic countries, Levi discovered that women are discouraged from wearing tight-fitting attire, so the firm made a line of loose-fitting jeans. When Levi entered Japan, management assessed the firm's ability to make its famous blue jeans tighter and slimmer, to fit the smaller physique of many Japanese. When targeting consumers in hot climates, Levi evaluated its ability to produce shorts and thinner denim in bright colors.[5]

 ## Task Two: Assess the Suitability of Products and Services for Foreign Markets

Once management has confirmed the firm's readiness to internationalize, it next determines the suitability of its products and services for foreign markets. Most companies produce a portfolio of offerings, some or all of which may hold the potential for generating international sales.

Factors Contributing to Product Suitability for International Markets

The products or services with the best international prospects tend to have the following four characteristics:

1. *Sell well in the domestic market.* Offerings received well at home are likely to succeed abroad, especially where similar needs and conditions exist.

2. *Cater to universal needs.* For example, buyers worldwide demand personal-care products, medical devices, and banking services. International sales may be promising if the product or service is unique or has important features that are appealing to foreign customers and are hard for foreign firms to duplicate.

3. *Address a need not well served in particular foreign markets.* Potential may exist in countries where the product or service does not currently exist, or where demand is just starting to emerge.

4. *Address a new or emergent need abroad.* Demand for some products and services can suddenly emerge after a disaster or emergent trend. For example, a major earthquake in Haiti created an urgent need for easy-to-build housing. An increase in AIDS cases in South Africa suggests a need for drugs and medical sup-

plies. Growing affluence in emerging markets is spurring demand for restaurants and hospitality services.

Key Issues to Resolve in Measuring Product Potential

Here are some key questions managers should answer to help measure the international market potential of a product or service:

- *Who initiates purchasing?* Homemakers are usually the chief decision makers for household products. Professional buyers make purchases on behalf of firms.

- *Who uses the product or service?* Children consume various products, but their parents may be the actual buyers. Employees consume products their company purchases.

- *Why do people buy the product or service?* What specific needs does it fulfill? Such needs vary worldwide. For example, while consumers in advanced economies use Honda's gas-powered generators for recreational purposes, in developing economies households may buy them for everyday heating and lighting.

- *Where do people purchase the product or service?* Once the researcher understands where the offering is typically purchased, it is useful to visit likely vendors in order to determine sales potential as well as whether the offering should be adapted for the market and how best to price, promote, and distribute it.

- *What economic, cultural, geographic, and other factors in the target market may limit sales?* Countries vary substantially in terms of buyer income levels, preferences, climate, and other factors that can inhibit or facilitate purchasing behavior.

Products that already sell well at home are among those most likely to succeed abroad. As a manager, given Starbuck's success in the United States, would you have supported opening this store in Shanghai, China?

One of the simplest ways to find out whether a product or service can sell abroad is to ask intermediaries in the target market about the likely local demand for it. Another is to attend an industry trade fair in the target market or region and interview prospective customers or distributors there. Since trade fairs often draw participants from entire regions, such as Asia or Europe, this approach is efficient for learning about the market potential of several countries at once.

 ## Task Three: Screen Countries to Identify Target Markets

Screening to identify the best countries is a fundamental task, especially in the early stages of internationalization. For most firms, it is also the most time-consuming part of opportunity assessment. Yet failure to choose the right countries not only results in financial loss; it also incurs opportunity costs, tying up resources the firm might have used more profitably elsewhere. Exporting, foreign direct investment (FDI), and sourcing each require a different set of screening criteria. Let's see why.

Screening Countries for Exporting

Exporters first examine such criteria as population, income, demographic characteristics, government stability, and nature of the general business environment in individual countries. Statistics that span several years help determine which markets are growing and which are shrinking. The exporter can purchase research reports from professional market research firms that provide assessments of and key statistics for particular markets. National governments also provide much useful information, typically free of

When deciding on target markets, internationalizing firms often choose regional hubs, which serve as critical entry points for important national or regional markets. Pictured here is Hong Kong, an important entry hub for China.

charge. In the United States, for example, the Department of Commerce (www.export.gov) conducts and publishes numerous market surveys, such as *The Water Supply and Wastewater Treatment Market in China, Automotive Parts and Equipment Industry Guide in France*, and *Country Commercial Guide for Brazil*.

Some firms target countries that are psychically near—that is, countries similar to the home country in language, culture, legal environment, and other factors. Such countries fit management's comfort zone. Australian firms often choose Britain, New Zealand, or the United States as their first target markets abroad. As managerial experience, knowledge, and confidence grow, firms expand into more complex and culturally distant markets, such as China or Japan.

Other firms are more venturesome and target nontraditional, higher-risk countries. The born-global companies exemplify this trend. Ongoing globalization, as well as advances in communication and transportation technologies, have reduced the foreignness of most countries, and hence the cost and risk of entering them. Even small firms now routinely reach out to culturally distant countries, including emerging markets and developing economies.

The information necessary for country screening varies by product type or industry. For example, in marketing consumer electronics, the researcher emphasizes countries with large populations having adequate discretionary income and ample energy production. For farming equipment, the best targets are countries with substantial agricultural land and large numbers of farmers. Health insurance companies target countries with many hospitals and doctors.

Read the *Global Trend* feature to learn about current trends that are spawning various international market opportunities.

Often, the firm may target a region or group of countries rather than individual countries. This approach is more cost effective, particularly in markets with similar characteristics. The European Union includes twenty-seven countries that are relatively similar in income levels, regulations, and infrastructure. When entering Europe, firms often devise a pan-European strategy that considers many EU member countries simultaneously, rather than planning separate efforts in individual countries.

In other cases, the firm may target so-called *gateway countries*, or regional hubs, that serve as entry points to nearby or affiliated markets. For example, Singapore is the gateway to southeast Asian countries, Hong Kong is an important gateway to China, Turkey is a good platform for the central Asian republics, Panama is a friendly entry to Latin America, and Finland provides easy access to Russia. Firms base their operations in a gateway country so they can serve the larger adjacent region.

Screening Methodology for Potential Country Markets   It is expensive and impractical to target all of the more than 200 countries worldwide. Management must choose markets that offer the best prospects. There are two basic methods for doing this: (i) gradual elimination and (ii) indexing and ranking.

Gradual elimination. The researcher that applies *gradual elimination* starts with a large number of prospective target countries and gradually narrows the choices by examining increasingly specific information. As indicated in Exhibit 13.1, the researcher aims to reduce the number of countries that warrant in-depth investigation as potential target markets to a manageable five or six. Because research is expensive, it is essential to eliminate unattractive markets quickly. Targeting a less-crowded economy with a prod-

GLOBAL TREND

Global Macro Trends That Affect International Business

Managers must regularly assess the long-term trends in their product markets, as well as in technology and globalization. Firms succeed when they ride these currents; those that swim against them usually struggle. In sectors like banking, telecommunications, and technology, almost two-thirds of Western firms' recent organic growth (that is, growth from increasing sales) has resulted from targeting the right markets and regions.

What current trends are international managers tracking that will make the future world very different from the world of today? A recent study by McKinsey consultants (www.mckinsey.com) identified the following.

Centers of economic activity are shifting. The locations of global economic activities are shifting due to economic liberalization, technological advances, capital market developments, and demographic changes. Today, Asia already accounts for more than 35 percent of the world GDP, exceeding the United States and the European Union. Clearly, global economic activity is shifting toward Asia. Some industries and functions in Asia— manufacturing and IT services, for example—will be the major beneficiaries. Emerging markets elsewhere are becoming centers of activity as well.

Need to increase organizational productivity. Populations are aging across the developed countries, leaving fewer young people to work and pay taxes. This demographic shift requires efficiency and creativity from both the public and private sectors to ensure that aging populations will not reduce the overall level of global wealth. Governments must provide services less expensively and with greater efficiency.

More consumers, especially in emerging markets. Almost a billion new consumers will enter the global marketplace through 2015, as economic growth in emerging markets pushes them beyond the threshold level of $5,000 in annual household income, a point when people begin to spend on discretionary goods. In the period through 2015, consumers' spending power in emerging economies will increase to more than $9 trillion, near the current spending power of Western Europe.

The shifting talent battlefield. The shift to knowledge-intensive industries highlights a growing scarcity of knowledge workers. Increasing integration of labor markets like China, India, and Eastern Europe is opening vast new talent sources. Emerging markets now have tens of millions of university-educated young profes-

sionals, more than double the number in advanced economies.

Growing demand for natural resources. As economic growth accelerates, especially in emerging markets, use of natural resources will grow at unprecedented rates. Demand for oil will rise substantially in coming years, bringing opportunities for firms in the global energy sector. In China, demand for copper, steel, and aluminum has tripled, suggesting opportunities for mining companies. Meanwhile, water shortages are increasingly common in much of the world.

Widespread access to information. Knowledge is increasingly accessible worldwide. Search engines such as Google make seemingly limitless information instantly available, and knowledge production itself is growing. Worldwide patent applications have been rising 20 percent a year as companies apply new models of knowledge production, access, distribution, and ownership.

SOURCES: Ian Davis, "The New Normal," *McKinsey Quarterly*, March 2009, retrieved from http://www.mckinseyquarterly.com; Ian Davis and E. Stephenson, "Ten Trends to Watch in 2006," *McKinsey Quarterly*, January 2006, retrieved from http://www.mckinsey.com; Warwick Grey, "Top Tech Trends 2009," *Chartered Accountants Journal of New Zealand* 88, no. 5 (2009): 88–95.

uct that is not yet widely available may be more profitable than targeting saturated and more competitive markets in Europe, Japan, and North America.

In the early stages, the researcher first obtains general information on macro-level indicators like population, income, and economic growth before delving into specific information. Broad screening data are readily available from sources such as globalEDGE™ (globalEDGE.msu.edu). The researcher then employs more specific indicators, such as import statistics, to narrow the choices. Import statistics help reveal the size of the market, the presence of competitors, and the market's viability for accepting new sales. The level of the country's exports also should be investigated, because some countries, such as Panama and Singapore, function as major transit points for international shipments and may not be actual product users. By analyzing research data and gradually narrowing the choices, the researcher identifies the most promising markets for further exploration.

Indexing and ranking. The second primary method for choosing the most promising foreign markets is *indexing and ranking,* in which the researcher assigns scores to countries for their overall market attractiveness. For each country, the researcher first identifies a comprehensive set of market-potential indicators and then uses one or more of them to represent a variable. Weights are assigned to each variable to establish its relative importance: The more important a variable, the greater its weight. The researcher uses the resulting weighted scores to rank the countries.

Assessing the Export Potential of Emerging Markets The indexing and ranking method is illustrated by the Market Potential Index for Emerging Markets, developed by Tamer Cavusgil[6] and featured at globalEDGE™ (www.globalEDGE.msu.edu).[7] Presented in Exhibit 13.2, the index ranks countries on a collection of variables for emerging markets. From it, a manager would conclude that China, Hong Kong, and Singapore are attractive markets. China has steadily risen in the index in recent years, as have Hungary, Poland, and the Czech Republic. The data are also helpful for decisions on entry via FDI and for sourcing.

Exhibit 13.3 defines the variables and relative weights in the index. The assigned weights can be adjusted up or down to fit the unique characteristics of any industry. For example, in evaluating market size, food industry firms may attach more weight to market size, while firms in the telecommunications equipment industry give more weight to infrastructure and country risk. The researcher can add variables or countries to refine the tool for greater precision.

The size and growth rate of the middle class are often critical indicators of promising targets. The *middle class* is measured by the share of national income available to middle-income households. These consumers are frequently the best prospect for a typical marketer because the wealthier class in most emerging markets is relatively small and the poorest segment has little disposable income. Exhibit 13.4 shows how the size of the middle class as a percentage of world population has consistently increased over time, thanks to rising affluence in emerging markets and developing economies.[8] Note, however, that measures of per-capita income may underestimate the true potential of emerging markets due to imprecise measurement methods and the existence of a large, informal economy in many countries.

The relative size of the middle class, and the pace of its growth, also indicate how national income is distributed in a country. If income distribution is particularly unequal, the size of the middle class will be limited and the market will be less attractive.

Exhibit 13.2 reveals some interesting patterns. Russia ranks third in market size but 24th in economic freedom. It also ranks low in market intensity and market receptivity, revealing there are always *trade-offs* in selecting target countries. No single country is attractive on all dimensions. Along with desirable features, the researcher also must contend with less desirable ones. For example, both Singapore and Hong Kong are favorable in terms of commercial infrastructure, but they are city-states with small populations.

The top four countries in the index in Exhibit 13.2 are all East Asian emerging economies. In recent years, these have made tremendous strides in market liberalization, industrialization, and modernization. South Korea is a champion of economic growth, with annual per-capita GDP growth often exceeding 5 percent (it has grown tenfold in the last 40 years). South Korean firms have become world leaders in many industries, such as shipbuilding, mobile communications, and flat-screen televisions. They use pioneering technologies years ahead of their competitors and are overtaking other countries in broadband and mobile technologies. Asia's rapid economic development is a primary factor in the current phase of globalization.[9]

Country rankings like those in Exhibit 13.2 are not static; they change over time with macroeconomic events or country-specific developments. While India ranks relatively high, it may dramatically fall if a new political regime reverses market liberalization. The recent accession of Bulgaria and Romania into the European Union will likely improve the economic prospects of these countries. The introduction of modern banking systems and legal infrastructure should increase Russia's attractiveness as an export market.

Exhibit 13.2 Market Potential Index for Emerging Markets, 2009

Country	Market Size		Market Growth Rate		Market Intensity		Market Consumption Capacity		Commercial Infrastructure		Economic Freedom		Market Receptivity		Country Risk		Overall Index	
	Rank	Index	Rank	Index	Rank	Index	Rank	Index	Rank	Index	Rank	Index	Rank	Index	Rank	Index	Rank	Index
Singapore	26	1	12	28	2	73	15	57	3	94	6	77	1	100	1	100	1	100
China	1	100	1	100	26	1	13	60	19	34	26	1	18	4	10	55	2	97
Hong Kong	24	1	14	27	1	100	18	48	1	100	2	93	2	69	2	89	3	93
South Korea	7	10	23	12	6	64	1	100	4	92	5	77	8	15	6	67	4	69
Czech Rep.	22	1	21	17	15	45	2	94	2	94	3	85	9	14	3	77	5	61
Israel	23	1	24	12	3	68	9	74	7	70	7	77	4	23	4	74	6	54
Poland	15	4	13	27	7	63	5	78	6	78	8	70	15	6	8	61	7	53
Hungary	25	1	26	1	4	67	3	90	5	82	4	81	5	16	15	43	8	48
Russia	3	25	8	38	21	29	8	75	8	65	24	7	21	3	12	48	9	40
Malaysia	19	3	17	26	22	27	10	73	9	64	16	45	3	24	9	55	10	36
India	2	38	3	54	23	25	11	60	25	2	17	44	24	3	23	24	11	36
Turkey	8	7	9	38	5	66	14	58	12	49	13	51	19	4	19	35	12	33
Chile	21	2	15	27	12	49	23	24	13	49	1	100	10	13	7	63	13	33
Mexico	6	10	22	16	10	58	22	38	15	46	10	63	6	15	11	51	14	31

NOTE: Only the top 14 countries are provided here; consult globalEDGE.msu.edu for the complete list.

SOURCE: Market Potential Index for Emerging Markets – 2009, globalEDGE™ [globalEDGE.msu.edu/resourcedesk/mpi].

Variable	Definition	Weight (out of 100)	Example Measurement Indicators
Market size	Proportion of country's population concentrated in cities	20	• Urban population
Market growth rate	Pace of industrialization and economic development	12	• Annual growth rate of commercial energy • Real GDP growth rate
Market intensity	Buying power of the country's residents	14	• Per-capita gross national income, based on purchasing power parity • Private consumption as a percentage of GDP
Market consumption capacity	Size and growth rate of the country's middle class	10	• Percentage share of middle-class income and consumption
Commercial infrastructure	Ease of access to marketing, distribution, and communication channels	14	• Telephones per 100 habitants • Paved road density • Internet hosts per million people • Population per retail outlet
Economic freedom	Degree to which the country has liberalized its economy	10	• Trade and tax policies • Monetary and banking policies • Capital flows and foreign investment • Property rights
Market receptivity to imports	Extent of country's openness to imports	12	• Per-capita imports • Trade as percentage of GDP
Country risk	Level of political risk	8	• Country risk rating
Total		**100**	

Exhibit 13.3 Variables Used in the Market Potential Index for Emerging Markets

SOURCE: Market Potential Index for Emerging Markets – 2009, globalEDGE™ (globalEDGE.msu.edu/resourcedesk/mpi)

Chile has achieved substantial progress in economic reforms and higher living standards, while economic stagnation has reduced Argentina's attractiveness.

The variables suggested by ranking indicators are only a general guide for identifying promising countries in the early stages of qualifying. The researcher should do much more detailed analyses once a handful of target markets are identified. Eventually, the researcher will supplement the indicators for specific industries. For medical equipment, for instance, the researcher should gather additional data on health care expenditures and the number of physicians and hospital beds per capita. Firms in the financial services sector require specific data on commercial risk, interest rates, and density of banks. Depending on the industry, researchers may also apply different weights to each market-potential indicator. Population size is relatively less important for a firm that markets yachts than for one that sells footwear.

Country Screening for Foreign Direct Investment

Because acquiring major productive assets such as land, plant, and equipment for FDI is costly and because FDI investments are usually undertaken for the long term, choosing the right market is critical, and different variables apply than for exporting. For example, with FDI the availability of skilled labor and managerial talent in the target market is more important. Researchers identifying the best locations for FDI normally consider the following variables:

- Long-term prospects for growth and substantial returns
- Cost of doing business, based on the price and availability of commercial infrastructure; tax rates and wages, and high-level skills and capital markets
- Country risk, including regulatory, financial, political, and cultural barriers, and the legal environment for intellectual property protection
- Competitive environment and intensity of competition from other firms
- Government incentives such as tax holidays, subsidized training, grants, or low-interest loans

Several sources of publicly accessible studies are available for screening countries for FDI, such as the United Nations Conference on Trade and Development (UNCTAD; www.unctad.org). Another is provided by the consulting firm A. T. Kearney, which prepares a *Foreign Direct Investment Confidence Index* (www.atkearney.com) that tracks how political, economic, and regulatory changes affect the FDI intentions and preferences of the world's top 1,000 firms. By surveying executives at these firms, the index captures the most important variables for the sixty-five countries that receive more than 90 percent of global FDI investments.

Exhibit 13.5 displays the A. T. Kearney Index. It reveals that investors have high confidence in traditional investment destinations such as Britain and the United States. Advanced economies engage in substantial cross-investments in each other's markets. For example, Europe and the United States are each other's most important partners for FDI. Their transatlantic economy represents more than $2.5 trillion in total foreign affiliate sales and mutually supports nearly a quarter of the world's entire foreign affiliate workforce employed by MNEs abroad. However, of particular interest in the Kearney Index are China and India, which top the list.

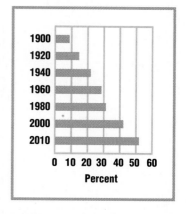

Exhibit 13.4 Middle Class Population in All Countries as a Percent of Total World Population

SOURCE: Based on "Burgeoning Bourgeoisie," by Surjit Bhalla © *The Economist* Newspaper Limited, London (February 12, 2009).

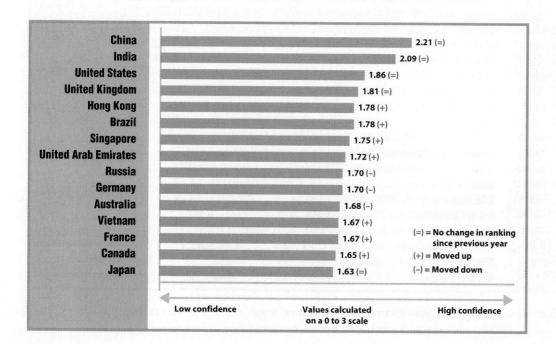

Exhibit 13.5 A. T. Kearney Foreign Direct Investment Confidence Index

SOURCE: Foreign Direct Investment Confidence Index®, *New Concerns in an Uncertain World*, Copyright A. T. Kearney, 2007. All rights reserved. Reprinted with permission.

Note that of the top ten destinations, seven are emerging markets: China, India, Hong Kong, Brazil, Singapore, United Arab Emirates, and Russia. Investors prefer China because of its huge size, fast-growing consumer market, and position as an excellent, low-cost manufacturing site. China also enjoys favorable government incentives and a stable macroeconomic climate. However, executives see India as the world's leader for business process and outsourcing IT services. India has a well-educated workforce, strong managerial talent, established rule of law, and transparent transactions and rules.

Country Screening for Sourcing

Global sourcing and offshoring describe the practice of procuring finished products, intermediate goods, and services from suppliers located abroad. When seeking foreign sources of supply, managers examine such factors as cost and quality of inputs, stability of exchange rates, reliability of suppliers, and the presence of a workforce with superior technical skills.

Firms increasingly source services from abroad to achieve various types of advantages. A. T. Kearney prepares a *Global Services Location Index* (www.atkearney.com), which lets managers compare the factors that make countries attractive as potential locations for offshoring service activities such as IT, business processes, and call centers. The index evaluates countries across forty-three criteria in three dimensions:

- *Financial attractiveness* accounts for compensation costs (average wages), infrastructure costs (for electricity and telecom systems), and tax and regulatory costs (tax burden, corruption, and fluctuating exchange rates).

- *People skills and availability* account for suppliers' experience and skills, labor-force availability, education and language proficiency, and employee-attrition rates.

- *Business environment* assesses economic and political aspects of the country, commercial infrastructure, cultural adaptability, and security of intellectual property.

Exhibit 13.6 presents the *Global Services Location Index*. Note that virtually all the top ten countries are emerging markets, such as India, China, and Malaysia. Although the

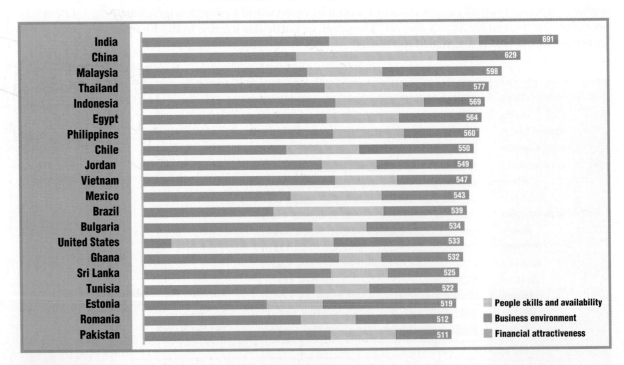

Exhibit 13.6 The 2009 A. T. Kearney Global Services Location Index

cost of labor is important, managers also cite productivity level, technical skills, and customer service skills as important factors. The index credits India and China (and to a lesser extent, Brazil and Mexico) with superior people skills.

 ## Task Four: Assess Industry Market Potential

The methods for screening countries we've discussed so far are most useful for gaining comparative insights into individual markets and for reducing the complexity of choosing appropriate foreign locations. Once the number of potential countries has been reduced to a manageable few, the next step is to conduct an in-depth analysis of each. In earlier stages, the researcher examined macro-level indicators. Now, because market potential is industry-specific, the researcher narrows the focus to examine industry-level indicators.

Industry market potential is an estimate of the likely sales for all firms in a particular industry over a specific period. It is different from *company sales potential*, the share of industry sales the focal firm itself can expect to achieve during a given year. Most firms forecast both industry market potential and company sales potential at least three years into the future.

Estimating industry market potential enables the researcher to refine the analysis and identify the most attractive countries for the firm's product or service, as well as gain industry-specific insights and understand how the firm needs to adapt its product and marketing approaches.

To estimate industry market potential, managers obtain data and insights on the following variables for each country:

- Size and growth rate of the market and trends in the specific industry
- Tariff and nontariff trade barriers to market entry
- Standards and regulations that affect the industry
- Availability and sophistication of distribution for the firm's offerings in the market
- Unique customer requirements and preferences
- Industry-specific market potential indicators

In addition to generic determinants of demand, each industry sector—from air conditioners to zippers—has its own *industry-specific potential indicators* or *distinctive drivers of demand*. Marketers of cameras, for example, examine climate-related factors such as the average number of sunny days in a typical year, given that most pictures are taken outdoors. In marketing laboratory equipment, the researcher might study the number of hospitals, clinics, hospital beds, and doctors, as well as the level of governmental expenditures on health care. A manufacturer of electric generators might examine the rate of industrialization and dependence on hydroelectricity. A marketer of cooling equipment and industrial filters will consider the number of institutional buyers, such as restaurants and hotels. These are all industry-specific market potential indicators.

The researcher also evaluates factors that affect marketing and use of the product, such as consumer characteristics, culture, distribution channels, and business practices. Because intellectual property rights and enforcement vary around the world, it is also important to protect the firm's critical assets by looking into regulations, trademark rules, and product liability. The researcher should also investigate subsidy and incentive programs from home and foreign governments that reduce the cost of foreign market entry.

Industry market potential An estimate of the likely sales for all firms in a particular industry over a specific period.

Camera makers account for climate in their estimates of demand, since most pictures are taken outdoors. What other industry-specific variables might they consider?

More British pubs are serving food, creating a new market potential for firms in the food catering industry.

Growth rates tend to be relatively high in new or rapidly innovating industries. The researcher should bear in mind that the product is likely to be in a different phase of its life cycle in each country. Countries in which the product is not currently available or in which competitors have only recently introduced it may be especially promising targets.

Practical Methods for Managers to Assess Industry Market Potential

Managers use a variety of methods to estimate industry market potential:

- *Simple trend analysis.* This method quantifies the total likely amount of industry market potential by examining aggregate production for the industry as a whole, adding imports from abroad and deducting exports. Trend analysis provides a rough estimate of the size of current industry sales in the country.

- *Monitoring key industry-specific indicators.* The manager examines unique industry drivers of market demand by collecting data from various sources. For example, Caterpillar, a manufacturer of earth-moving equipment, examines the volume of announced construction projects, number of issued building permits, growth rate of households, infrastructure development, and other pertinent leading indicators as a way of anticipating countrywide sales of its construction equipment.

- *Monitoring key competitors.* Here, the manager investigates the degree of major competitor activity in the countries of interest. If Caterpillar is considering Chile as a potential market, its managers investigate the current involvement of its number-one competitor, the Japanese firm Komatsu, in Chile and gather competitive intelligence to anticipate Komatsu's likely future moves in Chile.

- *Following key customers around the world.* Automotive suppliers can anticipate where their services will be needed next by monitoring the international expansion of their customers such as Honda or Mercedes-Benz. Caterpillar follows its current customers such as Bechtel and Fluor as they bid for contracts or establish operations in specific foreign markets.

- *Tapping into supplier networks.* Many suppliers serve multiple clients and can be a major source of information about competitors. Firms can gain valuable leads from current suppliers by asking them about the activities of competitors, as long as the questions are ethical and don't expose competitors' trade secrets and other proprietary information.

- *Attending international trade fairs.* By attending a trade fair in the target country, a manager can learn a great deal about market characteristics that help indicate industry sales potential. Trade fairs are also helpful for identifying potential distributors and other business partners.

Data Sources for Estimating Industry Market Potential

For each target country, the manager seeks data that directly or indirectly report levels of industry sales and production, as well as the intensity of exports and imports in the product category of interest. Exhibit 13.7 summarizes numerous sites useful for estimat-

Site	Address	Description
globalEDGE™	globalEDGE.msu.edu	Data, information, search engines, and diagnostic tools on a full range of international business topics
Export.gov	www.export.gov	Country commercial guides and other U.S. government resources to support international sales and marketing
UK Trade and Investment	www.uktradeinvest.gov.uk	United Kingdom data and resources to support international business
Industry Canada	www.ic.gc.ca	Canada data and resources to support international business
United Nations Commission on Trade and Development (UNCTAD)	www.unctad.org	Country fact sheets and statistics for analysis of international trade, FDI, and economic trends
World Trade Organization (WTO)	www.wto.org	Statistics on tariffs, government intervention, and economic conditions worldwide
World Bank	www.worldbank.org	National and international statistics, financial and technical information, sectoral data, trends in the world economy
World Bank Doing Business	www.doingbusiness.org	Reports on doing business in various countries
International Monetary Fund (IMF)	www.imf.org	Data and statistics on countries, and economic and financial indicators
A.T. Kearney	www.atkearney.com	Various indices, including the Foreign Direct Investment Confidence Index

Exhibit 13.7
A Sampling of Sites for Conducting International Business Research

ing industry market potential, as well as accessing various statistics for conducting market opportunity assessment and other international business research.

One useful source in the United States is the market research section at export.gov (www.export.gov/mrktresearch). Specific reports available at this site include:

- *Best Market* and *Market Update* reports provide extensive industry, country, and market research to pinpoint the best export markets and develop entry strategies.
- *Country Commercial Guides* comprehensively profile the political, economic, and commercial environment of some 150 countries.
- *Industry Overviews* and *Industry/Regional Reports* describe conditions in specific industries.

Recent Grad in IB

Javier's major: Business

Objectives: Integrating business skills with social planning in a public agency and pursuing a career in politics

Jobs held since graduating:
- United Nations World Food Programme in Guatemala and Honduras
- Director of Research, Bates Advertising, Dominican Republic
- Director of a major charity in Mexico

Javier Estrada

Javier Estrada graduated from a state university several years ago with a bachelor's degree in business. Upon graduation, Javier went to work for the United Nations World Food Programme (WFP) in Guatemala and Honduras and was given the task of monitoring the functioning and execution of all WFP projects. The experience taught Javier about international management and logistics in the high-pressure environment of disaster relief that the United Nations has faced in Central America.

Ever adventurous, Javier next moved to the Dominican Republic, where, at the age of 24, he took a position as director of research in the local office of Bates Advertising, a global ad agency that handled accounts such as Wendy's, Purina, and Bell South. In this position, Javier investigated the local target market—how the market responded to key brands, the level of market share, and the most effective way of reaching target markets with advertising and other marketing communications tools. According to Javier, "The real challenge in international advertising is not in the large, established brands, but in the small, poorly positioned one."

A typical day for Javier included meeting with colleagues to discuss the progress of research projects and assessing the next steps on behalf of his clients. Javier implemented consumer surveys to find out what specific benefits Latin American consumers were seeking. He used the information from this research to craft advertising campaigns ideally tailored to customer needs and attitudes. In creating surveys, Javier researched various secondary data sources on the Internet and in Bates's private library. He visited Santo Domingo to get a more authentic feel for the market and to meet with local experts. He also used a comprehensive report prepared by the United States Department of Commerce International Trade Administration on the target market. Javier developed Spanish-language questionnaires to gain an even deeper understanding of the market. He sent out questionnaires to random samples of typical consumers throughout the Dominican Republic. He then analyzed the completed questionnaires and presented the results to his superiors. Findings from these studies helped Javier prepare reports with recommendations on the most appropriate advertising strategies for the Dominican Republic.

Success Factors

"My parents felt strongly that our lives should be influenced not only by the quality of our education, but also by our travels. . . . In school we were far from the wealthiest kids, but we were definitely among the most traveled." Javier was lucky enough to visit several countries during his teens and twenties. He comments: "You really get to know yourself when you are completely alone in a whole new culture and establishing a network of friends and work contacts." International experience contributed to Javier's independent spirit and his ability to function successfully anywhere in the world.

In his market research position, Javier enjoyed going to other countries and meeting different people. "My job provided the chance to help companies develop marketing programs that were really appropriate for their customers. If you really understand your customer, you have tremendous responsibility to use the information wisely and honestly.... Of course, I wouldn't have received the job if I hadn't worked hard in school. Good management training provided me with the skills to perform effectively. Sensitivity is important, since you need to be able to communicate with people who are culturally different from you. You need a strong empathy for your customers, and you need to try to identify exactly which research questions they are trying to address."

What's Ahead?

Javier has ever-higher goals for his career. He has been long concerned about poverty issues in Latin America, and his experiences with the United Nations had a profound effect on him. Javier earned a master's degree in social policy and planning from the London School of Economics. Having worked in both business and development, Javier found his passion in integrating his business skills with social planning at the governmental level. Recently, Javier headed a major charity organization in Mexico. Eventually he wants to pursue a political career. He says, "I need to dream big."

Managers must be creative in finding and consulting resources that shed light on the task at hand. Data and resources in international research are rarely complete or precise. Consider Teltone Inc. The firm wished to enter Mexico with its inexpensive brand of cellular telephones and needed to estimate industry-wide demand. It consulted numerous sources, including reports by the International Telecommunications Union (in Geneva, Switzerland), Export.gov, and several United Nations publications. Managers researched the size of the Mexican upper class and its average income, the nature of support infrastructure for cellular systems in Mexico, and the nature and number of retail stores that could handle cell phones. They also found some statistics from the National Telecommunications Trade Association on the number of competitors already active in Mexico and their approximate sales volumes. From these sources, the firm was able to arrive at a rough estimate of market size for telephones and prevailing prices in Mexico.

The *Recent Grad in IB* feature profiles Javier Estrada, who found exciting opportunities in his young career in international market research and working in emerging markets.

 ## Choosing Foreign Business Partners

Business partners are critical to success in international business. These partners include distribution-channel intermediaries, facilitators, suppliers, and collaborative venture partners such as joint venture partners, licensees, and franchisees. Once the firm has selected a target market, it must identify the types of partners it needs for its foreign-market venture, negotiate terms with chosen partners, and support and monitor their conduct.

Exporters tend to collaborate with foreign-market intermediaries such as distributors and agents. Firms that choose to sell their intellectual property, such as know-how, trademarks, and copyrights, tend to work through foreign licensees. These **licensing** partners are independent businesses that apply intellectual property to produce products in their own country. In **franchising**, the foreign partner is a franchisee, an independent business abroad that acquires rights and skills from the focal firm to conduct operations in its own market (such as in the fast-food or car-rental industries). The focal firm can also internationalize by initiating an **international collaborative venture**, a business activity undertaken jointly with other firms. These collaborations may be project-based or require equity investments. Other types of international partnerships include global sourcing, contract manufacturing, and supplier partnerships. We describe these in greater detail in later chapters.

Criteria for Choosing a Partner

One of the most important decisions for the focal firm is to identify the ideal qualifications of potential foreign partners. The firm should seek a good fit in terms of both strategy (common goals and objectives) and resources (complementary core competencies and value-chain activities). It is helpful to anticipate the potential degree of synergy with the prospective partner for the intermediate-term, three to six years into the future.

Brunswick Corporation (www.brunswick.com), a leading manufacturer of recreational goods such as boats and bowling equipment, looks for the following when screening for potential foreign distributors:

- Financial soundness and resourcefulness, to ensure the venture receives the appropriate level of support initially and in the long run
- Competent and professional management, with qualified technical and sales staff
- Solid knowledge of the industry, with access to distribution channels and end users in the marketplace
- Reputation in the marketplace and good connections with local government (political clout is often helpful, especially in emerging markets)
- Commitment, loyalty, and willingness to invest in the venture and grow it over time

Licensing Arrangement in which the owner of intellectual property grants a firm the right to use that property for a specified period of time in exchange for royalties or other compensation.

Franchising Arrangement in which the firm allows another the right to use an entire business system in exchange for fees, royalties, or other forms of compensation.

International collaborative venture Cross-border business alliance whereby partnering firms pool their resources and share costs and risks to undertake a new business venture; also referred to as an "international partnership" or an "international strategic alliance".

Firms seeking a foreign business partner look for a variety of qualifications, including common goals and objectives and competent management.

Firms also seek partners with complementary expertise. For example, while the focal firm may bring engineering and manufacturing expertise to the partnership, the local distributor may bring knowledge of local customers and distribution channels.

Desirable characteristics are not always available in prospective partners. If a company enters a foreign market late, it may have to pick the second-best or even less-qualified partner. The firm should then be ready and able to strengthen the partner's capabilities by transferring appropriate managerial skills, technical know-how, and other resources over time.

Searching for Prospective Partners

The process of screening and evaluating business partners can be overwhelming. Commercial banks, consulting firms, and trade journals, as well as country and regional business directories such as *Kompass* and *Dun and Bradstreet*, are helpful in developing a list of partner candidates. National governments offer inexpensive services that assist firms in finding partners in specific foreign markets. The knowledge portal globalEDGE™ (www.globalEDGE.msu.edu) provides additional resources, including diagnostic tools, to help managers make systematic choices among partner candidates.

Onsite visits and research from independent sources and trade fairs are crucial in the early stages of assessing a partner. Companies also find it useful to ask prospective partners to prepare a formal business plan before entering into an agreement. The quality and sophistication of such a plan provides insights into the capabilities of the prospective partner and serves as a test of the partner's commitment.

 Task Six: Estimate Company Sales Potential

Once managers have identified several promising country markets, verified industry market potential, and assessed the availability of qualified business partners, the next step is to determine company sales potential in each country. **Company sales potential** is an estimate of the share of annual industry sales the firm expects to generate in a particular target market. Arriving at it is often more challenging than earlier tasks, because the researcher typically needs to obtain highly refined information from the market and make some fundamental assumptions to project the firm's revenues and expenses three to five years into the future. These estimates are never precise and require quite a bit of judgment and creative thinking.

Company sales potential   An estimate of the share of annual industry sales that the firm expects to generate in a particular target market.

For example, research suggests that fewer than 10 percent of people in Vietnam have a banking relationship. But demand for banking is growing rapidly, by as much as 25 percent annually. It is highest among Vietnamese 21–29 years old, who are less wary of banking and more open to foreign banks than their elders. Vietnam's economy is growing rapidly, with rising household income, and there are few competitors in the marketplace.[10] Suppose a bank from your country is considering entering the market in Vietnam. How would it estimate its sales potential there? We address such issues next.

Determinants of Company Sales Potential

In arriving at an estimate of company sales potential in the foreign market, managers will collect and review various research findings and assess the following:

- *Intensity of the competitive environment.* Local or third-country competitors are likely to intensify their own marketing efforts when confronted by new entrants. Their actions are often unpredictable and not easily observed.

- *Pricing and financing of sales.* The degree to which pricing and financing are attractive to both customers and channel members is critical to initial entry and ultimate success.

- *Financial resources.* Sufficient capital is a prerequisite for any project. International ventures often require substantial financial outlays.

- *Human resources.* Management must ensure it has personnel with sufficient capabilities in language, culture, and other areas to do business in target markets.

- *Partner capabilities.* The competencies and resources of foreign partners, including channel intermediaries and facilitators, influence how quickly the firm can enter and generate sales in the target market.

- *Access to distribution channels.* The ability to establish and make best use of channel intermediaries and distribution infrastructure in the target market determines sales.

- *Market penetration timetable.* A key decision is whether managers opt for gradual or rapid market entry. Gradual entry gives the firm time to develop and leverage resources and strategies but may cede market share to competitors. Rapid entry can ensure first-mover advantages but also tax the firm's resources and capabilities.

- *Risk tolerance of senior managers.* Results depend on the level of resources top management is willing to commit, which in turn depends on management's tolerance for risk.

- *Special links, contacts, and capabilities of the firm.* The extent of the focal firm's network in the market—its existing relationships with customers, channel members, and suppliers—can strongly affect venture success.

- *Reputation.* The firm can succeed faster in the market if target customers are already familiar with its brand name and reputation.

Such a comprehensive assessment should lead to general estimates of potential sales, which managers can compare to actual sales of incumbent firms in the market, when such data are available.

Thus, the process of estimating company sales is more like starting from multiple angles, then converging on an ultimate estimate that relies heavily on judgment. Exhibit 13.8 provides a framework to estimate company sales. Managers combine information about customers, intermediaries, and competition and see whether the result points to a reasonable estimate. Managers may make multiple estimates based on best-case, worst-case, and most-likely case scenarios. They will usually make assumptions about the degree of firm effort, price aggressiveness, possible competitive reactions, degree of intermediary effort, and so on. The firm's sales prospects also hinge on factors both controllable by management (like prices charged to intermediaries and customers) and uncontrollable (like intensity of competition). Ultimately, the process of estimating company sales potential is more art than science.

Practical Approaches to Estimating Company Sales Potential

The manager should begin with the factors suggested in Exhibit 13.8. Experienced managers also find the following activities especially helpful:

- *Survey of end users and intermediaries.* The firm can survey a sample of customers and distributors to determine the level of potential sales.

- *Trade audits.* Managers may visit retail outlets and question channel members to assess relative price levels of competitors' offerings and perceptions of competitor strength. In this approach, managers estimate market potential through the eyes of intermediaries (distributors) responsible for handling the product in the market. The trade audit can also indicate opportunities for new modes of distribution, identify types of alternative outlets, and provide insights into company standing relative to competitors.

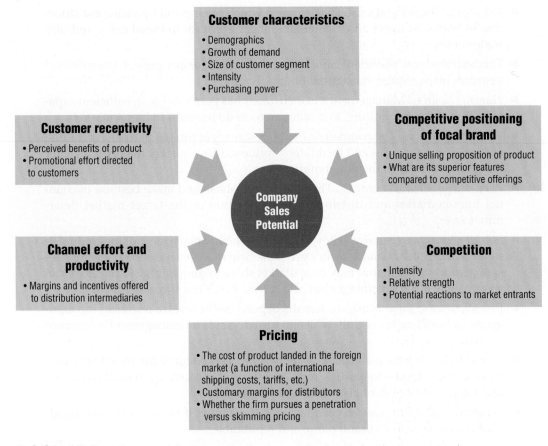

Exhibit 13.8 A Framework for Estimating Company Sales Potential in the Foreign Market

- *Competitor assessment.* The firm may benchmark itself against principal competitor(s) in the market and estimate the level of sales it can attract away from them. What rival firms will it have to outperform? If key competitors in a given market are large and powerful, competing head-on could prove costly and lead to failure. Even in countries dominated by large firms, however, research may reveal untapped or underserved market segments that can be attractive, particularly for smaller firms with modest sales goals.

- *Estimates from local partners.* Collaborators such as distributors, franchisees, or licensees already experienced in the market are often best positioned to develop estimates of market share and sales potential.

- *Limited marketing efforts to test the waters.* Some companies may choose to engage in a limited entry in the foreign market—a sort of test market—as a way of gauging long-term sales potential or gaining a better understanding of the market. From these early results, it is possible to forecast longer-term sales.

In developing economies and emerging markets, where information sources are especially limited, two other techniques are useful for estimating company sales potential. These are *analogy* and *proxy indicators*. We illustrated these approaches in the opening vignette.

- *Analogy.* In the analogy method, the researcher draws on known statistics from one country to gain insights into the same phenomenon for another, similar country. For example, if the researcher knows the total consumption of citrus drinks in India, then—assuming citrus drink consumption patterns do not vary much in neighboring Pakistan—a rough estimate of Pakistan's consumption can be made, adjusting, of course, for the difference in population. If a firm knows X number of bottles of antibiotics are sold in a country with Y number of physicians per thousand people, it can assume the same ratio (of bottles per 1,000 physicians) will apply in a similar country.

■ *Proxy indicators.* With proxy indicators, the researcher uses known information about one product category to infer potential about another product category, especially if the two are complementary. A proxy indicator of demand for professional hand tools might be the level of construction activity in the country; for a particular piece of surgical equipment, it might be the total number of surgeries performed.

A firm contemplating a major market entry via FDI should make its market research especially comprehensive. When Britain's huge retailer Tesco assessed its entry into the United States, researchers investigated every detail of the country's in-store offerings and grocery buyer behavior. The firm set up a mock store in Los Angeles and invited groups of 250 customers in to watch how they shopped, then asked for feedback. The researchers moved into sixty California families' homes for two weeks, sifting through their cupboards and refrigerators, shopping and cooking with them, and keeping diaries of their every movement, from how they got their kids to school to what they did at night. The research has paid off, making Tesco the world's most successful international food retailer, outpacing Walmart.[11]

In Conclusion

The decision to internationalize is never easy. Some firms are attracted to foreign markets by the promise of revenues and profits, others by the prospect of increasing production efficiency. Still others internationalize to quell competitive pressures or keep pace with rivals. Whatever the rationale, when companies fail in international ventures, it is often because they neglect to conduct a systematic and comprehensive assessment of global market opportunity.

Although we've presented the six tasks of global market opportunity assessment in a sequence, firms do not necessarily pursue them that way. Indeed, they often pursue two or more simultaneously. And the process is dynamic: Market conditions change, partner performance fluctuates, and competitive intensity may increase. These events require managers to constantly evaluate their decisions and commitments, remaining open to course changes as circumstances dictate.

Some choices managers make are interrelated. For example, the choice of business partner is a function of the country. The type of distributor to use varies from market to market—say, for example, between the Netherlands and Nigeria. The degree of country risk may imply a need for a politically well-connected business partner. In nontraditional markets, such as Vietnam, the firm may need a partner that can serve as both distributor and cultural adviser.

Seasoned executives contend that even the most attractive country cannot compensate for a poor partner. While the quantity and quality of market information about individual countries have increased substantially, firms often struggle to identify qualified and interested business partners, especially in emerging markets. The most qualified partners are likely to be already subscribed and representing other foreign firms. This necessitates recruiting second- or even third-best candidates and then committing adequate resources to ensure their success.

Advanced Biomedical Devices: Assessing Readiness to Export

Dr. Richard Bentley, a well-known British surgeon who developed a medical device that helps the wound-healing process, was so committed to the ground-breaking technology that he left his surgical practice to found Advanced Biomedical Devices, Inc. (ABD), headquartered in the eastern United States. ABD plans to initiate exporting activities and just completed the process of assessing its readiness, using CORE (**CO**mpany **R**eadiness to **E**xport).

ABD's product line includes several innovative devices called Speedheal that promote healing and also reduce postsurgical pain by keeping the wound area from swelling. Speedheal oxygenates the wound area by pulsing electrons through the bandage covering the wound. The devices are very small and portable. Versions exist for different types of surgeries: hand surgery, face lifts, abdominal procedures, and so on.

Dr. Bentley launched ABD with a skillful management team whose members have worked extensively in the European market, the Pacific Rim, and Latin America. ABD's manufacturing director is from Germany, and another manager lived in France and Malaysia for several years.

Thanks to high demand, Speedheal sales increased rapidly, primarily through medical product distributors that sold to hospitals and clinics throughout the United States. Growth approached 20 percent in some years, and the staff grew to 85 people. The firm's success stimulated the entry of competitors offering similar products, but rivals never achieved the degree of miniaturization in ABD's products. Miniaturization thus remains one of Speedheal's competitive advantages. Management's projections for ABD's future growth remain positive.

Dreams of International Expansion

ABD had received unsolicited orders from abroad and learned a great deal about handling international transactions, including foreign exchange, letters of credit, and logistics. Though ABD's plan to internationalize was in its early stages, management intended to expand beyond occasional export sales to target key world markets. Its managers preferred dealing with psychically close markets—those with familiar culture, business customs, and legal and banking systems. But they were willing to consider others, especially large and fast-growing markets and those promising superior profitability.

One expected benefit was the opportunity for ABD to learn from global competitors and markets. Many trends that start in foreign markets eventually reach the home country, and often the best way to track them is to do business internationally. Management also believed it could reduce ABD's overall risks by diversifying sales to various foreign markets. Finally, internationalization would help preempt competitors in particular foreign markets.

International Strategic Intent

Dr. Bentley and his management team formulated some questions to clarify ABD's internationalization goals. They knew that answering the questions would help clarify ABD's strategic intent for going international. Management also wanted to develop a comprehensive strategic plan that would lay the foundation for international success. Following a series of meetings, the team reached consensus on the following key elements of ABD's initial strategic direction:

- Top management will strongly commit to internationalization, and ABD will pursue foreign markets aggressively. The firm will hire a vice president for international sales in the coming year.

- ABD will invest up to 20 percent of company earnings in export opportunities.

- ABD will begin building distributor relationships in a number of countries.

- ABD will establish a marketing subsidiary in at least one foreign location within three to five years and hire salespeople who select and manage the distributors in their market area.

- Management will seek to ensure that all international ventures reach profitability within two years of their launch.

- Management will develop international marketing plans for each target market, each with its own budget.

- Plans call for international sales to reach 35 percent of total sales within four years.

- ABD will establish an annual budget of $220,000 to finance international activities for each of the first three years. Of that, about $60,000 will be devoted to market research to determine the best target markets and to understand competitors.

Product Readiness for Export

Following approval of ABD's strategic intent, Dr. Bentley and his management team addressed questions about the challenges of internationalization. The first dealt with training sales representatives in foreign markets to sell medical devices to hospitals and clinics, the primary end markets for ABD products. Sales reps require training because they deal with doctors, nurses, and other professionals who are deeply involved in decision making about purchases of hospital supplies. Because training costs can be high in foreign markets, Dr. Bentley wanted to ensure ABD was prepared to make this investment.

Dr. Bentley also raised the issue of after-sales service, which can be challenging in foreign markets. Because ABD's products were seldom defective, the solution for a defective product was to replace it rather than trying to make a repair. U.S. customers counted on a ready backup stock in the event of product defects. ABD planned to employ the same solution for its foreign operations, and management assumed there would be no need for a separate staff to deal with after-sales service. Because Speedheal devices are small and lightweight (though valuable), per-unit transportation costs are very low. In fact, in urgent situations abroad, ABD already made it a practice to ship a replacement device by air.

While management well understood pricing in the United States, there was much it did not know about foreign pricing. Dr. Bentley and several managers had attended trade fairs in Europe and concluded that ABD's prices were not too high, particularly since no other firms offered similar products. In fact, ABD had filled unsolicited orders from Europe and found that customers never challenged its pricing. In the end, however, management decided research was needed to refine ABD's pricing approach.

Next, the team discussed foreign inventory management. Because the devices were cheap to transport by air freight, distributors could replenish inventories quickly and economically, a significant benefit because they would not have to maintain much inventory to support sales. On the other hand, Speedheal devices were sensitive to changes in temperature and humidity and functioned best when warehoused in climate-controlled facilities. Such warehousing was increasingly common, so ABD should have no problem locating the right warehousing in Europe and elsewhere.

ABD's management realized the firm's flexible packaging put them in a good position to enter foreign markets, and they were also prepared to modify the product in various ways to meet worldwide standards and regulations. Two in particular were the CE mark, a mandatory safety mark required on toys, machinery, and low-voltage equipment, and ISO standards, which aim to make development and manufacturing of products efficient, safe, and clean.

Knowledge, Skills, and Resources

In a subsequent meeting, the ABD team considered less tangible aspects of the firm's readiness to internationalize. Management knew critical self-assessment was vital to long-term success, and internationalization would require additional working capital for foreign warehousing, longer shipping times, and larger inventories abroad. Other costs included legal help, freight forwarding, international transportation, customs duties, bank charges, rent for foreign offices, and approval for certain regulatory issues. ABD's management was not completely clear on the amount of these costs, but they were willing to learn. While it would use letters of credit when first opening new markets, ABD would opt for open-account payment systems (payable in 30 or 60 days, depending on the market).

Dr. Bentley also considered the appropriate growth rate for the firm. A company's business could increase rapidly, demanding more product than the firm could reasonably supply. Or domestic sales could drop sharply, requiring management to divert all efforts to rescuing domestic operations, thus disrupting the export program.

Competitive intelligence was another concern. A key incentive for venturing abroad was to learn more about foreign competitors. Some major medical device manufacturers marketed their products in the United States, while others were based strictly abroad. ABD would have to research and understand the strategies and marketing practices of the important competitors. Dr. Bentley recognized the importance of getting patent coverage on his inventions around the world and of protecting the intellectual property rights of his firm. He planned to retain legal counsel, at home and abroad, to protect ABD's critical assets from patent infringements; to develop suitable distribution and agent agreements, sales agreements, and licensing; and to ensure compliance with local employment laws.

Management believed ABD's initial foreign markets would be Australia, Canada, Western Europe, and Japan, because of their large proportion of affluent consumers with the ability to pay for sophisticated medical care. Thus, ABD had gathered information about the markets and competition in those countries but recognized that it needed to do much more.

Managerial Capabilities for Long-Term Internationalization

One concern was whether management would be able to cope with deepening internationalization. In the end, the ABD team recognized that they were right to take painstaking efforts to determine the firm's readiness to export. Extensive meetings and preliminary research provided the basis for developing initial strategies and action programs, as well as for identifying improvements to make the company stronger in the coming years.

AACSB: **Reflective Thinking Skills, Analytic Skills**

Case Questions

1. Do you believe ABD's products are in a state of readiness to begin exporting to Europe? Why or why not? Are the products ready for exporting to emerging markets (e.g., China, Mexico, Russia)? Why or why not? What factors suggest Speedheal products might enjoy demand in all types of foreign markets?

2. Does management at ABD possess the appropriate knowledge, skills, and capabilities for internationalization? Justify your answer. What steps should management take to better prepare the firm, managers, and employees to internationalize?

3. How well did ABD complete the key tasks in global market opportunity assessment? Evaluate whether it accomplished each task well or poorly. Did ABD achieve each of the objectives set out for the tasks?

4. If you were a member of ABD's management team, what countries would you recommend targeting first? As a manager, you would need to justify your recommendation. A good approach is to investigate key characteristics of specific countries via globalEDGE™ (globalEDGE.msu.edu) or similar Web sites.

5. What approaches could ABD employ to estimate the firm's sales potential for markets in Europe and other affluent economies? Justify your answer.

NOTE: This case was written by Myron M. Miller, Michigan State University (retired), in association with Professor S. Tamer Cavusgil.

CHAPTER ESSENTIALS

Key Terms

company sales potential, p. 390
franchising, p. 389
global market opportunity, p. 372

industry market potential, p. 385
international collaborative venture,
    p. 389

licensing, p. 389

Summary

In this chapter, you learned about:

1. Assessing global market opportunities

A **global market opportunity** is a favorable combination of circumstances, locations, or timing that offer prospects for exporting, investing, sourcing, or partnering in foreign markets. The firm may perceive opportunities to sell, establish factories, obtain inputs of lower cost or superior quality, or enter collaborative arrangements with foreign partners that support the focal firm's goals. Global market opportunities help the firm improve its performance. Managers continuously seek the most relevant data and knowledge to make the most of international opportunities. There are six key tasks that managers perform in defining and pursuing global market opportunities.

2. Analyzing organizational readiness to internationalize

As the first task, management assesses the firm's readiness to internationalize. Management assesses the strengths and weaknesses in the firm's ability to do international business. It assesses the external business environment by conducting formal research on the opportunities and threats that face the firm. The firm must develop resources it lacks. Diagnostic tools, such as *CORE* (**CO**mpany **R**eadiness to **E**xport), facilitate a self-audit of readiness to internationalize.

3. Assessing the suitability of products and services for foreign markets

Products and services that are good candidates for selling abroad sell well in the domestic market, cater to universal needs, address a need not well served in the target market, or address a new or emergent need abroad. Management should ask the following questions: Who initiates purchasing in the market? Who uses the offering? Why do people buy it? Where is the product or service purchased? What economic, cultural, geographic, and other factors can limit sales?

4. Screening countries to identify target markets

Whether the firm is engaged in importing (sourcing from abroad), investing, or exporting, the choice of country is critical, particularly in the early stages of internationalization. The best markets are large and fast-growing. The nature of information necessary for country screening varies by product type and industry. There are two basic screening methods: gradual elimination and ranking and indexing.

5. Assessing industry market potential

Once a firm reduces the number of potential country targets to five or six, the next step is to conduct in-depth analyses of each. **Industry market potential** is an estimate of the likely sales for all firms in the particular industry for a specific period. Each industry sector also has its own *industry-specific potential indicators*. Among the methods for assessing industry market potential are performing simple trend analysis, monitoring key industry-specific indicators, monitoring key competitors, following key customers around the world, tapping into supplier networks, and attending international trade fairs.

6. Choosing foreign business partners

International business partners include distribution channel intermediaries, facilitators, suppliers, joint venture partners, licensees, and franchisees. Some partners undertake **licensing**, **franchising**, and **international collaborative ventures**. Management in the focal firm must decide the types of partners it needs, identify suitable partner candidates, negotiate the terms of relationships with chosen partners, support the partners, and monitor their performance.

7. Estimating company sales potential

Company sales potential is the share of annual industry sales the firm can realistically achieve in the target country. Estimating company sales potential requires the researcher to obtain highly refined market information. Among the most influential determinants of company sales potential are: partner capabilities, access to distribution channels in the market, intensity of the competitive environment, pricing and financing of sales, quality of human and financial resources, timetable for market entry, risk tolerance of senior managers, the firm's contacts and capabilities, and its reputation in the market.

Test Your Comprehension AACSB: Reflective Thinking Skills

1. What is a global market opportunity? What types of opportunities do firms seek abroad?

2. Identify and explain the six major tasks in global market opportunity assessment.

3. Identify the issues managers consider when they analyze organizational readiness to internationalize.

4. Describe the characteristics of products or services most likely to sell well in foreign markets.

5. Summarize the screening methodology for potential country markets.

6. What are the typical variables used in indexing and ranking?

7. What types of variables should the researcher consider when screening for each of the following: export markets, foreign direct investment, and global sourcing?

8. What tasks does assessing industry market potential entail?

9. What are the major issues to consider when selecting foreign business partners?

10. How can firms estimate company sales potential?

Apply Your Understanding AACSB: Communication Abilities, Reflective Thinking Skills, Ethical Understanding and Reasoning Abilities

1. Target® is a large retailer with about 1,500 stores in the United States, but very few in other countries. It has a reputation for merchandising thousands of chic yet inexpensive products for the home, including apparel, furniture, electronics, toys, and sporting goods. Management wants to open stores in major European cities but will have limited floor space there. Target hires you as a consultant to decide which products to offer in Europe. Write a brief report in which you describe the selection criteria you will use and offer some examples to back up your ideas. Be sure to justify your answer using the advice and other information included in this chapter.

2. Upon graduation, you are hired by Cuesta Corporation, an SME manufacturer of accessories for luxury cars. Management wants you to conduct research to locate foreign markets with the best potential for sales. You discover that markets are fairly saturated in advanced economies, but you are aware of numerous *emerging markets* the industry has overlooked. Using your knowledge of Exhibit 13.2, Emerging Market Potential Indicators, develop a list of the top five emerging markets Cuesta should target. Be sure to justify your choice, based on indicators from this chapter such as market size, market growth rate, market intensity, and market consumption capacity.

3. *Ethical Dilemma:* Steve Kilmeade is the Export Manager at Braveheart Industries, a manufacturer of office furnishings. He has identified Russia as a promising market and decides to attend a furniture trade fair in Moscow. As he prepares for the fair, a consultant suggests hiring two female models in revealing clothing to work the company's booth. The consultant says the models will "create buzz" and increase Braveheart's visibility at the crowded fair. Kilmeade is skeptical and seeks advice from two colleagues. One colleague says the idea "amounts to exploiting women and could invite sexual harassment charges. . . . It is sex discrimination. The booth workers' gender and good looks are a condition for their employment." Another colleague tells Steve that hiring the models is no problem. He says those who oppose such a practice "perpetuate stereotypes of women as delicate creatures who cannot decide what's best for themselves." Besides, he continues, "Russia is a male-dominated society and people are not offended by such practices." What do you think? Using the Ethical Framework in Chapter 5, analyze the issue and make a recommendation.

globalEDGE Internet Exercises

(http://globalEDGE.msu.edu)

AACSB: Reflective Thinking Skills, Use of Information Technology

Refer to Chapter 1, page 62, for instructions on how to access and use globalEDGE™.

1. China is a huge attractive market, with growing affluence. Before exporting to China, most firms conduct market research to acquire a fuller understanding of the country's market situation. Two useful research sites are the China Business Information Center (CBIC; www.export .gov/china) and UK Trade and Investment (www.uktradeinvest.gov.uk). At the CBIC, for example, firms can find out if they are "China Ready." They can access trade leads and read current news about business in China. Suppose you are hired by a firm that wants to begin exporting to China three products: (a) breakfast cereal, (b) popular music on CDs, and (c) laptop computers. For each of these product categories, using the above Web sites and globalEDGE™, prepare a list of the information that the firm should gather prior to making a decision to export to China.

2. Walmart is a huge retailer, but gets only about a quarter of its sales from outside the United States. Coles is one of the largest retailers in Australia and gets very little of its sales outside Australia. Assess the international retailing sector using online resources, such as globalEDGE™ and A. T. Kearney (www.atkearney.com). Based on your research: (a) What factors should these top retailers consider in choosing countries for internationalizing their operations? (b) What are the best markets for these firms to target for foreign expansion? (c) What types of questions should management at each firm ask in assessing their readiness to internationalize?

3. The United States Census Bureau tracks foreign trade statistics. Visit the site at www.census .gov/foreign-trade and find the most recent versions of the report "Profile of U.S. Exporting Companies" by entering this title in the search engine. Peruse the report and address the following questions: (a) What types of firms export from the United States? That is, what is the breakdown by company type of U.S. exporters? For example, are the exporters mainly large or small firms? Do they operate mainly in the manufacturing, agricultural, or services sectors? (b) What is the role of small and medium-sized exporters in U.S. trade? What percent of U.S. exporters are these types of firms, and for what proportion of total exports do they account? (c) What countries are the three favorite targets of U.S. exporters? According to the report, what factors make these countries the top markets for U.S. firms?

LEARNING OBJECTIVES In this chapter, you will learn about:

1. An overview of foreign market entry strategies
2. Internationalization of the firm
3. Exporting as a foreign market entry strategy
4. Managing export-import transactions
5. Payment methods in exporting and importing
6. Export-import financing
7. Identifying and working with foreign intermediaries
8. Countertrade: A popular approach for emerging markets and developing economies

Exporting and Countertrade

Exporter's Dogged Pursuit of International Customers

Is your pet having a bad hair day? Is your horse's mane looking dull? Sharon Doherty, president of Vellus Products, Inc., can help. Vellus is a small U.S. firm that makes shampoos, conditioners, brushes, and other grooming products for pets. According to Doherty, shampoos for people don't work well on pets because animals' skin is sensitive and easily irritated.

Vellus' first export sale was to a Taiwanese importer who purchased $25,000 worth of products to sell at dog shows. The word was out. "I started receiving calls from people around the world who heard of our products and asked how they could buy them," Doherty recalls. "But I needed to do market research and learn more about ways of doing business in these countries." Vellus had to adapt some of its marketing for foreign markets to meet local conditions.

Vellus has become very familiar with the cultural aspects of pet care. In England, dog exhibitors prefer less poofed-out topknots than those in show dogs in the United States, where owners prefer more exotic topknots. In England, dog exhibitors prefer Shih-Tzus with a big head, long back, and stature somewhat lower to the ground, while U.S. exhibitors prefer Shih-Tzus with more leg and a shorter back. These preferences determine the types of shampoos and brushes that each country needs.

Exporting benefits firms such as Vellus by increasing their sales and profits and diversifying their customer base. As an entry strategy, exporting is low cost, low risk, and uncomplicated. These are big advantages for smaller firms like Vellus that typically lack substantial financial and human resources. Exporting also helps stabilize fluctuations in sales volume. For example, because dog shows take place abroad during different parts of the year, exporting helps stabilize Vellus' sales levels.

Firms like Vellus take advantage of support provided by intermediaries located abroad. Doherty often gives advice and guidance to her foreign-based distributors, sharing her knowledge and understanding of importing along with marketing in the dog-show network. She says the advice is much appreciated and goes far in building long-term relationships. Doherty also makes sure to do her homework on potential distributors. "Gather as much information as you can," she advised. "Don't make any assumptions—the wrong choice can cost your business valuable time and money."

Exporters like Vellus locate foreign distributors using various methods. One approach is to attend a trade fair in the target country. Vellus' management discovered potential distributors by attending foreign dog shows. Other companies consult country and regional business directories, foreign yellow pages, industry trade associations, and government sources.

Vellus received guidance from government agencies that support small-firm exporting. "They provided lots of help and excellent information," Doherty said. Because she's done her homework, it's no wonder Vellus continues to flourish. The firm has a wide range of clients, from the rich and famous to breeders and individual pet owners around the world. The president of the United Arab Emirates is a regular customer; his stables buy Vellus products for his horses twice a year.

To date, Vellus has sold its products in more than thirty countries, including Australia, Canada, China, England, Finland, New Zealand, Norway, Singapore, South Africa, and Sweden. Roughly half the firm's revenues come from exports. All told, more

than 300 breeds of pampered pooches are strutting their stuff with the help of Vellus Products. Management has registered the firm's trademark in fifteen countries and looks to expand export sales.

SOURCES: J. Judy, "Worldwise Women," *Small Business News*, July 1, 1998, p. 21; S. Pavilkey, "Pet Product Maker Gives International Clients Royal Treatment," *Business First*, January 19, 2001, p. A20; C. Cultice, "Best in Show: Vellus Products," *World Trade*, January 2007, p. 70; company Web site at http://www.vellus.com; H. Shoemack and P. Rath, *Essentials of Exporting and Importing* (New York: Fairchild Publications, 2009).

An Overview of Foreign Market Entry Strategies

The choice of entry strategy is one of the key decisions management makes in international business. Let's review the options. Recall Chapter 3 and Exhibit 3.5, where we discussed three categories of internationalization strategies for the focal firm:

Importing or **Global sourcing** The procurement of products or services from independent suppliers or company-owned subsidiaries located abroad for consumption in the home country or a third country.

Exporting The strategy of producing products or services in one country (often the producer's home country), and selling and distributing them to customers located in other countries.

Countertrade An international business transaction where all or partial payments are made in kind rather than cash.

1. *Trade of products and services* are generally *home-based* international exchange activities, such as *global sourcing, exporting,* and *countertrade.* **Importing** or **Global sourcing**, also known as *global procurement,* or *global purchasing,* is the strategy of buying products and services from foreign sources and bringing them into the home country or a third country. While sourcing and importing represent an inbound flow, exporting represents *outbound* international business. Thus, **exporting** refers to the strategy of producing products or services in one country (often the producer's home country) and selling and distributing them to customers located in other countries. In both global sourcing and exporting, the firm manages its international operations largely from the home country. We discuss global sourcing in greater detail in Chapter 17. **Countertrade** refers to an international business transaction in which full or partial payments are made in kind rather than cash. That is, instead of receiving money as payment for exported products, the firm receives other products or commodities.

2. *Equity or ownership-based international business activities* typically are *foreign direct investment (FDI)* and equity-based *collaborative ventures.* In contrast to home-based international operations, here the firm establishes a presence in the foreign market by investing capital in and securing ownership of a factory, subsidiary, or other facility there. Collaborative ventures include joint ventures in which the firm makes similar equity investments abroad, but in partnership with another company. We discuss FDI and collaborative ventures in Chapter 15.

3. *Contractual relationships* usually take the form of *licensing* and *franchising,* in which the firm allows a foreign partner to use its intellectual property in return for royalties or other compensation. Firms such as McDonalds, Dunkin Donuts, and Century 21 Real Estate use franchising to serve customers abroad. We discuss contractual strategies for foreign market entry in Chapter 16.

Each foreign market entry strategy has advantages and disadvantages, and each places specific demands on the firm's managerial and financial resources. Exporting, licensing, and franchising require a relatively low level of managerial commitment and dedicated resources. By contrast, FDI and equity-based collaborative ventures necessitate a high level of commitment and resources.

When undertaking foreign market entry, the focal firm must consider numerous factors, including:

- Its *goals* and *objectives*, such as desired profitability, market share, or competitive positioning
- The degree of *control* the firm wants to maintain over the decisions, operations, and strategic assets involved in the venture
- The specific financial, organizational, and technological *resources* and *capabilities* available to the firm (for example, capital, managers, technology)
- The degree of *risk* the firm is willing to tolerate in each proposed foreign venture, relative to the firm's goals
- The *characteristics of the product or service* to be offered
- *Conditions in the target country*, such as legal, cultural, and economic circumstances and the nature of business infrastructure such as distribution and transportation systems
- The nature and extent of *competition* from existing rivals and from firms that may enter the market later
- The availability and capabilities of *partners* in the market
- The *value-adding activities* the firm is willing to perform itself in the market and what activities it will leave to partners
- The long-term *strategic importance* of the market

While all these factors are relevant, perhaps none is more critical than the degree of control the firm wants to maintain over the venture. *Control* is the ability to influence the decisions, operations, and strategic resources involved in the foreign venture. Without control, the focal firm "will find it more difficult to coordinate actions, carry out strategies . . . and resolve the disputes that invariably arise when two parties . . . pursue their own interests."[1]

Exhibit 14.1 illustrates another useful way to organize foreign market entry strategies based on the degree of control each strategy affords the focal firm over foreign operations.

On the continuum of control in Exhibit 14.1, the arm's-length buyer-seller relationships of exporting represent little or no control at one extreme, while FDI, through a wholly owned subsidiary, represents maximum control at the other extreme.

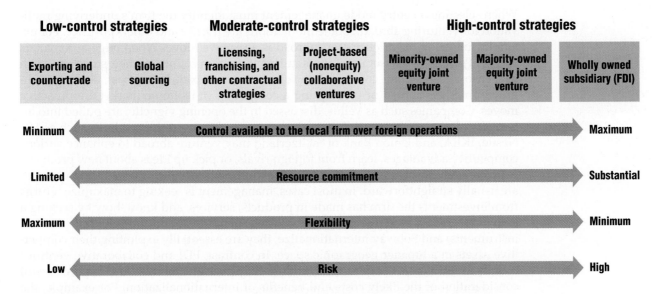

Exhibit 14.1   A Classification of Foreign Market Entry Strategies Based on Degree of Control Afforded by the Focal Firms

- *Low-control strategies* are exporting, countertrade, and global sourcing. They provide the least control over foreign operations, because the focal firm delegates considerable responsibility to foreign partners, such as distributors or suppliers.
- *Moderate-control strategies* are contractual relationships such as licensing and franchising and project-based collaborative ventures.
- *High-control strategies* are equity joint ventures and FDI. The focal firm attains maximum control by establishing a physical presence in the foreign market.

The particular arrangement of entry strategies in Exhibit 14.1 also highlights trade-offs, other than control, that the focal firm makes when entering foreign markets. First, high-control strategies require substantial *resource commitments* by the focal firm. Second, because the firm becomes anchored or physically tied to the foreign market for the long term, it has less *flexibility* to reconfigure its operations there as conditions in the country evolve over time. Third, longer-term involvement in the market also implies considerable *risk* due to uncertainty in the political and customer environments. Especially important are political risk, cultural risk, and currency risk, which we discussed earlier.

In addition to control, the specific characteristics of the product or service, such as fragility, perishability, and ratio of value to weight, can strongly influence the choice of internationalization strategy. For example, products with a low value/weight ratio (such as tires and beverages) are expensive to ship long distances, suggesting the firm should internationalize through a strategy other than exporting. Similarly, fragile or perishable goods (such as glass and fresh fruit) are expensive or impractical to ship long distances because they require special handling or refrigeration. Complex products (such as copy machines and computers) require significant technical support and after-sales service, which can necessitate a substantial presence in the foreign market.

 ## Internationalization of the Firm

In this chapter, we explore home-based international trade activities: exporting, importing, and countertrade. Exporting is the typical foreign market entry strategy for most firms, and thus it deserves greater attention. Before discussing exporting in detail, let's consider the nature and characteristics of firm internationalization.

Diverse Motives for Pursuing Internationalization

When selecting an entry mode, management must identify the firm's underlying motivation for venturing abroad.[2] Some motivations are *reactive* and others *proactive*. For example, following major customers abroad is a reactive move. When large automakers such as Ford or Toyota set up manufacturing in foreign countries, their suppliers, such as Denso and Lear, are compelled to follow them abroad. In contrast, seeking high-growth markets abroad or preempting a competitor in its home market are proactive moves. Companies such as Vellus, discussed in the opening vignette, are pulled into international markets because of the unique appeal of their products. MNEs such as HP, Nestlé, IKEA, and Union Bank of Switzerland may venture abroad to enhance various competitive advantages, learn from foreign rivals, or pick up ideas about new products.

The motives of companies that launch exporting, licensing, or franchising ventures are usually straightforward. In most cases, management is seeking to maximize returns from investments the firm has made in products, services, and know-how by seeking a larger customer base in foreign markets. When such firms as Boston Scientific (medical instruments) and Subway internationalize, they are essentially exploiting their competitive assets in a broader geographic space. In contrast, FDI and collaborative ventures usually involve more complex motivations. They pose greater risks and require careful consideration of the likely costs and benefits of internationalization. For example, the

Swedish appliance maker Electrolux (www.electrolux.com) recently built assembly operations in such diverse markets as Hungary, Mexico, and Thailand. Home appliances represent a complex global industry in which profit margins are tight and competition is intense. By undertaking product development, manufacturing, supply-chain coordination, and workforce management in relatively risky markets, Electrolux has assumed formidable challenges.[3]

Characteristics of Firm Internationalization

We can identify certain patterns and characteristics associated with the process of international expansion:[4]

1. *Push and pull factors serve as initial triggers.* Typically a combination of triggers, internal to the firm and in its external environment, is responsible for initial international expansion. *Push factors* include unfavorable trends in the domestic market that compel firms to explore opportunities beyond national borders, such as declining demand, growing competition at home, and arrival at the mature phase in a product's life cycle. *Pull factors* are favorable conditions in foreign markets that make international expansion attractive, such as the potential for faster growth and higher profits, foreign government incentives, or increased opportunities to learn from competitors.

Vellus Products Inc. is a U.S.-based producer of grooming products for dogs, and exports to countries worldwide. It is one of many examples of SMEs that find success by internationalizing their unique products.

2. *Initial international expansion can be accidental or unplanned.* DLP, Inc., a manufacturer of medical devices for open-heart surgery, made its first major sale to foreign customers its managers met at a trade fair. Without any deliberate plans, DLP got started in international business right from its founding. Vellus Products, the firm in the opening vignette, started exporting because a foreign distributor decided to showcase the firm's products at a dog show in Taiwan.

3. *Risk and return must be balanced.* Managers weigh the potential profits, revenues, and goal achievement of internationalization against the investment of money, time, and other company resources. Because of higher costs and greater complexity, international ventures often take much time to become profitable. Managers' risk-taking preferences determine the firm's initial investments and its tolerance for delayed returns. Risk-averse managers prefer entering safe markets using conservative entry strategies. They usually target markets with a culture and language similar to the home country. For example, a risk-averse U.S. firm would favor Canada over China. A risk-averse Australian firm would prefer Britain over Saudi Arabia.

4. *Internationalization is an ongoing learning experience.* By interacting in a variety of national environments, management encounters ample opportunities to learn and adapt how to do business. Internationalization exposes managers to new ideas and valuable lessons they can apply to the home market and to other foreign markets.[5] For example, while developing fuel-efficient automobiles for the United States, General Motors (GM) turned to its European operations, where it had been marketing smaller cars for some time. GM leveraged ideas it had acquired in Europe to develop fuel-saving cars for the U.S. market.

5. *Firms may evolve through stages of internationalization.* Historically, most firms opted for a gradual, incremental approach to international expansion. Even today, most firms internationalize in stages, employing relatively simple and low-risk

Stages of internationalization	Critical management activity or orientation	How the firm behaves
Domestic market focus	Exploit home market opportunities	Firm operates only in its home market due to limited resources or lack of motivation
Pre-internationalization stage	Research and evaluate the feasibility of undertaking international business activity	*Typical triggers from outside the firm:* • The firm receives unsolicited orders from foreign customers. • The firm is contacted by change agents (such as distributors), who want to represent it abroad. *Typical triggers from inside the firm:* • Managers seek to increase the firm's profits or other advantages. • Managers are proactive about international expansion.
Experimental involvement	Initiate limited international business activity, typically through exporting	• Managers consider foreign market opportunities attractive.
Active involvement	Explore international expansion, including entry strategies other than exporting	• Managers' accumulated experience reinforces expectations about the benefits of international business. • Managers commit further resources to international expansion. • Managers dedicate more resources to expand into new foreign markets.
Committed involvement	Allocate resources based on international opportunities	• The firm performs well in various international ventures. • The firm overcomes barriers to doing international business.

Exhibit 14.2 Typical Stages in Firm Internationalization

SOURCE: Adapted from S. Tamer Cavusgil (1980) "On the Internationalization Process of Firms," *European Research* 8 (6): 273–281.

strategies early on and progressing to more complex strategies as they gain experience and knowledge. Exhibit 14.2 illustrates the typical firm's internationalization stages and the justifications for each. Initially, management focuses on only the home market. As it begins to internationalize, the firm targets low-risk, culturally close markets, using simple entry strategies such as exporting or licensing. With growing experience and competence, the firm will then target increasingly complex markets, using more challenging entry strategies such as FDI and collaborative ventures.

While firms generally follow the pattern described in Exhibit 14.2 when expanding abroad, today *born global* firms internationalize much earlier than companies did in the past. Born globals reach a stage of active engagement in international business within the first few years of their founding.

 Exporting as a Foreign Market Entry Strategy

Because it entails limited risk, expense, and knowledge of foreign markets and transactions, exporting is what most companies prefer as their primary foreign market entry strategy. Typically, the focal firm retains its manufacturing activities in its home market but conducts marketing, distribution, and customer service activities in the export market, either itself or through an independent distributor or agent.

Exporting and the Global Economy

Exporting is the entry strategy responsible for the massive inflows and outflows that constitute global trade and generates substantial foreign-exchange earnings for nations. Japan has benefited from export earnings for years. China has become the leading exporter in various sectors, providing enormous revenues to its economy. Smaller economies such as Belgium and Finland also add much to their foreign-exchange reserves from exporting and use them to pay for their sizable imports of foreign goods.

When government agencies cite statistics on trade deficits, trade surpluses, and the volume of merchandise trade for individual countries, these data generally refer to firms' collective exporting and importing activities. For example, the United States is the primary export market for Canadian goods and accounts for some three-quarters of Canadian exports each year. The two-way trade between Canada and the United States represents the largest bilateral trade relationship in the world. China recently surpassed Europe, Japan, and the United States to become the world's top exporter of information technology (IT) products. The speed of China's ascent has been startling. In 1996, its exports of computers, mobile phones, and other IT goods amounted to only $36 billion. By 2008, the figure exceeded $300 billion. In the intervening years, almost all major Western IT firms had located much of their hardware production in China, primarily because of its low-cost manufacturing and capable factory workers. China's success has occurred particularly at the expense of the United States, from which direct IT exports have declined substantially in recent years.[6]

Exporting is the entry strategy responsible for global trade, and generates enormous earnings for nations. Exporting serves the internationalization goals of firms, small and large. Aircraft manufacturer Boeing is one the world's leading exporters.

Exporting: A Popular Entry Strategy

Beyond initial entry, most firms, large and small, use exporting as part of their internationalization portfolio. For example, some of the largest exporters in the United States include aircraft manufacturers Boeing and Lockheed Martin Aero. Big trading companies that deal in commodities, such as Cargill and Marubeni, are also large-scale exporters. Large manufacturing firms typically account for the largest overall value of exports and make up about three-quarters of the total value of exports from the United States. However, the vast majority of exporting firms—more than 90 percent in most countries—are SMEs with fewer than 500 employees.

As an entry strategy, exporting is very flexible. The exporter can both enter and withdraw from markets fairly easily, with minimal risk and expense. Exporting may be employed repeatedly during the firm's internationalization process, generally at the early stages and again from production facilities that the firm eventually establishes at various foreign locations, destined for markets in other countries. Experienced international firms usually export in combination with other strategies, such as joint ventures and FDI. Toyota has used FDI to build factories in key locations in Asia, Europe, and North America from which it exports cars to neighboring countries and regions.

Exhibit 14.3 shows the degree to which various manufacturing industries, and firms within those industries, depend on international sales. The analysis is limited to large, publicly traded manufacturing companies in the United States. The data represent international sales from both the headquarters country and the firm's foreign subsidiaries.

Industry	Average International Sales in the Industry (as percentage of total sales)	Example of a Leading Firm in the Industry	Example Firm's International Sales (as percentage of total sales)
Computers & other electronic products	60%	Fairchild Semiconductor International Inc.	92%
Chemicals	44	OM Group Inc.	84
Medical instruments & equipment	42	Bio-Rad Laboratories Inc.	66
Motor vehicle parts	42	TRW Automotive Holdings Corp.	70
Communications equipment	40	3Com Corp.	90
Pharmaceuticals	37	Merck & Co.	70
Aerospace & defense	36	Boeing Corp.	39
Food	32	Chiquita Brands International Inc.	41
Plastics	32	Tupperware Corp.	73
Apparel	31	Nike Inc.	66
Beverages	30	Coca-Cola Co.	75
Electrical equipment & appliances	28	Exide Technologies	61
Publishing & printing (including software)	27	Oracle Corp.	56
Motor vehicles	26	Paccar Inc.	68

Exhibit 14.3 International Sales Intensity of Various United States-Based Industries

SOURCES: Industry Week, http://www.industryweek.com, Industry Week 500; Hoovers corporate profiles at http://www.hoovers.com

The exhibit suggests that firms in industries such as computers, chemicals, and medical equipment are more dependent on international sales than firms in electrical equipment, publishing, and autos. What are the common features of the most geographically diversified industries? Many are high value-added, high-technology industries subject to globalization.

Service Sector Exports

In most advanced economies, services are the largest component of economic activity. Services marketed abroad include travel, construction, engineering, education, banking, insurance, and entertainment. Hollywood film studios earn billions by exporting their movies and videos. Construction firms send their employees abroad to work on major construction projects. Accountants and engineers often provide their services via the Internet, by telephone and mail, and by visiting customers directly in their home countries. Insurance packages can be created in a central location, such as London, and then exported via mail and the Internet to customers in other countries. The U.S. firm PMI Mortgage Insurance Co. exports mortgage insurance packages to various foreign markets and enjoys considerable success in Asia and various European countries.[7]

However, many *pure* services cannot be exported because they cannot be transported. You cannot box up a haircut and ship it overseas. Most retailing firms, such as Carrefour and Marks & Spencer, offer their services by establishing retail stores in their target markets—that is, they internationalize via FDI because retailing requires direct contact with customers. Many services firms can export *some* of what they produce but rely on other entry strategies to provide other offerings abroad. For example, while Ernst & Young (www.ey.com) can export *some* accounting services by sending its employees abroad, in other cases it will establish a physical presence abroad by setting up an office and hiring local personnel to perform local accounting services.

Most services are delivered to foreign customers either through local representatives or agents or in conjunction with other entry strategies such as FDI, franchising, or licensing. The Internet provides the means to export some types of services, from airline tickets to architectural services, helping to make the service sector one of the fastest-growing areas of exports in international business.[8]

Services can also promote and maintain product exports, many of which would not take place without their support. Few people would buy a car if there were no repair services available to maintain it. Thus, firms that export cars must also provide a means for the vehicles to be repaired in the recipient countries. They establish customer service facilities in target markets through FDI, or they contract with local shops to provide such services.

Advantages of Exporting

Exporting is a beneficial growth strategy. Exhibit 14.4 illustrates the advantages for the firm. The low-cost, low-risk nature of exporting, combined with the ability to leverage foreign partners, makes it especially suitable for SMEs. In the $1 billion U.S. wine export industry, small California wineries sell nearly 20 percent of their total output abroad. They also face the challenge at home of imports from cost-effective wine-producing countries like Chile and South Africa.[9] The *Global Trend* feature describes how SMEs are increasingly active in exporting.

Limitations of Exporting

As an entry strategy, exporting also has some drawbacks. First, because it does not require the firm to have a physical presence in the foreign market (in contrast to FDI), it offers management fewer opportunities to learn about customers, competitors, and other unique aspects of the market. The firm may thus fail to optimally perceive opportunities and threats or miss some knowledge it needs for long-term success in the market.

Exhibit 14.4
Advantages of Exporting

- Increase overall sales volume, improve market share, and generate profit margins that are often more favorable than in the domestic market

- Increase economies of scale, reducing per-unit cost of manufacturing

- Diversify customer base, reducing dependence on home markets

- Stabilize fluctuations in sales associated with economic cycles or seasonality of demand

- Minimize the cost of foreign market entry; the firm can use exporting to test new markets before committing greater resources through FDI.

- Minimize risk and maximize flexibility, compared to other entry strategies

- Leverage the capabilities and skills of foreign distributors and other business partners located abroad

SOURCES: U.S. Department of Commerce at http://www.export.gov/comm_svc/press_room/news/articles; Igor Filatotchev, Xiaohui Liu, Trevor Buck, and Mike Wright, "The Export Orientation and Export Performance of High-Technology SMEs in Emerging Markets," *Journal of International Business Studies* 40, no. 6 (2009): 1005–22; Kent Neupert, C. Christopher Baughn, and T. Dao, "SME Exporting Challenges in Transitional and Developed Economies," *Journal of Small Business and Enterprise Development* 13, no. 4 (2006): 535–44; K. Thuermer, "Small Business Takes to Export," *World Trade* 21, no. 12 (2008): 40–43; U.S. International Trade Commission, *Small and Medium-Sized Enterprises: Overview of Participation in U.S. Exports*, USITC Publication 4125 (Washington, DC: U.S. International Trade Commission, 2010).

GLOBAL TREND

The Emergence of SME Exporters

The role of small and medium-sized enterprises (SMEs) in exporting continues to grow. From 1995 to 2007, SMEs represented almost 100 percent of the growth in the U.S. exporter population, swelling from fewer than 150,000 firms in 1995 to 260,000 by 2007. SMEs accounted for more than 90 percent of all exporters in the United States in 2010. Many are wholesalers, distributors, and other nonmanufacturing firms.

Australia, Britain, Canada, China, New Zealand, and the United States have undertaken aggressive campaigns to help more SMEs become exporters. Governments sponsor trade fairs and trade missions that connect SMEs with distributors and other facilitators in promising foreign markets. The World Bank assists SME exporters from emerging markets by increasing access to capital and developing their international business skills. While most SMEs export to advanced economies, an increasing number also target emerging markets. These firms do not necessarily require large markets since they tend to cater to smaller niches.

E.J. Ajax is a small manufacturer of complex metal stampings (three-dimensional metal parts for assembling cars, appliances, and machinery). Looking to expand its export sales, the firm established relationships with distributors in Mexico, China, and Saudi Arabia. Another SME, Optical Xport, exports optical lenses and frames to customers in West and Central Africa from its low-cost manufacturing base in Senegal. These efforts increase the flow of medical supplies and eyeglasses to the poor in Latin America and Africa.

Certain advantages differentiate SMEs from larger and more experienced firms:

- *Flexibility*—the ability to rapidly adapt to foreign market opportunities.
- *Quick response*—faster decision making and implementation of new operating methods.
- *Customization*—the ability to customize products to foreign buyers, with greater ease and smaller production runs.
- *Risk taking*—an entrepreneurial spirit, high-growth aspirations, and a strong determination to succeed.

SMEs bring these advantages to bear in markets worldwide. They benefit numerous emerging markets, which typically lack access to a wide range of products and services.

Second, exporting requires the firm to acquire new capabilities and dedicate organizational resources to properly conduct complex export transactions, putting a strain on its resources. Exporters must acquire proficiency in international sales contracts and transactions, new financing methods, and logistics and documentation.

Third, compared to other entry strategies, exporting is much more sensitive to tariff and other trade barriers, as well as fluctuations in exchange rates. Exporters run the risk of being priced out of foreign markets if shifting exchange rates make their products too costly to foreign buyers. For instance, the U.S. dollar gained 25 percent against the euro and the pound in 2008–2009. This slowed growth of some U.S. exports, harming firms that rely heavily on exporting for generating international sales.

A Systematic Approach to Exporting

Experienced managers use a systematic approach to successful exporting by assessing potential markets, organizing the firm to undertake exporting, acquiring appropriate skills and competencies, and implementing export operations. Exhibit 14.5 highlights the steps in this process. Let's examine each in detail.

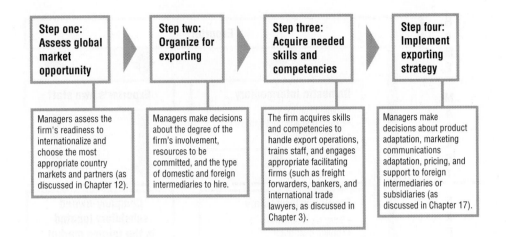

Exhibit 14.5
A Systematic Approach
to Exporting
SOURCE: Reprinted by permission of
American Marketing Association. All rights
reserved.

Step One: Assess Global Market Opportunity   As a first step, management assesses the various global market opportunities available to the firm. It analyzes the readiness of the firm and its products to carry out exporting, screens for the most attractive export markets, identifies qualified distributors and other foreign business partners, and estimates industry market potential and company sales potential. Managers often visit the most promising countries to develop a deeper understanding of them. Participating in foreign trade shows and trade missions is useful for identifying market potential and foreign intermediaries. We explained Global Market Opportunity Assessment (GMOA) in detail in Chapter 13.

Step Two: Organize for Exporting   Next, managers ask: What types of managerial, financial, and productive resources should the firm commit to exporting? What timetable should the firm follow for achieving export goals and objectives? To what degree should the firm rely on domestic and foreign intermediaries to implement exporting?

Exhibit 14.6 illustrates alternative organizational arrangements in exporting. **Indirect exporting** is accomplished by contracting with intermediaries located in the firm's home market. Smaller exporters, or those new to international business, typically hire an export management company or a trading company based in their home country. These intermediaries assume responsibility for finding foreign buyers, shipping products, and getting paid. The principal advantage of indirect exporting for most firms is that it provides a way to penetrate foreign markets without the complexities and risks of more direct exporting. The novice international firm can start exporting with no incremental investment in fixed capital, low startup costs, and few risks, but with prospects for incremental sales.

In contrast, **direct exporting** is typically achieved by contracting with intermediaries located in the foreign market. The foreign intermediaries serve as an extension of the exporter, negotiating on behalf of the exporter and assuming such responsibilities as local supply-chain management, pricing, and customer service. The main advantage of direct exporting is that it gives the exporter greater control over the export process and potential for higher profits, as well as allowing a closer relationship with foreign buyers and the marketplace. However, the exporter also must dedicate substantial time, personnel, and corporate resources to developing and managing export operations.

Indirect exporting
Exporting that is accomplished by contracting with intermediaries located in the firm's home market.

Direct exporting
Exporting that is accomplished by contracting with intermediaries located in the foreign market.

Firms engage trading companies to organize their exporting activities. AJC International was founded in Atlanta by Eric Joiner (pictured here) and Gerald Allison. The firm is a world leader in marketing chilled food products, and providing logistics and distribution services. AJC brings together suppliers and customers in more than 140 countries and employs a multicultural workforce.

Exhibit 14.6
Alternative Organizational
Arrangements for Exporting

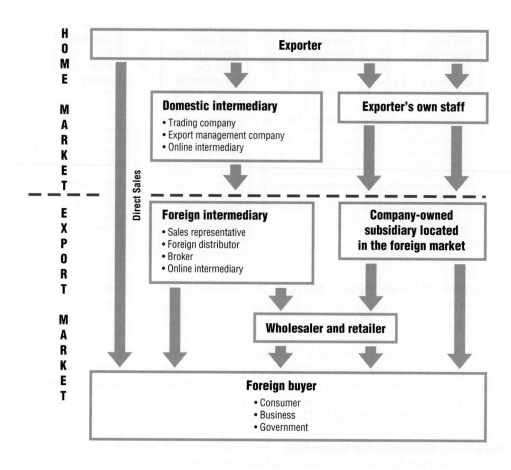

Direct and indirect exporting are not mutually exclusive, and many firms use both, but for different markets. Key considerations for choosing direct or indirect are: (1) the time, capital, and expertise that management is willing to commit; (2) the strategic importance of the foreign market; (3) the nature of the firm's products, including the need for after-sales support; and (4) the availability of capable foreign intermediaries in the target market.

Another exporting arrangement occurs when the firm sets up a sales office or a **company-owned subsidiary** in the foreign market to handle marketing, physical distribution, promotion, and customer service activities. The firm undertakes major tasks directly in the foreign market, such as participating in trade fairs, conducting market research, searching for distributors, and finding and serving customers. Management may pursue this route if the foreign market is likely to generate a high volume of sales or has substantial strategic importance. At the extreme, the firm may establish distribution centers and warehouses or a full-function marketing subsidiary staffed with a local sales force. For example, exports of Australia-based Webspy company's (www.webspy.com) Internet software make up 80 percent of the firm's annual revenue. Initially the firm exported exclusively through independent foreign distributors. However, Webspy eventually established sales subsidiaries in London and Seattle to serve its two most important regional markets, Europe and North America (www.austrade.gov.au).

Step Three: Acquire Needed Skills and Competencies Export transactions require specialized skills and competencies in areas such as product development, distribution, logistics, finance, contract law, and currency management. Managers may also need to acquire foreign language skills and the ability to interact with customers

Company-owned subsidiary A representative office of the focal firm that handles marketing, physical distribution, promotion, and customer service activities in the foreign market.

from diverse cultures. Fortunately, numerous facilitators, such as those described in Chapter 3, are available to assist firms that lack specific competencies.

Step Four: Export Management   In the final stage, the firm implements and manages its exporting strategy, often requiring management to refine approaches to suit market conditions. *Product adaptation* means modifying a product to make it fit the needs and tastes of the buyers in the target market. When Microsoft markets computer software in Japan, it must ensure the software is written in Japanese. Even Vellus, the firm discussed in the opening vignette, must vary the dog-grooming products it sells abroad because U.S. exhibitors prefer dogs with poofed-out topknots while British exhibitors prefer less hair. The dog brushes and shampoos that Vellus sells in the United States may not sell in Britain. In export markets with many competitors, the exporter needs to adapt its products to gain competitive advantage.

Marketing communications adaptation refers to modifying advertising, selling style, public relations, and promotional activities to suit individual markets. *Price competitiveness* keeps foreign pricing in line with that of competitors. SMEs often lack the resources to compete with larger rivals on pricing. In order to succeed, they compete not by charging low prices, but by emphasizing the nonprice benefits of their products such as quality, reliability, and brand leadership. *Distribution strategy* often hinges on developing strong and mutually beneficial relations with foreign intermediaries.[10] We address details of export marketing strategy in Chapter 18.

Importing

The counterpart of exporting is *importing*, in which the firm chooses to buy products and services from foreign sources and bring them into the home market. The sourcing may be from independent suppliers abroad or from company-owned subsidiaries or affiliates.

Manufacturing firms often import raw materials and parts used for assembling finished products. Many retailers secure a substantial portion of their merchandise from foreign suppliers. In the United States, retailers such as Walmart, Home Depot, Best Buy, and Target are among the largest importers. By itself, Walmart accounts for about 10 percent of U.S. imports from China, over $20 billion per year. Other large importers include electronics firms like Philips and food wholesalers including Chiquita.

The fundamentals of exporting, payments, and financing also apply to importing. Exporting and importing collectively refer to *international trade*. Exhibit 14.7 reveals the top trading partners of selected countries and the European Union (EU), counting their combined imports and exports. The exhibit reveals some interesting patterns. As single countries, Canada and the United States are each others' top trading partners. The chart for Canada reveals its heavy dependence on trade with the United States. China is a top trading partner with the United States, mostly due to its massive merchandise exports. The EU trades most with China and the United States. Overall, the exhibit reveals that most international trade occurs

The United States imports enormous amounts of goods from China. As one of the largest U.S. importers, Walmart alone accounts for about 10% of the country's imports of toys and other products from China, worth more than $20 billion a year.

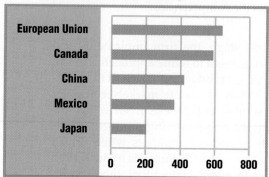

United States: Top Trading Partners

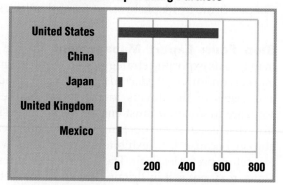

Canada: Top Trading Partners

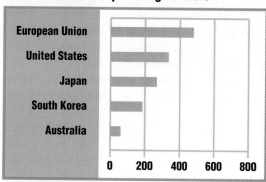

China: Top Trading Partners

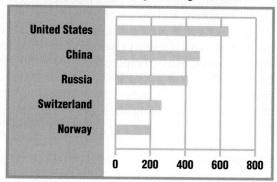

European Union: Top Trading Partners

Exhibit 14.7 Top Trading Partners of Selected Countries

NOTE: Values shown represent the sum of merchandise exports and imports in billions of U.S. dollars, in 2008.

SOURCES: CIA World Factbook, at http://www.cia.gov; European Commission, Trade, at http://ec.europa.eu; Industry Canada, at http://www.ic.gc.ca; US-China Business Council, at http://www.uschina.org

among the advanced economies and increasingly between the advanced economies and emerging markets.

 ## Managing Export-Import Transactions

When comparing domestic and international business transactions, key differences arise in documentation and shipping.

Documentation

Documentation Official forms and other paperwork required in export transactions for shipping and customs procedures.

Documentation refers to the official forms and other paperwork required in export transactions for shipping and customs procedures. The exporter usually first issues a *quotation* or *pro forma invoice* upon request by potential customers. It informs them about the price and description of the exporter's product or service. The *commercial invoice* is the actual demand for payment issued by the exporter when a sale is made.

Firms typically distribute exported goods by ocean transport, although some use air transport. The *bill of lading* is the basic contract between exporter and shipper. It authorizes a shipping company to transport the goods to the buyer's destination and also serves as the importer's receipt and proof of title for purchase of the goods. The shipper's *export declaration* lists the contact information of the exporter and the buyer (or importer), as well as a full description of the products being shipped. Government authorities use the export declaration to ascertain the content of shipments, control exports, and compile statistics on the goods entering and leaving the country. The *certificate of origin* is the "birth certificate" of the goods being shipped and indicates the country where they originate. Exporters usually purchase an *insurance certificate* to protect the exported goods against damage, loss, pilferage (theft), and, in some cases, delay.

The exporter typically entrusts the preparation of documents to an international freight forwarder. As we saw in Chapter 3, freight forwarders are among the key facilitators in international business, functioning like travel agents for cargo. They assist exporters with tactical and procedural aspects of exporting such as logistics, packing, and labeling and arrange to have exported products cleared through customs and shipped to the buyer.

Another important document is the *license*, a permission to export. National governments sometimes require exporters to obtain a license for reasons of national security and foreign policy. Governments usually don't allow firms to export nuclear materials or harmful biological agents that can be used to create weapons. In addition, some governments impose sanctions on trade with certain countries as part of their foreign policy. Lastly, governments may forbid the export of certain types of essential goods, such as petroleum products, if they are in short supply in the home country. In 2010, Russia halted exports of certain grains, due to a shortage of foodstuffs in the country.

Shipping and Incoterms

International shipping exposes the exporter's goods to adverse conditions and handling by various facilitators. Logistics agents ensure the goods arrive in good condition. Most export transactions involve shipping products from the exporter's factory to a nearby seaport or airport, and from there by ship or airplane to a foreign port, to be transferred to land-based transportation and conveyed to the customer. Of course some shipments to bordering countries are transported entirely overland by rail or truck. Throughout the delivery process the exporter incurs transportation costs and carries insurance against damage or loss during transit.

In the past, disputes sometimes arose over who should pay the cost of freight and insurance in international transactions: the seller (that is, the exporter) or the foreign buyer. To eliminate such disputes, a system of universal, standard terms of sale and delivery, known as **Incoterms** (short for "International Commerce Terms"), was developed by the International Chamber of Commerce (www.iccwbo.org). Commonly used in international sales contracts, Incoterms specify how the buyer and the seller share the cost of freight and insurance, and at which point the buyer takes title to the goods. Exhibit 14.8 illustrates the implications of the three most commonly used Incoterms.

Incoterms Universally accepted terms of sale that specify how the buyer and the seller share the cost of freight and insurance in an international transaction and at which point the buyer takes title to the goods.

Export transactions generally ship products through seaports and other maritime facilities. Pictured here is a container ship passing through the Panama Canal.

Incoterms	Definition	Key Points	Arrangement of Shipping
EXW Ex works (named place)	Delivery takes place at the seller's premises or another named place (i.e., works, factory, or warehouse).	EXW represents minimal obligation for the seller; the buyer bears all costs and risks involved in claiming the goods from the seller's premises.	Buyer arranges shipping.
FOB Free on board (named port of shipment)	Delivery takes place when the goods pass the ship's rail at the named port of shipment.	The buyer bears all the costs and risks of loss or damage upon delivery. The seller clears the goods for export.	Buyer arranges shipping.
CIF Cost, insurance and freight (named port of destination)	Delivery takes place when the goods pass the ship's rail in the port of shipment.	The seller pays for freight and insurance to transport the goods to the named port of destination. At that point, responsibility for the goods is transferred from the seller to the buyer.	Seller arranges shipping and insurance.

Exhibit 14.8   Incoterms: Examples of How Transport Obligations, Costs, and Risks Are Shared between the Buyer and the Seller

SOURCE: International Chamber of Commerce, http://www.iccwbo.org

 ## Payment Methods in Exporting and Importing

Receiving payment can be more complicated in international business. Foreign currencies may be unstable, and/or governments may be reluctant to allow funds to leave the country. In the event of disputes, local laws and enforcement mechanisms may favor local companies over foreign firms. Some customers in developing economies may lack payment mechanisms such as credit cards and checking accounts.

In advanced economies and many emerging markets, firms often extend credit to buyers with the assurance they will be paid. It is typical for exporters to allow these customers several months to make payments or to structure payment on *open account*. If payment is not forthcoming, a legal system is usually in place to compel creditors to meet their obligations. In trading with some developing economies, however, exporters extend credit cautiously. They evaluate new customers carefully and may decline a request for credit if the risk is too great.

There are several methods for getting paid in international business. Listed roughly in order from most to least secure, they are: *cash in advance, letter of credit, open account,* and *countertrade*. While the last method, countertrade, can serve as a method of payment in international transactions, it is also a distinct form of foreign market entry that deserves extensive treatment. We discuss it separately in this chapter. We explain each of the other three payment methods next.

Cash in Advance

When the exporter receives cash in advance, payment is collected before the goods are shipped to the customer. The main advantage is that the exporter need not worry about collection problems and can access the funds almost immediately upon concluding the sale. From the buyer's standpoint, however, cash in advance is risky and may cause cash-flow problems. The buyer may hesitate for fear the exporter will not follow through with shipment, particularly if the buyer does not know the exporter well. For these reasons, cash in advance is unpopular with buyers and tends to discourage sales. Exporters who insist on it tend to lose out to competitors who offer more flexible payment terms.

Letter of Credit

A documentary letter of credit, or simply a letter of credit, resolves some of the problems associated with cash in advance. Because it protects the interests of both seller and buyer, it has become the most popular method for getting paid in export transactions. Essentially, a **letter of credit** is a contract between the banks of the buyer and seller that ensures payment from the buyer to the seller upon receipt of an export shipment. It amounts to a substitution of each bank's name and credit for the name and credit of the buyer and seller. The system works because virtually all banks have established relationships with correspondent banks around the world.

Once established, an *irrevocable letter of credit* cannot be canceled without agreement of both buyer and seller. The selling firm will be paid as long as it fulfills its part of the agreement.

The letter of credit immediately establishes trust between buyer and seller. Among the countless firms that use it is Pinewood Healthcare (www.pinewood.ie), a pharmaceutical firm. Exports account for 70 percent of Pinewood's sales. When the firm first started exporting to Africa, it sometimes experienced difficulties getting paid. The situation improved greatly when it began contracting sales via letter of credit.[11]

The letter of credit also specifies the documents the exporter is required to present, such as a bill of lading, commercial invoice, and certificate of insurance. Before making a payment, the buyer's bank verifies that all documents meet the requirements the buyer and seller agreed to in the letter of credit. If not, the discrepancy must be resolved before the bank makes the payment.

Exhibit 14.9 presents the typical cycle of an international sale through a letter of credit.

1. An "Exporter" signs a contract for sale of goods to a foreign buyer, the "Importer."

2. The Importer asks its bank (the "Importer's Bank") to open a letter of credit in favor of the Exporter, the beneficiary of the credit.

3. The Importer's Bank notifies the "Exporter's Bank" that a letter of credit has been issued.

Letter of credit
Contract between the banks of a buyer and a seller that ensures payment from the buyer to the seller upon receipt of an export shipment.

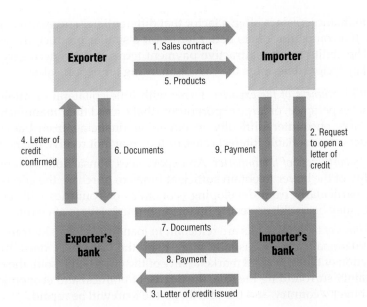

Exhibit 14.9 Letter of Credit Cycle

4. The Exporter's Bank confirms the validity of the letter of credit.

5. The Exporter prepares and ships the products to the Importer as specified in the letter of credit.

6. The Exporter presents the shipment documents to its bank, the Exporter's Bank, which examines them to ensure they fully comply with the terms of the letter of credit. The documents typically include an invoice, bill of lading, and insurance certificate, as specified in the letter of credit.

7. The Exporter's Bank sends the documents to the Importer's Bank, which similarly examines them to ensure they comply fully with the letter of credit.

8. Upon confirmation that everything is in order, the Importer's Bank makes full payment for the goods to the Exporter, via the Exporter's Bank.

9. The Importer makes full payment to its bank within the time period granted, which, in many countries, can extend to several months.

A related payment method is the *draft*. Similar to a check, the draft is a financial instrument that instructs a bank to pay a precise amount of a specific currency to the bearer on demand or at a future date. For both letters of credit and drafts, the buyer must make payment upon presentation of documents that convey title to the purchased goods and confirm that specific steps have been taken to prepare the goods and their shipment to the buyer. Letters of credit and drafts can be paid immediately or at a later date. In addition, the exporter can sell any drafts and letters of credit in its possession, to avoid having to wait weeks or months to be paid for its exports.

Open Account

When the exporter uses an *open account*, the buyer pays the exporter at some future time following receipt of the goods, in much the same way a retail customer pays a department store on account for products he or she has purchased. Because of the risk involved, exporters use this approach only with customers of longstanding or excellent credit, or with a subsidiary owned by the exporter. The exporter simply bills the customer, who is expected to pay under agreed terms at some future time. However, in international transactions, open account is risky, and the firm should structure such payment methods with care.

Export-Import Financing

The ability to finance a sale is often a factor that differentiates successful exporters from other firms. If a competitor offers better terms for a similar product, the exporter may lose sales. The ability to offer attractive payment terms is often necessary to generate sales. Four key factors determine the cost of financing for export sales:

1. *Creditworthiness of the exporter.* Firms with little collateral or minimal international experience, or large export orders that exceed their manufacturing capacity, may encounter difficulty in obtaining financing from banks and other lenders at reasonable interest rates, or they may not receive financing at all.

2. *Creditworthiness of the importer.* An export sales transaction often hinges on the ability of the buyer to obtain sufficient funds to purchase the goods. Some buyers, particularly from developing economies or countries with currency controls, may be unable to secure financing through letters of credit.

3. *Riskiness of the sale.* Banks are reluctant to loan funds for risky transactions, and international sales are usually more risky than domestic ones. Riskiness is a function of the value and marketability of the good being sold, the extent of uncertainty surrounding the sale, the degree of political and economic stability in the buyer's country, and the likelihood the loan will be repaid.

4. *Timing of the sale* influences the cost of financing. In international trade, the exporter usually wants to be paid as soon as possible, while the buyer prefers to delay payment, especially until it has received or resold the goods. In some industries, the length of time to complete a sale may be considerable. A common challenge arises when the firm receives an unusually large order from a foreign buyer and needs to draw on substantial working capital to fill it. This is particularly burdensome for resource-constrained SMEs.

Ultimately, the cost of financing affects the pricing and profitability of a sale as well as the payment terms the exporter can offer. Fortunately, there are various sources for financing international sales, which we discuss next.

Commercial Banks

The same commercial banks that finance domestic activities can often finance export sales. A logical first step for the exporter is to approach the local commercial bank with which it already does business, or a commercial bank with an international department that is familiar with exporting and may also provide international banking services such as letters of credit. Another option is to have the bank make a loan directly to the foreign buyer to finance the sale.

Factoring, Forfaiting, and Confirming

Factoring is the discounting of a foreign account receivable by transferring title of the sold item and its account receivable to a *factoring house* (an organization that specializes in purchasing accounts receivable) for cash at a discount from the face value. *Forfaiting* is the selling, at a discount, of long-term accounts receivable of the seller or promissory notes of the foreign buyer. Numerous forfaiting houses specialize in this practice. *Confirming* is a financial service in which an independent company confirms an export order in the seller's country and makes payment for the goods in that country's currency.

Distribution Channel Intermediaries

In addition to acting as export representatives, many intermediaries such as trading and export management companies provide short-term financing or simply purchase exported goods directly from the manufacturer, eliminating the need for financing and any risks associated with the export transaction.

Buyers and Suppliers

Foreign buyers of expensive products often make down payments that reduce the need for financing from other sources. In addition, buyers may make incremental payments as production of the goods or project is completed. Some industries use letters of credit that allow for progress payments upon inspection by the buyer's agent or receipt of a statement by the exporter that a certain percentage of the product has been completed. In addition, vendors from whom the exporter buys input goods or supplies may be willing to offer more favorable payment terms to the exporter if they are confident they will receive payment.

Intracorporate Financing

Large multinational enterprises with foreign subsidiaries have many more options for financing exports. The MNE may allow its subsidiary to retain a higher-than-usual level of its own profits in order to finance export sales. The parent firm may provide loans, equity investments, and trade credit (such as extensions on accounts payable) as funding for the international selling activities of its subsidiaries. The parent can also guarantee loans obtained from foreign banks by its subsidiaries. Finally, large MNEs can often access equity financing by selling corporate bonds or shares in stock markets.

Government Assistance Programs

Numerous government agencies offer programs to assist exporters with their financing needs. Some provide loans or grants to the exporter, while others offer guarantee programs that require the participation of a bank or other approved lender. Under such arrangements, the government pledges to repay a loan made by a commercial bank in the event the importer is unable to repay.

In the United States, the *Export-Import Bank* (Ex-Im Bank; www.exim.gov) is a government agency that issues credit insurance to protect firms against default on exports sold under short-term credit. The U.S. Small Business Administration (www.sba.gov) helps small exporters obtain trade financing. Canada's Export Development Corporation (www.edc.ca), India's Export Credit & Guarantee Corporation (www.ecgc.in), and Argentina's Compania Argentina de Seguros de Credito (www.casce.com.ar) provide services similar to those of the Ex-Im Bank.

Multilateral Development Banks (MDBs)

Multilateral development banks (MDBs) | International financial institutions owned by multiple governments within world regions or other groups.

Multilateral development banks (MDBs) are international financial institutions owned by multiple governments within world regions or other groups. Their individual and collective objective is to promote economic and social progress in their member countries, many of which are developing countries. MDBs include the African Development Bank (www.afdb.org), the Asian Development Bank (www.adb.org), the European Bank for Reconstruction and Development (www.ebrd.com), the Inter-American Development Bank (www.iadb.org), and the World Bank Group (www.worldbank.org). These institutions fulfill their missions by providing loans, technical cooperation, grants, capital investment, and other types of assistance to governments and agencies in the member countries.

Identifying and Working with Foreign Intermediaries

As the opening vignette emphasizes, success in exporting usually depends on establishing strong relationships with distributors, sales representatives, and other foreign market intermediaries. Trade fairs are a good way to meet potential intermediaries, become familiar with key players in the industry, and pick the brains of other, more experienced exporters. Firms can also obtain recommendations from freight forwarders and trade consultants. In other cases, to find suitable foreign intermediaries, exporters may consult the following sources:

- Country and regional business directories, such as *Kompass* (Europe), *Bottin International* (worldwide), *Nordisk Handelskelander* (Scandinavia), and the *Japanese Trade Directory*. Other directories include: Dun and Bradstreet, Reuben H. Donnelly, Kelly's Directory, and Johnson Publishing, as well as foreign *Yellow Pages* (often available online).

- Trade associations that support specific industries, such as the National Furniture Manufacturers Association or the National Association of Automotive Parts Manufacturers.

- Government departments, ministries, and agencies charged with assisting economic and trade development, such as Austrade in Australia (www.austrade.gov.au), Export Development Canada (www.edc.ca), and the International Trade Administration of the U.S. Department of Commerce (www.trade.gov).

- Commercial attachés in embassies and consulates abroad.

- Branch offices of certain foreign government agencies located in the exporter's country, such as JETRO, the Japan External Trade Organization (www.jetro.org).

Often, the best way to identify and qualify intermediaries is to visit the target market. On-site visits afford managers direct exposure to the market and opportunities to meet prospective intermediaries. Managers can also inspect the facilities as well as gauge the capabilities, technical personnel, and sales capabilities of prospective intermediaries. Once they have narrowed the choices to one or two, experienced exporters can request a prospective intermediary to prepare a business plan for the proposed venture. Its quality and sophistication provide a basis for judging the candidate's true capabilities.

Working with Foreign Intermediaries

In exporting, the most typical intermediary is the foreign-based independent distributor. The exporter relies on the distributor for much of the marketing, physical distribution, and customer service activities in the export market and greatly depends on his or her capabilities. Therefore, effective managers go to great lengths to build *relational assets*—that is, high-quality, enduring business and social relationships with key intermediaries and facilitators abroad that provide competitive advantages. Sharon Doherty (in the opening vignette) succeeded in exporting by developing close relationships with qualified foreign distributors. While competitors can usually replicate the exporter's other competitive attributes, such as product features or marketing skills, strong ties with competent foreign intermediaries are built over time and provide the exporter with an enduring competitive advantage.

Firms develop relationships with their intermediaries in various ways. They can cultivate mutually beneficial, bonding relationships; genuinely respond to intermediary needs; and build solidarity by demonstrating solid commitment, remaining reliable, and building trust.[12] Capstone Turbine Corporation (www.capstoneturbine.com) is a manufacturer of clean-technology microturbine energy systems. When exporting to a particular country, Capstone initially develops a close working relationship with the country's top importer, which then becomes Capstone's conduit to other companies in the country. The recipe is a success: Capstone now receives nearly two-thirds of its revenues from abroad, much of it from developing economies.[13]

To create a positive working relationship, the exporter should be sensitive to the intermediary's objectives and aspirations. This requires developing a good understanding of the intermediary's needs and working in earnest to address them. In general, foreign intermediaries expect exporters to provide:

- Good, reliable products for which there is a ready market
- Products that provide significant profits
- Opportunities to handle other product lines
- Support for marketing communications, advertising, and product warranties
- A payment method that does not unduly burden the intermediary
- Training for intermediary staff and the opportunity to visit the exporter's facilities (at the exporter's expense) to gain first hand knowledge of the exporter's operations
- Help establishing after-sales service facilities, including training of local technical

Working closely with foreign intermediaries helps green energy manufacturer Capstone Turbine Corporation earn nearly two-thirds of its revenues from abroad. This Ford was transformed into a hybrid vehicle by Langford Performance Engineering in England, using a Capstone microturbine.

representatives and the means to replace defective parts, as well as a ready supply of spare parts, to maintain or repair the products

The exporter in turn has expectations its intermediaries should meet. Exhibit 14.10 summarizes the selection criteria that experienced exporters use to qualify prospective intermediaries.

When Intermediary Relations Go Bad

Despite good intentions, disputes can arise between the exporter and its intermediaries about such issues as:

- Compensation arrangements (e.g., the intermediary may wish to be compensated even if not directly responsible for a sale in its territory)
- Pricing practices
- Advertising and promotion practices and the extent of advertising support
- After-sales service
- Return policies
- Adequate inventory levels
- Incentives for promoting new products
- Adapting the product for local customers

In anticipation of such disagreements, exporters generally establish a contract-based, legal relationship with the partner. Some firms require candidate intermediaries

Exhibit 14.10 Criteria for Evaluating Export Intermediaries

SOURCE: From S. Tamer Cavusgil, Poh-Lin Yeoh, and Michel Mitri (1995), "Selecting Foreign Distributors: An Expert Systems Approach," *Industrial Marketing Management*, 24 (4), pp. 298–304. Copyright © 1995, with permission from Elsevier.

Intermediary Dimension	Evaluation Criteria
Organizational Strengths	• Ability to finance initial sales and subsequent growth in the market • Ability to provide financing to customers • Quality of management team • Reputation among current and past customers • Connections with influential people or government agencies in the market
Product factors	• Familiarity with the exporter's product • Quality and sophistication of all product lines handled by the intermediary • Ability to ensure security for patents and other intellectual property rights • Willingness to drop competing product lines
Marketing skills	• Experience with target customers • Extent of geographic coverage provided in the target market • Quality and quantity of sales force • Ability to formulate and implement marketing plans
Commitment	• Percent of intermediary's business accounted by a single supplier • Willingness to maintain inventory sufficient to fully serve the market • Commitment to achieving minimum sales targets

to undergo a probationary period during which they evaluate performance. If it is suboptimal or if disputes appear likely to emerge, the exporter may impose special requirements or even terminate the relationship.

In a typical contract, the exporter binds the intermediary to achieve certain performance objectives and handle the product in a specified manner. The contract clarifies the tasks and responsibilities of both parties, specifies the duration of the relationship, defines the intermediary's sales territory, and explains the dispute resolution and termination processes if, for instance, the intermediary falls short of performance requirements such as sales targets.

Exporters need to ascertain the legal requirements for termination in advance and specify the intermediary's rights for compensation. In many countries, commercial regulations favor local intermediaries and may require the exporter to indemnify—that is, compensate—the intermediary even if there is just cause for termination. In some countries, legal contracts may prove insufficient to protect the exporter's interests. Many countries in Africa and Latin America lack strong legal institutional frameworks, which can make contracts hard to enforce.

Just as in their domestic operations, exporters occasionally encounter problems with buyers or intermediaries who default on payment. As a rule, problems with bad debt are easier to avoid than to correct after they occur. Before entering an agreement, the exporter should perform a credit and other background checks on potential intermediaries and large-scale buyers. In terms of payment mechanisms, cash in advance or a letter of credit is usually best. In addition to ensuring payment, the letter of credit encourages a high degree of trust between buyer and seller. The exporter can also buy insurance from insurance companies specialized in international transactions to cover commercial credit risks.

Eventually, however, some buyers default on payment. When this happens, the exporter's best recourse is to negotiate with the offending party. With patience, understanding, and flexibility, conflicts can often be resolved to the satisfaction of both sides. If negotiations fail and the cost of termination is substantial, the exporter may need to seek assistance from its bank or attorney. At the extreme, the exporter may pursue litigation, arbitration, or other legal means for enforcing payment on a sale.

Countertrade: A Popular Approach for Emerging Markets and Developing Economies

Countertrade activities, in which goods and services are traded for other goods and services when conventional means of payment are difficult, costly, or nonexistent, are especially prevalent in dealing with developing-country governments. Thus, barter is a form of countertrade.

Consider Caterpillar, which exported earth-moving equipment to Venezuela. In exchange, the Venezuelan government gave Caterpillar 350,000 tons of iron ore. Middle Eastern countries occasionally pay for imported goods with crude oil, as when Saudi Arabia purchased jets from Boeing. Also called two-way or reciprocal trade, countertrade operates on the principle, "I'll buy your products if you'll buy mine."

Exhibit 14.11 illustrates the multiple transactions in countertrade deals. Typically, the focal firm is a Western company, say General Electric (GE), that wishes to sell its products or technology—for example, jet engines—to a developing-country government. In one case, the Indonesian government experienced a shortage of convertible currencies (for example, the U.S. dollar, the euro, the pound). Unable to pay in cash, it asked GE to accept some local products as partial payment.

Typically the products developing countries offer are commodities (for example, agricultural grains, minerals, or manufactured goods with limited international sales potential). If a firm agrees to take these products, it must sell them in order to get paid

Exhibit 14.11
A Countertrade Transaction Where Products Are Received from the Customer as Partial or Full Payment

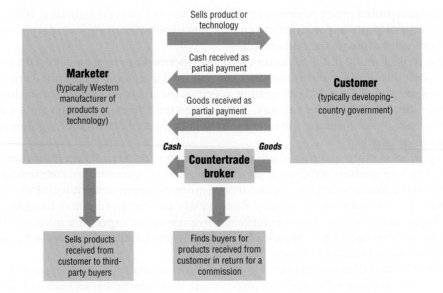

or ask a countertrade broker to sell them on its behalf. Countertrade transactions are generally more complicated than conventional cash-for-goods trade. Multiple transactions may take years to complete.

Philip Morris exported cigarettes to Russia for which it received industrial chemicals as payment. It shipped the chemicals to China and received glassware in exchange that it then sold for cash in North America. As payment for its exports, Coca-Cola at one point received tomato paste from buyers in Turkey and beer from buyers in Poland.

Magnitude and Drivers of Countertrade

Many MNEs have pursued nontraditional trade deals since the 1960s, not only in developing economies that lack hard currencies but also in industrialized nations. While the exact extent of countertrade is unknown, some observers estimate it accounts for as much as one-third of all world trade. Countertrade deals are common in large-scale government procurement projects. For example, countertrade has been mandatory for all Australian federal government foreign purchases of more than 2.5 million Australian dollars. In South Korea, countertrade is mandated for government telecommunications and defense procurement exceeding $1 million. In Asia, Indonesia led the way early by requiring countertrade for large-scale public sector purchases. Eastern European nations and Russia have practiced barter and countertrade transactions for many years.

Countertrade occurs in response to two primary factors. First is the chronic shortage of hard currency which is common to developing economies. Second is the lack of international marketing prowess among developing economy firms. Countertrade enables such firms to generate hard currency and access markets that might otherwise be inaccessible to them.

Types of Countertrade

There are four main types of countertrade: barter, compensation deals, counterpurchase, and buy-back agreements.

Barter—the oldest form of trade—is the direct exchange of goods without any money. Though less common today, barter is still exercised (even in domestic trade) in straightforward, one-shot deals. It requires a single contract (rather than two or more contracts typical of other forms), has a short time span (other countertrade deals may stretch over several years), and is less complicated (other forms usually require managerial commitment and additional resources).

Barter A type of countertrade in which goods are directly exchanged without the transfer of any money.

Compensation deals include payment in both goods and cash. For example, a company may sell its equipment to the government of Brazil and receive half the payment in hard currency and the other half in merchandise.

Counterpurchase, also known as a back-to-back transaction or offset agreement, requires two distinct contracts. In the first, the seller agrees to a set price for goods and receives cash from the buyer. However, this first deal is contingent on a second contract wherein the seller also agrees to purchase goods from the buyer (or produce and assemble a certain proportion of goods in the buyer's country) for the same cash amount as the first transaction or a set percentage of it. If the two exchanges are not of equal value, the difference can be paid in cash. Counterpurchase is common in the defense industry, where a government purchasing military hardware might require a defense contractor to purchase some local products or contribute to local employment.

Finally, in a product **buy-back agreement**, the seller agrees to supply technology or equipment to construct a facility and receives payment in the form of goods produced by the facility. For example, the seller might design and construct a factory in the buyer's country to manufacture tractors. The seller is compensated by receiving finished tractors from the factory it built, which it then sells in world markets. In essence, the original transaction trades goods and services that produce other goods and services, which are then received in payment. Product buy-back agreements may require several years to complete and therefore entail substantial risk.

Risks of Countertrade

Firms can encounter five problems in countertrade.

1. The goods the customer offers may be inferior in quality, with limited sales potential in international markets.

2. It is often difficult to put a market value on goods that the customer offers, because they are typically commodities or low-quality manufactured products. In addition, the buyer may not have the opportunity to inspect the goods or analyze their marketability.

3. Each party to the transaction will tend to pad its prices, anticipating that their counterpart will do the same. The seller may then experience difficulty re-selling the commodities it receives as payment. In a typical scenario, General Electric (GE) will place the products it receives as payment in countertrade (furniture, tomato paste) with a broker who sells them in world markets for a commission. Consequently, GE will build the cost of disposing of the goods into the price it quotes to the buyer. The buyer, anticipating that GE will quote a price on the high end, will pass the extra cost on to its customers. Thus, the resulting transaction between GE and the buyer is inefficient.

4. Countertrade is usually complex, cumbersome, and time-consuming. Deals are often difficult to bring to fruition.

5. Government rules can make countertrade highly bureaucratic and often prove frustrating for the exporting firm.

Why Consider Countertrade?

Although most firms avoid countertrade, there are five reasons to consider it.

1. The alternative may be no trade at all, as in the case of mandated countertrade.

2. Countertrade can help the firm get a foothold in new markets, leading to new customer relationships. For example, in the mining industry, certain types of minerals are available only in developing economies. Mining rights may be available only to firms willing to countertrade.

Compensation deals
A type of countertrade in which payment is in both goods and cash.

Counterpurchase
A type of countertrade with two distinct contracts. In the first, the seller agrees to a set price for goods and receives cash from the buyer. This first deal is contingent on a second wherein the seller agrees to purchase goods from the buyer for the same amount as in the first contract or a set percentage of same.

Buy-back agreement
A type of countertrade in which the seller agrees to supply technology or equipment to construct a facility and receives payment in the form of goods produced by the facility.

3. Many firms use countertrade creatively to develop new sources of supply. The firm may develop new suppliers in the process.

4. Firms have used countertrade as a way of repatriating profits frozen in a foreign subsidiary operation's blocked accounts. Otherwise unable to access its funds, the firm will scout the local market for products it can successfully export. General Motors' former Motors Trading subsidiary was created to generate trade credits—that is, sell its vehicles in return for contributing to exports of merchandise originating from that country.

5. Firms may succeed in developing managers comfortable with a trading mentality. Multinational enterprises such as GM, GE, Siemens, and Toshiba have set up separate divisions to develop global managers who are entrepreneurial, innovative, politically connected, and highly knowledgeable about a range of commodities and tradable goods. These firms recognize the value of such attributes for pursuing international deals and attempt to foster them by engaging their managers in countertrade. Acquired skills contribute to international performance, not only in countertrade deals, but in various other cross-border transactions as well.

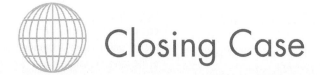 Closing Case

Barrett Farm Foods: A Small Firm's International Launch

Philip Austin, general manager of Barrett Farm Foods, was thrilled after returning from the food industry trade fair in Cologne, Germany—the largest food and beverage fair in the world. Barrett Farm Foods, based in Melbourne, Victoria, is Australia's sixth-largest food company. It distributes both bulk agricultural commodities and processed food products. Among others, it sells macadamia nuts, cereal bars, garlic, ginger, dried fruits, and honey throughout Australia. Barrett has had a healthy rate of growth over the past decade, and its sales reached USD $215 million last year. While Barrett is well known in the domestic market, its international experience has been limited to responding to occasional, unsolicited orders from foreign customers. In completing these export orders, Barrett has relied on intermediaries in Australia that provided assistance for international logistics and payments. Yet Austin is enthusiastic about substantially expanding the export business over the next few years.

Recognizing an Opportunity

What prompted Austin to attend the Cologne fair was a report from Austrade, the Australian government's trade promotion agency, which highlighted the potential of Australian foodstuffs exports. According to Austrade, Australian food exports exceeded AU $30 billion last year. Austrade believes processed foodstuffs are the coming trend and wants to boost exports.

But this raises a dilemma: Much of current exports are primarily raw foods, not *processed* foods. If just 10 percent of processed food value-adding were done in Australia, the country's balance of trade would improve. For example, instead of exporting raw grains to Europe, Austrade wants Australian producers to process the grains into bread and other bakery products, thereby creating jobs for Australians. Austrade believes meat, cereal, sugar, dairy commodities, and marine products have the most potential for food processing.

Meeting with Potential Export Customers at the Cologne Fair

At the Cologne fair, Barrett's nut-and-honey cereal bars and butter-like spread were a hit. Luigi Cairati, a senior executive with the Italian supermarket chain Standa, was keen on doing business with Barrett. He pointed out that, over the past decade, there has been an explosion of interest among European supermarkets for exotic foods and vegetables, with each group competing to display produce from around the world. Standa was seeking new products from other countries, partly to meet off-season demand for fruit and vegetables. Gabrielle Martin, purchasing manager for French food group Fauchon, also confirmed her interest in showcasing exotic and high-quality food in Fauchon stores. She added that Europeans view Australia as exotic and pollution-free and as a producer of quality products. In addition, the market for canned fruit is opening up as the fruit crop from trees in Europe declines over time.

Austin also met Peter Telford, an agent from the United Kingdom who showed interest in representing Barrett in the European Union (EU). Telford emphasized his knowledge of the market, extensive contacts, and prior business experience. He noted that other Australian firms, such as Burns Philip, Elders-IXL, and Southern Farmers, are already doing business in the region. He pointed to several success stories, including Sydney-based pastry manufacturer, C & M Antoniou, which established a small plant in Britain to avoid the wall of agricultural duties surrounding the EU market. The company now supplies several British supermarket chains, including Marks & Spencer, Tesco, and Sainsbury's. Another Australian group, Buderim Ginger, expanded its operations from Britain into continental Europe by opening an office in Germany.

Creating a Task Force

After the fair, Austin created a three-person task force among his senior managers and charged them with implementing an export drive. He felt an export volume of USD $30 million for the first year was reasonable. To identify the most promising exports, Barrett would examine its current product offerings. It would appoint an agent, such as Peter Telford, to facilitate EU sales. The people Austin met at the Cologne fair were potential customers to contact for immediate sales. Barrett could also forward some product and company literature to European importers, identify and appoint one or more distributors in Europe that have access to supermarkets and other large-scale buyers, and revamp its Web site to attract export business.

While Barrett senior managers shared Austin's enthusiasm about exporting to Europe, they did not share his optimism. Barrett had little internal expertise to deal with the complexities of international shipping, export documentation, and receiving payments from export customers. In addition, they knew export transactions take time to complete, and the firm would have to arrange for financing of export sales. Most importantly, senior managers felt they would have to invest in creating a small export team and hire or train employees in export operations.

Food is a complex business, in part because it is perishable, often requiring special equipment for distribution. Europe also has many differences in national tastes, regulations, and market structures. While Australians love Vegemite—a brown, salty breakfast spread made from yeast—the product enjoys little popularity outside Australia. With no name recognition in Europe, Barrett may have to resort to store branding, which will generate lower profit margins.

Barrett would have to rely on foreign intermediaries with access to well-known supermarket chains to distribute its products. Is Peter Telford the right choice? What is the appropriate commission structure for compensating intermediaries? With many larger, more experienced competitors in the EU, Barrett must keep its pricing competitive, although the complexity of pricing can overwhelm inexperienced managers. Barrett's senior managers also realize that prices strongly affect sales and profits. The euro, Europe's common currency, simplified pricing strategy, but numerous challenges remain. Prices are affected by transportation costs, buyer demand, exchange rates, tariffs, competitors' pricing, regulatory compliance, and the costs of marketing and physical distribution.

AACSB: Reflective Thinking Skills, Analytic Skills

Case Questions

1. Do you see any problems with Philip Austin's plan for European expansion? Do you support his entrepreneurial approach to exporting? What should be the features of a more systematic approach to exporting?

2. Why did Barrett choose exporting as its entry strategy for Europe, as opposed to foreign direct investment or licensing? What advantages does exporting provide to Barrett? What are the potential drawbacks of exporting for Barrett?

3. What challenges can Barrett expect in its export drive? What types of new capabilities does the firm need to acquire to manage its export transactions?

4. How should Barrett choose between direct and indirect exporting? What are the ideal characteristics of European intermediaries for Barrett? Where can Barrett turn for financing its export sales?

5. There are already numerous companies selling processed foods in Europe. What can Barrett do to compete successfully against these firms?

6. Why does Austrade want Australian firms to focus on exporting *processed* foods? Why is exporting high value-added products good for Australia?

CHAPTER ESSENTIALS

Key Terms

barter, p. 424
buy-back agreement, p. 425
company-owned subsidiary, p. 412
compensation deals, p. 425
counterpurchase, p. 425
countertrade, p. 402

direct exporting, p. 411
documentation, p. 414
exporting, p. 402
global sourcing, p. 402
importing, p. 402
Incoterms, p. 415

indirect exporting, p. 411
letter of credit, p. 417
multilateral development bank
(MDB), p. 420

Summary

In this chapter, you learned about:

1. **An overview of foreign market entry strategies**

   Market entry strategies consist of *exporting, sourcing,* and *foreign direct investment,* as well as *licensing, franchising,* and *non-equity alliances.* Each strategy has advantages and disadvantages. To select a strategy, managers must consider the firm's resources and capabilities, conditions in the target country, risks inherent in each venture, competition from existing and potential rivals, and the characteristics of the product or service to be offered in the market. **Importing** is buying products and services from sources located abroad for use at home. It is also called **global sourcing**, global purchasing, or global procurement.

2. **Internationalization of the firm**

   Firms internationalize due to *push factors* and *pull factors.* Initial internationalization may be unplanned. Management must balance risk against return. Each international venture provides learning experiences that encourage further internationalization. Firms generally pass through stages of internationalization, going from relatively simple to more complex entry strategies.

3. **Exporting as a foreign market entry strategy**

   Exporting is producing at home and then shipping products abroad, to be sold and delivered to foreign customers via intermediaries. It is the strategy most firms favor when they first internationalize. It is also a relatively flexible entry strategy, allowing the firm to readily withdraw in case of problems in the target market. A systematic approach to exporting requires managers to perform a global market opportunity assessment, make organizational arrangements for exporting, acquire needed skills and competencies, and design and implement the export strategy. Among the organizational arrangements for exporting are **indirect exporting**, **direct exporting,** and establishing a **company-owned subsidiary**.

4. **Managing export-import transactions**

   Management must become familiar with customs clearance, international goods transportation, and **documentation**, the required forms and other paperwork used to conclude international sales. The exporter typically entrusts preparation of documents to a freight forwarder. **Incoterms** are universally accepted terms of sale that effectively specify what is and is not included in the price of a product sold internationally.

5. Payment methods in exporting and importing

Exporting also requires knowledge of payment methods, such as cash in advance, **letter of credit**, open account, and countertrade. For most firms, letter of credit is best because it establishes immediate trust and protects both buyer and seller.

6. Export-import financing

Intense competition in export markets mandates that exporters offer attractive payment terms to their customers. Sources of finance for export transactions include commercial banks; *factoring, forfaiting,* and *confirming;* distribution channel intermediaries; intercompany financing; government assistance programs; and **multilateral development banks**.

7. Identifying and working with foreign intermediaries

Managers can identify intermediaries, such as sales representatives and distributors, from a variety of public and private information sources. It is best to develop long-term relationships with these business partners, who perform a variety of functions abroad on behalf of the exporter, by cultivating mutually beneficial bonds, genuinely responding to distributor needs, and encouraging loyalty.

8. Countertrade: A popular approach for emerging markets and developing economies

Countertrade is an international business transaction in which full or partial payment is made in kind (goods or services) rather than in cash. There are four types of countertrade. **Barter** is the direct exchange of goods without any money. **Compensation deals** include payment in both goods and cash. With **counterpurchase**, the seller agrees to sell its product at a set price and receive cash payment from the buyer. The deal is contingent on a second transaction in which the seller agrees to purchase goods from the buyer for the same amount as the first sale or a set percentage of it. **Buy-back agreements** commit the seller to supply technology or equipment to construct a facility and receive payment in the form of goods produced by the facility.

Test Your Comprehension AACSB: Reflective Thinking Skills

1. What are the major foreign market entry strategies? What are the characteristics of each?

2. Describe the typical internationalization process a firm may use in expanding abroad.

3. What is exporting? What are its advantages and disadvantages?

4. Describe the organizing framework for exporting. What steps should the firm follow to ensure exporting success?

5. What are the major tasks involved in managing export transactions?

6. Explain the payment methods that exporters typically use. What is the most reliable payment method, and how do exporters carry it out?

7. What are Incoterms, and why do firms follow them?

8. How would you go about identifying suitable foreign intermediaries?

9. What steps should the exporter take to ensure success in working with intermediaries?

10. Explain the nature, role, and risks involved in countertrade.

Apply Your Understanding AACSB: Communication Abilities, Reflective Thinking Skills, Ethical Understanding and Reasoning Abilities

1. Suppose you've been hired by a young, small firm that manufactures office furniture. The firm needs to generate more sales and wants to expand abroad. Given that internationalization is risky, particularly for smaller firms, what advice would you give to top management? In particular, what systematic approach to exporting and managing export-import transactions would you recommend?

2. Moose & Walrus (M&W) is a manufacturer of a popular line of clothing for young people. M&W is firmly established in its home market, which is relatively saturated and has little prospects for future sales growth. Top management has decided to export M&W's clothing line to Japan and various European countries. Suppose you are hired by M&W to assist with internationalization. Prepare a briefing for senior managers that describes the advantages and disadvantages of exporting. Recommend and describe payment methods.

3. Antenna Communications Technologies, Inc. (ACT) is a small satellite technology communications firm. Its product is a multibeam antenna that allows customers in the broadcast industry to receive signals from up to thirty-five satellites simultaneously. The firm has little international business experience. ACT recently hired you as its export manager and, based on extensive research, you ascertain that substantial export markets exist for the product in Africa, China, Russia, and Saudi Arabia. Having followed most of the steps in the organizing framework for exporting, you decide direct exporting is the best entry strategy for ACT. Your next task is to find distributors in the target markets. How will you approach this task? What resources should you access to find distributors in these markets? Once established, what is the best way to maintain solid relations with foreign distributors? Finally, what payment method should ACT use for most of its prospective markets?

4. *Ethical Dilemma:* You are hired by EcoPure Industries, a manufacturer of components for hybrid motor vehicles. EcoPure emphasizes social responsibility in its international dealings and regularly employs three foreign market entry strategies: exporting, joint ventures, and FDI. Exporting implies the sale of products to customers located abroad, usually via contract with local independent intermediaries that organize marketing and distribution activities in target markets. Using joint ventures, EcoPure partners with foreign firms to access their technology, expertise, production factors, or other assets. Using FDI, EcoPure invests funds to establish factories or other subsidiaries overseas. Each of the strategies—exporting, joint venture, and FDI—is vulnerable to particular types of ethical dilemmas, and top management has directed you to identify and describe the most typical ones. Using the Ethical Framework and other material in Chapter 5 as a guide, what types of ethical problems might arise in each type of entry strategy? Which entry strategy most likely gives rise to ethical problems? Be sure to justify your answer.

globalEDGE Internet Exercises
(http://globalEDGE.msu.edu)

AACSB: Communication Abilities, Reflective Thinking Skills

Refer to Chapter 1, page 62, for instructions on how to access and use globalEDGE™.

1. You work for a firm that manufactures children's toys. Despite little international experience, management wants to start exporting. Your boss understands the importance of using strong distributors abroad but knows little about how to find them. You are aware that many national governments offer programs that help new exporters find intermediaries in foreign countries. Examples include trade missions, trade shows, and matchmaker programs (in which the exporter is matched with foreign intermediaries). In the United States, the International Trade Administration (ITA) provides various services to help exporters find foreign distributors. Visit the ITA Web site (www.ita.doc .gov), or the main trade support agency of your country (via globalEDGE™), and see what programs are available. Then prepare a memo to your boss in which you describe specific programs to help your firm get started in exporting.

2. Suppose you work for a major trading company exporting timber from Canada; petroleum from Britain; and processed food products from the United States. To enhance your career prospects, you want to learn more about the export of these goods from their respective countries. Visit globalEDGE™ and research current international news about these industries in the countries indicated. Based on your findings, prepare a brief report on the current status of each in the context of your firm's exporting efforts.

3. Suppose your employer wants to export its products and get paid through letter of credit (LC). You have volunteered to become the company's LC expert. One way to accomplish this is to visit globalEDGE™ and do a search on the keywords "letter of credit." Another is to visit the Web sites of major banks to learn about procedures and instructions for getting paid via LC. Visit the Web sites of CIBC (www.cibc.com), the National Australia Bank (www.national.com .au), and Wachovia (www.wachovia.com) to see what you can learn about LCs. For each bank, what are the requirements for getting an LC? What services does the bank offer in regard to LCs? Can you get training in LCs from these banks?

CHAPTER *15*

LEARNING OBJECTIVES In this chapter, you will learn about:

1. International investment and collaboration
2. Motives for FDI and collaborative ventures
3. Characteristics of foreign direct investment
4. Types of foreign direct investment
5. International collaborative ventures
6. Managing collaborative ventures
7. The experience of retailers in foreign markets

Foreign Direct Investment and Collaborative Ventures

Deutsche Post DHL's Rapid International Expansion

As cross-border trade increases, so does the demand for supply chain, logistics, and express delivery services from firms that move raw materials, parts, finished goods, packages, and documents around the world. Specialized logistics facilitators organize, coordinate, and control supply chains using technological advancements and a physical presence that spans the world. Couriers such as UPS, FedEx, and DHL have global networks of offices and warehouses, trucks and aircraft, and extensive information tracking systems to serve firms' global delivery and logistics needs.

Deutsche Post DHL is a leading mail and logistics group. The Deutsche Post and DHL corporate brands include logistics (DHL) and communications (Deutsch Post) services. Deutsche Post DHL offers integrated services and customer-focused solutions for transporting and managing letters, information, and goods. It accomplishes this through its four divisions: Mail, Express, Global Freight Forwarding and Supply Chain.

Deutsche Post DHL has more than 500,000 employees in a network of over 4,700 offices in some 200 countries. Deutsche Post DHL (www.dp-dhl.com) generates roughly half its sales in Europe, 19 percent in the Americas, and 11 percent from the Asia/Pacific region. Annual revenues exceed $70 billion.

Deutsche Post DHL established its many offices through either foreign direct investment (FDI) or collaborative ventures with partner firms in foreign markets.

Firms like Deutsche Post DHL use FDI to establish a physical presence abroad by building or acquiring a production or assembly facility, sales office, or other type of local facility. The parent firm in this relationship may own 100 percent of the foreign operation, or it may exercise only partial ownership in a joint venture or other collaboration with a foreign partner.

Like many other firms in recent years, Deutsche Post DHL has used foreign acquisitions to expand internationally. It paid $2.7 billion to acquire the U.S. firm DHL and $1 billion for the ground-delivery network of U.S.-based Airborne. The acquisition of 81 percent of the Indian express company Blue Dart strengthened Deutsche Post's ability to serve customers in Asia. Buying Britain's Exel, with its 110,000 employees in 130 countries, increased Deutsche Post DHL's control of express delivery and logistics operations across Europe and the United States. DHL became Deutsche Post DHL's main arm for global express delivery, offering express services, international air and ocean freight, contract logistics, and value-added services for such customers as BMW, PepsiCo, and Standard Chartered Bank.

In addition to acquisitions, Deutsche Post DHL entered various collaborative ventures. The firm formed an alliance with Amazon.com to handle Amazon's huge delivery needs for its export customers. DHL entered a 50/50 joint venture with Sinotrans to serve the huge Chinese market. In Japan, Deutsche Post DHL formed a joint venture with Yamato, Japan's biggest private postal company. FDI and collaborative ventures allowed Deutsch Post DHL to expand abroad quickly. FDI was critical to the firm's internationalization in order to establish an extensive network of offices, warehouses, and other facilities necessary to offer express delivery services.

Deutsche Post DHL faced formidable challenges in absorbing acquisitions and producing strong financial returns. In the United States, it struggled to build a reliable transportation network. Late deliveries sparked customer defections and forced Deutsche Post to offer price discounts. The huge cost of absorbing DHL and Airborne reduced management's ability to make needed improvements to operations and service standards.

As a former German state enterprise, much of the early success of Deutsche Post DHL stemmed from subsidies and other support received from the German government. Competitors in the United States, such as FedEx and UPS, as well as labor unions and national security bodies, argued that

Deutsche Post DHL should not be allowed to acquire major transportation infrastructure in the United States. Despite substantial legal wrangling, regulators ruled in favor of DHL and Deutsche Post.

FDI poses various challenges, and Deutsche Post DHL has struggled to skillfully manage all its far-flung operations. During the most recent global financial crisis, the firm lost billions of dollars. In 2010, it terminated its air and ground services in the United States, eliminating thousands of jobs. Deutsche Post DHL's wide-ranging experience highlights both the opportunities and challenges of foreign direct investment.

SOURCES: Deutsche Post DHL Web sites at http://www.dp-dhl .com and http://www.deutschepost.de; Deutsche Post corporate profile at http://www.hoovers.com; "Amazon Expands Alliance with Deutsche Post Global Mail," *Direct Marketing*, November 2001, p. 7; Mike Esterl, "Deutsche Post Struggles to Deliver in the U.S.," *Wall Street Journal*, April 12, 2006, p. C.5; A. Hahn, "Deutsche Post Unique Route," *The Investment Dealers' Digest*, March 31, 2003, p. 1; William Hoffman, "Post-Merger Indigestion," *Traffic World*, March 27, 2006, p. 1; "Deutsche Post Says US Exit of DHL on Schedule," *Journal of Commerce Online*, January 19, 2009; Alex Roth and Mike Esterl, "DHL Beats a Retreat From the U.S.: Deutsche Post Unit's Campaign Foiled by Souring Economy, Management Missteps," *Wall Street Journal*, November 11, 2008, p. B1.

Foreign direct investment (FDI) An internationalization strategy in which the firm establishes a physical presence abroad through acquisition of productive assets such as capital, technology, labor, land, plant, and equipment.

International collaborative venture Cross-border business alliance whereby partnering firms pool their resources and share costs and risks to undertake a new business venture; also referred to as an "international partnership" or an "international strategic alliance".

The cross-border spread of capital and ownership is one of the most remarkable facets of globalization. Consider a recent example. Tata Motors (www.tatamotors .com) is India's largest automaker and obtains a substantial proportion of its sales from abroad. In 2008, Tata paid $2.3 billion to purchase Jaguar and Land Rover from Ford Motor Company. In addition to Jaguar and Land Rover factories in the United Kingdom, Tata owns numerous other car plants around Asia and Europe. Recently, Renault and Nissan partnered with Tata to distribute the Nano in Europe, which Tata unveiled in 2008 as the world's cheapest car. The first Nanos were sold in March 2009 and delivered in July 2009. Tata also acquired 70 percent of Miljo, a Norwegian electric vehicle maker. In South Korea, Tata purchased Daewoo Commercial Vehicle Company, a leading manufacturer of trucks and tractors.[1] These examples illustrate the important phenomena of foreign direct investment and international collaborative ventures.

International Investment and Collaboration

Foreign direct investment (FDI) is an internationalization strategy where the firm establishes a physical presence abroad through direct ownership of productive assets such as capital, technology, labor, land, plant, and equipment.

An **international collaborative venture** is a cross-border business partnership where collaborating firms pool their resources and share costs and risks of a new venture. Here the focal firm partners with one or more companies to pursue a joint project or initiative. International collaborative ventures are also sometimes called "international partnerships" or "international strategic alliances."

Consider the following recent example from the beer industry. South African Breweries (SAB; www.sabmiller.com) established a major presence in the U.S. beer market through its 2002 purchase of Miller Brewing, changing its name to SABMiller plc. In 2005, the firm acquired 97 percent of Bavaria S.A., the second-largest brewer in South America. In 2006, SABMiller acquired Foster's India for $120 million, gaining control of nearly 50 percent of the Indian beer market. Meanwhile, in China, the firm entered a joint venture with CR Snow Breweries, helping to make SABMiller the largest brewer in China. In the United States, SABMiller owns 58 percent of MillerCoors, a joint venture with Canada's Molson Coors. A **joint venture** is a form of collaboration between two or more firms to create a new, jointly owned enterprise. Unlike collaborative arrangements where no new entity is created, the partners in a joint venture typically invest money to create a new enterprise, which may endure for many years. A partner in a joint venture may enjoy minority, equal, or majority ownership. Through numerous FDI and collaborative ventures in the 2000s, SABMiller has become the world's third-largest brewer, with operations in more than sixty countries.[2] Both FDI and international collaborative ventures are fundamental strategies that focal firms employ to expand abroad.

Joint venture A form of collaboration between two or more firms to create a new, jointly owned enterprise.

Trends in Foreign Direct Investment and Collaborative Ventures

FDI is the most advanced and complex foreign market entry strategy. It entails establishing manufacturing plants, marketing subsidiaries, or other facilities in target countries. Because this involves investing substantial resources to establish a physical presence abroad, FDI is riskier than other entry strategies.

In 2008, there were 251 cross-border acquisitions valued at more than $1 billion.[3] The top three recipient countries were Britain, Canada, and the United States. Here are recent examples of typical cross-border investments:

- General Motors invested more than $3 billion in Mexico to build manufacturing capacity, including a new factory in San Luis Potosi.
- Japan's Daiichi Sankyo pharmaceutical paid $4.6 billion to acquire Ranbaxy Laboratories, India's largest producer of generic medications.
- The Dutch manufacturer AkzoNobel spent $338 million to build a chemical factory in China.
- SABIC Corporation, a Saudi Arabia firm, paid $11.6 billion to acquire GE Plastics from General Electric.
- Yildiz, a Turkish holding company that owns the confectionary company Ulker, acquired chocolatier Godiva from Campbell Soup Company. Campbell Soup had earlier acquired Godiva from a Belgium-based firm.

These and numerous other examples illustrate several trends in the contemporary global economy. First, companies from both advanced economies and emerging markets are active in FDI. Second, destination or recipient countries for such investments include both advanced economies and emerging markets. Third, companies employ multiple strategies to enter foreign markets as investors, including acquisitions and collaborative ventures. Fourth, companies from all types of industries, including services, are active in FDI and collaborative ventures. For example, major retailers began expanding abroad in the 1970s, including Walmart (United States), Carrefour (France), Royal Ahold (Netherlands), Metro AG (Germany), and Tesco (United Kingdom).

Finally, direct investment by foreign companies occasionally raises patriotic sentiments among citizens. For example, the possibility of a Haier takeover of Maytag Corporation in 2005 stirred anxiety in the United States over East Asian companies gobbling up U.S. businesses. A bid by Chinese oil company CNOOC Ltd. to buy California-based Unocal Corporation for $18.5 billion raised concerns over the possibility of a Chinese state enterprise gaining control in the critical U.S. energy sector. Consequently, the U.S. Congress banned the deal.

Motives for FDI and Collaborative Ventures

While the ultimate goal of FDI and international collaborative ventures is to enhance company competitiveness in the global marketplace, managers pursue these strategies for complex reasons. As shown in Exhibit 15.1, we classify the reasons into three categories: market-seeking motives, resource- or asset-seeking motives, and efficiency-seeking motives.[4] In any one venture, several motives may apply simultaneously, one more dominant than others. Let's examine them in greater detail.

Market-Seeking Motives

Managers may seek new market opportunities as a result of either unfavorable developments in their home market (that is, they may be pushed into international markets) or attractive opportunities abroad (they may be pulled into international markets). There are three primary market-seeking motivations:

1. *Gain access to new markets or opportunities.* The existence of a substantial market motivates many firms to produce offerings at or near customer locations. Local production improves customer service and reduces the cost of transporting goods to buyer locations. Coca-Cola, Samsung, and Siemens all generate more sales abroad than in their home markets. The giant chip-maker Intel expects big sales from China, where incomes are still rising and few Chinese families have bought a computer yet.[5]

2. *Follow key customers.* Firms often follow their key customers abroad to preempt other vendors from serving them. Establishing local operations also positions the firm to better serve customer needs. Tradegar Industries supplies the plastic that its customer Procter & Gamble uses to manufacture disposable diapers. When P&G built a plant in China, Tradegar established production there as well.

3. *Compete with key rivals in their own markets.* Some MNEs may choose to confront current or potential competitors directly, in the competitors' home market. The strategic purpose is to weaken the competitor by forcing it to expend resources to defend its market. In the earth-moving equipment industry, Caterpillar entered a joint venture with Mitsubishi to put pressure on the market share and profitability of their common rival, Japan's Komatsu. The expenditure of substantial resources to defend its home market hampered Komatsu's ability to expand its activities abroad.[6]

Exhibit 15.1 Firm Motives for Foreign Direct Investment and Collaborative Ventures

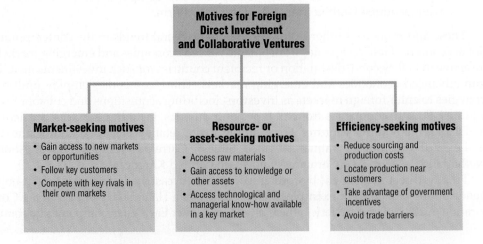

Resource- or Asset-Seeking Motives

Firms frequently want to acquire production factors that are more abundant or less costly in a foreign market. They may also seek complementary resources and capabilities of partner companies headquartered abroad. Specifically, FDI or collaborative ventures may be motivated by the firm's desire to attain the following assets.

1. *Raw materials needed in extractive and agricultural industries.* Firms in the mining, oil, and crop-growing industries have little choice but to go where the raw materials are located. In the wine industry, companies establish wineries in countries suited for growing grapes, such as France and Chile. Oil companies establish refineries in countries with abundant petroleum reserves such as Kuwait.

2. *Knowledge or other assets.*[7] By establishing a local presence through FDI, the firm is better positioned to deepen its understanding of target markets. FDI provides the foreign firm better access to market knowledge, customers, distribution systems, and control over local operations. By collaborating in R&D, manufacturing, and marketing, the focal firm can benefit from the partner's know-how. When Whirlpool entered Europe, it partnered with Philips to benefit from the latter's well-known brand name and distribution network. General Motors and Toyota jointly established NUMMI, Inc., in California to build vehicles for the U.S. market. Through this venture, GM learned about Toyota's production techniques for manufacturing high-quality vehicles. Toyota obtained technology and design expertise from GM that allowed it to develop cars better suited for U.S. consumers. Due to changed circumstances, the partners ended the NUMMI venture in 2010.

3. *Technological and managerial know-how.*[8] The firm may benefit by establishing a presence in a key industrial cluster, such as the robotics industry in Japan, chemicals in Germany, fashion in Italy, or software in the United States. Companies can obtain many advantages from locating at the hub of knowledge development and innovation in a given industry. Denmark, Finland, Israel, New Zealand, Sweden, and the United States are considered ideal for R&D in the biotechnology industry because they all have abundant pools of biotech knowledge workers.[9] Many firms enter a collaborative venture abroad as a prelude to operating wholly owned FDI. Collaboration with a local partner reduces the risks of entry while allowing the entrant to gain local expertise before launching operations of its own in the market.

Efficiency-Seeking Motives

In expanding abroad, many firms seek to create economies of scale as well as economies of scope—that is, to reduce business costs by employing the same corporate assets across a larger number of products and markets. Similarly, MNEs usually concentrate production in only a few locations as a way to increase the efficiency of manufacturing.[10] Firms typically disseminate their best practices in production and other activities to all their foreign subsidiaries to increase the efficiency of their operations worldwide. Many develop global brands to increase the efficiency of marketing activities. There are four major efficiency-seeking motives:

Firms in the petroleum industry internationalize to access raw materials; in this case, oil reserves in areas with appropriate natural resources such as the Middle East. Pictured is an oil refinery in Saudi Arabia.

1. *Reduce sourcing and production costs by accessing inexpensive labor and other cheap inputs to the production process.*[11] This motive accounts for the massive investment by foreign firms in factories and service-producing facilities in China, Mexico, Eastern Europe, and India. MNEs establish factories in such locations to reduce production costs.

2. *Locate production near customers.* In industries that need to be especially sensitive to customer needs or in which tastes change rapidly, managers often locate factories or assembly operations near important customers. Zara and Forever 21 locate much of their garment production in key fashion markets such as Europe. Production is more expensive, but the clothing gets into shops faster and more closely represents the latest fashion trends.[12]

3. *Take advantage of government incentives.*[13] In addition to restricting imports, governments frequently offer subsidies and tax concessions to foreign firms to encourage them to invest locally. Governments encourage inward FDI because it provides local jobs and capital, increases tax revenue, and transfers skills and technologies.

4. *Avoid trade barriers.* Companies often enter markets via FDI to avoid tariffs and other trade barriers, as these usually apply only to exporting. By establishing a physical presence inside a country or an economic bloc, the foreign company obtains the same advantages as local firms. Partnering with a local firm also helps overcome regulations or trade barriers and satisfy local content rules. The desire to avoid trade barriers helps explain why numerous Japanese automakers established factories in the United States. However, this motive is declining in importance because trade barriers have fallen substantially in many countries.

 ## Characteristics of Foreign Direct Investment

Internationalizing through FDI enables the firm to maintain a physical presence in key markets, secure direct access to customers and partners, and perform critical value-chain activities in the market. FDI is an equity or ownership form of foreign market entry. It is the entry strategy most associated with large MNEs—such as Bombardier, Ford, and Unilever—that have extensive physical presences around the world. As they venture abroad, firms that specialize in products usually establish manufacturing plants. Firms that offer services, such as banks, cruise lines, and restaurant chains, usually establish agency relationships and retail facilities.

KONE is a major manufacturer based in Finland. You may have used KONE's products without knowing it, because KONE is one of the leading producers of elevators and escalators. Read the *Recent Grad in IB* profile featuring Jennifer Knippen, who went to work for KONE after college. Her case illustrates that you can acquire valuable international business experience by working for a foreign-owned company in your home country.

Samsung (www.samsung.com), the South Korean electronics giant, first entered the United States through FDI in the 1980s and also used FDI to establish low-cost factories in Mexico, Southeast Asia, and Eastern Europe. In the 1990s, Samsung acquired capabilities, via acquisition, for developing and producing semiconductors. The firm then used FDI to establish numerous R&D centers—in Britain, China, India, Israel, Japan, and the United States—that drive the development of leading technologies in digital media and appliances, telecommunications, and semiconductors. Most of Samsung's sales are from international operations—in Asia (51 percent), Europe (28 percent), and the United States (15 percent)—which are facilitated through the firm's roughly sixty-four foreign sales affiliates. Samsung also has thirty-eight manufacturing sites and three logistics centers located abroad, all established via FDI. Samsung has now surpassed Motorola to become the biggest-selling brand of mobile phone in the United States.[14]

International portfolio investment Passive ownership of foreign securities such as stocks and bonds for the purpose of generating financial returns.

Do not confuse FDI with **international portfolio investment**, which refers to passive ownership of foreign securities, such as stocks and bonds, for the purpose of generating financial returns. International portfolio investment is a form of international investment, but it is not FDI, which seeks ownership control of a business abroad and represents a long-term commitment. The United Nations uses the benchmark of at least 10 percent ownership in the enterprise to differentiate FDI from portfolio investment.

Recent Grad in IB

Jennifer's majors: Economics and International Business

Jobs held since graduating:
- Sales Engineer, KONE, Inc.

Jennifer Knippen

Jennifer Knippen was inspired to pursue an international career after participating in a study-abroad program in Valencia, Spain. After graduating with dual majors in economics and international business, she returned to Spain for five months of intensive training in Spanish and traveled through various regions to broaden her education.

When she returned home, Jennifer attended a career fair, which led to a sales engineer position with the U.S. subsidiary of KONE, Inc., a leading manufacturer of elevators and escalators based in Finland. Her experience at KONE was both challenging and inspiring. Jennifer had to learn a technical product in the demanding construction industry.

As a sales engineer, she consulted architects in the design stages of a project—cost analysis, equipment specifications, building integration, and code compliance. She next generated a proposal to the general contractor working on the project. If accepted, she managed the project through completion (usually more than a year). Jennifer managed multiple projects at a time while still meeting annual and quarterly sales budgets.

Managers at KONE praised Jennifer's strong presentations and relationship-building skills. She began working on high-rise projects with some of the top architectural and construction firms. Through preselling, with KONE's global support and resources, Jennifer stimulated substantial demand. Eventually she was awarded "Best in Class" for the highest-volume sales in her region.

Jennifer experienced the benefits and challenges that come with working for a local subsidiary of an international parent company. KONE has enjoyed big success in Europe and other parts of the world and has applied a similar approach in the United States. One of the challenges Jennifer faced was strict U.S. building code regulations. She also had to monitor fluctuations in the euro–dollar exchange rate, because these greatly affect the sales price of imported equipment.

What's Ahead?

The elevator business has its ups and downs, and Jennifer returned to school to complete an MBA in international business. She thought her experience, coupled with an advanced degree in international management, would position her well for an exciting international career. Jennifer is excited about what lies ahead.

Success Factors for a Career in International Business

Foreign travel and a study-abroad program in college inspired Jennifer to pursue an international career. Learning Spanish enhanced her credentials to secure an international business job. Jennifer set career goals and worked hard to achieve them.

However, this percentage may be misleading, because control is not usually achieved unless the investor owns at least 50 percent of a foreign venture.

Key Features of Foreign Direct Investment

FDI has several key features, which we consider next.

FDI represents substantial resource commitment. As the ultimate internationalization strategy, it is far more taxing on the firm's resources and capabilities than any other entry strategy. For example, the U.S. firm General Electric owns more than $400 billion in factories, subsidiaries, and other operations outside the United States.[15]

FDI implies local presence and operations. By using FDI, management chooses to have local presence and establish direct contact with customers, intermediaries, facilitators, and the government sector. Some firms concentrate their operations in one or a handful of locations; other firms disperse their FDI among numerous countries. Often, MNEs' networks of operations become so extensive that the nationality of individual firms is not always clear. For example, although based in Switzerland, Nestlé generates more than 90 percent of its sales from abroad. The Indian MNE Tata Consultancy Services generates most of its revenues in North America, while rival IBM, a U.S. company, obtains nearly two-thirds of its sales from abroad.[16]

Firms invest in countries that provide specific comparative advantages. Managers choose particular countries in which to invest, based on the advantages these locations offer. Thus, firms tend to: perform R&D activities in those countries with leading-edge knowledge and experience for their industry; source from countries where suppliers provide the best-value products; build production facilities at locations that provide the best ratio of productivity to labor costs; and establish marketing subsidiaries in countries with the greatest sales potential.

FDI entails substantial risk and uncertainty. Compared to other entry strategies, establishing a permanent, fixed presence in a foreign country makes the firm vulnerable to country risk and intervention by local government on issues such as wages, hiring practices, and product pricing. We discussed country risk and government intervention in Chapters 7 and 8, respectively. Direct investors also must contend with inflation, recessions, and other local economic conditions. French automaker Renault recently paid $1 billion to obtain a 25 percent stake in AvtoVAZ (www.lada-auto.ru), a car factory in Russia. Renault management wants to produce Lada brand cars for the local market. However, the AvtoVAZ plant is 40 years old and plagued by inefficient operations and a slow-moving workforce with origins in the Soviet era of communism. It even has a history of organized crime, including criminal gangs who once roamed the plant freely, stealing cars.[17] Business deals in Russia often require paying expensive bribes, and the country has a long history of high inflation and other macroeconomic concerns. Russian government intervention in the private sector complicates business planning and operations.

Direct investors must deal more intensively with specific social and cultural variables in the host market. MNEs with high-profile, conspicuous operations are especially vulnerable to close public scrutiny of their actions. To minimize potential problems, managers often favor investing in countries that are culturally and linguistically familiar. When setting up shop in continental Europe, for example, U.S. firms frequently choose the Netherlands because English is widely spoken there.[18]

Vodafone is one of the most international firms due to its very extensive FDI activities. The firm invests abroad to establish retail outlets, such as this store in Safaga, Egypt.

These features of FDI pose formidable challenges for the firm. Even a large, well-established company like Disney (www.disney.com) experienced several failures in its foreign investing. As *Fortune* magazine noted, "The company's record in operating theme parks overseas is spottier than 101 Dalmatians."[19] When Disney established Tokyo Disneyland, its management incorrectly assumed the Disneyland experience could not be successfully transferred to Japan. So instead of investing, Disney opted to license rights in Japan for nominal profits. Tokyo Disneyland proved to be a huge success. Not wanting to repeat the same mistake, management opted to retain an FDI stake in its next theme park—Disneyland Paris. But it proved to be a financial sinkhole. Having learned from these experiences, Disney has made the latest theme park, Hong Kong Disneyland, more successful. Disney owns just 46 percent of the venture, making the Hong Kong government the major partner. Management wants to expand the park, but negotiations with the Hong Kong government have been tense and complicated. In

2009, China gave Disney the go-ahead for plans to develop Shanghai Disneyland. However, management is worried about intellectual property violations in China, which may reduce profits from licensing Disney movies, animated characters, and other valuable properties.[20]

Corporate Social Responsibility and FDI

Multinational firms increasingly strive to behave in *socially responsible* ways in host countries. Many are investing in local communities and seeking to establish global standards of fair treatment for workers. Unilever (www.unilever.com), the giant Dutch-British producer of consumer products, operates a free community laundry in a São Paulo slum, provides financing to assist tomato growers to convert to environmentally friendly irrigation, and recycles 17 million pounds of waste annually at one of its toothpaste factories. In Bangladesh, where there are relatively few doctors, Unilever funds a hospital that offers free medical care to the needy. In Ghana, the company teaches palm oil producers to reuse plant waste while providing drinkable water to deprived communities. In India, Unilever provides small loans to help women in remote villages start small-scale enterprises. In all the countries where it operates, Unilever discloses how much carbon dioxide and hazardous waste it produces.[21]

Unilever is not alone in being socially responsible in its host countries. Many other MNEs are responding to such global agendas as *sustainability*, or meeting humanity's needs without harming future generations. For example, automakers such as Toyota, Renault, and Volkswagen are investing in fuel-efficient and clean technologies. Nokia is a leader in phasing out toxic materials. Dell was among the first to accept old PC hardware from consumers and recycle it for free. GlaxoSmithKline and Merck offer AIDS drugs at cost in numerous impoverished countries. Suncor Energy assists Native Americans to deal with social and ecological issues in Canada's far north.

Most Active Firms in FDI

Exhibit 15.2 provides a sample of leading MNEs engaged in FDI. General Electric, Vodafone, and other firms in the exhibit are listed based on the volume of factories, subsidiaries, and other assets they own in foreign countries, ranked by asset value. For example, U.K.-based Vodafone is a mobile phone supplier with sales offices in cities around the world. The most internationally active MNEs are in the automotive, oil, and telecommunications industries.

Service Firms and FDI

Companies in the services sector, such as retailing, construction, and personal care, must offer their services where they are consumed. This requires establishing either a permanent presence through FDI (as in retailing) or a temporary relocation of the service company personnel (as in the construction industry).[22] Management consulting is a service usually embodied in experts who interact directly with clients to dispense advice. To reach their customers, firms such as McKinsey and Cap Gemini have established numerous offices in foreign markets. Many support services, such as advertising, insurance, accounting, legal work, and overnight package delivery, are also best provided at the customer's location. FDI is vital for internationalizing services.[23]

Intrawest, Inc., which is building several ski resorts in China, has offices at various locations in China. Banks establish branches around the world because banking services are usually provided directly to customers wherever they do business. Exhibit 15.3 portrays the world's most international financial institutions and the breadth of their operations abroad. The firms are ranked based on the number of foreign subsidiaries and affiliates and the number of countries where the MNEs do business. For example, Citigroup has representative offices in seventy-five countries.

Rank	Company	Home Country	Industry	Assets (billions of U.S. dollars)		Sales (billions of U.S. dollars)		Approximate Number of Subsidiaries and Affiliates	
				Foreign	Total	Foreign	Total	Foreign	Total
1	General Electric	United States	Electrical & electronic equipment	$400	$798	$98	$183	787	1,157
2	Vodafone	United Kingdom	Telecommunications	205	223	52	60	70	198
3	Royal Dutch Shell	Netherlands & United Kingdom	Petroleum	222	282	262	458	328	814
4	BP	United Kingdom	Petroleum	187	228	284	366	445	611
5	Exxon Mobil	United States	Petroleum	161	228	322	460	237	314
6	Toyota Motor	Japan	Motor vehicles	183	320	144	226	129	341
7	Total	France	Petroleum	141	165	190	250	410	576
8	Electricité De France	France	Electricity, gas & water	129	279	42	90	204	264
9	Ford Motor	United States	Motor vehicles	103	223	76	129	130	216
10	E.ON	Germany	Electricity, gas & water	141	219	50	121	303	596

Exhibit 15.2 World's Most International Non-Financial MNEs, Based on Volume of Foreign Assets

SOURCE: UNCTAD, World Investment Report 2009 (New York: United Nations, 2009, p. 225, "Annex table A.1.9. The World's Top 100 non-financial TNCs, ranked by foreign assets, 2007a"), accessed June 4, 2010 at http://unctad.org/en/docs/wir2009_en.pdf.

Exhibit 15.3 World's Most International Financial MNEs, Based on Breadth of Worldwide Operations

SOURCE: UNCTAD, World Investment Report 2009 (New York: United Nations, 2009, p. 225, "Annex table A.1.12. The top 50 financial TNCs ranked by Geographical Spread Index (GSI), 2008"), accessed June 4, 2010 at http://unctad.org/en/docs/wir2009_en.pdf.

Company	Home Country	Number of Subsidiaries and Affiliates		Number of Host Countries
		Foreign	Total	
Citigroup, Inc.	United States	723	1,020	75
Allianz SE	Germany	612	823	52
ABN AMRO	Netherlands	703	945	48
Generali	Italy	342	396	41
HSBC	United Kingdom	683	1,048	54
Société Générale	Italy	345	526	53
Zurich Financial Services	Switzerland	383	393	34
UBS	Switzerland	432	465	35
Unicredito Italiano	Italy	1,052	1,111	34
Axa	France	464	575	39

Leading Destinations for FDI

Advanced economies such as Australia, Britain, Canada, Japan, Netherlands, and the United States have long been popular destinations for FDI because of their strong GDP per capita, GDP growth rate, density of knowledge workers, and superior business infrastructure, such as telephone systems and energy sources.[24] However, in recent years, emerging markets are also gaining appeal as FDI destinations. According to A. T. Kearney's Global Location Index, the top destinations for foreign investment today are China and India (www.atkearney.com). China is popular because of its size, rapid growth rate, and low labor costs. It is an important platform where MNEs manufacture products for export to key markets in Asia and elsewhere. India is popular because of its managerial talent, well-educated workforce, and relatively fewer cultural barriers.[25] China and India are also attractive for strategic reasons: They have much long-term potential as target markets and new sources of competitive advantage.

Factors to Consider in Choosing FDI Locations

Exhibit 15.4 lists the criteria firms use to evaluate countries as potential targets for FDI projects. Suppose Taiwan-based Acer (www.acer.com) wants to build a new computer factory. Its managers will research the best country in which to build it, looking at country and regional factors, infrastructural factors, political factors, profit retention factors, and human resource factors.

Consider the attractiveness of Eastern European nations as FDI destinations. Several of the selection criteria noted in Exhibit 15.4 have attracted foreign firms to these countries. In the Czech Republic, giant Chinese electronics manufacturer Sichuan Changhong (www.changhong.com) built a $30 million factory that produces up to one million

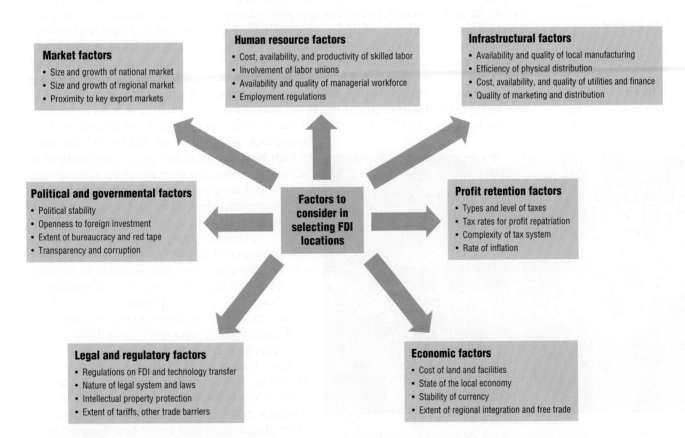

Exhibit 15.4   Factors to Consider in Selecting Foreign Direct Investment Locations

SOURCE: From *Entry Strategies for International Markets* by Franklin R. Root. Copyright © 1994 by John Wiley & Sons, Inc. Reprinted by permission of John Wiley & Sons, Inc.

flat-screen televisions per year. Numerous automakers, from Ford to Nissan, have built factories in the region. Firms find the region attractive for various reasons. First, wages in Eastern Europe are relatively low; engineers in Slovakia earn half of what Western engineers make, and assembly line workers one-third to one-fifth. Second, East European governments offer incentives, from financing to low taxes, as in Slovakia where all taxes are a simple 19 percent. By comparison, personal income tax rates often exceed 30 percent in Germany. Third, local manufacturing allows firms to avoid trade barriers. Sichuan Changhong's presence in the Czech Republic helps it avoid tariffs the European Union imposes on imports from China. Fourth, companies prefer Eastern Europe because of its physical proximity to the huge EU market. Many Eastern European countries are EU members themselves. Just as Eastern Europe has become a popular FDI destination, production of cars and other products is falling in much of Western Europe due to higher manufacturing costs, taxes, and strict labor rules.[26] As these examples imply, managers examine a combination of criteria when making decisions about where in the world to establish operations via FDI.

 ## Types of Foreign Direct Investment

We can classify FDI activities by form (greenfield versus mergers and acquisitions), nature of ownership (wholly owned versus joint venture), and level of integration (horizontal versus vertical).

Greenfield Investment versus Mergers and Acquisitions

Greenfield investment
Direct investment to build a new manufacturing, marketing, or administrative facility, as opposed to acquiring existing facilities.

Acquisition   Direct investment to purchase an existing company or facility.

Greenfield investment occurs when a firm invests to build a new manufacturing, marketing, or administrative facility, as opposed to acquiring existing facilities. As the name *greenfield* implies, the investing firm typically buys an empty plot of land and builds a production plant, marketing subsidiary, or other facility there for its own use. This is exactly what Ford did, for example, when it established its large factory outside Valencia, Spain.

An **acquisition** is the purchase of an existing company or facility. When Home Depot entered Mexico, it acquired the stores and assets of an existing retailer of building products, Home Mart.[27] The Chinese personal computer manufacturer Lenovo made an ambitious acquisition of IBM's PC business, which now accounts for some two-thirds of its annual revenue. The deal provided Lenovo with valuable strategic assets such as brands and distribution networks and helped it rapidly extend its market reach and become a global player.[28]

Multinational enterprises may favor acquisition over greenfield FDI because, by acquiring an existing company, they gain access to its accumulated assets. They gain ownership of existing assets such as plant, equipment, and human resources, as well as access to existing suppliers and customers. Unlike greenfield FDI, acquisition provides an immediate stream of revenue and accelerates the MNE's return on investment. However, host-country governments usually want MNEs to undertake greenfield FDI because it creates new jobs and production capacity, facilitates technology and know-how transfer to locals, and improves linkages to the global marketplace. Many governments offer incen-

The Chinese computer maker Lenovo, whose Beijing factory is shown here, purchased IBM's personal computer business for $1.25 billion and now earns more than two-thirds of its revenue from this ambitious acquisition.

tives to encourage greenfield investments, which may be sufficient to offset the advantages of acquisition-based entry.

A **merger** is a special type of acquisition in which two companies join to form a new, larger firm. Mergers are more common between companies of similar size because they are capable of integrating their operations on a relatively equal basis. One example is the merger between Lucent Technologies in the United States and Alcatel in France. This deal created the world's largest firm in the global telecommunications equipment industry (Alcatel-Lucent). Like joint ventures, mergers can generate many positive outcomes, including interpartner learning and resource sharing, increased economies of scale, cost savings from elimination of duplicative activities, a broader range of products and services for sale, and greater market power. Cross-border mergers confront many challenges due to national differences in culture, competition policy, corporate values, and operating methods. Success requires substantial advance research, planning, and commitment.

Merger A special type of acquisition in which two firms join to form a new, larger firm.

The Nature of Ownership in FDI

Foreign direct investors also choose their degree of control in the venture. This is accomplished through full or partial ownership, resulting in a commensurate degree of control over decision making on such issues as product development, expansion, and profit distribution. Firms can choose between a wholly owned or joint venture to secure control, which also determines the extent of their financial commitment. If the focal firm is pursuing partial ownership in an existing firm, this is known as **equity participation**.

Wholly owned direct investment is FDI in which the investor assumes 100 percent ownership of the business and secures complete managerial control over its operations. For example, many foreign automotive firms have established fully owned manufacturing plants in the United States to serve this large market from within. Exhibit 15.5 maps the location of Toyota's U.S. plants and the year of establishment. In contrast to wholly owned direct investment, an **equity joint venture** is a type of partnership in which a separate firm is created through the investment or pooling of assets by two or more parent firms that gain joint ownership of the new legal entity.[29] A partner in a joint venture may hold majority, equal (50–50), or minority ownership. Minority ownership provides little control over the operation.

Equity participation Acquisition of partial ownership in an existing firm.

Wholly owned direct investment A foreign direct investment in which the investor fully owns the foreign assets.

Equity joint venture A type of partnership in which a separate firm is created through the investment or pooling of assets by two or more parent firms that gain joint ownership of the new legal entity.

Many firms find joint ventures attractive because of the complexity of foreign markets. Collaborating with a local partner increases the foreign entrant's ability to navigate the local market. Collaborative ventures also benefit small and medium-sized enterprises by providing them with needed capital and other assets. For example, Shanghai-based Tri Star International acquired a majority stake in Illinois-based Adams Pressed Metals, a manufacturer of parts for tractors and other earth-moving equipment. The cash infusion saved forty jobs at Adams and gave Tri Star access to the U.S. market and marketing know-how.[30]

A joint venture with a local partner may sometimes be the only entry strategy available to the focal firm, as when the government of a target country seeks to protect its important industries by prohibiting 100 percent foreign ownership in local enterprises. However, governments are relaxing such regulations in most industries, and they are now relatively receptive to FDI.

Vertical versus Horizontal Integration

A third way of classifying FDI is by whether integration takes place vertically or horizontally. **Vertical integration** is an arrangement whereby the firm owns, or seeks to own, multiple stages of a value chain for producing, selling, and delivering a product or service. Vertical FDI takes two forms. In *forward* vertical integration, the firm develops the capacity to sell its outputs by investing in downstream value-chain facilities—that is, in marketing and selling operations. Forward vertical integration is less common than *backward* vertical integration, in which the firm acquires the capacity abroad to provide

Vertical integration An arrangement whereby the firm owns, or seeks to own, multiple stages of a value chain for producing, selling, and delivering a product or service.

Exhibit 15.5 Toyota's Direct Investments in Manufacturing Plants in the United States

SOURCE: *Toyota United States Operations 2010,* retrieved from http://www.toyota.com and *Fortune,* © 2007 Time Inc. All rights reserved. Used by permission and protected by the Copyright Laws of the United States. The printing, copying, redistribution, or retransmission of the Material without express written permission is prohibited.

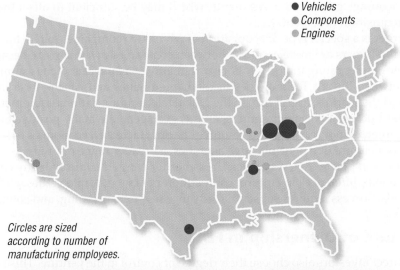

● Vehicles
● Components
● Engines

Circles are sized according to number of manufacturing employees.

Vehicle plants currently operating	Start of production	Models produced	Manufacturing employees
1. Long Beach, California	1972	Hino trucks, various parts	800
2. Georgetown, Kentucky	1988	Avalon, Camry, Solara	7,000
3. Princeton, Indiana	1999	Sequoia, Sienna, Highlander	4,500
4. San Antonio, Texas	2003	Tundra, Tacoma	1,850
5. Blue Springs, Mississippi	2010	Prius	2,000

More companies are investing in Africa to develop dams and power plants. In addition to providing capital for local economies, such investments supply needed infrastructure. Pictured here is the Jozini Dam in Kwazulu Natal Province, South Africa.

inputs for its foreign or domestic production processes by investing in upstream facilities, typically factories, assembly plants, or refining operations. Firms can own both backward and forward vertical integration. In various countries, Honda owns both suppliers of car parts and dealerships that sell and distribute cars.

Horizontal integration is an arrangement whereby the firm owns, or seeks to own, the activities performed in a single stage of its value chain. Microsoft's primary business is developing computer software. In addition to producing operating systems, word processing, and spreadsheet software, it has also developed subsidiaries abroad that make other types of software, such as a Montreal-based firm that produces software for creating movie animations. As this example suggests, companies invest abroad in their own industry to expand their capacity and activities. A firm may acquire another firm engaged in an identical value-chain activity to achieve economies of scale, expand its product line, increase its profitability, or, in some cases, eliminate a competitor. The *Global Trend* feature describes the progress of FDI in the recent global recession.

GLOBAL TREND
FDI in the Global Financial Crisis

More than 82,000 multinational enterprises operate worldwide. Collectively, they control some 800,000 foreign subsidiaries and affiliates critical to the world economy. Foreign affiliates of MNEs account for about one-third of world exports of goods and services and employ more than 75 million people. These firms produce the FDI flows vital to the world economy. However, FDI flows declined substantially during the recent recession and global financial crisis.

The crisis cost millions of people their jobs, reduced profits, and delayed internationalization projects for countless firms. The decline in FDI harmed poorer countries in Africa, Asia, and Latin America, which depend heavily on inward investment for financing. Global FDI flows fell below $1.2 trillion in 2009, down substantially from their historic high of $2 trillion in 2007.

The drop resulted from declines in three major categories of investment: equity investments, other capital (mainly intra-company loans), and reinvested earnings. As company profits fell, firms had less capital to invest in foreign operations. The recession also produced sharp declines in cross-national merger and acquisition (M&A) activity. One exception was the 2008 purchase for $52 billion of beer producer Anheuser Busch by the Belgian firm Stichting Interbrew.

Global portfolio investments in the form of private equity funds were hit especially hard, because equity capital (money invested in stock markets) is very fluid. Thus, international investors were able to withdraw their investments quickly from countries. As lenders and investors became more risk-conscious, capital flows in global portfolio investments shrank.

One of the bright spots in FDI trends is Africa, where investment inflows have grown in the recent past, increasing from $22 billion to $30 billion between 2007 and 2008 alone. Much of the inflows were for prospecting projects in search of oil and base metals. Other investments were made in infrastructure development, such as the construction of dams and plants for generating power. The main sources of FDI to Africa were firms based in advanced economies, such as Britain, France, and the United States. Chinese firms also have undertaken substantial investment activities in Africa. One factor that encourages the inward FDI is increased political and economic stability in African governments in recent years.

SOURCES: J. Espinoza, "Investment Outlook Is Mixed for Europe," *Wall Street Journal*, March 11, 2010, retrieved from http://www.wsj.com; "Global Outlook: FDI Trends—Emerging from Crisis," *Foreign Direct Investment*, February/March 2010, retrieved from http://www.fdimagazine.com; A. Hawser, "Africa Leads the Way to a New Era," *Global Finance*, December 2009, pp. 47–49; UNCTAD, *World Investment Report 2009* (New York: United Nations, 2009).

International Collaborative Ventures

Collaborative ventures, sometimes called *international partnerships* or *international strategic alliances*, are essentially partnerships between two or more firms.[31] They help companies overcome together the often substantial risks and costs involved in achieving international projects that might exceed the capabilities of any one firm operating alone. Groups of firms sometimes form partnerships to accomplish large-scale goals such as developing new technologies or completing major projects such as power plants. By collaborating, the focal firm can draw on a range of complementary technologies, accessible only from other firms, to innovate and develop new products. Advantages like these help explain why the volume of such partnerships has grown substantially in the last few decades.[32]

While collaboration can take place at similar or different levels of the value chain, it is typically focused on R&D, manufacturing, or marketing. International collaborative ventures have been on the rise and have led to joint R&D in knowledge-intensive, high-technology sectors such as robotics, semiconductors, aircraft manufacturing, medical instruments, and pharmaceuticals.

There are two basic types of collaborative ventures: equity joint ventures and project-based, nonequity ventures. *Equity joint ventures* are traditional collaborations of a type that has existed for decades. In recent years, however, there has been a proliferation of newer, *project-based collaborations*.

Horizontal integration
An arrangement whereby the firm owns, or seeks to own, the activities performed in a single stage of its value chain.

Equity Joint Ventures

Joint ventures are normally formed when no one party possesses all the assets needed to exploit an available opportunity. In a typical international deal, the foreign partner contributes capital, technology, management expertise, training, or some type of product. The local partner contributes the use of its factory or other facilities, knowledge of the local language and culture, market navigation know-how, useful connections to the host country government, or lower-cost production factors such as labor or raw materials. Western firms often seek joint ventures to gain access to markets in Asia. The partnership allows the foreign firm to access key market knowledge, gain immediate access to a distribution system and customers, and attain greater control over local operations.

Procter & Gamble (P&G) is in a joint venture with Dolce & Gabbana, an Italian fashion house. Under the deal, P&G produces perfumes, while the Italian firm markets them in Europe, leveraging the local strength of its brand name.[33] The partnership provides both firms superior access to each other's strategic assets in R&D, production, branding, distribution, and market knowledge.

Samsung, the Korean electronics firm, began internationalizing in the 1970s through joint ventures with foreign-technology suppliers such as NEC, Sanyo, and Corning Glass Works. The partnerships allowed Samsung to acquire product designs and marketing outlets and gave management increasing confidence in foreign operations. As its capabilities grew, Samsung ventured into international production. Its earliest foreign manufacturing effort was a joint venture in Portugal, launched in 1982. In the 1990s, Samsung formed a joint venture with British supermarket chain Tesco to establish a chain of hypermarkets in South Korea. In 2010, Samsung set up a joint venture in China to manufacture liquid crystal display panels.[34]

Project-Based, Nonequity Ventures

Project-based, nonequity venture A collaboration in which the partners create a project with a relatively narrow scope and a well-defined timetable, without creating a new legal entity.

Increasingly common in cross-border business, the **project-based, nonequity venture** is a collaboration in which the partners create a project with a relatively narrow scope and a well-defined timetable, without creating a new legal entity. Combining staff, resources, and capabilities, the partners collaborate on new technologies or products until the venture bears fruit or they no longer consider collaboration valuable. Such partnering reduces the enormous fixed costs of R&D, especially in technology and knowledge-intensive industries, and helps firms catch up with rivals. Sony developed the microprocessor used in Playstation 3 in partnership with IBM and Toshiba. The venture led to the creation of the Cell chip, which is ten times faster than Intel's most powerful Pentium chip and permits more graphics-intensive gaming.[35]

IBM entered a strategic partnership for a limited period in which it provided outsourcing services to NTT, the Japanese telecommunications carrier, and NTT in turn provided outsourcing services and contacts for IBM to offer computer services sales to customers in Japan.[36] Germany's Siemens teamed with Motorola to develop the next generation of 300-mm 12-inch wafers, an important innovation in the global semiconductor industry. Motorola provided its expertise in advanced logic products and leading-edge manufacturing; Siemens contributed superior knowledge of random-access memory.

Differences between Equity and Project-Based, Nonequity Ventures

Project-based collaborations differ from traditional equity joint ventures in four important ways. First, no new legal entity is created. Partners carry on their activity within the guidelines of a contract. Second, parent companies do not necessarily seek ownership of an ongoing enterprise. Instead, they contribute their knowledge, expertise, staff, and monetary resources to derive knowledge or other benefits. Third, collaboration tends to

	Advantages	*Disadvantages*
Equity joint ventures	• Afford greater control over future directions • Facilitate transfer of knowledge between the partners • Common goals drive the joint venture	• Complex management structure • Coordination between the partners may be a concern • Difficult to terminate • Greater exposure to political risk
Project-based, nonequity ventures	• Easy to set up • Simple management structure; can be adjusted easily • Takes advantage of partners' respective strengths • Can respond quickly to changing technology and market conditions • Easy to terminate	• Knowledge transfer may be less straightforward between the partners • No equity commitment; thus, puts greater emphasis on trust, good communications, and developing relationships • Conflicts may be harder to resolve • Division of costs and benefits may strain relationship

Exhibit 15.6 Advantages and Disadvantages of International Collaborative Ventures

have a well-defined timetable and end date; partners go their separate ways once they have accomplished their objectives or have no further reason for continuation. Fourth, collaboration is narrower in scope than in equity joint venturing, typically emphasizing a single project, such as development, manufacturing, marketing, or distribution of a new product.

Exhibit 15.6 highlights advantages and disadvantages of the two types of international collaborative ventures.

Consortium

A **consortium** is a project-based, usually nonequity venture initiated by multiple partners to fulfill a large-scale project. It is typically formed with a contract, which delineates the rights and obligations of each member. Work is allocated to the members on the same basis as profits. Thus, each partner in a three-partner consortium performs one-third of the work and earns one-third of the resulting profits. Consortia are popular for innovation in industries such as commercial aircraft, computers, pharmaceuticals, and telecommunications, where the costs of developing and marketing a new product often reach hundreds of millions of dollars and require sweeping expertise. For example, Boeing, Fuji, Kawasaki, and Mitsubishi joined forces to design and manufacture major components of the Boeing 767 aircraft.

Often, several firms pool their resources to bid on a major project, such as building a power plant or a high-tech manufacturing facility. Each brings a unique specialty to the project but would be unable to win the bid on its own. No formal legal entity is created; each firm retains its individual identity. In this way, if one party withdraws, the consortium can continue with the remaining participants. iNavSat is a consortium formed among several European firms to develop and manage Europe's global satellite navigation system.

Cross-Licensing Agreements

A **cross-licensing agreement** is a type of a project-based, nonequity venture whose partners each agree to access licensed intellectual property developed by the other on preferential terms. For example, Microsoft entered such an agreement with Japan's JVC to share patented knowledge on software and other products. Two firms also might enter

Consortium A project-based, nonequity venture initiated by multiple partners to fulfill a large-scale project.

Cross-licensing agreement A type of project-based, nonequity venture where partners agree to access licensed technology developed by the other on preferential terms.

a cross-distribution agreement, in which each partner has the right to distribute products or services produced by the other on preferential terms. For instance, the Star Alliance is an agreement among over twenty-five airlines—including Air Canada, United, Lufthansa, SAS, Singapore Airlines, and Air New Zealand—to market each others' airline flights (www.staralliance.com).

 ## Managing Collaborative Ventures

In FDI and exporting, the focal firm emphasizes competing skillfully against rival companies. In collaborative ventures, however, the focal firm must cooperate with one or more other firms that, in different circumstances or other countries, may actually be its competitors. This requires managers to acquire skills in developing and consummating partnerships with other firms around the world.[37] Let's review the key managerial tasks in successful collaboration.

Understand Potential Risks in Collaboration

Firms that collaborate have decided partnering is preferred to going it alone. In short, the potential benefits outweigh potential risks. In analyzing a possible collaboration, management should address the following questions:

- As a firm, are we likely to grow dependent on our partner?
- By partnering, will we stifle growth and innovation in our own organization?
- Will we share our competencies excessively, to the point where corporate interests are threatened? How can we safeguard our core competencies?
- Will we be exposed to significant commercial, political, cultural, or currency risks?
- Will we close off certain growth opportunities by participating in this venture?
- Will managing the venture place an excessive burden on our corporate resources, such as managerial, financial, or technological resources?

The potential partner may be a current or potential competitor, is likely to have its own agenda, and will likely gain important competitive advantages from the relationship.[38] Management must protect its hard-won capabilities and other organizational assets to preserve its bargaining power and ability to compete. Harmony is not necessarily the most important goal, and accepting some conflict and tension between the partners may be preferable to surrendering core skills. The firm does not want to become too dependent on its partner. In collaborations with partners in China, Intel has been careful not to share too much of its proprietary technology. It has avoided building computer chip factories there because Intel's microprocessor devices are the heart of its intellectual property. In a country known for weak intellectual property rights, management worries about theft of not only its chip designs but also of its design and manufacturing methods.[39]

Pursue a Systematic Process for Partnering

The initial decision in internationalization is to choose the most appropriate target market, because the market determines the characteristics needed in a business partner. If the firm is planning to enter an emerging market, for example, it may want a partner with political clout or connections. Thus, country targeting and partner selection are ideally interdependent choices.

Exhibit 15.7 outlines the process for identifying and working with a suitable business partner.[40] It reveals that managers need to draw on their cross-cultural competence, legal expertise, and financial planning skills.

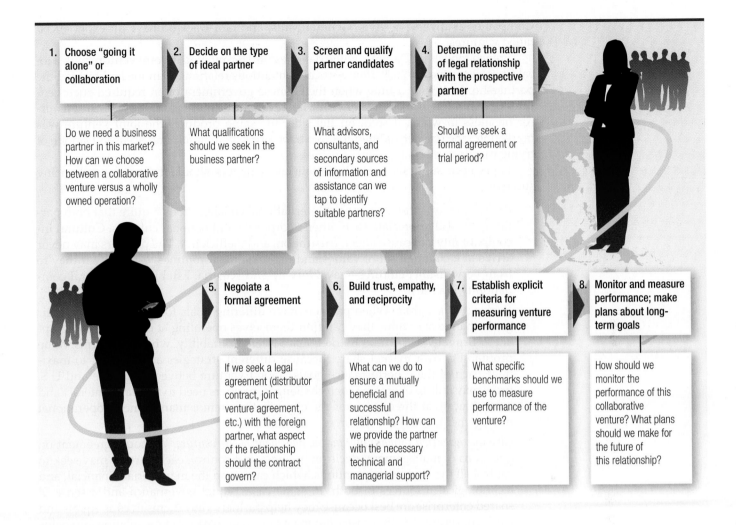

1. Choose "going it alone" or collaboration

    Do we need a business partner in this market? How can we choose between a collaborative venture versus a wholly owned operation?

2. Decide on the type of ideal partner

    What qualifications should we seek in the business partner?

3. Screen and qualify partner candidates

    What advisors, consultants, and secondary sources of information and assistance can we tap to identify suitable partners?

4. Determine the nature of legal relationship with the prospective partner

    Should we seek a formal agreement or trial period?

5. Negoiate a formal agreement

    If we seek a legal agreement (distributor contract, joint venture agreement, etc.) with the foreign partner, what aspect of the relationship should the contract govern?

6. Build trust, empathy, and reciprocity

    What can we do to ensure a mutually beneficial and successful relationship? How can we provide the partner with the necessary technical and managerial support?

7. Establish explicit criteria for measuring venture performance

    What specific benchmarks should we use to measure performance of the venture?

8. Monitor and measure performance; make plans about long-term goals

    How should we monitor the performance of this collaborative venture? What plans should we make for the future of this relationship?

Exhibit 15.7 A Systematic Process to International Business Partnering

When managers first contemplate internationalization via FDI, they usually think in terms of a wholly owned operation. Many are accustomed to retaining the control and sole access to profits that come with 100 percent ownership. The nature of the industry or product may also make partnering less desirable. But management should consider collaboration an option. Typically, the firm enters a collaborative venture when it discovers a weak or missing link in its value chain and chooses a partner that can remedy the deficiency. China is an increasingly popular venue for collaboration in the Internet service-provider industry. Both Microsoft and Google entered this huge market via joint ventures with local partners. But eBay and Yahoo entered China primarily via wholly owned FDI. Each firm chose the entry strategy most appropriate for its situation.[41]

Ensure Success with Collaborative Ventures

About half of all collaborative ventures fail within the first five years of operation because of unresolved disagreements, confusion about venture goals, and other problems. International ventures are particularly challenging because, in addition to facing complex business issues, managers must contend with differences in culture and language, as well as in political, legal, and economic systems. Collaborative ventures in developing economies have an even higher failure rate than those in advanced economies.[42]

Companies as diverse as Avis, General Mills, and GM-Daewoo have all experienced failed ventures.

French food giant Danone (www.danone.com) terminated its joint venture with a local Chinese partner in 2009 after years of contentious relations. Danone had formed the partnership in 1996 at a time when the Chinese government often required such ventures from foreign firms.[43] In later years, however, the Chinese partner established a mirror business in which it sold, on the side, the same products the joint venture was marketing. The partner claimed that contract terms were unfair and accused Danone of trying to gain control of its other businesses.

Experience suggests several guidelines managers should follow for enhancing success:

Be cognizant of cultural differences. International collaborations require that both parties learn and appreciate each other's corporate and national cultures. Cultural incompatibility can cause anger, frustration, and inefficiency. The partners may never arrive at a common set of values and organizational routines, especially if they're from very distinct cultures—say, Norway and Nigeria. Establishing cultural compatibility is a must.

Pursue common goals. When partners have differing goals for the venture, or their goals change over time, they can find themselves operating at cross-purposes. Japanese firms tend to value market share over profitability, while U.S. firms value profitability over market share. Because different strategies are required to maximize each of these performance goals, a joint venture between Japanese and U.S. firms may fail. To overcome such challenges, partners need to regularly interact and communicate at three levels of the organization: senior management, operational management, and the workforce.

Give due attention to planning and management of the venture. Without agreement on questions of management, decision making, and control, each partner may seek to control all the venture's operations, which can strain the managerial, financial, and technological resources of both. In some cases, equal governance and a sense of shared enterprise are best because they help partners view themselves as equals and reach consensus. In other cases, having a dominant partner in the relationship helps ensure success. When one of the partners is clearly the driver or the leader in the relationship, there is less likelihood of a stalemate or prolonged negotiations.

Safeguard core competencies. Collaboration takes place between current or potential competitors that must walk a fine line between cooperation and competition. Volkswagen and General Motors succeeded in China by partnering with the Chinese firm, Shanghai Automotive Industry Corporation (SAIC; www.saicmotor.com). The Western firms transferred much technology and know-how to their Chinese partner. Having learned much from them, SAIC is now poised to become a significant player in the global automobile industry and even a competitor to its earlier partners.[44]

Adjust to shifting environmental circumstances. When environmental conditions change, the rationale for a collaborative venture may weaken or disappear. An industry or economic downturn may shift priorities in one or both firms. Cost overruns can make the venture untenable. New government policies or regulations can increase costs or eliminate anticipated benefits. Managers should maintain flexibility to adjust to changing conditions.

 ## The Experience of Retailers in Foreign Markets

Retailers represent a special case of international service firms that internationalize substantially through FDI and collaborative ventures. Retailing takes various forms and includes department stores (Marks & Spencer, Macy's), specialty retailers (Body Shop,

Gap), supermarkets (Sainsbury, Safeway), convenience stores (7-Eleven, Tom Thumb), discount stores (Zellers, Target), and big-box stores (Home Depot, IKEA). Walmart has more than 240 stores and tens of thousands of employees in China. It sources almost all its merchandise locally, providing jobs for thousands more Chinese.[45]

The major drivers of retailer internationalization have been saturation of home country markets, deregulation of international investment, and opportunities to benefit from lower costs abroad. Home Depot expanded abroad because the home improvement market in Canada and the United States is becoming increasingly saturated.[46] Most emerging markets exhibit pent-up demand, fast economic growth, a growing middle class, and increasingly sophisticated consumers. In densely populated developing countries, consumers are flocking to discount retailers that sell a wide selection of merchandise at low prices.

Retailers usually choose between FDI and franchising as a foreign market entry strategy. The larger, more experienced firms, such as Carrefour, Royal Ahold, and Walmart, tend to internationalize via FDI; that is, they typically own their stores and maintain direct control over operations and proprietary assets. Smaller and less internationally experienced firms such as Borders bookstores tend to rely on networks of independent franchisees. In franchising, the retailer adopts a business system from, and pays an ongoing fee to, a franchise operator. Other firms may employ a dual strategy—using FDI in some markets and franchising in others. While franchising facilitates rapid internationalization, compared to FDI, it affords the firm less control over its foreign operations, which can be risky in countries with unstable political or economic situations or weak intellectual property laws.

Many retailers have floundered in foreign markets. When the French department store Galleries Lafayette opened in New York City, it could not compete with the city's numerous posh competitors. In its home market in Britain, Marks & Spencer succeeds with store layouts that blend food and clothing offerings in relatively small spaces, a formula that translated poorly in Canada and the United States. IKEA experienced problems in Japan, where consumers value high-quality furnishings, not the low-cost products IKEA offers.

Walmart (www.walmart.com) is the world's largest retailer but failed in Germany because it could not compete with local competitors and eventually exited the market. In Mexico, Walmart constructed massive U.S.-style parking lots for its new super centers. But most Mexicans don't have cars and city bus stops were too far away, so shoppers could not haul their goods home. In Brazil, most families do their big shopping once a month on payday. Walmart built aisles too narrow and crowded to accommodate the rush and stocked shelves in urban São Paulo with unneeded leaf blowers. In Argentina, Walmart's red, white, and blue banners, reminiscent of the U.S. flag, offended local tastes. Sam's Club, Walmart's food discounting operation, flopped in Latin America partly because its huge multipack items were too big for local shoppers with low incomes and small apartments.[47]

Challenges of International Retailing

As these examples reveal, foreign markets pose big challenges for retailers. Retailing depends for much of its success on the store environment and the shopping experience and is strongly affected by factors in each national environment. Four barriers stand in the way of successfully transplanting home market success to international markets.

First, *culture and language* are a significant obstacle. Compared to most businesses, retailers are close to customers. They must respond to local market requirements by customizing their product and service portfolio, adapting store hours, modifying store size and layout, training local workers, and meeting labor union demands.

Second, consumers tend to develop strong *loyalty to indigenous retailers*. As Galleries Lafayette in New York and Walmart in Germany discovered, local firms usually enjoy great allegiance from local consumers.

Third, managers must address *legal and regulatory barriers* that can be idiosyncratic. Germany limits store hours, and retailers must close on Sundays. Japan's Large-Scale Store Law required foreign warehouse and discount retailers to get permission from existing small retailers before setting up shop. Although it has been relaxed in recent years, the law presented a major obstacle to the entry of stores like Toys "R" Us. In 2009, IKEA abandoned efforts to expand in India, due to restrictions imposed on foreign retailers.[48]

Fourth, when entering a new market, retailers must develop *local sources* for thousands of products, including some that local suppliers may be unwilling or unable to provide. When Toys "R" Us entered Japan, local toy manufacturers were reluctant to work with the U.S. firm. Some retailers end up importing many of their offerings, which requires establishing complex and costly international supply chains.

International Retailing Success Factors

The most successful retailers pursue a systematic approach to international expansion. First, advanced research and planning is essential. A thorough understanding of the target market, combined with a sophisticated business plan, allows the firm to anticipate potential problems and prepare for success. In the run-up to launching stores in China, management at the giant French retailer Carrefour spent 12 years building up its business in Taiwan, where it developed a deep understanding of Chinese culture. It also learned how to forge alliances with local governments. These preparations helped Carrefour become China's biggest foreign retailer, rapidly developing a network of hypermarkets in twenty-five cities.[49]

Second, international retailers need to establish efficient logistics and purchasing networks in each market where they operate. Scale economies in procurement are especially critical. Retailers need to organize sourcing and logistical operations to ensure they always maintain adequate inventory while minimizing the cost of operations.

Third, international retailers should assume an entrepreneurial, creative approach to foreign markets. Virgin Megastore is a good example. Starting from one London location in 1975, founder Richard Branson expanded Virgin to numerous markets throughout Europe, North America, and Asia. The stores were big, well lit, and stocked music albums in a logical order. Consequently, sales turnover was much faster than that of smaller music retailers.

Fourth, retailers must be willing to adjust their business model to suit local conditions. Home Depot offers merchandise in Mexico that suits the small budgets of do-it-yourself builders. It has introduced payment plans and promotes the do-it-yourself mind-set in a country where most cannot afford to hire professional builders.[50] The major dimensions along which retailers differentiate themselves abroad include selection, price, marketing, store design, and the ways in which goods are displayed. They must proceed cautiously while adapting to local conditions, to avoid diluting or destroying the unique features that first made them successful.

IKEA, the world's largest furniture retailer, has enjoyed great success, launching over 200 furniture megastores in dozens of countries. Superior performance derives from strong leadership and skillful management of human resources, and from the careful balancing of global integration of operations with responsiveness to local tastes. In each store, IKEA (www.ikea.com) offers as many standardized products as possible while maintaining sufficient flexibility to accommodate specific local conditions. It tests the waters first and learns in smaller markets before entering big markets. For instance, IKEA perfected its retailing model in German-speaking Switzerland before entering Germany.

AUTOLATINA: A Failed International Partnership

Autolatina, a joint venture between Ford and Volkswagen (VW), was created in Brazil with several goals in mind:

- Serve the highly protected car markets of Brazil and Argentina from within.
- Establish an unbeatable presence in Latin America.
- Share the risk of operating in a volatile market.
- Offer a wide range of car models to Latin American customers.

Soon after Autolatina founded the venture, its market share reached 60 percent in the Brazilian market and 30 percent in Argentina.

Germany's Volkswagen was originally founded with the goal of offering popular cars that anyone could afford. The company achieved this goal with the Beetle, at one time the world's best-selling car. Early on, the Beetle became a mascot of Brazil's economic miracle, accounting for nearly half of Brazilian car sales. Volkswagen had launched the Gol some years before. It was assembled at Volkswagen do Brazil, which employed more than 45,000 people, becoming the largest industrial corporation in Latin America. Eventually, the Gol surpassed the Beetle as Brazil's best-selling car.

Ford was the first car company to assemble in Brazil. Early on, Ford resisted government demands to establish complete automotive operations, including assembly and full manufacturing, in Brazil. Ford's resistance worked to VW's advantage—the German firm eventually prevailed and became number one in Brazil.

Meanwhile, Brazil's own car industry, coddled by years of high tariffs and other protectionism, was moving quickly to modernize. For decades, the country banned imported cars or did not allow expensive, foreign parts to be fitted to locally made cars. In the 1970s, the auto industry was a symbol of the "Brazilian miracle." A ban on imports meant that Brazil's underdeveloped industry faced little foreign competition. Local manufacturers became complacent and failed to keep up with the latest car styles and technological innovations. At around the same time, Ford management was renewing its interest in Brazil and aimed to reestablish its former dominance there.

Autolatina: A Perfect Marriage

The partners' objective in the Ford-VW joint venture was to combine operations in order to overcome obstacles in the Brazilian market. Eventually, Ford and Volkswagen had a total of fifteen vehicle, engine, and parts plants in Brazil and Argentina, employing 75,000 people. Their combined annual production capacity was 900,000 cars and trucks, distributed through 1,500 dealerships. Their automotive and credit operations achieved total sales of USD $4 billion.

In a market protected from foreign imports, Autolatina became a big success. It offered inexpensive models, including the Escort XR3, Sierra, VW's Gol, Beetle, and midsized Ford Falcons. The partners organized plant operations by size of vehicles: VW focused on building small cars, while Ford supplied the larger Escort and a line of pickup trucks. The two partners also produced shared products. For instance, Volkswagen made the Ford Versailles (derived from the VW Santana), and Ford produced the VW Logus (derived from the Ford Escort). The firms unified their marketing and sales staffs and hired specialists and consultants to accommodate the two different company cultures.

Production of Autolatina cars grew rapidly over time. It seemed that both companies had succeeded in identifying the key factors contributing to Autolatina's success: inexpensive, noncompeting models, a growing market, and sharing manufacturing and profits. Autolatina enabled Ford and VW to serve an important region from within while reducing the partners' operational costs.

New Competition and the Emergence of MERCOSUR

Eventually, however, conditions shifted in Brazil, and Autolatina was caught unprepared by renewed economic growth. In addition to the popular car policy, Brazil reduced tariffs on car imports. Over the course of five years, import tariffs fell from 85 percent to as low as 20 percent.

In 1991, MERCOSUR (Mercado Comun del Sur, the region's free trade agreement) went into effect. Eventually MERCOSUR came to include Argentina, Bolivia, Brazil, Chile, Paraguay, and Uruguay. With 150 million of MERCOSUR's 200 million inhabitants, Brazil was ready to become the region's car-making center. The formation of MERCOSUR coincided with a rise in domestic demand, industrial modernization, and the internationalization of numerous firms from the region. Local companies such as Autolatina began to target the greatly enlarged market.

At the same time, MERCOSUR opened new opportunities for foreign multinationals. Numerous carmakers entered Brazil and Argentina, including Fiat, GM, Honda, Mercedes-Benz, Renault, and Toyota. They used FDI to launch local production of various popular car models. Gradually Brazil became the world's 10th-largest producer of motor vehicles.

Meanwhile, Autolatina's products, built for a protected market, fell out of step with the rapidly evolving marketplace. Brazilian consumers began to show a preference for lower-cost small cars, and price competition intensified. Both GM and Fiat launched popular cars (Corsa and Uno, respectively) for less than $7,000. The accompanying table presents the variety of offerings by four leading firms. Although Autolatina had succeeded in reviving the VW Beetle, customers opted instead for lower-priced competing brands. With increased competition, customers' choices expanded beyond low cost, increasing the pressure on manufacturers to improve quality and offerings.

Offerings by Four Leading Car Firms in Brazil

Company	Market Segment	Products
Volkswagen	Small	Beetle, Gol
	Midsized	Logus, Pointer, Voyage
	Large	Santana
Ford	Midsized	Escort, Verona
	Large	Versailles
General Motors	Small	Corsa
	Midsized	Kadett, Monza, Vectra
	Large	Omega
Fiat	Small	Uno
	Large	Tempra

Conflicts between the Partners

In addition to dynamic changes in the market, conflicts arose in the strategies of Ford and VW. Ford dealers in Brazil had been begging for smaller cars, better suited to Latin American consumers. But Ford avoided the erosion of Autolatina's profits by competing with VW's Gol (from which it was receiving half the profits). Volkswagen management, on the other hand, avoided sharing its subcompact designs with Ford. Mutual willingness to share technological knowledge and other key competencies declined over time.

Differences in the organizational cultures of the two partners also contributed to deteriorating relationships. The German and the U.S. organizations had different history and origins and differing management styles.

Within the boundaries of Autolatina, VW and Ford were reasonably well integrated operationally, even exchanging model fabrication. But outside the relationship, suppliers continued to serve the two companies independently, as well as the dealerships. Autolatina was not fully integrated with suppliers or dealers, leading to inefficiencies in the supply chain. Although consolidation reduces cost of administration and value-chain activities, the two firms failed to consolidate their supply bases and dealerships.

VW and Ford continued to compete with each other in the worldwide market, which hindered the sharing of technical knowledge and potential gains from joint R&D. Outside the Autolatina collaboration, the partners even competed against each other by launching new cars in the same category.

The End of Autolatina

In 1995, Ford and VW dissolved their alliance. The parting was so amicable that the employees were allowed to choose for which company they would continue to work.

Because the sale of subcompact vehicles, known as popular cars in Latin America, took off rapidly, Volkswagen's smaller cars benefited from the demise of the joint venture. Volkswagen held one-third of the regional market. The firm invested $2.5 billion to expand capacity by one-third (up to 2,500 vehicles a day) and launched a new truck plant and a line of new engines.

Ford continued to specialize in midsized cars but was unable to respond to the regional demand for small cars. Eventually its image in Brazil was hurt and it acquired a reputation for producing cars few wanted to buy. Ford began a $1.1 billion investment on its own to build Fiestas in Brazil and Escorts in Argentina. But by then VW, Fiat, and GM had attained big market shares in Brazil. Ford's fell to just 11 percent. Ford now builds the Fiesta, Focus, and a few other small cars in Brazil and Argentina. Each plant exports in large volumes to neighboring countries. Both Ford and Volkswagen see a bright future for the growing Brazilian car market. In 2010, both firms announced they are investing billions of dollars to add new production capacity there.

AACSB: Reflective Thinking Skills

Case Questions

1. What were Ford's motives and objectives for entering its collaborative venture with Volkswagen? Evaluate the extent to which Ford accomplished these objectives.

2. What type of collaborative venture did Ford enter with Volkswagen? What were the advantages and disadvantages of this venture from Ford's perspective?

3. What strengths did Ford and VW bring to the Auto-latina venture? Did these firms have any weaknesses? Elaborate.

4. Did Ford commit any blunders in its Latin American operations? Specify.

5. What can other managers learn from Ford's experience regarding international collaborative ventures? What should Ford do now?

SOURCES: Rebecca Blumenstein, "Head of Ford Unit in Brazil Expects a Narrower Loss," Wall Street Journal, May 14, 1997, p. B8; K. Bradsher, "Messy Latin Divorce Splits Ford and VW," International Herald Tribune, May 18, 1997, p. 8; S. T. Cavusgil, "International Partnering: A Systematic Framework for Collaborating with Foreign Business Partners," Journal of International Marketing 6, no. 1, (1998): 91–108; E. Corcoran, "Special Report—The Global Automobile: Cooper-ating to Compete," IEEE Spectrum 24, no. 10 (1987): 53–56; "The Bugs from Brazil," Economist, August 21, 1993, p. 54; "Brazil's Car Industry: Party Time," Economist, September 17, 1994, p. 76; "Ford to Invest $2.2 Billion in Brazil through 2011," FinancialWire, January 5, 2007, p. 1; Thomas Kamm, "Beetles Could Give Power to the People of Brazil Once Again—President Wants Auto-latina to Revive the VW Bug, But Price Won't Be Retro," Wall Street Journal, February 1, 1993, p. A1; Thomas Kamm, "Pedal to the Metal: Brazil Swiftly Becomes Major Auto Producer as Trade Policy Shifts," Wall Street Journal, April 20, 1994, p. A1; I. Katz, G. Smith, and A. Mandel-Campbell, "Brazil's Neighbors Are Very Nervous," Business Week, November 17, 1997, p. 64; M. Kotabe, "MERCOSUR and Beyond." Austin: Center for International Business Education and Research, University of Texas at Austin, 1997; M. Moffett, "Bruised in Brazil: Ford Slips as Market Blooms," Wall Street Journal, December 13, 1996, p. A10; J. Reed, "Fiat Cracks Brazil, But Rivals Follow," Financial Times, May 25, 2010, p. 25; H. Shapiro, "Determinants of Firm Entry into the Brazilian Automobile Manufacturing Industry, 1956–1968." Business History Review 65 (1991): 876–948.

NOTE: This case was prepared by Alexandre M. Rodrigues and Elvin Zung under the direction of Professor S. Tamer Cavusgil.

CHAPTER ESSENTIALS

Key Terms

acquisition, p. 444
consortium, p. 449
cross-licensing agreement, p. 449
equity joint venture, p. 445
equity participation, p. 445
foreign direct investment (FDI), p. 434
greenfield investment, p. 444

horizontal integration, p. 447
international collaborative venture, p. 434
international portfolio investment, p. 438
joint venture, p. 435
merger, p. 445

project-based, nonequity venture, p. 448
vertical integration, p. 445
wholly owned direct investment, p. 445

Summary

In this chapter, you learned about:

1. International investment and collaboration

Foreign direct investment (FDI) is an internationalization strategy where the firm establishes a physical presence abroad through ownership of productive assets such as capital, technology, labor, land, plant, and equipment. An **international collaborative venture** is a cross-border business alliance where partnering firms pool their resources and share costs and risks of the venture. A **joint venture** is a form of collaboration between two or more firms that leads to minority, equal, or majority ownership.

2. Motives for FDI and collaborative ventures

Firms employ FDI for various reasons, including *market-seeking motives*, to enter new markets and gain new customers; *resource/asset-seeking motives*, to acquire production factors that may be cheaper or more abundant in foreign markets; and *efficiency-seeking motives*, to enhance the efficiency of the firm's value-adding activities. These motives often occur in combination. Motivations for international collaborative ventures include the ability to gain access to new markets, opportunities, or knowledge; to undertake international activities too costly or risky for one firm alone; to reduce costs; to meet government requirements; and to prevent or reduce competition.

3. Characteristics of foreign direct investment

FDI is the most advanced and complex entry strategy and involves establishing manufacturing plants, marketing subsidiaries, or other facilities abroad. For the firm, FDI requires substantial resource commitment, local presence and operations in target countries, and the ability to access comparative advantages. It also entails greater risk as compared to other entry modes. FDI is most commonly used by MNEs—large firms with extensive international operations. Services are intangible and typically cannot be exported. Services are usually location-bound and require firms to establish a foreign presence, generally via FDI. **International portfolio investment** is passive ownership of foreign securities such as stocks and bonds.

4. Types of foreign direct investment

FDI can be **wholly owned direct investment**, in which the firm owns 100 percent of foreign operations, or an **equity joint venture** with one or more partners. Firms may engage in **greenfield investment** by building a facility from scratch or by acquiring an existing facility from another firm through **acquisition**. With **vertical integration**, the firm seeks to own multiple stages of its value chain. With **horizontal integration**, the firm seeks to own activities involved in a single stage of its value chain. A **merger** is a special type of acquisition in which two companies join together to form a new, larger firm.

5. International collaborative ventures

Joint ventures (JVs) are normally formed when no one party possesses all the assets needed to exploit an opportunity. Joint ventures are an example of ownership-based collaborations. The **project-based, nonequity venture** emphasizes a contractual relationship between the partners and is formed to pursue certain goals or meet an important business need while the partners remain independent. A **consortium** is a project-based, nonequity venture initiated by multiple firms to undertake a large-scale activity that is beyond the capabilities of the individual members.

6. Managing collaborative ventures

Collaboration requires management to clearly define its goals and strategies. It requires much research and analysis up-front, as well as strong negotiation skills. Decisions are made regarding allocation of responsibilities in management, production, finance, and marketing, as well as how to handle day-to-day operations and plans for the future. At least half of all collaborative ventures fail prematurely. Firms should choose their partners carefully and follow a systematic process for managing ventures.

7. The experience of retailers in foreign markets

Because retailing requires intensive customer interaction, it is particularly susceptible to culture, income levels, and other conditions abroad. Success depends on adapting to local conditions while maintaining the retailer's unique features and value proposition. International retailers face cultural and language barriers, strong customer loyalty to local retailers, legal and regulatory barriers, and the need to develop local supply sources. Retailer success also depends on advanced research and planning, establishing efficient logistics and purchasing networks, using an entrepreneurial and creative approach to foreign markets, and adjusting the business model to suit local needs.

Test Your Comprehension AACSB: Reflective Thinking Skills, Analytic Skills

1. What are the various types of FDI? Distinguish between acquisition and greenfield.

2. What are the major motivations for undertaking FDI?

3. Delineate the types of firms involved in FDI. Are there any types of companies that can internationalize only via FDI? Elaborate.

4. Identify the different types of collaborative ventures. What type of venture is best for entering a culturally distant market like Malaysia? For the next generation of products in its industry? For undertaking a short-term project, such as building infrastructure (e.g., highway, dam) abroad.

5. What are the major motives for undertaking FDI for a small firm whose sales are dwindling in its home market? For a firm that wants to enter a country with high trade barriers? For a firm with high manufacturing costs in its home market? For a hotel chain? For a large, diversified firm seeking to enter various markets worldwide for a variety of reasons?

6. What factors should management consider when deciding where in the world to establish a factory? A marketing subsidiary? A regional headquarters?

7. Governments often provide incentives to encourage foreign firms to invest within their national borders. Why do governments encourage inward FDI?

8. What steps should the firm take to ensure the success of its international collaborative ventures?

9. Explain what steps a firm should take to successfully launch a collaborative venture with a foreign partner.

10. What are the risks of international retailing? What can a retailer—such as a department store or a restaurant—do to maximize its chances of succeeding in foreign markets?

Apply Your Understanding AACSB: Communication Abilities, Reflective Thinking Skills, Ethical Understanding and Reasoning Abilities

1. Suppose you get a job at MobileTV, a small manufacturer of TV sets installed in cars and boats. Business has declined recently, foreign rivals from emerging markets are increasing competition, and management is worried. Because MobileTV does all its manufacturing in Britain and Canada, it lacks cost advantages and its prices are relatively high. After studying the problem, you conclude MobileTV should move much of its production to Mexico. But top management knows little about FDI. Prepare a report to management detailing the advantages of establishing a production base in Mexico. Why should the firm be interested in foreign manufacturing? Finally, recommend which type of FDI MobileTV should use in Mexico.

2. Suppose you work for Aoki Corporation, a producer of processed foods. Your boss, Hiroshi Aoki, heard there is a big market for processed foods in Europe but does not know how to enter or do business there. You recommend entering Europe through a joint venture with a local European firm. Prepare a memo to Aoki explaining the objectives and risks of internationalizing via collaborative ventures. Explain why a collaborative venture might be a better entry strategy than wholly owned FDI. Keep in mind that processed food is a culturally sensitive product that entails various complexities in marketing and distribution. What type of European partner should Aoki seek?

3. *Ethical Dilemma:* Media censorship standards vary worldwide. What is acceptable in some countries, such as nudity on television, criticizing authority, or revealing government secrets that affect national security, is unacceptable in others. Google is an Internet service multinational that used FDI to establish operations in China, a fast-growing market of 200 million Internet users. Google enjoyed growing market success for several years. In 2010, however, Chinese government officials blocked Google from the market because management refused to censor links to Web sites on sensitive topics, such as independence for Taiwan and criticism of the Chinese government. Government censorship requirements eventually forced Google to withdraw from mainland China, a move that ceded market share to Chinese competitors and hurt Google's profits. Suppose you're an international manager at Google. Should Google have exited China, or should it re-establish its presence there and comply with Chinese censorship rules? Using the Ethical Framework in Chapter 5, analyze the arguments for and against Google's withdrawal from China. What can Google do to address the problem effectively?

globalEDGE Internet Exercises
(http://globalEDGE.msu.edu)

AACSB: Communication Abilities, Reflective Thinking Skills, Use of Information Technology

Refer to Chapter 1, page 62, for instructions on how to access and use globalEDGE™.

1. Suppose your company wants to establish a factory in Latin America to make and sell products in the region. It has narrowed the pool of candidate countries to Argentina, Brazil, and Chile. Your task is to write a report that compares the FDI environments of these countries. One approach is to obtain the Country Fact Sheet for each nation from UNCTAD (www.unctad.org), the United Nations Conference on Trade and Development, an agency that gathers FDI data. You can access this data either through globalEDGE™ or the UNCTAD site. By examining the fact sheets, answer each of the following questions individually for Argentina, Brazil, and Chile:

   a. What nations are the major trading partners of each country in the region? (This indicates the size and stability of existing trading relationships with key partners.)

   b. Which companies are the leading firms now doing FDI in each country? (This can identify key competitors.)

   c. What is each country's rating on the FDI Performance Index? (This rating indicates the performance that typical firms have experienced when investing in each country.)

   d. What is the level of merger and acquisition activity in each country?

   (This shows the maturity of each country for acquisition-based FDI.) Elaborate and justify your findings.

2. Suppose your firm aims to identify prospective countries for direct investment. Your boss has requested a report on the attractiveness of alternative locations based on their potential FDI return. A colleague mentions a tool called the "FDI Confidence Index." Consult this resource and write a report in which you identify the top FDI destinations, as well as the criteria used to construct the index. The Confidence Index is published by the consulting firm A. T. Kearney, based on an annual survey of CEOs at the world's top MNEs. Access the index by entering "FDI Confidence Index" at globalEDGE™ or directly at www.atkearney.com. Download the PDF file to do your research.

3. Assume you own a company that manufactures medical products in the biotechnology industry. You want to establish a foreign plant to manufacture your products and are seeking countries with a high concentration of knowledge workers. Thus, you decide to collect information about the "knowledge economy" abroad. The World Bank highlights the state of the knowledge economy in various countries. The data are accessible by visiting the World Bank site (www.worldbank.org) and entering the keywords "Knowledge Economy Index" in the search engine. You will be able to find several articles and retrieve information about these countries. Visit the site and prepare a report on the knowledge economy for each of the following: Singapore, South Korea, and Spain.

CHAPTER 16

LEARNING OBJECTIVES In this chapter, you will learn about:

1. Contractual entry strategies
2. Licensing as an entry strategy
3. Advantages and disadvantages of licensing
4. Franchising as an entry strategy
5. Advantages and disadvantages of franchising
6. Other contractual entry strategies
7. Guidelines for protecting intellectual property

Licensing, Franchising, and Other Contractual Strategies

Harry Potter: The Magic of Licensing

One of the hottest properties in merchandise licensing is Harry Potter (harrypotter.warnerbros.com), the literary phenomenon that has grossed billions of dollars in retail sales globally to date. Not bad for a bespectacled 11-year-old boy. The fictional Harry has come a long way since he appeared in a 1997 children's book, the first of seven, by then-unknown author J. K. Rowling. In novels that appeal to both children and adults, Harry has evolved from unhappy orphan to confident young wizard. Young people love Harry because he's a fantastic combination of cool kid and good kid. Adults like the series' classic theme of good versus evil. Globally, Potter books have sold more than 400 million copies in sixty-seven languages in 200 countries.

Warner Brothers, which purchased exclusive licensing rights to the series, produced and released six Harry Potter movies prior to 2010. The movie version of the seventh book is scheduled to be released in two parts in late 2010 and mid-2011. All of the movies rank among the twenty-five top-grossing films of all time. Warner allows companies worldwide to use Potter-related images on manufactured products like game software, children's furniture, school supplies, toys, and clothing in exchange for a *royalty*, a percentage of the sale generated by the licensed product that the manufacturer pays to the licensor. The ability to associate these images with manufactured products greatly increases the products' sales potential and allows them to command high prices. Li-

censing deals (and book sales) have made Rowling one of the wealthiest women in Britain.

Warner licenses Harry Potter to a number of companies. Some produce *artifacts,* products seen in the films that do not have Harry's name on them. California's Jelly Belly Candy Company created Harry's favorite candy, Bertie Bott's Every Flavour Beans, in flavors such as earwax and sardine. LEGO makes construction kits for kids to build their own Hogwarts castle, and Mattel makes Harry Potter toys, including card games, play sets, chess sets, and action figures.

Electronic Arts (EA), the popular software game producer, paid Warner for a license to develop and market video games played on the Internet, video game consoles such as Sony's PlayStation, and cell phones. Fans can play a virtual version of Quidditch, which is like aerial polo with contestants flying on broomsticks. In 2009, EA released the video game version of *Harry Potter and the Half-Blood Prince,* selling millions of copies worldwide.

Goodwin Weavers, a home furnishings company, also has a Harry Potter license and produces Potter tapestry throws, wall hangings, decorative pillows, "pillow buddies," and fleece. P.J. Kids made a line of Potter beds that sold extremely well despite a price tag of nearly $2,000, demonstrating the magic of licensing a popular brand. Warner also sells licenses to service firms. For example, in 2010 the theme park attraction, The Wizarding

Contractual entry strategies in international business Cross-border exchanges where the relationship between the focal firm and its foreign partner is governed by an explicit contract.

Intellectual property Ideas or works created by individuals or firms, including discoveries and inventions; artistic, musical, and literary works; and words, phrases, symbols, and designs.

Intellectual property rights The legal claim through which the proprietary assets of firms and individuals are protected from unauthorized use by other parties.

Licensing Arrangement in which the owner of intellectual property grants a firm the right to use that property for a specified period of time in exchange for royalties or other compensation.

Royalty A fee paid periodically to compensate a licensor for the temporary use of its intellectual property, often based on a percentage of gross sales generated from the use of the licensed asset.

Franchising Arrangement in which the firm allows another the right to use an entire business system in exchange for fees, royalties, or other forms of compensation.

World of Harry Potter, opened at Universal Orlando Resort in Florida.

The licensing process has been self-generating—each new Harry Potter book yielded a movie, which boosted book sales, which promoted sales of Potter-licensed products and services. Warner reports the top markets for Potter-licensed products are the United States, Britain, Germany, Japan, France, South Korea, Russia, and China.

Rowling and Warner have exercised restraint: They don't want to license Potter to just anyone, though experts estimate the hot property could have generated 200 to 300 product licenses in the United States alone. Warner wants to ensure overexposure doesn't kill the golden goose.

One risk licensors such as Warner face is intellectual property violations. These occur when a firm or individual uses the licensed item to generate profits without permission of the property's owner. For example, some 80 percent of recorded music

and business software sold in China is counterfeit. Pirated DVD versions of Potter movies are sold on the streets of Chinese cities for as little as one dollar, often before the films have their official premieres there. Unauthorized foreign translations of the books posted on the Internet diminish future book sales. To combat book counterfeiting, the series' official Chinese publisher printed the Potter books on green paper and advised the local media—newspapers, magazines, television—how to recognize the real version.

SOURCES: Ben Charny, "EA Bets on Harry Potter to Help Sell More Games," *Wall Street Journal*, May 13, 2009, p. B1; Stuart Derrick, "Brands Cash in on Literary Scene," *Promotions & Incentives*, July/August 2005, pp. 13–14; "Harry Potter: Is Warner Bros. Brewing Licensing Magic?" *DSN Retailing Today*, August 21, 2000, p. A8; "Harry Potter and the Publishing Goldmine," *Economist.com/Global Agenda*, June 23, 2003, p. 1; Alexandra Jardine, "Marketing Magic," *Marketing*, November 15, 2001, p. 20; Sheila O'Mara, "Harry—Licensing's Golden Child," *Home Textiles Today*, January/February 2002, p. 10; Tony Lisanti, "Warner Bros. and the Magic World of Harry Potter," *License! Global*, June 2009, pp. 66–70.

In this chapter, we address various types of cross-border contractual relationships, including licensing and franchising. **Contractual entry strategies in international business** are cross-border exchanges in which the relationship between the focal firm and its foreign partner is governed by an explicit contract. **Intellectual property** describes ideas or works created by individuals or firms, including discoveries and inventions; artistic, musical, and literary works; and words, phrases, symbols, and designs. As explained in Chapter 5, intellectual property is safeguarded through **intellectual property rights**, the legal claim through which proprietary assets are protected from unauthorized use by other parties.[1]

 ## Contractual Entry Strategies

Two common types of contractual entry strategies are *licensing* and *franchising*. **Licensing** is an arrangement in which the owner of intellectual property grants another firm the right to use that property for a specified period of time in exchange for *royalties* or other compensation. As described in the opening vignette, a **royalty** is a fee paid periodically to compensate a licensor for the temporary use of its intellectual property, often based on a percentage of gross sales generated from the use of the licensed asset. As an entry strategy, licensing requires neither substantial capital investment (FDI) nor involvement of the licensor in the foreign market. Licensing is a relatively inexpensive way for the firm to gain a presence in the market without having to resort to expensive FDI.

Franchising is an advanced form of licensing in which the firm allows another the right to use an entire business system in exchange for fees, royalties, or other forms of compensation.

Contractual relationships are fairly common in international business and allow companies to routinely transfer their knowledge assets to foreign partners. Professional service firms such as those in architecture, engineering, advertising, and consulting extend their international reach through contracts with foreign partners. Similarly, retailing, fast food, car rental, television programming, and animation firms rely on licensing and franchising agreements. 7-Eleven (www.7-eleven.com) runs the world's largest chain of convenience stores, with about 37,000 locations in eighteen countries. While the parent firm in Japan owns most of them, several thousand in Canada, Japan, Mexico, and the United States are operated by entrepreneurs through franchising arrangements.

Unique Aspects of Contractual Relationships

Cross-border contractual relationships share several common characteristics.

- *They are governed by a contract that provides the focal firm with a moderate level of control over the foreign partner.* A formal agreement specifies the rights and obligations of both partners. *Control* refers to the ability of the focal firm to influence the decisions, operations, and strategic resources of the foreign venture and ensure the partner undertakes assigned activities and procedures. The focal firm also maintains ownership and jurisdiction over its intellectual property. However, as indicated in Exhibit 14.1, contractual agreements do not afford the same level of control as foreign direct investment, since they require the focal firm to rely on independent businesses abroad.

- *They typically include the exchange of intangibles (intellectual property) and services.* Intangibles that firms exchange include various intellectual property, technical assistance, and know-how. Firms may also exchange products or equipment to support the foreign partner.

- *Firms can pursue them independently or in conjunction with other foreign market entry strategies.* In responding to international opportunities, firms may employ contractual agreements alone, or they may combine them with FDI and exporting.[2] The use of such agreements is context specific; that is, the firm may pursue a contractual relationship with certain customers, countries, or products, but not others. For example, while licensing is common for certain types of products, it is not appropriate for others.

- *They provide dynamic, flexible choice.* Some focal firms use contractual agreements to make their initial entry in foreign markets. Then, as conditions evolve, they switch to another, often more advanced entry strategy. For example, franchisors such as McDonald's or Coca-Cola occasionally acquire some of their franchisees and bottlers. In doing so, they switch from a contractual approach to an ownership-based entry strategy.

- *They often reduce local perceptions of the focal firm as a foreign enterprise.* A contractual relationship with a local firm allows the focal firm to blend into the local market, attracting less attention and less of the criticism often directed at firms that enter through more visible entry strategies such as FDI.

- *They generate a consistent level of earnings from foreign operations.* In comparison to FDI, contractual relationships are less susceptible to volatility and risk, bringing both parties a more predictable stream of revenue.[3]

Types of Intellectual Property

A *patent* provides an inventor the right to prevent others from using or selling an invention for a fixed period—typically, up to 20 years.[4] It is granted to those who invent or discover a new and useful process, device, manufactured product, or an improvement on these. A *trademark* is a distinctive design, symbol, logo, word, or series of words placed on a product label. It identifies a product or service as coming from a common source and having a certain level of quality. Examples include Honda's H-shaped symbol,

McDonald's golden arches, and Nike's swoosh mark. A *copyright* protects original works of authorship, giving the creator the exclusive right to reproduce the work, display and perform it publicly, and authorize others to perform these activities. Copyrights cover music, art, literature, films, and computer software.

An *industrial design* describes the appearance or features of a product. The design is intended to improve the product's aesthetics and usability as well as increase its production efficiency, performance, or marketability. The Apple iPod is a well-known industrial design. A *trade secret* is confidential know-how or information that has commercial value.[5] Trade secrets include production methods, business plans, and customer lists. The formula to produce Coca-Cola is a trade secret. A *collective mark* is a logo belonging to an organization whose members use it to identify themselves and associate their products with a level of quality or accuracy, geographical origin, or other positive characteristic. 'DIN' is the collective mark for the German Institute for Standardization, typically found on home appliances in Europe.

Intellectual property rights (IPRs) are the legal claims that protect the proprietary assets of firms and individuals from unauthorized use by other parties. They derive from patents, trademarks, copyrights, and other protections associated with intellectual property. IPRs provide inventors with a monopoly advantage for a specified period of time, so they can exploit their inventions not only to recoup their investment costs and create commercial advantage, but also to acquire power and market dominance free of direct competition. The availability and enforcement of these rights vary from country to country. Without such legal protection and the assurance of commercial rewards, most firms and individuals would have little incentive to invent.

Licensing as an Entry Strategy

A licensing agreement specifies the nature of the relationship between the owner of intellectual property, the *licensor,* and the user of the property, the *licensee.* High-technology firms routinely license their patents and know-how to foreign companies. For example, Intel has licensed the right to a new process for manufacturing computer chips to a chip manufacturer in Germany.

Warner (in the opening vignette) licenses images from the Harry Potter books and movies to companies worldwide. Disney (disney.go.com) licenses the right to use its cartoon characters to shirt and hat manufacturers in Hong Kong. It also licenses its trademark names and logos to manufacturers of apparel, toys, and watches for sale worldwide. Licensing allows Disney to create synergies with foreign partners, which can adapt materials, colors, and other design elements to suit local tastes and market a product similar to one Disney may already produce in the United States.

Exhibit 16.1 illustrates the nature of the licensing agreement.[6] Upon signing a licensing contract, the licensee pays the licensor a fixed amount up front *and* an ongoing royalty of typically 2 to 5 percent of gross sales generated from using the licensed asset. The fixed amount covers the licensor's initial costs of transferring the licensed asset to the licensee, including consultation, training in how to deploy the asset, engineering, or adaptation. Certain types of licensable assets, such as copyrights and trademarks, may have lower transfer costs. The royalty percentage may escalate with increasing sales.

A typical licensing contract runs five to seven years and is renewable at the option of the parties. Initially, the licensor provides technical information and assistance to the licensee. Once the relationship has been established and the licensee fully understands its role, the licensor usually plays an advisory role but has no direct involvement in the market and provides no ongoing managerial guidance. Most firms enter into *exclusive agreements*, in which the licensee is not permitted to share the licensed asset with any other company within a prescribed territory. In addition to operating in its domestic market, the licensee may also be permitted to export to other countries.

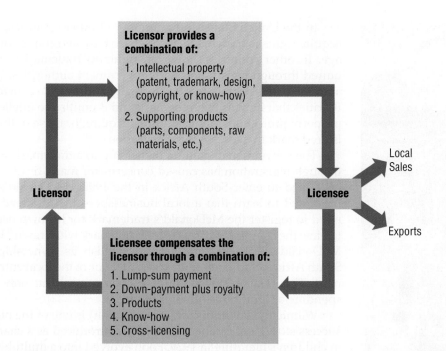

Exhibit 16.1   Licensing as a Foreign Market Entry Strategy

SOURCE: Adapted from Welch and Welch (1996) and personal correspondence with Lawrence Welch.

If the licensor is an MNE, it may enter a licensing arrangement with its own wholly or partly owned foreign affiliate. In this case, licensing is an efficient way to compensate the foreign affiliate, especially when it is a separate legal entity, and transfer intellectual property to it within a formal legal framework.

In the fashion industry, firms with strong brands such as Bill Blass, Hugo Boss, and Pierre Cardin generate substantial profits from licensing deals for jeans, fragrances, and watches. Saks Inc. entered China by licensing its Saks Fifth Avenue name for a flagship department store in Shanghai. Saks generates revenue from the agreement and controls which merchandise is sold in China but has no other involvement. Licensing brings greater awareness of Saks Fifth Avenue to Asia without requiring Saks itself to operate the store, thereby reducing its risk.[7]

The national origin of some popular brands might surprise you. Switzerland-based Nestlé sells its KitKat brand of chocolate bars in the United States under license through Hershey Foods. Planters and Sunkist are brands owned by U.S. companies and sold in Britain and Singapore through licensing agreements with local companies. Evian bottled water is owned by the French company Danone and distributed in the United States under license by Coca-Cola. Indeed, a review of annual reports from 120 of the largest multinational food companies revealed that at least half engage in some form of international product licensing.[8]

There are two major types of licensing agreements: (1) trademark and copyright licensing and (2) know-how licensing. Let's review each in detail.

Trademark and Copyright Licensing

Trademark licensing grants a firm permission to use another firm's proprietary names, characters, or logos for a specified period of time in exchange for a royalty. Trademarks appear on such merchandise as clothing, games, food, beverages, gifts, novelties, toys, and home furnishings. Organizations and individuals with name-brand appeal benefit from trademark licensing, such as Coca-Cola, Harley-Davidson, Laura Ashley, Disney, Michael Jordan, and even your favorite university. A famous trademark like Harry Potter can generate millions of dollars to the owner with little effort. U.S. companies derive trademark-licensing revenues well in excess of $100 billion annually.

The Japanese firm Sanrio licenses its trademark characters to apparel and accessory manufacturers worldwide, generating substantial revenue. Shown here is the Hello Kitty store in Osaka, Japan.

In the United States and a number of other countries, firms acquire rights to trademarks through first use and continuous usage. In other countries, however, rights to trademarks are acquired through registration with government authorities. When a firm registers its trademark, it formally notifies government authorities that it owns the trademark and is entitled to intellectual property protection. Many countries require local use of the registered mark to maintain the registration.

The convention of gaining ownership to a trademark simply through registration has caused concerns for many firms. When it wanted to enter South Africa in the 1990s, McDonald's was frustrated to learn that a local businessperson had already applied to register the McDonald's trademark for his own use and to have the company's rights to the trademark withdrawn.[9] When McDonald's protested in court to establish its ownership, the South African Supreme Court ruled in favor of the local entrepreneur. The company eventually won on appeal but only after spending a significant sum on legal fees.

Winnie the Pooh (disney.go.com/pooh) is one of the biggest success stories of trademark licensing. Introduced as a character in children's literature in 1926, Pooh evolved into a multi-billion-dollar licensing property. Acquired by Disney in 1961, it is the second-highest earning fictional character of all time, behind only Mickey Mouse. The Pooh image is licensed to many manufacturers for inclusion on a range of products from baby merchandise to textiles to gardening products. There are roughly 1,000 Pooh licensees in Europe alone.[10]

In many countries, a *copyright* gives the owner the exclusive right to reproduce the work, prepare derivative works, distribute copies, or perform or display the work publicly. Original works include art, music, and literature, as well as computer software. The term of protection varies by country, but the creator's life plus 50 years is typical. Because many countries offer little or no copyright protection, it is wise to investigate local copyright laws before publishing a work abroad.[11]

Know-How Licensing

Know-how agreement

Contract in which the focal firm provides technological or management knowledge about how to design, manufacture, or deliver a product or a service.

Gaining access to technology is an important rationale for licensing. A **know-how agreement** is a contract in which the focal firm provides technological or management knowledge about how to design, manufacture, or deliver a product or a service to a licensee in exchange for a royalty. The royalty may be a lump sum, a *running royalty* based on the volume of products produced from the know-how, or a combination of both.

In some industries, such as pharmaceuticals and semiconductors, inventions and other intellectual property are acquired in reciprocal licensing arrangements between firms in the same or similar industries. Known as *cross-licensing*, the practice is common in industries with rapid technological advances that often build on each other. Technology licensing from competitors reduces the cost of innovation by avoiding duplication of research, while reducing the risk of excluding any one firm from access to new developments.

AT&T (www.att.com) once held most of the key patents in the semiconductor industry. As more firms entered the industry and the pace of research and development (R&D) quickened, AT&T risked being surpassed by competitors in Europe, Japan, and the United States, where thousands of semiconductor patents were being awarded. In such a complex network of patents, few firms would have succeeded without obtaining licenses from competitors. AT&T, Intel, Siemens, and numerous other competitors began licensing their patents to each other, creating synergies that greatly accelerated innovation in semiconductors.

Rank	Firm Name	Annual Licensing Revenues (U.S. $ billions)	Typical Deals
1	Disney Consumer Products	$30.0	Toy and apparel licensing for Disney movies such as *Little Mermaid* and *Hannah Montana: The Movie*, and characters such as Winnie the Pooh and Mickey Mouse
2	ICONIX	6.5	Apparel licensing for such brands as OP, Starter, and Danskin
3	Warner Bros. Consumer Products	6.0	Toy and apparel licensing from movies such as *Batman*, *Scooby-Doo*, and *Harry Potter*
4	Marvel Entertainment	5.7	Toy, game, and apparel licensing for Marvel comic characters such as *Iron Man*, *Fantastic Four*, and *X-Men*
5	Nickelodeon & Viacomm Consumer Products	5.5	Toy and apparel licensing for TV programs such as *SpongeBob SquarePants* and *Dora the Explorer*
6	Major League Baseball	5.1	Baseball-related video games, apparel, toys
7	Phillips-Van Heusen	5.0	Apparel and accessories licensing for such brands as *Arrow*, *Izod* and *Van Heusen*
8	Sanrio (Japan)	4.5	Toys and apparel tied to the *Hello Kitty* character
9	The Collegiate Licensing Company	4.3	Licensed merchandise for universities and collegiate sports teams
10	The Cherokee Group	4.0	Apparel and shoes tied to Cherokee and Sideout brands

Exhibit 16.2   Leading Licensors Ranked by Licensing Revenues

SOURCE: *License! Global* (2009). "Top 100 Global Licensors," April, pp.19–41.

In the pharmaceutical industry, the R&D expense to develop new drugs can reach billions of dollars. Pharmaceutical firms want to launch new drugs quickly in order to recoup these costs and expedite product development. Thus, the firms frequently cross-license technologies to each other, exchanging scientific knowledge about producing specific products, as well as the right to distribute them in certain geographic regions.[12] In other industries, firms may license technology and know-how from competitors to compensate for insufficient knowledge, fill gaps in their product line-ups, enter new businesses, or save time and money.

The World's Top Licensing Firms

Exhibit 16.2 lists the world's leading licensing firms by annual revenues. All but one (Sanrio) are based in the United States. The greatest amount of licensing occurs in the apparel, games, and toy industries. In late 2009, Disney acquired Marvel Entertainment for $4 billion, greatly expanding Disney's inventory of licensed assets. Licensing sales have benefited immensely from the emergence of large-scale retailers, such as Walmart and Carrefour, and Internet-based selling.

 ## Advantages and Disadvantages of Licensing

Exhibit 16.3 summarizes the advantages and disadvantages of licensing from the per-spective of the licensor. Let's highlight some key points.

Advantages	Disadvantages
• Does not require capital investment or presence of the licensor in the foreign market	• Revenues are usually more modest than with other entry strategies
• Ability to generate royalty income from existing intellectual property	• Difficult to maintain control over how the licensed asset is used
• Appropriate for entering markets that pose substantial country risk	• Risk of losing control of important intellectual property, or dissipating it to competitors
• Useful when trade barriers reduce the viability of exporting or when governments restrict ownership of local operations by foreign firms	• The licensee may infringe the licensor's intellectual property and become a competitor
• Useful for testing a foreign market prior to entry via FDI	• Does not guarantee a basis for future expansion in the market
• Useful as a strategy to preemptively enter a market before rivals	• Not ideal for products, services, or knowledge that are highly complex
	• Dispute resolution is complex and may not produce satisfactory results

Exhibit 16.3 Advantages and Disadvantages of Licensing to the Licensor

Advantages of Licensing

Licensing requires neither substantial capital investment nor direct involvement of the licensor in the foreign market. Unlike other entry strategies, the licensor need not establish a physical presence in the market or maintain inventory there. Simultaneously, the licensee benefits by gaining access to a key technology at a much lower cost and in less time than if it had developed the technology on its own.[13] Licensing makes entry possible in countries that restrict foreign ownership in security-sensitive industries, such as defense and energy. Licensing also facilitates entry in markets that are difficult to enter because of trade barriers, tariffs, and bureaucratic requirements, which usually apply only to exporting or FDI. Licensing can be used as a low-cost strategy to test the viability of foreign markets. By establishing a relationship with a local licensee, the foreign firm can learn about the target market and devise the best future strategy for establishing a more durable presence there. For example, Swiss pharmaceutical manufacturer Roche entered a licensing agreement with Chugai Pharmaceuticals in Japan, where success requires substantial knowledge of the local market and the drug approval process. The relationship accelerated Roche's penetration of the huge Japanese market.[14] Licensing can also help the firm develop its brand name in a target market and preempt the later entry of competitors.

Disadvantages of Licensing

From the licensor's standpoint, licensing is a relatively passive entry strategy. Profits tend to be lower than those from exporting or FDI, and licensing does not guarantee a basis for future expansion. To earn royalties, the licensor must rely on the licensee's sales and marketing prowess. A weak partner will provide only meager royalties. Also, licensing provides limited control over how the licensor's asset is used. If the licensee produces a substandard product, the licensor's reputation can be harmed. To avoid such problems, experienced firms require foreign licensees to meet minimum quality and performance standards. For example, Budweiser beer is made and distributed in Japan through a licensing arrangement with Kirin (www.kirin.co.jp/english). Kirin is one of Japan's most reputable brewers and produces the beer according to Budweiser's strict standards.

If the licensee is very successful, the licensor may regret not entering the market through a more lucrative entry strategy. This happened to Disney, which developed Disneyland Tokyo through a licensing arrangement with a Japanese partner. When the theme park proved more successful than originally forecast, Disney management wished it had used FDI to develop Disneyland Tokyo itself. In Mexico, Televisa (www.televisa.com), the largest producer of Spanish-language TV programming, opted for a licensing arrangement with California-based Univision to enter the U.S. market. Although there are more than 35 million native Spanish speakers in the United States, Televisa receives only 9 percent of Univision's Spanish market advertising revenue.

Because licensing requires sharing intellectual property with other firms, the risk of creating a future competitor is substantial.[15] The rival may exploit the licensor's intellectual property by entering third countries or creating products based on knowledge gained in the relationship. This scenario has played out in the auto, computer chip, and consumer electronics industries in Asia as Western firms have transferred process technologies to firms in China, Japan, and South Korea. Japan's Sony (www.sony.net) originally licensed transistor technology from U.S. inventor Bell Laboratories to make hearing aids. But instead Sony used the technology to create small, battery-powered transistor radios and soon grew to become a global leader in this product.[16]

The U.S. toymaker Mattel licensed rights to distribute the Barbie doll to the Brazilian toymaker Estrela (www.estrela.com.br). Once the agreement expired, Estrela developed its own Barbie look-alike –"Susi"—which surpassed Brazilian sales of Barbie dolls. Estrela then launched the Susi doll throughout South America to great success. In Japan, Mattel entered a licensing agreement with local toymaker Takara (www.takaratomy.co.jp), which adapted the Barbie doll for Japanese girls. When the agreement expired, Takara continued to sell the doll under the name "Jenny," becoming a competitor to Mattel in the world's second-biggest toy market.[17]

Licensors run the risk of creating competitors, as Mattel discovered when it granted a license to a Brazilian firm to market Barbie dolls. The latter firm went on to create a competitor to Barbie, the Susi doll.

 Franchising as an Entry Strategy

Franchising is an advanced form of licensing in which the focal firm, the *franchisor,* allows an entrepreneur, the *franchisee,* the right to use an entire business system in exchange for compensation. As with licensing, an explicit contract defines the terms of the relationship. McDonald's, Subway, Hertz, and FedEx are well-established international franchisors. Others that use franchising to expand abroad include Benetton, Body Shop, Yves Rocher, and Marks & Spencer. Franchising is common in international retailing. However, some retailers such as IKEA and Starbucks have a strong preference for internationalizing through company-owned outlets. Ownership provides these firms with greater control over foreign operations but also typically restricts their ability to expand more rapidly abroad.

Although there are various types of franchising, the most typical arrangement is *business format franchising* (sometimes called *system franchising*).[18] Exhibit 16.4 shows the nature of the franchising agreement. The franchisor transfers to the franchisee a total business method, including production and marketing methods, sales systems, procedures, and management know-how, as well as the use of its name and usage rights for products, patents, and trademarks.[19] The franchisor also provides the franchisee with training, ongoing support, incentive programs, and the right to participate in cooperative marketing programs.

Exhibit 16.4
Franchising as a Foreign
Market Entry Strategy

SOURCE: Adapted from Welch (1992)
and personal correspondence with
Lawrence Welch.

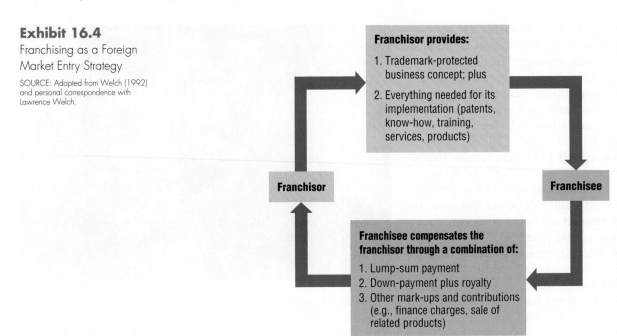

Franchisor provides:

1. Trademark-protected business concept; plus

2. Everything needed for its implementation (patents, know-how, training, services, products)

Franchisor

Franchisee

Franchisee compensates the franchisor through a combination of:

1. Lump-sum payment
2. Down-payment plus royalty
3. Other mark-ups and contributions (e.g., finance charges, sale of related products)

In return, the franchisee pays some type of compensation to the franchisor, usually a royalty representing a percentage of the franchisee's revenues. The franchisee may be required to purchase certain equipment and supplies from the franchisor to ensure standardized products and consistent quality. Burger King and Subway require franchisees to buy food preparation equipment from specified suppliers.

While licensing relationships are often short-lived, franchising parties normally establish an ongoing relationship that may last many years, making for a more stable long-term entry strategy. In addition, franchisors often combine franchising with other entry strategies. For example, about 70 percent of the more than 2,400 Body Shop stores worldwide are operated by franchisees, while the rest are owned by Body Shop headquarters (www.thebodyshop.com). Large retailers such as Carrefour often employ both franchising and FDI when expanding abroad.

Franchising is more comprehensive than licensing because the franchisor prescribes virtually all of the business activities of the franchisee. The franchisor tightly controls the business system to ensure consistent standards. International franchisors employ globally recognized trademarks and attempt to guarantee the customer a uniform retail experience and consistent product quality. Completely standardized business activities, however, are difficult to replicate across diverse markets. Differences in franchisee resources, key ingredients, worker qualifications, and physical space may necessitate changes to the franchise formula. Space restrictions in Japan forced KFC to reconfigure its cooking equipment from a wide horizontal design, common in the United States, to a narrower, more vertical design that saves space. Japanese KFCs also tend to be multistoried restaurants to save on the high cost of land. The challenge is to strike the right balance, adapting the format to respond to local markets without affecting the overall image and service of the franchise.[20]

Some focal firms may choose to work with a single, coordinating franchisee in a particular country or region. In this **master franchise** arrangement, an independent company is licensed to establish, develop, and manage the entire franchising network in its market. The master franchisee has the right to subfranchise to other independent businesses and thus assume the role of the local franchisor. McDonald's is organized this way in Japan. From the focal firm's perspective, the arrangement is the least capital- and time-intensive. By delegating the responsibilities of identifying and working with its franchisees directly, the focal firm gives up considerable control over its foreign market operations.

Master franchise Arrangement in which an independent company is licensed to establish, develop, and manage the entire franchising network in its market and has the right to subfranchise to other franchisees, assuming the role of local franchisor.

Master franchisees prefer this arrangement because it provides them with an exclusive, large, predefined territory (often an entire country) and substantial economies of scale based on operating numerous sales outlets simultaneously. They gain access to a proven retailing and marketing concept and partnership with a corporate headquarters and master franchisees in other territories, which typically provide support, know-how, and the latest innovations in the field. Master franchising accounts for as much as 80 percent of international franchising deals. Sbarro, Inc., the pizza chain, operates via master franchises in Belgium, Britain, Canada, Guatemala, Kuwait, and the Philippines.[21]

Franchisors are internationalizing rapidly. The *Global Trend* feature discusses the internationalization of franchisors, particularly in emerging markets.

Who Are the Top Global Franchisors?

Franchising is a global phenomenon and accounts for a large proportion of international trade in services, especially fast-food outlets, professional business services, home improvement, and various types of retailers.[22]

U.S. firms dominate international franchising, especially in the fast-food industry. Although McDonald's has been operating in Russia for more than 20 years, Russia's first Burger King opened in Moscow in January 2010. What competitive advantages do you think Burger King might have over McDonald's in Russia?

GL BAL TREND

Internationalization of Franchising: Emerging Markets

International franchising has a prosperous history going back to the 1970s, when U.S. brands such as McDonald's, Burger King, KFC, and Pizza Hut became familiar sights in cities around the world. Australia, Britain, Canada, Japan, the United States, and countries in Europe have long been popular franchise destinations. Historically, U.S. franchisors have targeted Europe as their initial market abroad, and within Europe, Britain is often the first choice because of its linguistic and cultural familiarity.

Franchisors view international expansion as an important way to diversify their portfolios. One survey found that nearly two-thirds of franchisors currently franchise or operate in international locations. Top management at almost three-quarters of them indicate they plan to start or accelerate international ventures. When expanding abroad, franchisors need to consider the economic health of a country or region, availability of qualified labor, and other factors that will lead to sustained growth.

Most firms, especially fast-food franchisors, prefer entering a new national market via a master franchising approach. The advantages are increased speed of market development, relatively small capital outlay, and access to knowledgeable local entrepreneurs to help navigate the often-complex conditions in foreign markets.

As markets in Europe and other advanced economies become saturated, franchisors look increasingly to emerging markets, such as Brazil, China, India, Mexico, and Russia.

Subway is doing big business in Eastern Europe. Avis car rental has enjoyed much success in Latin America. Ben & Jerry's is dishing up ice cream in Thailand and Turkey. Emerging markets account for half the world's population and present the most dynamic potential for long-term growth.

SOURCES: Stephen Choo, Tim Mazzarol, and Geoff Soutar, "The Selection of International Retail Franchisees in East Asia," *Asia Pacific Journal of Marketing and Logistics* 19, no. 4 (2007): 380–89; A. Kazmin, "Attention to Local Palates Pays Off," *Financial Times*, January 29, 2010, p. 3; G. Knack, "Strategies for International Development in Uncertain Times," *Franchising World*, November 2008, pp. 75–76; M. Shay, "Franchising Is Key to Global Economic Recovery," *Franchising World*, March 2009, p. 6; Dianne Welsh, Ilan Alon, and Cecilia Falbe, "An Examination of International Retail Franchising in Emerging Markets," *Journal of Small Business Management* 44, no. 1 (2006): 130–49.

Subway (www.subway.com) is the third-largest U.S. fast-food chain in China, where its fish and tuna salad sandwiches are top sellers. Exhibit 16.5 profiles several other leading global franchisors.[23]

The United States is home to the largest number of franchisors and dominates international franchising. U.S. franchisors and their franchisees account for roughly $1 trillion in annual U.S. retail sales—an astonishing 40 percent of total U.S. retail sales. Approximately one in every twelve retail establishments in the United States is a franchised business.[24] The United Kingdom is home to numerous home-grown franchisors, like Eden Delicious and Perfect Pizza. Annual franchised sales of fast food in Britain are said to account for 30 percent of all food eaten outside the home.

The ability to exchange information instantaneously through the Internet enhances the franchisor's ability to control international operations and saves time and money. Some franchisees use electronic point-of-sale equipment that links their sales and inventory data to the franchisor's central warehouse and distribution network. Information technology also allows the franchisor to serve customers or franchisees with central accounting and other business process functions.

Franchisor	Type of Business	International Profile	Major Markets
Subway	Submarine sandwiches & salads	32,239 shops in 90 countries	Canada, Australia, UK, New Zealand, Germany
McDonald's	Fast-food restaurants	32,000 restaurants in 120 countries	Canada, France, UK, Australia, China
7-Eleven	Convenience stores	35,141 stores in 15 countries	Japan, Thailand, Mexico, United States
Dunkin Donuts	Coffee and donuts	8,924 restaurants in 30 countries	China, Japan, Taiwan
Jani-King	Commercial cleaning	13,046 franchisees in 18 countries	Canada, Australia, Brazil, France, Malaysia
Kumon Math & Reading Centers	Supplemental education	26,311 franchises in 40 countries	Canada, Japan, United States
Pizza Hut	Pizza, pasta, chicken wings	13,500 outlets in 98 countries	China, Brazil, Canada, Japan
Curves	Women's fitness & weight-loss	10,000 centers in 60 countries	Brazil, France, Mexico, Australia, Ireland, UK
UPS Store / Mail Boxes Etc.	Postal, business, and communications services	6,000 locations in 40 countries	Canada, Germany, China, India
WSI Internet	Internet services	1,700 franchises in 87 countries	Canada, UK

Exhibit 16.5   Leading International Franchisors

SOURCES: Entrepreneur.com; Hoovers.com; company Web sites and reports.

Advantages and Disadvantages of Franchising

In an ideal relationship, franchisor and franchisee complement each other. The franchisor possesses economies of scale, a wealth of intellectual property, and know-how about its industry, while the franchisee has entrepreneurial drive and substantial knowledge about the local market and how to run a business there. A large pool of well-chosen franchisees greatly enhances the speed and quality of the franchisor's performance abroad.[25] For example, KFC internationalized quickly and performed well worldwide by developing franchisees in 109 countries with more than 20,000 restaurants serving more than 12 million customers per day.

The Franchisor Perspective

Exhibit 16.6 highlights the advantages and disadvantages of franchising to the franchisor. Firms prefer franchising when they lack the capital or international experience to get established abroad through FDI, or when offering the product through exporting or basic licensing is ineffective as an internationalization strategy. Foreign markets often provide greater profitability than the home market. For example, the Beijing KFC store has generated more sales than any other KFC outlet worldwide partly due to the novelty and popularity of the offering and the lack of direct competition. Governments in host countries often encourage franchising by foreign entrants because most of the profits and investment remain in the local economy.

For the franchisor, franchising is a low-risk, low-cost entry strategy. It offers the ability to develop international markets relatively quickly and on a larger scale than possible for most nonfranchise firms. The franchisor can generate profit with only incremental investments in capital, staff, production, and distribution.

The major disadvantages include the need to maintain control over potentially thousands of outlets worldwide and the risk of creating competitors. When the franchising agreement is terminated, some franchisees leverage their newly acquired knowledge to remain in business, often by slightly altering the franchisor's brand name or trademark. Franchisees may also jeopardize the franchisor's image by not upholding its standards. Dunkin' Donuts experienced problems in Russia when it discovered some franchisees were selling vodka along with donuts.

When the franchisor depends heavily on a foreign partner as master franchisee, it is critical to cultivate friendly, durable relationships. However, even experienced franchisors sometimes encounter major challenges. In 2010, nearly 30 years after opening its first outlet in Japan, restaurant chain Wendy's could not reach a new agreement with its Japanese master franchisee, Zensho Company, and chose to close its seventy-one restaurants there.

Advantages	*Disadvantages*
• Entry into numerous foreign markets can be accomplished quickly and cost effectively	• Maintaining control over franchisee may be difficult
• No need to invest substantial capital	• Conflicts with franchisee are likely, including legal disputes
• Established brand name encourages early and ongoing sales potential abroad	• Preserving franchisor's image in the foreign market may be challenging
• The firm can leverage franchisees' knowledge to efficiently navigate and develop local markets	• Requires monitoring and evaluating performance of franchisees, and providing ongoing assistance
	• Franchisees may take advantage of acquired knowledge and become competitors in the future

Exhibit 16.6

Advantages and Disadvantages of Franchising to the Franchisor

The move disappointed countless Japanese fans, who formed long lines in front of Wendy's outlets in the days before the hamburger chain was shuttered.[26]

Another major challenge is to become familiar with foreign laws and regulations. The European Union has strict laws that favor the franchisee, which sometimes hamper the franchisor's ability to maintain control over operations. Laws and foreign exchange circumstances affect the payment of royalties.

Franchising emphasizes standardized products and marketing, but this does not imply 100 percent uniformity. Local franchisees exercise some latitude in tailoring offerings to local needs and tastes. McDonald's offers a McPork sandwich in Spain, a spicy chicken burger in China, teriyaki burgers in Japan, and wine in France. In its Beijing outlets, KFC offers shredded carrots, fungus, and bamboo shoots instead of the coleslaw it sells in Western countries. Also in China, Starbucks offers a Green Tea Cream Frappuccino, TCBY sells sesame-flavored frozen yogurt, and Mrs. Fields markets mango muffins.[27]

The Franchisee Perspective

Exhibit 16.7 highlights the advantages and disadvantages of franchising from the franchisee's side. Franchising is especially beneficial to SMEs, many of which lack substantial resources and strong managerial skills. The big advantage is the ability to launch a business using a tested business model. In essence, franchising amounts to cloning best practices. It greatly increases the small firm's chances for success by duplicating a tried-and-true business format.[28]

Managerial Guidelines for Licensing and Franchising

Licensing and franchising are complex undertakings and require skillful research, planning, and execution. The focal firm must conduct advance research on the host country's laws on intellectual property, repatriation of royalties, and contracting with local partners. Key challenges of the focal firm include establishing whose national law takes precedence for interpreting and enforcing the contract, deciding whether to grant an exclusive or nonexclusive arrangement, and determining the geographic scope of territory to be granted to the foreign partner.

As with other entry strategies, the most critical success factor is often finding the right partner abroad. The focal firm should carefully identify, screen, and train potential partners who are unlikely to become competitors in the future. The most qualified franchisees tend to have entrepreneurial drive, access to capital and prime real estate, a successful

---

Exhibit 16.7
Advantages and Disadvantages of Franchising to the Franchisee

Advantages	Disadvantages
• Gain a well-known, recognizable brand name	• Initial investment or royalty payments may be substantial
• Acquire training and know-how; receive ongoing support from the franchisor	• Franchisee is required to purchase supplies, equipment, and products from the franchisor only
• Operate an independent business	• The franchisor holds much power, including superior bargaining power
• Increase likelihood of business success	• Franchisor's outlets may proliferate in the region, creating competition for the franchisee
• Become part of an established international network	• Franchisor may impose inappropriate technical or managerial systems on the franchisee

business track record, good relationships with local and national government agencies, strong links to other firms (including facilitators), a pool of motivated employees, and a willingness to accept oversight and follow company procedures. In emerging markets, a knowledgeable, locally connected partner can help sort through various operational problems. In China and Russia, partnering with a state-owned enterprise may be necessary to gain access to key resources and navigate legal and political environments.

For franchisors, developing capable partners in local supply chains is also a prerequisite. Franchisees need a reliable supply chain to obtain input products and supplies. In developing economies and emerging markets, host-country suppliers may be inadequate for providing a sufficient quantity or quality of input goods. In Turkey, Little Caesars pizza franchisees found it difficult to locate dairy companies that could produce the cheese varieties they required. In other countries, KFC developed its own supply-chain network, ensuring dependable delivery of chicken and other critical inputs. In Russia and Thailand, McDonald's had to develop its own supply lines for potatoes to ensure the quality of its French fries. When McDonald's first entered India, it faced resistance from the government. Relations improved as the government recognized McDonald's would work with Indian farmers to improve the country's agricultural practices and was committed to being a good corporate citizen.

 ## Other Contractual Entry Strategies

In addition to licensing and franchising, several other types of contractual agreements in international business cover building major construction projects, manufacturing products under contract, providing management and marketing services, or leasing major assets. We devote Chapter 17 to global sourcing, a specific form of international contracting. Here, we discuss turnkey contracting, build-operate-transfer arrangements, management contracts, and leasing.

Turnkey Contracting

Turnkey contracting is an arrangement in which the focal firm or a consortium of firms plans, finances, organizes, manages, and implements all phases of a project abroad and then hands it over to a foreign customer after training local workers. Contractors are typically firms in construction, engineering, design, and architectural services. In a typical turnkey project, a contractor builds a major facility (such as a nuclear power plant or a subway system), puts it into operation, and then hands it over to the project sponsor, often a national government. The contractor may provide follow-up services such as testing and operational support.

Among the most popular turnkey projects are extensions and upgrades to metro systems, such as bridges, roadways, and railways, and the construction of airports, harbors, refineries, and hospitals. Financed largely from public budgets, most metro projects are in Asia and Western Europe, where demand is driven by intensifying urbanization and worsening congestion. In Abu Dhabi, a collection of companies received a multi-billion-dollar contract to build an integrated processing plant for natural gas. The team included JGC of Japan, Tecnimont of Italy, and Hyundai Engineering & Construction (HDEC; en.hdec.kr) of South Korea. HDEC has built industrial, infrastructure, commercial, and multifamily residential projects in about fifty countries.[29]

Another example is Hochtief AG of Germany and Skanska AB of Sweden. (See Exhibit 3.6 on page 106 for a list of leading firms.) They have undertaken some of the world's most important construction projects, such as the Three Gorges Dam in China and the Chunnel linking England to France. California-based Bechtel participated in projects such as the renovation of London's 140-year-old subway, the cleanup of the Chernobyl nuclear plant in Russia, and construction of nuclear power plants in South Korea.[30] In Hong Kong, a consortium of firms, including the French giant Bouygues

Turnkey contracting
Arrangement in which the focal firm or a consortium of firms plans, finances, organizes, manages, and implements all phases of a project abroad and then hands it over to a foreign customer after training local workers.

The spectacular Petronas Twin Towers complex in Kuala Lumpur, Malaysia, was a seven-year turnkey project built by Bovis Lend Lease, one of the world's leading project management and construction companies. Among the firms with offices in the Towers are Accenture, Al Jazeera English, Huawei Technologies, Microsoft, and Reuters.

(www.bouygues-construction.com), signed a $550 million contract to build the main highway running from Hong Kong into mainland China.[31]

Build-Operate-Transfer Arrangements (BOT)

Under a **build-operate-transfer (BOT)** arrangement, a firm or consortium of firms contracts to build a major facility abroad, such as a dam or water treatment plant; operates it for a specified period; and then transfers ownership to the project sponsor, typically the host-country government or public utility. This is a variation of turnkey contracting in which, instead of turning the completed facility over to the project sponsor, the builder first operates it for a number of years.

While the consortium operates the facility, it can charge user fees, tolls, and rentals to recover its investment and generate profits. Or the host-country government can pay the BOT partner for services provided by the facility, such as water from a treatment plant, at a price calculated over the life of the contract, to cover its construction and operating costs and provide a reasonable return.

Governments often grant BOT concessions to get needed infrastructure built cost effectively. Typical projects include sewage treatment plants, highways, airports, mass transit systems, and telecommunications networks. In Vietnam, rapid growth in industry and tourism has greatly increased demand for electric power. The Vietnamese government commissioned the construction of the 720 megawatt *Phu My 3* power plant, the country's first privately owned major energy facility, as a BOT project by Siemens Power Generation (Germany). It is owned by a consortium that includes BP (Britain) and Kyushu Electric Power (Japan).[32]

Build-operate-transfer (BOT) Arrangement in which the firm or a consortium of firms contracts to build a major facility abroad, operate it for a specified period, and then hand it over to the project sponsor, typically the host-country government or public utility.

Management contract Arrangement in which a contractor supplies managerial know-how to operate a hotel, hospital, airport, or other facility in exchange for compensation.

Management Contracts

Under a **management contract**, a contractor supplies managerial know-how to operate a hotel, hospital, airport, or other facility in exchange for compensation. The client organization receives assistance in managing local operations, while the management company generates revenues without having to make a capital outlay. Much of Disney's income from its theme parks in France and Japan comes from providing management services for the parks, which are largely owned by other interests. BAA Limited manages the retailing and catering operations of various airports in Europe and the United States. Both the Marriott and Four Seasons corporations run numerous luxury hotels around the world through management contracts without owning them.

Management contracts can help foreign governments with infrastructure projects when the country lacks local people with the skills to run them. Occasionally the offering of a management contract is the critical element in winning a bid for other types of entry strategies, such as BOT deals and turnkey operations. A key disadvantage of management contracts is they involve training foreign firms that may become future competitors.[33]

Leasing

In international leasing, another contractual strategy, a focal firm (the lessor) rents out machinery or equipment to corporate or government clients abroad (lessees), often for several years at a time. The lessor retains ownership of the property throughout the lease period and receives regular payments from the lessee. From the perspective of the lessee, leasing helps reduce the costs of using needed machinery and equipment. A major advantage for the lessor is the ability to gain quick access to target markets, while putting assets to use earning profits. Leasing can be more profitable in international than in domestic markets because of tax regulations.[34] International leasing benefits developing economies that may lack the financial resources to purchase needed equipment.

Amsterdam-based ING Lease International Equipment Management owns and leases Boeing commercial aircraft to clients such as Brazil's Varig airlines. Dubai-based Oasis Leasing leases aircraft to Air New Zealand, Virgin Express, and Macedonian Airlines. One of the top leasing firms is Japan's ORIX (www.orix.co.jp), which leases everything from computers and measuring equipment to aircraft and ships. The firm operates 1,500 offices worldwide and generated $10.6 billion in revenues in 2009.

The Special Case of Internationalization by Professional Service Firms

Professional services include accounting, advertising, market research, consulting, engineering, legal counsel, and IT services. Firms in these industries have rapidly internationalized over the past three decades. Some simply follow their key clients abroad. The Internet has greatly aided the international spread of some business process services such as software engineering, which is increasingly centralized in cost-effective locations such as India and Eastern Europe.

Professional service firms encounter three unique challenges when going international. First, professional qualifications that allow firms to practice law, dentistry, medicine, or accounting in the home country are rarely recognized by other countries. If you are licensed as a Certified Public Accountant in the United States and want to practice accounting in Argentina, you must earn local certification in that country. Second, professionals who work abroad for long periods generally must obtain employment visas in the countries where they are employed. Third, professional services often require intensive interaction with the local public, which necessitates language and cultural skills.[35]

What international market entry strategies do professional service firms employ? Typically, they use a mix of direct investment and contractual strategies. An advertising agency such as Publicis Groupe, based in France, will maintain a network of company-owned branches around the world while simultaneously entering contractual relationships with independent local firms. Focal firms in professional services are likely to serve their major markets with direct investment and operate company-owned offices there. In small markets, however, they will enter contractual relationships with independent partner firms in the same line of business, typically known as *agents, affiliates,* or *representatives*. PriceWaterhouseCooper, a leading international accounting firm, can contract with indigenous accounting firms in smaller markets where it chooses not to have its own offices. Focal firms with limited international experience often prefer to employ foreign partners that can provide international business know-how.

 Guidelines for Protecting Intellectual Property

We've seen that working with independent partners through contractual arrangements provides the focal firm with only moderate control over foreign partners. Safeguarding intellectual property and foreign operations thus becomes a challenge. Laws that govern contractual obligations are not always clear, conflicts arise due to cultural and language differences, and contract enforcement abroad is often costly or unattainable. Ultimately, the best way to ensure foreign partners comply with contractual provisions and produce successful outcomes is to ensure their satisfaction with the relationship. Thus, management in the focal firm should seek close and trusting relationships with foreign partners by providing strong support and superior resources.

Infringement of intellectual property
Unauthorized use, publication, or reproduction of products or services protected by a patent, copyright, trademark, or other intellectual property right.

Infringement of intellectual property is the unauthorized use, publication, or reproduction of products and services protected by a patent, copyright, trademark, or other intellectual property right. Such a violation amounts to piracy and takes the form of production and distribution of counterfeit goods. See Exhibit 5.2 on page 161 for a list of losses from piracy in selected countries. For example, annual piracy losses in CDs and music are $117 million in Brazil, and losses in business software exceed $1 billion in Russia.

The total value of counterfeit and pirated goods crossing borders and traded online worldwide exceeds $600 billion annually.[36] Counterfeiters create knockoffs of clothing, fashion accessories, watches, medicines, appliances, and other products. Some use a product name that differs only slightly from that of a well-known brand; it is close enough that buyers inadvertently associate it with the genuine product but just different enough so that prosecution is hampered. While firms such as Rolex and Tommy Hilfiger are well-known victims, counterfeiting is also common in such industrial products as medical devices and car parts. Counterfeiters have even faked entire motor vehicles.[37]

Cisco Systems sued its Chinese joint venture partner, Huawei Technologies Co., for pirating its networking software and infringing patents. The lawsuit also cited Huawei, the largest telecommunications equipment manufacturer in China, for illegally using technical documentation that Cisco copyrighted in its own product manuals.[38] Although Microsoft's Windows and Office products dominate the software market, the firm receives no payment when its software is copied and distributed by unauthorized parties. Up to 90 percent of computer software in Russia may be pirated. As a result, Microsoft sells its products only to corporate customers. The firm battles piracy even among the employees in its Russian subsidiary.[39]

However, don't assume counterfeiting is confined only to lower-income countries. Raids of retail outlets in the United States net millions of dollars worth of counterfeit products every year. In one week in 2009, investigators closed thirty-one stores in New York City for selling counterfeit designer goods.[40]

The Internet has added a new dimension to international counterfeiting. In Russia, Web sites sell popular music downloads for as little as 5 cents each, or less than $1 for an entire CD. The sites are easily accessed by shoppers in countries where they are outlawed under intellectual property laws and use low prices to attract music fans worldwide.[41]

Counterfeiting and piracy erode the firm's competitive advantage and brand equity.[42] They can be particularly troublesome in emerging markets and developing economies, where intellectual property laws are usually weak or poorly enforced. Small and medium-sized enterprises are particularly vulnerable because they typically lack the resources to prosecute violators.

In advanced economies, intellectual property is usually protected within established legal systems and methods of recourse. A firm can initiate legal action against someone who infringes on its intellectual assets and will usually achieve a satisfactory remedy. Advanced economies have taken the lead in signing treaties that support international protection of intellectual property, including the Paris Convention for the Protection of Industrial Property, the Berne Convention for the Protection of Literary and Artistic Works, and the Rome Convention for the Protection of Performers and Broadcasting Organizations. The World Intellectual Property Organization (WIPO; www.wipo.int)—an agency of the United Nations—administers these multilateral agreements.

Recently, the World Trade Organization (WTO; www.wto.org) created the Agreement on Trade Related Aspects of Intellectual Property Rights (TRIPS), a comprehensive international treaty that lays out remedies, dispute-resolution procedures, and enforcements to protect intellectual property. The WTO is pressuring member countries to comply with the accord and can discipline violators through the dispute settlement mechanism. At the same time, TRIPS provides exceptions that benefit developing economies, such as the ability to access needed patent medication for ailments such as AIDS.

Firms working in countries that are not signatories to WIPO, TRIPS, or other treaties still face challenges. Rights granted by a patent, trademark registration, or copyright apply only in the country where they are obtained; they confer no protection abroad. Enforcement depends on the attitudes of local officials, substantive requirements of the law, and court procedures. As a result, former licensees and franchisees can launch illicit businesses using proprietary knowledge to which they are no longer entitled.

Experienced firms devise sophisticated strategies to reduce the likelihood of intellectual property violations and help avoid their adverse effects, especially in countries with weak property rights. Exhibit 16.8 illustrates such a set of strategies.[43] Let's elaborate further on key strategies:

- Understand local intellectual property laws and enforcement procedures, especially when exposed assets are valuable.

- Register patents, trademarks, trade secrets, and copyrights with the government in each country where the firm does, or intends to do, business. Also register in countries known to be sources of counterfeit products.

- Ensure that licensing and franchising agreements provide for oversight to ensure intellectual property is used as intended.

- Include a provision in licensing contracts that requires the licensee to share any improvements or technological developments on the licensed asset with the licensor.[44]

- Pursue criminal prosecution or litigation against those who infringe on protected assets, such as logos and proprietary processes. Mead Data Central, Inc., owner of the Lexis-Nexis brand of computerized legal research services, sued Toyota when the Japanese firm began selling its new luxury automobiles under the name "Lexus." The suit failed, but it shows Mead's determination to protect its assets.[45]

- Monitor franchisee, distribution, and marketing channels for any asset infringements. Monitor the activities of local business partners for potential leaks of vital information and assets.[46]

- Include in franchise contracts a requirement that the franchisee, suppliers, and distributors report infringements of products or processes, if discovered.

- Guard trade secrets closely. Use password-based security systems, surveillance, and firewalls to limit access to intellectual property. Intel and Microsoft release only limited information about key technologies to partner firms.

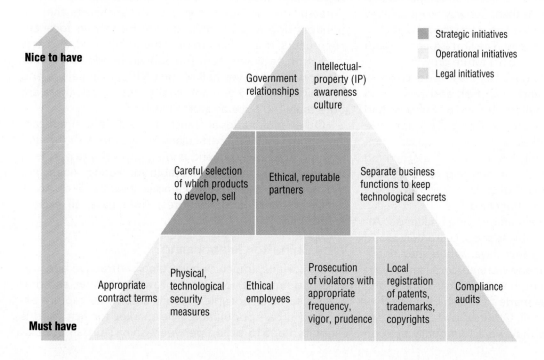

Exhibit 16.8 The Pyramid of Intellectual Property Protection

SOURCE: Meagan Dietz, Sarena Shao-Tin Lin, and Lei Yang. (2005). "Protecting Intellectual Property in China," *The McKinsey Quarterly,* number 3.

- Include noncompete clauses in employee contracts for all positions to prevent employees from serving competitors for up to three years after leaving the firm.[47]
- Use contemporary technology to minimize counterfeiting. Many firms build biotech tags, electronic signatures, or holograms into their products to differentiate them from fakes.
- Continuously update technologies and products. The firm that regularly renews its technology can stay ahead of counterfeiters by offering products that counterfeiters cannot imitate fast enough. Also differentiate products by emphasizing a strong brand name. Customers usually prefer established brands that feature the latest technology.

In the long run, the best way to cope with the consequences of infringement is to sustain competitiveness through innovation and constant technological advances. Then, even when licensing violations occur, the firm is protected because the stolen property rapidly becomes obsolete. Firms also lobby national governments and international organizations for stronger intellectual property laws and more vigilant enforcement, with limited success. Ultimately, when contractual strategies prove undesirable or ineffective, management may opt to enter target markets via FDI, through which the firm acquires ownership, and thus greater control, over important assets.

Closing Case

Subway and the Challenges of Franchising in China

Subway, the fast-food marketer of submarine sandwiches and salads, has more than 32,000 stores in ninety-one countries and generates some $12 billion in annual revenues. The franchising chain opened its first international restaurant in Bahrain in 1984. Since then, Subway (www.subway.com) has expanded worldwide and generates about one-fifth of its annual revenues abroad. The firm expects foreign markets to contribute to much of its future growth.

Subway is the third-largest U.S. fast-food chain in China, after McDonald's and KFC. Fish and tuna salad sandwiches are the top sellers. By 2006, Subway had opened fewer than forty stores in China. The franchise had its share of initial setbacks. Subway's master franchisee in Beijing, Jim Bryant, lost money to a scheming partner and had to teach the franchising concept to a country that had never heard of it. Until recently, there was no word in Chinese for "franchise."

Cultural problems remain an ongoing challenge. After Bryant opened his first Subway shop, customers stood outside and watched for a few days. When they finally tried to buy a sandwich, many were so confused Bryant had to print signs explaining how to order. Some didn't believe the tuna salad was made from fish because they could not see the head or tail. Others didn't like the idea of touching their food, so they would gradually peel off

the paper wrapping and eat the sandwich like a banana. To make matters worse, few customers liked sandwiches.

But Subway—or Sai Bei Wei (Mandarin for "tastes better than others")—is forging ahead. Bryant managed to recruit a few highly committed franchisees that he monitors closely to maintain quality. He recruits local entrepreneurs, trains them to become franchisees, and acts as a liaison between them and Subway headquarters. For this work, he receives half of their $10,000 initial fee and one-third of their 8 percent royalty fees. Today, there are more than 140 Subway stores in China.

Other multinational franchisors still face significant challenges in China, particularly in dealing with the ambiguous legal environment, finding appropriate partners, and identifying the most suitable marketing, financing, and logistics strategies. Famous brands like A&W, Dunkin' Donuts, and Rainforest Cafe have all experienced these issues.

Why China for Franchising?

On the surface, franchising in China is attractive because of its huge market, long-term growth potential, and dramatic rise in disposable income among its rapidly expanding urban population. The market for fast food is estimated at $15 billion per year. China's urban population, the target market for casual dining, has expanded at a 5 percent compound annual growth rate over the past several years, a trend expected to continue. Increasingly hectic lifestyles have led to an increase in meals the Chinese eat outside the home. Surveys reveal that Chinese consumers are interested in sampling non-Chinese foods.

Market researchers have identified several major benefits to franchising in China:

- *A win-win proposition.* Restaurants were one of the first industries the government opened to private ownership in the early 1980s. Franchising in China combines the Western know-how of franchisors with the local market knowledge of franchisees. Many Chinese have strong entrepreneurial instincts and are eager to launch their own businesses.

- *Minimal entry costs.* Because much of the cost of launching a restaurant is borne by local entrepreneurs, franchising minimizes the costs to franchisors of entering the market.

- *Rapid expansion.* By leveraging the resources of numerous local entrepreneurs, the franchisor can get set up quickly. Franchising is superior to other entry strategies for rapidly establishing many outlets throughout any new market.

- *Brand consistency.* Because franchisors are required to strictly adhere to company operating procedures and policies, brand consistency is easier to maintain.

- *Circumvention of legal constraints.* Franchising allows the focal firm to avoid trade barriers associated with exporting and FDI, common in China.

Challenges of Franchising in China

China's market also poses many challenges for franchisors:

- *Knowledge gap.* Despite the likely pool of potential franchisees, realistically, few Chinese have significant knowledge about how to start and operate a business. There is still much confusion about franchising among lawmakers, entrepreneurs, and consumers. Focal firms must educate government officials, potential franchisees, and creditors on the basics of franchising, a process that consumes energy, time, and money.

- *Ambiguous legal environment.* Franchisors need to closely examine China's legal system regarding contracts and intellectual property rights. The Chinese government introduced regulations permitting franchising in 1997. The legal system is evolving and has numerous loopholes and ambiguities. Some critical elements are not covered. The situation has led to diverse interpretations of the legality of franchising in China. Franchisors must be vigilant about protecting trademarks. A local imitator can quickly dilute or damage a trademark a focal firm has built up through much expense and effort. Branding is important to franchising success, but consumers become confused if several similar brands are present. For instance, Starbucks fought a Shanghai coffee shop, which had copied its logo and name. The fast-food hamburger chain "Merry Holiday" uses a yellow color scheme and emphasizes the letter "M" in its signage, similar to McDonald's. There have been reports about fake Burger King restaurants operating in China. Large franchisors such as KFC and Pizza Hut are struggling to root out counterfeiters.

- *Escalating start-up costs.* Ordinarily, entry through franchising is cost-effective. However, various challenges, combined with linguistic and cultural barriers, can increase the up-front investment and resource demands of new entrants in China and delay profitability. Given the shortage of restaurant equipment in China, the franchisor may have to invest in store equipment and lease it to the franchisee, at least until the franchisee can afford to buy it. Franchisors must be patient. McDonald's has been in China since the early 1990s and has devoted substantial resources to building its brand. But few firms have its resources.

Perhaps the biggest challenge of launching franchises in China is finding the right partners. It is paradoxical that entrepreneurs with the capital to start a restaurant often lack the business experience or entrepreneurial drive, while entrepreneurs with sufficient drive and expertise often lack the start-up capital. Subway's franchise fee of $10,000 is equivalent to more than two years' salary for the average Chinese. China lacks an adequate system of banks and other capital sources for small business, so entrepreneurs often borrow funds from family members and friends to launch business ventures. Fortunately, Chinese banks are increasingly open to franchising. The Bank of China established a comprehensive credit line of $12 million for Kodak franchisees.

Availability and financing of suitable real estate are major considerations as well, particularly for initial showcase stores where location is critical. According to real estate laws enacted in 1990, local and foreign investors are allowed to develop, use, and administer real estate. But in many cases, the Chinese government owns real estate that is not available for individuals to purchase. Private property laws are underdeveloped, and franchisees occasionally risk eviction. Fortunately, a growing number of malls and shopping centers are good locations for franchised restaurants.

The Chinese authorities maintain restrictions on the repatriation of profits to the home country. Strict rules discourage repatriation of the initial investment, making this capital rather illiquid. To avoid this problem, firms make initial capital investments in stages to minimize the risk of not being able to withdraw overinvested funds. Fortunately, China is gradually relaxing its restrictions, and franchisors have been reinvesting their profits back into China to continue to fund the growth of their operations. Reinvesting profits also provides a natural hedge against exchange rate fluctuations.

Learning from the Success of Others

Experience has shown that new entrants to China often benefit from establishing a presence in Hong Kong and then moving inland to the southern provinces. Before it was absorbed by mainland China, Hong Kong was one of the world's leading capitalist economies. It is an excellent pro-business location to gain experience for doing business in China. In other cases, franchisors have launched stores in smaller Chinese cities, gaining experience there before expanding into more costly, competitive urban environments such as Beijing and Shanghai.

Adapting offerings to local tastes appears to be a prerequisite. Suppliers and business infrastructure in the country are often lacking. Franchisors spend much money to develop supplier and distribution networks. They may also need to build logistical infrastructure to move inputs from suppliers to individual stores. McDonald's has replicated its supply chain, bringing its key suppliers, such as potato supplier Simplot, to China. There is no one best approach in China. For instance, TGI Friday's imports roughly three-quarters of its food supplies, which helps maintain quality. But heavy importing is expensive and exposes profitability to exchange rate fluctuations.

AACSB: Reflective Thinking Skills, Multicultural and Diversity Understanding

Case Questions

1. Subway brings to China various intellectual property in the form of trademarks, patents, and an entire business system. What are the specific threats to Subway's intellectual property in China? What can Subway do to protect its intellectual property in China?

2. What do you think about Subway's method and level of compensating its master franchisee and regular franchisees in China? Is the method satisfactory? Is there room for improvement?

3. What are the advantages and disadvantages of franchising in China from Jim Bryant's perspective? What can Bryant do to overcome the disadvan-

tages? From Subway's perspective, is franchising the best entry strategy for China?

4. Subway faces various cultural challenges in China. What are these challenges, and what can Subway and its master franchisee do to overcome them?

SOURCES: Carlye Adler, "How China Eats a Sandwich," *Fortune*, March 21, 2005, pp. F210B–D; Ilan Alon, "Interview: International Franchising in China with Kodak," *Thunderbird International Business Review* 43, no. 6 (2001): 737–46; Bob Burke and Carol Wingard, "The Big Chill," *China Business Review* 24, no. 4 (1997): 12–18; Mark Clifford, "Companies: And They're Off," *Far Eastern Economic Review* 156, no. 48 (1998): 76–79; A. Dayal-Gulati and Angela Lee, *Kellogg on China: Strategies for Success* (Evanston, IL: Northwestern University Press, 2004); Richard Gibson, "Foreign Flavors: When Going Abroad, You Should Think of Franchising as a Cookie-Cutter Business; Unless, of Course, You Want to Succeed," *Wall Street Journal*, September 25, 2006, p. R8; Subway corporate Web site at http://www.subway.com.

CHAPTER ESSENTIALS

Key Terms

build-operate-transfer (BOT), p. 478
contractual entry strategies in international business, p. 464
franchising, p. 464
infringement of intellectual property, p. 480

intellectual property, p. 464
intellectual property rights, p. 464
know-how agreement, p. 468
licensing, p. 464

management contract, p. 478
master franchise, p. 472
royalty, p. 464
turnkey contracting, p. 477

Summary

In this chapter, you learned about:

1. **Contractual entry strategies**

   Contractual entry strategies in international business grant foreign partners permission to use the focal firm's **intellectual property** in exchange for a continuous stream of payments. **Intellectual property rights** are the legal claims through which the proprietary assets of firms and individuals are protected from unauthorized use by other parties. Firms run the risk of disclosing their intellectual property to outside partners. **Licensing** grants a firm the right to use another firm's intellectual property for a specified period of time in exchange for royalties or other compensation. **Franchising** allows one firm the right to use another's entire business system in exchange for fees, royalties, or other forms of compensation. A **royalty** is a fee paid to the licensor at regular intervals to compensate for the temporary use of intellectual property. Under a **know-how agreement,** the focal firm provides technological or managerial knowledge about how to design, manufacture, or deliver a product or service.

2. **Licensing as an entry strategy**

   The agreement between the licensor and the licensee is for a specific time period in a specific country or region. The licensor may enter an exclusive agreement with the licensee to minimize competition with other licensees in the same territory. Once the relationship is established and the licensee fully understands its role, the licensor has little additional input. Licensing is widely used in the fashion and toy industries.

3. **Advantages and disadvantages of licensing**

   Licensing's main advantage to the licensor is it does not require substantial capital investment or physical presence in the foreign market. The licensor can avoid political risk, government regulations, and other risks associated with FDI. However, licensing generates lower profits and limits the firm's ability to control its intellectual property. The licensee may become a competitor once the licensing agreement expires.

4. **Franchising as an entry strategy**

   Franchisors employ widely identifiable trademarks and attempt to guarantee the customer a consistent retail experience and product quality. A **master franchise** is an arrangement whereby a franchisee obtains the rights to, and is responsible for, developing franchised outlets to serve a country or a region. Franchising is common in international retailing but difficult to replicate across diverse markets.

5. **Advantages and disadvantages of franchising**

   Franchising allows franchisees to gain access to well-known, well-established brand names and business systems, allowing them to launch successful businesses with minimal risk. The franchisor can rapidly internationalize by leveraging the drive and knowledge of local franchisees but risks disseminating its intellectual property to unauthorized parties.

6. **Other contractual entry strategies**

   Under **build-operate-transfer (BOT)** arrangements, the firm contracts to build a major facility, such as a power plant, which it operates for a period of years and then transfers to the host-country government or other public entity. In **turnkey contracting,** one or several firms plan, finance, organize, and manage all phases of a project which, once completed, they hand over to a host-country customer. **Management contracts** occur when a company contracts with another to supply management know-how in the operation of a factory or service facility, such as a hotel. With leasing, the firm rents machinery or equipment, usually for a long period, to clients located abroad.

7. **Guidelines for protecting intellectual property**

   Infringement of intellectual property rights takes place through counterfeiting and piracy, which cost companies billions of dollars per year. Managers must proactively safeguard their proprietary assets by registering patents, trademarks, and other assets in each country and minimize operations in major counterfeiting countries and countries with weak intellectual property laws. Managers must also train employees and licensees in the proper legal use of intellectual property and vigilantly track down and prosecute violators.

Test Your Comprehension AACSB: **Reflective Thinking Skills**

1. Distinguish between the major types of intellectual property: trademarks, copyrights, patents, industrial designs, and trade secrets.

2. What are the major characteristics of licensing? What are the major characteristics of franchising?

3. What are the advantages and disadvantages of licensing?

4. What are the advantages and disadvantages of franchising from the perspective of franchisors and franchisees?

5. Name the industry sectors that rely the most on franchising to tap foreign markets?

6. Define and distinguish the following contractual entry strategies: build-operate-transfer, turnkey projects, management contracts, and leasing.

7. What are the best practices in managing international contractual relationships?

8. Suppose you work for a firm that holds valuable intellectual property and is contemplating various international business projects. What strategies would you recommend to management for protecting the firm's intellectual property?

Apply Your Understanding AACSB: **Communication Abilities, Reflective Thinking Skills**

1. Warner Brothers is doing a thriving business by licensing images of Harry Potter characters on its manufactured products, such as software, games, and clothing. However, illicit operators worldwide produce their own books, shirts, games, and other products that feature the Potter images—without entering a licensing agreement with Warner. What steps can Warner take to address this problem? How can it protect Harry Potter from intellectual property infringement around the world?

2. Suppose upon graduation you get a job with Hitachi America, Ltd. (www.hitachi.us), the U.S. subsidiary of the giant Japanese firm. Hitachi uses various contractual entry strategies in its international operations. These include build-operate-transfer and turnkey projects in the infrastructure development sector, management contracts to run nuclear power plants, and leasing of heavy earthmoving equipment to foreign governments. Hitachi America wants to extend its reach into Latin America. Prepare a brief report for senior management in which you explain the various ways to implement its existing entry strategies in this region.

3. *Ethical Dilemma:* You are the president of Dynamic Publishing, a firm that publishes textbooks. During a trip to various countries you assess the prospects for marketing Dynamic's textbooks abroad. Visiting a university in a developing country, you discover that many students use photocopied or locally reproduced versions of Dynamic's books. Upon investigation, you are advised that most students could not afford to attend college if they were required to pay full price for the books. You are appalled by the clear violation of intellectual property rights. You believe Dynamic cannot maintain profitability if its intellectual property is infringed. You also feel obligated to protect the rights of the authors of Dynamic's textbooks. At the same time, however, you are sympathetic to the students' plight. Using the Ethical Framework in Chapter 5, analyze the dilemma presented here. Should you try to enforce Dynamic's intellectual property rights, or should you look the other way and allow the illicit photocopying to continue? Is there a creative solution to this problem?

globalEDGE Internet Exercises
(http://globalEDGE.msu.edu)

AACSB: Reflective Thinking Skills

Refer to Chapter 1, page 62, for instructions on how to access and use globalEDGE™.

1. Suppose you've just started working in the office of the International Intellectual Property Alliance (IIPA; www.iipa.com). You learn that worldwide piracy of products is rampant. Your boss assigns you to draft a brief policy memo in which you address the following questions:

   - What is the worldwide scope of piracy? What industries are most affected by piracy, and what is the financial loss from piracy in each of these industries?
   - What are the top five countries that are the greatest sources of piracy?
   - What strategies do you recommend for combating piracy?

   In addition to globalEDGE™ and the IIPA portal, other useful sites for this exercise are the Office of the United States Trade Representative (www.ustr.gov), United Nations (www.un.org), and the Business Software Alliance (www.bsa.org).

2. Suppose you are an international entrepreneur and want to open your own franchise somewhere in Europe. You decide to conduct research to identify the most appropriate franchise and to learn how to become a franchisee. Entrepreneur.com publishes an annual list of the top 200 franchisors seeking international franchisees. Visit www.entrepreneur.com for the list or search for "franchising" at globalEDGE™. Choose the franchise that interests you most (for example, Subway, ServiceMaster, Century 21), and visit its corporate Web site. Based on information from the Web site, as well as globalEDGE™ and Hoovers.com, address the following questions:

   - How many franchised operations does this firm have outside its home country?

   - What are the major countries in which the firm has franchises? Are there any patterns in terms of the countries where this firm is established?
   - According to the application information provided at the corporate site, what qualifications is the firm seeking in new franchisees?
   - What types of training and support does the firm provide for its franchisees?

3. The International Licensing Industry Merchandisers' Association (LIMA; www.licensing.org) is an organization with offices worldwide. It fosters the growth and expansion of licensing by helping members network, educating members about licensing, and establishing standards of ethical and professional conduct in intellectual property licensing. Suppose you work for a small animation company that has developed several popular cartoon characters that have licensing potential, in the same way that Disney licenses its cartoon characters. Management would like to learn more about becoming a licensor of its cartoon characters. To begin licensing the characters to interested garment makers, school supply manufacturers, and similar firms, visit the LIMA Web site and write a memo that addresses the following:

   - Who are the major members of LIMA?
   - What are the major trade shows that your firm can attend to exhibit its licensable products and learn more about licensing?
   - What types of seminars and training are available to learn more about becoming a licensor?
   - Based on the information provided at the site, what can you learn about anti-counterfeiting activities and challenges in licensing?

CHAPTER 17

LEARNING OBJECTIVES In this chapter, you will learn about:

1. Outsourcing, global sourcing, and offshoring
2. Benefits of global sourcing
3. Risks of global sourcing
4. Strategies for minimizing the risks of global sourcing
5. Implementing global sourcing through supply-chain management
6. Global sourcing and corporate social responsibility

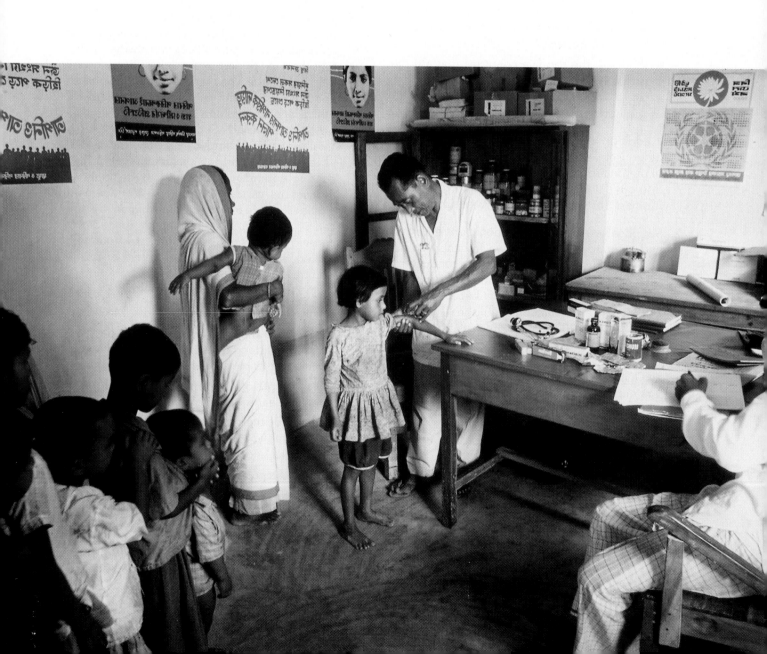

Global Sourcing

Global Sourcing of Pharmaceutical Drug Trials

In 2010, some two million people in India took part in human clinical trials for new drugs. Pharmaceutical firms now conduct nearly 40 percent of such trials in emerging markets because such countries offer numerous advantages: (1) lower costs for recruitment of physicians and patients, (2) large potential patient populations, (3) diversity of patients and medical conditions, and (4) less likelihood of patients taking other medicines that could interact with the drug under study. Clinical trials also provide a means to enter and learn about emerging markets, which pharmaceutical firms consider increasingly promising for future sales growth.

It currently costs more than $1 billion to develop and bring a new drug to market in the United States. More than half the cost is incurred in confirming drug safety and effectiveness in human drug trials required by the U.S. Food and Drug Administration (FDA; www.fda.gov) and similar agencies worldwide. Because recruiting patients accounts for approximately 40 percent of the trial budget, testing in emerging markets greatly reduces recruitment costs. According to GlaxoSmithKline, a drug trial costs about $30,000 on a per-patient basis in the United States versus about $3,000 in Romania. Lowering costs has become especially important in recent years, due to the recent global recession and pressures from governments worldwide to reduce health care expenditures.

Pharmaceutical firms typically outsource human drug trials to contract research organizations (CROs), which in turn hire physicians in local communities and hospitals to recruit patients. For example, almost every major Western pharmaceutical firm is conducting some of the required clinical trials in hospitals across Russia. The country's centralized hospital system recruits patients for trials quickly, which saves millions of dollars and several months of effort in the drug development process.

Offshoring of clinical trials can raise questions about ethics and oversight. While most trials in emerging markets have been conducted without problems, and patients there often consider them a way to access advanced medical treatment, some breakdowns have occurred. One study found a quarter of all trials in developing economies did not receive adequate official oversight to ensure compliance and safety. The FDA inspects only a small proportion of these trial sites. In a recent year, more than 500 drug trials were conducted in Russia at some 3,000 sites. In that same year, the FDA was able to inspect only about 100 sites worldwide. It criticized more than 30 percent of those inspected for failure to follow protocol and cited nearly 10 percent for failure to report adverse patient reactions of the trial drugs. The European Medicines Agency (EMA; www.ema.europa.eu), the EU's drugs regulator, made only a few dozen inspections for "good clinical practice" in 2009.

Numerous physicians in Russia triple or quadruple their monthly incomes by operating as trial investigators and recruiting patients. This financial incentive raises potential conflicts for doctors, some of whom may induce patients to participate. Some trials have endangered patients or been conducted without proper ethical review. Pfizer was sued for testing a meningitis drug on Nigerian children without their parents' consent, resulting in five deaths. A Nigerian human clinical trial for an antiretroviral drug was shut down amid concerns that researchers did not store the drugs or handle the scientific data properly.

SOURCES: Dinesh Sharma, "Outsourcing Big Pharma," *Health Affairs*, March 2010, pp. 563–64; Geeta Anand and Shirley Wang, "New Concern for Drug Tests Abroad," *Wall Street Journal*, March 23, 2009, p. B2; M. Bloch, A. Dhankhar, and S. Narayanan, "Pharma Leaps Offshore," *McKinsey Quarterly*, July 2006, p. 12; A. T. Kearney, "Make Your Move: Taking Clinical Trials to the Best Location," 2010, retrieved from http://www.atkearney .com; Pete Engardio, Arlene Weintraub, and Nandini Lakshman, "Outsourcing the Drug Industry," *Business Week*, September 15, 2008, p. 48; Philip Fiscus, "Global Risks for Drug Manufacturers," *Risk Management*, May 2009, p. 55; Andrew Jack, "Drugs Company Ethics on Trial in Developing World," *Financial Times*, June 8, 2009, retrieved from http://www.ft.com; PhRMA, *Pharmaceutical Industry Profile 2009*, retrieved from http://www.phrma .org; D. Ramesh, "Cost Cutting Becomes the Pharma Industry's Mantra," *Chemical Week*, September 28–October 5, 2009, pp. 24–27; Shirley Wang, "Most Clinical Trials Done Abroad," *Wall Street Journal*, February 19, 2009, p. D3.

As the opening vignette suggests, companies in the pharmaceutical industry frequently reduce product development costs and increase speed to market by sourcing a portion of their human clinical trials in emerging markets. Global sourcing has changed the way companies do business in all kinds of industries. Focal firms shop the world for inputs or finished products to meet efficiency and strategic objectives and to remain competitive. The search for the best sources of products and services is an ongoing task for managers. Many of the products sold by general retailers such as Best Buy and Marks & Spencer are sourced from low-cost suppliers in emerging markets. Steinway procures parts and components from a dozen foreign countries to produce its grand pianos. HP provides much of its technical support to customers from call centers in India.

In many cases, firms move entire sections of their value chains abroad, such as R&D, manufacturing, or technical support. In the sports apparel industry, firms such as Nike and Reebok contract out nearly all their athletic shoe production to lower-cost foreign manufacturers. Today, Nike and Reebok function primarily as brand owners and marketers, not as manufacturers. Apple sources some 70 percent of its production abroad while focusing internal resources on continuously improving its software platforms. This allows Apple management to optimize usage of the firm's finite capital resources and focus on its core competencies.

The total worldwide sourcing market for product manufacturing and services exceeded $300 billion in 2009. The total *potential* market is estimated to be nearly $1 trillion. The IT industry alone in India now employs more than two million people. Worldwide, the most frequently outsourced business processes include logistics and procurement, sales and marketing, and customer service, followed by finance and accounting.[1] Global sourcing by the private sector now accounts for more than half of all imports by major countries.[2]

 ## Outsourcing, Global Sourcing, and Offshoring

Outsourcing   The procurement of selected value-adding activities, including production of intermediate goods or finished products, from independent suppliers.

Business process outsourcing (BPO)   The outsourcing to independent suppliers of business service functions such as accounting, payroll, human resource functions, travel services, IT services, customer service, or technical support.

Outsourcing refers to the procurement of selected value-adding activities, including production of intermediate goods or finished products, from external independent suppliers. Firms outsource because they generally are not superior at performing *all* value-chain activities and it is more cost effective to outsource these activities. **Business process outsourcing (BPO)** occurs when firms procure, from an external supplier, such services as accounting, payroll, human resource functions, travel services, IT services, customer service, and/or technical support.[3] Firms contract with third-party service providers to reduce the cost of performing service tasks that are not part of the firm's core competencies or not critical to maintaining its competitive position in the market-place. BPO can be divided into two categories: *back-office activities*, which include internal, upstream business functions such as payroll and billing, and *front-office activities*, which include downstream, customer-related services such as marketing or technical support.

In undertaking outsourcing, managers face two key decisions: (1) which, if any, value-chain activities should be outsourced, and (2) where in the world these activities should be performed. Let's consider these choices.

Decision 1: Outsource or Not?

Managers must decide between *internalization* and *externalization*—whether each value-adding activity should be conducted in house or by an external, independent supplier. In business, this is traditionally known as the *make or buy* decision: "Should we make a product or perform a value-chain activity ourselves, or should we source it from an outside contractor?"

Firms usually internalize those value-chain activities they consider part of their *core competencies*, those that require the use of proprietary knowledge and trade secrets they want to control. Canon uses its core competencies in precision mechanics, fine optics, and microelectronics to produce some of the world's best cameras, printers, and copiers. It usually performs R&D and product design itself to reduce the risk of divulging proprietary knowledge to competitors and to generate continuous improvement in these competencies. By contrast, firms will usually source from *external* suppliers when they can obtain non-core products or services at lower cost or from suppliers specialized in providing them.

Decision 2: Where in the World Should Value-Adding Activities Be Located?

A second key decision firms face is whether to keep each value-adding activity in the home country or locate it in a foreign country. **Configuration of value-adding activity** refers to the pattern or geographic arrangement of locations where the firm carries out value-chain activities.[4] Instead of concentrating value-adding activities in their home country, many firms configure them across the world to save money, reduce delivery time, access factors of production, or extract maximum advantages relative to competitors.

This helps explain the migration of manufacturing industries from Europe, Japan, and the United States to emerging markets in Asia, Latin America, and Eastern Europe. Depending on the firm and the industry, management may decide to concentrate certain value-adding activities in just one or a handful of locations, while dispersing others to numerous countries. External suppliers are typically located in countries characterized by low-cost labor, competent production processes, and specific knowledge about relevant engineering and development activities.[5]

To run its global network of package shipping, DHL established offices in countries and cities worldwide. It also set up high-tech tracking centers in Arizona, Malaysia, and the Czech Republic. This configuration allows DHL staffers to track the locations of shipments worldwide, 24 hours a day. DHL management chose these specific locations for shipment tracking because, in a world of twenty-four time zones, they are each about 8 hours distant from each other.

German automaker Bayerische Motoren Werke AG (BMW; www.bmw.com) employs 70,000 factory workers at twenty-three sites in thirteen countries to manufacture sedans, coupes, and convertibles. Workers at the Munich plant build the BMW 3 Series and supply engines and key body components to other BMW factories abroad. In the United States, BMW has a plant in South Carolina that makes 240,000 vehicles annually for the world market. In northeast China, BMW makes cars in a joint venture with Brilliance China Automotive Holdings Ltd. In India, BMW has a manufacturing presence to

Configuration of value-adding activity The pattern or geographic arrangement of locations where the firm carries out value-chain activities.

serve the needs of the rapidly growing South Asia market. Management must configure BMW's sourcing at the best locations worldwide to minimize costs (for example, by producing in China), hire skilled people (by producing in Germany), remain close to key markets (by producing in China, India, and the United States), and succeed in the intensely competitive global car industry.[6]

Global Sourcing

Global sourcing The procurement of products or services from independent suppliers or company-owned subsidiaries located abroad for consumption in the home country or a third country.

Global sourcing is the procurement of products or services from independent suppliers or company-owned subsidiaries located abroad for consumption in the home country or a third country. Also called *global procurement* or *global purchasing*, global sourcing amounts to importing—an inbound flow of goods and services. It is an entry strategy that relies on a contractual relationship between the buyer (the focal firm) and a foreign source of supply. Dell (www.dell.com) relies extensively on a manufacturing network, composed largely of independent suppliers located around the world. Exhibit 17.1 details how Dell assembles components from suppliers in numerous locations for its Dell Inspiron notebook computer.[7]

Global sourcing is a low-control strategy in which the focal firm sources from independent suppliers through contractual agreements, as opposed to the high-control strategy of buying from company-owned subsidiaries. Global sourcing frequently represents the firm's initial involvement in international business. For many firms, it increases management's awareness about other international opportunities. Based on experience

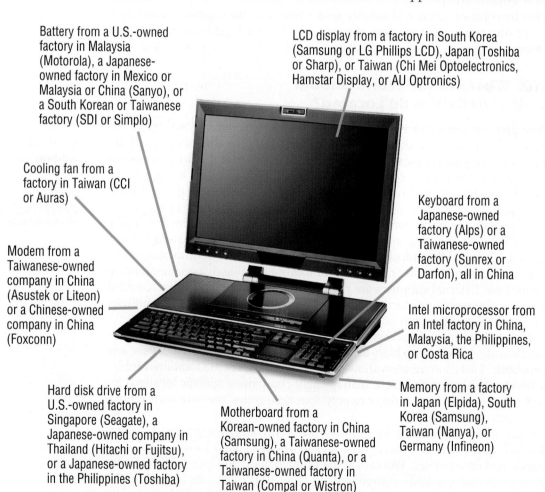

Exhibit 17.1   Sourcing for the Dell Inspiron Notebook Computer

SOURCE: Adapted from Friedman, Thomas. (2007). *The World s Flat 3.0: A Brief History of the Twenty-first Century*, New York: Picado.

it gains through such *inward internationalization*, the firm may progress to exporting, direct investment, or other forms of *outward internationalization*.

Global sourcing has been an established international business activity since the 1980s and has gained momentum in the current phase of globalization.[8] Contractors such as Softtek in Mexico help U.S. banks develop customized software, manage IT systems, and perform support and maintenance for commercial finance operations. Softtek (www.softtek.com) has 3,500 employees, mostly engineers. Its outsourcing facilities are located in Brazil, Colombia, Peru, and Venezuela. Argentina boasts one of the best-educated workforces in Latin America and is aggressively promoting its software development centers. The low salaries of software engineers (typically less than $12,000 a year) have persuaded such companies as Disney, Peugeot, and Repsol to have Web site design and software development performed in Argentina.

Three key drivers are especially responsible for the growth of global sourcing in recent years:

- *Technological advances in communications, especially the Internet and international telephony.* Access to vast online information means focal firms can quickly find suppliers that meet specific needs, anywhere in the world. Firms can communicate continuously with foreign suppliers at very low cost.

- *Falling costs of international business.* Tariffs and other trade barriers have declined substantially. Efficient communication and transportation systems have made international procurement cost effective and accessible to any firm.

- *Entrepreneurship and rapid economic transformation in emerging markets.* China, India, and other emerging markets have quickly developed as important suppliers of various products and services. Entrepreneurial suppliers aggressively pursue sourcing partnerships with foreign buyers.

The decisions about whether and where to outsource lead to the framework in Exhibit 17.2. The focal firm can source from independent suppliers, from company-owned subsidiaries and affiliates, or from both. In the Exhibit, Cells C and D represent the global sourcing scenarios. While global sourcing implies procurement from foreign locations, in some cases the focal firm may source from its own wholly owned subsidiary or an affiliate jointly owned with another firm (Cell C). This is **captive sourcing**. Genpact was a captive sourcing unit of General Electric (GE), with annual revenues of more than $1 billion and more than 37,000 employees worldwide. Now an independent company based in India, Genpact (www.genpact.com) is one of the largest providers of business-process outsourcing services.[9]

The relationship between the focal firm and its foreign supplier (Cell D in Exhibit 17.2) may take the form of **contract manufacturing**, an arrangement in which the focal firm

Captive sourcing
Sourcing from the firm's own production facilities.

Contract manufacturing
An arrangement in which the focal firm contracts with an independent supplier to manufacture products according to well-defined specifications.

	Value-adding activity is internalized	Value-adding activity is externalized (outsourced)
Value-adding activity kept in home country	*A* Keep production in-house, in home country	*B* Outsource production to third-party provider at home
Value-adding activity conducted abroad (global sourcing)	*C* Delegate production to foreign subsidiary or affiliate (captive sourcing)	*D* Outsource production to a third-party provider abroad (contract manufacturing or global sourcing from independent suppliers)

Exhibit 17.2 The Nature of Outsourcing and Global Sourcing

SOURCES: B. Kedia and D. Mukherjee, "Understanding Offshoring: A Research Framework Based on Disintegration, Location and Externalization Advantages," *Journal of World Business* 44, no. 3 (2009): 250–261; *Information Economy Report 2009* (New York: United Nations, 2009); *World Investment Report 2004* (New York: UNCTAD, 2004).

contracts with an independent supplier to manufacture products according to well-defined specifications. Once it has manufactured the products or components, the supplier delivers them to the focal firm, which then markets, sells, and distributes them. In essence, the focal firm "rents" the manufacturing capacity of the foreign contractor. Contract manufacturing is especially common in the apparel, shoe, furniture, aerospace, defense, computer, semiconductor, energy, medical, pharmaceutical, personal care, and automotive industries.

Patheon is a leading global pharmaceutical contract manufacturer (www.patheon.com). It operates eleven production facilities in Europe and North America, producing over-the-counter drugs and several top-selling prescription medications on contract to many of the world's twenty-largest pharmaceutical firms. Patheon generates about half its sales in North America and the other half in Europe.[10]

You may never have heard of Taiwan's Hon Hai Precision Industry Co., a leading contract manufacturer in the global electronics industry. Hon Hai (www.foxconn.com) works under contract for many well-known companies, churning out PlayStations for Sony; iPods, iPhones, and iPads for Apple; printers and PCs for Hewlett-Packard; and thousands of other products. In 2009, Hon Hai generated sales of $60 billion. The firm employs some 360,000 people in scores of contract factories worldwide, from Malaysia to Mexico.[11]

Offshoring

Offshoring The relocation of a business process or entire manufacturing facility to a foreign country.

Offshoring is the relocation of a business process or entire manufacturing facility to a foreign country. It is common in the service sector, including banking, software code writing, legal services, and customer-service activities.[12] Large legal hubs have emerged in India that provide services such as drafting contracts and patent applications, conducting research and negotiations, and performing paralegal work, all on behalf of Western clients. With lawyers in Europe and North America costing $300 an hour or more, law firms in India can cut Western companies' legal bills by up to 75 percent.[13]

In each of the business functions—human resources, accounting, finance, marketing, and customer service—certain tasks are considered routine and discrete. Many are candidates for offshoring as long as their performance by independent suppliers does not threaten or diminish the focal firm's core competencies or strategic assets. Examples of functions successfully offshored to foreign providers include billing and credit card processing in finance, creating customer databases and recording sales transactions in marketing, and payroll maintenance and benefits administration in human resources.

India is the current leader in the processing of advanced economies' relocated business services. Its market share has grown dramatically in the 2000s and is expected to increase by several hundred percent between 2010 and 2020, thanks to India's huge pool of qualified labor working for as little as 25 percent of what comparable workers get in the advanced economies.[14] The recent economic turndown is expected to pressure advanced-economy firms to seek further ways to reduce costs, to the benefit of service suppliers in India. Firms in Eastern Europe perform support activities for architectural and engineering firms from Western Europe and the United States. Accountants in the Philippines perform support

Running a business as far-flung as DHL's package delivery service requires support offices around the world. This delivery boat travels the Amstel River in Amsterdam. DHL has tracking centers in three time zones that are 8 hours apart, allowing it to offer 24-hour worldwide tracking service.

work for major accounting firms. Accenture has back-office operations and call centers in Costa Rica. Many IT support services for customers in Germany are actually based in the Czech Republic and Romania. Boeing, Nissan, and Nortel do much of their R&D in Russia. South Africa is the base for technical and user-support services for English-, French-, and German-speaking customers throughout Europe.[15]

Scope of Global Sourcing

Not all business activities or processes lend themselves to global sourcing. Many jobs in the service sector cannot be separated from their place of consumption. People normally do not travel abroad to see a banker, doctor, dentist, or accountant.[16] Personal contact is vital at the downstream end of virtually all value chains. By 2008, fewer than 5 percent of jobs in the United States that require substantial customer interaction (such as in retailing) had been transferred to low-wage economies. Fewer than 15 percent of all service jobs have moved from advanced economies to emerging markets.[17]

Many firms, such as Harley-Davidson (www.harley-davidson.com) in the United States, have their own reasons for keeping production at home. Harley both assembles its motorcycles and procures key components such as the engine, transmission, gas tank, brake system, and headlight assembly in the United States.[18] Harley customers view the product as a U.S. icon and highly value its "Made in the U.S.A." character.

However, countless other firms benefit from global sourcing. Jobs most conducive to being sourced abroad tend to be in industries characterized by:

- Large-scale manufacturing whose primary competitive advantage is efficiency and low cost

- High labor intensity in product and service production, such as garment manufacturing and call centers

- Uniform customer needs and standardized technologies and processes in production and other value-chain activities, such as automobiles and machine parts

- Established products with a predictable pattern of sales, such as components for consumer electronics.

- Information intensity whose functions and activities can be easily transmitted via the Internet, such as accounting, billing, and payroll.

- Outputs that are easily codified and transmitted over the Internet or by telephone, such as software preparation, technical support, and customer service.

Diversity of Countries That Initiate and Receive Outsourced Work

The *Global Trend* feature highlights the ongoing rivalry between China and India as they compete to be the world's leading destinations for global sourcing. For example, diamond processing is a labor-intensive industry that uses standardized processes to make diamond jewelry and equipment used for fine cutting. For five centuries, the industry was concentrated in Antwerp, Belgium. However, diamond cutting is increasingly outsourced to firms in India that perform the work more cost-effectively and provide other advantages. China is also emerging as an important participant in diamond cutting.

In addition to China and India, numerous other countries are active players as well. As for buyer countries, global sourcing is practiced by firms around the world. Insourcing supports a variety of relatively high-skilled jobs in engineering, management consulting, banking, legal services, and other areas.[19]

Firms based in advanced economies outsource the most services by volume. U.S. firms have led by offshoring over 50 percent of their service projects. More than 75 percent of major U.S. financial institutions send a portion of their IT work offshore. In Europe and Japan, the majority of large firms outsource some of their services, most often

GL⊕BAL TREND

China and India: Chief Rivals in the Global Sourcing Game

India is perhaps the world's leading offshoring destination for software development and back-office services such as telephone call centers and financial accounting activities. It is one of the leading world centers in the IT industry, thanks in part to the emergence of indigenous MNEs such as Infosys (www.infosys.com) and Wipro (www.wipro.com). Infosys rivals Microsoft as one of the top software firms worldwide.

China has a long history as a center of manufacturing for countless Western firms. Typical is the case of U.S. firm Keurig. After management found its single-serving coffee-makers were overpriced at $250 due to high manufacturing costs, it outsourced manufacturing to a partner in China. The move allowed Keurig to offer new models for as little as $99 and greatly increase its sales.

China aims to surpass India in services outsourcing, and the Chinese government is making huge investments to upgrade worker training and the quality of its universities. China has several major advantages. First, it is home to a large pool of skilled, low-cost labor. It produces 350,000 graduate engineers every year, almost four times as many as the United States. Second, China has become a world leader in R&D and innovation. Third, it has a huge domestic market with rapid and sustainable economic growth. Finally, the attitude of the Chinese government, long an obstacle to foreign firms, is increasingly pro-business, with a range of policies favoring foreign firms that manufacture in China.

Nevertheless, China also has several disadvantages. It is weak in intellectual property protection, has a language and culture foreign firms find challenging, and lacks consistently high-quality infrastructure. Dealing with the Chinese government is complicated because of bureaucracy and infighting among its various agencies. The resulting chaos hampers the ability of Chinese entrepreneurs to launch and manage companies. Finally, the cost of labor in China will rise over time and make the country less competitive for supplying numerous goods.

India has better intellectual property protection, a workforce with English language skills, and infrastructure that, although poor by advanced-economy standards, is often superior to that of China. India has become an enabler of growth in various global industries through expansion of its own offshoring firms into other countries. It is likely to remain the global-sourcing leader in the services sector for some time to come.

SOURCES: A. T. Kearney, "Geography of Offshoring Is Shifting, According to A.T. Kearney Study," May 18, 2009, retrieved from http://www.atkearney.com; Alan Beattie, "Ethical Rules Impose Perverse Incentives," *Financial Times,* January 30, 2009, retrieved from http://www.ft.com; A. Bhattacharya, "China and India: New Innovation and Talent Forces," *Business Week,* November 17, 2008, retrieved from http://www.businessweek.com; Pete Engardio, "China's Eroding Advantage," *Business Week,* June 15, 2009, pp. 54–55; Rahul Sachitanand, "IT Morphs Yet Again," *Business Today,* December 27, 2009, retrieved from http://businesstoday.intoday.in/.

to China and India, followed by countries in Eastern Europe, Latin America, and the Middle East. In Asia, the Philippines is a successful recent entrant in global services sourcing. It draws on solid English skills and long-standing cultural ties with the West to attract call-center work.[20]

Exhibit 17.3 identifies key players in global sourcing by four geographic regions. Russia is aiming at high-end programming jobs. With its strong engineering culture, it offers an abundant pool of talent at wages about one-fifth those of the United States. In Egypt, Xceed Contact Center (www.xceedcc.com) handles calls in Arabic and European languages on behalf of Carrefour, Microsoft, and Oracle.

Singapore and Dubai assert that their safety and advanced legal systems give them an edge in handling high-security and business-continuity services. Central and South American countries seek call-center contracts for the Spanish-speaking Hispanic market in the United States.[21] With Europe as its largest export market, Vietnam dramatically increased outsourced production in the 2000s because it offers modern but low-cost operations, skilled but inexpensive labor, and access to local sources unburdened by trade restrictions.[22]

A. T. Kearney's Global Services Location Index (www.atkearney.com) is topped by emerging markets and developing economies: India, China, Malaysia, Thailand, Indonesia, Egypt, Chile, and the Philippines. Canada and the United States are the only

	Central and Eastern Europe	*Central and South Asia*	*Latin America and the Caribbean*	*Middle East and Africa*
Top-Ranked Countries	Czech Republic, Bulgaria, Slovakia, Poland, Hungary	India, China, Malaysia, Philippines, Singapore, Thailand	Chile, Brazil, Mexico, Costa Rica, Argentina	Egypt, Jordan, United Arab Emirates, Ghana, Tunisia, Dubai
Up-and-Comers	Romania, Russia, Ukraine, Belarus	Indonesia, Vietnam, Sri Lanka	Jamaica, Panama, Nicaragua, Colombia	South Africa, Israel, Turkey, Morocco
Emerging Local Providers	*Luxoft* (Russia, software development); *EPAM Systems* (Belarus, software development); *Softengi* (Ukraine, software engineering)	*NCS* (Singapore, business processes); *Bluem* (China, IT services); *BroadenGate* (China, software development)	*Softtek* (Mexico, business processes); *Neoris* (Mexico, IT services); *Politec* (Brazil, IT services)	*Xceed* (Egypt, software development); *Ness Technologies* (Israel, IT services); *Jeraisy Group* (Saudi Arabia, IT services)

Exhibit 17.3 Key Players in Global Sourcing by Region

SOURCES: Crosman, Penny. (2008). "Worldsourcers," *Wall Street & Technology*, July, p. 26; Engardio, Pete. (2006). "The Future of Outsourcing: How It's Transforming Whole Industries and Changing the Way We Work," *Business Week*, January 30, p. 58.

advanced economies in the top 30 destinations. To help firms identify countries for outsourcing value-chain activities, the index emphasizes various criteria: the country's financial structure (compensation costs, infrastructure costs, tax and regulatory costs), the availability and skills of its people (cumulative business-process experience and skills; labor force availability, education, and language; and worker attrition rates), and the nature of the business environment (the country's political and economic environment, physical infrastructure, cultural adaptability, and security of intellectual property).[23]

Strategic Choices in Global Sourcing

Exhibit 17.4 explains the strategic implications of the two choices firms face: whether to perform specific value-adding activities themselves or to outsource them, and whether to concentrate each activity in the home country or disperse it abroad. The exhibit portrays a typical value chain, ranging from R&D and design to customer service. The first row indicates the degree to which management considers each value-adding activity a strategic asset to the firm. The second row indicates whether the activity tends to be internalized inside the focal firm or outsourced to a foreign supplier. The third row indicates where management typically locates an activity.

In addition to large firms, global sourcing provides big benefits for small and medium-sized enterprises (SMEs). Main Street businesses from car dealerships to real estate firms increasingly farm out accounting, support services, and design work to suppliers in Brazil, Hungary, India, and other top destinations. Outsourcing brokers and international online sites such as www.guru.com and www.rentacoder.com do big business serving the global sourcing needs of countless SMEs. Internet search engines allow small firms to find service vendors anywhere in the world. An auto dealership in

	R&D, Design	Manufacturing of Parts, Components	Manufacturing or Assembly of Finished Products	Marketing and Branding	Sales and Distribution	Customer Service
Importance of this activity to the firm as a strategic asset	High importance	Low importance	Low to medium importance	High importance	Medium importance	Medium importance
Likelihood of internalizing rather than outsourcing this activity	High	Low	Low to medium	High	Low to medium	Low to medium
Geographic configuration: Overall tendency to locate activity at home or abroad	Usually concentrated at home	Usually dispersed across various markets	Usually concentrated in a few markets	Branding concentrated at home; Marketing concentrated or dispersed to individual markets	Dispersed to individual markets	Dispersed to individual markets, except call centers, which are often concentrated

Exhibit 17.4 Typical Choices of Outsourcing and Geographic Dispersion of Value-Chain Activities among Firms

New York hired an Internet developer in Brazil to design a multimedia Web site to sell cars online. A real estate agent in California uses suppliers in Hungary, India, and Portugal to design graphics, manage databases, and update online information.[24]

Benefits of Global Sourcing

Like other international entry strategies, global sourcing offers both benefits and risks. Exhibit 17.4 provides an overview. The exhibit lists two primary reasons to pursue global sourcing: cost efficiency and the ability to achieve strategic goals. Let's consider these in detail.

Cost Efficiency

Cost efficiency is the traditional rationale for sourcing abroad. The firm takes advantage of the large wage gap between advanced economies and emerging markets. Exhibit 17.6 reveals typical salary levels of BPO and IT workers in various countries. One study found that firms expect to save an average of more than 40 percent off baseline costs as a result of offshoring, particularly in R&D, product design activities, and back-office operations such as accounting and data processing.[25] A worker in business process outsourcing in Egypt or the Philippines earns less than $5,000 per year. A call center worker in India earns roughly $500 per month, while the same worker in Europe or the United States earns $2,000 to $3,000 monthly. This wage discrepancy explains why firms like HP, Accenture, Citicorp, Dell, and HSBC grew their Indian operations 30 to 50 percent a year during the 2000s.[26]

Ability to Achieve Strategic Goals

The strategic view of global sourcing—called *transformational outsourcing*—suggests that just as the firm achieves gains in efficiency, productivity, quality, and revenues by leveraging offshore talent, it also obtains the means to turn around failing businesses, speed

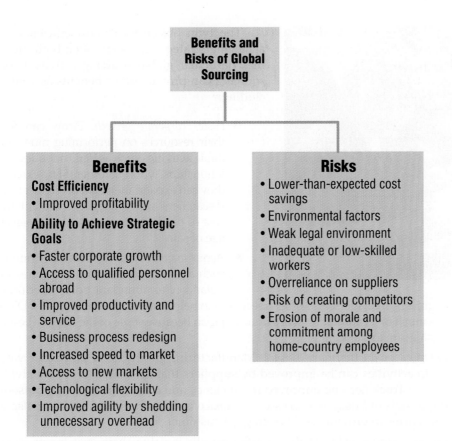

Exhibit 17.5 Benefits and Risks of Global Sourcing

Benefits and Risks of Global Sourcing

Benefits

Cost Efficiency
• Improved profitability

Ability to Achieve Strategic Goals
• Faster corporate growth
• Access to qualified personnel abroad
• Improved productivity and service
• Business process redesign
• Increased speed to market
• Access to new markets
• Technological flexibility
• Improved agility by shedding unnecessary overhead

Risks
• Lower-than-expected cost savings
• Environmental factors
• Weak legal environment
• Inadequate or low-skilled workers
• Overreliance on suppliers
• Risk of creating competitors
• Erosion of morale and commitment among home-country employees

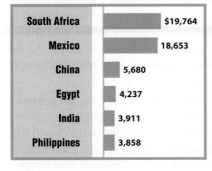

Business-process outsourcing
Annual average entry-level salary, in U.S. dollars

South Africa	$19,764
Mexico	18,653
China	5,680
Egypt	4,237
India	3,911
Philippines	3,858

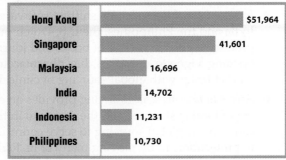

IT professionals
Annual average salary, in U.S. dollars

Hong Kong	$51,964
Singapore	41,601
Malaysia	16,696
India	14,702
Indonesia	11,231
Philippines	10,730

Exhibit 17.6 Annual Salaries of Typical Outsourcing Workers in Various Countries

SOURCE: James Hookway and Josephine Cuneta, "World News: Philippine Call Centers Ring Up Business," *Wall Street Journal*, May 30, 2009, p. A14. Reprinted with permission of *Wall Street Journal*, Copyright © 2009 Dow Jones.

up innovation, restructure operations, and fund otherwise-unaffordable development projects.[27] Global sourcing allows the firm to free expensive analysts, engineers, and managers from routine tasks to spend more time researching, innovating, managing, and generally undertaking high-value-adding activities that contribute more productively to increasing company performance.[28] In this way, global sourcing becomes a catalyst to overhaul organizational processes and company operations and increase the firm's overall competitive advantages. It allows the firm to achieve large, longer-term strategic goals.

In 2009, the clothing company Liz Claiborne sold its sourcing operations, which handle all aspects of production from finding materials to manufacturing garments, to Li & Fung Group, based in Hong Kong. Li & Fung (www.lifunggroup.com) specializes in managing the supply chains of dozens of brands and retailers worldwide. Claiborne management took the step to dramatically shift the firm's business model and focus on its core competencies, such as marketing and distribution.[29]

Toy companies like Lego and Mattel outsource much of their production to manufacturers in China. Global sourcing helps reduce costs, improves productivity, and facilitates the redesign of critical value-chain activities.

The twin objectives of cost efficiency and achieving strategic goals are often both present in a particular global sourcing activity. Global sourcing can provide other benefits as well, including:

- *Faster corporate growth.* Firms can focus their resources on performing more profitable activities such as R&D or building relationships with customers. For example, they can expand their staff of engineers and researchers while keeping constant their cost of product development as a percentage of sales.[30]

- *Access to qualified workers abroad.* Countries such as China, India, the Philippines, and Ireland offer abundant pools of educated engineers, managers, and other specialists to help firms achieve their goals. Disney has much of its animation work done in Japan because some of the world's best animators are located there.

- *Improved productivity and service.* Manufacturing productivity and other value-chain activities can be improved by suppliers that specialize in these activities. Penske Truck Leasing improved its efficiency and customer service by outsourcing dozens of business processes to Mexico and India. Global sourcing also enables firms to provide 24/7 coverage of customer service.

- *Business process redesign.* By reconfiguring their value-chain systems or reengineering their business processes, companies can improve their production efficiency and resource utilization. Multinational firms see offshoring as a catalyst for a broader plan to overhaul outdated company operations.[31]

- *Increased speed to market.* By shifting software development and editorial work to India and the Philippines, the U.S.-Dutch publisher Walters Kluwer was able to produce a greater variety of books and journals and publish them faster. As the opening vignette describes, big pharmaceutical firms get new medications to market faster with global sourcing of clinical drug trials.

- *Access to new markets.* Sourcing provides an entrée to the market, an understanding of local customers, and the means to initiate marketing activities there. Firms can also use global sourcing to serve countries that may be otherwise closed due to protectionism. By moving many of its R&D operations to Russia, the telecommunications firm Nortel gained an important foothold in a market that desperately needs telephone switching equipment and other communications infrastructure. Indian conglomerate Tata Group (www.tata.com) established a call center in the United States to expand its growing presence in the U.S. market.[32]

- *Technological flexibility.* Leveraging independent suppliers abroad provides firms the flexibility to quickly change sources of supply, employing whichever suppliers offer the most advanced technologies. In this way, sourcing provides greater organizational flexibility and faster responsiveness to evolving buyer needs.

- *Improved agility by shedding unnecessary overhead.* Unburdened by a large bureaucracy and administrative overhead, companies can be more responsive to opportunities and adapt more easily to environmental changes, such as new competitors.

Combined, these benefits give firms the ability to continuously renew their strategic positions. Outsourcing specialists such as Accenture and Genpact meticulously dissect the workflow of other firms' human resources, finance, or IT departments. This helps the specialists build new IT platforms, redesign all processes, and administer programs, acting as virtual subsidiaries to their client firms. The specialists then disperse work among global networks of staff from Asia to Eastern Europe and elsewhere.[33]

 ## Risks of Global Sourcing

In addition to potential benefits, global sourcing can also bring unexpected complications. Studies show that as many as half of all outsourcing arrangements are terminated earlier than planned. As summarized in Exhibit 17.5, global sourcing introduces the following major risks.[34]

- *Lower-than-expected cost savings.* International transactions are often more complex and costly than expected. Conflicts and misunderstandings may arise from differences in the national and organizational cultures between the focal firm and foreign supplier. Initial or ongoing costs can be substantial. Establishing an outsourcing facility can be surprisingly expensive, due to the need to upgrade poor infrastructure or locate it in a large city to attract sufficient skilled labor.

- *Environmental factors.* Environmental challenges include currency fluctuations, tariffs and other trade barriers, high energy and transportation costs, adverse macroeconomic events, and labor strikes. Many countries suffer from poor public infrastructure, as exemplified by power outages and poor road and rail networks. Workers in India occasionally stage violent labor protests. A weakening home currency makes foreign-sourced products more costly to import. If the Chinese yuan increases in value, for example, then China's exports will likely decrease because it will be more expensive for foreign customers to buy Chinese products. In a similar way, firms that source from China will experience higher costs.

- *Weak legal environment.* Many popular locations for global sourcing (for example, China, India, and Russia) have weak intellectual property laws and poor enforcement, which can erode key strategic assets. Inadequate legal systems, red tape, convoluted tax systems, and complex business regulations complicate local operations in many countries.

- *Inadequate or low-skilled workers.* Some foreign suppliers may be staffed by employees who lack appropriate knowledge about the tasks with which they are charged. Other suppliers suffer rapid turnover of skilled employees. Typical Indian operations in business processing may lose 20 percent or more of their workers each year, and good managers are often in short supply. In 2009, customer complaints about the quality of service led Delta Airlines to move its corporate call centers from India back to the United States.[35]

- *Overreliance on suppliers.* Unreliable suppliers may put earlier work aside when they gain a more important client. Suppliers occasionally encounter financial difficulties or are acquired by other firms with different priorities and procedures. When such events occur, management at the focal firm may find itself scrambling to find alternate suppliers. Overreliance can shift control of key activities too much in favor of the supplier and reduce the focal firm's control of important value-chain tasks.

- *Risk of creating competitors.* As the focal firm shares its intellectual property and business-process knowledge with foreign suppliers, it also runs the risk of creating future rivals. Schwinn, long the leader in the global bicycle industry, transferred much of its production and core expertise to lower-cost foreign suppliers, which acquired sufficient knowledge to become competitors, eventually forcing Schwinn into bankruptcy (from which it later recovered).

■ *Erosion of morale and commitment among home-country employees.* Global sourcing can leave employees caught in the middle between their employer and their employer's clients. At the extreme, workers find themselves in a psychological limbo, unclear who their employer really is. When outsourcing forces retained and outsourced staff to work side by side, tensions and uncertainty may evolve into an "us-versus-them" syndrome and diminish employee commitment and enthusiasm.

 ## Strategies for Minimizing the Risks of Global Sourcing

Experience suggests seven managerial guidelines for achieving success in global sourcing:

■ *Go offshore for the right reasons.* The best rationale is strategic. The vast majority of companies cite cost cutting as the main reason for global sourcing. After the first year, however, most firms encounter diminishing returns in the amount of money saved. Cost cutting is often a distraction from more beneficial, long-term goals such as enhancing the quality of offerings, improving overall productivity, and freeing up knowledge workers and other core resources that can be redeployed to improve long-term performance. To maximize returns, management should examine tasks and activities in each of the firm's value chains and outsource those in which the firm is relatively weak, that offer relatively little value to the bottom line, or that can be performed more effectively by others, yet are not critical to the firm's core competencies.

■ *Get employees on board.* Global sourcing can invite opposition from employees and other organizational stakeholders. Disaffected middle managers may undermine projects and other goals that offshoring seeks to achieve. Poorly planned sourcing projects can create unnecessary tension and harm employee morale. Thus, management should seek to gain employee support by reaching a consensus of middle managers and employees, developing alternatives for redeploying laid-off workers, and including employees in the selection of foreign partners. Managers can also seek the counsel of labor unions and incorporate their views. For example, when Dutch bank ABN Amro (www.abnamro.com) decided to offshore accounting and finance functions, it set up a full-time communications department to explain the move to middle managers and staff in advance. Senior executives held town hall-style meetings with employees and involved unions in managing the shift. These steps allowed offshoring to proceed more smoothly, enhancing company performance.[36]

■ *Choose carefully between a captive operation and contracting with outside suppliers.* Managers should be vigilant about striking the right balance between the organizational activities they retain inside the firm and those they source from outside. Many firms establish their own sourcing operations abroad to maintain control of outsourced activities and technologies. When Boeing sought to outsource key value-chain tasks, management established a company-owned center in Moscow where it employs 1,100 skilled but relatively low-cost aerospace engineers. The Russian team is working on a range of projects, including the design of titanium parts for the new Boeing 787 Dreamliner jet.[37]

■ *Choose suppliers carefully.* Finding and managing foreign suppliers is complex. The focal firm may have limited influence over suppliers' manufacturing and processes. Suppliers may engage in opportunistic behavior or act in bad faith. To ensure the success of sourcing ventures, the focal firm must exercise great care to identify and screen potential suppliers and then monitor the activities of those suppliers from which it sources.

- *Emphasize effective communications with suppliers.* A common reason for global sourcing failure is that buyers and suppliers spend too little time getting well acquainted. They rush into a deal before clarifying each other's expectations, giving rise to misunderstandings and inferior results. Because production quality in an emerging market may vary over time, managers at the focal firm may need to closely monitor manufacturing processes. To avoid mistakes and frustration, partners must share necessary information.[38] Where differing business philosophies and practices lead partners to approach the same issue differently, effective communication helps minimize misunderstandings that diminish buyer–supplier relationships.

Minimizing the risks of global sourcing entails several, critical strategies. Following a careful selection process, the focal firm should invest in collaborating and communicating with suppliers. Pictured is a call center in New Delhi, India.

- *Invest in supplier development and collaboration.* When a business function is delegated to a supplier, the parties need to exchange information, transfer knowledge, troubleshoot, coordinate, and monitor. Over the long haul, benefits emerge when the focal firm adjusts its processes and product requirements to match the capabilities of foreign suppliers. Management should collaborate closely with suppliers in codevelopment and codesign activities. Close supplier cooperation also enables the focal firm to tap into a stream of ideas for new products, processes, technologies, and improvements. Efforts to build strong relationships help create a moral contract between the focal firm and the supplier, one that is often more effective than a formal legal contract.

- *Safeguard interests.* The focal firm should take specific actions to safeguard its interests in the supplier relationship. First, it can advise the supplier against engaging in potentially destructive acts that jeopardize the firm's reputation. Second, it can escalate commitments by making partner-specific investments (such as sharing knowledge with the supplier) on an incremental basis, allowing for ongoing review, learning, and adjustment. Third, it can share costs and revenues by building a stake for the supplier so that, in case of failure to meet expectations, the supplier also suffers costs or foregoes revenues. Fourth, it can maintain flexibility by keeping open its options for finding alternate partners if needed. Finally, the focal firm can keep the partner at bay by withholding access to intellectual property and key assets. If conflicts are unresolved by negotiations, one option is to acquire full or partial ownership of the supplier.

Implementing Global Sourcing Through Supply-Chain Management

A key reason sourcing products from distant markets has become a major business phenomenon is the efficiency with which goods can be physically moved from one part of the globe to another.

Global supply chain
The firm's integrated network of sourcing, production, and distribution, organized on a worldwide scale and located in countries where competitive advantage can be maximized.

A **global supply chain** is the firm's integrated network of sourcing, production, and distribution, organized on a worldwide scale and located in countries where competitive advantage can be maximized. Global supply-chain management includes both upstream (supplier) and downstream (customer) flows.

The concepts of supply chain and value chain are related but distinct. Recall that the value chain is the collection of activities intended to design, produce, market, deliver, and support a product or service. By contrast, the supply chain is the collection of logistics specialists and activities that provides inputs to manufacturers or retailers.

Skillful supply-chain management serves to optimize value-chain activities. Sourcing from numerous suppliers scattered around the world is neither economical nor feasible without an efficient supply-chain system. Casual observers are impressed by the vast collection of products in a supermarket or department store that originated from dozens of different countries. The speed with which these products are delivered to end users is equally impressive.

Consider a customer in Canada who orders a Dell laptop computer. The order is typically routed to the Dell factory in Malaysia, where workers must access thirty distinct component parts that originate with Dell suppliers scattered around the world. Indeed, the total supply chain for a typical Dell computer, including multiple tiers of suppliers, typically includes some 400 companies in Asia, Europe, and the Americas. Dell is so skilled at managing all this complexity that customers typically receive their computers within two weeks of submitting an order.[39]

You probably heard about Boeing's new 787 Dreamliner, a fuel-saving, medium-sized passenger aircraft that uses carbon composite for the fuselage instead of aluminum. It is lightweight and has spacious interiors and higher cabin pressure than other models, for a more comfortable journey. However, the most remarkable aspect of the Dreamliner is the extent of outsourcing. Boeing (www.boeing.com) is responsible for manufacturing only about 10 percent of the jet's value—the tail fin and final assembly. Some forty suppliers worldwide contribute the remaining 90 percent. The wings are built in Japan, the carbon composite fuselage in Italy, and the landing gear in France (see Exhibit 17.7). The global dispersion of manufacturing responsibility has allowed Boeing to transform itself into a systems integrator and focus on its core capabilities—design, marketing, and branding.

Nevertheless, the execution of this global manufacturing network has been far from flawless. The 787's inaugural flight and deliveries were delayed more than two years. Production delays resulted in lost earnings estimated to exceed $11 billion. Much of the difficulty is attributable to the complexity of coordinating a global supply-chain network.[40]

Networks of supply-chain hubs and providers of global delivery service are an integral part of global supply chains. Many focal firms delegate supply-chain activities to such independent logistics service providers as DHL, FedEx, and TNT. Consulting firms that manage the logistics of other firms are called *third party logistics providers (3PLs)*. Using a 3PL is often the best solution for international logistics, especially for firms that produce at low volumes or lack the resources and expertise to create their own logistics network.

A good example of evolving supply-chain management is the integration of the European Union. The removal of border controls allowed supply-chain managers to redraw the maps of their sourcing and distribution activities throughout Europe. Warehousing and distribution centers were consolidated and centralized. In another instance, the computer chip company Intel significantly reduced shipping costs by consolidating its freight expenditures into four transportation suppliers. As a result, from its fourteen manufacturing sites around the world, Intel considerably improved on-time delivery and customer-service performance.[41]

Exhibit 17.8 illustrates the stages, functions, and activities in the supply chain. It reveals how suppliers interact with the focal firm and how these, in turn, interact with distributors and retailers.

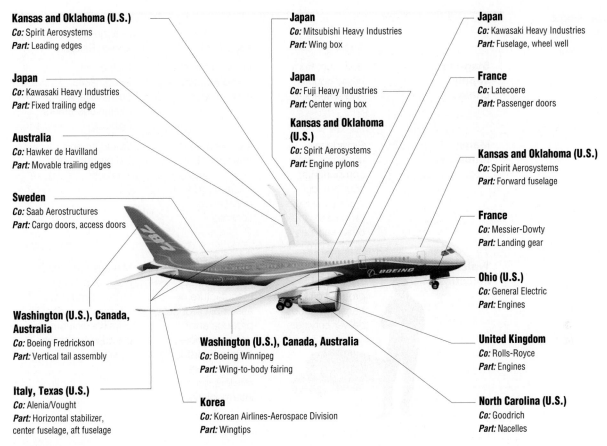

Kansas and Oklahoma (U.S.)
Co: Spirit Aerosystems
Part: Leading edges

Japan
Co: Kawasaki Heavy Industries
Part: Fixed trailing edge

Australia
Co: Hawker de Havilland
Part: Movable trailing edges

Sweden
Co: Saab Aerostructures
Part: Cargo doors, access doors

Washington (U.S.), Canada, Australia
Co: Boeing Fredrickson
Part: Vertical tail assembly

Italy, Texas (U.S.)
Co: Alenia/Vought
Part: Horizontal stabilizer, center fuselage, aft fuselage

Japan
Co: Mitsubishi Heavy Industries
Part: Wing box

Japan
Co: Fuji Heavy Industries
Part: Center wing box

Kansas and Oklahoma (U.S.)
Co: Spirit Aerosystems
Part: Engine pylons

Washington (U.S.), Canada, Australia
Co: Boeing Winnipeg
Part: Wing-to-body fairing

Korea
Co: Korean Airlines-Aerospace Division
Part: Wingtips

Japan
Co: Kawasaki Heavy Industries
Part: Fuselage, wheel well

France
Co: Latecoere
Part: Passenger doors

Kansas and Oklahoma (U.S.)
Co: Spirit Aerosystems
Part: Forward fuselage

France
Co: Messier-Dowty
Part: Landing gear

Ohio (U.S.)
Co: General Electric
Part: Engines

United Kingdom
Co: Rolls-Royce
Part: Engines

North Carolina (U.S.)
Co: Goodrich
Part: Nacelles

Exhibit 17.7   Where Boeing Sources the Components for Its New 787 Aircraft

SOURCE: Tatge, Mark (2006), "Global Gamble," *Forbes* (April 17), pp. 78–80.

Information and Communications Technology

Costs of physically delivering a product to an export market may account for as much as 40 percent of the good's total cost. Skillful supply-chain management reduces this cost while increasing customer satisfaction. Experienced firms use information and communications technologies (ICTs) to streamline supply chains, reducing costs and increasing distribution efficiency. For example, *electronic data interchange (EDI)* automatically passes orders directly from customers to suppliers through a sophisticated ICT platform. Britain's Tesco supermarket chain (www.tesco.com) greatly reduced inventory costs by using an EDI system to link point-of-sale data to logistics managers. Tesco tracks product purchases down to the minute, and many canned foods that once sat in its warehouses for days or weeks now come directly from suppliers to Tesco stores.[42]

Specialized software enhances information sharing and improves efficiency by allowing the firm to track international shipments and clear customs. Many firms digitize key documents such as customs declarations and invoices, which improves speed and reduces order processing costs and shipping procedures. The most sophisticated supply chains are characterized by reliable, capable partners connected through automated, real-time communications. In an efficient system, the focal firm and its supply-chain partners continuously communicate and share information to constantly meet the demands of the marketplace. The Spanish retailer Zara uses EDI technology to optimize supply-chain management, inventory management, and responsiveness to consumer demands. Store managers use wireless personal digital assistants and instantaneous communications to help headquarters conduct ongoing market research. Such technologies have allowed Zara to become the leader in rapid-response retailing.[43]

Exhibit 17.8 Stages, Functions, and Activities in the Global Supply Chain

	Suppliers	Focal Firm	Intermediaries and/or Retailers
Stage in supply chain	Sourcing, from home country and abroad	Inbound materials; outbound goods and services	Distribution to domestic customers or foreign customers (exports)
Major functions	Provide raw materials, parts, components, supplies, as well as business processes and other services to focal firm	Manufacture or assemble components or finished products, or produce services	Distribute and sell products and services
Typical activities	Maintain inventory, process orders, transport goods, deliver services	Manage inventory, process orders, manufacture or assemble products, produce and deliver services, distribute products to customers, retailers, or intermediaries	Manage inventory, place or process orders, produce services, manage physical distribution, provide after-sales service

Logistics and Transportation

Logistics physically moves goods through the supply chain. It incorporates information, transportation, inventory, warehousing, materials handling, and similar activities associated with the delivery of raw materials, parts, components, and finished products. Managers seek to reduce moving and storage costs by using just-in-time inventory systems. Internationally, logistics are complex due to wide geographic distances, multiple legal environments, and the often inadequate and costly nature of distribution infrastructure in individual countries. The more diverse the firm's global supply chain, the greater the cost of logistics.

Competent logistics management is critical, especially for just-in-time inventory systems. The California ports of Los Angeles (www.portoflosangeles.org) and Long Beach (www.polb.com) handle more than 40 percent of imports into the United States, processing over 24,000 shipping containers per day. Infrastructure deficiencies and increasing demand can result in long delays, which translate into longer transit times and higher costs for U.S. importers. Because of delays, Toys "R" Us had to build 10 extra days into its supply chain. MGA Entertainment lost $40 million in revenues when it could not deliver its best-selling Bratz dolls to retailers on time.[44] As a result of poor supply-chain planning, Microsoft's Xbox 360 games console sold out soon after launch. Scarcity led to high prices in unofficial channels. On eBay, Xbox consoles sold for as much as $1,000, compared with the official price of about $400.[45]

Transportation Modes

International logistics usually make use of multiple *transportation modes,* including land, ocean, and air transport. Land transportation is conducted via highways and railroads, ocean transport is via container ships, and air transport is via commercial or cargo aircraft. Transportation modes involve several trade-offs. The three main considerations are *cost, transit time* to deliver the goods, and *predictability*, the match between anticipated and actual transit times.

Land transport is usually more expensive than ocean transport but cheaper than air. Exporters often opt for ocean shipping even when land transport is available. For example, some Mexican firms send goods to Canada by ship.

Ocean transport is slower than air, but far cheaper. Ocean transport was revolutionized by the development of 20- and 40-foot shipping containers, the big boxes that sit atop seagoing vessels. The ability of a modern ship to carry thousands of containers yields economies of scale, which makes ocean transport very cost effective, often accounting for less than 1 percent of a product's final price.

Air transport is fast and extremely predictable, but expensive. Given its high cost, it is used mostly to transport perishable products (like food and flowers), products with a high value-to-weight ratio (like fine jewelry and laptop computers), and urgently needed goods (like medicines and emergency supplies). While the use of air freight has increased because of gradually declining cost, it still accounts for only 1 percent of international shipments.

 ## Global Sourcing and Corporate Social Responsibility

The business community sees global sourcing as a way of maintaining or increasing business competitiveness. Others view it negatively, focusing on the loss of local jobs. After IBM workers in Europe went on strike against offshoring, shareholders at IBM's annual meeting argued for an anti-offshoring resolution. In the United States, 27,000 machinists went on strike at Boeing to protest the aircraft company's resolve to globally outsource jobs in the production of the 787 Dreamliner jet.[46]

The general public has also criticized offshoring. When the state of Indiana awarded a $15 million IT services contract to a supplier that planned to use technicians from India to do some of the work, the Indiana Senate intervened and cancelled the deal. However, the state recently leased management of the Indiana Toll Road to an Australian-Spanish partnership for 75 years for $3.8 billion. The city of New Orleans has outsourced management of its mass transit system to the French firm Veolia Environnement.[47]

Potential Harm to Local and National Economy from Global Sourcing

Critics of global sourcing point to three potentially major problems. Global sourcing can result in (1) job losses in the home country, (2) reduced national competitiveness, and (3) declining standards of living. Regarding the last two concerns, critics worry that, as more tasks are performed at lower cost with comparable quality in other countries, high-wage countries will eventually lose their national competitiveness. Long-held knowledge and skills will eventually drain away to other countries, they fear, and the lower wages paid abroad will eventually pull down wages in the home country, leading to lower living standards.

A major concern is job losses. The number of jobs in the U.S. legal industry outsourced to foreign contractors now exceeds 25,000 per year.[48] Some estimate that more than 400,000 jobs in the United States IT industry have moved offshore.[49] Projections are that more than three million jobs will be outsourced from the United States by 2015.[50] Critics say this amounts to exporting jobs.

Global sourcing has sparked protests in many countries. Here, trade union members in Britain protest about jobs at Lloyds TSB bank being outsourced to India.

Job losses also increase when companies increase their sourcing of input and finished goods from abroad. Walmart sources as much as 70 percent of its finished merchandise from abroad. This has led concerned citizens to form a protest group called Walmartwatch.com, which claims millions of U.S. jobs have been lost due to Walmart's global sourcing.[51] Job losses are occurring in developing economies as well. For example, in the textile industry, El Salvador, Honduras, Indonesia, and Turkey have seen jobs gradually being transferred to China, India, and Pakistan.[52]

Consider the potentially devastating effect of job losses on a small community. For nearly 40 years Electrolux (www.electrolux.com), the Swedish home-appliance company, manufactured refrigerators in Greenville, Michigan, providing 2,700 jobs. Once the world's largest refrigerator factory, the plant developed weak financial performance and high labor costs. Electrolux closed the factory and established a *maquiladora* plant in Juarez, Mexico, seeking to profit from lower wages and the El Paso Foreign Trade Zone just across the border in Texas. Management believed it was acting in the firm's best interest and strengthening its global competitiveness. From Greenville's standpoint, however, the decision was devastating. How could so many jobs be replaced in such a small community? What would happen to the town's social and economic landscape? Wage concessions by the labor union and over $100 million in grants and tax breaks in Michigan were insufficient to halt the closure.[53]

From such examples, it is easy to see the clash of interests between firms and local communities. It takes considerable time for laid-off workers to find new jobs. According to one estimate, as many as one-third of U.S. workers who have been laid off cannot find suitable employment within a year.[54] Older workers in particular struggle to learn the skills needed for new positions. The rate of redeployment is likely to be even lower in Europe, where unemployment rates are already high, and in Japan, where employment practices are less flexible. In Germany, the percentage of workers who are not reemployed within a year of losing their jobs is as high as 60 percent. Under such circumstances, global sourcing may increase unemployment rates, reduce income levels, and harm the local community and national economy.

Public Policy on Global Sourcing

The consequences of global sourcing for the national economy and workers are not yet fully known. A recent comprehensive study carried out for the United States argues that official statistics understate the impact of offshoring on national economies.[55] The study found that import growth, adjusted for inflation, is faster than the official numbers show. The study author concluded that more of the gain in living standards in recent years has come from cheap imports and less from increased domestic productivity. U.S. consumers may thus enjoy an even better standard of living from imports than previously thought.

Offshoring is a process of *creative destruction*, a concept first proposed by the Austrian economist Joseph Schumpeter.[56] According to this view, firms' innovative activities tend to make mature products obsolete over time: The introduction of personal computers essentially eliminated the typewriter industry, the DVD player eliminated the VCR, and so on. Just as offshoring results in job losses and adverse effects for particular groups and economic sectors, it also creates new advantages and opportunities for firms and consumers alike. New industries created through creative destruction will create new jobs and innovative products.

Public policy should strive to mitigate the potential harm global sourcing can cause.[57] Governments can use economic and fiscal policies to encourage the development of new technologies by helping entrepreneurs reap the financial benefits of their work and keeping the cost of capital for financing R&D low. Another useful policy is to ensure the nation has a strong educational system, including technical schools and well-funded universities that supply engineers, scientists, and knowledge workers. A strong educational system helps provide firms with pools of high-quality labor. And, as firms restructure through global sourcing efforts, flexibility acquired through education ensures that many who lose jobs can be redeployed in other positions.

Closing Case

Good Hopes for Global Outsourcing

Good Hope Hospitals of California, Inc. ("Good Hope") is a chain of nine hospitals in or near Los Angeles, San Diego, and San Francisco. Founded in 1976, Good Hope is run on a for-profit basis and management continuously strives for efficient operations. Andy Delgado is Good Hope's Vice President for Finance and Accounting, and Joy Simmons is the senior manager in Information Technology. The two executives needed to make significant cuts in operational costs in their respective areas. Extremely reluctant to lay off workers, they mutually agreed on a plan to outsource some work now done by contractors in California to suppliers located abroad.

Delgado and Simmons believed that some of Good Hope's ongoing business processes could be outsourced, including data processing for accounts receivable and accounts payable, certain customer service applications, transcription of medical records, and some data processing. Both managers had heard about the benefits of global sourcing but neither knew how to proceed. So, they began to research their options.

The Downside of Global Sourcing

In the course of their research, Delgado and Simmons also learned that services are frequently more challenging to outsource than manufacturing. This is partly because it is usually more difficult to judge the quality of services than that of manufactured products. Firms that use global sourcing sign legal contracts with suppliers binding themselves to deliver promised levels of service. In reality, there is much variation in the quality of services delivered. To achieve satisfactory outcomes, the contracting firm should emphasize developing trust and understanding with the supplier, especially critical in cross-cultural settings. Delgado and Simmons wondered about the enforceability of legal agreements in different country settings.

Another potential concern was the quality of workers. Some foreign suppliers cannot hire a sufficient number of skilled managers to oversee the work performed by their staffs. Workers must be trained, supervised, and properly motivated. Could Good Hope provide such support and technical assistance?

Delgado and Simmons also read troubling stories about firms whose offshore operations proved to be more costly than originally planned. They read about firms that lost customers and jeopardized their reputations because of poor customer service received from abroad. Delgado and Simmons also worried about breach of confidentiality—to what extent could they rely on foreign organizations to keep patient data confidential? The various risks implied that

Good Hope would need to interact closely and frequently with the external supplier, which would add substantial costs in terms of negotiating, transacting, and monitoring, as well as international travel. Delgado and Simmons realized they would need to approach global sourcing very carefully.

Offshoring Destinations

Delgado and Simmons next focused their research on identifying the most promising foreign locations for offshoring. Their investigation revealed that India was the most popular choice for many types of services. The country's outsourcing sector had been growing at 25 to 50 percent per year. India's labor costs are 25 to 40 percent of those in the United States and English is widely spoken. The team learned that reputable firms such as IBM, Dell, and Citicorp had offshored numerous service operations to India.

Their investigation revealed that China was also a potential destination. The country has millions of suitable workers and soon is expected to rival India as a provider of services such as insurance underwriting and back-office operations. Outsourcing costs are currently lower in China than in India. However, a concern is China's reputation for excessive regulation and bureaucracy. Delgado and Simmons wondered if they could develop sufficient trust and understanding with partners in an unfamiliar and distant culture with language differences.

Eastern Europe also emerged as a promising location. The region is culturally similar to the United States, and wages in much of the region are on par with those in India. For example, while Indian accountants earn roughly $10 an hour, wages are substantially lower in Bulgaria and Romania. The Czech Republic is a popular location and is the site of business-process centers for firms such as DHL, Siemens, and Lufthansa. One expert claimed the quality of work in the Czech Republic sometimes surpasses the best available in India. Even Infosys, the giant Indian IT firm, has major support operations in the Czech Republic. But Eastern European countries sometimes have a shortage of qualified labor, particularly among middle managers. As the region's economies develop, social and health insurance costs are also increasing. Taxes can be high and bureaucratic governments hinder efficient business operations. Corruption is a problem in some countries.

Delgado and Simmons also considered sites in Latin America such as Chile, Mexico, and Costa Rica. Latin America offered various attractions. In addition to being cost effective, it is much closer to the United States and generally in the same time zone. Outsourcing customer service to Latin America also makes sense to Californians, many of whom speak Spanish as their first language. But Latin America's outsourcing infrastructure is still young, and Delgado and Simmons worried about whether they could find an appropriate supplier. Numerous other outsourcing locations were possible around the world. For Delgado and Simmons, the number of options was bewildering. Somehow they had to reach a decision.

Help from an Outsourcing Broker

The executives sought the assistance of an outsourcing broker, a consultant with expertise in finding subcontractors and services suppliers abroad. Brokers are especially useful for firms new to outsourcing or those that lack the resources to find foreign suppliers on their own. Eventually the broker found a supplier in India that appeared well suited to meet Good Hope's needs. For example, for transcribing doctor's notes and other medical documents, Simmons learned that Good Hope would pay 12 cents per word, 5 cents less than charged by the firm's current supplier in California. Simmons determined that Good Hope would save about $640,000 a year on medical transcriptions alone. When the accounting and customer service work were added to the mix, the executives discovered that Good Hope would save roughly $1.4 million annually. Delgado was elated: "How else could we shave so much from our expenses with so little effort? And best of all, we don't have to lay off any of our own workers."

The Supplier Firm

To meet all their outsourcing needs, Delgado and Simmons settled on a firm in Bangalore, India, known as BangSource. According to the outsourcing broker, BangSource had a good reputation and was already handling accounting, data processing, transcription, and customer service operations for several large U.S. hospitals. BangSource expects to pick up many new accounts in Australia, Canada, and Europe. BangSource is located in one of the fastest-growing areas of Bangalore and buses in workers from all around the region. The outsourcing broker confided that although BangSource's employee turnover rate was 25 percent, this was consistent with the rate at other outsourcing firms.

The consultant put Good Hope in touch with Mr. Singh, a manager at BangSource and recent graduate of one of India's numerous MBA programs. Mr. Singh explained that BangSource had been in business for about 4 years and had quickly achieved considerable expertise in various business processes. BangSource had recently begun to hire computer engineers and marketing personnel, as the firm was planning to increase its outsourcing capabilities to include software development and telemarketing.

The Situation One Year Later

In the year following the signing of a contract with BangSource, Good Hope encountered various problems. The cost of BangSource's services proved to be significantly higher than what Mr. Singh had originally forecast. Processing of accounting and other data was more complex than anticipated, so costs had escalated. Also, BangSource proved less efficient in addressing Good Hope's customer service queries, and required more telephone time and phone calls to address customer needs. Although the Indian customer service workers generally spoke perfect English, some had hard-to-understand accents and a few of Good Hope's customers had complained. Various misunderstandings arose between BangSource and Good Hope as management at the respective firms attempted to refine activity processing. The problem was exacerbated by recent fluctuations in the rupee-dollar exchange rate, which sometimes inflated the cost of BangSource's services even further.

In addition, while BangSource's business had increased substantially in the previous year, provision of electrical power by the local energy utility had not kept pace, and BangSource occasionally experienced power outages and downtime of computer systems. Growing demand for workers in the Bangalore area delayed hiring efforts, and BangSource was sometimes late in performing promised services due to a shortage of skilled workers. BangSource also faced problems hiring enough qualified managers, which further impaired the quality of its accounting and call-center services.

Delgado and Simmons were disappointed and unsure whether Good Hope was better off today than a year earlier. Top management was pressing the team to solve the problems. As the pair prepared to fly to India to meet with BangSource management, they knew that outsourcing could succeed but they had to figure out how to overcome the various challenges.

AACSB: **Reflective Thinking Skills, Ethical Understanding and Reasoning Abilities**

Case Questions

1. What motives and specific strategic goals can Good Hope achieve by outsourcing to India? Identify strategic goals that Good Hope could potentially achieve in the future.

2. What are the specific risks that Good Hope faced and potentially faces in outsourcing the activities to India?

3. What specific guidelines should management at Good Hope have taken into account as it ventured into global sourcing? What should Good Hope do now to resolve the problems it faces in outsourcing to BangSource?

4. Suppose that thousands of additional firms in California decided to outsource their back-office activities

(such as accounting, finance, and data analysis) to India. What would be the implications of such a trend to California's workers and economy? What steps could California take to reduce the potential harm to its citizens of widespread global sourcing?

SOURCES: Dahl, Darren. (2005). "Outsourcing the Outsourcing," *Inc. Magazine*, December, pp. 55–56; *Economist*. (2004). "A World of Work: A Survey of Outsourcing," November 13, special section; *Economist*. (2005). "The Rise of Nearshoring," December 3, pp. 65–67; *Economist*. (2005). "India: The Next Wave," December 17, pp. 57–58; Engardio, Pete. (2006). "The Future of Outsourcing: How It's Transforming Whole Industries and Changing the Way We Work," *Business Week*, January 30, p. 58; Ewing, Jack, and Gail Edmondson. (2005). "The Rise of Central Europe," *Business Week*, December 12, pp. 50–56; Human Resources Outsourcing Association Europe. (2007). "Outsourcing's Future Holds Major Surprises for Global Providers," April 13, at www.hroaeurope.com.

CHAPTER ESSENTIALS

Key Terms

business process outsourcing (BPO), p. 490
captive sourcing, p. 493
configuration of value-adding activity, p. 491

contract manufacturing, p. 493
global sourcing, p. 492
global supply chain, p. 504

offshoring, p. 494
outsourcing, p. 490

Summary

In this chapter, you learned about:

1. Outsourcing, global sourcing, and offshoring

Global sourcing refers to the procurement of products or services from suppliers or company-owned subsidiaries located abroad for consumption in the home country or a third country. **Outsourcing** is the procurement of selected value-adding activities, including production of intermediate goods or finished products, from external independent suppliers. **Business process outsourcing** refers to the outsourcing of business functions such as finance, accounting, and human resources. Procurement can be from either independent suppliers or via company-owned subsidiaries or affiliates. **Offshoring** refers to the relocation of a business process or entire manufacturing facility to a foreign country. Managers make two strategic decisions regarding value-adding activities: whether to *make or buy* inputs and where to locate value-adding activity—that is, the geographic **configuration of value-adding activity**. **Contract manufacturing** is an arrangement in which the focal firm contracts with an independent supplier to have the supplier manufacture products according to well-defined specifications.

2. Benefits of global sourcing

Global sourcing aims to reduce the cost of doing business or to achieve other strategic goals. For some entrepreneurs, global outsourcing has provided the means to turn around failing businesses, speed up the pace of innovation, or fund development projects that are otherwise unaffordable. Other benefits of global sourcing include faster corporate growth, the ability to access qualified personnel, improved productivity and service, redesigned business processes, faster foreign market entry, access to new markets, and technological flexibility. Global sourcing also allows firms to focus on their core activities and continuously renew their strategic assets.

3. Risks of global sourcing

Risks include failing to realize anticipated cost savings, dealing with environmental uncertainty, creating competitors, engaging suppliers with insufficient training, relying too much on suppliers, and eroding the morale of existing employees.

4. Strategies for minimizing the risks of global sourcing

Firms should develop a strategic perspective in making global sourcing decisions. Although cost cutting is usually the first rationale, global sourcing is also a means to create customer value and improve the firm's competitive advantages. It is a tool to enhance the quality of offerings, improve productivity, and free up resources that can be redeployed to improve long-term performance. To make global sourcing succeed, management should gain employee cooperation, emphasize strong supplier relations, safeguard its interests in the supplier relationship, and choose the right foreign suppliers.

5. Implementing global sourcing through supply-chain management

The efficiency with which goods can be physically moved from one part of the globe to another makes global sourcing feasible. **Global supply chain** refers to the firm's integrated network of sourcing, production, and distribution, organized on a world scale and located in countries where competitive advantage can be maximized.

6. Global sourcing and corporate social responsibility

Global sourcing is a means to sustain or enhance firm competitiveness but can also contribute to job losses and declining living standards. Some firms outsource to suppliers that employ low-cost labor. Attempts to prohibit global sourcing are impractical. Governments should enact policies in the home country that encourage job retention and growth by reducing the cost of doing business, by encouraging entrepreneurship and technological development, and by developing a strong educational system and upgrading the modern skills of the population.

Test Your Comprehension AACSB: Reflective Thinking Skills, Ethical Understanding and Reasoning Abilities

1. Distinguish between outsourcing, global sourcing, and offshoring.

2. What is business process outsourcing? What are its implications for company strategy and performance?

3. What are the two strategic decisions that managers face regarding the firm's international value chain, and what are their implications for company performance?

4. Identify the benefits that companies receive from global sourcing. Why do firms outsource to foreign suppliers?

5. What two countries are the most important global sourcing destinations today? What are the basic differences between these two countries, and what activities are typically outsourced to each?

6. What are the characteristics that make countries attractive as global sourcing destinations?

7. In what service industries are jobs commonly outsourced to foreign suppliers?

8. What are the risks that firms face in global sourcing?

9. What steps can managers take to minimize the risks of global sourcing?

10. What are the major guidelines for strategic global sourcing? What actions can management take to make global sourcing succeed?

11. What are the advantages and disadvantages of global sourcing to the nation? What public policy initiatives are likely to reduce the disadvantages of global sourcing?

Apply Your Understanding AACSB: Reflective Thinking Skills, Ethical Understanding and Reasoning Abilities

1. *Ethical Dilemma:* Revisit the opening vignette at the beginning of this chapter. Assume you have started a new job as a junior manager at a pharmaceutical firm. Management is considering having clinical trials of a new medication performed by a subcontractor in Russia. What are the benefits and specific strategic goals that your firm can achieve by undertaking global sourcing? According to the opening vignette, conducting clinical trials in Russia can be risky because quality control is sometimes lax. Testing is occasionally done without adequate oversight. Some breakdowns in ethical and scientific processes may compromise the reliability of findings from clinical trials. What should you do?

Using the Ethical Framework in Chapter 5, analyze the ethical consequences of subcontracting clinical trials to the Russian firm.

2. Suppose your new job is at Intel, the world's largest semiconductor company and the inventor of the microprocessors found in many personal computers. Intel combines advanced chip design capability with a leading-edge manufacturing capability. The firm is well known for advanced R&D and innovative products. Intel has much of its manufacturing done in China, to take advantage of low-cost labor and an educated workforce capable of producing Intel's knowledge-intensive products. Intel has been stepping up its R&D

activity in China and collaborates with Chinese firms in new-technology development. Identify the risks that Intel faces in its operations in China. What strategies and proactive measures can Intel management take to safeguard its interests? What long-term strategic goals does Intel achieve by offshoring from China?

3. *Ethical Dilemma:* You work for a congressman or member of parliament at your national legislature who must decide how to vote on a bill making its way through the legislative process. The bill is a new law that would restrict the ability of firms in your country to outsource work to countries that pay lower average wages than in your country. Proponents of the legislation note that foreign suppliers frequently operate sweatshops, factories where people work long hours for very low wages, often in harsh conditions. Some outsourced work is performed using child labor. Many factories have poor environmental standards and generate excessive pollution. However, opponents of the new legislation point to the benefits of global sourcing. They argue that outsourced work provides needed jobs that help decrease poverty in developing economies. By reconfiguring value chains to the most cost-efficient locations, companies in your country can reduce production costs, allowing them to hire more workers and reduce prices charged to customers. What recommendation will you make on how to vote on the proposed bill? Use the Ethical Framework in Chapter 5 to analyze the pros and cons of global sourcing.

globalEDGE Internet Exercises
(http://globalEDGE.msu.edu)

AACSB: Reflective Thinking Skills, Ethical Understanding and Reasoning Abilities, Use of Information Technology, Analytic Skills

Refer to Chapter 1, page 62, for instructions on how to access and use globalEDGE™.

1. You work for a software company that aims to outsource some of its software development to a foreign supplier. At present, you are considering three countries: Hungary, Mexico, and Russia. You need to learn more about the capabilities of these countries as sites for the outsourcing of software development. One approach is to visit the research section of the World Bank (www.worldbank.org). At the World Bank Web site, go to Topics, then to Information & Communication Technologies (ICT), then to ICT Tables. For each of the three countries, find and analyze variables that indicate the quality of the local software and IT environment. Based on your findings, which country appears strongest for meeting the needs of your firm?

2. International labor standards are complex and closely related to global sourcing. In particular, the use of sweatshops has attracted much attention. A sweatshop is a factory characterized by very low wages, long hours, and poor working conditions. Some sweatshops employ children in unsafe conditions. Prolabor groups advocate for minimum labor standards in foreign factories. Suppose your future employer wants to outsource a portion of its production to certain developing countries, but is concerned about the possibility of employing sweatshop labor. Visit the Web sites of groups that encourage minimum standards in labor conditions (for example, www.workersrights.org, www.usas.org, www.corpwatch.org, or enter the keywords "labor conditions" at globalEDGE™) and prepare a memo to your employer that discusses the major concerns of those who advocate minimum labor standards.

3. Your firm just decided to outsource to India such back-office operations as accounting and basic finance functions. Unclear on how to proceed, management has asked you to find candidate suppliers in India. As a first step, you decide to check the online Yellow Pages (such as yahoo.com or superpage.com) and search for appropriate Indian firms. Find three firms in India that specialize in business-process outsourcing and examine their Web sites. Describe and compare the business-process services that each firm provides. What selection criteria should you use? Which firm seems most qualified and reputable for providing outsourcing of business-process services?

PART 5

CHAPTER *18*

LEARNING OBJECTIVES In this chapter, you will learn about:

1. Global marketing strategy
2. Standardization and adaptation of international marketing
3. Global branding and product development
4. International pricing
5. International marketing communications
6. International distribution

Marketing in the Global Firm

Zara's Unique Model for International Marketing Success

The Spanish multinational Inditex has transformed itself into Europe's leading apparel retailer. Inditex's flagship store is Zara, the fashion chain that specializes in up-to-date clothing at affordable prices. Headquartered in northern Spain, Zara generated about $5 billion in sales in 2006 across its stores in some 60 countries. In Asia, Zara has some 40 stores from Bangkok to Tokyo, and opened its first shop in Shanghai in 2006.

Zara is a leader in rapid-response retailing. In-house teams produce fresh designs twice a week. While competitors typically have up to an 11–month lead time to move a garment from design to manufacturing, total turn-around time at Zara is just 2 weeks. None of its styles last in stores more than a month. Zara is fast and flexible in meeting market needs by integrating design, production, distribution, and sales within its own stores. Zara created about 20,000 different items in 2006, roughly triple what Gap produced. Because textiles are a labor-intensive business, most retailers source from low-cost shops in Asia. Zara, on the other hand, produces its most fashionable items—50 percent of all its merchandise—at a dozen company-owned factories in Spain. Clothes with longer shelf life are outsourced to low-cost suppliers in Turkey and Asia.

Zara's supply chain is lightning fast. Once clothing is produced, it is shipped to stores in 24 to 36 hours. Using the latest information technology, garments are continuously scanned as they pass through the distribution channel. Distributors immediately know what is needed for restocking. Predetermined fabrics await design instructions, and suppliers provide other needed materials, such as thread, zippers, and buttons just-in-time. Rapid-response retailing means fashions go straight from the factory to stores. Nevertheless, the Spain-based production and distribution model has its limitations. Rapid-response retailing becomes harder to manage the farther away from Spain the firm's outlets are located.

Stores are both uncluttered and colorful, creating a high-end luxury shopping environment. Management emphasizes product innovation and value pricing. Adapted to individual markets, prices are higher in high-income countries and more competitive in low-income or low-demand countries. Much of the firm's promotional activities depend on creating buzz, generating word-of-mouth, and setting up stores in prominent locations. Zara's flashy outlets are on some of the world's priciest streets: Fifth Avenue in New York, Ginza in Tokyo, Via Condotti in Rome, and the Champs-Elysees in Paris.

Zara's positioning differentiates the firm from key competitors based on pricing (low to moderate) and fashion (slightly formal, chic). For instance, the United States-based chain Gap and Italy's Benetton are positioned as moderately high-priced but not particularly fashion-forward. Sweden's H&M offers merchandise that is casual and targeted to younger people. A key competitive advantage of Zara is that it stays at the very leading edge of fashion.

The retailer follows a unique approach to eliciting consumer feedback. Management reacts quickly to daily sales figures. Using wireless organizers, managers and salespeople in Zara's stores advise headquarters daily about constantly changing consumer tastes. Stores employ retail

515

specialists with a strong sense of fashion who advise on which items move fastest. Fast-moving items are replicated quickly, in a myriad of colors or styles, and slow-moving items are removed. Zara's researchers also visit college campuses, clubs, and other hotspots. Magazines like Vogue as well as fashion shows provide additional inspiration.

In a fickle industry, often characterized by sluggish growth, Zara has been growing fairly rapidly. The firm is expanding in Asia and North America and penetrating deeper into Europe. Managers intend to apply the same strategies that have proven successful thus far.

SOURCES: *Business Week*, (2007). "Retailers Need to Boost Product Turnover," January 16. Retrieved from www.business week.com; *Business Week*, (2006). "Fashion Conquistador,''' September 4. Retrieved from www.businessweek.com; *Business Week*, (2006). "Zara: Taking the Lead in Fast-Fashion," April 4. Retrieved from www.businessweek.com; Echikson, William. (2000). "The Mark of Zara," *Business Week*, May 29, pp. 98–100; *Economist*, (2005). "The Future of Fast Fashion," June 18, p. 63; Fraiman, Nelson, and Medini Singh. (2002). *Zara*. Case study. New York: Columbia Business School, Columbia University; Heller, Richard. (2001). "Galician Beauty," *Forbes*, May 28, p. 98; Hoovers.com entry on Zara International, Inc.; Inditex press kit, June 2007. www.inditex.com; Inditex Press Release "Business Week Ranks Inditex as the Seventh Best Performing European Company," May 14, 2007; Maitland, Alison. (2005). "Make Sure You Have Your Christmas Stock In," *Financial Times*, December 19, p. 11.

Global Marketing Strategy

In internationalizing firms, marketing is concerned with identifying, measuring, and pursuing customer needs and market opportunities abroad. Exhibit 18.1 provides a framework for these activities and previews the topics of this chapter. The outer layer

Exhibit 18.1
Organizing Framework for Marketing in the International Firm

represents the cultural, social, political, legal, and regulatory environment of foreign markets. These environmental conditions constrain the firm's ability to price, promote, and distribute a product. For example, the firm will need to review prices frequently in high-inflation countries, adapt the positioning or selling propositions of the product to suit local customer expectations, and ensure products comply with mandated government standards.

The middle layer in Exhibit 18.1 represents **global marketing strategy**—a plan of action the firm develops for foreign markets that guides its decision-making on (1) how to position itself and its offerings, (2) which customer segments to target, and (3) to what degree it should standardize or adapt its marketing program elements.[1]

Targeting Customer Segments and Positioning

Market segmentation refers to the process of dividing the firm's total customer base into homogeneous clusters in a way that allows management to formulate unique marketing strategies for each group. Within each market segment, customers exhibit similar characteristics, including income level, lifestyle, demographic profile, and desired product benefits. For example, in selling its earthmoving equipment, Caterpillar develops distinct marketing approaches for several major market segments, including construction firms, farmers, and the military. In setting prices, Caterpillar creates value-priced tractors for farmers, moderately priced earthmoving equipment for construction firms, and high-priced, heavy-duty trucks and other vehicles for the military.

In international business, firms frequently form market segments by grouping countries based on macro-level variables, such as level of economic development or cultural dimensions. Many MNEs group Latin American countries based on a common language (Spanish) or the European countries based on shared economic conditions. This approach has proven most effective for product categories in which governments play a key regulatory role (such as telecommunications, medical products, and processed foods) or where national characteristics prevail in determining product acceptance and usage.[2]

Today, firms increasingly target global market segments. A **global market segment** is a group of customers who share common characteristics across many national markets. Firms target these buyers with relatively uniform marketing programs. For example, MTV and Levi Strauss both target a largely homogenous youth market that exists around most of the world. This segment generally follows global media, is quick to embrace new fashions and trends, and has significant disposable income. Another global market segment is frequent business travelers. They tend to be more affluent and are eager consumers of premium products that represent luxury and sophisticated style.

The firm's objective in pursuing global market segments is to uniquely position its offerings in the minds of target customers. *Positioning* is a marketing strategy in which the firm develops both the product and its marketing to evoke a distinct impression in the customer's mind, emphasizing differences from all competitive offerings. In the theme park business, Disney positions itself as standing for family values and "good, clean fun" to attract families around the world.[3] Starbucks aims for customers with sophisticated tastes who do not mind paying several dollars for a cup of coffee. BMW wants to compete in the premium car market segment.

Positioning may also evoke the specific *attributes* consumers associate with a product.

Global marketing strategy   A plan of action for foreign markets that guides the firm in deciding how to position itself and its offerings, which customer segments to target, and the degree to which it should standardize or adapt its marketing program elements.

Global market segment   A group of customers who share common characteristics across many national markets.

MTV has a global market segment of young adults who enjoy music. Here, Alicia Keys greets fans at the MTV Asia awards.

Diet Coke elicits an image of someone who needs to lose or maintain weight. When Coca-Cola first entered Japan, research revealed that Japanese women do not like products labeled "diet," nor is the population considered overweight. Thus, management altered the product's positioning in Japan by changing the name to Coke Light.

Internationalizing firms aim for a *global positioning strategy*, which positions the offering similarly in the minds of buyers worldwide. Starbucks, Volvo, and Sony successfully use this approach. Consumers around the world view these strong brands in the same way. Global positioning strategy reduces international marketing costs by addressing the shared expectations of a global customer market segment.[4]

Standardization and Adaptation of International Marketing

In addition to guiding targeting and positioning, global marketing strategy also articulates the degree to which the firm's marketing program should vary between different foreign markets. With **adaptation** the firm modifies one or more elements of its international marketing program to accommodate specific customer requirements in a particular market. **Standardization** makes the marketing program elements uniform, with a view to targeting entire regions, or even the global marketplace, with the same product or service.

In the innermost layer in Exhibit 18.1, we identify the key elements of the marketing program (sometimes referred to as the *marketing mix*) affected by the standardization/adaptation decision. These are: global branding and product development, international pricing, international marketing communications, and international distribution. In the international context, marketing strategy tackles the complexity of having both global and local competitors, as well as cross-national differences in culture, language, living standards, economic conditions, regulations, and quality of business infrastructure. A key challenge is to resolve the trade-offs between standardization and adaptation.

When they enter international markets, managers undertake a broad corporate strategy in which they attempt to strike the ideal balance between *global integration* and *local responsiveness*. As we discussed in Chapter 12, global integration seeks cross-national synergy in the firm's value-chain activities in order to take maximum advantage of similarities between countries, while local responsiveness aims to meet the specific needs of buyers in individual countries. How the firm resolves the balance between global integration and local responsiveness also affects how it makes standardization and adaptation decisions in its marketing program elements.

Exhibit 18.2 highlights the trade-offs between standardization and adaptation in international marketing. Let's examine the advantages of each approach.

Standardization

Representing a tendency toward global integration, standardization is more likely to be pursued in global industries such as aircraft manufacturing, pharmaceuticals, and credit cards. Airbus, Pfizer, and MasterCard use a standardized marketing strategy with great success. Their offerings are largely uniform across many markets worldwide. A standardized marketing approach is most appropriate when:

- Similar market segments exist across countries.
- Customers seek similar features in the product or service.
- Products have universal specifications.
- Business customers have converging expectations or needs regarding specifications, quality, performance, and other product attributes.

The viability of standardization varies across industries and product categories. Commodities, industrial equipment, and technology products lend themselves to a high

Adaptation Firm's efforts to modify one or more elements of its international marketing program to accommodate specific customer requirements in a particular market.

Standardization Firm's efforts to make its marketing program elements uniform, with a view to targeting entire regions, or even the global marketplace, with the same product or service.

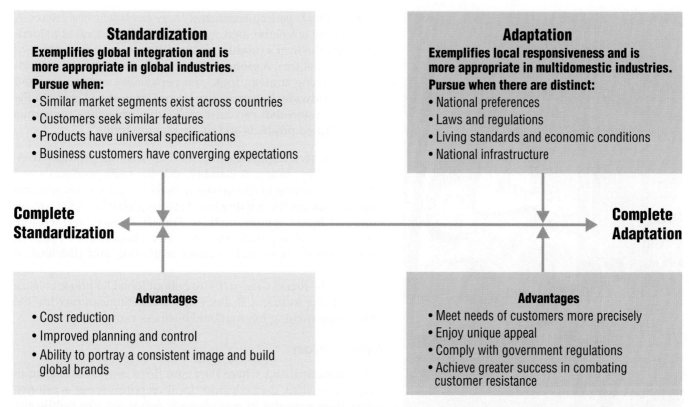

Standardization
Exemplifies global integration and is more appropriate in global industries.
Pursue when:
- Similar market segments exist across countries
- Customers seek similar features
- Products have universal specifications
- Business customers have converging expectations

Adaptation
Exemplifies local responsiveness and is more appropriate in multidomestic industries.
Pursue when there are distinct:
- National preferences
- Laws and regulations
- Living standards and economic conditions
- National infrastructure

Complete Standardization ←→ **Complete Adaptation**

Advantages
- Cost reduction
- Improved planning and control
- Ability to portray a consistent image and build global brands

Advantages
- Meet needs of customers more precisely
- Enjoy unique appeal
- Comply with government regulations
- Achieve greater success in combating customer resistance

Exhibit 18.2   Trade-offs between Adaptation and Standardization of International Marketing Program

degree of standardization. Popular consumer electronics like Sony's PlayStation, Apple's iPod, and Canon digital cameras, as well as well-known fashion accessories like Rolex watches and Louis Vuitton handbags, are largely standardized around the world. Automotive parts, building materials, dinnerware, and basic food ingredients are other products that require little or no adaptation.

When managers build on commonalities in customer preferences and attempt to standardize their international marketing program, they can expect at least three types of favorable outcomes.

■ *Cost reduction.* Standardization reduces costs by making possible economies of scale in design, sourcing, manufacturing, and marketing. Offering a similar marketing program to the global marketplace or across entire regions is more efficient than having to adapt products for each of the numerous individual markets. Electrolux (based in Sweden, www.electrolux.com) once made hundreds of refrigerator models to accommodate the diverse tastes and regulatory requirements of each country in Europe. As product standards and tastes gradually harmonized across the European Union, Electrolux was able to reduce the number of its refrigerator models to a few dozen, consolidate manufacturing facilities, and streamline its marketing activities across the EU. The resulting consolidation saved Electrolux millions of euros. With fewer offerings, the company now focuses its R&D activities on advanced features and superior technology.

■ *Improved planning and control.* Standardization provides for improved planning and control of value-adding activities. Fewer offerings simplify quality control and reduce the number of replacement parts Electrolux needs to stock. Marketing activities are also simplified. Instead of designing a unique marketing campaign for each country in Europe, the firm is able to simultaneously offer a largely standardized campaign for numerous countries.

Popular consumer products like Sony's PlayStation, Rolex watches, and Louis Vuitton handbags are largely standardized around the world. Here shoppers stroll in front of a Louis Vuitton store in Tokyo, Japan.

Global brand A brand whose positioning, advertising strategy, look, and personality are standardized worldwide.

- *Ability to portray a consistent image and build global brands.* A brand is a name, sign, symbol, or design intended to identify the firm's product and to differentiate it from those of competitors. A **global brand** is one whose positioning, advertising strategy, look, and personality are standardized worldwide. It increases customer interest and reduces the confusion that can arise when the firm offers numerous adapted products and marketing programs.[5]

Gillette (www.gillette.com), the U.S. shaving products division owned by Procter & Gamble, sells the same products using uniform marketing in all the countries where it does business and often introduces them with simultaneous global launches, under universal brand names such as Trak II, Sensor, and Fusion. Gillette's global approach has achieved an impressive 70 percent global market share and reduced marketing and distribution costs.[6]

Read the *Recent Grad in IB* story about John Dykhouse to learn how working in brand strategy and marketing can provide the basis for an exciting international business career.

Adaptation

While standardizing where they can, firms may also engage in adaptation when they consider local responsiveness a priority. Adaptation is useful in *multidomestic industries*, like publishing and software, which tailor their offerings to suit individual markets. It may be as straightforward as translating labels, instructions, or books into a foreign language or as complex as completely modifying a product to fit unique market conditions. Local adaptation can provide the marketer with important advantages. Managers consider several different rationales when adapting marketing program elements, which we explore next.

- *Differences in national preferences.* Adaptation may be carried out to modify the offering to the specific, unique wants and needs of customers in individual markets. The dairy producer New Zealand Milk adds ginger and papaya flavoring to its milk products to suit the tastes of Chinese customers. The Netherlands' Foremost Friesland Co. sells green tea-flavored fresh milk in Thailand.[7]

When *The Simpsons* cartoon series was broadcast in Saudi Arabia, it was substantially adapted for language and local Islamic sensibilities. The show was renamed *Al Shamshoon*, Homer Simpson's name was changed to "Omar," and Bart Simpson became "Badr." The program aims to win coveted young viewers, who constitute much of the Arab world. In addition to translating the show into Arabic, producers had to address the way the Simpson daughter and mother dress. Producers removed references to practices forbidden by the Qur'an or considered potentially offensive, such as consuming pork and beer. They changed Homer Simpson's Duff beer to soda, hot dogs to Egyptian beef sausages, and donuts to the popular Arab cookies called *kahk*. Moe's Bar was edited out of the show. As one Arab viewer told ABC News, "We are a totally different culture, so you can't talk about the same subject in the same way."[8]

McDonald's has been able to standardize its hamburgers across most world markets, but not all. Some cultures and religions shun consumption of beef. McDonald's substitutes lamb or chicken in its burgers in some markets such as India. It also adds additional items such as Kofte burgers (hamburger with special spices) in Turkey. In Hong Kong, burgers are sandwiched between buns made of glutinous rice. McDonald's outlets in Norway serve "McLaks," a grilled salmon

RECENT GRAD IN IB

John's major: Bachelor of Business Administration (International Business, Marketing)

Objectives: Inspiration, business success, adventure, a global outlook on life, community involvement, and helping others achieve their goals

Internships during college: Non-profit marketing; business innovations for a large consumer packaged goods firm

Jobs held since graduating:
- Associate Brand Manager, Amway Corporate Marketing, Nutrition Brands
- Brand Manager, Amway Corporate Marketing, Nutrition Brands
- Trade Development Manager, Amway Global, Health Brands

John Dykhouse: Trade Development Manager

A single decision made in the blink of an eye can shape your life. As an undergraduate, John Dykhouse decided to study abroad in Grenoble, France, for one year. John notes, "For the first time, I understood that learning a new culture and language doesn't open doors just to communication, but to a new way of thinking."

Upon his graduation, the combination of international experience and several marketing-related internships helped John obtain a position at Amway Corporation. Over time, he became Associate Brand Manager with Nutrilite, a brand of vitamins, minerals, and dietary supplements sold in many countries around the world. His job responsibilities included the management of several product categories within the brand, managing a global product portfolio, communications, and pricing, to name a few.

Within two years, John was offered the position of Brand Manager. With this new role came a shift into the world of athletic sponsorships. The position gave John the chance to work with professional athletes and their agencies to further develop their brands through awareness-generating sponsorships and events around the world. His work brought John back to Europe many times, as well as to Korea and Japan, to support local efforts rooted in a corporate strategy he helped create. In his newest position, John is working in Trade Development to create training tools, product campaigns, and digital strategies.

John's Advice for Career Success

"First, it's important to be a good communicator. With international work, think about when to use simplified English, and in all things understand the importance of brevity. Second, be persistent. Many people give up on the first, second, or even third try. The chances are good that you will make at least a few blunders during an international career. Embrace these as learning experiences, and move on—just don't make them again. Third, do what it takes to find a great mentor, and learn from him or her. Fourth, be a team player. You will likely work with people who come from cultures you don't completely understand. Make sure you explore what is behind their opinions, be respectful, and at times, be cautious. Fifth, be curious. The best international businesspeople are always curious, taking in the sights, sounds, people, and even some smells of the places they visit. Lastly, learn the power of the lunch break. While it's tempting to sit at a desk to work through lunch, consider using the time to lunch with mentors and colleagues—you will likely have some of the most productive discussions of your career, helping you navigate through many challenges."

In the coming years, John plans to complete an MBA, with an emphasis on Brand Management and International Business.

sandwich with dill sauce. In Berlin, consumers can savor a beer with their double cheeseburgers and fries. In some Arab countries, the "McArabia," a spicy chicken filet on flatbread, has been a success. Customers in Chile dress their burgers with avocado paste.[9]

- *Differences in living standards and economic conditions.* Because income levels vary substantially around the world, firms attempt to adjust both the pricing and the complexity of their product offerings for individual markets. Microsoft has lowered the price of its software for Thailand, Malaysia, and Indonesia to bring it in line with local purchasing power.[10] Dell sells inexpensive simplified versions of its computers in developing economies. Inflation and economic recessions also influence pricing policy. A recession signals a drop in consumer confidence, and the firm may need to reduce prices to generate sales. High inflation can rapidly erode profits, even as prices rise. Exchange rate fluctuations also necessitate adjustments. When the importing country currency is weak, the purchasing power of its consumers is reduced.

■ *Differences in laws and regulations.* Germany, Norway, and Switzerland are among the countries that restrict advertising directed at children. Packaged foods in Europe are often labeled in several different languages, including English, French, German, and Spanish. In Quebec, Canada's French-speaking province, local law requires product packaging to be in both English and French. In some markets, the use of certain sales promotion activities like coupons and sales contests is restricted.

■ *Differences in national infrastructure.* The quality and reach of transportation networks, marketing intermediaries, and overall business infrastructure influence the marketing communications and distribution systems that firms employ abroad. Infrastructure is especially poor in the rural parts of developing economies, necessitating innovative approaches for getting products to customers. Road and rail networks in western China are underdeveloped, so firms use small trucks to reach retailers in outlying communities. Undeveloped media also require substantial adaptations to carry marketing communications. In rural Vietnam, most consumers cannot access television, magazines, or the Internet. Radio, billboards, and brochures are favored for targeting low-income buyers.

In light of the above rationale, we can identify four primary advantages of adapting an international marketing program to the local market:

1. Meet the needs of local customers more precisely
2. Create unique appeal for the product
3. Comply with local or national government regulations
4. Achieve greater success in combating local and global competitors

Adaptation also provides managers an opportunity to explore alternate ways of marketing the product or service. What they learn in the process can guide R&D efforts, often leading to superior products for sale abroad and at home. Products developed or modified for foreign markets sometimes prove so successful that they are launched as new products in the firm's home market. Toyota originally designed the Lexus for the U.S. market. After perfecting the luxury car during 15 years in the United States, the firm launched it in Japan. In 2009, after developing an inexpensive, battery-powered electrocardiograph machine for doctors in China and India, General Electric realized the device's potential for advanced economies and began marketing it to rural clinics and visiting nurses in the United States.[11]

Standardization and Adaptation: A Balancing Act

A managerial decision about standardization and adaptation is not an either/or decision but rather a balancing act. There are good arguments and outcomes that favor both options; it is up to senior marketing managers and the global new-product planning team to sort out the trade-offs in light of the distinctive environments in which the firm operates.

Perhaps the most important distinction between standardization and adaptation is that standardization helps the firm reduce its costs, while local adaptation helps the firm more precisely cater to local needs and requirements. Adaptation frequently requires adding marketing expertise in local subsidiaries. It is also time-consuming and costly. It may require substantial redesign of products and modifications to manufacturing, pricing, distribution, and communications. Thus, managers usually err on the side of standardization because it is easier and less costly than adaptation. Many firms adapt marketing program elements *only when necessary* to respond to local customer preferences and mandated regulations. Unilever (www.unilever.com) streamlined the number of its brands from more than 1,600 to about 400 and focused attention on a dozen or so global ones. However, the firm had to retain many local adaptations to suit individual markets. In nutrition-conscious countries, it is adapting its food products by lowering the levels of sugar, salt, trans-fats, and saturated fats.[12]

Typically, for a given product or service, managers both standardize and adapt in varying degrees. Some marketing mix elements are standardized, some are localized, and others require a compromise among corporate, regional, and local decision makers. For instance, management might offer a standardized product worldwide but modify its pricing and advertising for different markets. Management decides not only *what* elements to adapt, but also *how much* to adapt them. IKEA maintains uniform product designs across markets while modifying, say, the size of beds or chests of drawers in individual countries. Similarly, it emphasizes its catalog as the principal promotional tool worldwide but supplements it with TV advertising in mass-media oriented markets like the United States.

Firms rarely find it feasible or practical to follow a "one offering-one world" strategy across *all* dimensions of the marketing program. Automotive companies tried for years to market a "world car" that meets customer preferences everywhere and complies with various governments' safety specifications. Ambitious experiments such as the Ford Mondeo failed to meet the approval of customers and regulatory bodies around the world. Flexibility and adaptability in design became necessary due to climate and geography (which affected engine specifications), government emissions standards, customer preferences for frills like cupholders, and gas prices. In 2010, as part of its "One Ford" vision, the Ford Motor Company once again attempted to position its Focus car for customers in every world region and sold it under one name.

As a compromise, some firms pursue standardization as part of a *regional* strategy, formulating international marketing elements to exploit commonalities across a geographic region instead of across the world. General Motors (www.gm.com) markets distinctive car models for China (Buick, HRV), Europe (Opel, Vauxhall), and North America (Cadillac, Chevrolet). Convergence of regional preferences, regional economic integration, harmonization of product standards, and growth of regional media and distribution channels all make regional marketing more feasible than pursuing global marketing approaches.[13]

Popular consumer electronics such as Apple's iPod can gain a worldwide following and require little adaptation from country to country. This fan is using his iPod at the Louvre Museum in Paris, France.

Global Branding and Product Development

Global marketing strategy poses unique challenges and opportunities for managers, particularly in branding and product development. Let's examine these topics.

Global Branding

A key outcome of global positioning strategy is the development of a global brand. Well-known global brands include Hollywood movies (*Ice Age*), pop stars (Rain), sports figures (David Beckham), personal care products (Gillette Sensor), toys (Barbie), credit cards (Visa), food (Cadbury chocolate), beverages (Heineken), furniture (IKEA), and consumer electronics (iPod).[14] Consumers prefer globally branded products because branding provides a sense of trust and confidence in the purchase decision.[15] A strong global brand enhances the efficiency and effectiveness of marketing programs, stimulates brand loyalty, allows the firm to charge premium prices, increases its leverage with intermediaries and retailers, and generally enhances its competitive advantage in global markets.[16] The firm can reduce its marketing and advertising costs by concentrating on a single global brand instead of a number of national brands.

The strength of a global brand is best measured by its brand equity—the market value of a brand. Exhibit 18.3 provides brand equity figures for selected global brands, as calculated by Interbrand (www.interbrand.com), a European-based company. *BusinessWeek* devotes a special issue each year to Interbrand's list of the top 100 global brands (www.businessweek.com/brand). To qualify for the list, a brand must first generate worldwide sales exceeding $1 billion, at least a third of which should come from outside the home market. Then, Interbrand estimates the projected brand earnings and deducts a charge for the cost of owning the tangible assets from these earnings. Finally, Interbrand calculates the net present value of future brand earnings, ending with an estimate of brand value.

Look up the entire list of 100 global brands on the *BusinessWeek* web site. What allows these brands to capture such a worldwide following? Here are the underlying factors that make global brands succeed:

- Some are highly visible, conspicuous consumer products, such as consumer electronics and jeans.
- Some serve as status symbols worldwide, such as cars and jewelry.
- Many have widespread appeal because of innovative features that seem to fit everyone's lifestyle, such as mobile phones, credit cards, and cosmetics.
- Some are identified with the country of origin and command a certain degree of country appeal, such as Levi's (U.S. style) and IKEA furniture (Scandinavian style).

Exhibit 18.3   Top Global Brands, by Region

SOURCES: *Business Week* (http://www.businessweek.com/brand) and *Interbrand* (http://www.interbrand.com), data for 2009.

Company	Brand Value U.S. $ Billions	Country of Origin	Main Product or Service
Asian Brands			
Toyota	$31.3	Japan	Cars
Honda	17.8	Japan	Cars
Samsung	17.5	South Korea	Consumer electronics
Sony	12.0	Japan	Consumer electronics
Canon	10.4	Japan	Copiers, cameras
European Brands			
Nokia	34.8	Finland	Cell phones
Mercedes-Benz	23.9	Germany	Cars
BMW	21.7	Germany	Cars
Louis Vuitton	21.1	France	Fashion accessories
H&M	15.4	Sweden	Clothing
U.S. Brands			
Coca-Cola	68.7	United States	Soft drinks
IBM	60.2	United States	IT services and consulting
Microsoft	56.7	United States	Software
GE	47.8	United States	Appliances, jet engines
McDonald's	32.3	United States	Fast food

Still, in other cases, global brands are reaping the benefits of first-mover advantages in offering new and novel products or services. In 1971, the first Starbucks opened in Seattle, Washington, and offered freshly brewed coffee in a comfortable setting that encouraged people to sit and relax. Nokia, originally founded as a Finnish wood-processing plant in 1865, reengineered itself in the 1990s to become one of the world's leading mobile phone companies. It has distanced itself from competitors by investing in new technologies and design. Samsung Electronics, part of a larger South Korean conglomerate, also propelled itself into consumer electronics with unique design and leading-edge technology.

Developing and maintaining a global brand name is one of the best ways for firms to build global recognition. The Eveready Battery Co. consolidated its various national brand names—such as Ucar, Wonder, and Mazda—into one global brand name, Energizer. The move greatly increased the efficiency of Eveready's marketing efforts around the world. While most managers conceive brands for a national market and then internationalize them, the preferred approach is to build a global brand from the beginning with input from all major markets. Several firms have succeeded in this approach, including Japan's Sony Corporation. "Sony" was derived from the Latin for "sound." The Japanese car company Datsun switched its name to Nissan to create a unified global brand worldwide.[17]

Global branding also helps the MNE compete more effectively with popular local brands that appeal to buyers' sense of local tradition, pride, and preference. Market leaders Coca-Cola and Pepsi face many local brands around the world. In Europe, popular local brands include Virgin Cola (Britain), Afri-Cola (Germany), Kofola (Czech Republic), and Cuba Cola (Sweden). Cola Turka was developed to challenge the dominance of Coca-Cola and Pepsi in its native Turkey. In Peru, Inca Kola was long a successful local brand that established itself as "Peru's Drink." Its experience reveals how local brands can be vulnerable to the market power of strong global brands. In 1999, Coca-Cola purchased 50 percent of the Inca Kola Corporation. Coke and Inca Cola each have about 30 percent of the Peruvian market, giving Coca-Cola an edge since it owns half the other brand.

Global Product Development

In developing products with multi-country potential, managers emphasize their commonalities across countries rather than the differences between them.[18] A basic product will incorporate only core features into which the firm can inexpensively implement variations for individual markets. For instance, while the basic computers Dell sells worldwide are essentially identical, the letters on its keyboards and the languages used in its software are unique to countries or major regions. Many firms design products using *modular architecture*, a collection of *standardized* components and subsystems they can rapidly assemble in various configurations to suit the needs of individual markets. Honda and Toyota design models like the Accord and Corolla around a standardized platform to which modular components, parts, and features are added to suit specific needs and tastes.

General Motors created its *Global Product Development Council* in Detroit to improve efficiency. Concerned about duplication of effort across its divisions, GM top management took authority away from regional engineering operations and charged the council with overseeing $8 billion in annual spending on new model development. The council promotes company-wide use of GM's best car platforms, wherever they are developed worldwide. It adapted the Holden Monaro from GM's Australian subsidiary for North American use as the GTO rather than creating a totally new model. As a result, development cost a modest $50 million instead of the $500 million typical for creating a new model.[19]

A *global new-product planning team* is a group within a firm that determines which elements of the product will be standardized and which will be adapted locally. The team also decides how to launch products—with simultaneous release across countries or

GLOBAL TREND

Growing Role for Marketing in Developing Economies

Some four billion people live in developing economies that suffer severe poverty. Bottom of the pyramid (BOP) countries represent the poorest segment of humanity, often living on less than $2,000 per year. BOP consumers lack the financial resources to buy products and services that raise their standard of living. Inadequate distribution and marketing infrastructure also hamper their access. For daily necessities, BOP consumers typically pay high prices, contributing to their poverty.

In the private sector, companies have historically targeted advanced economies. During the last decade, countless companies have invested in emerging markets. Recently, some leading firms have begun to revise their traditional business models and are profitably targeting BOP markets as well. This is partly due to advances in information and communications technologies that facilitate a larger reach at lower costs, lower marketing transaction costs, better pricing, and distribution channel management. When they do business in BOP countries, firms often hire local citizens to assist in developing products and services, distribution channels, and other infrastructure that improve economic conditions and the lives of consumers. In all these ways, firms can play a substantial role in addressing global poverty.

But how do companies succeed in developing economies? First, they need to recognize the long-term potential of BOP markets, which can be large and fast-growing. By developing a complete line of appropriate health and home care products, packaging, and pricing for BOP customers in India, Unilever created a $2.6 billion portfolio of products that generate a high return on investment.

Second, entry should be preceded by opportunity assessment and market research. Management must be careful to adapt products appropriately and ensure pricing is suited to local income levels. This often requires firms to get "embedded" in the local market to develop insights unique to BOP countries.

Third, the MNE should be careful not to underestimate the intensity of local competition. Local firms know and understand local consumers and often demonstrate a strong capability to develop and successfully implement well-thought-out marketing strategies. Moreover, firms native to BOP countries may enjoy financial and other support from local authorities and banks that are not available to foreign firms.

Fourth, in BOP countries, it is generally important to establish appropriate partners and other connections at the national and local levels to develop effective business operations. Often, this means recruiting employees with the right connections.

Finally, foreign firms should not be seduced by the time-honored attractiveness of "middle-class" market segments where premium pricing, strong brands, and heavy promotion are perceived as the only path to success. Rather, today many firms target the lower-income segment, which is generally much larger in size. They need to devise creative strategies, including competitively priced products and innovative promotion and distribution methods.

SOURCES: Vijay Mahajan and Kamini Banga, *The 86% Solution: How to Succeed in the Biggest Market Opportunity of the 21st Century* (Upper Saddle River, NJ: Wharton School Publishing, 2006); C. K. Prahalad, *The Fortune at the Bottom of the Pyramid* (Upper Saddle River, NJ: Wharton School Publishing, 2006); Peter Walters and Saeed Samiee, "Executive Insights: Marketing Strategy in Emerging Markets," *Journal of International Marketing* 11, no. 1 (2003): 97–106.

with sequential release. Sequential release implies launching a product one country at a time and is often preferred for products requiring substantial local adaptation.

Global new-product planning teams are assigned to formulate best practices a firm would implement in all its worldwide units. These teams assemble employees with specialized knowledge and expertise from various geographically diverse units of the MNE, who collaborate in a project to develop workable solutions to common problems.

You may wish to do a quick online search for creative product designs that benefited from global new-product planning teams. The iXi Bike was designed by a team from Britain, France, and the United States for France's iXi Bicycle Company. The bike fits easily into the trunk of a small car. The Logiq & Vivid E9 is a mobile ultrasound system developed by a global team from France, Japan, and the United States. Used for medical examinations, the ergonomic equipment offers substantial efficiency with minimal environmental impact. A global new-product planning team from Israel and the United States created the Charge Spot, an award-winning compact electricity charging station for electric vehicles that can be embedded in sidewalks, next to parking spaces.[20]

Increasingly, managers understand the role marketing can play in targeting developing economies, where the firm can contribute to raising the living standards of local residents. Read the *Global Trend* box to learn more about this development.

International Pricing

Pricing is complex. It is even more difficult in international business, with multiple currencies, trade barriers, additional cost considerations, potential government regulation, and typically longer distribution channels.[21] Prices often invite competitive reaction, which can drive down a price. Conversely, prices can escalate to unreasonable levels because of tariffs, taxes, and higher markups by foreign intermediaries. Price variations among different markets can lead to **gray market activity**—legal importation of genuine products into a country by intermediaries other than authorized distributors (also known as parallel imports). We discuss gray markets later in this chapter.

Prices influence customers' perception of value, determine the level of motivation of foreign intermediaries, affect promotional spending and strategy, and compensate for weaknesses in other elements of the marketing mix. Let's explore the unique aspects of international pricing.

Gray market activity
Legal importation of genuine products into a country by intermediaries other than authorized distributors (also known as parallel imports).

Factors That Affect International Pricing

Factors that influence international pricing fall into four categories.

1. *Nature of the market.* Buyers' income level and demographic profile are major factors that influence their ability to pay for products and services. Most countries are emerging markets or developing economies where the majority of consumers lack significant disposable income. Thus, prices must be set lower. Regulation, climate, infrastructure, and other factors in foreign markets may also require the firm to spend money to modify a product or its distribution. Food items shipped to hot climates require refrigeration, which drives up costs. In countries with many rural residents or those with a poor distribution infrastructure, delivering products to widely dispersed customers necessitates higher pricing because of steeper shipping costs. Foreign government intervention is also a factor. Governments impose tariffs that lead to higher prices. They also enforce health rules, safety standards, and other regulations that increase the cost of doing business locally. Canada imposes price limits on prescription drugs, which reduces pharmaceutical firms' pricing flexibility.

2. *Nature of the product or industry.* Products with substantial added value—such as cars or high-end computers—usually necessitate charging relatively high prices. A specialized product, or one with a technological edge, gives a company greater price flexibility. When the firm holds a relative monopoly in a product (such as Microsoft's operating system software), it can generally charge premium prices.

3. *Type of distribution system.* Exporting firms rely on independent distributors based abroad. Some of these distributors occasionally modify export pricing to suit their own goals. Some distributors mark up prices substantially—up to 200 percent in some countries—which may harm the manufacturer's image and pricing strategy in the market. By contrast, when the firm internationalizes via FDI by establishing company-owned marketing subsidiaries abroad, management maintains control over their pricing strategy. Firms that make direct sales to end users also control their pricing and can make rapid adjustments to suit evolving market conditions.

4. *Location of the production facility.* Locating manufacturing in those countries with low-cost labor enables a firm to charge lower prices. Locating factories in or near major markets cuts transportation costs and may reduce problems created by foreign exchange fluctuations. During the 1980s, Toyota and Honda built car factories in the United States, their most important foreign market. Mazda retained much of its manufacturing in Japan, exporting its cars to the United States. As the Japanese yen appreciated against the dollar, Mazda had to raise its prices, which hurt U.S. sales.

Exhibit 18.4 provides a comprehensive list of internal and external factors that influence how firms set international prices. Internally, management accounts for its own objectives regarding profit and market share, the cost of goods sold, and the degree of control desired over pricing of the firm's products abroad. Externally, management must account for customer characteristics, competitor prices, exchange rates, tariffs, taxes, and costs related to generating international sales, as well as transporting and distributing the goods. Many countries in Europe and elsewhere charge value-added taxes (VATs) on imported products. Unlike a sales tax, which is calculated based on the retail sales price, the VAT is determined as a percentage of the gross margin—the difference between the sales price and the cost to the seller of the item sold. In the EU, for example, VAT rates range between 15 and 25 percent.

A Framework for Setting International Prices

Managers examine the suitability of prices at several levels in the international distribution channel—importers, wholesalers, retailers, and end users—and then set prices accordingly. Exhibit 18.5 presents a systematic approach for managers to use in setting international prices.[22]

Exhibit 18.4 Internal and External Factors That Affect International Pricing

Internal to the Firm
- Management's profit and market share expectations
- Cost of manufacturing, marketing, and other value-chain activities
- The degree of control management desires over price setting in foreign markets

External Factors
- Customer expectations, purchasing power, and sensitivity to price increases
- Nature of competitors' offerings, prices, and strategy
- International customer costs
  - Product/package modification; labeling and market requirements
  - Documentation (certificate of origin, invoices, banking fees)
  - Financing costs
  - Packing and container charges
  - Shipping (inspection, warehousing, freight forwarder's fee)
  - Insurance
- Landed cost
  - Tariffs (customs duty, import tax, customs clearance fee)
  - Warehousing charges at the port of import; local transportation
- Importer's cost
  - Value-added tax and other applicable taxes paid by the importer
  - Local intermediary (distributor, wholesaler, retailer) margins
  - Cost of financing inventory
- Anticipated fluctuations in currency exchange rates

Step 1. Estimate the "landed" price of the product in the foreign market by totaling all costs associated with shipping the product to the customer's location.

Step 2. Estimate the price the importer or distributor will charge when it adds its profit margin.

Step 3. Estimate the target price range for end users. Determine:
- Floor price (lowest acceptable price to the firm, based on cost considerations)
- Ceiling price (highest possible price, based on customer purchasing power, price sensitivity, and competitive considerations)

Step 4. Assess the company sales potential at the price the firm is most likely to charge (between the floor price and ceiling price).

Step 5. Select a suitable pricing strategy based on corporate goals and preferences from:
- Rigid cost-plus pricing
- Flexible cost-plus pricing
- Incremental pricing

Step 6. Check consistency with current prices across product lines, key customers, and foreign markets (in order to deter potential gray market activity).

Step 7. Implement pricing strategy and tactics, and set intermediary and end-user prices. Then, continuously monitor market performance and make pricing adjustments as necessary to accommodate evolving market conditions.

Exhibit 18.5   Key Steps in International Price Setting

Let's illustrate the international pricing framework with an example. Suppose a leading U.S. musical instrument manufacturer, Melody Corporation, wants to begin exporting electric guitars to Japan and needs to set prices. Melody decides to export its John Mayer brand of guitar, which retails for $2,000 in the United States. Initial research reveals that additional costs of shipping, insurance, and a 5 percent Japanese tariff will add a total of $300 to the price of each guitar, bringing the total landed price to $2,300. Melody has identified an importer in Japan, Aoki Wholesalers, which wants to add a 10 percent profit margin to the cost of each imported guitar. Thus, the total price once a guitar leaves Aoki's Japan warehouse is $2,530. This is the *floor price*, the lowest acceptable price to Melody, since management doesn't want Japanese earnings to dip below those in the United States.

Next, market research on income levels and competitor prices reveals that Japanese musicians are willing to pay prices about 30 percent above typical U.S. prices for high-quality instruments. Given this information, Melody management believes Japan can sustain a ceiling price for the Mayer guitar of $2,600. Additional research provides estimates for Melody's sales potential at the floor price and at the ceiling price. Managers eventually decide on a suggested price of $2,560. Research has revealed this is the most appropriate price in light of factors in Japan such as local purchasing power, size of the market, market growth, competitors' prices, and Japanese attitudes on the relationship of price to product quality. Management also feels the price is reasonable given Melody's pricing in other markets, such as Hawaii and Australia. Accordingly, the firm implements the price level for end users and the corresponding price for Aoki, the importer. Melody begins shipping guitars to Japan and monitors the marketplace, keeping track of actual demand and the need to adjust prices in light of demand, economic conditions, and other emergent factors.

Let's review the three pricing strategies in Step 5 of Exhibit 18.5. *Rigid cost-plus pricing* refers to setting a fixed price for all export markets. It is an approach favored by less experienced exporters. In most cases, management simply adds a flat percentage to the domestic price to compensate for the added costs of doing business abroad. The export customer's final price includes a mark-up to cover transporting and marketing the product, as well as profit margins for both intermediaries and the manufacturer. A key disadvantage of this method is that it often fails to account for local market conditions, such as buyer demand, income level, and competition.

In *flexible cost-plus pricing*, management includes any added costs of doing business abroad in its final price. At the same time, management also accounts for local market and competitive conditions, such as customer purchasing power, demand, competitor prices, and other external variables, as identified in Exhibit 18.4. This approach is more sophisticated than rigid cost-plus pricing because it accounts for specific circumstances in the target market. For example, the fashion retailer Zara uses this approach, adapting prices to suit conditions in each of the countries where it does business.

In highly competitive markets, the firm may set prices to cover only its variable costs, but not its fixed costs. This is known as *incremental pricing*. Here, management assumes fixed costs are already paid from sales of the product in the firm's home country or other markets. The approach enables the firm to offer competitive prices, but it may result in suboptimal profits.

When carried to an extreme, incremental pricing may invite competitors to accuse a firm of dumping. As we discussed in Chapter 8, *dumping* is the practice of charging a lower price for exported products, sometimes below manufacturing cost—potentially driving local suppliers out of business. The seller may compensate for the low price by charging higher prices in other markets. Many national governments regard dumping as a form of unfair competition and impose antidumping duties or initiate legal action through the World Trade Organization (www.wto.org).

Managing International Price Escalation

International price escalation The problem of end-user prices reaching exorbitant levels in the export market, caused by multilayered distribution channels, intermediary margins, tariffs, and other international customer costs.

International price escalation refers to the problem of end-user prices reaching exorbitant levels in the export market, caused by multilayered distribution channels, intermediary margins, tariffs, and other international customer costs (identified in Exhibit 18.4). International price escalation means the retail price in the export market can be significantly higher than the domestic price, creating a competitive disadvantage for the exporter. Corporations can use five key strategies to combat export price escalation abroad, which is reviewed next.[23]

1. *Shorten the distribution channel* to establish a more direct route to reach the final customer by bypassing some intermediaries in the channel. With a shorter channel, there are fewer intermediaries to compensate, which reduces the product's final price.

2. *Redesign the product* to remove costly features. Whirlpool developed a no-frills, simplified washing machine that it manufactures inexpensively and sells for a lower price in developing economies.

3. *Ship products unassembled,* as parts and components, to qualify for lower import tariffs. Then perform final assembly in the foreign market, ideally by using low-cost labor. Some firms have their product assembled in Foreign Trade Zones, where import costs are lower and government incentives may be available.[24]

4. *Reclassify the exported product* to qualify for lower tariffs. Suppose Motorola faces a high tariff when exporting "telecommunications equipment" to Bolivia. By having the product reclassified as "computer equipment," Motorola might be able to export the product under a lower tariff. The practice is possible because imported products often fit more than one product category for determining tariffs.

5. *Move production or sourcing to another country* to take advantage of lower production costs or favorable currency rates.

Managing Pricing under Varying Currency Conditions

In export markets, a strong domestic currency can reduce competitiveness, while a weakening domestic currency makes the firm's foreign pricing more competitive. Exhibit 18.6 presents various firm responses to a weakening or appreciating domestic currency.[25]

Exhibit 18.6
Strategies for Dealing with
Varying Currency Conditions

When the exporter gains a price advantage because its home-country currency is WEAKENING relative to the customer's currency, then it should:	When the exporter suffers from a price disadvantage because its home-country currency is APPRECIATING relative to the customer's currency, then it should:
Stress the benefits of the firm's low prices to foreign customers.	Accentuate competitive strengths in nonprice elements of its marketing program, such as product quality, delivery, and after-sales service.
Maintain normal price levels, expand the product line, or add more costly features.	Consider lowering prices by improving productivity, reducing production costs, or redesigning the product to eliminate costly features.
Exploit greater export opportunities in markets where this favorable exchange rate exists.	Concentrate exporting to those countries whose currencies have not weakened in relation to the exporter.
Speed repatriation of foreign-earned income and collections.	Maintain foreign-earned income in the customer's currency and delay collection of foreign accounts receivable (if there is an expectation that the customer's currency will regain strength over a reasonable time period).
Minimize expenditures in the customer's currency (for example, for advertising and local transportation).	Maximize expenditures in the customer's currency.

Transfer Pricing

Transfer pricing, or intracorporate pricing, refers to the practice of pricing intermediate or finished products exchanged among the subsidiaries and affiliates of the same corporate family located in different countries.[26] For example, when the Ford parts plant in South Africa sells parts to the Ford factory in Spain, it charges a transfer price for this intracorporate transaction. This price generally differs from the market prices Ford charges its external customers.

MNEs like Ford attempt to manage internal prices primarily for two reasons.[27] First, it gives them a way to repatriate—that is, bring back to the home country—the profits from a country that restricts MNEs from taking their earnings out, often due to a shortage of its own currency. High prices charged to its foreign affiliate serve as an alternative means of transferring money out of the affiliate's country. The strategy works because controls imposed on money transferred in this way are not normally as strict as controls imposed on straight repatriation of profits.

Second, transfer pricing can help MNEs shift profits out of a country with high corporate income taxes into a country with low corporate income taxes to increase company-wide profitability. In this case, the MNE may opt to maximize the expenses (and therefore minimize the profits) of the foreign-country affiliate by charging high prices for goods sold to the affiliate. MNEs typically centralize transfer pricing under the direction of the chief financial officer at corporate headquarters.

Consider Exhibit 18.7 for a simple illustration of transfer pricing. A subsidiary may buy or sell a finished or intermediate product from another affiliate below cost, at cost, or above cost. Suppose the MNE treats Subsidiary A as a favored unit. That is, Subsidiary

Transfer pricing   The practice of pricing intermediate or finished products exchanged among the subsidiaries and affiliates of the same corporate family located in different countries.

Exhibit 18.7 How Transfer Pricing Can Help Maximize Corporate-Wide Reported Earnings

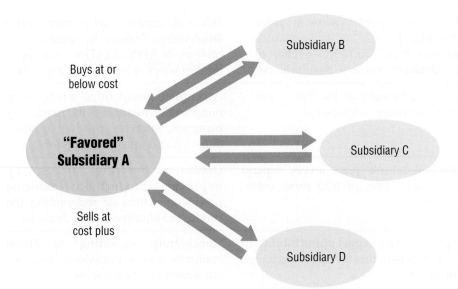

A is allowed to *source at or below cost* and *sell at a relatively high price* when transacting with other subsidiaries. Over time, Subsidiary A will achieve superior financial results at the expense of Subsidiaries B, C, and D. Why would the MNE headquarters allow this? In general, this would be done to optimize profits of the firm as a whole. A subsidiary would receive such a favorable treatment if it is located in a country with:

- Lower corporate income-tax rates,
- High tariffs for the product in question,
- Favorable accounting rules for calculating corporate income,
- Political stability,
- Little or no restrictions on profit repatriation, or
- Strategic importance to the MNE.

While the subsidiary's financial performance has been boosted in an artificial way, the earnings of the MNE as a whole are optimized. This benefit frequently comes at a cost. First, there is the complication of internal control measures. Manipulating transfer prices may make it more difficult to determine the true profit contribution of a subsidiary. Second, morale problems typically surface at a subsidiary whose profit performance has been made to look worse than it really is. Third, some subsidiary managers may react negatively to price manipulation. Fourth, as local businesses, subsidiaries must abide by local accounting rules. Legal problems will arise if they follow accounting standards not accepted by the host government. Indeed, governments often scrutinize MNE transfer pricing practices to ensure foreign firms pay their fair share of taxes by reporting accurate earnings.

Gray Market Activity (Parallel Imports)

What do companies such as Caterpillar, Duracell, Gucci, and Sony have in common? They are all MNEs with established brand names that have been the target of gray market activity. Exhibit 18.8 illustrates the nature of flows and relationships in gray market activity—the legal importation of genuine products into a country by intermediaries other than authorized distributors.[28]

Consider a manufacturer that produces its products in one country and exports them to another, illustrated by the green arrow between countries A and B in Exhibit 18.8. If the going price of the product happens to be sufficiently lower in Country B, then gray market brokers can exploit arbitrage opportunities—buy the product at a low price in

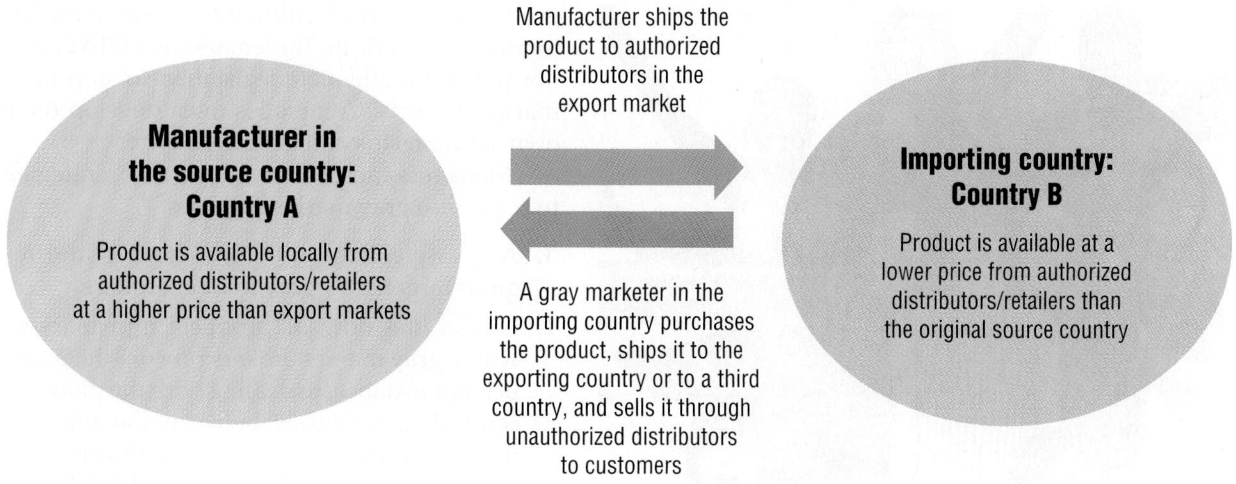

Exhibit 18.8 Illustration of Gray Market Activity

Country B, import it into the original source country, and sell it at a high price there, illustrated by the orange arrow.

In this scenario, the first transaction, illustrated by the green arrow, is carried out by authorized channel intermediaries. The second transaction, illustrated by the orange arrow, is carried out by unauthorized intermediaries. Often referred to as *gray marketers*, the unauthorized intermediaries are typically independent entrepreneurs. Because their transactions parallel those of authorized distributors, gray market activity is also called *parallel importation*.

In Canada, drug prices are determined by the government, which essentially imposes price controls. Consequently, drug prices are often lower there than in the United States. Because of this difference, some U.S. consumers purchase their prescription drugs from online pharmacies in Canada with savings. The U.S. Food and Drug Administration discourages such imports, suggesting the authenticity, efficacy, or safety of these purchases are not guaranteed.[29] Gray market activity is also common in automobiles, cameras, watches, computers, perfumes, and even construction equipment.

The root cause of gray market activity is a large enough difference in price of the same product between two countries. Such price differences arise due to: (i) the manufacturer's inability to coordinate prices across its markets; (ii) deliberate efforts by the firm to charge higher prices in some countries when competitive conditions permit; or (iii) exchange rate fluctuations that result in a price gap between products priced in two different currencies.

Manufacturers of branded products are concerned about gray market activity because it can lead to:

1. *A tarnished brand image* when customers realize the product is available at a lower price through alternative channels, particularly less-prestigious outlets.

2. *Strained manufacturer-distributor relations* that can arise when parallel imports result in lost sales to authorized distributors.

3. *Disruptions in company planning* that occur in regional sales forecasting, pricing strategies, merchandising plans, and general marketing efforts.

Laws regarding gray market activity are ambiguous in much of the world. In the United States, the legality of parallel imports had not been initially clarified (hence the term *gray* markets) until the U.S. Supreme Court ruled in 1988 that trademark owners cannot prevent parallel importation. By ruling in favor of the gray market brokers, the Supreme Court acted to serve the best interests of the consumer, who has access to *genuine* (not counterfeit) products at substantially lower prices. Lobbying by industry

Many firms use a standardized approach to international advertising. Benetton's standardized 'United Colors of Benetton' ad campaign has enjoyed much success worldwide.

groups such as the Coalition to Preserve the Integrity of American Trademarks (COPIAT) has not produced adequate legislation to stop gray market imports. Companies must develop their own solutions to combat such activity.

Managers can pursue at least four strategies to cope with gray market imports.[30]

1. Aggressively cut prices in countries and regions targeted by gray market brokers.
2. Hinder the flow of products into markets where gray market brokers procure the product. For instance, in dealing with the pharmaceutical gray market between Canada and the United States, the U.S. firm Pfizer could reduce shipment of its cholesterol drug Lipitor to Canada to levels just sufficient for local use by Canadians.
3. Design products with exclusive features that strongly appeal to customers. Adding distinctive features unique to each market reduces the likelihood that products will be channeled elsewhere.
4. Publicize the limitations of gray market channels. Trademark owners publicize the disadvantages of buying gray market goods to potential buyers. In the United States, consumers who fill their prescriptions via online pharmacies from Canada have been warned the products may be counterfeit. Indeed, this is a legitimate concern, since counterfeit drugs do make their way into pharmacies in Canada and the United States.[31]

International Marketing Communications

Companies use *marketing communications* (also known as *marketing promotion*) to provide information to, and communicate with, existing and potential customers, with the ultimate aim of stimulating demand. International marketing and communications vary substantially around the world. Let's examine them in more detail.

International Advertising

Firms conduct advertising via *media*, which includes direct mail, radio, television, cinema, billboards, transit, print media, and the Internet. *Transit* refers to ads placed in buses, trains, and subways; they are particularly useful in large cities. *Print media* are newspapers, magazines, and trade journals. Managers assess the availability and viability of media by examining the amount and types of advertising spending already occurring in each market. In 2009, advertising expenditures on major media amounted to approximately USD $100 billion in both Western Europe and the Asia-Pacific region. In the United States, advertising expenditures exceeded $160 billion.[32] Five western firms—Yum Brands, Pernod Ricard, Avon Products, Colgate-Palmolive, and P&G—spend more than 10 percent of their ad budgets in just one country, China.[33]

The availability and quality of media closely determine the feasibility and nature of marketing communications. Exhibit 18.9 provides statistics on media for various countries. The literacy rate indicates the number of people who can read, which is critical for understanding most ads. Other data reveal the diversity of communication media in selected countries. In developing economies, TV, radio, newspapers, and the

	Literacy Rate (percentage of population)	Households with Television (percentage of all households)	Radio Stations per One Million People	Daily Newspapers per One Million People	Internet Users (percentage of population)
Argentina	98%	97%	31.0	2.7	27%
Australia	99	96	29.0	2.4	72
China	93	91	0.5	0.7	23
Ethiopia	36	2	0.1	0.1	0
India	66	37	0.2	4.8	1
Japan	99	99	2.4	0.9	37
Mexico	93	93	12.6	2.9	21
Netherlands	99	99	34.2	2.1	86
Nigeria	72	26	0.8	0.2	7
Saudi Arabia	85	99	2.6	2.0	27
United Kingdom	99	98	14.8	3.0	80
United States	99	98	44.8	5.0	75

Exhibit 18.9 Media Characteristics in Selected Countries

NOTE: Data are for the most recent year available.

SOURCES: *CIA World Factbook* at http://www.cia.gov; World Bank at http://www.worldbank.org

Internet are often quite limited. The firm must use creative approaches to advertise in countries with low literacy rates and limited media infrastructure. Certain media selections make sense for some countries but not others. Marketers in Mexico and Peru emphasize television advertising, in Kuwait and Norway they concentrate on print media, and in Bolivia firms use a lot of outdoor advertising on billboards and buildings. About half of all advertising funds in Italy are spent on television, more than double the figure for Britain, where newspapers attract the largest proportion of ad spending.[34]

International advertising expenditures vary depending on the size and extent of the firm's foreign operations. Smaller firms often lack the resources to advertise on TV or to develop a foreign sales force. Differences in culture, laws, and media availability mean it is seldom possible to duplicate in foreign markets the type and mix of advertising used in the home market. For example, the Italian government limits television advertising on state channels to 12 percent of airtime per hour and 4 percent per week. Mexico and Peru require that firms produce commercials for the local audience in their respective countries and use local actors.

Culture determines buyer attitudes toward the role and function of advertising, humor content, the depiction of characters (such as the roles of men and women), and decency standards. Advertising conveys a message encoded in language, symbols, colors, and other attributes, each of which may have distinctive meanings. Buyer receptiveness differs as a function of culture and language. In China, Nike ran an ad in which NBA basketball star LeBron James battles—and defeats—a computer-generated Chinese Kung Fu master. Chinese consumers were offended and China's national government banned the ad.[35]

Exhibit 18.10 The Largest Global Ad Agencies

SOURCE: *Advertising Age* (2009). "Top 15 Consolidated Agency Networks," April 27, 2009, accessed at http://adage.com.

Rank	Agency	Headquarters	Worldwide Revenue, Millions of Dollars, 2008
1	Dentsu	Tokyo	$2,472
2	BBDO Worldwide	New York	1,986
3	McCann Erickson Worldwide	New York	1,741
4	DDB Worldwide	New York	1,509
5	TBWA Worldwide	New York	1,357
6	Euro RSCG Worldwide	New York	1,170
7	JWT	New York	1,157
8	Young & Rubicam	New York	1,100
9	Publicis	Paris	1,071
10	OgilvyOne Worldwide	New York	1,054

Many MNEs employ relatively standardized advertising around the world, an approach that simplifies the communications strategy and saves money. Benetton, the Italian clothing manufacturer, has enjoyed much success by using essentially the same "United Colors of Benetton" ad campaigns in markets worldwide. Levi Strauss's (www.levi.com) advertising approach is similar around the world, stressing the all-American image of its jeans. One TV ad in Indonesia showed teenagers cruising around a U.S. town in 1960s convertibles. In Japan, Levi Strauss frequently used James Dean, the 1950s U.S. film star, as the centerpiece of its advertising. The dialogue in Levi's ads is often in English worldwide.[36] The most effective ad campaigns are based on a full understanding of the target audience's buying motivations, values, behavior, purchasing power, and demographic characteristics.

Most MNEs employ advertising agencies to create promotional content and select media for foreign markets. The choice is usually between a home-country-based agency with international expertise, a local agency based in the target market, or a *global advertising agency* that has offices in the target market. Exhibit 18.10 identifies the leading global advertising agencies. These firms maintain networks of affiliates and local offices around the world. They can create advertising that is both global and sensitive to local conditions while offering a range of additional services such as market research, publicity, and package design.

International Promotional Activities

Promotional activities are short-term marketing activities intended to stimulate an initial purchase, immediate purchase, or increased purchases of the product and to improve intermediary effectiveness and cooperation. They include tools such as coupons, point-of-purchase displays, demonstrations, samples, contests, gifts, and Internet interfacing.

Greece, Portugal, and Spain permit virtually every type of promotion, and Germany, Norway, and Switzerland forbid or restrict some. Couponing is illegal or restricted in some countries. Other promotional activities, such as giveaways, may be considered unethical or distasteful. In much of the world, such activities are uncommon and may be misunderstood. Promotions usually require a high level of intermediary or retailer sophistication to succeed.

International Distribution

Distribution refers to the processes of getting the product or service from its place of origin to the customer. Distribution is the most inflexible of the marketing program elements—once a firm establishes a distribution channel, it may be difficult to change it. As we discussed in Chapters 3 and 14, the most common approaches to international distribution include engaging independent intermediaries (for exporting firms), or establishing marketing and sales subsidiaries directly in target markets (an FDI-based approach). The exporting firm ships goods to its intermediary, which moves the product through customs and the foreign distribution channel to retail outlets or end users.

By contrast, the foreign direct investor establishes its own operations in the market, working directly with customers and retailers to move offerings through the channel into the local marketplace. Using this approach, the firm will lease, acquire, or set up a sales office, warehouse, or an entire distribution channel, directly in the target market. Direct investment provides various advantages. First, it helps ensure control over marketing and distribution activities in the target market. Second, it facilitates monitoring the performance of employees and other actors in the local market. Third, it allows the firm to get close to the market, which is especially helpful when the market is complex or rapidly changing. A key disadvantage of direct investment is that it is costly.

Some firms bypass traditional distribution systems altogether by using *direct marketing*—selling directly to end users. It typically implies using the Internet to provide detailed product information and the means for foreigners to buy offerings. Some firms such as Amazon.com are entirely Internet based, with no retail stores. Others, such as Coles, Tesco, and Home Depot, combine direct marketing with traditional retailing.

Channel length refers to the number of distributors or other intermediaries that it takes to get the product from the manufacturer to the market. The longer the channel, the more intermediaries the firm must compensate, and the costlier the channel. For example, Japan is characterized by long distribution channels involving numerous intermediaries. High channel costs contribute to international price escalation, creating a competitive disadvantage for the firm.

Global Account Management

In a gradually globalizing world, foreign customers increasingly seek uniform and consistent prices, quality, and customer service. **Global account management (GAM)** means serving a key global customer in a consistent and standardized manner, regardless of where in the world it operates. Walmart is a key global account for Procter & Gamble, purchasing a substantial amount of P&G products. Walmart expects consistent service, including uniform prices for the same P&G product regardless of where in the world it is delivered.

Key accounts such as Migros, Zellers, and Walmart typically purchase from a collection of preferred suppliers that meet their specifications. Suppliers target these key customers by shifting resources from national, regional, and function-based operations to GAM, whose programs feature dedicated cross-functional teams, specialized coordination activities for specific accounts, and formalized structures and processes. Private IT-based portals facilitate the implementation of such systems. Each global customer is assigned a global account manager, or team, who provides the customer with coordinated marketing support and service across various countries.[37]

Global account management (GAM)
Serving a key global customer in a consistent and standardized manner, regardless of where in the world it operates.

H&M: International Marketing Success Story

H&M is a Swedish clothing retailer specializing in "fast fashion" and "cheap chic" styles for men, women, and children. The firm generated around $8.5 billion in global sales in 2009, making it the world's third largest fashion retailer, after Gap Inc. (#1) and Zara (#2). When H&M opens a new store, it is accompanied by much attention and interest. From New York to Berlin to Tokyo, store openings typically receive massive media coverage. The Pasadena, California, store launch was covered from news helicopters, and numerous people slept outside the store the night before it opened. Such excitement is typical of H&M store launches worldwide.

The firm began as a women's clothing retailer, Hennes, in 1947 and later merged with the Swedish men's store Mauritz. Management changed the name to H&M to simplify worldwide perception of the brand.

Initially, H&M was cautious with international expansion, restricting its reach to nearby European countries, where Germany, France, and Britain became top markets. In 2000, H&M opened its first U.S. store on Fifth Avenue in New York. Most recently, the firm expanded into China, Japan, Russia, South Korea, and the Middle East. Today, H&M has 75,000 employees operating more than 2,000 stores in thirty-seven countries.

Internationalization has not proceeded without missteps. On the heels of the spacious Fifth Avenue store launch, H&M opened several more outlets in the United States. Nevertheless, the success of its Manhattan store did not consistently translate to other locations. Some new stores were too big, forcing management to downsize them. In the United States, H&M quickly learned that styles vary between cities and suburban locales. Management focused trendy fashions in city stores and maintained more conservative items at suburban mall stores. A decision to launch a colorful apparel collection backfired, forcing retreat to traditional styles with subdued shades. Compared to Europe, top management noted that U.S. stores need to be more inviting, and U.S. salespeople prefer focusing on a single segment, like children's wear or men's clothing.

Rapid Response Retailing

H&M emphasizes fast turnaround, the ability to take a garment from design to store shelf in three weeks. Though this falls short of competitor Zara's two-week turnaround, H&M's prices are usually lower. Known for its flexibility, H&M constantly monitors sales, restocking stores daily to quickly replenish popular merchandise.

Another cost-saving measure comes from outsourcing apparel manufacturing to 700 independent suppliers via twenty production offices, primarily in Asia and Europe. Large quantities of materials are ordered from suppliers, allowing economies of scale that are passed on to consumers.

Rapid response retailing means that H&M ensures the right product gets to the right stores at the right time. It requires careful cost control and management of lead times with suppliers, factories, and distributors. The approach results in prices substantially lower than competitors.

Market Segments and Branding

The H&M brand symbolizes "fashion and quality at the best price." Men's and women's collections emphasize innovative styling for fashion-minded people of all ages. Strong branding increases marketing effectiveness, stimulates brand loyalty, and enhances customer confidence in purchase decisions. It helps customers know what H&M stands for—simple, stylish fashions offered at popular prices. The brand drives management decisions on how to design products and where and how to launch new stores.

Most H&M stores are located in Europe, where brand awareness is substantial. However, brand awareness is still limited in other parts of the world. In some markets, building a strong brand remains challenging. Weak brand image limits H&M's sales potential and its ability to recruit and retain employees, who are crucial to long-term success.

Marketing

H&M has more than 100 in-house designers who interpret apparel trends and create fashions accessible to everyone. H&M collaborates with well-known designers, offering limited edition clothing lines in some stores. For example, collaboration with Chanel design chief Karl Lagerfeld drew large crowds to H&M stores, selling out the exclusive line in only three days. Other design partners include Stella McCartney, Madonna, and Roberto Cavalli. At the Tokyo store opening, H&M introduced a collection with Comme des Garçons, one of Japan's most respected fashion houses. The initial response exceeded expectations, with customers waiting in line for three days before the launch.

H&M employs unique strategies to reach target markets and attract customers to new stores. Management is careful to choose the location of stores in each city, preferring exclusive shopping districts with high traffic. Stores are intended to be fun, inspiring, and inviting, with interior design and displays that communicate what H&M stands for. Together, the products, shop floors, displays, and staff make up the whole package that communicates the H&M brand.

The firm employs conventional promotional tactics such as print advertisements and catalogues, as well as more novel approaches. *H&M Magazine* offers readers a mix of fashion and the latest lifestyle trends. The firm has its own Facebook page and sends out "tweets" on Twitter, maintaining a social network with fans around the world. The H&M YouTube site offers Fashion TV and inspirational films.

Use of celebrities like Benicio Del Toro and Molly Sims helps maintain a trendy image. H&M experiments with nontraditional methods to communicate with customers. Partnering with marketing agencies Mobiento and Adiento, H&M launched a mobile marketing campaign targeted to 20- to 40-year-old women. The campaign included banner ads placed on carrier portals and media sites, and a Web site with click-through slideshows and animated images of the firm's latest designs. Beyond promoting new additions to its apparel collection, the campaign drove customers to the H&M Club and its loyalty rewards program. Consumers received alerts and mobile coupons redeemable at nearby stores.

Recently, the firm expanded beyond traditional apparel by venturing into the home textiles business. H&M Home's products, including pillows, towels, curtains, and other textile products, are sold online and by mail. With this addition, H&M now competes with Spanish retailer Zara in the home textile market.

Global Strategy and Localization

H&M management follows a global approach by emphasizing a uniform global brand and similar apparel in all its stores. Company designers at headquarters draw inspiration from key markets so that different regions' styles are incorporated into apparel designs. The product assortment is 80 percent the same in all markets, and local managers adjust the remaining 20 percent to fit local tastes. Apparel offered in the Tokyo stores is essentially the same as that offered in Europe, but the presentation is modified.

The head office provides substantial guidance on global strategy, while store managers localize tactics to their markets. At individual stores, local managers can adapt pricing, advertising, and product range to suit local conditions. The firm offers smaller sizes in Asia, con-servative apparel in Islamic countries, and garments adjusted for seasonal differences between the northern and southern hemispheres. In a fickle industry, H&M has been a smashing success. The firm has applied skillful marketing to triumph in markets around the world.

Case Questions

1. Visit H&M's Web site at www.hm.com. What are the characteristics of H&M's global market segment(s)? How does H&M position itself in the minds of target customers around the world?

2. How does management at H&M use global branding and global product development to create and offer its fashions? How does the firm use marketing mix elements to market its offerings around the world?

3. A key aspect of H&M's strategy is to provide value to customers by maximizing perceived product benefits, minimizing prices, or both. Given this, how can H&M further increase the value of its offerings to customers? That is, what steps can management take to increase the benefits and reduce the prices that its customers encounter when shopping for H&M products?

4. How does H&M strike a balance between standardization and adaptation of its marketing program? What advantages does H&M gain from standardization? From adaptation? What factors drive management to adapt offerings in particular markets?

5. Increasingly, H&M targets emerging markets like China, Russia, and Saudi Arabia, which are often characterized by distinctive cultures, lower incomes, and inexperience with leading-edge fashion. Thinking in terms of marketing program elements, what can management do to ensure H&M succeeds in these markets?

SOURCES: "H&M: It's the Latest Thing—Really," *BusinessWeek,* March 27, 2006, p. 70; Dan Butcher, "Retail Giant H&M Runs Multifaceted Mobile Marketing Campaign," 2009, retrieved from http://www.mobilemarketer.com; Kerry Capell, "H&M: Bringing *Haute* to the Hoi Polloi," *BusinessWeek,* May 30, 2005, retrieved from http://www.businessweek.com; Patricia Cheng, "H&M Customers, Lured by Madonna Line, Flock to Asia Store Debut," 2009, retrieved from http://www.bloomberg.com; Ellen Groves, "H&M Asia Push to Move Ahead in South Korea in 2010," *Womens Wear Daily* 197, no. 42 (February 26, 2009): 18; H&M corporate Web site at http://www.hm.com; "Clothing Culture: International Designers Cut Their Cloth to Suit Local Tastes: Management Briefing: Japan," *Just-Style,* October 2009, pp. 13–16; Ola Kinnander, "H&M Launches Home Textile in Bid to Offset Fashion Slowdown," *Wall Street Journal,* March 2, 2009, p. B3; Ana Roncha, "Nordic Brands Towards a Design-Oriented Concept," *Journal of Brand Management* 16, no. 1-2 (2008): 21–29; Valerie Seckler, "Gauging Their Worth: H&M, Vuitton, Wal-Mart Top Brand Value Study," *Women's Wear Daily,* July 1, 2009, retrieved from http://www.wwd.com; Marina Strauss, "H&M's Next Move: Taking It to the Streets," *The Globe and Mail,* May 22, 2009, retrieved from http://www.theglobeandmail.com; Stephen Wigley and C. R. Chiang, "Retail Internationalisation in Practice: Per Una in the UK and Taiwan," *International Journal of Retail & Distribution Management* 37, no. 3 (2009): 250–70; Stephen Wigley and Christopher Moore, "The Operationalisation of International Fashion Retailer Success," *Journal of Fashion Marketing and Management* 11, no. 2 (2007): 281–96.

NOTE: This case was prepared by Professor Erin Cavusgil, University of Michigan Flint, for classroom discussion.

CHAPTER ESSENTIALS

Key Terms

Summary

In this chapter, you learned about:

1. Global marketing strategy

Developing a marketing strategy requires managers to assess the unique foreign market environment and then make choices about market segments, targeting, and positioning. A **global marketing strategy** is a plan of action that guides the firm in how to position itself and its offerings in foreign markets, which customer segments to pursue, and to what degree its marketing program elements should be standardized and adapted.

2. Standardization and adaptation of international marketing

How management balances **adaptation** and **standardization** determines the extent to which the firm must modify a product and its marketing to suit foreign markets. On the whole, firms prefer to standardize their products to achieve scale economies and minimize complexity. A **global market segment** is a group of customers that shares common characteristics across many national markets. *Positioning* strategy involves using marketing to create a particular image of a product or service, especially relative to competitor offerings, among the firm's customers worldwide.

3. Global branding and product development

A **global brand** is perceived similarly in all the firm's markets and increases marketing strategy effectiveness, allowing the firm to charge higher prices and deal more effectively with channel members and competitors. In developing products with multicountry potential, managers emphasize the commonalities across countries rather than the differences. The development of global products facilitates economies of scale in R&D, production, and marketing. Innovation and design in international product development are increasingly performed by *global teams*—internationally distributed groups of people with a specific mandate to make or implement decisions that are international in scope.

4. International pricing

International prices are determined by factors both internal and external to the firm that often cause prices to inflate abroad. A special challenge for exporters in pricing is **international price escalation**—the problem of end-user prices reaching exorbitant levels in the export market, caused by multilayered distribution channels, intermediary margins, tariffs, and other international customer costs. **Transfer pricing** is the practice of pricing intermediate or finished products exchanged among the subsidiaries and affiliates of the same corporate family located in different countries. **Gray market activity**, also known as parallel imports, refers to legal importation of genuine products into a country by intermediaries other than authorized distributors.

5. International marketing communications

International marketing communications involves the management of advertising and promotional activities across national borders. Managers are often compelled to adapt their international communications due to unique legal, cultural, and socioeconomic factors in foreign markets. Firms must also accommodate literacy levels, language, and available media.

6. International distribution

Firms usually engage foreign intermediaries or foreign-based subsidiaries to reach customers in international markets. Some firms bypass traditional distribution systems by using *direct marketing*. *Channel length* refers to the number of distributors or other intermediaries it takes to get the product from the manufacturer to the market. Long channels are relatively costly. In working with key business customers, firms may undertake **global account man-**agement (GAM)—servicing key global customers in a consistent and standardized manner, regardless of where in the world they operate.

Test Your Comprehension AACSB: Reflective Thinking Skills, Ethical Understanding and Reasoning Abilities

1. Describe the marketing program elements and how each influences sales and performance in international business.

2. Audrey Corp. has historically adapted its offerings for all its foreign markets, leading to a proliferation of product variations. Explain why Audrey Corp. might want to consider a global marketing strategy. What are the benefits of a global marketing strategy?

3. Distinguish between adaptation and standardization in international marketing.

4. Consider Toshiba's laptop computer division. In terms of the marketing program elements, what attributes of laptop computers does the firm need to adapt and which attributes can it standardize for international markets?

5. What is the role of market segmentation and positioning in international marketing? What is a global market segment?

6. William Corporation is a manufacturer of high-quality men's and women's fashions. What steps should you take to transform William into a well-recognized global brand?

7. What are the most important factors to consider when formulating international pricing strategies? What steps would you follow in arriving at international prices?

8. Suppose export customers of a consumer product are highly sensitive to price. However, the firm is experiencing substantial price escalation in the market. What factors may be causing this situation? What can management do to reduce the harmful impact of international price escalation?

9. What are the most important factors to consider when designing strategy for international marketing communications?

10. Describe the role of distribution in international business.

Apply Your Understanding AACSB: Reflective Thinking Skills, Analytic Skills, Ethical Understanding and Reasoning Abilities

1. Products must be adapted to accommodate national differences arising from customer preferences and each market's economic conditions, climate, culture, and language. Think about the following products: packaged flour, swimsuits, textbooks, and automobiles. For each of these products, describe how a firm would need to adapt marketing to suit conditions in China, Germany, and Saudi Arabia. In particular, think about the nature of the product, its pricing and distribution, and the marketing communications associated with it. Keep in mind that China is an emerging market with low per-capita income, Saudi Arabia is an emerging market with a conservative culture rooted in Islam, and Germany is an advanced and liberal economy. You may wish to consult globalEDGE™ (globalEDGE.msu.edu) to learn more about these specific markets.

2. Office Depot, the supplier of office equipment and supplies, has stores in countries throughout Asia, Europe, and Latin America. Suppose the firm has decided to launch its own line of notebook computers and wants to know how to price them in various markets. What would be the most important factors Office Depot should consider when setting prices in foreign markets? Suggest a step-by-step approach to international pricing.

3. *Ethical Dilemma:* You just assumed a senior management position with Philip Morris (PM), a major manufacturer of cigarettes. As cigarette sales have declined in the advanced economies, PM has increased its marketing efforts in developing economies and emerging markets, where demand for smoking tobacco remains strong. Because of the

enormous population in such countries, PM expects to generate huge sales over time. At the same time, many of the countries are characterized by substantial illiteracy and lack of awareness about the harmful health effects of smoking cigarettes, and people often become addicted to tobacco products. Given these factors, is it ethical to target such countries with cigarettes? Using the Ethical Framework in Chapter 5, analyze the arguments for and against marketing cigarettes to developing economies and emerging markets. As a senior manager, what steps should you take, if any, to address the dilemma?

globalEDGE Internet Exercises

(http://globalEDGE.msu.edu)

AACSB: Reflective Thinking Skills

Refer to Chapter 1, page 26, for instructions on how to access and use globalEDGE™.

1. Global branding is key to international marketing success. Every year *BusinessWeek* and *Interbrand* publish a ranking of the top 100 global brands. The ranking can be accessed by searching the term "global brand" at globalEDGE™, or by entering "global brands scorecard" in a Google search. For this exercise, locate and retrieve the most current ranking and answer the following questions:

   a. What do you consider the strengths and weaknesses of the methodology *Interbrand* uses to estimate brand equity?

   b. What patterns do you detect in terms of the countries and industries most represented in the top 100 list?

   c. According to the article *BusinessWeek* publishes in conjunction with the ranking, what managerial guidelines will help a company develop a strong global brand?

2. Procter and Gamble (P&G) and Unilever are the two leading firms in the consumer products industry for offerings such as soap, shampoo, and laundry detergent. P&G (www.pg.com) is based in the United States, and Unilever (www.unilever.com) is based in Europe. What are the major regional markets of each firm? What products does each firm offer through a global marketing strategy? Structure your answer in terms of the marketing-mix elements. That is, what global strategy approaches does each firm apply for the product, its pricing, communications, and distribution?

3. A *third-party logistics provider (3PL)* provides outsourced or "third-party" logistics services to companies for part or all of their distribution activities. Examples include C.H. Robinson Worldwide, Maersk Logistics, and FedEx. Your firm needs to find a 3PL to handle its distribution efforts abroad. Your task is to locate two 3PLs online and address the following questions:

   a. What logistical services does each firm provide?

   b. What types of customers does each 3PL serve?

   c. Where are their headquarters and branch offices located?

   d. Based on the information provided, which of the two 3PLs would you most likely choose? Why?

CHAPTER 19

LEARNING OBJECTIVES In this chapter, you will learn about:

1. The strategic role of human resources in international business
2. International staffing policy
3. Preparation and training of international employees
4. International performance appraisal
5. Compensation of employees
6. International labor relations
7. Diversity in the international workforce

Human Resource Management in the Global Firm

Johnson & Johnson: A Leader in International Human Resource Management

Johnson & Johnson (J&J) is a leading global manufacturer of pharmaceutical and consumer health care products, with well-known brands such as Band-Aid, Tylenol, Neutrogena, Listerine, and Rolaids. Worldwide sales in 2009 topped $60 billion, about half of which came from North America, one quarter from Europe, 15 percent from the Asia-Pacific region and Africa, and the rest from Latin America and other regions. J&J's decentralized workforce includes more than 118,000 employees in over 250 business units worldwide.

J&J (www.jnj.com) pays special attention to the care and management of human resources. For more than six decades, J&J's Credo has articulated the firm's commitment to employees. A section of the Credo reads:

> We are responsible to our employees worldwide. Everyone must be considered as an individual. We must respect their dignity and recognize their merit. They must have a sense of security in their jobs. Compensation must be fair and adequate, and working conditions clean, orderly and safe. We must be mindful of our employees' family responsibilities. Employees must feel free to make suggestions and complaints. There must be equal opportunity for employment, development and advancement. We must provide competent, ethical management.

Riddhi Parikh, Assistant Manager for Human Resources at J&J in India, relies on the Credo whenever employee action is needed, such as authorizing employee expenses, without having to consult her manager. Riddhi says the Credo gives her the freedom to make her own decisions and to learn and advance at her own pace in the firm. Thanks to J&J's high regard for human resources, the average tenure of employees at the Indian subsidiary is 15 years. J&J managers worldwide are empowered to make important decisions within their scope of operations.

Johnson & Johnson attempts to hire "the best and the brightest" to fill its leadership pipeline. All J&J leaders are responsible for developing managers for global operations. The company chairman is evaluated in part on his ability to develop managers. The executive committee spends much of its time seeking and nurturing talent. In Canada, J&J's Leadership Development Program drives company culture and superior business performance. As part of the development process, employees learn new skills to move across functional boundaries and take up new international assignments.

Many firms link merit increases and discretionary bonuses to the new skills their managers acquire. J&J's sophisticated evaluation system uses a "total rewards" compensation approach in which management considers all the rewards available. These include opportunities worldwide for learning and development such as attending the J&J Law School, an online curriculum, or the J&J Leadership Development Program, which rotates participants through classroom and on-the-job training on various parts of the business.

J&J also emphasizes diversity in hiring. Managers are rewarded for their efforts to hire minorities, women, and people from varied cultural backgrounds, which is crucial to expanding the firm's global markets. J&J's vice president for human resources is Kaye Foster-Cheek, a woman and native of Barbados. J&J is pursuing its Women's Leadership Initiative in its international units, even in emerging markets like India.

SOURCES: Cindy Crosby and Greg Zlevor, "Johnson & Johnson's Transformational Leadership Program Prepares

Quality Leaders for Global Challenges," *Global Business and Organizational Excellence* 29, no. 2 (2010): 19–25; Desda Moss, "The Value of Giving," *HRMagazine*, December 2009, pp. 22–26; Carolynn Cameron, "Johnson & Johnson Canada's Design, Development and Business Impact of a Local Leadership Development Program," *Organization Development Journal* 25, no. 2 (2007), pp. 65–70; Johnson & Johnson company profile retrieved from http://www.hoovers.com; Shivani Lath, "Johnson & Johnson: Living by Its Credo," *Business Today*, November 5, 2006, p. 126; Jessica Marquez, "Business First," *Workforce Management*, October 23, 2006, pp. 1–6; Daisy Maxey, "CEO Compensation Survey," *Wall Street Journal*, April 9, 2007, p. R.4; Steven Rumpel and John Medcof, "Total Rewards: Good Fit for Tech Workers," *Research Technology Management*, September/October 2006, pp. 27–36.

 ## The Strategic Role of Human Resources in International Business

Today, leading firms often refer to their employees as "human talent," "human capital," or "intangible assets," emphasizing that they represent a strategic investment rather than a cost. This is especially apparent in knowledge-intensive industries such as management consulting, banking, advertising, engineering, and architecture. Without designers, problem solvers, knowledge workers, and other creative people, firms such as McKinsey, Pixar, Gucci, Nokia, and many others would have great difficulty in competing globally.

Managers at Johnson & Johnson recognize their employees and the knowledge they possess are among their most important strategic assets. Recruiting, managing, and retaining human resources are especially challenging at a firm with global operations. Take Siemens (www.siemens.com), the German MNE. In 2010, Siemens employed more than 400,000 people in some 190 countries: 230,000 throughout Europe, 90,000 in North and South America, 70,000 in the Asia-Pacific region, and 12,000 in Africa, the Middle East, and Russia. Like Siemens, Anglo American, Hutchison Whampoa, IBM, Mittal Steel, Nestlé, Matsushita, McDonald's, Unilever, Volkswagen, and Walmart each has more than 150,000 employees working outside their home countries.

International human resource management (IHRM) refers to the planning, selection, training, employment, and evaluation of employees for international operations.[1] Management grapples with a wide range of challenges in hiring and managing workers within the distinctive cultural and legal frameworks that govern employee practices around the world. International human resource managers, usually located at corporate or regional headquarters, support subsidiary managers by providing IHRM guidelines and by hiring, training, and evaluating employees for international operations.

Three Employee Categories

In a firm with multicountry operations, international managers operate at three levels:

1. **Parent-country nationals (PCNs).** Citizens of the country where the MNE is headquartered. Also called home-country nationals.

2. **Host-country nationals (HCNs).** Citizens of the country where the MNE's subsidiary or affiliate is located. They typically constitute the largest proportion of workers hired abroad. They usually work in manufacturing, assembly, basic service activities, clerical work, and other nonmanagerial functions.

3. **Third-country nationals (TCNs).** Citizens of countries other than the home or host country. Most work in management and are hired because they possess special knowledge or skills.[2]

International human resource management (IHRM) The planning, selection, training, employment, and evaluation of employees for international operations.

Parent-country national (PCN) An employee who is a citizen of the country where the MNE is headquartered.

Host-country national (HCN) An employee who is a citizen of the country where the MNE subsidiary or affiliate is located.

Third-country national (TCN) An employee who is a citizen of a country other than the home or host country.

A Canadian MNE may employ Italian citizens in its subsidiary in Italy (HCNs), send Canadian citizens to work in the Asia-Pacific region on assignment (PCNs), or assign Swiss employees to its subsidiary in Turkey (TCNs).

Employees in any of the three categories assigned to work and reside in a foreign country for an extended period, usually a year or longer, are called **expatriates** (sometimes shortened to "expat"). A U.S. firm might employ a German manager in its subsidiary in France or transfer a Japanese executive to its U.S. headquarters.[3] Both these managers are expatriates. While expatriates comprise only a small percentage of the workforce in most MNEs, they perform many critical functions.

For IHRM managers, the ultimate challenge is to ensure the right person is in the right position at the right location with the right pay scale. In some countries it is easier to get work visas for employees with specific specialized skills. For example, the financial services and information technology sectors in southern India have experienced a shortage of mid- and senior-level managerial talent. Consequently, managers from as far away as Eastern Europe are being posted to India to take advantage of compensation packages that are now competitive by advanced economy standards.[4]

Expatriate An employee assigned to work and reside in a foreign country for an extended period, usually a year or longer.

Differences between Domestic and International HRM

International human resource management is usually more complex than domestic human resource management. Exhibit 19.1 illustrates six factors that drive this complexity.[5] Let's examine each in turn.

1. *New HR responsibilities.* IHRM managers encounter numerous factors not necessarily present at home, including foreign taxation issues for expatriates, international relocation and orientation, administrative services for expatriates, host government relations, language translation services, and repatriation (returning the expatriate to his or her home country).

2. *The need for an international perspective in compensation policy.* Management must account for all its PCNs, HCNs, and TCNs, who may be nationals of numerous countries. In an emerging market like Vietnam, compensation may need to include allowances for housing, education, and other facilities not readily available there. Establishing a fair and comparable compensation scale, regardless of nationality, is a frequent challenge in large MNEs. For instance, an Australian national posted to Brazil can be subject to income taxation by both governments. Thus, tax equalization—ensuring there is no tax disincentive associated with an international assignment—is a complicating aspect.

3. *Greater involvement in employees' personal lives.* Human resource professionals help expatriates and their families with housing arrangements, health care, children's schooling, safety, and security, as well as proper compensation given higher living costs in some foreign locations.

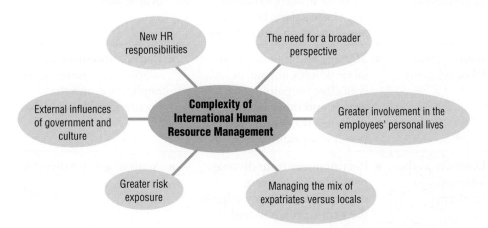

Exhibit 19.1 Factors Contributing to the Complexity of Human Resource Management in the International Context

4. *The mix of expatriates versus locals.* Foreign subsidiaries are frequently staffed from the home country, the host country, and/or third countries. The mix of staff depends on several factors, including the international experience of the firm, cost of living in the foreign location, and availability of qualified local staff.

5. *Greater risk exposure.* When employee productivity falls below acceptable levels, when workers go on strike, or when key managers quit the firm, the consequences are often more pronounced in international business. Exposure to political risk and terrorism are major concerns for IHRM professionals and may require greater compensation and security arrangements for employees and their families.

6. *External influences of the government and national culture.* Employees must be hired, evaluated, and compensated in ways consistent with country and regional customs and regulations. Laws govern work hours, the firm's ability to dismiss or lay off employees, and severance compensation. In many European countries, labor unions are active in managing the firm. In France, Germany, and Spain, employees may work no more than a set number of hours per week, sometimes as few as 35.

Exhibit 19.2 Key Tasks and Challenges of International Human Resource Management

Task	Strategic Goals	Illustrative Challenges
International staffing policy	■ Choose between home-country nationals, host-country nationals, and third-country nationals ■ Develop global managers ■ Recruit and select expatriates	■ Avoid country bias, nepotism, and other local practices ■ Cultivate global mind-set
Preparation and training of international employees	■ Increase effectiveness of international employees, leading to increased company performance ■ Train employees with an emphasis on area studies, practical information, and cross-cultural awareness	■ Minimize culture shock and the occurrence of early departure by expatriates
International performance appraisal	■ Assess, over time, how effectively managers and other employees perform their jobs abroad	■ Establish uniform, organization-wide performance benchmarks while remaining sensitive to customary local practices.
Compensation of employees	■ Develop guidelines and administer compensation (e.g., base salary, benefits, allowances, and incentives)	■ Avoid double taxation of employees
International labor relations	■ Manage and interact with labor unions, engage in collective bargaining, handle strikes and other labor disputes, wage rates, and possible workforce reduction	■ Reduce absenteeism, workplace injuries due to negligence, and the occurence of labor strikes
Diversity in the international workforce	■ Recruit talent from diverse backgrounds to bring experience and knowledge to the firm's problems and opportunities	■ Achieve gender diversity

Key Tasks in International Human Resource Management

Exhibit 19.2 outlines six key tasks of international human resource managers. First is international staffing—the activities directed at recruiting, selecting, and placing employees. Second is preparing and training workers. Third is international performance appraisal, providing feedback necessary for employees' professional development. Fourth is formulating compensation and benefits packages that may vary greatly from country to country. Fifth is interacting with labor unions and collective bargaining. Sixth is achieving diversity in the international workforce. The remainder of this chapter is devoted to examining these tasks.

 ## International Staffing Policy

One of the critical tasks for MNEs is to determine the ideal mix of employees in the firm's foreign subsidiaries and affiliates.[6] The optimal mix varies by location, industry, stage in the value chain, and availability of qualified local workers. Country laws may also dictate how many employees can come from nonlocal sources.

Exhibit 19.3 illustrates the criteria and rationale for hiring each type of employee.[7] Firms usually post PCNs abroad to take advantage of their specialized knowledge,

Staff with Parent-Country Nationals (PCNs) When...	Staff with Host-Country Nationals (HCNs) When...	Staff with Third-Country Nationals (TCNs) When...
Headquarters wants to maintain strong control over its foreign operations.	The country is distant in terms of culture or language (such as Japan), or when local operations emphasize downstream value-chain activities such as marketing and sales, as HCNs usually understand the local business environment best.	Top management wants to create a global culture among the firm's operations worldwide.
Headquarters wants to maintain control over valuable intellectual property that is easily dissipated when accessible by HCNs or TCNs.	Local connections and relations are critical to operational success (such as relations with the government in Russia).	Top management seeks unique perspectives for managing host-country operations.
Knowledge sharing is desirable among headquarters and the subsidiaries, particularly for developing local managers or the host-country organization.	The local government requires the MNE to employ a minimum proportion of local personnel, or tough immigration requirements prevent the long-term employment of expatriates.	Headquarters wants to transfer knowledge and technology from third countries to host-country operations.
Foreign operations emphasize R&D and manufacturing, because PCNs are usually more knowledgeable about such upstream value-chain activities.	Cost is an important consideration; salaries of PCNs, especially those with families, can be up to four times those of HCNs.	The firm cannot afford to pay the expensive compensation typical of PCNs.

Exhibit 19.3 Criteria for Selecting Employees for Foreign Operations

A western family and a young Muslim woman feed pigeons in front of an Istanbul mosque. Successful expatriates have family members who cope well in new environments.

especially in upstream value-chain operations, or to maintain local control over foreign operations. PCNs can also help develop local managers.

By contrast, firms prefer HCNs when the host-country environment is complex and their specialized knowledge or local connections are required in the local marketplace. HCNs often perform downstream value-chain activities, such as marketing and sales, which require extensive local knowledge.[8] It is usually less costly to compensate them than PCNs or TCNs.

Firms often prefer TCNs when senior management wants to transfer specific knowledge or corporate culture from third countries to host-country operations. Worldwide staffing with TCNs helps firms develop an integrated global enterprise.

Recruiting, Selecting, and Developing Talent

Recruitment is searching for and locating potential job candidates to fill the firm's needs. *Selection* is gathering information to evaluate and decide who should be employed in particular jobs.

For most multinational firms, it's challenging to find talented managers willing and qualified to work outside their home countries. Schlumberger Ltd. (www.slb.com) is a Texas oil company with operations worldwide. To maintain a sufficient team of engineers, Schlumberger has turned its human resources department into a strategic asset for finding and developing talent around the world. Among other initiatives, Schlumberger has assigned high-level executives as "ambassadors" to forty-four important engineering schools, such as Kazakhstan's Kazakh National Technical University, Beijing University, Massachusetts Institute of Technology, and Universidad Nacional Autónoma de México. IBM, Nokia, and Unilever are also proactive in finding and developing international talent.[9]

Developing talent is a multistep collaboration between human resource managers and executive management. Together, they need to:

- Analyze the firm's growth strategies and the mission-critical roles needed to achieve them;
- Define the desired skills, behaviors, and experiences for each role;
- Examine the firm's current supply of talent and create a plan to acquire needed talent;
- Develop talent internally and acquire existing or potential talent from outside the firm; and
- Assess current and potential talent according to each individual's performance over time, willingness to learn, learning skills, and commitment to career advancement.[10]

Cultivating Global Mind-Sets

In some firms ethnocentric headquarters staff believe their ways of doing business are superior and can be readily transferred to other countries.[11] More progressive MNEs have a *geocentric orientation*—they staff headquarters and subsidiaries with the most competent people, regardless of national origin. As we discussed in Chapter 4, a geocentric orientation is synonymous with a global mind-set. Managers with a *global mind-set* are open to multiple cultural and strategic realities on both global and local levels.[12]

Not everyone has the skills, traits, or global mind-set needed for an expatriate position. Many employees prefer to remain at home. Those adept at working effectively in foreign environments tend to have the following characteristics:[13]

- *Technical competence.* In distant locations, managers need sufficient managerial and technical capabilities to fulfill the firm's goals and objectives.

- *Self-reliance.* Having an entrepreneurial orientation, a proactive mind-set, and a strong sense of innovativeness are important because expatriate managers frequently function with increased independence abroad and limited support from headquarters.

- *Adaptability.* The manager should adjust well to foreign cultures. The most important traits are cultural empathy, flexibility, diplomacy, and a positive attitude for overcoming stressful situations.

- *Interpersonal skills.* The best candidates get along well with others. Building and maintaining relationships is key, particularly for managers who interact with numerous colleagues, employees, local partners, and government officials.[14]

- *Leadership ability.* The most successful managers view change positively. They skillfully manage threats and opportunities that confront the firm. They collaborate with employees to implement strategies and facilitate successful change.

- *Physical and emotional health.* Living abroad can be stressful. Expatriates must learn to adapt to the local culture. Medical care is often different and may be difficult to access.

- *Spouse and dependents prepared for living abroad.* The candidate's spouse and other family members need the desire and ability to cope with unfamiliar environments and cultures.

Employees with a global mind-set strive to understand organizational and group dynamics to create consensus on a team.[15] Members of a *global team* (see Chapter 12) require specialized training to work effectively with others from different cultures and life experiences.

Successful expatriates cope well in new environments. Cultural intelligence implies the ability to function effectively in situations characterized by cultural diversity, including the ability to adopt appropriate local behaviors.

Cultural Intelligence

Human resource managers need to prepare expatriates and their families to live and work effectively in new cultural environments. Employees should be trained to understand local government regulations, cultural norms, and language differences, and to adapt to local customs such as gift giving and business dining.

Cultural intelligence is an employee's ability to function effectively in situations characterized by cultural diversity.[16] It has four dimensions: (1) *strategy* describes how an employee makes sense of cross-cultural experiences through her or his judgments; (2) *knowledge* is the employee's understanding of cultural dimensions such as values, social norms, religious beliefs, and language; (3) *motivation* measures the employee's interest in interacting with people from different cultures and confidence in doing so effectively; and (4) *behavioral flexibility* is the employee's ability to adopt verbal and nonverbal behaviors appropriate in different cultures.[17]

Cultural intelligence
An employee's ability to function effectively in situations characterized by cultural diversity.

Expatriate Assignment Failure and Culture Shock

Expatriate assignment failure An employee's premature return from an international assignment.

Culture shock Confusion and anxiety experienced by a person who lives in a foreign culture for an extended period.

Area studies Factual knowledge of the historical, political, and economic environment of the host country.

Practical information Knowledge and skills necessary to function effectively in a country, including housing, health care, education, and daily living.

Cross-cultural awareness Ability to interact effectively and appropriately with people from different language and cultural backgrounds.

What happens when things go awry for the employee working abroad? **Expatriate assignment failure,** the employee's premature return from an international assignment, may occur because an employee is unable to perform well or because his or her family has difficulty adjusting. Such failure is costly to company productivity and goals, and adds to the costs of relocating. Failure can also affect expatriates themselves, leading to diminished careers or problems in their family lives. As many as one-third of foreign assignments end prematurely due to expatriate assignment failure. The rate is particularly high among employees assigned to countries with substantial culture and language differences.

A leading cause of expatriate assignment failure is **culture shock**—confusion and anxiety experienced by a person who lives in a foreign culture for an extended period.[18] It can affect the expatriate or family members and results from an inability to cope with the differences experienced in a foreign environment. Inadequate language and cross-cultural skills tend to exacerbate culture shock, as the expatriate is unable to function effectively in the foreign environment or fails to communicate well with locals.[19] Most expatriates and their families who experience culture shock overcome it, usually within a few months. But a few give up and return home early.

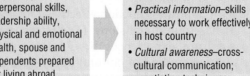 Preparation and Training of International Employees

What can firms do to help employees better understand, adapt, and perform well in foreign environments?[20] Proper preparation and training are crucial. International human resource managers must assist subsidiary management in assessing the needs of host-country workers and devise training programs that enable them to successfully achieve their work objectives, whether in manufacturing, marketing, sales, after-sales services, or business processes such as accounting and records management.

Exhibit 19.4 highlights key features of preparation and training programs for international workers. Training consists of three components: (1) **area studies**—factual knowledge of the historical, political, and economic environment of the host country; (2) **practical information**—knowledge and skills necessary to function effectively in a country, including housing, health care, education, and daily living; and (3) **cross-cultural awareness**—the ability to interact effectively and appropriately with people from different language and cultural backgrounds.[21]

Employees benefit from training in the host-country language and learning to communicate more effectively with local colleagues and workers, suppliers, and customers. Language skills allow them to monitor competitors, recruit local talent, and improve

Goal	Desirable employee qualities	Training emphasizes	Training methods
Increase manager's effectiveness abroad; increase company performance	Technical competence, self-reliance, adaptability, interpersonal skills, leadership ability, physical and emotional health, spouse and dependents prepared for living abroad	• *Area studies*–host-country historical, political, economic, and cultural dimensions • *Practical information*–skills necessary to work effectively in host country • *Cultural awareness*–cross-cultural communication; negotiation techniques; reduction of ethnocentric orientation and self-reference criterion; language skills	Videos, lectures, assigned readings, case studies, critical incident analysis, simulations and role-playing, language training, field experience, long-term immersion

Exhibit 19.4 Key Features of Preparation and Training for International Employees

relationships with host-country officials and organizations. Language ability also increases employees' insights into and enjoyment of the local culture.[22]

Cross-cultural awareness training increases intercultural sensitivity and effectiveness. Managers need to be well versed in how best to supervise and communicate with local employees, negotiate with customers and suppliers, and adapt to the local culture. Training should aim to help employees avoid the *self-reference criterion*—the tendency to view other cultures through the lens of your own.

Training methods vary. In order of increasing rigor, they include: videos, lectures, assigned readings, case studies, books, Web-based instruction, critical incident analyses, simulations, role-playing, language training, field experience, and long-term immersion. In role-playing and simulations, the employee acts out typical encounters with foreigners. As Chapter 4 showed, critical incident analysis examines an episode in which tension arises between employee and foreign counterpart due to a cross-cultural misunderstanding. Field experience is a visit to the host country, usually for one or two weeks. Long-term immersion puts the employee in the country for several months or more, often for language and cultural training. In choosing training methods, the firm must strike a balance between rigor and the degree of interaction required abroad as well as consider the distance between the employee's native and new cultures.[23]

Preparing Employees for Repatriation

Repatriation is the expatriate's return to his or her home country following completion of a foreign assignment. Like expatriation, it requires advance preparation, this time to help the employee avoid problems upon returning home. Some expatriates report financial difficulties upon returning, such as higher housing costs. Some find their international experience is not valued, and they may be placed in lesser positions than they held abroad. Others experience "reverse culture shock," difficult readjustment to home-country culture. For those who have spent several years abroad and for their families, adjustment to life back home may be stressful. As many as one-quarter of expatriates leave their firm within one year of returning home. Others refuse to undertake subsequent international assignments.[24]

International human resource managers can help reduce repatriation problems by providing counseling on the types of problems employees face upon returning home. While the expatriate is abroad, the firm can monitor his or her compensation and career path. After repatriation, the firm can provide bridge loans and other interim financial assistance, as well as counseling, to address both career and psychological needs. The firm needs to ensure the expatriate has a career position equal to, or better than, the one held before going abroad.[25]

Repatriation The expatriate's return to his or her home country following the completion of a foreign assignment.

Training in cultural awareness, host-country history and politics, and practical and leadership skills is critical for helping ensure expatriates' success in their assignments abroad and preparing their families for the challenge. Foreign language fluency or training is usually a must.

Charting Global Careers for Employees

Many firms create career development programs that provide high-potential employees with opportunities to gain experience both at headquarters and in the firm's operations around the world. They do this because, as the firm generates an increasing proportion of sales and earnings from abroad, it needs globally experienced employees capable of managing company operations worldwide. This approach broadens the pool of global talent for managerial positions and visibly demonstrates top management's commitment to their global strategy.

For example, employees at Unilever (www .unilever.com) cannot advance far professionally

Global talent pool
A searchable database of employees, profiling their international skill sets and potential for supporting the firm's global aspirations.

Performance appraisal
A formal process for assessing how effectively employees perform their jobs.

without substantial international experience. This Anglo-Dutch firm has numerous programs to develop international leadership skills. Managers are rotated through various jobs and locations around the world, especially early in their careers. Unilever maintains a **global talent pool**—a searchable database of employees that profiles their international skill sets and potential for supporting the firm's global aspirations. Human resource managers search the database for the recruit with ideal qualifications, regardless of where he or she works in Unilever's global network. They identify the best global talent and present candidates to the appropriate managers for final selection.[26]

 ## International Performance Appraisal

Performance appraisal is a formal process for assessing how effectively employees perform their jobs. Appraisals help a manager identify problem areas where an employee needs to improve and where additional training is warranted. Performance appraisals are typically conducted annually.

In appraising performance, managers compare mutually agreed-upon objectives with actual performance. MNEs typically devise diagnostic procedures to assess the performance of individual employees, see whether problems are attributable to inadequate skill levels, provide additional training and resources as needed, and terminate employees who consistently fail to achieve prescribed goals.

Firms may give employees a variety of organizational goals that vary from unit to unit. A new foreign subsidiary might be charged with establishing relationships with key customers and rapidly increasing sales. A manufacturing plant might be tasked with ensuring high productivity or maintaining high-quality output. Occasionally a subsidiary performs poorly, and the local manager's task is simply to resolve problems and get the unit back on track.

The following factors make performance evaluations more complex in the international context:[27]

- The problem of *noncomparable outcomes* arises because of differences in economic, political, legal, and cultural variables. For example, the firm should not punish a Mexican subsidiary manager because worker productivity is half that of the average in home-country operations. Firms need to take into account worker conditions, factory equipment, and other factors in Mexico that may result in lower productivity levels.[28] Differing accounting rules may make financial results appear more favorable than under stricter rules used at home.

- *Incomplete information* results because headquarters is separated from foreign units by both time and distance. Headquarters staff usually cannot directly observe employees working in foreign subsidiaries. To address this problem, subsidiary managers may be assessed by two evaluators—one from headquarters and one based abroad. The firm may send managers to visit subsidiaries in order to meet staff and observe local conditions firsthand.

- Performance outcomes may be affected by the *maturity* of foreign operations. Relatively new subsidiaries usually do not achieve the same level of results as older subsidiaries staffed with experienced personnel. New international operations may require more time to achieve results than those in the home market.

To avoid inaccurate or biased assessments, management needs to consider such unique challenges when appraising the performance of foreign subsidiaries, affiliates, and employees.[29]

 ## Compensation of Employees

Compensation packages vary across nations because of differences in legally mandated benefits, tax laws, cost of living, local tradition, and culture. Employees posted at foreign sites frequently expect to be compensated at a level that allows them to maintain their usual home country standard of living. This can add substantially to company costs. Exhibit 19.5 presents the cost of living in selected cities. You can see that some world business capitals are expensive. Managers typically consider four elements when developing compensation packages for employees working internationally: (1) base remuneration or wages, (2) benefits, (3) allowances, and (4) incentives.

The *base remuneration* represents the salary or wages the employee typically receives in his or her home country. A local factory worker in Poland would receive wages equivalent to what average factory workers receive in the particular industry in Poland. A Japanese manager working in the United States would receive a base salary comparable to that paid to managers at the same level in Japan. Expatriate salaries are usually paid in the home currency, the local currency, or some combination of both.

Benefits include health care plans, life insurance, unemployment insurance, and a certain number of paid vacation days. They typically make up a third of the total compensation package but vary greatly as a function of local regulation, industry practice, and taxability. Expatriates usually receive the benefits normally accorded to home-country employees.

Allowance is an additional payment that allows the expatriate to maintain a standard of living similar to that at home. It usually pays for housing, and sometimes food and clothing. Additional support may be provided to cover relocation, children's education, travel, and business-related entertainment. Housing is costly in many locations. International relocation is also potentially costly. Firms provide hardship allowances to compensate employees who work in countries with civil strife or other dangers, or in developing economies that lack essential housing, education, and other facilities.[30]

Given the potential hardships of working abroad, many MNEs also provide *incentives* to expatriate employees. The incentive is like a bonus intended to motivate the employee to undertake extraordinary efforts to accomplish company goals abroad, particularly in new foreign markets. It is typically a one-time, lump-sum payment.[31]

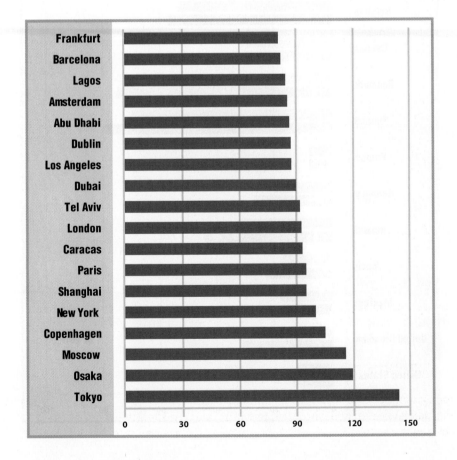

Exhibit 19.5 Cost of Living in Selected Cities, 2009 (Index scale; New York = 100)

SOURCE: Mercer LLC, *Worldwide Cost of Living Survey, 2009—City Ranking*, accessed at http://www.mercer.com. Reprinted with permission.

In expatriate compensation, tax equalization is a special consideration. Expatriates may face two tax bills for the same pay, one from the host country and one from the home country. Most parent-country governments have devised regulations that allow the expatriate to minimize double taxation or pay income tax in only one country. When the employee incurs additional taxes, the employer will usually reimburse him or her for this extra tax burden.

 International Labor Relations

Collective bargaining
Joint negotiations between management and hourly labor and technical staff regarding wages and working conditions.

Labor relations is the process through which management and workers identify and determine job relationships that will apply in the workplace. *Labor unions* (also called trade unions) provide a means for **collective bargaining**—joint negotiations between management and hourly labor and technical staff regarding wages and working conditions. When the firm and labor union negotiate a relationship, they formalize it with a contract. Labor regulations vary substantially, from minimal rules in Africa and the Indian subcontinent to highly detailed laws and regulations in countries such as Germany and Sweden.

Exhibit 19.6 illustrates the percentage of workers in each country that have formal union memberships. Note the recent gradual decline of union membership in many advanced economies. It has fallen to less than 15 percent of workers in France and the United States and less than 25 percent in Australia, Germany, Japan, and Mexico. However, union membership is relatively high in Belgium, Denmark, and Finland, where more than 50 percent of workers, mostly government employees, are unionized.[32]

Exhibit 19.6
Percentage of Workers Who Belong to Labor Unions, 1997 and 2007

SOURCES: *Organisation for Economic Cooperation and Development,* "Trade Union Density," accessed at http://www.oecd.org; Bureau of Labor Statistics (2010), "Union Membership," United States Department of Labor: Washington DC, accessed at http://www.bls.gov, May 12, 2010; Visser, Jelle "Union Membership Statistics in 24 Countries," *Monthly Labor Review,* January, 2006.

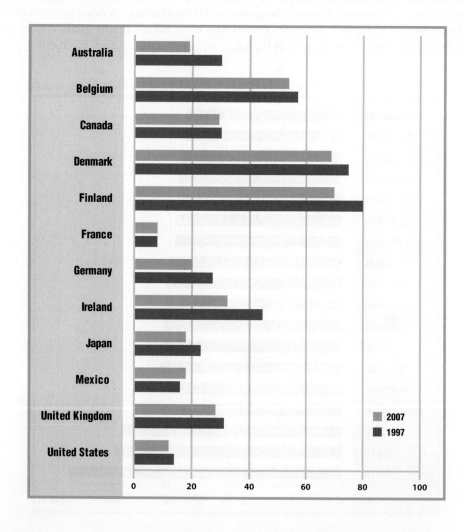

In many countries, younger workers are less interested in joining unions, and labor laws have become less union-friendly than in the past.[33] The trend toward outsourcing manufacturing and business processes to foreign suppliers also contributes to declining membership. Germany, a nation with a strong tradition of unionized labor, has seen a net outflow of FDI in recent years as German firms have established manufacturing facilities in Eastern Europe and Southeast Asia.

When management and labor fail to reach agreement, the union may declare a *strike*—an organized, collective refusal to work with the aim of pressuring management to grant union demands. Exhibit 19.7 shows the average annual number of days per 1,000 employees not worked due to strikes and other labor disputes for various countries. Worldwide, the incidence of strikes has declined over the last decade, but they remain a powerful weapon with important implications for business. In 2009 labor unions throughout France held strikes to protest job cuts and falling pay. The strikes by transportation workers, automakers, oil workers, and even supermarket cashiers shut down trains and air travel, halted work in key industries, and led to the closure of numerous schools throughout the nation. In 2010, a strike by 1,200 workers at a Nokia plant in India seriously delayed production of mobile telephones.[34]

If a strike lasts more than a few days, a *mediator* or an *arbitrator* may be called in to negotiate between labor and management in an attempt to end the dispute. A mediator is an expert in labor-management relations who brings both sides together and helps them reach a mutually acceptable settlement. An arbitrator is an expert third party who delivers a judgment in favor of one side or the other, after assessing arguments presented by both sides.

Distinctive Features of Labor around the World

Each world region has a distinctive approach to labor influenced by its history, tradition, and other local factors. In the United States, unionization is concentrated in such industries as automobiles and steel and among public-sector employees such as police and teachers. Union membership in the United States peaked in the 1950s, and the unionized labor force in various traditional industries has fallen in recent years. Globalization, capital mobility, and mass immigration from Mexico have substantially affected the power of organized labor, leading to continued workforce restructuring. Nevertheless, U.S. labor unions remain an important political force. Their activities center on collective

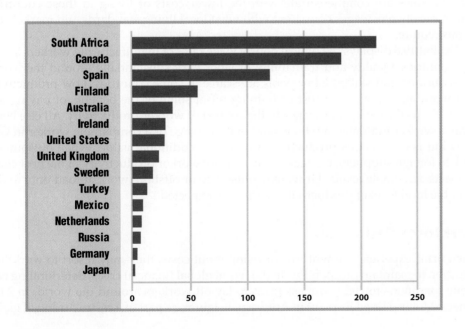

Exhibit 19.7 Average Annual Days Not Worked Due to Labor Disputes (per 1,000 employees, 1998–2008)

SOURCE: The International Labour Organization (ILO), accessed at http://www.ilo.org

bargaining over wages, benefits, and workplace conditions and on representing members if management attempts to violate contract provisions.[35]

Labor activism and dispute resolution through unions have grown significantly in China in recent years. Given close ties between Chinese labor and government, Western managers usually deal extensively with China's national and local governments in managing labor relations. Walmart had to officially recognize unions in China—something it does not normally do. China also has a developing independent labor movement. In recent years, workers have staged thousands of strikes and protests there to demand better wages and working conditions.

Unions are a factor in reducing the occurrence of sweatshops and other poor working conditions in China.[36] The government has launched several initiatives to better protect workers' rights, including new legislation. A campaign by the All-China Federation of Trade Unions (ACFTU), the world's largest labor federation with over 150 million members, is seeking to unionize workers at all foreign firms operating in China. The ACFTU functions largely to bridge labor demands and the interests of the Chinese government.[37]

Unions in Europe often represent not only factory workers but white-collar workers such as physicians, engineers, and teachers. They hold much political power and may be allied with a particular political party, usually the Labor Party. A unique feature in Europe, especially in Germany and the Scandinavian countries, is labor union participation in determining wage rates, bonuses, profit sharing, holiday leaves, dismissals, and plant expansions and closings. In 2006, the European Union passed new legislation that requires even small enterprises to inform and consult employees about a range of business, employment, and work organization issues.[38] In Sweden, labor plays a significant role in shop-floor decisions and participates in such issues as product quality standards and how to organize the factory for greater efficiency and safety. In Sweden and Germany, labor participation in management may be mandated, and workers often sit on corporate boards, a practice known as **codetermination**.[39] By contrast, in Britain, South Korea, and the United States, relations between management and labor unions are often adversarial.

Codetermination An industrial relations practice in which labor representatives sit on the corporate board and participate in company decision making.

Cost, Quality, and Productivity of Labor

Worker wages vary greatly worldwide. So do the quality and productivity of worker efforts. Advanced economies tend to pay relatively higher wages. Hourly wages are particularly high in Northern Europe. Lower wages in emerging markets and developing economies are commensurate with the lower costs of living in those countries; firms typically pay wages consistent with what local living standards and market conditions require.

Exhibit 19.8 displays the typical hourly wage rates of manufacturing workers in various countries. Quality and trainability of labor vary substantially around the world. Well-educated and skilled labor pools are scarce in some countries. Low productivity, poor work quality, and the cost of training offset some of the benefits of paying low wages. Firms must consider wages in the context of worker productivity. All else being equal, a worker in Romania who is paid half the wage of a comparable worker in Germany but is only half as productive provides no additional value. When outsourcing work to foreign suppliers, managers must ensure worker productivity in the host country meets acceptable levels. Firms may outsource or offshore work abroad only to discover the local level of productivity is less than expected.

Workforce Reduction

When firms experience downturns or rising input costs, they may resort to workforce reduction to maintain profitability. In the recent global financial crisis, deteriorating economic conditions forced countless firms to lay off workers around the world. In 2010, General Motors closed its plant in Antwerp, Belgium, as part of a restructuring of global

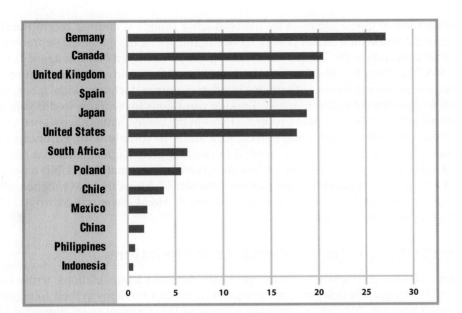

Exhibit 19.8 Wage Rate of Manufacturing Labor, in US Dollars per Hour, 2008

SOURCE: The International Labour Organization (ILO), accessed at http://www.ilo.org

operations. The factory had employed more than 2,600 workers who manufactured the Opel for the European market. Management also announced plans to lay off 4,000 employees in Germany.[40]

Laying off workers (or making them "redundant," as it is called in some countries) requires management to consider various factors, including local norms, regulations, and the presence of strong labor unions. Local custom obligates firms in Japan to avoid lay-offs or find positions for dismissed workers in supplier organizations. Most European countries have regulations that restrict management's ability to lay off workers.

International human resource and legal managers must possess a full understanding of local labor laws and regulations regarding worker dismissal. In the United States, declaring bankruptcy enables firms to shed labor in the process of reorganization. In this way auto parts manufacturer Delphi Corporation gained concessions from the United Auto Workers union on wages, benefits, and plant closings in 2007. Delphi was able to reduce hourly wages from about $27 per hour to a $14–$18.50 range.[41]

Many countries require "just cause" to terminate an employee. In most cases, just cause is satisfied if the employee becomes permanently disabled, is terminated within a probationary period (usually one to six months), or is found guilty of incompetence, theft, or disclosure of confidential information. If the firm cannot demonstrate just cause, local courts may require it to pay an indemnity, a sum of money upon termination that can be substantial. In most countries, the employee is considered the weaker party; thus, ambiguous cases are usually settled in the employee's favor.[42]

Trends in International Labor

Labor is increasingly mobile across national borders thanks to the growing integration of national economies, the rapid expansion of multinational firms, and the rise of international collaborative ventures. As more countries liberalize their economies, governments are also shedding protectionist policies that restrict work permits for foreigners.

Many countries must cope with an influx of immigrants, both legal and illegal, who compete with established workers by providing low-cost labor. Some nations, particularly those with labor shortages or rapidly growing economies, encourage immigration. Immigration bolsters the pool of needed labor in Canada and the United States. Several million Polish workers have sought jobs in Britain since Poland became a member of the European Union. Persian Gulf countries have long retained large labor pools from abroad. By contrast, Japan discourages worker immigration, a policy that, combined with a low birth rate, will produce labor shortages in the future.

Formation of global alliances by national labor unions is another recent trend. To help counter weakening union power, labor organizations have lobbied supranational organizations, such as the International Labour Office (a United Nations agency), to require MNEs to comply with labor standards and practices worldwide. Some national labor unions are joining forces with unions in other countries, forming global labor/trade unions to equalize compensation and working conditions for workers in different geographical areas.[43] Subsidiaries of European firms in the United States have signed union-organizing agreements that compel their U.S. units to comply with European labor standards.[44] A few unions have succeeded in creating global agreements that affect all the subsidiaries of numerous MNEs. The Union Network International (UNI) represents 900 unions with 15 million members around the world. Firms that have signed global agreements with the UNI include Carrefour (France), H&M (Sweden), Metro AG (Germany), and Telefonica (Spain).[45]

Firm Strategy in International Labor Relations

Because national differences produce markedly different labor relations across countries, MNEs frequently delegate the management of labor relations to their foreign subsidiaries. However, this can be a mistake because of the potential *global* impact of labor relations in any one country. Today, cross-border linkages give rise to complex interactions among differing national labor systems. Wage levels or labor unrest in one country affect the firm's activities in other countries. For instance, a strike by 1,800 workers at an auto-parts factory in India forced management at Ford and General Motors to temporarily shut factories in North America due to a parts shortage.[46] Because unions influence the cost of labor, productivity, worker morale, and firm performance, and because labor agreements made by foreign subsidiaries can create precedents for negotiations in other countries, it is critical to maintain cohesive labor relations.

Skillful development and management of international human resource policies at headquarters helps ensure consistency. A centralized information system, ideally on the company's intranet, can provide continuous data on labor developments among subsidiaries to help managers anticipate employee concerns and resolve potential threats in cross-national labor relations. The intranet is also useful for communicating with employees worldwide and regularly informing them of the firm's mission, objectives, ongoing challenges, and future threats. It is often easier to negotiate with labor unions when they understand what confronts the firm.

IHRM assists global corporate and country executives in fulfilling their corporate social responsibility objectives. The *Global Trend* feature details how Nike is rising to this challenge.

 Diversity in the International Workforce

Leading firms in global business embrace employees from diverse backgrounds who bring a wealth of experience and knowledge. We saw in the chapter opener that Johnson & Johnson links managers' compensation to efforts to hire minorities, women, and people from varied cultural backgrounds and sponsors the Women's Leadership Initiative in its international units. Diverse groups are active in the international workforce and accepted around the world.

Women in International Business

Societies impose a range of roles on men and women. Some restrict women to a limited set of work roles and grant them fewer legal rights than men, upon whom women are often economically dependent. In Latin America, employers might consider a woman's

GLOBAL TREND

Global Corporate Social Responsibility and the Role of International Human Resource Management

Corporate actions affect employees, whether they work directly or indirectly for the firm. Heightened interest in this impact is compelling firms to become better corporate citizens abroad. Corporate social responsibility (CSR) means the firm should be responsive to all its stakeholders and operate in socially acceptable ways, including when hiring, contracting with, and managing employees.

Apparel and footwear is a low-tech industry, employing low-cost labor in emerging markets and developing economies. Firms like Nike and Reebok are primarily designers, marketers, and distributors of athletic footwear and apparel. They outsource nearly all their production to independent contractors located abroad. Nike (www.nike.com) relies on numerous suppliers that employ some 800,000 workers, mainly in China, Vietnam, Indonesia, and Thailand. These suppliers usually have limited bargaining power and often lack human resource policies to prevent labor exploitation.

Nike had long been accused of caring little for the welfare of its contract workers abroad. In the early 1990s, employees in some Nike factories in Asia were paid wages insufficient to sustain even basic nutritional needs. Many plants were operated like sweatshops, where workers labored for long hours in difficult conditions. Nike executives deflected the accusations by arguing that because Nike did not own the factories, it was not responsible for conditions in them. Over time, however, negative publicity became a major public relations problem, and activist groups made Nike a major target for anti-globalization and anti-sweatshop movements.

To better understand the situation, Nike systematically assessed its suppliers' foreign factories. Then, in the mid-2000s, it announced CSR goals to integrate corporate responsibility into its business strategies and long-term growth. Nike demanded improved working conditions from its suppliers. It set benchmarks to improve labor conditions and eliminate long work hours. It developed auditing tools to measure compliance with new labor standards and approved supplier plans to invest in worker development and ensure its standards were followed.

Nike also developed a process to select suppliers based on their meeting minimal environmental, health, and safety standards and to monitor them for compliance. Today, Nike examines country-level factors such as quality of infrastructure, human rights, and economic and political conditions and aims to ensure that workers in its supply chains are paid fair wages. It is introducing collective bargaining training in all contract factories. Minimum wages are to be determined through negotiations between labor and management.

Despite all these efforts, improvements are still needed. In some Nike contract factories, local managers are not yet fully complying with the firm's standards. Factory managers have sometimes denied inspectors access, and others have provided false information about work conditions. Some employees continue to work very long hours, some suppliers are still using child labor, and auditors have found evidence of physical abuse. Nike is working hard to meet its CSR obligations.

SOURCES: Eugenia Levenson, "Citizen Nike," *Fortune*, November 24, 2008, p. 165; Richard Locke, *The Promise and Perils of Globalization: The Case of Nike* (Cambridge: Massachusetts Institute of Technology, 2007); Khalid Nadvi, "Global Standards, Global Governance and the Organization of Global Value Chains," *Journal of Economic Geography* 8 (2008): 323–43; Nike, "Nike CSR," 2007 press release retrieved from http://www.nike.com; Nike, "Workers in Contract Factories," 2007 company report retrieved from http://www.nike.com; Michael Skapinker, "Nike Ushers in a New Age of Corporate Responsibility," *Financial Times*, April 20, 2005, p. 11.

marital status in hiring. Some firms consider young married women with no children a risky investment based on the assumption they will soon leave to start a family. In Asia and the Middle East, female managers are often mistaken for the wife or secretary of a male manager. In other countries women have few opportunities to work outside the home and advance their own economic interests.

Female managers in international business are still more the exception than the norm.[47] Consider the proportion of women working in top management positions, as presented in Exhibit 19.9. The data are based on an annual survey of 7,200 privately held firms headquartered in thirty-six countries.[48] Note the unique position of the Philippines, where representation by women in senior management is highest. Women's

Exhibit 19.9 Average Percentage of Women in Senior Management Positions

SOURCE: Grant Thornton International Ltd. (2010), *Privately Held Businesses; The Lifeblood of the Global Economy, International Business Report* 2010, at http://www.grantthorntonibos.com. Reprinted with permission.

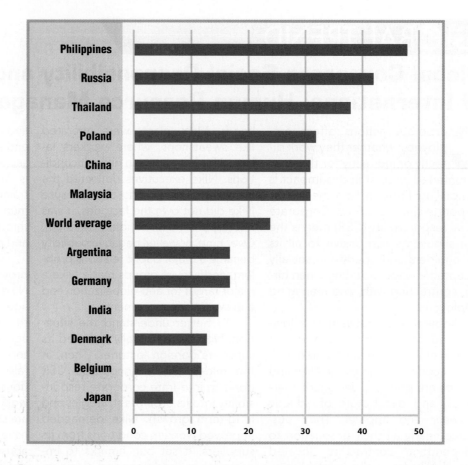

rights have never been a contentious issue there, religious practices do not clash with a woman's right to work outside the home, and women have refined their entrepreneurial and leadership skills over many decades.

Exhibit 19.9 suggests women still do not enjoy equal access to senior management positions in most countries. Even in the advanced economies, they are sometimes not afforded the same opportunities for education and training as their male colleagues. Although evidence suggests just as many women seek international positions as men, relatively few are asked to fill expatriate positions.[49]

There are several reasons for this. First, senior managers may assume women do not make suitable leaders abroad or that foreign men do not like reporting to female managers. Firms are reluctant to send women to locations where the demarcation between male and female roles is sharp. Even obtaining a work visa can prove problematic in certain male-dominated countries. In many countries, male managers drink together, go to sports events, or enjoy the night life. Some women may feel uncomfortable in such all-male settings.[50]

Having children and other family obligations can disrupt career paths. Although flexible and part-time work policies are often beneficial to women's progress up the corporate ladder, not all companies provide such opportunities. Finally, because women currently occupy relatively few top management positions (in Europe, they hold only 15 percent of senior executive posts), there are fewer women with sufficient experience to be sent abroad for important jobs.[51]

Today, many more women are obtaining university degrees in business. Women account for about one-third of students in MBA programs in Europe and the United States. About one-half of recruits who join European firms are female university graduates.[52] In the United States, 140 women enroll in higher education each year for every 100 men; in Sweden, the rate is as high as 150.[53] Businesswomen increasingly form their own networks. In the United Kingdom, a group of women established *Women Directors on*

Boards, which aims to improve prospects for women to reach top management jobs. The *Association of Women in International Trade* is a U.S. organization that promotes the interests of women working in international business (www.wiit.org).

In 2003, females accounted for only 6 percent of seats on Norwegian boards of directors. Under an initiative by the Norwegian government, however, new legislation requires listed and state-owned companies to ensure that women hold at least 40 percent of seats on the board. The legislation has been effective; female board representation now exceeds 45 percent in such companies. New companies also have to comply with the rules, and the government is considering extending them to family-owned companies as well. Since the Norwegian legislation was introduced, Spain has followed suit with rules for female board representation and France has proposed similar laws.

A survey by Mercer Human Resource Consulting (www.mercer.com) found companies worldwide are substantially increasing the number of women on foreign assignments. About half the surveyed firms believe the number of female expatriates will continue rising in the future. At the same time, 15 percent of companies said they would not send women to hardship locations such as the Middle East. The survey included more than 100 multinational companies with nearly 17,000 male and female expatriates.[54]

Success Strategies for Women Managers in International Business

In many countries, being a female expatriate can be an advantage for developing and leveraging strengths as a woman and as a manager. Women stand out more, and competent women earn much respect. In the long run, managerial competence wins out over prejudice.

Many women have found ways of overcoming senior management bias against sending females abroad. It is easier to get foreign assignments if you speak a foreign language or have other international skills. Gaining substantial experience as a domestic manager or in short international assignments can greatly improve prospects for working abroad. Garnering strong support from senior management increases credibility. Once abroad, most women report the first reaction of surprise is often replaced by professionalism and respect. Some female graduates highlighted in the *Recent Grads in IB* feature in this book fit this trend.

Firms can ensure women achieve greater equality in international business. They can provide training programs to develop female managerial talent. They can fill leadership roles in foreign assignments with qualified women. They can fill a minimal percentage of senior executive posts with female employees. They can set targets for the number of women on executive boards. Many female executives are now serving as mentors and role models for aspiring women. Leading firms understand the need to forge a new paradigm of diverse and internationally successful female managers. Organizations like Accenture, Ernst & Young, and Vinson & Elkins all sponsor programs that assist women to advance in the global workplace.

Evolving Human Resource Challenges at Sony

The Japanese electronics giant Sony employs 170,000 people worldwide, making and marketing the PlayStation home video game systems, televisions, digital and video cameras, laptop computers, personal music players, and semiconductors. Europe, Japan, and North America each generate about a quarter of its sales; the remainder comes from the rest of the world. The firm has several entertainment divisions, including Epic and Sony Pictures Entertainment, and plants in Britain, China, Japan, Malaysia, Mexico, Spain, and the United States.

Sony has struggled in recent years because of the impact of the strong yen and the global recession. The PlayStation is facing serious competition from Nintendo's Wii system. The Sony Reader has been pressured by Amazon's Kindle and now iPad. Sony's music-player business was undone by the iPod and iPhone.

The Manufacturing Workforce

Sony's CEO is Sir Howard Stringer, a native of Wales who ran CBS in New York for many years. Recently, he reorganized Sony, closing a dozen factories, cutting 18,000 jobs, and shifting component manufacturing to low-cost countries. For example, management closed an audio-equipment plant in Indonesia, laying off some 1,000 workers.

Sony tries to avoid worker lay-offs, however. Factories in Britain, where 4,000 people once made cathode ray tubes, gradually lost their competitiveness after introduction of the flat-screen TV. Sony worked with unions to create enhanced severance packages and find new job opportunities in the region, and over time it restructured the plants to produce high-definition broadcast cameras. Sony built strong customer relationships, developed new talent, created a new corporate culture, and aligned employees to the new strategy. The plants reinvented themselves by emphasizing best-in-class efforts to achieve preferred supplier status.

Sony has numerous plants and R&D centers in China and has relocated scores of expatriates there. Initially, the firm was attracted to China because of its low-cost labor, but today it also benefits from the superior skills of the local workforce, particularly for high-technology projects. Sony's R&D center in northern China employs over 20,000 software engineers. Nearby universities and technical institutes churn out thousands more engineering graduates each year. The high concentration of foreign firms in China (including Dell, Hitachi, IBM, and NEC) has created much competition for local talent.

Human Resource Philosophy

Sony has a highly developed approach to international human resource management. When recruiting new employees, executives look for candidates who have an entrepreneurial spirit, think creatively, and have strong communications skills. Sony's former chairman, Norio Ohga, was also an opera singer, an orchestral conductor, and a licensed jet pilot. His education in music and the arts, alongside science and engineering, strongly influenced the development of the firm's most successful products. In all areas, Sony encourages employees to structure their roles to make best use of their individual strengths.

In Sony's foreign subsidiaries, human resource managers spend time with executives and employees, linking the firm's objectives and strategies to employee capabilities. Senior managers identify key jobs for realizing the firm's objectives and analyze whether they have the best people in the most strategically important jobs and what talent they need to acquire.

When Sony Europe had to reinvent itself, human resource managers focused on identifying and leveraging the key strengths of managers and other employees as a means to enhance corporate performance. The firm introduced mentoring projects that encouraged employees to focus on what they do best and maximize their contribution to increasing firm performance.

Training and Talent Development

Sony offers management trainee programs for its most promising recruits. Trainees are counseled to do what they are passionate about and find ways to use their talents to advance the firm. They complete formal courses and training, increasingly tailored to individual demands and career aspirations. The firm established a mentoring and coaching network across all its talent pools. Executives coach their potential successors, who in turn act as mentors to younger upper-management candidates.

Sony is putting more emphasis on developing global managers and ensuring succession planning for top management jobs. Senior management grooms executives with strong analytical and intellectual qualities who are driven and not shy about taking risks. Programs stress strong people skills and the ability to interact with and influence others. The firm's senior leadership development programs emphasize visionary leadership and leading with emotional intelligence.

Sony implemented an extensive talent pipeline running vertically through the organization, developing and supporting high-potential employees from entry level all the way to senior levels of the firm. Management has a system of exhaustive interviews and assessments for identifying potential talent within Sony's own ranks. Executive fast-track candidates must be fluent in English and two other languages, have significant international experience, and possess the drive and ambition to take on international leadership roles.

Senior managers are required to continuously scan the employee pool to identify and groom potential talent. Recently the firm, long bound by its Japanese culture, has launched initiatives to groom more English-speaking executives as a way to transform itself and remain on the cutting edge. Stringer has appointed numerous non-Japanese leaders who are much younger than the traditional, seasoned Japanese management. The mere presence of a non-Japanese CEO at Sony points to the firm's geocentric staffing policy.

Each year, Stringer hosts a closed-door management conference in Tokyo, attended by over 1,000 Sony managers from around the world. The conference aims to in-spire management, convey the firm's strategic vision, and build cohesiveness for the global organization.

Corporate Social Responsibility

Sony pursues an "integrity approach" to foreign manufacturing operations and attempts to maintain workplace standards that exceed local requirements. As the firm expands internationally, management knows that actions today may be crucial for entry to new markets tomorrow. Exploiting low workplace standards in one country can ruin a reputation and jeopardize entry to new markets. Sony learned a lesson from its experiences in Mexico, where human rights groups accused it of violating workers' rights to organize and associate freely.

Managers appear to have learned that simply doing what is required by the standards of the host country can result in inconsistencies in firm operations. The result may be fragmentation and difficulty in establishing effective quality control. The firm has taken steps to standardize workplace norms so management can benchmark internal performance, transfer expertise between countries, and provide coherent management to worldwide operations. It is attempting to establish a universal standard of employment, offering superior working conditions and locally relevant wages and benefits at all locations. Managers want to ensure that wages in foreign factories provide a fair standard of living to all workers.

AACSB: Reflective Thinking Skills, Ethical Understanding and Reasoning Abilities, Multicultural and Diversity Understanding

Case Questions

1. Traditionally, Japanese MNEs followed an ethnocentric orientation in international staffing, in which managers from headquarters hold key subsidiary positions. Sony is shifting away from this model. What approach should Sony follow for staffing its subsidiaries? When recruiting expatriates for foreign operations, what characteristics should Sony emphasize to ensure its managers are adept at living and working abroad?

2. Sony faces challenges in finding suitable talent for its operations in China and Europe. What steps should it take to ensure it has an adequate pool of international managers and other talent for worldwide operations? What should Sony do to promote global mind-sets?

3. What is your view of Sony's training efforts? What steps could Sony take to improve its training in light of its multicountry operations?

4. Sony has experienced labor relations problems in Indonesia and elsewhere. What strategies should management follow to improve labor relations? What can it do to reduce the number and severity of labor difficulties the firm might face in the future?

5. What is your view of Sony's efforts at corporate social responsibility (CSR) in international operations? What steps can Sony take to improve CSR in organizing and managing its operations around the world, particularly in developing countries and emerging markets?

SOURCES: Frederick Balfour and Hiroko Tashiro, "Golf, Sushi—and Cheap Engineers," *BusinessWeek*, March 28, 2005, p. 54; Richard Siklos, "Sony: Lost in Transformation," *Fortune*, July 6, 2009, p. 68; "Game On," *Economist*, March 7, 2009, p. 73; Hoover's profile of Sony retrieved from http://www.hoovers.com; Rebecca Johnson, "Can You Feel It?" *People Management* 13, no. 17 (2007), pp. 1–4; Simon Kent, "Pooling Its Resources," *Personnel Today*, September 2005, pp. 23–24; David Turner, "Personality, Not University, Key to Job Hunting in Japan," *Financial Times*, September 22, 2005, p. 7; "Labor Department to Study Complaint Against Sony," *Wall Street Journal*, October 20, 1994, p. B2; Roy White, "Building on Employee Strengths at Sony Europe," *Strategic HR Review*, July/August 2006, pp. 28–31.

CHAPTER ESSENTIALS

Key Terms

area studies, p. 552
codetermination, p. 558
collective bargaining, p. 556
cross-cultural awareness, p. 552
cultural intelligence, p. 551
culture shock, p. 552

expatriate, p. 547
expatriate assignment failure, p. 552
global talent pool, p. 554
host-country national (HCN), p. 546
international human resource
    management (IHRM), p. 546

parent-country national (PCN), p. 546
performance appraisal, p. 554
practical information, p. 552
repatriation, p. 553
third-country national (TCN), p. 546

Summary

In this chapter, you learned about:

1. The strategic role of human resources in international business

International human resource management (IHRM) is the selection, training, employment, and motivation of employees for international operations. IHRM is more complex than its domestic counterpart. The firm must develop procedures, policies, and processes appropriate for each country where it does business. A **parent-country national (PCN)** is an employee who is a citizen of the country where the MNE is headquartered. A **host-country national (HCN)** is an employee who is a citizen of the country where the MNE subsidiary or affiliate is located. A **third-country national (TCN)** is an employee who is a citizen of a country other than the home or host country. An **expatriate** is an employee who is assigned to work and reside in a foreign country for an extended period, usually a year or longer. There are six key tasks in IHRM: international staffing policy; preparation and training of international employees; international **performance appraisal**; compensation, including formulation of benefit packages that vary from country to country; international labor relations; and managing diversity in the international workplace.

2. International staffing policy

IHRM managers determine the ideal mix of employees to work in the firm's subsidiaries and affiliates abroad. Managers best suited for working abroad typically have technical competence, self-reliance, adaptability, interpersonal skills, leadership ability, physical and emotional health, and, if present, a family prepared for living abroad. **Expatriate assignment failure** is the unplanned early return home of an employee or the failure of an expatriate to function effectively abroad. It is not unusual for expatriates to experience **culture shock**.

3. Preparation and training of international employees

Proper training and orientation of managers improves firm performance. Training for foreign assignments includes **area studies, practical information,** and **cross-cultural awareness**. Training includes methods such as videos, lectures, readings, simulations, and field experience. Acquiring language skills provides managers with numerous advantages. **Repatriation** is the return of the expatriate to the home country and requires advance preparation. Training is also important for the nonmanagerial workforce abroad.

4. International performance appraisal

International performance appraisals involve providing feedback on how well employees are doing their jobs, identifying problems and areas where more training is needed, and providing a basis to reward superior performance. Firms must develop systems for measuring the performance of foreign units. Various factors in the foreign environment can impede effective performance appraisal.

5. Compensation of employees

Compensation packages vary internationally because of differences in legally mandated benefits, tax laws, cost of living, local tradition, and culture. Expatriates expect to be compensated at a level that allows them to maintain their usual standard of living, which can be costly in some locations. Typical expatriate compensation includes four components: base salary, benefits, allowances, and incentives. Tax equalization must be considered because expatriates may face two tax bills for the same pay, from the host and home countries.

6. **International labor relations**

   MNEs employ many nonmanagerial employees abroad, often represented by *labor unions*, to work in factories and perform other tasks. Management must ensure effective labor relations and take care when reducing the workforce. Along with the cost of labor, the quality and productivity of the workforce are important considerations. **Codetermination**, the participation of workers on boards of directors, is common in some countries. Labor unions are sometimes at odds with the realities of global competition and the influx of immigrants in many countries. Leading MNEs establish an information system on labor developments, communicate with all employ-

ees, and formulate a standard policy on employment and working conditions worldwide.

7. **Diversity in the international workforce**

   Progressive MNEs include people from diverse backgrounds, nationalities, and gender who bring a wealth of experience and knowledge to addressing the firm's problems and opportunities. Employee cultural diversity increases the complexity of interaction. Success comes from understanding and accepting differences, and then using them to enhance planning, strategy, and the firm's operations. In most countries, female managers in international business are still somewhat rare. Firms can take several steps to ensure women achieve more equality in international business.

Test Your Comprehension AACSB: Reflective Thinking Skills,
Ethical Understanding and Reasoning Abilities

1. What is international human resource management (IHRM)? Why is it important to internationalizing firms? What is the role of IHRM in company strategy?

2. Under what circumstances would an MNE staff itself with (a) parent-country nationals, (b) host-country nationals, and (c) third-country nationals?

3. What steps can senior managers take to develop global managers?

4. What are the characteristics of managers adept at working abroad?

5. In what ways might an employee experience expatriate assignment failure?

6. What are the major components of training for foreign assignments?

7. What approaches can human resource managers follow to prepare expatriates for returning home?

8. What factors should human resource managers consider when appraising the performance of an employee working abroad?

9. Suppose you are working abroad as an expatriate for an MNE. What are typical components you would expect to have in your compensation package?

10. What are some key trends affecting international labor?

11. What measures can firms take to enhance the prospects of placing women in international business jobs?

Apply Your Understanding AACSB: Communication Abilities,
Reflective Thinking Skills, Ethical Understanding and Reasoning Abilities

1. Nissan Motor Co. is Japan's second-largest automotive company, with annual sales of around USD $100 billion. The firm makes Maxima and Sentra cars, Altima and Infiniti upscale sedans, Frontier pickups, and the Xterra and Pathfinder SUVs. A few years ago, Nissan was on the verge of bankruptcy. Then

Carlos Ghosn was installed as the firm's CEO. He closed inefficient factories, curbed purchasing costs, and introduced new products. Suppose Nissan asked you to advise them on IHRM issues. What specific human resource strategies would you recommend to Nissan top management to further enhance the firm's performance? In particular, how would you advise top management on international staffing policy, development of global managers, preparation and training of employees, and company strategy for international labor?

2. Global Wannabe (GW), a manufacturer of musical instruments, is eager to internationalize. While it conducts almost no international business now, the board of directors believes that in the coming four years, GW should generate at least a third of its sales from abroad by establishing foreign marketing subsidiaries and setting up production bases in low-cost countries to reduce manufacturing costs. GW's president, Larry Gerber, has placed you on the task force charged with recruiting managers who can run GW's operations abroad. What guidelines would you offer to GW for recruiting and selecting expatriates, avoiding the problem of expatriate assignment failure, and evaluating the performance of employees posted abroad?

3. *Ethical Dilemma:* Recently the U.S. Congress pushed for legislation that would make it easier for workers to form unions. The measure was strongly supported by the Teamsters, a powerful international labor union. Management at FedEx, a leading express delivery firm, contended that the new legislation would inflate its labor costs and make it vulnerable to strikes and disruptions in its global transport network. FedEx is a major aircraft buyer, and some suggested the firm might purchase more airplanes from lower-cost foreign suppliers if business expenses rose due to the proposed legislation. Unionization could also reduce FedEx's ability to compete against top rivals DHL (Germany) and TNT (Netherlands). Meanwhile, labor unions in FedEx's foreign markets are trying to unionize company workers. For example, Teamsters launched efforts to unionize FedEx workers in Canada. Is it acceptable for FedEx to prevent its workers from forming a union? What factors should management consider when determining the appropriateness and role of unions? To whom is FedEx most accountable—its employees or its shareholders (who expect FedEx to maximize profits)? Analyze this dilemma by using the Ethical Framework in Chapter 5.

globalEDGE Internet Exercises
(http://globalEDGE.msu.edu)

AACSB: Communication Abilities, Reflective Thinking Skills, Use of Information Technology

Refer to Chapter 1, page 62, for instructions on how to access and use globalEDGE™.

1. The cost of living and other lifestyle factors vary considerably around the world. It is critical to develop an appropriate compensation package for managers working abroad. The U.S. Department of State provides information firms can use to calculate compensation around the world. Prepare a report on the factors relevant to developing a compensation package for expatriates working in Prague and Tokyo, including "Living Costs Abroad," by accessing the State Department via globalEDGE™ (keywords "Travel/Living Abroad") or directly at aoprals.state.gov.

2. Stryker Corp., a manufacturer of medical devices based in the United States, is considering establishing an assembly facility in France, Germany, or the Netherlands, so it can better serve its European customers. You have the task of choosing the most appropriate country from the three choices by researching the following statistics: the cost of labor ("manufacturing hourly compensation index") and level of productivity ("manufacturing output per hour"). Essentially, management wants to pick the country that has the best overall profile of low labor cost and high productivity. A good source for this data is the U.S. Department of Labor, Bureau of Labor Statistics (www.bls.gov). After conducting your research and analysis, prepare a recommendation on which country—France, Germany, or the Netherlands—would be the best choice to locate the factory. (Note: Such decisions are normally much more complex than implied here, but a preliminary analysis is a starting point for decision making.)

3. Executive Planet™ is just one of numerous portals that provide information for traveling managers and expatriates on how to live and do business in various countries. Suppose that you work for Virgin, the British airline, and are assigned to work in Virgin's office in an emerging market (choose an emerging market such as Argentina, India, Russia, Mexico, South Africa, or Turkey). You need to learn how to be effective in your dealings with customers and colleagues in the chosen country. Select three topics (such as making appointments, business dress guidelines, or gift giving) and prepare an executive summary on how to behave regarding the topics that you have selected for your chosen country. You can find Executive Planet™ online via globalEDGE™ or by visiting the site directly at www.executiveplanet.com.

CHAPTER 20

LEARNING OBJECTIVES In this chapter, you will learn about:

1. Key tasks in international financial management
2. International capital structure
3. Raising funds for the firm's international activities
4. Management of working capital and cash flow
5. Capital budgeting for international operations
6. Management of currency risk
7. Management of international accounting and tax practices

Financial Management and Accounting in the Global Firm

A Small Firm Rides the Waves of Foreign Exchange

Markel Corporation is a Pennsylvania-based SME that makes wire and tubing for the automotive and fluid-handling industries. The firm exports to Germany, Spain, Japan, and numerous other countries, generating much of its more than $20 million in annual sales from abroad. Markel thus faces the recurring challenges of fluctuating international currencies. Every day, CEO Kim Reynolds scans the financial news to stay abreast of how exchange rates are affecting sales and profits. In the early 2000s, an appreciating dollar made Markel's products more expensive to European and Japanese customers, resulting in a decrease in demand for Markel products. But the currency game works both ways. By the late-2000s both the euro and yen had strengthened, increasing the buying power of European and Japanese customers and boosting Markel's sales.

When the euro was introduced in 2000, however, its value relative to the U.S. dollar bottomed out at 83 cents, making each euro that Markel received in sales worth less in U.S. dollars than expected. In 2001 and 2002, the firm suffered more than $625,000 in currency losses, forcing management to rethink its strategies for currency exchange planning.

Swings in the $3.2 trillion-a-day world currency market can make or break a small firm. Markel's problem arose because the firm quoted prices in its customers' currencies. The approach helped Markel capture 70 percent of the world market for its products because customers prefer to pay in their own currencies. At the same time, the approach exposed Markel to currency risk because translating foreign currency sales into the U.S. dollar can result in losses if the customer's currency is significantly weaker than the dollar. Suppose Markel sells merchandise to its Spanish importer for €50,000, payable in 90 days. The delay in getting paid exposes Markel to currency risk: If the euro depreciates during the 90-day period, Markel will receive fewer dollars.

To deal with fluctuating currency rates, Markel developed a three-part strategy:

- Quote prices in the customer's currency, which translates to more consistent prices for the customer and helps generate more sales.
- Purchase *forward contracts* to stabilize future dollar-denominated revenues.
- Emphasize efficient company operations to make it through the times when exchange rates move in the wrong direction and hurt sales.

A *forward contract* is an agreement to buy or sell currency at an agreed-upon exchange rate for delivery at a specific future date. Firms like Markel buy forward contracts from banks to hedge exchange-rate exposure. For example, Markel might enter a forward agreement to sell €50,000, at a date 90 days in the future and an exchange rate agreed upon today, ensuring it receives a known dollar amount. The goal of such *hedging* is to balance purchases and sales of foreign currencies to minimize exposure to future currency risk.

When Markel's chief financial officer thinks the dollar is on its way up, he or she hedges the firm's expected euro revenue stream with a forward contract. But Markel's forecast isn't always correct. Suppose Markel buys a €50,000 contract at $1.05 per euro, or $52,500, but when the contract is exercised at the end of the 90-day period, the euro is actually trading at $1.08. Had Markel estimated correctly, it could have made an extra $1,500. Like most international firms, however, Markel is not in the business of trying to make money on foreign exchange

trading. Its goal instead is to minimize its international currency risks.

SOURCES: Barry Goss and Joost Pennings, "Reducing the Likelihood and Impact of Currency Crises," *The Banker*, January 2010, p. 8; Robert Wade, "The Perils of Cross-Border Payments," *World Trade*, June 2009, p. 8; Mark Landler and Simon Romero, "Diverging Fortunes, Tied to the Dollar," *New York Times*, December 11, 2004, retrieved from http://www.nytimes.com; Michael M. Phillips, "How a Small Firm Rides Foreign-Exchange Waves," *Wall Street Journal*, February 7, 2003, retrieved from http://www.wsj.com.

International financial management is the acquisition and use of funds for cross-border trade, investment, R&D, manufacturing, marketing, outsourcing, and other commercial activities. It is a complex but critical business function. Firms face many still-new challenges: increasing globalization, the integration of financial markets, the rise of global e-commerce, expanding opportunities to profit from financial activities, and, most recently, the global financial crisis. Financial managers access funds from investors, foreign bond markets, local stock exchanges, foreign banks, venture capital firms, and intracorporate financing—wherever in the world capital is cheapest. Their ability to minimize risk and seize opportunities depends on their financial management skills and their understanding of the laws and regulations governing financial exchanges worldwide.

Key Tasks in International Financial Management

Motorola (www.motorola.com) has facilities in nearly fifty countries, and its network of subsidiaries and strategic business units raises funds in financial markets around the world. The international financial manager at a firm like Motorola acquires and allocates financial resources for the firm's current and future activities and projects to help maximize company value. Such managers must be competent in six financial management tasks, highlighted in Exhibit 20.1:

1. *Decide on the capital structure.* Determine the ideal long-term mix of financing for the firm's international operations.

Exhibit 20.1
International Financial
Management Tasks

2. *Raise funds for the firm.* Obtain financing for funding value-adding activities and investment projects. Financing might come from selling stocks, borrowing money, or using internally generated funds.

3. *Manage working capital and cash flow.* Administer funds passing in and out of the firm's value-adding activities.

4. *Perform capital budgeting.* Assess the financial attractiveness of major investment projects, such as foreign expansion.

5. *Manage currency risk.* Oversee transactions in various foreign currencies and manage risk exposure resulting from exchange rate fluctuations.

6. *Manage the diversity of international accounting and tax practices.* Learn to operate in a global environment with diverse accounting practices and international tax regimes.

The relevance of these tasks increases as the firm expands the scale of its international operations and must dedicate more attention to efficient cross-border acquisition and use of funds. Yet, it is precisely this scale of global operations that gives the firm strategic flexibility thanks to increased opportunities to tap capital at lower cost, minimize tax obligations, achieve efficient scale of financial operations, and gain bargaining power with lenders.

The six tasks also serve as the basis for organizing this chapter. Let's delve more deeply into each.

Task One: Decide on the Capital Structure

A *capital structure* is the mix of long-term equity financing and debt financing that firms use to support their international activities. Capital structure affects the profitability and stability of the firm and its international operations. Companies obtain capital in two basic ways: by borrowing it or by selling shares of ownership in the firm. **Equity financing** is selling shares of stock to investors, which provides them with an ownership interest— that is, *equity*—in the firm. The firm can also retain earnings—that is, reinvest profit rather than paying it out as dividends to investors. In new companies, founders often provide equity financing from their personal savings. **Debt financing** comes from either of two sources: loans from banks and other financial intermediaries or the sale of corporate bonds to individuals or institutions.

Debt service payments—the periodic principal and interest payments to pay off a loan—are a fixed cost. Using debt financing can add value to the firm because some governments allow firms to deduct interest payments from their taxes. To minimize the possibility of bankruptcy and maintain a good credit rating, most MNEs keep the debt proportion of their capital structure below a threshold they can service even in adverse conditions. Too much debt can force companies into financial distress. Before the recent global financial crisis, private debt instruments such as bonds became significantly more common in world financial markets. Financial institutions in the United States relied on levels of debt amounting to many times the value of their assets. Some undertook risky investments in the growing real estate market. When high valuations in the real estate market proved unsustainable, the risky bets taken with borrowed funds brought many financial institutions to the point of financial distress.[1]

How much debt a firm should hold partly depends on the nature of its industry and target markets. For instance, an insurance company with relatively stable sales to affluent foreign markets can sustain a higher debt ratio than a consumer goods firm that sells to mostly poor countries with cyclical sales.

Not all countries view substantial debt as risky. The average debt ratio in Germany, Italy, Japan, and numerous developing economies typically exceeds 50 percent. This may arise because the country lacks a well-developed stock market or other systems for

Equity financing The issuance of shares of stock to raise capital from investors and the use of retained earnings to reinvest in the firm.

Debt financing The borrowing of money from banks or other financial intermediaries, or the sale of corporate bonds to individuals or institutions, to raise capital.

obtaining capital from equity sources. Hence, firms may have little choice but to borrow money from banks. In other nations, firms maintain close relationships with banks. In Japan, large MNEs are often part of a conglomerate or holding company that includes a bank. Sony Corporation has its own bank, Sony Bank.

Task Two: Raise Funds for the Firm's International Activities

Lufthansa Airlines raised several hundred million euros by issuing stock shares to acquire A380 airplanes, the double-decker aircraft from Airbus. Grupo Mexico, a giant producer of copper and silver, issued millions of peso-denominated shares to honor debts and other commitments incurred by its foreign subsidiaries. Stanley Works, the U.S. toolmaker, funds part of its Japanese operations by selling shares on the Tokyo Stock Exchange.

Global money market
The collective financial markets where firms and governments raise short-term financing.

Global capital market
The collective financial markets where firms and governments raise intermediate and long-term financing.

Companies can obtain financing in the **global money market,** the collective financial markets where firms and governments raise *short-term* financing. Alternatively, companies may obtain financing from the **global capital market,** the collective financial markets where firms and governments raise *intermediate and long-term* financing. Since funding for most projects comes from instruments whose maturity period is over one year, we refer to all such funding as *capital*. In this chapter, we focus on the global capital market.

The great advantage for international investors of participating in the global capital market is the ability to access a wide range of investment opportunities. The benefit for corporations is the ability to access funds from a large pool of sources at a competitive cost. Access to capital is one of the main criteria businesses consider when deciding to expand abroad.[2]

Financial Centers

The global capital market is concentrated in major *financial centers*: New York, London, and Tokyo. Major secondary centers include Frankfurt, Hong Kong, Paris, San Francisco, Singapore, Sydney, and Zurich. At these locations, firms can access the major suppliers of capital through banks, stock exchanges, and venture capitalists. Exhibit 20.2 lists the share of major financial markets held by Europe, the United States, and the rest of the world. Europe is home to the largest share of over-the-counter derivatives turnover (54 percent of the world total), the United States is home to the largest share of foreign equities turnover, and countries outside Europe and the United States have sizeable market shares in marine insurance and foreign exchange (60 percent and 50 percent, respectively). Europe's global share of financial markets has been rising in recent years, although the United States remains dominant in many markets.

The global capital market is huge and growing rapidly, despite significant shrinkage during the recent global financial crisis. In 2009:

- International issues of equity in world securities markets amounted to about $400 billion, up from $83 billion in 1996 and just $14 billion in 1986.

- The stock of cross-national bank loans and deposits exceeded $22,000 billion, up from $11,000 billion 10 years earlier.

- There were more than $23,000 billion in outstanding international bonds and notes, up from around $4,000 billion in 1998.[3]

Why did global capital markets grow so rapidly in the past decade? We can count at least four reasons. First, governments' deregulation of financial markets eased movement of capital across national borders. Second, innovation in information and communication technologies accelerated the ease and speed of global financial transactions. Third, globalization of business compelled firms to seek new cost-effective ways to finance global operations and conduct financial management activities. Fourth is the

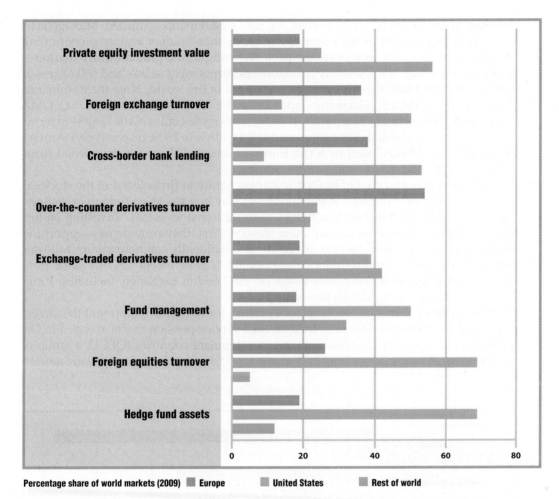

Percentage share of world markets (2009) ■ Europe   ■ United States   ■ Rest of world

Exhibit 20.2   Share of Financial Markets in Major World Regions

SOURCE: International Financial Markets in the UK, November 2009. International Financial Services London. Accessed at http://www.ifsl.org.uk.

widespread *securitization* of financial instruments, which resulted in conversion of illiquid financial instruments, such as bank loans, into tradable securities, such as bonds.

Some of these factors also contributed to the recent global financial crisis. Fueled by large-scale availability of credit and easy movement of capital across national borders, speculative ventures led to asset bubbles in commodities and real estate markets. As market participants realized that valuations in credit markets did not rest on solid fundamentals, asset prices quickly declined. In fact, the value of financial assets in the world declined from \$194 trillion in 2007 to \$178 trillion in 2008. Further declines occurred in 2009 and 2010.[4]

The global capital market provides three key advantages for the firm. First is a broader base from which to draw funds. Second is the ability to access funding at reduced cost. Third is the variety of investment opportunities for MNEs, professional investment firms, and individuals.

Sources of Funds for International Operations

We now consider in more detail the three primary sources of funds: equity financing, debt financing, and intracorporate financing.

Equity Financing   In equity financing, the firm obtains capital by selling stock, which gives shareholders a percentage of ownership in the firm and, often, a stream of dividend payments. The main advantage is that the firm obtains capital without debt.

Global equity market
The worldwide market of funds for equity financing—stock exchanges around the world where investors and firms meet to buy and sell shares of stock.

However, whenever new equity is sold, the firm's ownership is diluted. Management also risks losing control in the event one or more shareholders acquire a controlling interest. Internationally, firms obtain equity financing in the **global equity market**—stock exchanges worldwide where investors and firms meet to buy and sell shares of stock. Exhibit 20.3 lists the largest stock exchanges in the world. Note the dominance of exchanges in Britain, Germany, Japan, and the United States. NASDAQ OMX (www.nasdaq.com) and NYSE Euronext (U.S.; www.nyse.com) are the largest in terms of volume of shares traded ($29 trillion and $17.8 trillion in 2009, respectively). Among the roughly 3,200 firms listed in NYSE Euronext, about 500 are foreign-owned firms from Europe, Canada, Asia, and Latin America.

As an investor, you are not limited to buying equity in firms listed in the stock exchanges of your home country. Many investors today buy stocks on foreign exchanges, a trend driven by the large-scale activities of institutional investors.[5] Investing on foreign exchanges makes sense for two main reasons. First, they provide new opportunities for lucrative investing. Second, investing internationally can help minimize losses during slumps in the local economy. For example, U.S. investors can buy stock from among several hundred companies listed on the London exchange, including Kingfisher, Canon, and South African Breweries.[6]

Pension funds, which invest employee savings for retirement, represent the largest segment of international investing. In 2009, total private pension assets invested in Organisation for Economic Co-operation and Development countries (OECD, a group of thirty leading advanced economies and emerging markets; www.oecd.org) were around

Exhibit 20.3 Largest Stock Exchanges in the World, 2009–2010

SOURCE: World Federation of Exchanges, accessed at http://www.world-exchanges.org.

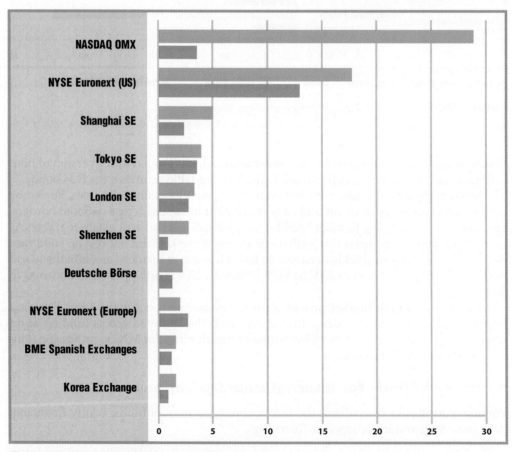

■ Total Value of Share Trading (trillions of U.S. dollars)
■ Domestic Equity Market Capitalization (trillions of U.S. dollars)

$22 trillion, more than the GDP of the United States.[7] At one point, CALPERS, the pension fund of the state of California, held investments in France's stock exchange that totaled some 5 percent of the exchange. In the five years through 2015, U.S. pension funds are expected to invest some $100 billion in portfolios of emerging market nations.[8]

Mergers and collaborations between exchanges facilitate international trading. The 2006 merger of the NYSE (New York Stock Exchange) and the Euronext—a pan-European exchange with subsidiaries in Belgium, France, the Netherlands, Portugal, and the United Kingdom—contributed to increased transatlantic trading.[9] Thanks to the Internet, investors now trade on world stock markets at low cost. Even a small market like the Cayman Islands Stock Exchange (www.csx.com.ky) offers full online investing opportunities. Read the *Global Trend* feature to learn about the development of stock exchanges in emerging markets.

Debt Financing

In debt financing, a firm borrows money from a creditor (or sells bonds) in exchange for repayment of principal and an agreed-upon interest amount in the future. The main advantage is that the firm does not sacrifice any ownership to obtain needed capital.

GLOBAL TREND

Emerging Markets as International Investment Destinations

Many investors view stocks in emerging markets as a good bet because of the formation there of numerous fast-growth firms. While some political regimes do not consistently respect shareholder rights and the rule of law, their economies often are geared for global growth.

Emerging-market stocks often entail considerable risk. Investors were burned by the Asian financial crisis in 1997, when countries such as Thailand and Malaysia saw their currencies devalued because local banks could not service their debt obligations. Shockwaves prompted a sell-off in stock markets in various countries due to the cross-national interconnectedness of financial markets.

In 1998, the Russian government devalued its currency and defaulted on its debt. Equity markets in Argentina and Turkey also have experienced considerable volatility. Share-price indices

on the Shanghai and Shenzhen exchanges have been volatile.

During the most recent global financial crisis, industrial production and exports declined in numerous emerging markets, leading to currency devaluation as well. Investment flows declined significantly as banks reduced cross-border loans and equity portfolio investors withdrew funds from the markets. As the panic began to subside in 2009, investors reevaluated their positions and positive growth returned to exchanges in many emerging markets.

As opportunities arise in emerging markets to invest in stock markets and undertake FDI, firms and governments there understand the cost of capital goes hand in hand with good governance and respect for shareholder rights. Firms that abuse shareholders by not providing periodic earnings reports find it hard to raise money from the public.

To accommodate demand to invest in emerging markets, local stock exchanges are becoming increasingly sophisticated. Those in Brazil and China have several hundred corporate listings, worth hundreds of billions of dollars. In smaller countries, the stock exchange may be a one-room operation with a blackboard and a telephone. Bhutan, Oman, and Kazakhstan have established primitive exchanges in the hope of becoming the next Chile or Singapore.

SOURCES: Evrim Turgutlu and Burcu Ucer, "Is Global Diversification Rational? Evidence from Emerging Equity Markets through Mixed Copula Approach," *Applied Economics*, 42 (2010): 647–58; Steve Johnson, "Pensions to Pour into EM Debt," *Financial Times*, January 25, 2010, p. 1; Bank for International Settlements, "80th Annual Report," June 28, 2010, retrieved from http://www.bis.org; McKinsey Global Institute, *Global Capital Markets: Entering a New Era*, 2009; "Global Markets," *Forbes*, March 27, 2006, p. 150; "China's Stock Market: A Marginalized Market," *Economist*, February 26, 2005, pp. 71–72.

Eurodollars are deposited in banks such as Barclays Plc., Britain's third-largest bank. Eurocurrencies, funds banked outside their country of origin, are a key source of loanable funds for international business.

International Loans The firm may borrow from banks in its home market or foreign markets. However, borrowing internationally is complicated by differences in national banking regulations, inadequate banking infrastructure, shortage of loanable funds, macroeconomic difficulties, and fluctuating currency values.[10] Banks are often reluctant to extend credit to small and medium-sized enterprises (SMEs), so these firms may turn to government agencies such as the Export Import (Ex-IM) Bank (www.exim.gov), a U.S. federal agency for loans and loan guarantees. Governments in the developing world often provide loans to promote inward direct investment projects such as the construction of dams, power plants, and airports. Finally, many subsidiaries of large MNEs obtain loans from their parent firm or a sister subsidiary.

The Eurocurrency Market Another key source of loanable funds is money deposited in banks outside its country of origin. Although its role has declined in favor of the euro, the U.S. dollar accounts for the largest proportion of these funds.[11] **Eurodollars** are U.S. dollars held in banks outside the United States, including foreign branches of U.S. banks. Thus, a U.S. dollar-denominated bank deposit in Barclays Bank in London or Citibank in Tokyo is a Eurodollar deposit. More broadly, any currency deposited in a bank outside its origin country is called **Eurocurrency.** Eurodollars account for roughly two-thirds of all Eurocurrencies. Interestingly, more than two-thirds of U.S. banknotes are often held outside the United States as a reserve currency. Matsushita and Hitachi borrowed Eurodollars in Japan to finance much of their worldwide operations. Other Eurocurrencies include euros, yen, and British pounds, as long as they are banked outside their home country.

The Eurocurrency market is attractive to firms because these funds are not subject to the government regulations of their home-country banking systems. U.S. dollars in French banks and euros in U.S. banks are free of the reserve requirements of their home countries. Banks typically offer higher interest rates on Eurocurrency deposits and charge lower interest rates for Eurocurrency loans, contributing to the emergence of a huge Eurocurrency market.

Eurodollars U.S. dollars held in banks outside the United States, including foreign branches of U.S. banks.

Eurocurrency Any currency deposited in a bank outside its country of origin.

Bond A debt instrument that enables the issuer (borrower) to raise capital by promising to repay the principal along with interest on a specified date (maturity).

Global bond market The international marketplace in which bonds are bought and sold, primarily through bond brokers.

Foreign bond A bond sold outside the issuer's country and denominated in the currency of the country where issued.

Eurobond A bond sold outside the issuer's home country but denominated in its own currency.

Bonds A major source of debt financing is bonds. A **bond** is a debt instrument that enables the issuer (borrower) to raise capital by promising to repay the principal along with interest on a specified date (maturity). Along with firms, governments, states, and other institutions also sell bonds. Investors purchase bonds and redeem them at face value in the future. The **global bond market** is the international marketplace in which bonds are bought and sold, primarily through bond brokers.

Foreign bonds are sold outside the bond issuer's country in the currency of the country where issued. When Mexican cement giant Cemex sells dollar-denominated bonds in the United States, it is issuing foreign bonds. **Eurobonds** are sold outside the bond issuer's home country but denominated in its own currency. When Toyota sells yen-denominated bonds in the United States, it is issuing Eurobonds. The telecommunications giant AT&T has issued hundreds of millions of dollars in Eurobonds to support its international operations. Pharmaceutical firms Eli Lilly and Merck have funded much of their multinational operations with Eurobonds. Eurobonds are typically issued in denominations of $5,000 or $10,000, pay interest annually, and are sold in major financial centers, especially London.

Intracorporate Financing

Funding for international operations can also be obtained from within the firm's network of subsidiaries and affiliates. At times, when some units of an MNE are cash-rich and others are cash-poor, they can lend each other money. **Intracorporate financing** is funds from sources inside the firm (both headquarters and subsidiaries) in the form of equity, loans, and trade credits. Trade credit arises in the firm when a supplier unit grants a buyer unit the option to pay at a later date.

What are some advantages of loaning funds to the firm's own foreign subsidiaries? First, it can reduce the borrowing subsidiary's income tax burden because interest payments are often tax deductible. Second, an intracorporate loan has little effect on the parent's balance sheet, because the funds are simply transferred from one area of the firm to another. Third, a loan within the MNE may save bank transaction costs (fees banks charge to exchange foreign currencies and transfer funds between locations). Fourth, a loan avoids the ownership dilution of equity financing.

IBM's global financing division invests in international financing assets and obtains and manages international debt to support IBM's global operations. The division provides loan financing to internal users for terms of two to five years. It provides inventory and accounts receivable financing to IBM's dealers and subsidiaries in various countries.[12]

Intracorporate financing Funds from sources inside the firm (both headquarters and subsidiaries) such as equity, loans, and trade credits.

Task Three: Manage Working Capital and Cash Flow

Recall that *working capital* refers to the current assets of a company. *Net working capital* is the difference between current assets and current liabilities. As part of working capital management, firms manage all current accounts, such as cash, accounts receivable, inventory, and accounts payable. Cash comes from various sources, especially sales of goods and services. In the MNE, an important task of working capital management is ensuring cash is available where and when needed. Cash-flow needs arise from everyday activities, such as buying labor and materials, paying interest on debt, and paying taxes and shareholder dividends. To optimize global operations, international finance managers devise strategies for transferring funds among the firm's operations worldwide.

The volume and complexity of intracorporate transfers depends on the number of headquarters, subsidiaries, alliances, and business relationships the firm maintains worldwide. For firms with extensive international operations, the network of funds transfers can be vast. Roughly *one-third* of world trade results from collective trading activities within individual MNE networks.

Methods for Transferring Funds within the MNE

Financial managers employ various methods for transferring funds within the MNE. Funds must be moved efficiently, minimizing transaction costs and tax liabilities while maximizing returns the funds can earn. Exhibit 20.4 depicts a typical firm with subsidiaries in Mexico and Taiwan. Within its network, this firm can transfer funds through trade credit, dividend remittances, royalty payments, fronting loans, transfer pricing, and multilateral netting. Here is how each works:

- Through *trade credit*, a subsidiary can defer payment for goods and services received from the parent firm. The 30-day credit is the U.S. norm, while 90-day credit is typical in Europe, with longer terms elsewhere.

- *Dividend remittances* are common for transferring funds from foreign subsidiaries to the parent but vary depending on tax levels and currency risks. Some host governments levy high taxes on dividend payments or limit how much MNEs can remit.

Exhibit 20.4 Typical Methods for Transferring Funds within the MNE

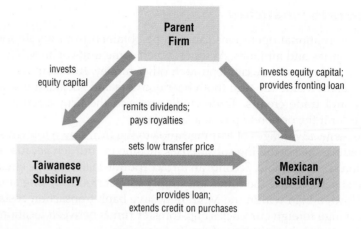

- *Royalty payments* are compensation paid to owners of intellectual property, as explained in Chapter 16. Assuming the subsidiary has licensed technology, trademarks, or other assets from the parent or other subsidiaries, royalties can be an efficient way to transfer funds and are tax deductible in many countries. A parent MNE can collect royalties from its own subsidiaries as a way of generating funds.

Fronting loan A loan between the parent and its subsidiary, channeled through a large bank or other financial intermediary.

- In a **fronting loan**, the parent deposits a large sum in a foreign bank, which transfers it to a subsidiary as a loan. Fronting allows the parent to circumvent restrictions that foreign governments impose on direct intracorporate loans. If the loan is made through a bank in a **tax haven**—a country hospitable to business and inward investment because of its low corporate income taxes—the parent can minimize taxes that might be due if the loan were made directly. While some countries restrict the amount of funds MNEs can transfer abroad, such restrictions usually do not apply to repayment of bank loans.

Tax haven A country hospitable to business and inward investment because of its low corporate income taxes.

- *Transfer pricing* (also known as *intracorporate pricing*) is the means by which subsidiaries and affiliates charge each other as they exchange goods and services. Recall from Chapter 18 that firms can use transfer pricing to shift profits from high-tax to low-tax countries, optimizing internal cash flows.[13]

Multilateral Netting

In the past, cash was frequently held in each foreign subsidiary responsible for funding its own short-term needs. Today, MNE managers use a method known as *pooling* to bring surplus funds together in a regional or global *centralized depository*. They then direct these funds to needy subsidiaries or invest them to generate income.

A centralized depository lets managers reduce the size of highly liquid accounts and invest the funds, generally at the higher interest rates offered for large deposits, to generate maximal returns. If the depository is in a financial center (London, New York, Sydney, or Toronto), management can also access a variety of short-term investments that pay higher rates of return. Finally, the depository centralizes expertise and financial services, providing subsidiaries with more benefits at lower cost.

Large MNEs conduct numerous international transactions, each of which generates transaction costs. Suppose a firm's Japanese subsidiary owes the Spanish subsidiary $8 million and the Spanish subsidiary owes the Japanese subsidiary $5 million. While the firm could cancel these debts in separate transactions, a more intelligent solution that reduces transaction costs has the Japanese subsidiary pay the Spanish subsidiary $3 million. Transferring an amount considerably lower than either of the two original amounts greatly reduces transactions costs such as fees and delays in funds transfers.

Multilateral netting Strategic reduction of cash transfers within the MNE family through the elimination of offsetting cash flows.

At a more sophisticated level, **multilateral netting** is the strategic reduction of cash transfers within the MNE family through the elimination of offsetting cash flows involving three or more subsidiaries that hold accounts payable or accounts receivable with another subsidiary. MNEs with numerous subsidiaries usually establish a netting center, a central exchange, that headquarters supervises. Philips, a leading Dutch consumer electronics firm (www.philips.com), has operating units in some sixty countries and a netting center to which subsidiaries regularly report all intracorporate balances on the same date. The center then advises each subsidiary of the amounts to pay and receive from other subsidiaries on a specified date, helping save Philips considerable money.

Task Four: Perform Capital Budgeting

How do firms decide whether to launch a major exporting effort, acquire a distribution center, build a new factory, or refurbish industrial equipment? Companies have limited resources and cannot afford to invest in every project opportunity. The purpose of *capital budgeting* is to help managers decide which international projects provide the best financial return.

The decision depends on the project's initial investment requirement, its cost of capital, and the incremental cash flow or other advantages it can provide. Many variables affect the potential profitability of a venture. Investors in the fast-food industry consider the cost of alternate locations and the level of local competition, as well as the distance to highways, availability of public transportation, and amount of traffic at each location.[14]

Net Present Value Analysis of Capital Investment Projects

Managers typically employ net present value (NPV) analysis to evaluate domestic and international capital investment projects. NPV is the difference between the present value of a project's incremental cash flows and its initial investment requirement.[15] Four considerations complicate international capital budgeting for an MNE. First, project cash flows are usually in a currency other than the reporting currency of the parent firm. Second, tax rules in the project location and the parent's country usually differ. Third, governments may limit the transfer of funds from the project to the parent firm. Finally, the project may be exposed to country risk, such as government intervention, high inflation, or adverse exchange rates.

Managers employing NPV address these in two ways. One is to estimate the incremental after-tax operating cash flows in the subsidiary's local currency and *then* discount them at the project's cost of capital, or required rate of return, appropriate for its risk characteristics. If the NPV is positive, the project is expected to earn its required return and add value to the subsidiary. This approach takes the *project's perspective* in capital budgeting, and managers can use it as a first screening method.[16]

The second approach, called the *parent's perspective*, estimates future cash flows from the project in the *functional currency* of the parent— that is, the currency of the primary economic environment in which it operates. Thus, U.S.-based firms' functional currency is the U.S. dollar; for Japan-based firms it is the yen. This conversion forecasts *spot exchange rates*, or forward rates, and calculates their present value using a discount rate in line with the required return on projects of similar risk. Managers then compute the NPV in the parent's functional currency by subtracting the initial investment cash flow from the present value of the project cash flows. To be acceptable the project must add value to the parent company; it should therefore have positive NPV from the parent's perspective.

Headquarters of the Anglo-Dutch consumer products giant Unilever in Rotterdam, Netherlands. MNEs such as Unilever conduct capital budgeting to determine which foreign locations are economically desirable. Managers account for various costs and revenue factors, including the cost of land and facilities, the nature of taxation, and local wages and salaries.

Estimating project cash flows is complex and requires forecasting a range of variables that contribute to anticipated revenues and costs over several years. The largest component of revenue is usually sales. Initial and ongoing costs typically include R&D, development of essential project resources, labor, factor inputs, and marketing. Read the *Recent Grad in IB* feature on Chip Besse to learn about the variety of tasks young managers undertake in international finance.

 ## Task Five: Manage Currency Risk

Shifting currency values are among the biggest day-to-day challenges facing international firms, like Markel in the chapter opening vignette. Foreign direct investors face currency risk because they receive payments and incur obligations in foreign currencies. Managers of foreign investment portfolios also face currency risk. A Japanese stock might gain 15 percent in value, but if the yen falls 15 percent, the stock gain is zero.

Currency crises affect other local asset prices, including debt, equipment, and real estate markets. Firms face currency risk when their cash flows and the value of their assets and liabilities change as a result of unexpected changes in foreign exchange rates. Exporters and licensors face currency risk—from unexpected fluctuations in exchange rates—because foreign buyers typically pay in their own currency. If the firm could quote its prices and get paid in its home-country currency, it could eliminate its currency risk, but the risk would still exist for its foreign customers. To accommodate foreign buyers, companies frequently quote their prices in the buyer's currency. In international transactions, either the buyer or the seller incurs currency risk.

Three Types of Currency Exposure

Currency fluctuations result in three types of exposure for the firm: transaction exposure, translation exposure, and economic exposure.[17]

Transaction exposure is currency risk firms face when outstanding accounts receivable or payable are denominated in foreign currencies. Suppose Gateway (www.gateway.com) imports three million Taiwan dollars' worth of computer keyboards and pays in the foreign currency. At the time of the purchase, suppose the exchange rate was US$1 = T$30, but Gateway pays on credit terms three months after the purchase. If during the three-month period the exchange rate shifts to US$1 = T$27, Gateway will have to pay an extra US$11,111 as a result of the rate change ([3,000,000/27] −[3,000,000/30]). From Gateway's standpoint, the Taiwan dollar has become more expensive. Such gains or losses are real. They affect the firm's value directly by affecting its cash flows and profit.

Translation exposure results when an MNE translates financial statements denominated in a foreign currency into the functional currency of the parent firm, as part of *consolidating* international financial results. **Consolidation** is the process of combining and integrating the financial results of foreign subsidiaries into the parent firm's financial records. Accounting practices usually require the firm to report consolidated financial results in the functional currency.

Translation exposure occurs because, as exchange rates fluctuate, so do the functional-currency values of exposed assets, liabilities, expenses, and revenues. Translating quarterly or annual foreign financial statements into the parent's functional currency results in gains or losses on the date financial statements are consolidated. When translated into dollars, the quarterly net income of the Japanese subsidiary of a U.S. MNE may drop if the Japanese yen depreciates against the dollar during the quarter. Note that gains or losses in translation exposure are "paper" or "virtual" changes and do not affect cash flows directly. This contrasts with transaction exposure, in which gains and losses are real.

Economic exposure (also known as *operating exposure*) results from exchange-rate fluctuations that affect the pricing of products and inputs, and the value of foreign

---

Transaction exposure The currency risk firms face when outstanding accounts receivable or payable are denominated in foreign currencies.

Translation exposure The currency risk that results when a firm translates financial statements denominated in a foreign currency into the functional currency of the parent firm, as part of consolidating international financial results.

Consolidation The process of combining and integrating the financial results of foreign subsidiaries into the financial statements of the parent firm.

Economic exposure The currency risk that results from exchange rate fluctuations affecting the pricing of products, the cost of inputs, and the value of foreign investments.

Recent Grad in IB

International Financial Specialist

Maria's majors: Finance, International Business, and Spanish

Objectives: Move into the executive suite at Motorola or other multinational firm

Maria's jobs since graduation: Various jobs at Motorola – Credit Analyst (U.S.); Finance Manager (U.K.); Financial Controller (Dubai, United Arab Emirates)

Maria Keeley

In college, Maria Keeley spent a year in Spain and served as the president of the international business club. She majored in Finance, International Business, and Spanish. After graduation, she took a job as a credit analyst with Motorola (www.motorola.com), a leading producer of cell phones and other wireless handsets. Maria used analytical, problem-solving, and communication skills acquired in college to serve Motorola clients and subsidiaries throughout Latin America.

At Motorola, Maria analyzed risk levels of various customers and countries. She managed accounts receivables and conducted audits in Motorola's international operations. These duties required her to travel often to Latin America. Within her first year on the job, she became the primary contact for financial analysis support to northern Latin America, the Caribbean, and Central America. Her tasks included the analysis, tracking, and reconciliation of Motorola's funds for regional marketing activities.

Eager to gain experience in Europe, Maria volunteered to transfer to Motorola's London office, where she served as a finance manager in the firm's $160 million mobile phone business for the Middle East, North Africa, and Turkey. She also sought her CIMA certification, the British equivalent of certified public accountant (CPA). After two years in London, Maria transferred to Dubai, the United Arab Emirates, as Financial Controller in Motorola's Middle East region. In this role, she coordinated the management of Motorola's financial activities in the Islamic world.

Lessons Learned

Maria commented on her experience in the world of international financial management. "One of my big challenges was increased regulations that required stricter auditing of financial records in the wake of accounting scandals. It's critical to ensure that all of Motorola's legal entities are compliant worldwide. Local regulations also must be assimilated and integrated. The time I allocated to compliance activities greatly increased. Simultaneously, competition in the mobile devices industry grew, and I had to enhance the level of support to our sales and marketing operations as well.

"When based in England, I supported a big region with multiple time zones and work schedules. The work week in the Middle East varies from Saturday to Thursday, or from Sunday to Friday. Due to time differences, the region starts the day at least three hours before Britain. I was often on the phone with colleagues in the Middle East at 6 a.m. London time.

"The languages in my region are French (North Africa), Arabic (Middle East), and Turkish (Turkey). Although I studied Arabic, I still cannot carry a business conversation in Arabic and only manage to use my Spanish while visiting a particular distributor in Morocco that is partially owned by Telefonica (www.telefonica.com), Spain's telecom provider. Luckily, most of our business partners spoke English. There is definitely a disadvantage to not speaking the local language. In Turkey, for instance, some of our business partners do not speak English and so I relied on the sales team to translate conversations. Even when

colleagues speak fluent English, particularly in North Africa, they often revert to their most comfortable language, in this case French.

"Much of the Islamic world has specific norms for women, who usually do not participate in professional business activities. But people generally treat me with respect. I have found that, if I establish myself as a knowledgeable professional, people in the Middle East generally treat me as well as they do their male colleagues. There is one last cultural difference that puts me at a disadvantage: being a non-smoker in countries where people still smoke a lot. Most of the debriefing after a challenging meeting happens during cigarette breaks. Given the relaxed atmosphere, the parties are more likely to discuss issues in a candid manner. But I'm not willing to take up smoking to be more effective in my job. It is a cultural difference that I accept."

Maria's Advice

The qualities that contributed most to Maria's success include "hard work, having a deliberate career strategy, and cultivating relationships with helpful people both when I was in college and in the professional world. You really have to plan. Set goals for yourself and work hard to meet them." As for the future, Maria hopes to move into the executive suite at a multinational firm. But having a career, especially an international one, is still challenging these days for women who also want to start a family. Maria looks forward to fulfilling both her career and personal goals.

investments. Exchange rate fluctuations help or hurt sales by making the firm's products relatively more or less expensive for foreign buyers. If the yen appreciates against the euro, a European firm can expect to sell more goods in Japan because the Japanese have more buying power for buying euros. But if the yen weakens against the euro, the European firm's sales will likely drop in Japan unless management lowers its Japanese prices by an amount equivalent to the fall in the yen. Similarly, the firm may be harmed by currency shifts that raise the price of inputs sourced from abroad. The value of foreign investments can also fall, in home currency terms, with exchange rate changes.

While transaction exposure is a factor in ongoing contractual transactions, economic exposure affects long-term profitability through changes in revenues and expenses and thus appears in the firm's financial statements. For example, weakening of the U.S. dollar against the euro gradually reduces the value of U.S. investments in Europe, increases the cost of Euro-denominated input goods, but improves the prospects for U.S. firms to sell their dollar-denominated products in the EU.

The three types of currency exposure can produce positive results when exchange rates fluctuate favorably for the firm. Managers are more concerned with fluctuations that harm the firm. Such problems help explain why many countries in Europe use a single currency, the euro. With a single medium of exchange, currency risk is eliminated in trade among the countries using the euro. For international firms operating outside the euro zone, however, currency risk is still a significant problem.

Foreign Exchange Trading

Centuries ago, people used gold and silver as a medium of exchange and for reserve currencies. In 2006, two Swedish farmers digging holes on a farm in Gotland, an island off the Swedish coast, discovered a pile of 10th-century silver coins, weighing about seven pounds. The silver coins were minted in Baghdad, Iraq—over 2,000 miles from Sweden—and apparently served as a source of currency for Vikings.[18] Today, a relatively limited number of currencies still facilitate cross-border trade and investment. Around 64 percent of official foreign reserves are in U.S. dollars, 27 percent in euros, 4 percent in British pounds, 3 percent in Japanese yen, and only 2 percent in the world's remaining national currencies.[19]

What is different today is the sheer volume of currencies exchanged and the speed with which these transactions occur. In 2010, the daily volume of global trading in foreign exchange amounted to some $3.2 trillion.[20] To put this in perspective, that is more than 100 times the daily value of global trade in products and services.

Also impressive is the role of information technology in currency trading. Consider UBS (www.ubs.com), the large Swiss investment bank, which offers a range of currency-related products. The bank's clients transact nearly all their spot, forward, and currency-swap trades online using UBS's computer platforms in dozens of countries. Technology allows customers in remote areas to enjoy currency trading services that until recently were accessible only in large cities via big banks.[21] Citibank (www.citibank.com) leverages its comprehensive customer portal, CitiFX Interactive, to provide clients a wide range of services, including library research, currency trading, and analytical tools. Online bill payment is important to executives and others who frequently travel abroad.[22]

Large banks are the primary dealers in the currency markets, and they quote the prices at which they will buy or sell currencies. If an importer wants to buy $100,000 in euros to finance a purchase from Austria, the currency exchange will typically be handled through the importer's bank. Large banks such as Citibank maintain reserves of major currencies and work with foreign *correspondent banks* to facilitate currency buying and selling. Currency transactions between banks occur in the *interbank market*.

Currency also can be bought and sold through brokers that specialize in matching up buyers and sellers. They are especially active in major financial centers such as London, New York, and Sydney. Trading can also be done through online brokers and dealers at sites like www.forex.com and Everbank (www.everbank.com).

The foreign-exchange market uses specialized terminology to describe the functions currency dealers perform. The **spot rate** is the exchange rate applied when the current

Spot rate The exchange rate applied when the current exchange rate is used for immediate receipt of a currency.

exchange rate is used for immediate receipt of a currency. The rate applies to transactions between banks for delivery within two business days, or immediate delivery for over-the-counter transactions involving nonbank customers—for example, when you buy currencies at airport kiosks.

The **forward rate** is the exchange rate applicable to the collection or delivery of foreign currencies at some future date. Dealers in the forward exchange market promise to receive or deliver foreign exchange at a specified time in the future, but at a rate determined at the time of the transaction. The primary function of the forward market is to provide protection against currency risk.

Dealers quote currency exchange rates in two ways. The **direct quote,** also known as the *normal quote,* is the number of units of domestic currency needed to acquire one unit of foreign currency. For example, on September 1, 2010, it cost $1.27 to acquire one euro (abbreviated as `€'). The **indirect quote** is the number of units of foreign currency obtained for one unit of domestic currency. For example, on September 1, 2010, it cost €0.79 to acquire $1.00. Please review the book's Appendix to learn more about currency trading.

You may have observed at airports that when foreign-exchange dealers quote prices, they always quote a *bid* (buy) rate and an *offer* (sell) rate at which they will buy or sell any particular currency. The difference between the bid and offer rates—*the spread*—is the margin on which the dealer earns a profit.

A currency trader in London monitors the latest news to guide his buying and selling of world currencies. Multinational firms must skillfully manage multiple-currency transactions and the risk associated with exchange rate fluctuations.

Types of Currency Traders

The three main types of currency traders are hedgers, speculators, and arbitragers. **Hedgers,** typically MNEs and other international trade or investment firms, seek to minimize their risk of exchange rate fluctuations, often by entering into forward contracts or similar financial instruments. They are not necessarily interested in profiting from currency trading.

Speculators are currency traders who seek profits by investing in currencies with the expectation their value will rise in the future and then sell them later at the higher value. A speculator might purchase a certificate of deposit denominated in Mexican pesos or a money market account tied to the Chinese yuan, believing the value of these currencies will rise. The speculator can also bet on a currency's downturn by taking a *short position* in that currency. When investors take a short position, they sell a currency that they previously borrowed from a third party (usually a broker) with the intention of buying the identical currency back at a later date to return to the lender. In so doing, the short seller hopes to profit from a decline in the value of the currency between the sale and the repurchase, as the seller will pay less to buy the currency than the seller received on selling it. Exhibit 20.5 shows an example speculation in the foreign exchange market through a forward contract.

Arbitragers are currency traders who buy and sell the same currency in two or more foreign-exchange markets to profit from differences in the currency's exchange rate. But unlike the speculator who bets on the future price of a currency, the arbitrager attempts to profit from a current disequilibrium in currency markets based on known prices. If the euro-dollar exchange rate quoted in New York on Monday morning is €1 = $1.25, but the quoted exchange rate in London at that moment is €1 = $1.30, a trader could buy €1 million for $1.25 million in New York and simultaneously sell those euros in London for $1.3 million, yielding a riskless profit of $50,000 before commission and expenses. But don't get too excited! When such arbitrage opportunities exist, they quickly

Forward rate The exchange rate applicable to the collection or delivery of a foreign currency at some future date.

Direct quote The number of units of domestic currency needed to acquire one unit of foreign currency; also known as the normal quote.

Indirect quote The number of units of foreign currency obtained for one unit of domestic currency.

Hedgers Currency traders who seek to minimize their risk of exchange rate fluctuations, often by entering into forward contracts or similar financial instruments.

Speculators Currency traders who seek profits by investing in currencies with the expectation their value will change in the future.

Exhibit 20.5 An Example of Speculation in the Foreign Exchange Market

Scenario: A speculator is offered a forward contract by a bank to be able to sell the bank €1 in exchange for $1.45 one year from now. Suppose that the speculator expects the spot exchange rate to be €1 = $1.40 a year from now. The speculator may try to profit from the difference between the expected spot exchange rate and the quoted forward exchange rate by entering into a forward contract with the offering bank. In this case, the speculator is taking a risk by attempting to make a profit based on an uncertain future spot exchange rate.

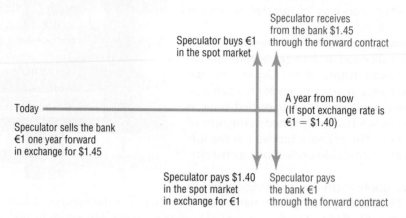

Speculator receives from the bank $1.45 through the forward contract

Speculator buys €1 in the spot market

Today

Speculator sells the bank €1 one year forward in exchange for $1.45

A year from now (If spot exchange rate is €1 = $1.40)

Speculator pays $1.40 in the spot market in exchange for €1

Speculator pays the bank €1 through the forward contract

Outcome: If the spot exchange rate is actually €1 = $1.40 a year from now, the speculator earns a profit of $0.05. However, if the spot exchange rate turns out to be €1 = $1.50, the speculator will lose $0.05 as a result of having to sell the bank, through the forward contract, €1 for $1.45 instead of its actual spot value of $1.50.

Arbitragers Currency traders who buy and sell the same currency in two or more foreign-exchange markets to profit from differences in the currency's exchange rate.

disappear because the very actions of the arbitragers force the exchange rates to adjust to the equilibrium level.

Exchange Rate Forecasting

Losses due to exchange rate risk are common in international business. In the 1980s, the Japanese automaker Subaru (www.subaru.com) manufactured nearly all its vehicles in Japan, although three-quarters of its sales were in the United States. Between 1985 and 1987, the Japanese yen appreciated almost 50 percent against the dollar. This caused the dollar price of Subaru cars to rise substantially, resulting in a decline in U.S. sales of Subarus.[23]

Financial managers monitor currency trading daily, paying particular attention to the potential for momentum trading or herding behavior. *Momentum trading* is accomplished via computers programmed to conduct massive buying or selling when prices reach certain levels. *Herding* is the tendency of investors to mimic each others' actions. In 2008, fears about geopolitical tensions and a declining Russian economy triggered a sell-off of some $20 billion of shares in the Russian stock market. In rapid succession, as foreign investors liquidated holdings in the stock exchange, billions of dollars worth of Russian roubles were converted to foreign currencies, prompting a depreciation of the rouble by some 30 percent between August 2008 and February 2009.[24] In most countries, exchange rates respond immediately to economic information, such as the election of a new government, labor disputes, and major supply shocks (for example, when oil-exporting countries suddenly announce a drop in supply). In addition to forecasting such events, managers must assess the likely actions of foreign-exchange traders.

Firms with extensive international operations develop sophisticated capabilities to forecast exchange rates that combine in-house forecasting with reports provided by major banks and professional forecasters. *Technical analysis* looks at recent movements in exchange rates and *fundamental analysis* studies involving macroeconomic data.

SMEs usually lack the resources to do substantial in-house forecasting and rely on forecasts provided by banks and from business news sources. A table in each issue of the *Economist* magazine describes recent exchange rate trends. Other useful information sources include the Bank for International Settlements (www.bis.org), the World Bank (www.worldbank.org), and the European Central Bank (www.ecb.int).

Managing Exposure to Currency Risk through Hedging

Suppose you want to buy a Toyota and the local car dealer insists you pay in Japanese yen. You probably wouldn't buy the car, partly because you'd need to acquire yen and partly because other dealers let you pay in your own currency. Customers around the world prefer to deal in their own currency. If firms insist on quoting prices and getting paid in their own currency, the burden is on foreign buyers to monitor and manage foreign exchange. Even small exporters learn to operate in foreign currencies to remain competitive. In so doing, they also learn to minimize their exposure to currency risk.

The most common method for managing exposure is **hedging,** using financial instruments and other measures to lock in guaranteed foreign exchange positions. If the hedge is perfect, the firm is protected against the risk of adverse changes in the price of a currency. Banks offer forward contracts, options, and swap agreements to facilitate hedging and charge fees and interest payments on amounts borrowed to carry out the transactions. The firm must balance these costs against expected benefits.

In *passive hedging*, each exposure is hedged as it occurs and the hedge stays in place until maturity. In *active hedging*, the firm frequently reviews total exposure and hedges only a subset of its total exposures, usually those that pose the greatest risk. Hedges may be withdrawn before they reach maturity. Some active hedgers seek to profit from hedging, even maintaining active in-house trading desks. However, most firms are conservative and simply try to cover all exposures—or their most important ones—and leave hedges in place until maturity.

Hedging Instruments   Having assessed its level of currency risk exposure, the firm attempts to balance exposed assets and exposed liabilities. The four most common hedging instruments are forward contracts, futures contracts, currency options, and currency swaps.

A **forward contract** is an agreement to exchange two currencies at a specified exchange rate on a set future date. No money changes hands until the delivery date of the contract. Banks quote forward prices in the same way as spot prices—with bid and ask prices at which they will buy or sell currencies. The bank's bid-ask spread is a cost for its customers.

Forward contracts are especially appropriate for hedging transaction exposure. Suppose Dow Chemical (www.dow.com) sells merchandise to a German importer for €100,000, payable in 90 days. During the 90 days, Dow has a transaction exposure to currency risk: It will receive fewer dollars if the euro depreciates during that time. To hedge against this risk, Dow executes a forward contract with a bank to sell €100,000 in 90 days at an exchange rate agreed upon today, ensuring it receives a known dollar amount in the future. Exhibit 20.6 illustrates the cash flows of Dow Chemical's forward market hedge.

Like a forward contract, a **futures contract** represents an agreement to buy or sell a currency in exchange for another at a specified price on a specified date. Unlike forward contracts, futures contracts are standardized to enable trading in organized exchanges, such as the Chicago Mercantile Exchange. While the terms of forward contracts are negotiated between a bank and its customer, futures contracts have standardized maturity periods and amounts. Futures contracts are especially useful for hedging transaction exposure.

A **currency option** differs from forward and futures contracts in that it gives the purchaser the right, but not the obligation, to buy a certain amount of foreign currency at a set exchange rate within a specified amount of time. The seller of the option must sell the currency at the buyer's discretion, at the price originally set. Currency options typically are traded on organized exchanges, such as the London Stock Exchange (www.londonstockexchange.com) and the Philadelphia Stock Exchange (PHLX; www.nasdaqtrader.com), and only for the major currencies.[25]

Hedging   Using financial instruments and other measures to reduce or eliminate exposure to currency risk by locking in guaranteed foreign exchange positions.

Forward contract   A contract to exchange two currencies at a specified exchange rate on a set future date.

Futures contract   An agreement to buy or sell a currency in exchange for another at a specified price on a specified date.

Currency option   A contract that gives the purchaser the right, but not the obligation, to buy a certain amount of foreign currency at a set exchange rate within a specified amount of time.

Scenario: Dow Chemical sells merchandise to a German importer for €100,000, payable in 90 days. Given that the U.S. dollar - euro spot exchange rate 90 days from now is not known today, Dow faces uncertainty regarding how much it will be receiving from its German customer in U.S. dollar terms. To hedge against this risk, Dow enters into a forward contract with a bank to sell €100,000 90 days from now at an exchange rate of €1 = $1.45 agreed upon today, ensuring that it receives a known dollar amount in future.

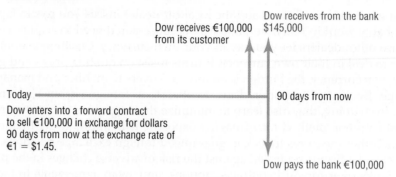

Outcome: Today, Dow is able to see that the €100,000 it will be receiving from its European customer will be worth $145,000 regardless of how much the actual spot price of the euro is 90 days from now.

Exhibit 20.6 An Example of Hedging in the Foreign Exchange Market

There are two types of options. A *call option* is the right, but not the obligation, to buy a currency at a specified price within a specific period (called an *American option*) or on a specific date (called a *European option*).[26] A *put option* is the right to sell the currency at a specified price. Each option is for a specific amount of currency. On a recent date, Australian dollar option contracts were offered with a contract size of 50,000 Australian dollars on the NASDAQ OMX PHLX. Options are useful as an insurance policy or disaster hedge against adverse currency movements.

Currency swap
An agreement to exchange one currency for another, according to a specified schedule.

In a **currency swap**, two parties agree to exchange a given amount of one currency for another and, after a specified period of time, give back the original amounts. Thus, a swap is a simultaneous spot and forward transaction. When the agreement is activated, the parties exchange principals at the current spot rate. Usually each party must pay interest on the principal as well. If Party A loaned dollars and borrowed euros, it pays interest in euros and receives interest in dollars. Consider the following example: An MNE agrees to pay 4 percent compounded annually on a euro principal of €1,000,000 and receive 5 percent compounded annually on a U.S. dollar principal of $1,300,000 every year for two years. As a result it will receive €1,000,000 and pay $1,300,000 today. It will then pay €40,000 annual interest and receive $65,000 annual interest for 2 years. At the end of the second year, the MNE will receive $1,300,000 and pay €1,000,000.

Best Practice in Minimizing Currency Exposure

Managing currency risk across many countries is challenging because management must keep abreast of the firm's evolving exposures, as well as shifting laws, regulations, and market conditions. Managers need to pursue a systematic approach to minimize currency risk.

Exhibit 20.7 presents guidelines that managers can use to minimize currency risk. The last recommendation, maintaining strategic flexibility in manufacturing and sourcing, is an ultimate solution. If the firm operates in numerous markets, each with varying degrees of currency, economic, and political stability, it will be well positioned to optimize its operations. For example, Dell outsources parts and components from various countries and can quickly shift sourcing from one country or supplier to another, depending on the favorability of exchange rates and other factors.

Managerial Guidelines for Minimizing Currency Risk

Exhibit 20.7
Managerial Guidelines
for Minimizing Currency Risk

1. **Seek expert advice.** Initially, management should obtain expert help from banks and consultants to establish programs and strategies that minimize risk.

2. **Centralize currency management within the MNE.** While some currency management activities may be delegated to local managers, company headquarters should set basic guidelines for the subsidiaries to follow.

3. **Decide on the level of risk the firm can tolerate.** The level varies depending on the nature of the project, amount of capital at risk, and management's tolerance for risk.

4. **Devise a system to measure exchange rate movements and currency risk.** The system should provide ongoing feedback to help management develop appropriate risk-minimizing strategies.

5. **Monitor changes in key currencies.** Exchange rates fluctuate constantly. Continuous monitoring can avert costly mistakes.

6. **Be wary of unstable currencies or those subject to exchange controls.** The manager should deal in stable, readily convertible currencies. Be wary of government restrictions that affect the ability to exchange currencies.

7. **Monitor long-term economic and regulatory trends.** Exchange rate shifts usually follow evolving trends such as rising interest rates, inflation, labor unrest, and the coming to power of new governments.

8. **Distinguish economic exposure from transaction and translation exposures.** Managers often focus on reducing transaction and translation exposures. However, the long-run effects of economic exposure on company performance can produce even greater harm.

9. **Emphasize flexibility in international operations.** A flexible production and outsourcing strategy means the firm can shift production and outsourcing to various nations, to benefit from favorable exchange rates.

Task Six: Manage the Diversity of International Accounting and Tax Practices

Accounting systems differ around the world, with dozens of approaches for determining company profits, R&D expenditures, and cost of goods sold.[27] Balance sheets and income statements vary internationally, not just in language, currency, and format, but also in their underlying accounting principles. Financial statements prepared according to the rules of one country may be difficult to compare with those of another.

Transparency in Financial Reporting

Local accounting practices determine the degree of transparency in the reporting of financial information. **Transparency** is the degree to which companies regularly reveal substantial information about their financial condition and accounting practices. The more transparent a nation's accounting systems, the more regularly, comprehensively,

Transparency The degree to which companies regularly reveal substantial information about their financial condition and accounting practices.

Transparency is the degree to which companies regularly reveal information about their financial condition and accounting practices. Pictured here is the stock exchange in Santiago, Chile, one of several countries attracting more inward investment by improving transparency in their business sectors.

and reliably the nation's public firms report their financial results to creditors, stockholders, and the government. Transparency facilitates better managerial decision making and lets investors accurately evaluate company performance. Chile, Costa Rica, and the Czech Republic have attracted greater FDI by increasing the transparency of their regulatory systems. By contrast, most developing economies are characterized by confusing accounting systems, delayed financial reporting, and published information that is unreliable or incomplete.

Transparency is an issue even in the advanced economies. The Sarbanes-Oxley Act of 2002 was enacted to improve U.S. accounting standards. It emerged in the wake of accounting scams at large corporations like Enron and Worldcom. Sarbanes-Oxley makes corporate CEOs and CFOs personally responsible for the accuracy of annual reports and other financial data. Foreign affiliates of U.S. firms and foreign firms with significant U.S. operations are also required to comply with the act's provisions. A major challenge, however, is the cost of compliance.

In the wake of the recent global financial crisis, governments and central banks in Asia, Europe, and the Americas are increasing the transparency and strictness of accounting standards and strengthening their supervision of banks and other financial institutions.[28]

Trends toward Harmonization

The growth of international business has pressured multinational firms and international organizations such as the International Accounting Standards Board (IASB), the United Nations, the European Union, and the Asociación Interamericana de Contabilidad (Interamerican Association of Accounting) to harmonize world accounting systems, particularly regarding measurement, disclosure, and auditing standards. The IASB is attempting to develop a single set of high-quality, understandable, and enforceable global accounting standards that emphasize transparent and comparable information.

The IASB favors harmonization for several reasons. First, comparability and transparency of accounting practices will enhance the reliability of financial reporting. Second, harmonization will help reduce the cost of preparing financial statements. Third, it will increase the efficiency of consolidating financial information from various countries. Fourth, by facilitating investment analysis, it will reduce risk for investors and help managers make better decisions. Harmonization is particularly important to MNEs that seek foreign investors by listing on foreign stock exchanges. In the United States, firms must comply with Generally Accepted Accounting Practices (GAAP). By contrast, more than 100 countries in Europe and elsewhere apply International Financial Reporting Standards (IFRS; www.ifrs.com). In 2009, a milestone was reached when the U.S. Securities and Exchange Commission ended the requirement that foreign firms operating in the United States reconcile their accounts according to GAAP. Numerous U.S. firms, such as Procter & Gamble, use IFRS standards in many of their foreign subsidiaries. Europe's IASB and the U.S. Financial Accounting Standards Board have worked closely to harmonize GAAP and IFRS. The next ambitious goal is to permit U.S. companies that operate globally to file only under the IFRS.[29]

Consolidating the Financial Statements of Subsidiaries

A critical task in international accounting is *foreign currency translation,* or translating data denominated in foreign currencies into the firm's functional currency. Each of the firm's subsidiaries abroad normally maintains its financial records in the currency of the country where it is located. When subsidiary results are consolidated into headquarters' financial statements, they must be expressed in the parent's functional currency. Consolidation also facilitates headquarters' efforts to plan, evaluate, and control the firm's activities around the world.

When headquarters consolidates financial records, foreign currencies are translated into the functional currency using one of two methods: the current rate method or the temporal method. The **current rate method** translates foreign currency balance sheets and income statements at the *current* exchange rate—the spot exchange rate in effect on the day (in the case of balance sheets) or for the period (in the case of income statements) the statements are prepared. This method is typically used when translating records of foreign subsidiaries that are considered separate entities, rather than part of the parent firm's operations. Consider Computershare, an Australian firm that markets financial software through its network of subsidiaries worldwide. The company translates the financial statements of its subsidiaries using the current rate method because these subsidiaries are stand-alone legal entities. Amounts payable and receivable in foreign currencies are converted to Australian dollars at the exchange rate in effect on the day of consolidation.[30]

The current rate results in gains and losses, depending on the exchange rates in effect during the translation period. For example, the value of income received in a foreign currency six months earlier may differ substantially from its value on the day it is translated. For firms with extensive international operations, the accounting translation method can strongly influence company performance and valuation.

In the **temporal method**, the choice of exchange rate depends on the underlying method of valuation. If assets and liabilities are normally valued at historical cost, then they are translated at the historical rates—that is, the rates in effect when the assets were acquired. If assets and liabilities are normally valued at market cost, they are translated at the current rate of exchange. Thus, monetary items such as cash, receivables, and payables are translated at the current exchange rate. Nonmonetary items such as inventory and property, plant, and equipment are translated at historical rates.

According to U.S. accounting standards, if the functional currency of the subsidiary is that of the local operating environment (for example, if the yen is the main currency used by the Japanese subsidiary of a U.S. multinational firm), the company must use the current rate method. If the functional currency is the parent's currency, the MNE must use the temporal method. The choice of method can give rise to different profitability and other performance outcomes, and firms must adhere to accepted accounting practices and laws.

Current rate method
Translation of foreign currency balance sheet and income statements at the current exchange rate—the spot exchange rate in effect on the day or for the period when the statements are prepared.

Temporal method
Translation of foreign currency balance sheet and income statements at an exchange rate that varies with the underlying method of valuation.

International Taxation

In the countries where they operate, companies pay direct taxes, indirect taxes, sales taxes, and value-added taxes, among others. *Direct taxes* are typically imposed on income from profits, capital gains, intracorporate transactions, royalties, interest, and dividends. *Indirect taxes* apply to firms that license or franchise products and services or that charge interest. In effect, the local government withholds some percentage of royalty payments or interest charges as tax. A *sales tax* is a flat percentage tax on the value of goods or services sold, paid by the ultimate user. A *value-added tax* (VAT) is payable at each stage of processing in the value chain of a product or service. VAT is calculated as a percentage of the difference between the sale and purchase price of a product and is common in Canada, Europe, and Latin America. Each business in a product's value chain is required to bill the VAT to its customers and pay the tax on its purchases, crediting the amounts it

Exhibit 20.8

Corporate Income Tax Rates Around the World (as a percent of corporate income, rounded to the nearest whole percent)

SOURCE: Information reprinted from KPMG International. KPMG is a Swiss cooperative. Member firms of the KPMG network of independent firms are affiliated with KPMG International. KPMG International provides no client services. No member firm has any authority to obligate or bind KPMG International or any member from vis-a-vis third parties, nor does KPMG International have any such authority to obligate or bind any member firm. All rights reserved. Reprinted with permission of KPMG International.

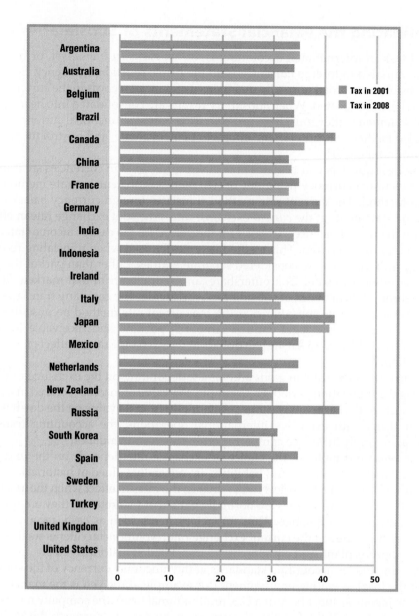

paid against the amounts due on its own activities. The net result is a tax on the added value of the good.

The most common form of direct tax is the *corporate income tax*. Exhibit 20.8 provides rates for a sample of countries. Called "corporation tax" in some localities, it is a major factor in international planning because it encourages managers to organize business operations in ways that minimize the tax, usually by deducting business expenses from revenues. Thus, income tax influences the timing, magnitude, and composition of company investment in plant and equipment, R&D, inventories, and other assets. The exhibit reveals that many countries have reduced tax rates because they recognize high taxes can discourage investment.[31] In Russia, the corporate income tax rate decreased from 43 percent in 2001 to 24 percent in 2008. In Canada, the rate decreased from 42 percent to 36 percent. Ireland has the lowest income tax rate, 13 percent—one of the pillars of its economic revitalization policy.

The U.S. automaker Ford has sold cars in Canada, Japan, and several other countries almost since its founding in 1903. At one time, whenever Ford sold cars in Canada, it was required to pay direct taxes on its income in both Canada and the United States.[32] Because of a lack of harmony in international tax rules, many MNEs were subject to double taxation, which reduced company earnings and discouraged firms from investing abroad. To resolve the problem, most countries signed tax treaties with their trading partners that help ensure firms pay an appropriate amount of tax. A typical tax treaty between country A and country B states that, if the firm pays income tax in A, it need not pay the tax in B (or vice versa) if the taxes are similar amounts. This result is accomplished with foreign tax credits—an automatic reduction in domestic tax liability when the firm can prove it has already paid income tax abroad. Or the firm may be liable to pay tax in each country, but the amount is prorated so the total is no more than the maximum tax in either country. Most tax treaties also obligate nations to assist each other in tax enforcement, ensuring that MNEs pay taxes in one country or the other to deter tax evasion.

Tax Havens   Because tax systems vary around the world, MNEs have an incentive to structure their global activities in ways that minimize taxes. They take advantage of tax havens like the Bahamas, Luxembourg, Singapore, and Switzerland, either by establishing operations in them or by funneling business transactions through them. Nissan and Kraft Foods moved their European headquarters to Switzerland to take advantage of lower corporate taxes. The Irish rock bank U2 moved its music-publishing business to the Netherlands to shelter its songwriting royalties from taxation.[33] The use of tax havens for tax reduction is generally legal but is restricted by some governments. The United States limited firms' ability to move major operations to such countries.[34] Corporations sometimes use tax havens to "park" revenues until needed elsewhere for trade or investment.

The OECD, World Bank, and other international organizations discourage the wrongful use of tax havens and lobby countries to develop transparent tax systems. The EU and OECD also pressure countries to reduce harmful tax competition. In Europe, foreign investors tend to establish operations in countries with low taxes and avoid countries with high taxes. Because this discourages European unity and economic development, EU governments are seeking to harmonize taxation throughout Europe.

Managing International Finance to Minimize Tax Burden   Taxation affects managerial decisions about the type of entry modes, the legal form of foreign operations, transfer pricing, methods for obtaining capital, and even the choice of target markets. Financial managers seek to legally minimize their tax obligations. In Japan, the government imposes a high tax on malt, a key beer ingredient. Partly to avoid the tax, firms that brew beer in Japan employ a distillation technology that eliminates the need for malt. The end product tastes like beer but is actually a type of liquor. Occasionally, governments may create tax breaks on income earned abroad. In the United States, for example, the American Jobs Creation Act of 2004 provided a one-time opportunity for U.S. MNEs to repatriate foreign subsidiary earnings at the maximum rate of 5.25 percent, instead of the typical 35 percent. The act triggered the repatriation of several hundred billion dollars.

Many techniques described in this chapter for transferring funds within the MNE and managing currency exposure are also useful for legally minimizing the firm's tax burdens. Minimizing taxes is typically a key goal of transfer pricing strategies, for instance. MNEs also benefit from differences in tax rates and systems between countries. They establish holding companies or finance corporations in particular countries or operate in government-designated low-tax zones (Foreign Trade Zones), structuring production and selling activities to minimize tax obligations.

Closing Case

International Financial Operations at Tektronix

An oscilloscope is a measuring device with a display screen that checks the condition of electronic equipment. In 1946, founders of U.S.-based Tektronix, Inc. (www.tek .com) built their first oscilloscope from electronic parts purchased from government surplus sales. TEK, as the firm is known, went public in 1963. Its oscilloscopes and other measuring devices contributed immensely to the development of computers and communications equipment.

TEK employs several thousand employees in dozens of countries and earns roughly half its $1 billion in annual sales from North America, 25 percent from Europe, 15 percent from Japan, and the rest from other countries. TEK owes part of its original success to venture capital funding. However, the majority of its capital comes from equity financing and debt sources. TEK was acquired by Danaher Corporation in 2007.

International Operations

TEK launched its first foreign distributor in Sweden in 1948. In later years, the firm set up many sales subsidiaries abroad. It developed joint ventures in Japan (Sony-Tek) and China to distribute TEK products in those countries. It also established manufacturing plants in Germany, Italy, and Malaysia. TEK still manufactures most of its products in the United States, while competitors HP, Kodak, and Xerox have manufacturing plants in numerous countries around the world. TEK management prefers to centralize manufacturing to synchronize production with R&D, ensure quality control, and exploit economies of scale.

Because TEK manufactures in the United States and sells abroad, it has substantial foreign exchange exposure. Most of TEK's foreign sales are invoiced in local currencies. If the U.S. dollar strengthens against those currencies, TEK's profits are reduced when it converts these local revenues into U.S. dollars. TEK also sources many inputs from abroad, which creates currency risks in its accounts payable.

For financial accounting, many of TEK's non-U.S. subsidiaries use their local currencies as the functional currency. Thus, assets and liabilities are translated into U.S. dollars at end-of-period exchange rates. Income and expense items are translated at the average rate during the accounting period. To minimize currency risk, management deals proactively with transaction, translation, and economic exposures.

Tax-Related Decisions

While one goal of every MNE is to legally minimize domestic and foreign taxes, in recent years countries such as France and Germany have increased their tax audits of foreign firms' local subsidiaries. To help address these and other tax challenges, TEK centralized all its European treasury functions, including cash management, inventory, and receivables, to the firm's subsidiary in England. In addition, the firm sets all the pricing for its markets worldwide at company headquarters. Such approaches provide efficiencies in company financial activities, simplify tax preparation, and enhance TEK's ability to use foreign tax credits. The goal is to legally minimize TEK's average tax rate across all its markets, which had been running at 32 percent.

Currency Risk Management

TEK has employed currency hedging selectively. Not all risks can be profitably hedged because of the high cost of banking fees and interest charges. As a result, TEK has experienced foreign exchange losses in the past. To help minimize these losses, management established a unit at headquarters responsible for assessing and managing currency risk. TEK managers obtain intelligence from online sources and the forecasting departments of large banks and regularly monitor changes in key currencies. Among the approaches that TEK applies are multilateral netting, offsetting cash flows, a centralized depository, forward contracts, and currency options.

Multilateral Netting

TEK has many ongoing transactions with and among its subsidiaries. Its financial managers can strategically reduce cash transfers, transaction costs, and bank fees by eliminating offsetting cash flows between headquarters and the subsidiaries. In TEK's multilateral netting process, all subsidiaries report to headquarters what is owed in foreign currencies to other subsidiaries, customers, suppliers, and headquarters. Financial managers then advise each subsidiary how much to pay to minimize the number and amount of inter-subsidiary cash transfers. Management also matches hedging instruments with the firm's most pressing currency exposures. The launch of the euro greatly simplified international transactions and reduced the need for some netting operations in Europe.

Offsetting Cash Flows

Whenever possible, management consolidates accounts receivable and accounts payable, matching them against one another. If TEK owes a French supplier 800,000 euros, it can grant a trade credit in the amount of 800,000 euros to a German customer, making the receivable and payable offset each other in the same currency. TEK also has some flexibility to change the invoicing currency of its subsidiaries and affiliates—for example, by denominating some invoices from its Japan subsidiary in yen instead of dollars. Cash flows are also offset with counterbalanced investments in Asia and Europe and skillful transfer pricing and other intracorporate financing activities. If headquarters wants to spend $1 million to establish a new subsidiary in Europe, it will direct existing European subsidiaries to retain a similar amount of their earnings in euros. Then, instead of converting the foreign earnings into U.S. dollars, TEK uses the retained euro earnings to build the new subsidiary.

Centralized Depository

While some currency management is delegated to local managers, headquarters in the United States is in charge and sets guidelines for the subsidiaries to follow. Management pools funds into centralized depositories and directs them to subsidiaries where needed or invests them to generate income. Management also pools accounts receivable for some European subsidiaries into a regional depository, which makes receipt and dispersal of cash more manageable, creates economies of scale in the investment and other uses of excess cash, and reduces the need for local borrowing. The centralized approach also concentrates managerial expertise and financial services at one location. Finally, the firm employs a reinvoicing center that invoices foreign subsidiaries in the local currency but receives invoices in U.S. dollars.

Forward Contracts and Currency Options

TEK hedges against currency risk by taking positions in forward contracts. These instruments allow financial managers to buy or sell currency at a specific future date at an agreed-upon exchange rate. If there is much uncertainty about the value of a future receivable, management can guarantee a fixed exchange rate and minimize currency risk. The firm also employs currency options, contracts that grant the holder the right to buy or sell currency at a specified exchange rate during a specified period of time. TEK uses currency futures contracts with maturities of one to three months to mitigate currency risk. At any time, the firm's currency contracts can exceed $100 million. The downside is that TEK must pay substantial trading fees and other costs for its currency hedging activities.

Other Financial Developments

Some years ago, TEK undertook a major restructuring of company operations. The sale of a major division generated proceeds of more than $900 million. Management used the funds partly to pay down the firm's corporate debt. In comparison to its equity holdings, the firm's debt is modest and manageable. Management favors a low debt-to-equity ratio.

While TEK regularly experiences fluctuations in sales and currency values, management has developed substantial expertise to weather difficult challenges. Careful planning and implementation of financial operations will help the firm continue to reign as the leader in oscilloscopes and other measuring equipment.

AACSB: Reflective Thinking Skills, Analytic Skills

Case Questions

1. What are the implications for currency risk of TEK focusing its manufacturing in the United States but generating most of its sales abroad? Competitors like HP and Kodak are more geographically diversified in their sourcing. What advantages does this create for them?

2. The case lists various approaches TEK follows to minimize its exposure to currency risk. If hired by TEK, what other strategies and tactics would you recommend to reduce the firm's exposure even further? Justify your answer.

3. TEK management attempts to maintain a reasonable ratio of debt to equity. Most firms prefer relatively low levels of debt in their capital structures. Why? What other approaches could TEK use to generate financing for its international operations? What approaches can TEK use to transfer funds within its operations worldwide?

4. The case describes approaches TEK follows to minimize its international tax liability. Based on your reading of the chapter, how would you advise TEK management to further reduce its taxes around the world?

SOURCES: "Tektronix Finds Surprising Results from Net Promoter Scores," *B to B*, June 9, 2008, p. 14; "Danaher to Acquire Tektronix," *Canadian Electronics*, November/December 2007, p. 1; Danaher, Inc., 2008 Annual Report, Washington, DC; Joseph Epstein, "Did Rip Van Winkle Really Lift Its Head?" *Financial World*, April 8, 2006, pp. 42–45; Lori Ioannou, "Taxing Issues," *International Business*, March 1995, pp. 42–45; Marshall Lee, *Winning with People: The First 40 Years of Tektronix* (Beaverton, OR: Tektronix, Inc., 1986); Richard J. Maturi, "Take the Sting Out of the Swings," *Industry Week*, September 3, 1990, p. 96; Tim McElligott, "This Way Out: Rick Wills, Tektronix," *Telephony*, June 4, 2001, pp. 190–191; Arthur Stonehill, Jerry Davies, Randahl Finnessy, and Michael Moffett, "Tektronix (C)," *Thunderbird International Business Review* 46, no. 4 (July/August 2004): 465–469; Sony Corp., "History of Sony," retrieved from http://www.sony.net; Tektronix, Inc., "Tektronix Named Finalist for 'Best in Test' 2010 Awards," press release retrieved from http://www.tek.com; Tektronix corporate profile retrieved from http://www.hoovers.com; Tektronix corporate Web site at http://www.tek.com; Tektronix, Inc., 2000 Annual Report and Form 10-K to U.S. Securities and Exchange Commission (2005), Beaverton, OR.

CHAPTER ESSENTIALS

Key Terms

arbitragers, p. 586
bond, p. 578
consolidation, p. 582
currency option, p. 587
currency swap, p. 588
current rate method, p. 591
debt financing, p. 573
direct quote, p. 585
economic exposure, p. 582
equity financing, p. 573
Eurobond, p. 578
Eurocurrency, p. 578

Eurodollars, p. 578
foreign bond, p. 578
forward contract, p. 587
forward rate, p. 585
fronting loan, p. 580
futures contract, p. 587
global bond market, p. 578
global capital market, p. 574
global equity market, p. 576
global money market, p. 574
hedgers, p. 585

hedging, p. 587
indirect quote, p. 585
intracorporate financing, p. 579
multilateral netting, p. 580
speculators, p. 585
spot rate, p. 584
tax haven, p. 580
temporal method, p. 591
transaction exposure, p. 582
translation exposure, p. 582
transparency, p. 589

Summary

In this chapter, you learned about:

1. Key tasks in international financial management

International financial management involves the acquisition and use of funds for cross-border trade and investment activities. Participants include firms, banks, and brokerage houses. Managers such as Chief Financial Officers (CFOs) organize financial activities inside the focal firm. CFOs decide on the firm's capital structure, raise capital, manage working capital and cash flows, do capital budgeting, manage currency risk, and deal with diverse accounting and tax practices.

2. International capital structure

The capital structure is the mix of long-term financing—**equity financing** and **debt financing**—that the firm uses to support its international activities. Equity financing is obtained by selling shares in stock markets and by retaining earnings. Debt financing is obtained by borrowing money from banks and other financial institutions or by selling **bonds**.

3. Raising funds for the firm's international activities

Companies can raise money in the **global capital market**. Equity financing can be obtained in the **global equity market**—the stock exchanges throughout the world where investors and firms meet to buy and sell shares of stock. In terms of debt financing, firms may borrow in the **Eurocurrency** market, which uses currency banked outside its country of origin. Firms also sell bonds—often **foreign bonds** or **Eurobonds**—in the **global bond market**. In addition, MNEs can support the operations of their subsidiaries through **intracorporate financing**.

4. Management of working capital and cash flow

Net working capital is the difference between current assets and current liabilities. Firms often manage intracorporate funds by developing a *centralized depository*, into which funds are pooled from the firm's network of subsidiaries and affiliates to distribute to units that need funds. The various methods for transferring funds within the MNE include *dividend remittances, royalty payments, transfer pricing,* and *fronting loans*. A **fronting loan** is a loan from a parent firm to its subsidiary, channeled through a bank or other financial intermediary. **Multilateral netting** is the process of strategically reducing the number of cash transfers between the parent and subsidiaries by eliminating the offsetting cash flows between these entities.

5. Capital budgeting for international operations

Capital budgeting rests on analyses that management undertakes to evaluate the viability of proposed international projects. Management calculates the *net present value* of a proposed project to decide whether it should be implemented.

6. Management of currency risk

There are three main types of currency exposure: transaction exposure, economic exposure, and translation exposure. A firm faces **transaction exposure** when outstanding accounts receivable or payable are denominated in foreign currencies. **Economic exposure** results from exchange rate fluctuations affecting the pricing of products, the cost of inputs, and the value of foreign investments. **Translation exposure** arises as the firm combines the financial statements of foreign subsidiaries into the parent's financial statements, a process called **consolidation**. Currency trading takes place between banks and currency brokers, often on behalf of multinational firms. Currency traders include **hedgers, speculators,** and **arbitragers**. Managers attempt to forecast exchange rates to minimize their firm's exposure to currency risk. Approaches for minimizing exposure to currency risk include centralizing currency management, measuring currency risk, monitoring long-term trends, and emphasizing flexibility in international operations. Firms also employ **hedging**, the use of specialized financial instruments to balance positions in foreign currencies. Key hedging tools include **forward contracts, futures contracts, currency options,** and **currency swaps**.

7. Management of international accounting and tax practices

Financial statements prepared in one country may be difficult to compare with those from other countries. Through **transparency**, firms regularly and comprehensively reveal reliable information about their financial condition and accounting practices. Various factors account for differences in national accounting systems. Several international organizations are aiming to harmonize cross-national accounting practices. Managers use the **current rate method** and the **temporal method** for currency translation. Internationally, firms seek to minimize taxes, which consist of direct taxes, indirect taxes, sales taxes, and value-added taxes. Governments use two major methods for eliminating multiple taxation: the foreign tax credit and tax treaties. **Tax havens** are countries with low taxes that are friendly to business and inward investment.

Test Your Comprehension AACSB: Reflective Thinking Skills

1. What are the major tasks in international financial management?

2. What are the components of the capital structure in the typical MNE? What about MNEs in Japan and Germany? What about a typical firm in your country?

3. From a managerial perspective, what are the advantages and disadvantages of financing obtained from each of the following: equity, debt, and intracorporate sources?

4. Suppose you had to raise capital to fund international value-adding activities and investment projects. From what types of sources (e.g., stock markets) would you most likely obtain each type of financing? What are financial centers and where are they located?

5. What are the major tasks in managing working capital and cash flow for international operations?

6. What are the major steps in capital budgeting? For what types of ventures do international managers typically engage in capital budgeting?

7. What are the types of currency exposure? Why is currency exposure potentially harmful to the firm's

international operations? How can managers forecast currency exposure? What steps could you take to minimize currency exposure?

8. Who are the major players in foreign-exchange trading?

9. What are the major methods for translating foreign-currency denominated financial statements into the financial statements of the parent firm?

10. As an international tax consultant to an MNE, what steps would you take to minimize tax obligations around the world?

Apply Your Understanding AACSB: Reflective Thinking Skills, Analytic Skills, Ethical Understanding and Reasoning Abilities

1. Marite Perez is CEO of Havana, Inc., a large manufacturer of high-tech medical equipment based in North Miami Beach, Florida. The firm makes vital signs monitors, MRIs, X-ray machines, and other equipment for exploratory medical diagnostics. Marite wants to rapidly expand the firm into foreign markets. To accomplish this, she plans to invest much money in developing new products and establishing production and marketing subsidiaries abroad. What can Marite do to raise capital for these projects? What are the various methods that Marite might employ to raise capital for her firm? What are the advantages and disadvantages associated with each?

2. Michael Norton is the president of Liberty Enterprises, a large MNE based in Singapore that makes computers and related peripherals. The firm has many subsidiaries around the world. Demand for Liberty's products has been growing in Asia and Europe, especially in Indonesia, Japan, France, and Spain. Michael has always used external sources to finance the firm's working capital needs. Currently, with rapidly expanding business, he needs to access more working capital. What is the feasibility of raising funds through intracorporate sources? What methods can Michael use to transfer funds within the firm? What should Michael know about multilateral netting?

3. *Ethical Dilemma:* Suppose you are the president of West Turner Bank (WTB), a major financial institution. WTB has made numerous loans for major construction projects in Indonesia and several countries in Eastern Europe. However, during the global financial crisis, like many banks, WTB faced financial ruin. In order to shore up its deteriorating finances, WTB's executive committee decided to call in loans made to these countries. That is, management decided to force borrowers in the construction projects to immediately repay their loans. You know that by calling the loans, economic conditions in the affected countries will worsen and thousands of workers will likely lose their jobs. What should you do? Use the Ethical Framework in Chapter 5 to analyze this situation. Can you find any "creative" solutions to the dilemma?

globalEDGE Internet Exercises

(http://globalEDGE.msu.edu)

AACSB: Reflective Thinking Skills, Analytic Skills

Refer to Chapter 1, page 62, for instructions on how to access and use globalEDGE™.

1. The World Federation of Exchanges is the organization that represents major stock exchanges around the world. Visit the online portal at www.world-exchanges.org and use the annual report of the Federation as well as detailed statistics available on individual exchanges to answer the following questions:

   a. What percentage of the world market capitalization is represented by the top 10 exchanges?

   b. For the most recent year, what exchanges accounted for the largest increases in market capitalization?

   c. Which exchanges have seen the greatest increase recently in the number of firms listed?

   d. Worldwide consolidation trends have also affected the stock exchanges. A good example is the merger of Paris-based Euronext with the NYSE. What are the underlying causes of these cross-border mergers?

2. Suppose your job is to ensure your firm has enough foreign exchange on hand to pay outstanding accounts payable. Assume your firm owes 1 million yen to a Japanese supplier, which is due exactly 60 days from now. Your task is to exchange dollars for the right amount of yen. To do this, you can enter a contract with a bank today to buy 1 million yen 60 days forward, or wait 60 days and buy 1 million yen at the then-prevailing spot exchange rate. Which alternative do you prefer, and why? If you expect the spot rate 60 days from now will be the same as it is today, what is the expected dollar cost of buying 1 million yen in the spot market 60 days from now? How many dollars will it cost you to obtain 1 million yen if you entered the forward contract? To obtain the spot exchange rates, go to www.ft.com and click on Markets, then Currencies; or go to globalEDGE™ and enter "exchange rates" in the search engine.

3. Many corporate Web sites provide financial information, including financial statements, as well as other information about companies' status and progress. As an institutional investor, you are thinking of investing in one of the following firms: Diageo (www.diageo.com), the premium drinks firm; Vivendi (www.vivendi.com), a French telecom; Grupo Carso (www.gcarso.com.mx), a major Mexican retailing conglomerate; and SK Telecom (www.sktelecom.com), the largest wireless communication services provider in South Korea. Look up each firm's corporate Web site. Based on the information provided, answer the following questions:

   a. How would you rate the transparency of each firm?

   b. How inclined are you to invest in each firm, based on the information provided? Justify your answer.

   c. In terms of transparency and investor-oriented information, which site is best?

   d. Based on the best site, what recommendations would you make to the firm that owns the weakest site to improve its transparency and attract investors?

> Appendix

The Math of Currency Trading

News outlets such as the *Financial Times* and the *Wall Street Journal*, as well as online sources, publish bilateral exchange rate tables that list currency values in terms of other currencies. These tables report bid-ask midpoints and so do not represent prices that can actually be traded in the market. Here is an example.

	£	€	¥	$
U.K. pound (£)	1	0.9051	0.006865	0.6329
Euro (€)	1.1049	1	0.007585	0.6993
Japanese yen (¥)	145.68	131.85	1	92.20
U.S. dollar ($)	1.5800	1.4300	0.010846	1

The numeric cells contain the number of units of the currency in the left-most column that equal one unit of the currencies along the top row of the table (e.g., £0.9051/€1). Rather than trying to remember this convention, it is usually easier to infer the convention used in these tables from the values of your domestic currency. In the example above, Japanese and U.S. residents are likely to know that the dollar/yen price of 92.20 reflects a yen-per-dollar exchange rate of ¥92.20/$1, rather than a dollar-per-yen price. This is a direct price for a U.S. resident and an indirect price for a Japanese resident. The yen-per-dollar price is then simply the reciprocal of the dollar-per-yen price:

$$1/(¥92.20/\$) = \$0.010846/¥.$$

Note that the values in this table are internally consistent. Thus, the yen-per-pound exchange rate must equal the yen-per-dollar rate times the dollar-per-pound rate:

$$¥145.68/£ = (¥92.20/\$) = (\$1.5800/£).$$

Alternatively, the yen-per-pound rate can be calculated by dividing the yen-per-dollar rate by the pound-per-dollar rate:

$$¥145.68/£ = (¥92.20/\$)/(£0.6329/\$).$$

Keeping track of the currency units ensures that the answer has the correct units.

Exchange rates that do not involve the domestic currency are called cross rates. Cross rates for infrequently traded currencies can be calculated by comparing them against an actively traded currency such as the dollar. For example, the cross rate between the Chilean peso (CLP) and Japanese yen can be calculated by combining the CLP-per-dollar rate with the yen-per-dollar rate. If one U.S. dollar is worth 507.15 Chilean pesos, then the CLP-per-yen rate must be

$$(CLP\ 507.15/\$)/(¥92.20/\$) = CLP\ 5.5005/¥.$$

Again, it is important to keep track of the currency units to ensure the desired result.

> Glossary

Absolute advantage principle A country benefits by producing only those products in which it has an absolute advantage or that it can produce using fewer resources than another country.

Acculturation The process of adjusting and adapting to a culture other than one's own.

Acquisition Direct investment to purchase an existing company or facility.

Adaptation Firm's efforts to modify one or more elements of its international marketing program to accommodate specific customer requirements in a particular market.

Advanced economies Post-industrial countries characterized by high per-capita income, highly competitive industries, and well-developed commercial infrastructure.

Agent An intermediary (often an individual or a small firm) that handles orders to buy and sell commodities, products, and services in international business transactions for a commission.

Antidumping duty A tax imposed on products deemed to be dumped and causing injury to producers of competing products in the importing country.

Arbitragers Currency traders who buy and sell the same currency in two or more foreign-exchange markets to profit from differences in the currency's exchange rate.

Area studies Factual knowledge of the historical, political, and economic environment of the host country.

Balance of payments The annual accounting of all economic transactions of a nation with *all* other nations.

Barter A type of countertrade in which goods are directly exchanged without the transfer of any money.

Bond A debt instrument that enables the issuer (borrower) to raise capital by promising to repay the principal along with interest on a specified date (maturity).

Born global firm A young entrepreneurial company that initiates international business activity very early in its evolution, moving rapidly into foreign markets.

Build-operate-transfer (BOT) Arrangement in which the firm or a consortium of firms contracts to build a major facility abroad, operate it for a specified period, and then hand it over to the project sponsor, typically the host-country government or public utility.

Business process outsourcing (BPO) The outsourcing to independent suppliers of business service functions such as accounting, payroll, human resource functions, travel services, IT services, customer service, or technical support.

Buy-back agreement A type of countertrade in which the seller agrees to supply technology or equipment to construct a facility and receives payment in the form of goods produced by the facility.

Capital flight The rapid sell-off by residents or foreigners of their holdings in a nation's currency or other assets, usually in response to a domestic crisis that causes investors to lose confidence in the country's economy.

Captive sourcing Sourcing from the firm's own production facilities.

Central bank The monetary authority in each nation that regulates the money supply and credit, issues currency, and manages the exchange rate of the nation's currency.

Codetermination An industrial relations practice in which labor representatives sit on the corporate board and participate in company decision making.

Collective bargaining Joint negotiations between management and hourly labor and technical staff regarding wages and working conditions.

Commercial risk Firm's potential loss or failure from poorly developed or executed business strategies, tactics, or procedures.

Common market A stage of regional integration in which trade barriers are reduced or removed, common external barriers are established, and products, services, and *factors of production* are allowed to move freely among the member countries.

Company-owned subsidiary A representative office of the focal firm that handles marketing, physical distribution, promotion, and customer service activities in the foreign market.

Company sales potential An estimate of the share of annual industry sales that the firm expects to generate in a particular target market.

Comparative advantage Superior features of a country that provide unique benefits in global competition, typically derived from either natural endowments or deliberate national policies.

Comparative advantage principle It can be beneficial for two countries to trade without barriers as long as one is relatively more efficient at producing goods or services needed by the other. What matters is not the absolute cost of production but rather the relative efficiency with which a country can produce the product.

Compensation deals A type of countertrade in which payment is in both goods and cash.

Competitive advantage Distinctive assets or competencies of a firm that are difficult for competitors to imitate and are typically derived from specific knowledge, capabilities, skills, or superior strategies.

Configuration of value-adding activity The pattern or geographic arrangement of locations where the firm carries out value-chain activities.

Consolidation The process of combining and integrating the financial results of foreign subsidiaries into the financial statements of the parent firm.

Consortium A project-based, nonequity venture initiated by multiple partners to fulfill a large-scale project.

Contagion The tendency of a financial or monetary crisis in one country to spread rapidly to other countries, due to the ongoing integration of national economies.

Contract manufacturing An arrangement in which the focal firm contracts with an independent supplier to manufacture products according to well-defined specifications.

Contractual entry strategies in international business Cross-border exchanges where the relationship between the focal firm and its foreign partner is governed by an explicit contract.

Corporate governance The system of procedures and processes by which corporations are managed, directed, and controlled.

Corporate social responsibility (CSR) A manner of operating a business that meets or exceeds the ethical, legal, commercial, and public expectations of stakeholders, including customers, shareholders, employees, and communities.

Corruption The abuse of power to achieve illegitimate personal gain.

Counterpurchase A type of countertrade with two distinct contracts. In the first, the seller agrees to a set price for goods and receives cash from the buyer. This first deal is contingent on a second wherein the seller agrees to purchase goods from the buyer for the same amount as in the first contract or a set percentage of same.

Countertrade An international business transaction where all or partial payments are made in kind rather than cash.

Countervailing duty Tariff imposed on products imported into a country to offset subsidies given to producers or exporters in the exporting country.

Country risk Exposure to potential loss or adverse effects on company operations and profitability caused by developments in a country's political and/or legal environments.

Critical incident analysis (CIA) A method for analyzing awkward situations in cross-cultural encounters by developing objectivity and empathy for other points of view.

Cross-cultural awareness Ability to interact effectively and appropriately with people from different language and cultural backgrounds.

Cross-cultural risk A situation or event where a cultural misunderstanding puts some human value at stake.

Cross-licensing agreement A type of project-based, non-equity venture where partners agree to access licensed technology developed by the other on preferential terms.

Cultural intelligence An employee's ability to function effectively in situations characterized by cultural diversity.

Cultural metaphor A distinctive tradition or institution strongly associated with a particular society.

Culture The learned, shared, and enduring orientation patterns in a society. People demonstrate their culture through values, ideas, attitudes, behaviors, and symbols.

Culture shock Confusion and anxiety experienced by a person who lives in a foreign culture for an extended period.

Currency control Restrictions on the outflow of hard currency from a country or the inflow of foreign currencies.

Currency option A contract that gives the purchaser the right, but not the obligation, to buy a certain amount of foreign currency at a set exchange rate within a specified amount of time.

Currency risk Potential harm that arises from changes in the price of one currency relative to another.

Currency swap An agreement to exchange one currency for another, according to a specified schedule.

Current rate method Translation of foreign currency balance sheet and income statements at the current exchange rate—the spot exchange rate in effect on the day or for the period when the statements are prepared.

Customs Checkpoints at the ports of entry in each country where government officials inspect imported products and levy tariffs.

Customs brokers Specialist enterprises that arrange clearance of products through customs on behalf of importing firms.

Customs union A stage of regional integration in which the member countries agree to adopt common tariff and nontariff barriers on imports from nonmember countries.

Debt financing The borrowing of money from banks or other financial intermediaries, or the sale of corporate bonds to individuals or institutions, to raise capital.

Devaluation Government action to reduce the official value of its currency, relative to other currencies.

Developing economies Low-income countries characterized by limited industrialization and stagnant economies.

Direct exporting Exporting that is accomplished by contracting with intermediaries located in the foreign market.

Direct quote The number of units of domestic currency needed to acquire one unit of foreign currency; also known as the normal quote.

Distribution channel intermediary A specialist firm that provides various logistics and marketing services for focal firms as part of the international supply chain, both in the home country and abroad.

Documentation Official forms and other paperwork required in export transactions for shipping and customs procedures.

Dumping Pricing exported products at less than their normal value, generally less than their price in the domestic or third-country markets, or at less than production cost.

Economic exposure The currency risk that results from exchange rate fluctuations affecting the pricing of products, the cost of inputs, and the value of foreign investments.

Economic union A stage of regional integration in which member countries enjoy all the advantages of early stages, but also strive to have common fiscal and monetary policies.

Emerging markets Former developing economies that have achieved substantial industrialization, modernization, and rapid economic growth since the 1980s.

Equity financing The issuance of shares of stock to raise capital from investors and the use of retained earnings to reinvest in the firm.

Equity joint venture A type of partnership in which a separate firm is created through the investment or pooling of assets by two or more parent firms that gain joint ownership of the new legal entity.

Equity participation Acquisition of partial ownership in an existing firm.

Ethics Moral principles and values that govern the behavior of people, firms, and governments, regarding right and wrong.

Ethnocentric orientation Using our own culture as the standard for judging other cultures.

Eurobond A bond sold outside the issuer's home country but denominated in its own currency.

Eurocurrency Any currency deposited in a bank outside its country of origin.

Eurodollars U.S. dollars held in banks outside the United States, including foreign branches of U.S. banks.

Exchange rate The price of one currency expressed in terms of another; the number of units of one currency that can be exchanged for another.

Expatriate An employee assigned to work and reside in a foreign country for an extended period, usually a year or longer.

Expatriate assignment failure An employee's premature return from an international assignment.

Export control A government measure intended to manage or prevent the export of certain products or trade with certain countries.

Export department A unit within the firm charged with managing the firm's export operations.

Export management company (EMC) A domestically based intermediary that acts as an export agent on behalf of a client company.

Exporting The strategy of producing products or services in one country (often the producer's home country), and selling and distributing them to customers located in other countries.

Extraterritoriality Application of home country laws to persons or conduct outside national borders.

Facilitator A firm or an individual with special expertise in banking, legal advice, customs clearance, or related support services that assists focal firms in the performance of international business transactions.

Family conglomerate A large, highly diversified company that is privately owned.

Focal firm The initiator of an international business transaction, which conceives, designs, and produces offerings intended for consumption by customers worldwide. Focal firms are primarily MNEs and SMEs.

Foreign bond A bond sold outside the issuer's country and denominated in the currency of the country where issued.

Foreign direct investment (FDI) An internationalization strategy in which the firm establishes a physical presence abroad through acquisition of productive assets such as capital, technology, labor, land, plant, and equipment.

Foreign distributor A foreign market-based intermediary that works under contract for an exporter, takes title to, and distributes the exporter's products in a national market or territory, often performing marketing functions such as sales, promotion, and after-sales service.

Foreign exchange All forms of money that are traded internationally, including foreign currencies, bank deposits, checks, and electronic transfers.

Foreign exchange market The global marketplace for buying and selling national currencies.

Foreign trade zone (FTZ) An area within a country that receives imported goods for assembly or other processing and re-export. For customs purposes the FTZ is treated as if it is outside the country's borders.

Forward contract A contract to exchange two currencies at a specified exchange rate on a set future date.

Forward rate The exchange rate applicable to the collection or delivery of a foreign currency at some future date.

Franchising Arrangement in which the firm allows another the right to use an entire business system in exchange for fees, royalties, or other forms of compensation.

Franchisor A firm that grants another the right to use an entire business system in exchange for fees, royalties, or other forms of compensation.

Free trade Relative absence of restrictions to the flow of goods and services between nations.

Free trade agreement A formal arrangement between two or more countries to reduce or eliminate tariffs, quotas, and barriers to trade in products and services.

Free trade area A stage of regional integration in which member countries agree to eliminate tariffs and other barriers to trade in products and services within the bloc.

Freight forwarder A specialized logistics service provider that arranges international shipping on behalf of exporting firms.

Fronting loan A loan between the parent and its subsidiary, channeled through a large bank or other financial intermediary.

Functional structure An arrangement in which management of the firm's international operations is organized by functional activity, such as production and marketing.

Futures contract An agreement to buy or sell a currency in exchange for another at a specified price on a specified date.

Geocentric orientation A global mind-set in which the manager is able to understand a business or market without regard to country boundaries.

Geographic area structure An organizational design in which management and control are decentralized to the level of individual geographic regions.

Global account management (GAM) Serving a key global customer in a consistent and standardized manner, regardless of where in the world it operates.

Global bond market The international marketplace in which bonds are bought and sold, primarily through bond brokers.

Global brand A brand whose positioning, advertising strategy, look, and personality are standardized worldwide.

Global capital market The collective financial markets where firms and governments raise intermediate and long-term financing.

Global equity market The worldwide market of funds for equity financing—stock exchanges around the world where investors and firms meet to buy and sell shares of stock.

Global financial system The collective of financial institutions that facilitate and regulate investment and capital flows worldwide, such as central banks, commercial banks, and national stock exchanges.

Global industry An industry in which competition is on a regional or worldwide scale.

Global integration Coordination of the firm's value-chain activities across countries to achieve worldwide efficiency, synergy, and cross-fertilization in order to take maximum advantage of similarities between countries.

Global market opportunity Favorable combination of circumstances, locations, and timing that offers prospects for exporting, investing, sourcing, or partnering in foreign markets.

Global market segment A group of customers who share common characteristics across many national markets.

Global marketing strategy A plan of action for foreign markets that guides the firm in deciding how to position itself and its offerings, which customer segments to target, and the degree to which it should standardize or adapt its marketing program elements.

Global matrix structure An arrangement that blends the geographic area, product, and functional structures to leverage the benefits of a purely global strategy while keeping the firm responsive to local needs.

Global money market The collective financial markets where firms and governments raise short-term financing.

Global sourcing The procurement of products or services from independent suppliers or company-owned subsidiaries located abroad for consumption in the home country or a third country.

Global strategy An approach where headquarters seeks substantial control over its country operations in order to minimize redundancy and maximize efficiency, learning, and integration worldwide.

Global supply chain The firm's integrated network of sourcing, production, and distribution, organized on a worldwide scale and located in countries where competitive advantage can be maximized.

Global talent pool A searchable database of employees, profiling their international skill sets and potential for supporting the firm's global aspirations.

Global team An internationally distributed group of employees charged with a specific problem-solving or best-practice mandate that affects the entire organization.

Globalization of markets Ongoing economic integration and growing interdependency of countries worldwide.

Gray market activity Legal importation of genuine products into a country by intermediaries other than authorized distributors (also known as parallel imports).

Greenfield investment Direct investment to build a new manufacturing, marketing, or administrative facility, as opposed to acquiring existing facilities.

Hedgers Currency traders who seek to minimize their risk of exchange rate fluctuations, often by entering into forward contracts or similar financial instruments.

Hedging Using financial instruments and other measures to reduce or eliminate exposure to currency risk by locking in guaranteed foreign exchange positions.

High-context culture A culture that emphasizes nonverbal messages and views communication as a means to promote smooth, harmonious relationships.

Home replication strategy An approach in which the firm views international business as separate from and secondary to its domestic business.

Horizontal integration An arrangement whereby the firm owns, or seeks to own, the activities performed in a single stage of its value chain.

Host-country national (HCN) An employee who is a citizen of the country where the MNE subsidiary or affiliate is located.

Idiom An expression whose symbolic meaning is different from its literal meaning.

Import license Government authorization granted to a firm for importing a product.

Importing or global sourcing Procurement of products or services from suppliers located abroad for consumption in the home country or a third country.

Incoterms Universally accepted terms of sale that specify how the buyer and the seller share the cost of freight and insurance in an international transaction and at which point the buyer takes title to the goods.

Indirect exporting Exporting that is accomplished by contracting with intermediaries located in the firm's home market.

Indirect quote The number of units of foreign currency obtained for one unit of domestic currency.

Individualism versus collectivism Describes whether a person functions primarily as an individual or as part of a group.

Industrial cluster A concentration of businesses, suppliers, and supporting firms in the same industry at a particular location, characterized by a critical mass of human talent, capital, or other factor endowments.

Industry market potential An estimate of the likely sales for all firms in a particular industry over a specific period.

Infringement of intellectual property Unauthorized use, publication, or reproduction of products or services protected by a patent, copyright, trademark, or other intellectual property right.

Intellectual property Ideas or works created by individuals or firms, including discoveries and inventions; artistic, musical, and literary works; and words, phrases, symbols, and designs.

Intellectual property rights The legal claim through which the proprietary assets of firms and individuals are protected from unauthorized use by other parties.

Internalization theory An explanation of the process by which firms acquire and retain one or more value-chain activities inside the firm, minimizing the disadvantages of dealing with external partners and allowing for greater control over foreign operations.

International business Performance of trade and investment activities by firms across national borders.

International collaborative venture Cross-border business alliance whereby partnering firms pool their resources and share costs and risks to undertake a new business venture; also referred to as an "international partnership" or an "international strategic alliance."

International division structure An organizational design in which all international activities are centralized within one division in the firm, separate from domestic units.

International human resource management (IHRM) The planning, selection, training, employment, and evaluation of employees for international operations.

International investment The transfer of assets to another country or the acquisition of assets in that country.

International Monetary Fund (IMF) An international agency that aims to stabilize currencies by monitoring the foreign exchange systems of member countries and lending money to developing economies.

International monetary system Institutional framework, rules, and procedures by which national currencies are exchanged for one another.

International portfolio investment Passive ownership of foreign securities such as stocks and bonds for the purpose of generating financial returns.

International price escalation The problem of end-user prices reaching exorbitant levels in the export market caused by multilayered distribution channels, intermediary margins, tariffs, and other international customer costs.

International trade Exchange of products and services across national borders, typically through exporting and importing.

Intracorporate financing Funds from sources inside the firm (both headquarters and subsidiaries) such as equity, loans, and trade credits.

Investment incentive Transfer payment or tax concession made directly to foreign firms to entice them to invest in the country.

Joint venture A form of collaboration between two or more firms to create a new, jointly owned enterprise.

Joint venture partner A focal firm that creates and jointly owns a new legal entity through equity investment or pooling of assets.

Know-how agreement Contract in which the focal firm provides technological or management knowledge about how to design, manufacture, or deliver a product or a service.

Legal system A system for interpreting and enforcing laws.

Letter of credit Contract between the banks of a buyer and a seller that ensures payment from the buyer to the seller upon receipt of an export shipment.

Licensing Arrangement in which the owner of intellectual property grants a firm the right to use that property for a specified period of time in exchange for royalties or other compensation.

Licensor A firm that enters a contractual agreement with a foreign partner to allow the partner the right to use certain intellectual property for a specified period of time in exchange for royalties or other compensation.

Local responsiveness Management of the firm's value-chain activities on a country-by-country basis to address diverse opportunities and risks.

Logistics service provider A transportation specialist that arranges for physical distribution and storage of products on behalf of focal firms, and also controls information between the point of origin and the point of consumption.

Long-term versus short-term orientation Refers to the degree to which people and organizations defer gratification to achieve long-term success.

Low-context culture A culture that relies on elaborate verbal explanations, putting much emphasis on spoken words.

Management contract Arrangement in which a contractor supplies managerial know-how to operate a hotel, hospital, airport, or other facility in exchange for compensation.

Manufacturer's representative An intermediary contracted by the exporter to represent and sell its merchandise or services in a designated country or territory.

Maquiladoras Export-assembly plants in northern Mexico along the U.S. border that produce components and typically finished products destined for the United States on a tariff-free basis.

Masculinity versus femininity Refers to a society's orientation based on traditional male and female values. Masculine cultures tend to value competitiveness, assertiveness, ambition, and the accumulation of wealth. Feminine cultures emphasize nurturing roles, interdependence among people, and taking care of less fortunate people.

Master franchise Arrangement in which an independent company is licensed to establish, develop, and manage the entire franchising network in its market and has the right to sub-franchise to other franchisees, assuming the role of local franchisor.

Mercantilism The belief that national prosperity is the result of a positive balance of trade, achieved by maximizing exports and minimizing imports.

Merger A special type of acquisition in which two firms join to form a new, larger firm.

Monetary intervention The buying and selling of currencies by a central bank to maintain the exchange rate of a country's currency at some acceptable level.

Monochronic A rigid orientation to time, in which the individual is focused on schedules, punctuality, and time as a resource.

Multidomestic industry An industry in which competition takes place on a country-by-country basis.

Multidomestic strategy An approach to firm internationalization in which headquarters delegates considerable autonomy to each country manager, allowing him or her to operate independently and pursue local responsiveness.

Multilateral development banks (MDB) International financial institutions owned by multiple governments within world regions or other groups.

Multilateral netting Strategic reduction of cash transfers within the MNE family through the elimination of offsetting cash flows.

Multinational enterprise (MNE) A large company with substantial resources that performs various business activities through a network of subsidiaries and affiliates located in multiple countries.

National industrial policy A proactive economic development plan initiated by the government, often in collaboration with the private sector, that aims to develop or support particular industries within the nation.

New global challengers Top firms from emerging markets that are fast becoming key contenders in world markets.

Nontariff trade barrier A government policy, regulation, or procedure that impedes trade through means other than explicit tariffs.

Normativism The belief that ethical behavioral standards are universal, and firms and individuals should seek to uphold them around the world.

Offshoring The relocation of a business process or entire manufacturing facility to a foreign country.

Organizational culture The pattern of shared values, behavioral norms, systems, policies, and procedures that employees learn and adopt.

Organizational processes Managerial routines, behaviors, and mechanisms that allow the firm to function as intended.

Organizational structure Reporting relationships inside the firm that specify the links between people, functions, and processes.

Outsourcing The procurement of selected value-adding activities, including production of intermediate goods or finished products, from independent suppliers.

Parent-country national (PCN) An employee who is a citizen of the country where the MNE is headquartered.

Performance appraisal A formal process for assessing how effectively employees perform their jobs.

Political system A set of formal institutions that constitute a government.

Polycentric orientation A host-country mind-set in which the manager develops a strong affinity with the country in which she or he conducts business.

Polychronic A flexible, nonlinear orientation to time, whereby the individual takes a long-term perspective and emphasizes human relationships.

Power distance Describes how a society deals with the inequalities in power that exist among people.

Practical information Knowledge and skills necessary to function effectively in a country, including housing, health care, education, and daily living.

Privatization Transfer of state-owned industries to private concerns.

Product structure An arrangement in which management of international operations is organized by major product line.

Project-based, nonequity venture A collaboration in which the partners create a project with a relatively narrow scope and a well-defined timetable, without creating a new legal entity.

Protectionism National economic policies designed to restrict free trade and protect domestic industries from foreign competition.

Quota A quantitative restriction placed on imports of a specific product over a specified period of time.

Regional economic integration The growing economic interdependence that results when two or more countries within a geographic region form an alliance aimed at reducing barriers to trade and investment.

Regional economic integration bloc A geographic area consisting of two or more countries that have agreed to pursue economic integration by reducing barriers to the cross-border flow of products, services, capital, and, in more advanced states, labor.

Relativism The belief that ethical truths are not absolute but differ from group to group.

Repatriation The expatriate's return to his or her home country following the completion of a foreign assignment.

Royalty A fee paid periodically to compensate a licensor for the temporary use of its intellectual property, often based on a percentage of gross sales generated from the use of the licensed asset.

Rule of law A legal system in which rules are clear, publicly disclosed, fairly enforced, and widely respected by individuals, organizations, and the government.

Self-reference criterion The tendency to view other cultures through the lens of our own culture.

Small and medium-sized enterprise (SME) A company with 500 or fewer employees (as defined in Canada and the United States).

Socialization The process of learning the rules and behavioral patterns appropriate to one's given society.

Sovereign wealth fund (SWF) A state-owned investment fund that undertakes systematic, global investment activities.

Special Drawing Right (SDR) A unit of account or a reserve asset, a type of currency used by central banks to supplement their existing reserves in transactions with the IMF.

Speculators Currency traders who seek profits by investing in currencies with the expectation their value will change in the future.

Spot rate The exchange rate applied when the current exchange rate is used for immediate receipt of a currency.

Standardization Firm's efforts to make its marketing program elements uniform, with a view to targeting entire regions, or even the global marketplace, with the same product or service.

Stereotype Generalization about a group of people that may or may not be factual, often overlooking real, deeper differences.

Strategy A planned set of actions that managers employ to make best use of the firm's resources and core competencies to gain competitive advantage.

Subsidy Monetary or other resources that a government grants to a firm or group of firms, usually intended to encourage exports or to facilitate the production and marketing of products at reduced prices, to ensure the involved firms prosper.

Sustainability Meeting humanity's needs without harming future generations.

Tariff A tax imposed on imported products, effectively increasing the cost of acquisition for the customer.

Tax haven A country hospitable to business and inward investment because of its low corporate income taxes.

Temporal method Translation of foreign currency balance sheet and income statements at an exchange rate that varies with the underlying method of valuation.

Tenders Formal offers made by a buyer to purchase certain products or services.

Third-country national (TCN) An employee who is a citizen of a country other than the home or host country.

Trade deficit A condition in which a nation's imports exceed its exports for a specific period of time.

Trade surplus A condition in which a nation's exports exceed its imports for a specific period of time.

Trading company An intermediary that engages in import and export of a variety of commodities, products, and services.

Transaction exposure The currency risk firms face when outstanding accounts receivable or payable are denominated in foreign currencies.

Transfer pricing The practice of pricing intermediate or finished products exchanged among the subsidiaries and affiliates of the same corporate family located in different countries.

Transition economies A subset of emerging markets that evolved from centrally planned economies into liberalized markets.

Translation exposure The currency risk that results when a firm translates financial statements denominated in a foreign currency into the functional currency of the parent firm, as part of consolidating international financial results.

Transnational strategy A coordinated approach to internationalization in which the firm strives to be relatively responsive to local needs while retaining sufficient central control of operations to ensure efficiency and learning.

Transparency The degree to which companies regularly reveal substantial information about their financial condition and accounting practices.

Turnkey contracting Arrangement in which the focal firm or a consortium of firms plans, finances, organizes, manages, and implements all phases of a project abroad and then hands it over to a foreign customer after training local workers.

Turnkey contractors Focal firms or a consortium of firms that plan, finance, organize, manage, and implement all phases of a project and then hand it over to a foreign customer after training local personnel.

Uncertainty avoidance The extent to which people can tolerate risk and uncertainty in their lives.

Value chain The sequence of value-adding activities performed by the firm in the course of developing, producing, marketing, and servicing a product.

Vertical integration An arrangement whereby the firm owns, or seeks to own, multiple stages of a value chain for producing, selling, and delivering a product or service.

Visionary leadership A quality of senior management that provides superior strategic guidance for managing efficiency, flexibility, and learning.

Wholly owned direct investment A foreign direct investment in which the investor fully owns the foreign assets.

World Bank An international agency that provides loans and technical assistance to low- and middle-income countries with the goal of reducing poverty.

World Trade Organization (WTO) A multilateral governing body empowered to regulate international trade and investment.

> Notes

Chapter 1

[1] We use the term *international business* to refer to the cross-border business activities of individual firms, while economists use *international trade* to refer to aggregate cross-border flows of products and services between nations. While international business describes an enterprise-level phenomenon, international trade describes the macrophenomenon of aggregate flows between nations.

[2] Dave Shellock, "Signs of Deepening Recession Dent Confidence," *Financial Times*, February 14, 2009, p. 14; Gabriele Parussini, "World News: Euro-Zone Economic Outlook Darkens," *Wall Street Journal*, January 17, 2009, p. A7.

[3] "Numbers: International Trade Hits a Wall," *BusinessWeek*, January 26/February 2, 2009, p. 15.

[4] Nick Wingfield, "eBay Sets Sights on Indian Market with Acquisition," *Wall Street Journal*, June 23, 2004, p. A3.

[5] "Desert Song," *The Economist*, October 7, 2004, p. 88; "News: The Banker Country Awards 2007," *The Banker*, December, 2007, p. 1.

[6] Marc A. Miles et al., *2008 Index of Economic Freedom* (Washington, DC: The Heritage Foundation).

[7] Gabriele Parussini, "World News: Euro-Zone Economic Outlook Darkens," *Wall Street Journal*, January 17, 2009, p. A7; Dave Shellock, "Signs of Deepening Recession Dent Confidence," *Financial Times*, February 14, 2009, p. 14.

[8] Organisation for Economic Co-operation and Development, *Globalization and Small and Medium Enterprises (SMEs)*, (Paris: OECD, 1997).

[9] Gary Knight and S. Tamer Cavusgil, "Innovation, Organizational Capabilities, and the Born-Global Firm," *Journal of International Business Studies* 35, no. 2 (2004): 124–41; Patricia McDougall, Scott Shane, and Benjamin Oviatt, "Explaining the Formation of International New Ventures: The Limits of Theories from International Business Research," *Journal of Business Venturing* 9, no. 6 (1994): 469–87; OECD (1997).

[10] U.S. Department of Commerce (2009), http://www.commerce.gov.

[11] World Bank, *World Development Indicators* (Washington, DC: The World Bank, 2008).

[12] Sidney Weintraub, *NAFTA at Three: A Progress Report* (Washington, DC: Center for Strategic and International Studies, 1997).

[13] Christopher Bartlett and Sumantra Ghoshal, *Transnational Management: Text, Cases, and Readings in Cross-Border Management* (Homewood, IL: Irwin, 1992).

[14] Kerry Capell, "McDonald's Offers Ethics with Those Fries," *BusinessWeek*, January 9, 2007, retrieved from http://www.businessweek.com.

Chapter 2

[1] Thomas L. Friedman, "It's a Flat World, After All," *New York Times Magazine*, April 3, 2005, pp. 33–37.

[2] *Ibid.*

[3] *Ibid.*

[4] Thomas L. Friedman, *The Lexis and the Olive Tree* (New York: Anchor Books, 2000).

[5] This discussion is based on Lawrence Beer, *Tracing the Roots of Globalization, It's Not A New Event*, unpublished manuscript, W. P. Carey School of Business, Arizona State University, 2006.

[6] The word *trade* comes from the Anglo-Saxon term *trada*, which means to walk in the footsteps of others. Ancient trade routes were the foundation for a high level of cross-cultural exchange of ideas that led to the development of religion, science, economic activity, and government. The phrase "all roads lead to Rome" is not so much a metaphorical reference to Rome's dominance of the world 2,000 years ago, but to the fact that Rome's territorial colonies were constructed as commercial resource centers to serve the needs of the Roman Empire and increase its wealth. In an empire that stretched from England to Israel and from Germany to Africa, the Romans created more than 300,000 kilometers of roads. Roman roads were the lifeblood of the state that allowed trade to flourish. The Roman Empire was so concerned with the interruption of its shipping lanes for imported goods that it dispatched army legions to protect those lanes.

In the Middle Ages, the Knights Templar acted as guardians for pilgrims making the hazardous journey to pay homage to the birthplace of the Christian religion. In addition to protecting tourists, this warrior order created the first international banking system with the use of rudimentary traveler's checks, eliminating the need for travelers to carry valuables on their person.

In 1100, Genghis Khan not only united the Mongols but created an empire beyond the Chinese border that included Korea and Japan in the East, Mesopotamia (modern day Iraq and Syria), Russia, Poland, and Hungary. He instituted common laws and regulations over his domain, most notably the preservation of private property, to enhance and protect international trade.

Arab merchants traded in spices along land routes reaching from northern Arabia across modern-day Turkey, through Asia Minor, and finally reaching China. By concealing the origins of cinnamon, pepper, cloves, and nutmeg, traders gained a monopoly and controlled prices. Europeans came to believe that the spices came from

Africa, when in fact they had merely changed hands in the region. Under the traditional trading system, spices, linen, silk, diamonds, pearls, and opium-based medicines reached Europe via indirect routes over land and sea. Representing one of the earliest systems of international distribution, the products passed through many hands on their long voyage. At every juncture, prices increased several fold. (This discussion is based on Lawrence Beer, *Ibid.*)

[7] C. Chase-Dunn, Yukio Kawano, and Benjamin D. Brewer, "World Globalization Since 1795: Waves of Integration in the World-System," *American Sociological Review* 65, no. 1 (2000): 77–95.

[8] Lawrence Franko, *The European Multinationals* (Stamford, CN: Greylock Publishers, 1976).

[9] Louis Emmerij, "Globalization, Regionalization, and World Trade," *Columbia Journal of World Business* 27, no. 2 (1992): 6–13.

[10] "The Death of Distance: A Survey of Telecommunications," *The Economist*, September 30, 1995.

[11] Company profile of Vodafone, 2007, at http://www.hoovers.com/.

[12] "The Phenomenal Growth of Vodafone: Rapid Rise through an Aggressive Leadership Style," *Strategic Direction* 19, no. 7 (2003): 25–26.

[13] "Operating Profit," *The Economist*, August 16, 2008: 74–76.

[14] Marcos Aguiar et al., *The New Global Challengers: How Top 100 Rapidly Developing Economies Are Changing the World*, Boston Consulting Group, May 25, 2006.

[15] GNI refers to the total value of goods and services produced within a country after taking into account payments made to, and income received from, other countries.

[16] Jeremy Siegel, *The Future for Investors* (New York: Crown Business, 2005).

[17] Michael E. Porter and Victor E. Millar, "How Information Gives You Competitive Advantage," *Harvard Business Review* 63 (July–August 1985): 149–60; S. Tamer Cavusgil, "Extending the Reach of E-Business," *Marketing Management* 11, no. 2 (2002): 24–29; Janice Burn and Karen Loch, "The Societal Impact of the World Wide Web—Key Challenges for the 21st Century," *Information Resources Management Journal* 14, no. 4 (2001): 4–12.

[18] Cliff Wymbs, "How E-Commerce Is Transforming and Internationalizing Service Industries," *Journal of Services Marketing* 14, no. 6 (2000): 463–71.

[19] Jack Ewing, "Upwardly Mobile in Africa," *BusinessWeek*, September 24, 2007, pp. 64–71.

[20] Dave Shellock, "Signs of Deepening Recession Dent Confidence," *Financial Times*, February 14, 2009, p. 14; Gabriele Parussini, "World News: Euro-Zone Economic Outlook Darkens," *Wall Street Journal*, January 17, 2009, p. A7.

[21] "When Fortune Frowned," *The Economist*, October 11, 2008, pp. 3–5; Shellock (2009).

[22] "A Monetary Malaise," *The Economist*, October 11, 2008, pp. 20–25.

[23] Shellock (2009); Parussini (2009).

[24] Bin Jiang, Timothy Koller, and Zane Williams, "Mapping Decline and Recovery Across Sectors," *McKinsey on Finance*, (Winter 2009): 21–25.

[25] "When Fortune Frowned," pp. 3–5; International Monetary Fund, http://www.imf.org; Shellock (2009).

[26] Martin Wolf, *Why Globalization Works* (New Haven, CN: Yale University Press, 2004).

[27] "The Day the Factories Stopped," *The Economist*, October 23, 2004, p. 70.

[28] Pete Engrail et al., "The New Global Job Shift," *BusinessWeek*, February 3, 2003, p. 50.

[29] Tara Radon and Martin Calkins, "The Struggle Against Sweatshops: Moving Toward Responsible Global Business," *Journal of Business Ethics* 66, no. 2–3 (2006): 261–69.

[30] S. L. Bachman, "The Political Economy of Child Labor and Its Impacts on International Business," *Business Economics* (July 2000): 30–41.

[31] Wolf (2004).

[32] Michael Smith, "Trade and the Environment," *International Business* 5, no. 8 (1992): 74.

[33] "Rise of the Sushi King," *Business 2.0*, December 1, 2004, p. 80.

[34] "A Glimmer of Light at Last? Africa's Economy," *The Economist*, June 24, 2006, p. 71.

[35] Dambisa Moyo, *Dead Aid* (New York: Farrar, Straus and Giroux, 2009).

[36] Moyo (2009); Robert Farzad, "Can Greed Save Africa?" *BusinessWeek*, December 10, 2007, pp. 46–54; C. K. Prahalad, *The Fortune at the Bottom of the Pyramid* (Upper Saddle River, NJ: Wharton School Publishing, 2004).

[37] Robert Farzad (2007); Organisation for Economic Co-operation and Development and African Development Bank.

Chapter 3

[1] UNCTAD, *World Investment Report 2008* (New York: United Nations, 2008).

[2] Carol Matlack, "Europe: Go East, Young Man," *BusinessWeek*, October 30, 2006, pp. 46–47.

[3] Alison Coleman, "How to Be an Expert at Export," *Financial Times*, October 26, 2005, p. 9.

[4] Farok Contractor, Chin-Chun Hsu, and Sumit Kundu, "Explaining Export Performance: A Comparative Study of International New Ventures in Indian and Taiwanese Software Industry," *Management International Review* 45, Special Issue no. 3 (2005): 83–110; G. Knight and S. T. Cavusgil, "The Born Global Firm: A Challenge to Traditional Internationalization Theory," in *Advances in International Marketing* vol. 8, ed. Tage Koed Madsen (Greenwich, CN: JAI Press, 1996): 11–26; A. Rebecca Reuber and Eileen Fischer, "The Influence of the Management Team's International Experience on the Internationalization Behaviors of SMEs," *Journal of International Business Studies* 28, no. 4 (1997): 807–19.

[5] Y. Ono, "Beer Venture of Anheuser, Kirin Goes Down Drain on Tepid Sales," *Wall Street Journal*, November 3, 1999, p. A23.

[6] C. Macdonald, "Toy Story," *Canadian Plastics* 61, no. 2 (2003): 17–18.

[7] W. Alsakini, K. Wikstrom, and J. Kiiras, "Proactive Schedule Management of Industrial Turnkey Projects in Developing Countries," *International Journal of Project Management* 22, no. 1 (2004): 75–82; Christian Hicks and Tom McGovern, "Product Life Cycle Management in Engineer-to-Order Industries," *International Journal of Technology Management*, 48, no. 2 (2009): 153–61.

[8] Peter M. Reina, "Public Funds and Turnkey Contracts Fuel Growing Global Subway Work," *ENR*, October 25, 2004, p. 32.

[9] Engineering News-Record, "The Top 225 International Contractors," August 18, 2008: 32.

[10] "Hitachi Ltd.: Joint Venture to Promote Smart-Card Operating System," *Wall Street Journal*, November 26, 2005, p. A9.

[11] D. Kealey, D. Protheroe, D. MacDonald, and T. Vulpe, "International Projects: Some Lessons on Avoiding Failure and Maximizing Success," *Performance Improvement* 45, no. 3 (2006): 38–47; H. Ren, B. Gray, and K. Kim, "Performance of International Joint Ventures: What Factors Really Make a Difference and How?," *Journal of Management* 35, no. 3 (2009): 805–14.

[12] Charles Waltner, "Cisco Forms Strategic Alliance with Fujitsu," December 5, 2004, http://www.newsroom.cisco.com/dlls/2004/prod_120604c.html; Cisco, "China's ZTE Forms Strategic Alliance with Cisco Systems," http://www.newsroom.cisco.com/dlls/2004/prod_120604c.html; Italtel, "Italtel and Cisco Systems Alliance Mission," http://www.italtel.com/ShowContent?item=1028.

[13] "Managing Global Supply Chains," *McKinsey Quarterly*, July 2008, http://www.mckinseyquarterly.com.

[14] U.S. Department of Commerce, *A Basic Guide to Exporting* (Washington, DC: U.S. Government Printing Office, 1992).

[15] S. Tamer Cavusgil, Lyn S. Amine, and Robert Weinstein, "Japanese Sogo Shosha in the U.S. Export Trading Companies," *Journal of the Academy of Marketing Science* 14, no. 3 (1986): 21–32.

[16] Andrew Rettman, "EU Welcomes New U.S. CO_2-Reduction Plan," *BusinessWeek*, April 2, 2009, http://www.businessweek.com.

[17] Dave Shellock, "Signs of Deepening Recession Dent Confidence," *Financial Times*, February 14, 2009, p. 14; Gabriele Parussini, "World News: Euro-Zone Economic Outlook Darkens," *Wall Street Journal*, January 17, 2009, p. A7.

[18] Chris Giles, "Big Ideas Fail to Mop up Europe's Current Mess," *Financial Times*, February 26, 2009, p. 2.

[19] Stanley Reed, "G-20 Summit: Thorny Issues, a Soothing Outcome?" *BusinessWeek*, 2009, http://www.businessweek.com.

[20] Harvey Morris, "Dollar Reserve Reform Urged," *Financial Times*, March 27, 2009, p. 7.

[21] "Sovereign-Wealth Funds," *The Economist*, May 24, 2007, p. 54; "Capital Markets," *The Economist*, January 17, 2008, p. 62; Nuno Fernandes and Arturo Bris, "Sovereign Wealth Revalued," *Financial Times*, February 12, 2009, http://www.ft.com.

[22] Bjorn Lomborg, "Help the Poor with Free Trade," *Forbes*, March 16, 2009, p. 12.

Chapter 4

[1] R. Rosmarin, "Mountain View Masala," *Business 2.0* (March 2005): 54–56.

[2] Howard Perlmutter, "The Tortuous Evolution of the Multinational Corporation," *Columbia Journal of World Business* 4, no. 1 (1969): 9–18.

[3] V. Govindarajan and A. Gupta, *The Quest for Global Dominance* (San Francisco: Jossey-Bass/Wiley, 2001).

[4] Robert Boyd and Peter Richerson, *Culture and Evolutionary Process* (Chicago: University of Chicago Press, 1985).

[5] Harry C. Triandis, *Culture and Social Behavior* (New York: McGraw-Hill, 1994).

[6] M. J. Herskovits, *Cultural Anthropology* (New York: Knopf, 1955).

[7] Geert Hofstede, *Culture's Consequences* (Beverly Hills, CA: Sage, 1980).

[8] Harry C. Triandis, *Culture and Social Behavior* (New York: McGraw-Hill, 1994).

[9] Vern Terpstra and Kenneth David, *The Cultural Environment of International Business*, 3rd ed. (Cincinnati, OH: Southwestern, 1991).

[10] Sengun Yeniyurt and Janell Townsend, "Does Culture Explain Acceptance of New Products in a Country? An Empirical Investigation," *International Marketing Review* 20, no. 4 (2003): 377–96; Yong Zhang and James Neelankavil, "The Influence of Culture on Advertising Effectiveness in China and the USA: A Cross-Cultural Study," *European Journal of Marketing* 31, no. 2 (1997): 134–42.

[11] "Here Comes a Whopper," *The Economist*, October 25, 2008, p. 78; David A. Griffith, Michael Y. Hu, and John K. Ryans, Jr., "Process Standardization across Intra- and Intercultural Relationships," *Journal of International Business Studies* 31, no. 2 (2000): 303–24; Thomas Head, Clara Gong, Chunhui Ma et al., "Chinese Executives' Assessment of Organization Development Interventions," *Organization Development Journal* 24, no. 1 (2006): 28–40; K. Hille, "Haier Focuses on Marketing Instead of Takeovers," *Financial Times*, February 18, 2009, p. 7; Joel D. Nicholson and Yim-Yu Wong, "Culturally Based Differences in Work Beliefs," *Management Research News* 24, no. 5 (2001): 1–10.

[12] David Aviel, "American Managers and Their Asian Counterparts," *Industrial Management* 38, no. 2 (1996): 1–2; Richard Linowes, Yoshi Tsurumi, and Toro Nakamura, "The Japanese Manager's Traumatic Entry into the United States: Understanding the American Japanese Cultural Divide; Executive Commentary," *Academy of Management Executive* 7, no. 4 (1993): 21–40.

[13] Martin Gannon and Associates, *Understanding Global Cultures: Metaphorical Journeys through 17 Countries* (Thousand Oaks, CA: Sage, 1994).

[14] Nancy Adler, *International Dimensions of Organizational Behavior* (Cincinnati, OH: South-Western, 2002).

[15] Edward T. Hall, *Beyond Culture* (New York: Anchor, 1976).

[16] Hofstede (1980).

[17] *Ibid.*

[18] Richard Priem, Leonard Love, and Margaret Shaffer, "Industrialization and Values Evolution: The Case of Hong Kong and Guangzhou, China," *Asia Pacific Journal of Management* 17, no. 3 (2000): 473–82.

[19] F. Kluckhohn and F. Strodbeck, *Variations in Value Orientations* (Evanston, IL: Row Peterson, 1961).

[20] Alice Eagly and Shelly Chaiken, *The Psychology of Attitudes* (New York: Harcourt Brace Jovanovich, 1993).

[21] Joyce Osland, Silvio De Franco, and Asbjorn Osland, "Organizational Implications of Latin American Culture: Lessons for the Expatriate Manager," *Journal of Management Inquiry* 8, no. 2 (1999): 219–38.

[22] Roger Axtell, *The Do's and Taboos of International Trade* (New York: Wiley, 1994).

[23] Meg Carter, "Muslims Offer a New Mecca for Marketers," *Financial Times,* August 11, 2005, p. 13.

[24] "Babel Runs Backwards," *The Economist,* January 1, 2005, pp. 58–60.

[25] Edward T. Hall, *The Silent Language* (Garden City, NY: Anchor, 1981).

[26] P. Dicken, *Global Shift: Transforming the World Economy* (New York: Guilford, 1998).

[27] T. Clark and D. Rajaratnam, "International Services: Perspectives at Century's End," *Journal of Services Marketing* 13, nos. 4/5 (1999): 298–302.

[28] B. Kogut, "Country Capabilities and the Permeability of Borders," *Strategic Management Journal* 12 (Summer 1991): 33–47.

[29] T. Clark, D. Rajaratnam, and T. Smith, "Toward a Theory of International Services: Marketing Intangibles in a World of Nations," *Journal of International Marketing* 4, no. 2 (1996): 9–28.

[30] S. Lorge, "Federal Express," *Sales and Marketing Management* 149, no. 11 (1997): 63.

[31] J. M. Greig, "The End of Geography? Globalization, Communications, and Culture in the International System," *The Journal of Conflict Resolution* 46, no. 2 (2002): 225–44.

[32] R. Rosmarin, "Text Messaging Gets a Translator," *Business 2.0* (March 2005): 32; Nitish Singh, Vikas Kumar, and Daniel Baack, "Adaptation of Cultural Content: Evidence from B2C E-Commerce Firms," *European Journal of Marketing* 39, nos. 1/2 (2005): 71–86.

[33] Russell Belk, "Hyperreality and Globalization: Culture in the Age of Ronald McDonald," *Journal of International Consumer Marketing* 8, nos. 3/4 (1996): 23–37.

[34] Tyler Cowen, *Creative Destruction: How Globalization Is Changing the World's Cultures* (Princeton, NJ: Princeton University Press, 2002).

[35] Laszlo Tihanyi, David A. Griffith, and Craig J. Russell, "The Effect of Cultural Distance on Entry Mode Choice, International Diversification, and MNE Performance: A Meta-Analysis," *Journal of International Business Studies* 36, no. 3 (2005): 270–83.

[36] Tomasz Lenartowicz and James P. Johnson, "A Cross-National Assessment of the Values of Latin America Managers: Contrasting Hues or Shades of Gray?" *Journal of International Business Studies* 34, no. 3 (2003): 266–81.

[37] James Johnson, Tomasz Lenartowicz, and Salvador Apud, "Cross-Cultural Competence in International Business: Toward a Definition and a Model," *Journal of International Business Studies* 37, no. 4 (2006): 525–35; Soon Ang, Linn Van Dyne, and Christine Koh, "Personality Correlates of the Four-Factor Model of Cultural Intelligence," *Group & Organization Management* 31, no. 1 (2006): 100–123.

Chapter 5

[1] We are grateful to Professor Larry Beer, Arizona State University Emeritus, for his helpful comments regarding this chapter.

[2] John Sullivan, *The Moral Compass of Companies: Business Ethics and Corporate Governance as Anti-Corruption Tools* (Washington, DC: International Finance Corporation, World Bank, 2009).

[3] O. C. Ferrell and L. Gresham, "A Contingency Framework for Understanding Ethical Decision Making in Marketing," *Journal of Marketing* 49, no. 3 (1985): 87–96; Naresh Malhotra and G. Miller, "An Integrated Model for Ethical Decisions," *Journal of Business Ethics* 17, no. 3 (1998): 263–80; D. McAlister, O. C. Ferrell, and L. Ferrell, *Business and Society* (Boston: Houghton Mifflin, 2003).

[4] Marco Celentani, Juan-Jose Ganuza, and Jose-Luis Peydros, "Combating Corruption in International Business Transactions," *Economica* 71, no. 283 (2004): 417–49; David Zussman, "Fighting Corruption Is a Global Concern," *Ottawa Citizen,* October 11, 2005, p. A15.

[5] Tara Radin and Martin Calkins, "The Struggle against Sweatshops: Moving toward Responsible Global Business," *Journal of Business Ethics* 66 (2006): 261–68.

[6] Brian Grow et al., "Bitter Pills," *Business Week,* December 18, 2006, p. 110.

[7] Transparency International, *Progress Report: OECD Anti-Bribery Convention 2009*, retrieved from http://www.transparency.org.

[8] Sarah McBride and Loretta Chao, "Disney Fights Pirates at China Affiliate," *Wall Street Journal,* November 21, 2008, p. B1; Michael Schuman and Jeffrey Ressner, "Disney's Great Leap into China," *Time,* July 18, 2005: 52–54.

[9] "Business: The Reluctant Briber," *The Economist,* November 4, 2006, p. 79; Vara Vauhini, "Russian Web Sites Offer Cheap Songs, But Piracy Is Issue," *Wall Street Journal,* January 26, 2005, p. D10.

[10] Larry Beer, *Business Ethics for the Global Business and the Global Manager: A Strategic Approach* (New York: Business Expert Press, 2010; Sheila Bonini, Lenny Lendonca, and Jeremy Oppenheim, "When Social Issues Become Strategic," *The McKinsey Quarterly* 2 (2006), retrieved from http://www.mckinseyquarterly.com; Erin Cavusgil, "Merck and Vioxx: An Examination of an Ethical Decision-Making Model," *Journal of Business Ethics* 76, no. 4 (2007): 451–61; L. Kaufmann, F. Reimann, M. Ehrgott, and J. Rauer, "Sustainable Success," *Wall Street Journal,* June 22, 2009, retrieved from http://www.wsj.com; Malhotra and Miller (1998); McAlister, Ferrell, and Ferrell (2003); Michael Porter and Mark Kramer, "Strategy & Society: The Link Between Competitive Advantage and Corporate Social Responsibility," *Harvard Business Review,* December 2006, pp. 178–92.

[11] Sullivan (2009); Alan Muller and Ans Kolk, "Extrinsic and Intrinsic Drivers of Corporate Social Performance: Evidence from Foreign and Domestic Firms in Mexico," *Journal of Management Studies* 47, no. 1 (2010): 1–26.

[12] Ferrell and Gresham (1985); McAlister, Ferrell, and Ferrell (2003).

[13] Beer (2010); United Nations Conference on Trade and Development (UNCTAD), *World Investment Report 2009* (New York: UNCTAD, 2009).

[14] Transparency International (2009).

[15] Beer (2010).

[16] Alan Muller and Gail Whiteman, "Exploring the Geography of Corporate Philanthropic Disaster Response: A Study of Fortune Global 500 Firms," *Journal of Business Ethics* 84, no. 4 (2009): 589–603; UNCTAD (2009); N. Isdell, *21st Century Capitalism,* speech to Council on Foreign Relations, New York, 2009, retrieved from http://fora.tv/2009/03/06/Neville_Isdell_ 21st_Century_Capitalism; K. Rehbein, S. Waddock, and S. Graves, "Understanding Shareholder Activism: Which Corporations Are Targeted?" *Business and Society* 43, no. 3 (2004): 239–67.

[17] Nanette Byrnes and Frederik Balfour, "Philip Morris Unbound," *BusinessWeek,* May 4, 2009, pp. 39–42; Betsy McKay, "Where There's Smoke: Emerging World," *Wall Street Journal,* February 7, 2008, pp. B1–B2.

[18] V. Agarwal and Krishna Pokharel, "India's Populists Resist Big Retail; Fear of Chains Displacing Local Shops Stirs Backlash in Rapidly Growing Market," *Wall Street Journal,* October 9, 2007, p. A6; Chip Cummins, "Shell, Chevron to Cut Deliveries of Oil amid Protests in Nigeria," *Wall Street Journal,* December 23, 2004, p. A2; Stephen Fidler and John Labate, "Sudan Ties Jeopardise Chinese Oil Listing," *Financial Times,* October 6, 1999, p. 8; U. Idemudia, "Oil Extraction and Poverty Reduction in the Niger Delta: A Critical Examination of Partnership Initiatives," *Journal of Business Ethics* 90 (May 2009): 91–116; Kris Maher, "Wal-Mart Tops Global Agenda for Labor Leaders," *Wall Street Journal,* August 18, 2005, p. A2.

[19] UNCTAD (2009).

[20] Center for Corporate Citizenship, "In Good Company: Motorola," Boston College, Carroll School of Management, 2007, retrieved from http://www.bcccc.net.

[21] S. Bachman, "The Political Economy of Child Labor and Its Impacts on International Business," *Business Economics,* July 2000, pp. 30–41; C. Bhattacharya, S. Sen, and D. Korschun, "Using Corporate Social Responsibility to Win the War for Talent," *MIT Sloan Management Review* 49, no. 2 (2008): 37–44; V. Friedman, "Luxury Brands Fail to Make Ethical Grade," *Financial Times,* November 29, 2007, p. 2; M. Orlitzky, F. Schmidt, and S. Rynes, "Corporate Social and Financial Performance: A Meta-analysis," *Organization Studies* 24, no. 3 (2003), pp. 403–41; Porter and Kramer (2006); Transparency International (2009); R. Trudel and J. Cotte, "Does Being Ethical Pay?" *Wall Street Journal,* May 12, 2008, p. R4.

[22] Beer (2010); Philip Kotler and Nancy Lee, *Up and Out of Poverty: The Social Marketing Solution* (Upper Saddle River, NJ: Wharton School Publishing, 2009); Hildy Teegen, Jonathan Doh, and Sushil Vachani, "The Importance of Nongovernmental Organizations (NGOs) in Global Governance and Value Creation: An International Business Research Agenda," *Journal of International Business Studies* 35, no. 4 (2004): 463–83.

[23] "Green Is Good," *Fortune,* April 2, 2007, pp. 43–56.

[24] Transparency International (2009).

[25] Jo Johnson and Aline van Duyn, "Forced Child Labour Claims Hit Clothes Retailers," *Financial Times,* October 29, 2007, p. 3; Kaufmann, Reimann, Ehrgott, and Rauer (2009); Nancy Landrum and Sandra Edwards, *Sustainable Business: An Executive's Primer* (New York: Business Expert Press, 2009).

[26] Daniel Vermeer and Robert Clemen, "Why Sustainability Is Still Going Strong," *Financial Times,* February 12, 2009, retrieved from http://www.ft.com.

[27] Bonini, Lendonca, and Oppenheim (2006); Muller and Kolk (2010).

[28] Ferrell and Gresham (1985); T. Low, L. Ferrell, and P. Mansfield, "A Review of Empirical Studies Assessing Ethical Decision Making in Business," *Journal of Business Ethics* 25, no. 3 (2000): 185–204; Malhotra and Miller (1998); McAlister, Ferrell, and Ferrell (2003).

[29] Sullivan (2009).

[30] This framework appeared originally in *Issues in Ethics* 1, no. 2 (1988). It was developed at the Markkula Center for Applied Ethics at Santa Clara University, California. See also: Bonini, Lendonca, and Oppenheim (2006); Cavusgil (2007); Ferrell and Gresham (1985); Low, Ferrell, and Mansfield (2000); Malhotra and Miller (1998); McAlister, Ferrell, and Ferrell (2003); UNCTAD, *World Investment Report* 2006 (New York: UNCTAD, 2006); Sullivan (2009).

[31] Transparency International (2009).

[32] Vermeer and Clemen (2009).

[33] Beer (2010).

[34] *Ibid.*

Chapter 6

[1] We thank Professors Attila Yaprak, Wayne State University, and Heechun Kim, Georgia State University, for their helpful comments on this chapter.

[2] David Ricardo, *Principles of Political Economy and Taxation* (London: Everyman Edition, 1911; first published in 1817).

[3] John Romalis, "Factor Proportions and the Structure of Commodity Trade," *The American Economic Review* 94, no. 1 (2004): 6–97.

[4] Raymond Vernon, "International Investment and International Trade in the Product Cycle," *Quarterly Journal of Economics* 80 (May 1966): 190–207.

[5] Michael Porter, *The Competitive Advantage of Nations* (New York: Free Press, 1990).

[6] Mourad Dakhli and Dirk De Clercq, "Human Capital, Social Capital, and Innovation: A Multi-Country Study," *Entrepreneurship and Regional Development* 16, no. 2 (2004), 10–115.

[7] Richard Nelson and Sidney Winter, *An Evolutionary Theory of Economic Change* (Cambridge, MA: Belknap Press, 1982).

[8] Barry Jaruzelski and Kevin Dehoff, "Beyond Borders: The Global Innovation 1000," *Strategy+Business* 53 (2008): 52–67.

[9] Chalmers Johnson, *MITI and the Japanese Miracle: The Growth of Industrial Policy, 1925–1975* (Stanford, CA: Stanford University Press, 1982).

[10] Clyde Prestowitz, *Trading Places* (New York: Basic Books, 1989); Lester Thurow, *Head to Head: The Coming Economic Battle Among Japan, Europe, and America* (New York: William Morrow, 1992).

[11] "The Luck of the Irish: A Survey of Ireland," *The Economist*, special section, October 16, 2004.

[12] "The Party Is Definitely Over: Ireland's Economy," *The Economist*, March 21, 2009, p. 51.

[13] Warren Bilkey, "An Attempted Integration of the Literature on the Export Behavior of Firms," *Journal of International Business Studies* 9 (Summer 1978): 3–46; S. Tamer Cavusgil, "On the Internationalization Process of Firms," *European Research* 8, no. 6 (1980): 27–81; Jan Johanson and Jan-Erik Vahlne, "The Internationalization Process of the Firm—A Model of Knowledge Development and Increasing Foreign Commitments," *Journal of International Business Studies* 8 (Spring/Summer 1977): 2–32.

[14] Warren Bilkey, "An Attempted Integration of the Literature on the Export Behavior of Firms," *Journal of International Business Studies* 9 (Summer 1978): 3–46; S. Tamer Cavusgil, "On the Internationalization Process of Firms," *European Research* 8, no. 6 (1980): 27–81; Jan Johanson and Jan-Erik Vahlne, "The Internationalization Process of the Firm—A Model of Knowledge Development and Increasing Foreign Commitments," *Journal of International Business Studies* 8 (Spring/Summer 1977): 2–32.

[15] *Sony History*, 2009, retrieved from http://www.sony.net/Fun/SH.

[16] G. Knight and S. T. Cavusgil, "The Born Global Firm: A Challenge to Traditional Internationalization Theory," in *Advances in International Marketing*, vol. 8, ed. S. T. Cavusgil and T. Madsen (Greenwich, CT: JAI Press, 1996), pp. 11–26.

[17] S. T. Cavusgil and Gary Knight, *Born Global Firms: A New International Enterprise*, New York: Business Expert Press, 2009; Gary Knight and S. T. Cavusgil, "Innovation, Organizational Capabilities, and the Born-Global Firm," *Journal of International Business Studies* 35, no. 2 (2004): 12–41; Benjamin Oviatt and Patricia McDougall, "Toward a Theory of International New Ventures," *Journal of International Business Studies* 25, no. 1 (1994): 4–64; Michael Rennie, "Born Global," *McKinsey Quarterly* no. 4 (1993): 4–52.

[18] UNCTAD, *World Investment Report*, United Nations, New York, 2008, retrieved from http://www.unctad.org.

[19] Stephen Hymer, *The International Operations of National Firms* (Cambridge, MA: MIT Press, 1976).

[20] Peter Buckley and Mark Casson, *The Future of the Multinational Enterprise* (London: MacMillan, 1976); John Dunning, "The Eclectic Paradigm of International Production: A Restatement and Some Possible Extensions," *Journal of International Business Studies*, 19 (1988): 1–31.

[21] Dunning (1988).

[22] Dunning (1988).

[23] John Dunning, *International Production and the Multinational Enterprise* (London: Allen and Unwin, 1981); Bruce Kogut, "Joint Ventures: Theoretical and Empirical Perspectives," *Strategic Management Journal* 9 (1988): 319–332; P. Rajan Varadarajan and Margaret H. Cunningham, "Strategic Alliances: A Synthesis of Conceptual Foundations," *Journal of the Academy of Marketing Science* 23 (1995): 282–296.

[24] "For Starbucks, There's No Place Like Home," *BusinessWeek*, June 9, 2003, p. 48.

[25] James Lincoln, Christina Ahmadjian, and Eliot Mason, "Organizational Learning and Purchase-Supply Relations in Japan," *California Management Review* 40 no. 3 (1998): 244–64.

[26] Hakan Hakansson, *International Marketing and Purchasing of Industrial Goods: An Interaction Approach* (New York: Wiley, 1982).

[27] *Ibid.*

Chapter 7

[1] Jack Ewing, "Germany: A Cold Shoulder for Coca-Cola," *BusinessWeek*, May 2, 2005, p. 52.

[2] "Country Risk," *The Economist*, February 26, 2005, p. 102.

[3] "Getting Past Yukos," *BusinessWeek*, September 13, 2004, p. 52.

[4] S. Tamer Cavusgil, Pervez Ghauri, and Milind Agarwal, *Doing Business in Emerging Markets* (Thousand Oaks, CA: Sage, 2002).

[5] Steven Soper, *Totalitarianism: A Conceptual Approach* (Lanham, MD: University Press of America, 1985); Carl J. Friedrich and Zbigniew Brzezinski, *Totalitarian Dictatorship and Autocracy*, 2nd ed. (Cambridge, MA: Harvard University Press, 1965).

[6] Milton Friedman and Rose Friedman, *Free to Choose* (New York: Harcourt Brace Jovanovich, 1980).

[7] Joseph Johnson and Gerald Tellis, "Drivers of Success for Market Entry into China and India," *Journal of Marketing* 72 (May 2008): 1–13.

[8] Martin Schnitzer and James Nordyke, *Comparative Economic Systems* (Cincinnati, OH: Southwestern, 1983); Milton Friedman, "The Battle's Half Won," *Wall Street Journal*, December 9, 2004, p. A16; Statistical Abstract of the United States, Economics and Statistics Administration (Washington, DC: U.S. Census Bureau, 2004).

[9] Christopher Swan, "$400 Billion Industry: Japan's First Islamic Bond," *Bloomberg*, April 2007; Maha Khan Phillips, "Doing God's Work; Islamic Finance Is Meant to Reconcile Both Commercial and Religious Ideals," *Wall Street Journal*, March 1, 2010, retrieved from http://www.wsj.com; The Pew Forum, "Mapping the Global Muslim Population," 2009, retrieved from http://pewforum.org.

[10] Phyllis Berman, "The Three Marketeers," *Forbes*, July 25, 2005, p. 78.

[11] Raman Kumar, William Lamb, and Richard Wokutch, "The End of the South African Sanctions, Institutional Ownership, and the Stock Price Performance of Boycotted Firms," *Business and Society* 41, no. 2 (2002): 133–65.

[12] Seth Lubove, "Gas Attack," *Forbes*, May 23, 2005, pp. 54–56.

[13] Sharon Begley, "Good Cop/Bad Cop Goes Green," *Newsweek*, May 4, 2009, retrieved from http://www.newsweek.com.

[14] P. Green, "Risky Business," *Global Finance*, October 2008, pp. 38–39.

[15] J. Blas and C. Hoyos, "Oil Wrestling," *Financial Times*, May 5, 2006, p. 15.

[16] Charles Forelle, "EU Investigates Breakup of Fortis," *Wall Street Journal*, April 9, 2009, p. C3; Patrick Jenkins and Kiran Stacey, "Bank 'Brainstorm' Marks Loan Drive," *Financial Times*, July 1, 2010, p. 2.

[17] David Wernick and Sumit Kundu, "Terrorism, Political Risk and International Business: Conceptual Considerations," in *Proceedings: 2008 Annual Conference, Academy of International Business* (East Lansing, MI: Academy of International Business, 2008).

[18] *Ibid.*

[19] Jason Bush, "Russia's Raiders," *BusinessWeek*, June 16, 2008, pp. 67–71.

[20] N. Vardi, "Power Putsch," *Forbes*, June 2, 2008, pp. 84–92.

[21] V. Nair, "Tata Nano, World's Cheapest Car, Won't Help Pay Debt," *Bloomberg*, 2009, retrieved from http://www.bloomberg.com.

[22] Yonah Alexander, David Valton, and Paul Wilkinson, *Terrorism: Theory and Practice* (Boulder, CO: Westview, 1979).

[23] M. Srivastava and N. Lakshman, "How Risky Is India?" *BusinessWeek*, December 4, 2008, retrieved from http://www.businessweek.com.

[24] Jonathan Laing, "Aftershock," *Barron's*, September 9, 2002, p. 23.

[25] Cavusgil, Ghauri, and Agarwal (2002).

[26] J. Fox, "New World Order," *Time*, February 16, 2009, p. 29; "Krise des Bankensystems: Zu viel Finanzinnovationen, zu wenig Regulierung?" *Ifo Schnelldienst*, November 14, 2008, pp. 3–15; Laura Kodres, "What Is to Be Done," *Finance & Development*, March 2009, pp. 23–27.

[27] International Chamber of Commerce, "Policy Statement: Extraterritoriality and Business," July 13, 2006.

[28] Kurt Stanberry, Barbara C. George, and Maria Ross, "Securities Fraud in the International Arena," *Business and Society* 30, no. 1 (1991): 27–36.

[29] Randall Hess and Edgar Kossack, "Bribery as an Organizational Response to Conflicting Environmental Expectations," *Academy of Marketing Science* 9, no. 3 (1981): 206–26; Judith Scott, Debora Gilliard, and Richard Scott, "Eliminating Bribery as a Transnational Marketing Strategy," *International Journal of Commerce & Management* 12, no. 1 (2002): 1–17.

[30] Alan Field, "Long Arm, Getting Longer," *Journal of Commerce*, December 21, 2009, p. 2; Dionne Searcey, "Small-Scale Bribes Targeted by OECD," *Wall Street Journal*, December 10, 2009, p. A4.

[31] Hank Boerner, "Europe Faces Eagle Eye of U.S. Financial Regulation," *European Business Forum* 21 (2005): 46–49.

Chapter 8

[1] Jeffrey D. Sachs and Andrew Warner, "Economic Reform and the Process of Global Integration," *Brookings Papers on Economic Activity*, Issue no. 1 (Washington, DC: Brookings Institute, 1995); Heritage Foundation, retrieved from the Heritage Foundation Web site at http://www.heritage.org/research/features/index/.

[2] David Dollar and Aart Kraay, "Trade, Growth, and Poverty," Policy Research Working Paper no. WPS 2615, June 2001, Washington, DC: World Bank, Development Research Group; United Nations, *World Economic and Social Survey*, 2005, retrieved from http://www.un.org.

[3] "Bush Move Marks U.S. Trade Policy Turning Point," *Financial Times*, March 6, 2002, p. 6.

[4] Jim Carlton, "U.S. Nears Mexican Cement Pact," *Wall Street Journal*, August 29, 2005, p. A7.

[5] Stefanie Lenway, Kathleen Rehbein, and Laura Starks, "The Impact of Protectionism on Firm Wealth: The Experience of the Steel Industry," *Southern Economic Journal* 56, no. 4 (1990): 1079–93.

[6] G. Chazan and G. White, "Kremlin Weighs on Growth," *Wall Street Journal*, October 17, 2005, p. A16.

[7] Robert Reich, *The Work of Nations: Preparing Ourselves for 21st Century Capitalism* (New York: Knopf, 1991); Lester Thurow, *Head to Head: The Coming Economic Battle among Japan, Europe, and America* (New York: William Morrow, 1992).

[8] United Nations, 2009, retrieved from the United Nations Web site on financial statistics at http://www.un.org/reports/financing/profile.htm.

[9] World Trade Organization, *Tariff Profile* on the European Union, 2009, retrieved from http://www.wto.org.; Dustin Smith, "The Truth about Industrial Country Tariffs," *Finance and Development* 39, no. 3 (2002), Washington, DC, International Monetary Fund, retrieved from http://www.imf.org.

[10] "Textiles: Knickers in a Twist," *The Economist*, August 27, 2005, p. 50.

[11] Jessica Vascellaro and Loretta Chao, "Google Defies China on Web: Search Giant Stops Censoring Its Results," *Wall Street Journal*, March 23, 2010, p. A1.

[12] World Bank, *Doing Business: Benchmarking Business Regulations*, 2009, retrieved from http://www.doingbusiness.org.

[13] U.S. Trade Representative, "National Trade Estimate Report," 2009, retrieved from http://www.ustr.gov.

[14] Frederik Balfour, "The State's Long Apron Strings," *BusinessWeek*, August 22, 2005, p. 74.

[15] M. Kripalani, "India Takes a Bath on Oil Subsidies," *BusinessWeek*, June 16, 2008, p. 36.

[16] World Trade Organization, Glossary, 2009, retrieved from http://www.wto.org.

[17] *Ibid.*

[18] "World Trade: Barriers to Entry," *The Economist*, December 20, 2008, p. 121.

[19] William Beach and Marc Miles, "Explaining the Factors of the Index of Economic Freedom," *2005 Index of Economic Freedom* (Washington, DC: Heritage Foundation), retrieved from http://www.heritage.org.

[20] Heritage Foundation, *2010 Index of Economic Freedom* (Washington, DC: Heritage Foundation), retrieved from http://www.heritage.org.

[21] Smith (2002).

22 C. Giles, "Big Ideas Fail to Mop Up Europe's Current Mess," *Financial Times*, February 26, 2009, p. 2.

23 United Nations Conference on Trade and Development, *The Global Economic Crisis: Systemic Failures and Multilateral Remedies* (Geneva, Switzerland: United Nations, 2009).

24 G. Rachman, "When Globalisation Goes into Reverse," *Financial Times*, February 2, 2009, retrieved from http://www.ft.com.

25 J. Miller, "Nations Rush to Establish New Barriers to Trade," *Wall Street Journal*, February 6, 2009, pp. A1, A6.

26 R. Wright, "Financial Crises and Reform: Looking Back for Clues to the Future," *The McKinsey Quarterly*, December 2008.

27 "In the Shadow of Prosperity," *The Economist*, January 20, 2007, pp. 32–34.

28 N. King, "Tale of the Tuna: Grocery Rivalry Fuels Tariff Spat," *Wall Street Journal*, April 20, 2002, p. B1.

29 Militiades Chacholidades, *International Economics* (New York: McGraw-Hill, 1990); James Ingram, *International Economics* (New York: Wiley, 1983); William McDaniel and Edgar Kossack, "The Financial Benefits to Users of Foreign-Trade Zones," *Columbia Journal of World Business* 18, no. 3 (1983): 33–41.

30 Eugene Salorio, Jean Boddewyn, and Nicolas Dahan, "Integrating Business Political Behavior with Economic and Organizational Strategies," *International Studies of Management & Organization* 35, no. 2 (2005): 28–35; Scott Kennedy, "The Barbarians Learn How to Lobby at the Gates of Industry," *Financial Times*, September 28, 2005, p. 5.

Chapter 9

1 Bela Balassa, *The Theory of Economic Integration* (Homewood, IL: Irwin, 1961); Jacob Viner, *The Customs Union Issue* (New York: Carnegie Endowment for International Peace, 1950).

2 J. Crawford and R. Fiorentino, *The Changing Landscape of Regional Trade Agreements*, Discussion Paper no. 8 (Geneva, Switzerland: World Trade Organization, 2005).

3 European Union, Web site at http://europa.eu.

4 "Transformed: EU Membership Has Worked Magic in Central Europe," *The Economist*, June 25, 2005, pp. 6–8.

5 "European Carmakers: Driving Out of the East," *The Economist*, March 5, 2005, p. 60.

6 R. Smyser, "The Core of the Global Economy," *The World & I*, April 2001, pp. 26–31.

7 World Trade Organization, 2009 statistics from the WTO Web site at http://www.wto.org.

8 "Happy Birthday, NAFTA," *BusinessWeek*, December 22, 2003, p. 112.

9 Alan Rugman, *The End of Globalization: Why Global Strategy Is a Myth and How to Profit from the Realities of Regional Markets* (New York: American Management Association, 2001).

10 P. Engardio, "This Would Be Bigger than NAFTA," *BusinessWeek*, October 27, 2008, p. 66.

11 Central Intelligence Agency, *CIA World Factbook*, 2009, retrieved from http://www.cia.gov/library/publications/the-world-factbook.

12 George Garman and Debora Gilliard, "Economic Integration in the Americas: 1975–1992," *The Journal of Applied Business Research* 14, no. 3 (1998): 1–12.

13 Viner (1950); Franklin Root, *International Trade and Investment*, 5th ed. (Cincinnati, OH: South-Western Publishing, 1984); Emile Dreuil, James Anderson, Walter Block, and Michael Saliba, "The Trade Gap: The Fallacy of Anti World-Trade Sentiment," *Journal of Business Ethics* 45, no. 3 (2003): 269–78.

14 EIU ViewsWire, "Ukraine Politics: The Viktor and Yulia Show, Continued," April 24, 2009, retrieved from http://viewswire.eiu.com; Oleg Riabokon, "Trade Liberalization for the Second Largest Country in Europe: Going West or East or Can It Be Both?" *Journal of World Trade*, February 2006: 69–112.

15 "A Divided Union," *The Economist*, September 23, 2004, p. 64.

16 Subhash Jain and John K. Ryans, "A Normative Framework for Assessing Marketing Strategy Implications of Europe 1992," in *Euromarketing*, E. Kaynak and P. Ghauri, eds. (New York: International Business Press, 1994).

17 "Transformed: EU Membership Has Worked Magic in Central Europe," *The Economist*, June 25, 2005, pp. 6–8.

18 "Beyond Doha," *The Economist*, October 11, 2008, pp. 30–33.

19 "The EU and India," *Financial Times*, September 23, 2008, p. 12; "Odd Man Out," *Forbes*, November 17, 2008, p. 20.

20 European Union Web site at http://europa.eu.

Chapter 10

1 "The Luck of the Irish: A Survey of Ireland," *The Economist*, October 16, 2004, pp. 4–6.

2 World Bank, *World Bank Development Indicators* (Washington, DC: World Bank, 2009).

3 *Ibid.*

4 World Bank, *Doing Business: Benchmarking Business Regulations*, 2009, retrieved from http://www.doingbusiness.org.

5 Jack Behrman and Dennis Rondinelli, "The Transition to Market-Oriented Economies in Central and Eastern Europe," *European Business Journal* 12 (2000): 87–99.

6 M. Bartiromo, "Power Player Naguib Sawiris," *BusinessWeek*, December 8, 2008, p. 23; Profile of Orascom at http://www.hoovers.com; Stanley Reed, "This Mobile Upstart Really Gets Around," *BusinessWeek*, July 31, 2006, p. 49.

7 "Creative Destruction," *Forbes*, April 21, 2008, p. 170; "Fortune Global 500" for 2008, *Fortune*, retrieved from http://money.cnn.com/magazines/fortune/global500.

8 "Britain's Lonely High-Flier," January 10, 2009, *The Economist*, pp. 60–61.

9 "Two Billion More Bourgeois: The Middle Class in Emerging Markets," *The Economist*, February 14, 2009, p. 18.

10 Michael Deneen and Andrew Gross, "The Global Market for Power Tools," *Business Economics*, July 2006, pp. 66–73.

11 L. Lee, "Thank Heaven for Emerging Markets," *BusinessWeek*, January 7, 2008, pp. 62–63.

12 "Racing Down the Pyramid," *The Economist*, November 15, 2008, p. 76.

13 S. Tamer Cavusgil and Lyn S. Amine, "Demand Estimation in a Developing Country Environment: Difficulties, Techniques, and Examples," *Journal of the Market Research Society* 28 (1986): 43–65.

14 "Big Mac Index," *The Economist*, February 4, 2009, retrieved from http://www.economist.com.

[15] The "percent of income held by middle class" refers to the percentile distribution of income in a nation. In particular, it represents the proportion of national income earned by the middle 60 percentile of the population when the top 20 percentile (the wealthiest) and the bottom 20 percentile (the poorest) are excluded. For example, the middle class—60 percent of the population sandwiched between the wealthiest and the poorest—in Brazil accounted for only 35 percent of national income, suggesting a relatively unequal distribution of national income.

[16] Surjit Bhalla, *Second among Equals: The Middle Class Kingdoms of India and China* (Washington, DC: Peterson Institute for International Economics, Washington, forthcoming); "Burgeoning Bourgeoisie: A Special Report on the New Middle Classes in Emerging Markets," *The Economist*, February 14, 2009, Special Section.

[17] Ariel Cohen, "Putin's Crisis: Dealing with Russia's Political Upheaval," WebMemo #671, February 20, 2005, retrieved from http://www.doingbusiness.org; World Bank, *Doing Business 2010* (Washington, DC: The World Bank, 2010).

[18] United States Trade Representative, *National Trade Estimate Report on Foreign Trade Barriers*, 2006, retrieved from http://www.ustr.gov.

[19] World Bank, *Doing Business 2009* (Washington, DC: The World Bank, 2009).

[20] World Bank, *Doing Business in China 2008* (Washington, DC: The World Bank, 2008).

[21] Transparency International, *Corruption Perceptions Index 2009*, retrieved from http://www.transparency.org.

[22] "Creaking, Groaning: Infrastructure Is India's Biggest Handicap," *The Economist*, December 13, 2008, pp. 11–13.

[23] M. Valente and A. Crane, "Private, but Public," *Wall Street Journal*, March 23, 2009, p. R6.

[24] Daekwan Kim, Destan Kandemir, and S. Tamer Cavusgil, "The Role of Family Conglomerates in Emerging Markets: What Western Companies Should Know," *Thunderbird International Business Review* 46 (2004): 13–20.

[25] A. Bhattacharya and D. Michael, "How Local Companies Keep Multinationals at Bay," *Harvard Business Review*, March 2008, pp. 85–95.

[26] Peter Marsh, "Toyota Gears Up for Production Drive in India," *Financial Times*, March 5, 2007, p. 21.

[27] G. Edmondson, "Renault's Race to Replace the Rickshaw," *BusinessWeek*, 2007, retrieved from http://www.businessweek.com.

[28] "The World of the Internet," *Business 2.0*, August 2007, pp. 20–21.

[29] Ted London and Stuart Hart, "Reinventing Strategies for Emerging Markets: Beyond the Transnational Model," *Journal of International Business Studies* 35 (2004): 350–63; Valente & Crane (2009).

[30] A. Bhattacharya and D. Michael, "How Local Companies Keep Multinationals at Bay," *Harvard Business Review*, March 2008, pp. 85–95.

[31] Jeffrey Garten, *The Big Ten: The Big Emerging Markets and How They Will Change Our Lives* (New York: Basic Books, 1997); G. Kolodko, ed., *Emerging Market Economics: Global-ization and Development* (Aldershot, Hants, England: Ashgate, 2003); Kim, Kandemir, and Cavusgil (2004).

[32] Pete Engardio, "Emerging Giants," *BusinessWeek*, July 31, 2006, pp. 40–49.

[33] C. K. Prahalad, "Aid Is Not the Answer," *Wall Street Journal*, August 31, 2005, p. A8; C. K. Prahalad, *The Fortune at the Bottom of the Pyramid: Eradicating Poverty Through Profits* (Philadelphia: Wharton School Books, 2005).

[34] M. Bahree, "Cheaper Sleeper," *Forbes*, October 13, 2009, p. 100.

[35] International Telecommunications Union, "Africa Has 300 Million Mobile Phone Subscribers," 2009 press release retrieved from http://www.itu.int; "Mobile Phone Growth Biggest in Africa," *African Business*, April 2009, p. 8.

[36] Brigit Helms, *Access for All: Building Inclusive Financial Systems* (Washington, DC: The World Bank, 2006).

[37] Jay Greene, "Taking Tiny Loans to the Next Level," *BusinessWeek*, November 27, 2006, pp. 76–82; Muhammad Yunus, *Creating a World Without Poverty* (New York: PublicAffairs, 2009).

[38] Christopher Beshouri, "A Grassroots Approach to Emerging-Market Consumers," *The McKinsey Quarterly* 4 (2006), retrieved from http://www.mckinseyquarterly.com.

[39] "Opportunity Knocks," *The Economist*, October 11, 2008, pp. 33–35.

[40] "Opportunity Knocks" (2008); R. Farzad, "Can Greed Save Africa?" *BusinessWeek*, December 10, 2007, pp. 46–54.

[41] Farzad (2007); J. Nocera, "Diamonds Are Forever in Botswana," *New York Times*, August 9, 2008, p. C1.

[42] L. Enriquez, S. Schmitgen, and G. Sun, "The True Value of Mobile Phones to Developing Markets," *McKinsey Quarterly*, February, 2007, retrieved from http://www.mckinseyquarterly.com; J. Ewing, "Upwardly Mobile in Africa," *BusinessWeek*, September 24, 2007, pp. 64–71.

[43] Farzad (2007).

[44] M. Conway, S. Gupta, and K. Khajavi, "Addressing Africa's Health Workforce Crisis," *McKinsey Quarterly*, November 2007, retrieved from http://www.mckinseyquarterly.com.

[45] Dambisa Moyo, *When Help Does Harm* (New York: Farrar, Straus and Giroux, 2009); D. Zeng, ed., *Knowledge, Technology, and Cluster-Based Growth in Africa* (Washington, DC: The World Bank Group, 2008).

Chapter 11

[1] C. Belton, "Moscow Sees End to Capital Flight as Rouble Stabilises," *Financial Times*, February 27, 2007, p. 3; "The Chavez Play; Venezuela and Argentina," *The Economist*, October 28, 2006, p. 109; "The Weakening of the 'Strong Bolivar'; Venezuela's Devaluation," *The Economist*, January 16, 2010, p. 39; J. Lyons, "Polo-Loving Banker Lives Really Large in Chavez Socialism," *Wall Street Journal*, January 29, 2008, p. A1.

[2] *Federal Reserve Bulletin*, various years, at http://www.federalreserve.gov.

[3] "E-Shoppers of the World Unite—Around the Weak Greenback," *BusinessWeek*, December 24, 2007, p. 21;

Bradley Davis, "Euro Touches a Nine-Month High on the Dollar," *Wall Street Journal*, September 15, 2009, p. C2.

[4] Richard Ajayi and Mbodja Mougoue, "On the Dynamic Relation between Stock Prices and Exchange Rates," *The Journal of Financial Research* 19 (1996): 193–207.

[5] Kenneth Maxwell, "Wii Sales Slump Hits Nintendo," *Wall Street Journal*, July 31, 2009, p. B5.

[6] "Pakistan Economy: Crisis Averted?" *EIU ViewsWire*, July 10, 2009; "Pakistan," *Oxford Economic Country Briefings*, December 3, 2008, pp. 1–5.

[7] Abdul-Hamid Sukar and Seid Hassan, "U.S. Exports and Time-Varying Volatility of Real Exchange Rate," *Global Finance Journal* 12 (2001): 109–14.

[8] Josef Brada, Ali Kutan, and Su Zhou, "The Exchange Rate and the Balance of Trade: The Turkish Experience," *The Journal of Development Studies* 33 (1997): 675–84.

[9] International Monetary Fund, *Global Financial Stability Report*, 2004, retrieved from http://www.imf.org.

[10] U.S. Department of the Treasury, *Report on Foreign Portfolio Holdings of U.S. Securities*, April 2009, retrieved from http://www.treas.gov.

[11] Alan Greenspan, "The Globalization of Finance," *The Cato Journal* 17 (1997), retrieved from http://www.cato.org.

[12] International Monetary Fund, "Effects of Financial Globalization on Developing Countries: Some Empirical Evidence," 2003, retrieved from http://www.imf.org.

[13] T. Mahalingam, "East Meets Western Union: Remittances to India Could Hit $35 Billion in 2007," *Business Today*, March 23, 2008, p. 12; Adam Thomson, "Families Struggle to Survive as Flow of Dollars Dries Up," *Financial Times*, August 19, 2009, p. 4.

[14] "Telcos Offer Incentives to Lure Bond Investors," *Corporate Finance*, July 2000, p. 4.

[15] "Open Wider: A Survey of International Banking," *The Economist*, May 21, 2005, special section.

[16] "AFRICA: Mobile Banking Prospects Remain Positive," Oxford Analytica Daily Brief Service, October 3, 2008, p. 1; Moin Siddiqi, "Banking in Africa," *African Business*, April 2000, pp. 25–27.

[17] Bank for International Settlements, *Consultative Document: The New Basel Capital Accord*, 2001, retrieved from http://www.bis.org.

[18] International Monetary Fund, *Financial Statements*, for the years ending April 30, 2009, and April 30, 2010, retrieved from http://www.imf.org.

Chapter 12

[1] S. Tamer Cavusgil, Sengun Yeniyurt, and Janell Townsend, "The Framework of a Global Company: A Conceptualization and Preliminary Validation," *Industrial Marketing Management* 33 (2004): 711–16; G. T. Hult, S. Deligonul, and S. Tamer Cavusgil, "The Hexagon of Market-Based Globalization: An Empirical Approach Towards Delineating the Extent of Globalization in Companies," in *New Perspectives in International Business Thought*, A. Lewin, ed. (London: Palgrave, 2006); George Yip, *Total Global Strategy II* (Upper Saddle River, NJ: Prentice Hall, 2003).

[2] Christopher A. Bartlett and Sumantra Ghoshal, *Managing Across Borders: The Transnational Solution* (Boston, MA: Harvard Business School Press, 1989).

[3] Christopher A. Bartlett and Sumantra Ghoshal, *Transnational Management: Text, Cases, and Readings in Cross-Border Management*, 3rd ed. (Boston, MA: Irwin/McGraw-Hill, 2000), p. 273.

[4] *Ibid.*

[5] Bruce Kogut, "Designing Global Strategies: Profiting from Operational Flexibility," *Strategic Management Journal* 27 (1985): 27–38.

[6] L. Bryan and D. Farrell, "Leading through Uncertainty," *The McKinsey Quarterly*, December 2008, retrieved from http://www.mckinseyquarterly.com.

[7] Cavusgil, Yeniyurt, and Townsend (2004); Hult, Deligonul, and Cavusgil (2006); Yip (2003).

[8] Hult, Deligonul, and Cavusgil (2006); Ben L. Kedia and Akuro Mukherji, "Global Managers: Developing a Mindset for Global Competitiveness," *Journal of World Business* 34 (1999): 230–51; Robert Waterman, Tom Peters, and J. R. Philips, "Structure Is Not Organization," *Business Horizons* 23, no. 3 (1980): 14–26.

[9] Haig Simonian, "Climber Scales the Health Peak," *Financial Times*, August 21, 2006, p. 8.

[10] Stephen Rhinesmith, *A Manager's Guide to Globalization* (Homewood, IL: Business One Irwin, 1998).

[11] Gary A. Knight and S. Tamer Cavusgil, "Innovation, Organizational Capabilities, and the Born-Global Firm," *Journal of International Business Studies* 35 (2004): 124–41; Jeffrey Covin and Dennis Slevin, "Strategic Management of Small Firms in Hostile and Benign Environments," *Strategic Management Journal* 10 (January 1989): 75–87; G. T. Lumpkin and Gregory Dess, "Clarifying the Entrepreneurial Orientation Construct and Linking It to Performance," *Academy of Management Review* 21 (1996): 135–72.

[12] Gary Hamel and C. K. Prahalad, "Strategic Intent," *Harvard Business Review*, May–June 1989, pp. 63–76.

[13] "The Grey Market: Hey, Big Spender," *The Economist*, December 3, 2005, pp. 59–60.

[14] Cavusgil, Yeniyurt, and Townsend (2004).

[15] "What You Can Learn from Toyota," *Business 2.0*, January/February 2005, pp. 67–72; Suman Layak, "Can Tata Put India on Wheels?," *Business Today*, April 19, 2009, pp. 2–3; J. Soble, "Toyota Appoints Founder's Grandson as Next Chief Executive," *Financial Times*, January 21, 2009, p. 18.

[16] Joel Nicholson and Yim-Yu Wong, "Culturally Based Differences in Work Beliefs," *Management Research News* 24, no. 5 (2001): 1–10; Edgar H. Schein, *Organizational Culture and Leadership*, 2nd ed. (San Francisco: Jossey-Bass, 1997).

[17] Clay Chandler, "Canon's Big Gun," *Fortune*, February 6, 2006, pp. 92–98.

[18] A. Shameen, "Hyundai's Hitting Its Stride," *Barron's*, July 20, 2009, p. M7; A. Taylor III, "Hyundai Smokes the Competition," *Fortune*, January 18, 2010, pp. 62–71.

[19] Cavusgil, Yeniyurt, and Townsend (2004); Rhinesmith (1998); George S. Yip, Johny K. Johansson, and J. Roos, "Effects of Nationality on Global Strategy," *Management International Review* 37 (1997): 365–85.

[20] Björn Ambos and Bodo Schlegelmilch, "In Search of Global Advantage," *European Business Forum* 21 (Spring 2005): 23–24; Stephen Chen, Ronald Geluykens, and Chong Ju Choi, "The Importance of Language in Global Teams," *Management International Review* 46, no. 6 (2006): 679–96; Jay R. Galbraith, *Designing the Global Corporation* (San Francisco: Jossey-Bass, 2000); Robert T. Keller, "Cross-Functional Project Groups in Research and New Product Development: Diversity, Communications, Job Stress, and Outcomes," *Academy of Management Journal* 44 (2001): 547–55; Mary Maloney and Mary Zellmer-Bruhn, "Building Bridges, Windows and Cultures," *Management International Review* 46 (2006): 697–720.

[21] Martha L. Maznevski and Nicholas A. Athanassiou, "Guest Editors' Introduction to the Focused Issue: A New Direction for Global Teams Research," *Management International Review* 46 (2006): 631–46.

[22] Terence Brake, *Managing Globally* (New York: Dorling Kindersley, 2002).

[23] Bartlett and Ghoshal (1989); Gary Hamel and C. K. Prahalad, "Do You Really Have a Global Strategy?" *Harvard Business Review* 63 (July–August 1985): 139–49; T. Hout, Michael Porter, and E. Rudden, "How Global Companies Win Out," *Harvard Business Review* 60 (September–October 1982): 98–105; Theodore Levitt, "The Globalization of Markets," *Harvard Business Review* 61 (May–June 1983): 92–102; Robert T. Moran and John R. Riesenberger, *The Global Challenge* (London: McGraw-Hill, 1994); Kenichi Ohmae, "Planning for a Global Harvest," *Harvard Business Review* 67 (July–August 1989): 136–45.

[24] Bartlett and Ghoshal (1989); Timothy M. Devinney, David F. Midgley, and Sunil Venaik, "The Optimal Performance and the Global Firm: Formalizing and Extending the Integration-Responsiveness Framework," *Organization Science* 11 (2000): 674–95; Yves L. Doz, Christopher Bartlett, and C. K. Prahalad, "Global Competitive Pressures and Host Country Demands: Managing Tensions in MNCs," *California Management Review* 23 (1981): 63–74; Yadong Luo, "Determinants of Local Responsiveness: Perspectives from Foreign Subsidiaries in an Emerging Market," *Journal of Management* 26 (2001): 451–77; C. K. Prahalad, *The Strategic Process in a Multinational Corporation*, Unpublished doctoral dissertation (Graduate School of Business Administration, Harvard University, Cambridge, MA, 1975).

[25] Bartlett and Ghoshal (1989); Moran and Riesenberger (1994).

[26] Bartlett and Ghoshal (2000).

[27] Bartlett and Ghoshal (2000); G. Ghislanzoni, R. Penttinen, and D. Turnbull, "The Multilocal Challenge: Managing Cross-Border Functions," *The McKinsey Quarterly*, 2008, retrieved from http://www.mckinseyquarterly.com.

[28] L. Chang, "Nestlé Stumbles in China's Evolving Market," *Wall Street Journal*, December 8, 2004, p. A10; G. Chazan, "Foreign Products Get Russian Makeovers," *Wall Street Journal*, January 16, 2001, p. A23; Nestlé Corporation, "Key Facts and History," 2009, retrieved from http://www.nestle.com; Greg Steinmetz and Tara Parker-Pope, "All Over the Map: At a Time When Companies Are Scrambling to Go Global, Nestlé Has Long Been There," *Wall Street Journal*, September 26, 1996, p. R4.

[29] Moran and Riesenberger (1994).

[30] Bartlett and Ghoshal (2000).

[31] Bartlett and Ghoshal (1989); Hamel and Prahalad (1985); Hout, Porter, and Rudden (1982); Levitt (1983); Moran and Riesenberger (1994); Ohmae (1989).

[32] "Whirlpool Corp," *Appliance Manufacturer*, 2004, p. 10; Peter Marsh and Nikki Tait, "Whirlpool Platform for Growth: Management Product Development," *Financial Times*, March 26, 2008, p. 8; Tom Stundza, "Whirlpool Aims to Cut Costs 5% Annually," *Purchasing*, August 9, 2001, pp. 17–21; Whirlpool Corporation profile at http://www.hoovers.com.

[33] Bartlett and Ghoshal (2000).

[34] Shaoming Zou and S. Tamer Cavusgil, "The GMS: A Broad Conceptualization of Global Marketing Strategy and Its Effect on Firm Performance," *Journal of Marketing* 58 (January 2002): 1–21; Yip (2003).

[35] Katrin Hille, "Back to the Future for Lenovo," *Financial Times*, February 12, 2009, p. 17; Chuan Zhi Liu, "Lenovo: An Example of Globalization of Chinese Enterprises," *Journal of International Business Studies* 38, no. 4 (2007): 573–77; Huaichuan Rui and George Yip, "Foreign Acquisitions by Chinese Firms: A Strategic Intent Perspective," *Journal of World Business* 43, no. 2 (2008): 213–26; Jane Spencer and Loretta Chao, "Lenovo Goes Global, But Not Without Strife," *Wall Street Journal*, November 4, 2008, p. B1.

[36] Pankaj Ghemawat, "Regional Strategies for Global Leadership," *Harvard Business Review* 83 (December 2005): 98–106.

[37] Moran and Riesenberger (1994); Franklin Root, *Entry Strategies for International Markets* (San Francisco: Jossey-Bass, 1998).

[38] Moran and Riesenberger (1994).

[39] Alfred D. Chandler, *Strategy and Structure* (Cambridge, MA: MIT Press, 1962).

[40] Moran and Riesenberger, 1994.

[41] *Ibid.*

[42] *Ibid.*

[43] *Ibid.*

[44] *Ibid.*

[45] Bartlett and Ghoshal, 1989; Moran and Riesenberger, 1994; G. T. Hult, Deligonul, and Cavusgil (2006).

[46] Deborah Ball, "Despite Revamp, Unwieldy Unilever Falls behind Rivals," *Wall Street Journal*, January 3, 2005, pp. A1, A5; Unilever corporate profile at http://www.hoovers.com.

[47] Philip Atkinson, "Managing Chaos in a Matrix World," *Management Services*, November 2003, p. 8; Jennifer Pellet, "Fine-Tuning Philips," *Chief Executive*, March/April 2009, pp. 12–13.

[48] Moran and Riesenberger, 1994.

Chapter 13

[1] Jeen-Su Lim, Thomas Sharkey, and Ken Kim, "Competitive Environmental Scanning and Export Involvement: An Initial Inquiry," *International Marketing Review* 13 (1996): 65–80.

2 L. Bryan and D. Farrell, "Leading through Uncertainty," *The McKinsey Quarterly*, December 2008, retrieved from http://www.mckinseyquarterly.com.

3 Jenny Mero, "John Deere's Farm Team," *Fortune*, April 14, 2008, pp. 119–26.

4 F. Cunningham, "Commerce Department Helps Franchisors Go Global," *Franchising World*, December 2005, pp. 63–67.

5 D. Vrontis and P. Vronti, "Levi Strauss: An International Marketing Investigation," *Journal of Fashion Marketing and Management* 8 (2004): 389–98.

6 S. Tamer Cavusgil, "Measuring the Potential of Emerging Markets: An Indexing Approach," *Business Horizons* 40 (January–February 1997): 87–91.

7 GlobalEDGE™, "Market Potential Index for Emerging Markets–2009," retrieved from http://globaledge.msu.edu/resourcedesk/mpi.

8 "Burgeoning Bourgeoisie: A Special Report on the New Middle Classes in Emerging Markets," *The Economist*, February 14, 2009, Special Section.

9 Moon Ihlwan and Amey Stone, "Special Report: Emerging Tech Markets: South Korea: Tech's Test Market," *BusinessWeek*, March 4, 2003; Evan Ramstad, "South Korea Surges toward a Recovery," *Wall Street Journal*, August 3, 2009, p. A7.

10 N. Andrade, J. Lottner, and C. Roland, "How Young Consumers Could Shape Vietnam's Banks," *The McKinsey Quarterly*, March 2008, retrieved from http://www.mckinseyquarterly.com.

11 C. Miller and P. Olson, "Tesco's Landing," *Forbes*, June 4, 2007, pp. 116–18.

Chapter 14

1 Erin Anderson and Hubert Gatignon, "Modes of Foreign Entry: A Transaction Cost Analysis and Propositions," *Journal of International Business Studies* 17 (Fall 1986): 1–26; William H. Davidson, *Global Strategic Management* (New York: Wiley, 1982).

2 Tao Gao, "The Contingency Framework of Foreign Entry Mode Decisions: Locating and Reinforcing the Weakest Link," *Multinational Business Review* 12 (2004): 37–68.

3 "Escaping the Middle Market Trap: An Interview with the CEO of Electrolux," *McKinsey Quarterly* 4 (2006): 73–79.

4 S. Tamer Cavusgil, "On the Internationalization Process of Firms," *European Research* 8 (1980): 273–81.

5 Jan Johanson and J.-E. Vahlne, "The Internationalization Process of the Firm—A Model of Knowledge Development and Increasing Foreign Commitments," *Journal of International Business Studies* 8 (Spring–Summer 1977): 23–32; Robert Salomon and J. Myles Shaver, "Learning by Exporting: New Insights from Examining Firm Innovation," *Journal of Economics & Management Strategy* 14 (2005): 431–42.

6 "Digital Dragon," *The Economist*, December 17, 2005, p. 58; A. Porter, N. Newman, J. Roessner, D. Johnson, and X. Jin, "International High Tech Competitiveness: Does China Rank Number 1?" *Technology Analysis & Strategic Management* 21, no. 2 (2009): 173–83.

7 David Liu, "Exporting Mortgage Insurance Beyond the United States," *Housing Finance International* 14 (2000): 32–41.

8 Javalgi Rajshekhar, Charles Martin, and Patricia Todd, "The Export of E-Services in the Age of Technology Transformation: Challenges and Implications for International Service Providers," *The Journal of Services Marketing* 18 (2004): 560–73.

9 Institute for International Business, "The Global vs. Domestic Wine Industry," *Global Executive Forum*, Spring–Summer 2005, p. 12.

10 S. Tamer Cavusgil and Shaoming Zou, "Marketing Strategy-Performance Relationship: An Investigation of the Empirical Link in Export Market Ventures," *Journal of Marketing* 58 (January 1994): 1–21.

11 M. O'Flanagan, "Case Study: Exporting Gives Businesses a Healthy Outlook," *Sunday Business Post*, April 6, 2003.

12 Chun Zhang, S. Tamer Cavusgil, and Anthony Roath, "Manufacturer Governance of Foreign Distributor Relationships: Do Relational Norms Enhance Competitiveness in the Export Market?" *Journal of International Business Studies* 34 (2003): 550–63.

13 Capstone Turbine Corporation 2009 Annual Report, retrieved from http://www.capstoneturbine.com.

Chapter 15

1 Company profile of Tata at http://www.hoovers.com; P. Beckett, "Tata Chairman Doesn't Sweat the Timing on Global Expansion," *Wall Street Journal*, November 18, 2009, p. B1.

2 B. Bhavna, "The Beer Market in India," *Just—Drinks*, March 2007, pp. 65–87; company profile of SABMiller at http://www.hoovers.com.

3 UNCTAD, *World Investment Report* (New York: United Nations, 2009).

4 John Dunning, *International Production and the Multinational Enterprise* (London: Allen and Unwin, 1981).

5 Fred Vogelstein, "How Intel Got Inside," *Fortune*, October 4, 2004, pp. 127–36.

6 Farok Contractor and Peter Lorange, eds., *Cooperative Strategies in International Markets* (Lexington, MA: Lexington Books, 1988); Gary Hamel, Yves Doz, and C. K. Prahalad, "Collaborate with Your Competitors—and Win," *Harvard Business Review* 67 (January–February 1989): 133–39; Katherine Harrigan, "Strategic Alliances: Their New Role in Global Competition," *Columbia Journal of World Business* 22 (Summer 1987): 67–69; Vern Terpstra and Bernard Simonin, "Strategic Alliances in the Triad," *Journal of International Marketing* 1 (1993): 4–25.

7 Lilach Nachum and Srilata Zaheer, "The Persistence of Distance? The Impact of Technology on MNE Motivations for Foreign Investment," *Strategic Management Journal* 26 (2005): 747–67.

8 Wilbur Chung and Juan Alcacer, "Knowledge Seeking and Location Choice of Foreign Direct Investment in the United States," *Management Science* 48 (2002): 1534–42.

9 Anders Lotsson, "Tomorrow: A Sneak Preview," *Business 2.0* (August 2005): 77–84.

10 Lilach Nachum and Cliff Wymbs, "Product Differentiation, External Economies and MNE Location Choices: M&As

in Global Cities," *Journal of International Business Studies* 36 (2005): 415–23.

[11] Nachum and Zaheer (2005).

[12] "Retailing: Storm Clouds Over the Mall," *The Economist*, October 8, 2005, pp. 71–72.

[13] Barbara Katz and Joel Owen, "Should Governments Compete for Foreign Direct Investment?" *Journal of Economic Behavior & Organization* 59 (2006): 230–38.

[14] Samsung, *Step Forward: Samsung Profile 2009*, retrieved from http://www.samsung.com; UNCTAD, *World Investment Report 2006* (New York: United Nations, 2006).

[15] "Biggest Transnational Companies," *The Economist*, October 3, 2009, p. 121.

[16] Steve Hamm, "IBM vs. Tata: Which Is More American?" *BusinessWeek*, May 5, 2008, p. 28.

[17] Carol Matlack, "Carlos Ghosn's Russian Gambit," *BusinessWeek*, March 17, 2008, pp. 57–58.

[18] Thomas C. Head and P. Sorensen, "Attracting Foreign Direct Investment: The Potential Role of National Culture," *The Journal of American Academy of Business* 6 (2005): 305–309.

[19] Clay Chandler, "Mickey Mao," *Fortune*, April 18, 2005, pp. 170–78.

[20] Chandler (2005); Jane Leung and Kate Nicholson, "Disney Seeks to Consolidate Reputation in China," *Media*, November 19, 2009, p. 16.

[21] "Beyond the Green Corporation," *BusinessWeek*, January 29, 2007, pp. 50–64.

[22] M. K. Erramilli and C. P. Rao, "Service Firms' International Entry-Mode Choice: A Modified Transaction-Cost Analysis Approach," *Journal of Marketing* 57 (July 1993): 19–38; J. Li and S. Guisinger, "The Globalization of Service Multinationals in the 'Triad' Regions: Japan, Western Europe, and North America," *Journal of International Business Studies* 23 (1992): 675–96; United Nations, *The Transnationalization of Service Industries* (New York: Transnational Corporations and Management Division, Department of Economic and Social Development, 1993).

[23] Rajshekhar Javalgi, David A. Griffith, and D. Steven White, "An Empirical Examination of Factors Influencing the Internationalization of Service Firms," *Journal of Services Marketing* 17 (2003): 185–201.

[24] UNCTAD (2006).

[25] A. T. Kearney, *FDI Confidence Index* (Alexandria, VA: Global Business Policy Council, 2004).

[26] John Tagliabue, "Would Stalin Drive a Peugeot?" *New York Times*, November 25, 2006, pp. B1, B9; David Rocks, "Made in China—Er, Veliko Turnovo," *BusinessWeek*, January 8, 2007, p. 43.

[27] Andrew Ward, "Home Depot in Mexico," *Financial Times*, April 6, 2006, p. 8.

[28] UNCTAD (2006).

[29] In this book, we adopt the customary definition of "joint venture" where it is assumed to carry equity interest by the parent firms that founded it. That is, a joint venture is always an equity venture. Nevertheless, in the popular literature the term "equity venture" is incorrectly used to refer to all types of collaborative ventures, including project-based collaborations. Therefore, we will use the term "equity joint venture" rather than simply "joint venture" to avoid miscommunication.

[30] Paul Kaihla, "Why China Wants to Scoop Up Your Company," *Business 2.0*, June 2005, pp. 29–30.

[31] Farok Contractor and Peter Lorange, *Cooperative Strategies and Alliances* (Oxford, England: Elsevier Science, 2002); Janell Townsend, "Understanding Alliances: A Review of International Aspects in Strategic Marketing," *Marketing Intelligence & Planning* 21 (2003): 143–58.

[32] Donald Fites, "Make Your Dealers Your Partners," *Harvard Business Review* 74 (1996): 84–91; Masaaki Kotabe, Hildy Teegen, Preet Aulakh, Maria Cecilia Coutinho de Arruda, Roberto Santillan-Salgado, and Walter Greene, "Strategic Alliances in Emerging Latin America: A View from Brazilian, Chilean, and Mexican Companies," *Journal of World Business* 35 (2000): 114–32.

[33] Ellen Byron and Rachel Dodes, "P&G Flirts with Luxury Cosmetics," *Wall Street Journal*, March 9, 2009, p. B1.

[34] K. Hille and Song Jung-a, "LCD TV Makers Flock to China," *Financial Times*, October 17, 2009, p. 9; Y. Kim and K. Ahn, "Samsung Tesco Homeplus and Corporate Social Responsibility," *Richard Ivey School of Business Case Collection*, July 29, 2009; UNCTAD (2006).

[35] Daniel Lyons, "Holy Chip!" *Forbes*, January 30, 2006, pp. 76–82.

[36] Robert A. Guth, "IBM Announces Deal with Japan's NTT," *Wall Street Journal*, November 1, 2000, p. A23.

[37] Contractor and Lorange (2002); Gary Hamel, "Competition for Competence and Inter-Partner Learning within International Strategic Alliances," *Strategic Management Journal* Special Issue: Global Strategy, 12 (Summer 1991): 83–103; Gary Hamel, Yves Doz, and C. K. Prahalad, "Collaborate with Your Competitors—and Win," *Harvard Business Review* 67 (January–February 1989): 133–39; S. Tamer Cavusgil, "International Partnering: A Systematic Framework for Collaborating with Foreign Business Partners," *Journal of International Marketing* 6 (1998): 91–107; Destan Kandemir, Attila Yaprak, and S. Tamer Cavusgil, "Alliance Orientation: Conceptualization, Measurement and Impact on Market Performance," *Journal of the Academy of Marketing Science* 34 (2006): 324–40.

[38] *Ibid.*

[39] Fred Vogelstein, "How Intel Got Inside," *Fortune*, October 4, 2004, pp. 127–36; Bruce Heimana and Jack Nickerson, "Empirical Evidence Regarding the Tension Between Knowledge Sharing and Knowledge Expropriation in Collaborations," *Managerial and Decision Economics* 25 (2004): 401–20.

[40] S. Tamer Cavusgil, "International Partnering: A Systematic Framework for Collaborating with Foreign Business Partners," *Journal of International Marketing* 6 (1998): 91–107.

[41] "Asian Alliances: New Ties for VW, GM and Peugeot Citroen," *The Economist*, December 12, 2009, p. 72; "China: The Great Internet Race," *BusinessWeek*, June 13, 2005, pp. 54–55; Sing Keow Hoon-Halbauer, "Managing Rela-

tionships within Sino-Foreign Joint Ventures," *Journal of World Business* 34 (1999): 334–70.

42 Cavusgil (1998); Kandemir, Yaprak, and Cavusgil (2006).

43 James Areddy, "Danone Pulls Out of Disputed China Venture," *Wall Street Journal*, October 1, 2009, p. B1.

44 "Asian Alliances" (2009).

45 Dorinda Elliott and Bill Powell, "Wal-Mart Nation," *Time*, June 27, 2005, pp. 37–39; Mei Fong, "Retailers Still Expanding in China," *Wall Street Journal*, January 22, 2009, p. B1.

46 Andrew Ward, "Home Depot in Mexico," *Financial Times*, April 6, 2006, p. 8.

47 Adrienne Sanders, "Yankee Imperialist," *Forbes*, December 13, 1999, p. 56.

48 Amy Kazmin, "Ikea Axes Push After India Refuses to Alter Law," *Financial Times*, June 12, 2009, p. 16.

49 Clay Chandler, "The Great Wal-Mart of China," *Fortune*, July 25, 2005, pp. 104–16.

50 Andrew Ward, "Home Depot in Mexico," *Financial Times*, April 6, 2006, p. 8.

Chapter 16

1 International Centre for Trade and Sustainable Development (ICTSD), *Property Rights: Implications for Development Policy, Policy Discussion Paper,* Intellectual Property Rights & Sustainable Development Series (Geneva, Switzerland: ICTSD and New York: UNCTAD, 2003).

2 Farok J. Contractor, "Strategic Perspectives for International Licensing Managers: The Complementary Roles of Licensing, Investment and Trade in Global Operations," Working Paper no. 99.002 (Rutgers, NJ: Rutgers University, 1999).

3 *Ibid.*

4 ICTSD (2003).

5 Kay Millonzi and William Passannante, "Beware of the Pirates: How to Protect Intellectual Property," *Risk Management* 43 (1996): 39–42.

6 D. E. Welch and L. S. Welch, "In the Internationalization Process and Networks: A Strategic Management Perspective," *Journal of International Marketing* 4 (1996): 11–28.

7 Vanessa O'Connell and Mei Fong, "Saks to Follow Luxury Brands into China," *Wall Street Journal*, April 18, 2006, p. B1.

8 Dennis Henderson, Ian Sheldon, and Kathleen Thomas, "International Licensing of Foods and Beverages Makes Markets Truly Global," *FoodReview* (September 1994): 7–12.

9 "Management Brief: Johannesburgers and Fries," *The Economist*, September 27, 1997, pp. 113–14.

10 "History of Merchandising," *The Licensing Journal*, April 2009, p. 23; U.S. Department of Commerce, *A Basic Guide to Exporting* (Washington, DC: U.S. Government Printing Office, 1992).

11 Graham Pomphrey, "Pooh at 80," *License Europe!*, April 1, 2006, retrieved from http://www.licensemag.com/licensemag.

12 Piero Telesio, *Technology Licensing and Multinational Enterprises* (New York: Praeger, 1979).

13 *Ibid.*

14 "Roche Gains a Stronghold in Elusive Japanese Market," *Chemical Market Reporter*, December 17, 2001, p. 2.

15 Telesio (1979).

16 Akio Morita, Edwin Reingold, and Mitsuko Shimomura, *Made in Japan: Akio Morita and Sony* (New York: EP Dutton, 1986).

17 Jan Golab, "King Barbie: How I Gussied Up America's Favorite Toy and Turned My Struggling Company into a Megatoyopoly," *Los Angeles Magazine*, August 1, 1994, p. 66; Mattel, Inc., annual reports (various years).

18 F. Burton and A. Cross, "International Franchising: Market versus Hierarchy," in *Internationalisation Strategies*, G. Chryssochoidis, C. Millar, and J. Clegg, eds., pp. 135–52 (New York: St. Martin's Press, 2001).

19 L. S. Welch, "Internationalization by Australian Franchisors," *Asia Pacific Journal of Management* 7 (1990): 101–21.

20 K. Fladmoe-Lindquist, "International Franchising," in *Globalization of Services*, Y. Aharoni and L. Nachum, eds., pp. 197–216 (London: Routledge, 2000).

21 *Ibid.*; C. Steinberg, "A Guide to Franchise Strategies," *World Trade* 7 (1994): 66–70.

22 John Stanworth and Brian Smith, *The Barclays Guide to Franchising for the Small Business* (Oxford, UK: Basil Blackwell, 1991).

23 Carlye Adler, "How China Eats a Sandwich," *Fortune Small Business*, March 2005, pp. 72–76.

24 David Kaufmann, "The Big Bang: How Franchising Became an Economic Powerhouse the World Over—Franchise 500®," *Entrepreneur*, January 2004, retrieved at http://www.entrepreneur.com.

25 Barry Quinn and Anne Marie Doherty, "Power and Control in International Retail Franchising," *International Marketing Review* 17 (2000): 354–63.

26 Adler (2005), pp. F210B–D.

27 "Wendy's Shuts Doors in Japan," *The New York Times*, January 2, 2010, p. B3.

28 Stanworth (1991).

29 "Public Funds and Turnkey Contracts Fuel Growing Global Subway Work," *ENR*, October 25, 2004, p. 32; "Abu Dhabi Awards $9 Billion in Gas Project Contracts," *Oil & Gas Journal*, July 27, 2009, pp. 32–33.

30 "Full Steam Ahead with Nuclear Power," *Euromoney*, December 1980, p. 36.

31 "BOT Group Awards Major Hong Kong Road Contract," *ENR*, July 3, 1995, p. 30.

32 Robert Peltier, "Phu My 3 Power Plant, Ho Chi Minh City, Vietnam," *Power*, August 2004, p. 42.

33 Farok Contractor and Sumit Kundu, "Modal Choice in a World of Alliances: Analyzing Organizational Forms in the International Hotel Sector," *Journal of International Business Studies* 29 (1998): 325–56; V. Panvisavas and J. S. Taylor, "The Use of Management Contracts by International Hotel Firms in Thailand," *International Journal of Contemporary Hospitality Management* 18 (2006): 231–40.

34 David A. Ricks and Saeed Samiee-Esfahani, "Leasing: It May Be Right Abroad Even When It Is Not at Home," *Journal of International Business Studies* 5 (1974): 87–90.

35 Lloyd Downey, "Marketing Services: How TPOs Can Help," *International Trade Forum* 4 (2005): 7–8; Geoffrey

Jones and Alexis Lefort, "McKinsey and the Globalization of Consultancy," Harvard Business School case study 9–806–035 (Cambridge, MA: Harvard Business School, 2006).

[36] International Chamber of Commerce, "OECD Study a Vital Step to Understanding the Global Scope of Counterfeiting," 2007, retrieved from http://www.iccwbo.org.

[37] Murray Hiebert, "Chinese Counterfeiters Turn Out Fake Car Parts," *Wall Street Journal*, March 3, 2004, p. A14; Joon Muller, "Stolen Cars," *Forbes*, February 16, 2004, p. 58.

[38] Matthew Hamblen, "Cisco, Huawei Look to Settle Software-Copying Lawsuit," *Computer World*, October 6, 2003, p. 19.

[39] B. Cassell, "Microsoft Battles Piracy in Developing Markets," *Wall Street Journal*, December 23, 2004, p. B4.

[40] Jane O'Donnell, "Raids Crack Down on Counterfeit Goods," *USA Today*, December 18, 2009, retrieved from http://www.usatoday.com.

[41] Vauhini (2005), p. 59; Jack Goldsmith and Tim Wu, *Who Controls the Internet: Illusions of a Borderless World* (Oxford, England: Oxford University Press, 2006).

[42] Xiaobai Shen, "Developing Country Perspectives on Software," *International Journal of IT Standards & Standardization Research* 3 (2005): 21–43.

[43] Meagan Dietz, Sarena Shao-Tin Lin, and Lei Yang, "Protecting Intellectual Property in China," *The McKinsey Quarterly* 3 (2005): 6–10.

[44] A. Dayal-Gulati and Angela Lee, *Kellogg on China: Strategies for Success* (Evanston, IL: Northwestern University Press, 2004).

[45] Millonzi and Passannante (1996).

[46] Dietz, Shao-Tin Lin, and Yang (2005).

[47] Ibid.

Chapter 17

[1] Rupa Chanda, "India and Services Outsourcing in Asia," *The Singapore Economic Review* 53, no. 3 (2008), 419–47; Rahul Sachitanand, "IT Morphs Yet Again," *Business Today*, December 27, 2009, p. 7; Amol Sharma and Ben Worthen, "Indian Tech Outsourcers Aim to Widen Contracts," *Wall Street Journal*, October 5, 2009, p. B1; Ning Wright, "China's Emerging Role in Global Outsourcing," *The China Business Review*, November/December 2009, pp. 44–49.

[2] Duke University CIBER/Archstone Consulting, *Second Biannual Offshore Survey Results*, 2005; UNCTAD, *World Investment Report 2005* (New York: United Nations, 2005).

[3] "Outsourcing: Time to Bring It Back Home?" *The Economist*, March 5, 2005, p. 63.

[4] Michael E. Porter, *Competition in Global Industries* (Boston: Harvard Business School Press, 1986).

[5] Benito Arrunada and Xose H. Vazquez, "When Your Contract Manufacturer Becomes Your Competitor," *Harvard Business Review*, September 2006, pp. 135–45.

[6] Jamil Anderlini, "BMW Plans to Boost China Output after Demand Surge," *Financial Times*, November 13, 2009, p. 19.

[7] Thomas Friedman, *The World Is Flat 3.0: A Brief History of the Twenty-First Century* (New York: Picador, 2007).

[8] Geri Smith, "Can Latin America Challenge India?" *BusinessWeek*, January 30, 2006, Online Extra, retrieved from http://www.businessweek.com.

[9] Andrew Baxter, "GE Unit Plugs into the Outside World," *Financial Times*, September 28, 2005, p. 8; Corporate profile of Genpact at http://www.hoovers.com.

[10] "Patheon Inc.: Contract Drug Manufacturing and Development," *Shareowner*, November–December 2003, p. 36.

[11] Bruce Einhorn, "A Juggernaut in Electronics," *BusinessWeek*, June 18, 2007, p. 46.

[12] Masaaki Kotabe, Janet Murray, and Rajshekhar Javalgi, "Global Sourcing of Services and Market Performance: An Empirical Investigation," *Journal of International Marketing* 6 (1998): 10–31; Masaaki Kotabe and Janet Murray, "Outsourcing Service Activities," *Marketing Management* 10 (2001): 40–46.

[13] "India: The Next Wave," *The Economist*, December 17, 2005, pp. 57–58; Amy Kazmin, "Outsourcing: Law Firms Fuel the Demand for Offshore Services," *Financial Times*, January 30, 2009, retrieved from http://www.ft.com.

[14] Institute for International Business, "Globalization of Work: Outsourcing and Offshoring," *Global Executive Forum*, Spring–Summer 2005, pp. 6–7; Niraj Sheth, "India Calls Are Now Taken at Home," *Wall Street Journal*, July 1, 2009, p. B6.

[15] A. T. Kearney, "Geography of Offshoring Is Shifting, According to A. T. Kearney Study," May 18, 2009, retrieved from http://www.atkearney.com; "Is Your Job Next?" *BusinessWeek*, February 3, 2003, retrieved from http://www.businessweek.com; Norihiko Shirouzu, "Engineering Jobs Become Car Makers New Export," *Wall Street Journal*, February 7, 2008, pp. B1–B2.

[16] Murray Weidenbaum, "Outsourcing: Pros and Cons," *Executive Speeches* 19 (2004): 31–35.

[17] Peter Marsh, "Foreign Threat to Service Jobs 'Overblown,' says Study'" *Financial Times*, June 16, 2005, p. 12.

[18] Kerry Capelli, "Zara Thrives by Breaking All the Rules," *BusinessWeek*, October 20, 2008, p. 66; "If You Can Make It Here . . . How Some Companies Manage to Keep Building Things in America," *New York Times*, September 4, 2005, section 3, p. 1.

[19] Chanda (2008); Kazmin (2009); Abdul Rasheed and K. Matthew Gilley, "Outsourcing: National- and Firm-Level Implications," *Thunderbird International Business Review* 47 (2005): 513–28.

[20] Chanda (2008); Penny Crosman, "Worldsourcers," *Wall Street & Technology*, July 2008, p. 26; Kazmin (2009); Everest Global, Inc., *Global Sourcing Market Vista*, Everest Research Institute, 2009, retrieved from http://www.everestresearchinstitute.com.

[21] *BusinessWeek* (2003).

[22] Patrick Burnson, "Strained," *Logistics Management*, May 2009, p. 36.

[23] A. T. Kearney (2009).

[24] Pete Engardio, "Mom-and-Pop Multinationals," *BusinessWeek*, July 14 & 21, 2008, pp. 77–78.

[25] Duke University CIBER/Archstone Consulting (2005).

[26] James Hookway and Josephine Cuneta, "World News: Philippine Call Centers Ring Up Business," *Wall Street Journal*, May 30, 2009, p. A14; Paulo Prada and Niraj Sheth, "Delta Air Ends Use of India Call Centers," *Wall Street Journal*, April 18, 2009, p. B1; Sheth (2009).

[27] *BusinessWeek* (2003).

[28] Pete Engardio, "The Future of Outsourcing," *Business-Week*, January 30, 2006, pp. 50–64.

[29] Bruce Einhorn, "How Not to Sweat the Retail Details," *BusinessWeek*, May 25, 2009, pp. 52–54.

[30] Duke University CIBER/Archstone Consulting (2005).

[31] *BusinessWeek* (2003).

[32] "Indian Call Center Lands in Ohio," *Fortune*, August 6, 2007, p. 23.

[33] Engardio (2006).

[34] Masaaki Kotabe and Janet Murray, "Global Sourcing Strategy and Sustainable Competitive Advantage," *Industrial Marketing Management* 33 (2004): 7–14.

[35] Prada and Sheth (2009); Jackie Range, "India Faces a Homegrown Staffing Issue: Not Enough Talent," *Wall Street Journal*, July 16, 2008, p. B8.

[36] Manjeet Kripalani, "Five Offshore Practices That Pay Off," *BusinessWeek*, January 30, 2006, pp. 60–61.

[37] *BusinessWeek* (2003).

[38] David Craig and Paul Willmott, "Outsourcing Grows Up," *The McKinsey Quarterly* (February 2005), Web exclusive, retrieved at http://www.mckinseyquarterly.com.

[39] Ben Charny, "Dell Widens U.S. Computer-Share Lead," *Wall Street Journal*, January 17, 2008, p. B4; Thomas Friedman, *The World Is Flat* (New York: Farrar, Straus, & Giroux, 2005).

[40] Judith Crown and Carol Matlack, "Boeing Delays Dreamliner Again," *BusinessWeek*, April 9, 2008, retrieved at http://www.businessweek.com; Dominic Gates, "Latest Delay of Boeing 787 Pushes Back First Delivery to Third Quarter of 2009," *Seattle Times*, April 10, 2008, retrieved from www.seattletimes.com; Jon Ostrower, "One Year On: The Story of the 787," *Flightglobal*, May 5, 2008, retrieved from www.flightglobal.com; Peter Sanders "Boeing Confronts New Woes in 787 Jet," *Wall Street Journal*, June 25, 2010, p. B1.

[41] George Yip, *Total Global Strategy II* (Upper Saddle River, NJ: Prentice Hall, 2003).

[42] James Womack and Daniel Jones, *Lean Solutions* (New York: Free Press, 2005).

[43] Capelli (2008).

[44] Barney Gimbel, "Yule Log Jam," *Fortune*, December 13, 2004, pp. 164–70.

[45] Alison Maitland, "Make Sure You Have Your Christmas Stock In," *Financial Times*, December 19, 2005, p. 11.

[46] J. Lynn Lunsford, "Outsourcing at Crux of Boeing Strike," *Wall Street Journal*, September 8, 2008, pp. B1, B4.

[47] Christopher Conkey, "Strapped Cities Outsource Transit Lines," *Wall Street Journal*, July 13, 2009, p. A6; Celeste Pagano, "Proceed with Caution: Avoiding Hazards in Toll Road Privatizations," *St. John's Law Review*, 83, no. 1 (2009): 351–94.

[48] Eric Bellman and Nathan Koppel, "More U.S. Legal Work Moves to India's Low-Cost Lawyers," *Wall Street Journal*, September 28, 2005, p. B1; Kazmin (2009).

[49] Weidenbaum (2004).

[50] Chanda (2008); J. McCarthy, "3.3 Million U.S. Service Jobs to Go Offshore," *Forrester Research, Inc.*, 2002, retrieved from http://www.forrester.com.

[51] "To Start Up Here, Companies Hire Over There," *USA Today*, February 11, 2005, pp. 1B–2B.

[52] John Thoburn, Kirsten Sutherland, and Thi Hoa Nguyen, "Globalization and Poverty: Impacts on Households of Employment and Restructuring in the Textiles Industry of Vietnam," *Journal of the Asia Pacific Economy* 12, no. 3 (2007): 345–62.

[53] Ryan Jeltema, "Electrolux Plant Walls Come Tumbling Down," *The Daily News*, June 7, 2007, retrieved from http://www.thedailynews.cc.

[54] L. D. Tyson, "Offshoring: The Pros and Cons for Europe," *BusinessWeek*, December 6, 2004, p. 32.

[55] Michael Mandel, "The Real Cost of Offshoring," *Business-Week*, June 18, 2007, p. 29.

[56] Joseph A. Schumpeter, *Capitalism, Socialism, and Democracy* (New York: Harper, 1942).

[57] Tyson (2004).

Chapter 18

[1] Shaoming Zou and S. Tamer Cavusgil, "The GMS: A Broad Conceptualization of Global Marketing Strategy and Its Effect on Firm Performance," *Journal of Marketing* 66 (2002): 40–56.

[2] H. Gatignon, J. Eliashberg, and T. Robertson, "Modeling Multinational Diffusion Patterns: An Efficient Methodology," *Marketing Science* 8 (1989): 231–43.

[3] G. Fowler and M. Marr, "Disney's China Play," *Wall Street Journal*, June 16, 2005, pp. B1, B7.

[4] George Yip, *Total Global Strategy II* (Upper Saddle River, NJ: Prentice Hall, 2003).

[5] Roger Calantone, S. Tamer Cavusgil, Jeffrey Schmidt, and Geon-Cheol Shin, "Internationalization and the Dynamics of Product Adaptation—An Empirical Investigation," *Journal of Product Innovation Management* 21 (2004): 185–98.

[6] Yip (2003); Ellen Byron, "Gillette Sharpens Its Pitch for Expensive Razor," *Wall Street Journal*, October 6, 2008, p. B9.

[7] Cris Prystay, "Milk Industry's Pitch in Asia: Try the Ginger or Rose Flavor," *Wall Street Journal*, August 9, 2005, p. B1.

[8] J. Tapper and A. Miller, "'The Simpsons' Exported to Middle East," October 18, 2005, *ABC News*, retrieved from http://abcnews.go.com/wnt.

[9] Brian Bremner, "McDonald's Is Loving It in Asia," *BusinessWeek*, January 24, 2007, retrieved from http://www.businessweek.com.

[10] "Microsoft to Offer Budget Windows Program in Asia," *Wall Street Journal*, August 11, 2004, p. B2.

[11] Reena Jana, "Inspiration from Emerging Economies," *BusinessWeek*, March 23, 2009, p. 38; Ian Rowley, "Will Japan Fall in Love with Lexus?" *BusinessWeek*, July 11, 2005, p. 49.

[12] Gabriele Suder and David Suder, "Strategic Megabrand Management: Does Global Uncertainty Affect Brands?" *The Journal of Product and Brand Management* 17, no. 7 (2008): 436–45.

[13] Janell Townsend, S. Tamer Cavusgil, and Marietta Baba, "Global Integration of Brands and New Product Development at General Motors," *The Journal of Product Innovation Management* 27, no. 1 (2010): 49–62; Yip (2003).

[14] Douglas Holt, John Quelch, and Earl Taylor, "How Global Brands Compete," *Harvard Business Review* (September 2004), pp. 68–75.

[15] Rajshekhar Javalgi, Virginie Pioche Khare, Andrew Gross, and Robert Scherer, "An Application of the Consumer Ethnocentrism Model to French Consumers," *International Business Review* 14 (2005): 325–44.

[16] David A. Aaker, *Managing Brand Equity* (New York: The Free Press, 1991); James Gregory and Jack Wiechmann, *Branding Across Borders* (Chicago: McGraw-Hill, 2002).

[17] Yip (2003).

[18] *Ibid.*

[19] "General Motors: 2009 Company Profile Edition 3: Chapter 9 Product Development," *Just-Auto* (September 2009), pp. 28–29; Townsend, Cavusgil, and Baba (2010).

[20] Helen Walters, "IDEA 2009: Designing a Better World," *BusinessWeek*, July 29, 2009, retrieved from http://www.businessweek.com.

[21] Matthew B. Myers, "Implications of Pricing Strategy-Venture Strategy Congruence: An Application Using Optimal Models in an International Context," *Journal of Business Research* 57 (2004): 591–690.

[22] S. Tamer Cavusgil, "Pricing for Global Markets," *Columbia Journal of World Business* (Winter 1996): 66–78.

[23] S. Tamer Cavusgil, "Unraveling the Mystique of Export Pricing," *Business Horizons* 31 (1988): 54–63.

[24] William McDaniel and Edgar Kossack, "The Financial Benefits to Users of Foreign-Trade Zones," *Columbia Journal of World Business* 18 (1983): 33–41.

[25] Cavusgil (1988).

[26] Thomas Pugel and Judith Ugelow, "Transfer Prices and Profit Maximization in Multinational Enterprise Operations," *Journal of International Business Studies* 13 (Spring–Summer 1982): 115–19.

[27] Ralph Drtina and Jane Reimers, "Global Transfer Pricing: A Practical Guide for Managers," *S.A.M. Advanced Management Journal* 74, no. 2 (2009): 4–12.

[28] S. Tamer Cavusgil and Ed Sikora, "How Multinationals Can Counter Gray Market Imports," *Columbia Journal of World Business* 23 (1988): 75–86; Reza Ahmadi and B. Rachel Yang, "Parallel Imports: Challenges from Unauthorized Distribution Channels," *Marketing Science* 19 (Summer 2000): 281; Matthew B. Myers, "Incidents of Gray Market Activity Among U.S. Exporters: Occurrences, Characteristics, and Consequences, *Journal of International Business Studies* 30 (1999): 105–26.

[29] Ernst Berndt, "A Primer on the Economics of Re-Importation of Prescription Drugs," *Managerial and Decision Economics* 28 (2007): 415–35.

[30] S. Tamer Cavusgil and Ed Sikora, "How Multinationals Can Counter Gray Market Imports," *Columbia Journal of World Business* 23 (1988): 75–86.

[31] Chris Hansen, "Inside the World of Counterfeit Drugs," June 9, 2006, *MSNBC Interactive*, retrieved from http://www.msnbc.msn.com.

[32] Colin Macleod, "Global Economy and Adspend Prospects," *International Journal of Advertising* 28, no. 1 (2009): 187–89.

[33] Laurel Wentz and Bradley Johnson, "Top 100 Global Advertisers Heap Their Spending Abroad," *Advertising Age*, November 30, 2009, pp. 1–2.

[34] Macleod (2009).

[35] F. Balfour and D. Kiley, "Ad Agencies Unchained," *BusinessWeek*, April 25, 2005, pp. 50–51.

[36] Yip (2003).

[37] Linda Shi, Shaoming Zou, J. Chris White, Regina McNally, and S. Tamer Cavusgil, "Executive Insights: Global Account Management Capability," *Journal of International Marketing* 13 (2005): 93–113; Sengun Yeniyurt, S. Tamer Cavusgil, and Tomas Hult, "A Global Market Advantage Framework: The Role of Global Market Knowledge Competencies," *International Business Review* 14 (2005): 1–19.

Chapter 19

[1] Peter Dowling, Marion Festing, and Allen Engle, *International HRM: Managing People in a Multinational Context*, 5th ed. (London: Thomson Learning, 2008).

[2] *Ibid.*

[3] *Ibid.*

[4] Jo Johnson, "More Westerners Take Top Posts in India as Locals' Pay Demand Soars," *Financial Times*, May 30, 2007, p. 1.

[5] Dowling, Festing, and Engle (2008).

[6] James Neelankavil, Anil Mathur, and Yong Zhang, "Determinants of Managerial Performance: A Cross-Cultural Comparison of the Perceptions of Middle-Level Managers in Four Countries," *Journal of International Business Studies* 31, no. 1 (2000): 121–41.

[7] Dowling, Festing, and Engle (2008); Anne-Wil Harzing, "Of Bears, Bumble-Bees, and Spiders: The Role of Expatriates in Controlling Foreign Subsidiaries," *Journal of World Business* 36, no. 4 (2008): 366–79.

[8] Anne-Wil Harzing, "Who's in Charge? An Empirical Study of Executive Staffing Practices in Foreign Subsidiaries," *Human Resource Management* 40, no. 2 (2001): 139–45.

[9] Debbie Lovewell, "Employer Profile: World Order," *Employee Benefits*, September 2009, p. 50.

[10] Nanette Byrnes, "Star Search," *BusinessWeek*, October 10, 2005, p. 68; David Pollitt, "Unilever 'Raises the Bar' in Terms of Leadership Performance," *Human Resource Management International Digest* 14, no. 5 (2006): 23–25; Philip Harris, Robert Moran, and Sarah Moran, *Managing Cultural Differences*, 6th ed. (Burlington, MA: Elsevier Buttermann-Heinemann, 2007).

[11] Robert T. Moran and John R. Riesenberger, *The Global Challenge* (London: McGraw-Hill, 1994).

[12] Ben L. Kedia and Akuro Mukherji, "Global Managers: Developing a Mindset for Global Competitiveness," *Journal*

of World Business 34, no. 3 (1999): 230–51; Orly Levy, Schon Beechler, Sully Taylor, and Nakiye Boyacigiller, "What We Talk about When We Talk about 'Global Mindset'— Managerial Cognition in Multinational Corporations," *Journal of International Business Studies* 38, no. 2 (2007): 231–58.

[13] Dowling, Festing, and Engle (2008).

[14] Harris, Moran, and Moran (2007).

[15] Jeanne Brett, Kristin Beyfar, and Mary Kern, "Managing Multicultural Teams," *Harvard Business Review* 84, no. 11: 84–92.

[16] S. Ang, L. Van Dyne, and C. K. S. Koh, "Personality Correlates of the Four Factor Model of Cultural Intelligence," *Group and Organization Management* 31 (2006): 100–23.

[17] *Ibid.*

[18] Dowling, Festing, and Engle (2008).

[19] Anne-Wil Harzing and Claus Christensen, "Expatriate Failure: Time to Abandon the Concept?" *Career Development International* 9, no. 6/7 (2004): 616–20.

[20] M. Mendenhall, E. Dunbar, and G. Oddou, "Expatriate Selection, Training and Career Pathing: A Review and Critique," *Human Resources Management* 26 (1987): 331–45.

[21] Harris, Moran, and Moran (2007).

[22] Stephen Rhinesmith, *A Manager's Guide to Globalization* (Homewood, IL: Business One Irwin, 1998).

[23] Rosalie Tung, "Expatriate Assignments: Enhancing Success and Minimizing Failure," *Academy of Management Executive* 1 (1987): 117–26.

[24] J. Black, H. Gregersen, and M. Mendenhall, "Toward a Theoretical Framework of Repatriation Adjustment," *Journal of International Business Studies* 23 (1992): 737–60.

[25] Harris, Moran, and Moran (2007).

[26] George Yip, *Total Global Strategy II* (Upper Saddle River, NJ: Prentice Hall, 2003).

[27] Peter Dowling, Denice Welch, and Randall Schuler, *International Human Resource Management*, 3rd ed. (Cincinnati, OH: South-Western, 1999).

[28] *Ibid.*

[29] *Ibid.*

[30] Richard Hodgetts and Fred Luthans, *International Management: Culture, Strategy, and Behavior*, 5th ed. (Boston: McGraw-Hill Irwin, 2003).

[31] *Ibid.*

[32] David Blanchflower, "International Patterns of Union Membership," *British Journal of Industrial Relations* 45, no. 1 (2007): 1–28.

[33] *Ibid.*; Guglielmo Meardi, "Multinationals' Heaven? Uncovering and Understanding Worker Responses to Multinational Companies in Post-Communist Central Europe," *International Journal of Human Resource Management* 17, no. 8 (2006): 1366–78.

[34] "Paris in the Spring; Unrest in France," *The Economist*, March 21, 2009, p. 52; R. Jai Krishna, Dhanya Ann Thoppil, and Romit Guha, "Strike Disrupts Work at Nokia's Chennai Plant," *Wall Street Journal*, January 21, 2010, retrieved from http://www.wsj.com.

[35] M. Dubofsky and F. R. Dulles, *Labor in America: A History*, 7th ed. (Wheeling, IL: Harlan Davidson, 2004).

[36] "Business: Membership Required; Trade Unions in China," *The Economist*, August 2, 2008, p. 55; Dexter Roberts, "Waking Up to Their Rights," *BusinessWeek*, August 22–29, 2005, pp. 123–28.

[37] Jian Qiao, "Between the State and Market: Multiple Roles of the Chinese Trade Unions from the Perspectives of Shop Stewards," *Employee Relations* 32, no. 1 (2010): 28–41; Victorien Wu, "Labor Relations in Focus," *The China Business Review* 33, no. 6 (2006): 40–44.

[38] John Gennard, "Development of Transnational Collective Bargaining in Europe," *Employee Relations* 31, no. 4 (2009): 341–46; Stephen Hardy and Nick Adnett, "Breaking the ICE: Workplace Democracy in a Modernized Social Europe," *The International Journal of Human Resource Management* 17, no. 6 (2006): 1021–31.

[39] Alberto Alesina and Francesco Giavazzi, *The Future of Europe: Reform or Decline* (Boston: MIT Press, 2006).

[40] Stanley Pignal, John Reed, and Daniel Schafer, "GM Opel Confirms Antwerp Factory Will Shut," *Financial Times*, January 22, 2010, p. 24.

[41] Ashby Monk, "The Knot of Contracts: The Corporate Geography of Legacy Costs," *Economic Geography* 84, no. 2 (2008): 211–35.

[42] Lawrence Koslow and Robert Scarlett, *Global Business*, (Houston, TX: Cashman Dudley, 1999).

[43] C. Mako, P. Csizmadi, and M. Illessy, "Labour Relations in Comparative Perspective," *Journal for East European Management Studies* 11, no. 3 (2006): 267–87.

[44] Jessica Marquez, "Unions' Global End Run," *Workforce Management*, January 30, 2006, pp. 1–4.

[45] John Gennard, "A New Emerging Trend? Cross Border Trade Union Mergers," *Employee Relations* 31, no. 1 (2009): 5–8.

[46] Krishna, Thoppil, and Guha (2010).

[47] Dowling, Welch, and Schuler (1999); "The Conundrum of the Glass Ceiling," *The Economist*, July 23, 2005, pp. 63–65; Price Waterhouse, *International Assignments: European Policy and Practice 1997/1998*, London: Price Waterhouse, 1997.

[48] Grant Thornton International Ltd., *Privately Held Businesses: The Lifeblood of the Global Economy*, International Business Report 2009, retrieved from http://www.grantthorntonibos.com.

[49] Nancy Adler, *International Dimensions of Organizational Behavior*, 4th ed. (Cincinnati, OH: South-Western, 2002); Harris, Moran, and Moran (2007).

[50] Robert T. Moran, Phillip R. Harris, and Sarah V. Moran, *Managing Cultural Differences, Global Leadership Strategies for the 21st Century*, 7th ed. (Oxford, UK: Elsevier, 2007); Jeanine Prime, Karsten Jonsen, Nancy Carter, and Martha Maznevski, "Managers' Perceptions of Women and Men Leaders: A Cross Cultural Comparison," *International Journal of Cross Cultural Management* 8, no. 2 (2008): 171–80.

[51] Georges Desvaux, Sandrine Devillard-Hoellinger, and Mary Meaney, "A Business Case for Women," *McKinsey Quarterly* September, 2008, retrieved from www.mckinseyquarterly.com; Lynda Gratton, "Steps That Can Help Women Make It to the Top," *Financial Times*, May 23, 2007, p. 13.

52 *Ibid.*; "Conundrum of the Glass Ceiling" (2005); Ruth Simpson and Afam Ituma, "Transformation and Feminisation: The Masculinity of the MBA and the 'Un-Development' of Men," *Journal of Management Development* 28, no. 4 (2009): 301–16.

53 "Women and the World Economy: A Guide to Womenomics," *Economics*, April 12, 2006, p. 80; Matthew Brannan and Vincenza Priola, "Between a Rock and a Hard Place: Exploring Women's Experience of Participation and Progress in Managerial Careers," *Equal Opportunities International* 28, no. 5 (2009): 378–97.

54 Mercer Human Resource Consulting, "More Females Sent on International Assignment Than Ever Before, Survey Finds," October 12, 2006, retrieved from http://www.mercerhr.com.

Chapter 20

1 Peter Yeoh, "Causes of the Global Financial Crisis: Learning from the Competing Insights," *International Journal of Disclosure and Governance* 7, no. 1 (2010): 42–69.

2 Ernst and Young, "Globalisation Act II: Team Europe Defends Its Goals," results of 2006 survey on the attractiveness of Europe (Paris: Ernst & Young, 2006).

3 Bank for International Settlements, Statistics Division, retrieved from http://www.bis.org.

4 McKinsey Global Institute, "Global Capital Markets: Entering a New Era," September 2009, retrieved from http://www.mckinsey.com/mgi.

5 K. Lewis, "Trying to Explain Home Bias in Equities and Consumption," *Journal of Economic Literature* 37 (1999): 571–608.

6 Robert Cottrell, "Thinking Big: A Survey of International Banking," *The Economist*, May 20, 2006, survey section.

7 Organisation for Economic Co-operation and Development (OECD), *Private Pensions and Policy Responses to the Crisis*, 2009, retrieved from http://www.oecd.org; OECD, *Private Pensions Outlook 2008* (Paris: OECD, 2009).

8 Steve Johnson, "Pensions to Pour into EM Debt," *Financial Times*, January 25, 2010, p. 1; Daniel Yergin and Joseph Stanislaw, *The Commanding Heights: The Battle for the World Economy* (New York: Touchstone, 2002).

9 "Battle of the Bourses," May 27, 2006, *The Economist*, pp. 83–85.

10 Cottrell (2006).

11 Steve Hanke, "When Currencies Falter," *Forbes*, June 8, 2009, p. 106; Michael Sesit and Craig Karmin, "How One Word Haunts the Dollar," *Wall Street Journal*, March 17, 2005, p. C16.

12 IBM, Inc., *2008 Annual Report*, retrieved from http://www.ibm.com.

13 Here is an example of how transfer pricing works: Consider an MNE with subsidiaries in three countries. Suppose that subsidiary A operates in country A with high corporate income taxes, and subsidiary B operates in country B, a tax haven. One way to minimize taxes is for subsidiary A to sell merchandise to subsidiary B for a low transfer price. Subsidiary B then resells the merchandise to subsidiary C in the

third country at a high transfer price. This results in lower overall taxes for subsidiary A because of its low profits, for subsidiary B because of country B's low tax rates, and for subsidiary C because the high cost of its purchase reduces its profits.

While this approach to transferring funds within the MNE is quite common, transfer pricing has some drawbacks. First, while transfer pricing between members of the corporate family is legal when carried out within reasonable limits, governments strongly disapprove of the practice of avoiding tax obligations. Thus, many governments impose policies that restrict transfer pricing. Coca-Cola's Japan subsidiary was fined 15 billion yen for making royalty payments from trademarks and products to its U.S. parent that Japan's National Tax Administration judged as too high. Second, transfer pricing can distort the financial results of foreign subsidiaries. For instance, a subsidiary that is required to charge low prices for its exports may experience unusually low profitability, which harms its performance and can demoralize local staff. Third, some MNEs use artificial transfer prices to hide the poor results of a badly performing subsidiary or achieve other goals aimed at concealing the true performance of the firm.

14 Timor Mehpare and Seyhan Sipahi, "Fast-Food Restaurant Site Selection Factor Evaluation by the Analytic Hierarchy Process," *The Business Review* 4 (2005): 161–67.

15 Here is an illustration of net present value analysis: A U.S.-based MNE is considering an expansion project through its subsidiary in Mexico. The project requires an initial investment of 220 million Mexican pesos (MXP) and has an economic life of five years. The project is expected to generate annual after-tax cash flows of MXP120 million, MXP125 million, MXP150 million, MXP155 million, and MXP200 million, which will be remitted to the parent company during the next five years. The current spot exchange rate is MXP11/$1 and the spot rates are expected to be MXP11.10/$1, MXP11.25/$1, MXP11.50/$1, MXP11.55/$1, and MXP11.75/$1 for the next five years. Assuming that the appropriate discount rate for this project is 10%, what is the NPV of the project from the parent company's perspective? Should the MNE accept this project based on its NPV? Let's analyze. The U.S. cash flows of the project can be calculated as follows:

	0	1	2	3	4	5
Mexican peso cash flows	−MXP 220 Million	MXP 120 Million	MXP 125 Million	MXP 150 Million	MXP 155 Million	MXP 200 Million
Prevailing spot exchange rate	MXP 11/$1	MXP 11.10/$1	MXP 11.25/$1	MXP 11.50/$1	MXP 11.55/$1	MXP 11.75/$1
U.S. dollar cash flows	−$20,000,000	$10,810,811	$11,111,111	$13,043,478	$13,419,913	$17,021,277

The NPV of the project can be calculated as follows:
$$NPV = -\$20,000,000 + \$10,810,811/(1 + 0.10)^1 + \$11,111,111/(1 + 0.10)^2 + \$13,043,478/(1 + 0.10)^3 + \$13,419,913/(1 + 0.10)^4 + \$17,021,277/(1 + 0.10)^5$$
$$NPV = \$28,545,359$$
The MNE can accept the project because it has a positive NPV.

[16] The discount rate used in the NPV analysis of international projects may be higher due to a premium for additional risks involved in doing business internationally. Management may insist on a higher level of required return in the net present value calculation because higher country/political and currency risks indicate a higher probability of venture failure. A firm might apply a 7% discount rate to potential investments in Germany and Japan because those countries enjoy political and economic stability. But the same firm might use a 14% discount rate for similar potential investments in Pakistan and Russia because those countries experience political and economic turmoil. The higher the discount rate, the higher the projected net cash flows must be for the investment to have a positive net present value contribution. Occasionally, the discount rate for international projects can be lower than for domestic ones. Risk arises from various sources, and management must systematically assess the range of potentially influential factors.

[17] Robert Aliber, *Exchange Risk and International Finance* (New York: Wiley, 1979).

[18] "Viking-Era Silver Coins Found in Sweden," *Washington Post*, November 1, 2006, retrieved from http://www.washingtonpost.com.

[19] Hanke (2009).

[20] Bank for International Settlements, "Monetary and Economic Department: Detailed Tables on Provisional Locational and Consolidated Banking Statistics," January 2010, retrieved from http://www.bis.org; Robert Wade, "The Perils of Cross-Border Payments," *World Trade*, June 2009, p. 8.

[21] Gordon Platt, "World's Best Foreign Exchange Banks 2005," *Global Finance* 19 (2005): 24–33.

[22] Adam Rombel, "The World's Best Internet Banks," *Global Finance* 16 (2002): 37–38.

[23] Richard Rescigno, "At the Crossroads: Subaru Strives to Get Back into Gear," *Barron's*, March 28, 1988, pp. 15–19.

[24] Catherine Belton, "Moscow Facing Lending Crisis in Cash Exodus," *Financial Times*, September 10, 2008, p. 5; "Russia: Currency Forecast," *EIU ViewsWire*, March 31, 2009.

[25] Ariful Hoquea, Felix Chana, and Meher Manzur, "Efficiency of the Foreign Currency Options Market," *Global Finance Journal* 19, no. 2 (2008): 157–70.

[26] Here is a simple example of an option transaction from a familiar context: Say you are in the market to buy a house. You find one that you like, but you are not sure if you want to buy it. At this stage, you opt to put a deposit down to have the seller keep his for-sale house for you for two weeks. Later, if you buy the house, the deposit counts toward the purchase price. If you do not buy the house, you lose your deposit. You have the option to buy the house at an agreed-upon price but not the obligation to do so.

[27] W. Wallace and J. Walsh, "Apples to Apples: Profits Abroad," *Financial Executive*, May–June, 1995, pp. 28–31.

[28] Hank Boerner, "Europe Faces Eagle Eye of US Financial Regulation," *European Business Forum* 21 (2005): 46–49.

[29] American Institute of Certified Public Accountants, "International Financial Reporting Standards," 2010, retrieved from http://www.ifrs.com; Deborah Lindberg and Deborah Seifert, "A New Paradigm of Reporting," *The CPA Journal* 80, no. 1 (2010): 36–39.

[30] Computershare, *2003 Annual Report*, retrieved from http://www.computershare.com.

[31] Alan J. Auerbach and Martin Feldstein, *Handbook of Public Economics*, 3rd ed. (Amsterdam: North-Holland, 2001).

[32] Joseph Froomkin and Ira Wender, "Revenue Implications of United States Income Tax Treaties," *National Tax Journal* 7, no. 2 (1954): 177–81.

[33] Kerry Capell, "Lower Your Taxes: Move to Switzerland," *BusinessWeek*, September 21, 2009, p. 62; Timothy Noah, "Bono, Tax Avoider," *Slate*, October 31, 2006, retrieved from http://www.slate.com.

[34] Dries Lesage, David McNair, and Mattias Vermeiren, "From Monterrey to Doha: Taxation and Financing for Development," *Development Policy Review* 28, no. 2 (2010): 155–62; Brody Mullins, "Accenture Lobbyists Near Big Win on Securing Tax-Haven Status," *Wall Street Journal*, July 14, 2005, p. A2.

> Photo Credits

Cover

Tan Wei Ming/Shutterstock; Adrian Lindley/Shutterstock; Stanislav Komogorov/Shutterstock; Andy Heyward/Shutterstock

Chapter 1

page 38: © Yadid Levy/Alamy Images; **page 51:** Maciej Dakowicz/Alamy Images; **page 52:** Bartek_chiny/Dreamstime LLC-Royalty Free; **page 54:** © Jack Hollingsworth/CORBIS All Rights Reserved; **page 55:** Tan Wei Ming/Shutterstock; **page 56:** © Ashley Lumb

Chapter 2

page 64: © Steve Raymer/CORBIS All Rights Reserved; **page 72:** © Daniel Karmann/CORBIS All Rights Reserved; **page 78:** Robert Hardholt/Shutterstock; **page 79:** Jeff Greenberg/PhotoEdit Inc.; **page 83:** F. Bettex—Mysterra.org/Alamy Images; **page 87:** Henry M. Trotter/Wikimedia Commons

Chapter 3

page 94: Dam D'Cruz/Shutterstock; **page 100:** http://www.thecoca-colacompany.com/ourcompany/board_kent.html; **page 102:** Jank1000/Dreamstime LLC-Royalty Free; **page 105:** © Reuters/CORBIS/CORBIS All Rights Reserved; **page 108:** Tristar Photos/Alamy Images; **page 109:** © Eric Joiner; **page 113:** © Cynthia Asoka; **page 114:** G P Bowater/Alamy Images

Chapter 4

page 122: Julio Etchart/Alamy Images; **page 126:** iStockphoto.com; **page 127:** © Maurice Dancer; **page 129:** r.nagy/Shutterstock; **page 131:** Alamy Images; **page 132:** © Zhibo (Lawrence) Yu; **page 138:** © Erico Sugita/CORBIS All Rights Reserved; **page 146:** Getty Images-Photodisc-Royalty Free

Chapter 5

page 154: Eye Ubiquitous/Alamy Images; **page 157:** AP Wide World Photos; **page 162:** Paul Prescott/Shutterstock; **page 163:** Photoroller/Shutterstock; **page 166:** Paul Prescott/Shutterstock

Chapter 6

page 176: Peter and Georgina Bowater c/o Mira; **page 181:** Speedfighter17/StockPhotos, Inc./Globe Photos, Inc.; **page 182:** Alamy/Ali Mubarak/Grapheast; **page 183:** Picsfive/Shutterstock; **page 185:** AP Wide World Photos; **page 190:** Getty Images, Inc.; **page 191:** Getty Images, Inc.

Chapter 7

page 208: Demetrio Carrasco © Dorling Kindersley; **page 215:** Jeff Greenberg/The Image Works; **page 220:** Mark Shenley/Alamy Images; **page 223:** Philippe Bataille/AP Wide World Photos; **page 225:** Haruyoshi Yamaguchi/*The New York Times*

Chapter 8

page 236: © Dan White/Alamy Images; **page 241:** Carsten Medom Madsen/Shutterstock; **page 247:** Robert Fried/Alamy; **page 248:** Jim Young/CORBIS—NY; **page 254:** Robert Harding Picture Library Ltd/Alamy

Chapter 9

page 262: Getty Images, Inc.; **page 277:** © Krista Kennell/ZUMA/CORBIS All Rights Reserved; **page 278:** kycstudio/iStockphoto.com; **page 280:** Andia/Alamy/Monasse Th; **page 282:** Wikimedia Commons

Chapter 10

page 288: Getty Images, Inc.; **page 294:** NASA\NASA Headquarters; **page 299:** Rainer Unkel/ Alamy Images; **page 307:** Zeber/Shutterstock; **page 308:** © Andrew and Jamie Waskey; **page 309:** Shutterstock; **page 310:** Charles O. Cecil/Alamy Images

Chapter 11

page 318: Yao Wei/© Panorama Media (Beijing)Ltd/ Alamy; **page 329:** ZAP ART/Getty Images, Inc.—Taxi; **page 330:** Sigurdur Jokull Olafsson/© Icelandic photo agency/Alamy; **page 333:** © Maria Keeley; **page 334:** Lou Linwei/Alamy; **page 335:** Wig Worland/Alamy

Chapter 12

page 342: Paul Souders/DanitaDelimont.com/"Danita Delimont Photography"/Newscom; **page 347:** Herve Lavigne/Alamy; **page 354:** Getty Images, Inc.; **page 355:** Lou Linwei/Alamy Images; **page 356:** Jenny Matthew/Alamy; **page 360:** Martin Barlow/Alamy Images; **page 363:** Getty Images, Inc.

Chapter 13

page 370: Bojan Pavlukovic/Shutterstock; **page 376:** David Pearson/Alamy Images; **page 377:** Tim Graham/Alamy Images; **page 378:** Jon Arnold Images Ltd/Alamy Images; **page 385:** Ints Vikmanis/Shutterstock; **page 386:** © Steve

Raymer / CORBIS All Rights Reserved; **page 388**: © Javier Estrada; **page 390**: Yuri Arcurs/Shutterstock

Chapter 14

page 400: © Hitoshi Yamada/Andia/Alamy Images; **page 405**: Seth Wenig/AP Wide World Photos; **page 407**: Randy Duchaine/Alamy Images; **page 411**: © Eric Joiner; **page 413**: Getty Images, Inc.; **page 415**: Rolf Richardson/Alamy Images; **page 421**: Capstone Turbine Corporation/Newscom

Chapter 15

page 432: © Anthony Kay/Flight/Alamy Images; **page 437**: Art Directors & Trip/Alamy; **page 439**: © Jennifer Knippen; **page 440**: Caro/Alamy Images; **page 444**: Getty Images, Inc.; **page 446**: Getty Images, Inc.

Chapter 16

page 452: Getty Images, Inc.; **page 468**: Malcolm Fairman/Alamy Images; **page 471**: Eddie Gerald/Alamy Images; **page 473**: Getty Images, Inc.; **page 478**: Getty Images, Inc.

Chapter 17

page 488: UN/DPI Photo by Philip Teuscher; **page 494**: Danita Delimont/Alamy Images; **page 500**: Alamy/Mark Henley/Imagestate Media Partners Limited-Impact

Photos; **page 502**: Mira/Alamy Images; **page 503**: Fredrik Renander/Alamy Images; **page 507**: Roger Bamber/Alamy Images

Chapter 18

page 514: Daniel Berehulak/Getty Images, Inc - Liaison; **page 517**: MJ Kimm/Staff/Getty Images AsiaPac; **page 520**: Iain Masterton/Alamy Images; **page 521**: © John Dykhouse; **page 523**: Tom Craig/Alamy Images; **page 534**: newscom/foto Agencia EL UNIVERSAL/Archivo

Chapter 19

page 544: © Rupert Conant/Alamy Images; **page 551**: © Owen Franken/CORBIS All Rights Reserved; **page 552**: Neil McAllister/Alamy Images; **page 554**: Jonathan Littlejohn/Alamy Images

Chapter 20

page 570: © Tan Kian Khoon/Shutterstock; **page 578**: © Paul Doyle/Alamy Images; **page 581**: Jochen Tack/Alamy Images; **page 583**: © Chip Besse; **page 585**: Alex Segre/Alamy Images; **page 590**: ImageState/Alamy Images

> Author Index

This index includes names of authors cited.
For names of companies, see the Company Index.
For terms and topics, see the Subject Index.
Page references with "e" refer to exhibits. Page
references with "n" refer to notes cited by number.

A

Aaker, David A., 524n
Adler, Carlye, 474n, 476n, 484
Adler, Nancy, 133n, 562n
Adnett, Nick, 558n
Adolph, G., 290
Agarwal, Milind, 211n, 226n
Agarwal, V., 163n
Aguiar, Marcos, 73n, 315
Ahmadi, Reza, 532n
Ahmadjian, Christina, 201n
Ahn, K., 448n
Ajayi, Richard, 324n
Alcacer, Juan, 437n
Alesina, Alberto, 558n
Alexander, Yonah, 224n
Aliber, Robert, 582n
Alon, Ilan, 473, 484
Alsakini, W., 105n
Ambos, Björn, 349n
Amine, Lyn S., 109n, 300n, 372
Anand, Geeta, 490
Anderlini, Jamil, 492n
Anderson, Erin, 403n
Anderson, James, 277n
Andrade, N., 390n
Ang, Soon, 148n, 551n
Apud, Salvador, 148n
Areddy, James, 320, 452n
Arrunada, Benito, 491n
Athanassakos, G., 59
Athanassiou, Nicholas A., 349n
Atkinson, Philip, 363n
Auerbach, Alan J., 592n
Aulakh, Preet, 447n
Aviel, David, 131n
Axtell, Roger, 138n

B

Baack, Daniel, 145n
Baba, Marietta, 523n, 525n
Bachman, S. L., 86n, 164n
Bahree, M., 310n
Balassa, Bela, 264n, 266e
Balfour, Frederik, 163n, 247n, 298, 535n, 565
Banga, Kamini, 526
Barel, R., 59
Barnard, B., 117
Bartiromo, M., 297n
Bartlett, Christoper A., 55n, 345n, 350n, 351n,
    352n, 353n, 354n, 355n, 362n
Batson, Andrew, 320
Baughn, C. Christopher, 410
Baxter, Andrew, 493n
Beach, William, 249n
Beattie, Alan, 496
Beaver, G., 59
Beckett, P., 434n
Beechler, Schon, 550n
Beer, Lawrence, 67n, 160n, 161n, 162n, 165n,
    170n, 171n
Begley, Sharon, 221n
Behrman, Jack, 295n
Belk, Russell, 145n

Bell, Deborah, 363n
Bellman, Eric, 237, 507n
Belton, Catherine, 322n, 586n
Berman, Phyllis, 221n
Berndt, Ernst, 533n
Beshouri, Christopher, 311n
Beyfar, Kristin, 551n
Bhalla, Surjit, 303n
Bhattacharya, A., 290, 306n, 307n, 496
Bhattacharya, C., 164n
Bhavna, B., 435n
Bilkey, Warren, 193n, 194n
Black, J., 553n
Blanchflower, David, 556n, 557n
Blas, J., 222n
Bloch, M., 490
Block, Walter, 277n
Blumenstein, Rebecca, 457
Boddewyn, Jean, 256n
Boerner, Hank, 229n, 590n
Bonini, Sheila, 160n, 167n, 168n
Borneman, J., 284
Bornon, J., 150
Boyacigiller, Nakiye, 550n
Boyd, Robert, 126n
Brada, Josef, 326n
Bradsher, K., 457
Brake, Terence, 349n
Brannan, Matthew, 562n
Bremner, Brian, 521n
Brett, Jeanne, 551n
Brewer, Benjamin D., 67n
Bris, Arturo, 115n
Bronson, J., 59
Bryan, L., 346n, 372n
Brzezinski, Zbigniew, 214n
Buck, Trevor, 410
Buckley, Peter, 199n
Burke, Bob, 484
Burn, Janice, 77n
Burnson, Patrick, 496n
Burton, F., 471n
Bush, Jason, 223n, 344
Butcher, Dan, 539
Byrnes, Nanette, 163n, 550n
Byron, Ellen, 448n, 520n

C

Calantone, Roger, 520n
Calkins, Martin, 83n, 157n
Cameron, Carolynn, 546
Canterbery, E., 150
Capell, Kerry, 57n, 344, 495n, 505n, 539, 593n
Carlton, Jim, 240n
Carter, Meg, 139n
Carter, Nancy, 562n
Cassell, B., 480n
Casson, Mark, 199n
Cavusgil, Erin, 160n, 168n
Cavusgil, S. Tamer, 51n, 77n, 103n, 109n, 193n,
    194n, 211n, 226n, 300n, 306n, 307n, 345n,
    346n, 347n, 348n, 355n, 362n, 372, 380n,
    396, 405n, 406e, 411e, 413n, 421n, 422e,
    450n, 451n, 457, 517n, 520n, 523n, 525n,
    528n, 530n, 532n, 534n, 537n
Celentani, Marco, 156n
Chaiken, Shelly, 137n
Champion, M., 273
Chana, Felix, 587n
Chanda, Rupa, 490n, 495n, 496n, 507n
Chandler, Alfred D., 357n

Chandler, Clay, 348n, 440n, 441n, 454n
Chang, L., 353n
Chao, Loretta, 160n, 246n, 355n
Charny, Ben, 99e, 464, 504n
Chase-Dunn, C., 67n
Chazan, G., 210, 241n, 353n
Chen, Stephen, 349n
Cheng, Patricia, 539
Chiang, C. R., 539
Choi, Chong Ju, 349n
Choo, Stephen, 473
Christensen, Claus, 552n
Chryssochoidis, G., 471n
Chung, Wilbur, 437n
Clark, D., 284
Clark, T., 144n
Clegg, J., 471n
Clemen, Robert, 166n, 170n
Clifford, Mark, 484
Cohen, Ariel, 303n
Coleman, Alison, 102n
Colvin, G., 284
Conkey, Christopher, 507n
Contractor, Farok J., 103n, 436n, 447n, 450n,
    465n, 478n
Conway, M., 312n
Corcoran, E., 457
Cotte, J., 164n
Cottrell, Robert, 576n, 578n
Coutinho de Arruda, Maria Cecilia, 447n
Covin, Jeffrey, 347n
Cowen, Tyler, 145n
Coy, P., 253
Craig, David, 503n
Crane, A., 304n, 306n
Crawford, D., 172
Crawford, J., 265n
Crosby, Cindy, 546
Crosman, Penny, 496n, 497e
Cross, A., 471n
Crown, Judith, 258, 504n
Csizmadi, P., 560n
Cultice, C., 402
Cummins, Chip, 163n
Cuneta, Josephine, 498n, 499e
Cunningham, F., 375n
Cunningham, Margaret H., 200n

D

Dahan, Nicolas, 256n
Dahl, Darren, 511
Dakhli, Mourad, 188n
Dalton, M., 258
Dao, T., 410
Dass, M., 210
David, Kenneth, 129e, 129n
Davidson, William H., 403n
Davies, Jerry, 596
Davis, Bradley, 323n
Davis, Ian, 379
Day, K., 150
Dayal-Gulati, A., 481n, 484
De Clercq, Dirk, 188n
De Franco, Silvio, 138n
Debroux, P., 91
Dehoff, Kevin, 188n
Delacroix, J., 150
Deligonul, S., 345n, 346n, 362n
Deneen, Michael, 299n
Derrick, Stuart, 464
Dess, Gregory, 347n

> Company Index

This index includes names of companies and commercial banks.
For names of authors, see the Author Index. For terms and topics, see the Subject Index.
Page numbers with "e" refer to exhibits.

> Subject Index

This index includes terms and topics. For names of companies, see the Company Index. For authors cited, see the Author Index. Page numbers with "e" refer to exhibits.

A

Absolute advantage principle, 181–182e
Abu Dhabi, 477–478, 555e
Accountants, 114, 479
Accounting practices, 228–229, 589–593, 592e. *See also* Financial management
Acculturation, 127. *See also* Culture
Acquisitions
  foreign direct investment, 444–445
  global financial crisis 2008, 447
  regional economic integration, 282
  trends, 435
Active hedging, 587–589, 588e
Adaptation, marketing, 518–523, 519e
Administrative procedures, 243e, 246
Ad valorem tariffs, 242
Advanced Biomedical Devices, Inc., case study, 394–396
Advanced economies
  characteristics of, 296e
  overview of, 290–291, 292e, 293e, 294e
  trade conditions, 295
Advertising, 225, 465, 479, 534–536e, 535e. *See also* Marketing
Afghanistan, legal environment, 218e
Africa
  communications technology, 78
  corruption, 155, 156, 158e, 159e
  debt, 291
  economic development of, 311–312
  emerging markets, 294–295
  ethical standards, 160
  foreign direct investment, 43–44e
  globalization and, 87–88
  gross national income, 73, 75e
  legal environment, 218e
  regional economic integration, 277
  stock of inward/outward FDI, 196e, 197e
  tariffs, 244
After-sales service, 97e–99e, 98e. *See also* Services
Agents, defined, 107
Agreement on Subsidies and Countervailing Measures (ASCM), 257–258
Agreement on Trade Related Aspects of Intellectual Property Rights, 480
Agricultural goods, 108, 247–248, 279–280
AIDS crisis, 312
AIG (American International Group), case study, 337–339
Airbus, case study, 257–258
Algeria, 277
All-China Federation of Trade Unions (ACFTU), 558
Allowance, compensation packages, 555
Amae, 131
Ambiguity, tolerance for, 146
American football in Europe, 123–124
American option, 588
Amsterdam, cost of living, 555e
Analogy indicators, 392–393
An Inquiry into the Nature and Causes of the Wealth of Nations (Smith), 181
Antidumping duty, 244e, 248
APEC (Asia Pacific Economic Cooperation), 71–72, 254
Apocalypse Now, 148

Arabic language, 143e
Arab Maghreb Union, 277
Arbitragers, 585–586e
Arbitrators, labor negotiations, 557
Architectural services, 105–106e, 465, 477–478
Area studies, employee training, 552e–554
Argentina. *See* El Mercado Comun del Sur (MERCOSUR)
  currency crisis, 577
  debt, 336
  GDP, 297e
  global financial crisis, 254
  inflation, 325e
  media characteristics, 535e
  per capita GDP, 301e
  tax rate, 592e
ASEAN (Association of Southeast Asian Nations), 221, 275–276e
Asia. *See also* specific country name
  emerging markets, 294–295
  foreign direct investment, 43–44e
  global recession, 41
  gross national income, 73, 75e
  stock of inward/outward FDI, 196e, 197e
Asian financial crisis, 2033, 327, 577
Asia-Pacific Economic Cooperation (APEC), 71–72, 254, 276
Asociación Interamericana de Contabilidad, 590
Assets, 222–224, 228–229
Association of Southeast Asian Nations (ASEAN), 221, 275–276e
Association of Women in International Trade, 562–563
A.T. Kearney, 387e
Attitudes, culture and, 130–131, 137
Austrade, 420
Australia
  Closer Economic Relations Agreement (CER), 276
  currency, 321e
  ethical standards, 161–162
  foreign direct investment, 383e
  GDP, 297e
  labor disputes, 557e
  labor unions, 556e
  legal environment, 218e
  media characteristics, 535e
  regional economic integration, 276
  small and medium-sized enterprises, 49
  stock of inward/outward FDI, 196e, 197e
  tariffs, 244e
  tax rate, 592e
Austria, 271e. *See also* European Union
AUTOLATINA, case study, 455–457
Autonomy, regional economic integration, 280
Avoidance, cultural differences, 136

B

Bahrain, 277
Balance of payments, 326
Bangladesh, 218e, 311
Bank for International Settlements, 322–323e, 329, 335, 586
Banking, international. *See also* Currency; Financial systems
  case study, regulation of, 338
  central banks, 115, 324–325, 329, 335
  commercial banks, 332, 334
  export-import financing, 420
  facilitator role, 96, 111–114
  international monetary system, overview, 329

  investment banks, 334
  overview, 45
  regulations, 115
Banking crisis 2044, 72
Banking crisis, defined, 336
Bank of England, 335
Bank of Japan, 335
Bankruptcy, 559
Banque de France, 335
Barcelona, 555e
Barrett Farm Foods, case study, 426–427
Barter, 424
Basel Capital Accord, 335
Base remuneration, 555
Belgium. *See also* European Union
  GDP, 271e
  international trade, 42–43e
  labor unions, 556e
  stock of inward/outward FDI, 196e, 197e
  tax rate, 592e
Benefits packages, 549, 554–556, 555e
Bengali language, 143e
Bentley, Richard, 394
Berne Convention for the Protection of Literary and Artistic Works, 480
Best Market Reports, 387
Bias, cultural, 146
Big Mac Index, 301–302e
Bill and Melinda Gates Foundation, 311
Bill of lading, 414–415
BME Spanish Exchanges, 576e
Boeing, case study, 257–258
Bolivia. *See* El Mercado Comun del Sur (MERCOSUR)
Bond market, 72, 332, 577–578
Born global firm, 49, 95–96, 102–103, 194
Boycotts, 223–224, 227
Brabeck, Peter, 347
Branding, 71, 523–527, 524e. *See also* Marketing
Brazil. *See also* El Mercado Comun del Sur (MERCOSUR)
  currency, 321e
  foreign direct investment, 383e
  GDP, 297e, 371
  global financial crisis, 254
  Global Services Location Index, 384e
  inflation, 325e
  middle class, 303e
  per capita GDP, 301e
  piracy and counterfeits, 161e
  stock of inward/outward FDI, 196e, 197e
  tax rate, 592e
Bretton Woods Conference, 68, 327
Bribery, 155–156, 209–210, 304
Bridges
  international entry strategies, 105, 106e
Britain. *See* United Kingdom
Brokers, goods and services, 104–106e, 107
Brunei. *See* Association of Southeast Asian Nations (ASEAN)
Buddhism, 139–142, 140e, 141e
Build-operate-transfer (BOT) arrangements, 478
Build-own-transfer ventures, 105, 106e
Bulgaria, 271e, 301e, 384e. *See also* European Union
Business directories, 420
Business format franchising, 471–474e, 472e
Business partners, selecting, 389–390
Business process outsourcing, 490–491, 501–502
Business Week, 524e
Buy-back agreements, 425
Buyers, export-import financing, 419